UNIVERSITY CASEBOOK SERIES®

FEDERAL INCOME TAXATION OF CORPORATIONS

FOURTH EDITION

by

MARTIN J. MCMAHON, JR.
Professor of Law and
James J. Freeland Eminent Scholar in Taxation
University of Florida

DANIEL L. SIMMONS
Professor of Law Emeritus
University of California at Davis

PAUL R. MCDANIEL
Late Professor of Law and
James J. Freeland Eminent Scholar in Taxation
University of Florida

FOUNDATION
PRESS

University Casebook Series is a trademark registered in the U.S. Patent and Trademark Office.

© 1997, 1999, 2006 FOUNDATION PRESS
© 2014 LEG, Inc. d/b/a West Academic
    444 Cedar Street, Suite 700
    St. Paul, MN 55101
    1-877-888-1330

Printed in the United States of America

ISBN: 978-1-60930-189-7

Mat #41309435

PREFACE

This book covers the federal income taxation of corporations and their shareholders. It is for use in courses that cover only corporate taxation, separately from the study of taxation of partnerships. In a course, or coordinated sequence of courses, covering partnerships, S corporations, and C corporations, *Federal Income Taxation of Business Organizations, 5th Ed.* should be used for comprehensive coverage. Chapters 1-16 of this volume are substantially identical to chapters 10-25 in *Federal Income Taxation of Business Organizations*, with the exception of the elimination of some cross references.

Depending on the level of detail covered, this volume can be used in a variety of courses covering corporate taxation at either the J.D. or LL.M. level. The arrangement in outline format of both the subdivisions within the chapters and the *DETAILED ANALYSIS* following the principal cases is intended to facilitate the assignment by the instructor of only selected portions of the material on any particular topic when the book is employed in survey course on corporate taxation. At the same time, the text presents detailed discussion of complex issues in the proper statutory structural context for coverage in more advanced courses.

We recognize that teachers approach their courses with different objectives in mind and use different techniques for handling the materials. In selecting and organizing the materials, we have attempted to maximize the usefulness of these materials for whatever approach the teacher wishes to adopt—an intensive technical analysis, a problem oriented method, a consideration of the policies that underlie the technical tax structure, or a survey of the principal elements of the federal income taxation of corporations. While the selection of principal cases and the numerous examples discussed in the *DETAILED ANALYSIS* can, in effect, serve as problems for students and class discussion, many instructors choose to cover corporate taxation by using a series of detailed problems for class discussion. We have published an accompanying separately bound set of Class Discussion Problems keyed to the materials in this volume, together with an accompanying teacher's manual.

This book charts a course between those books that employ primarily textual explanation and those that rely for the most part on cases. Most chapters and sections of chapters are introduced by a textual discussion or outline of the basic issues and structure of the statute governing treatment of the particular item or transaction covered in the chapter or section. Principal cases have been included to illustrate key concepts not governed by a detailed statutory provision, as well as to illustrate how the courts have utilized the technical tools at their disposal. Numerous important changes in the statutory structure over the past few decades—the changing magnitude of the capital gain preference, repeal of the *General Utilities* rule providing nonrecognition of gain upon the distribution of property by a corporation, the flattening of the personal income tax rates resulting in a maximum individual rate only slightly higher than the maximum corporate rate, preferential rates for dividends, and the passive activity loss rules — have changed dramatically the important issues. Multiple statutory changes have made it impossible to include a judicial decision as a principal case to illustrate the application of a significant number of Code provisions. As a result, many cases long used in teaching materials are no longer helpful to students, even though they remain valid precedents. Accordingly, in many chapters the "principal case" is an excerpt from a congressional committee report or a Revenue Ruling, which helps the student understand the reasons underlying changes in the statute, as well as providing a road map to assist in mastering the detailed statutory provisions.

In the *DETAILED ANALYSIS,* which follows the principal cases or textual intorduction, we have attempted to provide sufficient discussion of rulings and cases to give an insight into the endless variety of factual situations to which the highly technical provisions of the Internal Revenue Code governing corporate and partnership taxation must be applied. The *DETAILED ANALYSIS* also provides important historical background and discussion of sequential amendments to particular sections of the Code and Regulations necessary to understand the significance of the current Code provisions. The breadth and detail of the *DETAILED ANALYSIS* is such that many instructors may wish to assign only portions of it depending on the scope of the particular course. To assist in selective use of *DETAILED ANALYSIS,* we have endeavored to arrange the *DETAILED ANALYSIS* from the general to the more specific as the outline format progresses, and have numbered the issues addressed in the *DETAILED ANALYSIS* in a "European" outline format, which facilitates selective inclusion (or omission) in the syllabus.

Of course, the Internal Revenue Code and Treasury Regulations are the centerpiece of any course in federal taxation. This text is intended to be used in conjunction with either a complete set of the Code and Regulations or one of the several available edited versions of the Code and Regulations. The statutory and regulatory references at the head of each topic are not intended to be exhaustive. Rather, they represent only the essential sections of the Code and Regulations that the student must understand to obtain the framework for the cases and materials under the particular topic. We have not undertaken completely to explain the operation of the Code and Regulations in the text. The student must work with the statute and regulatory material before undertaking the examination of its application in the materials in this volume, as well as attempting to solve the problems in the accompanying Class Discussion Problems.

This book is divided into seven Parts, which are further subdivided into chapters. Each Part, in general, represents a block of material in which we think most instructors in a particular course will chose to cover all of the chapters, although the depth of the coverage within each chapter may differ with the overall scope of the course

Part 1 (Chapters 1- 7) covers basic corporate taxation: the corporate income tax, classification, formation, capital structure, dividends, redemptions, and liquidations (except in connection with acquisitions). These materials generally will be combined with other Parts as one element in a broader course, although they may be used for a separate two hour course in basic corporate taxation. Part 2 (Chapter 8) covers Subchapter S. This Part typically will be combined with Part 1 in course in basic corporate taxation, but in an LL.M. program, it might be combined with material from subsequent parts in an advanced corporate tax course.

Part 3 (Chapter 9) covers affiliated corporations and consolidated returns. Most books, if they cover this material at all, include it near the end of the book. We have placed the material on consolidated returns immediately following Subchapter S because we believe both Parts reflect a common theme—application of aggregate theory as opposed to separate entity theory in the taxation of corporate income, albeit in differing manners and to limited extents. Thus, it might be logical to close a course in basic corporate taxation with some discussion of both Subchapter S and consolidated returns. Alternatively, a basic course might close with Subchapter S and an advanced course, dealing primarily with acquisitions, might begin with consolidated returns, the rules respecting which play an important part in structuring acquisition transactions. (The authors generally have begun their courses on corporate acquisitions and reorganizations with consolidated returns). Finally, some instructors may choose to skip this Chapter.

Part 4 (Chapters 10 through 12) covers taxable and tax free mergers and acquisitions. This Part (particularly Chapter 11 dealing with bootstrap acquisitions) relates back to, and builds upon, concepts explored in Part 1. Part 5 (Chapters 13 and 14) covers single-corporation reorganizations and corporate divisions (§ 355). Part 6 (Chapter 15) covers carryover of corporate attributes in acquisitions and reorganizations. These three Parts (as well as Part 3) may be combined into a two or three credit hour course in advanced corporate taxation. Alternatively portions of Parts 3, 4, and 5 may be combined with Part I (and possibly Part II) in a four hour course covering corporate taxation generally. Experience has proven, however, that it is difficult to cover all of the topics discussed in these Parts in a four credit hour course. To facilitate selective use of the materials on tax-free acquisitive reorganizations, the first two sections of Chapter 12 provide an overview of corporate reorganizations and the important judicial and administrative limitations superimposed on the statute, while the remaining sections individually examine in detail each different form of acquisition technique. Some instructors may choose to cover only the first two sections in a basic corporate taxation course.

Part 7 (Chapter 16) covers penalty taxes. We expect that only a few courses, primarily advanced corporate taxation courses in LL.M. programs, will cover this Part in conjunction with more discrete division of the earlier parts into a greater number of courses having a more narrowly focused scope. Some limited reference to these materials may be in order in J.D. level courses in corporate taxation.

As to editorial matters, the statutory references throughout are to the 1986 Code, except where the text expressly indicates otherwise. References in the cases and other primary sources to the 1954 and 1939 Codes and prior statutes have been edited to conform them to the 1986 Code. Generally the practice is to omit the earlier citation and instead refer to the matter as "the former version," or "the predecessor," or to give the current relevant 1986 Code section if there has been no significant change in the statutory language. But if a significant change has occurred, that fact is noted and the prior language is given. Footnotes in cases and materials frequently have been omitted. Where retained the original numbering of the footnotes has been kept so that, in many instances, the footnote numbers are not consecutive. Editorial footnotes for cases and materials are so designated and are indicated by an asterisk. References to Tax Court Memorandum decisions are to the number assigned by the Tax Court and not to any particular commercial publication. In general, references to the Code, Regulations, cases and rulings are current as of January 31, 2014.

We are indebted to Matt Evans and Darius Rodriguez, both of whom are graduates of the University of Florida College of Law Graduate Tax Program, for research and editorial assistance.

March 2014

Martin J. McMahon, Jr.
Daniel L. Simmons

Paul R. McDaniel
In Memoriam

This edition of *Federal Income Taxation of Corporations* is the first new edition since the death of Paul McDaniel on July 16, 2010. We will miss greatly his intellect, insights, guiding hand, humor, and personal warmth. This text traces its origins back to Volume II of Surrey, Warren, McDaniel & Ault, Federal Income Taxation, published in 1972. We were invited to join the team of authors in 1987, after the passing of Stanley Surrey and William Warren, and worked first with both Paul and Hugh Ault and later only with Paul on successor volumes and annual supplements for nearly twenty-five years

We have endeavored to carry forward crucial lessons taught to us by Paul about describing the Code, regulations, cases, and rulings. Paul always believed that the purpose of a law school classroom tax textbook was not to completely describe the rules for the students, but rather provide for them a framework for reading the Code and regulations themselves and to provide illustrations of the application of the rules of the Code and regulations that the students could use as tools to answer in class questions beyond those clearly addressed by the Code and regulations. That is a methodology that we have since always endeavored to apply, although in the era of constant tax acts and a flood of new complex regulations, it is becoming ever-increasingly more difficult. We will miss Paul greatly, but his indelible mark on this text and much of his remarkable input will be present in every edition to come.

SUMMARY OF CONTENTS

TABLE OF CONTENTS

TABLE OF CASES

The principal cases are in bold type.

TABLE OF STATUTES

TABLE OF RULINGS

TABLE OF TREASURY REGULATIONS

TABLE OF PROPOSED TREASURY REGULATIONS

TABLE OF TEMPORARY TREASURY REGULATIONS

UNIVERSITY CASEBOOK SERIES ®

FEDERAL INCOME TAXATION OF CORPORATIONS

FOURTH EDITION

PART 1

TAXATION OF CORPORATIONS AND SHAREHOLDERS

CHAPTER 1

TAXATION OF CORPORATE INCOME AND IDENTIFYING TAXABLE CORPORATE ENTITIES

SECTION 1.   THE CORPORATE INCOME TAX

Corporations are taxpaying entities that are separate and distinct from their shareholders. Except in certain limited situations, a corporation must pay an income tax on its profits even if the corporation currently or subsequently distributes those profits to its shareholders as dividends taxable to them individually as a part of their taxable income. Thus, corporations differ from partnerships, which are not taxpaying entities, but which generally are treated as an aggregate of the partners who pay tax on their shares of partnership income.

The corporate income tax predates the current individual income tax. The modern corporate income tax originated in 1909, four years before the adoption of the Sixteenth Amendment and the broad based individual income tax which it made possible. In Flint v. Stone Tracy Company, 220 U.S. 107 (1911), the Supreme Court upheld the 1909 corporate income tax against a constitutional challenge, which alleged that the corporate income tax was a direct tax that was not apportioned among the states according to population as required by Article I, Section 9, Clause 4 of the Constitution. Rather, the Court held that the corporate income tax was an excise tax on the privilege of doing business in the corporate form.

Ever since the enactment of the individual income tax in 1913, corporate income generally has been taxed twice, first when earned by the corporation and again when distributed to the shareholders as dividends or in liquidation. Historically, there have been some exceptions. Prior to 1936 there was a partial exclusion of dividends under the individual income tax, and during 1936 and 1937 corporations were allowed a deduction for the amount of dividends paid out to shareholders. From 1954 through 1986, individuals were permitted by former § 116 to exclude from income a relatively small portion of dividends received (the original exclusion was $50; this amount had increased to $100 per taxpayer immediately prior to repeal of the exclusion). In addition, from 1954 until 1963 shareholders were allowed a credit equal to 4 percent of dividends received (in excess of the exclusion).[1] For taxable years after 2003 § 1(h)(11) generally taxes dividends at the same rate as long-term capital gains—currently zero

---

[1]   See Shoup, The Dividend Exclusion and Credit in the Revenue Code of 1954, 8 Nat'l Tax J. 136 (1955).

percent for capital gains and dividends that would have been taxed in the 10 and 15 percent brackets if they had been taxed at ordinary income rates, 15 percent for capital gains and dividends that would have been taxed in the tax brackets higher than 15 percent but below the 39.6 percent bracket if they had been taxed at ordinary income rates, and 20 percent for capital gains and dividends that would have been taxed in the 39.6 percent bracket if they had been taxed at ordinary income rates.

Under current law the most significant exception to taxation of the corporation as a separate entity is the election under Subchapter S (§§ 1361–1379) to treat the corporation as a pass-through entity with gains and losses being reported on the shareholders' individual returns.[2] A number of restrictive conditions limit the availability of this election. Corporations that do not make an election under subchapter S are called "C corporations;" corporations which make the election are called "S corporations." Approximately sixty percent of all corporations elect to be treated as S corporations. These corporations generally are very small, both in terms of assets and revenues, and usually have only a few shareholders.

The policy decision to treat a corporation as a tax-paying entity separate and distinct from its shareholders entails certain structural requirements. A separate rate structure, currently specified in § 11, is applicable to corporations. The rate of tax on corporate income has varied over the years.[3] Currently, the rates are15 percent on the first $50,000 of taxable income, 25 percent on the next $25,000, 34 percent on taxable income between $75,000 and $10 million, and 35 percent of taxable income in excess of $10 million. If taxable income exceeds $100,000, a five percent surtax is imposed on the excess over $100,000 up to a maximum additional tax of $11,750, which occurs when taxable income reaches $335,000. If a corporation has taxable income over $15 million, a three percent surtax is imposed on the excess over $15 million, up to a maximum additional tax of $100,000, which occurs when taxable income reaches $18.33 million. The purpose of these surtaxes is to phase-out the benefit of the graduated rates for corporations having taxable incomes in excess of $100,000, so that corporations with taxable income exceeding $18.33 million pay a 35 percent flat rate. As with any phase-out technique, corporations in the phase-out ranges are subject to a marginal rate in excess of the statutory rate that would otherwise apply. The marginal rate structure of the regular corporate tax, as a result of the phase-outs, is as follows:

15% on first $50,000

25% on next $25,000 ($75,000)

---

[2]   Subchapter S applies only to "small business corporations" having a limited number of shareholders. While Subchapter S is loosely referred to as permitting a corporation to elect to be taxed as a partnership, the operational effects under the Subchapter differ somewhat from partnership treatment. Subchapter S is discussed in Chapter 8.

[3]   In 1909, when the corporate income tax was introduced, the rate was 1%. During World War I, it reached 12%; a 40% top rate was applicable during World War II; and a 52% rate was imposed during the Korean War. In 1964, the rate was reduced to 50% for that year and to 48% beginning in 1965. The rates and brackets were modified several times during the 1970's and 1980's. See J. Pechman, Federal Tax Policy, 135–137, 302–305, 321–322 (5th ed. 1987).

34% on next $25,000 ($100,000)

39% on next $235,000 ($335,000)

34% on next $9,665,000 ($10 million)

35% on next $5,000,000 ($15 million)

38% on next $3,333,333 ($18.333 million)

35% above $18,333,333

Section 11(b)(2) imposes a flat-rate 35 percent corporate income tax (rather than the normal graduated corporate rates in § 11(b)(1)) on "qualified personal service corporations." Generally, "qualified personal service corporations" are corporations engaged in health, law, engineering, architecture, accounting, actuarial science, performing arts, and consulting businesses, if substantially all of the stock is owned directly or indirectly by employees performing such services. See I.R.C. § 448(d)(2). In Grutman-Mazler Engineering Inc. v. Commissioner, T.C. Memo. 2008–140, the taxpayer corporation had two shareholders, a 60 percent shareholder was a licensed engineer who performed engineering services for the corporation and oversaw its activities, and a forty percent shareholder who had an engineering degree, but was not a licensed civil engineer, and worked in a "planning division." In determining whether the taxpayer corporation was a "qualified personal service corporation" as defined under § 448(d)(2), the court held that state law is relevant to determine whether an activity is within a qualifying field. Under the relevant state law (California) civil engineering includes submitting designs, plans, tentative tract maps, grading plans, and engineering reports to local governments and coordinating other professionals. Therefore, because both shareholders performed services that constituted "engineering" under California law and the other conditions of § 448 were met, the corporation's income was taxed under § 11(b)(2), not at graduated rates. See also Rainbow Tax Service, Inc. v. Commissioner, 128 T.C. 42 (2007) (because tax return preparation and bookkeeping services constitute accounting services under § 448(d)(2)(A) and Temp.Reg. § 1.448–1T(e)(5)(vii), Ex. (1)(i), the taxpayer employee-owned-corporation was subject to the 35% flat-rate corporate tax under § 11(b)(2)).

Taxable income of a corporation is basically determined by applying the same rules that govern taxation of individuals. Thus, the gross income rules, the deduction rules, the accounting provisions, and the capital gain and loss provisions are all pertinent.[4] However, there are a number of important variations from these basic income tax provisions that are applicable only to corporations. For example, application of the deduction sections, such as § 162(a) and § 165(a), to corporations is generally guided by the premise that all corporations are engaged in trade or business. In addition, there are a number of special provisions that apply only to corporations, such as the dividends received deduction in § 243 for intercorporate dividends, which effectively excludes all or part of such dividends from a corporation's

---

[4] As with individuals, corporations are subject to the alternative minimum tax provided by § 55 through § 59 in any year in which the alternative minimum tax exceeds the regular tax. The alternative minimum tax rate for corporations is 20 percent, and the tax is imposed on "alternative minimum taxable income," a tax base that differs substantially from "taxable income."

taxable income. The treatment of capital gains and losses recognized by corporations also differs. Under § 1212(a), capital losses are allowed only to the extent of capital gains, with a five-year carryover and a three-year carryback of any excess losses. Section 1201 provides that for any year in which the maximum tax rate under § 11 exceeds 35 percent (excluding the 5 percent and 3 percent surtaxes), the maximum rate of tax on long term capital gains is limited to 35 percent. At present, corporate rates do not exceed 35 percent so this provision has no impact.[5]

Section 199, added by the 2004 Jobs Act, provides a special deduction for taxpayers operating a trade or business that engages in domestic manufacturing activities. Generally, for corporations, the effect of the deduction is to reduce the statutory tax rate applied to manufacturing by nine percent. For example, for a corporation normally subject to the 35 percent rate, the effective tax rate on manufacturing income would be only 31.85 percent. See page 8.

The non-applicability to most corporations of the passive activity loss rules of § 469 is a significant difference between individual and corporate taxation. Section 469 applies to a closely held C corporation, defined in §§ 469(j)(1) and 465(a)(1)(B) as a C corporation more than 50 percent of the stock of which is held at some time during the last half of the taxable year by five or fewer persons, taking into account certain attribution rules. It also applies to "personal service corporations" defined in § 469(j)(2). Section 469 does not apply to S corporations, but it does apply to the shareholders in taking into account their shares of S corporation income or loss. Special rules govern the determination of whether a closely held C corporation or personal service corporation "materially participates" in an activity. See I.R.C. § 469(h)(4).

The rules governing choice of accounting methods and taxable years also differ for corporations. Most C corporations are required to use the accrual method of accounting. Exceptions are provided for corporations with average annual gross receipts of less than $5 million and for personal service corporations. See I.R.C. § 448. Although most C corporations are free to choose any taxable year, personal service corporations and S corporations generally are required to adopt a calendar year. See I.R.C. §§ 441(i), 1378(b). A personal service corporation or S corporation may adopt a fiscal year, however, if the corporation can establish a business purpose for the fiscal year, or if it makes an election under § 444, which requires that the corporation make an advance deposit of taxes.

Special problems also result from transactions unique to the corporate form, such as the tax consequences to a corporation of the issuance of its stock or of dealings by it in its stock. Section 1032 solves this problem by providing that a corporation does not realize income upon the sale or issuance of its own shares for money, property, or services. Further, securities issued by a corporation must be classified as either stock or debt because payment of interest on debt generates a

---

[5]   Of course, there is nothing to prevent Congress from amending § 1201 to provide a higher maximum rate of tax on capital gains at the same time it amends § 11 to increase the general rate. Conversely, § 1201 might be amended to provide, as it did prior to the 1986 Act, for a maximum tax rate on capital gains lower than the then current maximum rate under § 11.

deduction to the corporation under § 163 while the distribution of a dividend on stock does not. This classification issue, which is considered in Chapter 3, is a matter of considerable controversy.

Because the corporation is a separate tax entity, rules must be provided to specify the tax treatment for various events in the life of the corporation that involve the transfer of property or money to or from shareholders, e.g., upon the formation of the corporation. In general, if an individual, group of individuals, or partnership desires to incorporate a business and transfers the business's assets to a corporation formed for that purpose, no gain or loss will be recognized from the change in the form of the ownership of the assets. The transferor now owns stock of a corporation holding the assets instead of holding the assets themselves; but the Code expressly provides that any gain or loss inherent in those assets is not to be recognized when they are so exchanged for stock. The transferor's basis for the assets now becomes the basis for the stock, and this asset basis likewise carries over to the corporation and becomes its basis for the assets. The rules governing formation of a corporation are discussed in Chapter 2.

Problems also arise as to the proper tax relationship between the ongoing corporation and its shareholders. The corporation may distribute cash, property, or its own stock. It is necessary to establish a standard for ascertaining the extent to which distributions represent corporate earnings, which should be taxed to the shareholders as dividends, or a return of capital which should be applied against the basis of the shareholder's stock and taxable as gain if the distribution exceeds that basis. It also is necessary to decide whether the distribution of property by the corporation is an event that should result in the recognition of gain or loss to the corporation when the property is either appreciated or depreciated. The rules governing the tax treatment of dividends are considered in Chapter 4. Special problems presented by dividends paid in the distributing corporation's own stock are discussed in Chapter 6.

Some of the shares of a shareholder, or all of the shares of some shareholders, may be redeemed by the corporation for cash or other property. In this case it is necessary to determine whether the transaction more nearly resembles a sale of the stock, thereby giving rise to recovery of basis and capital gain treatment, or a dividend with the attendant ordinary income consequences. It is also necessary to determine whether it is appropriate for the corporation to recognize gain or loss if property, rather than cash, is distributed to the shareholder in such a transaction. The rules required to determine the proper tax treatment of these transactions at the corporate and the shareholder level are considered in Chapter 5.

The shareholders later may decide to sell or liquidate the corporation. Again, it is necessary to provide rules for determining the gain or loss realized in such cases, and whether that gain or loss will be recognized at the corporate level, the shareholder level, or both. Special rules may be appropriate if the liquidated corporation is a subsidiary corporation, most of the stock of which is owned by another corporation. In this case nonrecognition of gain and loss to both corporations may be appropriate. Furthermore, consideration must be given to treatment of sales and purchases of corporate assets in connection with a liquidation.

The purchase of all of the stock of a corporation and the purchase of all of its assets as a going business may be alternatives from a non-tax perspective. Chapters 10 and 12 consider the extent to which the tax system treats these transactions identically and to what extent the form chosen by the parties governs the transaction.

It would be possible to "integrate" the tax treatment of the corporation with the tax treatment of its shareholders. It is not essential to an income tax system that corporations be subject to a separate tax structure, in the sense that both the corporation and its shareholders bear tax on the same income. The tax systems of some countries have varying degrees of integration of the corporate and individual income taxes. The policy arguments for a separate corporate income tax versus integration of the taxation of corporations and their shareholders are discussed later in this Section. The limited integration offered by Subchapter S is considered in Chapter 8.

Since the 2003 Act, the double taxation of corporate profits has been partially mitigated. For taxable years after 2003, § 1(h)(11) generally taxes dividends at the same rate as long-term capital gains—currently zero percent for capital gains and dividends that would have been taxed in the 10 and 15 percent brackets if they had been taxed at ordinary income rates, 15 percent for capital gains and dividends that would have been taxed in the tax brackets higher than 15 percent but below the 39.6 percent bracket if they had been taxed at ordinary income rates, and 20 percent for capital gains and dividends that would have been taxed in the 39.6 percent bracket if they had been taxed at ordinary income rates. However, most of subchapter C, as well as certain related penalty taxes found elsewhere in the Code, was developed in the context of, and frequently to deal with transactions designed to exploit, capital gains being taxed at rates substantially lower than the rate at which dividends were taxed. As you study the materials in the following chapters consider the extent to which the need for various provisions might have been obviated by equalizing the tax rates for dividends and long-term capital gains.

Another way of viewing the materials is from the standpoint of business planning requirements. What are the various routes to implement a given business decision when tax consequences are taken into consideration? Which are more or less expensive from a tax standpoint? In which situations do business needs appear to have shaped the tax rules, and conversely, in which situations has the development of the tax law determined the manner in which business transactions are carried out? The materials on the sale and purchase of the corporate business in Chapters 10 and 11, acquisitive tax-free reorganizations in Chapter 12, single corporation reorganizations in Chapter 13, and corporate divisions in Chapter 14 raise planning as well as structural questions.

DETAILED ANALYSIS

1. DEDUCTION FOR QUALIFIED PRODUCTION ACTIVITIES INCOME

Section 199 provides a special deduction for taxpayers operating a trade or business that engages in manufacturing activities. For corporations, the deduction allowed by § 199 is 9 percent of the lesser of "qualified production activities income" or taxable income, but the deduction cannot exceed 50 percent of the wages paid by the taxpayer during the year for which the deduction is sought. I.R.C. § 199(a) and (b). Qualified production activities income is defined as the excess of "domestic production gross receipts" over the sum of (1) the cost of goods sold allocable to domestic production gross receipts, (2) other deductions, expenses, or losses directly allocable to domestic production gross receipts, and (3) a ratable portion of other deductions, expenses, and losses not directly allocable to domestic production gross receipts or to any other class of income. I.R.C. § 199(c)(1).

Domestic production gross receipts are gross receipts derived from (1) the lease, rental, license, or sale, exchange, or other disposition of (a) "qualifying production property," defined as tangible personal property, computer software, and sound recordings, produced (in whole or in significant part) by the taxpayer in the United States, (b) a "qualified film" produced by the taxpayer, or (c) electricity, natural gas, or potable water produced by the taxpayer in the United States, (2) construction performed within the United States, or (3) architectural or engineering services performed in the United States for United States construction projects. Section 199(c)(4)(B) excludes from the definition of domestic production gross receipts any receipts from (1) the sale of food and beverages prepared by the taxpayer at a retail establishment, or (2) the transmission or distribution (as contrasted with the production) of electricity, natural gas, or potable water.

Because the deduction is a percentage of a specified type of net income, rather than an allowance for actual expenses incurred by the taxpayer, its effect can be viewed as reducing the effective tax rate on qualified production activities income. (Indeed, it originated in a proposal to reduce the corporate tax rate generally, but through the legislative process metamorphosed into its current structure.) Suppose a corporation has $50,000,000 of qualified production activities income (sufficient income to be subject to a marginal rate of 35 percent beyond the surtax brackets). The § 199 deduction reduces the corporation's taxable income derived from qualified production activities from $50,000,000 to $45,500,000. At 35 percent, the tax on $45,500,000 is $15,925,000, which is an effective tax rate of only 31.85 percent on the $50,0000,000 of qualified production activities income.

2. THE ALTERNATIVE MINIMUM TAX

2.1. *Generally*

The alternative minimum tax (AMT) applies to both individuals and corporations (other than S Corporations and small business corporations), but certain structural features of the AMT make it a much more important consideration for corporate taxpayers than for individual taxpayers. At present, most individuals do not have to make AMT computations each year. On the other hand, the possibility that a corporation may be liable for the AMT is so significant that most corporations must make annual AMT computations even though no AMT liability may arise for that year. The purpose of the AMT is to assure that a taxpayer with substantial economic income cannot escape significant tax liability through exclusions, deductions, and credits that are provided under the regular tax as incentives for economic behavior that Congress intends to encourage rather than serve to measure economic income accurately. See S.Rep. No. 99–313, 99th Cong. 2d Sess. 518–20 (1986).

Mechanically, under § 55(a) the AMT is an "add on" tax, but structurally the AMT is a "shadow" tax system that applies a lower uniform rate to a more broadly defined tax base than is used in computing the regular income tax. The corporation generally is required to pay the greater of the regular income tax or the AMT.

2.2. *AMT Rate and Exclusion*

In general, the tax base for the AMT is the corporation's regular taxable income increased by the "tax preferences" specified in § 57 and adjusted as required under § 56 by recomputing certain deductions, such as MACRS depreciation under § 168, to negate to some extent the acceleration of these deductions which is provided under the regular income tax. The resulting tax base is termed "alternative minimum taxable income" (AMTI) and, after an allowance of an exemption, AMTI is taxed at a flat 20 percent rate. I.R.C. § 55(b)(1)(B). The exemption allowed to a corporation is $40,000, but it is reduced by 25 percent of the amount by which the corporation's AMTI exceeds $150,000. I.R.C. § 55(d)(2), (3). Thus, no exemption is available for a corporation with AMTI of $310,000 or more. As a result of the phase-out of the $40,000 AMT exemption, the corporate AMT marginal rate structure is as follows:

0% on first $40,000

20% on next $110,000 ($150,000)

25% on next $160,000 ($310,000)

20% above $310,000

The amount of tax resulting from this computation is termed "tentative minimum tax" by § 55(b). Technically, the AMT liability is the amount by which this tentative minimum tax exceeds regular tax liability for the year. Thus in a year in which the corporation is liable for AMT it also is liable for regular tax.

2.3. *Alternative Minimum Taxable Income*

AMTI is computed by adding back to taxable income the preference items listed in § 57 including the following: (1) solid mineral (but not oil and gas) depletion allowances under § 611 to the extent that the deductions exceed the taxpayer's basis for the property at the end of the year (this applies only to percentage depletion, but not to all percentage depletion over cost depletion); (2) a portion of the amount by which intangible drilling and development costs deducted under § 263(c) for drilling oil, gas or geothermal steam wells exceeds net income from such wells for the year; (3) interest on private activity bonds exempt from tax under § 103; and (4) certain accelerated depreciation taken on property placed in service before 1987.

Regular taxable income is also adjusted by the items described in § 56. The complex adjustments of § 56 may either increase or decrease AMTI relative to taxable income, and may produce different results in different years. For example, § 56(a)(1) prescribes that in computing AMTI, taxable income is "adjusted" by recomputing depreciation of tangible personal property applying the 150 percent declining balance method, switching to

enacting § 7704, discussed at page 24, which taxes unincorporated publicly traded business entities as corporations.

This declining interest in integration also coincided with a growing appreciation of the extraordinarily complex and difficult technical issues which would be entailed in implementing any form of integration system. See McLure, A Status Report on Tax Integration in the United States, 31 Nat'l Tax J. 313 (1978). Moreover, it became apparent that various political interests had strongly differing views about the extent and characteristics of any form of integration that might be adopted. See McLure and Surrey, Integration of Income Taxes: Issues For Debate, 55 Harv.Bus.Rev. 169 (Sept.–Oct. 1977). Academic interest in corporate integration, however, has continued. Furthermore, as a practical matter, integration is rapidly becoming relevant only with respect to publicly traded businesses. With the enactment of limited liability company statutes in virtually every state, owners of a closely held business can enjoy the important attributes of a corporation for state law purposes while achieving pass-through single level tax status. See page 19. Nevertheless, the issue continues to be important because the relatively small number of publicly traded corporations earn a dominant share of overall business profits.

Political interest in corporate integration in the United States came to a crescendo in the first few years of the twenty-first century. The administration of President George W. Bush asked Congress to enact a full exclusion for dividends received by all shareholders, provided the distribution had been subject to corporate tax at the full 35 percent corporate tax rate. Congress responded by enacting § 1(h)(11). Rather than actually integrating the corporate and individual income taxes, for taxable years after 2003, § 1(h)(11) generally taxes dividends at the same preferential rates as long-term capital gains.

The issue of who economically bears the burden of the corporate tax— an issue on which there is disagreement among economists—relates to the desirability of integration. Some analysts believe that integration is less appropriate if the burden is shifted primarily to workers or consumers than it would be if the burden is borne primarily by shareholders, while others believe that even if the burden is shifted primarily to workers or consumers, integration is desirable because it would mitigate the shifting of the burden to workers or consumers.

3.2. *American Law Institute Study Reporter's Proposals*

Among the arguments made in favor of integration is that the current double taxation system distorts the corporation's choice as to whether to fund new investment by issuing shares to raise equity capital or by borrowing. This problem was addressed by Professor William Andrews, the Reporter for the American Law Institute, Federal Income Tax Project, Subchapter C: Proposals on Corporate Acquisitions and Dispositions (1980), in his Study on Distributions (1980), published with the adopted ALI proposals. Professor Andrews adopted a different approach to the proper relationship between the corporate and individual tax systems as reflected in the following excerpt:

> Most of the troubles with existing law arise from two main uncompensated biases: 1) the bias against new equity investment, and 2) the bias in favor of nondividend distributions. The main proposals in this Study are to alleviate those biases by providing

relief for the former and imposing a compensatory excise on the latter. If these proposals were adopted, all distributions would be subjected to more nearly comparable tax burdens, and contributions to corporate equity (negative distributions) would attract a comparable benefit (negative burden). In such a system, the difficult definitional problems with which present law struggles would be eliminated or reduced substantially in significance.

While the proposals complement one another in important ways, an effort has been made to analyze and present them separately, as follows:

1) *Relief for new equity.* Reporter's Proposal R1 is to relieve the bias against new equity by provision of a deduction based on newly contributed equity capital. The main proposal is for a corporate dividends-paid deduction, limited to a specified rate on the amount of net newly contributed equity capital, akin to the interest deduction that would have resulted from a debt investment. Adoption of this proposal would move a long way toward eliminating problems of differentiation between debt and equity, since it would attach comparable tax consequences to any investment of outside funds.

The main problem in implementing this proposal is defining net newly contributed investment in a manner that will exclude mere refinancing of accumulated earnings or previously contributed capital. This problem would be minimized if an appropriate tax burden were imposed generally on nondividend distributions.

2) *Nondividend distributions.* Reporter's Proposal R2 would deal with the present bias in favor of nondividend distributions by imposing some increased tax on them. One possibility would be to impute redemption distributions pro rata to continuing shareholders, as if they had received a dividend and used it to buy out redeeming shareholders. The proposal offered is simply to impose a flat-rate, compensatory excise on nondividend distributions, to be withheld and paid over to the government by the distributing corporation.

Adoption of this proposal would take much of the pressure off questions of dividend equivalence, with which present law struggles, and make it possible to be much more lenient about stock dividends and spin-offs, and the bailout opportunities they generate under existing law.

3) *Intercorporate investments and distributions.* A corporation can now purchase dividend-paying stock of another corporation and enjoy 85 or 100 percent exemption from corporate income tax on the dividends received from this investment. A purchase of shares from noncorporate shareholders represents an indirect way of distributing funds out of corporate solution, and the intercorporate dividend deduction operates to contract the corporate income tax base accordingly, but all without any

distribution, as such, by either corporation. Reporter's Proposal R3 would distinguish between direct and mere portfolio investment. In the case of portfolio investment, the dividend-received deduction and cognate provisions would be made inapplicable; with respect to direct investment those provisions would continue in effect, but purchases of shares would be treated as nondividend distributions subject to the compensatory excise in Reporter's Proposal R2.

Note how the ALI Subchapter C Study Reporter's proposals deal with the transition problem that would arise if an integration proposal were adopted. Assuming that the shareholders bear some substantial portion of the corporate tax and that such tax burden is capitalized into, i.e., depresses, the value of corporate stock and hence the price at which the current owners purchased the stock, adoption of full integration or dividend relief would give rise to a windfall economic gain for those shareholders. By limiting relief to the portion of the yield on new equity which approximates interest, the Reporter's approach eliminates this problem. How does the proposal for a corporate level excise tax on nondividend distributions increase the fairness or the efficiency of taxation of corporate income? It appears that the perceived problem is that a greater price can be obtained for shares sold back to the corporation than for shares sold to another investor because the other investor could be expected to discount the value of the shares to an amount below the value of a proportionate amount of the corporation's assets to reflect the double taxation of a flow of dividends from those assets. Are the ALI Reporter's proposals intended to solve the same problems as are perceived by those who favor integration?

3.3. *Treasury Department Study*

In January of 1992 the Treasury Department released a comprehensive study on integration of the corporate and individual income tax systems. United States Department of the Treasury, Report on Integration of The Individual and Corporate Tax Systems: Taxing Business Income Once (1992). The Report concluded that integration of the corporate and individual taxes would reduce three economic distortions inherent in the classical corporate tax system. First, the current incentive to invest in non-corporate rather than corporate businesses would be reduced. A correlative effect would be the elimination of "self-help integration" through disincorporation. Second, elimination of the double taxation of earnings from corporate equity investment would reduce the tax incentive to finance new corporate investment with debt rather than equity. Finally, integration would reduce the incentive to retain earnings in some cases, and in other cases to repurchase shares with borrowed funds in order to avoid the double tax on distribution of corporate profits.

The Report focused on the basic operation of three prototype systems: (1) a dividend exclusion system; (2) a shareholder allocation system; and (3) a Comprehensive Business Income Tax (CBIT) system. An imputation credit system was discussed but was not proposed. The Treasury Department recommended further study of the relatively simple dividend exclusion model and the CBIT prototype.

Under the dividend exclusion prototype, the corporate income tax would continue in effect much in its current form. Distributions to shareholders, however, would be tax-free. The primary technical complexity of the dividend exclusion model is the need to maintain an Excludable Distributions Account (EDA) at the corporate level. The EDA would be credited with an amount equal to the income on which the corporation paid taxes and only distributions charged against the EDA would be eligible for exemption at the shareholder level. Such a rule is necessitated, in part, by the existence of tax preferences, such as accelerated depreciation and expensing of certain capital outlays, in the corporate income tax. These preferences sometimes are viewed as effectively reducing the rate of corporate taxation, or, alternatively, as effectively exempting some of the corporation's income from taxation. Since income sheltered from corporate taxation by preferences would not augment the EDA, distributions of such income would be taxable to shareholders. In addition, because gains from the sale of stock in some part generally represent retained earnings, some mechanism is necessary to ameliorate double taxation caused by taxing gains from the sale of stock. To deal with this issue, the Treasury Report proposed a Dividend Reinvestment Plan (DRIP) election under which the corporation and shareholders could deem earnings to have been distributed by the corporation and recontributed by the shareholders, thereby effecting an increase in the shareholders' bases in their stock. By recommending a dividend exclusion model, the report avoids the need to reexamine some basic policy decisions regarding the treatment of distributions to tax-exempt organizations. If relief from double taxation were effected at the corporate level rather than at the shareholder level, tax-exempt organizations, such as charities and pension funds owning stock in a taxable corporation, might have to be taxed in order to insure that all corporate income is taxed at least once.[7]

Presumably because the dividend exclusion prototype, while eliminating the double tax on corporate income, does not eliminate all differences between debt and equity financing,[8] the Treasury Report sets forth the more radical CBIT prototype. The distinctive feature of the CBIT is the denial of the interest deduction for both corporate and unincorporated businesses, coupled with an exemption for interest income. Under the CBIT, corporations, partnerships, and proprietorships all would pay an entity level tax on their profits, but both dividends and interest would be tax exempt to the recipient.[9] It appears that the Treasury Department's CBIT prototype does not provide for a deduction for reasonable compensation to owner/employees, such as partners and proprietors, instead relying on an exemption from the CBIT for small businesses "[b]ecause it is difficult to separate returns to capital from returns to labor in the case of very small businesses." Failure to provide such a deduction is a problem whenever the owner-employee is in a marginal tax bracket less than the CBIT rate, which was proposed to be 31

---

[7] The Report recommends that the exclusion of interest and dividend income be extended to nonresident alien shareholders only through tax treaties. See Ault, Corporate Integration and Tax Treaties: Where Do We Go From Here?, 4 Tax Note Int'l 545 (March 16, 1992); Doernberg, International Aspects of Individual and Corporate Tax Integration, 4 Tax Notes Int'l 535 (March 26, 1992).

[8] Under the dividend exclusion prototype system, dividends are not deductible by the corporation but are excludable by the shareholder. Interest, however, is deductible by the corporation but includable by the creditor. While facially there appears to be a single level of tax on both interest and dividends, when a tax exempt organization is the lender the interest income escapes taxation at both the corporate and investor levels.

[9] The Report recommends that the exemption for interest and dividend income be extended to nonresident alien shareholders and bondholders only through tax treaties.

percent (equal to the then maximum individual rate). In such cases the CBIT could overtax the owner/employee unless the small business exception applied.

The Treasury Department Report examines, but recommends against adoption of a full imputation model, in other words, treating all corporations the same as partnerships and taxing the shareholders currently on their respective shares of corporate income, without regard to distributions. Such a system, the report concludes, would be too complex to administer. The Treasury Department likewise rejected an imputation credit system, which in effect treats the corporate income tax largely as a refundable withholding tax on corporate distributions, as too complex. Since the latter is the mechanism employed by most industrialized countries that have adopted integration systems, the Treasury's conclusion is somewhat puzzling.

In opting to recommend two systems that levy a flat rate entity level tax on business profits and exempt from tax distributions representing the yield on capital investment, the Treasury Department appears to have decided implicitly that income from capital should be taxed at a flat rate, rather than at progressive rates. This conclusion is re-enforced by the Treasury's rejection of the shareholder allocation and imputation credit systems, both of which can be structured to preserve principles of progressive taxation. Indeed, the arguments in favor of either of the systems include the preservation of taxation of dividends at the shareholder's personal tax rate. The traditional equity criterion of tax policy has been subordinated in the Treasury Report. Instead, the Treasury Department appears to have given primacy to administrability and economic efficiency criteria.

The concept of taxing some types of income at flat rates, whether higher or lower than the maximum marginal rate applying to other types of income, previously had not received an imprimatur of approval from any branch of the government. Some analogy might lie, however, in the provisions that between 1969 and 1981 imposed a maximum rate of 50 percent on income from services, and the provisions in effect from 1954 until 1978 imposing a maximum rate of 25 percent on capital gains (limited to $50,000 of gains after 1969).

Notwithstanding the rejection by the Treasury Department of the imputation credit system for integration of the corporate and individual income taxes, the American Law Institute developed a report concerning an imputation credit prototype for integration. Under the ALI's model, the corporate income tax would be converted into a withholding tax on shareholder income taxes on corporate distributions. For purposes of computing shareholders' incomes, distributions would be grossed-up by the amount of taxes "withheld" by the corporation. Because the withholding tax would be creditable against income from other sources and refundable to the extent it exceeded taxes on income from other sources, progressivity at the shareholder level could be preserved. Unlike the Treasury Department proposals, the ALI draft proposals provide for a limited pass-through to shareholders of certain tax preferences. Like the Treasury Department Report, the ALI proposal recognizes that some relief for capital gains realized on the sale of corporate stock may be appropriate to relieve the double tax on retained earnings. Thus the ALI also recommends a constructive dividend-reinvestment rule. In addition, the ALI report proposed other rules to coordinate the imputation credit system with the capital loss limitation rules, which should be relaxed, and the § 1014 step-up in basis at death, which should be denied in an amount (roughly speaking) equal to any dividends (grossed-up by withholding taxes) that could be distributed to the heirs on which taxes had been withheld.

Finally, because the ALI proposals, unlike the Treasury Department Report, tax corporate earnings at the shareholder's rate, the elimination of even a single level of tax on corporate earnings distributed to tax-exempt shareholders must be considered. Although the ALI proposals take no position on the treatment of tax-exempt organizations generally, the proposals include the imposition of tax on both the interest and dividend income of tax-exempt entities, while allowing them the credit for corporate taxes paid with respect to the dividend income and another credit for taxes withheld on the interest income. The ALI proposals include a separate corporate interest withholding tax with respect to interest paid by corporations; although interest would remain deductible in computing taxable income, corporations would pay a flat rate tax on interest payments made and recipients of interest would receive a credit for this tax although their interest income would not be grossed-up by the withholding tax paid by the corporation. The purpose of this rather complex rule is to equalize the treatment of debt and equity investments by tax-exempt entities. Because of this limited goal, the ALI proposals make no recommendation regarding the tax rate that should be imposed on tax-exempt entities, and note that if the rate were set at zero and, as recommended, both credits are refundable, no tax would be imposed on corporate earnings distributed as either dividends or interest to tax-exempt shareholders. Rules dealing with foreign shareholders and bondholders in domestic corporations would be similarly structured, with a Foreign Investor's Tax imposed at the corporate level on interest and dividends paid to foreign investors (and gains realized by foreign investors on sales of securities in domestic corporations) and a refundable credit against that tax at the shareholder level. Again, the ALI proposes no recommendation regarding the tax rate.

SECTION 2.   IDENTIFYING TAXABLE CORPORATE ENTITIES

Under current law, corporate income in the highest income bracket is taxed at a marginal rate of 35 percent (although surtax rates applicable to certain lower income brackets result in effective marginal rates as high as 39 percent), while the maximum individual marginal tax rate is 39.6 percent. At differing income levels, however, a significant rate differential may exist between the corporate and individual rates, but the relationship cannot be described as systematic. A maximum corporate tax rate that is the same as the maximum individual tax rate, coupled with the double taxation of corporate earnings, even though the portion of the double tax imposed at the shareholder level is only 20 percent (the maximum rate on both dividends received from a corporation and long-term capital gains on the sale of corporate stock), serves as a disincentive to organizing businesses in the corporate form unless nontax factors strongly indicate that the corporate form is necessary or desirable or an election under subchapter S is available.

Prior to 1987, the maximum individual rate exceeded the maximum corporate rate by a substantial amount. In addition, although corporate earnings were taxed twice, if the distribution of earnings was delayed until liquidation of the corporation or of the shareholder's entire interest in the corporation, the shareholder level tax was incurred at preferential rates for long-term capital gains that were even more generous than the current preference. These factors, coupled with the pre-1987 statutory provisions that permitted corporations to distribute appreciated property to shareholders without recognizing a corporate level taxable gain on the appreciation, served as a strong tax inducement to incorporate a profitable business venture that was going to accumulate and reinvest earnings, even if no nontax factors indicated that incorporation was preferable to the partnership or sole proprietorship form. Conversely, if the venture was expected to produce a tax loss, for example a business experiencing tax losses in its early years attributable in part to tax preferences, it was advantageous to be taxed as a partnership or sole proprietorship, even though the use of the corporate form would have been desirable to accomplish some nontax objective.

The pre-1987 incentive for individuals to shift income to a corporation (or obtain other tax benefits available only in corporate form) gave rise to controversies regarding whether income should be taxed to the corporation or directly to its owners. The materials in this chapter examine the resolution of this issue in several contexts. Under the current rate structure, however, in many instances the positions of the government and the taxpayer may be reversed, i.e., the government may seek to tax income at the corporate rather than the individual rate; individual taxpayers may have the opposite objective.

A. WHAT IS A "CORPORATION" UNDER THE INCOME TAX

INTERNAL REVENUE CODE: Sections 7701(a)(3); 7704.

REGULATIONS: Sections 301.7701–1(a) and (b), –2(a), (b)(1)–(7), –3(a), (b)(1), (c)(1)(i)–(iv), –4(a)–(c).

A business may be conducted by an entity that under the law of the state or foreign nation in which the entity is organized is a corporation, a partnership, or neither a corporation nor a partnership, for example, a limited liability company (LLC) or a business trust. For federal income tax purposes, however, Treas.Reg. § 301.7701–2 provides that a business entity with two or more members is classified as either a partnership or a corporation. For this purpose the term "business entity" is very broad. See Treas.Reg. § 301.7701–1(a)(2). It includes not only corporations, partnerships (both limited and general), and limited liability companies formally organized as such under state law, but also less formally organized associations as well as business trusts. Under Treas.Reg. § 301.7701–2(b), any business organized as a "corporation" under relevant state or federal law automatically is classified as a corporation for federal income tax purposes, as are insurance companies and most banks. Treas.Reg. § 301.7701–2(b)(8) lists specified foreign entities that are *per se* corporations for federal income tax purposes.

A "business entity" that is not listed in Treas.Reg. § 301.7701–2(b) as a corporation is classified as a partnership if it has two or more members. Treas.Reg. § 301.7701–3(a) and   (b). An entity that is classified as a partnership may elect to be taxed as a corporation, Treas.Reg. § 301.7701–3(a), but if no election is made, the entity is by default classified as a partnership. Treas.Reg. § 301.7701–3(b). Treas.Reg. § 301.7701–4 distinguishes businesses, financial operations, and ventures taxed as partnerships from trusts established for the protection and conservation of property (which may include a trade or business operated by the trust as a sole proprietor). A business entity with one member, for example, a single member limited liability company, that is not a corporation, is disregarded for tax purposes. Treas.Reg. § 301.7701–2(c)(2), –3(b)(1)(ii).

Rules and Regulations, Department of the Treasury, Internal Revenue Service, Simplification of Entity Classification Rules

T.D. 8697, 1997–1 C.B. 215.

Explanation of Provisions

Section 7701(a)(2) of the Code defines a partnership to include a syndicate, group, pool, joint venture, or other unincorporated organization, through or by means of which any business, financial operation, or venture is carried on, and that is not a trust or estate or a corporation. Section 7701(a)(3) defines a corporation to include associations, joint-stock companies, and insurance companies.

The existing regulations for classifying business organizations as associations (which are taxable as corporations under section 7701(a)(3)) or as partnerships under section 7701(a)(2) are based on the historical differences under local law between partnerships and corporations. Treasury and the IRS believe that those rules have become increasingly formalistic. This document replaces those rules with a much simpler approach that generally is elective.

As stated in the preamble to the proposed regulations, in light of the increased flexibility under an elective regime for the creation of organizations classified as partnerships, Treasury and the IRS will continue to monitor carefully the uses of partnerships in the international context and will take appropriate action when partnerships are used to achieve results that are inconsistent with the policies and rules of particular Code provisions or of U.S. tax treaties.

A. *Summary of the Regulations*

Section 301.7701–1 provides an overview of the rules applicable in determining an organization's classification for federal tax purposes. The first step in the classification process is to determine whether there is a separate entity for federal tax purposes. The regulations explain that certain joint undertakings that are not entities under local law may nonetheless constitute separate entities for federal tax purposes; however, not all entities formed under local law are recognized as separate entities for federal tax purposes. Whether an organization is treated as an entity for federal tax purposes is a matter of federal tax law, and does not affect the rights and obligations of its owners under local law. For example, if a domestic limited liability company with a single individual owner is disregarded as an entity separate from its owner under § 301.7701–3, its individual owner is subject to federal income tax as if the company's business was operated as a sole proprietorship.

An organization that is recognized as a separate entity for federal tax purposes is either a trust or a business entity (unless a provision of the Code expressly provides for special treatment, such as the Qualified Settlement Fund rules (§ 1.468B) or the Real Estate Mortgage Investment Conduit (REMIC) rules, see section 860A(a)). The regulations provide that trusts generally do not have associates or an objective to carry on business for profit. The distinctions between trusts and business entities, although restated, are not changed by these regulations.

Section 301.7701–2 clarifies that business entities that are classified as corporations for federal tax purposes include corporations denominated as such under applicable law, as well as associations, joint-stock companies, insurance companies, organizations that conduct certain banking activities, organizations wholly owned by a State, organizations that are taxable as corporations under a provision of the Code other than section 7701(a)(3), and certain organizations formed under the laws of a foreign jurisdiction (including a U.S. possession, territory, or commonwealth).

* * *

Any business entity that is not required to be treated as a corporation for federal tax purposes (referred to in the regulation as an eligible entity) may choose its classification under the rules of § 301.7701–3. Those rules provide that an eligible entity with at least two members can be classified as either a partnership or an association, and that an eligible entity with a single member can be classified as an association or can be disregarded as an entity separate from its owner.

* * *

In order to provide most eligible entities with the classification they would choose without requiring them to file an election, the regulations provide default classification rules that aim to match taxpayers' expectations (and thus reduce the number of elections that will be needed). The regulations adopt a passthrough default for domestic entities, under which a newly formed eligible entity will be classified as a partnership if it has at least two members, or will be disregarded as an entity separate from its owner if it has a single owner. The default for foreign entities is based on whether the members have limited liability. Thus a foreign eligible entity will be classified as an association if all members have limited liability. A foreign eligible entity will be classified as a partnership if it has two or more members and at least one member does not have limited liability; the entity will be disregarded as an entity separate from its owner if it has a single owner and that owner does not have limited liability. Finally, the default classification for an existing entity is the classification that the entity claimed immediately prior to the effective date of these regulations. An entity's default classification continues until the entity elects to change its classification by means of an affirmative election.

An eligible entity may affirmatively elect its classification on Form 8832, Entity Classification Election. The regulations require that the election be signed by each member of the entity or any officer, manager, or member of the entity who is authorized to make the election and who represents to having such authorization under penalties of perjury. An election will not be accepted unless it includes all of the required information * * *.

Taxpayers are reminded that a change in classification, no matter how achieved, will have certain tax consequences that must be reported. For example, if an organization classified as an association elects to be classified as a partnership, the organization and its owners must recognize gain, if any, under the rules applicable to liquidations of corporations.

B. Discussion of Comments on the General Approach and Scope of the Regulations

Several comments requested clarification with regard to the rules for determining when an owner of an interest in an organization will be respected as a bona fide owner for federal tax purposes. Some commentators * * * relying on Rev.Rul. 93–4, 1993–1 C.B. 225, suggested that if two wholly-owned subsidiaries of a common parent were the owners of an organization, those owners would not be respected as bona fide owners and the organization would be treated as having only one owner (the common parent). Although the determination of whether an organization has more than one owner is based on all the facts and circumstances, the fact that some or all of the owners of an organization are under common control does not require the common parent to be treated as the sole owner. Consistent with this approach, Rev.Rul. 93–4 treated two wholly owned subsidiaries as associates and then classified the foreign entity based on the four corporate characteristics under section 7701. While these four factors will no longer apply with the adoption of the regulations, determining whether the subsidiaries are associates continues to be an issue.

* * *

C. Discussion of Comments Relating to the Elective Regime

Most of the commentators agreed that the default rules included in the proposed regulations generally would match taxpayers' expectations. * * *

Some commentators requested that taxpayers be allowed to make classification elections with their first tax returns. The regulations retain the requirement that elections be made at the beginning of the taxable year. Treasury and the IRS continue to believe that it is appropriate to determine an entity's classification at the time that it begins its operations. Taxpayers can specify the date on which an election will be effective, provided that date is not more than 75 days prior to the date on which the election is filed (irrespective of when the interest was acquired) and not more than 12 months after the date the election was filed. * * *

The regulations limit the ability of an entity to make multiple classification elections by prohibiting more than one election to change an entity's classification during any sixty month period. * * * [T]he regulations permit the Commissioner to waive the application of the sixty month limitation by letter ruling. However, waivers will not be granted unless there has been more than a fifty percent ownership change. The sixty month limitation only applies to a change in classification by election; the limitation does not apply if the organization's business is actually transferred to another entity.

* * *

DETAILED ANALYSIS

1. LIMITED LIABILITY COMPANIES

A businesses may be conducted through a limited liability company (LLC) organized under state law, rather than through a partnership, corporation, or through direct ownership. Although state law recognizes an LLC as a distinct type of entity, as discussed in the preamble to the check-a-box entity classification regulations, there is no single federal tax regime specifically dealing with LLCs. Rather, for federal tax purposes, an LLC can be treated as a corporation, a partnership, or be "disregarded" depending on the specific facts.

An LLC that has two or more members (owners) is an entity separate and distinct from its members and is treated either as a corporation or a partnership. Treas.Reg. § 301.7701–2(a). An LLC with two or more members that does not elect to be taxed as a corporation will be treated as a partnership for purposes of federal income taxation. Treas.Reg. § 301.7701–3(b)(1)(i). The LLC is taxed as a corporation only if it affirmatively elects to be so treated for federal tax purposes. Treas.Reg. § 301.7701–3(a). An LLC with a single owner (whether the owner is an individual, corporation, or partnership) may elect to be taxed as a corporation, but if it does not so elect, it will disregarded as an entity separate and distinct from its owner. Treas.Reg. § 301.7701–3(b)(1)(ii). When an LLC is disregarded as an entity, its assets, liabilities, income items, and deduction items will be treated as owned, owed, received, and incurred directly by its owner. Thus, for example, if a corporation is the sole owner of a LLC that has not elected to be taxed as a corporation, the business conducted by the LLC will be treated as a division of the corporation, the income of which is reportable directly on the corporation's income tax return. In practice, LLCs rarely, if ever, elect to be taxed as corporations, and virtually every LLC is either treated as a partnership or is disregarded for federal tax purposes.

A single member LLC that is a disregarded entity provides a corporation with a vehicle to insulate other assets against the risks of the business in the LLC while allowing the corporation to offset losses from one line of business against profits from another line of business on its federal income tax return. A corporation that has a subsidiary cannot offset the losses from its subsidiaries' business against its profits in computing federal income taxes, unless the corporations file a consolidated return pursuant to the complex rules discussed in Chapter 9. Through the use of multiple LLCs that are disregarded entitles, an incorporated business can manage the risk of loss in its various lines of business without suffering adverse federal tax consequences. Thus, the practice is becoming increasingly common.

2. PUBLICLY TRADED PARTNERSHIPS AND LIMITED LIABILITY COMPANIES

2.1. *General*

Section 7704 generally treats as a corporation any partnership the interests in which are traded on an established securities market or are readily tradable on a secondary market or a substantial equivalent of a secondary market. The provision in fact only applies to limited partnerships and limited liability companies, because under state law general partnership interests cannot be traded. The legislative history explains that a secondary market for partnership interests exists if prices are regularly quoted by brokers or dealers who are making a market for such interest. Occasional accommodation trades of partnership interests, a buy-sell agreement between the partners (without more), or the occasional repurchase or redemption by the partnership or acquisition by a general partner of partnership interests will not be treated as a secondary market or the equivalent thereof. However, if the partners have regular and ongoing opportunities to dispose of their interests, the interests are tradable on the equivalent of a secondary market. Meaningful restrictions imposed on the right to transfer partnership interests may preclude classification as a corporation, even if some interests are actually traded. See H.Rep. 100–495, 100th Cong., 1st Sess. 943–950 (1987).

2.2. *Meaning of "Publicly Traded"*

Treas.Reg. 1.7704–1(b) and (c) provide definitions of the statutory terms "established securities market" and "readily tradable on a secondary market or the substantial equivalent of a secondary market." Established securities markets include not only exchanges, but also interdealer quotation systems. A secondary market or a substantial equivalent of a secondary market exists if the partners are readily able to buy, sell, or exchange their interests in a manner that is economically comparable to trading on an established securities market. Interests are readily tradable on a secondary market or its equivalent if (1) firm quote trading exists, even if only one person makes available bid or offer quotes; (2) the holder of an interest has a readily available, regular and ongoing opportunity to sell or exchange such interest through a public means of obtaining or providing information of offers to buy, sell, or exchange interests; or (3) buyers and sellers have the opportunity to buy, sell, or exchange interests in a time frame and with the regularity and continuity that the existence of a market maker would provide. Interests are not readily tradable, however, unless the partnership participates in establishing the market or recognizes transfers by admission of purchasers to the partnership or recognizes their rights as transferees. Treas.Reg. § 1.7704–1(d). A redemption or repurchase plan can result in partnership interests being publicly traded.

The Regulations provide several "safe harbors." In determining whether there is public trading of the partnership interests, Treas.Reg. § 1.7704–1(e) disregards transfers in which the transferee has a transferred basis, transfers at death, transfers between family members, transfers pursuant to certain redemption agreements, and certain other transfers. The most broadly applicable safe harbor excludes from the definition of publicly traded partnership so-called "private placements"—that is, any partnership whose interests are not required to be registered under the

Securities Act of 1933, but only if the partnership does not have more than 100 members. Treas.Reg. § 1.7704–1(h).

In addition, a partnership will not be considered to be traded on the substantial equivalent of a secondary market for any year in which no more than 2 percent of the total interests in partnership capital or profits is sold or disposed of in transactions other than private transfers, qualifying redemptions, certain other safe harbors. Treas.Reg. § 1.7704–1(j). It is clear from § 7704(f), dealing with the effect of a partnership becoming a corporation, that § 7704 contemplates the possibility that a partnership which is initially recognized as such might in a subsequent year become a corporation under § 7704. The "lack of actual trading" safe harbor, which applies on a year-by-year basis, suggests further that a partnership might be considered to be a corporation in one year and a partnership in the next, when it meets the safe harbor. This result could give rise to a constructive liquidation of the "corporation" with tax consequences to the entity and the investors or, conversely, the constructive formation of a new corporation.

2.3. *Exceptions*

A broad exception to § 7704 allows publicly traded limited partnerships more than 90 percent of whose gross income is from certain "passive sources" to continue to be treated as partnerships. Qualified income for this purpose, with some narrow exceptions, includes interest, dividends, real property rents, gain from the sale of real property, and income and gains from the exploration, development, extraction, processing, refining, etc. of oil and gas or any other natural resource. While the legislative history is silent as to the reason for this exception, it presumably is based on the historic use of limited partnerships in organizing such ventures and the availability of conduit taxation for other entity forms (e.g., real estate investment trusts) making investments of this type. See I.R.C. § 7704(c) and (d).

An additional exception permits publicly traded partnerships that were in existence on December 31, 1987 to continue to be treated as partnerships as long as they do not add a "substantial new line of business." See I.R.C. § 7704(g).

3. FOREIGN BUSINESS ENTITIES

Treas.Reg. § 301.7701–2(b)(8) lists certain foreign business entities (including entities organized in U.S. possessions, territories, and commonwealths) that are classified as *per se* corporations. The listed organizations are limited liability entities, such as the British Public Limited Company, the French Societe Anonyme, the German Aktiengesellschaft, and the Sociedad Anonima in South American countries (Sociedade Anonima in Brazil). Other foreign entities can elect under Treas.Reg. § 301.7701–3(a) whether to be treated as a partnership or as a corporation. In contrast to the partnership default classification rules for domestic organizations, under Treas.Reg. § 301.7701–3(b)(2), the default rule for foreign entities is based on whether the members have limited liability. For a foreign entity that provides limited liability for its members and which is not a per se corporation (listed in Treas.Reg. § 301.7701–2(b)(8)(i)), the default rule is that the entity is a corporation unless it elects to be a partnership (if it has two or more members) or a disregarded entity (if it has only one member). A foreign entity is classified as a partnership if it has two or more members and at least one member does not have limited liability. If a foreign entity has only one owner, who does not have limited liability, the entity is disregarded unless it elects to be regarded as a corporation.

4.   BUSINESS TRUSTS

4.1. *General*

Treas.Reg. § 301.7701–4(a) though (c) distinguish between "ordinary" trusts, the purpose of which are the protection or conservation of trust property, and trusts which are in effect a joint enterprise of the beneficiaries to conduct a business for profit and which will be classified as either a partnership or a corporation under Treas.Reg. § 301.7701–2 and – 3. No cases have been decided or rulings issued under the current version of Treas.Reg. § 301.7701–4, but a number of cases were decided under the prior version of the classification regulations. In most of those cases the question of whether the trust was an "ordinary trust" or a business association taxable as a corporation turned on whether the trust beneficiaries were in fact business associates. For example, in Outlaw v. United States, 494 F.2d 1376 (Ct.Cl.1974), a trust was formed to own and manage some 10,000 acres of farm land and employed 18 to 20 full-time and 60 to 70 temporary workers to engage in a full scale agricultural operation. The trust had 27 original investors, which increased over time to 41 investors; its objective was to carry on a business of owning, developing and exploiting agricultural lands for income; its existence continued notwithstanding the withdrawal, death, bankruptcy, etc. of an investor; all decisions were made by an operating committee akin to a corporate board of directors; the investor-beneficiaries were liable only to the extent of their proportionate interests in the trust assets; and the investors could freely transfer their interests after giving notice to the trustee. Based on these facts, the trust was classified as a business entity taxable as a corporation.

See also Rev.Rul. 80–75, 1980–1 C.B. 314 (trust established by promoter to conduct business activity and to which beneficiaries contributed cash in exchange for income interests and a remainder to person designated by the holder of income interest was classified as a business association); Estate of Bedell v. Commissioner, 86 T.C. 1207 (1986) (testamentary trust which conducted a manufacturing business lacked "associates" because the beneficiaries had "not planned a common effort or entered into a combination for the conduct of a business enterprise," only a few of the beneficiaries participated in trust affairs, and their interests were not transferrable); Elm Street Realty Trust v. Commissioner, 76 T.C. 803 (1981) (Acq.) (inter vivos estate planning trust which received rent from net lease of real estate had business objective because trustee had the power to sell real estate and purchase and improve other real estate; the trust, however, lacked associates because donee beneficiaries had no role in creation of trust, only limited powers to participate in the trust's activities, and beneficial interests were transferable only under restrictive conditions). Hynes v. Commissioner, 74 T.C. 1266 (1980), held that a trust created to develop and sell real estate was to be taxed as an association even though the grantor held 100 percent of the beneficial interest; the term "associates" in the regulations encompasses "one-person corporations."

Under current Treas.Reg. § 301.7701–4, trusts such as those involved in *Outlaw* and *Estate of Bedell* would be classified as business entities rather than as ordinary trusts, and under Treas.Reg. § 301.7701–2 and –3 then would be classified as partnerships unless the trusts elected to be taxed as corporations.

4.2. *Liquidating Trusts*

Treas.Reg. § 301.7701–4(d) provides a special rule for "liquidating" trusts which will not be held to be associations taxable as corporations as long as the primary purpose of the trust is the liquidation and distribution of the assets transferred to it. See Abraham v. United States, 406 F.2d 1259 (6th Cir.1969), where the court found the trust to be an association taxable as a corporation and not a liquidating trust; the trustees were given broad powers to conduct the prior business, although the powers were not actually exercised. In Walker v. United States, 194 F.Supp. 522 (D.Mass.1961), an irrevocable trust was set up to hold an office building as part of a family settlement of a dispute over the property. The court found the arrangement was a trust; it had centralized management but no transferability of interests or continuity of life because of the power of the beneficiaries to revoke the arrangement. The purpose of the trust was the liquidation of the property and not the carrying on of business for profit. See also Rev.Rul. 75–379, 1975–2 C.B. 505, and Rev.Rul. 63–228, 1963–2 C.B. 229, finding certain trusts which engaged in business activities to fall within the "liquidation" exception; Rev.Proc. 82–58, 1982–2 C.B. 847, amplified by Rev.Proc. 91–15, 1991–1 C.B. 484 (guidelines for advance rulings on classification of liquidation trusts), modified and amplified by Rev. Proc. 94–45, 1994–2 C.B. 684 (income reporting requirements and checklist for ruling requests).

5.   SPECIAL CLASSES OF CORPORATIONS

5.1. *Conduit Corporations Relieved of Federal Tax*

Regulated investment companies investing in securities (mutual funds) are in effect relieved of corporate tax liability as respects the dividends and capital gains from their stock investments if they currently distribute this income to their shareholders. A mutual fund to this extent is thus treated as a conduit rather than a taxable entity. See I.R.C. §§ 851–855.

In 1960 Congress extended conduit treatment to real estate investment trusts (REITs) otherwise taxable as corporations (see §§ 856–860); and in 1986 conduit treatment was extended to real estate mortgage investment conduits (REMICs) (§§ 860A–860G).

5.2. *Other Special Corporate Treatment*

Certain classes of corporations are given special treatment as respects the computation or treatment of taxable income, e.g., banks, insurance companies, and foreign corporations; or exemption from tax, e.g., the various tax-exempt organizations (as to which, however, the corporate income tax is applicable to the extent of "unrelated business taxable income," I.R.C. §§ 511–514).

B. REGARD AND DISREGARD OF THE CORPORATE ENTITY

Prior to the late 1980s, a combination of tax and nontax factors led many individuals to choose to operate businesses, whether closely held or publicly held, as C corporations subject to the double tax regime.

More recently, the development of the limited liability company business form, coupled with the adoption of the check-a-box classification regulations, and the current rate structure have strongly influenced individuals to conduct closely held businesses in a form subject to the partnership taxation rules of Subchapter K, particularly if capital is a material income producing factor. Even if a corporate structure is desired, the shareholders often elect to be taxed under Subchapter S, which eliminates the corporate level tax and results in the corporation's income being taxed directly to the shareholders. In both of these instances, the question of whether business income or deductions properly are attributable to the entity or directly to the owners does not frequently arise. In the classic C corporation, however, the question of whether particular items of income or deduction are properly attributable to the corporation or directly to the shareholders is very important. Under the current rate structures (taking into account the preferential treatment of capital gains and dividends) and statutory scheme, the C corporation is the form of choice only for publicly traded businesses, which are forced into the C corporation regime, and businesses whose income is derived primarily from personal services of the shareholders (largely because the C corporation form has certain, but limited, advantages over the other forms with regard to the provision of tax-free fringe benefits to the shareholder-employees). Most of the case law regarding this issue, however, developed in the context of closely held businesses in which capital was a material income producing factor.

Strong v. Commissioner[*]

United States Tax Court, 1976.
66 T.C. 12.

■ TANNENWALD, JUDGE: * * *

Petitioners formed a partnership for the purpose of constructing and operating an apartment complex on real estate contributed by several partners. In order to obtain financing for the project, it was necessary to transfer the property to a corporation wholly owned by the partnership so that mortgage loans could be made at an interest rate in excess of the limit imposed by State usury laws on loans to individuals. Construction and operation of the apartments generated net operating losses during the years in issue which were reported on the partnership's returns and as distributive shares on the individual returns of the petitioners. The respondent determined that the corporation, as owner of the property, was the proper party to report those losses. Petitioners allege that the corporation was a nominee whose ownership should be disregarded for tax purposes. The crux of petitioners' case is that the corporation was merely a sham or device used for the purpose of avoiding the New York usury statute, that it performed no acts other than those essential to that function, and that to treat it as the actual owner of the property would be to exalt form over substance.

---

[*]   [Ed.: The decision was affirmed by order, 553 F.2d 94 (2d Cir.1977).]

The use of sham or dummy corporations to avoid application of the usury laws is a recognized practice in New York. Hoffman v. Lee Nashem Motors, Inc., 20 N.Y.2d 513, 231 N.E.2d 765, 285 N.Y.S.2d 68 (1967) * * *. There is no doubt that petitioners sought to do business in partnership form and that the corporation was, at least in their eyes, a mere tool or conduit. Their argument is not without some appeal, but we conclude that it should not be accepted.

The principal guidepost on the road to recognition of the corporate entity is Moline Properties v. Commissioner, 319 U.S. 436 (1943). In that case, a corporation was organized as part of a transaction which included the transfer of mortgaged property to it by the shareholder, the assumption by it of the outstanding mortgages, and the transfer of its stock to a voting trustee named by the mortgagee as security for additional advances. Later the indebtedness was repaid and the shareholder reacquired control of the corporation. Thereafter it mortgaged and sold some of the property it held, and leased another portion. The Court held that the corporation was a separate entity from its inception, and stated its rule of decision as follows:

> The doctrine of corporate entity fills a useful purpose in business life. Whether the purpose be to gain an advantage under the law of the state of incorporation or to avoid or to comply with the demands of creditors or to serve the creator's personal or undisclosed convenience, *so long as that purpose is the equivalent of business activity or is followed by the carrying on of business by the corporation,* the corporation remains a separate taxable entity. * * * In Burnet v. Commonwealth Improvement Co., 287 U.S. 415, this Court appraised the relation between a corporation and its sole stockholder and held taxable to the corporation a profit on a sale to its stockholder. This was because the taxpayer had adopted the corporate form for purposes of his own. The choice of the advantages of incorporation to do business, it was held, required the acceptance of the tax disadvantages. [319 U.S. at 438–439. Fn. refs. omitted; emphasis supplied.]

Cases following *Moline Properties* have generally held that the income from property must be taxed to the corporate owner and will not be attributed to the shareholders, unless the corporation is a *purely passive dummy* or is used for a tax-avoidance purpose. Harrison Property Management Co. v. United States, 475 F.2d 623 (Ct.Cl.1973); Taylor v. Commissioner, 445 F.2d 455 (1st Cir.1971); National Investors Corp. v. Hoey, 144 F.2d 466 (2d Cir.1944) * * *. This is particularly true where the demand that the corporate entity be ignored emanates from the shareholders of a closely held corporation. See Harrison Property Management Co. v. United States, supra at 626; David F. Bolger, 59 T.C. 760, 767 n. 4 (1973).[8] It has been suggested that the prevailing approach misses the point by focusing (as do the parties herein) on the viability of the corporate entity rather than the situs of real beneficial

---

[8] See also Higgins v. Smith, 308 U.S. 473 (1940). Cf. Colin v. Altman, 39 App.Div.2d 200, 333 N.Y.S.2d 432, 433–434 (1st Dept.1972): "the corporate veil is never pierced for the benefit of the corporation or its stockholders. * * * [The sole stockholder] is not the corporation either in law or fact and, having elected to take the advantages [of incorporation], it is not inequitable to subject him to the disabilities consequent upon his election."

or economic ownership. Kurtz & Kopp, "Taxability of Straw Corporations in Real Estate Transactions," 22 Tax Lawyer 647 (1969). However, the thrust of the case law, as we read it, is to leave the door open to the argument that a corporation played a purely nominal or "straw" role in a transaction, while closing it firmly against any contention that a corporation may be disregarded simply because it is the creature of its shareholders. * * *

The Supreme Court has held that shareholder domination, even to the extent that a corporation could be said to lack beneficial ownership of its assets and income, is insufficient to permit taxpayers to ignore the corporation's existence. National Carbide Corp. v. Commissioner, 336 U.S. 422, 433–434 (1949); Moline Properties v. Commissioner, supra. The Court of Appeals for the Second Circuit, to which appeal will lie herein, has similarly refused to disregard the interposition of a corporate entity between shareholders and their property, except where the corporation has not purported to deal with the property in its own right. The focus is on business purpose or activity with respect to the particular property whose ownership is in question.

In Paymer v. Commissioner, 150 F.2d 334 (2d Cir.1945), two brothers formed a pair of corporations (Raymep and Westrich) to which they transferred legal title to certain real estate. Their purpose was to deter execution against the property by their individual creditors. Neither corporation engaged in any business activity except that Raymep obtained a loan and as part security "assigned to the lender all the lessor's rights, profits and interest in two leases on the property and covenanted that they were in full force and effect and that it was the sole lessor." 150 F.2d at 336. Westrich was disregarded on the ground that it "was at all times but a passive dummy which did nothing but take and hold title to the real estate conveyed to it. It served no business purpose *in connection with the property.*" 150 F.2d at 337. (Emphasis added.) Raymep, however, was not disregarded, because it did perform a business function as the owner of the property.

In Jackson v. Commissioner, 233 F.2d 289 (2d Cir.1956), affg. 24 T.C. 1 (1955), the Court of Appeals disregarded holding companies which lacked separate business purpose or activity, stating that the situation was encompassed within the foregoing language in its opinion in *Paymer* and further observing:

> A natural person may be used to receive income which in fact is another's. So, too, a corporation, although for other purposes a jural entity distinct from its stockholders, may be used as a mere dummy to receive income which in fact is the income of the stockholders or of someone else; in such circumstances, the company will be disregarded. [233 F.2d at 290 n. 2.]

Finally, in Commissioner v. State-Adams Corp., 283 F.2d 395 (2d Cir.1960), revg. 32 T.C. 365 (1959)(which involved a different factual situation), the court characterized its holding in *Paymer* as "nothing more than a restatement of the fundamental rule that income from real estate held in the name of a nominee will be taxed to the beneficial owner, not to the nominee." 283 F.2d at 398 (fn. ref. omitted). The mere fact that some of the documents herein speak in terms of a corporate nominee is not sufficient to bring petitioners within the exception to the general rule. Harrison Property Management Co. v. United States, supra.

In short, a corporate "straw" may be used to separate apparent from actual ownership of property, without incurring the tax consequences of an actual transfer; but to prevent evasion or abuse of the two-tiered tax structure, a taxpayer's claim that his controlled corporation should be disregarded will be closely scrutinized. If the corporation was intended to, or did in fact, act in its own name with respect to property, its ownership thereof will not be disregarded.

The degree of corporate purpose and activity requiring recognition of the corporation as a separate entity is extremely low. Thus, it has been stated that "a determination whether a corporation is to be considered as doing business is not necessarily dependent upon the quantum of business" and that the business activity may be "minimal." See Britt v. United States, 431 F.2d 227, 235, 237 (5th Cir.1970).

In this case, the corporation's purpose and activities were sufficient to require recognition of its separate ownership of the property in question and, a fortiori, of its existence as a taxable entity. The purpose to avoid State usury laws is a "business purpose" within the meaning of *Moline Properties.* Collins v. United States, supra; David F. Bolger, supra. The corporation had broad, unrestricted powers under its charter. Compare Collins v. United States, supra. Its activities were more extensive than those which required recognition of Raymep in Paymer v. Commissioner, supra. Like Raymep, it borrowed money on the security of rents; in addition, it mortgaged the property itself and it received and applied the loan proceeds. It engaged in the foregoing activities on more than one occasion and is more vulnerable than was the corporation in Collins v. United States, supra, which was also formed to avoid usury law restrictions and placed only a single mortgage. These activities, carried out in its own name, go beyond "transactions essential to the holding and transferring of title." See Taylor v. Commissioner, 445 F.2d at 457. The fact that the corporation in this case, unlike those in other cases, did not enter into any leases does not, in our opinion, constitute a sufficient basis for distinguishing their thrust.[10]

Furthermore, the corporation was otherwise treated by the partnership in a manner inconsistent with petitioners' contention that the two were the same entity. The partnership agreement required that deeds, loan agreements, and mortgages "executed by or on behalf of the partnership" be signed by both Jones and Strong; property standing in the corporate name was so dealt with on Jones' signature alone. Separation of title to the various parcels permitted the creation of mutual easements, an act which would have been prevented by the doctrine of merger had the properties been under common ownership. See Parsons v. Johnson, 68 N.Y. 62 (1877); Snyder v. Monroe County, 2 Misc.2d 946, 153 N.Y.S.2d 479, 486 (1956), affd. mem. 6 A.D.2d 854,

---

[10] In Raymep Realty Corp., 7 T.C.M. 262 (1948), relied upon by petitioners we held the execution of a lease in the name of a corporate nominee titleholder did not require the corporation to be recognized as a taxable entity. We characterized that single act as "a purely nominal adjunct to the holding of title." Here, by contrast, the business activity was the raison d'être of the corporation.

175 N.Y.S.2d 1008 (4th Dept.1958). The corporation applied for and received insurance on the property in its own name.

Finally, although not determinative, an element to be considered is the fact that the corporate vehicle in this case, whatever the parties' intentions, carried with it the usual baggage attending incorporation, including limitation of the shareholders' personal liability during construction. Jones alone was potentially responsible (as guarantor) for repayment of the construction loans.

In the final analysis, the corporation herein fits the mold articulated in Collins v. United States, supra:

> The fact remains, however, that the corporation did exist and did perform the function intended of it until the permanent loan was consummated. It was more than a business convenience, it was a business necessity to plaintiffs' enterprise. As such, it came into being. As such, it served the purpose of its creation. [386 F.Supp. at 21.]

The fact that the purpose and use of the corporation was limited in scope is beside the point. See Sam Siegel, 45 T.C. 566, 577 (1966).

The tide of judicial history is too strong to enable petitioners to prevail, albeit that the activities of the corporation were substantially less than those involved in most of the decided cases with the exception of Collins v. United States, supra.

Having set up a separate entity through which to conduct their affairs, petitioners must live with the tax consequences of that choice. Indeed, the very exigency which led to the use of the corporation serves to emphasize its separate existence. See Moline Properties v. Commissioner, 319 U.S. at 440; David F. Bolger, 59 T.C. at 766. Our conclusion is not based upon any failure of the petitioners to turn square corners with respondent; they consistently made clear their intention to prevent separate taxation of the corporation if legally possible. They took most precautions consistent with business exigency to achieve that end. We simply hold that their goal was not attainable in this case.

Reviewed by the Court.

Decisions will be entered for the respondent.

Commissioner v. Bollinger

Supreme Court of the United States, 1988.
485 U.S. 340.

■ JUSTICE SCALIA delivered the opinion of the Court.

Petitioner the Commissioner of Internal Revenue challenges a decision by the United States Court of Appeals for the Sixth Circuit holding that a corporation which held record title to real property as agent for the corporation's shareholders was not the owner of the property for purposes of federal income taxation. 807 F.2d 65 (1986). * * *

I

Respondent Jesse C. Bollinger, Jr., developed, either individually or in partnership with some or all of the other respondents, eight apartment complexes in Lexington, Kentucky. (For convenience we will refer to all the ventures as "partnerships.") Bollinger initiated development of the first apartment complex, Creekside North Apartments, in 1968. The Massachusetts Mutual Life Insurance Company agreed to provide permanent financing by lending $1,075,000 to "the corporate nominee of Jesse C. Bollinger, Jr." at an annual interest rate of eight percent, secured by a mortgage on the property and a personal guaranty from Bollinger. The loan commitment was structured in this fashion because Kentucky's usury law at the time limited the annual interest rate for noncorporate borrowers to seven percent. Ky.Rev.Stat. §§ 360.010, 360.025 (1972). Lenders willing to provide money only at higher rates required the nominal debtor and record title holder of mortgaged property to be a corporate nominee of the true owner and borrower. On October 14, 1968, Bollinger incorporated Creekside, Inc., under the laws of Kentucky; he was the only stockholder. The next day, Bollinger and Creekside, Inc., entered into a written agreement which provided that the corporation would hold title to the apartment complex as Bollinger's agent for the sole purpose of securing financing, and would convey, assign, or encumber the property and disburse the proceeds thereof only as directed by Bollinger; that Creekside, Inc., had no obligation to maintain the property or assume any liability by reason of the execution of promissory notes or otherwise; and that Bollinger would indemnify and hold the corporation harmless from any liability it might sustain as his agent and nominee.

Having secured the commitment for permanent financing, Bollinger, acting through Creekside, Inc., borrowed the construction funds for the apartment complex from Citizens Fidelity Bank and Trust Company. Creekside, Inc., executed all necessary loan documents including the promissory note and mortgage, and transferred all loan proceeds to Bollinger's individual construction account. Bollinger acted as general contractor for the construction, hired the necessary employees, and paid the expenses out of the construction account. When construction was completed, Bollinger obtained, again through Creekside, Inc., permanent financing from Massachusetts Mutual Life in accordance with the earlier loan commitment. These loan proceeds were used to pay off the Citizens Fidelity construction loan. Bollinger hired a resident manager to rent the apartments, execute leases with tenants, collect and deposit the rents, and maintain operating records. The manager deposited all rental receipts into, and paid all operating expenses from, an operating account, which was first opened in the name of Creekside, Inc., but was later changed to "Creekside Apartments, a partnership." The operation of Creekside North Apartments generated losses for the taxable years 1969, 1971, 1972, 1973, and 1974, and ordinary income for the years 1970, 1975, 1976, and 1977. Throughout, the income and losses were reported by Bollinger on his individual income tax returns.

Following a substantially identical pattern, seven other apartment complexes were developed by respondents through seven separate partnerships. For each venture, a partnership executed a nominee agreement with Creekside, Inc., to obtain financing. (For one of the ventures, a different Kentucky corporation, Cloisters, Inc., in which Bollinger had a 50 percent interest, acted as the borrower and titleholder. For convenience, we will refer to both Creekside and Cloisters as "the corporation.") The corporation transferred the construction loan proceeds to the partnership's construction account, and the partnership hired a construction supervisor who oversaw construction. Upon completion of construction, each partnership actively managed its apartment complex, depositing all rental receipts into, and paying all expenses from, a separate partnership account for each apartment complex. The corporation had no assets, liabilities, employees, or bank accounts. In every case, the lenders regarded the partnership as the owner of the apartments and were aware that the corporation was acting as agent of the partnership in holding record title. The partnerships reported the income and losses generated by the apartment complexes on their partnership tax returns, and respondents reported their distributive share of the partnership income and losses on their individual tax returns.

The Commissioner of Internal Revenue disallowed the losses reported by respondents, on the ground that the standards set out in National Carbide Corp. v. Commissioner, 336 U.S. 422, 69 S.Ct. 726, 93 L.Ed. 779 (1949), were not met. The Commissioner contended that *National Carbide* required a corporation to have an arm's length relationship with its shareholders before it could be recognized as their agent. Although not all respondents were shareholders of the corporation, the Commissioner took the position that the funds the partnerships disbursed to pay expenses should be deemed contributions to the corporation's capital, thereby making all respondents constructive stockholders. Since, in the Commissioner's view, the corporation rather than its shareholders owned the real estate, any losses sustained by the ventures were attributable to the corporation and not respondents. Respondents sought a redetermination in the United States Tax Court. The Tax Court held that the corporations were the agents of the partnerships and should be disregarded for tax purposes. Bollinger v. Commissioner, 48 TCM 1443 (1984), ¶ 84,560 PBH Memo TC. On appeal, the United States Court of Appeals for the Sixth Circuit affirmed. 807 F.2d 65 (1986). We granted the Commissioner's petition for certiorari.

II

For federal income tax purposes, gain or loss from the sale or use of property is attributable to the owner of the property. See Helvering v. Horst, 311 U.S. 112, 116–117, 61 S.Ct. 144, 147 (1940); Blair v. Commissioner, 300 U.S. 5, 12, 57 S.Ct. 330 (1937) * * *. The problem we face here is that two different taxpayers can plausibly be regarded as the owner. Neither the Internal Revenue Code nor the regulations promulgated by the Secretary of the Treasury provide significant guidance as to which should be selected. It is common ground between the parties, however, that if a corporation holds title to property as agent for a partnership, then for tax purposes the partnership and not the corporation is the owner. Given agreement on that premise, one would suppose that there would be agreement upon the conclusion as well. For each of respondents' apartment complexes, an agency agreement expressly provided that the corporation would "hold such property as nominee and agent for" the partnership, App. to Pet. for Cert. 21a, n. 4, and that the partnership would have sole control of and responsibility for the apartment complex. The partnership in each instance was identified as the principal and owner of the property during financing, construction, and operation. The lenders, contractors, managers, employees, and tenants—all who had contact with the development—knew that the corporation was merely the agent of the partnership, if they knew of the existence of the corporation at all. In each instance the relationship between the corporation and the partnership was, in both form and substance, an agency with the partnership as principal.

The Commissioner contends, however, that the normal indicia of agency cannot suffice for tax purposes when, as here, the alleged principals are the controlling shareholders of the alleged agent corporation. That, it asserts, would undermine the principle of Moline Properties v. Commissioner, 319 U.S. 436, 63 S.Ct. 1132 (1943), which held that a corporation is a separate taxable entity even if it has only one shareholder who exercises total control over its affairs. Obviously, *Moline*'s separate-entity principle would be significantly compromised if shareholders of closely held corporations could, by clothing the corporation with some attributes of agency with respect to particular assets, leave themselves free at the end of the tax year to make a claim—perhaps even a good-faith claim—of either agent or owner status, depending upon which choice turns out to minimize their tax liability. The Commissioner does not have the resources to audit and litigate the many cases in which agency status could be thought debatable. Hence, the Commissioner argues, in this shareholder context he can reasonably demand that the taxpayer meet a prophylactically clear test of agency.

We agree with that principle, but the question remains whether the test the Commissioner proposes is appropriate. The parties have debated at length the significance of our opinion in *National Carbide Corp. v. Commissioner,* supra. In that case, three corporations that were wholly owned subsidiaries of another corporation agreed to operate their production plants as "agents" for the parent, transferring to it all profits except for a nominal sum. The subsidiaries reported as gross income only this sum, but the Commissioner concluded that they should be taxed on the entirety of the profits because they were not really agents. We agreed, reasoning first, that the mere fact of the parent's control over the subsidiaries did not establish the existence of an agency, since such control is typical of all shareholder-corporation relationships, id., 336 U.S. at 429–434, 69 S.Ct., at 730–732; and second, that the agreements to pay the parent all profits above a nominal amount were not determinative since income must be taxed to those who actually earn it without regard to anticipatory assignment, id., at 435–436, 69 S.Ct., at 733–734. We acknowledged, however, that there was such a thing as "a true corporate agent * * * of [an] owner-principal," id. at 437, 69 S.Ct., at 734, and proceeded to set forth four indicia and two requirements of such status, the sum of which has become known in the lore of federal income tax law as the "six *National Carbide* factors":

"[1] Whether the corporation operates in the name and for the account of the principal, [2] binds the principal by its actions, [3] transmits money received to the principal, and [4] whether receipt of income is attributable to the services of employees of the principal and to assets belonging to the principal are some of the relevant considerations in determining whether a true agency exists. [5] If the corporation is a true agent, its relations with its principal must not be dependent upon the fact that it is owned by the principal, if such is the case. [6] Its business purpose must be the carrying on of the normal duties of an agent." Id., at 437, 69 S.Ct., at 734 (footnotes omitted).

We readily discerned that these factors led to a conclusion of nonagency in *National Carbide* itself. There each subsidiary had represented to its customers that it (not the parent) was the company manufacturing and selling its products; each had sought to shield the parent from service of legal process; and the operations had used thousands of the subsidiaries' employees and nearly $20 million worth of property and equipment listed as assets on the subsidiaries' books. * * *

The Commissioner contends that the last two *National Carbide* factors are not satisfied in the present case. To take the last first: The Commissioner argues that here the corporation's business purpose with respect to the property at issue was not "the carrying on of the normal duties of an agent," since it was acting not as the agent but rather as the owner of the property for purposes of Kentucky's usury laws. We do not agree. It assuredly was not acting as the owner in fact, since respondents represented themselves as the principals to all parties concerned with the loans. Indeed, it was the lenders themselves who required the use of a corporate nominee. Nor does it make any sense to adopt a contrary-to-fact legal presumption that the corporation was the principal, imposing a federal tax sanction for the apparent evasion of Kentucky's usury law. To begin with, the Commissioner has not established that these transactions were an evasion. Respondents assert without contradiction that use of agency arrangements in order to permit higher interest was common practice, and it is by no means clear that the practice violated the spirit of the Kentucky law, much less its letter. It might well be thought that the borrower does not generally require usury protection in a transaction sophisticated enough to employ a corporate agent—assuredly not the normal *modus operandi* of the loan shark. That the statute positively envisioned corporate nominees is suggested by a provision which forbids charging the higher corporate interest rates "to a corporation, the principal asset of which shall be the ownership of a one (1) or two (2) family dwelling," Ky.Rev.Stat. § 360.025(2)(1987)—which would seem to prevent use of the nominee device for ordinary home-mortgage loans. In any event, even if the transaction did run afoul of the usury law, Kentucky, like most States, regards only the lender as the usurer, and the borrower as the victim. See Ky.Rev.Stat. § 360.020 (1987) (lender liable to borrower for civil penalty), § 360.990 (lender guilty of misdemeanor). Since the Kentucky statute imposed no penalties upon the borrower for allowing himself to be victimized, nor treated him as *in pari delictu,* but to the contrary enabled him to pay back the principal without any interest, and to sue for double the amount of interest already paid (plus attorney's fees), see Ky.Rev.Stat. § 360.020 (1972), the United States would hardly be vindicating Kentucky law by depriving the usury victim of tax advantages he would otherwise enjoy. In sum, we see no basis in either fact or policy for holding that the corporation was the principal because of the nature of its participation in the loans.

Of more general importance is the Commissioner's contention that the arrangements here violate the fifth *National Carbide* factor—that the corporate agent's "relations with its principal must not be dependent upon the fact that it is owned by the principal." The Commissioner asserts that this cannot be satisfied unless the corporate agent and its shareholder principal have an "arm's-length relationship" that includes the payment of a fee for agency services. The meaning of *National Carbide's* fifth factor is, at the risk of understatement, not entirely clear. Ultimately, the relations between a corporate agent and its owner-principal are *always* dependent upon the fact of ownership, in that the owner can cause the relations to be altered or terminated at any time. Plainly that is not what was meant, since on that interpretation all subsidiary-parent agencies would be invalid for tax purposes, a position which the *National Carbide* opinion specifically disavowed. We think the fifth *National Carbide* factor—so much more abstract than the others—was no more and no less than a generalized statement of the concern, expressed earlier in our own discussion, that the separate-entity doctrine of *Moline* not be subverted.

In any case, we decline to parse the text of *National Carbide* as though that were itself the governing statute. As noted earlier, it is uncontested that the law attributes tax consequences of property held by a genuine agent to the principal; and we agree that it is reasonable for the Commissioner to demand unequivocal evidence of genuineness in the corporation-shareholder context, in order to prevent evasion of *Moline*. We see no basis, however, for holding that unequivocal evidence can only consist of the rigid requirements (arm's-length dealing plus agency fee) that the Commissioner suggests. Neither of those is demanded by the law of agency, which permits agents to be unpaid family members, friends, or associates. See Restatement (Second) of Agency §§ 16, 21, 22 (1958). It seems to us that the genuineness of the agency relationship is adequately assured, and tax-avoiding manipulation adequately avoided, when the fact that the corporation is acting as agent for its shareholders with respect to a particular asset is set forth in a written agreement at the time the asset is acquired, the corporation functions as agent and not principal with respect to the asset for all purposes, and the corporation is held out as the agent and not principal in all dealings with third parties relating to the asset. Since these requirements were met here, the judgment of the Court of Appeals is

Affirmed.

DETAILED ANALYSIS

1.   APPLICATION OF THE BUSINESS ACTIVITY TEST

1.1. *General*

In cases involving the issue whether a corporation should be taxed as a separate entity, the taxpayer and the IRS may be on different sides, depending on the tax stakes involved. For example, a taxpayer whose personal tax bracket exceeds the corporate rate will urge that the corporation be recognized for tax purposes so as to postpone imposition of his higher individual rate on the income; the IRS may seek to disregard the corporate entity. Conversely, as in *Strong* and *Bollinger*, the taxpayer who seeks to deduct directly losses that result from activities of the "corporation" or who utilizes the corporate form only for nominal purposes, will urge that the formal existence of the corporation be ignored; the IRS will assert that the activities of the corporation warrant its recognition as a separate taxable entity. Historically, taxpayers generally had little success in attempts to assert that the corporation which they created should be disregarded for tax purposes; the courts generally have upheld the IRS's position that the activities of the corporation were sufficient to warrant it being regarded as a separate entity for tax purposes. (Note that even in *Bollinger*, in which the taxpayer prevailed, the corporation was not ignored for tax purposes; it was treated as the shareholders' agent.) On the other hand, in certain cases the corporate entity should be disregarded to prevent tax avoidance. The following cases illustrate the results reached by the courts in this area.

1.2. *Insufficient Business Activity—Corporate Entity Disregarded*

In Greenberg v. Commissioner, 62 T.C. 331 (1974), aff'd per curiam, 526 F.2d 588 (4th Cir.1975), two individuals formed five corporations to develop large residential subdivisions. All the corporations performed identical functions. Following a disagreement between the two shareholders, four corporations were liquidated, and one of the shareholders was redeemed out of the remaining corporation. The taxpayer was left as the sole shareholder of the remaining corporation. The taxpayer reported capital gains on the amounts received in liquidation of the four corporations. The court held that the four liquidated corporations were merely shams; all the income earned by those corporations was the income of the continuing corporation; and the amounts distributed to the taxpayer were simply a dividend: "These [liquidated] corporations served no purpose except to obtain a tax benefit which is not 'business' sufficient to grant them recognition as separate 'taxworthy' entities for Federal tax purposes." See also Kimbrell v. Commissioner, 371 F.2d 897 (5th Cir.1967) (IRS's contention upheld that corporations involved were "mere depositories" for the individual shareholder's income where the corporation engaged in no business activities but merely received the income for the services performed by the individual taxpayer); Patterson v. Commissioner, T.C. Memo. 1966–239, aff'd per curiam, 68–2 U.S.T.C. ¶ 9471 (2d Cir.1968) (the corporation performed no useful function and the taxpayer, a professional boxer, "simply did not put flesh on the bones of the corporate skeleton").

In Robucci v. Commissioner, T.C. Memo 2011–19, the Tax Court disregarded the entity status of two corporations formed by a practicing psychiatrist on the advice of an accountant in order to avoid federal employment taxes. The psychiatrist was the sole shareholder of both corporations. One corporation was formed as a professional services corporation and was a five percent limited partner in a limited liability company (LLC) in which 95 percent of the partnership interests were held by the psychiatrist and through which he conducted his practice. The corporation entered into a management agreement with the LLC, but it did not have any assets, employees, contracts, or customers other than the

LLC, and it did not actually perform any services. The court concluded that the corporation "was not formed for a purpose that 'is the equivalent of a business activity' within the meaning of Moline Props., Inc. v. Commissioner, 319 U.S. at 429." The second corporation was formed purportedly to manage reimbursements of various expenses of the LLC, including a medical reimbursement plan, but while it maintained a bank account to which and from which some deposits and withdrawals were made, there was "scant evidence" of regular transfers of funds related to the purported activity of the corporation. The transfers of funds "to the extent they occurred, were the equivalent of taking money from one pocket and putting it into another. Such a procedure hardly qualifies as a 'business activity' within the contemplation of *Moline Props., Inc.*" The court concluded that both corporations were hollow shells, neither of which carried on any business after incorporation. Thus, their income was the taxpayer's income. Because the professional services corporation was disregarded as an entity, the limited liability company was treated as a sole member disregarded entity and all of its income was taxed directly to the taxpayer.

In Noonan v. Commissioner, 52 T.C. 907 (1969), aff'd per curiam, 451 F.2d 992 (9th Cir.1971), a corporation received income as a limited partner from a business enterprise in which the sole shareholder was a general partner. The Tax Court acknowledged that the corporation had been properly organized, but it refused to recognize the separate corporate entity where the record was devoid of evidence showing any active business purpose.

1.3. *Sufficient Business Activity—Corporate Entity Respected*

1.3.1.   *General*

In situations similar to that in Strong v. Commissioner, the courts have rejected taxpayers' attempts to have a corporation holding title to real estate disregarded and treated as a "mere dummy" for tax purposes. In Bolger v. Commissioner, 59 T.C. 760 (1973), the taxpayer was engaged in real estate investment and finance. The taxpayer would locate a building which a business desired to lease. The following transactions would take place, often all on the same day: Taxpayer would organize a nominally capitalized corporation with the shareholders being himself and other individuals; the corporation would purchase the building and enter into a lease with the user; and the corporation would then issue its notes, secured by a mortgage on the property and an assignment of the lease, to an institutional lender to obtain funds for the purchase. The term of the mortgage notes and the primary term of the lease were usually coextensive. The mortgage provided that the property could be transferred, with the transferees being obligated to fulfill the terms of the mortgage and the lease except that the transferees would assume no personal financial obligation for the payment of principal and interest on the note. Such transferees were also obligated to keep the corporation in existence. Immediately after these transactions, the corporation would then convey the property to its shareholders subject to the lease and mortgage and without any cash payment to the corporation. The transferee shareholders would assume the corporation's obligation under the lease and mortgage, but they had no personal liability thereon except to the extent of the property they received. The taxpayers claimed that they were entitled to the depreciation deductions generated by the properties. The IRS asserted that only the corporation had a depreciable interest in the property. The court first held that both at the time the corporation was created and after the transfer of the property to the shareholders, the corporation was a viable business entity. Although at the latter point the corporation was stripped of its assets and, by virtue of its various agreements could not engage in any business activity, the court held it was sufficient that the corporation continued to be liable on its obligations to the lender and remained in existence with full powers to own property and transact business. The court went on to hold, however, that because of the transfer of the property to the shareholders, the individual taxpayers were entitled to the depreciation deductions. The case presaged the Tax Court's position in *Strong* that there is very little room for a taxpayer successfully to assert disregard of the corporate form which the taxpayer has adopted.

Weekend Warrior Trailers, Inc. v. Commissioner, T.C. Memo. 2011–105, involved the formation of a corporation solely to engage in a series of transactions designed to reduce income taxes using a strategy to shift income to an employee stock ownership plan (ESOP), a scheme that no longer is possible because the relevant statutory rules that produced the results were amended after the years in question in the case. The sole shareholder of the taxpayer, Weekend Warrior Trailers, which manufactured travel trailers, established a sibling corporation, Leading Edge, to provide design and management services, to be performed by the taxpayer's shareholder as an employee of Leading Edge (while he also continued to serve as a managerial employee of the taxpayer), for the taxpayer's manufacturing operations. The taxpayer also transferred its employees to Leading Edge, which then leased the employees to the taxpayer. The taxpayer made substantial payments (millions of dollars) to Leading Edge for management services. The IRS disallowed a deduction for the taxpayer's management fee on the grounds that (1) Leading Edge " 'should be disregarded for Federal income tax purposes as Leading Edge Design, Inc. lacked both economic substance and economic purpose and was formed for the primary purpose of obtaining tax benefits', and (2) 'Transactions entered into between Leading Edge Design, Inc. and Weekend Warrior Trailers, Inc. should be disregarded for Federal Income tax' purposes because they lacked economic substance and economic purpose and were entered into for the primary purpose of obtaining tax benefits.' " Applying the *Moline Properties* doctrine, the Tax Court rejected the IRS's arguments, stating as follows:

> Even if a corporation was not formed for a valid business purpose, it nevertheless must be respected for tax purposes if it actually engaged in business activity. See Moline Props., Inc. v. Commissioner, 319 U.S. at 438–439; Bass v. Commissioner, [50 T.C. 595, 602 (1968)]. The prongs of the test under Moline Props. are alternative prongs. See Moline Props., Inc. v. Commissioner, supra at 438–439; Bass v. Commissioner, supra at 602; see also Rogers v. Commissioner, T.C. Memo. 1975–289 ("Moline establishes a two-pronged test, the first part of which is business purpose, and the second, business activity. * * * Business purpose or business activity are alternative requirements."). Accordingly, the issue turns on whether Leading Edge engaged in business activity. Whether a corporation is carrying on sufficient business activity to require its recognition as a separate entity is a question

of fact. Bass v. Commissioner, supra at 602 (status of a corporation respected when testimony established that "the corporation was managed as a viable concern, and not as simply a lifeless facade.")

The court concluded that, on the record, Leading Edge was not a "lifeless facade." Nevertheless, the taxpayer's scheme failed because the court went on to hold that the evidence did not prove that the management fees paid by Weekend Warrior to Leading Edge were necessary or reasonable.

See also Tomlinson v. Miles, 316 F.2d 710 (5th Cir.1963) (corporation formed to hold title to real estate to facilitate its ultimate sale held taxable on the gain from such sales although the corporation held title "for the use and benefit" of the shareholders); Taylor v. Commissioner, 445 F.2d 455 (1st Cir.1971) (opening of a checking account and the execution of deeds and a mortgage constituted "business activity"; "If [the corporation] were to serve only as a straw, it should have only performed those transactions essential to the holding and transferring of title."); Commissioner v. State-Adams Corp., 283 F.2d 395 (2d Cir.1960) (court rejected the taxpayer's argument that the holding of title did not warrant recognition of the corporate entity since the corporate functions of collecting money with respect to the land constituted "business activity"); Britt v. United States, 431 F.2d 227 (5th Cir.1970) (where the court held, for the taxpayer, that the corporation was a separate entity since the corporate activity in signing notes and collecting dividends constituted "business activity").

Recognition of the corporate entity because the corporation conducts sufficient business activity does not preclude a *Bollinger* type argument that the corporation nevertheless was acting merely as the agent of its shareholders.

1.3.2.   *Investment Activity*

Taxpayers have sometimes been successful in having their corporations recognized as separate entities under the *Moline Properties* concept of "business activity" even though the corporate function consisted only of a single investment asset rather than active business operations. In Siegel v. Commissioner, 45 T.C. 566 (1966) (Acq.), the taxpayer, wishing to limit his potential liability, established a Panamanian corporation to invest in a farm joint venture in Cuba. The taxpayer had no immediate need for the profits and his plan at the time of the incorporation was ultimately "to obtain the fruits of the venture through liquidation of the corporation." Although the other members of the joint venture actively participated in the farming operation, the corporation's only activity was to receive money from the venture, deposit it in its account, and periodically invest and reinvest the funds in the Cuban farming venture. The Tax Court concluded that there was a sufficient amount of business activity: "Nor may it be said that [the corporation's] minimal activity did not constitute the conduct of business. The point is that [the corporation] was formed for only a limited purpose, namely, to invest in the joint venture * * *."[10] See also Bateman v. United States, 490 F.2d 549 (9th Cir.1973) (corporation which owned a limited partnership interest in a partnership in which its sole shareholder was active and conducted no business other than this passive investment

---

[10] Section 951, added in 1962, would now deal with the situation in *Siegel* to the extent that the utilization of a foreign rather than a domestic corporation was involved.

was treated as a separate taxable entity based on the trial court's finding that the business purpose for the corporation was to build a cash reserve fund to buy out retiring or deceased partners' interests).

2.   IRRELEVANCE OF ACTUAL DIRECTION OF CORPORATE ACTIVITIES

In attempting to have the corporation disregarded for tax purposes, the IRS has argued unsuccessfully that the corporation is not engaged in "business activity" in cases in which the shareholder-owner has completely dominated the corporate activities. For example, in Bass v. Commissioner, 50 T.C. 595 (1968), the taxpayer organized a Swiss corporation to which he transferred working interests in oil and gas leases. The IRS attempted to discount the business actions of the corporation on the theory that the taxpayer "actually made the business decisions for the corporation." The Tax Court concluded that the corporation was a viable business entity since it had "acted" like a genuine corporation in paying the expenses of the business and filing returns. The *Bass* opinion emphasized the Supreme Court's language in National Carbide Corp. v. Commissioner, 336 U.S. 422 (1949), that "the fact that the owner retains direction of its affairs down to the minutest detail * * * [makes] no difference tax-wise." A like result was reached in Ross Glove Co. v. Commissioner, 60 T.C. 569 (1973) (Acq.).

After failing to prevent the classification of professional service corporations as corporations for tax purposes, see, e.g., Kurzner v. United States, 413 F.2d 97 (5th Cir. 1969), the IRS began to attack professional service corporations generally on the basis that such corporations were shams that did not actually earn their incomes. However, as long as corporate formalities were followed and the shareholder-employees respected the corporate form in conducting business, the IRS met with little success. Compare Achiro v. Commissioner, 77 T.C. 881 (1981) (corporate form of management services company respected at taxpayer's behest even though shareholders were sole employees and primary purpose of forming corporation was to reduce income taxes) with Jones v. Commissioner, 64 T.C. 1066 (1975) (court reporter who formed personal service corporation taxed individually because court rules required reporter to be an individual rather than a corporation).

3.   APPLICATION OF THE AGENCY RATIONALE

The *Moline Properties* doctrine makes it difficult to disregard the corporate entity if the corporation conducts any business, particularly because the requisite activity threshold is low. Taxpayers have sought to achieve the same result as is produced by the disregard of corporate entity theory on the ground that a principal-agent relationship exists between the shareholder and the corporation. Therefore the income involved is the shareholder's rather than the corporation's. As explained in the *Bollinger* opinion, this argument was based on language in National Carbide Corp. v. Commissioner, 336 U.S. 422, 437–39 (1949).

Prior to the *Bollinger* decision, most cases turned on application of the fifth *National Carbide* factor, whether the relations between the principal and the agent depended on the principal's ownership of the agent. For example, in Harrison Property Management Co., Inc. v. United States, 475 F.2d 623 (Ct.Cl.1973), three partners transferred title to oil-bearing property to the corporation, retaining all beneficial rights and interests in the property in themselves. The primary reason for the formation of the corporation was the orderly management of the property in the event of the death of one of the individuals. The corporation received the income from oil leases, paid expenses incident thereto, and filed a fiduciary income tax return showing all net income distributed to the three individuals. The individuals reported the amounts in their individual returns. The IRS contended that the corporation should be treated as a separate entity and was taxable on the income. The court first held that the corporation was a taxable entity under the *Moline Properties* test and then rejected the taxpayer's alternative contention that an agency relationship existed between the corporation and the three individuals:

> *National Carbide* makes it clear that the formal designation of "agency agreement" is not conclusive; the significant criteria, as we understand them, are whether the so-called "agent" would have made the agreement if the so-called "principals" were not its owners, and conversely whether the "principals" would have undertaken the arrangement if the "agent" were not their corporate creature. * * *

> [W]e do not doubt that the present plaintiffs fail the test. It is inconceivable that Harrison Property Management Co., Inc. would have made its alleged "agency" contract with property owners other than its own shareholders, the Harrisons, or that the latter would have agreed to such an arrangement with the corporation if they did not own and control it. Obviously the agreement was deliberately drawn, in conjunction with the special provisions of the corporate charter, so that the company would service its owners alone, and was made solely because they were its owners. The entire operating arrangement was custom-made for that very purpose. * * * In other words, all of the corporation's relations with the beneficial owners of the managed property were wholly dependent on the fact that they were the sole shareholders. * * *

The Courts of Appeals decisions preceding *Bollinger* viewed the six *National Carbide* factors as being of greater importance than did the Supreme Court in *Bollinger,* and also emphasized the fifth factor. Roccaforte v. Commissioner, 708 F.2d 986 (5th Cir.1983), rev'g, 77 T.C. 263 (1981), held that while the first four factors were relevant, in order to establish an agency relationship it was mandatory that the final two factors—relations between the principal and agent must be arms' length and the business purpose of the corporation must be to carry on the normal duties of an agent—be met. Because the Tax Court had found that the relations between the shareholders and the corporation were dependent on the fact that the "agent" was owned by the principals, the court held that a true agency had not been established. The facts upon which the non-arms' length relationship conclusion was based were that the corporation was owned by its shareholders in the same percentages which the shareholders held their interests in the partnership which they claimed owned the property for tax purposes, the sole function of the "agent" was to borrow money in avoidance of state usury laws, and it was not compensated for its services. Similar results were reached in Ourisman v. Commissioner, 760 F.2d 541 (4th Cir.1985); Vaughn v. United States, 740 F.2d 941 (Fed.Cir.1984); Jones v. Commissioner, 640 F.2d 745 (5th Cir.1981); Frink v. Commissioner, 798 F.2d 106 (4th Cir.1986), vacated 485 U.S. 973 (1988);

George v. Commissioner, 803 F.2d 144 (5th Cir.1986), vacated 485 U.S. 973 (1988). In all of these cases the court concluded that a corporation is not compensated and which is owned by one or more of its principals could not be a true agent under the fifth *National Carbide* factor.

Several Courts of Appeals decisions, however, applied an agency rationale to avoid corporate taxation. In general, these decisions focused on the fact that the corporation was not owned proportionately by the principals. The Sixth Circuit in its opinion in *Bollinger* distinguished *Roccaforte* because in *Bollinger* the corporation's stock was not owned by the same individuals who claimed to be the principals. 807 F.2d 65 (6th Cir.1986). See also Moncrief v. United States, 730 F.2d 276 (5th Cir.1984) (corporation wholly owned by 25 percent partner was true agent of partnership; *Roccaforte* distinguished); Raphan v. United States, 759 F.2d 879 (Fed.Cir.1985) (principals owned no stock of agent corporation).

The above Courts of Appeals decisions might be of less relevance after *Bollinger* if the *Bollinger* opinion signals that form will control. The opinion stresses that a written agency agreement, the terms of which are respected, should be sufficient to establish the agency. Apparently these facts should suffice even in the case of an individual claiming that a wholly owned corporation is the shareholder's agent. If so, the analysis in *Harrison Property Management Co.,* at page 42, is no longer valid. From the perspective of preventing tax avoidance through self-serving labeling of transactions, the *Harrison Property Management Co.* analysis is preferable to the *Bollinger* rule. On the other hand, the *Bollinger* rule appears to be more administrable than the *Harrison Property Management Co.* analysis. Some cases after *Bollinger* have confronted the situation where no written agreement exists, and the issue is whether the agency argument should be rejected on the ground that form has not been followed, or whether the court should engage in a facts and circumstances search for a "real" agency relationship. Heaton v. Commissioner, T.C. Memo. 1989–459, held that under *Bollinger* the absence of a written agency agreement was fatal to the taxpayer's agency claim, but the court also examined other factors to find that the taxpayer failed to satisfy every one of the *Bollinger* standards. The importance of form under the *Bollinger* standards also was emphasized in Greenberg v. Commissioner, T.C. Memo. 1989–12.

In re LeBlanc, 79 A.F.T.R.2d 97–754 (Bkrtcy.E.D.La.1997), held that *Bollinger* did not merely establish a safe harbor but established a definite standard, although less stringent than the *National Carbide* test, that must be met for a genuine agency relationship to exist. According to the *LeBlanc* court, the tripartite *Bollinger* test requires: "(1) 'the fact that the corporation is acting as agent for its shareholders with respect to a particular asset is set forth in a written agreement at the time the asset is acquired'; (2) 'the corporation functions as agent . . . with respect to the asset for all purposes'; and (3) 'the corporation is held out as the agent . . . in all dealings with third parties relating to the asset.' "

In First Chicago Corp. v. Commissioner, 96 T.C. 421 (1991), the Tax Court returned to the *National Carbide* factors to reject the taxpayer's argument that stock of a foreign corporation owned by various subsidiary members of an affiliated group of corporations was owned by the subsidiaries as agents for the parent corporation (which claimed a foreign tax credit under § 902 of the Code which is only available to a 10% stockholder of a foreign corporation). The Tax Court focused specifically on the last two *National Carbide* factors. In Bramblett v. Commissioner, 960 F.2d 526 (5th Cir.1992), a partnership sold land to a corporation owned by the partners. The corporation then developed and sold the land. The IRS denied the partnership capital gains treatment on the sale of the land, claiming that the corporation was acting as the partnership's agent in developing the land. In holding that the corporation was not the agent of the partnership, the Court of Appeals treated the *National Carbide* factors as the primary test for an agency relationship, and described *Bollinger* as a case involving additional factors that may indicate an agency relationship exists.

Apart from the broader issue of what factors generally establish a true agency relationship or, conversely, preclude a true agency relationship, the *Bollinger* opinion arguably is flawed on its particular facts in finding an agency relationship. The sole purpose and activity of the corporation was to obtain a loan at a rate that would have been usurious under state law if the loan had been made to an individual. According to the opinion in *Bollinger,* the individual rather than the corporation was taxed because the corporation was a genuine agent. If that is true, then the principal—an individual—was the true borrower, and the loan was usurious under state law. Thus the lender would have violated state law. In Commissioner v. First Security Bank of Utah, N.A., 405 U.S. 394 (1972), the Supreme Court refused to apply § 482, discussed below, to tax a bank on income received by a commonly controlled insurance company. A key element in the Court's reasoning was that it would have been illegal for the bank to have received the income. From this perspective, *Bollinger* is inconsistent with *First Security Bank of Utah*.

C. REALLOCATION OF INCOME

INTERNAL REVENUE CODE: Section 482.

Section 482 authorizes the IRS to reallocate items of income, deduction, or credit among two or more organizations, trades or businesses under common control when necessary to prevent evasion of taxes or clearly to reflect income. This provision may apply in a variety of contexts, but the common theme is that when related entities deal with one another at less than arm's length the IRS can adjust their taxable incomes to reflect the income that each would have earned had they dealt at arm's length. Thus an increase in the income of one of the related parties, reflecting a payment which would have been made in an arm's length relationship but which was not made, must be accompanied by a correlative deduction or capitalized item for the other related party. Treas.Reg. § 1.482–1(g)(2).[11]

The extensive regulations under § 482 are intended to ensure that taxpayers clearly reflect income attributable to controlled transactions by placing commonly controlled taxpayers on "a tax parity with an uncontrolled taxpayer by determining the true taxable income of the controlled taxpayer." Treas.Reg. § 1.482–1(a)(1). True taxable income resulting from a transaction is computed by applying an "arm's length" standard, which attempts to equate the results of a controlled

---

[11] Treas.Reg. § 1.482–1(g) permits taxpayers whose incomes have been adjusted under § 482 to make payments or setoffs reflecting the adjustments without further tax consequences. See Rev.Proc. 99–32, 1999–2 C.B. 296.

transaction with the result that would have occurred if uncontrolled taxpayers had engaged in the same transaction under similar circumstances. Treas.Reg. § 1.482–2(b)(1). The regulations provide various methods which, if followed, are deemed to result in an arm's length price. See Treas. Regs. § 1.482–2 (loans, services, and rents), 1.482–3 (sales of tangible property), and 1.482–4 (sales of intangible property). Although § 482 does not authorize taxpayers to invoke its terms to reallocate income or deductions, Treas.Reg. § 1.482–1(a)(3) permits a taxpayer to report income on a return using prices that vary from the prices actually charged in a controlled transaction in order to reflect an arm's length result. A § 482 reallocation makes sense only if the parties involved are subject to significantly different tax rates or regimes. Thus, § 482 is employed primarily in the international context. In some instances, however, the provision is invoked by the IRS in the purely domestic context, but there have been virtually no reported judicial decisions involving the application of § 482 in a domestic context in over 30 years. That fact could reflect that the IRS's application of § 482 domestically is moribund.

DETAILED ANALYSIS

1. APPLICATION TO TRANSACTIONS INVOLVING INDIVIDUAL SHAREHOLDERS AND THEIR CONTROLLED CORPORATIONS

In the context of transactions involving individual shareholders and their controlled corporations, § 482 has been applied to dealings such as leases at inadequate or excessive rent and to dealings between commonly controlled corporations at an inadequate or at an excessive price, such as the sale of goods or services from X Corporation to Y Corporation, both of which are owned by the same shareholders. See, e.g., Fegan v. Commissioner, 71 T.C. 791 (1979) (79 percent shareholder of a corporation leased a motel to the corporation for less than its fair rental value); Peck v. Commissioner, 752 F.2d 469 (9th Cir.1985) (reallocation due to less than arm's length rental).

Virtually all of the case law involving the domestic application of § 482 arose prior to the dramatic changes in the rate structure in 1986. Accordingly, most of the cases involved an allocation of income from a corporation to individual shareholders. Under the rate structure of the late 1980s and early 1990s, in which corporate rates exceeded the maximum individual rate, the situations that were likely to raise § 482 issues were different. Between 1986 and 1993, the IRS had the incentive only to allocate income from the individual shareholders to the corporation. More recent changes to the rate structure, including a significant capital gains preference, however, may lead to a renewal of the historic pattern. The following cases (involving both income allocations to and from corporations) illustrate how the IRS and the courts have applied § 482 in the individual shareholder-corporation context.

In Cooper v. Commissioner, 64 T.C. 576 (1975), the taxpayer transferred a construction business to a corporation and retained the depreciable assets. The taxpayer did not charge the corporation with any rent. The court upheld the IRS's allocation of the fair rental value of the depreciable assets to the individual taxpayer under § 482; the taxpayer was still engaged in a trade or business by virtue of retention of assets essential to the conduct of the construction business. See also Powers v. Commissioner, 724 F.2d 64 (7th Cir.1983) (shareholder leased property from one corporation at greater than arm's length rental and subleased to another corporation at less than arm's length rental; reallocations from both corporations to shareholder upheld).

Section 482 can be applied to allocate gross income between related taxpayers regardless of whether one or both of them have taxable income or loss for the year. Treas.Reg. § 1.482–1(f)(1)(ii). In Procacci v. Commissioner, 94 T.C. 397 (1990), a partnership leased a golf course to a corporation controlled by the partners. Because the corporation's operating expenses to third parties exceeded its available funds, the corporation paid no rent to the partnership. The IRS invoked § 482 to allocate rental income to the partnership. The court rejected the taxpayer's argument that § 482 could not be applied to reallocate income from a taxpayer with net operating losses, but nevertheless held that the IRS's § 482 allocation was improper. At the time the partnership acquired the golf course, it had physically deteriorated. The partnership's goals were to improve the course to "championship status," to enhance the value of adjacent land that the partnership planned to develop, and to enable the partnership profitably to develop golf condominiums on the golf course property. Since, under the circumstances, operating expenses of the golf course were too high to permit its profitable operation, an unrelated lessee would have demanded a subsidy from the partnership. Accordingly, on the facts, the court found that a zero rental was an arm's length amount.

In some situations in which § 482 might be invoked, other principles are applied. These other rules do not necessarily require correlative adjustments such as those required under § 482. Thus, when an employee-shareholder is paid an excessive salary, the IRS often simply disallows a deduction to the corporation under § 162(a)(1) rather than invoking § 482. When a shareholder purchases or leases property from a corporation at a bargain price, the IRS asserts that the bargain element is a dividend to the shareholder. See page 219. Finally, below market rate of interest loans are subject to the rules of § 7872, although § 482 also may be relevant. See Treas.Reg. § 1.482–2(a).

2. THE EXISTENCE OF "CONTROL"

The existence of control is a practical rather than formalistic question. In Hall v. Commissioner, 32 T.C. 390 (1959) (Acq.), aff'd, 294 F.2d 82 (5th Cir. 1961), the taxpayer as a sole proprietorship sold goods manufactured by him to a foreign corporation at a price considerably below his usual list price, the stock of the corporation according to the taxpayer being owned by his son and another. The Tax Court said that § 482 was applicable regardless of the legal ownership of the stock, since the taxpayer in fact exercised control over the corporation and dominated it. The court therefore allocated a part of the corporation's income to the taxpayer by treating the sales as if made in accordance with the taxpayer's list prices. In Ach v. Commissioner, 358 F.2d 342 (6th Cir.1966), the proprietor of a profitable clothing business sold the assets of a dress business to a corporation with loss carryovers controlled by her son. The Government argued that the sale should be ignored completely and the income from the dress business taxed directly to the proprietor. The Tax Court refused to take this approach, ("The corporation was actually in existence, and there was a genuine transfer of assets to it that were actually used in the conduct of the dress business," 42 T.C. 114, 123 (1964)), but went on to allocate 70 percent of the profits of the dress business to the proprietor because of her continuing management activities. The Court of Appeals sustained the allocation.

In a case in which two unrelated taxpayers each owned 50 percent of the stock in a subsidiary corporation, the Tax Court originally held that the predecessor of § 482 was not applicable since the subsidiary was not "controlled" by the same interests despite the fact that the taxpayers were acting in furtherance of their common purposes. Lake Erie & Pittsburg Railway Co. v. Commissioner, 5 T.C. 558 (1945). The IRS initially acquiesced in this decision (1945 C.B. 5), but in 1965 reexamined its position and indicated that it would no longer follow the *Lake Erie* holding. Rev.Rul. 65–142, 1965–1 C.B. 223. *Lake Erie* was likewise rejected by B. Forman Co. v. Commissioner, 453 F.2d 1144 (2d Cir.1972). In that case, two unrelated corporations formed a subsidiary, in which they each owned 50 percent of the stock, to build and operate a shopping center next to their department stores. The court held § 482 was applicable to allow the IRS to allocate to the shareholders interest income on non-interest bearing loans made to the subsidiary: "Whether [the two shareholders] are regarded as a partnership or joint venture, *de facto,* in forming [the subsidiary], the conclusion is inescapable that they acted in concert in making loans without interest to a corporation, all of whose stock they owned and all of whose directors and officers were their alter egos. They were not competitors in their dealings with one another or with [the subsidiary]. Their interests in [the subsidiary] were identical. When the Commissioner withdrew his acquiescence in *Lake Erie,* he gave reality of control as one of the reasons for doing so * * *. We agree."

3.   INADEQUATE SALARY PAID TO SHAREHOLDERBEMPLOYEES

3.1. *Background*

When individual rates substantially exceed corporate tax rates, as was the case prior to 1987, a sole shareholder, who is also the principal officer of his corporation, might not take any salary from the corporation, planning instead to build up the value of the corporation and then sell the stock, paying tax at capital gain rates. This raises the question of whether § 482 permits the IRS to allocate a fair salary to the shareholder (which the employee is then treated as having been recontributed to the corporation) on which the shareholder-employee must pay tax. An important issue is whether the IRS can also apply the principles of § 61 and Lucas v. Earl, 281 U.S. 111 (1930), to tax the corporation's income to the shareholder-employee. Similar issues have arisen in situations in which the corporation is a personal services corporation through which the shareholder-employee renders services that he previously performed as a sole proprietor. Since 1986, however, an individual has had a much reduced incentive to avoid taking a salary from his wholly-owned corporation except to the extent of the benefit provided by the 15 and 25 percent corporate rate brackets.

3.2. *Application of Section 482*

In some cases the IRS has successfully applied § 482 to a shareholder serving as an employee of a controlled corporation for an inadequate salary, thereby artificially inflating the corporation's income. See, e.g., Rubin v. Commissioner, 429 F.2d 650 (2d Cir.1970), on remand, 56 T.C. 1155 (1971) (Acq.), aff'd per curiam, 460 F.2d 1216 (2d Cir.1972); Borge v.

Commissioner, 405 F.2d 673 (2d Cir.1968). However, the IRS has not always been successful.

In Foglesong v. Commissioner, T.C. Memo. 1976–294, the taxpayer was a sales representative for a pipe company. He formed a corporation which issued 98 percent of its common stock to him. The taxpayer's children were issued preferred stock with a stated value of $400. Thereafter the corporation entered into an employment contract with the taxpayer and into contracts with the pipe manufacturers for whom the taxpayer sold pipe products; commissions earned on sales were paid by the manufacturers directly to the corporation, from which the taxpayer received a salary. The taxpayer's compensation over the next several years was less than two-thirds of the commissions paid to the corporation, which had no other employees or sources of income. During that period dividends of $32,000 were paid on the preferred stock; no dividends were paid on the common stock. The Tax Court weighed the legitimate business purposes for the arrangement against its tax avoidance potential and held that the taxpayer so controlled and directed the earning of the income of the corporation that he was personally taxable on 98 percent of such income under the principles of Lucas v. Earl.

On appeal, the Seventh Circuit Court of Appeals vacated and remanded the case. 621 F.2d 865 (7th Cir.1980). The Court of Appeals concluded that applying § 61 was imprecise and directed the Tax Court to reconsider the case based on the IRS's power to reallocate income under § 482. On remand, the Tax Court held that § 482 was properly applied to allocate 98 percent of the corporation's income to the taxpayer because his salary was unreasonably low. 77 T.C. 1102 (1981). The Tax Court applied its earlier decision in Keller v. Commissioner, 77 T.C. 1014 (1981), to hold that the requisite "two organizations" existed: Foglesong was in the trade or business of selling pipe as an employee of the corporation, and the corporation was in the trade or business of selling pipe (through the efforts of Foglesong). The taxpayer appealed again, and the Court of Appeals vacated and remanded the decision a second time. A different panel held that § 482 could not be invoked to allocate income from a personal service corporation to its shareholder-employee who performs services solely for the corporation. The Court of Appeals did not consider the "two organizations" requirement to have been met.

The IRS does not follow the second Court of Appeals decision in *Foglesong*. Rev.Rul. 88–38, 1988–1 C.B. 246. Similarly, notwithstanding the reversal by the Seventh Circuit in *Foglesong*, the Tax Court continues to hold that § 482 can be applied to allocate income between a corporation and a shareholder-employee who performs services solely for a controlled corporation, at least where appeal does not lie to the Seventh Circuit. See Haag v. Commissioner, 88 T.C. 604 (1987) (income of professional service corporation reallocated to physician-sole shareholder who drew nominal salary).

In determining whether a reallocation of income is appropriate under § 482, the inquiry is whether the shareholder-employee's total compensation (including salary, bonuses, deferred compensation, and other fringe benefits) approximates the amount he would have received absent incorporation of the business. See Keller v. Commissioner, 77 T.C. 1014 (1981), aff'd, 723 F.2d 58 (10th Cir.1983) (§ 482 applicable, but on facts no

Suppose A transfers a building worth $100,000, with an adjusted basis of $10,000, to a newly created corporation in return for 100 shares of its stock, and as part of the same planned transaction B transfers land worth $50,000, with a basis of $40,000, to the corporation in exchange for 50 shares of its stock. Because A and B together control the corporation, neither A nor B recognizes any gain. Under § 358(a), A's basis for the 100 shares of stock is $10,000, and B's basis for the 50 shares of stock is $40,000. Under § 362(a)(1), the corporation's basis for the building is $10,000, and its basis in the land is $40,000.

If the corporation had been in existence and was owned by both A and B and it had issued to A both 70 shares of stock and $30,000 cash for the building, while issuing only an additional 50 shares of stock to B, A would have had realized a gain of $90, but would have been required to recognize a gain of only $30,000 (the extent of the boot, assuming that the value of the stock was $70,000 and assuming that no dividend was involved); A's basis in the stock would be $10,000; the corporation would have had a basis in the building of $40,000 ($10,000 basis in transferor A's hands plus gain of $30,000 recognized by A). The consequences to B would be unchanged.

If A and B lacked control of the corporation immediately after the transfer—for example, because A and B had a pre-existing obligation to sell the stock received in the exchange to a third-party—the incorporation transfers would not be governed by § 351 at all; their entire gain would be recognized, and the basis of the building and land in the corporation's hands under general cost basis principles would be the fair market value of the stock issued for the assets. Treas.Reg. § 1.1032–1(d). The fair market value of the assets would be relevant in determining that value, though it would not be controlling. Rev.Rul. 56–100, 1956–1 C.B. 624.

The corporation's basis in an asset under § 362(a) is thus dependent only on the basis of the transferring stockholder and the amount of gain, if any, that is recognized by the stockholder. It does not depend upon nor is it affected by any actual cost that the corporation may incur. Hence, in the immediately preceding example, where the corporation paid out $30,000 cash as well as stock, if the stockholder's basis for the building had been exactly equal to the value of the stock and the cash received, so that the stockholder realized and recognized neither gain nor loss, the corporation's basis for the building would still be the same as that of the stockholder. The corporation's basis for the building would not be increased by the $30,000 cash that it paid.

If § 351 is applicable, the combined effect of the two basis provisions, §§ 358(a) and 362(a)(1), is to produce the possibility of two gains—the gain on the sale of the stock and the gain on the sale of the property transferred to the corporation—where only one existed before. However, a subsequent recognition of the stockholder's gain may be postponed if the stock is later transferred in a tax-free transaction, e.g., a reorganization. Furthermore, if the stock is held by the transferor until death, one of the two gains or losses is eliminated by the rule of § 1014, which provides for a basis equal to the value of the stock at the date of death. Although at first blush, the combined effect of §§ 358(a) and 362(a)(1) also appears to raise possibility of two losses—the gain on the sale of the stock and the loss on the sale of the property transferred to the corporation—where only one existed before, § 362(e)(2), discussed below, generally prevents this from occurring.

Where the shareholder transfers a capital asset or a § 1231 asset in exchange for stock, § 1223(1) provides that the shareholder's holding period for the stock includes the period for which the shareholder held the capital asset or § 1231 asset. Similarly, § 1223(2) provides the that the corporation's holding period for any capital asset or § 1231 asset received in an exchange to which § 351 applies to the shareholder includes the period for which the transferor shareholder held the capital or § 1231 asset. If a mix of assets only some of which qualify for a tacked holding period for the shareholder under § 1223(1) are transferred to the corporation, a proportionate number of shares (by value) should be assigned a tacked holding period and the remaining shares should take a holding period beginning with the exchange. See Runkle v. Commissioner, 39 B.T.A. 458 (1939).

DETAILED ANALYSIS

1. "PROPERTY": CASH AND PROMISSORY NOTES

For purposes of § 351, "property" includes cash. Rev.Rul. 69–357, 1969–1 C.B. 101. Since gain and loss never can be recognized on the purchase of stock for cash, the importance of Rev.Rul. 69–357 lies in the principle that a transferor of cash can be included in the control group along with transferors of appreciated or depreciated property.

A shareholder who issues the shareholder's own promissory note to the corporation in exchange for stock should be treated in the same manner as one who pays cash to the corporation for stock for purposes of determining the control group. However, there really has not been any "exchange" of "property" because the shareholder cannot "own" the shareholder's promissory note prior to giving it to the corporation—the note does not exist until an item of property until ownership vests in the corporation. Thus, the transaction should be considered a stock purchase for purposes of determining the obligor-shareholder's tax consequences. The issuance of the shareholder's note to acquire the stock is not a realization event for the shareholder issuing the note. See Treas.Reg. § 1.61–12(c)(1). As a result, § 351 is not necessary to provide nonrecognition to the shareholder who gives the corporation a promissory note for the stock.

The term "property" also includes accounts receivable, regardless of whether the transferor used the cash or accrual method of accounting, Rev.Rul. 80–198, 1980–2 C.B. 113, as well as § 453 installment notes owned by the transferor that were received from another person in a prior transaction. Under Treas.Reg. § 1.453–9(c)(2), in general no gain or loss results from the transfer of installment obligations to a corporation in an exchange to which § 351 applies despite the fact that part of the tax on the installment gain may in effect be shifted to the other shareholders.

Section 351 may apply to transfers to a preexisting corporation as well as to transfers to a newly organized corporation, provided the control requirement is met. Thus, the question can arise of whether a transfer of outstanding indebtedness of an existing corporation in exchange for stock of that corporation can qualify for nonrecognition under § 351. This will be particularly important if the transferor purchased the indebtedness at less than face value, and the value of the stock received in exchange for the debt instrument exceeds its basis to the shareholder. The question also arises if the corporation's obligation is a § 453 installment obligation in the hands of the shareholder. Sections 351(d)(2) and (3) provide that stock issued to satisfy an indebtedness of the issuing corporation not evidenced by a security, or to pay interest on indebtedness of the issuing corporation, is not considered as issued in return for property. Rev.Rul. 73–423, 1973–2 C.B. 161, following dicta in Jack Ammann Photogrammetric Engineers, Inc. v. Commissioner, 341 F.2d 466 (5th Cir.1965), held that where the obligor on the installment obligation is the corporation itself, then the § 351 transaction constitutes a "satisfaction" of the installment obligation under § 453B(a) and results in a tax to the transferor. Furthermore, § 351(e)(2) provides that § 351 is not applicable if a corporation in a bankruptcy or insolvency proceeding transfers assets to another corporation and then distributes the stock received to its creditors. The transaction is treated as if the assets had first been distributed to the creditors and the creditors had then transferred the property to the new corporation.

Furthermore, if the corporation is solvent and not in bankruptcy,[3] and the sum of the principal amount of the debt, whether or not represented by a security, plus accrued but unpaid interest, exceeds the fair market value of the stock issued in the transaction, then pursuant to § 108(e)(8), the corporation is treated as having satisfied the indebtedness with an amount of money equal to the fair market value of the stock. As a result, the transaction produces cancellation of debt income for the corporation under § 61(a)(12) to the extent the amount of the debt exceeds the value of the stock. Section 1032 does not apply in this instance.

2. SHAREHOLDER'S STOCK BASIS

2.1. *Generally*

If the stockholder receives stock of different classes, e.g., some common stock and some preferred stock, the stockholder's aggregate basis in all of the stock must be allocated among the stock of different classes in proportion to the fair market values of the stock in each class. I.R.C. § 358(b)(1); Treas.Reg. § 1.358–2(b)(2). Thus, for example, if A transfers real property with a basis of $20 and fair market value of $100 to X, a controlled corporation, in a nonrecognition transaction under § 351, and A receives in exchange common stock with a value of $80 and preferred stock with a value of $20, A's substituted basis in the common stock is $16 ($20 × $80/$100) and A's substituted basis in the preferred stock is $4 ($20 × $20/100). The stockholder cannot allocate the basis of some transferred assets to one block of stock, for example, preferred stock, and the lower basis of other assets to another block of stock. See Rev.Rul. 85–164, 1985–2 C.B. 117. Prop.Reg. § 1.358–2(g)(1) (2009) would adopt the principles in Rev.Rul. 85–164 to provide that as long as none of the property transferred to the corporation was itself corporate stock, the aggregate basis of the stock received, i.e., the aggregate basis of the property transferred, as adjusted for any gain recognized, must be allocated among all of the shares of stock received in proportion to the fair market values of each share of stock.

---

[3] Any cancellation of debt income realized by an insolvent or bankrupt debtor is excluded from gross income pursuant to § 108(a)(1).

Under general principles of taxation, stock in a corporation acquired in exchange for the shareholder's promissory note takes a § 1012 cost basis equal to the principal amount of the note. See Rev.Rul. 2004–37, 2004–1 C.B. 583.

2.2. *Special Rule For Stock Received in Exchange for Stock of Another Corporation*

Adopting the tracing principles of Treas.Reg. § 1.358–2 applicable to stock-for-stock exchanges in corporate reorganizations, page 604, Prop.Reg. § 1.358–2(g)(2) (2009) would provide that in the case of a § 351 exchange in which stock of another corporation is transferred to the corporation, and no liabilities are assumed, the basis of each share of stock received in the exchange will be the same as the basis of the share or shares transferred in exchange. Under this rule, if shares representing different blocks of stock are transferred to the corporation in exchange for more than one share, the basis of the different blocks of stock will be reflected in the bases of the stock received for each block. If more than one share is received in exchange for a share transferred, then the basis of the transferred share would be apportioned to the shares received by the fair market value of the shares received. Treas.Reg. § 1.358–2(a)(2)(i), Prop.Reg. 1.358–2(b)(2) (2009). If fewer shares are received than the number of shares transferred, the allocation of the basis of the transferred shares would be made in some manner that reflects the fact that each share received was acquired on the same date and with the same basis as the shares transferred. Treas.Reg. § 1.358–2(a)(2)(i), Prop.Reg. § 1.358–2(b)(3) (2009).

3.   TAX CONSEQUENCES TO THE CORPORATION ISSUING STOCK

Section 1032, which applies both to newly-issued stock and treasury stock, provides that the issuance of its own stock is not a taxable event for the corporation. Thus, § 1032 provides nonrecognition of the "profit" realized by a corporation purchasing and reissuing its own shares.

If the transaction does not fall under § 351 or the reorganization nonrecognition sections, which pursuant to § 362 generally result in a transferred basis, Treas.Reg. § 1.1032–1(d) provides that the basis of the property acquired by the corporation in exchange for its stock is a "cost" basis under § 1012. Rev.Rul. 56–100, 1956–1 C.B. 624, interpreted this provision to require that the property received by the corporation in a taxable exchange not subject to § 351 be assigned a basis in the corporation's hands equal to the fair market value of the stock exchanged for the property, and not the fair market value of property received, if those values differed. Case law also has consistently reached this result. See, e.g., FX Systems Corp. v. Commissioner, 79 T.C. 957 (1982). The ruling notes that, "[e]vidence as to the fair market value of the assets received is admissible to show the fair market value of the stock used in making the acquisition, but is of less weight than available direct evidence of the fair market value of such stock." Pittsburgh Terminal Corp. v. Commissioner, 60 T.C. 80, aff'd by order, 500 F.2d 1400 (3d Cir. 1974), is to the same effect regarding valuation of stock that cannot be otherwise valued.

4.   THE CORPORATION'S ASSET BASIS

4.1. *Multiple Asset Transfers*

When a shareholder exchanges more than one item of property solely for stock in a § 351 transfer, the corporation's basis in each item of property is the same as it was in the hands of the shareholder. See P.A. Birren & Son v. Commissioner, 116 F.2d 718 (7th Cir.1940); Gunn v. Commissioner, 25 T.C. 424, 438 (1955), aff'd per curiam, 244 F.2d 408 (10th Cir.1957). Thus, for example, if the shareholder transfers Blackacre, with a basis of $100 and a fair market value of $300 and Whiteacre with a basis of $200 and a fair market value of $300, the basis of each property remains the same. The aggregate basis of $300 is not reallocated among the properties. The problems encountered in allocating a basis increase attributable to the transferor's recognized gain when multiple assets are involved are discussed at page 72.

4.2. *Limitations on Built-in Losses*

4.2.1. *Anti-loss Duplication Rules for Transferred Built-in Loss Property*

Section 362(e)(2) prevents taxpayers from transmuting a single economic loss into two (or more) tax losses by taking advantage of the dual application of the substituted basis rules in § 358 for stock received in a § 351 transaction and in § 362 for assets transferred to a corporation in a § 351 transaction. If the aggregate basis of the property transferred to a corporation by any one transferor in a § 351 transaction exceeds the aggregate fair market value, the aggregate basis of the property must be reduced to its fair market value. Thus, for example, if A transfers Blackacre, with a basis of $1,000 and a fair market value of $600 to newly formed X Corporation in exchange for all of the X Corporation stock, X Corporation's $1,000 basis in Blackacre, determined under § 362(a), will be reduced to $600 under § 362(e)(2). Alternatively, pursuant to § 362(e)(2)(C),[4] A and X Corporation may jointly elect to reduce A's basis in the X Corporation stock, which here is otherwise an exchanged basis of $1,000 pursuant to § 358, to its fair market value, here presumably $600, with the transferee, X Corporation, taking a normal transferred basis under § 362(a)—here $1,000.

The operation of § 362(e)(2) is more complex where multiple assets are involved. When some appreciated property also is transferred to the corporation, § 362(e)(2) does not necessarily result in the basis of every item of loss property being reduced to its fair market value. Section 362(e)(2)(A) requires that the aggregate basis of the transferred property be reduced by the excess of the aggregate basis over the aggregate fair market value, and § 362(e)(2)(B) requires that the aggregate basis reduction be allocated among the transferred properties in proportion to the built-in losses in the properties before taking into account § 362(e)(2). Assume, for example, that B transferred three properties to newly formed Y Corporation in exchange for all of the stock: a copyright, fair market value $4,500, basis $3,000; land, fair market value $7,000, basis $9,000; and a machine, fair market value $4,000, basis $5,000. The aggregate fair market

---

4   Treas.Reg. § 1.362–4(d) provides details on how to make the § 362(h)(2)(C) election to reduce the transferor's stock basis in lieu of the corporation reducing asset basis. For an election to be effective: (1) prior to filing "a Section 362(e)(2)(C) Statement" the transferor and transferee must enter into a written, binding agreement to elect to apply § 362(e)(2)(C), and (2) detailed requirements for filing the "Section 362(e)(2)(C) Statement," which is required to contain extraordinarily detailed information about the transfer, must be followed. The transferor must include the "Section 362(e)(2)(C) Statement" on or with its timely filed (including extensions) original return for the taxable year in which the transfer occurred. A § 362(e)(2)(C) election is irrevocable. It may be made protectively and will have no effect to the extent it is determined that § 362(e)(2) does not apply.

value of the three properties is $15,500 and their aggregate basis is $17,000, thus requiring a basis reduction of $1,500 ($17,000 − $15,500) with respect to the land and the machine, the two properties with a basis that exceeds fair market value. The land has a built-in loss of $2,000 and the machine has a built-in loss of $1,000. The $1,500 basis reduction is allocated 2/3 to the land ($2,000/($2,000 + $1,000)), and 1/3 to the machine ($1,000/($2,000 + $1,000)). Thus the basis of the land is reduced by $1,000 (2/3 × $1,500), from $9,000 to $8,000, leaving an unrealized loss of $1,000 ($8,000 basis − $7,000 fair market value) inherent in the land and the basis of the machine is reduced by $500 (1/3 × $1,500), from $5,000 to $4,500, leaving an unrealized loss of $500 ($4,500 basis − $4,000 fair market value) inherent in the machine.

Section 362(e)(2) applies transferor-by-transferor. Thus, if the copyright, land, and machine described above were transferred to the corporation by C, D, and E, respectively, the $2,000 built-in loss with respect to the land and the $1,000 built-in loss with respect to the machine would be taken into account separately, and would not be offset by the $1,500 built-in gain with respect to the copyright. As a result, the basis of the land would be reduced from $9,000 to $7,000 and the basis of the machine would be reduced from $5,000 to $4,000. Alternatively, D could elect (jointly with the corporation) to reduce the basis of the stock received in exchange for the land from $9,000 to $7,000, leaving the corporation with a $9,000 basis in the land; and E could separately elect (jointly with the corporation) to reduce the basis of the stock received in exchange for the machine from $5,000 to $4,000, leaving the corporation with a $5,000 basis in the machine.

When a § 362(e)(2)(C) election is made, the basis reduction is allocated among the shares of stock received by the transferor in proportion to the fair market value of each share. Treas.Reg. § 1.362–4(d)(2). This rule is of greatest significance when the transferor receives shares of more than one class, for example, both common and preferred.

4.2.2.   *Limitations on Importation of Built-in Losses*

Section 362(e)(1) applies property-by-property to reduce the corporation's basis of transferred property from the normal § 362(a) transferred basis to its fair market value, if (1) there is net built-in loss in the aggregate transferred properties and (2) gain or loss realized by the transferor with respect to the property was not subject to U.S. income tax immediately prior to the transfer. This provision applies principally to transfers by foreign shareholders to U.S. corporations and transfers by tax exempt organizations to U.S. corporations.

5.   TRANSFER OF PROPERTY TO AN EXISTING CORPORATION WITHOUT ISSUANCE OF ADDITIONAL STOCK

5.1. *Transfer to a Controlled Corporation*

Section 351 also applies when a controlling shareholder transfers property to a controlled corporation without any additional stock being issued to the transferor. Lessinger v. Commissioner, 872 F.2d 519 (2d Cir. 1989); Rev.Rul. 64–155, 1964–1 C.B. 138. This most commonly occurs when property is transferred to a wholly owned corporation, since the issuance of additional stock would be a meaningless gesture. In such a case, the transferor adds the basis of the transferred property to the basis of stock already owned, and the corporation takes a transferred basis in the property under § 362(a), subject to the limitations in § 362(e).

5.2. *Contributions to Capital of a Corporation not Controlled by the Transferor*

If a stockholder who does not control the corporation contributes additional capital to the corporation in the form of assets that have appreciated or depreciated in value without receiving additional shares of stock in return, presumably no gain or loss will be realized because nothing is received in return. The transferor simply adds the basis of the contributed property to the basis for his stock. Pursuant to § 362(a)(2) the corporation takes a transferred basis from the transferor, subject to § 362(e). If property is transferred as a contribution to capital by persons other than stockholders, as in situations in which a community organization transfers property to a corporation to induce it to locate in the area, the corporation may exclude the contribution under § 118 and under § 362(c) the corporation's basis in the property is zero.

6.   BUSINESS PURPOSE REQUIREMENT

In circumstances that evidence overly aggressive tax planning, the courts sometimes impose a business purpose requirement as a prerequisite for obtaining nonrecognition under § 351. West Coast Marketing Corp. v. Commissioner, 46 T.C. 32 (1966) is an example of such a case. In that case, West Coast Marketing owned an interest in a tract of land and, its sole stockholder, owned an interest in two adjacent tracts. At a time when a taxable exchange of the lands for stock in a publicly held corporation was imminent, West Coast Marketing and its shareholder organized another corporation, Manatee, and transferred their interests in the land to Manatee in exchange for stock of Manatee. Soon thereafter, all of the stock of Manatee was transferred to a publicly held corporation, Universal, in exchange for Universal stock in a transaction that was tax-free under §§ 354 and 368(a)(1)(B), discussed at page 614. Shortly thereafter Manatee was liquidated and its assets transferred to Universal in a tax-free transaction, see text at pages 342–352. The Tax Court held that Manatee was not organized or used for any bona fide business purpose, and that the substance of the transaction was a taxable exchange of an interest in land for stock of Universal. Rev.Rul. 70–140, 1970–1 C.B. 73, reached the same result on similar facts.

Estate of Kluener v. Commissioner, 154 F.3d 630 (6th Cir.1998), also imposed a business purpose requirement, which was not met. Kluener owned all of the stock of APECO, which had over $4 million of net operating loss carryovers and was in financial straits. Kluener also directly owned highly leveraged real estate and thoroughbred horses, both of which activities were losing substantial amounts of money. To help stem his losses, he decided to sell some horses. On the advice of his accountants, Kluener transferred the horses to APECO to shelter the gains (approximately $1.2 million) with APECO's net operating loss carryovers. Kluener hid the transfer from APECO's directors and did not use the $2.5 million sales proceeds to alleviate APECO's financial straits, but instead caused the corporation shortly after the sale to distribute most of the funds to himself for personal use—mostly repayment of personal debts. The Sixth Circuit affirmed the Tax Court's holding that the transfer to APECO lacked a business purpose. Accordingly, the transfer to APECO was not respected for tax purposes and the gain was taxed directly to Kluener because Kluener himself was the true seller of the horses.

Notwithstanding these cases, there are no authorities requiring that there be a business purpose for organizing an corporation actually to conduct a business, as opposed to conducting a business in an unincorporated form, or for transferring to an existing corporation additional assets to be used in a trade or business conducted or to be conducted by the corporation.

7. RECEIPT OF STOCK DISPROPORTIONATE TO PROPERTY TRANSFERRED

The 1939 Code predecessor of § 351 required that for the provision to be applicable the nonrecognition property received by each transferor had to be substantially in proportion to the transferor's interest in the transferred property prior to the exchange. The 1954 Code dropped the proportionate interest requirement as a factor in the nonrecognition of gain, but retained it as a factor indicating the possible existence of compensation or a gift. See the cross-references in § 351(h)(3) and (4). Treas.Reg. § 1.351–1(b)(1) states that "in appropriate cases" the stock will be treated as if first received in proportion to assets transferred, and then transferred to the ultimate recipients by way of gift or compensation if the facts so warrant. However, Rev.Rul. 76–454, 1976–2 C.B. 102, applied Treas.Reg. § 1.351–1(b)(1) to find a dividend in a situation in which a stockholder and his controlled corporation formed a new corporation with the stockholder receiving a disproportionately large amount of the stock of the newly formed corporation. The dividend was in the form of stock of the newly formed corporation constructively received by the original corporation in the § 351 transaction and constructively distributed to the shareholder.

8. SECURITIES "SWAP FUNDS"

Section 351(e) provides that § 351 does not apply to transfers to investment companies, which are corporations holding a diverse investment portfolio that are operated to permit an exchange of a single investment for a diverse portfolio. Suppose that an individual owns a large amount of a particular stock that has greatly appreciated in value. The taxpayer would like to diversify that investment but feels that the tax on capital gains is too high a price to pay for diversification. There are many other individuals in a similar situation, but with different stocks. An investment house forms a regulated investment company (mutual fund)— which is a corporation for federal tax purposes—and invites an exchange of the stocks of the individuals in return for stock of the fund. This exchange would provide the individuals with the desired diversification, since they would now have, through their participation in the mutual fund, an interest in many different stocks, including their former shares. During the early 1960s, such swap funds flourished. In 1966, however, Congress enacted the statutory predecessor of § 351(e), which provides that § 351 does not apply to transfers to investment companies. As a result, gain or loss is recognized by the transferors in such transactions.[5]

---

[5] Section 683 provides similar rules for transfers to trusts used as swap funds, and § 721(b) deals with diversification through partnership formation.

Treas.Reg. § 1.351–1(c) provides that a transfer will be considered to be to an "investment company" if the transaction results, directly or indirectly, in a diversification of the transferor's interest and the transferee is a regulated investment company, a real estate investment trust, or a corporation more than 80 percent of the value of the assets of which is held in readily marketable stocks or securities or similar transferable interests. Under Treas.Reg. § 1.351–1(c)(5), a transaction ordinarily results in diversification "if two or more persons transfer nonidentical assets to a corporation in the exchange." The IRS has taken the position that the requirement that two or more persons transfer nonidentical assets to the corporation is satisfied if one group of transferors transfers the stock of a single corporation and another group transfers cash to a newly organized corporation that is a regulated investment company, i.e., a mutual fund. Rev.Rul. 87–9, 1987–1 C.B. 133.

In Rev.Rul. 88–32, 1988–1 C.B. 113, the IRS ruled that a transfer of stock does not result in diversification unless diversification is the result of a nonrecognition transaction. Thus, there is no proscribed diversification if the transferor transfers stock of a single corporation to a controlled investment company that sells the stock in a taxable transaction and reinvests the sales proceeds in a diverse portfolio of stock.

B. "PROPERTY" AND MIDSTREAM TRANSFERS OF INCOME ITEMS

Foster v. Commissioner

United States Court of Appeals, Ninth Circuit, 1985.
756 F.2d 1430.

■ J. BLAINE ANDERSON, CIRCUIT JUDGE:

In 1955, Jack Foster and his three sons formed a partnership, T. Jack Foster and Sons (Partnership), for the general purpose of dealing in property, with Jack as the managing partner. In 1958, the Partnership began to investigate the reclamation potential of Brewer's Island, a 2,600 acre undeveloped and partially submerged tract of land located about 12 miles south of San Francisco. After commissioning engineering studies, the Partnership determined that the tract could be transformed into a self-contained city (Foster City) of 35,000.

In December, 1959, the Partnership acquired an option to purchase the property for $12.8 million; in May, 1960, it secured enabling legislation from the California legislature for a municipal improvement district known as Estero, which was coterminus with Brewer's Island; and, in August, 1960, it exercised its option to purchase the tract. Thereafter, the Partnership and Estero began developing the property by neighborhood.

* * *

C. *Application of § 482 to the Disposition of Property Acquired in a Nonrecognition Transaction*

The first of the nine neighborhoods to be developed was Neighborhood One. In October, 1962, before any sales to builders were consummated, the Partnership transferred an undivided one-quarter interest in 127 acres of Neighborhood One to each of four newly formed corporations as tenants in common. Each of the four corporations, referred to collectively by the Tax Court as the Alphabets, was solely owned by one of the Fosters.

In August, 1966, the Partnership transferred 311 lots in Neighborhood Four, which had been improved to a lesser extent than Neighborhood One, to Foster Enterprises, a corporation owned by the Fosters in equal shares. Foster Enterprises, which was incorporated in 1960 to take title to a hotel in Hawaii, had accumulated a net operating loss of $1.2 million.

The Neighborhood One transaction was an exchange of property for stock under § 351. The Neighborhood Four transaction was a contribution to capital under § 1032. Under both sections, neither the transferor nor the transferee recognize gain or loss on the transfer, and the basis of the property does not change. The transferee therefore inherits the potential gain or loss inherent in the property at the time of its transfer.

The Tax Court was correct in its determination that the Commissioner may employ § 482 to reallocate income derived from the disposition of property previously acquired in a nonrecognition transaction. Rooney v. United States, 305 F.2d 681, 686 (9th Cir.1962) (Section 482 will control when it conflicts with § 351 as long as the discretion of the Commissioner in reallocating is not abused.); Treas.Reg. § 1.482–1(d)(5)(1984). * * *

D. *Section 482 Reallocation*

The Tax Court, pursuant to § 482, reallocated all the income from the sale of the lots in Neighborhood One and Neighborhood Four from the Alphabets and Foster Enterprises to the Partnership. The income reallocated was divided into two parts, income due to appreciation in value before the transfers and income due to appreciation after the transfers.

1. *Pre-transfer Appreciation*

The Tax Court reallocated the income attributable to appreciation before the transfers on the ground that the purpose of the transfers was to avoid taxes. It found that A.O. Champlin, the Fosters' long-time tax advisor, decided it was advantageous from a tax standpoint for the Fosters to undertake the development of Foster City in a partnership form. Losses incurred during the early years could then be used by the partners to reduce income on their personal tax returns. Later, as the land was developed, certain lots were transferred from the Partnership to its controlled entities in an effort to shift income. As noted by the Tax Court, "only highly appreciated inventory pregnant with income was conveyed." Foster, 80 T.C. at 179. Moreover, according to the testimony of Champlin, the value of money on hand to the Fosters far exceeded any interest that might eventually have to be paid on a tax deficiency, particularly when the rate of interest charged by the Government was less than that charged by commercial banks.

In the case of the Alphabets, which were formed within a month of the transfer, the Tax Court determined that the object was to shift from the Partnership the income from the sale of the lots and split it among taxpayers subject to a lower rate of tax. The Fosters argue that the transfer could not have been tax motivated because it would have increased taxes; the income reported by the Alphabets was not offset by any losses, whereas if the income had been reported by the Partnership, it would have been offset by the operating losses which the Partnership claimed on its returns. The Tax Court, however, found that "the tax savings to an individual realized by preserving a partnership loss may very well exceed the tax cost to his corporation incurred by reporting the income." Id., 80 T.C. at 173.

The Fosters contend that although the Neighborhood Four transfer may have resulted in a tax saving, it was made for a business purpose. There was evidence that Rex Johnson, a senior vice president of Republic National Bank who was in charge of monitoring the Fosters' account, insisted that the lots be conveyed to Foster Enterprises as a condition to Republic's renewing the Partnership's loans. The Tax Court discounted this as the motivation behind the transfer, and we find its reasoning persuasive.

Foster Enterprises was not indebted to Republic. It had borrowed money from Likins-Foster Honolulu Corporation and Roy Turner Associates, Ltd., a subsidiary of Likins-Foster. Both Likins-Foster and the Partnership were indebted to Republic.

According to Johnson, the transfer was necessary to improve the liquidity of Foster Enterprises and thereby (1) enhance the collectibility of the indebtedness of Likins-Foster to Republic, (2) improve the bank's security in the Likins-Foster stock, and (3) insulate the bank from the fortunes of the Foster partnership. The Tax Court, however, found that a special audit report prepared by the bank stated that the Likins-Foster loans were being paid according to schedule. Moreover, if Johnson were concerned about the ability of Likins-Foster to repay its loan, it would have made more sense to transfer the lots directly to that corporation because it was the Likins-Foster stock that had been pledged as security. The transfer of the lots obviously weakened the Partnership's ability to repay its loan to Republic, noted the Tax Court, and certainly exacerbated its cash flow problem.

The sales proceeds were not used by Foster Enterprises to liquidate its debts to Likins-Foster and Turner Associates. Rather, they were loaned to the Partnership to further develop Foster City. Although Foster Enterprises still had an asset, it was now, continued the Tax Court, an unsecured receivable from the Partnership. Collectibility was therefore dependent upon the Partnership's overall success with the Foster City undertaking, precisely the risk against which Johnson ostensibly wanted to protect.

The Tax Court found that the purpose of the Neighborhood Four transaction was to shift to Foster Enterprises the income earned from the sale of the lots so that it could be absorbed by that corporation's losses. The record contains ample evidence to support the Tax Court's conclusions concerning both the Neighborhood Four and the Neighborhood One transactions. We therefore find that the Commissioner did not abuse his discretion in reallocating to the Partnership that portion of the sales income due to appreciation before the date of transfer. * * *

2. *Post-transfer Appreciation*

Because Neighborhoods One and Four were both further developed after the transfers, a part of the income derived from the sale of lots was created after the transfer date. The Tax Court concluded that Estero was controlled by the Partnership, and was used by it as its instrument for the development of Foster City. Thus Estero's efforts were to be viewed as those of the Partnership, and the gain was to be attributed to it.

Estero, a Municipal Improvement District, was created in 1960 by a special act of the California legislature. It was authorized to tax and to issue tax-exempt bonds to finance its activities in reclaiming and improving Brewer's Island. * * *

Foster, 80 T.C. at 58.

We agree with the Tax Court that during the years in issue, the Fosters, as the principal landowners and developers, controlled Estero. Indeed, the California Supreme Court has recognized that the Estero Act was designed by the California legislature to place control of the district in the landowner/developer. Cooper v. Leslie Salt Co., 70 Cal.2d 627 * * *. The Tax Court stated:

> There is no question that Estero added value to Brewer's Island. However, it never realized that value because it did not own the land or receive the proceeds from its sale. All we are deciding here is whether the value added by Estero is allocable to the Foster partnership because of the legislatively conferred control that the partnership exercised over the district. To answer that question in the affirmative does not require that we ignore Estero's legal identity as a public agency.

Foster, 80 T.C. at 169. Estero was the Partnership's creature, used by it to improve the land and thus increase its value. That is what it was designed to be and do. Because it is a public body, validly created, its own income, if any, belongs to it, and would not be allocable to some other entity.

* * *

The Tax Court stated that its finding that the Partnership controlled Estero did not conflict with the district's status as a "juristic entity." * * * We agree. The primary question here is not whether Estero is an independent entity. The primary question is whether the Commissioner can allocate to the Partnership the income arising from value created by Estero that would have gone to the Partnership but for the transfers to the Alphabets and Foster Enterprises. The Alphabets' and Foster Enterprises' function was to divert what would normally be the income of the Partnership away from it and to the Alphabets and Foster Enterprises. If the transfers had not been made, the income in question would not have been Estero's; it would have been that of the Partnership. The relationship between the Partnership and its creatures, the Alphabets and Foster Enterprises, was precisely the same, whether the appreciation in value occurred before the transfers or after them. Under section 482, the Commissioner may allocate income earned subsequent to the income evading event or transfer. The fact that some of it is attributable to a time following the transfers makes no difference. Because Estero did not own the land, the gain in value would never accrue to Estero, but would have accrued to the Partnership, the landowner, but for the transfers. By the transfers, the Partnership shifted that income away from itself and to the Alphabets, which had nothing, and to Foster Enterprises, which had large losses from unrelated ventures. By that device, the Partnership sought to get out from under large tax liabilities and yet retain control of Foster City. Under § 482, the Commissioner could reallocate to the Partnership the income that the Partnership had shifted to the Alphabets and Foster Enterprises. The transfers had no business function; their purpose was tax avoidance. The Tax Court properly upheld the Commissioner's reallocation.

* * *

DETAILED ANALYSIS

1. SECTION 482 ALLOCATIONS

Treas.Reg. § 1.482–1(f)(1)(iii) now expressly provides that § 482 may be applied to override § 351. Although the Ninth Circuit held in *Foster* that § 482 overrides § 351, allowing the IRS to allocate subsequent income back to the transferor or previously incurred expenses to the transferee corporation, some earlier court decisions had held that § 482 could not be applied to override a nonrecognition provision. See, e.g., Ruddick Corp. v. United States, 643 F.2d 747 (Ct.Cl.1981).

2. ASSIGNMENT OF INCOME

In the case of a transfer to the corporation of contract rights or other property with accrued but uncollected income, the IRS has invoked assignment of income principles to force the transferor to recognize earned income on the transfer of the right to collect that income. See Weinberg v. Commissioner, 44 T.C. 233 (1965), aff'd per curiam sub nom. Commissioner v. Sugar Daddy, Inc., 386 F.2d 836 (9th Cir.1967). However, where a cash method taxpayer transfers all of the assets of a going business to a corporation in exchange for stock of the corporation, the assignment of income doctrine will not be invoked to tax the transferor on the income realized from collection of the receivables. Hempt Bros., Inc. v. United States, 490 F.2d 1172 (3d Cir.1974), held that in such circumstances, application of the assignment of income doctrine to tax the transferor of receivables would frustrate the policy of § 351, which is to facilitate incorporation of a going business. Rev.Rul. 80–198, 1980–2 C.B. 113, adopts the holding of *Hempt Brothers* where all of the assets of a going business are transferred to a corporation for a valid business reason, but adds that assignment of income principles will apply to tax the transfer of receivables if that is the only asset transferred to the corporation. Pursuant to § 362(a), the corporation will have a zero basis in the receivables and will thus be required to recognize on collection the full amount as income, provided that neither the assignment of income doctrine nor § 482 taxes the collected amounts to the transferor.

3. TAX BENEFIT RULE

In general, the tax benefit rule requires current inclusion in income of previously deducted items when a subsequent event is inconsistent with the prior deduction. However, Hillsboro National Bank v. Commissioner, 460 U.S. 370 (1983), held that the tax benefit rule did not apply to the transferor of previously expensed property transferred to another party in a transaction in which the transferee took a transferred basis (a corporate liquidation governed by a now repealed provision). This result is appropriate in a § 351 transaction because the corporation takes a transferred basis under § 362(a). If, on the other hand, the transaction provides the transferee with a stepped-up basis, then application of the tax benefit rule to "recapture" the prior deduction is appropriate. See United States v. Bliss Dairy, Inc., a case consolidated with *Hillsboro National Bank.*

C. "SOLELY FOR STOCK"—THE RECEIPT OF OTHER PROPERTY

INTERNAL REVENUE CODE: Sections 351(b), (g); 358(a), (b); 362(a); 453(a)–(c), (f)(6), (g); 1239(a), (b)(1), (c)(1)(A).

REGULATIONS: Sections 1.301–1(a); 1.351–2.

PROPOSED REGULATIONS: Section 1.453–1(f)(1)(iii), (f)(3)(ii).

The nonrecognition rule of § 351(a) is limited to an exchange of property "solely for stock" of the controlled corporation. Section 351(b) permits the receipt of other property, but requires that the transferor recognize gain to the extent of the fair market value of other property plus the amount of money received. The basis rules of § 358 adjust the transferor's basis in the stock of the controlled corporation to account for boot by decreasing basis in an amount equal to the fair market value of property and the amount of money received, and increasing basis by the amount of any gain recognized. The transferee corporation's basis in transferred assets is also increased under § 362(a) by the amount of gain recognized by the transferor on the § 351 exchange.

[handwritten note in right margin: 358 adjusts transferor basis in stock when boot]

In some circumstances, a taxpayer may desire to treat the transfer of property to a controlled corporation as a "sale" rather than as an exchange governed by § 351. If the taxpayer has property that has declined in value, a "sale" may be desirable to enable the transferor to recognize a loss on the depreciated assets. Sale treatment may be achieved only if the property is transferred in exchange for property other than stock or only for nonqualified preferred stock (as defined in § 351(g)). If the transaction qualifies as a § 351 transaction, even where boot is received, no loss can be recognized in the transaction.

Under certain circumstances, if there is a significant differential between the individual capital gains rate and the corporate tax rate, a transferor might be willing to pay a capital gain tax on the sale of appreciated assets to permit the corporation to obtain a step-up in basis for the assets, thereby providing the corporation higher depreciation or capital recovery deductions against ordinary income (but see § 1239). The receipt of "property" other than stock in a § 351 transaction also would provide the corporation a basis increase under § 362(a) to the extent of gain recognized by the shareholder under § 351(b).

Where property is transferred to a controlled corporation for stock and debt obligations, whether or not the debt is a security, no part of the transaction constitutes a sale with a resulting recognition of loss.

The debt instrument constitutes "other property" (boot) and the tax consequences thus are governed by § 351(b). Under § 351(g), certain types of preferred stock that have characteristics that cause the stock more nearly to resemble debt also are treated as boot. When the shareholder receives boot in addition to stock, any gain realized on the exchange is recognized to the extent of the fair market value of other property, but no loss is recognized. The taxpayer cannot alter these tax consequences by attempting to denominate part of the transaction as a "sale" of some assets and the balance as a transfer under § 351. See, e.g., Nye v. Commissioner, 50 T.C. 203 (1968).

Where the transferor receives only cash or property, including debt securities (and no stock), the transaction is a sale or exchange and gain or loss will be recognized accordingly. Thus the taxpayer can achieve sale treatment by transferring property for debt instruments ("securities") rather than stock. However, if the transferor is in control of the corporation, sale treatment will not be accorded the transaction if the purported debt instrument is in fact "equity" (see page 121), thus bringing § 351 into play. In addition, a shareholder who transfers depreciated property to the corporation and who receives only nonqualified preferred stock (as defined in § 351(g)) may recognize the loss, notwithstanding that for some other purposes, the preferred stock might be "equity."

The method of computing gain upon the receipt of stock and boot in exchange for two or more different assets is explained in Rev.Rul. 68–55, which follows. Prop.Reg. § 1.351–2(b) (2009) would promulgate the holding of Rev.Rul. 68–55 in regulations. The proposed regulation would provide that in determining the amount of gain recognized in a § 351 transaction, the fair market value of each category of consideration received is allocated to the transferred properties in proportion to the relative fair market value of each of the transferred properties.

Revenue Ruling 68–55
1968–1 C.B. 140.

Advice has been requested as to the correct method of determining the amount and character of the gain to be recognized by Corporation *X* under section 351(b) of the Internal Revenue Code of 1954 under the circumstances described below.

Corporation *Y* was organized by *X* and *A*, an individual who owned no stock in *X*. *A* transferred 20*x* dollars to *Y* in exchange for stock of *Y* having a fair market value of 20*x* dollars and *X* transferred to *Y* three separate assets and received in exchange stock of *Y* having a fair market value of 100*x* dollars plus cash of 10*x* dollars.

In accordance with the facts set forth in the table below if *X* had sold at fair market value each of the three assets it transferred to *Y*, the result would have been as follows:

	Asset I Capital asset held more than 6 months.	*Asset II* Capital asset held not more than 6 months.	*Asset III* Section 1245 property.
Character of asset.			
Fair market value.	$22x	$33x	$55x
Adjusted basis.	40x	20x	2x
Gain (loss).	($18x)	$13x	$30x
Character of gain or loss.	Long-term capital loss.	Short-term capital gain.	Ordinary income.

The facts in the instant case disclose that with respect to the section 1245 property the depreciation subject to recapture exceeds the amount of gain that would be recognized on a sale at fair market value. Therefore, all of such gain would be treated as ordinary income under section 1245(a)(1) of the Code.

Under section 351(a) of the Code, no gain or loss is recognized if property is transferred to a corporation solely in exchange for its stock and immediately after the exchange the transferor is in control of the corporation. If section 351(a) of the Code would apply to an exchange but for the fact that there is received, in addition to the property permitted to be received without recognition of gain, other property or money, then under section 351(b) of the Code gain (if any) to the recipient will be recognized, but in an amount not in excess of the sum of such money and the fair market value of such other property received, and no loss to the recipient will be recognized.

The first question presented is how to determine the amount of gain to be recognized under section 351(b) of the Code. The general rule is that each asset transferred must be considered to have been separately exchanged. See the authorities cited in Revenue Ruling 67–192, C.B. 1967–2, 140, and in Revenue Ruling 68–23, [1968–1 C.B. 144] * * *. Thus, for purposes of making computations under section 351(b) of the Code, it is not proper to total the bases of the various assets transferred and to subtract this total from the fair market value of the total consideration received in the exchange. Moreover, any treatment other than an asset-by-asset approach would have the effect of allowing losses that are specifically disallowed by section 351(b)(2) of the Code.

The second question presented is how, for purposes of making computations under section 351(b) of the Code, to allocate the cash and stock received to the amount realized as to each asset transferred in the exchange. The asset-by-asset approach for computing the amount of gain realized in the exchange requires that for this purpose the fair market value of each category of consideration received must be separately allocated to the transferred assets in proportion to the relative fair market values of the transferred assets. See section 1.1245–4(c)(1) of the Income Tax Regulations which, for the same reasons, requires that for purposes of computing the amount of gain to which section 1245 of the Code applies each category of consideration received must be allocated to the properties transferred in proportion to their relative fair market values.

Accordingly, the amount and character of the gain recognized in the exchange should be computed as follows:

	Total	Asset I	Asset II	Asset III
Fair market value of asset transferred.............	$110x	$22x	$33x	$55x
Percent of total fair market value.................	—	20%	30%	50%
Fair market value of *Y* stock received in exchange....	$100x	$20x	$30x	$50x
Cash received in exchange..	10x	2x	3x	5x
Amount realized.......	$110x	$22x	$33x	$55x
Adjusted basis............	—	40x	20x	25x
Gain (loss) realized....	—	($18x)	$13x	$30x

Under section 351(b)(2) of the Code the loss of 18x dollars realized on the exchange of Asset Number I is not recognized. Such loss may not be used to offset the gains realized on the exchanges of the other assets. Under section 351(b)(1) of the Code, the gain of 13x dollars realized on the exchange of Asset Number II will be recognized as short-term capital gain in the amount of 3x dollars, the amount of cash received. Under sections 351(b)(1) and 1245(b)(3) of the Code, the gain of 30x dollars realized on the exchange of Asset Number III will be recognized as ordinary income in the amount of 5x dollars, the amount of cash received.

DETAILED ANALYSIS

1. THE CORPORATION'S BASIS

If no gain is recognized, the corporation takes a transferred basis from the shareholder in each separate asset under § 362(a)(1). This transferred basis is increased by the transferor's recognized gain, which requires an allocation of the gain to different assets. Rev.Rul. 68–55 applies the principle of Williams v. McGowan, 152 F.2d 570 (2d Cir.1945), now codified in § 1060, requiring the seller of multiple assets to compute gain or loss on an asset-by-asset basis, to § 351 transactions involving boot. See also Rev.Rul. 67–192, 1967–2 C.B. 140; Treas.Reg. § 1.1245–4(c). Although the regulations under § 362 are silent on the issue, and no Revenue Ruling directly addresses the point, this comminution rule also should apply to determine adjustments to the corporation's basis in the transferred assets. The amount of gain allocated to each asset for purposes of the basis adjustment required by § 362(a) should be the amount of gain recognized by the seller with respect to that asset under Rev.Rul. 68–55. Thus the corporation's basis in each of the assets involved in Rev.Rul. 68–55 should be as follows:

	Asset I	Asset II	Asset III
Transferor's Basis	$40x	$20x	$25x
Transferor's Gain		$ 3x	$ 5x
Corporation's Basis	$40x	$23x	$30x

Note that there is no basis adjustment to Asset I, because with respect to that asset the transferor realized an unrecognized loss.

2.   EXCHANGE OF PROPERTY FOR CORPORATE DEBT

2.1. *Installment Sale Treatment*

The receipt of corporate debt obligations as boot by the shareholder might result in installment sale treatment subject to deferred recognition of gain under the rules of § 453. An installment sale is defined as a disposition of property for payments that are received from the transferee of the property after the close of the taxable year in which disposition occurs. However, generally speaking, § 453 installment sale treatment is available only with respect to capital and § 1231 assets. Even with respect to § 1231 assets, § 453 installment sale treatment is not available with respect to the portion of the gain that is § 1245 or § 1250 recapture, which is taxed as ordinary income. I.R.C. § 453(i). But § 453 installment reporting is available for unrecaptured § 1250 gain, within the meaning of § 1(h)(6), for appreciated real property with respect to which depreciation deductions previously have been claimed. Section 453 installment reporting is not available for boot debt obligations allocable to transfers of inventory or property held primarily for sale to customers in the ordinary course of business. I.R.C. § 453(b)(2). Nor is § 453 installment sale reporting available if the corporation's debt obligations issued to the transferor shareholder are payable on demand or are readily tradable. I.R.C. § 453(f)(5).

Under § 453(c) the gain recognized with respect to any payment in an installment sale is an amount that bears the same ratio to the payment as the gross profit on the installment sale bears to the total contract price. Section 453(f)(6) provides, with respect to a like-kind exchange under § 1031(b), that payments and total contract price do not include property that may be received without recognition of gain. Prop.Reg. § 1.453–1(f)(3)(ii) (1984) applies the rules of § 453(f)(6) to a § 351 exchange in which the transferor shareholder receives boot in the form of a debt obligation of the corporation. Prop.Reg. § 1.453–1(f)(1)(iii) (1984) allocates the transferor's basis in transferred property first to the stock received without recognition under § 351, to the extent of the fair market value of the stock. Any remaining basis is used to offset gain recognized on the installment sale. In effect, neither payments nor total contract price include stock permitted to be received under § 351 without recognition of gain.

Assume, for example, that A transfers property with an adjusted basis of $40 and a fair market value of $100 to a corporation controlled by A in exchange for stock worth $70 and a note for $30, payable in three annual installments, with adequate interest, beginning in the year following the transfer. Because under Treas.Reg. § 1.1001–1(g) the amount realized upon receipt of the note is $30, § 351(b) requires that A recognize $30 of A's $60 realized gain. Under § 453, however, since "payments" do not include the stock received in the year of the exchange, no gain is recognized immediately. Under the proposed regulations, A's $40 basis is allocated to the stock, leaving no basis to reduce gain on the installment sale. Recognition is deferred until the receipt of each $10 payment, whereupon A recognizes the full $10 ($10 × $30/$30). Alternatively, if A's basis in the property transferred were $85 dollars, $70 of basis would be allocated to the stock, leaving $15 of basis to offset A's installment gain. A would recognize $15 of gain under § 351(b) but the recognition would be deferred under § 453. A would recognize $5 of gain on each $10 payment ($10 × $15/$30). Installment reporting does not apply if the boot the shareholder

Gerdau MacSteel, Inc. v. Commissioner, 139 T.C. 67 (2012), is the only case to have dealt with whether a particular class of preferred stock was nonqualified preferred stock. The issue arose when a corporation transferred high basis, low value property to its wholly owned subsidiary, with which it filed a consolidated return, solely in exchange for the preferred stock. When the corporation shortly thereafter sold the preferred stock received in the exchange, it claimed a § 358 exchanged basis in the stock rather than a low cost basis equal to the value of the stock. (The purpose of the transaction was to create a capital loss to shelter capital gains recognized on the sale of two other subsidiary corporations.) The stock in question was voting preferred stock with (a) "an assumed" $100 per share issue price, (b) cumulative dividends of 9.5 percent, payable quarterly, (c) which the parent had rights to call after five years and which the shareholders could put to the parent after seven years, and (d) providing for a liquidation value equal to the greater of (i) $125 or (ii) an amount equal to the lesser of (a) a percent of certain tax savings determined formulaically or (b) the subsidiary's book net equity. The Tax Court held that the preferred stock was nonqualified preferred stock and that pursuant to § 351(g)(1)(A), since the parent had received no other stock in the transaction, the transaction was not governed by § 351(a); the preferred stock thus took a cost basis. The court found the transactions were structured in such a way that it was highly likely when the preferred stock was issued that it would be redeemed within the five-and seven-year periods and that the redemption payment would be $125 per share. Although the stock had an assumed issue price of $100 per share and would be redeemed at $125 per share, because of the ceiling on the redemption price, the court concluded that the stock " 'does not participate in corporate growth to any significant extent' within the meaning of I.R.C. sec. 351(g)(3)(A)."

4. THE RECEIPT OF STOCK OPTIONS AND OTHER CONTINGENT INTERESTS

The last sentence of Treas.Reg. § 1.351–1(a)(1)(ii) provides that stock rights or stock warrants are not "stock" for § 351 purposes. This provision raises the issue of whether stock options received along with stock in a § 351 transaction constitute boot subject to § 351(b). In Hamrick v. Commissioner, 43 T.C. 21 (1964) (Acq. in result only, 1966–2 C.B. 5), the taxpayer transferred property to a controlled corporation in exchange for stock plus a contingent right to additional stock dependent upon the performance of the corporation. The Tax Court held that the taxpayer's subsequent receipt of the contingent stock qualified for nonrecognition treatment under § 351. The Tax Court followed the decision in Carlberg v. United States, 281 F.2d 507 (8th Cir.1960), holding that transferable contingent rights to receive stock were stock for purposes of § 354 (nonrecognition treatment for an exchange of stock for stock in corporate reorganizations). In both cases, the opinions concluded that the contingent rights received by the taxpayers could represent either stock or nothing at all. The IRS has indicated that it will follow the result of *Hamrick,* but only because the rights received by the taxpayer were nonassignable and nonmarketable, and could only give rise to the receipt of additional stock by one who was a party to the transfer. Rev.Rul. 66–112, 1966–1 C.B. 68, 70.

5.　TRANSFERS OF DEPRECIABLE PROPERTY: DEPRECIATION RECAPTURE AND SECTION 1239

Section 1245(b)(3) provides that there is no recapture of depreciation in § 351 transactions except to the extent of the gain required to be recognized by § 351(b). Treas.Reg. § 1.1245–4(c)(1) provides that if a taxpayer transfers both § 1245 property and other property to a corporation in a § 351 transaction and receives boot in addition to stock, the amount of the recognized gain that is § 1245 depreciation recapture ordinary income is determined under principles identical to those applied in Rev.Rul. 68–55.

If there is a significant differential between the individual capital gains rate and the corporate tax rate, a taxpayer owning an asset with a low basis but a high value, but with little or no recapture ordinary income potential, might attempt to step-up the basis for depreciation by selling the asset to another taxpayer under the taxpayer's control, with the larger depreciation deductions offsetting the capital gain. When the sale is between a corporation and a more than 50 percent stockholder, § 1239 meets this problem by providing ordinary income treatment on the sale. Section 1239 applies to the gain recognized under § 351(b) (boot) and thus also to the gain required to be recognized under § 357(c) (liabilities in excess of basis). Rev.Rul. 60–302, 1960–2 C.B. 223; Alderman v. Commissioner, 55 T.C. 662 (1971). Section 1239 does not apply, however, to sales or boot taxed under § 351(b) if the shareholder involved in the transaction owns 50 percent or less of the corporation's stock.

6.　TRANSFERS TO EXISTING CONTROLLED CORPORATIONS

6.1.　*Dividend Distributions*

Since § 351 applies to transfers to an existing corporation, as well as to transfers to form a new corporation, a taxpayer might be tempted to combine a transfer of property with a distribution of cash. For example, a sole stockholder transfers a capital asset worth $10,000 to a corporation for additional shares of stock plus $1,000 cash. Rather than being treated as boot in a § 351 transaction, resulting in capital gain, the $1,000 cash could be classified as a dividend under § 301. While § 351(h) does not include a cross-reference to the dividend sections, it would seem that dividend treatment is appropriate in such a case. See Treas.Reg. §§ 1.351–2(d) and 1.301–1(*l*).

If property worth $10,000 is sold by a sole stockholder to an existing corporation for $10,000 cash, the transaction presumably is a sale. However, if the stockholder cannot establish a business purpose for the transfer, the stockholder might be regarded as making a contribution to capital of $10,000 and receiving a dividend of $10,000. But see Curry v. Commissioner, 43 T.C. 667 (1965) (Nonacq.), where the court summarily disposed of the IRS's contention that there was no "business purpose" for a sale of real estate to a controlled corporation: "It would seem that the mere desire to sell, even if the sole purpose was to realize capital gains, should be a sufficient business purpose (assuming always that the substance complies with the form). * * * Indeed, it is difficult to imagine what added business purpose respondent would require for a sale of property."

6.2.　*Treatment of Corporation Transferring Appreciated Property as Boot*

Section 351(f) provides that if in addition to its own stock a corporation transfers appreciated property to a shareholder as boot in a § 351 exchange, the corporation must recognize gain under § 311(b) with respect to the boot property it transfers to the shareholder. Section 311(b) requires recognition of gain as if the property transferred by the corporation had been sold for its fair market value. Thus, corporate level gain will be recognized on a transfer of appreciated property to a stockholder as boot in a § 351 exchange.

This provision is most likely to come into play when transfers are made to a preexisting corporation, but it could apply in a formation as well. Suppose A and B want to form a corporation that they will own equally to operate Blackacre, which is owned by A and has a fair market value of $1,000 and Whiteacre, which is owned by B and has a fair market value of $800. To incorporate with equal contributions, in addition to contributing Whiteacre, B also contributes marketable securities with a basis of $20 and a fair market value of $100, which the corporation distributes to A. (As a result of the contribution of the marketable securities by B and their distribution to A, each of A and B has contributed a net amount of $900.) In addition to A being required to account for $100 of boot under § 351(b), the corporation will recognize a gain of $80 under § 351(f).

SECTION 2.   "SOLELY" FOR STOCK: ASSUMPTION OF LIABILITIES

INTERNAL REVENUE CODE: Sections 357; 358(d).

REGULATIONS: Sections 1.357–1,–2; 1.358–3.

A. BASIC PRINCIPLES

Under § 357(a), the assumption of a liability, or receipt of property subject to a liability, is not treated as the receipt of money or other property by the transferor. Section 357(a) is subject to two exceptions. Section 357(b), enacted in 1939 as part of the original provision, treats liabilities as boot if either (1) a tax avoidance purpose is present or (2) there is no bona fide business purpose for transferring the liabilities. The structure of § 351(b) thus requires the transferor to demonstrate a business purpose for the assumption of the liabilities by the corporation. Second, under § 357(c), enacted in 1954, if the amount of liabilities assumed exceeds the basis of the property transferred, gain results to the extent of such excess, regardless of the purpose of the debt or the assumption. For purposes of determining the transferor's basis in nonrecognition property received in the exchange, § 358(d) treats the assumption of a liability of the transferor or a transfer of property subject to a liability as the receipt of cash by the transferor, without regard to how the debt is treated under § 357. The result is a reduction in the transferor's basis in the stock to the extent of the liability.

DETAILED ANALYSIS

1.   SECTION 357(b) SITUATIONS

Under § 357(b) the total amount of liabilities assumed or to which transferred property is subject is treated as money received unless the taxpayer can show that the principal purpose of the assumption or transfer subject to liabilities was not tax avoidance and that the purpose was a bona fide business purpose. Section 357(b)(2) adds that the taxpayer must meet the burden of proof by "the clear preponderance of the evidence." Under the express terms of the statute, if any liability is found to have been assumed by the corporation for the forbidden tax avoidance purpose, or without a bona fide business purpose, all liabilities are treated as money. Treas.Reg. § 1.357–1(c). Because its application depends on the facts relating to "business purpose" and "tax avoidance purpose," however, the precise scope of the application § 357(b) is not always clear.

1.1. *Purchase Money Liabilities Relating to Transferred Assets*

An assumption of liabilities incurred initially to acquire business assets transferred to the transferee should satisfy the bona fide business purpose requirement. See Jewell v. United States, 330 F.2d 761 (9th Cir.1964) (not applying the predecessor of § 357(b) to the transfer of assets to a corporation that assumed transferor's purchase money indebtedness incurred to acquire the assets). In Rev.Rul. 79–258, 1979–2 C.B. 143, the IRS concluded that in a type (D) reorganization (discussed at page 651), a nonrecognition transaction that is also subject to § 357(a) and (b), there was no tax avoidance motive where the transferor refinanced a portion of an existing long-term debt on the eve of assumption of the debt by the transferee corporation. The refinanced indebtedness was attributable to business assets received by the transferee.

1.2. *Liabilities Unrelated to Acquisition of Transferred Assets*

Section 357(b) has been applied to treat assumed debt as boot in cases involving the assumption of personal nonbusiness liabilities of the transferor. In Estate of Stoll v. Commissioner, 38 T.C. 223 (1962), the taxpayer transferred all the assets of a newspaper business to a corporation, which assumed $1,015,000 of the taxpayer's debts. To the extent of $600,000, the liability represented a refinancing of debt related to the newspaper business that took place just prior to the incorporation and was secured by property transferred to the corporation. The $415,000 balance of the liability was secured by life insurance policies on the taxpayer's life that were not transferred to the corporation. The Tax Court held that the 1939 Code predecessor of § 357(b) applied to treat the $415,000 of indebtedness as boot because there was no business purpose for the assumption of the liability by the corporation and the liability was not related to the transferred business. However, the predecessor of § 357(b) did not apply to treat as boot the $600,000 liability that related to the transferred business. Note that unlike its 1939 Code predecessor, § 357(b)(1) requires that the *total liability* be treated as boot if there is a tax avoidance purpose or if there is no bona fide business purpose for the assumption of any liability.

If a liability, such as a bank loan, is incurred just before a transfer of property to a controlled corporation so that the stockholder obtains the cash loan proceeds, the corporation assumes the debt, and subsequently pays the bank, the transaction viewed as a whole is the equivalent of a payment of cash by the corporation to the stockholder in exchange for the property. The assumption of the liability in such cases generally is found to fall under § 357(b), because of the presence of a tax avoidance purpose, whether or not the liability is secured by the transferred property. In Campbell v. Wheeler, 342 F.2d 837 (5th Cir.1965), the taxpayer transferred a partnership interest to a corporation subject to liabilities that had been incurred just prior to the transfer in order to pay the personal income tax liability of the taxpayer. The court held that the transaction was governed by § 357(b) and the amount of the liabilities assumed constituted boot. Similarly, in Thompson v. Campbell, 64–2 U.S.T.C. ¶ 9659 (N.D.Tex.1964), aff'd per curiam, 353 F.2d 787 (5th Cir.1965), the taxpayer borrowed money with the loan secured by corporate stock and other intangible assets that he already owned. The next day, he transferred the assets, but not the cash proceeds of the loan to a wholly owned corporation that assumed the debt. The transfer to the controlled corporation of assets subject to liabilities incurred the day before incorporation resulted in boot under § 357(b). See also Bryan v. Commissioner, 281 F.2d 238 (4th Cir.1960) (finding a tax avoidance purpose and lack of business purpose on transfer of real estate to a controlled corporation subject to liabilities incurred just prior to the transfer; the court, however, treated as boot only the amount of the liabilities in excess of basis, although the case arose prior to the enactment of § 357(c)).

On the other hand, when a liability secured by the transferred property predates the inception of the plan to incorporate, the assumption by the corporation of the liability in connection with the transfer of assets generally has been found not to run afoul of § 357(b), regardless of the application of the loan proceeds, because there is a business purpose for the debt assumption, i.e., the debts follow the encumbered asset, and no tax avoidance plan. In Simpson v. Commissioner, 43 T.C. 900 (1965) (Acq.), the taxpayer transferred the assets of two department stores, cash, and publicly traded securities to a corporation in a § 351 transaction. The corporation also assumed liabilities in an amount that was slightly less than the aggregate basis of the assets transferred. Most of the liabilities were liens against the publicly traded stock. An admitted purpose of transferring the stock to the corporation was to reduce the income taxes incurred with respect to the dividends received from the stock. In addition, however, ownership of its own marketable securities would make it easier for the corporation to obtain financing, income from the securities would enable the business to weather hard times, and the business would have adequate working capital for expansion and other purposes, all of which the court found to constitute a valid business reason to transfer the securities to the corporation. The IRS asserted that § 357(b) applied, but the court held that the arrangement for the assumption of liabilities was not subject to § 357(b) because the liabilities were secured by transferred property and the loans were not incurred in anticipation of the transfer. Furthermore, the fact that the transferred securities were selected with a view to avoid § 357(c)—the aggregate basis of the stock slightly exceeded the amount of the debt assumed—also was not a tax avoidance purpose either.

In Drybrough v. Commissioner, 376 F.2d 350 (6th Cir.1967), the taxpayer in 1957 transferred real estate to four corporations, each assuming a portion of the mortgage debt on the property that had been incurred in 1953. Another property was transferred to a fifth corporation subject to a mortgage that had been placed on the property in 1957, just three months prior to the transfer. The proceeds of the 1957 mortgage had been invested in tax-exempt bonds. About one-half of the 1953 mortgage proceeds had been used to pay off a loan incurred in 1946 secured by the properties, and most of the balance was also invested in tax-exempt bonds. The court held that the assumption of the 1953 indebtedness was not governed by § 357(b); the use to which the proceeds of the mortgage were put was not relevant in determining whether there was a tax avoidance purpose on the exchange. There was a valid business purpose for placing the real estate subject to the mortgage in the corporation. On the other hand, the assumption of the 1957 indebtedness was governed by § 357(b); the creation of the debt was directly in anticipation of having the corporation assume the indebtedness and constituted a plan to avoid recognition of gain. Note that the application of § 357(b) to the 1957 loan did not result in the application of § 357(b) to the 1953 loan in *Drybrough* because the 1957 loan was assumed by a different corporation from the one that assumed the 1953 loan.

In some cases a borrowing immediately before the transfer has been found not to run afoul of the business purpose requirement. In Easson v. Commissioner, 33 T.C. 963 (1960), rev'd on other grounds, 294 F.2d 653 (9th Cir.1961), the Tax Court construed the 1939 Code predecessor of § 357(b) not to apply on the facts of the case to a mortgage debt placed on the assets shortly before incorporation because the taxpayer had a valid business purpose for the corporate assumption of the mortgage (i.e., insulation of personal assets from potential liabilities and facilitation of management of the real estate and estate planning by obtaining liquidity), and the corporation was an active business entity. The *Easson* case appears to be an aberration, and it is unlikely that it would be followed currently.

2. ASSUMPTION OF TRANSFEROR'S DEBT TO TRANSFEREE CORPORATION

In Kniffen v. Commissioner, 39 T.C. 553 (1962) (Acq.), the taxpayer transferred assets and liabilities of a sole proprietorship to a pre-existing corporation. Among the liabilities assumed by the corporation was a debt from the taxpayer to the corporation. The assumption eliminated the taxpayer's debt by operation of law. The IRS asserted that the taxpayer realized cancellation of debt income as boot under § 351(b) and that there was no assumption of debt to bring § 357 into play. The court held for the taxpayer; the debt was assumed and then discharged so that § 357 applied. Under the current statutory pattern, however, it appears that § 108(e)(4) would require the recognition of cancellation of indebtedness income (unless otherwise not recognized under § 108) if the transferor "controls" the transferee corporation (control for this purpose being defined in § 267(b), which provides a more than 50 percent of value test for control).

3. TRANSFER OF NET VALUE REQUIREMENT

Proposed amendments to Treas.Reg. § 1.351–1 would add requirements that there be both (1) a contribution of net value and (2) a receipt of net value as a prerequisite for § 351 to apply. Prop.Reg. § 1.351–1(a)(1)(iii)(A) (2005) would provide that stock will not be treated as issued for property if either (1) the fair market value of the transferred property does not exceed the sum of the amount of liabilities of the transferor that are assumed by the transferee in connection with the transfer and the amount of any money and the fair market value of any other property (other than stock permitted to be received under § 351(a) without the recognition of gain) received by the transferor in connection with the transfer, or (2) the fair market value of the assets of the transferee does not exceed the amount of its liabilities immediately after the transfer. Prop.Reg. § 1.351–1(a)(2), Ex. 4 (2005), illustrates the rule by concluding that a transfer of real property encumbered by a nonrecourse mortgage in excess of the property's fair market value to a wholly owned corporation, which remains solvent after the transaction, in exchange for additional stock is not subject to § 351. Although the example does not recharacterize the transaction, it presumably is a sale on which gain or loss is recognized and which gives rise to a purchase price basis under § 1012 for the corporation.[7]

B. LIABILITIES IN EXCESS OF BASIS

(1) GENERAL RULES

INTERNAL REVENUE CODE: Sections 357(c); 358(d); 362(d)(1).

REGULATIONS: Sections 1.357–2; 1.358–3.

Section 357(c)(1) requires the recognition of gain to a transferor if in connection with a transfer subject to § 351 the transferee corporation assumes liabilities of the transferor in excess of the adjusted basis of the property transferred to the corporation. Suppose that A owned an asset worth $100,000, which cost $10,000 and was subject to a mortgage of $50,000 to secure a bank loan of $50,000 obtained by A in a separate transaction. If A were permitted to transfer the asset to a controlled corporation subject to the liability without recognition of gain, A would avoid tax on $40,000, the difference between A's original investment of $10,000 and the $50,000 cash received by A from the borrowing. The problem is resolved by § 357(c)(1). The gain recognized under § 357(c)(1) is capital or ordinary according to the ratio of capital assets to ordinary assets transferred. Treas.Reg. § 1.357–2(b).

In calculating the shareholder's basis in the stock received in the exchange, § 358(d)(1) requires that the full amount of the transferor's debts assumed by the corporation be treated as boot received by the transferor for purposes of applying § 358(a). Thus, in the above example, the shareholder's basis in the stock is $0: the $10,000 basis of transferred property—$50,000 debt assumed by the corporation + $40,000 gain recognized. Under § 362(a), the corporation's basis in the property is increased by the gain recognized to the transferor. Thus, in the above example, the corporation takes the property with a $50,000 basis ($10,000 + $40,000).

Section 357(c) applies with respect to the aggregate amount of the transferor's liabilities assumed by the corporation and the aggregate amount of the bases of the properties transferred to the corporation by a particular transferor. Treas.Reg. § 1.357–2(a). Thus, in the above situation, A could avoid recognition of gain under § 357(c) by transferring to the corporation along with the property, cash in the amount of $40,000 or other property with a basis of at least $40,000. The following case deals with the question of whether the same result is obtained when the transferor gives the corporation a promissory note rather than cash or additional property in which the transferor has a basis.

---

[7]   A realized loss, however, might be disallowed under § 267(a)(1) if the transferor owns more than 50 percent of the value of the stock of the transferee corporation.

Peracchi v. Commissioner

United States Court of Appeals, Ninth Circuit, 1998.
143 F.3d 487.

■ KOZINSKI, CIRCUIT JUDGE:

We must unscramble a Rubik's Cube of corporate tax law to determine the basis of a note contributed by a taxpayer to his wholly-owned corporation.

The Transaction

The taxpayer, Donald Peracchi, needed to contribute additional capital to his closely-held corporation (NAC) to comply with Nevada's minimum premium-to-asset ratio for insurance companies. Peracchi contributed two parcels of real estate. The parcels were encumbered with liabilities which together exceeded Peracchi's total basis in the properties by more than half a million dollars. As we discuss in detail below, under section 357(c), contributing property with liabilities in excess of basis can trigger immediate recognition of gain in the amount of the excess. In an effort to avoid this, Peracchi also executed a promissory note, promising to pay NAC $1,060,000 over a term of ten years at 11% interest. Peracchi maintains that the note has a basis equal to its face amount, thereby making his total basis in the property contributed greater than the total liabilities. If this is so, he will have extracted himself from the quicksand of section 357(c) and owe no immediate tax on the transfer of property to NAC. The IRS, though, maintains that (1) the note is not genuine indebtedness and should be treated as an unenforceable gift; and (2) even if the note is genuine, it does not increase Peracchi's basis in the property contributed.

The parties are not splitting hairs: Peracchi claims the basis of the note is $1,060,000, its face value, while the IRS argues that the note has a basis of zero. If Peracchi is right, he pays no immediate tax on the half a million dollars by which the debts on the land he contributed exceed his basis in the land; if the IRS is right, the note becomes irrelevant for tax purposes and Peracchi must recognize an immediate gain on the half million. The fact that the IRS and Peracchi are so far apart suggests they are looking at the transaction through different colored lenses. To figure out whether Peracchi's lens is rose-tinted or clear, it is useful to take a guided tour of sections 351 and 357 and the tax law principles undergirding them.

Into the Lobster Pot: Section 351[2]

The Code tries to make organizing a corporation pain-free from a tax point of view. A capital contribution is, in tax lingo, a "nonrecognition" event: A shareholder can generally contribute capital without recognizing gain on the exchange. * * * See I.R.C. § 351. So long as the shareholders contributing the property remain in control of the corporation after the exchange, section 351 applies: It doesn't matter if

---

[2] "Decisions to embrace the corporate form of organization should be carefully considered, since a corporation is like a lobster pot: easy to enter, difficult to live in, and painful to get out of." Boris I. Bittker & James S. Eustice, Federal Income Taxation of Corporations and Shareholders ¶ 2.01[3] (6th ed.1997) (footnotes omitted) (hereinafter Bittker & Eustice).

the capital contribution occurs at the creation of the corporation or if—as here—the company is already up and running. * * *

Gain Deferral: Section 358(a)

* * * [W]hen a shareholder like Peracchi contributes property to a corporation in a nonrecognition transaction, * * * the shareholder must substitute the basis of that property for what would otherwise be the cost basis of the stock.[6] This preserves the gain for recognition at a later day: The gain is built into the shareholder's new basis in the stock, and he will recognize income when he disposes of the stock.

The fact that gain is deferred rather than extinguished doesn't diminish the importance of questions relating to basis and the timing of recognition. In tax, as in comedy, timing matters. Most taxpayers would much prefer to pay tax on contributed property years later-when they sell their stock-rather than when they contribute the property.[7] Thus what Peracchi is seeking here is gain deferral: He wants the gain to be recognized only when he disposes of some or all of his stock.

Continuity of Investment: Boot and section 351(b)

* * * [T]he central exception to nonrecognition for section 351 transactions comes into play when the taxpayer receives "boot"—money or property other than stock in the corporation—in exchange for the property contributed. See I.R.C. § 351(b). Boot is recognized as taxable income because it represents a partial cashing out. * * *

Peracchi did not receive boot in return for the property he contributed. But that doesn't end the inquiry: We must consider whether Peracchi has cashed out in some other way which would warrant treating part of the transaction as taxable boot.

Assumption of Liabilities: Section 357(a)

The property Peracchi contributed to NAC was encumbered by liabilities. Contribution of leveraged property makes things trickier from a tax perspective. When a shareholder contributes property encumbered by debt, the corporation usually assumes the debt. And the Code normally treats discharging a liability the same as receiving money: The taxpayer improves his economic position by the same amount either way. See I.R.C. § 61(a)(12). NAC's assumption of the liabilities attached to Peracchi's property therefore could theoretically be viewed as the receipt of money, which would be taxable boot. See United States v. Hendler, 303 U.S. 564 * * * (1938).

The Code takes a different tack. Requiring shareholders like Peracchi to recognize gain any time a corporation assumes a liability in connection with a capital contribution would greatly diminish the nonrecognition benefit section 351 is meant to confer. Section 357(a) thus takes a lenient view of the assumption of liability: A shareholder engaging in a section 351 transaction does not have to treat the assumption of liability as boot, even if the corporation assumes his obligation to pay. * * *

---

[6]   See I.R.C. § 358(a) * * *.

[7]   Of course, should the taxpayers be lucky enough to die before disposing of the stock, their heirs would take a stepped-up basis in the stock equal to its fair market value as of the date of death. See I.R.C. § 1014.

This nonrecognition does not mean that the potential gain disappears. Once again, the basis provisions kick in to reflect the transfer of gain from the shareholder to the corporation: The shareholder's substitute basis in the stock received is decreased by the amount of the liability assumed by the corporation. See I.R.C. § 358(d), (a). The adjustment preserves the gain for recognition when the shareholder sells his stock in the company, since his taxable gain will be the difference between the (new lower) basis and the sale price of the stock.

Sasquatch and The Negative Basis Problem: Section 357(c)

Highly leveraged property presents a peculiar problem in the section 351 context. Suppose a shareholder organizes a corporation and contributes as its only asset a building with a basis of $50, a fair market value of $100, and mortgage debt of $90. Section 351 says that the shareholder does not recognize any gain on the transaction. Under section 358, the shareholder takes a substitute basis of $50 in the stock, then adjusts it downward under section 357 by $90 to reflect the assumption of liability. This leaves him with a basis of minus $40. A negative basis properly preserves the gain built into the property: If the shareholder turns around and sells the stock the next day for $10 (the difference between the fair market value and the debt), he would face $50 in gain, the same amount as if he sold the property without first encasing it in a corporate shell.[8]

But skeptics say that negative basis, like Bigfoot, doesn't exist. Compare Easson v. Commissioner, 33 T.C. 963, 970 (1960) (there's no such thing as a negative basis) with Easson v. Commissioner, 294 F.2d 653, 657–58 (9th Cir.1961) (yes, Virginia, there is a negative basis). Basis normally operates as a cost recovery system: Depreciation deductions reduce basis, and when basis hits zero, the property cannot be depreciated farther. At a more basic level, it seems incongruous to attribute a negative value to a figure that normally represents one's investment in an asset. Some commentators nevertheless argue that when basis operates merely to measure potential gain (as it does here), allowing negative basis may be perfectly appropriate and consistent with the tax policy underlying nonrecognition transactions. See, e.g., J. Clifton Fleming, Jr., The Highly Avoidable Section 357(c): A Case Study in Traps for the Unwary and Some Positive Thoughts About Negative Basis, 16 J. Corp. L. 1, 27–30 (1990). Whatever the merits of this debate, it seems that section 357(c) was enacted to eliminate the possibility of negative basis. * * *

Section 357(c) prevents negative basis by forcing a shareholder to recognize gain to the extent liabilities exceed basis. Thus, if a shareholder contributes a building with a basis of $50 and liabilities of $90, he does not receive stock with a basis of minus $40. Instead, he takes a basis of zero and must recognize a $40 gain.

Peracchi sought to contribute two parcels of real property to NAC in a section 351 transaction. Standing alone the contribution would

---

[8] If the taxpayer sells the property outright, his amount realized includes the full amount of the mortgage debt * * * and the result is as follows: Amount realized ($10 cash + $90 debt) — $50 Basis = $50 gain.

have run afoul of section 357(c): The property he wanted to contribute had liabilities in excess of basis, and Peracchi would have had to recognize gain to the extent of the excess, or $566,807:

	Liabilities	Basis
Property #1	1,386,655	349,774
Property #2	161,558	631,632
	1,548,213	981,406
Liabilities	1,548,213	
Basis	981,406	
Excess (357(c))	566,907	

The Grift: Boosting Basis with a Promissory Note

Peracchi tried to dig himself out of this tax hole by contributing a personal note with a face amount of $1,060,000 along with the real property. Peracchi maintains that the note has a basis in his hands equal to its face value. If he's right, we must add the basis of the note to the basis of the real property. Taken together, the aggregate basis in the property contributed would exceed the aggregate liabilities:

	Liabilities	Basis
Property #1	1,386,655	349,774
Property #2	161,558	631,632
Note	0	1,060,000
	1,548,213	2.041,406

Under Peracchi's theory, then, the aggregate liabilities no longer exceed the aggregate basis, and section 357(c) no longer triggers any gain. The government argues, however, that the note has a zero basis. If so, the note would not affect the tax consequences of the transaction, and Peracchi's $566,807 in gain would be taxable immediately.

Are Promises Truly Free?

Which brings us (phew!) to the issue before us: Does Peracchi's note have a basis in Peracchi's hands for purposes of section 357(c)?[12] The language of the Code gives us little to work with. The logical place to start is with the definition of basis. Section 1012 provides that "[t]he basis of property shall be the cost of such property. . . ." But "cost" is nowhere defined. What does it cost Peracchi to write the note and contribute it to his corporation? The IRS argues tersely that the "taxpayers in the instant case incurred no cost in issuing their own note to NAC, so their basis in the note was zero." Brief for Appellee at 41. See Alderman v. Commissioner, 55 T.C. 662, 665 (1971); Rev.Rul. 68–629, 1968–2 C.B. 154, 155.[13] Building on this premise, the IRS makes

---

[12] Peracchi owned all the voting stock of NAC both before and after the exchange, so the control requirement of section 351 is satisfied. * * * Peracchi did not receive any stock in return for the property contributed, so it could be argued that the exchange was not "solely in exchange for stock" as required by section 351. Courts have consistently recognized, however, that issuing stock in this situation would be a meaningless gesture: Because Peracchi is the sole shareholder of NAC, issuing additional stock would not affect his economic position relative to other shareholders. See, e.g., Jackson v. Commissioner, 708 F.2d 1402, 1405 (9th Cir.1983).

[13] We would face a different case had the Treasury promulgated a regulation interpreting section 357(c). A revenue ruling is entitled to some deference as the stated litigating position of the agency which enforces the tax code, but not nearly as much as a

Peracchi out to be a grifter: He holds an unenforceable promise to pay himself money, since the corporation will not collect on it unless he says so.

IRS argues he's "paying" himself.

It's true that all Peracchi did was make out a promise to pay on a piece of paper, mark it in the corporate minutes and enter it on the corporate books. It is also true that nothing will cause the corporation to enforce the note against Peracchi so long as Peracchi remains in control. But the IRS ignores the possibility that NAC may go bankrupt, an event that would suddenly make the note highly significant. Peracchi and NAC are separated by the corporate form, and this gossamer curtain makes a difference in the shell game of C Corp organization and reorganization. Contributing the note puts a million dollar nut within the corporate shell, exposing Peracchi to the cruel nutcracker of corporate creditors in the event NAC goes bankrupt. And it does so to the tune of $1,060,000, the full face amount of the note. Without the note, no matter how deeply the corporation went into debt, creditors could not reach Peracchi's personal assets. With the note on the books, however, creditors can reach into Peracchi's pocket by enforcing the note as an unliquidated asset of the corporation.

The key to solving this puzzle, then, is to ask whether bankruptcy is significant enough a contingency to confer substantial economic effect on this transaction. If the risk of bankruptcy is important enough to be recognized, Peracchi should get basis in the note: He will have increased his exposure to the risks of the business—and thus his economic investment in NAC—by $1,060,000. If bankruptcy is so remote that there is no realistic possibility it will ever occur, we can ignore the potential economic effect of the note as speculative and treat it as merely an unenforceable promise to contribute capital in the future.

When the question is posed this way, the answer is clear. Peracchi's obligation on the note was not conditioned on NAC's remaining solvent. It represents a new and substantial increase in Peracchi's investment in the corporation.[14] The Code seems to recognize that economic exposure of the shareholder is the ultimate measuring rod of a shareholder's investment. * * * Peracchi therefore is entitled to a step-up in basis to the extent he will be subjected to economic loss if the underlying investment turns unprofitable. * * *

The economics of the transaction also support Peracchi's view of the matter. The transaction here does not differ substantively from others that would certainly give Peracchi a boost in basis. For example, Peracchi could have borrowed $1 million from a bank and contributed the cash to NAC along with the properties. Because cash has a basis equal to face value, Peracchi would not have faced any section 357(c) gain. NAC could then have purchased the note from the bank for $1

---

regulation. Ruling 68–629 offers no rationale, let alone a reasonable one, for its holding that it costs a taxpayer nothing to write a promissory note, and thus deserves little weight.

[14] We confine our holding to a case such as this where the note is contributed to an operating business which is subject to a non-trivial risk of bankruptcy or receivership. NAC is not, for example, a shell corporation or a passive investment company; Peracchi got into this mess in the first place because NAC was in financial trouble and needed more assets to meet Nevada's minimum premium-to-asset ratio for insurance companies.

million which, assuming the bank's original assessment of Peracchi's creditworthiness was accurate, would be the fair market value of the note. In the end the corporation would hold a million dollar note from Peracchi—just like it does now—and Peracchi would face no section 357(c) gain.[15] The only economic difference between the transaction just described and the transaction Peracchi actually engaged in is the additional costs that would accompany getting a loan from the bank. Peracchi incurs a "cost" of $1 million when he promises to pay the note to the bank; the cost is not diminished here by the fact that the transferor controls the initial transferee. The experts seem to agree: "Section 357(c) can be avoided by a transfer of enough cash to eliminate any excess of liabilities over basis; and since a note given by a solvent obligor in purchasing property is routinely treated as the equivalent of cash in determining the basis of the property, it seems reasonable to give it the same treatment in determining the basis of the property transferred in a § 351 exchange." Bittker & Eustice ¶ 3.06[4][b].

We are aware of the mischief that can result when taxpayers are permitted to calculate basis in excess of their true economic investment. * * * [W]e do not believe our holding will have such pernicious effects. First, and most significantly, by increasing the taxpayer's personal exposure, the contribution of a valid, unconditional promissory note has substantial economic effects which reflect his true economic investment in the enterprise. * * * Peracchi will have to pay the full amount of the note with after-tax dollars if NAC's economic situation heads south. Second, [i]t is the pass-through of losses that makes artificial increases in equity interests of particular concern. * * * We don't have to tread quite so lightly in the C Corp context, since a C Corp doesn't funnel losses to the shareholder.[16] * * *

We find further support for Peracchi's view by looking at the alternative: What would happen if the note had a zero basis? The IRS points out that the basis of the note in the hands of the corporation is the same as it was in the hands of the taxpayer. Accordingly, if the note has a zero basis for Peracchi, so too for NAC. See I.R.C. § 362(a).[17] But what happens if NAC—perhaps facing the threat of an involuntary petition for bankruptcy—turns around and sells Peracchi's note to a third party for its fair market value? According to the IRS's theory,

---

[15] * * * We readily acknowledge that our assumptions fall apart if the shareholder isn't creditworthy. Here, the government has stipulated that Peracchi's net worth far exceeds the value of the note, so creditworthiness is not at issue. But we limit our holding to cases where the note is in fact worth approximately its face value.

[16] Our holding therefore does not extend to the partnership or S Corp context.

[17] But see Lessinger v. Commissioner, 872 F.2d 519 (2d Cir.1989). In *Lessinger*, the Second Circuit analyzed a similar transaction. It agreed with the IRS's (faulty) premise that the note had a zero basis in the taxpayer's hands. But then, brushing aside the language of section 362(a), the court concluded that the note had a basis in the corporation's hands equal to its face value. The court held that this was enough to dispel any section 357(c) gain to the taxpayer, proving that two wrongs sometimes do add up to a right.

We agree with the IRS that *Lessinger's* approach is untenable. Section 357(c) contemplates measuring basis of the property contributed in the hands of the taxpayer, not the corporation. Section 357 appears in the midst of the Code sections dealing with the effect of capital contributions on the shareholder; sections 361 et seq., on the other hand, deal with the effect on a corporation, and section 362 defines the basis of property contributed in the hands of the corporation. Because we hold that the note has a face value basis to the shareholder for purposes of section 357(c), however, we reach the same result as *Lessinger*.

NAC would take a carryover basis of zero in the note and would have to recognize $1,060,000 in phantom gain on the subsequent exchange, even though the note did not appreciate in value one bit. That can't be the right result.

Accordingly, we hold that Peracchi has a basis of $1,060,000 in the note he wrote to NAC. The aggregate basis exceeds the liabilities of the properties transferred to NAC under section 351, and Peracchi need not recognize any section 357(c) gain.

Genuine Indebtedness or Sham?

The Tax Court never reached the issue of Peracchi's basis in the note. Instead, it ruled for the Commissioner on the ground that the note is not genuine indebtedness. The court emphasized two facts which it believed supported the view that the note is a sham: (1) NAC's decision whether to collect on the note is wholly controlled by Peracchi and (2) Peracchi missed the first two years of payments, yet NAC did not accelerate the debt. These facts certainly do suggest that Peracchi paid imperfect attention to his obligations under the note, as frequently happens when debtor and creditor are under common control. But we believe the proper way to approach the genuine indebtedness question is to look at the face of the note and consider whether Peracchi's legal obligation is illusory. And it is not. First, the note's bona fides are adequate: The IRS has stipulated that Peracchi is creditworthy and likely to have the funds to pay the note; the note bears a market rate of interest commensurate with his creditworthiness; the note has a fixed term. Second, the IRS does not argue that the value of the note is anything other than its face value; nothing in the record suggests NAC couldn't borrow against the note to raise cash. Lastly, the note is fully transferable and enforceable by third parties, such as hostile creditors. On the basis of these facts we hold that the note is an ordinary, negotiable, recourse obligation which must be treated as genuine debt for tax purposes. * * *

The IRS argues that the note is nevertheless a sham because it was executed simply to avoid tax. Tax avoidance is a valid concern in this context; section 357(a) does provide the opportunity for a bailout transaction of sorts. For example, a taxpayer with an unencumbered building he wants to sell could take out a nonrecourse mortgage, pocket the proceeds, and contribute the property to a newly organized corporation. Although the gain would be preserved for later recognition, the taxpayer would have partially cashed out his economic investment in the property: By taking out a nonrecourse mortgage, the economic risk of loss would be transferred to the lender. Section 357(b) addresses this sort of bailout by requiring the recognition of gain if the transaction lacks a business purpose.

Peracchi's capital contribution is not a bailout. Peracchi contributed the buildings to NAC because the company needed additional capital, and the contribution of the note was part of that transaction. The IRS, in fact, stipulated that the contribution had a business purpose. Bailout potential exists regardless of whether the taxpayer contributes a note along with the property; section 357(b), not 357(c), is the sword the Service must use to attack bailout transactions.

* * *

The Aftermath

We take a final look at the result to make sure we have not placed our stamp of approval on some sort of exotic tax shelter. We hold that Peracchi is entitled to a step up in basis for the face value of the note, just as if he contributed cash to the corporation. See I.R.C. § 358. If Peracchi does in fact keep his promise and pay off the note with after tax dollars, the tax result is perfectly appropriate: NAC receives cash, and the increase in basis Peracchi took for the original contribution is justified. Peracchi has less potential gain, but he paid for it in real dollars.

But what if, as the IRS fears, NAC never does enforce the note? If NAC goes bankrupt, the note will be an asset of the estate enforceable for the benefit of creditors, and Peracchi will eventually be forced to pay in after tax dollars. Peracchi will undoubtedly have worked the deferral mechanism of section 351 to his advantage, but this is not inappropriate where the taxpayer is on the hook in both form and substance for enough cash to offset the excess of liabilities over basis. By increasing his personal exposure to the creditors of NAC, Peracchi has increased his economic investment in the corporation, and a corresponding increase in basis is wholly justified.[20]

Conclusion

We hold that Peracchi has a basis of $1,060,000 in the note, its face value. As such, the aggregate liabilities of the property contributed to NAC do not exceed its basis, and Peracchi does not recognize any § 357(c) gain. The decision of the Tax Court is REVERSED. The case is remanded for entry of judgment in favor of Peracchi.

■ FERNANDEZ, CIRCUIT JUDGE, Dissenting:

Is there something that a taxpayer, who has borrowed hundreds of thousands of dollars more than his basis in his property, can do to avoid taxation when he transfers the property? Yes, says Peracchi, because by using a very clever argument he can avoid the strictures of 26 U.S.C. § 357(c). He need only make a promise to pay by giving a "good," though unsecured, promissory note to his corporation when he transfers the property to it. That is true even though the property remains subject to the encumbrances. How can that be? Well, by preparing a promissory note the taxpayer simply creates basis without cost to himself. But see 26 U.S.C. § 1012; Rev.Rul. 68–629, 1968–2 C.B. 154; Alderman v. Commissioner, 55 T.C. 662, 665 (1971). Thus he can extract a large part of the value of the property, pocket the funds, use them, divest himself of the property, and pay the tax another day, if ever at all.

But as with all magical solutions, the taxpayer must know the proper incantations and make the correct movements. He cannot just transfer the property to the corporation and promise, or be obligated, to pay off the encumbrances. That would not change the fact that the

---

[20] What happens if NAC does not go bankrupt, but merely writes off the note instead? Peracchi would then face discharge of indebtedness income to the tune of $1,060,000. This would put Peracchi in a worse position than when he started, since discharge of indebtedness is normally treated as ordinary income. Peracchi, having increased his basis in the stock of the corporation by $1,060,000 would receive a capital loss (or less capital gain) to that extent. But the shift in character of the income will normally work to the disadvantage of a taxpayer in Peracchi's situation.

property was still subject to those encumbrances. According to Peracchi, the thaumaturgy that will save him from taxes proceeds in two simple steps. He must first prepare a ritualistic writing—an unsecured promissory note in an amount equal to or more than the excess of the encumbrances over the basis. He must then give that writing to his corporation. That is all.[1] But is not that just a "promise to pay," which "does not represent the paying out or reduction of assets?" Don E. Williams Co. v. Commissioner, 429 U.S. 569, 583 * * * (1977). Never mind, he says. He has nonetheless increased the total basis of the property transferred and avoided the tax. I understand the temptation to embrace that argument, but I see no real support for it in the law.

Peracchi says a lot about economic realities. I see nothing real about that maneuver. I see, rather, a bit of sortilege that would have made Merlin envious. The taxpayer has created something—basis—out of nothing.

Thus, I respectfully dissent.

DETAILED ANALYSIS

1. DETERMINATION OF AMOUNT OF LIABILITY ASSUMED

Section 357(d) provides statutory rules for determining the extent to which a debt of the transferor has been assumed by the transferee corporation for purposes of determining the transferor's gain under § 357(c) and the corporate transferee's step-up in basis under § 362(a) that results from the transferor's recognition of gain.[8] Recourse debt is treated as having been assumed only if, based on all the facts and circumstances, the transferee corporation has agreed to pay the debt and is expected to pay the debt, regardless of whether or not the transferor shareholder has been relieved of liability vis-à-vis the creditor. The transferee corporation is treated as assuming any nonrecourse debt encumbering property it receives, but the amount of the debt assumed is reduced by the lesser of: (1) the amount of the debt secured by assets not transferred to the corporation that another person or corporation has agreed (and is expected) to satisfy, or (2) the fair market value of the other assets secured by the debt.

Seggerman Farms v. Commissioner, 308 F.3d 803 (7th Cir. 2002), held that § 357(c) requires gain recognition when the liabilities assumed by the corporation exceed the transferor shareholder's basis in the property even if the transferor remains liable as a guarantor. The shareholders argued that because they had personally guaranteed the debt, they were not relieved of their obligations on the transferred property, and, thus, no gain should be recognized on the transfer. The court rejected the taxpayers' argument that under "the emerging equitable interpretation of § 357(c)" their guarantees should be treated in the same manner as the shareholders' promissory notes to the corporations in Peracchi v. Commissioner, supra, and

---

[1] What is even better, he need not even make payments on the note until after the IRS catches up with him. I, by the way, am dubious about the proposition that the Tax Court clearly erred when it held that the note was not even a genuine indebtedness.

[8] In REG–100818–01, Liabilities Assumed in Certain Transactions, 68 F.R. 23931 (May 6, 2003), the IRS and Treasury announced that they are concerned that §§ 357(d) and 362(d) do not always produce appropriate results and that it might be desirable to modify certain rules by regulation, as permitted by § 357(d)(3). The notice explains the issues and the rules the IRS and Treasury are considering proposing.

Lessinger v. Commissioner, page 93, reasoning that the guarantee, standing alone, does not constitute an "economic outlay." Although the case arose prior to the enactment of § 357(d), the court noted in its opinion that the result would not be different under the current statute.

On the other hand, § 357(d) has changed the results in Rosen v. Commissioner, 62 T.C. 11 (1974), aff'd by order, 515 F.2d 507 (3d Cir.1975), and Owen v. Commissioner, 881 F.2d 832 (9th Cir.1989), cited in footnote 10 of the *Peracchi* opinion. Both of those cases held that § 357(c) applied in situations in which the transferor remained personally liable on recourse debts secured by property transferred to a corporation where the corporation did not expressly assume the obligations but merely took the property subject to the encumbrances. Prior to the enactment of § 357(d), 357(c) applied as long as the property received by the corporation was subject to the debt.

2. CONTRIBUTION OF SHAREHOLDER'S PROMISSORY NOTE: DETERMINATION OF TRANSFEROR'S BASIS

Peracchi was not the first case to consider the question whether a transferor of encumbered property could eliminate recognized gain under § 357(c) by the transfer of the transferor's own promissory note. Several courts have confronted the issue, and each has analyzed it differently. In Rev.Rul. 68–629, 1968–2 C.B. 154, the IRS held that for purposes of applying § 357(c) a shareholder's note contributed to the corporation had a zero basis because the shareholder "incurred no cost in making the note." The Tax Court first faced the issue in Alderman v. Commissioner, 55 T.C. 662 (1971), where, as in *Peracchi*, the taxpayers transferred assets to their corporation, which assumed liabilities in excess of the transferors' basis for the assets. In order to increase the assets of the corporation and avoid gain under § 357(c), the taxpayers executed a note payable to the corporation in an amount slightly in excess of the amount by which the assumed liabilities exceeded the basis of the transferred assets. Following Rev.Rul. 68–629, the Tax Court held that because the taxpayers incurred no cost in making the note, their basis in the note was zero. Thus, gain resulted under § 357(c). Presumably, however, the note should give rise to an immediate adjustment to the obligor-shareholder's basis for the stock. If there is no immediate basis adjustment for the note, the stockholder should receive an increased basis for the stock for additional capital contributed to the corporation as the note is paid. Pursuant to § 1032, the corporation would not be required to recognize gain either when the note itself was received or when payment was received. (However, in dictum, the court gratuitously— erroneously in the opinion of the authors of this text—added that corporation's basis in the note also was zero).

In Lessinger v. Commissioner, 872 F.2d 519 (2d Cir.1989), the Court of Appeals for the Second Circuit refused to follow *Alderman*. Lessinger transferred the assets of a sole proprietorship to his wholly owned corporation in a transaction to which § 351 applied. The proprietorship was insolvent in that its liabilities exceeded the value of the transferred assets. The liabilities assumed by the corporation also exceeded Lessinger's basis in the transferred assets. The transferee corporation created a "loan receivable" due from Lessinger on the corporate books in the amount that the liabilities of the proprietorship exceeded the value of the transferred assets. Reversing the Tax Court (85 T.C. 824 (1985)), the Court of Appeals held that Lessinger was not required by § 357(c) to recognize gain, but followed a different path of reasoning than the Ninth Circuit Court of Appeals did in *Peracchi*. The Second Circuit agreed with the *Alderman* holding that a taxpayer has no basis in the taxpayer's own promise to pay, but also concluded that the basis of Lessinger's obligation in the hands of the corporate transferee was equal to the face amount of the obligation. The court reasoned that the transferee corporation "incurred a cost in the transaction involving the transfer of the obligation by taking on the liabilities of the proprietorship that exceeded its assets." The court also pointed out that unless the corporation had a basis in Lessinger's obligation, it would have to recognize gain on payment of the debt. The court then held that "where the transferor undertakes genuine personal liability to the transferee, 'adjusted basis' in § 357(c) refers to the transferee's basis in the obligation which is its face amount." Finally, the court also noted that Lessinger did not avoid recognition of economic gain on the transaction because he undertook "genuine personal liability" to the corporation for the liabilities exceeding the basis of the assets.

The Second Circuit's reasoning in *Lessinger* is unsupportable. First, in total disregard of § 362(a), the court concluded that the corporation took a basis in the transferor's promissory note equal to its face amount. (That result might be true for other reasons, but it does not occur by reason of § 362(a).) Second, since the payments on the note should be treated as capital contributions, the corporation will not recognize any gain as it receives payments. Third, the court's reasoning that gain under § 357(c) is computed with reference to the transferee's basis in the transferred property rather than the transferor's basis is contrary to the otherwise universally accepted rule that gain is computed with reference to the transferor's basis.

The courts' reasoning in each of *Peracchi* and *Lessinger*, as well as the Tax Court's reasoning in *Alderman* and the IRS's reasoning in Rev.Rul. 68–629, are misguided, but ultimately the court in *Peracchi* reaches the correct conclusion, at least where the debt obligation is genuine. All of these authorities focus on determining whether the transferor shareholder's basis in the shareholder's own note is zero or its principal (face) amount in applying § 357(c). All of the court decisions, including *Peracchi*, as well as the IRS, miss the point that the statutory rule in § 357(c) is inadequate to deal with the issue because the statute focuses on the transferor's basis in property "transferred." To transfer property the transferor must own the property prior to the transfer. However, the transferor never owned his own promissory note. It did not come into existence as "property" until it was owned by the corporation. The shareholder "issued" the note to the corporation; he did not "transfer" it; the note was created by its issuance. *Alderman* and the IRS attempt to follow the statutory pattern of Subchapter C quite literally, without resort to general principles of taxation. *Peracchi*, on the other hand, superimposes on Subchapter C the general principle that payment with a promissory note is treated the same as payment in cash. For basis purposes, the acquisition of property for a note is the same as the acquisition of property for cash. See Rev.Rul. 2004–37, 2004–1 C.B. 583, holding that under general principles of taxation, stock in a corporation acquired in exchange for the shareholder's promissory note takes a § 1012 cost basis equal to the principal amount of the note, just as it would if cash had been paid. From this perspective it should not matter whether a taxpayer, on the one hand, transfers property and cash to a corporation in exchange for stock or, on the other hand, transfers property and a promissory note in exchange for stock. If the exchange were a taxable transaction, the tax consequences to both the shareholder and corporation would be identical in each case. Thus, the issuance of shareholder's promissory note to the corporation in addition to the transfer of property in connection with which the corporation assumes debts of the shareholder should be treated in the same manner as a contribution of cash equal to the principal amount of the debt. Perhaps this is the reason that no case, Revenue Ruling, or any informal IRS guidance has applied or cited either *Alderman* or Rev.Rul. 68–629 since *Peracchi* was decided.

3.   THE CORPORATION'S BASIS

When a single asset is transferred in a situation to which § 357(c) applies, determination of the corporation's basis is not difficult. But where multiple assets are transferred—a common situation because the contribution of improved real estate involves two separate assets, the building and the land under it—determining the basis of each asset to the corporation under § 362(a) is very difficult. If § 357(b) applies to treat liabilities as boot, the recognition of gain is no different than in the case of cash or other property. Thus the basis increase for the corporation with respect to each asset equals the gain recognized to the transferor with respect to that asset. Allocation of gain recognized by the transferor under § 357(c), however, presents different issues.

The principle of Rev.Rul. 68–55, page 70, upon which the allocation of § 351(b) gain among assets for purposes of the basis adjustment in § 362(a)(1) is based, does not help because, unlike § 351(b) gain, § 357(c) gain is not computed asset-by-asset. Gain under § 357(c) results only when aggregate liabilities assumed by the corporation exceed the aggregate basis of all transferred assets. If a liability is secured by a particular asset, however, gain recognized by the transferor under § 357(c) with respect to the liability reasonably might be allocated solely to the encumbered asset. But in many cases this simplified allocation method will be unavailing. For example, assume that A transfers two assets to X, a controlled corporation. One asset is real property with a fair market value of $75 and a basis of $15, and the second asset is equipment with a value of $25 and a basis of $30. X assumes unsecured liabilities of $50, which requires that A recognize $5 of gain under § 357(c). Here the recognized gain occurs because in the aggregate the basis of transferred assets is less than liabilities. Unlike the case in which boot is received, the recognized gain is not attributable to specific assets. Nonetheless, an allocation of A's $5 gain to the real property rather than an apportionment between the two assets has some appeal because the allocation will not result in increasing the difference between the fair market value and the adjusted basis of any asset. This same logic would indicate that if a single transferor transfers two or more appreciated assets and recognizes gain under § 357(c), the basis adjustment should be made by apportioning the gain among the assets relative to the amount by which the fair market value of each asset exceeds its basis. The regulations are silent regarding these question, however, and the IRS has never issued a revenue ruling on point. Treas.Reg. § 1.357–2(b), which deals with determining the character of the transferor's gain, suggests that the basis increase should be allocated in proportion to the fair market values of the assets, but Treas.Reg. § 1.357–

2(b) is deeply flawed from a theoretical perspective because it can allocate gain to an asset that is not appreciated.

Section 362(d)(1) provides that under § 362(a) the basis of any property transferred to the corporation cannot be increased to an amount above its fair market by reason of any gain recognized to the transferor as are result of the assumption of a liability.

4.   INTERACTION OF SECTIONS 351(b) and 357

Rev.Rul. 60–302, 1960–2 C.B. 223, illustrates the simultaneous application of § 351(b) and § 357(c) to a transfer. In the ruling, A transferred property with a fair market value of $500 and a basis of $200 to a corporation in a transaction subject to § 351. In addition to issuing stock, the corporation assumed a $210 liability secured by the property and gave the transferor a note for $80. The ruling held that A recognized a $10 gain under § 357(c) and an $80 gain under § 351(b), for a total of $90.

The application of these principles is more complex where multiple assets are transferred. Suppose that B transfers two assets to X Corporation: (1) Blackacre, with a fair market value of $700 and a basis of $250, subject to a mortgage debt of $350, and (2) publicly traded stock with a fair market value of $300 and a basis of $300, subject to a lien debt of $150. In exchange, B receives all of the common stock of X Corporation (fair market value $300), a promissory note for $200, and X Corporation assumes the $500 of debt encumbering the transferred assets. Because the $500 of debt does not exceed the aggregate basis of Blackacre and the stock ($550), no gain is recognized under § 357(c). Applying the principles of Rev.Rul. 68–55, under § 351(b), B recognizes a gain of $140 with respect to Blackacre, but does not recognize any gain or loss with respect to the stock.

	Blackacre	Stock
Fair market value	$700	$300
Percent of Fair market value	70%	30%
Amount realized		
Fair market value of stock		
received in exchange ($300)	$210	$ 90
Promissory Note ($200)	$140	$ 60
Debt assumption ($500)	$350	$150
	$700	$300
Basis	$250	$300
Gain (loss) realized	$450	($ 0)
Gain (loss) recognized	$140	$ 0

B's basis in the stock of X Corporation, as determined under § 358 is negative $10, computed as follows:

Basis of transferred property		
Blackacre	$250	
Stock	$300	
		$550
Minus boot & debt		
Note	$200	
Debt assumed	$500	
		($700)
Plus gain recognized		$140
Basis of Stock		($ 10)

Properly applying the Code to this fact pattern, there is no way around negative basis. Notwithstanding what Judge Kozinski might have said about it in *Peracchi*, negative basis, unlike Bigfoot, does exist.

(2) ASSUMPTION OF DEBTS THAT WOULD BE DEDUCTIBLE WHEN PAID: SECTION 357(c)(3)

INTERNAL REVENUE CODE: Sections 357(c); 358(d), (h).

Revenue Ruling 95–74

1995–2 C.B. 36.

ISSUES

(1) Are the liabilities assumed by S in the § 351 exchange described below liabilities for purposes of §§ 357(c)(1) and 358(d)?

(2) Once assumed by S. how will the liabilities in the § 351 exchange described below be treated?

FACTS

Corporation P is an accrual basis, calendar-year corporation engaged in various ongoing businesses, one of which includes the operation of a manufacturing plant (the Manufacturing Business). The plant is located on land purchased by P many years before. The land was not contaminated by any hazardous waste when P purchased it. However, as a result of plant operations, certain environmental liabilities, such as potential soil and groundwater remediation, are now associated with the land.

In Year 1, for bona fide business purposes, P engages in an exchange to which § 351 of the Internal Revenue Code applies by transferring substantially all of the assets associated with the Manufacturing Business, including the manufacturing plant and the land on which the plant is located, to a newly formed corporation S, in exchange for all of the stock of S and for S's assumption of the liabilities associated with the Manufacturing Business, including the environmental liabilities associated with the land. P has no plan or intention to dispose of (or have S issue) any S stock. S is an accrual basis, calendar-year taxpayer.

P did not undertake any environmental remediation efforts in connection with the land transferred to S before the transfer and did not deduct or capitalize any amount with respect to the contingent environmental liabilities associated with the transferred land.

In Year 3, S undertakes soil and groundwater remediation efforts relating to the land transferred in the § 351 exchange and incurs costs (within the meaning of the economic performance rules of § 461(h)) as a result of those remediation efforts. Of the total amount of costs incurred, a portion would have constituted ordinary and necessary business expenses that are deductible under § 162 and the remaining portion would have constituted capital expenditures under § 263 if there had not been a § 351 exchange and the costs for remediation efforts had been incurred by P. See Rev.Rul. 94–38, 1994–1 C.B. 35 (discussing the treatment of certain environmental remediation costs).

LAW AND ANALYSIS

Issue 1: Section 351(a) provides that no gain or loss shall be recognized if property is transferred to a corporation solely in exchange for stock and immediately after the exchange the transferor is in control of the corporation.

Section 357(a) provides a general rule that a transferee corporation's assumption of a transferor's liability in a § 351 exchange will not be treated as money or other property received by the transferor. Section 357(b) provides an exception to the general rule of § 357(a) when it appears that the principal purpose of the transferor in having the liability assumed was avoidance of Federal income tax on the exchange or, if not such purpose, was not a bona fide business purpose.

Section 357(c)(1) provides a second exception to the general rule of § 357(a). Section 357(c)(1) provides that if the sum of the liabilities the transferee corporation assumes and takes property subject to exceeds the total of the adjusted basis of the property the transferor transfers to the corporation pursuant to the exchange, then the excess shall be considered as gain from the sale or exchange of the property.

For purposes of applying the exception in § 357(c)(1), § 357(c)(3)(A) provides that a liability the payment of which would give rise to a deduction (or would be described in § 736(a)) is excluded. This special rule does not apply, however, to any liability to the extent that the incurrence of the liability resulted in the creation of, or an increase in, the basis of any property. Section 357(c)(3)(B).

Section 358(a)(1) provides that in a § 351 exchange the basis of the property permitted to be received under § 351 without the recognition of gain or loss shall be the same as that of the property exchanged, decreased by (i) the fair market value of any other property (except money) received by the transferor, (ii) the amount of any money received by the transferor, and (iii) the amount of loss to the transferor which was recognized on such exchange, and increased by (i) the amount which was treated as a dividend and (ii) the amount of gain to the transferor which was recognized on such exchange (not including any portion of such gain which was treated as a dividend).

Section 358(d)(1) provides that where, as part of the consideration to the transferor, another party to the exchange assumed a liability of the transferor, such assumption (in the amount of the liability) shall, for purposes of § 358, be treated as money received by the transferor on the exchange. Section 358(d)(2) provides that § 358(d)(1) does not apply to any liability excluded under § 357(c)(3).

* * *

A number of cases concerning cash basis taxpayers were litigated in the 1970s with respect to the definition of "liabilities" for purposes of § 357(c)(1), with sometimes conflicting analyses and results. * * * In response to this litigation, Congress enacted § 357(c)(3) to address the concern that the inclusion in the § 357(c)(1) determination of certain deductible liabilities resulted in "unforeseen and unintended tax difficulties for certain cash basis taxpayers who incorporate a going business." S.Rep. No. 1263, 95th Cong., 2d Sess. 184–85 (1978), 1978–3 C.B. 482–83.

Congress concluded that including in the § 357(c)(1) determination liabilities that have not yet been taken into account by the transferor results in an overstatement of liabilities of, and potential inappropriate gain recognition to, the transferor because the transferor has not received the corresponding deduction or other corresponding tax benefit. Id. To prevent this result, Congress enacted § 357(c)(3)(A) to exclude certain deductible liabilities from the scope of § 357(c), as long as the liabilities had not resulted in the creation of, or an increase in, the basis of any property (as provided in § 357(c)(3)(B)). * * *

While § 357(c)(3) explicitly addresses liabilities that give rise to deductible items, the same principle applies to liabilities that give rise to capital expenditures as well. Including in the § 357(c)(1) determination those liabilities that have not yet given rise to capital expenditures (and thus have not yet created or increased basis) with respect to the property of the transferor prior to the transfer also would result in an overstatement of liabilities. Thus, such liabilities also appropriately are excluded in determining liabilities for purposes of § 357(c)(1). Cf. * * * Rev.Rul. 88–77, 1988–2 C.B. 129 (accrued but unpaid expenses and accounts payable are not liabilities of a cash basis partnership for purposes of computing the adjusted basis of a partner's interest for purposes of § 752).

In this case, the contingent environmental liabilities assumed by S had not yet been taken into account by P prior to the transfer (and therefore had neither given rise to deductions for P nor resulted in the creation of, or increase in, basis in any property of P). As a result, the contingent environmental liabilities are not included in determining whether the amount of the liabilities assumed by S exceeds the adjusted basis of the property transferred by P pursuant to § 357(c)(1).

Due to the parallel constructions and interrelated function and mechanics of §§ 357 and 358, liabilities that are not included in the determination under § 357(c)(1) also are not included in the § 358 determination of the transferor's basis in the stock received in the § 351 exchange. * * * Therefore, the contingent environmental liabilities assumed by S are not treated as money received by P under § 358 for purposes of determining P's basis in the stock of S received in the exchange.

Issue 2: In Holdcroft Transp. Co. v. Commissioner, 153 F.2d 323 (8th Cir.1946), the Court of Appeals for the Eighth Circuit held that, after a transfer pursuant to the predecessor to § 351, the payments by a transferee corporation were not deductible even though the transferor partnership would have been entitled to deductions for the payments had the partnership actually made the payments. The court stated generally that the expense of settling claims or liabilities of a predecessor entity did not arise as an operating expense or loss of the business of the transferee but was a part of the cost of acquiring the predecessor's property, and the fact that the claims were contingent and unliquidated at the time of the acquisition was not of controlling consequence.

In Rev.Rul. 80–198, 1980–2 C.B. 113, an individual transferred all of the assets and liabilities of a sole proprietorship, which included accounts payable and accounts receivable, to a new corporation in exchange for all of its stock. The revenue ruling holds, subject to certain limitations, that the transfer qualifies as an exchange within the meaning of § 351(a) and that the transferee corporation will report in its income the accounts receivable as collected and will be allowed deductions under § 162 for the payments it makes to satisfy the accounts payable. In reaching these holdings, the revenue ruling makes reference to the specific congressional intent of § 351(a) to facilitate the incorporation of an ongoing business by making the incorporation tax free. The ruling states that this intent would be equally frustrated if either the transferor were taxed on the transfer of the accounts receivable or the transferee were not allowed a deduction for payment of the accounts payable. * * *

The present case is analogous to the situation in Rev.Rul. 80–198. For business reasons, P transferred in a § 351 exchange substantially all of the assets and liabilities associated with the Manufacturing Business to S, in exchange for all of its stock, and P intends to remain in control of S. The costs S incurs to remediate the land would have been deductible in part and capitalized in part had P continued the Manufacturing Business and incurred those costs to remediate the land. The congressional intent to facilitate necessary business readjustments would be frustrated by not according to S the ability to deduct or capitalize the expenses of the ongoing business.

Therefore, on these facts, the Internal Revenue Service will not follow the decision in Holdcroft Transp. Co. v. Commissioner, 153 F.2d 323 (8th Cir.1946). Accordingly, the contingent environmental liabilities assumed from P are deductible as business expenses under § 162 or are capitalized under § 263, as appropriate, by S under S's method of accounting (determined as if S has owned the land for the period and in the same manner as it was owned by P).

HOLDINGS

(1) The liabilities assumed by S in the § 351 exchange described above are not liabilities for purposes of § 357(c)(1) and § 358(d) because the liabilities had not yet been taken into account by P prior to the transfer (and therefore had neither given rise to deductions for P nor resulted in the creation of, or increase in, basis in any property of P).

(2) The liabilities assumed by S in the § 351 exchange described above are deductible by S as business expenses under § 162 or are capital expenditures under § 263, as appropriate, under S's method of accounting (determined as if S has owned the land for the period and in the same manner as it was owned by P).

DETAILED ANALYSIS

1.   CASH METHOD ACCOUNTS PAYABLE

As described in Rev.Rul. 95–74, prior to the Revenue Act of 1978 special problems were present when accounts receivable and accounts payable were transferred by a cash method taxpayer in a § 351 transaction. Since the accounts receivable would not have been included in income at the time of the transfer, their tax basis in the hands of the transferor is zero. On the other hand, the accounts payable, by definition not yet paid or deducted by a cash method taxpayer, would, under the literal language of § 357(c), constitute "liabilities" assumed by the corporation in the incorporation transaction. As a result, a cash method taxpayer could realize income in a § 351 transaction if the accounts payable were transferred to a corporation in connection with accounts receivable or other assets with a low tax basis. Raich v. Commissioner, 46 T.C. 604 (1966). The courts struggled with different approaches to avoid this result until the Revenue Act of 1978 added § 357(c)(3), providing that liabilities which would give rise to a deduction on payment are not considered for purposes of § 357(c)(1). See, e.g., Focht v. Commissioner, 68 T.C. 223 (1977) (Acq.) (the Tax Court abandoned its position in *Raich* and held that cash method payables are not liabilities under § 357(c) to the extent the payables would be deductible when paid). The 1978 Act also enacted § 358(d)(2), which provides that such liabilities are not treated as cash received for purposes of determining the transferor's basis in stock or securities received.

Accounts payable that are treated as not being liabilities by § 357(c)(3) typically include cash method trade accounts payable and other cash method liabilities, such as interest and taxes, which relate to the transferred trade or business. Whether a transferor is a cash method taxpayer is determined separately for each item. For example, a taxpayer using a hybrid method of accounting, which utilizes inventories and the accrual method in computing income from purchases and sales and which utilizes the cash method in computing all other items of income and expenses, is considered a cash method taxpayer for purposes of applying § 357(c) to accounts payable for items computed on the cash method of accounting, but not with respect to liabilities relating to inventory. See Staff of the Joint Committee on Taxation, General Explanation of the Revenue Act of 1978, 218–20 (Comm.Print 1978).

Not all of the potential problems with payables are resolved by § 357(c)(3). In Orr v. Commissioner, 78 T.C. 1059 (1982), which arose before the effective date of § 357(c)(3), the taxpayer transferred to a newly formed corporation customers' cash deposits for travel received in the course of taxpayer's business as a travel agent. The deposits were refundable and had not been taken into income by the taxpayer. The taxpayer's liability to refund deposits exceeded the amount of cash, and hence the basis of property, transferred to the new corporation. The Tax Court held that the taxpayer recognized gain under § 357(c)(1) to the extent the liabilities exceeded the taxpayer's basis in transferred property. The Tax Court refused to allow nonrecognition under its decision in *Focht* because refunds of the deposits would not have been deductible by the taxpayer. Presumably the same result would be reached under § 357(c)(3).

2. BASIS REDUCTION FOR CERTAIN LIABILITIES DESCRIBED IN SECTION 357(c)(3) WHERE STOCK BASIS EXCEEDS FAIR MARKET VALUE

As illustrated by Rev.Rul. 95–74, § 357(c)(3) applies not only to cash method accounts payable, but also to liabilities of accrual method transferors that have not yet been allowed as a deduction under the economic performance rules of § 461(h) or because the liability is too contingent. As a result, § 358(d)(2) applies and the transferor shareholder's basis in the stock received in the exchange is not reduced by the liability. Prior to the enactment of § 358(h), aggressive tax planners took advantage of this pattern of interaction of the various statutory provisions to create artificial double deductions.

Coltec Industries v. United States, 454 F.3d 1340 (Fed. Cir. 2006), rev'g 62 Fed. Cl. 716 (2004), which arose prior to the enactment of § 358(h), is an example of such an attempt to create double deductions. In a transaction subject to § 351, one corporation, Garlock, contributed to another corporation, Garrison, cash, a $375 million promissory note to Garlock from a related corporation, and certain other property. In connection with the transfer Garrison assumed $371.2 million of Garlock's contingent liabilities for asbestos product liability damage claims, which under Garlock's accounting method were not yet deductible. Shortly thereafter, Garlock sold a significant number of the shares of Garrison and claimed approximately $370 million of losses, having determined the basis of the Garrison stock with reference to an exchanged basis under § 358 that was not reduced to reflect the assumption of the contingent asbestos liabilities. Since the liabilities were contingent and the liabilities would have been deductible by the transferor upon payment, the Court of Federal Claims held that the liabilities were within those described in §§ 357(c)(3)(A) and 358(d)(2), and thus neither § 357(c)(1), requiring the recognition of gain to the extent that the amount of liabilities exceed the basis of the contributed assets, nor § 358(d)(1), requiring the reduction of the transferred basis assigned to the stock, applied. Therefore, Garlock's basis in Garrison properly was the exchanged basis of the transferred property, unreduced by the amount of liabilities assumed by Garrison, and the loss was allowed. The Claims Court decision was reversed by the Federal Circuit. The Court of Appeals agreed that there was nothing in §§ 358(d) and 357(c)(3) that required Garlock to reduce its basis in the stock by the amount of the liabilities assumed by the controlled corporation, Garrision. However, the Court of Appeals held that the lower court erred by failing to apply the economic substance doctrine in order to recognize that the transaction had no meaningful purpose except for the tax benefits. The court thus held that the transactions should be disregarded for tax purposes.

Black & Decker Corp. v. United States, 436 F.3d 431 (4th Cir.2006), involved a similar transaction. In 1998, Black & Decker sold three of its businesses and realized significant capital gains. That same year, Black & Decker created Black & Decker Healthcare Management Inc. (BDHMI), to which it transferred approximately $561 million, with BDHMI assuming

$560 million in contingent employee healthcare claims against Black & Decker. Black & Decker then sold the BDHMI stock to a third-party for $1 million dollars, and claimed a $560 million loss on the ground that its basis in the BDHMI stock was $561 million dollars. The court concluded that §§ 357(c)(3) and 358(d)(2) applied and that Black & Decker's basis in the BDHMI stock properly was not reduced by the amount of the contingent employee healthcare claims. It rejected the government's contention that the claims had to be deductible by the transferee (BDHMI) and, based upon the legislative history of § 357(c)(3), concluded that § 357(c)(3) and § 358(d)(2) apply in cases in which the claims would have been deductible by the transferor shareholder if it had paid the claims. The Court of Appeals affirmed the district court's decision with respect to the computation of Black & Decker's basis in the stock of BDHMI, but vacated the summary judgment in the taxpayer's favor and remanded the case for a determination of whether Black & Decker's loss should be disallowed under the "sham transaction" doctrine.

Even before the decisions in *Black & Decker* and *Coltec Industries* were handed down, Congress became concerned about the possibility of inappropriate duplication of deductions and losses, and in 2000 responded by enacting § 358(h) to prevent the recognition of the artificial losses allowed to be claimed in such transactions. (Section 358(h) did not apply in those cases because the transactions occurred prior to its enactment.) If the basis of stock received in a § 351 transaction otherwise would exceed its fair market value, § 358(h) requires that the basis of the stock be reduced (but not below the fair market value) by the amount (determined as of the date of the exchange) of any § 357(c)(3) liability that was assumed by the corporation. For this purpose, "liability" is broadly defined to include "any fixed or contingent obligation to make payment, without regard to whether the obligation is otherwise taken into account for purposes of [the income tax]." Under this definition, a liability that is not cognizable under § 357—for example, a cash method account payable, a contingent liability, or an obligation of an accrual method taxpayer that is not yet deductible because of the operation of the economic performance rules of § 461(h)—nevertheless will be taken into account under § 358(h) to reduce the transferor shareholder's stock basis. Section 358(h) does not apply in all instances, however. Section 358(h)(3) provides that, except as provided in regulations, § 358(h) does not apply if, as part of the exchange (1) "the trade or business with which the liability is associated is transferred to the person assuming the liability," or (2) "substantially all of the assets with which the liability is associated are transferred to the person assuming the liability." Treas.Reg. § 1.358–5 narrows this exception by providing that the exception for a transfer of "substantially all of the assets with which the liability is associated" to the corporation assuming the liability is inoperative. Thus, the exception in § 358(h)(3) actually applies if, and only if, the trade or business with which the liability is associated is transferred to the corporation assuming the liability, for example, the specific fact pattern in Rev.Rul. 95–74. The exception in § 358(h)(3) does not apply to selective transfers of assets that may bear some relationship to the liability, but that do not represent the full scope of the trade or business (or substantially all the assets) with which the liability is associated.

The operation of § 358(h) is illustrated by the following examples.

(1) Assume that X Corporation transferred $10,000,000 in cash to newly formed Y Corporation in exchange for all of the stock of Y Corporation, and in connection with the exchange, Y Corporation assumed a future $8,000,000 environmental remediation obligation of X Corporation with respect to mining property owned by X Corporation. The $8,000,000 environmental remediation obligation is a liability described in § 357(c)(3) and does not result in a basis reduction under § 358(d). Thus, before the application of § 358(h), the basis of X Corporation's stock in Y Corporation is $10,000,000. Because the liability is a liability described in § 358(h)(3), is not subject to § 357(c)(1), and the business in connection with which the liability was incurred was not transferred to Y Corporation, § 358(h)(1) requires that the basis of X Corporation's stock in Y Corporation be reduced by the $8,000,000 liability, from $10,000,000 to $2,000,000.

(2) Assume alternatively that X Corporation transferred investment securities with a basis of $9,000,000 and a fair market value $10,000,000 to Y Corporation in exchange for all of the stock of Y Corporation, and in connection with the exchange, Y Corporation assumed the future $8,000,000 environmental remediation obligation of X Corporation with respect to mining property owned by X Corporation. Before the application of § 358(h), the basis of X Corporation's stock in Y Corporation is $9,000,000. Again, the basis of the stock must be reduced by the amount of the liability, but because the fair market value of the stock is $2,000,000 ($10,000,000 value of the securities transferred minus the $8,000,000 obligation assumed), the $9,000,000 basis cannot be reduced by the full $8,000,000 liability; the basis can only be reduced to $2,000,000 under the statutory rule. Note that there is no theoretical reason for the statutory rule so limiting the basis reduction. Indeed the statutory purpose of § 358(h) would be better served not only by reducing the basis of the stock by the full amount of the obligation, but by triggering gain recognition under § 357(c) as well if the amount of the obligation exceeded the basis of the transferred property.

(3) Assume alternatively that X Corporation transferred an *operating* mining property with a basis of $9,000,000 and a fair market value $10,000,000 to Y Corporation in exchange for all of the stock of Y Corporation, and in connection with the exchange, Y Corporation assumed the future $8,000,000 environmental remediation obligation of X Corporation with respect to the mining property transferred from X Corporation to Y Corporation. In this case the exception in § 358(h)(2) applies because the business with which the liability is associated has been transferred to Y Corporation. Thus, no basis adjustment is required under § 358(h) and the basis of X Corporation's stock in Y Corporation remains $9,000,000. This example follows the fact pattern in Rev.Rul. 95–74, page 96.

SECTION 3. THE "CONTROL" REQUIREMENT

INTERNAL REVENUE CODE: Sections 351(a), (c)(1); 368(c).

REGULATIONS: Section 1.351–1(a), (b).

Section 351 provides nonrecognition of gain or loss only if *immediately after the transfer* the transferor or transferors of property are in "control" of the corporation as defined in § 368(c), which requires ownership of 80 percent of the combined voting power of all stock and 80 percent of all other classes of stock. Thus, for example, if individual A transfers property to a pre-existing corporation, in which A previously owned no stock, in exchange for 25 percent of the only class of voting common stock, § 351 does not apply to provide nonrecognition of gain or loss. This rule raises the question of the meaning of "immediately after" in situations in which at the time of the transfer it is contemplated that the transferor will dispose of the stock or that additional stock will be issued to a person who is not also a transferor of property. This question, in turn, raises the issue of the principles that will be applied to determine when two putatively separate transactions will be viewed together as a single transaction under the "step transaction doctrine," which is discussed in the following case and revenue ruling.

American Bantam Car Co. v. Commissioner[*]

Tax Court of the United States, 1948.
11 T.C. 397.

* * *

The basic issue in this case is whether the exchange on June 3, 1936, whereby petitioner's assets were acquired, was one in which gain or loss is to be recognized for tax purposes. If gain or loss is to be recognized, then the proper basis for the assets is their cost to petitioner on the date of their acquisition, as is contended by the petitioner. If the exchange is one in which no recognition is given to gain or loss, then the proper basis for the assets is their basis in the hands of the transferors, as contended by the respondent.

* * *

[A group of individuals called the "associates," purchased the assets of a bankrupt automobile company in 1935. The "associates" then organized the taxpayer corporation, American Bantam Car Co., in 1936. Pursuant to a plan, the associates were to transfer the assets (subject to certain liabilities) to the corporation in return for 300,000 shares of no par common stock, which would constitute all of the corporation's common stock to be issued at that time. Ninety thousand shares of the preferred stock of the corporation (each share having three votes) were to be sold to the public through underwriters at $10 a share. The underwriters were to receive as compensation, in addition to discounts and commissions, certain amounts of the common stock issued to the associates based on a schedule determined by the progress of the sale of the preferred stock. The transfer of the assets to the corporation was made on June 3, 1936, in return for the common stock. At that time the

---

[*]   Ed.: The decision was affirmed per curiam, 177 F.2d 513 (3d Cir.1949).

corporation had no working capital, no labor force, and no sales organization. On June 8, 1936, the associates and the underwriters agreed on the details of the compensation schedule. On August 16, 1936, the associates placed their 300,000 common stock shares in escrow until the public offering of the preferred stock was completed. In October 1937, the associates, pursuant to the agreement, transferred to the underwriters 87,900 common stock shares and the underwriters sold 1,008 of these shares to the public. As a consequence of the underwriters' stock sales, the associates held 212,100 shares of the common stock (less than 80%), the underwriters held 86,892 shares of the common stock (28.96%), and the public 1,008 shares. The public also held 83,618 shares of preferred stock. The issue before the court was the corporation's basis for depreciation of the acquired assets in the years 1942 and 1943. The taxpayer corporation claimed that depreciation should be based on cost to the taxpayer in 1936, i.e., the market value of the assets in 1936. The Commissioner claimed that depreciation should be based on the basis of the assets in the hands of the associates prior to the transfer to the taxpayer, which basis was lower than the 1936 fair market value. The determination of the basis turned on the question whether the original transfer qualified under the statutory predecessor of § 351. If the 1936 and 1937 transactions were treated as separate, then the associates were in control "immediately after" the initial stock transaction and predecessors to §§ 351 and 362 would apply to transfer the old basis of the assets to the corporation. Under the taxpayer's view, if all the elements of the transaction were taken together under a step transaction approach, the associates were not in control of the corporation immediately after the transfer of the assets, and the corporation received a stepped-up basis for the assets; the associates ownership of only 212, 100 shares of common stock—less than 80 percent—after the transfer of the 87,900 shares of common stock to the underwriter would fail to satisfy the control requirement.]

The first question, then, is whether the associates had * * * "control" over the petitioner immediately after the exchange on June 3, 1936. Prima facie, when the various steps taken to organize the new corporation and transfer assets to it are considered separately, the associates did have "control" of the petitioner immediately after the exchange within the statutory definition of the word. We think that from June 3 to June 8, 1936, they owned 100 per cent of all the issued stock, and from June 8, 1936, until October 1937 they owned stock possessing at least 80 per cent of the total combined voting power of all classes of stock. On June 3, 1936, the associates were issued absolutely and unconditionally 300,000 shares of no par common stock. The resolution of the board of directors of petitioner accepting the associates' offer * * * attached no strings whatsoever to the issuance of the stock to them. It is true that on June 2, 1936, petitioner had an authorized capital stock of 700,000 shares, 600,000 common shares and 100,000 preferred shares, but in determining control only stock actually issued is considered. * * * On June 8 no other common stock had been issued, and a contract regarding possible future assignment of those 300,000 shares already issued was not entered into before that date. No preferred stock had been issued on June 3, nor was a contract for its sale provided until June 8. The statutory words "immediately after the exchange" require control for no longer period; in fact, momentary control is sufficient. Evans Products Co., 29 B.T.A. 992. Certainly, therefore, the associates had absolute control over the corporation from June 3 to June 8, 1936, due to their complete ownership of all outstanding stock.

It is true that, by virtue of their agreement with the associates on June 8, 1936, the underwriters did at that time acquire the right to earn shares of the common stock issued to the associates by the sale of certain percentages of preferred stock, but the ownership of the 300,000 shares remained in the associates until such sales were completed. * * *

During all of 1936 the associates retained ownership over the 300,000 shares of common stock and during that interval the underwriters sold only 14,757 shares of preferred stock which did not entitle them to any common stock under the agreement of June 8, 1936. The corporation's by-laws provided that each share of preferred stock should have three votes while each share of common stock should have one vote. Therefore, at the end of 1936, out of 344,271 possible stock votes, the total combined voting power of all outstanding stock, the associates owned 300,000 or over 80 per cent. It was not until October 1937 when the [underwriters] received 87,900 shares of the associates' common stock in fulfillment of the underwriting agreement that the associates lost "control" of petitioner within the statutory definition of the word. Retention of "control" for such a duration of time satisfies the governing provision of [section 351].

Petitioner, however, contends that the series of steps organizing the new corporation, transferring assets to it, and arranging for the sale of its preference stock must be considered as parts of the integrated plan formulated in May 1936, and, therefore, considered as parts of a single transaction. It argues that this unified transaction started on June 2, 1936, when petitioner was incorporated, and ended in October 1937, when the public offering of the preferred stock by the underwriters ceased and Grant was awarded 87,900 shares of common stock; that the transfer of common stock to Grant in 1937 was the final step of an indivisible operation and must be viewed concurrently with the preceding steps. On this theory the associates did not obtain control of petitioner, for on consummation of this final step in the general plan the associates had only 212,100 shares of common stock, while Grant had 86,892 shares and the public had 1,008 and there were 83,618 shares of outstanding preferred stock owned by the public. The 212,100 stock votes held by the associates in October 1937 fell shy of the required 80 per cent to give the requisite control.

In determining whether a series of steps are to be treated as a single indivisible transaction or should retain their separate entity, the courts use a variety of tests. * * * Among the factors considered are the intent of the parties, the time element, and the pragmatic test of the ultimate result. An important test is that of mutual interdependence. Were the steps so interdependent that the legal relations created by one transaction would have been fruitless without a completion of the series?

Using these tests as a basis for their decisions the courts in Hazeltine Corp. v. Commissioner, 89 F.2d 513, and Bassick v. Commissioner, 85 F.2d 8, treated the series of steps involved in each case as parts of a unified transaction and therefore determined that the transferors of assets to the new corporation did not acquire the requisite control. An analysis of the fact situations involved shows salient distinguishing features from the present facts. In each of the above cases there was a written contract prior both to the organization of the new corporation and the exchange of assets for stock which bound the transferors unconditionally to assign part of the stock acquired to third parties after the exchange. Thus at the moment of the exchange the recipient of the stock did not own it, but held it subject to a binding contractual obligation to transfer a portion. The court in each case thought that the incorporation and exchange would never have been agreed upon without the supplemental agreement turning over stock to a third party. In such situations it is logical for the courts to say that the exchange and the subsequent transfer are part of one and the same transaction so that the transferor never actually owned the shares he later assigned.

A close examination of the facts surrounding the exchange in the present case makes it clear that the exchange of assets for stock and the subsequent transfer of a portion of that stock to [the underwriters] therein involved should not be considered part of the same transaction so as to deprive the associates of "control" immediately after the exchange. The facts are distinguishable from those existing in the *Hazeltine* and *Bassick* cases on three grounds. First, there was no written contract prior to the exchange binding the associates to transfer stock to the underwriters. At the most there was an informal oral understanding of a general plan contemplating the organization of a new corporation, the exchange of assets for stock, and marketing of preferred stock of the new corporation to the public. A written contract providing for the transfer of shares from the associates to the underwriters did not come until five days after the exchange. Secondly, when the transfer of shares to the underwriters was embodied specifically in a formal contract, the underwriters received no absolute right to ownership of the common stock, but only when, as and if, certain percentages of preferred stock were sold. How clearly contingent was the nature of their rights is illustrated by the fact only one underwriter, Grant, met the terms of the agreement and became entitled to any shares. Thirdly, the necessity of placing the 300,000 shares in escrow with a bank is indicative of complete ownership of such stock by the associates following the exchange.

The standard required by the courts to enable them to say that a series of steps are interdependent and thus should be viewed as a single transaction do not exist here. It is true all the steps may have been contemplated under the same general plan of May 1936; yet the contemplated arrangement for the sale of preferred stock to the public was entirely secondary and supplemental to the principal goal of the plan—to organize the new corporation and exchange its stock for the Austin assets. * * *

Thus we conclude that in the present case the exchange of assets for stock between the associates and petitioner on June 3, 1936, was a separate completed transaction distinct from the subsequent transfer of common stock to [the underwriters] so that the associates were in control of petitioner immediately after the exchange within the provisions of [section 351]. * * *

Revenue Ruling 2003–51

2003–1 C.B. 938.

ISSUE

Whether a transfer of assets to a corporation (the "first corporation") in exchange for an amount of stock in the first corporation constituting control satisfies the control requirement of § 351 of the Internal Revenue Code if, pursuant to a binding agreement entered into by the transferor with a third party prior to the exchange, the transferor transfers the stock of the first corporation to another corporation (the "second corporation") simultaneously with the transfer of assets by the third party to the second corporation, and immediately thereafter, the transferor and the third party are in control of the second corporation.

FACTS

Corporation W, a domestic corporation, engages in businesses A, B, and C. The fair market values of businesses A, B, and C are $40x, $30x, and $30x, respectively. X, a domestic corporation unrelated to W, also engages in business A through its wholly owned domestic subsidiary, Y. The fair market value of X's Y stock is $30x. W and X desire to consolidate their business A operations within a new corporation in a holding company structure. Pursuant to a prearranged binding agreement with X, W forms a domestic corporation, Z, by transferring all of its business A assets to Z in exchange for all of the stock of Z (the "first transfer"). Immediately thereafter, W contributes all of its Z stock to Y in exchange for stock of Y (the "second transfer"). Simultaneous with the second transfer, X contributes $30x to Y to meet the capital needs of business A after the restructuring in exchange for additional stock of Y (the "third transfer"). After the second and third transfers, Y transfers the $30x and its business A assets to Z (the "fourth transfer"). After the second and third transfers, W and X own 40 percent and 60 percent, respectively, of the outstanding stock of Y. Viewed separately, each of the first transfer, the combined second and third transfers, and fourth transfer qualifies as a transfer described in § 351.

LAW

Section 351(a) provides that no gain or loss shall be recognized if property is transferred to a corporation by one or more persons solely in exchange for stock in such corporation and immediately after the exchange such person or persons are in control (as defined in § 368(c)) of the corporation.

Section 368(c) defines control to mean the ownership of stock possessing at least 80 percent of the total combined voting power of all classes of stock entitled to vote and at least 80 percent of the total number of shares of all other classes of stock of the corporation.

Section 1.351–1(a)(1) of the Income Tax Regulations provides that the phrase "immediately after the exchange" does not necessarily require simultaneous exchanges by two or more persons, but comprehends a situation where the rights of the parties have been previously defined and the execution of the agreement proceeds with an expedition consistent with orderly procedure.

Courts have held that the control requirement of § 351 is not satisfied where, pursuant to a binding agreement entered into by the transferor prior to the transfer of property to the corporation in exchange for stock, the transferor loses control of the corporation by a taxable sale of all or part of that stock to a third party who does not also transfer property to the corporation in exchange for stock. See, e.g., S. Klein on the Square, Inc. v. Commissioner, 188 F.2d 127 (2d Cir.), cert. denied, 342 U.S. 824 (1951); Hazeltine Corp. v. Commissioner, 89 F.2d 513 (3d Cir. 1937); Intermountain Lumber Co. v. Commissioner, 65 T.C. 1025 (1976). The IRS has reached the same conclusion when addressing similar facts. See Rev.Rul. 79–194, 1979–1 C.B. 145; Rev.Rul. 79–70, 1979–1 C.B. 144; Rev.Rul. 70–522, 1970–2 C.B. 81.

In Rev.Rul. 70–140, 1970–1 C.B. 73, A, an individual, owns all of the stock of corporation X and operates a business similar to that of X through a sole proprietorship. Pursuant to an agreement between A and Y, an unrelated, widely held corporation, A transfers all of the assets of the sole proprietorship to X in exchange for additional shares of X stock. A then transfers all his X stock to Y solely in exchange for voting common stock of Y. The ruling reasons that because the two steps of the transaction are parts of a prearranged plan, they may not be considered independently of each other for Federal income tax purposes. The ruling concludes that A's receipt of the X stock in exchange for the sole proprietorship assets is transitory and without substance for tax purposes because it is apparent that the assets of the sole proprietorship are transferred to X to enable Y to acquire those assets without the recognition of gain to A. Accordingly, the ruling treats A as transferring its sole proprietorship assets directly to Y in a transfer to which § 351 does not apply, and Y as transferring these assets to X, independently of A's transfer of the X stock to Y in exchange for Y voting stock. The exchange by A of the stock of X solely for voting stock of Y constitutes an exchange to which § 354 applies. * * *

In Rev.Rul. 77–449, 1977–2 C.B. 110, amplified by Rev.Rul. 83–34, 1983–1 C.B. 79, and Rev.Rul. 83–156, 1983–2 C.B. 66, a corporation transfers assets to a wholly owned subsidiary, which in turn transfers, as part of the same plan, the same assets to its own wholly owned subsidiary. The ruling states that the transfers should be viewed separately for purposes of § 351. Because each transfer satisfies the requirements of § 351, no gain or loss is recognized by the transferor.

In Rev.Rul. 83–34, corporation P owns 80 percent of the stock of a subsidiary, S1. An unrelated corporation owns the remaining 20 percent. P transfers assets to S1 solely in exchange for additional shares of S1 stock. As part of the same plan, S1 transfers the same assets to S2, a newly formed corporation of which S1 will be an 80 percent shareholder. An unrelated corporation will own the remaining 20 percent of the S2 stock. Citing Rev.Rul. 77–449, the ruling concludes that the transfers should be viewed separately for purposes of § 351 and that each transfer satisfies the requirements of § 351.

In Rev.Rul. 84–111, 1984–2 C.B. 88, Situation 1, a partnership transfers all of its assets to a newly formed corporation in exchange for all the outstanding stock of the corporation and the assumption by the corporation of the partnership's liabilities. The partnership then terminates by distributing all the stock of the corporation to the partners in proportion to their partnership interests. The steps undertaken by the partnership were parts of a plan to transfer the partnership operations to a corporation organized for valid business reasons in exchange for its stock and were not devices to avoid or evade recognition of gain. The ruling concludes that, under § 351, the partnership recognizes no gain or loss on the transfer of its assets to the corporation in exchange for the corporation's stock and the corporation's assumption of the partnership's liabilities, notwithstanding the partnership's subsequent distribution of the corporation's stock to the partners and consequent loss of control within the meaning of § 368(c) of the corporation.

ANALYSIS

As described above, if the first transfer were viewed as separate from each of the other transfers, the first transfer would satisfy the technical requirements of a transfer under § 351 because W transfers property to Z in exchange for stock in Z and, immediately after the exchange, W is in control of Z. However, because the first and second transfers are undertaken pursuant to a prearranged binding agreement, it is necessary to determine whether the second transfer causes the first transfer to fail to satisfy the control requirement of § 351.

"Section 351 has been described as a deliberate attempt by Congress to facilitate the incorporation of ongoing businesses and to eliminate any technical constructions which are economically unsound." Hempt Bros., Inc. v. United States, 490 F.2d 1172, 1177 (3d Cir.), cert. denied, 419 U.S. 826 (1974). Section 351(a) is intended to apply to "certain transactions where gain or loss may have accrued in a constitutional sense, but where in a popular and economic sense there has been a mere change in the form of ownership and the taxpayer has not really 'cashed in' on the theoretical gain, or closed out a losing venture." Portland Oil Co. v. Commissioner, 109 F.2d 479, 488 (1st Cir.), cert. denied, 310 U.S. 650 (1940). See S. Rep. No. 67–275, at 12 (1921) (explaining that the predecessor to § 351 was enacted in 1921 to "permit business to go forward with the readjustments required by existing conditions"). A transaction described under § 351 "lacks a distinguishing characteristic of a sale, in that, instead of the transaction having the effect of terminating or extinguishing the beneficial interests of the transferors in the transferred property, . . . the transferors continue to be beneficially interested in the transferred property and have dominion over it by virtue of their control of the new corporate owner of it." American Compress & Warehouse Co. v. Bender, 70 F.2d 655, 657 (5th Cir.), cert. denied, 293 U.S. 607 (1934).

As described above, courts have held that the control requirement of § 351 is not satisfied where, pursuant to a binding agreement entered into by the transferor prior to the transfer of property to the corporation in exchange for stock, the transferor loses control of the corporation by a taxable sale of all or part of that stock to a third party that does not also transfer property to the corporation in exchange for stock. Treating a transfer of property that is followed by such a prearranged sale of the stock received as a transfer described in § 351 is not consistent with Congress' intent in enacting § 351 to facilitate the rearrangement of the transferor's interest in its property. Treating a transfer of property that is followed by a nontaxable disposition of the stock received as a transfer described in § 351 is not necessarily inconsistent with the purposes of § 351. Accordingly, the control requirement may be satisfied in such a case, even if the stock received is transferred pursuant to a binding commitment in place upon the transfer of the property in exchange for stock. For example, in Rev.Rul. 84–111, Situation 1, the partnership's transfer of property to the transferee corporation qualified as a transfer described in § 351, even though the partnership relinquished control of the transferee corporation within the meaning of § 368(c) pursuant to a prearranged plan to transfer the transferee stock.

In Rev.Rul. 70–140, the transfer of assets to the transferor's wholly owned subsidiary followed by an exchange of stock of the wholly owned subsidiary for stock of another corporation was recast as a direct transfer of assets to the unrelated, widely held corporation in a taxable transaction. In Rev.Rul. 70–140, there was no alternative form of transaction that would have qualified for nonrecognition treatment. In contrast, in this case, W's transfer of the business A assets to Z was not necessary for W and X to combine their business A assets in a holding company structure in a manner that would have qualified for nonrecognition of gain or loss under § 351. A transfer of W's business A assets to Y in exchange for Y stock as part of a plan that included X's transfer of $30x to Y in exchange for Y stock, and Y's transfer of the business A assets and $30x to Z in exchange for all of the Z stock, would have qualified as successive transfers described in § 351. See Rev.Rul. 83–34; Rev.Rul. 77–449. Accordingly, in these circumstances, Rev.Rul. 70–140 is distinguishable.

In this case, even though the first transfer is followed by a transfer of the stock received, treating the first transfer as a transfer described in § 351 is not inconsistent with the purposes of § 351. Accordingly, the second transfer will not cause the first transfer to fail to satisfy the control requirement of § 351.

HOLDING

A transfer of assets to the first corporation in exchange for an amount of stock in the first corporation constituting control satisfies the control requirement of § 351 even if, pursuant to a binding agreement entered into by the transferor with a third party prior to the exchange, the transferor transfers the stock of the first corporation to the second corporation simultaneously with the transfer of assets by the third party to the second corporation, and immediately thereafter, the transferor and the third party are in control of the second corporation.

DETAILED ANALYSIS

1.   CONTROL IMMEDIATELY AFTER THE TRANSFER

1.1. *Stock Transfers or Issuance to Nontransferors of Property*

Commissioner v. National Bellas Hess, Inc., 220 F.2d 415 (8th Cir.1955), is similar to the *American Bantam* case, in that a sale of stock to the public within three months after the transfer of property to a corporation did not prevent control from residing in the transferors of property immediately after the transfer; nor did the existence of unexercised stock options held by the employees of the transferee corporation to purchase some stock from the transferors affect the transferors' ownership immediately after the transfer. In Federal Grain Corp. v. Commissioner, 18 B.T.A. 242 (1929), an agreement that the transferors would place the stock of the corporation in a voting trust for five years was said not to defeat the "control" of the transferors, since the definition of "control" relates to ownership of stock rather than actual control through the exercise of voting rights.

Rev.Rul. 70–140, 1970–1 C.B. 73, discussed in Rev.Rul. 2003–51, supra, held that § 351 did not apply to the transfer of assets of a sole proprietorship to a controlled corporation followed immediately by a prearranged exchange of the stock of the controlled corporation for the stock of another corporation "in an integrated transaction." Because of the integrated nature of the two transactions, the original transferor was not in control of the transferee immediately after the transfer.

Intermountain Lumber Co. v. Commissioner, 65 T.C. 1025 (1976), held that the requisite control immediately after the exchange was not present where, as part of the incorporation transaction, the transferor was obligated under an agreement of sale to sell almost half of the shares of the corporation to a third party. The court formulated the control requirement of § 351 as follows:

> A determination of "ownership," as that term is used in section 368(c) and for purposes of control under section 351, depends upon the obligations and freedom of action of the transferee with respect to the stock when he acquired it from the corporation. * * * If the [stockholder], as part of the transaction by which the shares were acquired, has irrevocably foregone or relinquished at that time the legal right to determine whether to keep the shares, ownership in such shares is lacking for purposes of section 351. By contrast, if there are no restrictions upon freedom of action at the time he acquires the shares, it is immaterial how soon thereafter the [stockholder] elects to dispose of his stock or whether such disposition is in accord with a preconceived plan not amounting to a binding obligation.

Since the stockholder was under an obligation to sell the shares, § 351 was not applicable and the corporate transferee obtained a stepped-up basis in the property involved in the transaction.

In Mojonnier & Sons, Inc. v. Commissioner, 12 T.C. 837 (1949) (Nonacq.), a father had agreed that if his sons and a foreman worked in his business they would receive some stock when he incorporated his business a few years later. On that later incorporation, shares of stock were issued directly to the sons and foreman, so that the father received less than 80 percent of the stock. The court held, as argued by the taxpayer corporation, that § 351 did not apply to the formation due to the lack of the required control. It rejected the IRS's argument that the father should be regarded as receiving all of the stock and then making gifts to the others, the court stating that the transfers of stock were not gifts but rewards for past services and, moreover, had been made directly to the others in accordance with the prior agreement.

A different result was reached in D'Angelo Associates, Inc. v. Commissioner, 70 T.C. 121 (1978), which involved a situation in which the incorporators of the taxpayer, a closely-held corporation, deliberately attempted to avoid the application of § 351 in an effort to recognize individual capital gains on the transfer of a building while providing the corporation with a stepped-up basis for depreciation purposes.[9] To this end, Dr. and Mrs. D'Angelo transferred property to a newly formed corporation, which issued one-quarter of its stock to each of Dr. and Mrs. D'Angelo and their two minor children. D'Angelo Associates, Inc. then claimed that it had acquired the property in a taxable transaction and thus was entitled to depreciation calculated with reference to a § 1012 cost basis rather than a transferred basis under § 362, on the ground that Dr. and Mrs. D'Angelo, the sole transferors of property to the corporation, were not in control of the corporation immediately after the transfer because they had never received at least 80 percent of the stock as required by § 351(a). The court rejected this argument.

> We view the events before us as equivalent to the formation and capitalization of the corporation, followed by a gift to the D'Angelo children of the controlling interest when Dr. and Mrs. D'Angelo caused petitioner to directly issue the 50 shares to the children. * * * The D'Angelo children did not purchase the stock issued in their names, but were simply the beneficiaries of a gift from their parents.

> The loss of control of petitioner resulting from the gift of stock does not preclude the application of section 351(a), which requires that the transferors be in control of the transferee corporation "immediately after the exchange." This requirement is satisfied where, as here, the transferors transfer by gift the stock they were entitled to receive in exchange for the property they transferred to the corporation, regardless of whether such disposition was planned before or after acquiring control. See Wilgard Realty Co. v. Commissioner, 127 F.2d 514, 516 (2d Cir.1942), affg. 43 B.T.A. 557 (1941), cert. denied 317 U.S. 655 (1942); Stanton v. United States, 512 F.2d 13, 17 (3d Cir.1975) * * *. The issuance of the stock by petitioner to the D'Angelo children is the direct consequence of "the absolute right" of Dr. and Mrs. D'Angelo to designate who would receive all of the stock. * * * Since it is possession of this power which is essential under section 351 for control, it follows that the transferors herein, Dr. and Mrs. D'Angelo were in control of petitioner immediately after the exchange. * * *

> Petitioner nevertheless argues that since the stock was issued directly to Mrs. D'Angelo and the children, Dr. D'Angelo never held any stock in the corporation. We recognize that * * * in Mojonnier & Sons, Inc. v. Commissioner, 12 T.C. 837 (1949) * * * this Court stated:

>> In the instant proceeding, however, the stock, exclusive of the 1,490 shares issued to Mojonnier and his wife, was not

[9] Although the result that was sought by the taxpayers in D'Angelo represented desirable tax planning under the rate structure and provisions of Subchapter C in effect at the time of the transaction, under current law the transaction is not nearly as desirable from the perspective of the founders of a closely held corporation.

issued to the transferors and then conveyed by them to members of their family, but was issued directly to the members of the family in accordance with the plan and offer of F.E. Mojonnier. Thus, the transferors were never the owners or holders of a sufficient amount of stock to place them in "control" of the corporation within the meaning of [the predecessor of section 351]. * * *

Nevertheless, the decisions in both *Wilgard* and *Stanton* were clearly predicated on the power of the transferor to designate who will receive the stock rather than the precise moment that the power was exercised. These cases do not turn on whether the tune Dr. D'Angelo called was written in two/four time, but on his power to call the tune. And it is on this score that both Florida Machine & Foundry Co. and Mojonnier & Sons, Inc., are distinguishable from *Wilgard, Stanton,* and the facts before us.

1.2. *Transfer of Assets to Subsidiary in Exchange for Stock of Parent Corporation*

Rev.Rul. 84–44, 1984–1 C.B. 105, held that § 351 is not applicable to the transfer of property to a corporate subsidiary in exchange for stock of the transferee subsidiary's parent corporation, which is in turn controlled by the transferor. However, the same result can be accomplished by restructuring the transaction first as a transfer of the property to the controlled parent corporation in exchange for its stock, followed by a transfer of the property by the parent corporation to its controlled subsidiary. Rev.Rul. 83–34, 1983–1 C.B. 79, holds that although these transfers may be undertaken pursuant to an integrated plan, each transfer is treated as a separate transaction that satisfies § 351. See also Rev.Rul. 83–156, 1983–2 C.B. 66, holding that § 351 applies to a transfer of assets to a wholly owned subsidiary that then transfers the assets to a partnership. Although nonrecognition of gain or loss under § 351 is based in principle on the transferors' continued investment in the transferred property, and requires a continued proprietary interest in the transferee corporation through the receipt of stock representing control, there is no express requirement that the transferors maintain a continued interest in the transferred assets.

2.   WHO ARE THE TRANSFERORS?

2.1. *General*

Section 351 applies when one or more persons who transfer property to the corporation are in control immediately after the transfer. The control requirement thus requires identification of the group of transferors who are to be counted.

In some cases taxpayers have attempted to count existing stockholders as members of the control group in order to classify an exchange of appreciated property for stock by non-controlling persons as a nonrecognition transaction under § 351. For example, in Estate of Kamborian v. Commissioner, 469 F.2d 219 (1st Cir.1972), taxpayers holding 76 percent of the stock of a corporation transferred appreciated property to the corporation in exchange for additional stock. A trust that held 13 percent of the stock of the transferee corporation purchased a small number of shares for cash in an attempt to qualify the transfer under § 351.

The taxpayers claimed that the trust was a transferor so that together the combined holdings of transferors exceeded 80 percent. The court held that it is "permissible to consider transfers by other owners only if those transfers were, in economic terms, sufficiently related to * * * make all of the transfers parts of a single transaction." The court added that, "[t]he trustees' desire to help the [other] stockholders avoid taxes, warrantably found by the Tax Court to have been the primary motive for the trust's purchase cannot be used to make a single transaction out of otherwise unrelated transfers."

The issue in *Kamborian* is addressed in Treas.Reg. § 1.351–1(a)(1)(ii), which provides that if the primary purpose of the transfer of property to a corporation by an existing shareholder is to qualify for § 351 treatment a transfer of property to the corporation by another person, and the stock newly received by the existing shareholder is of "relatively small value" in comparison to the value of that shareholder's stock owned before the transfer, the newly received stock of the existing shareholder will not be counted in determining the control group. Rev. Proc. 77–37, § 3.07, 1977–2 C.B. 568, indicates that the property transferred will not be considered to be of "relatively small value" if it has a value equal to at least 10 percent of the value of the stock owned by the existing shareholder before the transfer.

Rev.Rul. 79–194, 1979–1 C.B. 145, held that a pre-arranged sale between two transferors of property for stock does not affect the control requirement. Z Corporation transferred property to Newco for 80 percent of Newco stock. A group of investors transferred property for 20 percent of Newco stock. Following the transfers to Newco, Z sold stock to the investors. At the end of the transaction, Z owned 49 percent of the Newco stock. The Ruling held that since Z and the investors were transferors, the persons transferring property to Newco in exchange for Newco stock owned 100 percent of Newco stock immediately after the exchange. However, where the investor group transferred property in exchange for only 1 percent of the Newco stock, with Z receiving 99 percent, the investors' stock ownership was not sufficient to qualify them as transferors of property and thus the control requirement was not satisfied because of the subsequent sale of stock by Z to the investors. Previously, in May Broadcasting Co. v. United States, 200 F.2d 852 (8th Cir.1953), a transfer of a radio station to a newly formed corporation for its stock and then a sale of one-fourth of the stock to a third party, who also contributed cash to the corporation, was held not to be a § 351 exchange since the sale was pursuant to a contract existing at the time of incorporation, although the requirement of Federal Communications Commission approval delayed the sale until nine months after the first transaction. Rev.Rul. 79–194 appears to reject the holding in this case.

In contrast to Rev.Rul. 79–194, Rev.Rul. 79–70 1979–1 C.B. 144, held that the requirements of § 351 had not been met where the prearranged sale of stock was to a creditor of the corporation. In Rev.Rul. 79–70, X Corporation transferred property to newly organized Y Corporation and, pursuant to a prearranged binding contract, sold 40 percent of the Y stock to Z Corporation. Simultaneously, Z purchased securities for cash from Y. The Ruling held that Z Corporation was not a transferor of property because it received only debt securities from Y. Z's ownership of the Y stock acquired by purchase from X Corporation could not be counted in determining whether the control requirement of § 351 was satisfied. Since Z therefore received only securities for cash and was not a stockholder prior to the exchange, it was not a member of the control group for § 351 purposes. X was the only transferor of property, it received only 60 percent of the stock, and the transaction therefore did not qualify under § 351.

2.2. *Underwriting Situations*

Treas.Reg. § 1.351–1(a)(3) provides that if a person acquires stock from an underwriter in exchange for cash in a "qualified underwriting transaction," for purposes of § 351 the person who purchases the stock from the underwriter is treated as transferring the cash directly to the corporation in exchange for the stock and the underwriter's role in the transaction is disregarded. A "qualified underwriting transaction" is an underwriting in which a corporation issues stock for cash in which either the underwriter is an agent of the corporation or the underwriter's ownership of stock is transitory.

3.   CONTROL WHEN THERE ARE MULTIPLE CLASSES OF STOCK

The existence of multiple classes of voting stock requires a determination regarding the relative voting power of each class in order to determine whether the transferors of property are in control. There is little available guidance regarding the meaning of "total combined voting power of all classes of stock entitled to vote." In Rev.Rul. 63–234, 1963–2 C.B. 148, the IRS ruled under § 368(c) (in a type (B) reorganization) that preferred stock that entitled its holders to elect two of twelve directors was voting stock in that "it conferred upon the holders of such stock the right to significant participation in the management of the affairs of the corporation." The IRS relied on its earlier ruling in I.T. 3896, 1948–1 C.B. 72 (declared obsolete in Rev.Rul. 68–100, 1968–1 C.B. 572), which considered voting control for purposes of membership in an affiliated group, holding that the voting power of preferred stock was in proportion to the number of directors elected by the preferred stockholders. Thus preferred stock with the right to elect two of twelve directors possessed 2/12, or 16.7 percent of voting control. See also Rev.Rul. 69–126, 1969–1 C.B. 218, applying the same analysis for purposes of defining voting control under § 1504. Under this standard, a stockholder who receives common stock for services might receive more than 20 percent of the common stock by value without defeating § 351 nonrecognition treatment for transferors of property if the common stock transferred to the service stockholder represents a separate class of stock with limited voting rights.

The IRS also has ruled in Rev.Rul. 59–259, 1959–2 C.B. 115, that "control" under § 368(c) requires that in addition to 80 percent of the combined voting power of all classes of voting stock, the transferor stockholders must also own 80 percent of the number of shares of *each* class of nonvoting stock. Ownership of 80 percent of the total number of shares outstanding is not sufficient.

Nonqualified preferred stock, as defined in § 351(g), is treated as property other than stock for purposes of determining whether the transferor who receives such stock in exchange for property recognizes gain or loss in a § 351 transaction. See page 75. Nevertheless, except to the extent otherwise provided by regulations, nonqualified preferred stock is treated as stock for purposes of determining whether the control requirement has been met and the transaction as a whole qualifies under § 351(a). See S.Rep. No. 174, 105th Cong., 2d Sess. 206 (1998).

SECTION 4.　　RECEIPT OF STOCK FOR SERVICES

INTERNAL REVENUE CODE: Section 83(a)—(c)(2), (h); 351(d)(1).

REGULATIONS: Sections 1.83–1(a)(1),–6(a)(1); 1.351–1(a)(1), (2), Exs. (2) and (3).

Section § 351 applies only to the transfer of "property" in exchange for stock. Section 351(d)(1) specifically provides that stock issued for services is not issued for property. Section 83 applies to stock issued for services. Thus, the shareholder who receives stock for services realizes ordinary income equal to the fair market value of the stock. If the stock is subject to a substantial risk of forfeiture or other restrictions that prevent it from being fully vested, § 83 provides rules for determining the year in which the value of the stock interest must be included in income. Pursuant to § 83(h), the corporation will be able to deduct the fair market value of the stock if the services provided by the transferee were not capital in nature. See also Treas.Reg. § 1.83–6. Otherwise the corporation must capitalize the value of the stock.

If a single transferor transfers both property and services for stock, the transaction must be bifurcated and treated as the receipt of stock for property of equivalent value and the receipt of stock for services. Thus the transferor may be accorded nonrecognition under § 351 with respect to the stock received for property even though the receipt of the remainder of the stock is taxable under § 61 and § 83.

If a person who only provides services to the corporation and does not transfer any property to a newly formed corporation receives more than twenty percent of the voting stock or more than twenty percent of any particular class of nonvoting stock upon the formation of a new corporation, the transferors of property will not be in "control" of the corporation immediately after the transfer. In such a case, the issuance of stock for services will preclude § 351 nonrecognition treatment for the transferors of property. See Mojonnier & Sons, Inc. v. Commissioner, 12 T.C. 837 (1949) (Nonacq.) (§ 351 did not apply to the transferor of property where upon incorporation of a sole proprietorship former employees received more than 20 percent of stock in consideration for past services), discussed at page 111.

However, a transferor of services who receives more than 20 percent of the stock for his services and who also transfers some property to the corporation for stock can qualify as a "transferor of property," so that both the stock received for services and the stock received for property will be counted in determining whether the control test is met. However, Treas.Reg. § 1.351–1(a)(1)(ii) warns that if the primary purpose of the property transfer is to qualify the stock received for services and the property transferred constitutes only a "relatively small value" in comparison to the value of the services stock, the services stock will not be counted in determining the control group. Rev. Proc. 77–37, § 3.07, 1977–2 C.B. 568, indicates that the property transferred will not be considered to be of "relatively small value" if it has a value equal to at least 10 percent of the value of the stock received for services by the person providing services (i.e., the value of the property is at least 9.09 percent of the total value of the stock received by the person who provided both property and services).

DETAILED ANALYSIS

1.   "PROPERTY" DISTINGUISHED FROM SERVICES AND SERVICE FLAVORED ASSETS

"Property" for § 351 purposes does not include all interests that may be considered property interests for other purposes. The question of whether assets that have been produced as the result of the taxpayer's personal efforts constitute "property" for purposes of § 351 is identical to that encountered in exchanges of property for a partnership interest accorded nonrecognition treatment under § 721, and is similar, but not identical, to that encountered in connection with whether an asset constitutes "property" for purposes of capital gain treatment under § 1221. Thus, the term "property" includes secret processes and formulae whether patentable or not. Rev.Rul. 64–56, 1964–1 (Part 1) C.B. 133. Under that ruling, if the transferred information qualifies as property, then § 351 applies even though services are to be performed in connection with the transfer; the services, however, must be ancillary and subsidiary to the property transfer. Continuing technical assistance, employee training, and construction assistance will ordinarily be considered services for purposes of § 351 transfers. Rev.Rul. 71–564, 1971–2 C.B. 179, holds that trade secrets are property for purposes of § 351 transfers as long as the transferee corporation receives an exclusive right to the trade secret until it becomes public knowledge and is no longer protectable under applicable law. E.I. Du Pont de Nemours & Co. v. United States, 471 F.2d 1211 (Ct.Cl.1973), held, however, that the transfer of a royalty-free, nonexclusive license qualified as a transfer of "property" in a § 351 exchange. The fact that a taxable transfer of the nonexclusive license would not have qualified for capital gain treatment did not prevent § 351 from applying.

Rev.Rul. 70–45, 1970–1 C.B. 17, provides that business goodwill is property. In Rev.Rul. 79–288, 1979–2 C.B. 139, the IRS ruled further that a corporate name registered in a foreign country and protected under the laws of the foreign country is property for § 351 purposes, but that an unregistered, unprotected name with no goodwill value is not property.

In United States v. Frazell, 335 F.2d 487 (5th Cir.1964), a geologist entered into an agreement under which he was to identify potentially productive oil and gas properties, using several oil maps that he owned. Frazell was paid for his services and was to receive a specified interest in the properties after the other venturers had recovered certain costs. Eventually, instead of an interest in the properties, he received stock in a corporation to which the properties had been transferred. One of the court's alternative holdings was that Frazell realized ordinary income under § 351 on the theory that, if the stock were a substitution for the partnership interest originally contemplated, it would be compensation for services (and not received in exchange for "property"), and hence taxable under § 351. To the extent that the geological maps constituted "property," the taxpayer was entitled to § 351 nonrecognition treatment as to these items.

In James v. Commissioner, 53 T.C. 63 (1969), the taxpayer and one Talbot entered into an agreement to develop a real estate project. Talbot was to contribute land and the taxpayer was to promote the project and obtain the necessary FHA commitment and financing for the project. The taxpayer obtained the commitments in the name of the corporation and the taxpayer and Talbot then transferred the land and financing commitments to a corporation. The stock of the corporation was issued 50–50 to the taxpayer and Talbot. The taxpayer argued that he had transferred contract rights (analogous to patents or secret processes) to the corporation and therefore § 351 controlled. Following *Frazell,* the court held that the stock was received for services and was therefore ordinary income to the taxpayer. Furthermore, the only transferor of "property" was Talbot, who owned only 50 percent of the stock after the transaction. Thus § 351 did not apply to Talbot's transfer because the 80 percent control test was not met and taxable gain resulted.

James was distinguished in United States v. Stafford, 727 F.2d 1043 (11th Cir.1984), which held that an unenforceable letter of intent to provide financing was property under § 721, which provides for nonrecognition of gain or loss on the contribution of property to a partnership. The court indicated that it would reach the same result under § 351. The court pointed out that Stafford had developed the letter of intent for his own account and owned the letter of intent individually. The financing commitment in *James* was in the name of the corporation.

In Hospital Corp. of America v. Commissioner, 81 T.C. 520, 587–590 (1983), the Tax Court held that the transfer of an opportunity to negotiate a management contract in Saudi Arabia was not the transfer of "property". In Roberts Company, Inc. v. Commissioner, 5 T.C. 1 (1945), however, a contingent fee agreement in favor of attorneys conveying an interest in land in the event of a successful litigation was held to constitute a property interest in the land involved, so that the attorneys could qualify as transferors of property.

2. TREATMENT OF THE CORPORATION

Whether a corporation issues stock in exchange for services in a § 351 transaction upon its formation or after the corporation is formed, the corporation recognizes no gain under § 1032 and is entitled either to a deduction under § 162 or to capitalize the value of the stock as the cost of the asset to which the services for which the stock was issued are related. Justification for the corporation claiming a deduction or acquiring basis while not recognizing any income is not self-evident.

If a corporation pays an employee a bonus in the form of its stock and the value of the stock would otherwise be a deductible expense (see § 83(h)), the nonrecognition treatment of § 1032 relieving the gain from inclusion (Treas.Reg. § 1.1032–1(a) (last sentence)) arguably might bring into play § 265, which disallows expenses allocable to income "wholly exempt." In Hercules Powder Co. v. United States, 180 F.Supp. 363 (Ct.Cl.1960), after holding that stock so distributed did not result in gain to the corporation under the pre-§ 1032 regulations, the court then allowed the deduction as against the IRS's assertion of the rule of § 265: "We think that the words 'gives rise to neither taxable gain nor deductible loss' in the regulation concerning the original issue of shares did not create an exemption of income from taxation. That could not be accomplished by regulation. That language must mean that such an issue does not give rise to income, within the meaning of [§ 61]." Subsequently, the IRS ruled that a transfer of appreciated stock or newly issued stock to employees as compensation for services is fully deductible under § 162. Although not discussing § 265, the rulings stated that the nonrecognition provisions of § 1032 have no effect on business expense deductions otherwise allowable under § 162. Rev.Rul. 62–217, 1962–2 C.B. 59; Rev.Rul. 69–75, 1969–1 C.B. 52.

CHAPTER 3

THE CAPITAL STRUCTURE OF THE CORPORATION

SECTION 1.　DEBT VERSUS EQUITY

The tax treatment of the various forms that an investment in a corporation can take is a central issue in the pattern of corporate taxation. Unlike in the partnership situation, the return on capital invested in ownership interests in the corporation, i.e., corporate stock, is subject to two levels of tax, once in the hands of the corporation and again when dividends are distributed to individual shareholders. On the other hand, the return on an investment in a corporation as a creditor, i.e., the interest paid by the corporation for the funds advanced, is only subject to a single level of tax since the interest payment, unlike a dividend, is deductible by the corporation and thus avoids the corporate level tax. Moreover, if the investor is a tax-exempt entity, such as a pension fund, debt classification generally eliminates the yield from the corporate tax base entirely. The tax "bias" in favor of investment as a creditor has been a source of great strain on the tax system. Taxpayers and their advisors have attempted to structure obligations that qualify as debt for tax purposes, with the attendant single level of tax on the return, while at the same time giving the investor an opportunity to participate in the growth of the business enterprise—a typical aspect of an ownership or equity investment.

Whether an investment is treated as equity or debt also affects the tax consequence of recognition of loss in disposition of the investment. Gain or loss recognized by a corporate or individual stockholder on the sale, exchange or retirement of stock will be capital gain or loss. Loss incurred on worthless stock also is a capital loss. However, § 1244 allows individuals an ordinary loss deduction on stock in certain small business companies, and a corporation is allowed an ordinary loss deduction on the worthless stock of a controlled subsidiary. Gain or loss recognized on the sale, exchange or retirement of a debt obligation is also capital to a corporate or individual holder (unless there is an element of original issue or market discount involved). Loss on a worthless debt obligation that is classified as a "security" is treated as a capital loss to both the corporate and individual holder. For this purpose, a debt obligation is a "security" if it is in registered form or has coupons attached. No loss is allowed in the case of a worthless debt which is a "registration required debt" but which has not been registered. I.R.C. § 165(j). An individual's loss on a debt obligation that is not a security is a short-term capital loss, unless the debt arose in the individual's trade or business, in which case the loss is ordinary. Loss incurred by a corporate holder on a nonsecurity debt obligation is ordinary. See I.R.C. §§ 165(g), 166(a) and (d). Loss incurred by a corporate holder with respect to worthless securities of a controlled subsidiary generally is ordinary. I.R.C. § 165(g)(3).

The debt/equity equation is further complicated by the preferential tax rate accorded to most dividends on stock. Since 2003, § 1(h)(11) generally taxes dividends received by individuals at the same preferential rates enjoyed by long-term capital gains—currently zero percent for capital gains and dividends that would have been taxed in the 10 and 15 percent brackets if they had been taxed at ordinary income rates, 15 percent for capital gains and dividends that would have been taxed in the tax brackets higher than 15 percent but below the 39.6 percent bracket if they had been taxed at ordinary income rates, and 20 percent for capital gains and dividends that would have been taxed in the 39.6 percent bracket if they had been taxed at ordinary income rates. As a result, the tax bias in favor of debt financing is ameliorated to some extent. While interest remains deductible to the corporation, the lender is taxed on interest received at the lender's normal marginal rate—up to 39.6 percent. Dividends, on the other hand, while not deductible to the corporation have been taxed to the investor at a substantially lower rate. Thus, an individual investor who is concerned only with the investor's own tax situation preferred to receive dividends on a stock investment rather than interest on a loan, if the before-tax yields are similar. But if the investor is wearing the hats of both a lender and a shareholder, and is concerned with the corporation's overall tax picture, the financial interests of the investor and the corporation may be intertwined, thus shifting the balance somewhat in the direction of debt rather than equity financing.

Aside from the tax consequence of variable rates, an investor generally is indifferent to the formal classification of the investment instrument. From the investment perspective, the question is the yield on the investment in relation to the level of risk involved and the formal classification of the return as "interest" or "dividend" is not a matter of concern (except, of course, from a tax point of view). As a general matter, the higher the level of legal and economic protection provided in the instrument, the lower the investment return. Historically an equity investment was considered as riskier than debt, with its promised return of principal plus interest, and thus an investor in equity expected a higher rate of return. However, given the imagination of the marketers of financial products, the possible combinations of ownership and creditor interests in a particular financial instrument are almost infinite.

The development of tax principles in this area has lagged far behind the development of investment products. This lag may be traceable to two causes. In the first place, the legal rules for the classification of investment instruments as debt or equity have developed primarily in the context of small, closely held corporations in cases in which the investors were both shareholders and "lenders." The method of analysis developed by the courts in that context has been largely inadequate to deal with situations such as large venture capital firms investing in an emerging business or the issuance of highly complex and sophisticated financial instruments by publicly traded companies. Secondly, and closely related, is the fact that, in developing the debt-equity rules, the courts generally have applied an "all or nothing" approach. That is, a particular instrument is either a debt instrument in its entirety for tax purposes or an equity instrument in its entirety. This approach is totally at odds with the various combinations of debt and equity features which can be employed in a particular financial instrument. Nonetheless, except when Congress has been willing to provide a legislative alternative (which in a few situations it has been forced to do), the all-or-nothing approach continues to prevail. This approach has made it relatively easy for sophisticated investors and their equally sophisticated tax advisors to craft instruments that combine the desirable legal features of ownership and creditor status with the most advantageous tax treatment.

The material in this chapter first considers the "traditional" debt-equity classification issues primarily as they have developed in the context of closely-held corporations. It then deals with the classification issues that are raised by more complex financial instruments and the more specific Congressional responses to those issues.

The present distinction between debt and equity capital presents the corporation and its investors with different tax issues and planning possibilities. As respects the corporation issuing the obligation,[1] if the obligation is debt, interest is deductible, retirement at a discount may result in cancellation of indebtedness income, or retirement at a premium may provide an additional interest deduction. If the obligation is stock, dividends are not deductible and generally the corporation does not recognize income or loss on retirement. Retention of earnings to retire debt generally will not run afoul of the § 531 penalty tax on improperly accumulated earnings, see page 849, but such retention might result in that tax in the case of stock. Also the availability of the deduction for original issue discount requires that the obligation be classified as debt; no such deduction is allowed for the issuance of stock.

Payments on an obligation will also produce different tax results for the holder depending on the character of the obligation. If the payment constitutes interest it will be includible in the recipient's income whether or not the corporation has earnings and profits, whereas inclusion as a dividend depends on the presence of earnings and profits. If a corporation holds the obligation, the intercorporate dividends received deduction under § 243 (see page 223) depends on the presence of a "dividend," which requires that the obligation be treated as stock. If the advances to the corporation are regarded as contributions to capital, i.e., additional stock investment, repayment usually will be a dividend to the stockholder, but if regarded as loans, the repayment will not be taxable. Where the obligation is retired, if it is stock, the retirement under some circumstances will be a dividend under § 301; if a debt, retirement will produce capital gain or loss (in the absence of original issue discount or premium).

The preceding discussion is not exhaustive, and there are other facets to the problem. For example, the classification of the obligation as stock or debt is important under the reorganization provisions to both the investor and the corporation. Also, if a foreign subsidiary is involved, the classification will be important, for example, with respect to the foreign tax credit. Classification of the obligation as stock or debt

---

[1] The term "obligation" is used in the following materials to include stock, debt, and instruments with attributes of both stock and debt whose proper classification is in doubt.

also is important in determining the applicability of the personal holding company tax. See page 859.

A. GENERAL PRINCIPLES GOVERNING CLASSIFICATION AS DEBT OR EQUITY

Indmar Products Co., Inc. v. Commissioner

United States Court of Appeals for the Sixth Circuit, 2006.
444 F.3d 771

■ McKEAGUE, CIRCUIT JUDGE.

Indmar Products Co., Inc. ("Indmar") appeals the decision of the Tax Court to disallow interest deductions the company claimed for tax years 1998–2000, and to assess accuracy-related tax penalties for those years. The interest deductions relate to a number of advances made to Indmar by its majority stockholders over several years. Indmar argued at trial that the advances were legitimate loans made to the company, and thus it could properly deduct the interest payments made on these advances under 26 U.S.C. § 163(a). The Tax Court, following the position taken by the Commissioner of Internal Revenue (the "Commissioner"), disagreed, concluding that the advances were equity contributions and therefore the company could not deduct any purported interest payments on these advances. The court imposed penalties on Indmar based on the deductions. *Indmar Prods. Co., Inc. v. Comm'r*, T.C.M.2005–32.

Upon review of the record, we conclude that the Tax Court clearly erred in finding the advances were equity. The Tax Court failed to consider several factors used by this court for determining whether advances are debt or equity, ignored relevant evidence, and drew several unsupported inferences from its factual findings. We reverse and find that the stockholder advances were bona fide debt.

I. BACKGROUND

A. Stockholder Advances to Indmar

Indmar, a Tennessee corporation, is a marine engine manufacturer. In 1973, Richard Rowe, Sr., and Marty Hoffman owned equal shares of Indmar. In 1987, after Hoffman passed away, Richard and his wife, Donna Rowe, together owned 74.44% of Indmar, with their children and children's spouses owning the rest. By all accounts, Indmar has been a successful company. From 1986 to 2000, Indmar's sales and costs-of-goods sold increased from $5m and $3.9m to $45m and $37.7m, respectively. In addition, Indmar's working capital (current assets minus current liabilities) increased from $471,386 to $3.8m. During this period, Indmar did not declare or pay formal dividends.

Since the 1970s, Indmar's stockholders have advanced funds to it, receiving a 10% annual return in exchange. Hoffman started the practice in the 1970s. Beginning in 1987, the Rowes (as well as their children) began to make advancements on a periodic basis. Indmar treated all of the advances as loans from stockholders in the corporate books and records, and made monthly payments calculated at 10% of the advanced funds. Indmar reported the payments as interest expense deductions on its federal income tax returns. Consistent with Indmar's reporting, the Rowes reported the payments as interest income on their individual income tax returns.

The parties did not initially document the advances with notes or other instruments. Beginning in 1993, the parties executed notes covering all of the advances at issue. Specifically, Indmar executed a promissory note in 1993 with Donna Rowe for $201,400 (i.e., her outstanding balance). The note was payable on demand and freely transferable, had no maturity date or monthly payment schedule, and had a fixed interest rate of 10%. In 1995, Indmar executed a similar promissory note with Richard Rowe for $605,681 (i.e., his outstanding balance). In 1998, when the outstanding transfers totaled $1,222,133, Indmar executed two line of credit agreements with the Rowes for $1m and $750,000. The line of credit agreements provided that the balances were payable on demand and the notes were freely transferable. In addition, the agreements provided a stated interest rate of 10% and had no maturity date or monthly payment schedule. None of the advances were secured.

Repayments of the advances were paid on demand, based on the needs of the stockholders, and not subject to set or predetermined due dates. The record indicates that between 1987 and 2000, the total advance balances ranged from $634,000 to $1.7m, and Indmar made purported interest payments between $45,000 and $174,000 each year.

The parties structured the advances as demand loans to give the Rowes flexibility as creditors. Moreover, as demand loans, the advances were treated by the Rowes as short-term debt under Tennessee law, thereby excepting interest payments from a 6% state tax on dividends and interest on long-term debts. Tenn.Code Ann. §§ 67–2–101(1)(B)(i), 67–2–102 (2005). Indmar, however, reported the advances as long-term liabilities on its financial statements to avoid violating loan agreements with First Tennessee Bank ("FTB"), its primary creditor, who required a minimum ratio of current assets to current liabilities.

In order to reconcile the treatment and execution of the advances as demand loans versus listing them as long-term debt in its financial reports, Indmar received waivers from the Rowes agreeing to forego repayment on the notes for at least 12 months. From 1989 to 2000, the notes to Indmar's financial statements disclosed that "The stockholders have agreed not to demand payment within the next year," and in 1992 and 1993, the Rowes signed written agreements stating that they would not demand repayment of the advances. Indmar did all of this under the direction of its accountant.

Despite the annual waivers, the Rowes demanded and received numerous partial repayments of the advances. Specifically, in 1994 and 1995, Richard Rowe demanded repayment of $15,000 and $650,000, respectively, to pay his taxes and purchase a new home. He also demanded repayment of $84,948, $80,000, $25,000, and $70,221 from 1997–2000 to pay litigation expenses, boat repairs, and tax expenses. Donna Rowe demanded repayment of $180,000 in 1998 for boat repairs. The Rowes made additional advances in 1997 and 1998 of $500,000 and $300,000, respectively. The balance of notes payable to stockholders on December 31, 2000, totaled $1,166,912.

As Indmar was a successful, profitable company, numerous banks sought to lend money to it. FTB worked hard to retain Indmar's business, made funds immediately available upon request, and was willing to lend Indmar 100% of the stockholder advances.

In its loan agreements with Indmar, FTB required the company to subordinate all transfers, including stockholder advances, to FTB's loans. FTB did not strictly enforce the subordination provision, however, as Indmar repaid—with FTB's knowledge—some of the stockholder advancements at the same time FTB loans remained outstanding. As an example, when Richard demanded repayment of $650,000 to purchase a new home, Indmar borrowed the entire amount from FTB at 7.5% (the prime lending rate was 8.75%). Indmar secured the loan with inventory, accounts and general intangibles, equipment, and the personal guarantee of the Rowes. Richard Moody, the FTB lending officer who worked with Indmar on the loan, testified that he knew Indmar used the proceeds to repay Richard. Indmar had loans outstanding with FTB at the time.

As stipulated by the parties, the prime lending rate ranged from a low of 6% to a high of 10.5% between 1987–1998. In 1997, Indmar and FTB executed a promissory note for $1m that was modified in 1998. The interest rate on the note (7.85%) was below the prime lending rate. Indmar also had a collateralized line of credit with FTB. Similar to the stockholder advances, the bank line of credit was used for short-term working capital. . . .

B.   Claimed Deductions at Issue

On its tax returns for 1998–2000, Indmar claimed deductions for the purported interest payments paid on the stockholder advances. The Commissioner issued a notice of deficiency. Indmar filed a petition in the Tax Court challenging the Commissioner's decision. After trial, the Tax Court concluded that the advances did not constitute genuine indebtedness and thus the payments to the stockholders were not deductible. The Tax Court calculated a total tax deficiency of $123,735 and assessed $24,747 in penalties. Indmar timely appealed.

II.   LEGAL ANALYSIS

A.   Determining Whether Advance Is Debt or Equity

As a general matter, the Commissioner's determination of a deficiency is entitled to a presumption of correctness. It is the taxpayer's burden to prove the determination to be incorrect or arbitrary. *Ekman v. Comm'r*, 184 F.3d 522, 524 (6th Cir.1999).

Issue

The basic question before us is whether the advances made to the company by the stockholders were loans or equity contributions. Under 26 U.S.C. § 163(a), a taxpayer may take a tax deduction for "all interest paid or accrued . . . on indebtedness." There is no similar deduction for dividends paid on equity investments. Thus, if the advances were loans, the 10% payments made by Indmar to the Rowes were "interest" payments, and Indmar could deduct these payments. If, on the other hand, the advances were equity contributions, the 10% payments were constructive dividends, and thus were not deductible.

Over the years, courts have grappled with this seemingly simple question in a wide array of legal and factual contexts. The distinction between debt and equity arises in other areas of federal tax law, *see, e.g., Roth Steel Tube Co. v. Comm'r*, 800 F.2d 625, 629–30 (6th Cir.1986) (addressing the issue in the context of the deductibility of advances as bad debt under 26 U.S.C. § 166(a)(1)), as well as bankruptcy law, *see, e.g.,* In re *AutoStyle Plastics, Inc.*, 269 F.3d 726, 750 (6th Cir.2001). The Second Circuit set out the "classic" definition of debt in *Gilbert v. Commissioner:* "an unqualified obligation to pay a sum certain at a reasonably close fixed maturity date along with a fixed percentage in interest payable regardless of the debtor's income or lack thereof." 248 F.2d 399, 402 (2d Cir.1957). "While some variation from this formula is not fatal to the taxpayer's effort to have the advance treated as a debt for tax purposes, . . . too great a variation will of course preclude such treatment." *Id.* at 402–03. The question becomes, then, what is "too great a variation"?

To determine whether an advance to a company is debt or equity, courts consider "whether the objective facts establish an intention to create an unconditional obligation to repay the advances." *Roth Steel,* 800 F.2d at 630 (citing *Raymond v. United States*, 511 F.2d 185, 190 (6th Cir.1975)). In doing so, courts look not only to the form of the transaction, but, more importantly, to its economic substance. *See, e.g., Fin Hay Realty Co. v. United States*, 398 F.2d 694, 697 (3d Cir.1968) ("The various factors . . . are only aids in answering the ultimate question whether the investment, analyzed in terms of its economic reality, constitutes risk capital entirely subject to the fortunes of the corporate venture or represents a strict debtor-creditor relationship."); *Byerlite Corp. v. Williams*, 286 F.2d 285, 291 (6th Cir.1960) ("In all cases, the prevailing consideration is that artifice must not be exalted over reality, whether to the advantage of the taxpayer, or to the government.").

[handwritten margin note: intention to create an unconditional obligation to repay the advances]

The circuit courts have not settled on a single approach to the debt/equity question. We elucidated our approach in *Roth Steel*, setting out eleven non-exclusive factors for courts to consider:

[handwritten margin note: Roth Steel factors]

> (1) the names given to the instruments, if any, evidencing the indebtedness; (2) the presence or absence of a fixed maturity date and schedule of payments; (3) the presence or absence of a fixed rate of interest and interest payments; (4) the source of repayments; (5) the adequacy or inadequacy of capitalization; (6) the identity of interest between the creditor and the stockholder; (7) the security, if any, for the advances; (8) the corporation's ability to obtain financing from outside lending institutions; (9) the extent to which the advances were subordinated to the claims of outside creditors; (10) the extent to which the advances were used to acquire capital assets; and (11) the presence or absence of a sinking fund to provide repayments. 800 F.2d at 630. No single factor is controlling; the weight to be given a factor (if any) necessarily depends on the particular circumstances of each case. *Id.; see also Universal Castings Corp.*, 37 T.C. 107, 114 (1961) ("It is not enough when examining such a precedential checklist to test each item for its presence or absence, but it is necessary also to weigh each item."), *aff'd*, 303 F.2d 620 (7th Cir.1962). In essence, the more a stockholder advance resembles an arm's-

length transaction, the more likely it is to be treated as debt. *AutoStyle Plastics*, 269 F.3d at 750.

800 F.2d at 630. No single factor is controlling; the weight to be given a factor (if any) necessarily depends on the particular circumstances of each case. *Id.; see also Universal Castings Corp.*, 37 T.C. 107, 114 (1961) ("It is not enough when examining such a precedential checklist to test each item for its presence or absence, but it is necessary also to weigh each item."), *aff'd,* 303 F.2d 620 (7th Cir.1962). In essence, the more a stockholder advance resembles an arm's-length transaction, the more likely it is to be treated as debt. *AutoStyle Plastics,* 269 F.3d at 750.

* * *

C. *Roth Steel Factors*

After discussing some, but not all, of the *Roth Steel* factors, the Tax Court concluded that the Rowes' advances were equity contributions. Specifically, it found the following factors weighed in favor of equity: (i) Indmar did not pay any formal dividends (although this is not one of the *Roth Steel* factors); (ii) there was no fixed maturity date or obligation to repay; (iii) repayment came from corporate profits and would not be paid if there were not sufficient profits; (iv) advances were unsecured; (v) there was no sinking fund; and (vi) at the time advances were made, there was no unconditional and legal obligation to repay. The court found that several factors weighed in favor of debt: (i) Indmar reported the advances on its federal income tax returns as interest expenses; (ii) external financing was available; (iii) Indmar was adequately capitalized; (iv) the advances were not subordinated to all creditors; and (v) the Rowes did not make the advances in proportion to their respective equity holdings. The court concluded that the factors favoring equity "certainly outweigh" those favoring debt. . . .

As explained below, we find that the Tax Court clearly erred in concluding that the advances were equity contributions rather than bona fide debt. The Tax Court failed to consider several *Roth Steel* factors. It also did not address in its analysis certain uncontroverted testimony and evidence upon which the parties stipulated. Consideration of all of the record evidence in this case leaves us "with the definite and firm conviction that a mistake has been committed." *Holmes,* 184 F.3d at 543.

1. *Fixed Rate of Interest and Interest Payments*

The first factor to which we look is whether or not a fixed rate of interest and fixed interest payments accompanied the advances. *Roth Steel,* 800 F.2d at 631. The absence of a fixed interest rate and regular payments indicates equity; conversely, the presence of both evidences debt. *Id.;* 7 Mertens Law of Fed. Income Tax'n § 26:28 ("A fixed interest rate is indicative of a deductible interest payment.") (collecting cases). In its findings of fact, the Tax Court determined that the advances were made with a 10% annual return rate. The court also found that Indmar made regular monthly interest payments on all of the advances.

The fixed rate of interest and regular interest payments indicate that the advances were bona fide debt. In its analysis, however, the Tax Court took a different view. Rather than analyzing these facts within the *Roth Steel* framework (i.e., as objective indicia of debt or equity), the Tax Court focused instead on why the Rowes made the advancements:

it concluded that the Rowes "characterized the cash transfers as debt because they wanted to receive a 10–percent return on their investment and minimize estate taxes." *Indmar*, 2005 T.C.M. LEXIS 31, at *11. Yet, neither of these intentions is inconsistent with characterizing the advances as loans.

For tax purposes, it is generally more important to focus on "what was done," than "why it was done." *United States v. Hertwig*, 398 F.2d 452, 455 (5th Cir.1968). "In applying the law to the facts of this case, . . . it is "clear that the objective factors . . . are decisive in cases of this type." " *Raymond*, 511 F.2d at 191 (quoting *Austin Village*, 432 F.2d at 745). It is largely unremarkable that the Rowes wanted to receive a return from their advances. Most, if not all, creditors (as well as equity investors) intend to profit from their investments. *Bordo Prods. Co. v. United States*, 476 F.2d 1312, 1322 (Ct.Cl.1973). As long as the interest rate is in line with the risks involved, a healthy return on investment can evidence debt.

Of course, "[e]xcessively high rates would . . . raise the possibility that a distribution of corporate profits was being disguised as debt. Were such the purpose of an exorbitant interest rate, the instrument involved would probably not qualify as debt in form." *Scriptomatic, Inc. v. United States*, 555 F.2d 364, 370 n.7 (3d Cir.1977) (citing William T. Plumb, Jr., *The Fed. Income Tax Significance of Corporate Debt: A Critical Analysis & A Proposal*, 26 Tax L.Rev. 369, 439–40 (1971)). The Tax Court found that the 10% rate exceeded the federal prime interest rate during most of the period at issue, as well as the rate charged by FTB on several of its loans to Indmar.

The record indicates that the 10% rate was not an "exorbitant interest rate" under the circumstances. Indmar had a collateralized line of credit with FTB, which, similar to the stockholder advances, was available for short-term working capital. The rate charged by FTB for the line of credit ranged between 8%–9.5%, a rate not much below the fixed rate of 10% charged by the Rowes. The rate differential makes financial sense when considering the differences in security—the FTB line of credit was secured while the Rowes' advances were not.[2]

As for the Rowes' desire to minimize their estate taxes, this also offers little to the analysis. "Tax avoidance is entirely legal and legitimate. Any taxpayer "may so arrange his affairs that his taxes shall be as low as possible; he is not bound to choose that pattern which will best pay the Treasury; there is not even a patriotic duty to increase one's taxes." " *Estate of Kluener v. Comm'r*, 154 F.3d 630, 634 (6th Cir.1998) (quoting *Helvering v. Gregory*, 69 F.2d 809, 810 (2d Cir.1934) (L.Hand, J.)). The desire to avoid or minimize taxes is not itself directly relevant to the question whether a purported loan is instead an equity investment. Rather, such a desire is only tangentially relevant, by acting as a flag to the Commissioner and courts to look closely at the transaction for any objective indicia of debt.

---

[2] The government took pains during trial to show that Indmar could have received a lower interest rate from FTB than its stockholders. Had the 10% rate been exorbitant, this would have been a useful line of inquiry. Under the circumstances here, the rate was not exorbitant, and whether Indmar could have received a better rate through FTB is of no import. To show bona fide debt, a taxpayer does not need to prove that it received the financially optimal rate, just a commercially reasonable one.

Far from proving the Commissioner's position, the existence and consistent payment of a fixed, reasonable interest rate strongly supports the inference that the advances were bona fide loans.

2.   *Written Instruments of the Indebtedness*

"The absence of notes or other instruments of indebtedness is a strong indication that the advances were capital contributions and not loans." *Roth Steel*, 800 F.2d at 631. In its analysis, the Tax Court found that Indmar "failed to establish that, at the time the transfers were made, it had the requisite unconditional and legal obligation to repay the Rowes (e.g., the transfers were *not documented*)." *Indmar*, 2005 T.C.M. LEXIS 31, at *15 (emphasis added).[3]

The Tax Court focused on only half the story. For years 1987–1992, the Rowes did make advancements without executing any notes or other instruments. Beginning in 1993, and for all the tax years at issue in this case, the parties executed notes of loans and lines of credit covering all of the advances at issue, as the Tax Court noted in its findings of fact. Yet, in its analysis of the *Roth Steel* factors, the Tax Court was silent as to the subsequent execution of notes. After-the-fact consolidation of prior advances into a single note can indicate that the advances were debt rather than equity contributions. *See, e.g., Dev. Corp. of Am. v. Comm'r*, T.C.M.1988–127. The Tax Court erred by focusing on the initial lack of documentation without addressing the subsequent history of executed notes.[4]

3.   *Fixed Maturity Date and Schedule of Payments*

"The absence of a fixed maturity date and a fixed obligation to repay indicates that the advances were capital contributions and not loans." *Roth Steel*, 800 F.2d at 631. Based on the Rowes' waivers, the Tax Court concluded that there was no fixed maturity date or fixed obligation to repay. While correct, we find that this factor carries little weight in the final analysis. The parties structured the advances as demand loans, which had *ascertainable* (although not fixed) maturity dates, controlled by the Rowes. *Piedmont Minerals*, 429 F.2d at 563 n. 5 ("The absence of a fixed maturity date is a relevant consideration, but it is far from controlling. The maturity of a demand note is always determinable by its holder."). Furthermore, the temporary waiver of payment does not convert debt into equity "since [the stockholders] still expected to be repaid." *AutoStyle Plastics*, 269 F.3d at 751.

Where advances are documented by demand notes with a fixed rate of interest and regular interest payments, the lack of a maturity date and schedule of payments does not strongly favor equity. To give any significant weight to this factor would create a virtual *per se* rule against the use of demand notes by stockholders, even though "[m]uch commercial debt is evidenced by demand notes." *Piedmont Minerals*,

---

[3]   The Tax Court did count in favor of debt the fact that Indmar consistently reported the payments as interest expense on its federal taxes.

[4]   The Tax Court was troubled by the treatment of the advances in the company's records as both demand debt and long-term debt. While we share the Tax Court's concerns, this was not the issue before the Tax Court or us on appeal. Importantly, regardless of whether it classified the payments as demand debt or long-term debt, the company *at all times* identified the advances as some form of debt. We leave it to the Tennessee authorities to determine whether Indmar owes any state taxes or penalties as a result of its reporting and accounting practices.

429 F.2d at 563 n. 5; *see also AutoStyle Plastics*, 269 F.3d at 750 (cautioning against a "rigid" rule that the factor always indicates equity).

4.   *The Source of Repayments*

"An expectation of repayment *solely* from corporate earnings is not indicative of bona fide debt regardless of its reasonableness." *Roth Steel*, 800 F.2d at 631 (emphasis added). Repayment can generally come from "only four possible sources . . . : (1) liquidation of assets, (2) profits from the business, (3) cash flow, and (4) refinancing with another lender." *Bordo Prods.*, 476 F.2d at 1326 (quoting Plumb, supra, at 526).

The Tax Court found that the "source of repayments" factor favored equity. It relied upon Richard Rowe's testimony that Indmar was expected to make a profit and that repayment "has to come from corporate profits or else the company couldn't pay for it." *Indmar*, 2005 T.C.M. LEXIS 31, at *14. The full colloquy from the testimony, however, is more equivocal:

> Q.   . . . [A]t the time that you made these advances, were you anticipating that the repayment was going to come from corporate profits?
>
> A.   Yes, sir. It has to come from corporate profits or else the company couldn't pay for it. Unless it made profit—and I have always believed from the first day we started, that we were going to be profitable.
>
> Q.   Was it your understanding and intent, at the time you made these advances, that if the company was not, in fact, profitable, you would not be repaid?
>
> A.   I had no intentions of not being repaid, sir.
>
> Q.   Why is that?
>
> A.   I believe it's me. It's my personality.
>
> Q.   Is that because you intended to make a profit?
>
> A.   Yes, sir.

There are at least two plausible ways to read this testimony. One can read it the way the Tax Court apparently did—Rowe's testimony was, at best, contradictory: repayment must come from profits, but he had no intention of not being repaid, regardless of the company's fortunes. Given the apparent contradiction, one should focus on the statement against Indmar's interest: Rowe admitted that repayment of the advances "has to come from corporate profits or else the company couldn't pay for it." If repayment "has" to come from profits, then this would imply that repayment was tied to the company's fortunes, suggesting the advances were equity contributions.

Another way to read the testimony, however, is that Rowe, as a small businessman and unsecured creditor, believed that full repayment of all of Indmar's debt required a thriving, successful business, which, ultimately, required profits. In other words, struggling companies near or at bankruptcy do not repay their debts, at least not dollar for dollar. Under this reading, his testimony is consistent with debt. In fact, we sounded a similar note in an earlier decision addressing the debt/equity issue: "One who makes a loan to a corporation also takes a risk, and while he may receive evidence of an obligation, payable in any event, often such obligation is never paid. . . . " All unsecured loans involve more or less risk." " *Byerlite*, 286 F.2d at 292 (quoting *Earle v. W.J. Jones & Son, Inc.*, 200 F.2d 846, 851 (9th Cir.1952)).

If there was no other evidence to support one view or the other, we could not say that the Tax Court's reading was clearly erroneous. Credibility determinations are left to the fact finder, and our review on appeal is strictly limited. The "Tax Court "is not bound to accept testimony at face value even when it is uncontroverted if it is improbable, unreasonable or questionable." " *Lovell & Hart, Inc. v. Comm'r*, 456 F.2d 145, 148 (6th Cir.1972) (quoting *Comm'r v. Smith*, 285 F.2d 91, 96 (5th Cir.1960)). On the other hand, the Tax Court cannot ignore relevant evidence in making its factual findings and any inferences from those findings.

Here, there is undisputed testimony by Rowe and the FTB lending officer, corroborated by stipulated evidence in the record, that clearly weighs in favor of debt on this factor. Indmar repaid a significant portion of the unpaid advances—$650,000—not from profits but by taking on additional debt from FTB. While the interest rate on the FTB loan was lower than 10%, Indmar had to secure the bank loan with inventory, accounts and general intangibles, equipment, and personal guarantees. Thus, Indmar repaid a significant portion of the unsecured stockholder advancements by taking on secured debt from a bank, rather than by taking the funds directly from earnings. This is important evidence that the parties had no expectation that Indmar would repay the advances "solely" from earnings. The Tax Court did not discuss or even cite this evidence in its *Roth Steel* analysis.

5. The Extent to Which the Advances Were Used to Acquire Capital Assets

Nor did the Tax Court address whether Indmar used the advances for working capital or capital expenditures. "Use of advances to meet the daily operating needs of the corporation, rather than to purchase capital assets, is indicative of bona fide indebtedness." *Roth Steel*, 800 F.2d at 632. Richard Rowe testified that Indmar always went to a bank for funds to buy capital equipment. He also testified that all of the advances he made to Indmar were used for working capital, as opposed to capital equipment. This is uncontroverted testimony. The government points, however, to Rowe's testimony that he advanced funds even when Indmar did not "need" the funds, and argues that this somehow cuts against his testimony that the advances were used as working capital.

The government's argument is unpersuasive. We do not find that Rowe's testimony on this subject was "improbable, unreasonable or questionable," especially in the absence of the Tax Court addressing this factor in its analysis.[5] A review of [pg. 2006–1965] Indmar's

---

[5] As the Tax Court did not address this factor, it made no credibility determinations with respect to Richard Rowe's testimony relating to the use of the advancements. At one point in its decision the Tax Court did find that Rowe's testimony was "contradictory, inconsistent, and unconvincing" and that the parties "manipulated facts," but this was in specific reference to its discussion about the inconsistent treatment of the advances as demand debt and long-term debt. *See Indmar*, 2005 T.C.M. LEXIS 31, at *12–13; *see also* supra note 4.

financial statements shows that it used all of the funds it received in various ways, including working capital and capital equipment expenditures. Thus, Indmar used the advances it received from the Rowes, even if not immediately upon receipt—i.e., Indmar identified a "need" for the advances at some point. There is nothing specific in the record, including Indmar's financial statements, that suggests the advances went to purchase capital equipment as opposed to being used for working capital. Accordingly, the government's supposition does not counter Rowe's testimony, and this factor squarely supports a finding of debt.

6.   Sinking Fund

"The failure to establish a sinking fund for repayment is evidence that the advances were capital contributions rather than loans." *Id.* The Tax Court was correct to point out that the lack of a sinking fund favors equity. This factor does not, however, deserve significant weight under the circumstances. First, a sinking fund (as a type of reserve) is a form of security for debt, and the Tax Court also counted the general absence of security for the stockholder advances as favoring equity. Second, the presence or absence of a sinking fund is an important consideration when looking at advances made to highly leveraged firms. In that case, the risk of repayment will likely be high on any unsecured loans, so any commercially reasonable lender would require a sinking fund or some other form of security for repayment. Where a company has sound capitalization with outside creditors ready to loan it money (as here), there is less need for a sinking fund. *See Bordo Prods.*, 476 F.2d at 1326.

7.   The Remaining Roth Steel Factors

On the remaining *Roth Steel* factors, the Tax Court determined that one favored equity (lack of security for the advances) and four favored debt (the company had sufficient external financing available to it; the company was adequately capitalized; the advances were not subordinated to all creditors; and the Rowes did not make the advances in proportion to their respective equity holdings). These findings are well-supported in the record.

8.   Failure to Pay Dividends

The Tax Court included in its discussion of *Roth Steel* a factor not actually cited in that case—Indmar's failure to pay dividends. In support, the Tax Court cited our decision in *Jaques v. Commissioner.*

The relevance of *Jaques* to this case is questionable. That case involved the withdrawal of funds by a controlling stockholder from his closely-held corporation. The stockholder argued that the withdrawal itself was a loan. We rejected the argument, relying in part on the fact that the corporation had never issued a formal dividend, and thus the withdrawal could have been a disguised dividend. *Jaques*, 935 F.2d at 107–08. The situation here is the exact opposite—the stockholders were advancing money to the corporation (not from), and it is the nature of those advances that we must determine.

Had the Rowes charged Indmar an exorbitant interest rate, the lack of any formal dividends might have been relevant to showing that the payments were not interest payments, but disguised dividends. As this was not the case, *see* supra Section II.C.1, we do not address further the relevance, if any, of the lack of dividend payments to the debt/equity question presented here.

D.   The Tax Court Committed Clear Error

To summarize, eight of the eleven *Roth Steel* factors favor debt. The three remaining factors suggest the advances were equity, but, as we explained above, two of the factors—the absence of a fixed maturity date and schedule of payments and the absence of a sinking fund—deserve little weight under the facts of this case. Moreover, the non-*Roth Steel* factor relied upon by the Tax Court—Indmar's failure to pay dividends—has questionable relevance to our inquiry. The only factor weighing in favor of equity with any real significance—the lack of security—does not outweigh all of the other factors in favor of debt.[6]

Accordingly, the trial evidence, when reviewed as a whole, conclusively shows that the Rowes' advances to Indmar were bona fide loans. The Tax Court committed clear error in finding otherwise.

III. CONCLUSION

For the foregoing reasons, we reverse the Tax Court's determination that the stockholders' advances were equity contributions. We find that the advances exhibited clear, objective indicia of bona fide debt. Accordingly, we also reverse the Tax Court's assessment of accuracy-related penalties.

■ ROGERS, CIRCUIT JUDGE, CONCURRING.

I concur fully in the majority opinion. I write separately to explain why the legal, non-factual components of the tax court's analysis are properly examined on appeal without deference to the tax court, notwithstanding the overall "clearly erroneous" standard that our court has stated to be applicable to the determination of whether a particular transaction is debt or equity.

Whether an issue to be determined by the courts is one of fact or law is sometimes pretty simple. But often, especially when the issue can be stated in the form of "Does the item before us fit within the legal definition of x?", the factual-versus-legal nature of the issue can be perplexing. This is because the seemingly single question really has two different components: "What is the nature of this item?" and "What is the legal meaning of x?" In a case where there is total agreement between the parties as to the nature of the item, the question whether the item is an x is a legal one. In a case where there is total agreement between the parties as to the meaning of x, but a dispute as to the nature of the item, the issue of whether the item is an x is totally

---

6   Judge Moore in her dissent suggests that we give "minimal deference" to the conclusions of the Tax Court. We respectfully disagree. Much of our analysis is expressly predicated on the Tax Court's findings of fact. *See, e.g.*, supra §§ II.C.1 & 2 (relying on the Tax Court's findings of a fixed 10% interest rate and regular interest payments, and documentation of advances from 1993–2000); 3 & 6 (accepting the Tax Court's findings of no fixed maturity date or schedule of payments, and no sinking fund, but concluding that these factors do not deserve significant weight under the circumstances); and 7 (accepting in full the Tax Court's findings on five of the *Roth Steel* factors). On the remaining two *Roth Steel* factors, we point to clear, uncontroverted evidence in the record favoring debt, evidence that the Tax Court unfortunately did not discuss in its *Roth Steel* analysis. On the issue of witness credibility, it is apparent from our analysis that we take issue not with any credibility determinations the Tax Court may have made as to Rowe's testimony on certain topics, but with the its failure to address evidence.

factual. Where there is some dispute on each of the two issues, the issue of whether the item is an x is a mixed question of law and fact.

* * *

Thus, in cases like the present one where the objective characteristics of a transaction have significant importance, our treatment of those objective characteristics does not require deference to the lower court. As we said in *Holmes v. Commissioner*, 184 F.3d 536, 543 (6th Cir. 1999) (emphasis added):

> On review, the Tax Court's *factual findings, and inferences drawn from the facts*, especially witness credibility determinations, are entitled to deference by the appellate court. . . . By contrast, the Tax Court's *application of legal standards*, and its legal conclusions, are reviewed *de novo*.

In my view, these cases are perfectly consistent with *not* deferring to the legal aspects of the lower court's reasoning, and avoidance of the fallacy described above requires us not to defer to such legal determinations. *See Livernois Trust*, 433 F.2d at 883 (McCree, J., concurring). Thus, while the majority opinion in this case cannot be faulted for stating that the overall scope of review in this case is "clear error," that conclusion must be interpreted to incorporate de novo review of legal questions necessary to our determination. Viewed in this way, the majority opinion's analysis is compelling.

In the instant case there is, to be sure, a limited factual aspect. One of the relevant *Roth* factors (the fourth) is whether repayment was intended to depend on company profit. 800 F.2d at 630. The tax court found that Indmar always intended to repay Mr. Rowe solely from profits because Mr. Rowe so testified. Clearly erroneous review requires substantial deference to this conclusion, but even applying such deference it is necessary to reject the factual conclusion: the undisputed facts show that it is not what happened. Indmar repaid advances on two occasions by tapping its line of credit (i.e., when there was not sufficient profits to cover the demand amount).

More importantly, however, the facts relevant to all the remaining factors are simply not in dispute. Even assuming that the payments were intended to be paid solely from profits, these other factors as a matter of law require the legal conclusion that the transactions represent debt rather than equity. There is no dispute as to the content of the transactions, form of the obligation, perfect repayment history, Indmar's solid creditworthiness, Indmar's equity-heavy capitalization, respective ownership interest of the parties, subordination of the notes, and applicable market interest rates. These undisputed facts make the tax court's legal conclusion that Indmar's obligation was equity erroneous. In other words, the extensive legal aspects of the question of whether these transactions amounted to debt are subject to our independent review, notwithstanding the applicability of a general "clearly erroneous" rubric to the overall question. Or stated differently, because the issue in dispute in this case is predominantly legal, cases requiring "clearly erroneous" review are pro tanto distinguishable. Either way, in a case like this one where a case that is largely factually indistinguishable could easily arise before a different lower court in the future, we must-to the extent that the facts are indeed objectively undisputed-rule in a way that insures consistent results. Applying "clearly erroneous" deference to lower court legal determinations, no matter how hidden or embedded such determinations are in overall determinations that are partly or even largely factual, is fundamentally at odds with the rule of law.

■ KAREN NELSON MOORE, CIRCUIT JUDGE, DISSENTING.

I respectfully dissent because I believe that the Tax Court's conclusion that the shareholder advances to taxpayer were equity contributions rather than genuine debt is not clearly erroneous. Far from being left "with the definite and firm conviction that a mistake has been committed," *Holmes v. Comm'r*, 184 F.3d 536, 543 (6th Cir. 1999) (internal quotation marks omitted), I believe that the record provides significant support for the Tax Court's conclusion, and I would affirm.

The majority is of course correct when it states that in reviewing Tax Court decisions, we review factual findings for clear error and conduct a more searching de novo inquiry into legal conclusions of the lower court.... Similarly, I share the concern expressed by Judge Rogers that we must take care to avoid being unduly deferential to trial court determinations of law, particularly when we are considering questions like this "where factual issues predominate, [and thus] the predominant scope of review is 'clearly erroneous.' " Concurrence at 14. However, we must not be so concerned about avoiding being overly deferential that we fail to afford due deference to a lower court's determinations when our standard of review so requires. While other courts have concluded that the ultimate issue of whether a shareholder advance constitutes equity or debt is a question of law or a mixed question of law and fact that is reviewed de novo, we have repeatedly held that this specific question is a question of fact reviewed for clear error, and we remain bound by this precedent.... I am therefore troubled by the robustness of the majority opinion's clear error review of several of the factual aspects of this case as well as the ultimate question of whether the payments were debt or equity, and I believe that the majority has "misapprehended and misapplied the clearly-erroneous standard." ...

* * *

Here the shareholder advances to Indmar are subject to "particular scrutiny" because, like advances between a controlling corporation and its subsidiary, "the control element suggests the opportunity to contrive a fictional debt." *Roth Steel*, 800 F.2d at 630 (internal quotation marks omitted). The taxpayer bears "the burden of establishing that the advances were loans rather than capital contributions." *Id.* (citing *Smith*, 370 F.2d at 180). The Tax Court's conclusion that Indmar failed to meet this burden was not clearly erroneous. While several of the *Roth Steel* factors support Indmar's claim that the shareholder advances were bona fide debt, several others instead favor equity. The unsecured nature of the shareholder advances "is a strong indication that the advances were capital contributions rather than loans." *Id.* at 631. Indmar's failure to establish a sinking fund is further "evidence that the advances were capital contributions rather than loans." *Id.* at 632. While the majority appears to view the absence of a sinking fund as redundant with the consideration that the transfers were unsecured, *Roth Steel* considers both as factors, and here both factors indicate equity. In addition, Indmar did not have any fixed maturity date or fixed obligation to repay the Rowes. This "indicates that the advances were capital contributions and not loans." *Id.* at 631. Nor did the Tax Court err in viewing Mr. Rowe's statement that repayment would have to come from corporate profits as a strong indicator of equity, because "an expectation of repayment solely from corporate earnings is not indicative of bona fide debt regardless of its reasonableness." *Id.*

* * *

In the particular circumstances of this case, which include the "contradictory, inconsistent, and unconvincing" testimony of the majority shareholder, I cannot conclude that it was clearly erroneous for the Tax Court to decide that the factors that favored equity were deserving of more weight than those that favored debt. Because I believe the record supports two permissible views of the evidence, I cannot join the majority's conclusion that the Tax Court's determination was clearly erroneous. *Anderson*, 470 U.S. at 574. I would affirm the decision of the Tax Court.

DETAILED ANALYSIS

1.   THE NATURE OF THE INQUIRY

1.1. *Generally*

Indmar Products is illustrative of a multitude of opinions involving classification of obligations issued by closely held corporations as debt or equity based on a list of factors developed by the courts to make the distinction. In Gilbert v. Commissioner, 248 F.2d 399 (2d Cir.1957), the court identified debt as an "unqualified obligation to pay a sum certain at a reasonably close fixed maturity date along with a fixed percentage in interest payable regardless of the debtor's income or lack thereof." *Gilbert* was one of the first cases to apply a multi-factor approach to separate a fixed obligation to pay from a payment that was dependent upon the fortunes of a corporate business. The courts, following the *Gilbert* analysis, began to search for factors that would help to distinguish the unqualified obligation to repay from an equity investment. As a result the courts began to develop formidable lists of factors, such as the *Roth* factors described in *Indmar Products,* against which obligations could be measured to determine if they more resembled debt or equity.

In Estate of Mixon v. United States, 464 F.2d 394, 402 (5th Cir.1972), the court enumerated a list of thirteen factors as follows:

(1)   the names given to the certificates evidencing the indebtedness;

(2)   the presence or absence of a fixed maturity date;

(3)   the source of payments;

(4)   the right to enforce payment of principal and interest;

(5)   participation in management flowing as a result;

(6)   the status of the contribution in relation to regular corporate creditors;

(7)   the intent of the parties;

(8)   "thin" or adequate capitalization;

(9)   identity of interest between creditor and stockholder;

(10) source of interest payments;

(11) the ability of the corporation to obtain loans from outside lending institutions;

(12) the extent to which the advance was used to acquire capital assets; and

(13) the failure of the debtor to repay on the due date or to seek a postponement.

At one point, the "factor check-off list" approach threatened to become as mechanical as the earlier obsession with debt-equity ratios.

Congress joined in the list making process with the Tax Reform Act of 1969. Section 385(a) directs the Secretary of the Treasury to promulgate regulatory guidelines to distinguish debt from equity. The legislative history contains the following non-exclusive list of factors to be included in the guidelines:

(1)   Whether there is a written unconditional promise to pay on demand or on a specified date a sum certain in money in return for an adequate consideration in money or money's worth, and to pay a fixed rate of interest;

(2)   Whether there is subordination to, or preference over, any indebtedness of the corporation;

(3)   The ratio of debt to equity of the corporation;

(4)   Whether there is convertibility into the stock of the corporation; and

(5)   The relationship between holdings of stock in the corporation and holdings of the interest in question.

GENERAL EXPLANATION OF THE TAX REFORM ACT OF 1969, Staff of the Joint Committee on Internal Revenue Taxation, 123–24 (1970). Final § 385 regulations were issued in December 1980, applicable to instruments issued after April 30, 1981. T.D. 7747, 1981–1 C.B. 141. The effective date was extended several times and the regulations were withdrawn on August 5, 1983. T.D. 7920, 1983–2 C.B. 69. The regulations focused primarily on proportionality and valuation as the keys to debt/equity distinctions. An instrument in the form of debt that was not held in proportion to stock was generally treated as debt. Proportionately held obligations were treated as debt if the debt was not excessive (thin capitalization), the interest rate was commercially reasonable, or if interest was not reasonable, the obligation was issued for money repayable at a fixed time. Although elegant in structure and theoretical underpinning, the regulations were difficult to apply in the myriad of situations that they were required to cover. The § 385 regulations expired under the weight of their complexity, particularly in the small business context, and because enterprising taxpayers developed financial instruments that would have successfully taken advantage of the regulations' bright line classification of hybrid instruments. See Rev.Rul. 83–98, 1983–2 C.B. 40 discussed at page 149, which was issued shortly before the proposed regulations were withdrawn. No new regulations have been issued under § 385, and the debt versus equity classification issue thus continues to turn on judicial authority.

The court's now generally avoid the "factor check-off list" approach, as a mechanical solution to the debt/equity conundrum. As the court noted in Slappey Drive Industrial Park v. United States, 561 F.2d 572 (5th Cir. 1977), "We have always recognized . . . that the various factors are not equally significant. 'The object of the inquiry is not to count factors, but to evaluate them.' Tyler v. Tomlinson, 414 F.2d 844, 848 (5th Cir.1969). Each case turns on its own facts; differing circumstances may bring different factors to the fore." Under this view, the trier of fact must weigh the various factors in the light of the entire evidence presented and not give undue weight to any one factor. Nonetheless, the courts' refusal to sanction a relatively mechanical test such as the debt-equity ratio, has resulted in a great deal of uncertainty for tax advisors and the government, with the inevitable consequence that a substantial amount of litigation has been generated in the debt-equity area.

Consistent with the view that the inquiry is inherently factual, the IRS will not "ordinarily" rule on whether advances to a corporation constitute debt or equity. See, e.g., Rev.Proc. 2014–3, § 4.02(1), 2014–1 I.R.B. 111.

1.2. *The Relevance of Evidentiary "Factors"*

The temptation to create legal shopping lists of factors should be resisted. It is the factors *in relationship* that appear to determine the results in debt-equity cases, even in those cases in which the court may emphasize particular factors. For instance, if a court considers subordination significant, it is generally subordination in relation to the absence of other factors that would demonstrate debt which is determinative, not subordination as such. Each of the factors considered by the courts contributes in varying degree to the resolution of the classification issue. For example, in Fin Hay Realty Co. v. United States, 398 F.2d 694 (3d Cir.1968), the court listed sixteen factors to be considered in distinguishing debt from equity, but described the factors as "only aids in answering the ultimate question whether the investment, analyzed in terms of its economic reality, constitutes risk capital entirely subject to the fortunes of the corporate venture or represents a strict debtor-creditor relationship. Since there is often an element of risk in a loan, just as there is an element of risk in an equity investment, the conflicting elements do not end at a clear line in all cases * * *."

The factors listed in the cases can best be understood in the context of the *Gilbert* language describing debt as an obligation to pay a fixed sum at a reasonably certain maturity date with fixed interest payments. Contrast a fixed obligation to repay debt with a discretionary corporate distribution of dividends at the behest of corporate management when the entity has sufficient earnings to permit a distribution to shareholders that is, therefore, dependent upon the success of the corporate enterprise. Thus, in Lane v. United States, 742 F.2d 1311 (11th Cir.1984), the court stated: "In order for an advance of funds to be considered a debt rather than equity, the courts have stressed that a reasonable expectation of repayment must exist which does not depend solely on the success of the borrower's business." The taxpayer who advanced funds to three failing corporations for demand notes testified in the trial court that he expected repayment when the corporations were in a position to retransfer the funds without damage to their ongoing businesses. The court concluded from the taxpayer's testimony that repayment was dependent upon the success of

the debt-equity ratio was only 14.6:1. The court declined to speculate on the business reasons for the nonpayment of interest.

2.2. *Thin Capitalization*

A high proportion of debt relative to shareholder equity is an indication that the corporation lacks reserves to pay interest and principal on debt when corporate income is insufficient to meet current payments. In such a case, the debt holders' potential recovery is subject to entrepreneurial risk as repayment is dependent on the success of the venture. Thus a high ratio of debt to equity is a factor favoring equity classification. See John Kelley Co. v. Commissioner, 326 U.S. 521 (1946) (subordinated convertible debentures were true debt because the corporation was not "thinly capitalized").

While generally the decisions mention the debt-equity ratio, they offer little discussion of the rules governing its determination. In Slappey Drive Industrial Park v. United States, supra page 139, the court looked at the relation of the debt both to the book value of the corporation's assets and to their actual fair market value. In Bauer v. Commissioner, 748 F.2d 1365 (9th Cir.1984), the court held that the debt to equity ratio compares total liabilities to the stockholders' equity that includes initial paid-in capital plus accumulated earnings. The court reversed the Tax Court's holding that shareholder loans were contributions to capital. The Tax Court had based its holding, in part, on a stipulation by the parties that the corporate debt/equity ratio was 92 to 1, the ratio of liabilities to the shareholders' initial capital contributions. Comparing liabilities with total shareholder equity, determined by including both paid in capital and accumulated earnings, produced debt to equity ratios ranging from 2 to 1 to 8 to 1.

In determining the ratio of debt to equity, courts may consider all of the outstanding indebtedness of the corporation even though it is typically shareholder debt that is being tested for equity equivalence. Thus an outstanding bank loan can have an influence on the "thinness" of the corporation's capital structure. See, e.g., Berkowitz v. United States, 411 F.2d 818 (5th Cir.1969).

A high ratio of debt to equity is not automatically fatal to debt status. In Bradshaw v. United States, 683 F.2d 365 (Ct.Cl.1982), notwithstanding a very high ratio of debt to equity (the corporation's capital consisted of an automobile valued at $4,500), the court classified as debt five notes, each in the face amount of $50,000, given to a sole shareholder of the debtor corporation in exchange for real property transferred to the corporation by the shareholder. The court emphasized the fact that the corporation's cash flow was sufficient to meet its obligations under the notes to pay interest and principal on fixed dates and that the corporation paid principal and interest on the notes when due. See also Delta Plastics, Inc. v. Commissioner, T.C. Memo. 2003–54 (pro-rata shareholder loans to a start-up corporation were respected as such, and an interest deduction allowed, even though the corporation's debt-equity ratio was 26:1, where the corporation made all scheduled payments when due).

2.3. *Subordination to Other Creditors*

In P.M. Finance Corp. v. Commissioner, 302 F.2d 786 (3d Cir.1962), the court held that shareholder "loans" were equity by placing heavy reliance on the fact that the loans were subordinated to all "present and future bank loans." Complete subordination, the court noted, "tends to wipe out a most significant characteristic of the creditor-debtor relationship, the right to share with general creditors in the assets in the event of dissolution or liquidation, * * * but it also destroys another basic attribute of creditor status: i.e., the power to demand payment at a fixed maturity date." (790) Subordination, however, is not invariably fatal to debt classification. See Jones v. United States, 659 F.2d 618 (5th Cir.1981) (debt status upheld despite state regulations requiring subordination to insurance corporation's policy holders); Federal Express Corp. v. United States, 645 F.Supp. 1281 (W.D.Tenn.1986) (debt status sustained for obligations subordinate only to senior debt; the challenged obligations were negotiated at arm's length by sophisticated institutional investors and were on a parity with trade debt).

2.4. *Intent, Business Purpose, and Tax Avoidance*

Although courts frequently list the taxpayer's "intent" as a factor in determining whether an obligation constitutes debt or equity, most cases recognize that "intent" is simply a way of stating the conclusion, and examine more objective factors to determine the debt-equity status of the particular obligation. In general, earlier cases in which taxpayer "intent" or "business purpose" appeared to take on an independent status have not been followed. See, e.g., Gooding Amusement Co. v. Commissioner, 236 F.2d 159 (6th Cir.1956); Tomlinson v. 1661 Corp., 377 F.2d 291 (5th Cir.1967). In Estate of Mixon v. United States, 464 F.2d 394 (5th Cir.1972), however, the court sustained the taxpayer's treatment of an interest-free shareholder advance to a bank, as required by bank examiners, as debt under its 13–factor analysis; the court indicated that where the objective signs point in all directions, the trial court was correct in looking to the subjective intent of the parties to decide which direction to follow.

2.5. *Absence of New Investment*

If a corporation has been in existence for some time, and then issues a dividend in the form of a debt obligation, or, by recapitalization, issues a debt obligation in exchange for previously outstanding stock, the IRS has attempted to treat the new obligation as stock on the ground that there is no new investment to permit the obligation to be considered as debt. Compare Sayles Finishing Plants, Inc. v. United States, 399 F.2d 214 (Ct.Cl.1968) (notes issued for stock in a reorganization constituted equity because no new funds were added to the corporation by issuing the debt and the only benefit to the business was the obtaining of the interest deduction) with Monon Railroad v. Commissioner, 55 T.C. 345 (1970) (Acq.) (debentures issued to acquire outstanding shares of stock were valid debt; it was not necessary that new funds be received by the corporation in exchange for the debt where other factors pointed to debt classification).

2.6. *Fixed Payments*

The court in Indmar Products Co., Inc. v. Commissioner, supra page 124, stated that, "The first factor to which we look is whether or not a fixed rate of interest and fixed interest payments accompanied the advances. . . . The absence of a fixed interest rate and regular payments indicates equity; conversely, the presence of both evidences debt." The court thus held that demand notes to corporate shareholders with a fixed rate of interest and regular payments were debt.

Payment of interest was of paramount significance to the District of Columbia Circuit in Cerand & Co. v. Commissioner, 254 F.3d 258 (D.C. Cir. 2001). The corporate taxpayer transferred funds to its three sister corporations through an "open accounts receivable" for each borrower without any formal documents describing the nature of the transfers. The taxpayer claimed bad debt deductions for the advances when the three "borrower" corporations went out of business. The Tax Court, T.C. Memo. 1998–423, originally held that the advances were contributions to capital, not loans, citing the absence of an agreement to memorialize the debt, the absence of a fixed maturity date or repayment schedule, the absence of a stated interest rate, and the Tax Court's ultimate conclusion that the repayment was inconsistent and appeared dependent on financial success. The Tax Court's conclusion also was based on the sister corporations' thin capitalization and lack of historical success, further indicating that the likelihood of repayment was low. In remanding the case back to the Tax Court, the D.C. Circuit held that the Tax Court "abused its discretion in assessing the evidence. The critical flaw in the tax court's analysis is its failure, despite the taxpayer having pressed the point, to consider Cerand's contemporaneous treatment of sums received from its sister corporations as in part the payment of 'interest,' taxable as income to Cerand." The Court of Appeals did not address the other factors considered by the Tax Court. On remand the Tax Court again denied the bad debt deduction, affirming its original holding that the advances were not debt. T.C. Memo. 2001–271. As a factual matter the Tax Court found that the purported interest payments were sporadic and varied as a percentage of the amount advanced. The Tax Court reiterated its reasoning that classification as debt or equity depends on an analysis of multiple factors and repeated its holding that, "In the overall setting of this case, however, the repayments and interest accruals are insufficient to overcome the weight of the evidence reflecting that, in form and substance, neither petitioner nor its sister corporations intended the advances to be loans, nor did they treat them as loans."

3.   SHAREHOLDER-GUARANTEED LOANS

Some arrangements have been structured to escape the debt-equity imbroglio by, instead of borrowing from a shareholder, the corporation borrows from a commercial lending institution, which agrees to make the loan only upon the condition that the shareholder personally guarantees the corporate obligation. In Plantation Patterns, Inc. v. Commissioner, 462 F.2d 712 (5th Cir.1972), Mrs. Jemison owned all the shares of stock of the taxpayer corporation, which had been capitalized at $5,000. Exercise of the elements of ownership of the shares, however, was dominated by Mr. Jemison, her husband. The taxpayer corporation acquired the business of another corporation and issued notes to the shareholders of the acquired corporation in a transaction that called for a purchase price of almost $650,000 in excess of the book net worth of the acquired corporation. All but $100,000 of the notes were subordinated to the corporate debt of the taxpayer, but the notes were personally guaranteed by Mr. Jemison. The debt-equity ratio of the taxpayer corporation was 100.5:1. The court held that the notes were in fact those of the guarantor, Mr. Jemison, which he contributed as capital to the corporation; therefore, the interest deduction was disallowed to the taxpayer corporation. Mrs. Jemison, the shareholder, correspondingly, received dividends on the note payments. The court based its decision on the facts that the notes were used to purchase capital assets of the taxpayer corporation; the guarantee by Mr. Jemison was essential to the transaction; subordination was present; the complete identity of interest between the shareholder and the guarantor, Mr. Jemison being regarded as the "constructive owner" of his wife's shares; and no value was given to the intangible financial skills of Mr. Jemison in determining the debt-equity ratio. On the last point the court stated: "[W]e conclude that intangible assets such as those claimed for Mr. Jemison have no place in assessing debt-equity ratio unless it can be shown by convincing evidence that the intangible asset has a direct and primary relationship to the well-being of the corporation. Additionally, it is clear to us that the assets sought to be valued must be something more than management skills and normal business contacts. These are expected of management in the direction of any corporation."

A contrary result was reached in Murphy Logging Co. v. United States, 378 F.2d 222 (9th Cir.1967), two partners formed a corporation that purchased logging equipment from the partnership. The corporation borrowed money from a bank to make the acquisition and the shareholders guaranteed the bank note. The IRS treated the transaction as if the bank loan had gone directly from the bank to the shareholders, who had then made a contribution to the capital of the corporation in a § 351 transaction. Payments by the corporation on the bank loan then were treated as constructive dividends to the shareholders (who presumably would also be treated as having made the bank payments, with possible corresponding interest deductions to the shareholders individually). The District Court upheld the IRS's treatment of the transaction, 239 F.Supp. 794 (D.Or.1965). The Court of Appeals, however, reversed and held that the debt ran from the bank to the corporation and allowed the corporate interest deduction. Although the shareholders had placed only $1,500 in the corporation and had sold the equipment to the corporation for $238,150, the court included the integrity and reputation of the shareholders as intangible assets to be considered in valuing the equity capital of the corporation. With this factor added, the court concluded that there was no thin capitalization. In addition, the transaction by which the corporation acquired the logging equipment was treated as a sale rather than a § 351 transaction, which permitted the corporation to use a cost basis for the equipment. See also Smyers v. Commissioner, 57 T.C. 189 (1971) (in the absence of thin capitalization, the shareholder guarantee did not convert a loan to equity even though it was "reasonable to assume that these unsecured loans would not have been made without petitioners' guarantee").

Comparison of the results in various cases reveals that the existence of a shareholder guarantee generally does not result in treating a bank loan to a corporation as a disguised equity contribution by the shareholder-guarantor whenever it can be established that the bank was looking primarily to the corporation for repayment, and the guarantee was only additional security for the bank or part of the bank's general policy of requiring shareholder guarantees on loans to closely held corporations.

4. LOANS BETWEEN RELATED CORPORATIONS

Transactions between parent and subsidiary corporations also give rise to debt-equity problems. In Jack Daniel Distillery v. United States, 379 F.2d 569 (Ct.Cl.1967), the taxpayer, a subsidiary, issued its $3.5 million note to its parent corporation to reflect an advance of that amount by the parent corporation. The parent corporation also contributed another $2 million in cash to the capital of the subsidiary. The court held that the subsidiary's note was a valid debt obligation because it was an unconditional obligation to pay regardless of earnings; interest was accrued for both book and tax purposes; the note was subordinated only to specific debts and not to creditors generally; the subsidiary had the ability to, and did in fact, borrow from unrelated banks (the parent having borrowed the $3.5 million contributed to the subsidiary with knowledge on the part of the lenders that the funds were going to be utilized by the subsidiary); further advances to the subsidiary were not necessary and the loan was repaid in full; despite the fact that the note was unsecured, there was a reasonable expectation that the amounts would be repaid; and substantial equity contributions had been made by the parent.

But in National Farmers Union Service Corp. v. United States, 400 F.2d 483 (10th Cir.1968), a parent's advance to a subsidiary was treated as an equity contribution where there was no acceleration clause, the note was unsecured, the funds were used to supply capital, some notes were canceled prior to maturity, the likelihood of repayment was remote, no sinking fund had been established, and a third party would not have made the loan. Although the parent had borrowed the money which was transferred to the subsidiary, the lenders did not know that the funds were going to be placed in the subsidiary, thus distinguishing the case from *Jack Daniel Distillery*, supra. On similar grounds, the court in Roth Steel Tube Co. v. Commissioner, 800 F.2d 625 (6th Cir.1986), upheld the Tax Court's ruling that advances to a 62 percent subsidiary, acquired by the taxpayer following a bankruptcy reorganization, were contributions to capital. The appellate court stated that neither the fact that 38 percent of the subsidiary's stock was owned by shareholders who did not make proportionate advances, nor the fact that the advances were used for operating funds, was sufficient justification for rejecting the Tax Court's determination that the advances were equity.

Related problems arise with respect to advances between brother-sister corporations. In Stinnett's Pontiac Service, Inc. v. Commissioner, 730 F.2d 634 (11th Cir.1984), the court denied the taxpayer corporation's bad debt deduction for advances to another corporation owned in part by the taxpayer's 74 percent shareholder. The purported loans lacked a fixed maturity date, no interest payments were made, there was no written evidence of indebtedness for a majority of the loans, repayment was subordinate to other creditors, and the borrower was thinly capitalized. The court held that the advances represented a contribution to capital. The court also held that the advances were taxable dividends to the taxpayer's major shareholder because the shareholder benefited from the advances in the form of an economic improvement in the shareholder's equity interest in the borrower. The court reached the opposite conclusion on similar facts in Mills v. Internal Revenue Service, 840 F.2d 229 (4th Cir.1988). The court was impressed with the group's regular history of repaying intercorporate advances and the testimony of the controlling shareholders that the advances were intended as loans.

Hubert Enterprises, Inc. v. Commissioner, 230 Fed. Appx. 526 (6th Cir. 2007), involved a similar but slightly different transaction. The taxpayer, a closely held family corporation, advanced $2.4 million to a limited liability company (a tax partnership) owned by family members.

The loan was represented by a demand note with no fixed maturity date, was not secured, and called for interest payable at the applicable federal rate. The borrower made only one payment of interest on the note. The court denied the taxpayer's claimed bad debt deduction under § 166 for the worthless note, finding that the note was equity under the factors specified in the Sixth Circuit's opinion in Roth Steel Tube Co. v. Commissioner, which are described in *Indmar Products* at page 124. Further, the Sixth Circuit also affirmed the Tax Court holding that the corporation was not entitled to deduct the amount advanced to the LLC as a loss of capital because the corporation had no ownership interest in the LLC. The advance represented a constructive dividend conferring an economic benefit on its shareholders (the owners of the LLC).

5. TRANSMUTATION OF DEBT TO EQUITY

Even if an obligation represents a valid debt obligation at the time of its issue, its character can change to equity as the result of the passage of time or a change in circumstances. For example, in Cuyuna Realty Co. v. United States, 382 F.2d 298 (Ct.Cl.1967), the taxpayer corporation between 1912 and 1914 incurred debt to its parent corporation of over $1.4 million. Interest was accrued but never paid. In 1956 the parent forgave the unpaid accrued interest and principal because the taxpayer had been insolvent since its organization and future repayment was impossible. The IRS disallowed the interest deduction to the taxpayer for the years beginning in 1952. The court upheld the IRS, concluding that, while the notes were intended to create a valid debt in the 1912–1914 period, they had changed their character to equity. No debtor-creditor relation existed long before 1956 since there was no maturity date, there was thin capitalization, no attempts were made to enforce the creditor's rights, and no outside lender would have made the loans: "A rule that the original intention of the parties should control the character of an instrument for all time would be completely inconsistent with the purpose of the statute. Interest, like an ordinary business expense, is allowed as a deduction from income because it is a cost of producing income. It ceases to be a real cost, if with the passage of time it becomes apparent that the parties had no intention of continuing the debtor-creditor relationship."

In Edwards v. Commissioner, 415 F.2d 578 (10th Cir.1969), the taxpayer acquired a corporation for $75,000, with $5,000 of the purchase price being allocated to acquisition of the stock of the acquired corporation and $70,000 to the acquisition of the corporation's notes in the face amount of $241,904 that had been issued by the acquired corporation to its previous sole shareholder. The acquired corporation proved successful and the notes were repaid out of earnings. The taxpayer treated the amounts received as long-term capital gains under the predecessor to § 1271(a). The IRS asserted that the payments constituted dividends. The IRS did not contest that the notes were originally valid corporate debt, but argued that they changed to equity in the hands of the taxpayer. The court held that the notes represented debt in the hands of the taxpayer and that the predecessor to § 1271(a) applied. The court found that there was no sham, no thin capitalization, and the purchase by the taxpayer did not convert the notes to equity. Under current law, the notes would have been market discount obligations, and the gain recognized upon retirement would have been taxed as ordinary income under § 1276, discussed at page 173. Thus, the incentive of the IRS to challenge the transactions on debt versus equity grounds would be lessened, but not completely eliminated.

Similarly, in Imperial Car Distributors, Inc. v. Commissioner, 427 F.2d 1334 (3d Cir.1970), four investors acquired the stock of the taxpayer corporation from the former owner for $2,000. For an additional $2,000 the investors also acquired notes of the corporation with a face value of $120,000 previously issued to the former owner. The corporation then issued new notes pro rata to the investors to replace the former notes. Payments to retire the notes were treated as capital gains by the investors under the predecessor to § 1271(a) and the taxpayer corporation deducted the interest on the notes. The IRS conceded that the original notes were valid debt, but urged that the notes became part of the capital of the taxpayer upon their transfer to the investors. The court held that the notes constituted valid debt obligations, reversing a Tax Court determination to the contrary, concluding that where a debt was valid when originally issued, the later transfer did not change its character to equity. Under current law, the new notes would have been original discount obligations, requiring current accrual of interest income by the holders over the term of the notes. See page 161.

6.   TAXPAYER EFFORTS TO RECLASSIFY OBLIGATIONS

The classification problem can be presented in reverse, with the taxpayer claiming that an instrument issued as stock is really debt or that an instrument that on its face is a debt instrument really is stock. Section 385(c)(1) provides that the characterization by the issuer of an instrument as stock or debt is binding on both the issuer and all of the holders of the instrument (but not on the IRS). However, § 385(c)(2) permits a holder of an instrument—but not the issuing corporation—to adopt an inconsistent treatment if the holder discloses the inconsistent treatment on the holder's tax return.

6.1. *Reclassification of Stock as Debt*

In Lee Telephone Co. v. Commissioner, 260 F.2d 114 (4th Cir.1958), which was decided before the enactment of § 385(c)(1), the court rejected the taxpayer's attempt to classify as debt shares of preferred stock issued to finance an expanding telephone business after a public utility commission thought that the debt ratio had grown too large; the shares had a sinking fund but otherwise closely resembled stock. Similarly, in Miele v. Commissioner, 56 T.C. 556 (1971) (Acq.), aff'd by order, 474 F.2d 1338 (3d Cir.1973), a corporation decided to purchase a new barge but needed a guarantee from the United States Maritime Commission on a first mortgage loan in order to make the acquisition. The Maritime Commission required $150,000 of additional capital from private sources before it would guarantee the loan and the corporation issued preferred stock to shareholders in proportion to their common stock holdings to secure the needed funds. Subsequently, the preferred stock was redeemed pro rata, and the taxpayer shareholder treated the preferred stock as debt in order to avoid dividend treatment under § 301. The court held the taxpayers to their classification.

6.2. *Reclassification of Debt as Equity*

Taxpayers sometimes have obtained a classification of debt instruments different from the formal characterization the parties themselves initially gave to the instruments. See, e.g., J.A. Maurer, Inc. v. Commissioner, 30 T.C. 1273 (1958) (Acq.) (corporation successfully asserted that advances by a shareholder in the form of debt constituted equity capital, so that no cancellation of indebtedness income resulted on the settlement of the advances for less than their face amount); Joseph Lupowitz Sons, Inc. v. Commissioner, 497 F.2d 862 (3d Cir.1974) (taxpayer successfully argued that open account advances were contributions to capital and not loans thus avoiding imputation of interest income).

7. CONVERTIBLE OBLIGATIONS, HYBRID SECURITIES, AND OTHER FINANCIAL INSTRUMENTS

7.1. *Convertible Obligations*

With debt instruments that are convertible into corporate stock, an investor may achieve both the certainty of a fixed payment of principal and interest, and the potential to share in economic growth if the corporation is successful. From the point of view of the corporation, hybrid securities are a way to attract investors interested in long term appreciation while providing deductible interest payments to the issuer. Convertibility is listed in § 385 as one of the facts and circumstances to be considered in determining whether a financial instrument is debt or equity.

Rev.Rul. 83–98, 1983–2 C.B. 40, considered a hybrid instrument referred to as an "adjustable rate convertible note" (ARCN). Under the facts of the ruling, X Corporation, with a single class of common stock outstanding, issued $10 million of ARCNs. An ARCN could be purchased for $1,000 of cash or 50 shares of X stock, which at the time of the offering was worth $1,000. At the option of the holder, each ARCN was convertible into 50 shares of stock. Otherwise, the ARCN would pay $600 at the end of the 20 year term of the note. The ARCN was callable for $600 by X at any time after the first two years. X was required to pay annual interest on each ARCN equal to the dividends paid on 50 shares of X stock, plus 2 percent of the issue price ($20). The interest was not to be less than $60 nor more than $175 in any year. In order to qualify the instrument as debt under the then § 385 regulations, the ARCN was designed so that the present value of its debt features was worth more than one-half of its $1,000 issue price. The IRS held that the ARCNs were equity. The IRS found that the ARCNs were structured so that under most likely eventualities they would be converted into common stock and therefore did not represent a promise to pay a sum certain. The IRS also noted that the guaranteed annual interest of $60 per $1,000 of capital was unreasonably low in comparison to the return available on nonconvertible, noncontingent instruments; based on the level of dividends on X common stock, more than 65 percent of the potential annual yield on the instruments was discretionary; and the instruments were subordinate to the claims of general creditors.

In Rev.Rul. 85–119, 1985–2 C.B. 60, the IRS allowed interest deductions for payments with respect to publicly traded subordinated notes with a mandatory conversion feature adopted to comply with banking regulations. At maturity the notes were convertible into stock of the issuing corporation with a value at the time of conversion equal to the principal of the notes. However, if a note holder elected not to accept stock, the issuer was required to undertake a secondary stock offering on the open market and deliver cash to the note holder in an amount equal to the note principal. The notes required quarterly interest payments in an amount that varied with the market rate payable on comparable subordinated instruments. Debt treatment was supported by the facts that the notes were publicly held and not in proportion to equity ownership; interest was payable without regard to earnings; the notes had a fixed maturity at the end of a limited period of time; the issuer was not thinly capitalized; note holders had no vote or participation in management; and, as distinguished from Rev.Rul. 83–98 supra, the amount of stock to be issued in exchange for the notes at maturity was based on the face amount of the notes rather than the value of stock. These debt factors outweighed the fact that the notes were subordinated to other creditors, but not equity interests, and were in form payable only in the issuer's stock.

Totally apart from the traditional debt versus equity classification standards, pursuant to § 163(*l*), interest payments are not deductible if conversion into equity is required by the terms of the debt obligation, or if the issuer or a related person has the option to make payments of a substantial portion of interest or principal in the form of equity interests in the issuer or a related entity, or in equity held by the issuer (or any related party) in any other entity. Interest or principal payable, at the option of the holder, in equity interests in the issuing corporation or a related party will be subject to § 163(*l*) if there is a "substantial certainty" that the option will be exercised. The basis of any such equity is increased by the amount of any disallowed interest. Dealers in securities are in general exempt from the disallowance rule of § 163(*l*). Rev.Rul. 2003–97, 2003–2 C.B. 380, approved a device adopted to avoid the limitation of § 163(*l*). The IRS ruled that interest was deductible on a five-year corporate note issued as part of a package—dubbed by the investment banking community as "Feline Pride"—that included a forward contract obligating the note holder to acquire stock of the issuer on a settlement date that was three years from the date of issue. The amount of the holder's obligation to purchase stock was the same as the principal amount of the note. The holder's obligation to purchase the stock was secured by the note. The ruling was based on the IRS's finding that the note and the futures contract constituted separate properties.

7.2. *Bifurcation of Debt and Equity Features*

7.2.1. *Court Decisions*

In two cases, the courts bifurcated the debt and equity components of a single financial instrument. In Helvering v. Richmond, F. & P. R.R. Co., 90 F.2d 971 (4th Cir.1937), the corporation was allowed an interest deduction for guaranteed 7 percent dividends paid on preferred stock, but payments in excess of the guarantee were treated as dividends, a return on equity. The preferred stock provided for participation in corporate earnings above the 7 percent guaranteed dividends and possessed full voting rights. The guaranteed dividends were a first lien on corporate assets and took precedence over all creditors, including general creditors.

In Farley Realty Corp. v. Commissioner, 279 F.2d 701 (2d Cir.1960), the corporation borrowed money from a nonshareholder to acquire a building. The obligation required fixed payments of interest and had a fixed maturity date. In addition, the obligation holder was entitled to 50 percent of the appreciation on sale of the building, whether this event occurred before or after the maturity date. The IRS allowed the corporation to deduct fixed interest payments on the loan but disallowed any deduction for payment in settlement of the creditor's interest in appreciation.

In contrast, in Rev.Rul. 83–51, 1983–1 C.B. 48, the IRS held that contingent interest in the form of shared appreciation paid by the borrower to the mortgagee on a home residence loan was deductible interest. The loans provided for a fixed interest rate plus 40 percent of the appreciation on sale of the residence or at the end of the 10 year term of the loan. The Ruling described the interest as ascertainable because it was dependent on fixed events. The Ruling expressly provides that it is not applicable in a commercial context.

7.2.2.   *Bifurcation by Statute*

7.2.2.1.   *Section 385*

Section 385(a) authorizes regulations classifying obligations as debt in part and equity in part. The legislative history indicates that "such treatment may be appropriate in circumstances where a debt instrument provides for payments that are dependent to a significant extent (whether in whole or in part) on corporate performance, whether through equity kickers, contingent interest, significant deferral of payment, subordination, or an interest rate sufficiently high to suggest a significant risk of default." H.Rep. No. 101–247, 101st Cong., 1st Sess. 1235–1236 (1989). No regulations have been promulgated under this provision.

7.2.2.2.   *Excess Interest Paid To Related Tax Exempt Persons*

Another example of a sort of bifurcation related to thin capitalization concepts is found in § 163(j). Under that section, "excess" interest paid to related parties who are tax-exempt may not be deducted currently by the paying corporation if the corporation has a debt-equity ratio in excess of 1.5 to 1. The provision is applicable to interest paid to more than 50 percent shareholders who are domestic tax-exempt organizations or foreign persons who are not subject to U.S. tax on interest payments. "Excess" interest is defined as interest in excess of 50 percent of the corporation's adjusted taxable income. Excess interest can be carried forward indefinitely and deducted in subsequent years to the extent the 50 percentage threshold is not met in those years. In addition, the 50 percent limitation itself can be carried forward for three years.

The congressional concern here was that the corporation's earnings were being "stripped" out in the form of deductible interest payments but not being taxed in the hands of the tax exempt recipients. In effect, the portion of the interest which is disallowed is included in the corporate tax base in the same way as earnings used to pay dividends.

8.   PLANNING CONSIDERATIONS

In view of the number of factors considered by the courts in resolving debt-equity cases and the unpredictable weight given to any particular factor, the tax advisor faces a difficult problem in advising clients as to the proper mix of debt and equity in determining the capital structure of a corporation. In some cases, the client simply may wish to avoid any problem and take his entire investment in the corporation in the form of equity interests. Where other corporate planning considerations—or the more adventurous nature of the client—indicate the use of debt, the tax planning problems are more difficult.

Some of the various factors in the debt-equity equation are clearly within the control of the taxpayer. Thus, proper attention to the form of the debt obligation can help to avoid problems. But how, for example, can the tax advisor establish that outside lenders would have made a loan, a factor which many of the cases consider significant? Here it would be important at the outset to determine through an analysis of the corporation's projected cash flow and operating capital requirements that a bank would have considered a loan under these circumstances and perhaps some documentation from a bank that it would have made such a loan. Other factors may be more difficult to control. For example, where shareholder debt is to be combined with some outside financing, a bank may insist on subordination of the shareholder debt and this factor cannot be "planned around."

Once the formalities indicating a debtor-creditor relationship between the corporation and its shareholders are established, it is important that the formalities be followed. For example, interest and principal should in fact be paid according to the terms of the instrument. But here the planning considerations become more complicated. While payment of principal may be helpful in establishing the debt character of the obligation, it also exposes the shareholder to the risk of dividend taxation should the tax advisor have "guessed wrong" on the debt-equity question. Would it be better to provide in the original instrument that no principal payments will be made for a period of time, with larger payments to be made later in the term of the note? If such a course is taken, however, the taxpayer loses the argument that principal payments were in fact made, a factor sometimes stressed by the courts. On the other hand, even if principal payments are postponed, complete assurance is still not possible. Even though the corporation has been audited and the loans accepted as debt for purposes of the interest deduction, the IRS could still challenge the status of the obligation in subsequent years when principal payments are made. In the end, there is no sure escape from the difficult decisions which the current status of the tax law on debt and equity require.

B. DEDUCTIONS FOR LOSS OF INVESTMENT IN A CORPORATION

INTERNAL REVENUE CODE: Sections 165(g); 166(a); (b), (d), (e); 1244; 1271(a)(1).

REGULATIONS: Sections 1.166–5, –9; 1.1244–1(a), (c), (d),–2(a)–(b).

The capital versus ordinary distinction is important to both individual and corporate taxpayers who suffer losses as well as to individuals who realize gains. Deduction of corporate capital losses is limited to the corporation's capital gains. I.R.C. § 1211(a). Capital loss deductions of noncorporate taxpayers are limited to the taxpayer's capital gains plus $3,000 annually. I.R.C. § 1211(b).

Section 165(g) in general treats a loss on worthless *"securities"* as a capital loss. In contrast, § 166(a) allows ordinary loss treatment on debts not represented by securities. Section 166(d), however, requires short-term capital loss treatment for *nonbusiness bad debt* held by a noncorporate taxpayer. For purposes of § 165(g), "securities" is defined to include stock, rights to acquire stock, and any bond, debenture, note, or other evidence of indebtedness issued by a corporation (or a governmental entity) which is in registered form or has interest coupons attached. I.R.C. § 165(g)(2). An obligation is in registered form if the rights to principal and stated interest are transferable through a book entry system maintained by the issuer. See, e.g., Treas.Reg. § 5f.103–1(c). Section 163(f) disallows an interest deduction with respect to obligations issued by a person other than an individual which are offered to the public unless the obligation is in registered form.[2] If a "registration required obligation" is not issued in registered form, § 165(j) further disallows a deduction for any loss sustained by the holder.

Section 1244 allows an individual stockholder to treat a loss on certain small business stock, called § 1244 stock, as an ordinary loss rather than a capital loss, whether the loss is attributable to worthlessness or realized upon a sale of the stock. This ordinary loss treatment is limited to $50,000 per year, or $100,000 on a joint return. The ordinary loss treatment is available only to the individual (or individuals who are members of a partnership) to whom the stock was issued.

Under § 165(g)(3), the corporate holder of a worthless security of an "affiliated corporation" is entitled to ordinary loss treatment. Whether a corporation is an affiliated corporation for this purpose is determined under § 1504, which, generally speaking, requires that the parent corporation directly or indirectly own at least 80 percent of the aggregate voting power and 80 percent of the aggregate value of the subsidiary, excluding nonvoting stock that is limited and preferred as to dividends and liquidating distributions. In addition, the affiliated corporation must have derived 90 percent of its aggregate gross receipts for all taxable years from sources other than passive investments such as rents, royalties, dividends and interest. Treas.Reg. § 1.165–5(d)(2)(iii) provides that the term gross receipts includes all corporate receipts without reduction for the cost of goods sold, except that gross receipts from the sale or exchange of stock or securities are taken into account only to the extent of the gains from such sales.

Section 1271(a)(1) provides that amounts received on the retirement of any debt instrument issued by a corporation are considered to have been received in an exchange, thus providing the exchange element prerequisite for capital gain or loss treatment. The provision does not independently characterize gain or loss. Under § 1271(a), gain or loss on retirement of a debt instrument that is a capital asset in the hands of the debt-holder will be treated as gain or loss on the exchange of the capital asset resulting in capital gain or loss treatment; gain or loss on retirement of a debt obligation that is not a capital asset is ordinary. A debt is "retired" for this purpose even if the debt is settled for less than its full amount. McClain v. Commissioner, 311 U.S. 527 (1941). Section 1272, however, requires current inclusion as ordinary income of original discount attributable to the bond; and § 1276 requires ordinary income treatment of any market discount realized upon retirement of a corporate bond. See Section 2 of this chapter.

---

[2]   There is an exception for obligations which are not held by a United States person on which interest is payable only outside of the United States. I.R.C. § 163(f)(2)(B).

As a result of these provisions, the following is the general pattern of loss treatment for *individuals* on the worthlessness of their investments in corporations:

1. Stocks, bonds, and other securities generally result in capital losses, allowable in full but only against capital gains plus $3,000 of ordinary income, with an unlimited carryover of excess losses.

2. Nonbusiness bad debts not represented by "securities", i.e., advances and notes not qualifying under § 165(g)(2)(C), result in short-term capital losses, also allowable in full but only against capital gains (and offset first against short-term gains) and $3,000 of ordinary income with an unlimited carryover of excess losses.

3. Business bad debts not represented by "securities" (as defined in § 165(g)(2)(C)), i.e., advances related to a trade or business of the investor, result in ordinary losses under § 166(a), allowable in full against ordinary income or capital gain and are included in the net operating loss deduction.

4. Section 1244 small business stock losses and § 1242 small business investment company stock losses result in ordinary losses, allowable in full against ordinary income or capital gain and are included in the net operating loss deduction.

The following is the general pattern of loss treatment for *corporations* when their investments in other corporations become worthless:

1. Stocks, bonds, and other securities (except those in certain subsidiaries) result in long-term capital losses, allowable in full but only against capital gains with a three year carryback and a five year carryforward.

2. Bad debts not represented by "securities," i.e., advances and notes not described in § 165(g)(2)(C), result in ordinary losses, allowable in full against ordinary income or capital gain and includable in the net operating loss deduction.

3. Stocks or securities in affiliated (80 percent owned) operating subsidiaries result in ordinary losses (under § 165(g)(3)), allowable in full against ordinary income or capital gain and includable in the net operating loss deduction. (If the stock is not worthless, then on liquidation of the subsidiary no loss is allowed on the stock under § 332 but the subsidiary's asset bases and its net operating losses are carried over to the parent.)

4. Certain corporations, such as small business investment companies and banks, have special rules providing ordinary losses in some situations.

Thus, classification of a loss as a bad debt for a corporation, or a business bad debt for an individual, remains important to obtain ordinary loss treatment. Deduction of a capital loss on an equity investment or a loss on a nonbusiness bad debt is limited by § 1211.

DETAILED ANALYSIS

1.   DEBT-EQUITY ASPECTS

The initial question in considering the loss character of shareholder advances to a corporation not represented by a security is whether the corporate obligation involved is classified as debt or equity. The rules of § 166 are applicable only if a true debt is created. If the advances are found to constitute a contribution to capital, the capital loss limitations of § 165(g) are generally applicable and the issue of business versus nonbusiness bad debt is not reached. As was the case in Gilbert v. Commissioner, page 127, the characterization of an advance as debt or equity for purposes of § 166 requires the same analysis used to determine whether payments with respect to an obligation are dividends or deductible interest, discussed in Section 1.A of this chapter. Compare Thompson v. Commissioner, 73 T.C. 878 (1980) (advances from shareholders evidenced by written demand notes treated as contributions to capital; small amount of initial capital compared to amounts claimed as debt indicated that the corporation was undercapitalized; no evidence that the holders had ever demanded payment; advances were proportionate to stockholdings); Recklitis v. Commissioner, 91 T.C. 874 (1988) (cash advances to controlled corporation held to be contributions to capital; the advances were interest free, contained no specific repayment terms, and were not evidenced by a written agreement) with Adelson v. United States, 737 F.2d 1569 (Fed.Cir.1984) (advances to client companies in which taxpayer held only minor equity interests held to be debt).

2.   BUSINESS VERSUS NONBUSINESS BAD DEBT

Loss incurred by a noncorporate debtor-investor on an advance that qualifies as a debt, and hence is not a contribution to capital, that is not evidenced by a security, is deductible as an ordinary loss only if advance qualifies as a business bad debt. A bad debt is a business bad debt only if the investor is engaged in a trade or business and has established the necessary degree of connection between the debt and the business to qualify the debt as a business bad debt. If these two tests are met, the loss falls under § 166(a) and (b) as a business bad debt and avoids the limitation of § 166(d).

2.1. *Protection of Employment Versus Protection of Investment*

Most frequently, the question of whether a debt is a business bad debt or a nonbusiness bad debt arises when a shareholder-employee makes a loan to the corporation. Employment by the corporation clearly constitutes a trade or business, so the crucial inquiry is whether the loan was "proximate" to the taxpayer's activity as an employee or the taxpayer's activity as a shareholder. See Treas.Reg. § 1.166–5. The seminal case on this issue is United States v. Generes, 405 U.S. 93 (1972).

In *Generes*, the Supreme Court held that a debt qualifies as a business bad debt only if the taxpayer's "dominant" motivation was preservation of the taxpayer's business, i.e., employment, rather than preservation of the value of the taxpayer's equity investment in the corporation. A "significant" business motivation, if not dominant, is not sufficient. The taxpayer in *Generes* lent several hundred thousand dollars to a corporation in which he owned 44 percent of the stock and from which he earned an annual salary of approximately $12,000 as a part-time employee. (He was a full time employee of a bank at a salary of $19,000.) He had invested approximately $39,000 in stock of the corporation. The Supreme Court held that it was unreasonable to think that the taxpayer's dominant motive was preservation of his salary, rather than his investment.

As one factor in the determination, the *Generes* opinion stressed the relation between the taxpayer's after-tax salary—$7,000 in that case—and the amount of his investment. In Adelson v. United States, 737 F.2d 1569 (Fed.Cir.1984), the court concluded that the dominant motive test of *Generes* required the trial court to compare the potential risk and reward of the taxpayer's equity interest in client companies to which the taxpayer advanced funds with the taxpayer's interest in his salary as a financial consultant. On remand, the Claims Court found that the taxpayer's dominant motive was business, but the Court of Appeals again remanded the case to the Claims Court for specific findings comparing the potential profits that might have inured to the taxpayer's business interest with the potential profits from the taxpayer's equity interests. The court stressed, however, that determination of dominant motive does not necessarily depend upon a mathematical analysis of relative benefits. Adelson v. United States, 782 F.2d 1010 (Fed.Cir.1986). On remand, after reevaluating the record, the Claims Court determined that the taxpayer established that advances to three corporations were business debts, but did not prove that loans to three other corporations had a dominant business motive. Adelson v. United States, 12 Cl.Ct. 231 (1987). The Claims Court based its determinations on a specific comparison of the taxpayer's potential fee income with the potential return on the taxpayer's equity investment in each corporation.

Litigated cases generally turn on the court's view of the taxpayer's dominant motive. See e.g., Tennessee Securities, Inc. v. Commissioner, 674 F.2d 570 (6th Cir.1982) (payments by taxpayers' stock brokerage corporation on taxpayers' guarantees of loans of a third-party lender to an unrelated corporation to an unrelated corporation that the taxpayers hoped would undertake a public stock offering utilizing the taxpayer's brokerage corporation as the underwriter were treated as dividends to the taxpayers and the payments on the guarantees were treated as a nonbusiness bad debt deductible by the taxpayers); Bowers v. Commissioner, 716 F.2d 1047 (4th Cir.1983) (business bad debt deduction allowed for advances to a major client real estate brokerage firm to protect the income of taxpayer's controlled corporation and thereby the taxpayer's own enhanced employment income); Estate of Mann, 731 F.2d 267 (5th Cir.1984) (business bad debt deduction allowed for advances to the taxpayer's brother's corporation in which the taxpayer had only a negligible stock interest and from which the taxpayer had earned substantial commissions as a broker in several corporate acquisitions); Litwin v. United States, 983 F.2d 997 (10th Cir.1993) (allowed bad debt deductions for advances and payments on guarantees with respect to the taxpayer's closely held corporation on the court's conclusion that taxpayer principally formed the corporation to earn a salary, be employed, and remain useful to society even though salary payments to the taxpayer had been deferred for the full three year existence of the corporation).

2.2. *Is the Taxpayer Engaged in a "Trade or Business"—The Promoter Cases*

In Whipple v. Commissioner, 373 U.S. 193 (1963), the Supreme Court considered whether an investor was engaged in a trade or business. The court denied a business bad debt deduction for advances made by the taxpayer to a company which he had formed and to which he had leased property he owned:

> Devoting one's time and energies to the affairs of a corporation is not of itself, and without more, a trade or business of the person so engaged. Though such activities may produce income, profit or gain in the form of dividends or enhancement in the value of an investment, this return is distinctive to the process of investing and is generated by the successful operation of the corporation's business as distinguished from the trade or business of the taxpayer himself. When the only return is that of an investor, the taxpayer has not satisfied his burden of demonstrating that he is engaged in a trade or business since investing is not a trade or business and the return to the taxpayer, though substantially the product of his services, legally arises not from his own trade or business but from that of the corporation. Even if the taxpayer demonstrates an independent trade or business of his own, care must be taken to distinguish bad debt losses arising from his own business and those actually arising from activities peculiar to an investor concerned with, and participating in, the conduct of the corporate business.

> If full-time service to one corporation does not alone amount to a trade or business, which it does not, it is difficult to understand how the same service to many corporations would suffice. To be sure, the presence of more than one corporation might lend support to a finding that the taxpayer was engaged in a regular course of promoting corporations for a fee or commission * * * or for a profit on their sale * * *, but in such cases there is compensation other than the normal investor's return, income received directly for his own services rather than indirectly through the corporate enterprise * * *. On the other hand, since the Tax Court found, and the petitioner does not dispute, that there was no intention here of developing the corporations as going businesses for sale to customers in the ordinary course, the case before us inexorably rests upon the claim that one who actively engages in serving his own corporations for the purpose of creating future income though those enterprises is in a trade or business. That argument is untenable * * *.

In many cases taxpayers have seized upon the suggestion in *Whipple* that promotional services provided to a number of corporations might constitute a trade or business. Although, as was observed by the court in Bell v. Commissioner, 200 F.3d 545 (8th Cir. 2000), "[t]axpayers have been litigating this theory for decades," taxpayer victories in these contests are few and far between. In *Bell,* the taxpayer failed to establish that he was engaged in the trade or business of "buying, rehabilitating, and reselling corporations" because he did not provide any services to the distressed companies that might result in a return exceeding a typical investor's return and there was no pattern of sales indicating that profits on resale were attributable to taxpayer's work to rehabilitate corporations. There is something of a "Catch-22" in the taxpayer's situation in these cases, in that the courts are prone to state that to prove that he was in the trade or business of "buying, rehabilitating, and reselling corporations" the taxpayer must introduce evidence that the sales of the corporations occurred "in a manner that confirms that the taxpayer's profits were * * * 'received directly for his own service'" or of "'an early and profitable sale' of the corporation." *Id.* Of course, the fact that a loan to the corporation has turned into a bad debt generally is factually inconsistent with either of these possibilities, unless the loan has continued to be outstanding for long after the sale. See also Townshend v. United States, 384 F.2d 1008 (Ct.Cl.1967) (over a 20–year period the taxpayer had investigated a number of business opportunities and had organized five corporations; although he was considered a "promoter" for securities law purposes, the court refused to allow a business bad debt deduction for advances made by the taxpayer; there was no showing that fees or commissions from promotional activities were received and the taxpayer realized no profits from a quick turnover of the investments).

2.3. *Shareholder Guarantee of Corporate Debts*

In Putnam v. Commissioner, 352 U.S. 82 (1956), the Supreme Court held that payments by a guarantor because of the default of the primary obligor are subject to the limitations of § 166 and are thus deductible only as capital losses unless the obligation can qualify as a business bad debt: "The familiar rule is that, *instanter* upon the payment by the guarantor of the debt, the debtor's obligation to the creditor becomes an obligation to the guarantor, not a new debt, but by subrogation, the result of the shift of the original debt from the creditor to the guarantor who steps into the creditor's shoes. Thus, the loss sustained by the guarantor unable to recover from the debtor is by its very nature a loss from the worthlessness of a debt."

Legislative history clarifies that one of the purposes of an amendment to § 166 in 1976 is to apply § 166 whether or not the guarantor has a right of subrogation. Thus, Treas.Reg. § 1.166–9 draws no such distinction. The only effect of a right of subrogation is to affect the timing of the guarantor's deduction. See Staff of the Joint Committee on Taxation, General Explanation of the Tax Reform Act of 1976, pp. 156–157 (Comm. Print 1976). See also Black Gold Energy Corporation v. Commissioner, 99 T.C. 482 (1992), aff'd by order, 33 F.3d 62 (10th Cir. 1994), in which the Tax Court held that only an actual payment made pursuant to a guarantee can give rise to a deduction under § 166; the accrual method taxpayer was not allowed a bad debt deduction in the year all events fixed the amount of the liability, nor was the taxpayer allowed to claim a bad debt deduction for the amount of a note given to the creditor as a result of the guarantee.

Because the guarantor's deduction is a bad debt deduction, it may be claimed only upon the worthlessness of the guarantor's right of subrogation against the primary obligor. Thus, in Intergraph Corp. v. Commissioner, 106 T.C. 312 (1996), aff'd by order, 121 F.3d 723 (11th Cir.1997), the taxpayer's deduction for paying a guarantee of its Japanese subsidiary's debt was denied because the subrogation right was not worthless. Even though the corporate primary obligor was insolvent at the time the guarantee was satisfied, the subsidiary continued to conduct business as a going concern.

The *Putnam* decision does not itself insure that payments made by a stockholder in satisfaction of a guarantee of corporate debt will be deductible as a nonbusiness bad debt under § 166. If a stockholder's guarantee of a loan from an outside lender is found to be a substitute for the infusion of additional equity capital, the stockholder's payment under the guarantee will be treated as a capital contribution. Treas.Reg. § 1.166–9(c). See Lane v. United States, 742 F.2d 1311 (11th Cir.1984) (applying the 13–factor test of *Slappey Drive Industrial Park* to distinguish debt from equity, the court concluded that the stockholder's intent at the time the guarantees were extended was to use the guarantees as short-term substitutes for more capital stock; the stockholder's payment was treated as a contribution to capital); Casco Bank & Trust Co. v. United States, 544 F.2d 528 (1st Cir.1976) (stockholder advances to corporation in order to avoid default on bonds guaranteed by the stockholder were held to be equity contributions; the stockholder's deduction of a nonbusiness bad debt was not allowed because at the time of the stockholder advances, there was little reasonable expectation that the stockholder would be repaid). In such a case the shareholder is allowed a bad debt deduction only when the shareholder's stock becomes worthless, not at the time the loan guarantee is satisfied. The amount of the § 165 loss deduction for worthless stock is augmented by the amount of the payment, which is added to the basis of the stock at the time the guarantee is satisfied.

Treas.Reg. § 1.166–9(a) and (b) expressly provides that § 166 and not § 163 applies to all payments made with respect to guarantees, including interest.

3.   ORDINARY LOSS ON STOCK

3.1. *Section 1244 Stock*

Section 1244 allows a stockholder to treat a loss recognized from the sale or worthlessness of stock in certain small corporations, called § 1244 stock, as an ordinary loss rather than a capital loss. The loss is also available in computing the stockholder's net operating loss deduction. This ordinary loss treatment is limited to $50,000 per year, or $100,000 on a joint return. Ordinary loss treatment under § 1244 is available only to the individual (not including a trust) or partnership to whom the stock was issued, and in the case of a partnership the loss may be passed through to the individual partners with the dollar limitations applying at the partner level.

Section 1244 stock is defined essentially as stock of a "small business corporation." The stock must be issued for money or other property, other than stocks or securities and, under Treas.Reg. § 1.1244(c)–1(d), other than for services. It is important that stock actually be issued in exchange for each separate contribution to the corporation. See Pierce v. Commissioner, T.C. Memo. 1989–647 (§ 1244 does not apply to the portion of basis of § 1244 stock attributable to additional capital contributions to corporation made after issuance of stock, even though § 1244 would have applied if additional shares had been issued in exchange for the additional contributions). In Adams v. Commissioner, 74 T.C. 4 (1980), § 1244 stock issued to a third party was reacquired by the corporation and then reissued to the taxpayer. Ordinary loss treatment was not allowed to the taxpayer when the stock became worthless. The taxpayer failed to demonstrate that the stock purchase price paid by the taxpayer was anything more than a substitution for capital paid out by the corporation on reacquisition of stock from the first holder. There was no net flow of funds into the corporation.

A corporation is a "small business corporation" if, at the time of the issuance of the stock for which an ordinary loss is claimed, the aggregate amount of equity capital received by the corporation does not exceed $1 million. If a qualified corporation issues common stock in excess of $1 million, Treas.Reg. § 1.1244(c)–2(b)(2) provides for designation of shares which were issued before the limit was exceeded as "§ 1244 stock."

If a corporation is a small business corporation when the stock was issued, it may lose that status thereafter without disqualifying the stock previously issued. The number of shareholders or the existence of several classes of stock is not material. In addition to being a small business corporation, however, the corporation also must have derived more than 50 percent of its gross receipts from operating income for a period up to five years prior to the loss on the stock, unless its deductions exceed its gross income. I.R.C. § 1244(c)(1)(C) and (2)(C). Treas.Reg. § 1.1244(c)–1(e)(2) provides that, even if deductions exceed gross income, ordinary loss treatment will be denied if the corporation is not "largely an operating company." The validity of the regulations was upheld and ordinary loss treatment denied in Davenport v. Commissioner, 70 T.C. 922 (1978), in which the corporation derived more than 50 percent of its aggregate gross receipts from interest during the five years preceding the loss, but during those years its deductions exceeded gross income; seven dissenters would have held for the taxpayer on the basis that the corporation was a small loan company and hence was an "operating company" even though its income was interest income. Special provisions regarding § 1244 stock cover stock dividends, recapitalizations, and reorganizations and disallow any loss attributable to property with a basis in excess of the value of property contributed to the corporation in exchange for § 1244 stock.

Since the benefits of § 1244 do not extend to debt, the provision creates an advantage for equity capital, which must be weighed against the present tax advantages accorded to debt obligations.

Taxpayer attempts to avoid the limitations of § 166 by having their insolvent corporate debtors issue § 1244 stock on which an ordinary loss was then claimed have been unsuccessful. See, e.g., Hollenbeck v. Commissioner, 50 T.C. 740 (1968), aff'd, 422 F.2d 2 (9th Cir.1970) (stock received in exchange for release of purported debt obligation did not qualify because the "debt" was found to be equity). In addition, notes issued in exchange for § 1244 stock do not receive ordinary loss treatment. Benak v. Commissioner, 77 T.C. 1213 (1981) (worthless note issued on redemption of § 1244 stock resulted in non-business bad debt treatment).

3.2. *Small Business Investment Company Stock*

The Small Business Investment Act of 1958 authorized the formation of small business investment companies organized to provide equity capital to small businesses through the purchase of their convertible debentures. These small business investment companies are private corporations with a paid-in capital and surplus of at least $300,000. The Small Business Administration is authorized to lend such a company up to $150,000 through the purchase of the latter's subordinated debentures. Under

§ 1242, if a stockholder investing in the stock of a small business investment company suffers a loss on the stock, the loss is treated as an ordinary loss and may be utilized in a net operating loss deduction. Also, under § 1243, if the small business investment company itself suffers a loss on stock acquired by it pursuant to the conversion privilege on convertible debentures, the loss is treated as ordinary.

4. LOSS ON SURRENDER OF STOCK VERSUS CONTRIBUTION TO CAPITAL

In Commissioner v. Fink, 483 U.S. 89 (1987), the Supreme Court held that controlling stockholders cannot recognize a loss on the surrender of a portion of their stock to the corporation. The taxpayers, husband and wife, owned 72.5 percent of the common stock of the corporation. They surrendered some of their shares, reducing their ownership interest to 68.5 percent in order to make the corporation's capital structure more attractive to outside investors. The taxpayers claimed an ordinary loss under § 165 to the extent of the basis in their surrendered shares. The Sixth Circuit allowed the taxpayers' loss deduction by treating each share of stock as a separate investment, adopting a "fragmented" view of stock ownership under which gain or loss is recognized separately on the sale or other disposition of each share of stock. Fink v. Commissioner, 789 F.2d 427 (6th Cir.1986). The Supreme Court, however, treated the controlling stockholders' stock as a unitary investment:

> A shareholder who surrenders a portion of his shares to the corporation has parted with an asset, but that alone does not entitle him to an immediate deduction. Indeed, if the shareholder owns less than 100 percent of the corporation's shares, any non-pro rata contribution to the corporation's capital will reduce the net worth of the contributing shareholder. A shareholder who surrenders stock thus is similar to one who forgives or surrenders a debt owed to him by the corporation; the latter gives up interest, principal, and also potential voting power in the event of insolvency or bankruptcy. But * * * such forgiveness of corporate debt is treated as a contribution to capital rather than a current deduction. * * * The Finks' voluntary surrender of shares, like a shareholder's voluntary forgiveness of debt owed by the corporation, closely resembles an investment or contribution to capital * * *.

SECTION 2.   BOND DISCOUNT AND PREMIUM

A. ORIGINAL ISSUE DISCOUNT

INTERNAL REVENUE CODE: Sections 163(e); 483; 1272(a); 1273; 1274(a)–
(d); 1274A; 1275(a)(1), (a)(2), (b), (c).

Tax Reform Act of 1984 General Explanation of the Revenue Provisions

Staff of the Joint Committee on Taxation 108 (1984).
[Pre-1984] Law

Timing of inclusion and deduction of interest: The OID rules

If, in a lending transaction, the borrower receives less than the amount to be repaid at the loan's maturity, the difference represents "discount." Discount performs the same function as stated interest; that is, it compensates the lender for the use of its money. Sections 1232A and 163(e) of [pre-1984] law (the "OID rules") generally required the holder of a discount debt obligation to include in income annually a portion of the original issue discount on the obligation, and allowed the issuer to deduct a corresponding amount, irrespective of whether the cash method or the accrual method of accounting was used.[7]

Original issue discount was defined as the excess of an obligation's stated redemption price at maturity over its issue price. This amount was allocated over the life of the obligation through a series of adjustments to the issue price for each "bond period" (generally, each one-year period beginning on the issue date of the bond and each anniversary). The adjustment to the issue price for each bond period was determined by multiplying the "adjusted issue price" (the issue price increased by adjustments prior to the beginning of the bond period) by the obligation's yield to maturity, and then subtracting the interest payable during the bond period. The adjustment to the issue price for any bond period was the amount of OID allocated to that bond period.

The OID rules did not apply to obligations issued by individuals,[8] obligations with a maturity of one year or less, or obligations issued in exchange for property where neither the obligation nor the property received for it was traded on an established securities exchange.

---

[7]   The premise of the OID rules was that an OID obligation should be treated in the same manner as a nondiscount obligation requiring current payments of interest for tax purposes. To accomplish this result, the rules in essence treated the borrower as having paid the lender the annual unpaid interest accruing on the outstanding principal balance of the loan, which amount the borrower was allowed to deduct as interest expense and the lender was required to include in income. The lender was then deemed to have lent this amount back to the borrower, who in subsequent periods was deemed to pay interest on this amount as well as on the principal balance. This concept of accruing interest on unpaid interest is commonly referred to as the "economic accrual" of interest, or interest "compounding."

[8]   Prior to 1982, the OID provisions applied only to corporate and taxable government obligations. The Tax Equity and Fiscal Responsibility Act of 1982 (TEFRA) extended these provisions to noncorporate obligations other than those of individuals.

Measurement of interest in deferred-payment transactions involving property: the imputed interest rules

A deferred-payment sale of property exempt from the OID rules was generally subject to the unstated interest rules of § 483. If the parties to the transaction failed to state a minimum "safe-harbor" rate of interest to be paid on the loan by the purchaser-borrower, § 483 recharacterized a portion of the principal amount as unstated interest. This "imputation" of interest was performed by assuming that interest accrued at a rate higher than the safe-harbor rate.

The safe-harbor rate was a simple interest rate; the imputation rate was a compound rate. The safe-harbor and imputation rates were 9 percent and 10 percent, respectively, when the Act became law. The safe-harbor interest rate applicable to certain transfers of land between members of the same family was 6 percent.

* * *

If interest was imputed under § 483, a portion of each deferred payment was treated as unstated interest. The allocation between unstated interest and principal was made on the basis of the size of the deferred payment in relation to the total deferred payments. Amounts characterized as unstated interest were included in the income of the lender in the year the deferred payment was received (in the case of a cash method taxpayer) or due (in the case of an accrual method taxpayer). The borrower correspondingly deducted the imputed interest in the year the payment was made or due.

Reasons for Change

Mismatching and noneconomic accrual of interest

Enacted in 1969, the OID rules were designed to eliminate the distortions caused by the mismatching of income and deductions by lenders and borrowers in discount lending transactions. Prior to that time, an accrual method borrower could deduct deferred interest payable to a cash method lender prior to the period in which the lender included the interest in income. Although the OID rules prevented mismatching in many situations, the potential for distortion continued to exist where the obligation was excepted from the OID rules. Some taxpayers attempted to exploit these exceptions, particularly the exception relating to nontraded obligations issued for nontraded property, to achieve deferral of tax on interest income and accelerated deductions of interest expense.

For example, in a typical transaction, real estate, machinery, or other depreciable property was purchased for a promissory note providing that interest accrued annually but was not payable until the note matured. The issuer, who used the accrual method of accounting, would claim annual interest deductions for accrued but unpaid interest. The holder, a cash method taxpayer, would defer interest income until it was actually received.

Such a mismatching of income and deductions had serious revenue consequences, since the present value of the income included by the lender in the later period was less than the present value of the deductions claimed by the borrower. The greater the length of time

more than five years after the obligation is issued, the obligation has accrued but unpaid interest in excess of the amount of the obligation's annual yield to maturity. I.R.C. § 163(i)(2). This disqualified portion of a high yield original issue discount obligation (the portion for which no current interest deduction is allowed and which is treated as a dividend to a corporate holder) is the lesser of the original issue discount of the obligation or the amount by which original issue discount exceeds the applicable federal rate plus six percent. I.R.C. § 163(e)(5)(C). Thus actual interest paid, plus original issue discount up to the applicable federal rate plus six percent, remains deductible as interest, but only when actually paid. The excess is given the equivalent of dividend treatment.

B. BOND PREMIUM

INTERNAL REVENUE CODE: Sections 171(a), (b); 249.

REGULATIONS: Sections 1.61–12(c)(2); 1.163–13(a), (c), (d).

DETAILED ANALYSIS

1. PREMIUM AT ORIGINAL ISSUE

The issuer of a bond with a stated interest rate in excess of prevailing market rates may be in a position to demand a premium for the bond, i.e., consideration in excess of the stated principal amount of the bond. This premium is not treated as income to the issuer at the time of receipt. Treas.Reg. § 1.61–12(c)(1). Instead, Treas. Regs. § 1.61–12(c)(3) and 1.163–13 generally require the issuer to include bond premium over the term of the bond, using the constant interest method, by reducing the issuer's interest deductions.

For the bondholder, § 171 provides an election to amortize premium over the term of the obligation using the constant interest method of § 1272(a). See Treas.Reg. § 1.1272–2. The premium reduces the interest income, although the creditor may also treat the premium as a deduction. I.R.C. § 171(e). The election is irrevocable without the consent of the Commissioner and applies to all bonds held by the taxpayer. See I.R.C. § 171(c). If the bondholder does not make the election with respect to fully taxable bonds, the premium paid is recovered as a loss on redemption of the bond for an amount less than its basis. Section 171(b) requires the creditor to amortize the bond premium over the full term to maturity, even though the bond may be callable at an earlier date.

Bond premium may also arise as the creditor pays an additional consideration for the privilege of converting the obligation into stock. Section 171(b)(1) excludes from bond premium "any amount attributable to the conversion features."

2. PREMIUM PAID BY THE ISSUER ON REDEMPTION

Bond premium paid by the issuer on redemption of an obligation is deductible by the issuer as additional interest on the obligation. In the case of convertible obligations, however, § 249 limits the deduction for redemption premium to an amount representing a "normal call premium" on obligations that are not convertible. The balance is a capital transaction. Thus, in the case of bond premium paid to redeem convertible bonds, the creditor is not allowed to amortize any portion of the premium attributable to the conversion feature, nor is the issuer allowed an interest deduction for that portion of a premium paid upon redemption of its bonds which is attributable to the conversion feature. This result presumably corresponds to the parallel treatment of original issue discount between issuer and holder, discussed at page 165. However, the treatment of the convertibility feature is different as between original issue discount and bond premium in the case of convertible bonds. The regulations adopt the view that in the case of convertible bonds, the conversion feature is not separable from the debt for purposes of determining original issue discount, hence preventing a larger original issue discount from resulting; on the other hand, in the case of bond premium the conversion feature is deemed under the Code to be a feature separable from the debt portion of the obligation and hence the amount, if any, attributable to the conversion element is not deductible as interest.

In Tandy Corp. v. United States, 626 F.2d 1186 (5th Cir.1980), the court denied a deduction under § 163 for premium on conversion of debt into stock. The taxpayer claimed that the excess of the fair market value of the stock issued over the face of the bonds was deductible as interest. The court concluded that under the terms of the indenture conversion extinguished the obligation to pay accrued interest or bond premium. Thus no accrued interest or bond premium was involved. The court did not consider the application of § 249.

In National Can Corp. v. United States, 687 F.2d 1107 (7th Cir.1982), an overseas finance subsidiary issued debentures convertible into the stock of its parent corporation. The parent redeemed its subsidiary's debentures with its own stock, the fair market value of which exceeded the issue price of the debentures. The parent claimed a deduction for the difference as premium under §§ 171 and 162. The parent corporation argued that the limitation of § 171(b)(1) applied only to obligations convertible into the stock of the issuing corporation, and not to obligations convertible into the stock of another. The court broadly interpreted § 171(b)(1) to limit deduction of premium attributable to any conversion feature. The court concluded that the premium was due to the unexercised conversion feature of the bonds so that amortization of premium was barred by § 171(b)(1) and Treas.Reg. § 1.171–2(c). The court also disallowed the taxpayer's claimed deduction under § 162, holding that under § 1032 the corporation recognizes no gain or loss when it issues stock in satisfaction of a conversion obligation of the bonds of a subsidiary. In the District Court the taxpayer also asserted that the value of the conversion feature at the time the bonds were issued reduced the issue price of the bonds thereby creating amortizable original issue discount in an amount equal to the value of the conversion rights. The District Court refused to treat the conversion rights as a separate asset capable of valuation apart from the debt component of the bonds. National Can Corp. v. United States, 520 F.Supp. 567 (N.D.Ill.1981). The taxpayer abandoned this claim on appeal.

CHAPTER 4

DIVIDEND DISTRIBUTIONS

SECTION 1. INTRODUCTION

The income tax treatment of corporate distributions to shareholders is a complex matter and the rules must be traced through many sections. The starting point is § 301(a), which generally covers all distributions of money or property by a corporation to its shareholders in their capacity as shareholders. As the general rule, § 301(a) is applicable to a broader range of distributions than just dividends in the corporate law sense. Section 301(a) provides that unless some other Code section provides a different treatment, the distribution will be treated as provided in § 301(c). Section 301(c), in turn, classifies distributions within the ambit of § 301 between dividends for tax purposes, which are included directly in gross income (§ 301(c)(1)), and distributions that are not dividends for tax purposes, which are treated as a return of capital applied against and reducing the stock basis (§ 301(c)(2)), and if in excess of that basis as gain from the sale or exchange of property (§ 301(c)(3)), thus bringing the capital gain provisions into play. Section 61(a)(7) also requires that dividends in the tax sense be included in gross income.

Before 2003, dividends were taxed at ordinary income rates, which were significantly higher than capital gains rates.[1] This historic pattern of taxation of dividends was changed in 2003, and dividends received by taxpayers other than corporations generally are taxed at the same preferential rates as long-term capital gains—currently zero percent for capital gains and dividends that would have been taxed in the 10 and 15 percent brackets if they had been taxed at ordinary income rates, 15 percent for capital gains and dividends that would have been taxed in the tax brackets higher than 15 percent but below the 39.6 percent bracket if they had been taxed at ordinary income rates, and 20 percent for capital gains and dividends that would have been taxed in the 39.6 percent bracket if they had been taxed at ordinary income rates. I.R.C. § 1(h)(11).

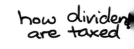
how dividends are taxed

Dividends received by a corporation are not accorded a special statutory rate. Instead, § 243(a)(1) provides a corporation that is a shareholder in another corporation with a deduction equal to 70 percent of intercorporate dividends received; § 243(c) increases the deduction to 80 percent if the shareholder corporation owns at least twenty percent of the stock of the payor corporation; and § 243(a)(3) extends this deduction to 100 percent for affiliated corporations that so elect. There are numerous limitations on the intercorporate dividends received deduction, which is discussed in Section 4 of this chapter.

Not all distributions by corporations that are subject to § 301(a) are dividends under § 301(c)(1) that must be included in gross income. Section 316(a) defines dividends for purposes of § 301(c)(1) with respect

---

[1]   Dividends were taxed at the same rate as capital gains from 1987 to 1991 because there was no preferential rate for long-term capital gains in those years.

to the "earnings and profits" of the corporation. The statutory dividend test is two-fold: any distribution to a shareholder is a dividend if it is out of either (1) earnings and profits accumulated after February 28, 1913, or (2) earnings and profits of the current year regardless of a lack of, or deficit in, accumulated earnings and profits. Earnings and profits differ substantially from taxable income, being more akin to net income in a financial accounting sense. But, because some significant adjustments to earned surplus in the corporate sense are not taken into account in computing earnings and profits, it is inaccurate to say that the taxability of the shareholder depends essentially on the earned surplus account of the corporation.

If the distributing corporation has neither current earnings and profits nor earnings and profits accumulated after February 28, 1913, so that the distribution is not a dividend for tax purposes, then the distribution is applied against the basis of the recipient shareholder's stock under § 301(c)(2), and any excess is taxed as a capital gain under § 301(c)(3).

Section 316(a) eliminates most tracing requirements by specifying in the second sentence that if any earnings and profits exist, the distribution is deemed to be out of such earnings and profits rather than from any other source, and first from the most recently accumulated earnings and profits. But while tracing difficulties are largely avoided, the problem of ascertaining the amount of a corporation's earnings and profits remains. If the earnings and profits of the current year exceed the distribution, the amount of the accumulated earnings and profits is irrelevant. If accumulated earnings and profits are present, the precise determination of the earnings and profits of the current year is likewise unnecessary. But in some situations the precise dollar amount of either current or accumulated earnings and profits may be crucial, and it is here that the exact scope of the statutory phrase "earnings and profits" must be determined. As will be seen, the phrase is only partially defined in § 312, thus requiring extensive judicial and administrative interpretation.

Section 301(b) determines the amount of the distribution in situations in which property or liabilities are involved, and § 301(d) establishes the basis of the distributed property in the shareholder's hands.

The scope of § 301(a) is qualified by various other sections dealing with corporate distributions, as the cross-references in § 301(f) indicate. Section 302 provides sale or exchange treatment for specified distributions *in redemption of stock*. If § 302 applies, capital gain or loss normally is recognized. Section 331 provides sale or exchange treatment for distributions in complete liquidation of the corporation; and § 302(b)(4) does the same for distributions to noncorporate shareholders in partial liquidation of the corporation. The definitions of complete and partial liquidations are tax words of art that are somewhat confusing. Certain distributions in corporate reorganizations also are specially treated (§§ 354 et seq.), as are certain distributions in redemption of stock to pay estate and inheritance taxes (§ 303) and distribution involving related corporations (§ 304).

Sections 305, 306, and 307 relate to the distribution of a "stock dividend." In general, these sections treat the distribution as a nontaxable event for the shareholder. However, there are many exceptions that can cause the receipt of the stock dividend to be taxable. In addition, some stock dividends, though they possess a nontaxable character on receipt, may on disposition generate ordinary income, although taxed at the same rate as dividends, to the extent of the amount realized rather than capital gain.

This statutory pattern provides many opportunities for controversies to flourish. Even though dividends received by individuals are taxed at capital gains rates, they remain ordinary income and cannot be offset by capital losses. Similarly, the shareholder's basis in his stock cannot be offset against dividend distributions. Liquidations, whether partial or complete, and certain stock redemptions achieve sale or exchange treatment in which the shareholder may apply the basis of the redeemed stock against the amount realized. Any gain is capital gain, against which capital losses may be deducted, and which may be taxed at a preferential rate if capital gains exceed capital losses for the year. But since a transaction cast in the form of a partial liquidation or other stock redemption may realistically amount to no more than the distribution of a dividend, the line is not crystal clear. Historically, because dividends generally have been subject to higher tax rates than capital gains, the differing treatment of dividends, on the one hand, and liquidations, partial liquidations, and redemptions, on the other hand, has been of great significance. The stakes of characterization of a transaction as a dividend, on the one hand, or as a redemption or liquidating distribution on the other hand, have been significantly reduced by the enactment of § 1(h)(11) in 2003. When dividends and capital gains are taxed at the same rate, the benefit to a noncorporate shareholder of characterization of a distribution as a redemption or liquidating distribution is limited to allowing recovery of basis under § 1001 and Treas.Reg. § 1.61–6(a)—which may result in offsetting a different amount of basis against the distribution than does § 301(c)(2)—and the ability to claim capital losses against capital gains. Furthermore, but now of importance primarily as a timing matter, the statutory exemption from taxation as current ordinary income of the receipt of many stock dividends historically provided the shareholder with the opportunity to create capital gain situations through the later sale of the dividend stock unless effective safeguards to prevent this tactic were placed in the statute.

Another facet of the taxation of corporate distributions that has shaped the historical development of Subchapter C should be noted at this point. The Tax Reform Act of 1986 amended § 311 and § 336 to require that gain be recognized by the corporation on the distribution of property, other than in liquidation of the corporation, and that both gain and loss be recognized on liquidating distributions. Before 1986, the predecessors of § 311 and § 336 provided for nonrecognition treatment to the corporation with respect to gain or loss inherent in distributed assets, whether by dividend, redemption, or liquidation. Where the corporate profits had not been realized but were represented by appreciation in value of corporate assets, distribution of appreciated assets in-kind permitted avoidance of corporate level tax on built-in gain. Over the years, numerous limitations were imposed on nonrecognition of gain with respect to distributed property culminating in the current recognition rules of §§ 311 and 336. Much of the logic behind the shape of the current provisions, and some of the historical cases to be encountered in the following chapters can be understood only if the former nonrecognition rules are kept in mind. As § 311 was tightened to limit nonrecognition on distributions of appreciated property, corporate taxpayers attempted to devise increasingly complex schemes to come within the remaining nonrecognition rules, and the courts and Congress were forced to respond. Since 1986, corporate taxpayers have continued to seek gaps in the recognition rules of § 311 to try to avoid the tax on appreciation at the corporate level.

The background of controversial areas involves two other statutory provisions, relating to the corporation rather than the shareholder, which appear in the Code outside of Subchapter C. If shareholders are taxed on distributions of corporate earnings, retention of corporate earnings and consequent postponement of the shareholder tax are the inevitable results of the treatment of the corporation as a taxpaying entity. As a force in the other direction, the Code contains in §§ 531–537 a special tax (at the maximum tax rate imposed on dividends) on a corporation that accumulates its earnings for the purpose of avoiding the imposition of the individual tax on its shareholders. Such a special tax presents its own problems of application. By its presence it also precipitates some of the controversial transactions mentioned above when the accumulation of earnings approaches the danger zone created by the § 531 accumulated earnings tax, since the shareholders will then usually act to draw some of the earnings out of the corporation. If the accumulation of earnings largely reflects passive investments of a closely-held corporation, such as the holding of stocks and other securities, even if the special § 531 tax can be avoided, another special 20 percent tax (the "personal holding company tax") may be imposed on the undistributed income if the passive income receipts meet the objective standards of §§ 541–547.

These penalty taxes were enacted at a time when the maximum rate of tax on individual income substantially exceeded the maximum rate of tax on corporate income, thereby giving rise to an incentive to earn income through a corporation that retained that income. Under the present rate structure, with the maximum individual rate being only slightly higher than the maximum corporate rate, there generally is little incentive to cause earnings that might otherwise be realized directly by an individual to be realized and accumulated by a corporation. In these circumstances, the reason for these penalty taxes has largely disappeared, although they remain as traps for the unwary. The provisions could perhaps be justified as enforcing a policy decision to impose a "double" tax on corporate profits on a reasonably current basis, but historically their function was to prevent accumulations at lower corporate rates.

The material in this chapter deals with cash and property dividend distributions by an ongoing corporation with respect to its continuing shareholders. Subsequent chapters deal with stock dividends, corporate distributions in redemption of stock, distributions in liquidation of the corporation, and the accumulated earnings tax and the personal holding company tax.

DETAILED ANALYSIS

1. DIVIDENDS ELIGIBLE FOR PREFERENTIAL RATES GENERALLY

The preferential rates for dividends under § 1(h)(11) apply only to dividends received by an individual shareholder from domestic and certain qualified foreign corporations. Payments in lieu of dividends, which are received by the lender of stock to a short-seller, are not eligible for the exclusion.[2] Although § 1(h)(11) treats dividends as "adjusted net capital gain" under § 1(h)(3), the dividend (unlike corporate stock) is not a capital asset as defined in § 1221, and dividends thus are not taken into account in the calculation of "net capital gain" under § 1222. As a result capital losses cannot be deducted against dividend income, except to the extent allowed by §§ 1211 and 1212.

2. ANTI-ABUSE RULES RELATING TO PREFERENTIAL RATES FOR DIVIDENDS

2.1. *Minimum Holding Period*

Section 1(h)(11)(B)(iii) is aimed at preventing taxpayers from obtaining unwarranted tax benefits in certain situations. The preferential rates for dividends, coupled with short-term holding of stock purchased in anticipation of receiving a dividend, creates the potential for inappropriate tax arbitrage benefits. Section 1(h)(11)(B)(iii) provides that the preferential rate for dividends does not apply to any dividends on any share of stock that is held for less than 61 days during the 121 day period beginning on the date that is 60 days before the date on which the stock becomes ex-dividend. (Under stock exchange rules, stock generally becomes ex-dividend three business days before the "record date" for paying dividends.) For preferred stock, if the dividends received are attributable to a period in excess of 366 days, the minimum holding period is 91 days during the 181 day period beginning 90 days before the ex-dividend date.

The effect of § 1(h)(11)(B)(iii) is illustrated by the following example. Assume that during the current tax year individual A realized a $200,000 short-term capital gain on the sale of X Corporation stock and no offsetting capital loss. Absent any other transactions, at a 39.6 percent marginal tax rate this $200,000 gain would result in a tax of $79,200. Now suppose that shortly before the end of the taxable year, A purchases 100,000 shares of Y Corporation stock for $5,000,000. Before the close of the taxable year, A (1) receives a $200,000 dividend on the Y Corporation stock, and (2) sells the Y Corporation stock for $4,800,000 (the value of the shares having declined as a result of the dividend). A realizes a $200,000 loss on disposition of the Y Corporation shares, because the basis in the stock was not reduced as a result of the dividend. This transaction is uneconomic, because the dividend income is exactly offset by the resulting capital loss. However, in the absence of § 1(h)(11)(B)(iii), at the 20 percent preferential rate, A would pay a tax of only $40,0000 on the $200,000 dividend received from Y Corporation, while using the $200,000 capital loss on the sale of the Y Corporation stock to offset the $200,000 short-term capital gain on the X Corporation stock that otherwise would have been taxed at the rate of 39.6 percent, saving $79,200 of tax. Thus, the transaction produces an after-tax

---

[2] Pursuant to § 6045(d), stock brokers generally must provide customers an information return that distinguishes payments in lieu of dividends from actual dividends. See Treas.Reg. § 1.6045–2.

benefit of $39,200, even though it produced a break-even before-tax cash flow. Under § 1(h)(11)(B)(iii), however, because the minimum holding period had not been met, the dividend would have been taxed at 39.6 percent—resulting in a $79,200 tax—instead of at 20 percent, and the $40,000 tax arbitrage benefit is eliminated.

2.2. Loss Recharacterization

Congress considered § 1(h)(11)(B)(iii) to be inadequate to deal with all of the tax avoidance possibilities created by the availability of the preferential rate for dividends as applied to extraordinarily large dividends. If an extraordinary dividend was expected to be paid on stock of a corporation, the investor owning the stock would be willing to hold the stock for the period required to avoid the limitation in § 1(h)(11)(B)(iii). Section 1(h)(11)(D)(ii) provides that if an individual receives an "extraordinary dividend," as defined in § 1059, taxed at the preferential rate, any loss on the sale of the stock on which the dividend is paid is treated as a long-term capital loss to the extent of the dividend, even if the actual holding period of the stock was short-term.

Section 1059(c) defines an extraordinary dividend in terms of the size of the dividend in relation to the shareholder's adjusted basis in its stock, subject to an alternative test using fair market value instead of basis at the taxpayer's election. A dividend is extraordinary if aggregate dividends received in any 85 day period exceed 10 percent of the basis of common stock, or 5 percent of the basis of preferred stock, with respect to which the dividends were paid. Furthermore, if aggregate dividends paid with respect to stock in any one year period exceed 20 percent of the corporate shareholder's basis for the stock, then all such dividends are aggregated and considered to be an extraordinary dividend.

Congress seems to have intended that under §§ 1222 and 1(h)(11)(D)(ii) the long-term capital loss on the sale of the stock with respect to which the dividend was received would reduce the amount of the dividend in determining adjusted capital gain eligible for the preferential rates. That is not how the language of the statute applies, however. Section 1(h)(11) provides that "net capital gain" means "net capital gain (determined without regard to this paragraph) increased by qualified dividend income." Under § 1222(11), "net capital gain" is the excess of net long-term capital gain over net short-term capital loss. Treating loss on the sale of stock with respect to which an extraordinary dividend is paid as a long-term capital loss may eliminate "net capital gain" (and indeed may create a "net capital loss"), but there is no provision in the Code for a negative "net capital gain." Net capital gain is either a positive number or non-existent. As a result, treating a loss as a long-term capital loss will reduce long-term capital gain, but once long term capital gain is exhausted, the "net capital gain" remains zero. Under § 1(h)(11), that zero amount is increased by the amount of a qualified dividend, which remains subject to tax at preferential capital gains rates.

Consider a variation of the preceding example. Suppose that early in the current tax year individual A realized a $700,000 short-term capital gain on the sale of X Corporation stock and no offsetting capital loss. Absent any other transactions, at a 39.6 percent marginal tax rate this $700,000 gain would result in a tax of $277,200. Now suppose that soon after the sale, A purchased 100,000 shares of Z Corporation stock for

$5,000,000, in anticipation of an extraordinary $700,000 dividend that will be paid later in the year. A holds the Z Corporation stock for more than the holding period required by § 1(h)(11)(B)(iii). Before the close of the taxable year, A (1) receives the $700,000 dividend on the Y Corporation stock, and (2) sells the Z Corporation stock, which has not been held for more than one year, for $4,300,000 (the value of the shares having declined as a result of the dividend). A realizes a $700,000 loss on disposition of the Z Corporation shares. Again, the transaction is uneconomic because the dividend income is exactly offset by the resulting capital loss. However, at the 20 percent preferential rate, A pays a tax of $140,000 on the $700,000 dividend. Applying § 1(h)(11)(D)(ii), A has $700,000 of net short-term capital gain and $700,000 of net long-term capital loss. I.R.C. § 1222(5) and (8). A has capital gain net income of zero (I.R.C. § 1222(9)), and zero net capital gain. I.R.C. § 1222(11). Under § 1(h)(11)(A), A's "net capital gain" subject to preferential rates is A's net capital gain of zero (as determined without regard to § 1(h)(11)), increased by A's $700,000 of qualified dividend income. Thus, A's extraordinary dividend remains subject to the preferential rate of § 1(h).

SECTION 2.   DIVIDEND DISTRIBUTIONS IN GENERAL

INTERNAL REVENUE CODE: Sections 61(a)(7); 301(a), (b), (c); 312(a), (c), (f)(1) (omitting subparagraph (A)), (k)(1)–(3), (*l*), (n)(2), (4), (5); 316(a); 317(a).

REGULATIONS: Sections 1.301–1(a), (c); 1.312–6(a), (b), (d); 1.312–7(b)(1); 1.316–1(a)(1), (e), Ex. (1); 1.316–2(a), (b), (c); 1.1016–5(a).

Mazzocchi Bus Co., Inc. v. Commissioner

United States Court of Appeals, Third Circuit, 1994.
14 F.3d 923.

■ BECKER, CIRCUIT JUDGE.

This appeal is from a decision of the United States Tax Court which upheld the Commissioner's determination of federal income tax deficiencies for the years 1974 through 1979 against Mazzocchi Bus Co., Inc. ("MBC"), a closely-held corporation; [and] Nicholas Mazzocchi ("Mazzocchi"), its controlling shareholder * * *. The Commissioner's determination stems from Mazzocchi's diversion of receipts totalling more than $700,000 from MBC for his personal use and benefit during the years in question, taken together with his failure to report that income on both his and MBC's tax returns.

The principal question presented by the appeal is whether MBC, a corporation using the cash method of accounting for computing its income taxes, should be entitled to use the accrual method for calculating its earnings and profits.[2] As applied to the facts, the

 Issue

---

[2] Under the cash method of accounting, the taxpayer reports income when received and expenditures when paid. In contrast, under the accrual method of accounting, the taxpayer reports income when the right to receive payment has accrued and the obligation to make payment has been established. Under § 446 the taxpayer may select one of several accounting methods, including the cash or accrual method, to compute taxable income, so long as it reflects income accurately and the taxpayer uses the same method to keep its books. But the

question is whether the tax court correctly held that the earnings and profits of MBC during the taxable years in question should not be reduced by income taxes, penalties, and interest owed but not paid by the corporation during those years. Relying on a reasonable Treasury regulation directly on point, we conclude that the tax court properly held that MBC must use the same accounting method for calculating its earnings and profits as it uses in calculating its income taxes. * * * [W]e will affirm.

I.   FACTS AND PROCEDURAL HISTORY

Mazzocchi was the president and controlling shareholder of MBC, which engaged in the school bus transportation business. During the years in question, MBC failed to record in its cash receipts books numerous checks constituting large payments for transportation services MBC provided several schools, and concomitantly failed to report those checks as receipts on its income tax returns. * * *

The omitted checks were mainly customer checks issued to Mazzocchi and/or MBC, 60 of which contained the single endorsement of Mazzocchi and 19 of which contained the initial endorsement of MBC followed by the second endorsement of Mazzocchi. As MBC's president, Mazzocchi was able surreptitiously (without the knowledge of corporate accountants or other officers) to negotiate these checks * * * thus affecting [sic] the diversion. * * *

The IRS ultimately commenced a criminal investigation of the business affairs of MBC and Mazzocchi, leading to Mazzocchi's indictment for income tax evasion [and subsequent guilty plea]. * * * Later, in 1986, the Commissioner determined that Mazzocchi had diverted money from MBC for his personal use and benefit and had failed to report it both on the joint returns he filed with his wife and on MBC's tax returns. Consequently, the Commissioner assessed the tax deficiencies and additions for fraud to the taxes against Mazzocchi and MBC which are at issue here.

The taxpayers challenged the Commissioner's deficiency determinations in the tax court, but the tax court rejected their efforts and held for the Commissioner. * * *

Mazzocchi additionally argued to the tax court that the earnings and profits of MBC, a cash basis taxpayer, should be reduced in the years at issue by the amount of accrued but unpaid taxes, penalties, and interest attributable to its income tax deficiencies for those years. This argument is premised on the Code's treatment of corporate distributions out of earnings and profits as ordinary income but its differing treatment of corporate distributions in excess of earnings and profits as either a return of capital or a capital gain, depending on the taxpayer's basis in the corporate securities. Had Mazzocchi prevailed on that point, then some unspecified portion of the income Mazzocchi diverted from MBC (depending on MBC's earnings and profits in the relevant tax years, an issue the tax court did not resolve) would represent some combination of a nontaxable return of capital and a capital gain with respect to Mazzocchi (in turn depending on his basis

---

Internal Revenue Code is mute about the accounting method a taxpayer must use for computing its earnings and profits.

in the corporate securities), instead of a constructive dividend taxable at ordinary income tax rates. The tax court, however, rejected his argument, reasoning that there was no basis to adjust earnings and profits for unpaid expenses incurred by MBC, a cash basis taxpayer.

* * *

[W]e chiefly focus on Mazzocchi's contention that a cash basis corporation should be allowed to deduct accrued but unpaid tax liabilities from its earnings and profits. * * *

II. DISCUSSION

A.

* * *

The Code generally treats corporate distributions (or dividends) out of earnings and profits as ordinary income to the shareholder taxpayer. But if a corporation pays a dividend which exceeds its earnings and profits (as measured by § 316(a)), the Code treats that portion of the dividend as a nontaxable return of capital to the shareholder taxpayer to the extent of the taxpayer's basis in the securities, and as a capital gain to the taxpayer once the taxpayer's basis is exhausted. See I.R.C. §§ 301(c), 316(a). * * * From the perspective of Mazzocchi's tax liability, characterizing the income as return of capital and/or capital gain is favorable since a return of capital is nontaxable and, as [capital gains, may be taxed at a lower rate than ordinary income].

The framework described above is relevant to this case because diverted corporate funds are treated as a constructive dividend to the taxpayer and, to the same extent, augment the corporation's taxable income (and hence its earnings and profits). See I.R.C. § 316(a) (defining a dividend as a distribution of property out of earnings and profits) * * *. In other words, the Code would treat the funds Mazzocchi diverted as income to MBC (inflating its earnings and profits), which income MBC then straightaway constructively disbursed to Mazzocchi as dividends.

Thus, assuming MBC did not suffer lost earnings and profits in the relevant years, a determination of a deficiency would increase MBC's earnings and profits by the amount of the deficiency and render all the diverted funds ordinary income to Mazzocchi. See I.R.C. § 301(c)(1). If MBC were able to reduce its earnings and profits by deducting therefrom the accrued (but unpaid) tax liabilities assessed against it in this action, the result would likely be to convert much of the constructive distribution to Mazzocchi into either a nontaxable return of capital or a capital gain, depending on Mazzocchi's basis in MBC shares. Thereby Mazzocchi's federal income tax deficiency and, correspondingly, the penalties and interest assessed against him, would be substantially reduced.

Of course, if MBC is not allowed to deduct the accrued tax liability from its earnings and profits in the relevant years, as a cash basis taxpayer it will be able to deduct those sums from its earnings and profits in the year it pays its back taxes. Accordingly, what is at issue here is only the timing of MBC's deduction of the income tax deficiency, penalties, and interest from its earnings and profits; under the cash basis method MBC would deduct it in the year paid (probably 1994), whereas under the accrual method it would deduct in each of the respective years 1975 through 1979 the amount accrued in that year.

To sustain his contention that a cash basis corporation may not employ the accrual method for determining its earnings and profits, the Commissioner principally relies on Treasury Regulation § 1.312–6 ("Earnings and Profits"[5]). Specifically, § 1.312–6 provides in relevant part:

> In determining the amount of earnings and profits * * * due consideration must be given to the facts, and, while mere bookkeeping entries increasing or decreasing surplus will not be conclusive, the amount of the earnings and profits in any case will be dependent upon the method of accounting properly employed in computing taxable income * * *. *For instance, a corporation keeping its books and filing its income tax returns * * * on the cash receipts and disbursement basis may not use the accrual basis in determining its earnings and profits. * * ***

Id. (emphasis added). As the Commissioner points out, we owe substantial deference to regulations issued by the agency Congress entrusted to administer the statute. * * *

We note in this regard that the Supreme Court approved a precursor to § 1.312–6(a) in Commissioner v. South Tex. Lumber Co., 333 U.S. 496 (1948), reh'g denied, 334 U.S. 813 (1948). Although that case arose under the excess profits tax, that tax used the same "accumulated earnings and profits" language which is contained in the current § 316. * * * In upholding a Treasury Regulation in pertinent respects remarkably similar to the one at issue here,[6] the Court rejected an attempt by a corporation which kept the relevant portion of its books using the installment method to use the accrual method in computing its earnings and profits[.] * * *

We owe the regulation heightened deference on account of its protracted history. * * * The Commissioner adhered to the IRS' longstanding practice when he first promulgated the regulation at issue here in 1955. See T.D. 6152, 1955–2 C.B. 61, 104–05 (promulgating the

---

[5] The term "earnings and profits" is used in various sections of the Code (its predominant use is in the treatment of dividend distributions by corporations), but is not defined therein. The Commissioner, however, has issued various regulations and revenue rulings in an effort to define it. * * * Briefly, earnings and profits are calculated by first adding to taxable income: "all income exempted by statute, income not taxable by the Federal Government under the Constitution [and] items includable in gross income under [the Code]," Treas.Reg. § 1.312–6(b); certain items which a corporation may deduct in computing taxable income (such as percentage depletion and dividends received); and deductions based on artificial timing (such as accelerated depreciation and deferred income). Then, earnings and profits are reduced by items like expenses and losses which a corporation may not deduct from its taxable income (for instance, federal income taxes and, notably, capital losses in past years disallowed as deductions from taxable income under Subchapter P of the Code, see Treas.Reg. § 1.312–7(b)(1)). Finally, various unusual financial transactions (for example, corporate distributions or changes in capital structure) may affect earnings and profits. * * *

[6] Compare § 29.115–3 of Regulations 111 ("In determining the amount of earnings or profits * * * due consideration must be given to the facts, and, while mere bookkeeping entries increasing or decreasing surplus will not be conclusive, the amount of the earnings or profits in any case will be dependent upon the method of accounting properly employed in computing net income."), reprinted in South Tex. Lumber, 333 U.S. at 500 n. 6, 68 S.Ct. at 698 n. 6 with Treas.Reg. § 1.312–6(a), quoted supra at 928.

regulation);[7] T.D. 5059, 1941–2 C.B. 125, 125–26 (Treasury decision issued to tax collectors containing virtually the identical language later incorporated into § 1.312–6(a)) * * *.

The tax court has also long adhered to the view that a cash basis taxpayer cannot deduct accrued but unpaid taxes from earnings and profits. * * *

Nonetheless, several old court of appeals opinions have come out otherwise, holding that a cash-basis corporation may deduct accrued but unpaid taxes from its earnings and profits. See Demmon v. United States, 321 F.2d 203, 204–06 (7th Cir.1963); Drybrough v. Commissioner, 238 F.2d 735, 738–40 (6th Cir.1956) * * *. The Commissioner's brief and the tax court, see, e.g., Webb v. Commissioner, 67 T.C. 1008, 1018 (1977), with whom we side, both provide incisive criticisms of the reasoning those appellate decisions utilized and advance cogent arguments why the applicable Treasury regulation is a reasonable construction of the Code which should govern the resolution of this question.[8]

B.

Drybrough primarily relied on cases which had allowed accrual method corporations to reduce earnings and profits by the amount of disputed federal taxes despite the fact that an accrual corporation generally cannot deduct disputed taxes from its income. Building on the reasoning those cases employed, the court in *Drybrough* engrafted a more discernible distortion onto the Code when it concluded that cash method corporations should also be permitted to reduce earnings and profits by the amount of accrued taxes. * * * We decline to brandish those ancient cases to fashion a similar rule * * *. The Commissioner forcefully argues, and we agree, that one objectionable departure from normal tax accounting practices does not justify another.[10]

We also take issue with the rationale expressed in *Drybrough* that general corporate law and accounting concepts of dividends and impairment of capital control the computation of earnings and profits for purposes of federal taxation. * * * As the tax court observed in *Webb*, *Drybrough* evidently "assumes that there must be some correlation between general corporate law concepts of capital and earning surplus and the Federal income tax concepts of capital and earnings and profits, an assumption which is not correct." *Webb*, 67 T.C. at 1020–21. * * * Given the disparate purposes behind the federal tax code and the corporate law impairment of capital doctrine, we agree.

---

[7] Treasury Regulation § 1.312–6 (1955) is, in all pertinent respects, identical to the current version.

[8] None of these appellate decisions considered the Treasury regulation which controls the outcome of this case, even though it was in effect when the later two decisions (*Demmon* and *Drybrough*) were handed down.

[10] Moreover, like the tax court, we discern no basis for differentiating between accrued taxes and other accrued liabilities when it comes to computing earnings and profits. See *Webb*, 67 T.C. at 1019. Besides our aforementioned deference to § 1.312–6, which contains no exception for tax liabilities, we believe that granting tax (as opposed to other) liabilities special treatment would institute inconsistent accounting methods (the cash method for most items but the accrual method for tax liabilities) for items taken into account in computing earnings and profits. Such special treatment would unnecessarily add complexity to the Code, undesirably distort earnings and profits, and unjustifiably engraft an unprincipled exception onto the Code.

* * *

The Seventh Circuit Court of Appeals in *Demmon*, supra, relied upon *Drybrough* * * * in resolving that "both reason and authority" support the argument that a cash basis corporation may deduct its accrued and unpaid taxes in computing earnings and profits. * * * [I]nsofar as we believe *Drybrough* to be flawed, we think so is *Demmon*.

* * *

C.

Finally, we consider Mazzocchi's assertion that "[c]ourts which have reduced earnings and profits by accrued but unpaid income tax liability have done so with the understanding that earnings and profits are intended to provide a measure of the ability of the Corporation to make distributions which are not out of its capital." That much is certainly true, but even if a Treasury regulation did not tie our hands, it is far from clear that the cash method does not accomplish that goal equally well. Earnings and profits ideally represent what the corporation has earned, whether during that fiscal year or since its inception, in excess of capital invested in it. But we think that in many cases, contrary to the suggestion of Mazzocchi, the cash method accurately reflects that amount, for it treats as earnings and profits the difference between the amount of cash received or gained and the amount of cash spent, depleted, or lost that year.

The cash basis method is not always meticulously accurate, as is illustrated by the case sub judice: a corporation may be deemed to have earnings and profits in one year although in a later year it has to pay taxes (or judgments, liabilities, or other losses) attributable to income earned in the earlier year, which exaggerates in the earlier year (but, by the same token, understates in the later year) the corporation's ability to distribute dividends. But the accrual system also has its drawbacks from an economic perspective. To take but one example, since the corporation has not yet collected the receipts it has accrued, it cannot distribute them (unless it takes out a loan with the accrued income as security, but economically that would be equivalent to selling the accrued income for present cash, rendering the modified accrual method akin to the cash method), and thus the accrual system may also overstate in the current year (and conversely understate in a later year) the corporation's ability to distribute dividends. In short, neither the cash nor the accrual method of accounting may accurately represent in an economic sense the amount of net assets that a corporation has available to distribute as dividends to its shareholders during any given year. Some inaccuracies inhere in the administrative necessity artificially to divide time into discrete years for tax purposes.

We find several significant drawbacks to Mazzocchi's suggested approach allowing a corporate taxpayer the freedom to choose which accounting system to use for calculating earnings and profits irrespective of the accounting method it uses to calculate its taxable income. First, it would tend to skew substantially the payment of taxes in favor of the taxpayer's shareholders, as the taxpayer will choose whichever method minimizes its shareholders' tax liability. * * * Second, to allow the choice would impose upon the Commissioner the burden of maintaining—and auditing—two sets of books for each taxpayer electing inconsistent accounting methods for income and earnings and profits purposes.

* * *

D.

In conclusion, we hold that the tax court correctly rejected Mazzocchi's argument that the earnings and profits of MBC, a cash basis corporation, should be reduced by the amount of accrued but unpaid taxes, penalties, and interest attributable to its income tax deficiencies for the years in issue. To preclude the distortion of tax liability and to spare the Commissioner the concomitant onerous bookkeeping tasks which would follow from a corporation's using one accounting method to compute income while using a different accounting method to calculate earnings and profits, § 1.312–6(a) of the Treasury regulations has long provided that a corporation must use the same accounting method in calculating earnings and profits as it uses in determining its taxable income. * * *

DETAILED ANALYSIS

1. DISTRIBUTIONS OUT OF EARNINGS AND PROFITS

1.1. *General*

Treas.Reg. § 1.316–2 provides rules for ascertaining the source of a distribution. Dividends are deemed to have been distributed first out of current earnings and profits for the year, to the extent thereof, without diminution by reason of the distributions during the year. It makes no difference that some of the earnings and profits accrued after the date of a distribution. Current earnings and profits are prorated among all distributions during the year. Suppose that as of January 1, Y Corporation had no accumulated earnings and profits. From January 1 through June 30 it had operating profits (for earnings and profits purposes) of $50,000, and on July 1 it distributed $40,000 in cash to its shareholders. As of December 31, Y Corporation had only $30,000 of current earnings and profits for the year. Only $30,000 of the July 1 distribution is taxable as a dividend because current earnings and profits always are determined at the end of the year without regard to distributions during the year, not at the time of the distribution. Accumulated earnings and profits are significant only if the earnings and profits of the current year do not cover the total distributions for the year. See Treas.Reg. § 1.316–1(a)(1). In the latter event, the current earnings and profits are prorated among all of the year's cash distributions and the remaining amount of the distributions is charged against accumulated earnings and profits as of the beginning of the year in the order in which the distributions were made. Although the regulations do not expressly apply this rule if one or more of the distributions is of property, no other rule is provided to govern such a case, and logically the same rule should be applied. See G.C.M. 36,138 (Jan. 15, 1975) (so interpreting Treas.Reg. § 1.316–2).

If the operating result for the current year is a loss, so no current earnings and profits exist, then a distribution during the year will be charged against accumulated earnings and profits computed to the date of

[handwritten margin note: Distribute 1st from CEP]

the distribution. If the actual current earnings and profits or loss to the date of the distribution cannot be ascertained, then the current loss of the year is prorated and applied to the accumulated earnings and profits as of the beginning of the year. See Rev.Rul. 74–164, 1974–1 C.B. 74. Suppose that as of January 1, X Corporation had $50,000 of accumulated earnings and profits. For the current year X Corporation had an operating loss of $80,000. On April 1 it distributed $40,000 in cash to its shareholders. Prorating X Corporation's $80,000 loss for the year (using a 30–day month convention for simplicity) results in treating $20,000 of the loss ($80,000 × 3/12) as occurring from January 1 through March 31. That leaves X Corporation with only $30,000 of accumulated earnings and profits on April 1 ($50,000–$20,000). Thus, only $30,000 of the $40,000 distribution on April 1 constituted a dividend. Pursuant to § 312(a), the dividend distribution reduced X Corporation's earnings and profits to $0 as of April 1. At the end of the year the $60,000 of X Corporation's $80,000 loss for the year that was prorated to the period April 1 to December 31 reduces X Corporation's accumulated earnings and profits to negative $60,000.

If there is no overall loss for the year, no proration is made. Suppose that on January 1, X Corporation had accumulated earnings and profits of $40,000. For the period January 1 through June 30, it had an operating loss (for earnings and profits purposes) of $50,000, but as of December 31, it had current earnings and profits for the year of $10,000. On July 1, X Corporation distributed $50,000 of cash to its shareholders. Even though as of July 1, the operating loss incurred during the first half of the year would have eliminated the accumulated earnings and profits if the corporate books had been closed at that time, the entire distribution is a dividend, $10,000 out of current earnings and profits and $40,000 out of accumulated earnings. Since the corporation did not in fact incur a loss for the year, but rather earned $10,000, the loss accrued as of July 1 did not reduce accumulated earnings and profits, which as of July 1 remained $40,000.

Allocation of earnings and profits among distributions with respect to different classes of stock presents more difficult problems where one class of stock has dividend priorities established by the corporate charter. Rev.Rul. 69–440, 1969–2 C.B. 46, involved a corporation that had three classes of stock, the first two of which had priority with respect to dividend payments. The corporation distributed amounts to the first two classes of stock in excess of earnings and profits. The ruling held that if the preferred stock, the first priority stock, had dividend priority under the corporate charter, then earnings and profits were first to be allocated to all of the dividends paid on the preferred stock. If this treatment exhausted earnings and profits and distributions were made with respect to other classes of stock, then those distributions simply reduced the basis of that stock.

1.2. *Timing of Dividend Inclusion*

A dividend is included in the shareholder's gross income when "received," regardless of whether the shareholder uses the cash receipts or accrual method. See Commissioner v. American Light & Traction Co., 156 F.2d 398 (7th Cir.1946), relying on the rule in Treas.Reg. § 1.301–1(b), and rejecting the other possible dates such as declaration or record; Rev.Rul. 64–290, 1964–2 C.B. 465. See also Caruth Corp. v. United States, 865 F.2d 644 (5th Cir.1989) (dividend on stock transferred by charitable gift after declaration date but before record date was taxable to charitable donee, not donor). Similarly, the date of payment (and not the date of declaration) is the date of distribution from the standpoint of the corporation and, accordingly, dividends are taken into account to reduce earnings and profits in the year of payment. Rev.Rul. 62–131, 1962–2 C.B. 94; Bush Bros. & Co. v. Commissioner, 73 T.C. 424 (1979), aff'd, 668 F.2d 252 (6th Cir.1982). Dividend checks payable and mailed on December 31 affect earnings and profits for the corporation in that year, even though the shareholder does not include the dividend in income until the following year. Rev.Rul. 65–23, 1965–1 C.B. 520.

2.   DISTRIBUTIONS NOT OUT OF EARNINGS AND PROFITS

A distribution that is not "out of earnings and profits," because there are neither earnings and profits of the current year nor accumulations since February 28, 1913, or because total distributions exceed available earnings and profits, is applied first to reduce the shareholder's basis for the stock to zero under § 301(c)(2), and any excess results in capital gain under § 301(c)(3).[3] Johnson v. United States, 435 F.2d 1257 (4th Cir.1971), held that a taxpayer who had several blocks of stock with different bases was required to treat a distribution on the stock not out of earnings and profits as made pro rata among the blocks of stock in order to determine the gain realized by the taxpayer on the distribution; the taxpayer was not allowed to aggregate the total basis in the stock and offset that total against the amount of the distribution. Prop.Reg. § 1.301–2 (2009) would adopt the rule of *Johnson* to provide that the portion of a distribution that is not a dividend will be applied to reduce the basis of each share within the class of stock on which the distribution is made pro rata on a share-by-share basis. As a consequence, the distribution may require recognition of gain under § 301(c)(3) with respect to some shares while the distributee shareholder retains basis in other shares.

3.   DETERMINATION OF EARNINGS AND PROFITS

3.1. *General*

The earnings and profits of a year are not synonymous with either taxable income or book net income. Accumulated earnings and profits is not earned surplus in the corporate sense, but the aggregate of annual earnings and profits, as adjusted for distributions and certain other transactions involving shareholders. Although the Code does not comprehensively define the term "earnings and profits," numerous statutory rules governing the determination of earnings and profits move the concept closer to economic income than to either taxable or book income. Nevertheless, the starting point for computing earnings and profits is taxable income, which must then be adjusted to take into account income items excluded from taxable income, expenses (not chargeable to a capital account) that are disallowed as deductions, and myriad differences regarding the timing of income and deductions. Taxable income is used as a starting point, in part, because it is an amount that must be computed in any event based on an ascertainable standard. However, taxable income must be adjusted to account for items of economic income and expenditure not reflected in the income tax base.

---

[3]   Distributions traceable to pre-March 1, 1913 profits are treated entirely as a return of capital. Since § 316(a) provides that for tax purposes all of the earnings and profits accumulated after February 28, 1913 must be distributed before a distribution may be regarded as out of the pre-March 1, 1913 profits, the latter type of distributions are unlikely to occur in the case of profitable corporations.

3.2. *Treatment of Special Income Items*

Most items of wholly or partially exempt income, such as tax-exempt interest, life insurance proceeds, and intercorporate dividends, are included in earnings and profits. Treas.Reg. § 1.312–6(b). But some items excluded from gross income also are excluded in the computation of earnings and profits. For example, those subsidies or payments to a corporation regarded as nontaxable contributions to capital under § 118 do not enter into earnings and profits, Rev.Rul. 66–353, 1966–2 C.B. 111. If receipts are treated as contributions to capital rather than as taxable income for services, and thus have no effect on earnings and profits, no depreciation deduction is allowed with respect to the property under Rev.Rul. 66–353, and hence earnings and profits in subsequent years would be increased correspondingly. Although there is no express authority on point, § 312(f)(1) should exclude from earnings and profits amounts received on the issuance of the corporation's own stock or stock options, which are excluded from income by § 1032.

A bad debt previously deducted without an income tax benefit, but which nevertheless reduced earnings and profits, increases earnings and profits on its recovery. Rev.Rul. 58–546, 1958–2 C.B. 143.

Cancellation of an indebtedness of the corporation increases earnings and profits if the cancellation results in taxable income. Schweppe v. Commissioner, 168 F.2d 284 (9th Cir.1948), aff'g 8 T.C. 1224 (1947). But if the cancellation is excluded from income under § 108 and there is a corresponding basis adjustment under § 1017, then no current increase in earnings and profits results from the cancellation. I.R.C. § 312(*l*); see also Rev.Rul. 58–546, supra. To the extent that there is no basis reduction, however, earnings and profits must be increased, even though other tax attributes are reduced under § 108(b).

3.3. *Treatment of Deduction Items*

Most expense items that are disallowed as deductions in computing taxable income are nonetheless subtracted in determining earnings and profits. Such items include federal income taxes, unreasonable compensation (to the extent not recharacterized as a dividend), excess charitable contributions, disallowed capital losses, and deductions disallowed on grounds of public policy under § 162(c), (e), (f), and (g). See Rev.Rul. 77–442, 1977–2 C.B. 264; see also Rev.Rul. 71–165, 1971–1 C.B. 111 (amortizable bond premium on tax-exempt bonds that is nondeductible under § 171(a)(2) reduces earnings and profits in the year to which the amortizable bond premium is attributable); Rev.Rul. 2009–25, 2009–28 C.B. 365 (interest paid by a corporation on a loan to purchase a life insurance policy on an individual for which a deduction has been disallowed under § 264(a)(4) reduces earnings and profits for the taxable year in which the interest would have been allowable as a deduction but for its disallowance under § 264(a)(4)).

A net operating loss carryover deduction does not reduce current earnings and profits because the adjustment to earnings and profits was made in the year the loss was incurred. The same is true with respect to capital loss carryovers under § 1212.

Some deductions permitted in computing taxable income are eliminated in computing earnings and profits. Treas.Reg. § 1.312–6(c) provides that a percentage depletion deduction allowed in computing taxable income must be adjusted to the cost depletion method for the computation of earnings and profits. Similarly, the intercorporate dividends received deduction under § 243 is disallowed. Although a charitable contribution deduction equal to the fair market value of property donated to charity may be allowable under § 170, Rev.Rul. 78–123, 1978–1 C.B. 87, held that a corporation's earnings and profits are reduced only by the adjusted basis of the property since the appreciation element had never entered into earnings and profits. Kaplan v. Commissioner, 43 T.C. 580 (1965) (Nonacq.), is to the contrary and in our view is incorrect.

3.4. *Treatment of Matters of Timing*

As discussed in *Mazzocchi Bus Co.*, except where the Code otherwise specifically so provides, the timing of earnings and profits adjustments is determined by the accounting method used by the corporation in computing taxable income. See Treas.Reg. § 1.312–6(a), first sentence; see also Bangor & Aroostook R. Co. v. Commissioner, 193 F.2d 827 (1st Cir.1951). Thus, for example, a reserve for estimated future expenses, while proper under accounting principles, would not reduce earnings and profits if not deductible for tax purposes. See also Rev.Rul. 66–35, 1966–1 C.B. 63 (amortizable bond premium and bond discount on taxable bonds are reflected in earnings and profits in the same year in which includible or deductible in computing taxable income); Rev.Rul. 60–123, 1960–1 C.B. 145 (corporation deducted interest and taxes for tax purposes, but capitalized such items on its books for regulatory purposes; held, such items are deductible in computing earnings and profits in the same manner and year as allowed for purposes of computing taxable income).

Section 312(f)(1) directs that realized gains and losses be taken into account in computing earnings and profits in the year that they are recognized. Thus, for example, gain deferred on a like-kind exchange under § 1031 does not increase earnings and profits. On the other hand, when gain realized on the sale of property is reported on the installment basis under § 453, § 312(n)(5) directs that the entire gain is added to earnings and profits in the year of the sale, rather than as each installment is received. If it later is determined that the taxpayer realized an overall loss on the transaction, earnings and profits are decreased in the subsequent year. Luckman v. Commissioner, 56 T.C. 1216 (1971).

In computing taxable income, accelerated depreciation deductions are allowed under § 168, and §§ 179, 179A, and 179B permit a limited amount of certain capital expenses to be deducted currently. In computing earnings and profits, however, § 312(k)(3) provides that: (1) amounts expensed under §§ 179, 179A, and 179B must be deducted ratably over a five-year period; and (2) depreciation deductions for tangible property to which § 168 applies must be computed under the less rapid alternative depreciation system of § 168(g)(2). Section 312(k) is designed to prevent the distribution of nontaxable dividends attributable to the excess of accelerated depreciation over the lesser amount of depreciation considered more accurately to reflect economic decline in value. See S.Rep. No. 91–552, 91st Cong., 1st Sess. 176 (1969). Under Treas.Reg. § 1.312–15(a), § 312(k) also applies to amortization under §§ 169, 184, 187, 188, or "any similar provision."

Because depreciation is allowed at a different rate for earnings and profits purposes, depreciable property has a different basis for this purpose.

Accordingly, the gain or loss on the sale of depreciable property for earnings and profits purposes will differ from the taxable gain or loss. I.R.C. § 312(f), flush language. Also, because depreciation on manufacturing plant and equipment must be treated as an inventory cost under § 263A, inventories will differ for earnings and profits purposes from those used in computing taxable income.

Section 312(n) requires a number of other adjustments to earnings and profits to reflect more accurately a corporation's economic gain or loss. Among the most significant are that: (1) earnings and profits be increased annually by the "LIFO recapture amount," which generally speaking is tantamount to requiring that earnings and profits be computed using only the first in-first out (FIFO) inventory method; and (2) deductible intangible drilling and development costs and solid mineral exploration and development costs be capitalized and amortized in future years.

3.5. *Effect of Stock Option Transactions*

In Luckman v. Commissioner, 418 F.2d 381 (7th Cir.1969), a shareholder received from a corporation a cash distribution that he treated as a nontaxable return of capital. In prior years, the corporation had sold stock to its employees under "restricted stock options" at a purchase price that was about $3.4 million less than the fair market value of the stock at the time of sale. Under a now repealed provision, the employees were not taxed on the discount. The taxpayer nevertheless argued that the difference between the option price and the fair market value reduced the earnings and profits of the corporation, creating a deficit in the corporation's earnings and profits account, and thus rendered the distributions received by the taxpayer nontaxable. The Tax Court held that earnings and profits were not reduced as the result of the exercise of the stock options (50 T.C. 619 (1968)), but the Court of Appeals reversed:

> As used in federal taxation, [the earnings and profits] concept represents an attempt to separate those corporate distributions with respect to stock which represent returns of capital contributed by the stockholders from those distributions which represent gain derived from the initial investment by virtue of the conduct of business. The crucial issue is whether a given transaction has a real effect upon the portion of corporate net worth which is not representative of distributed capital and which results from its conduct of business. In order to make this determination it is necessary to scrutinize the economic effects of the particular transaction as well as its character and relation to the corporate business. * * *

> Had the compensation been paid in cash and then used to purchase stock, there could be no question that the corporation had incurred a true economic expense which reduced earnings and profits. The amount of corporate assets available for distribution to those who owned the stock at the time of the transaction is reduced to the same extent in either case. The economic effect of the two transactions is identical.

418 F.2d at 383–83. Accord Divine v. Commissioner, 500 F.2d 1041 (2d Cir.1974), rev'g 59 T.C. 152 (1972).

Stock options that are governed by § 422 or by § 83 and Treas.Reg. § 1.421–6 should produce the same result as in *Luckman*. Rev.Rul. 2001–1, 2001–1 C.B. 726, confirmed that earnings and profits are reduced to reflect the corporation's deduction under §§ 83(h) and 162 when an employee receives stock upon the exercise of a nonstatutory stock option.

3.6. *Federal Income Tax Costs*

Following Treas.Reg. § 1.312–6(a), first sentence, which provides for computation of earnings and profits using the taxpayer's method of accounting, an accrual method corporation takes federal income taxes into account in determining earnings and profits in the year to which the taxes relate, even in the case of a deficiency that is not discovered and paid until a later year. Deutsch v. Commissioner, 38 T.C. 118 (1962). An income tax refund arising from a net operating loss carryback is taken into account for purposes of earnings and profits in the year in which the net operating loss occurred, not in the year to which it is carried back. *Deutsch,* supra; Rev.Rul. 64–146, 1964–1 (Part 1) C.B. 129.

As discussed in *Mazzocchi Bus Co.*, however, the treatment of federal income taxes for cash method corporations has proved troublesome. *Mazzocchi Bus Co.* followed Helvering v. Alworth Trust, 136 F.2d 812 (8th Cir.1943), Webb v. Commissioner, 67 T.C. 1008 (1977), aff'd per curiam, 572 F.2d 135 (5th Cir.1978), and Rev.Rul. 70–609, 1970–2 C.B. 78, in holding that a cash method corporation could not subtract the federal income taxes until the year paid, and refused to follow Drybrough v. Commissioner, 238 F.2d 735 (6th Cir.1956), and Demmon v. United States, 321 F.2d 203 (7th Cir.1963), which permitted subtraction in the year to which the taxes related. Since Congress has narrowed the types of C corporations that can use the cash method of accounting, the problem now is of diminished importance. But for those C corporations that can use the cash method of accounting, the *Mazzocchi Bus Co.* approach produces a result more consistent with the purposes of the earnings and profits concept.

3.7. *Effect of Distributions*

Accumulated earnings and profits represents a running account, which is based upon the algebraic sum of the yearly earnings and profits or loss figures from the commencement of the corporate life, reduced by distributions chargeable to earnings and profits. Thus, distributions of taxable dividends reduce the accumulated earnings and profits. I.R.C. § 312(a). Deficits in the accumulated earnings and profits resulting from operating losses must be made up by subsequent earnings and profits before the account will be on the plus side. But an impairment of capital resulting from capital distributions need not be restored. Hence a distribution treated as a dividend under corporation law but not constituting a dividend for tax purposes because the requisite earnings and profits do not exist, does not produce a deficit in the earnings and profits account and does not prevent subsequent earnings from producing positive accumulated earnings and profits. Meyer v. Commissioner, 7 T.C. 1381 (1946) (involving stock redemptions); Estate of Uris v. Commissioner, 605 F.2d 1258 (2d Cir.1979) (same result; deficit in earnings and profits can be created only by operating losses).

The cancellation by a corporation of a shareholder's debt to the corporation is a distribution of property to the shareholder that reduces

the shareholders could pay the corporation cash for the property. Alternatively, the corporation could declare a $6,000 cash dividend, thereby creating a debt to the shareholders, and then distribute the property in satisfaction of the debt. If the debt is bona fide and the subsequent transfer of property in satisfaction of the debt is an independent transaction, a loss should be allowed on the disposition of the property. But if the two distributions are related and the step transaction doctrine is applied to integrate the transactions, the loss would be disallowed by § 311(a).

If a sale is to a more than fifty percent shareholder, § 267(a)(1) disallows any loss at the corporate level. But if the shareholder later sells the property at a gain, pursuant to § 267(d) the gain will not be recognized to the extent of the previously disallowed loss. Section 311 does not permit the transferee in effect to use the disallowed loss in this fashion. If § 311 were amended to provide for recognition of loss to the distributing corporation, § 267 still could apply to disallow the loss in proper circumstances.

Congress did not explain why the 1986 revisions retained the *General Utilities* rule as to current distributions of depreciated property. Is there any sound policy reason for denying the loss deduction? Since under § 301(d) the sharcholder's basis for distributed property is its fair market value at the time of distribution, the loss is eliminated forever. The disallowance of the loss may be avoided by selling the property to a third party and distributing the proceeds to the shareholders or, assuming § 267 does not apply, by selling the property to the shareholders. In the first case, however, the shareholders may desire the actual property, not its equivalent value. In the second case, the transaction is economically different. Perhaps the unarticulated reason for disallowing the recognition of losses is Congressional concern with tax avoidance transactions in closely held corporations. If the tax avoidance potential of allowing corporations a loss on distributions of property to majority shareholders is the concern, it would appear that the problem could have been addressed by subjecting losses at the corporate level resulting from distributions to shareholders to the same rules that govern losses realized on sales to shareholders.

2.4. *Distributions of Encumbered Property*

The distribution of property subject to a lien, whether or not the shareholder expressly assumes the corporation's liability, results in realization of the same amount of gain as would have been realized if the property had been sold by the corporation. To deal with situations in which the amount of the lien exceeds the fair market value of the property, § 311(b)(2), through a cross reference to § 336(b), provides that for this purpose the fair market value of the property will be treated as not less than the amount of the liability. If the corporate debt secured by the property is nonrecourse, this rule is merely duplicative of § 7701(g).

3.   TREATMENT OF SHAREHOLDERS

Section 301(b)(1) provides that in the case of both corporate and individual shareholders the amount of any distribution that is a dividend is the fair market value of the distributed property. However, where the property is subject to a lien or the shareholder assumes a corporate indebtedness in connection with the distribution, § 301(b)(2) directs that the amount of the distribution be reduced by the amount of the debt. In all cases, nevertheless, the shareholder's basis in the distributed property is its fair market value. I.R.C. § 301(d). But see Tabbi v. Commissioner, T.C. Memo. 1995–463 (daughter of shareholder took a zero basis in property received from controlled corporation, as an indirect gift from father, because father did not report transfer as a constructive dividend to him). Suppose that a corporation with sufficient earnings and profits to support dividend treatment of the entire distribution distributes property having a fair market value of $100, subject to a mortgage of $60. The shareholder has a dividend of $40, but takes a basis in the distributed property of $100. If the shareholder then sells the property for $40 cash, with the purchaser assuming the $60 mortgage, the shareholder realizes no gain. This is the correct theoretical result because it treats the shareholder who receives a distribution of encumbered property in the same manner as a taxpayer who receives encumbered property in a fully taxable exchange of property, e.g., the receipt of land in exchange for publicly traded stock.

Treas.Reg. § 1.301–1(g) provides that the amount of indebtedness encumbering distributed property will reduce the amount of the distribution under § 301(b) only to the extent that the shareholder assumes the debt within the meaning of § 357(d), discussed at page 91. Suppose a corporation distributes to a shareholder a parcel of land with a fair market of $100, which is subject to a recourse mortgage lien of $35, and the shareholder does not expressly assume the debt. The amount of the distribution would be $100 unless, considering all the facts and circumstance, the shareholder has assumed the indebtedness. If the shareholder did assume the indebtedness, the amount of the distribution would be $65. If the indebtedness is a nonrecourse debt of the corporation, it generally is sufficient that the shareholder take the property subject to the indebtedness for it to be considered to have been assumed.

4. THE EFFECT OF DIVIDENDS IN KIND ON EARNINGS AND PROFITS

4.1. *Generally*

Accounting for the proper adjustments to earnings and profits as a result of dividends in kind entails several steps. Because a distribution in kind of appreciated property results in the recognition of gain to the corporation under § 311, earnings and profits automatically should be increased by the recognized gain under the normal rules basing earnings and profits on taxable income. See I.R.C. § 312(f)(1). Redundantly, § 312(b)(1) requires that earnings and profits be increased in the amount by which the fair market of the distributed property exceeds its basis. Read literally, § 312(b)(1) results in a double addition to earnings and profits; it is unlikely, however, that it will be so interpreted.

The distribution itself requires a downward adjustment to earnings and profits in an amount equal to the fair market value of the distributed property. See I.R.C. §§ 312(a)(3) and 312(b)(2). This reduction in earnings and profits, however, is taken into account only after all current earnings and profits, including the earnings and profits attributable to the gain recognized by reason of the distribution, have been allocated among *all* distributions during the year pursuant to Treas.Reg. § 1.316–2.

Section 312(b)(1) excepts from the rule requiring an increase in earnings and profits the distribution of the corporation's own promissory note. Similarly, § 311(b) excepts such a distribution from its gain recognition rule. The distribution, however, does effect a reduction in earnings and profits. The upward adjustment in effect occurs when the corporation earns the income used to pay the indebtedness; there is no downward adjustment when the note is paid.

If depreciated property is distributed, § 312(a)(3) allows earnings and profits to be reduced by the basis of the property, even though § 311(a) disallows recognition of the loss. As far as the net effect on earnings and profits is concerned, this treatment achieves the same result as allowing the loss and reducing earnings and profits by the fair market value of the distributed property, even though the loss is disallowed by § 311(a) in computing taxable income. Thus, earnings and profits accurately reflect economic income, even though taxable income does not. Like the reduction in earnings and profits for distributions of appreciated property, this reduction in earnings and profits is taken into account after current earnings and profits have been allocated among *all* distributions during the year.

In determining the extent to which any distributions (including that of the property itself) made during the year are taxable as dividends, the increase in current earnings and profits for the year resulting from the recognized gain attributable to the distribution of property is taken into account in the same manner as any other income item for the year as provided in Treas.Reg. § 1.316–2. Thus the current earnings and profits resulting from a distribution of appreciated property may be used to support dividend treatment of a portion of an unrelated cash distribution. Suppose that X Corporation has neither accumulated nor current earnings and profits except as generated by property distributions during the current year. During the year it distributes property having a fair market value of $100 and a basis of $20 to Shareholder A and $100 cash to Shareholder B. Forty dollars ($40) of the distribution to each shareholder is a dividend. In G.C.M. 36,138 (Jan. 15, 1975), the IRS so interpreted Treas.Reg. § 1.316–2.

4.2. *Distribution of Encumbered Property*

If the distributed property is subject to liens or the distributee shareholder assumes a corporate liability in connection with the distribution, § 312(c) requires that a "proper adjustment" be made. Treas.Reg. § 1.312–3 interprets the statutory language to mean that the downward adjustment to earnings and profits under § 312(a) or § 312(b) to reflect the distribution should be reduced by the amount of the liability. Because of the manner in which Treas.Reg. § 1.316–2 apportions earnings and profits among distributions during the year to determine the extent to which each distribution is a dividend, the result is not always the same as simply increasing current earnings and profits by the amount of the liability and then making the § 312(a) and § 312(b) adjustments to reflect the distribution.

The adjustments required by § 312(c) are illustrated by the following example derived from Treas.Reg. § 1.312–4.[5] In the current year, X Corporation distributed to its sole shareholder, B, a parcel of land. The property had a fair market value of $5,000, and was subject to a mortgage

---

[5]   Treas.Reg. § 1.312–4 itself does not reflect amendments to §§ 311 and 312(a) enacted in 1986 and thus is difficult to apply directly.

of $2,000. The adjusted basis of property was $1,000. X Corporation had no accumulated earnings and profits or current earnings and profits, except those attributable to the distribution. Pursuant to § 311(b), X Corporation recognizes a $4,000 gain on the distribution ($5,000 F.M.V. − $1,000 basis). As a result, X Corporation has $4,000 of current earnings and profits. Pursuant to § 311(b)(2), B has received a distribution of $3,000 ($5,000 F.M.V. − $2,000 mortgage), all of which is a dividend under §§ 301(a)(1) and 316 because the amount of the distribution does not exceed current earnings and profits. Finally, pursuant to §§ 312(a)(3), 312(b)(2), and 312(c), X Corporation reduces its earnings and profits by $3,000, the $5,000 fair market value of the property minus the $2,000 mortgage. As result, X Corporation commences the next year with $1,000 of accumulated earnings and profits ($4,000 current E & P − $3,000 distribution).

5. DISTRIBUTION OF RIGHTS TO PURCHASE STOCK OF ANOTHER CORPORATION

Under the broad definition of "property" provided in § 317(a), rights to purchase stock of another corporation are "property" and are currently taxable as a dividend under § 301. Rev.Rul. 70–521, 1970–2 C.B. 72; Weigl v. Commissioner, 84 T.C. 1192 (1985). Section 311(b) requires the distributing corporation to recognize gain in the amount by which the fair market value of the rights exceeds its basis in the rights; a correlative increase in earnings and profits is required. Under current § 312(a)(3) and 312(b)(2), the distributing corporation reduces earnings and profits by the fair market value of the rights.

6. DISTRIBUTION OF CORPORATION'S OWN SECURITIES

6.1. *Debt Instruments*

Suppose that a corporation distributes its own promissory note in the face amount of $10,000. As far as the shareholder is concerned, a distribution of the corporation's own debt instrument generally is treated in the same manner as any other distribution of property. Section 301(b), which appears to provide that the amount of the distribution is the fair market value of the instrument, and § 301(d), which appears to give the shareholder a fair market value basis in the distributed obligation, must be coordinated with the OID rules of §§ 1271–1275. (See Chapter 3, Section 2.) Pursuant to § 1275(a)(4) and Treas.Reg. § 1.1001–1(g), the "amount" of the distribution for purposes of § 301(b) is the "issue price" of the obligation determined under § 1273 or § 1274. If the instrument is publicly traded upon issue, its issue price equals its fair market value. I.R.C. § 1273(b); Treas.Reg. § 1.1273–2(b)(1). If the debt obligation is not publicly traded, the issue price is determined under § 1274 with reference to the sum of the present values (discounted at the appropriate AFR) of all payments due under the obligation. If the stated principal amount does not exceed the present value of the future payment at the appropriate AFR, then the stated principal amount is the issue price; otherwise, the issue price equals the discounted present value of the payments. The issue price, so determined, then becomes the shareholder's initial basis in the instrument. As long as the instrument bears interest, payable at least annually, at the appropriate AFR for its term, however, the issue price will be the stated principal amount of the obligation, which should be treated as its fair market value.

The distributing corporation receives substantially different treatment when it distributes its own debt instrument than it does when it distributes other property. Because its basis for its own promissory note presumably is zero, if the general rule applied, the distributing corporation might be required to recognize gain. However, the parenthetical in § 311(b)(1)(A) provides nonrecognition treatment to the distributing corporation. Earnings and profits adjustments are governed by § 312(a)(2), which reduces earnings and profits by the face amount of an obligation other than an obligation bearing original issue discount (OID). If the distributed instrument bears OID, then earnings and profits are reduced only by the "issue price." For purposes of applying § 312(a)(2), § 312(o) incorporates the OID rules. Section 1275(a)(4) treats an OID instrument distributed by a corporation with respect to its stock as an OID instrument issued in exchange for property. Therefore, as in the case of the shareholder, § 1274 applies. As a result, earnings and profits are reduced by the lesser of the "issue price" of the obligation or its face amount. See S.Rep. No. 98–169, 98th Cong., 2d Sess. 188–89 (1984).

Discount obligations distributed to shareholders in a § 301 distribution are thereafter subject to the OID rules, as if they had been issued for cash equal to their issue price at the time of distribution. When the corporation deducts interest on the obligation under § 163(e) as it economically accrues, earnings and profits eventually will be charged with the full face amount of the obligation.

6.2. *Stock or rights to acquire stock*

Distributions to shareholders of a corporation's own stock or rights to purchase such stock generally are not subject to the rules of § 301 and § 311. Special rules under § 305 apply to these situations. See Chapter 6.

SECTION 4.   DISGUISED DIVIDENDS

INTERNAL REVENUE CODE: Sections 61(a)(7); 301(a), (b); 316(a); 317(a).
REGULATIONS: Sections 1.162–7,–8; 1.301–1(c), (j), (m).

Ireland v. United States

United States Court of Appeals, Fifth Circuit, 1980.
621 F.2d 731.

■ AINSWORTH, CIRCUIT JUDGE:

Appellant Charles W. Ireland ("Ireland") used aircraft provided by his company to travel between his home and the firm's headquarters. The Internal Revenue Service ("IRS") assessed additional income to Ireland in the amount of the alleged value of the plane rides. After paying the resulting deficiency, Ireland brought suit in district court seeking a refund. The district court upheld the assessment and denied the refund. Ireland therefore appeals. We affirm the district court's holding that the value of the plane trips is taxable income to Ireland, but disagree, however, with the method used by the IRS and adopted by the district court in calculating the value. Accordingly, we remand for further proceedings in that regard.

Ireland was employed by Birmingham Slag Company in 1939. Virtually all of the stock in the company was owned by members of appellant's family. Working his way through the corporate ladder, appellant became the president of the firm in 1951. In 1956, Birmingham Slag merged with Vulcan Detinning Company to form Vulcan Material Company ("Vulcan"), with Ireland as its president. Since the merger, Vulcan has been a publicly held corporation with its principal office in Birmingham, Alabama.

* * *

[Eventually, Ireland became Chairman of the Board of Directors of Vulcan and Bernard Monaghan became President of Vulcan. Ireland and Monaghan differed in their views of corporate policy. Lower management personnel bypassed the corporate chain of command and brought problems directly to Ireland. The resulting conflict interfered with the efficient operation of the company. To resolve the deleterious effect of the conflict between Monaghan and Ireland, Monaghan was given sole control over the company's daily operations while Ireland concentrated on the development of long-range policies. To make Ireland less accessible to Vulcan's management personnel, thereby forcing them to deal directly with Monaghan, Ireland left Vulcan's Birmingham office.]

Ireland moved from Birmingham to Lynn Haven, Florida, in 1965, to a home owned by his wife. After the move, Vulcan paid for his long-distance calls to the Birmingham office as well as the cost of office supplies used in conjunction with a business office maintained in appellant's Lynn Haven home.

While in Lynn Haven, Ireland had frequent occasion to travel to Birmingham in order to attend meetings of the executive committee or the Board of Directors. Ireland also traveled to various other locations in conjunction with certain business deals * * *. Whenever Ireland desired, the company would arrange for one of its airplanes to fly to Panama City, the nearest airport to Lynn Haven, to pick up Ireland. The cost of these flights was borne by Vulcan. On occasion, Ireland's family or friends would travel with him on the flights on a space-available basis.

* * *

Ireland raises two issues on appeal. First, he challenges the district court's finding that the value of the airplane flights provided by Vulcan constituted income to him. Ireland contends that the flights were not regular commuting expenses because he was forced to move to Lynn Haven in order to solve the management crisis resulting from his personal conflict with Monaghan. Assuming the district court was correct on the first issue, Ireland also argues that the method of determining the value of the flights was improper. We address these issues in order.

The Value of the Flights as Income

* * * Under section 61(a)(7), gross income includes the receipt of any dividend. A dividend under the Code is "any distribution of property made by a corporation to its shareholders." 26 U.S.C. § 316(a). There is no requirement that the dividend be formally declared or even intended by the corporation. Loftin and Woodard, Inc. v. United States,

In Teymourian v. Commissioner, T.C. Memo. 2005–232, the Tax Court held that an advance from a corporation to a shareholder should be characterized as loan or a dividend based on the following objective factors: (1) whether the promise to repay is evidenced by a note or other instrument; (2) whether interest was charged; (3) whether a fixed schedule for repayments was established; (4) whether collateral was given to secure payment; (5) whether repayments were made; (6) whether the borrower had a reasonable prospect of repaying the loan and whether the lender had sufficient funds to advance the loan; and (7) whether the parties conducted themselves as if the transaction were a loan. In that case, although there was no promissory note, there was no fixed schedule for repayment, and there was no collateral, over $1.5 million of advances were characterized as a loan because adequate interest was paid, a substantial amount ($400,000) of principal was repaid, there was a reasonable prospect of repayment, and the parties, including minority shareholders, treated the advances as loans.

On the other hand, in Livernois Trust v. Commissioner, 433 F.2d 879 (6th Cir.1970), the existence of demand notes bearing six percent interest did not control the characterization of advances to a shareholder as loans rather than dividends. In Crowley v. Commissioner, 962 F.2d 1077 (1st Cir.1992), withdrawals by a minority shareholder were treated as constructive dividends rather than loans, even though the shareholder had made some repayments in a subsequent year; the shareholder's unrestricted withdrawal privilege was determinative.

4.2. *Below Market Rate of Interest Loans*

Section 7872 requires the imputation of a dividend if a corporation makes a below-market or interest-free loan to a shareholder. The shareholder may then be entitled to an offsetting interest deduction under § 163. The deductibility of such imputed interest by the shareholder, however, is subject to all of the limitations that generally apply to the deductibility of the interest depending on the use to which the loan proceeds are applied by the shareholder. See, e.g., § 163(d) (limiting deductions for investment interest); § 163(h) (disallowing deductions for personal interest); § 263A(f) (requiring capitalization of certain production period interest); § 265 (disallowing deduction of interest incurred with respect to tax-exempt bonds); § 469 (restrictions on deductions of passive losses). The corporation recognizes interest income but, of course, obtains no offsetting deductions for the imputed dividend. When the loan is payable on demand, both payments are deemed to have been made on December 31st of each year the loan is outstanding, and the amount of the dividend and the deemed interest payment equals the forgone interest for the year. I.R.C. § 7872(a). But if the loan is for a specified term, § 7872(b) provides that the dividend distribution is made on the date the loan is made, and its amount is determined by subtracting the net present value, using a specified discount rate, of the payment due to the corporation from the amount of the loan; the imputed interest payments are treated as occurring over the term of the loan by applying OID principles, discussed in Chapter 3, Section 2.

In KTA-Tator, Inc. v. Commissioner, 108 T.C. 100 (1997), a corporation made advances to its shareholders to finance the construction of real estate projects owned by the shareholders. No interest was charged during the construction period and the amounts were recorded on corporate books as "advances." Upon completion of the construction period, the advances were converted to interest bearing loans with a specific amortization schedule. Under § 7872, the advances were treated as interest free demand shareholder loans during the construction period, resulting in the realization of interest income by the corporation without any deduction for the deemed dividend distributions to the shareholders.

In Rountree Cotton Co. v. Commissioner, 113 T.C. 422 (1999), aff'd by order, 12 Fed. Appx. 641 (10th Cir. 2001), the taxpayer corporation had four related shareholders, none of whom owned more than approximately one-third of its stock. The corporation made interest-free loans to another corporation and to four partnerships in which one or more of its shareholders and their relatives owned stock or partnership interests in varying amounts. The court held that § 7872 applies to indirect corporation to shareholder loans effected by loans from a corporation to other corporations or partnerships in which its shareholders own stock or partnership interests. The facts that no one shareholder of the lender corporation held a majority interest in the lender and also held an interest in the borrower, or that other related individuals owned interests, even a majority interest, in two of the partnerships, did not affect the applicability of § 7872.

5.   BARGAIN TRANSACTIONS

A sale of property to a shareholder at a price below fair market value results in the "bargain" element being taxed as a dividend. In Honigman v. Commissioner, 466 F.2d 69 (6th Cir.1972), the shareholder purchased a hotel from the corporation for $661,000. The IRS on audit took the position that the hotel was worth $1,300,000 and asserted the tax on the excess of that amount over the actual purchase price as a dividend. Appraisal evidence submitted at the trial showed a range of values between $625,000 and $1,300,000. The Tax Court, affirmed by the Court of Appeals, found the fair market value of the property was $830,000 and accordingly taxed $169,000 as a dividend. The Court of Appeals rejected the taxpayer's argument that in a bargain purchase situation there must be an intent to distribute a dividend before dividend characterization of the bargain element is possible.

[handwritten note in margin: Savings from bargain buy are taxed as dividends]

Leases of corporate property to shareholders at less than fair rental value similarly result in constructive dividends. A lease by a corporation to a stockholder of a theater at a rental obviously too low in view of the profits from the property was held to result in the profits being taxed to the corporation and then to the shareholder as a dividend. 58th Street Plaza Theatre, Inc. v. Commissioner, 195 F.2d 724 (2d Cir.1952).

A lease of the shareholder's property to the corporation for a rental in excess of fair rental value also gives rise to a constructive dividend. For example, in Lucas v. Commissioner, 71 T.C. 838 (1979), aff'd 657 F.2d 841 (6th Cir.1981), the shareholders leased a coal deposit from a third party for a royalty of 25 cents per ton and subleased the coal to another party who agreed to pay royalties of 50 cents per ton on coal sold to the lessors' wholly owned corporation and 25 cents per ton on coal sold to unrelated parties. The additional 25 cents per ton royalty on coal sold to the corporation was held to be a dividend from the corporation. Accord Omholt v. Commissioner, 60 T.C. 541 (1973) (Acq.) (excessive royalty payments).

Cox Enterprises Inc. v. Commissioner, T.C. Memo. 2009–134, demonstrates that not all transactions that result in a diminution of corporate assets necessarily result in constructive dividend treatment, but the case is very unusual and probably does not provide support for avoiding constructive dividend treatment except on substantially similar facts. In that case, a corporation that was a member of the Cox Enterprises affiliated group of corporations transferred the assets of a television station to a partnership in exchange for a majority interest in the partnership in a transaction that normally would be tax-free under § 721. Two family partnerships, the partners of which were beneficiaries of three trusts that together held a 98 percent majority interest in the Cox Enterprises parent corporation, contributed cash to the partnership and received minority interests. The IRS asserted that under § 311(b), the Cox Enterprises corporate group recognized gain on the transfer to the trusts of a portion of the partnership interest it received in exchange for the assets because the partnership interest received by the Cox Enterprises group member that transferred the assets was worth $60.5 million less than the value of the transferred assets. The IRS's theory was that to the extent of the excess value of the contributed assets, the Cox Enterprises group had made a constructive distributed distribution "for the benefit of" the shareholder trusts. On the taxpayer's motion for summary judgment, for purposes of the motion, the $60.5 million disparity between the value of the assets and the value of the partnership interest it received in return was admitted. The Tax Court found that the undisputed facts established that Cox Enterprises' primary purpose was not to provide an economic benefit to the family partnerships and, derivatively, to the shareholder trusts. In summarizing the applicable case law, the court quoted Gilbert v. Commissioner, 74 T.C. 60, 64 (1980): "'[T]ransfers between related corporations can result in constructive dividends to their common shareholder if they were made primarily for his benefit and if he received a direct or tangible benefit.' If the benefit to the shareholder is 'indirect or derivative in nature, there is no constructive dividend.'" Applying this legal standard to the factual conclusion, there was not a constructive dividend to the shareholder trusts, even though an economic benefit was conferred on the beneficiaries of the shareholder trusts. Accordingly, no gain was recognized under § 311(b). The court rejected the IRS's argument that to find a constructive dividend "it is only necessary to establish that appreciated assets left the corporate solution . . . , for the benefit of its Shareholder Trusts, to establish that there has been a distribution with respect to [the] Shareholder Trusts' stock to which section 311 applies."

6. INDIRECT BENEFITS TO SHAREHOLDERS: PAYMENTS TO SHAREHOLDER'S RELATIVES

6.1. *General*

Dist. to relative

A distribution of money or property to a relative of a shareholder that serves a personal purpose of the shareholder rather than a corporate business purpose can be a constructive dividend to the shareholder, even though the shareholder personally did not receive anything. See, e.g., Snyder v. Commissioner, T.C. Memo. 1983–692 (shareholder received constructive dividends as a result of use of corporation's automobiles by shareholder's daughters for nonbusiness purpose, payment by corporation to shareholder's son of salary in excess of the amount deductible under § 162(a)(1) as reasonable compensation, payment by corporation of credit card charges incurred by shareholder's son to pay living expenses while at college, and payment of alimony to shareholder's ex-wife). Constructive dividends of this nature arise most commonly when a corporation pays excessive compensation to a relative of a shareholder and the corporation's deduction is disallowed under § 162(a)(1). The distributee relative is then treated as having received a tax free gift, and the shareholder may be liable for a gift tax as well. See Caledonian Record Publishing Co., Inc. v. United States, 579 F.Supp. 449 (D.Vt.1983) (excessive compensation paid to the controlling shareholder's son was a gift to the son; the IRS did not assert deficiency against father based on constructive dividend theory). But see Smith v. Manning, 189 F.2d 345 (3d Cir.1951) (excessive salaries paid by father to daughters taxed to daughters as compensation, notwithstanding disallowance of father's deduction).

In Speer v. Commissioner, T.C. Memo. 1996–323, the Home Shopping Network entered into a contract for data processing services with a corporation wholly owned by the son of the HSN's majority shareholder. The contract provided for fees to the son's corporation equal to one percent of HSN's gross profits. Because the son actually designed data processing software, the contract was on arm's-length terms, important unrelated minority HSN shareholders did not object, believing it to be fair, and the contract served a valid business purpose, the court rejected the IRS's argument that a constructive dividend to the HSN majority shareholder resulted from the contract. In Lanier v. Commissioner, T.C. Memo 1998–7, the court held that there was no constructive dividend from a contribution to a political campaign committee supporting the shareholders' son. The campaign committee was a separate legal entity. As a result, the contribution did not satisfy any direct obligations of the shareholders' son, and the economic benefit of the contribution accrued to a legal entity distinct from the shareholders or their family.

A bargain sale of property to a relative of a shareholder will be a constructive dividend to the shareholder if the transaction occurred by virtue of the shareholder's position as a shareholder and was personally motivated, as opposed to being an arm's length bargain between the corporation and the shareholder's relative. In Baumer v. United States, 580 F.2d 863 (5th Cir.1978), a corporation granted to the sole shareholder's son an option to purchase an undivided one-half interest in a tract of land for an amount equal to approximately one-half of the corporation's cost. At that time the possibility of developing the tract was ripe. The consideration for the option was substantially below its fair market value. The transaction was motivated by the sole shareholder's desire to make recompense for having advised his son not to purchase the property at a time prior to its purchase by the corporation. The court held that the dividend occurred at the time the option was granted, but because the value of the option was unascertainable at that time, the open transaction doctrine should be applied. Thus, the option was valued with reference to the amount received by the son on the sale of the property immediately after the exercise of the option in a later year. The amount of the distribution was the price paid by the ultimate buyer, minus the sum of the amount paid by the son to acquire the option plus the amount paid by the son to purchase the property upon exercise of the option. The distribution was taxable to the father in the later year.

7. TRANSACTIONS BETWEEN RELATED CORPORATIONS

Transactions between commonly controlled corporations, for example, the lease or sale of property or the provision of services for inadequate consideration, the making of a loan, etc., may involve constructive dividend issues. Most cases involve loans between related corporations in which the IRS attempts to treat the entire loan as a constructive distribution by the "lender" to the controlling shareholder coupled with a capital contribution by the shareholder to the "borrower." Not all loans between related corporations are susceptible to such recharacterization. The "loan" first must be found not to constitute bona fide indebtedness. Even then, a constructive dividend to the shareholder will be found only if the shareholder receives a direct benefit, distinct from an indirect benefit as a shareholder, from the making of the loan.

Transfers that discharge an obligation of the shareholder generally are found to serve a shareholder purpose. See, e.g., Gilbert v. Commissioner, 74 T.C. 60 (1980) (purported loan the proceeds of which were used to redeem stock of other 50 percent shareholder was constructive dividend to continuing shareholder); Stinnett's Pontiac Service, Inc. v. Commissioner, 730 F.2d 634 (11th Cir.1984) (loan to related corporation satisfying common shareholder's obligation to make additional capital contributions to "borrower" corporation was a constructive dividend). Transfers to a related corporation that serve a corporate business purpose generally escape constructive dividend treatment. See, e.g., Magnon v. Commissioner, 73 T.C. 980 (1980) (Acq.) (no constructive dividend because loan was bona fide and for purpose of improving relations with lender's largest customer, who desired that common shareholder of lender and borrower establish new, separate business); Mills v. Internal Revenue Service, 840 F.2d 229 (4th Cir.1988) (no constructive dividend because purpose of loan was to further financial stability of integrated business conducted through related corporations). In Davis v. Commissioner, T.C. Memo. 1995–283, the court articulated a four factor test to determine whether a purported loan from one corporation to another commonly controlled corporation is a constructive dividend to the common shareholder: (1) Was the common shareholder able to use the transferor as a source of risk capital for the transferee without using his or her personal resources; (2) could the common shareholder carry on a business with extremely thin capitalization without having his or her personal funds subordinated to the transferee's indebtedness; (3) was the value of the common shareholder's equity interest in the transferee enhanced by the transfer; and (4) was the common shareholder relieved of potential liability on personal guarantees or loans made to the transferee that were repaid with the transferred funds?

A sale of property from one commonly controlled corporation to another at less than an arm's-length price may be treated as if the selling corporation had made a distribution in an amount equal to the bargain element to its shareholders who in turn contributed that amount to the capital of the buying corporation. Rev.Rul. 69–630, 1969–2 C.B. 112, held that this result automatically followed if as a result of a tax avoidance transaction, § 482 was applied to reallocate income between the related corporations to reflect an arm's-length price. The case law usually has applied this approach when there has been an intentional diversion of funds from one corporation to the other. See Sparks Nugget, Inc. v. Commissioner, 458 F.2d 631 (9th Cir.1972) (constructive dividend found in a case where excessive rentals were paid in a transaction between related corporations); Arnold v. Commissioner, T.C. Memo. 1994–97 (constructive dividend to the owner of commonly controlled corporations resulted from a sale and leaseback between corporations at a bargain price because the transaction was structured to benefit the shareholder). Contra, White Tool and Machine Co. v. Commissioner, T.C. Memo. 1980–443, aff'd 677 F.2d 528 (6th Cir.1982) (no constructive dividend to common shareholder although corporation paid excessive rent to related corporation; reallocation of income under § 482 was adequate remedy).

Rev.Rul. 78–83, 1978–1 C.B. 79, involving the diversion of funds from one sister corporation to another to avoid foreign exchange control restrictions, indicated that the "constructive distribution-contribution to capital" analysis applies even though there was no motive to allocate income or deductions improperly.

SECTION 5.   INTERCORPORATE DIVIDENDS

INTERNAL REVENUE CODE: Sections 243(a), (b)(1) and (2), (c); 246(c); 246A; 301(e); 1059.

Corporate shareholders of domestic corporations may in effect exclude all or a portion of dividend income they receive. Prior to 1936 all intercorporate dividends were excluded in full. Taxation of a portion of intercorporate dividends was introduced in that year, reflecting a general policy in the early 1930's of discouraging complicated corporate structures. Under current law, however, the tax on intercorporate dividends affects primarily investments in public corporations by other corporations. These investments generally have little to do with corporate operating structures.

Without some exclusion, successive taxation of a dividend as it passed from corporation to corporation in a chain of corporations would result in multiple taxation of the dividend and leave very little for the ultimate individual shareholder. However, if the corporate shareholder has an insubstantial degree of ownership or control of the distributing corporation the argument in favor of relief from corporate taxation of dividend income is not as strong. For example, if a corporation has excess cash to invest on a short-term basis, it can be argued that the tax treatment of the corporation's investment return should not depend on whether the short-term investment is in portfolio stock or certificates of deposit. On the other hand, interest is deductible by the payor and dividends are not, so that if one believes that there should be only one tax imposed as long as earnings remain in corporate solution, the dividends received deduction is appropriate even in short-term investment situations.

If one corporation owns 80 percent or more of the voting stock and 80 percent or more in value of the stock of another corporation (excluding certain nonvoting, limited and preferred stock), these affiliated corporations may file a consolidated return, which eliminates dividends paid by the subsidiary to the parent in computing their consolidated taxable income. See I.R.C. §§ 1501–1505. See Chapter 9, Section 2. If affiliated corporations choose not to file consolidated returns, the parent nevertheless may deduct an amount equal to all dividends received from the subsidiary, subject to the conditions and limitations of § 243(b). See I.R.C. § 243(a)(2); Treas.Reg. § 1.243–4.

For many years prior to the 1986 Act, § 243(a) granted a deduction equal to 85 percent of intercorporate dividends received by any corporation that did not elect to file a consolidated return or qualify for the 100 percent deduction under § 243(b). The 1986 Act reduced this intercorporate dividend received deduction to 80 percent. The 1987 Act further amended § 243(a) and added § 243(c), thereby reducing the intercorporate dividend deduction to 70 percent for corporations that do not own 20 percent or more (in value and voting power) of the distributing corporation's stock. Thus, a higher rate of tax is imposed on dividends received on what might be broadly viewed as "portfolio" investments.

The maximum rate of tax on intercorporate dividends generally is 10.5 percent (35 percent times the 30 percent of the dividend included in income). However, the dividend received deduction creates a difference between earnings and profits and taxable income, thus potentially bringing the alternative minimum tax (AMT) into play even for corporations qualifying for a 100 percent dividend received deduction. See I.R.C. §§ 55 and 56(g), discussed at page 9. If the AMT applies, the maximum tax rate on intercorporate dividends is somewhat higher than under the regular tax.

The availability of the intercorporate dividend deduction creates a variety of tax arbitrage opportunities for corporations. Statutory provisions designed to limit the tax arbitrage benefits of transactions structured to take advantage of the dividends received deduction are explored in the following material.

DETAILED ANALYSIS

1. DEBT FINANCED PORTFOLIO STOCK

One tax arbitrage situation involves debt-financed acquisitions of dividend-paying stock. For example, X Corporation borrows $1,000,000, agreeing to pay 10 percent interest, and purchases, at par, $1,000,000 of preferred stock paying annual dividends of 10 percent. X Corporation will realize no pretax gain or loss because the interest expense equals the dividend income. However, if the interest paid to finance the acquisition and 70 percent of the dividends received from the debt-financed portfolio stock are both deductible, then the corporation will have an after-tax profit, even if the stock does not increase in value, because it will recognize income of $100,000, but claim $170,000 of deductions. For example, if X Corporation were in the 35 percent marginal tax bracket, the excess deductions would yield tax savings of $24,500 (35 percent $70,000).

Section 246A reduces the intercorporate dividend received deduction by the percentage of the corporation's portfolio stock that was debt financed during the applicable measuring period.[9] Thus, for example, if the

---

[9] H Enterprises International, Inc. v. Commissioner, T.C. Memo. 1998–97, held that § 246A may be applied in cases in which one member of an affiliated group of corporations incurs the borrowing and another member of the group purchases the portfolio stock. In that case a subsidiary corporation borrowed funds that it then distributed to its parent corporation, which in turn used the distributed loan proceeds to purchase the portfolio stock.

acquisition is three-quarters debt financed, the dividends received deduction is reduced by 75 percent. The dividends received deduction is never reduced, however, by an amount in excess of the interest deduction attributable to the debt that financed the portfolio stock. Section 246A(c)(2) defines "portfolio stock" in such a way that the provision generally does not apply to dividends received by a corporation that owns stock representing at least 50 percent of the total value and the total voting power of the outstanding stock of the distributing corporation. Section 246A also does not apply to dividends paid by certain closely-held corporations.

In OBH, Inc. v. United States, 397 F.Supp.2d 1148 (D. Neb. 2005), the court refused to apply § 246A to reduce OBH's (a subsidiary of Berkshire Hathaway) § 243 dividend received deduction with respect to dividends received on its portfolio stock investments, because the court found that OBH's indebtedness was not directly traceable to its acquisition of dividend-paying stock. Although an IRS agent testified that he was able to trace loan proceeds to stock purchases, the court concluded that there was no direct or immediate connection between the funds that OBH borrowed and the stock it purchased, and that the agent's findings were based on arbitrary allocations of funds among numerous transactions over a period of several months. The court's conclusion was reinforced by its acceptance as credible of Warren Buffett's uncontradicted testimony that the dominant purpose in incurring the indebtedness was to increase and fortify the corporation's capital base, and that at the time the taxpayer engaged in the borrowing transactions, Buffett, who personally made the investment decisions, did not know how the debt proceeds would be invested.

Is the problem addressed by § 246A created by the dividends received deduction or by the interest deduction? Compare the approach adopted in § 279, discussed at page 498, which disallows the interest deduction for certain acquisition indebtedness.

2. DIVIDEND-RELATED LOSSES: MINIMUM HOLDING PERIOD

A corporation's basis in stock generally is unaffected by the receipt of an intercorporate dividend. Section 301(c)(2) requires a reduction in basis for the portion of a distribution that is not a dividend and, therefore, is treated as a return of capital. However, § 301(c)(2) does not apply to the untaxed portion of intercorporate dividends. The intercorporate dividend deduction is intended to prevent double taxation at the corporate level, and reducing basis by the amount of the deduction would only postpone the exaction of such double tax.

Arguably, however, the intercorporate dividend deduction coupled with short-term holding of stock purchased in anticipation of receiving a dividend creates inappropriate tax arbitrage benefits. For example, suppose X Corporation realized a $500,000 capital gain and no offsetting capital loss during its current tax year. Shortly before the end of its taxable year, X Corporation purchases 10,000 shares of Z Corporation stock for $1,000,000. Before the close of its taxable year, X Corporation (1) receives a $200,000 dividend on its Z Corporation shares, and (2) sells its Z Corporation shares for $800,000 (the value of the shares having declined as a result of the dividend). X Corporation realizes a $200,000 loss on disposition of the Z Corporation shares because its basis in the stock was not reduced by the intercorporate dividend received. This transaction is uneconomic because the dividend income is offset by the resulting capital loss. However, X

Corporation pays tax at an effective rate of 10.5 percent on the $200,000 intercorporate dividend received (resulting in a tax of $21,000), while using the loss to offset a $200,000 capital gain that otherwise would have been taxed at the rate of 35 percent (saving $70,000 of tax). Thus, the transaction produces an after-tax benefit of $49,000.

Section 246(c) is aimed at such transactions and provides that the dividends received deduction is not allowed with respect to any dividends on any share of stock that is held for less than 46 days during the 91 day period beginning on the date that is 45 days before the date on which the stock becomes ex-dividend. (Under stock exchange rules, stock generally becomes ex-dividend three business days before the "record date" for paying dividends.) For preferred stock, if the dividends received are attributable to a period in excess of 366 days, the minimum holding period is extended to 91 days during the 181 day period beginning on the date that is 90 days before the date on which the stock becomes ex-dividend.

Section 246(c)(4) tolls the taxpayer's holding period of stock for any period in which its risk of loss is diminished through a put option, contract to sell, or short position. See Treas.Reg. § 1.246–5. In Progressive Corp. v. United States, 970 F.2d 188 (6th Cir.1992), the taxpayer acquired stock in anticipation of dividend distributions, and simultaneously held both put and call options on the stock at the same strike price. The taxpayer also acquired stock ex-dividend and simultaneously held in-the-money call options on the stock. The Sixth Circuit held that the taxpayer's holding period was tolled under § 246(c)(3) during the period it held the options. The District Court had misapplied Treas.Reg. § 1.246–3(d)(2) by concluding that the holding period is tolled only when the taxpayer is in a true "short position," i.e., had borrowed and sold the stock and did not own any similar shares with which to satisfy its outstanding obligation to return a like number of shares.

Debt-equity classification issues can be important under 246(c). Rev.Rul. 94–28, 1994–1 C.B. 86, involved an instrument that was classified as debt for state corporate law purposes but as stock for federal income tax purposes. The instrument provided for a payment of a fixed amount on a stated date. Accordingly, the corporate purchaser of this instrument had an "option to sell" or was under a "contractual obligation to sell" within the meaning of § 246(c)(4)(A). Thus, the 45–day holding period of § 246A(c)(1)(A) was stayed.

Would it be preferable to approach the basic problem addressed by § 243(c) by denying the loss deduction if the purchase and sale are closely related in time to a dividend payment?

3. BASIS REDUCTION FOR EXTRAORDINARY DIVIDENDS

3.1. *General*

Congress considered § 246(c) to be inadequate to deal with the tax avoidance possibilities created by the availability of the dividends received deduction for extraordinarily large dividends. If an extraordinary dividend was expected to be paid on stock of another corporation, the corporation owning the stock would be willing to hold the stock for the period required to avoid the limitation in § 246(c). In response, Congress enacted § 1059, which it justified as follows:

> When a stock pays an extraordinary dividend, the acquisition of the stock often may be viewed as the acquisition of two assets: the right to the distributions to be made with respect to the stock and the underlying stock itself. In instances in which the acquisition of stock is the acquisition of two assets, the committee concludes that it is appropriate to reduce the basis of the underlying stock to reflect the value of the distribution not taxed to the corporate distributee. In the committee's view, the failure of [prior] law to apply a two-asset analysis in cases of extraordinary distributions when the taxpayer's holding period in the stock is short, leads to tax arbitrage opportunities * * *.

H.Rep. No. 98–342, 98th Cong., 2d Sess. 1186 (1984).

Section 1059 requires that a corporate shareholder that receives an "extraordinary dividend" on stock that it has not held for more than two years before the dividend announcement date must reduce the basis of the stock (but not below zero) by the amount of the untaxed portion of the dividend. This basis reduction is treated as occurring at the beginning of the ex-dividend date of the extraordinary dividend. I.R.C. § 1059(d)(1). To the extent that the untaxed portion of any extraordinary dividend exceeds the shareholder's basis for the stock, the excess is taxed as gain on the sale of the stock in the taxable year in which the extraordinary dividend is received (in addition to gain otherwise recognized). I.R.C. § 1059(a)(2). The amount by which the basis of the stock is reduced is intended to represent the portion of the cost of the "two assets" allocated to the extraordinary dividend. The "basis" of the extraordinary dividend is never recovered because the dividends received deduction is allowed in its place. Because there is no untaxed portion of the dividend if § 246(c) applies, § 1059 operates only if the holding period requirement for avoiding § 246(c) has been met.

Section 1059(c) defines an extraordinary dividend in terms of the size of the dividend in relation to the shareholder's adjusted basis in its stock (after taking into any account prior basis reductions under § 1059), subject to an alternative test using fair market value instead of basis at the taxpayer's election. (For the application of the alternative test, see Rev.Rul. 88–49, 1988–1 C.B. 297.) A dividend is extraordinary if aggregate dividends received in any 85 day period exceed 10 percent of the basis of common stock, or 5 percent of the basis of preferred stock, with respect to which the dividends were paid. Furthermore, if aggregate dividends paid with respect to stock in any one year period exceed 20 percent of the corporate shareholder's basis for the stock, then all such dividends are aggregated and considered to be an extraordinary dividend.

Section 1059(e)(1) treats certain distributions as *per se* extraordinary dividends. This rule applies to any distribution (without regard to the holding period for the stock or the relative magnitude of the distribution) to a corporate shareholder in partial liquidation of the distributing corporation (as defined in § 302(e), discussed at page 261). Any redemption of stock that is non-pro rata (irrespective of the holding period of the stock or the relative size of the distribution) is treated as an extraordinary dividend.[10] Finally, § 1059(f) treats as extraordinary all dividends on

---

[10] Stock redemptions that are treated as dividends as a result of option attribution under § 318(a)(4), see page 238, also are *per se* extraordinary dividends, as are distributions in

preferred stock if according to the terms of the stock the dividend rate declines over time or the issue price exceeds the liquidation or redemption value.

3.2. *Exceptions*

There are a number of exceptions to § 1059. Section 1059(d)(6) generally exempts from the rules of § 1059 distributions to a corporate shareholder that has held the stock of the distributing corporation for the entire period the distributing corporation (and any predecessor corporation) has been in existence. Section 1059(e)(2) provides that the basis reduction rules do not apply to distributions between members of an affiliated group filing consolidated returns or to distributions that constitute qualifying dividends within the meaning of § 243(b)(1), except to the extent the dividends are attributable to pre-affiliation earnings or appreciation of the payor corporation. The § 1059(d)(6) and § 1059(e)(2) exceptions do not apply, however, to distributions in partial liquidations or non-pro rata redemptions treated as extraordinary dividends under § 1059(e)(1). Treas.Reg. § 1.1059(e)–1.

3.3. *Special Rules for Preferred Stock*

Under the general rule a preferred stock that pays a dividend of 5 percent or more within any period of 85 days or less is paying an extraordinary dividend. Thus, a 5 percent preferred stock dividend that is paid once annually would be extraordinary. On the other hand, a preferred stock that paid four quarterly 4.9 percent dividends, which on an annual basis is a substantially higher percentage, would not be subject to a basis adjustment under the general rule. To provide relief for preferred stock like the 5 percent preferred stock in the above example, § 1059(e)(3) applies a special rule to preferred stock that pays dividends at a fixed rate not less often than annually, provided the stock was not purchased when dividends were in arrears. If the taxpayer holds the stock for more than 5 years, no dividends received by the shareholder will be treated as extraordinary dividends, and therefore no basis reduction will be required, if during the period the shareholder held the stock the dividend rate did not exceed an annualized rate of 15 percent of the lower of (a) the taxpayer's adjusted basis or (b) the liquidation preference of the stock. However, if the actual rate of return from dividends on qualifying preferred stock during this period exceeds 15 percent, no relief is available and all of the dividends are extraordinary dividends.

If the corporate taxpayer does not hold the stock for 5 years, dividends announced during the two year period after the purchase (but not thereafter) are extraordinary to the extent they exceed the dividends "earned" by the taxpayer. I.R.C. § 1059(e)(3)(A)(ii). To determine whether the taxpayer's dividends received exceed the dividends it earned, the taxpayer's "actual dividend rate" is computed. The actual dividend rate is the average annual amount of dividends received (or deemed received under § 305 or any other provision) during the period the taxpayer owned the stock, computed as a return on the taxpayer's adjusted basis or, if less,

---

corporate reorganizations that are treated as dividends due to option attribution. The purpose of these two rules is to prevent the use of options to cause a distribution to a corporate shareholder that would otherwise result in sale or exchange treatment to benefit from the dividends received deduction.

the stock's liquidation preference. This is then compared to the stock's "stated dividend rate," which is the return represented by the annual fixed preferred dividends payable on the stock. If the actual dividend rate exceeds the stated dividend rate, a portion of each dividend received or deemed received will be an extraordinary dividend, and basis will be reduced by the untaxed portion of such dividend. The Conference Committee Report, Tax Reform Act of 1986, H.Rep. No. 99–841, 99th Cong., 2d Sess., Vol. II, 165 (1986) provides the following example of this determination:

> [A]ssume that on January 1, 1987, a corporation purchases for $1,000 ten shares of preferred stock having a liquidation preference of $100 per share and paying fixed preferred dividends of $6 per share to shareholders of record on March 31 and September 30 of each year. If the taxpayer does not elect to have the special rule apply, the basic rule would generally require the taxpayer to reduce the basis in the stock by the untaxed portion of each dividend received prior to the expiration of the two-year holding period. This is because a dividend exceeding 5 percent of adjusted basis (or fair market value, if shown to the satisfaction of the Secretary) paid semi-annually is an extraordinary dividend under the general rule. However, [the] special rule will apply to the preferred stock. Under this provision, the taxpayer's stated dividend rate is 12 percent ($12/$100). If the taxpayer sells the stock on October 1, 1988, (after holding the stock for 1.75 years) and no dividends in excess of the fixed preferred dividends have been paid, its actual dividend rate will be 13.7 percent ($240/$1,000 divided by 1.75). This 13.7 percent exceeds the 12 percent stated dividend rate by 1.7. This excess, as a fraction of the actual dividend rate, is 12.4 percent (1.7 divided by 13.7). Accordingly, each of the dividends will be treated as an extraordinary dividend described in § 1059(a) to the extent of 0.74 per share ($6 × 12.4 percent). However, if the corporation does not sell the stock until January 1, 1989, and no dividends in excess of the fixed preferred dividends have been paid, its "actual dividend rate" will be 12 percent ($240/$1000 divided by 2.0). This does not exceed the stated dividend rate; accordingly, no portion of any dividend will be treated as an extraordinary dividend.

4.   EARNINGS AND PROFITS RECALCULATION FOR DISTRIBUTIONS TO TWENTY PERCENT CORPORATE SHAREHOLDER

Section 301(e) provides a special rule for determining the portion of any distribution that is not a dividend to a corporate shareholder holding at least 20 percent, by either voting power or value, of the stock of the distributing corporation. When § 301(e) applies, earnings and profits of the distributing corporation are computed without regard to § 312(n), discussed at page 194, except the adjustments described in § 312(n)(7), relating to redemptions of corporate stock are taken into account. Section 312(n), in general, requires that certain income items that are deferred for purposes of computing taxable income, be taken into account in an earlier year in computing earnings and profits. Thus, the effect of § 301(e) is to convert a distribution that otherwise might have been wholly a dividend, subject to the intercorporate dividends received deduction, into a return of capital under § 301(c)(2), reducing the distributee's basis in its stock of the distributing corporation, or giving rise to a gain under § 301(c)(3). This narrow provision is aimed at certain manipulative devices involving the distribution of an extraordinary dividend followed by the sale of subsidiary stock after the subsidiary has realized an economic gain but before the subsidiary's corresponding taxable gain has been recognized, such as in the case of an installment sale under § 453. See H.Rep. No. 98–861, 98th Cong., 1st Sess. 842 (1984).

5.   DIVIDENDS DISTRIBUTED IN CONNECTION WITH THE SALE OF A CORPORATE BUSINESS

When a subsidiary corporation pays a dividend to its parent shortly before the sale of the stock of the subsidiary by the parent, the issue arises whether the distribution is a dividend eligible for the dividends received deduction under § 243 or is to be treated as a portion of the amount realized on the sale of the stock, and, therefore, ineligible for the deduction. The result can differ depending on the facts and circumstances surrounding the distribution. This matter is discussed in detail at page 517.

CHAPTER 5

STOCK REDEMPTIONS

SECTION 1.   INTRODUCTION

INTERNAL REVENUE CODE: Sections 302(a), (b)(1)–(4), (c)(1), (d), (e); 311; 317; 318.

REGULATIONS: Sections 1.302–1(a), –2.

When a shareholder sells stock back to the issuing corporation, it is necessary to determine whether the transaction more nearly resembles a sale of stock or a dividend distribution. If the transaction is thought more nearly to resemble a sale, the shareholder should be entitled to a recovery of basis with respect to the surrendered shares and capital gain or loss treatment. Since liquidating distributions generally are entitled to capital gain treatment under § 331, similar treatment clearly is appropriate if all of a shareholder's shares are sold back to the issuing corporation. Such treatment likewise appears to be appropriate if the shareholder's voting power and right to earnings are substantially reduced. But if there is no significant change in the voting rights or the share of earnings of the corporation to which a shareholder is entitled, the distribution is more like a normal dividend distribution and ordinary income treatment for the entire amount received, with no return of capital aspect, is appropriate.

Section 302(a) distinguishes those sales of stock back to the issuing corporation that are entitled to sale or exchange treatment, thus resulting in capital gain or loss, from those that more nearly resemble dividends. Section 302(a) provides that a redemption distribution to a shareholder is a "payment in exchange for the stock" if the transaction meets one of the tests of § 302(b). If the transaction does not meet one of those tests, then the amounts distributed by the corporation in redemption of the stock are treated by § 302(d) as distributions of property under § 301, and, if earnings and profits are present, constitute dividend distributions.

Historically, the stakes turning on the classification of a redemption under these rules were high as far as individual shareholders were concerned. Dividend treatment swept the entire distribution under the rates applicable to ordinary income. Redemption treatment resulted in no income to the extent of the shareholder's basis in the redeemed shares and taxation of the excess as capital gain, which could be offset by capital losses and which could be subject to tax at a lower preferential rate to the extent of net long-term capital gains for the taxable year.

Under current law, dividends received by noncorporate shareholder-taxpayers are taxed at the same rates as apply to long-term capital gains. The significance of characterizing a distribution as a dividend, on the one hand, or as a redemption, on the other hand, is greatly reduced under this approach. For a noncorporate shareholder receiving the distribution, the only important differences are that (1) all of a dividend distribution is includable in gross income, while only the

231

amount by which a redemption distribution exceeds the basis of the stock with respect to which the distribution has been made is includable, and (2) gains on redemption distributions can be offset by capital losses, while dividend income can be offset by capital losses only to a very limited extent under § 1211.

If the redeemed shareholder is a corporation, the consequences turning on characterization under § 302 can be important because dividend characterization qualifies the distribution for the intercorporate dividends received deduction under § 243 (see page 223), but the gain on a redemption (which is the distribution reduced by the basis of the redeemed stock) is taxed in full. If the redeemed corporate shareholder's basis for the redeemed stock is less than the dividend received deduction, dividend characterization results in less current tax liability than § 302 redemption characterization. Assume, for example, that X Corporation owns less than 20 percent of the stock of Y Corporation (and thus is eligible for the 70 percent dividends received deduction under § 243) and 10 shares of Y Corporation owned by X Corporation, having a basis of $60, are redeemed for $100. If § 302(a) applies, X Corporation recognizes a $40 gain, taxed at normal corporate tax rates (generally 35 percent). But if § 302(a) does not apply, and the $100 distribution is taxed as a dividend, after the resulting $70 dividend received deduction, only $30 is taxed at normal corporate tax rates. Thus, X Corporation would prefer the distribution to be characterized as a dividend. However, a disproportionate redemption that does not qualify for sale or exchange treatment under § 302(b), and which therefore is eligible for the § 243 dividends received deduction, is an extraordinary dividend with respect to which the basis of any remaining stock must be reduced under § 1059.

Subsections (b)(2) and (3) furnish two reasonably specific rules for identifying a redemption eligible for sale or exchange treatment: the § 302(b)(2) test of a substantially disproportionate redemption applicable if the particular shareholder retains some stock after the redemption, with the degree of disproportion specified in mathematical terms; and the § 302(b)(3) termination test applicable if all of the stock of the particular shareholder is redeemed. If these tests are not met, resort must be made to the vague, and possibly subjective, test of § 302(b)(1)—a redemption is treated as a capital transaction if it is not essentially equivalent to a dividend. In applying all three of these tests, shareholders are treated as owning not only those shares of stock actually owned by them, but also any shares in the corporation owned by certain family members and related entities. See I.R.C. §§ 302(c)(1), 318; Treas.Reg. § 1.301–1(a).

In addition, § 302(b)(4) provides that a redemption of stock held by an individual shareholder in partial liquidation of the corporation will be entitled to exchange treatment. Unlike §§ 302(b)(1) through (b)(3), which are applied by examining the effect of the distribution at the shareholder level, § 302(b)(4) examines the distribution from the perspective of the distributing corporation to determine whether a reduction in the size of the corporation justifies exchange treatment for the shareholders.

Finally, § 303, which is intended to relieve the perceived hardship of treating redemptions to pay estate taxes as a dividend, permits exchange treatment with respect to redemptions of certain stock held by a deceased shareholder's estate even though § 302(b) is inapplicable.

DETAILED ANALYSIS

1. EFFECT ON EARNINGS AND PROFITS

The impact on earnings and profits of a redemption distribution subject to § 302 is important because any reduction in earnings and profits caused by the distribution will reduce the potential "pool" of earnings and profits available for subsequent distributions taxable as dividends under §§ 301 and 316. If a redemption fails to qualify under § 302(a) and is treated as a § 301 distribution, earnings and profits are reduced under § 312(a) by the amount of the distribution. Calculating the reduction in earnings and profits is more complicated if the redemption qualifies for exchange treatment under § 302(a) or § 303.

Section 312(f) provides that if a distribution qualifies as a redemption under § 302(a) the amount by which earnings and profits is reduced for the distribution "shall be an amount which is not in excess of the ratable share of the earnings and profits of such corporation * * * attributable to the stock so redeemed." Assume, for example, that a corporation with $100,000 of earnings and profits redeemed 10 percent of its stock for $15,000. The maximum charge to earnings and profits is $10,000—ten percent of the total earnings and profits. The remaining $5,000 of the redemption proceeds represented payment for unrealized appreciation in the corporation's assets. That $5,000 should not reduce earnings and profits because the economic gains that it represented had not previously been taken into earnings and profits.

This formula ignores the amount of paid-in capital attributable to the redeemed stock on the corporation's books, which theoretically should be taken into account to reduce the amount by which earnings and profits is reduced. If this approach were followed and if in the preceding example the paid-in capital with respect to the stock had been $6,000, only $9,000 of the distribution would reduce earnings and profits. This charge to capital approach was followed in former § 312(e) before its repeal and replacement by § 312(n)(7) in 1984. See Rev.Rul. 70–531, 1970–2 C.B. 76, revoked by Rev.Rul. 79–376, 1979–2 C.B. 113.

The legislative history of § 312(n)(7) provides some guidelines for dealing with certain situations where the application of the statute is unclear. First, no amount of earnings and profits generally should be attributable to nonconvertible preferred stock, unless the distribution includes dividend arrearages. H.Rep. No. 98–861, 98th Cong., 2d Sess. 840 (1984). Presumably, however, the amount of any redemption premium might reduce earnings and profits. Second, earnings and profits are not reduced by more than the amount distributed. S.Rep. No. 98–169, 98th Cong., 2d Sess. 202 (1984). Thus, for example, if a corporation with $100,000 of accumulated earnings and profits redeemed 10 percent of its stock for $9,500, the *maximum* charge to earnings and profits would be $9,500. However, if the stock, again representing paid-in capital of $1,000, were redeemed in exchange for property having a basis of $12,000 and a fair market value of $9,500, § 312(a)(3) appears to permit earnings and profits to be reduced by $11,000; the additional $2,500 reduction in

Revenue Ruling 87-88

1987–2 C.B. 81.

ISSUE

If shares of both voting and nonvoting common stock are redeemed from a shareholder in one transaction, are the two classes aggregated for purposes of applying the substantially disproportionate requirement in section 302(b)(2)(C) of the Internal Revenue Code?

FACTS

X Corporation had outstanding 10 shares of voting common stock and 30 shares of nonvoting common stock. The fair market values of a share of voting common stock and a share of nonvoting common stock are approximately equal. A owned 6 shares of X voting common stock and all the nonvoting common stock. The remaining 4 shares of the X voting common stock were held by persons unrelated to A within the meaning of section 318(a) of the Code.

X redeemed 3 shares of voting common stock and 27 shares of nonvoting common stock from A in a single transaction. Thereafter, A owned 3 shares of X voting common stock and 3 shares of nonvoting common stock. The ownership of the remaining 4 shares of X voting common stock was unchanged.

LAW AND ANALYSIS

If a distribution in redemption of stock qualifies under section 302(b)(2) of the Code as substantially disproportionate, the distribution is treated under section 302(a) as a payment in exchange for the stock redeemed.

Under section 302(b)(2)(B) and (C) of the Code, a distribution is substantially disproportionate if (i) the shareholder owns less than 50 percent of the total combined voting power of the corporation immediately after the redemption, (ii) immediately after the redemption the ratio of voting stock owned by the shareholder to all the voting stock of the corporation is less than 80 percent of the same ratio immediately before the redemption, and (iii) immediately after the redemption the ratio of common stock owned by the shareholder to all of the common stock of the corporation (whether voting or nonvoting) is less than 80 percent of the same ratio immediately before the redemption.

Under section 302(b)(2)(C) of the Code, if more than one class of common stock is outstanding, the determination in (iii) above is made by reference to fair market value. Section 302(b)(2) applies to a redemption of both voting stock and other stock (although not to the redemption solely of nonvoting stock). Section 1.302–3(a) of the Income Tax Regulations.

With regard to requirements (i) and (ii) described above, after the redemption, A owned less than 50 percent of the voting power of X (43 percent), and A's voting power was reduced to less than 80 percent of the percentage of voting power in X that A owned before the redemption (from 60 percent to 43 percent for a reduction to 72 percent of the preredemption level).

With regard to requirement (iii) above, section 302(b)(2)(C) of the Code provides that, if there is more than one class of common stock outstanding, the fair market value of all of the common stock (voting and nonvoting) will govern the determination of whether there has been the requisite reduction in common stock ownership. The fact that this test is based on fair market value and is applied by reference to all of the common stock of the corporation suggests that the requirement concerning reduction in common stock ownership is to be applied on an aggregate basis rather than on a class-by-class basis. Thus, the fact that A has no reduction in interest with regard to the nonvoting common stock and continues to own 100 percent of this stock does not prevent the redemption of this class of stock from qualifying under section 302(b)(2) when the whole transaction meets section 302(b)(2) requirements. To conclude otherwise would require that, notwithstanding a redemption of one class of common stock in an amount sufficient to reduce the shareholder's aggregate common stock ownership by more than 20 percent in value, every other class of common stock owned by the shareholder must be subject to a redemption.

Prior to the redemption, A owned 90 percent of the total fair market value of all the outstanding X common stock (36 out of the 40 shares of voting and nonvoting common stock). After the redemption, A owned 60 percent of the total fair market value of all the X common stock (6 out of 10 shares). The reduction in ownership (from 90 percent to 60 percent) was a reduction to less than 80 percent of the fraction that A previously owned of the total fair market value of all the X common stock.

HOLDING

If more than one class of common stock is outstanding, the provisions of section 302(b)(2)(C) of the Code are applied in an aggregate and not a class-by-class manner. Accordingly, the redemption by X of 3 shares of voting common stock and 27 shares of nonvoting common stock qualifies as substantially disproportionate within the meaning of section 302(b)(2), even though A continues to own 100 percent of the outstanding nonvoting common stock.

DETAILED ANALYSIS

1. REDEMPTION OF STOCK OTHER THAN VOTING COMMON STOCK

Under Treas.Reg. § 1.302–3, a redemption of either common or preferred non-voting stock may qualify under § 302(b)(2) only if there is a simultaneous redemption of voting stock. A redemption of non-voting stock (preferred or common) alone, however, may not qualify under § 302(b)(2); such a transaction is governed by § 302(b)(1) and § 302(b)(3).

The next to last sentence of § 302(b)(2)(C) does not require that common stock be redeemed in all cases. Rev.Rul. 81–41, 1981–1 C.B. 121, held that § 302(b)(2) could apply to a redemption solely of voting preferred stock if the shareholder did not own any common stock before or after the redemption. If the shareholder owns common stock, however, even if nonvoting, sufficient common stock to meet the 80 percent test must be redeemed along with sufficient voting stock, whether common or preferred, to meet the 50 percent test. There is no requirement that after the redemption the shareholder hold less than 50 percent of the *value* of the common stock.

2.   CONSTRUCTIVE STOCK OWNERSHIP

Under § 302(c)(1), the attribution of stock ownership rules of § 318(a) respecting closely related family members and entities are applicable in determining whether the § 302(b)(2) tests have been met; the proportionate or disproportionate character of the distribution is tested by reference to the entire group of related parties. The network of attributed ownership can be quite wide under § 318(a). The attribution rules primarily deal with four situations:

(1) Section 318(a)(1) attributes stock ownership between *family members* standing in the specified familial relationships;

(2) Section 318(a)(2) attributes the ownership of stock held by *entities*—partnerships, estates, trusts, and corporations respectively—to the partners, beneficiaries, and shareholders owning 50 percent or more of the stock of a corporation;

(3) Section 318(a)(3) attributes stock owned by a partner, beneficiary, or shareholder owning 50 percent or more of the stock of a corporation to the "entity" if the stipulated relationships are present;

(4) Section 318(a)(4) treats a taxpayer as owning any stock that the taxpayer has an option to purchase.

In applying these rules, § 318(a)(5)(A) treats stock that is *constructively* owned by virtue of the application of the attribution rules as if it were *actually owned* for the purpose of reattribution. Thus, for example, if A is the beneficiary of a trust, stock owned by the trust would be attributed to A under § 318(a)(2)(B). Under § 318(a)(5)(A) that stock would then be considered as actually owned by A for "reattributing" the stock to A's parents under § 318(a)(1).

There are, however, some limits to the reattribution of constructively owned stock. Section 318(a)(5)(B) provides that the stock constructively owned by virtue of the application of the family attribution rules will not be considered as actually owned for purposes of its reattribution under those rules. Thus, pursuant to § 318(a)(5)(C), stock owned by A that is attributed to A's parents under § 318(a)(1) will not be reattributed through A's parents to A's brother or sister (there is no direct attribution between siblings). Similarly, if stock is attributed to a partnership, estate, etc., under § 318(a)(3), it will not then be reattributed to another partner, beneficiary, etc., under § 318(a)(2). These limitations on reattribution eliminate so-called "sideways" attribution.

Application of the attribution rules sometimes may help a taxpayer. Suppose that the husband owns voting common stock and the wife owns non-voting preferred stock. Some of the wife's preferred stock is redeemed in connection with a transaction in which part of the husband's common stock is redeemed and the husband's redemption meets the requirements of § 302(b)(2). Section 302(b)(2) applies to qualify the wife's redemption under Treas.Reg. § 1.302–3. Rev.Rul. 77–237, 1977–2 C.B. 88. On the other hand, if the attribution rules make another the constructive owner of stock actually held by the taxpayer, the attribution does not reduce the taxpayer's "real" ownership for purposes of testing the disproportionality of the distribution. Northwestern Steel and Supply Co. v. Commissioner, 60 T.C. 356 (1973). For example if A, who owns 50 shares of stock, and B, who owns 40 shares of stock, are parent and child, A is deemed to own B's 40 shares in addition to A's own 50 shares; correspondingly B is deemed to own A's 50 shares. Thus, in testing a redemption of shares from either or both of A and B under § 302(b)(2), both A and B are deemed to own 90 shares before the transaction.

In applying the option attribution rules, Treas.Reg. § 1.302–3(a) provides that options to purchase unissued stock from the corporation are disregarded. However, Rev.Rul. 68–601, 1968–2 C.B. 124, held that the holder of warrants and convertible debentures was deemed to hold the option shares, but that such shares were not to be counted in determining the percentage of stock owned by other shareholders. Henry T. Patterson Trust v. United States, 729 F.2d 1089 (6th Cir.1984), is to the contrary. In that case, a shareholder other than the shareholder whose stock was redeemed was treated as owning stock that he had an option to purchase from the corporation for purposes of determining the percentage of stock owned by the redeemed shareholder. As a result, as urged by the shareholder, § 302(b)(2) applied. See also Sorem v. Commissioner, 334 F.2d 275 (10th Cir.1964) (employees holding stock options on unissued stock treated as owning stock). Rev.Rul. 89–64, 1989–1 C.B. 91, held that the holder of an option to purchase shares from the corporation was deemed to hold the option shares even though the option was by its terms not exercisable until a future date.

3. SERIES OF DISTRIBUTIONS

Section 302(b)(2)(D) requires the taxpayer to treat a series of redemptions made pursuant to a plan as a single redemption in testing the disproportionality of the redemption. See Blount v. Commissioner, 425 F.2d 921 (2d Cir.1969). Rev.Rul. 85–14, 1985–1 C.B. 92, held that the existence of a "plan" does not require an agreement between two or more shareholders, but may be satisfied by "a design by a single redeemed shareholder to arrange a redemption as part of a sequence of events that ultimately restores to such shareholder the control that was apparently reduced in the redemption." In the ruling, A held 1,466 out of 2,031 shares of the corporation, or 72.18 percent. On January 1, B, who held 210 shares that were to be repurchased by the corporation upon his retirement pursuant to a stock repurchase agreement, announced that he would retire on March 22. A then caused the corporation to redeem 902 of his shares on March 15, reducing his interest to 49.96 percent. One week later, when B's shares were redeemed, A's interest was increased to 61.37 percent (564 out of 919 shares). The ruling held that the reduction in A's interest was not to be measured immediately following the redemption of his shares, but only after the redemption of B's shares. But Glacier State Electric Supply Co. v. Commissioner, 80 T.C. 1047 (1983), held that a possible future redemption upon the subsequent death of a shareholder pursuant to an executory buy-sell agreement should not be considered as part of a "plan" in testing whether a current redemption met the test of § 302(b)(2).

Because of the availability of the § 243 intercorporate dividend received deduction, a corporate shareholder frequently prefers to characterize a distribution as a dividend rather than as a § 302 redemption. In Bleily & Collishaw, Inc. v. Commissioner, 72 T.C. 751 (1979), aff'd by order, 647 F.2d 169 (9th Cir.1981), all of the shares of stock of another corporation held by a corporate shareholder were redeemed in seven installments over a six month period. Each of the first six installments left the shareholder with slightly more than 80 percent of the percentage ownership of stock that it held before that redemption. The shareholder claimed that each of the six distributions was a distribution under § 301 rather than § 302(a). Finding that there was a firm and fixed plan to eliminate the shareholder from the corporation, the Tax Court treated all of the installments as part of a single distribution in redemption of all of the taxpayer's shares under § 302(b)(3).

4.   BASIS CONSIDERATIONS

4.1. *Generally*

If a redemption fails to qualify for exchange treatment under § 302(a) and the distribution is a dividend, the basis of the redeemed stock is not relevant in computing the shareholder's income. Under Treas.Reg. § 1.302–2(c), the basis of the redeemed stock is added to the basis of the other stock held by the taxpayer. If the taxpayer does not actually own any stock after the transaction, but is attributed stock in the corporation by, for example, family attribution rules under § 318, then Treas.Reg. § 1.302–2(c), Ex. (2) suggests that the taxpayer's unrecovered basis in the stock shifts to the family member who actually owns the stock.

Redemption distributions to a shareholder that is a corporation and which are treated as dividends because of option attribution under § 318(a)(4) are extraordinary dividends under § 1059(e)(1)(A)(iii)(I). The corporate recipient is required to reduce the basis of its remaining stock to the extent that the dividend was not taxed by virtue of the § 243 dividends received deduction. See page 223.

In H.J. Heinz Co. v. United States, 76 Fed. Cl. 570 (2007), the taxpayer attempted to take advantage of the shift in basis of redeemed stock to other stock in order to generate a capital loss. Heinz Credit Company (HCC, a Delaware lending subsidiary formed to minimize state taxes on intercompany loans) purchased on the open market 3,500,000 shares of its parent's (H.J. Heinz) stock with cash acquired from commercial lenders. H.J. Heinz redeemed 3,325,000 of these shares giving HHC a subordinated zero coupon convertible note. H.J. Heinz and HHC treated the transaction as a dividend from H.J. Heinz to HCC under §§ 301 and 302(d). HCC thus asserted that its basis in the full 3,500,000 shares shifted to its remaining 175,000 H.J. Heinz shares. Thereafter, HHC sold the 175,000 shares to an unrelated party claiming a $124 million capital loss, which was reported on the H.J. Heinz consolidated return. See Chapter 9. At the end of three years, HHC converted the note into H.J. Heinz stock. The court found that HCC possessed the benefits and burdens of ownership of the H.J. Heinz stock and that its transfer of the stock to H.J. Heinz met the definition of a redemption under § 317(b). Nonetheless, the court concluded that the transaction was a sham because the only purpose of the transaction was to produce a capital loss to offset capital gains realized on another transaction, and the transaction had no business purpose. The court also applied the step transaction doctrine to disregard the HCC purchase and redemption of shares.

4.2. *Proposed Regulations*

The Treasury Department has proposed replacing the basis adjustment rules in Treas.Reg. § 1.302–2(c), which apply when a redemption is treated as a § 301 distribution, with an entirely different regime. Prop.Reg. § 1.302–5 (2009) would provide that the portion of a redemption distribution subject to § 301 but that is not treated as a dividend under § 301(c)(1), and thus results in a basis reduction under § 301(c)(2), will be applied to reduce the basis of each share of stock held by the redeemed shareholder in the same class of stock that is redeemed. Prop.Reg. § 1.302–5(a)(1) (2009). The basis reduction would be applied pro rata on a share-by-share basis. As a consequence of this share-by-share approach, gain may be recognized under § 301(c)(3) with respect to some shares while the distributee shareholder holds other shares with unrecovered basis. For example, suppose A owns all 100 shares of the common stock (the only class) of X Corporation. At different times, A acquired 50 shares for $100 (block 1) and 50 shares for $200 (block 2). The corporation, which has no earnings and profits, redeems all of A's block 2 shares for $300. Under §§ 302(d) and 301(c)(2) and (3), the redemption proceeds are treated as a recovery of basis then capital gain to the extent the distribution exceeds basis. The $300 distribution of property is applied on a pro rata, share-by-share basis with respect to each of the shares in the redeemed class owned by A before the redemption so that $150 is distributed with respect to each block of stock. A recognizes a $50 capital gain on block 1 ($150–100) under § 301(c)(3) and has $50 of basis remaining in block 2 ($150–200).

Prop.Reg. § 1.302–5(a)(2) (2009) would provide that after a reduction in basis under § 301(c)(2), the redeemed shareholder is treated as exchanging all of the shareholder's shares (including the redeemed shares) in a nonrecognition corporate recapitalization under § 368(a)(1)(E), discussed at page 676, for the number of shares retained after the redemption in which the basis of each share of stock received retains the same basis as the original shares deemed transferred. See Prop.Reg. § 1.358–2(b) (2009). This tracing rule preserves the basis of different blocks of shares in the shares remaining after redemption. Thus, in the example of the preceding paragraph, A's 100 shares will be treated as recapitalized with each block retaining its initial basis. A's basis in the 50 recapitalized shares remaining after the redemption determined from the shares deemed exchanged would be zero for 25 shares remaining from block 1 and $50 for 25 shares remaining from block 2.

In the case of redemption of all of the shares of the redeemed shareholder that is treated as a dividend distribution, Prop.Reg. § 1.302–5(a)(3) (2009) would provide that the shareholder's unrecovered basis in the redeemed shares is treated as a loss on the date of the redemption, but recognition of the loss is deferred to a subsequent "inclusion date." The inclusion date is the first date on which the redeemed shareholder would qualify for redemption status under § 302(b)(1), (2), or (3) if the facts on that date had been the facts on the date of the redemption (for example, a date on which a related party reduces an ownership interest), or a date on which all of the stock of the redeeming corporation becomes worthless. Prop.Reg. § 1.302–5(b)(4)(i) (2009). With respect to a corporate shareholder, the inclusion date includes the date on which the redeeming corporation disposes of its assets in a taxable transaction and ceases to exist for tax purposes. Prop.Reg. § 1.302–5(b)(4)(ii) (2009).

SECTION 3.   TERMINATION OF A SHAREHOLDER'S INTEREST

INTERNAL REVENUE CODE: Sections 302(b)(3), (c); 318.

REGULATIONS: Section 1.302–4.

Since the termination of a shareholder's interest is an example of a substantially disproportionate distribution, § 302(b)(3), treating a redemption in complete termination of a shareholder's interest as an exchange, initially appears to add little to the operation of § 302(b). It does, however, serve two major functions. First, it permits the redemption of non-voting stock to qualify for capital gain treatment without resort to the vague "not essentially equivalent to a dividend" test of § 302(b)(1). Second, if all of the stock actually owned by a shareholder is redeemed, § 302(c) permits the family attribution rules of § 318(a)(1) to be disregarded in determining if the shareholder's interest has been completely terminated. This waiver of the family attribution rules is not available under § 302(b)(2). No other attribution rules can be waived. All of the other attribution rules continue to apply when all of the stock actually owned by a shareholder has been redeemed and the application of those attribution rules can defeat the applicability of § 302(b)(3).

DETAILED ANALYSIS

1.   SERIAL REDEMPTIONS

A frequent issue under § 302(b)(3) is the treatment of redemptions of less than all of a shareholder's stock in each of a series of redemptions where the ultimate result is the complete termination of the shareholder's interest. If there is a firm and fixed plan to eliminate the shareholder from the corporation, the component redemptions will be treated as a single redemption of the shareholder's entire interest. The plan does not need to be enforceable or in writing, but it must be more than a handshake. "Generally, a gentleman's agreement lacking written embodiment, communication, and contractual obligations will not suffice to show a fixed and firm plan. * * * On the other hand, a plan need not be in writing, absolutely binding, or communicated to others to be fixed and firm although these factors all tend to indicate that such is the case." Bleily & Collishaw, Inc. v. Commissioner, 72 T.C. 751 (1979), aff'd by order, 647 F.2d 169 (9th Cir.1981). If the time frame for the redemption is vague and the redeemed shareholder retains control over corporate affairs in the interim, however, the individual transactions will not be aggregated; the preliminary redemptions will be treated as § 301 distributions. Benjamin v. Commissioner, 592 F.2d 1259 (5th Cir.1979). In Johnston v. Commissioner, 77 T.C. 679 (1981), a shareholder and a closely held family corporation agreed to the annual redemption of 40 shares. In each of the years 1976, 1977, and 1978, the corporation redeemed 40 shares, but no redemptions occurred in 1974, 1975, and 1979. The shareholder did not attempt to enforce the corporation's redemption obligation in the years when it failed to redeem her shares. The court held that the 1976 redemption was not an integrated step in a firm and fixed plan to redeem the taxpayer's shares, and thus the distribution was essentially equivalent to a dividend.

Merrill Lynch & Co., Inc. v. Commissioner, 386 F.3d 464 (2d Cir. 2004), aff'g 120 T.C. 12 (2003), is the most recent case to examine whether all of the individual transactions in series of redemptions should be viewed together as a complete termination for purposes of § 302(b)(3) or whether the preliminary transactions must be tested only under other subsections for qualification under § 302. Because the taxpayer-shareholder in that case was a corporation, it was to the taxpayer's advantage to classify the transactions as dividends rather than as redemptions. The IRS was arguing that § 302(b)(3) applied and that the distributions were not dividends. The Second Circuit affirmed the Tax Court's holding that the series of transactions should be viewed as a single complete redemption because they were effected pursuant to a "firm and fixed plan." Both the taxpayer and IRS argued that the "firm and fixed plan" test was the proper test, but they disagreed on how the test properly should be applied to the facts. In examining the prior case law and applying it to the facts at hand, the Second Circuit rejected the taxpayer's argument that a "firm and fixed plan" could be found to exist only when it was "absolutely binding" on the taxpayer, concluding that a plan did not have to be in writing, absolutely binding, and communicated to others in order to be firm and fixed. Instead, the court saw these as factors to be assessed in determining whether a plan was firm and fixed. Because "a significant amount of both documentary and circumstantial evidence that was available at the time of the [transactions] suggested there was a plan in place," the Court of Appeals concluded that the Tax Court correctly determined that a firm and fixed plan existed before the sales were executed. Furthermore, the court concluded that "while the plan was not binding in a legal sense, it certainly was binding economically," because, on the complex facts of the case, even though they involved significant transaction costs, the earlier transactions produced no economic benefit to the taxpayer unless the latter steps also were carried out.

Firm + fixed plan

If all of a shareholder's stock is redeemed for the corporation's promissory note, the question arises of whether the note is debt or equity. See Lisle v. Commissioner, T.C. Memo. 1976–140 (finding twenty year notes secured by escrow of stock to be true debt). If the note is found to be equity rather than a debt instrument, the "complete termination" required by § 302(b)(3) is not present. The receipt of the promissory note itself is not considered to be a distribution under either § 301 or § 302. Rather, each principal payment must be tested separately against the various § 302(b) tests to determine whether § 302 redemption treatment is available with respect to that payment or whether the payment represents a distribution under § 301.

2. WAIVER OF FAMILY ATTRIBUTION

2.1. *General*

Whether a shareholder's interest has been completely terminated as required by § 302(c)(1) is tested after applying the attribution rules of § 318(a). However, § 302(c)(2)(A) provides that the *family* attribution rules do not apply if the distributee has no further interest other than as a creditor and if the distributee files an agreement to notify the IRS of any subsequent acquisition of such an interest (which would retroactively disqualify the redemption if acquired within ten years from the distribution).

2.2. *Timely Filing of Waiver Agreement*

Treas.Reg. § 1.302–4(a)(1) provides that the agreement required by § 302(c)(2) must be filed with the tax return reporting the redemption distribution, but the courts have been much more lenient in their interpretation of the requirement. See, e.g., United States v. Van Keppel, 321 F.2d 717 (10th Cir.1963) (agreement filed over one year after the tax return was due, but not before issuance of a notice of deficiency, was timely); Fehrs v. United States, 556 F.2d 1019 (Ct.Cl.1977) (agreement filed seven years after redemption held timely). But Robin Haft Trust v. Commissioner, 62 T.C. 145 (1974), vacated on other grounds, 510 F.2d 43 (1st Cir.1975), held that agreements filed after an adverse Tax Court decision were not timely.

2.3. *Retention of Prohibited Interest*

Section 302(c)(2)(A) conditions the availability of the waiver of family attribution rules on the redeemed shareholder retaining no interest in the corporation, including an interest as an officer, director, or employee, other than an interest as a creditor. The IRS has been strict in its interpretation of what constitutes a prohibited "interest" in the corporation on the part of the redeemed shareholder. For example, Rev.Rul. 59–119, 1959–1 C.B. 68, held that if the shareholder retained the right to have a member of the law firm representing him serve on the board of directors of the corporation to protect his interests as a creditor and to determine that the conditions of the stock redemption agreement were being observed, the "limited" directorship by an agent prevented the application of § 302(c)(2)(A). Compare Rev.Rul. 76–524, 1976–2 C.B. 94 (continuing as director and officer does not prevent redemption from qualifying under § 302(b)(3) if waiver of family attribution is not necessary for complete termination). The courts have generally upheld the IRS's position involving prohibited interests.

2.3.1. *Employment*

Whether post-redemption employment of a former shareholder by the corporation precludes availability of the waiver may depend on the nature of the employment. A common law employment relationship invariably has been found to be a prohibited interest even though the former shareholder's compensation was not contingent on corporate profits and he did not manage the corporation. See Cerone v. Commissioner, 87 T.C. 1 (1986) (employment at significantly reduced salary as bartender and cashier in restaurant/bar); Seda v. Commissioner, 82 T.C. 484 (1984) (employment at fixed salary even though no fact finding as to role in management); Rev.Rul. 56–556, 1956–2 C.B. 177 (compensation is irrelevant; employment is *per se* a prohibited interest).

The answer is less certain if the employment is in the capacity of an independent contractor. Rev.Rul. 70–104, 1970–1 C.B. 66, held that a five-year "consulting contract" was a prohibited interest without examining the particular services to be provided and the terms of compensation. The Tax Court, however, applies a facts and circumstances test based on "whether the former stockholder has either retained a financial stake in the corporation or continued to control the corporation and benefit by its operations." Lynch v. Commissioner, 83 T.C. 597, 605 (1984), rev'd, 801 F.2d 1176 (9th Cir.1986). Compare Chertkof v. Commissioner, 72 T.C. 1113 (1979), aff'd, 649 F.2d 264 (4th Cir.1981), in which the Tax Court found a prohibited interest because the former shareholder had provided management services as an independent contractor, with Estate of Lennard v. Commissioner, 61 T.C. 554 (1974) (Nonacq.), in which the court held that rendering accounting services as an independent contractor was not a prohibited interest.

Lynch, supra, involved a taxpayer who, after the redemption of all of his stock, provided technical advice regarding the operation of sophisticated equipment used in the corporation's business. He initially received $500 per month, which was reduced to $250 per month after one year (while the corporation remained profitable), and the consulting arrangement was terminated after four years. The taxpayer provided no management services after the redemption. Applying the facts and circumstances test, the Tax Court found that the amount and nature of the payments the taxpayer received as a consultant were not "sufficient to give him a financial stake in the corporation." Furthermore, after the taxpayer's redemption, his son, the continuing shareholder, "in fact, assumed complete control over the corporation. After the redemption, the [taxpayer] may have given [his son] some advice with respect to the affairs of the corporation, but advice alone is not prohibited." The Ninth Circuit rejected the Tax Court's facts and circumstances test in favor of a *per se* prohibition on post-redemption provision of services to the corporation. This per se rule was then applied to deny waiver of family attribution. The Ninth Circuit expressly rejected the Tax Court's *Estate of Lennard* decision, supra, and held in *Lynch* that no qualitative judgments regarding the value of the retained interest are permissible. See also the concurring opinion in *Seda,* supra, in which eight Tax Court judges supported application of a *per se* rule.

2.3.2. *Creditor*

The statute allows the redeemed shareholder to remain as a "creditor" of the corporation, thus raising the issue whether obligations issued in the redemption constitute debt or equity. Treas.Reg. § 1.302–4(d) specifies conditions that must be met for the redeemed shareholder's interest as a creditor to be respected as such. See, e.g., Dunn v. Commissioner, 615 F.2d 578 (2d Cir.1980) (interest was as a "creditor" despite restrictions pursuant to automobile dealers franchise agreement on the payment of the obligations issued in the redemption if payment would leave inadequate working capital); *Estate of Lennard,* supra (subordination of the obligation to bank loans did not prevent "creditor" status notwithstanding Treas.Reg. § 1.302–4(d)). Treas.Reg. § 1.302–4(e) provides that the acquisition of the corporation's assets to enforce the redeemed shareholder's rights as a creditor is not a prohibited interest; but reacquisition of stock in enforcing the shareholder's creditor's rights is a prohibited interest. Even though reacquisition of the corporation's stock pursuant to a security agreement is the reacquisition of a prohibited interest, in Lynch v. Commissioner, 83 T.C. 597 (1984), rev'd on other grounds 801 F.2d 1176 (9th Cir.1986), the Tax Court held that a security interest in stock of the corporation, standing alone, does not constitute a prohibited interest.

2.3.3. *Other Contractual Rights*

Rev.Rul. 77–467, 1977–2 C.B. 92, held that a redeemed shareholder could lease real estate to the corporation and the lease would not be a prohibited interest if the rent was not dependent on corporate earnings. Rev.Rul. 84–135, 1984–2 C.B. 80, held that the right to receive a lifetime pension under a pre-existing unfunded nonqualified pension plan was not a prohibited interest. It is not readily apparent why these interests are any less a continuing interest in the corporation than employment in a nonmanagerial capacity for a fixed salary, but the IRS has nevertheless drawn the distinction.

2.3.4. *Multiple Retained Interests*

The question might arise whether a number of different retained contract rights, none of which alone constitutes a prohibited interest, might in their totality constitute a retained prohibited interest. Hurst v. Commissioner, 124 T.C. 16 (2005), illustrates that the "prohibited interest" test is based on analysis of each retained interest independently rather than on the number of different rights retained. If none of the retained rights alone is a prohibited interest, they cannot together be consolidated into an overall prohibited interest. In *Hurst* all of the taxpayer's stock in a corporation (HMI) in which his son continued as a 51 percent shareholder was redeemed for $2.5 million dollars payable quarterly, with 8 percent interest, over 15 years. The payment obligation was represented by a promissory note that was secured by all of the corporation's assets, as well as by a cross-collateralization pledge of the son's stock and the stock of the unrelated shareholders. In addition, HMI entered into a 10–year employment contract with the redeemed shareholder's wife, who personally had not owned any stock, giving her a small salary and fringe benefits, including medical insurance, and pursuant to which she performed "various administrative and clerical tasks." Finally, at time of the redemption the corporation signed a new lease on the building owned by the redeemed shareholder, in which it conducted its business, pursuant to which it paid rent of $8,500 per month, adjusted for inflation. Although the IRS "acknowledg[ed] that each relationship between the Hursts and their old company—creditor under the notes, landlord under the lease, employment of a non-owning family member—passes muster, he argue[d] that the total number of related obligations resulting from the transaction gave the Hursts a prohibited interest in the corporation by giving Richard Hurst a financial stake in the company's continued success." The Tax Court rejected this "holistic view," examining each obligation in turn, starting with the promissory notes.

> Neither the amount nor the timing of payments was tied to the financial performance of HMI. Although the notes were subordinate to HMI's obligation to its bank, they were not subordinate to general creditors, nor was the amount or certainty of the payments under them dependent on HMI's earnings. * * * All of these contractual arrangements had cross-default clauses and were secured by the buyers' stock. This meant that should any of the notes go into default, Mr. Hurst would have the right to seize the stock and sell it. The parties agree that the probable outcome of such a sale would be that Mr. Hurst would once again be in control of HMI. * * * But in Lynch v. Commissioner, 83 T.C.

597 (1984), revd. on other grounds 801 F.2d 1176 (9th Cir.1986), we held that a security interest in redeemed stock does not constitute a prohibited interest under section 302. We noted that "The holding of such a security interest is common in sales agreements, and * * * not inconsistent with the interest of a creditor." * * * Furthermore, at trial, the Hursts offered credible evidence from their professional advisers that these transactions, including the grant of a security interest to Mr. Hurst, were consistent with common practice for seller-financed deals. * * *

[T]he lease called for a fixed rent in no way conditioned upon the financial performance of HMI. Attorney Ron David, who was intimately familiar with the transaction, testified convincingly that there was no relationship between the obligations of the parties and the financial performance of HMI. The transactional documents admitted into evidence do not indicate otherwise. There is simply no evidence that the payment terms in the lease between the Hursts and HMI vary from those that would be reasonable if negotiated between unrelated parties. And the Hursts point out that the IRS itself has ruled that an arm's-length lease allowing a redeeming corporation to use property owned by a former owner does not preclude characterization as a redemption.

Furthermore, the court did not find the fact that subsequent to the redemption the parties modified both the lease and the note in a transaction in which the corporation surrendered an option to purchase the leased property in exchange for a reduction in the interest rate on the note issued for the stock indicated that Hurst's rights under the lease were in fact a retained interest.

The court then considered Mrs. Hurst's employment contract:

Mrs. Hurst did not own any HMI stock. Thus, she is not a "distributee" unable to have an "interest in the corporation (including an interest as officer, director, or employee), other than an interest as a creditor." * * * The Commissioner is thus forced to argue that her employment was a "prohibited interest" for Mr. Hurst. And he does, contending that through her employment Mr. Hurst kept an ongoing influence in HMI's corporate affairs. He also argues that an employee unrelated to the former owner of the business would not continue to be paid were she to work Mrs. Hurst's admittedly minimal schedule. And he asserts that her employment was a mere ruse to provide Mr. Hurst with his company car and health benefits, bolstering this argument with proof that the truck used by Mrs. Hurst was the same one that her husband had been using when he ran HMI. None of this, though, changes the fact that her compensation and fringe benefits were fixed, and again—like the notes and lease—not subordinated to HMI's general creditors, and not subject to any fluctuation related to HMI's financial performance. Her duties, moreover, were various administrative and clerical tasks—some of the same chores she had been doing at HMI on a regular basis for many years. And there was no evidence whatsoever that Mr.

Hurst used his wife in any way as a surrogate for continuing to manage (or even advise) HMI's new owners.

Somewhat surprisingly, perhaps, the court concluded that the fact that a default by the corporation on its obligations to Mrs. Hurst under the employment contract, as did a default under the lease, also constituted a default on the promissory note to Mr. Hurst, thereby triggering his right to reacquire the stock did not, under all of the facts and circumstances, constitute a prohibited retained interest. The IRS argued that "intertwin[ing] substantial corporate obligations with the employment contract of only one of 45 employees * * * [was] proof that the parties to this redemption contemplated a continuing involvement greater than that of a mere creditor." The court responded:

> [T]he proof at trial [demonstrated] that there was a legitimate creditor's interest in the Hursts' demanding [the cross collateralization provisions] * * * They were, after all, parting with a substantial asset (the corporations), in return for what was in essence an IOU from some business associates. Their ability to enjoy retirement in financial security was fully contingent upon their receiving payment on the notes, lease, and employment contract. * * * The value of that security, however, depended upon the financial health of the company. Repossessing worthless shares as security on defaulted notes would have done little to ensure the Hursts' retirement. The cross-default provisions were their canary in the coal mine. If at any point the company failed to meet any financial obligation to the Hursts, Mr. Hurst would have the option to retrieve his shares immediately, thus protecting the value of his security interest instead of worrying about whether this was the beginning of a downward spiral. This is perfectly consistent with a creditor's interest, and there was credible trial testimony that multiple default triggers are common in commercial lending.

Accordingly, the court held that:

> [T]he cross-default provisions protected the Hursts' financial interest as creditors of HMI, for a debt on which they had received practically no downpayment, and the collection of which (though not 'dependent upon the earnings of the corporation' as that phrase is used in section 1.302–4(d), Income Tax Regs.) was realistically contingent upon HMI's continued financial health. * * * The number of legal connections between Mr. Hurst and the buyers that continued after the deal was signed did not change their character as permissible security interests. Even looked at all together, they were in no way contingent upon the financial performance of the company except in the obvious sense that all creditors have in their debtors' solvency.

2.3.5. *Stock Ownership in Fiduciary Capacity*

Whether a redeemed shareholder who retains or reacquires voting power in a fiduciary capacity has a prohibited interest depends on the nature of the fiduciary position. Rev.Rul. 81–233, 1981–2 C.B. 83, held that a redeemed shareholder who within ten years became a custodian under the Uniform Gift to Minors Act with respect to stock given to his children by the shareholder's parents had acquired a prohibited interest because he had the power to vote the stock. See also Rev.Rul. 71–426, 1971–2 C.B. 173 (stock of the corporation was owned by a mother and her four children, with the children's stock held by a voting trust; retention by the mother of the position as voting trustee was a prohibited interest). If the fiduciary position is as an executor or testamentary trustee, however, the IRS has ruled that the exception for interests acquired by bequest or inheritance applies. Rev.Rul. 79–334, 1979–2 C.B. 127 (testamentary trustee); Rev.Rul. 72–380, 1972–2 C.B. 201 (executor of estate).

2.4. *Stock Acquired From a Related Party*

Under § 302(c)(2)(B), the waiver of family attribution rules might not be available if the redeemed stock was acquired by the distributee within the preceding 10–year period from a related person (a person whose stock would be attributable to the distributee). Thus, a complete termination under § 302(b)(3) is not available to a husband-distributee who received the redeemed stock from his wife within the 10–year period. Waiver of family attribution also is unavailable if within the 10–year period the distributee gave stock to a related person (e.g., the wife above is the distributee).

However, the limitation of § 302(c)(2)(B), does not apply unless one of the principal purposes of the acquisition or disposition was tax avoidance. See § 302(c)(2)(B), flush language, and Treas.Reg. § 1.302–4(g), last sentence. The IRS has issued a number of rulings dealing with the question of whether transfers of stock between related parties within ten years of the redemption were tax avoidance transactions. Rev.Rul. 77–293, 1977–2 C.B. 91, held that tax avoidance was not present in a case in which a father made a gift of a part of his stock to his son concurrently with a redemption of the remainder of the stock from the father. The purpose of the gift was to give the son control of the corporation in connection with the transfer to him of management responsibility. In Rev.Rul. 85–19, 1985–1 C.B. 94, a minority shareholder first sold to his father, the controlling shareholder, a number of shares received from the father by gift two years earlier, and the corporation then immediately redeemed the son's remaining shares, which he had acquired by bequest. The ruling held that there was no tax avoidance motive present and suggests that tax avoidance exists only if the transferor seeks to retain indirect control, such as by transferring stock to a spouse prior to a redemption of all of the shares actually owned, or if the transfer is in contemplation of a redemption of the shares from the transferee. See also Rev.Rul. 79–67, 1979–1 C.B. 128 (distribution of stock from estate to beneficiary to qualify redemption from beneficiary under § 302(b)(3) is not tax avoidance); Rev.Rul. 82–129, 1982–2 C.B. 76 (partition of stock held as community property is not a transfer).

2.5. *Waiver of Family Attribution By Entities*

Section 302(c)(2)(C) permits waiver of the family attribution rules by an entity to avoid attribution from a third party through the owner of an interest in the entity where the owner of the beneficial interest owns no stock directly. The attribution rules may be waived if after the redemption neither the entity (trust, estate, partnership, or corporation) nor the beneficiaries, partners, or shareholders hold an interest in the redeeming corporation and if both agree not to acquire such an interest in the stipulated ten-year period. Under § 302(c)(2)(C), only the *family* attribution rules may be waived; the attribution rules between entity and beneficiary may not be waived. For example, suppose A owns 50 percent of the stock of X Corporation and Trust T, created by a deceased aunt for the benefit of A's children, owns 50 percent. Under § 318, A's children are deemed to own A's stock and the trust is deemed to own the stock of the children. If all of the stock actually owned by the trust is redeemed, the trust can take advantage of the waiver of the family attribution rules provided in § 302(c)(2) and treat the redemption as a complete termination under § 302(b)(3).

3. BASIS OF STOCK REDEEMED IN NONQUALIFYING TRANSACTION

If a redemption is treated as a § 301 distribution under § 302(d), the basis of the redeemed shares is allocated to the shareholder's remaining shares. If the shareholder's actual interest is completely terminated but, due to the family attribution rules, the shareholder's entire interest has not been terminated, the basis of the redeemed shares should be added to the basis of the related person whose shares were attributed to the redeemed shareholder. Treas.Reg. § 1.302–2(c); see also, Levin v. Commissioner, 385 F.2d 521 (2d Cir.1967) (basis of parent's redeemed shares added to basis of son's shares).

Prop.Reg. § 1.302–5 (2009), discussed at page 241, would replace the basis adjustment rules in Treas.Reg. § 1.302–2(c). Under the proposed regulations, the redeemed shareholder's basis in the redeemed stock would not shift to the related person whose stock ownership precluded § 302(b)(3) from applying, but would be retained by the redeemed shareholder. That basis would then generate a loss deduction at some future date, for example, upon the sale by the related shareholder of his stock in the corporation or the resignation from continued employment of the board of directors of the shareholder whose stock had been redeemed.

SECTION 4. DISTRIBUTIONS NOT "ESSENTIALLY EQUIVALENT TO A DIVIDEND"

INTERNAL REVENUE CODE: Sections 302(b)(1), (c)(1); 318.

REGULATIONS: Section 1.302–2.

United States v. Davis

Supreme Court of the United States, 1970.
397 U.S. 301.

■ MR. JUSTICE MARSHALL delivered the opinion of the Court.

In 1945, taxpayer and E.B. Bradley organized a corporation. In exchange for property transferred to the new company, Bradley received 500 shares of common stock, and taxpayer and his wife similarly each received 250 such shares. Shortly thereafter, taxpayer made an additional contribution to the corporation, purchasing 1,000 shares of preferred stock at a par value of $25 per share.

The purpose of this latter transaction was to increase the company's working capital and thereby to qualify for a loan previously negotiated through the Reconstruction Finance Corporation. It was understood that the corporation would redeem the preferred stock when the RFC loan had been repaid. Although in the interim taxpayer bought Bradley's 500 shares and divided them between his son and daughter, the total capitalization of the company remained the same until 1963. That year, after the loan was fully repaid and in accordance with the original understanding, the company redeemed taxpayer's preferred stock.

In his 1963 personal income tax return taxpayer did not report the $25,000 received by him upon the redemption of his preferred stock as income. Rather, taxpayer considered the redemption as a sale of his preferred stock to the company—a capital gains transaction under § 302 of the Internal Revenue Code of 1954 resulting in no tax since taxpayer's basis in the stock equaled the amount he received for it. The Commissioner of Internal Revenue, however, did not approve this tax treatment. According to the Commissioner, the redemption of taxpayer's stock was essentially equivalent to a dividend and was thus taxable as ordinary income under §§ 301 and 316 of the Code. Taxpayer paid the resulting deficiency and brought this suit for a refund. The District Court ruled in his favor, 274 F.Supp. 466 (M.D.Tenn.1967), and on appeal the Court of Appeals affirmed. 408 F.2d 1139 (6th Cir.1969).

The Court of Appeals held that the $25,000 received by taxpayer was "not essentially equivalent to a dividend" within the meaning of that phrase in § 302(b)(1) of the Code because the redemption was the final step in a course of action that had a legitimate business (as opposed to a tax avoidance) purpose. That holding represents only one of a variety of treatments accorded similar transactions under § 302(b)(1) in the circuit courts of appeals.[2] We granted certiorari * * * in order to resolve this recurring tax question involving stock redemptions by closely held corporations. We reverse.

The Internal Revenue Code of 1954 provides generally in §§ 301 and 316 for the tax treatment of distributions by a corporation to its shareholders; under those provisions, a distribution is includable in a taxpayer's gross income as a dividend out of earnings and profits to the extent such earnings exist. There are exceptions to the application of these general provisions, however, and among them are those found in § 302 involving certain distributions for redeemed stock. The basic question in this case is whether the $25,000 distribution by the corporation to taxpayer falls under that section—more specifically, whether its legitimate business motivation qualifies the distribution under § 302(b)(1) of the Code. Preliminarily, however, we must consider the relationship between § 302(b)(1) and the rules regarding the attribution of stock ownership found in § 318(a) of the Code.

Issue

---

[2]   Only the Second Circuit has unequivocally adopted the Commissioner's view and held irrelevant the motivation of the redemption. See Levin v. Commissioner, 385 F.2d 521 (1967). * * *

The other courts of appeals that have passed on the question are apparently willing to give at least some weight under § 302(b)(1) to the business motivation of a distribution and redemption. See, e.g., Commissioner v. Berenbaum, 369 F.2d 337 (C.A.10th Cir.1966); Kerr v. Commissioner, 326 F.2d 225 (9th Cir.1964). * * * Even among those courts that consider business purpose, however, it is generally required that the business purpose be related, not to the issuance of the stock, but to the redemption of it. * * *

§318 applies to
§302(b)

Under subsection (a) of § 302, a distribution is treated as "payment in exchange for the stock," thus qualifying for capital gains rather than ordinary income treatment, if the conditions contained in any one of the four paragraphs of subsection (b) are met. In addition to paragraph (1)'s "not essentially equivalent to a dividend" test, capital gains treatment is available where (2) the taxpayer's voting strength is substantially diminished, (3) his interest in the company is completely terminated, or (4) certain railroad stock is redeemed. Paragraph (4) is not involved here, and taxpayer admits that paragraphs (2) and (3) do not apply. Moreover, taxpayer agrees that for the purposes of §§ 302(b)(2) and (3) the attribution rules of § 318(a) apply and he is considered to own the 750 outstanding shares of common stock held by his wife and children in addition to the 250 shares in his own name.

Taxpayer, however, argues that the attribution rules do not apply in considering whether a distribution is essentially equivalent to a dividend under § 302(b)(1). According to taxpayer, he should thus be considered to own only 25 percent of the corporation's common stock, and the distribution would then qualify under § 302(b)(1) since it was not pro rata or proportionate to his stock interest, the fundamental test of dividend equivalency. See Treas.Reg. 1.302–2(b) . However, the plain language of the statute compels rejection of the argument. In subsection (c) of § 302, the attribution rules are made specifically applicable "in determining the ownership of stock for purposes of this section." Applying this language, both courts below held that § 318(a) applies to all of § 302, including § 302(b)(1)—a view in accord with the decisions of the other courts of appeals, a longstanding treasury regulation,[6] and the opinion of the leading commentators.[7]

Against this weight of authority, taxpayer argues that the result under paragraph (1) should be different because there is no explicit reference to stock ownership as there is in paragraphs (2) and (3). Neither that fact, however, nor the purpose and history of § 302(b)(1) support taxpayer's argument. The attribution rules—designed to provide a clear answer to what would otherwise be a difficult tax question—formed part of the tax bill that was subsequently enacted as the 1954 Code. As is discussed further, infra, the bill as passed by the House of Representatives contained no provision comparable to § 302(b)(1). When that provision was added in the Senate, no purpose was evidenced to restrict the applicability of § 318(a). Rather, the attribution rules continued to be made specifically applicable to the entire section, and we believe that Congress intended that they be taken into account wherever ownership of stock was relevant.

Indeed, it was necessary that the attribution rules apply to § 302(b)(1) unless they were to be effectively eliminated from consideration with regard to §§ 302(b)(2) and (3) also. For if a transaction failed to qualify under one of those sections solely because of the attribution rules, it would according to taxpayer's argument nonetheless qualify under § 302(b)(1). We cannot agree that Congress intended so to nullify its explicit directive. We conclude, therefore, that the attribution rules of § 318(a) do apply; and, for the purposes of

---

[6]   See Treas.Reg. 1.302–2(b).

[7]   See B. Bittker & J. Eustice, Federal Income Taxation of Corporations and Shareholders 292 n. 32 (2d ed. 1966).

deciding whether a distribution is "not essentially equivalent to a dividend" under § 302(b)(1), taxpayer must be deemed the owner of all 1,000 shares of the company's common stock.

II

After application of the stock ownership attribution rules, this case viewed most simply involves a sole stockholder who causes part of his shares to be redeemed by the corporation. We conclude that such a redemption is always "essentially equivalent to a dividend" within the meaning of that phrase in § 302(b)(1)[8] and therefore do not reach the Government's alternative argument that in any event the distribution should not on the facts of this case qualify for capital gains treatment.[9]

The predecessor of § 302(b)(1) came into the tax law as § 201(d) of the Revenue Act of 1921, 42 Stat. 228 * * *.

By the time of the general revision resulting in the Internal Revenue Code of 1954, the draftsmen were faced with what has aptly been described as "the morass created by the decisions." Ballenger v. United States, 301 F.2d 192, 196 (4th Cir.1962). In an effort to eliminate "the considerable confusion which exists in this area" and thereby to facilitate tax planning, H.R.Rep. No. 1337, 83d Cong., 2d Sess., 35, the authors of the new Code sought to provide objective tests to govern the tax consequences of stock redemptions. Thus, the tax bill passed by the House of Representatives contained no "essentially equivalent" language. Rather, it provided for "safe harbors" where capital gains treatment would be accorded to corporate redemptions that met the conditions now found in §§ 302(b)(2) and (3) of the Code.

It was in the Senate Finance Committee's consideration of the tax bill that § 302(b)(1) was added, and Congress thereby provided that capital gains treatment should be available "if the redemption is not essentially equivalent to a dividend." Taxpayer argues that the purpose was to continue "existing law," and there is support in the legislative history that § 302(b)(1) reverted "in part" or "in general" to the "essentially equivalent" provision of § 115(g)(1) of the 1939 Code. According to the Government, even under the old law it would have been improper for the Court of Appeals to rely on "a business purpose for the redemption" and "an absence of the proscribed tax avoidance purpose to bail out dividends at favorable tax rates." See Northup v. United States, 240 F.2d 304, 307 (2d Cir.1957); Smith v. United States, 121 F.2d 692, 695 (3d Cir.1941) * * *. However, we need not decide that question, for we find from the history of the 1954 revisions and the purpose of § 302(b)(1) that Congress intended more than merely to re-enact the prior law.

In explaining the reason for adding the "essentially equivalent" test, the Senate Committee stated that the House provisions "appeared unnecessarily restrictive, particularly, in the case of redemptions of

---

[8]   Of course, this just means that a distribution in redemption to a sole shareholder will be treated under the general provisions of § 301, and it will only be taxed as a dividend under § 316 to the extent that there are earnings and profits.

[9]   The Government argues that even if business purpose were relevant under § 302(b)(1), the business purpose present here related only to the original investment and not at all to the necessity for redemption. See cases cited, n. 2, supra. Under either view, taxpayer does not lose his basis in the preferred stock. Under Treas.Reg. 1.302–2(c) that basis is applied to taxpayer's common stock.

preferred stock which might be called by the corporation without the shareholder having any control over when the redemption may take place." S.Rep. No. 1622, 83d Cong., 2d Sess., 44. This explanation gives no indication that the purpose behind the redemption should affect the result.[10] Rather, in its more detailed technical evaluation of § 302(b)(1), the Senate Committee reported as follows:

"The test intended to be incorporated in the interpretation of paragraph (1) is in general that currently employed under section 115(g)(1) of the 1939 Code. Your committee further intends that in applying this test for the future * * * the inquiry will be devoted solely to the question of whether or not the transaction by its nature may properly be characterized as a sale of stock by the redeeming shareholder to the corporation. For this purpose the presence or absence of earnings and profits of the corporation is not material. Example: X, the sole shareholder of a corporation having no earnings or profits causes the corporation to redeem half of its stock. Paragraph (1) does not apply to such redemption notwithstanding the absence of earnings and profits." S.Rep. No. 1622, supra, at 234.

The intended scope of § 302(b)(1) as revealed by this legislative history is certainly not free from doubt. However, we agree with the Government that by making the sole inquiry relevant for the future the narrow one whether the redemption could be characterized as a sale, Congress was apparently rejecting past court decisions that had also considered factors indicating the presence or absence of a tax-avoidance motive.[11] At least that is the implication of the example given. Congress clearly mandated that pro rata distributions be treated under the general rules laid down in §§ 301 and 316 rather than under § 302, and nothing suggests that there should be a different result if there were a "business purpose" for the redemption. Indeed, just the opposite inference must be drawn since there would not likely be a tax-avoidance purpose in a situation where there were no earnings or profits. We conclude that the Court of Appeals was therefore wrong in looking for a business purpose and considering it in deciding whether the redemption was equivalent to a dividend. Rather, we agree with the Court of Appeals for the Second Circuit that "the business purpose of a transaction is irrelevant in determining dividend equivalence" under § 302(b)(1). Hasbrook v. United States, 343 F.2d 811, 814 (1965).

Taxpayer strongly argues that to treat the redemption involved here as essentially equivalent to a dividend is to elevate form over

---

[10] See Bittker & Eustice, supra, n. 7 at 291: "It is not easy to give § 302(b)(1) an expansive construction in view of this indication that its major function was the narrow one of immunizing redemptions of minority holdings of preferred stock."

[11] This rejection is confirmed by the Committee's acceptance of the House treatment of distributions involving corporate contractions—a factor present in many of the earlier "business purpose" redemptions. In describing its action, the Committee stated as follows:

"Your committee, as did the House bill, separates into their significant elements the kind of transactions now incoherently aggregated in the definition of a partial liquidation. Those distributions which may have capital-gain characteristics *because they are not made pro rata* among the various shareholders, would be subjected, at the shareholder level, to the separate tests described in [§§ 301 to 318]. On the other hand, those distributions characterized by what happens solely at the corporate level by reason of the assets distributed would be included as within the concept of a partial liquidation."

S.Rep. No. 1622, supra, at 49. (Emphasis added.)

substance. Thus, taxpayer argues, had he not bought Bradley's shares or had he made a subordinated loan to the company instead of buying preferred stock, he could have gotten back his $25,000 with favorable tax treatment. However, the difference between form and substance in the tax law is largely problematical, and taxpayer's complaints have little to do with whether a business purpose is relevant under § 302(b)(1). It was clearly proper for Congress to treat distributions generally as taxable dividends when made out of earnings and profits and then to prevent avoidance of that result without regard to motivation where the distribution is in exchange for redeemed stock.

We conclude that that is what Congress did when enacting § 302(b)(1). If a corporation distributes property as a simple dividend, the effect is to transfer the property from the company to its shareholders without a change in the relative economic interests or rights of the stockholders. Where a redemption has that same effect, it cannot be said to have satisfied the "not essentially equivalent to a dividend" requirement of § 302(b)(1). Rather, to qualify for preferred treatment under that section, a redemption must result in a meaningful reduction of the shareholder's proportionate interest in the corporation. Clearly, taxpayer here, who (after application of the attribution rules) was the sole shareholder of the corporation both before and after the redemption, did not qualify under this test. The decision of the Court of Appeals must therefore be reversed and the case remanded to the District Court for dismissal of the complaint.

It is so ordered.

DETAILED ANALYSIS

1. GENERAL

If a shareholder is unable to meet the "safe haven" requirements of § 302(b)(2) or § 302(b)(3), the shareholder still may fall back on the general language of § 302(b)(1), allowing capital gain treatment to distributions found to be not essentially equivalent to a dividend. But the *Davis* case makes the task of the shareholder attempting to fit the transaction under § 302(b)(1) very difficult. First, the Court's holding that the attribution rules of § 318 apply to § 302(b)(1) situations means that in a family-held corporation context the shareholder almost invariably will be deemed to own a higher percentage of stock than is actually owned, and hence the distribution to the shareholder will more likely have or approach the pro rata character of a dividend distribution. See, e.g., Title Insurance and Trust Co. v. United States, 484 F.2d 462 (9th Cir.1973); Johnson v. United States, 434 F.2d 340 (8th Cir.1970); and Rev.Rul. 71–261, 1971–1 C.B. 108, all situations in which, by virtue of the application of the attribution rules, the shareholder was deemed to own 100 percent of the stock of the corporation and hence the distribution was treated as a dividend. (Indeed, in some cases the interaction of the attribution rules and the redemption can actually *increase* the redeemed shareholder's interest after the redemption, see, e.g., Sawelson v. Commissioner, 61 T.C. 109 (1973).) Second, the Court's elimination of the "business purpose" factor in determining dividend equivalence under § 302(b)(1) removes from consideration any argument based on the reasons for the redemption (presumably including "shareholder" purposes, see Nicholson v.

Commissioner, 17 T.C. 1399 (1952)), and focuses attention solely on the "effect" of the distribution. Here the factors discussed below, some of which were developed in the prior case law dealing with dividend equivalence, remain relevant after *Davis,* with the exception of those cases whose result turned on a finding of "business purpose" for the redemption.

Could the taxpayer in Davis have avoided the dividend result if, instead of receiving the preferred stock, he had made a subordinated loan to the corporation of $25,000?

2. "MEANINGFUL REDUCTION" IN THE SHAREHOLDER'S INTEREST

2.1. *Voting Stock*

2.1.1. *Effect on Control*

In attempting to give some content to the "meaningful reduction" standard set forth by the Supreme Court in *Davis,* subsequent cases and Revenue Rulings have focused principally on the effect that the redemption has on the shareholder's voting control of the corporation. Thus in Rev.Rul. 75–502, 1975–2 C.B. 111, a redemption that reduced the shareholder's voting stock interest in the corporation from 57 percent to 50 percent, the other 50 percent being held by a single unrelated shareholder, qualified as a meaningful reduction. The Ruling indicated that if the redemption had not reduced the shareholder's interest in the voting stock to 50 percent or less, then § 302(b)(1) would not have been applicable. See Rev.Rul. 77–218, 1977–1 C.B. 81 (8 percent reduction in actual and constructive ownership that left the shareholder with more than 50 percent of the voting stock because of the attribution rules was not a meaningful reduction even though all of the shares actually owned by the taxpayer were redeemed). Benjamin v. Commissioner, 66 T.C. 1084 (1976), aff'd, 592 F.2d 1259 (5th Cir.1979), involving a redemption of voting preferred stock, found that the redemption did not qualify under § 302(b)(1) because of the shareholder's continuing voting control over the corporation after the redemption. The facts that the shareholder's interest in the net worth of the corporation and the right to participate in its earnings were reduced were not sufficient since "the retention of absolute voting control in the present case outweighs any other considerations." (66 T.C. at 1111).

Roebling v. Commissioner, 77 T.C. 30 (1981), involved the redemption of voting preferred stock pursuant to a plan of the corporation to redeem all of its outstanding preferred stock over a number of years. Before the series of redemptions commenced, the shareholder held 91.94 percent of the preferred stock and 39.6 percent of the common stock, which gave her 57.12 percent of the total voting shares. If the plan had been carried out in full, the shareholder would have been left with less than forty percent of the voting stock of the corporation, which had approximately 500 shareholders. For the years in question, however, the shareholder's voting power was only reduced to 43.28 percent. Because the shareholder's voting power was reduced from majority control to less than 50 percent, the court concluded that the reduction was meaningful. This conclusion was reinforced by the reduction in the percentage of total dividend distributions that would be receivable by the taxpayer as a result of the redemption.

Rickey v. United States, 427 F.Supp. 484 (W.D.La.1976), aff'd on other grounds, 592 F.2d 1251 (5th Cir.1979), held that a reduction in voting stock from 72 percent to 58 percent was a qualifying redemption because the shareholder lost the ability to control the two-thirds vote necessary for certain corporate actions—amending the Articles of Incorporation, merger or consolidation, the voluntary sale, lease, exchange or disposition of all or substantially all of the assets of the corporation, or liquidation and dissolution—under the state corporation law. Henry T. Patterson Trust v. United States, 729 F.2d 1089 (6th Cir.1984), reached the same result in a case in which the shareholder's interest was reduced from 80 percent to 60 percent. This analysis was rejected by the IRS in Rev.Rul. 78–401, 1978–2 C.B. 127, which held that a reduction from 90 percent to 60 percent did not qualify under § 302(b)(1); the shareholder still had the right to control the day-to-day operations of the corporation and the fact that he gave up the right to control actions requiring a two-thirds vote under state corporation law was not sufficient.

Situations involving redemptions of voting stock held by minority shareholders are analyzed similarly. In Rev.Rul. 76–364, 1976–2 C.B. 91, the shareholder held 27 percent of the voting stock of the corporation and three other unrelated shareholders each had a 24.3 percent interest. A redemption that reduced the shareholder's 27 percent interest to 22.27 percent was held to be a meaningful reduction since through the redemption the shareholder lost the ability to control the corporation by acting in conjunction with only one of the other shareholders. See also Rev.Rul. 75–512, 1975–2 C.B. 112 (a reduction from 30 percent actual and constructive ownership to 24.3 percent constructive ownership qualified under § 302(b)(1) because all of the shares actually owned were redeemed). However, a small reduction in the interest of a minority shareholder who retains a large interest does not qualify. Rodgers P. Johnson Trust v. Commissioner, 71 T.C. 941 (1979) (Acq.), held that a reduction from 43.6 percent to 40.8 percent of the voting stock of the corporation was not meaningful. Furthermore, in Conopco, Inc. v. United States, 100 A.F.T.R.2d 2007–5296 (D. N.J. 2007), the court held that periodic redemptions of stock from an Employee Stock Ownership Plan (ESOP) trust, the largest of which reduced the trust's interest from 2.7884 percent to 2.7809 percent, which was a reduction of only 7.5 thousandths of one percent (0.0075%), qualified as a dividend (which permitted a corporate deduction for the distribution to the ESOP under § 404(k)(1)).[1] The court concluded that none of the redemption distributions meaningfully reduced the trust's interest in the corporation.

Redemptions from shareholders of publicly-traded corporations usually qualify under § 301(b)(1), but do not automatically do so. Rev.Rul. 76–385, 1976–2 C.B. 92, held that § 302(b)(1) applied to a redemption resulting in a 3.3 percent reduction in share ownership of a shareholder who had a .0001118 percent interest in a publicly held corporation. Because the shareholder effectively had no control at all with respect to the operation of the corporation, a 3.3 percent reduction in share ownership was meaningful. However, Rev.Rul. 81–289, 1981–2 C.B. 82, held that a redemption of 2 percent of the stock of a shareholder holding less than one percent of a publicly traded corporation's outstanding stock was essentially

---

[1]   The court also held that the dividend was not a deductible distribution to the ESOP under § 162(k), which bars a deduction for any expense incurred by a corporation in reacquisition of its stock. Accord, Ralston Purina Co. v. Commissioner, 131 T.C. 29 (2008), and General Mills v. United States, 103 A.F.T.R.2d 2009–589 (8th Cir. 2009).

equivalent to a dividend because simultaneous redemptions from other shareholders resulted in a total redemption of 2 percent of corporation's outstanding stock. Thus, the shareholder's proportionate interest was unchanged.

2.1.2.   Effect of "Family Hostility" on Application of Constructive Stock Ownership Rules

If, after the redemption, the shareholder's directly owned stock is insufficient to provide control but the shareholder is deemed to own over 50 percent of the voting stock because of the attribution rules, he shareholder is still treated as the controlling shareholder for purposes of testing the meaningful reduction in the shareholder's interest. See, e.g., Fehrs Finance Co. v. Commissioner, 487 F.2d 184 (8th Cir.1973); Rev.Rul. 77–218, supra. While *Davis* indicates that the attribution rules apply in such a situation, *Davis* could be viewed as permitting this shareholder to argue that where the related parties in fact were in disagreement, the attribution rules should not be applied in testing control. Several pre-*Davis* cases had adopted this approach. See, e.g., Estate of Squier v. Commissioner, 35 T.C. 950 (1961) (Nonacq.). In the first case to raise the issue following *Davis,* however, the Tax Court held that the *Davis* view of the attribution rules precluded applying a "family fight" exception. Robin Haft Trust v. Commissioner, 61 T.C. 398 (1973). The Court of Appeals, 510 F.2d 43 (1st Cir.1975), reversed and remanded the case for consideration of whether "the existence of family discord [tended] to negate the presumption that taxpayers would exert continuing control over the corporation despite the redemption." In Rev.Rul. 80–26, 1980–1 C.B. 66, the IRS announced that it would not follow the Court of Appeals decision in *Robin Haft Trust* on the theory that a "family hostility" exception to the attribution rules is inconsistent with both *Davis* and the legislative history of § 302(b)(1). Likewise, the Fifth Circuit, in David Metzger Trust v. Commissioner, 693 F.2d 459 (5th Cir.1982), held that there is no family hostility exception to the attribution rules.

The Tax Court rejected any possibility of a family hostility or "bad blood" exception to the application of the § 318 attribution rules in Niedermeyer v. Commissioner, 62 T.C. 280 (1974), aff'd per curiam 535 F.2d 500 (9th Cir.1976). Subsequently, however, in Cerone v. Commissioner, 87 T.C. 1, 22 (1986), the Tax Court described the relevance of family hostility as follows:

> First, the attribution rules are plainly and straightforwardly applied. Second, a determination is made whether there has been a reduction in the stockholder's proportionate interest in the corporation. If not, the inquiry ends because, if there is no change in the stockholder's interest, dividend equivalency results. If there has been a reduction, then all of the facts and circumstances must be examined to see if the reduction was meaningful under *United States v. Davis,* supra. It is at this point, *and only then,* that family hostility becomes an appropriate factor for consideration.

Since the shareholder's interest in *Cerone* was not reduced, this version of the family hostility doctrine was, on the facts, inapplicable.

The circumscribed family hostility doctrine of *Cerone* could lead to unusual results. Suppose the stock of X Corp. is held as follows: A, 41 shares; B, 34 shares; C, 17 shares; and D, 8 shares. A and B are parent and child, but the shareholders are otherwise unrelated. If there was "bad blood" between A and B, a redemption of as few as one of B's shares might qualify under § 302(b)(1). But if ten shares were redeemed from each of B and C, the redemption never could qualify because, taking into account the attribution rules, B's ownership increased from 75 percent to 81.25 percent, even though actual ownership was reduced from 34 percent to 24 percent and A alone now holds actual voting control of the corporation. See Henry T. Patterson Trust v. United States, 729 F.2d 1089 (6th Cir.1984), in which all of the stock actually owned by the taxpayer was redeemed; in an alternative holding the court concluded that due to family hostility there was a meaningful reduction even though after applying the attribution rules, the taxpayer's interest was reduced only from 97 percent to 93 percent.

2.2. *Non-Voting Stock*

If a redemption of non-voting stock is involved, the "meaningful reduction" is tested in terms of the change in the shareholder's rights with respect to the corporation's earnings and profits and assets on liquidation. See Himmel v. Commissioner, 338 F.2d 815 (2d Cir.1964), analyzing the "complex of shareholder rights" in a situation involving a multi-class capitalization. Rev.Rul. 75–502, 1975–2 C.B. 111, describes "a shareholder's interest to include (1) the right to vote and thereby exercise control: (2) the right to participate in current earnings and accumulated surplus; and (3) the right to share in net assets on liquidation." Rev.Rul. 77–426, 1977–2 C.B. 87, held that any redemption of non-voting preferred stock constituted a meaningful reduction for purposes of § 302(b)(1) in a situation in which the stockholder did not hold directly or indirectly any voting common stock. The rights given up in the redemption were permanently lost and not retained through continuing common stock ownership.

On the other hand, if a preferred shareholder continues to own common stock, achieving a meaningful reduction with respect to a redemption of nonvoting preferred stock is much more difficult. For example in Hays v. Commissioner, T.C. Memo. 1971–95, the taxpayer owned 80 percent of the common stock of the corporation and all of the preferred stock. A redemption of 10 percent of the preferred stock was found to result in a dividend to the shareholder: "The redemption of 300 out of 3,000 shares of preferred stock held by Hays could not be termed 'meaningful.' Also, whatever significance the reduction might have standing alone, its importance is diminished upon consideration of the fact that Hays remained owner of 80 percent of the common stock in [the corporation]. Thus while his right to earnings and profits via the preferred stock was reduced * * *, he continued to have access to 80 percent of that amount via his common stock. Since Hays owned the overwhelming majority of the common, the only voting stock, his ability to declare dividends was assured." Rev.Rul. 85–106, 1985–2 C.B. 116, involved a redemption of two-thirds of a shareholder's non-voting preferred stock. Prior to the redemption, the shareholder, which was a trust, held directly approximately 18 percent of each of the nonvoting preferred stock and nonvoting common stock and, by attribution from its sole beneficiary, approximately 18 percent of the voting common stock. The ruling held that the redemption was essentially equivalent to a dividend because, after taking into account attribution, the redeemed shareholder's potential for participating in a control group by aligning itself with two other stockholders, who together held 38 percent of the voting common stock, was not reduced.

2.3. *Comparative Dividend Analysis*

Another approach to the problem of dividend equivalence is to compare the distribution on redemption with the distribution of a similar amount as a hypothetical dividend. This approach was applied in Himmel v. Commissioner, 338 F.2d 815 (2d Cir.1964), to hold that a redemption of preferred stock was not essentially equivalent to a dividend because the taxpayer received a substantially larger distribution in the redemption than would have been received as dividend on the common stock. In contrast, Levin v. Commissioner, 385 F.2d 521 (2d Cir 1967), found that a redemption was essentially equivalent to a dividend where the redemption resulted in the shareholder receiving a distribution that was substantially less than would have been received had the distribution been a dividend on the common stock.

While the *Davis* opinion does not discuss this so-called "comparative dividend" method, it is not necessarily inconsistent with the Court's focus on the effect rather than the purpose of the distribution. In Grabowski Trust v. Commissioner, 58 T.C. 650 (1972), the Tax Court applied comparative dividend analysis, finding it consistent with *Davis*.

> In testing for dividend equivalency under this subsection, the Supreme Court in United States v. Davis, 397 U.S. 301 (1970), has now approved application of the "strict net effect" test * * *. This test considers whether the shareholders would have received the identical payments had the redemption been a dividend. In essence, the test measures whether the distribution has altered the shareholder's control over the corporation or the shareholder's rights to future earnings.

In that case the court held the redemption to be essentially equivalent to a dividend because (1) the redemption caused no reduction in the taxpayer's proportionate interest in the corporation, (2) had the distribution been instead a dividend, the taxpayer would have received more than it did in the actual redemption; and (3) the redemption caused an increase in the taxpayer's interest in the corporation's net worth.

Other cases decided after *Davis*, however, have rejected comparative dividend analysis. Brown v. United States, 477 F.2d 599 (6th Cir.1973), held the approach inconsistent with *Davis*. Similarly, in Rev.Rul. 85–106, 1985–2 C.B. 116, the IRS rejected the use of comparative dividend analysis, stating that "*Himmel* fails to reflect developments in the law represented by *Davis*." In that ruling, the nonvoting common stock of an 18 percent shareholder capable of forming a majority control block (56 percent) with two other 19 percent shareholders (the other 44 percent of the stock being widely held) was redeemed. The IRS ruled that § 302(b)(1) did not apply; because the shareholder's opportunity to act in concert with two other shareholders to form a control group was undiminished, there was no meaningful reduction of the shareholder's interest under *Davis*, notwithstanding the reduction in the shareholder's economic interest.

Do these developments since *Davis* indicate that in the redemption area Congress should rely exclusively on mechanical tests such as that in § 302(b)(2)?

3. INSUFFICIENT EARNINGS AND PROFITS

Suppose a distribution in redemption of stock is made under circumstances that would make it essentially equivalent to a dividend, but there are no current or accumulated earnings and profits. Treas.Reg. § 1.302–2(a) states that, despite the verbal difficulty of calling the distribution "essentially equivalent to a dividend," it should nevertheless be governed by §§ 302(d) and 301(c) rather than § 302(a). The distribution would thus be applied against the basis of *all* of the distributee's stock, rather than only the redeemed stock, and taxable gain results only if his entire basis is exceeded.

SECTION 5. PARTIAL LIQUIDATIONS

INTERNAL REVENUE CODE: Sections 302(b)(4), (e).

REGULATIONS: Section 1.346–1, –2, –3.

Section 302(b)(4) extends sale or exchange treatment to redemptions of stock from *individual* shareholders in "partial liquidation" of the distributing corporation. The term "partial liquidation" is defined in § 302(e), and that definition makes clear that unlike the redemptions described in § 302(b)(1) through (b)(3), which focus upon the effect of the distribution to the shareholder, whether a distribution qualifies as a partial liquidation is determined with reference to its effect on the corporation. Although the statutory language of § 302(e)(1) refers to a distribution "not essentially equivalent to a dividend (determined at the corporate level rather than at the shareholder level)," § 302(e) is concerned with the concept of a distribution in connection with a "corporate contraction." The lineage of § 302(e) can be traced through former § 346(a)(2) of the 1954 Code back to provisions of the 1939 Code. The provision was described in the Conference Committee Report accompanying its enactment as "continuing" the law under former § 346(a)(2). See S.Rep. No. 83–1622, 83rd Cong., 2d Sess. 49, 261–2 (1954). The case law under the 1939 Code had focused on corporate contraction as the test for a partial liquidation. See, e.g., Blaschka v. United States, 393 F.2d 983 (Ct.Cl.1968) (distribution was essentially equivalent to a dividend "in that there was no contraction of [the corporation's] business"); see also Treas.Reg. § 1.346–1(a) ("genuine contraction of the corporate business"). While there is relatively little recent case law with respect to the "contraction" doctrine, the IRS has issued a number of rulings that provide guidelines in the area, and the case law under the 1939 Code and former § 346(a)(2) of the 1954 Code continues to be relevant under § 302(e)(1). See H.Rep. No. 97–760, 97th Cong.2d Sess. 530 (1982).

Section 302(e)(2) provides a mechanical safe harbor rule that satisfies the not essentially equivalent to a dividend requirement under § 302(e)(1) if it is met. If the distribution consists of *all* of the assets, or the proceeds from the sale, of an *active* trade or business conducted for at least five years (which was not acquired by the corporation within the five year period in a taxable transaction), *and* after the distribution the corporation continues to conduct an *active* trade or business with a similar five year history, the distribution is not essentially equivalent to a dividend.

Whether the distribution is pro rata or not is immaterial for purposes of § 302(e)(2). I.R.C. § 302(e)(4). Thus, although technically the attribution of ownership rules apply, as a practical matter they are not a factor under § 302(e).

As in the other redemption situations, classification of a transaction as a partial liquidation is important to the shareholders to permit a recovery of basis, absorb otherwise realized capital losses, and take advantage of the preferential rates accorded long-term capital gains.

Estate of Chandler v. Commissioner*

Tax Court of the United States, 1954.
22 T.C. 1158.

[All of the petitioners were stockholders of Chandler-Singleton Company (hereinafter referred to as the Company), a Tennessee corporation organized on May 9, 1923. The capital stock of the Company consisted of 500 shares of common stock of $100 par value, all of which was outstanding until November 7, 1946. The stock was essentially all held by the Chandler family group. From its organization until February 28, 1946, the Company was engaged in the operation of a general department store in Maryville, Tennessee. It had a ladies' ready-to-wear department, men's department, children's department, piece goods department, and a bargain basement.

Chandler was the president and manager of the Company. At the beginning of 1944 he was in very poor health. John W. Bush was the secretary of the Company, but until 1944 he had not been particularly active in its affairs. On January 1, 1944, he became assistant manager of the Company. By profession he was a civil engineer, but at that time he was unemployed due to a change in the administration of the City of Knoxville, Tennessee. During 1944 and 1945 Chandler was sick most of the time. In his absence John W. Bush managed the department store.

John W. Bush did not like being a merchant and decided to return to engineering. In November 1945 he informed Chandler that he was resigning as manager at the end of the year. Chandler, feeling unable to manage the department store himself, decided to sell.

At a stockholders' meeting held on February 20, 1946, it was unanimously agreed that the Company should accept an offer to purchase its merchandise, furniture and fixtures, and lease. The sale was consummated and the Company ceased operating the department store on February 28, 1946. The purchaser, Arthur's Incorporated, moved in that night and began operating the store the following day.

Chandler had worked hard in the department store and had no outside interest. He wanted something to do and did not want to get out

---

* [Ed.: The Tax Court's decision was affirmed, 228 F.2d 909 (6th Cir.1955), the court stating that the finding as to dividend equivalence was a finding of fact sustained by the evidence. Some courts, however, would call this a conclusion of law.]

of business entirely. It was planned that a ladies' ready-to-wear store would be opened by the Company to be managed by Clara T. McConnell (now Clara M. Register) who had managed the ladies' ready-to-wear department of the department store. Thirty shares of stock in the Company owned by Chandler's wife were cancelled on April 5, 1946. Ten of these shares were issued to Clara McConnell on April 13, 1946, in order that she might have an interest in the Company whose store she was going to manage. A men's store, to be eventually taken over by the eldest son of John and Margaret Bush, was also contemplated. It was thought that approximately half of the assets of the Company would be needed for each of the two stores.

About the first of June, 1946, the Company obtained space for the ladies' ready-to-wear store about one-half block from the old department store and the store was opened on September 23, 1946.

The ladies' ready-to-wear store was about the same size as that department in the former department store. The department store had occupied 8,000 to 9,000 square feet of floor space, had employed 10 to 20 persons, and had carried fire insurance in the amount of $65,000 on its stock and fixtures. The new store had approximately 1,800 square feet of floor space, employed four to six persons, and carried fire insurance in the amount of $10,000.

A special meeting of the stockholders was held on September 28, 1946, the minutes of which read in part as follows:

"The Chairman explained that the purpose of the meeting was to authorize partial liquidation for the following reasons:

"The old business was sold and plans were developed to go back into business, operating two stores, a ladies' ready-to-wear business and a men's store. The ladies' ready-to-wear store has been opened and is now operating. Up to now, we have been unable to negotiate a lease for a suitable location, and, after considerable thought, it has been decided to abandon the idea of operating an exclusive men's shop and operate only the one store at the present time. It appears that requirements of the one store will be approximately one-half the capital now invested in Chandler's, Inc.

"Upon motion of Margaret Chandler Bush, seconded by J.W. Bush, and unanimously carried, the officials were authorized and instructed to redeem from each shareholder one-half of his stock, paying therefor the book value, which is approximately $269.00 per share."

On November 7, 1946, each stockholder turned in one-half of his stock in return for cash, the total distributed being $67,250.

The amount of cash and United States Bonds possessed by the Company at the beginning of 1946 exceeded the amount required for the current operation of the business by approximately $45,000. Between January 1 and February 28, 1946, the Company's earned surplus increased by $39,460.44 out of which the Company paid dividends in the amount of $12,500. To the extent of at least $58,027.91, the excess cash possessed by the Company prior to the November 7 distribution was not created by a reduction in the amount of capital needed to operate the Company's business.

Petitioners reported the excess of the payments received over the cost of the stock in their individual income tax returns as capital gain. Respondent treated the payments, to the extent of the earned surplus of $58,027.91, as dividends and taxed them to the petitioners as ordinary income.

The acquisition and cancellation of one-half the Company's stock in 1946 was done at such a time and in such a manner as to make the distribution and cancellation essentially equivalent to the distribution of a taxable dividend to the extent of $58,027.91.]

OPINION

■ BRUCE, JUDGE: Respondent contends that the Company's pro rata distribution in redemption of half its capital stock at book value was made at such a time and in such a manner as to make the distribution essentially equivalent to the distribution of a taxable dividend to the extent of earnings and profits. If respondent's contention is correct the distribution to the extent of earnings and profits loses [its capital gain status and is treated as a taxable dividend].

A cancellation or redemption by a corporation of all of the stock of a particular shareholder has been held not to be essentially equivalent to the distribution of a taxable dividend. Cf. Carter Tiffany, 16 T.C. 1443; Zenz v. Quinlivan, (C.A.6), 213 F.2d 914 * * *. However, "A cancellation or redemption by a corporation of its stock pro rata among all the shareholders will generally be considered as effecting a distribution essentially equivalent to a dividend distribution to the extent of the earnings and profits accumulated after February 28, 1913." Regs. 111, sec. 29.115–9. * * * But, as pointed out by the regulations, a pro rata distribution is not always "essentially equivalent to the distribution of a taxable dividend" and each case depends upon its own particular circumstances. Commissioner v. Sullivan, (C.A.5), 210 F.2d 607, affirming John L. Sullivan, 17 T.C. 1420. The circumstances in the instant case, however, do not warrant a finding that to the extent of earnings and profits the pro rata distribution was not essentially equivalent to a taxable dividend.

Being a question of fact, the decided cases are not controlling. However, in Joseph W. Imler, 11 T.C. 836, 840, we listed some of the factors which have been considered important, viz., "the presence or absence of a real business purpose, the motives of the corporation at the time of the distribution, the size of the corporate surplus, the past dividend policy, and the presence of any special circumstances relating to the distribution." * * *

An examination of the facts reveals that the Company had a large earned surplus and an unnecessary accumulation of cash from the standpoint of business requirement, both of which could have been reduced to the extent of earnings and profits by the declaration of a true dividend. The only suggested benefit accruing to the business by the distribution in cancellation of half the stock was the elimination of a substantial amount of this excess cash. Ordinarily such cash would be disposed of by the payment of a dividend. Coupled with the fact that the stockholders' proportionate interests in the enterprise remained unchanged, these factors indicate that [§ 115(a) of the 1939 Code respecting distributions essentially equivalent to a dividend, the predecessor of §§ 302 and 346] is applicable.

Petitioners seek to avoid application of [that section] by contending that the cash distribution and redemption of stock did not represent an artifice to disguise the payment of a dividend but was occasioned by a bona fide contraction of business with a resulting decrease in the need for capital. While important, the absence of a plan to avoid taxation is not controlling. A distribution in redemption of stock may be essentially equivalent to a taxable dividend although it does not represent an attempt to camouflage such a dividend. * * * Whether a cancellation or redemption of stock is "essentially equivalent" to a taxable dividend depends primarily upon the net effect of the distribution rather than the motives and plans of the shareholders or the corporation. * * * Moreover, we cannot find from the present record that the reduction of taxes was not the motivating factor causing the stockholders to make a distribution in redemption of stock rather than to declare a dividend to the extent of earnings and profits.

Petitioners' primary contention is that the sale of the department store and the opening of the smaller ladies' ready-to-wear store resulted in a contraction of corporate business. This is a vital factor to be considered, but a contraction of business per se does not render [the section in question] inapplicable. L.M. Lockhart, 8 T.C. 436. Furthermore, even though it is clear that there was a diminution in the size of the Company's business, there was no contraction such as was present in Commissioner v. Sullivan, Joseph W. Imler, and L.M. Lockhart, all supra. In those cases there was a contraction of business with a corresponding reduction in the amount of capital used. Here, although the business was smaller, the amount of capital actually committed to the corporate business was not reduced accordingly. On December 31, 1945, before the sale of the department store to McArthur's Incorporated, the Company had $32,736.53 tied up in fixed assets and inventories. On December 31, 1946, after the ladies' ready-to-wear store was opened, it had $31,504.67 invested in those items. Undoubtedly the department store required larger reserves than the ladies' ready-to-wear store for purchasing inventories and carrying accounts receivable. But to the extent of earnings and profits the excess cash distributed was not created by a reduction in the amount of capital required for the operation of the business. Most of the excess cash had existed since prior to the sale of the department store and did not arise from fortuitous circumstances, as petitioners contend, but from an accumulation of earnings beyond the needs of the business. This excess could have been eliminated by the payment of a taxable dividend, and its distribution in redemption of stock was essentially equivalent to a taxable dividend.

It is true that the entire $67,250 distribution could not have been made in the form of an ordinary dividend and to some extent a redemption of stock was required. But [the section] applies if the distribution is only "in part" essentially equivalent to a taxable dividend, and here the distribution was essentially equivalent to a taxable dividend to the extent of earnings and profits.

Decisions will be entered for the respondent.

DETAILED ANALYSIS

1. FIVE-YEAR SEPARATE BUSINESS SAFE HARBOR

Section 302(e)(2) deems a distribution consisting of *all* of the assets, or the proceeds from the sale, of an *active* trade or business conducted for at least five years and which was not acquired by the corporation within the five year period in a taxable transaction to be not essentially equivalent to a dividend if after the distribution the corporation continues to conduct an *active* trade or business with a similar five year history. Although the statute itself does not on its face require the distribution of all of the assets of the terminated business or all of the proceeds from the sale of the business, it has been interpreted by the IRS and the courts to so provide. See, e.g., Kenton Meadows, Inc. v. Commissioner, 766 F.2d 142 (4th Cir.1985); Rev.Rul. 79–275, 1979–2 C.B. 137. Furthermore, only the assets of the terminated trade or business, or the proceeds from the sale of such assets, or a combination thereof, can be distributed in a distribution qualifying as a partial liquidation. See Rev.Rul. 79–275, supra (distribution of unrelated assets rather than promissory notes received on sale of terminated business did not qualify).

Satisfaction of the mechanical test of § 302(e)(2) relates only to the "not essentially equivalent to a dividend" test of § 302(e)(1). It does not *per se* qualify the transaction under § 302(e)(1); the plan and timing tests of § 302(e)(1)(B) must be met even after satisfaction of § 302(e)(2). Rev.Rul. 77–468, 1977–2 C.B. 109; Baan v. Commissioner, 51 T.C. 1032 (1969), aff'd on other grounds, *sub nom.* Gordon v. Commissioner, 424 F.2d 378 (2d Cir.1970), and Baan v. Commissioner, 450 F.2d 198 (9th Cir.1971).

The concept of an active business separately conducted for five years also is utilized with respect to corporate divisions under § 355 and is discussed more fully in relation to that section (see page 718). The regulations under § 355 provide detailed examples of what constitutes the active conduct of a trade or business that are relevant for purposes of § 302(e). See Treas.Reg. §§ 1.346–1(c)(2); 1.355–3(c). There is, however, a significant difference between the test under § 355 and the test under § 302(e)(2). While the division of a single business may be accomplished under § 355, § 302(e)(2) requires the existence of two distinct, separate trades or businesses prior to the partial liquidation. Kenton Meadows, Inc. v. Commissioner, 766 F.2d 142 (4th Cir.1985); Krauskopf v. Commissioner, T.C. Memo. 1984–386. In Bilar Tool & Die Corp. v. Commissioner, 530 F.2d 708 (6th Cir.1976), the court held that the division of a single business because of shareholder disputes, carried out by the transfer of one-half the assets and liabilities of the business to a newly created corporation for its stock followed by the redemption of one of the shareholders' stock in the old corporation in exchange for stock of the new subsidiary, did not constitute a partial liquidation. (Such a transaction is a type (D) reorganization coupled with a split-off, discussed at page 709.) In determining whether the terminated activity constituted a separate trade or business, the inquiry focuses on (1) whether the activity produced a substantial part of the combined corporate income, and (2) whether there was separate supervision and control. Blaschka v. United States, 393 F.2d 983 (Ct.Cl.1968); Mains v. United States, 508 F.2d 1251 (6th Cir.1975).

The distributing corporation is not required to have conducted the terminated business throughout the five year predistribution period, as long as someone conducted the business and it was not acquired in a taxable transaction. Basically, this rule disqualifies acquisitions by purchase within the five year period but permits termination of a trade or business acquired in a tax free reorganization to qualify as a partial liquidation. The provision is designed to prevent the distributing corporation from temporarily "parking" excess funds in a trade or business for a short period prior to "termination" of the newly acquired business. Since tax free reorganizations entail acquisitions in exchange for stock of the acquiring corporation rather than cash, the same considerations do not apply.

2. CONTRACTION OF THE CORPORATE BUSINESS

As noted above, contraction of the corporate enterprise as the standard for testing nondividend equivalence originated under the 1939 Code, and that test has been carried forward through successive statutory revisions. It is available with respect to transactions that fail to come within the safe harbor of § 302(e)(2). See S. Rept. No. 1622, 83d Cong., 2d Sess. 49 (1954); Treas.Reg. § 1.346–1(a).

Imler v. Commissioner, 11 T.C. 836 (1948) (Acq.) is the leading case finding sufficient corporate contraction to constitute a partial liquidation. A corporation, whose stock was held by three stockholders, owned a seven story building and several smaller buildings and was engaged in retinning and soldering metals. It also rented its excess space. A fire destroyed the upper two floors of the seven story building in 1941. Because of the shortage of building materials, the corporation did not rebuild the two floors but reduced the building to a five-story building. Finding its facilities inadequate to store materials for the retinning and soldering activities and also that a scarcity of materials made those operations unprofitable, it discontinued those operations. The corporation distributed $15,000 pro rata in redemption of part of its stock, the cash in part representing the excess of insurance proceeds over repair costs. The redemption was held not to be a dividend, the court stressing the bona fide contraction of business operations, the consequent reduction in capital needed, and the fact that except for the fire no distribution would have been made.

In Lockhart v. Commissioner, 8 T.C. 436 (1947), the sole stockholder of a corporation in the business of oil production, drilling, and operation of a recycling plant desired to operate the business as an individual. He could not completely liquidate as some of the shares were pledged to secure an obligation; in addition, he desired to retain the corporate name and to obtain limited liability respecting the drilling business. The stockholder also needed about $220,000 to pay pending income tax liabilities. Accordingly, net assets of about one million dollars, including about $250,000 in cash, were transferred to him in exchange for 16,245 out of his 17,000 shares, so that the corporation retained only the drilling assets, worth about $34,000. The court held that the reasons for and the results of the redemption did not render it essentially equivalent to a dividend.

In a case in which a corporation did not want to incur the risks of developing certain oil leases, a pro rata distribution of the leases in cancellation of some of its stock was held not to be a dividend. Commissioner v. Sullivan, 210 F.2d 607 (5th Cir.1954). A dissent stressed the pro rata aspect as being almost conclusive and that there was no business purpose for the redemption of the stock instead of a mere distribution.

The IRS has carried the principles of the above cases forward in Revenue Rulings issued after the 1954 Code revision. Rev.Rul. 74–296, 1974–1 C.B. 80, held that there was a genuine corporate contraction where a corporation changed from operating a large department store to a small discount clothing store. In contrast, Rev.Rul. 57–333, 1957–2 C.B. 239, involved a corporation that distributed only a small parcel of land adjacent to its place of business, which it had acquired in contemplation of expansion and leased out in the interim. There was not a contraction where the rentals represented only 2 percent of the corporation's gross receipts. Similarly, a corporation in the quarrying business distributed a portion of a condemnation award received with respect to a taking of a portion of its mineral reserves; there was no contraction because the current operations of the corporation were unaffected. Rev.Rul. 67–16, 1967–1 C.B. 77.

The contraction must be represented by the disposition of all or part of the property used by the corporation in a trade or business. Rev.Rul. 56–512, 1956–2 C.B. 173 (distribution by corporation engaged in paper business of mineral land leased for royalties did not qualify because the corporation was not engaged in a trade or business with respect to the distributed property); Rev.Rul. 76–526, 1976–2 C.B. 101 (same as to distribution of parcel of land subject to net lease); Rev.Rul. 56–513, 1956–2 C.B. 191 (distribution of one-quarter of proceeds of contraction).

In Viereck v. United States, 3 Cl.Ct. 745 (1983), a corporation distributed to its sole shareholder real estate used in its flower business. Although the real estate constituted 80 percent of the net worth of the corporation before the distribution, the court found no partial liquidation because the corporation continued to conduct its flower business on the same scale as it had done previously. See also Rev.Proc. 2014–3, § 4.01(22), 2014–1 I.R.B. 111 (IRS will not issue ruling that redemption is a partial liquidation unless corporation reduces net fair market value of assets, gross revenues, and number of employees by 20 percent).

If the contraction of corporate business test is met, the partial liquidation distribution may include the working capital attributable to the discontinued activity. Rev.Rul. 60–232, 1960–2 C.B. 115. But funds transferred from another business into the terminated business shortly before the distribution may not constitute part of the working capital of the terminated business. Rev.Rul. 76–289, 1976–2 C.B. 100. Similarly, a distribution of cash reserves for future acquisitions of equipment that are no longer needed because of a change of business operations does not qualify as a contraction. Rev.Rul. 78–55, 1978–1 C.B. 88. In determining the amount of the distribution that will be considered attributable to a contraction, the proceeds from the sale of assets and the working capital must be reduced by corporate liabilities attributable to the discontinued activity (including taxes on the sale of the assets). Rev.Rul. 77–166, 1977–1 C.B. 90.

Rev.Proc. 81–42, 1981–2 C.B. 611, provides a checklist of information required by the IRS to obtain an advance ruling as to the qualification of a transaction as a partial liquidation.

3.   REQUIREMENTS OF "PLAN" AND "REDEMPTION"

3.1. *"Plan"*

Section 302(e)(1)(B) limits partial liquidation treatment to redemption distributions that (1) are "pursuant to a plan," and (2) occur within the taxable year in which the plan is adopted or in the succeeding taxable year. A formal plan is not required, Fowler Hosiery Co. v. Commissioner, 301 F.2d 394 (7th Cir.1962), Rev.Rul. 79–257, 1979–2 C.B. 136. But Blaschka v. United States, 393 F.2d 983 (Ct.Cl.1968), found that the total absence of a plan precluded partial liquidation treatment where the intention to redeem some of the shareholder's stock did not arise until after the sale of the corporation's business. Adherence to the time limitations for distributions, however, is crucial.

The strict enforcement of the two year window for distributions can be turned to the taxpayer's advantage if partial liquidation treatment is not desired. Section 302(e) is elective in the sense that its consequences may be avoided by failing to comply with the time requirements in § 302(e)(1)(B). See Rev.Rul. 77–468, 1977–2 C.B. 109. In some cases it may be important to determine precisely when the "plan" was adopted, a determination that may be difficult when the plan was not formally adopted. A number of cases and Revenue Rulings involving complete liquidations dealt with determining the date of adoption of an informal plan. See, e.g., Mountain Water Co. v. Commissioner, 35 T.C. 418 (1960) (Acq.); Rev.Rul. 65–235, 1965–2 C.B. 88.

To qualify a distribution as a partial liquidation under § 302(e), the proceeds from the sale of the assets meeting either the safe harbor of § 302(e)(2) or the general "contraction" test must be distributed as soon as possible within the permissible time window. See Treas.Reg. § 1.346–1(c)(2). The distribution need not be immediate; the proceeds may be invested in portfolio securities pending distribution, but investment profits are not treated as distributions in partial liquidation. Rev.Rul. 76–279, 1976–2 C.B. 99; Rev.Rul. 71–250, 1971–1 C.B. 112. Investment of the proceeds in additional assets for use in the corporation's remaining business, however, precludes a subsequent distribution of an amount equal to the proceeds from qualifying as a partial liquidation. Rev.Rul. 67–299, 1967–2 C.B. 138. See also Rev.Rul. 58–565, 1958–2 C.B. 140 (use of proceeds to pay debts precludes treatment of subsequent distribution of equivalent amount as partial liquidation).

3.2. *Redemption of Shares*

An actual surrender of the shares is not required in the case of a pro rata distribution. Rev.Rul. 90–13, 1990–1 C.B. 65; *Fowler Hosiery Co.,* supra. If there is a genuine contraction of a corporate business in partial liquidation, a surrender of shares would be meaningless; thus the shareholders are deemed to have surrendered a number of shares with a total fair market value equal to the amount of the distribution. If the corporation is not publicly traded, the number of shares deemed surrendered is considered to be the same ratio of total shares as the amount of the distribution bears to the value of all corporate assets prior to the distribution, regardless of actual shares surrendered. Rev.Rul. 56–513, 1956–2 C.B. 191. If the corporation is publicly traded, the number of shares deemed surrendered is considered to be the same ratio of total shares as the amount of the distribution bears to the fair market value of all of the outstanding stock immediately before the distribution. Rev.Rul. 77–245, 1977–2 C.B. 105. However, if the partial liquidation distribution was not pro rata, cases decided under the predecessor of § 302(e) have disqualified transactions if there was no actual redemption of the shares. E.g., Gordon v. Commissioner, 424 F.2d 378 (2d Cir.1970); Honigman v. Commissioner, 55 T.C. 1067 (1971), aff'd on this issue, 466 F.2d 69 (6th Cir.1972).

4. EFFECT OF OPERATION THROUGH A SUBSIDIARY

If a parent corporation operating a business also owns the stock of a subsidiary operating a five-year active business, a sale of the stock and distribution of the proceeds does not satisfy § 302(e). Rev.Rul. 79–184, 1979–1 C.B. 143. Nor would a direct distribution of the stock of the subsidiary qualify under § 302(e), § 355 being the controlling section in these situations. On the other hand, the parent could liquidate the subsidiary, sell its assets, and then make a qualifying distribution of the proceeds under § 302(e). Alternatively, the subsidiary could sell the assets prior to its liquidation with the parent in turn distributing the proceeds under § 302(e). Rev.Rul. 75–223, 1975–1 C.B. 109; Rev.Rul. 77–376, 1977–2 C.B. 107.

If a parent corporation does not operate any active business itself but is a holding company, the holding of the stock of two operating subsidiaries presumably would not satisfy the "trade or business" requirement of § 302(e)(2). See Blaschka v. United States, 393 F.2d 983 (Ct.Cl.1968) (management of a subsidiary did not establish a separate viable business for purposes of the two-business rule); Morgenstern v. Commissioner, 56 T.C. 44 (1971) (majority control of a corporation engaged in a business does not qualify the holder as engaged in that business for purposes of the two-active-businesses rule). The parent, however, could liquidate its operating subsidiaries and retain the assets of one while distributing the assets of the other to provide qualification under § 302(e)(2).

5. DISTRIBUTIONS TO CORPORATIONS

A partial liquidation distribution described in § 302(e) does not qualify as a redemption under § 302(b)(4) if received by a corporate shareholder. Thus, unless the redemption also is described in any of § 302(b)(1) through (3) with respect to the corporate shareholder, the redemption will be treated as a § 301 distribution. In determining whether the distributee is a corporation or an individual, § 302(e)(5) requires that stock owned by a trust or a partnership be treated as owned proportionately by the beneficiaries or partners.

Because a corporate distributee will be entitled to a § 243 dividends received deduction with respect to the distribution, denying partial liquidation treatment is not necessarily disadvantageous. The benefit of the dividends received deduction will be "recaptured," however, when the corporate shareholder later sells the stock with respect to which the partial liquidation distribution was received. Section 1059(e)(1) provides that a partial liquidation distribution is an "extraordinary dividend" regardless of the period for which the stock was held. See page 226. Thus, under § 1059(a) the corporate shareholder must reduce the basis of the stock by an amount equal to the dividends received deduction claimed with respect to the partial liquidation distribution. As a result, the gain on a taxable disposition will increase or the loss will be reduced. If the basis would have been reduced below zero if the full amount of the dividends received deduction had been subtracted from basis, the excess deduction, which did not reduce basis, is recaptured upon disposition of the stock. Thus, the § 243 deduction operates only to defer taxes when it is claimed with respect to partial liquidation distributions.

6.　EFFECT ON DISTRIBUTING CORPORATION

If the corporation distributes appreciated property in a partial liquidation, gain is recognized under § 311(b). No loss may be recognized on the distribution of depreciated property. I.R.C. § 311(a). This result is in contrast to the treatment of distributions in complete liquidation, discussed at page 329, in which losses are generally allowed by § 336.

Section 312(n)(7) governs the effect on earnings and profits of any redemption subject to § 302(a), including partial liquidations. These rules are discussed at page 233.

7.　OTHER ASPECTS OF PARTIAL LIQUIDATIONS

7.1.　*Qualification Under Section 302(b)(4) or Sections 302(b)(1)–(3)*

Treas.Reg. § 1.302–1(a) indicates that partial liquidation treatment controls if a distribution could be treated either as a partial liquidation or as a different redemption under § 302(b). If a distribution fails to qualify as a redemption under § 302(b)(4), it still may qualify under one of § 302(b)(1) through (3) and vice versa. Rev.Rul. 82–187, 1982–2 C.B. 80, held that a non-pro rata partial liquidation resulted in sale or exchange treatment, even though the redemption could not have qualified under any of § 301(b)(1) through (b)(3). See also Treas.Reg. § 1.346–2. Also, if a distribution may be either a complete termination under § 302(b)(3) only by virtue of the waiver of family attribution or a partial liquidation, § 302(b)(5) provides that the prohibition on the acquisition of a prohibited interest within ten years under § 302(c)(2)(A) does not apply.

7.2.　*Partial Liquidation Under Section 302(e) Versus Serial Installment in Complete Liquidation*

Distributions that are one of a series leading to complete liquidation are treated as distributions in complete liquidation under § 331, rather than as distributions in partial liquidation. See page 336. Characterization of a distribution in this regard may be important as respects the shareholder for two reasons. First, a loss may be realized and recognized (subject to the limitations in § 267) on a distribution in partial liquidation. See Rev.Rul. 56–513, 1956–2 C.B. 191. But in a complete liquidation, no loss may be claimed until the series of distributions is completed. Second, corporate distributees never qualify for exchange treatment under § 302(b)(4), but always will be accorded exchange treatment if the distribution is pursuant to a plan of complete liquidation. From the perspective of the distributing corporation, the difference is significant because the corporation under § 311 recognizes only gains (with realized losses being disallowed) on the distribution of property in a partial liquidation, but recognizes both gains and losses on the distribution of property in complete liquidation under § 336.

7.3.　*Other Recharacterizations*

If the shareholder, following the receipt of assets in a partial liquidation, transfers the assets to a new corporation, the liquidation-reincorporation issue, discussed at page 660, may be encountered; see, e.g.,

Rev.Rul. 76–429, 1976–2 C.B. 97 (subsidiary sold assets of one of two businesses and liquidated; parent placed assets of the other business in a newly created subsidiary; the liquidation and reincorporation were ignored and the transaction was treated as a partial liquidation). The characterization of the transaction is important with respect to whether the distributing corporation recognizes gain or loss on the distribution of the assets, and whether the shareholders currently recognize gain or loss with respect to the stock.

SECTION 6.   REDEMPTIONS THROUGH THE USE OF RELATED CORPORATIONS

INTERNAL REVENUE CODE: Sections 304 (omitting sections 304(b)(3)(C) and (D), (b)(4)—(b)(6)); 318.

REGULATIONS: Sections 1.304–2, –3, –5.

Section 304 provides that a sale of stock by the shareholder of one controlled corporation to another controlled corporation is to be treated as a redemption distribution. Section 304 is designed to prevent a shareholder from escaping dividend treatment on a transaction formally structured as a sale that has obvious similarities to a redemption. Because of the controlled nature of the corporations involved, there might not be a significant economic change in the shareholder's overall position. Section 304 requires that the sales proceeds received in such a transaction be treated as a corporate distribution that must meet the test of either § 302 or § 303 to qualify for sale or exchange treatment.[2] Section 304 deals with two basic factual patterns: sales between brother-sister corporations and sales involving parent-subsidiary corporations.

(1) Brother-Sister Corporations

Suppose that the shareholder owns all the stock of X Corporation and all of the stock of Y Corporation. If the shareholder sells some of the X Corporation stock to Y Corporation, § 304 restructures the transaction as a redemption distribution by Y Corporation. Dividend equivalence under § 302, however, is tested in terms of the shareholder's change in ownership in the corporation whose stock is sold, i.e., X Corporation. I.R.C. § 304(b)(1). The amount actually taxed as a dividend, however, is a function of the earnings and profits of *both* corporations, although § 304(b)(2) specifies that the earnings and profits of the purchasing corporation, i.e., Y Corporation, are attributed to the distribution before the earnings and profits of the corporation whose stock is sold, i.e., X Corporation. The X Corporation stock that was actually transferred to Y Corporation is treated as having been contributed to the corporation in a § 351 transaction by the shareholder who received the distribution.

Although § 304(b)(1) directs that the determination of whether the transaction is entitled to redemption treatment is made with respect to the stock of the issuing corporation, i.e., the corporation the stock of which was sold, the treatment of the transaction by § 304(a)(1) as a

---

[2]   For qualification for sale or exchange treatment under § 303 of a sale of stock subject to § 304, see Webb v. Commissioner, 67 T.C. 293 (1976), aff'd per curiam, 572 F.2d 135 (5th Cir.1978). Section 303 is discussed at page 287.

redemption by the *purchasing* corporation is important. If the combined earnings and profits of the issuing and purchasing corporations are not sufficient to support dividend treatment of the entire distribution, the excess distribution is applied against the basis of the purchasing corporation stock and, when that basis has been reduced to zero, the balance is taxable gain. The basis of the selling shareholder in any remaining shares of the issuer may not be applied against the distribution to avoid gain recognition.

(2) Parent-Subsidiary Situations

The second situation with which § 304 is concerned involves the purchase by a subsidiary of its parent's stock from the shareholders of its parent corporation (subsidiary being defined in terms of 50 percent or greater stock ownership). Under § 304(a)(2) the shareholders are treated as if the parent redeemed its stock from them. In testing for dividend equivalence under § 302, stock of the parent owned by the subsidiary after the transaction is attributed under § 318(a)(2)(C) first to the parent corporation and then again under § 318(a)(2)(C), to the shareholders of the parent. Assume, for example, that A owns 80 percent (80 out of 100 shares) of the stock of P Corporation, which in turn owns 70 percent (70 out of 100 shares) of S Corporation. If A sells 40 shares of P Corporation stock to S Corporation, A now actually owns only 40 of 100 shares, or 40 percent of P Corporation. But 70 percent of the 40 shares of P Corporation owned by S (28 shares) are attributed to P Corporation under § 318(a)(2)(C) and 40 percent of the 28 P Corporation shares thus constructively owned by P are attributed to A under § 318(a)(2)(C), with the result that A constructively owns 11.2 shares of P Corporation. A's total ownership of P has therefore been reduced only from 80 percent to 51.2 percent, and dividend treatment is likely. Because § 304(b)(2) permits the earnings and profits of both the issuer and the acquiring corporation to support dividend treatment, a dividend may result even though the parent corporation has no earnings and profits.

Because dividends currently are taxed at the same rate as long-term capital gains, the incentive for noncorporate shareholder-taxpayers to attempt to disguise dividends as stock sales—the avoidance transaction at which § 304 is directed—is greatly reduced. For a noncorporate shareholder, the only important differences between a dividend and a stock sale are that (1) all of a dividend distribution is includable in gross income, while only the amount by which sales proceeds exceed the basis of the stock is includable, and (2) gains on stock sales can be offset by capital losses, while dividend income can be offset by capital losses only to a very limited extent under § 1211.

Fehrs Finance Co. v. Commissioner*

Tax Court of the United States, 1972.
58 T.C. 174.

■ SIMPSON, JUDGE. [Mr. and Mrs. Fehrs owned all of the stock of Fehrs Rental Corporation (Rental). In December, 1964, Mr. Fehrs made gifts

---

* [Ed.: The decision of the Tax Court was affirmed in an opinion that essentially followed the reasoning of the Tax Court, 487 F.2d 184 (8th Cir.1973).].

of the Rental stock to members of his family and after the gifts Mr. Fehrs owned 982 shares, Mrs. Fehrs 177 shares and 221 shares were owned by his son-in-law, his daughters and his grandchildren. Approximately two months later, Fehrs Finance Company (Finance) was incorporated with two of the Fehrs daughters as its sole shareholders. Immediately thereafter Mr. and Mrs. Fehrs transferred all of the remaining Rental stock which they held to Finance in return for Finance's promise to pay them annuities totaling $70,000 per year for the rest of their lives. Finance immediately resold the Rental stock to Rental in exchange for $100,000 cash and an unsecured promissory note of $625,000. The Commissioner asserted a deficiency against Finance based on the gain it allegedly recognized on the disposition of the Rental stock.]

The issue ultimately to be decided in this case appears to be simple: Did the petitioner realize a capital gain on the sale of the Rental stock in 1965? However, to reach that ultimate issue, we must work our way through an amazing maze of preliminary issues. At no time has the respondent taken the position that Rental's acquisition of its stock constituted a redemption under section 302 and that the payments received by the petitioner should be treated as dividends; at all times, he has treated such payments as a capital gain. The controversy revolves about the petitioner's basis in the stock. The respondent contends that section 304 is applicable to the petitioner's acquisition of stock from Mr. and Mrs. Fehrs and that its basis in such stock is therefore determined under sections 304 and 362(a). He concedes that if section 304 is applicable to the petitioner's acquisition of such stock, the gain which it realized on the transfer of such stock to Rental is taxable as a long-term capital gain. Thus, the initial issue for us to consider is whether section 304 is applicable to the petitioner's acquisition of the stock.

Section 304(a)(1) provides in relevant part that, if one or more persons are in "control" of each of two corporations, and if one of those corporations acquires stock in the other corporation from the person or persons in control, then the transaction shall be treated as a redemption under section 302. The stock shall be treated by the acquiring corporation as having been received as a contribution to its capital. The term "control" is defined in section 304(c)(1) as "the ownership of stock possessing at least 50 percent of the total combined voting power of all classes of stock entitled to vote, or at least 50 percent of the total value of shares of all classes of stock." Furthermore, section 304(c)(2) states that the rules contained in section 318(a) with respect to the constructive ownership of stock shall apply for the purpose of determining "control," except that the 50-percent limitations of sections 318(a)(2)(C) and 318(a)(3)(C) shall be disregarded for such purpose. Section 318(a) provides that an individual shall be considered as actually owning the stock which is owned by his spouse, his children, and his grandchildren.

Section 304(a)(1) applies to what is commonly referred to as a "redemption by related or brother-sister corporations." It is clear that by its terms, such section applies to the factual situation in this case. Immediately prior to the transactions here in issue, Mr. and Mrs. Fehrs actually owned 1,159 of the 1,380 outstanding shares of Rental and their daughters and grandchildren owned 196 shares; thus, a total of 1,355 shares, or 98.2 percent of the outstanding stock, was actually or constructively owned by either Mr. Fehrs or Mrs. Fehrs. Only the 25 shares owned by Mr. Vlcek were not attributed to either of the Fehrses under section 318(a). All of the outstanding shares of the petitioner were owned by the daughters of the Fehrses, and were, therefore, similarly attributable to Mr. Fehrs or Mrs. Fehrs. Thus, either Mr. Fehrs or Mrs. Fehrs, or both, were regarded as the person or persons in control of both the petitioner and Rental prior to the transactions in issue. The transaction in which the petitioner acquired stock in Rental from Mr. and Mrs. Fehrs in return for the annuities must be treated as a redemption, and the stock of Rental so acquired must be treated as having been transferred by Mr. and Mrs. Fehrs to the petitioner as a contribution to its capital, under the express mandate of section 304(a)(1). See Rose Ann Coates Trust, 55 T.C. 501 (1970), [aff'd, 480 F.2d 468 (9th Cir. 1973).]. * * *

[W]e now reach the question as to what was the petitioner's basis for the Rental stock under section 304. The petitioner must treat the stock as if it received the stock from the Fehrses as a contribution to its capital; therefore, the petitioner's basis equals the basis of the transferred stock in the hands of Mr. and Mrs. Fehrs plus the amount of gain, if any, which was recognized by Mr. and Mrs. Fehrs upon the transfer. [Secs. 304(a)(1) and 362(a).] It has been stipulated that the basis of the transferred stock in the hands of the Fehrses was zero, so the only remaining question in computing the petitioner's basis in such stock is with respect to the amount of the gain, if any, which Mr. and Mrs. Fehrs recognized upon the transfer. According to the income tax regulations, there is no step-up in the petitioner's basis if the redemption is treated as essentially equivalent to a dividend under section 302 and if the payments to Mr. and Mrs. Fehrs are taxable as a dividend under sections 302(d) and 301, but if the redemption qualifies as an exchange under section 302(b), the petitioner's basis is increased by the gain recognized by Mr. and Mrs. Fehrs. Sec. 1.304–2(c), examples (1) and (3), Income Tax Regs. The validity of such rules has not been challenged. Thus, to determine whether there is any step-up in the petitioner's basis in the stock, it becomes necessary to determine first whether the redemption is essentially equivalent to a dividend under section 302 or whether it qualifies as an exchange under such section.

Section 302 sets forth in subsection (b) the conditions under which a redemption of stock shall be treated as an exchange, and provides in subsection (d) that if those conditions are not met, then the distribution is one to which section 301 applies. If the redemption meets any one of the four tests set forth in section 302(b), it is treated as an exchange, and the amount of the distribution is treated as payment for the stock. Neither party argues the applicability of section 302(b)(2) or 302(b)(4) in this case, but the petitioner argues that the redemption should be treated as an exchange because it meets the test of either section 302(b)(1) or 302(b)(3). We shall consider each such test.

Section 302(b)(1) states, in effect, that the redemption shall be treated as an exchange if it "is not essentially equivalent to a dividend." To meet this test, a redemption must result in a meaningful reduction of the shareholder's proportionate interest in the corporation, after applying the attribution rules of section 318(a) to the stock ownership interests as they existed both before and after the redemption. Secs. 1.302–1(a), 1.302–2(b), Income Tax Regs.; United States v. Davis, 397 U.S. 301, 90 S.Ct. 1041 (1970). * * *

After applying the attribution rules, Mr. and Mrs. Fehrs are considered as owning 98.2 percent of the outstanding shares of Rental—1,355 out of 1,380—both immediately before and immediately after the redemption by the petitioner. We discussed previously the method of computing the preredemption figure; the postredemption figure is reached by attributing to the Fehrses the shares owned by the petitioner as well as those owned by their descendants. The latter result obtains from attributing the petitioner's 1,159 shares to Mmes. Vlcek and May by virtue of section 318(a)(2)(C), the 50–percent requirement of which is not applicable here by reason of section 304(b)(1), and then attributing those shares in turn to the Fehrses under section 318(a)(1)(A)(ii).

The respondent contends that the correct comparison of the Fehrses' stock ownership before and after the redemption is to measure the percentage of the shares owned by them *immediately* before and *immediately* after the redemption; if such contention is accurate, it is clear that the Fehrses' stock ownership (as viewed through the prism of the attribution rules) was not changed at all by the redemption, and thus the redemption clearly fails to meet the test of section 302(b)(1) as articulated by the Supreme Court in United States v. Davis, supra, and as followed by this Court in the decisions previously cited.

* * *

The petitioner also argues that the attribution rules should be considered only for the purpose of "determining the ownership of stock," as prescribed by section 302(c)(1), but not for the purpose of determining control as part of a dividend equivalency test under section 302(b)(1); thus, the petitioner argues, we should take cognizance of the alleged fact that the redemption "eliminated the actual control of Edward J. Fehrs over the affairs of Fehrs Rental Co." However, in section 304, Congress expressly indicated that the attribution rules are to be applied in determining control. Section 304(a)(1) applies when one or more persons "control" each of two corporations; section 304(c)(1) defines control by stating that "control means the ownership" of stock possessing a specified percentage of voting rights or value; and section 304(c)(2) expressly provides, with one exception not here relevant, "Section 318(a)(relating to the constructive ownership of stock) shall apply for purposes of determining control under paragraph (1) [of section 304(c)]." The application of the attribution rules of section 318 to a redemption under section 304(a) can operate in such a way as to cause a person who actually owns no shares in a corporation to be treated as having 100–percent *control* of it. Coyle v. United States, 415 F.2d 488, 490 (C.A.4, 1968), reversing 268 F.Supp. 233 (S.D.W.Va.1967). In *Coyle,* there is no indication that the taxpayer exercised actual control over the affairs of such corporation; the Fourth Circuit regarded the attribution rules alone as sufficient to impute complete control to him. This Court, too, has applied the attribution rules to determine who controlled a corporation involved in a redemption under section 304. Ralph L. Humphrey, supra at 205.

* * * We hold that the redemption cannot be treated as an exchange under section 302(b)(1).

The next question is whether section 302(b)(3) is applicable. Such section provides that the redemption is to be treated as an exchange "if the redemption is in complete redemption of all of the stock of the corporation owned by the shareholder." However, under section 302(c)(1), the attribution rules of section 318 are applicable in determining whether a redemption has resulted in the complete termination of a shareholder's interest under section 302(b)(3), but section 302(c)(2) sets forth certain conditions under which the attribution rules are not applicable for such purposes. Obviously, Mr. and Mrs. Fehrs did actually transfer all of their stock in Rental, but whether the redemption can qualify under section 302(b)(3) depends upon whether the conditions of section 302(c)(2) have been met so that the attribution rules are not applicable.

[The court then held that section 302(b)(3) did not apply because the Fehrs had failed to file the agreements required by section 302(c)(2), discussed at page 243.]

For the foregoing reasons, the redemption in which the petitioner acquired the Rental stock from Mr. and Mrs. Fehrs does not qualify for treatment as an exchange under any of the provisions of section 302(b), and therefore, under section 302(d), the redemption shall be treated as a distribution of property governed by section 301.

Section 301(c)(1) provides in effect that, to the extent that it is made out of the corporation's earnings and profits, the distribution is treated as a dividend and is taxed as ordinary income to the recipient. Section 301(c)(2) goes on to provide that, to the extent that the distribution is not a dividend, it is first applied against the recipient's adjusted basis in the stock, and then, according to section 301(c)(3), the amount which exceeds such adjusted basis is treated as gain from the sale or exchange of property. The petitioner argues that, because it had no earnings and profits during its 1965 taxable year, the tax consequences to Mr. and Mrs. Fehrs of the annuity payments are governed by section 301(c)(2) and (3) and that the petitioner's basis in the stock acquired in the redemption should include, for purposes of computing its gain on the sale of the stock in 1965, the gains to be recognized in subsequent years by Mr. and Mrs. Fehrs as a result of the receipt of the annuity payments.

Initially, the respondent contends that there should be no increase in the petitioner's basis by reason of any gain recognized by the Fehrses under section 301. The respondent argues that section 362(a) provides for an increase in basis by reason of a gain recognized on the transfer and that such language does not apply to gains recognized under section 301(c)(3). There is nothing in the statute or the legislative history to support such contention. The words of section 362(a) are clearly broad enough to apply to a gain recognized under section 301(c)(3), and accordingly, we reject such contention of the respondent.

The petitioner's argument that the annuity payments to Mr. and Mrs. Fehrs will be taxable, after recovery of basis, as a gain under section 301(c)(3) rests on the propositions that it had no earnings and profits in its 1965 taxable year and that the tax treatment of the payments that Mr. and Mrs. Fehrs will receive in later years is determined by its earnings and profits, or lack thereof, in 1965. * * * Thus, we must first decide what constituted the property distributed to the Fehrses, when the distribution or distributions occurred, and for what year or years the earnings and profits of the petitioner are determinative of the tax treatment of such property.

The petitioner argues that the making of the annuity contracts in 1965 constituted distributions of property under section 301, but we do not agree. * * * Whatever the Fehrses may have considered the agreements to be worth to them, the agreements were in no way the equivalent of cash. Unlike the recipient of an ordinary promise to make a payment at a certain time in the future, the Fehrses did not receive anything in 1965 which they could have disposed of even at a substantial discount.

* * *

Since no annuity payments were made to Mr. and Mrs. Fehrs in 1965, and since we have concluded that the making of the annuity contracts did not constitute a distribution of property to them in that year, no amount of gain was recognized by them in 1965 as a result of the transfer of their stock to the petitioner. The petitioner argues that its basis should include the amount of gains to be recognized by Mr. and Mrs. Fehrs in subsequent years. Although there may be circumstances in which the acquiring corporation's basis in property should take into consideration the gains to be recognized by the transferors in later years—a question which we need not and do not decide—it seems clear that such a prediction of future gains could be appropriate only when there is a reasonably reliable method for ascertaining the amount of such gains. Here, it is utterly impossible to anticipate the amount of gains to be recognized in the future. * * * [I]t is impossible to forecast whether such payments will be treated as dividends under section 301(c)(1) or as gains under section 301(c)(3). * * * Thus, we conclude that the petitioner's basis in 1965 must be limited to any gain recognized by the transferors in that year; that is, zero. * * * Accordingly, we hold that in 1965, the petitioner's basis for the purpose of computing its gain on the sale of the Rental stock must be zero, and it must recognize as a gain the entire payment which it received in that year. * * *

Decision will be entered under Rule [155].

DETAILED ANALYSIS

1.   BROTHER-SISTER TRANSACTIONS

1.1. *"Control"*

Section 304(a)(1) applies to sales of stock in the brother-sister context only if "one or more persons are in control" of each corporation. "Control" for this purpose is defined in § 304(c)(1) as ownership of 50 percent *or* more of either combined voting power or value of all classes of stock. See Rev.Rul. 89–57, 1989–1 C.B. 90 (an individual who owned less than 50 percent of the voting stock, but more than 50 percent of the total value of the outstanding stock of a corporation, controlled the corporation). Control of the corporation the stock of which is sold (the issuer) is measured before the sale, while control of the corporation to which the stock is sold (the purchaser) is measured after the sale (to take account of the possibility that some of the consideration paid for the issuer's stock might be stock of the purchaser). I.R.C. § 304(c)(2); Treas.Reg. § 1.304–5(b). In measuring 50 percent ownership for testing control, the attribution rules of § 318 apply, but §§ 318(a)(2)(C) and 318(a)(3)(C)—dealing with attribution from and to corporations—are applied by substituting a greater than 5 percent threshold of ownership for the normal greater than 50 percent threshold. I.R.C. § 304(c)(3)(B). Moreover, there is no minimum ownership threshold for attribution to or from corporations when testing for dividend equivalency under § 302(b). I.R.C. § 304(b)(1). For example, if A owns 30 percent of X Corporation directly and A also owns 30 percent of Y Corporation, which owns the other 70 percent of X Corporation, A owns an additional 21 percent of X Corporation through Y Corporation (70% x 30%). Thus, A owns 51 percent of X Corporation solely for purposes of applying the control test. If A sold one-half of A's X Corporation stock to Z Corporation, of which A owned one-half of the stock and thus also controlled, after the sale A continues to own 21 percent of X corporation through Y corporation and 15 percent directly. A also now owns 7.5 percent of X corporation through Z corporation, for a total ownership of 43.5 percent of X corporation. Thus, A's ownership of X Corporation was reduced from 51 percent to 43.5 percent—15 percent directly, 21 percent through Y Corporation, and 7.5 percent through Z Corporation. The reduction in ownership of X Corporation fails the test of § 302(b)(2), but might meet the test of § 302(b)(1).

Related sales transactions involving a number of shareholders can be subject to § 304 using a control group concept. See Treas.Reg. § 1.304–2(b). In Bhada v. Commissioner, 89 T.C. 959 (1987), aff'd, 892 F.2d 39 (6th Cir.1989) and sub nom. Caamano v. Commissioner, 879 F.2d 156 (5th Cir.1989), an exchange of shares of a publicly traded corporation was, in part, subject to § 304. In determining whether the 50 percent threshold has been met, the attribution rules of § 318 apply, with certain modifications. Thus, as was the case in *Fehrs Finance Co.*, if A owns all of the stock of X Corporation, and A sells that stock to Y corporation, all of the stock of which is owned by A's child B, § 304 applies to the transaction. However, if the selling shareholder's entire *actual* interest in the corporation has been terminated, waiver of family attribution under § 302(c) may be available to avoid dividend treatment. In Fehrs v. United States, 556 F.2d 1019 (Ct.Cl.1977), the individual shareholders in *Fehrs Finance Co.,* who were not parties to the Tax Court litigation, and thus not collaterally estopped, argued in the Court of Claims that the § 302(c)(2) agreement was timely filed, thus qualifying the § 304(a)(1) constructive redemption for capital gain treatment under § 302(b)(3). The Court of Claims, refusing to follow the case involving the corporate taxpayer, found the filing of the agreements in "substantial compliance" with § 302(c)(2). It left open, however, the question whether a tax avoidance motive was present in the gifts of the stock by Fehrs to his family members which, if so, would prevent qualification under § 302(b)(3).

In Niedermeyer v. Commissioner, 62 T.C. 280 (1974), aff'd per curiam 535 F.2d 500 (9th Cir.1976), the taxpayers sold all of their common stock in a corporation controlled by two of their sons to another corporation, in which they actually owned no stock, controlled by three other sons. Although the selling shareholders filed a § 302(c) waiver agreement, the court held it invalid because they retained some preferred stock in the first corporation. In requiring dividend treatment, the Tax Court rejected the taxpayer's argument that due to hostility between the brothers controlling the two different corporations the attribution rules should not have been applied to determine control.

Suppose that A owned 50 percent of the stock of X Corporation and A's child B owned the other 50 percent and all of A's stock in X Corporation was redeemed in a transaction that qualified under § 302(b)(3) by virtue of a waiver of family attribution under § 302(c)(3). Subsequently, A sold all of the stock of Y Corporation to X Corporation. Section 304(a) applies to treat A's sale of the Y Corporation stock to X Corporation as an acquisition of X Corporation stock in exchange for stock of Y Corporation followed by an immediate redemption of the newly issued X Corporation stock for cash. Rev.Rul. 88–55, 1988–2 C.B. 45, held that the prior waiver of attribution for purposes of § 302(b)(3) did not affect application of the attribution rules in determining ownership of the Y stock held by X Corporation when applying § 304 to the sale of stock by A. Thus, since A continued to own by attribution 100 percent of Y Corporation after the sale, the transaction was treated as a redemption by X Corporation that was substantially equivalent to a dividend. The Ruling also held, however, that treatment of A as receiving a distribution with respect to X Corporation stock was not a prohibited interest in X Corporation in violation of the waiver of family attribution rules.

1.2. *Treatment of Distributions*

Section 304(a)(1) provides that if one or more persons are in control of each of two corporations, and one of the corporations acquires stock of the other from controlling shareholders, then the transaction is treated as a redemption of stock by the acquiring corporation. However, whether the redemption qualifies for sale or exchange treatment, rather than treatment as a § 301 distribution, is tested by applying § 302(b) with reference to the change in the selling shareholder's ownership in the stock of the corporation that issued the stock that was sold. I.R.C. § 304(b)(1). But if after the application of § 302(b) the transaction is characterized as a § 301 distribution, dividend status is determined with reference to the combined earnings and profits of both corporations, looking first to the earnings and profits of the acquiring corporation and then to the earnings and profits of the corporation that issued the stock that was sold. I.R.C. § 304(b)(2). Furthermore, if the transaction is treated as a § 301 distribution, for purposes of determining the transferor's basis in the stock of the acquiring corporation, as well as for purposes of determining the portion of the distribution, if any, that is a return of capital under § 301(c)(2) if the distribution is not wholly a dividend, the transferor is deemed to have contributed the exchanged stock to the acquiring corporation in exchange for stock of the acquiring corporation in a § 351 transaction following which that stock is promptly redeemed. The shareholder's basis of the issuing corporation stock deemed to have been contributed to the acquiring corporation in the § 351 transaction is transferred to the shares of stock of the acquiring corporation deemed to have been issued (I.R.C. § 358) and promptly redeemed. If the combined earnings and profits of the corporations are insufficient to support divided treatment for the entire amount received by the shareholder, the basis of all of the stockholder's shares of the acquiring corporation, and not merely the redeemed shares, is taken into account in determining the portion of the distribution that is a return of capital under § 301(c)(2). If the amount of the distribution exceeds the combined earnings and profits of the corporations, but is less than the sum of the combined earnings and profits of the corporations and the basis transferred from the issuing corporation stock to the acquiring corporation stock that is deemed to have been issued and redeemed, the excess transferred basis is add to the basis of the shareholder's remaining stock in the acquiring corporation. See Treas.Reg. §§ 1.302–2(c); 1.304–2(a).

The following examples illustrate the application of § 304(a)(1).

(1) Assume that A owned 80 of the 100 shares of stock of X Corporation and 50 of the 100 shares of stock of Y Corporation. Each share of X Corporation stock had a basis of $1 and each share of Y Corporation stock had a basis of $2. X Corporation had earnings and profits of $90, and Y Corporation had earnings and profits of $40. A sold 40 shares of X Corporation stock to Y Corporation for $300. After the sale, A owns 40 shares of X Corporation directly, and pursuant to § 318(a)(2)(C), A owns 20 shares of X Corporation through A's 50 percent ownership of Y Corporation. Thus, A's ownership interest in X Corporation was reduced from 80 percent to 60 percent (60/100) shares. (Note that unlike in the case of an actual redemption, in which the number of outstanding shares is reduced by the redemption, in the case of a transaction subject to § 304 the number of outstanding shares of the issuing corporation with respect to which § 302 is applied to test for sale or exchange treatment remains unchanged.) This reduction in ownership of X Corporation stock does not satisfy the requirements of § 302(b). Accordingly, the $300 is treated as a § 301 distribution by Y Corporation, but both Y Corporation's earnings and profits of $40, and X Corporation's earnings and profits of $90 support dividend treatment under § 301(c)(1) for $130 of the distribution. To determine the portion of the remaining $170 that is a return of capital, A is treated as having contributed the 40 shares of X Corporation stock with an aggregate basis of $40 (40 shares × $1) to Y Corporation in a § 351 transaction, thereby increasing A's basis in A's Y Corporation stock from $100 (50 shares × $2) to $140. Thus, $140 of the $170 of the distribution that exceeds the $130 dividend is a return of capital pursuant to § 301(c)(2) and $30 of capital gain is recognized under § 301(c)(3). A's basis in the Y Corporation stock is reduced to zero.

(2) Assume all of the same facts as in Example (1), except that A's basis in the X Corporation stock is $5 per share, for an aggregate basis of $200 in the 40 shares of X Corporation stock sold to Y Corporation. Again, the $300 is treated as a § 301 distribution by Y Corporation, of which $130 is a dividend. In this case, however, all of the remaining $170 of the distribution is a return of capital. A is treated as having contributed the 40 shares of X Corporation stock with an aggregate basis of $200 to Y Corporation in a § 351 transaction, thereby increasing A's basis in A's Y Corporation stock from $100 to $300. Those 40 shares are then treated as being redeemed (in a transaction subject to § 301 by virtue of § 302(d)) and under § 301(c)(2) the $170 is treated as a return of capital. The remaining $30 of the basis of the Y Corporation shares deemed to have been issued in exchange for the X Corporation shares and to have been redeemed is

transferred to A's 50 Y Corporation shares pursuant to Treas.Reg. § 1.302–2(c), which now have a basis of $130.

(3) Assume all of the same facts as in Example (1), except that A owned only 60 of the 100 shares of stock of X Corporation and A sold 30 shares of X Corporation stock to Y Corporation for $300. After the sale, A owns 30 shares of X Corporation directly, and pursuant to § 318(a)(2)(C) A owns 15 shares of X Corporation through A's 50 percent ownership of Y Corporation. Thus, A's ownership interest in X Corporation was reduced from 60 percent to 45 percent (45/100) shares. This reduction in ownership of X Corporation stock satisfies the requirements of § 302(b)(2) (45% < (60% × 80%)). Accordingly, the sale of the X Corporation stock by A to Y Corporation is treated as a sale or exchange, and A recognizes a $270 capital gain ($300 — $30). See Treas.Reg. § 1.304–2(a). The basis of A's 50 shares of Y Corporation stock is unaffected by the transaction. Id.

1.3. *Shareholder's Basis Issues*

What happens if the selling shareholder does not actually own any stock of the purchasing corporation after the transaction, but due to attribution rules constructively controls the purchasing corporation, for example, because the selling shareholder's child controls the purchasing corporation? Rev.Rul. 71–563, 1971–2 C.B. 175, held that the basis of the sold stock should be added to the selling shareholder's basis for any remaining stock of the issuer.

What is the effect on basis if, as in *Fehrs Finance Co.,* the selling shareholder actually owns no stock of either the issuer or the purchaser after the transaction? Coyle v. United States, 415 F.2d 488 (4th Cir.1968), suggests that in such a case the basis of the selling shareholder's stock could be added to the basis of the stock in the purchasing corporation held by the related person actually owning stock of the purchasing corporation. But Rev.Rul. 70–496, 1970–2 C.B. 74, held that the basis of the stock simply disappears. In that ruling, Y Corporation sold its wholly owned subsidiary, S Corporation, to Z Corporation. Both Y Corporation and Z Corporation were controlled by X Corporation. Due to the § 318 attribution rules, Y Corporation continued to own 100 percent of S Corporation after the sale and § 304(a)(1) recharacterized the transaction as a dividend. Because Y Corporation had no actual interest in Z Corporation, it had no basis to adjust, and X Corporation was denied a basis adjustment with respect to either Y Corporation or Z Corporation.

Prop.Reg. § 1.304–2(a)(3) (2009) would treat a deemed redemption that is subject to § 301 as a distribution subject to § 302(d) for all purposes of the tax law. To the extent that the deemed § 301 distribution exceeds earnings and profits, the basis of the common stock deemed issued in a § 351 exchange would be reduced on a share-by-share basis under the rules of Prop.Reg. § 1.302–5(a) (2009), discussed at page 241. Under that provision, any unrecovered basis would result in a loss that is not recognized until the occurrence of an inclusion event, which is an event that would qualify the deemed redemption as an exchange transaction under § 302(a) or the stock of the redeeming corporation becomes worthless.

1.4. *Purchasing Corporation's Basis in Stock*

Section 304(a)(1) provides that if a transaction tested under § 304 is treated as a § 301 distribution, the transferor is deemed to have contributed the exchanged stock to the acquiring corporation in exchange for stock of the acquiring corporation in a § 351 transaction. As a result, the acquiring corporation's basis in the stock is determined under § 362(a). Thus, the acquiring corporation's basis in the stock of the issuing corporation received in the transaction will be the same as the transferor's basis in the stock, increased by any gain recognized on the transfer. Prior to 1997, when *Fehrs Finance Co.* was decided and Treas.Reg. § 1.304–2(c), Ex. (3) was promulgated, the last sentence of § 304(a)(1) provided as follows: "To the extent that such distribution is treated as a distribution to which section 301 applies, the stock so acquired shall be treated as having been transferred by the person from whom acquired, and as having been received by the corporation acquiring it, as a contribution to the capital of such corporation." *Fehrs Finance Co.* interpreted the interaction of this statutory rule and § 362(a) as resulting in the acquiring corporation receiving a step-up in basis as a result of any § 301(c)(3) gain recognized by the redeemed shareholder on the overall transaction. In 1997, the last sentence of § 304(a)(1) was amended to read as it now does. If the last sentence of current § 304(a)(1) is read literally, it is difficult to discern how the shareholder can recognize any gain on the "transfer" of the issuing corporation's stock to the acquiring corporation—the gain is realized on the constructive redemption of the acquiring corporation's stock—and thus it is difficult to see how the acquiring corporation can obtain any step-up in the basis of the issuing corporation's stock. On the other hand, the same interpretative difficulties existed under the prior statutory language, which was interpreted to provide the basis step up, and that result appears to be theoretically correct.

If the transaction sufficiently reduces the selling shareholder's stock interest in the issuing corporation that the requirements of § 302(b) are met, the transaction is accorded sale of exchange treatment, and the purchasing corporation takes a § 1012 cost basis in the purchased stock. Although Treas.Reg. § 1.304–2(c), Ex. (3) indicates that in such a case the acquiring corporation's basis is the transferor's basis increased by the transferor's recognized gain, the regulation clearly misinterprets the statute, even though on its assumptions, the example inadvertently reaches the correct answer. In reality, the answer in the regulations virtually always will be incorrect, because the shareholder's amount realized (basis + gain) will not equal the corporation's cost basis—the shareholder's amount realized would be decreased by his transaction costs and the corporation's cost basis would be increased by its transaction costs.

1.5. *Effect of Sale of Stock for Promissory Notes*

Fehrs Finance Co. concluded that no gain was recognized under § 301(c)(3) in the year the annuity contracts were received because they could not be valued. That is not the result if the sale is for a promissory note. A promissory note will taken into account at its stated principal amount provided it bears interest at the applicable federal rate; if the obligation does not bear interest at the applicable federal rate, its principal amount will be determined under the OID rules discussed at page 162. Suppose that A controls both X Corporation and Y Corporation and sells all of the stock of X Corporation to Y Corporation for a $100,000 promissory note, bearing adequate interest, due in ten years. Suppose further, that the corporations' combined earnings and profits are only $20,000 and A's basis in the Y Corporation stock is zero. A recognizes an $80,000 gain under § 301(c)(3). Even though A received a promissory note, Cox v. Commissioner, 78 T.C. 1021 (1982), held that § 453 installment reporting of gains is not available for § 301(c)(3) gain because no "sale" occurs as a result of the distribution.

1.6. *Interaction With Section 351*

Section 304(b)(3) requires that a transaction in which §§ 304 and 351 overlap will be bifurcated, with § 304 controlling the distribution of property and § 351 controlling the distribution of the acquiring corporation's stock. Suppose, for example, A owns more than 50 percent of the stock of X Corporation and transfers the X Corporation stock to Y Corporation, in which A owns 80 percent of the stock, in exchange for additional Y Corporation stock and cash. The transaction would fall within the literal language of § 351. Under this approach, the cash received would be boot entitled to capital gain treatment. Section 304, however, treats the cash distribution as a § 301 distribution unless the change in A's ownership of X Corporation stock meets one of the tests of § 302(b).

If a shareholder transfers stock in a controlled corporation subject to a liability to a second controlled corporation, § 304(b)(3)(A) overrides § 357 and treats the assumption of the liability by the transferee corporation as a distribution of property. However, § 304(b)(3)(B) provides an exception for certain debt incurred to acquire the stock of a corporation that is assumed by a controlled corporation acquiring the stock; assumption of such debt is an alternative to a debt-financed direct acquisition by the acquiring company. In applying these rules, indebtedness includes debt to which the stock is subject as well as debt assumed by the acquiring company.

2.   PARENT-SUBSIDIARY SITUATIONS

2.1. *Control*

If a shareholder sells stock to a subsidiary of the issuer that is controlled by the issuer under the 50 percent test in § 304(c), § 304(a)(2) treats the transaction as a redemption of the issuer parent's own stock. Dividend equivalence under § 302 is tested by reference to the change in ownership of the parent's stock. In applying the tests of § 302(b), stock of the parent owned by the subsidiary is attributed under § 318(a)(3)(C) first to the parent corporation and then, under § 318(a)(2)(C), to the shareholders of the parent. Moreover, pursuant to § 304(b)(1), there is no minimum ownership threshold for applying § 318(a)(2)(C) attribution from a corporation in applying the § 302(b) tests.

Section 304(a)(2) is not limited to situations in which the selling shareholder controls the parent corporation. Assume that individual A owns 40 percent of the stock of P Corporation (40/100 shares), which in turn owns 80 percent of the stock of S Corporation. A sells 10 shares of P Corporation stock to S Corporation. After the transfer, A directly owns 30 percent of the outstanding shares of P Corporation. In addition, 80 percent of the 10 shares of P Corporation owned by S (8 shares) are attributed to P Corporation under § 318(a)(2)(C) and 30 percent of the 8 P Corporation shares thus constructively owned by P are attributed to A, with the result that A constructively owns 2.4 shares of P Corporation. A's total ownership of P Corporation thus is 32.4 percent. Because A's ownership of P has been reduced only from 40 percent to 32.4 percent, § 302(b)(2) does not apply, and unless the distribution is not essentially equivalent to a dividend under § 301(b)(1)—which depends on the distribution of ownership of the remaining 60 shares of P Corporation stock—dividend treatment is likely.

2.2. *Special Problems in Applying the Attribution Rules*

The attribution rules raise special problems under § 304(a) since two corporations, which, absent these rules, are in a brother-sister relationship, can be viewed by virtue of the attribution rules as being in a parent-subsidiary relationship. Similarly, in the converse situation, a real parent-subsidiary relationship can constructively become a brother-sister arrangement. Treas.Reg. § 1.304–2(c), without discussion, appears to take the position that "real" brother-sister corporations will not be characterized as parent-subsidiary for purposes of § 304. Broadview Lumber Co. v. United States, 561 F.2d 698 (7th Cir.1977), held in the converse situation that two corporations in a "real" parent-subsidiary relationship would not be recharacterized for purposes of § 304 as brother-sister corporations.

The application of the attribution rules in the § 304 context can create some unusual results. In Continental Bankers Life Insurance Co. v. Commissioner, 93 T.C. 52 (1989), P Corporation owned 100 percent of the stock of X Corporation and Y Corporation. P Corporation owned 56 percent of Z Corporation and Y Corporation owned 20 percent of the stock of Z Corporation. X Corporation purchased all of the stock of Z Corporation held by Y. Although Y Corporation held no X Corporation stock directly, by attribution through P Corporation, Y Corporation controlled both X Corporation and Z Corporation. Thus, the acquisition was a redemption of X Corporation stock pursuant to § 304(a)(1).

See also Rev.Rul. 74–605, 1974–2 C.B. 97, holding that the attribution rules did not cause § 304 to apply to situations involving a purchase by the parent of stock of a second tier subsidiary.

2.3. *Meaning of "Property" in Section 304(a)(2)*

Suppose that A controls P Corporation, which in turn owns all of the stock of S Corporation. To reverse the parent subsidiary relationship, A transfers to S Corporation more than 50 percent of the stock of P Corporation in exchange for newly issued shares constituting more than 50 percent (but less than 80 percent) of the stock of S Corporation. Does § 304(a)(2) apply to the transaction? Section 317(a) defines property so as to include all corporate stock other than "stock in the corporation making the distribution." Section 304(a)(2) recharacterizes transfers of stock to a subsidiary as a redemption by the issuer, i.e., the issuer is the distributing corporation. In the example, since P Corporation is the issuing corporation, which is deemed to make the distribution, and S Corporation stock was distributed, it is arguable that the S Corporation stock would be "property" as defined in § 317(a). However, Bhada v. Commissioner, 89 T.C. 959 (1987), aff'd 892 F.2d 39 (6th Cir.1989) and sub nom. Caamano v. Commissioner, 879 F.2d 156 (5th Cir.1989), held that the "distribution" in § 304(a) is not the deemed redemption, *but the actual transaction*. Thus, in the example, the distribution by S Corporation to A is a distribution of its own stock, which under § 317(a) is not property. The court reinforced its conclusion that the exchange was not subject to § 304 by noting that in receiving stock of the subsidiary, the shareholders of the parent did not withdraw assets from either the parent or the subsidiary. Rather, "[t]he transaction resulted in a change in the ownership structure of the two corporations. Congress did not intend to prevent such a change in corporate ownership by enacting section 304."

2.4. *Acquiring Corporation's Basis In Parent Corporation's Stock*

Regardless of whether the transaction is treated as a dividend or as a sale or exchange for the selling shareholder, the acquiring subsidiary takes a § 1012 cost basis in the parent corporation's stock purchased in the transaction. Rev.Rul. 80–189, 1989–2 C.B. 106. Furthermore, the purchase by the subsidiary is not treated as a constructive distribution to the parent. Id. Thus, there is no possibility of an adjustment to the parent's basis in the subsidiary stock.

3. RELATIONSHIP OF SECTION 304 TO PARTIAL LIQUIDATION RULES

Based upon a technical analysis of the language of a prior version of § 304 and the statutory predecessor of § 302(e), Blaschka v. United States, 393 F.2d 983 (Ct.Cl.1968), concluded that when § 304 overlaps with the partial liquidation rules of § 302(b)(4), discussed at page 261, qualification for sale and exchange treatment under § 304 is determined by applying the test for a partial liquidation with reference to the acquiring corporation, rather than with reference to the issuing corporation. Assume, for example, that A owns all of the stock of X Corporation, which in turn owns all of the stock of Y Corporation, and A transfers a portion of his shares in X Corporation to Y Corporation in exchange for the proceeds from the sale of all of the assets of one of Y Corporation's two operating divisions. This transaction is described by § 304 and is a partial liquidation of Y Corporation under § 302(b)(4). The partial liquidation of Y Corporation avoids the application of § 304. The court in *Blaschka* explained its reasoning as follows:

> The function of § 304, then is to complement § 302. To that end, § 304(b)(1) provides that such a sale is defined as a redemption of the stock of the acquiring corporation, and that for purposes of § 302(b), whether such stock acquisition is to be treated as a distribution in exchange for the stock is determined by reference to the stock of the issuing corporation. * * * The essential question is whether the distribution has affected the stockholder's proportionate interest and control in the issuing corporation, and for that reason the special rule of § 304(b)(1) points to the issuing corporation to apply § 304(a) to § 302. * * * [N]o mention is made of * * * any provision in § 304 or elsewhere in the 1954 Code, as to which corporation is to be tested to determine whether there has been a partial liquidation in a stock redemption through use of related corporations. * * * [H]owever, * * * the considerations underlying the tax treatment of partial liquidations requires that a § 304 stock redemption, involving the question of a partial liquidation under [§ 302(b)(4) and § 302(e)], be tested on the level of the acquiring corporation. * * * The very nature of a partial liquidation, at least as purportedly involved in this case, is a curtailment or contraction of the activities of the acquiring corporation, and the distribution to a stockholder of

unneeded funds in exchange for stock in a related corporation. It is concluded that the purported partial liquidation is not to be measured by § 302[(b)(1)–(3)], but that a general rule of § 304(a)— that the stock sale is to be treated as a redemption by the acquiring corporation—applies subject, however, to the statutory definition as to what constitutes a partial liquidation under [§ 302(b)(4)] and [§ 302(e)] * * *, applied to the acquiring corporation.

4.   EXTRAORDINARY DIVIDENDS

Under § 1059(e)(1)(A)(iii)(II), distributions to a corporate shareholder that are treated as § 301 distributions by virtue of § 304(a)(1), and thus are eligible for the dividends received deduction under § 243, are classified as extraordinary dividends. As a consequence, the corporate shareholder is required to reduce its basis in the stock of the acquiring corporation by the amount of the dividend that is not included in income. I.R.C. § 1059(a). Amounts in excess of basis are treated as exchange gain. See page 226.

SECTION 7.   STOCK REDEMPTION DISTRIBUTIONS TO PAY ESTATE AND INHERITANCE TAXES

INTERNAL REVENUE CODE: Section 303(a)–(c).

Revenue Ruling 87–132
1987–2 C.B. 82.

ISSUE

Whether the application of section 303 of the Internal Revenue Code to a stock redemption is precluded when the stock redeemed was newly distributed as part of the same transaction.

FACTS

X corporation had outstanding 300 shares of voting common stock that were owned equally by an estate and by *A*, an individual, who had no interest in the estate under section 318 of the Code. The value of the *X* stock held by the estate exceeded the amount specified in section 303(b)(2)(A). The estate wanted to effect a redemption pursuant to section 303 to pay death taxes.

In order to maintain relative voting power and to preserve continuity of management, *X* undertook the following two steps. First, *X* issued 10 shares of a new class of nonvoting common stock on each share of common stock outstanding. Thus, the estate and *A* each received 1,500 shares of this stock. Immediately thereafter, 1,000 shares of the non-voting common stock were redeemed by *X* from the estate in exchange for cash. The overall result of these two steps was that the estate obtained the cash it needed while giving up only nonvoting stock.

The redemption of the *X* nonvoting common stock occurred within the time limits prescribed by section 303(b)(1)(A) of the Code and did not exceed the amount permitted by section 303(a).

LAW AND ANALYSIS

Section 303(a) of the Code provides that a distribution of property to a shareholder by a corporation in redemption of stock of the corporation, which (for federal estate tax purposes) is included in determining the gross estate of a decedent, is treated as a distribution in full payment in exchange for the stock redeemed to the extent of the sum of certain taxes and expenses. These taxes and expenses are the estate, inheritance, legacy and succession taxes plus the amount of funeral and administrative expenses allowable as deductions for federal estate tax purposes.

Section 303(c) of the Code provides that if a shareholder owns stock of a corporation (new stock) the basis of which is determined by reference to the basis of stock of a corporation (old stock) that was included in determining the gross estate of a decedent, and section 303(a) would apply to a distribution in redemption of the old stock, then section 303(a) applies to a distribution in redemption of the new stock. Section 1.303–2(d) of the Income Tax Regulations specifically provides that section 303 applies to a distribution in redemption of stock received by an estate in a distribution to which section 305(a) applies.

Section 305(a) of the Code provides that, generally, gross income does not include the amount of any distribution of the stock of a corporation made by the corporation to its shareholders with respect to its stock. Section 305(b)(1), however, provides that if the distribution is, at the election of any of the shareholders (whether exercised before or after the declaration of the distribution), payable either in its stock or in property, then the distribution of stock is treated as a distribution to which section 301 applies. Section 305(b)(2) provides that if the distribution has the result of the receipt of property by some shareholders and an increase in the proportionate interest of other shareholders in the assets or earnings and profits of the corporation, then the distribution of stock is treated as a distribution to which section 301 applies.

Section 307(a) of the Code provides that if a shareholder already owning stock in a corporation ("old stock") receives additional stock ("new stock") in a distribution to which section 305(a) applies, then the basis of the old stock prior to the distribution is allocated between the old stock and new stock subsequent to the distribution.

Here, 3,000 shares of nonvoting common stock were distributed and 1,000 shares were subsequently redeemed by X as part of a plan designed to allow the estate to avail itself of the benefits of section 303 of the Code. The intent of Congress in enacting the statutory predecessor of section 303 was to provide an effective means whereby the estate of a decedent owning an interest in a family enterprise could finance the estate tax without being required to dispose of its entire interest in the family business in order to avoid the imposition of an ordinary dividend tax. H.R.Rep. No. 2319, 81st Cong., 2d Sess. 63–64 (1950). Given this intent, it follows that the estate should be able to obtain the benefits of section 303 without a substantially adverse effect on the estate's ownership of the family business.

Moreover, section 303(c) of the Code is a remedial provision that was added to expand the application of section 303 to the redemption of stock which, despite a technical change in the form of ownership, represents the same stock as that owned at death. S.Rep. No. 1622, 83rd Cong., 2nd Sess. 239 (1954). The sole requirement for application of section 303 to the redemption, under section 303(c), is that the basis of the stock redeemed ("new stock") be determined by reference to the basis of the "old stock" included in the estate. Section 1.303–2(d) of the regulations provides that stock received by an estate in a section 305(a) distribution is entitled to section 303 treatment. Rev.Rul. 83–68, 1983–1 C.B. 75, holds that a distribution of stock that is immediately redeemable at the option of a shareholder gives the shareholder an election to receive either stock or property within the meaning of section 305(b)(1) and, therefore, is a distribution to which section 301 applies. See also Rev.Rul. 76–258, 1976–2 C.B. 95.

The nature of section 303 of the Code and the limited time period for redemption provided in section 303(b)(1) are generally indicative of a Congressional intent that section 303 be applicable to stock issued as part of the same plan as the redemption. Consequently, for purposes of section 303 only, section 305 should be applied prior to, and without reference to, the subsequent redemption.

HOLDING

The exclusion from gross income provision of section 305(a) of the Code, and the carryover of basis provisions of section 307(a), apply to X's distribution of its new nonvoting common stock to A and the estate. Section 303(a) applies to X's distribution of cash to the estate in redemption of the 1,000 shares of its new nonvoting common stock. For the tax consequences to A (the nonredeeming shareholder) as a result of this transaction, see section 305.

* * *

DETAILED ANALYSIS

1. GENERAL

Section 303, whose provisions were first adopted in 1951, has a significant effect upon estate planning, since it permits certain redemptions for the purpose of paying estate taxes to qualify for sale or exchange treatment, even though the redemption does not meet any of the tests of § 302. In order to qualify under § 303 the stock must (1) have been included in the decedent's gross estate for Federal estate tax purposes; (2) have comprised the specified percentage of the gross estate (less certain expenses); (3) be redeemed from a person who bears the burden of the estate tax; and (4) be redeemed within a specified period of time after the decedent's death. A redemption that qualifies under § 303 generally produces limited tax consequences to the distributee as regards gain recognition because § 1014 provides the deceased shareholder's successor in interest with a basis in the stock equal to its value on the decedent's date of death. On the other hand, if § 303 is not satisfied, dividend treatment, which would generally be the case, would not allow tax-free basis recovery so the section in this regard gives the taxpayer a substantial advantage.

2.   POLICY BASIS FOR SECTION 303

By making the treasury of a closely-held corporation available as a source of funds at the death of a principal shareholder, the problem of meeting estate taxes may be substantially eased. The enactment of this provision was justified as follows:

> It has been brought to the attention of your committee that the problem of financing the estate tax is acute in the case of estates consisting largely of shares in a family corporation. The market for such shares is usually very limited, and it is frequently difficult, if not impossible, to dispose of a minority interest. If, therefore, the estate tax cannot be financed through the sale of the other assets in the estate, the executors will be forced to dispose of the family business. In many cases the result will be the absorption of a family enterprise by larger competitors, thus tending to accentuate the degree of concentration of industry in this country.

S.Rep. No. 81–2375, 81st Cong., 2d Sess. 54 (1951).

Since the enactment of § 303, the Code has been amended by the addition of § 6166, which provides an extension of time for payment of the estate tax if the estate consists largely of an interest in a closely held business. It would seem that the availability of relief under this provision should be sufficient to mitigate any hardship in paying estate taxes attributable to stock in closely held corporations and § 303 is, in fact, largely unnecessary.

3.   TECHNICAL ASPECTS OF SECTION 303

Suppose the stock redeemed to pay estate and inheritance taxes is "§ 306" preferred stock. Since the § 306 stock was included in the decedent's estate and its basis was determined under § 1014, it would lose its § 306 "taint" and can be redeemed under § 303 so as to receive exchange treatment at the shareholder level. See I.R.C. § 306(c)(1)(C).

Section 2035(c)(1)(A) includes in a decedent's gross estate for purposes of computing the § 303(b)(2) percentages (but not for purposes of computing Federal estate taxes) the value of any stock transferred by the decedent for less than adequate consideration within three years prior to death. Such transferred shares, however, may not be redeemed under § 303. Rev.Rul. 84–76, 1984–1 C.B. 91.

CHAPTER 6

STOCK DIVIDENDS

SECTION 1. TAXABLE VERSUS NONTAXABLE STOCK DIVIDENDS

A. JUDICIAL BACKGROUND

Eisner v. Macomber

Supreme Court of the United States, 1920.
252 U.S. 189.

[The taxpayer was the owner of 2,200 shares of common stock in the Standard Oil Company of California. The corporation declared a 50 percent stock dividend and the taxpayer received 1,100 additional shares of which 198.77 shares represented surplus of the corporation earned between March 1, 1913 and January 1, 1916, the latter date being the date of the stock dividend. The shares representing the post-March 1, 1913 surplus had a par value of $19,877 and the Commissioner treated the stock dividend as taxable income to the extent of the par value of such shares. Cash dividends in such an amount would have constituted taxable income. The applicable statute expressly included stock dividends in income. The taxpayer asserted that the stock dividend was not income within the meaning of the Sixteenth Amendment. The District Court rendered judgment against the Government.]

■ MR. JUSTICE PITNEY delivered the opinion of the Court. * * *

In Towne v. Eisner, [245 U.S. 418], the question was whether a stock dividend made in 1914 against surplus earned prior to January 1, 1913, was taxable against the stockholder under the Act of October 3, 1913, which provided that net income should include "dividends," and also "gains or profits and income derived from any source whatever." * * * When the case came here, after overruling a motion to dismiss made by the government upon the ground that the only question involved was the construction of the statute and not its constitutionality, we dealt upon the merits with the question of construction only, but disposed of it upon consideration of the essential nature of a stock dividend disregarding the fact that the one in question was based upon surplus earnings that accrued before the Sixteenth Amendment took effect. Not only so, but we rejected the reasoning of the District Court, saying (245 U.S. 366):

"Notwithstanding the thoughtful discussion that the case received below we cannot doubt that the dividend was capital as well for the purposes of the Income Tax Law as for distribution between tenant for life and remainderman. What was said by this court upon the latter question is equally true for the former. 'A stock dividend really takes nothing from the property of the corporation, and adds nothing to the interests of the shareholders. Its property is not diminished, and their interests are not increased. * * * The proportional interest of each shareholder remains the same. The only change is in the evidence which represents that interest, the new shares and the original shares together representing the same proportional interest that the original shares represented before the issue of the new ones.' Gibbons v. Mahon, 136 U.S. 549, 559, 560. In short, the corporation is no poorer and the stockholder is no richer than they were before. 255, 261 * * * If the plaintiff gained any small advantage by the change, it certainly was not an advantage of $417,450, the sum upon which he was taxed. * * * What has happened is that the plaintiff's old certificates have been split up in effect and have diminished in value to the extent of the value of the new."

This language aptly answered not only the reasoning of the District Court but the argument of the Solicitor General in this court, which discussed the essential nature of a stock dividend. And if, for the reasons thus expressed, such a dividend is not to be regarded as "income" or "dividends" within the meaning of the act of 1913, we are unable to see how it can be brought within the meaning of "incomes" in the Sixteenth Amendment; it being very clear that Congress intended in that act to exert its power to the extent permitted by the amendment. In Towne v. Eisner it was not contended that any construction of the statute could make it narrower than the constitutional grant; rather the contrary. * * * We adhere to the view then expressed, and might rest the present case there, not because that case in terms decided the constitutional question, for it did not, but because the conclusion there reached as to the essential nature of a stock dividend necessarily prevents its being regarded as income in any true sense.

Nevertheless, in view of the importance of the matter, and the fact that Congress in the Revenue Act of 1916 declared that a "stock dividend shall be considered income, to the amount of its cash value," we will deal at length with the constitutional question, incidentally testing the soundness of our previous conclusion.

* * *

[I]t becomes essential to distinguish between what is and what is not "income," as the term is there used, and to apply the distinction, as cases arise, according to truth and substance, without regard to form. Congress cannot by any definition it may adopt conclude the matter, since it cannot by legislation alter the Constitution, from which alone it derives its power to legislate, and within whose limitations alone that power can be lawfully exercised.

The fundamental relation of "capital" to "income" has been much discussed by economists, the former being likened to the tree or the land, the latter to the fruit or the crop; the former depicted as a reservoir supplied from springs, the latter as the outlet stream, to be measured by its flow during a period of time. For the present purpose we require only a clear definition of the term "income," as used in common speech, in order to determine its meaning in the amendment, and having formed also a correct judgment as to the nature of a stock dividend, we shall find it easy to decide the matter at issue.

After examining dictionaries in common use (Bouv.L.D.; Standard Dict.; Webster's Internat. Dict.; Century Dict.), we find little to add to the succinct definition adopted in two cases arising under the Corporation Tax Act of 1909 (Stratton's Independence v. Howbert, 231 U.S. 399, 415; Doyle v. Mitchell Bros. Co., 247 U.S. 179)—"Income may be defined as the gain derived from capital, from labor, or from both combined," provided it be understood to include profit gained through a sale or conversion of capital assets, to which it was applied in the Doyle Case, 247 U.S. 179, 185.

Brief as it is, it indicates the characteristic and distinguishing attribute of income essential for a correct solution of the present controversy. The government, although basing its argument upon the definition as quoted, placed chief emphasis upon the word "gain," which was extended to include a variety of meanings; while the significance of the next three words was either overlooked or misconceived. "*Derived—from—capital*"; "the *gain—derived—from—capital*," etc. Here we have the essential matter: *not* a gain *accruing to* capital; not a *growth* or *increment* of value *in* the investment; but a gain, a profit, something of exchangeable value, *proceeding from* the property, *severed from* the capital, however invested or employed, and *coming in,* being "*derived*"— that is, *received* or *drawn by* the recipient (the taxpayer) for his *separate* use, benefit and disposal—*that* is income derived from property. Nothing else answers the description.

The same fundamental conception is clearly set forth in the Sixteenth Amendment—"incomes, *from* whatever *source derived*"—the essential thought being expressed with a conciseness and lucidity entirely in harmony with the form and style of the Constitution.

Can a stock dividend, considering its essential character, be brought within the definition? To answer this, regard must be had to the nature of a corporation and the stockholder's relation to it. * * *

In the present case, the corporation had surplus and undivided profits invested in plant, property, and business, and required for the purposes of the corporation, amounting to about $45,000,000, in addition to outstanding capital stock of $50,000,000. In this the case is not extraordinary. The profits of a corporation, as they appear upon the balance sheet at the end of the year, need not be in the form of money on hand in excess of what is required to meet current liabilities and finance current operations of the company. Often, especially in a growing business, only a part, sometimes a small part, of the year's profits is in property capable of division; the remainder having been absorbed in the acquisition of increased plant, equipment, stock in trade, or accounts receivable, or in decrease of outstanding liabilities. When only a part is available for dividends, the balance of the year's profits is carried to the credit of undivided profits, or surplus, or some other account having like significance. If thereafter the company finds itself in funds beyond current needs it may declare dividends out of such surplus or undivided profits; otherwise it may go on for years conducting a successful business, but requiring more and more working capital because of the extension of its operations, and therefore unable to declare dividends approximating the amount of its profits. Thus the surplus may increase until it equals or even exceeds the par value of the outstanding capital stock. This may be adjusted upon the books in the mode adopted in the case at bar—by declaring a "stock dividend." This, however, is no more than a book adjustment, in essence not a dividend but rather the opposite; no part of the assets of the company is separated from the common fund, nothing distributed except paper certificates that evidence an antecedent increase in the value of the stockholder's capital interest resulting from an accumulation of profits by the company, but profits so far absorbed in the business as to render it impracticable to separate them for withdrawal and distribution. In order to make the adjustment, a charge is made against surplus account with corresponding credit to capital stock account, equal to the proposed "dividend"; the new stock is issued against this and the certificates delivered to the existing stockholders in proportion to their previous holdings. This, however, is merely bookkeeping that does not affect the aggregate assets of the corporation or its outstanding liabilities; it affects only the form, not the essence, of the "liability" acknowledged by the corporation to its own shareholders, and this through a readjustment of accounts on one side of the balance sheet only, increasing "capital stock" at the expense of "surplus"; it does not alter the preexisting proportionate interest of any stockholder or increase the intrinsic value of his holding or of the aggregate holdings of the other stockholders as they stood before. The new certificates simply increase the number of the shares, with consequent dilution of the value of each share.

A "stock dividend" shows that the company's accumulated profits have been capitalized, instead of distributed to the stockholders or retained as surplus available for distribution in money or in kind should opportunity offer. Far from being a realization of profits of the stockholder, it tends rather to postpone such realization, in that the fund represented by the new stock has been transferred from surplus to capital, and no longer is available for actual distribution.

The essential and controlling fact is that the stockholder has received nothing out of the company's assets for his separate use and benefit; on the contrary, every dollar of his original investment, together with whatever accretions and accumulations have resulted from employment of his money and that of the other stockholders in the business of the company, still remains the property of the company, and subject to business risks which may result in wiping out the entire investment. Having regard to the very truth of the matter, to substance and not to form, he has received nothing that answers the definition of income within the meaning of the Sixteenth Amendment. * * *

We are clear that not only does a stock dividend really take nothing from the property of the corporation and add nothing to that of the shareholder, but that the antecedent accumulation of profits evidenced thereby, while indicating that the shareholder is the richer because of an increase of his capital, at the same time shows he has not realized or received any income in the transaction.

It is said that a stockholder may sell the new shares acquired in the stock dividend; and so he may, if he can find a buyer. It is equally true that if he does sell, and in doing so realizes a profit, such profit, like any other, is income, and so far as it may have arisen since the Sixteenth Amendment is taxable by Congress without apportionment. The same would be true were he to sell some of his original shares at a profit. But if a shareholder sells dividend stock he necessarily disposes of a part of his capital interest, just as if he should sell a part of his old stock, either before or after the dividend. What he retains no longer entitles him to the same proportion of future dividends as before the sale. His part in the control of the company likewise is diminished. Thus, if one holding $60,000 out of a total $100,000 of the capital stock of a corporation should receive in common with other stockholders a 50 per cent. stock dividend, and should sell his part, he thereby would be reduced from a majority to a minority stockholder, having six-fifteenths instead of six-tenths of the total stock outstanding. A corresponding and proportionate decrease in capital interest and in voting power would befall a minority holder should he sell dividend stock; it being in the nature of things impossible for one to dispose of any part of such an issue without a proportionate disturbance of the distribution of the entire capital stock, and a like diminution of the seller's comparative voting power—that "right preservative of rights" in the control of a corporation. Yet, without selling, the shareholder, unless possessed of other resources, has not the wherewithal to pay an income tax upon the dividend stock. Nothing could more clearly show that to tax a stock dividend is to tax a capital increase, and not income, than this demonstration that in the nature of things it requires conversion of capital in order to pay the tax.

* * *

Conceding that the mere issue of a stock dividend makes the recipient no richer than before, the government nevertheless contends that the new certificates measure the extent to which the gains accumulated by the corporation have made him the richer. There are two insuperable difficulties with this: In the first place, it would depend upon how long he had held the stock whether the stock dividend indicated the extent to which he had been enriched by the operations of the company; unless he had held it throughout such operations the measure would not hold true. Secondly, and more important for present purposes, enrichment through increase in value of capital investment is not income in any proper meaning of the term. * * *

It is said there is no difference in principle between a simple stock dividend and a case where stockholders use money received as cash dividends to purchase additional stock contemporaneously issued by the corporation. But an actual cash dividend, with a real option to the stockholder either to keep the money for his own or to reinvest it in new shares, would be as far removed as possible from a true stock dividend, such as the one we have under consideration, where nothing of value is taken from the company's assets and transferred to the individual ownership of the several stockholders and thereby subjected to their disposal.

* * *

Thus, from every point of view we are brought irresistibly to the conclusion that neither under the Sixteenth Amendment nor otherwise has Congress power to tax without apportionment a true stock dividend made lawfully and in good faith, or the accumulated profits behind it, as income of the stockholder. The Revenue Act of 1916, in so far as it imposes a tax upon the stockholder because of such dividend, contravenes the provisions of article 1, § 2, cl. 3, and article 1, § 9, cl. 4, of the Constitution, and to this extent is invalid, notwithstanding the Sixteenth Amendment.

Judgment affirmed.

* * *

B. THE STATUTORY STRUCTURE

INTERNAL REVENUE CODE: Sections 305(a)–(d); 307(a).

REGULATIONS: Sections 1.305–1(a), (b); 1.305–2; 1.305–3(a)–(c), (e) Exs. 1–6; 1.305–5(a), (b)(1)–(3), (d), Exs. 4, 5; 1.305–6; 1.305–7; 1.307–1, –2.

Senate Finance Committee Report, Tax Reform Act of 1969

S.Rep. No. 91–552, 91st Cong., 1st Sess. 150–53 (1969).

[*Pre-1969*] *law.*—In its simplest form, a stock dividend is commonly thought of as a mere readjustment of the stockholder's interest, and not as income. For example, if a corporation with only common stock outstanding issues more common stock as a dividend, no basic change is made in the position of the corporation and its stockholders. No corporate assets are paid out, and the distribution merely gives each stockholder more pieces of paper to represent the same interest in the corporation.

On the other hand, stock dividends may also be used in a way that alters the interests of the stockholders. For example, if a corporation, with only common stock outstanding declares a dividend payable at the election of each stockholder, either in additional common stock or in cash, the stockholder, who receives a stock dividend is in the same position as if he received a taxable cash dividend and purchased additional stock with the proceeds. His interest in the corporation is increased relative to the interests of stockholders who took dividends in cash.

[Pre-1969] law (sec. 305(a)) provides that if a corporation pays a dividend to its shareholders in its own stock (or in rights to acquire its stock), the shareholders are not required to include the value of the dividend in income. There are two exceptions to this general rule. First, stock dividends paid in discharge of preference dividends for the current or immediately preceding taxable year are taxable. Second, a stock dividend is taxable if any shareholder may elect to receive his dividend in cash or other property instead of stock.

These provisions were enacted as part of the Internal Revenue Code of 1954. Before 1954 the taxability of stock dividends was determined under the "proportionate interest test," which developed out of a series of Supreme Court cases, beginning with Eisner v. Macomber, 252 U.S. 189 (1920). In these cases the Court held, in general, that a stock dividend was taxable if it increased any shareholder's proportionate interest in the corporation. The lower courts often had difficulty in applying the test as formulated in these cases, particularly where unusual corporate capital structures were involved.

Soon after the proportionate interest test was eliminated in the 1954 Code, corporations began to develop methods by which shareholders could, in effect, be given a choice between receiving cash dividends or increasing their proportionate interests in the corporation in much the same way as if they had received cash dividends and reinvested them in the corporation. The earliest of these methods involves dividing the common stock of the corporation into two classes, A and B. The two classes share equally in earnings and profits and in assets on liquidation. The only difference is that the class A stock pays only stock dividends and class B stock pays only cash dividends. The market value of the stock dividends paid on the class A stock is equated annually to the cash dividends paid on the class B stock. Class A stock may be converted into class B stock at any time. The stockholders can choose, either when the classes are established, when they purchase new stock, or through the convertibility option whether to own class A stock or class B stock.

In 1956, the Treasury Department issued proposed regulations which treated such arrangements as taxable (under sec. 305(b)(2)) as distributions subject to an election by the stockholder to receive cash instead of stock. In recent years, however, increasingly complex and sophisticated variations of this basic arrangement have been created. In some of these arrangements, the proportionate interest of one class of shareholders is increased even though no actual distribution of stock is made. This effect may be achieved, for example, by paying cash dividends on common stock and increasing by a corresponding amount the ratio at which convertible preferred stock or convertible debentures may be converted into common stock. Another method of achieving this result is a systematic periodic redemption plan, under which a small percentage, such as 5 percent, of each shareholder's stock may be redeemed annually at his election. Shareholders who do not choose to have their stock redeemed automatically increase their proportionate interest in the corporation.

On January 10, 1969, the Internal Revenue Service issued final regulations (T.D. 6990) under which a number of methods of achieving the effect of a cash dividend to some shareholders and a corresponding increase in the proportionate interest of other shareholders are brought under the exceptions in section 305(b), with the result that shareholders who receive increases in proportionate interest are treated as receiving taxable distributions.

General reasons for change.—The final regulations issued on January 10, 1969, do not cover all of the arrangements by which cash dividends can be paid to some shareholders and other shareholders can be given corresponding increases in proportionate interest. For example, the periodic redemption plan described above is not covered by the regulations, and the committee believes it is not covered by the present statutory language (of sec. 305(b)(2)).

Methods have also been devised to give preferred stockholders the equivalent of dividends on preferred stock which are not taxable as such under present law. For example, a corporation may issue preferred stock for $100 per share which pays no dividends, but which may be redeemed in 20 years for $200. The effect is the same as if the corporation distributed preferred stock equal to 5 percent of the original stock each year during the 20–year period in lieu of cash dividends. The committee believes that dividends paid on preferred stock should be taxed whether they are received in cash or in another form, such as stock, rights to receive stock, or rights to receive an increased amount on redemption. Moreover, the committee believes that dividends on preferred stock should be taxed to the recipients whether they are attributable to the current or immediately preceding taxable year or to earlier taxable years.

Explanation of [section 305].—The bill continues (in sec. 305(b)(1)) the provision of present law that a stock dividend is taxable if it is payable at the election of any shareholder in property instead of stock.

The bill provides (in sec. 305(b)(2)) that if there is a distribution or series of distributions of stock which has the result of the receipt of cash or other property by some shareholders and an increase in the proportionate interests of other shareholders in the assets or earnings and profits of the corporation, the shareholders receiving stock are to be taxable (under sec. 301).

For example, if a corporation has two classes of common stock, one paying regular cash dividends and the other paying corresponding stock dividends (whether in common or preferred stock), the stock dividends are to be taxable.

On the other hand, if a corporation has a single class of common stock and a class of preferred stock which pays cash dividends and is not convertible, and it distributes a pro rata common stock dividend with respect to its common stock, the stock distribution is not taxable because the distribution does not have the result of increasing the proportionate interests of any of the stockholders.

In determining whether there is a disproportionate distribution, any security convertible into stock or any right to acquire stock is to be treated as outstanding stock. For example, if a corporation has common stock and convertible debentures outstanding, and it pays interest on the convertible debentures and stock dividends on the common stock, there is a disproportionate distribution, and the stock dividends are to be taxable (under section 301). In addition, in determining whether there is a disproportionate distribution with respect to a shareholder, each class of stock is to be considered separately.

The committee has added two provisions to the House bill (secs. 305(b)(3) and (4)) which carry out more explicitly the intention of the House with regard to distributions of common and preferred stock on common stock, and stock distributions on preferred stock. The first of these provides that if a distribution or series of distributions has the result of the receipt of preferred stock by some common shareholders and the receipt of common stock by other common shareholders, all of the shareholders are taxable (under sec. 301) on the receipt of the stock.

The second of the provisions added by the committee (sec. 305(b)(4)) provides that distributions of stock with respect to preferred stock are taxable (under sec. 301). This provision applies to all distributions on preferred stock except increases in the conversion ratio of convertible preferred stock made solely to take account of stock dividends or stock splits with respect to the stock into which the convertible stock is convertible. * * *

The bill provides (in sec. 305(c)) that under regulations prescribed by the Secretary or his delegate, a change in conversion ratio, a change in redemption price, a difference between redemption price and issue price, a redemption treated as a section 301 distribution, or any transaction (including a recapitalization) having a similar effect on the interest of any shareholder is to be treated as a distribution with respect to each shareholder whose proportionate interest is thereby increased. The purpose of this provision is to give the Secretary authority to deal with transactions that have the effect of distributions, but in which stock is not actually distributed.

The proportionate interest of a shareholder can be increased not only by the payment of a stock dividend not paid to other shareholders, but by such methods as increasing the ratio at which his stock, convertible securities, or rights to stock may be converted into other stock, by decreasing the ratio at which other stock, convertible securities, or rights to stock can be converted into stock of the class he owns, or by the periodic redemption of stock owned by other shareholders. It is not clear under present law to what extent increases of this kind would be considered distributions of stock or rights to stock. In order to eliminate uncertainty, the committee has authorized the Secretary or his delegate to prescribe regulations governing the extent to which such transactions shall be treated as taxable distributions.
* * *

DETAILED ANALYSIS

1.   SCOPE OF SECTION 305

1.1. *General*

The blanket exclusion afforded stock dividends by § 305 prior to 1969 led to some difficulties as taxpayers probed for favorable tax techniques based on that exclusion. A variety of sophisticated schemes arose that in effect allowed shareholders to choose, sometimes on a year-to-year basis, whether to receive cash dividends or instead to obtain an increase in their equity participation in the corporation. These plans had the effect of allowing shareholders who chose the second course to substitute potential capital gain income for current ordinary income cash dividends which historically were subject to higher tax rates. The IRS attempted to reach some of these arrangements under regulations, but as the Senate Finance Committee Report indicates, the then existing statutory structure was not sufficiently broad to cover all of the situations. As a result, the 1969 legislation made some fundamental changes in the theory on which the taxation of stock dividends is based. Several related policies seem to lie behind the 1969 changes. The most dominant themes were to limit the possibility of converting ordinary income into capital gain and to limit the ability of taxpayers to defer income inclusion despite having received the economic equivalent of a dividend. With the current taxation of dividends and capital gain at the same rate, the first theme now has limited relevance.

1.2. *Stock in Lieu of Cash*

From the beginning, Congress wished to prevent a shareholder from having an obvious choice on a year-by-year basis whether to receive cash

distributions in the process of liquidation, and thus governed by § 336 at the corporate level and § 331 at the shareholder level, or a pre-liquidation dividend distribution, governed by § 311 at the corporate level and § 301 and/or § 302 at the shareholder level.

Nor do the regulations under §§ 331, 336, and 346 define a "liquidation," and thus whether a particular distribution is in "liquidation" of the corporation may be an issue. However, Treas.Reg. § 1.332–2(c), which defines the term "liquidation" in the context of liquidation of a corporate subsidiary, provides some guidance: "A status of liquidation exists when the corporation ceases to be a going concern and its activities are merely for the purpose of winding up its affairs, paying its debts, and distributing any remaining balance to its shareholders."

In Estate of Maguire v. Commissioner, 50 T.C. 130 (1968), the court formulated the test for determining whether a liquidation has in fact occurred as follows: "[T]here are three basic tests: (1) There must be a manifest intention to liquidate; (2) there must be a continuing purpose to terminate corporate affairs; and (3) the corporation's activities must be directed to such termination." Under these tests, distributions received in 1960 were held to be dividends and not liquidating distributions; although a plan of liquidation had been adopted in 1944, the corporation after the 1960 distributions still had assets of over $48 million and annual income of over $1.5 million, and liquidation had not been completed by 1964.

The factual nature of this inquiry is illustrated by contrasting *Estate of Maguire* with Olmsted v. Commissioner, T.C.Memo. 1984–381. During 1969 and 1970, the shareholders entered into contractual agreements to wind up the corporation's affairs and liquidate it. The board of directors began selling properties in 1970, but shareholders did not approve a plan of liquidation until December, 1973. Due to difficulties in selling mineral and timber properties, the corporation leased the properties to others and received almost $1,200,000 of income from mineral royalties, timber sales, and rents during the period 1973 through 1981. It distributed over $1,900,000 to shareholders over the same period. The Tax Court held that a status of liquidation existed during 1974 and 1975. Because the corporation would have had difficulty selling its properties, the leasing and royalty arrangements were substitutes for sales and were not inconsistent with the status of liquidation; the fact that the corporation ceased exploration and development of new mineral properties evidenced an intent to wind up business.

Formal action by the directors or shareholders is not necessarily required to effect a complete liquidation for tax purposes. Distributions may be treated as having been received in a *de facto* liquidation if the facts and circumstances indicate that notwithstanding a failure to comply with the formalities of corporate law, the corporation actually has ceased to be a going business. For example, in Rendina v. Commissioner, T.C. Memo. 1996–392, a corporation distributed all of its business assets to its sole shareholder, who in connection with the distribution assumed all of the corporation's liabilities. The corporation, however, did not formally dissolve. Relying on the tests for liquidation status in Treas.Reg. § 1.332–2(c), *Estate of Maquire,* and *Olmsted*, the court found that a *de facto* liquidation had occurred and declined to uphold the Commissioner's deficiency based on treatment of the distribution as a dividend.

1.2. *"Unchecking-the-Box" by Limited Liability Companies*

Treas.Reg. § 301.7701–3(g)(1) deals with situations in which an unincorporated entity, e.g., a limited liability company (LLC), that previously had elected to be taxed as a corporation under Treas.Reg. § 301.7701–3(c), discussed at page 19, revokes the election. In such a case, the entity is treated as if it had distributed all of its assets to its shareholders in a taxable liquidation. Section 336 applies to the entity taxed as a liquidating corporation and § 331 applies to the shareholders. If the entity has only one owner, the entity becomes a disregarded entity for tax purposes (see page 23), and it is deemed simply to have distributed its assets to its owner. If the entity has two or more owners, the liquidation is treated as if the owners immediately contributed all the assets to a newly formed partnership.

SECTION 2.   TREATMENT OF THE CORPORATION

INTERNAL REVENUE CODE: Sections 336(a)–(c), (d)(1)–(2); 6043.

Section 336(a) requires recognition to the corporation of gain or loss as if the property distributed in liquidation had been sold to the distributee for its fair market value. Gain and loss are computed separately on each asset. Generally the gain will be characterized with reference to the purpose for which the corporation held the property. Thus ordinary income will be recognized if inventory is distributed, capital gain will be recognized with respect to capital assets, § 1231 gain will be recognized with respect to depreciable property and land used in the corporation's business, and recapture income will be recognized where appropriate. As a result, in some cases the liquidating corporation may find itself with ordinary income and capital losses which may not be deducted against that income. See I.R.C. § 1211(a).

The treatment of liquidating distributions differs from current distributions in kind, which under § 311 result in recognition of gain but not of loss (see page 197). The legislative history of §§ 311 and 336 does not explain the reason for this differing treatment. Perhaps the answer is that Congress was concerned that allowing losses to be recognized on current distributions would have presented too much opportunity for manipulation, for example, by distributing an asset, such as portfolio securities, which had temporarily fallen in value but which was expected to regain its value. On the other hand, a liquidation terminates the corporate existence, and even though depreciated assets may regain value after the liquidation, the distribution is not a selective distribution subject to manipulation. Thus, it is appropriate to permit the corporation to recognize losses on liquidating distributions. To this end, § 267(a), which generally disallows deductions for losses incurred on sales and exchanges between certain related taxpayers, by its terms does not apply to losses recognized under § 336. However, Congress has provided for disallowance of losses that it considered to be artificial or duplicative of shareholder losses; § 336(d) imposes a complex web of limitations on losses that may be recognized with respect to certain distributions to majority shareholders and distributions of property that has been recently contributed to the corporation.

DETAILED ANALYSIS

1. ISSUES WITH RESPECT TO GAIN RECOGNITION UNDER SECTION 336

1.1. *Distributions of Encumbered Property*

Generally, distributions of encumbered property present no special problems under § 336(a). If a liquidating corporation distributes property having a basis of $200 and a fair market value of $1,000, subject to a $600 mortgage, the amount of the mortgage is irrelevant to the computation. The corporation recognizes a gain of $800. If the mortgage encumbering the distributed property exceeds the fair market value of the property, § 336(b) deems the value of the property to be not less than the amount of the liability. Thus, if the mortgage on the property in the immediately preceding example were $1,150, the corporation would recognize a $950 gain. Section 336(b) should apply on an asset-by-asset basis. Where a liability does not specifically encumber a particular property but a shareholder assumes the liability in connection with the distribution, the liability should be allocated among the distributed properties relative to their respective fair market values. See Rev.Rul. 80–283, 1980–2 C.B. 108 (applying now repealed version of former § 311(c), which was analogous to present § 336(b)).

1.2. *Distributions of Depreciable Property to Majority Shareholders*

Section 336(a) provides that gain is recognized "as if such property were sold to the distributee." Thus, in most cases the purpose for which the corporation held the property determines the character of the gain. Section 1239, however, treats as ordinary income any gain recognized with respect to any property distributed to a shareholder who owns more than 50 percent of the value of the stock (taking into account attribution under § 267(c), excluding § 267(c)(3)) if the shareholder holds the property as depreciable property. Thus, for example, if a corporation distributes to its sole shareholder a building, having an adjusted basis of $100,000 and a fair market value of $1,000,000, the entire $900,000 gain is ordinary income to the corporation, without regard to any applicable depreciation recapture, if the shareholder holds the building for use in a trade or business. The purpose for which the corporation held the building is not relevant under § 1239. Since corporate capital gains are not subject to preferential rates, this issue is important only if the distributing corporation has capital losses deductible under § 1211 only to the extent of capital gains.

2. LIMITATIONS ON LOSS RECOGNITION UNDER SECTION 336

2.1. *Distributions to Related Persons*

2.1.1. *Non-pro Rata Distributions to Related Shareholders*

If a specific item of loss property is distributed among the shareholders other than in undivided interests proportionate to their shareholdings, any loss attributable to the portion of the property distributed to a related person is disallowed. I.R.C. § 336(d)(1)(A)(i). This loss disallowance rule applies only with respect to property distributed to a shareholder who is "related" within the meaning of § 267, generally, a more than 50 percent shareholder. Assume, for example, that 60 percent of the stock of Y Corporation is held by B and 40 percent is held by C, who is unrelated to B. The corporation makes a liquidating distribution as follows: B receives

Blackacre, having a fair market value of $60 and a basis of $70; C receives Whiteacre, having a fair market value of $40 and a basis of $50. Y Corporation may recognize the loss on the distribution of Whiteacre to C because C is not a related person. But because B is a related person and B received 100 percent of the asset, none of the loss on Blackacre may be recognized. However, if Y Corporation had distributed an undivided 6/10th's of each asset to B and an undivided 4/10th's of each asset to C, it would have been allowed to recognize the loss with respect to both assets. Like the rule disallowing losses on distributions to related persons of property contributed within five years of the distribution (discussed below), this rule applies without regard to whether there was a valid business purpose for distributing the property non-pro rata. Furthermore, the disallowance rule applies regardless of how the corporation acquired the property.

The purpose of § 336(d)(1)(A)(i) is puzzling. If Y Corporation distributed Asset #1 and Asset #2 to B and C pro rata, under § 334(a) B and C each would have a basis in their respective interests in the property equal to fair market value. Thus, immediately after the distribution they could exchange the undivided interests received in the liquidating distribution without realization of gain or loss. (An undivided 4/10th's of Asset #1 is equal in value to an undivided 6/10th's of Asset #2, and each asset has a basis equal to its fair market value.) It would appear that B could end up with all of Asset #1 and C could receive all of Asset #2, and the corporation could recognize its losses. Could the IRS successfully apply the "step transaction" doctrine to treat the distribution as being made by the corporation non-pro rata? What if it made good business sense for B to own all of Asset #1 and C to own all of Asset #2?

2.1.2. *Distributions to a Related Shareholder of Recently Contributed Property*

Section 336(d)(1)(A)(ii) disallows any loss deduction to the corporation with respect to a distribution to a related shareholder if the property was acquired in a § 351 transaction or as a contribution to capital within the five year period ending on the date of the distribution. This rule was enacted in 1986, long before the enactment of § 362(e), discussed at page 60, to prevent "stuffing" property with built-in losses into the corporation in anticipation of the liquidation. At that time, in the absence of the rule in § 336(d)(1)(A)(ii), the corporation could recognize losses to offset gains on property held by the corporation; the shareholder also would recognize an additional loss on the liquidation because the basis of the stock would be increased under § 358 by the basis of the appreciated asset. At the same time, only the fair market value of the asset would be taken into account as an amount realized in computing gain or loss on the liquidation. This "double loss" situation was a corollary of the double taxation of gains. Congress has limited the availability of these double losses because of the tax avoidance potential. See H.Rep. No. 99–841, 99th Cong., 2d Sess. II–200 (1986). The importance of § 336(d)(1)(A)(ii) is reduced, but not completely eliminated by the enactment in 2004 of § 362(e), requiring that the corporation reduce the aggregate basis of the property transferred to a corporation in a § 351 transaction to its fair market value if the aggregate basis of the property in the hands of the transferor exceeds its aggregate fair market value. However, because § 362(e) compares the aggregate basis of contributed property with its aggregate fair market value, if both appreciated property and depreciated property are contributed to a corporation, the corporation's basis in a particular contributed asset can exceed the asset's fair market value thereby triggering application of § 336(d)(1)(A)(ii).

Suppose, for example, that A and B formed X Corporation, to which A contributed cash of $60 in exchange for 60 shares of common stock, and B contributed Whiteacre, with a fair market value of $25 and a basis of $10, and Blackacre with a fair market value of $15 and a basis of $30, in exchange for 40 shares of stock. Section 362(e) does not operate to reduce the basis of Blackacre to less than $30 because the aggregate basis of Blackacre and Whiteacre ($40) does not exceed their aggregate fair market value ($40). Four years later (when the bases and values of the properties are unchanged) X Corporation is liquidated. Blackacre, Whiteacre and cash are distributed to A; other property and cash are distributed to B. Although § 336(a) requires X Corporation to recognize the $15 gain with respect to Whiteacre, § 336(d)(1)(A)(ii) disallows recognition of the $15 loss with respect to Blackacre.

Furthermore, in operation, § 336(d)(1)(A)(ii) is mechanical and applies without regard to whether the property was appreciated or depreciated at the time it was contributed to the corporation. Suppose, for example, that for a valid business purpose C contributes two items of property to Y Corporation in exchange for all of its stock. The first asset has a basis of $500 and a fair market value of $1,000; the second has a basis of $1,000 and a fair market value of $1,600. Four years later Y Corporation is liquidated and both properties are distributed to C. At the time of the liquidation, the first property has appreciated in value to $2,000 and its basis remains $500; the second property has depreciated in value to $600 and its basis remains $1,000. Y Corporation must recognize the $1,500 gain on the first property, but may not recognize the $400 loss on the second property.

2.2. *Distributions and Sales of Recently Contributed Built-in Loss Property*

In cases where § 336(d)(1) is not applicable, § 336(d)(2), which applies without regard to the amount of stock of the corporation owned by a distributee shareholder, might disallow losses at the corporate level with respect to property distributed or sold to any person in the process of liquidation. Section 336(d)(2) applies to property acquired by the corporation in a § 351 transaction or as a contribution to capital if "the acquisition of such property by the liquidating corporation was part of a plan a principal purpose of which was to recognize loss by the liquidating corporation with respect to such property in connection with the liquidation." I.R.C. § 336(d)(2)(B)(i)(II). Section 336(d)(2), which also is intended to disallow built-in double losses, is more accurately targeted than § 336(d)(1)(A)(ii). Section 336(d)(2) disallows only that portion of the loss that is attributable to the excess of the adjusted basis of the property immediately after the acquisition over the fair market value of the property at that time. In other words, only the built-in loss is disallowed; any loss accruing while the property was owned by the corporation is allowed. Mechanically, this result is accomplished by reducing the basis of the contributed property in an amount equal to the built-in loss.

As is the case with respect to § 336(d)(1)(A)(ii), the subsequent enactment of § 362(e) has reduced, but not eliminated, the importance of

§ 336(d)(2). Suppose, for example, that D and E formed Z Corporation, to which D contributed cash of $40 in exchange for 40 shares of common stock, and E contributed $20 of cash, Whiteacre, with a fair market value of $25 and a basis of $10, and Blackacre with a fair market value of $15 and a basis of $30, in exchange for 60 shares of stock. Section 362(e) does not operate to reduce the basis of Blackacre to less than $30 because the aggregate basis of Blackacre and Whiteacre ($40) does not exceed their aggregate fair market value ($40). One year later (when the bases and values of the properties are unchanged) Z Corporation is liquidated. Blackacre and Whiteacre are distributed to D; cash is distributed to E. Section 336(d)(2) reduces the basis of Blackacre by $15, the amount of the built-in loss at the time of the contribution, from $30 to $15 before applying § 336(a). While § 336(a) requires Z Corporation to recognize the $15 gain with respect to Whiteacre, no gain or loss is realized with respect to Blackacre.

The basis reduction under § 336(d)(2) applies only for purposes of computing losses. For example, if an asset was contributed to the corporation at a time when its basis was $500 and its fair market value was $400 and the asset was distributed when its adjusted basis, without regard to § 336(d)(2), was $450 and its fair market value was $150, the adjusted basis would be reduced to $350, reflecting the $100 built-in loss, and only a $200 loss would be allowed, assuming that § 336(d)(1) does not also apply. However, because the basis reduction rule does not apply when computing gain, if the property had a fair market value of at least $350 but not more than $450 at the time it was distributed, the corporation would recognize neither a gain nor a loss.

Although the general applicability of the loss disallowance rule of § 336(d)(2) is based on intent, a timing element is introduced by § 336(d)(2)(B)(ii), which conclusively deems property contributed to the corporation within two years prior to adoption of the plan of liquidation to have been contributed as part of the proscribed plan, except as otherwise provided in regulations. However, the Conference Committee Report indicates that the regulations should provide that the presumption "will be disregarded *unless* there is no clear and substantial relationship between the contributed property and the conduct of the corporation's current or future business enterprises." H.Rep. No. 99–841, 99th Cong., 2d Sess. II–201 (1986). Stated affirmatively, the Committee Report suggests that the presumption should not apply to assets used in the corporation's trade or business and the question reverts to one of intent. Thus, for example, contributions of portfolio securities would be presumed to have been made for the prohibited purpose. Furthermore, the Conference Report indicates that the loss disallowance rule should not apply at all if a plan of liquidation is adopted within two years of formation of the corporation. Id. However, the statute on its face does not appear to be self-executing, and the rules for disregarding the presumption explained in the Committee Report thus are not in force until regulations are promulgated.

Technically, the loss disallowance rule of § 336(d)(2) applies to property transferred to the corporation more than two years prior to adoption of the plan of liquidation if the acquisition by the corporation was pursuant to a plan having the prohibited purpose. However, the Conference Committee Report indicates that § 336(d)(2) should be applied to property contributed more than two years prior to adoption of the plan of liquidation "only in the most rare and unusual cases." Id. at II–200.

The flush material of § 336(d)(2)(B)(i) includes within property subject to the basis adjustment any property the basis of which is determined with reference to property contributed pursuant to the proscribed plan. Thus, if contributed property is subject to a basis adjustment under § 336(d)(2), the taint cannot be purged by exchanging the property for other property which takes an exchanged basis (such as in a § 351 transaction or a § 1031 like-kind exchange).

3. EXCEPTIONS TO SECTION 336

Section 336 does not apply to distributions which are part of a corporate reorganization. I.R.C. § 336(c). However, § 361(c) may require recognition of gain, but not loss, with respect to property other than stock or securities of the acquiring corporation distributed in liquidations pursuant to a corporate reorganization. Corporate reorganizations are discussed in Chapter 12.

Section 337 displaces § 336 and provides nonrecognition in the case of liquidating distributions by an 80 percent controlled corporate subsidiary.

4. TRANSFERS TO TAX-EXEMPT ORGANIZATIONS

Pursuant to broad regulatory authority contained in § 337(d), Treas.Reg. § 1.337(d)–4(a)(1) requires recognition of built-in gain or loss by a taxable corporation on the transfer of substantially all of its assets to a tax-exempt entity. Recognition of loss is limited by Treas.Reg. § 1.337(d)–4(d) with respect to assets acquired in a § 351 exchange or as a contribution to capital and assets distributed to a shareholder or member of the taxable corporation's affiliated group if the transaction is part of a plan the principal purpose of which is to recognize a loss. Conversion of a taxable corporation into a tax-exempt entity is treated as a transfer of substantially all of its assets, thereby triggering recognition of gain or loss. Treas.Reg. § 1.337(d)–4(a)(2). Exceptions to the recognition rules are available for taxable corporations that were previously tax-exempt and which return to tax-exempt status within three years, and new corporations that acquire a tax exemption within three years of formation. Treas.Reg. § 1.337(d)–4(a)(3). In addition, assets transferred to a tax-exempt entity that are used in an activity subject to the tax on unrelated business taxable income of § 511(a) are excepted from the recognition rule until sold by the tax-exempt entity. Treas.Reg. § 1.337(d)–4(b).

SECTION 3.   TREATMENT OF SHAREHOLDERS

INTERNAL REVENUE CODE: Sections 331; 334(a); 346(a); 453(h)(1)(A)– (C), (2).

REGULATIONS: Section 1.331–1.

Section 331 treats a distribution in complete liquidation as being received in exchange for the stock of the liquidating corporation, resulting in recognition of capital gain or loss to the shareholder. The shareholder takes a basis in any property received in the liquidation equal to its fair market value. I.R.C. § 334(a). While these basic rules generally are not difficult to apply, certain situations may cause problems. Only distributions in *complete* liquidation are accorded sale or exchange treatment under § 331. Where a liquidation is accomplished through a series of distributions, § 346(a) provides that all distributions in the series pursuant to a plan to liquidate the corporation will be treated as liquidating distributions. Generally a distribution other than one in liquidation will be subject to § 301 and will be taxed as ordinary income to its full extent if the corporation has sufficient earnings and profits. Section 346(a) eliminates the necessity to distinguish between dividend distributions and liquidating distributions once the liquidation process begins, but determining when the liquidation process begins sometimes presents difficult factual questions. The status of liquidation is important to the tax treatment of the shareholder, since capital gain and recovery of basis with respect to the liquidating distribution result only if a "liquidation" exists; otherwise, the shareholder will generally be treated as having received an ordinary dividend.

Where property is distributed in liquidation and the shareholder assumes liabilities of the corporation in connection therewith, the shareholder's gain is computed by subtracting the basis of his stock from the fair market value of the property received less any liabilities assumed.[2] See Rev.Rul. 59–228, 1959–2 C.B. 59. For purposes of computing gain on a subsequent sale, the shareholder's basis for the property under § 334(a) is the fair market value of the property at the time of distribution without any adjustment to reflect the assumed liabilities. Ford v. United States, 311 F.2d 951 (Ct.Cl.1963). This failure to take liabilities directly into account in computing basis is appropriate because the liabilities were subtracted from the fair market value of the distributed property in computing the shareholder's amount realized on the liquidation. Since the shareholder must pay the liabilities, they are a cost of acquiring the property and properly should be reflected in basis. Since only the net fair market value of the property was taken into account in computing the shareholder's gain realized in the liquidation, providing the property with a basis equal to its fair market value undiminished by liabilities indirectly includes the liabilities in its basis. For this reason, it likewise is proper not to increase basis by the amount of the assumed liabilities; to do so would take them into account twice.

Section 331 provides that a liquidating distribution is received in *exchange* for the stock, thereby providing the vital link to § 1222 that produces capital gain or loss treatment. Suppose the stock of the corporation has become worthless prior to the liquidation and the shareholder receives nothing in the liquidation. Since there is no sale or exchange of the stock because there has been no liquidating distribution, see Aldrich v. Commissioner, 1 T.C. 602 (1943), it would appear that the loss would be an ordinary rather than capital loss. This result is foreclosed by § 165(g), which provides capital loss treatment upon the worthlessness of corporate stock and securities. However, § 1244, discussed at page 159, provides for ordinary loss treatment on

---

[2] If the amount of a liability is contingent at the time of the distribution and the shareholder later repays an amount in excess of the liability taken into account in computing his gain or loss on the distribution, the repayment will give rise to a capital loss, not an ordinary deduction. See Arrowsmith v. Commissioner, 344 U.S. 6 (1952).

the sale or exchange or worthlessness of certain stock in a "small business corporation," which is a narrowly defined term.

Section 267(a)(1) generally disallows loss deductions on the sale or exchange of property between a shareholder and a corporation of which the shareholder directly or through attribution owns more than 50 percent of the stock. Losses incurred on the complete liquidation of a corporation, however, are exempted from disallowance under § 267 by the express terms of that provision.

DETAILED ANALYSIS

1. ALLOCATION OF LIQUIDATING DISTRIBUTIONS AMONG SHARES

1.1. *Single Liquidating Distribution*

Where the shareholder of a liquidating corporation owns a single block of stock acquired at the same time and at the same cost, and receives a single liquidating distribution, the distribution is applied first to the basis of the stock. Gain is recognized to the extent the fair market value of the assets received exceeds the basis of the stock. However, where a series of liquidating distributions are received or where the shareholder owns different blocks of stock acquired at different times and at different costs, each distribution must be allocated to each block of stock and gain or loss is computed separately for each block of stock. Treas.Reg. § 1.331–1(e). Rev.Rul. 68–348, 1968–2 C.B. 141, amplified in Rev.Rul. 85–48, 1985–1 C.B. 126, provides examples of how to make the required allocations.

Assume that C purchased 200 shares of stock of X Corporation for $11,000 five years ago and also purchased 100 shares of stock of X Corporation for $1,000 three months ago. X Corporation liquidates and C receives $30 per share for a total of $9,000. C received a distribution of $6,000 with respect to the 200 shares purchased five years ago for $11,000, and recognizes a $5,000 long-term capital loss with respect to those shares. C received a distribution of $3,000 with respect to the 100 shares purchased three months ago for $1,000, and recognizes a $2,000 short-term capital gain with respect to those shares. These gains and losses are not directly netted, but are taken into account separately in calculating C's net long-term capital gain and net short-term capital loss for the year pursuant to § 1222.

Computation of gain and loss on a block-by-block basis when the shareholder receives a single liquidating distribution generally is relevant either if long-term capital gains are taxed differently than short-term capital gains or if liquidating distributions are made over the course of two or more years. Thus, block-by-block computations often are unnecessary. A block-by-block computation may have an impact, however, where the taxpayer holds a block of stock as a capital asset which has depreciated in value and holds an appreciated block as an ordinary income asset, as may be the case with a dealer in securities.

1.2. *Serial Liquidating Distributions*

Where the shareholder receives a series of distributions with respect to two or more blocks of stock, significant timing differences may occur as a result of the block-by-block computation. After each distribution has been allocated among the blocks of stock, gain is recognized with respect to a block of stock after its basis has been recovered. This treatment, ratified by Rev.Rul. 85–48, supra, reflects the "open transaction" doctrine of Burnet v. Logan, 283 U.S. 404 (1931), even though such treatment generally is not available for installment sales. See Treas.Reg. § 15a.453–1(c). However, no loss is recognized in a § 331 liquidation until after the corporation has made its final distribution. Rev.Rul. 68–348, 1968–2 C.B. 141; Schmidt v. Commissioner, 55 T.C. 335 (1970). Thus, gain may be recognized on a particular block before basis has been completely recovered on another block. Furthermore, where the series of distributions spans two or more years, it is possible for a shareholder with no overall gain to realize capital gain in one year and a capital loss in a subsequent year, without being able to offset the two.

Assume that B holds 300 shares of common stock of X Corporation. B's basis for 100 shares (Block 1) is $500; B's basis for the other 200 shares (Block 2) is $2,000. In 2013, X Corporation adopts a plan of liquidation pursuant to which it distributes $1,800 to B in 2013 and $900 in 2014. One-third of the $1,800 received in 2006, $600, is allocated to Block 1, and B recognizes a $100 gain with respect to Block 1. The remaining $1,200 received in 2012 is allocated to Block 2 and is applied against basis to reduce the basis of Block 2 from $2,000 to $800. When the $900 is received in 2014, $300 is allocated to Block 1, and B recognizes a $300 gain with respect to Block 1; $600 is allocated to Block 2, and B recognizes a $200 loss with respect to Block 2. Overall, B recognizes total net gain of $200, of which $100 is recognized in each of 2013 and 2014. Had B been permitted to aggregate the basis of both blocks and apply distributions against the aggregate basis before recognizing any gain, no gain would have been recognized in 2013, the entire $200 would have been recognized in 2013.

2. DISTRIBUTION OF INSTALLMENT NOTES

2.1. *Generally*

Where the corporation distributes in liquidation a § 453 installment note previously received from another person on the sale of property by the corporation, § 453B requires the corporation to include any remaining deferred gain in income. The shareholders generally are not entitled to use the installment method under § 453 with respect to the note. Instead, the shareholders must treat the fair market value of the note as an amount received from the corporation in a liquidating distribution. Any gain recognized is capital gain; and the note takes a basis in the hands of the shareholders equal to its fair market value at the time of the distribution. Rev.Rul. 66–280, 1966–2 C.B. 304. If the principal amount of the note exceeds its fair market value on the date of the distribution, the excess, when collected, is ordinary income, either pursuant to the market discount rules of § 1276 or judicial interpretation of the sale or exchange requirement of § 1222.

2.2. *Section 453(h)*

Section 453(h) provides a limited exception to the shareholder recognition rule (but not to the rules requiring recognition by the corporation upon distribution of the note) when the shareholders receive installment obligations arising from a sale or exchange of corporate assets occurring after the adoption of a plan of complete liquidation that is completed within twelve months after it was adopted,[3] and it applies whether the installment sale is pursuant to a complete acquisition of the seller's business or a dispersal sale. This provision applies only if the liquidation is completed within twelve months following adoption of the plan.[4] If this requirement is met, shareholders recognize gain on the liquidation with respect to the notes under the installment method of § 453 as they receive payments on the obligations. If an installment obligation arises from the sale of inventory, however, deferred recognition is available only if substantially all of the inventory attributable to a particular trade or business of the corporation was sold in bulk to a single purchaser.

Assume, for example, that C is the sole shareholder of Y Corporation. C's basis for the stock is $1,000. Y Corporation owns a factory and inventory. If Y Corporation sells the factory and inventory for a $10,000 promissory note, payable in five equal principal installments (with interest), and then distributes the note to C in complete liquidation, C recognizes no gain at the time of the liquidation, but instead recognizes $1,800 of gain under § 331 as each $2,000 installment is received (C also recognizes interest income). If the factory were sold for $6,000 cash and the inventory were sold in bulk for a $4,000 note, due in four equal principal installments (with interest), and Y Corporation liquidated, C would allocate a pro rata portion of the $1,000 basis in the stock, $600 ($1,000 × $6,000/($6,000 + $4,000)) to the cash distribution, and C would recognize a $5,400 gain upon receipt of the cash distribution; C would allocate $100 of basis to each $1,000 payment received on the note and recognize $900 of gain as each payment is received.

Section 453(h) has some limitations. If the property sold for an installment obligation is depreciable property and the purchaser is related to the shareholder (i.e., the shareholder's spouse, a trust of which the shareholder or the shareholder's spouse is a beneficiary, or a corporation or partnership more than 50 percent controlled by the shareholder of the selling corporation), installment reporting is not available to the shareholder. Where a corporation distributes cash or property (other than qualifying installment obligations) in one tax year and then in a subsequent tax year (but within 12 months) distributes installment obligations qualifying under § 453(h), the gain included in the first year must be recomputed—usually on an amended return—to reflect treatment of the earlier cash distribution as an installment payment. In turn, a portion of the basis for the stock originally used to offset the cash distribution must be allocated to the installment obligation, thereby increasing the gain recognized in the first year. Treas.Reg. § 1.453–11 provides detailed rules regarding the application of § 453(h).

---

[3]   Section 453(k)(2), denying installment sale treatment for sales of marketable stock and securities, might render § 453(h) unavailable in the liquidation of a publicly traded corporation, but it is highly unlikely that a publicly traded corporation ever would liquidate in a manner to which § 453(h) could apply.

[4]   Section 453(h) is a vestige of the pre-1987 rules under which a corporation did not recognize gain or loss on the sale or exchange of certain assets if the assets were sold after the adoption of a plan of liquidation and the liquidation was completed within twelve months. Although those rules were repealed by the Tax Reform Act of 1986, installment reporting of shareholder gain was continued.

3. DISTRIBUTIONS OF GOODWILL AND ASSETS WITH UNASCERTAINABLE VALUE

Where goodwill is distributed in a liquidation, the value of the goodwill is includible for purposes of determining shareholder gain. See Carty v. Commissioner, 38 T.C. 46 (1962) (Acq.) Section 1060 requires that in any "applicable asset acquisition," the value of acquired goodwill be determined by the "residual" method, which values goodwill as the excess of the purchase price over the fair market value of all other assets, including both tangible and intangible assets (other than going concern value and goodwill). See Treas.Reg. § 1.1060–1. The definition of "applicable asset acquisition" in § 1060(c), if read literally, might include corporate liquidations in which the shareholders acquire the assets of a trade or business of the corporation. In the context of liquidations of closely held corporations, application of the "residual" method to distributed goodwill is problematical because that valuation method contemplates that the consideration for the transferred assets is susceptible to valuation without reference to the assets themselves. In the case of a closely held corporation, the stock usually is valued with reference to the value of the assets, including the value of goodwill determined under a capitalization of earnings method. But see Treas.Reg. § 1.1060–1(b)(3), Ex. 3, requiring the application of § 1060 when assets are acquired from the corporation in a stock redemption transaction.

Nevertheless, in some cases a closely held corporation might not own goodwill apart from that of its shareholder employees. In Norwalk v. Commissioner, T.C. Memo 1998–279, an accounting services professional corporation dissolved and distributed its assets to its two CPA shareholders, who in turn contributed the assets to a partnership that they joined in the same year. The IRS asserted that in addition to its tangible assets, the corporation distributed to its shareholders customer based intangible assets, including the corporation's client base, client records, goodwill, and going concern value, which resulted in an additional gain to the corporation under § 336 and also increased the amount realized and thus the capital gain recognized by the shareholders on the liquidation. The court, however, upheld the taxpayer's argument that because any clients would have followed the individual CPAs, the corporation's earnings were entirely attributable to the CPA-shareholders. Thus it owned no goodwill or customer based intangibles that could be separately sold. Because clients sought the personal ability, personality, and reputation of the individual CPAs, these assets did not belong to the corporation. The corporation's name had no goodwill value. Martin Ice Cream Co. v. Commissioner, 110 T.C. 189 (1998), also suggests that business goodwill based on an individual shareholder's personal relationship with a supplier—specifically in that case, an importer's relationship with the management of Häagen-Dazs—remains property owned by the shareholder individually, even though the corporation avails itself of the goodwill to conduct business. Similarly, in H & M, Inc. v. Commissioner, T.C. Memo. 2012–290, the court rejected the IRS's assertion that a compensation agreement with the selling shareholder of an insurance agency that was dependent on customer relations with the shareholder represented goodwill of the corporation.

Thus, the court held that the corporation did not recognize additional gain on the sale under § 336 on distribution of appreciated goodwill.[5]

Suppose that a corporation liquidates and distributes to the shareholders a contractual right to receive royalties with respect to sales by a licensee of a product to which the corporation holds the patent. At the time of liquidation, there is no reasonable basis for estimating future sales. May the shareholders treat the liquidation as an open transaction, applying distributions and royalty payments against the basis of the stock and reporting gain only when the basis of the stock has been recovered fully? A number of cases allowed open transaction treatment for liquidating distributions of rights with a speculative or unascertainable value which occurred in years prior to the enactment of § 453(j)(2), which limited the use of the open transaction approach generally. See, e.g., Likins-Foster Honolulu Corp. v. Commissioner, 840 F.2d 642 (9th Cir.1988) (open transaction doctrine applied at Commissioner's behest to claims for condemnation of liquidated subsidiary's property); Cloward Instrument Corp. v. Commissioner, T.C. Memo. 1986–345, aff'd by order, 842 F.2d 1294 (9th Cir. 1988) (royalty contract). In other cases, income-producing intangibles were valued and the liquidation was taxed as a closed transaction. See, e.g., Waring v. Commissioner, 412 F.2d 800 (3d Cir.1969) (patent royalty contract). Whether § 453(j)(2) applies to liquidating distributions is unclear; literally a liquidation may fall within the definition of "installment" sale in § 453(b)(1). If § 453(j)(2) is applicable, open transaction reporting of a liquidating distribution generally will be foreclosed, and the shareholder will recover the basis of the stock ratably over fifteen years, unless a different basis recovery period can be established. See Temp.Reg. § 15a.453–1(c)(4).

4.   DISTRIBUTIONS IN PAYMENT OF SHAREHOLDER HELD DEBT

Payments of debts owed by the corporation to its shareholders are not treated as liquidating distributions. See, e.g., Braddock Land Co., Inc. v. Commissioner, 75 T.C. 324 (1980). Thus, a cash method shareholder generally will recognize ordinary income when in the course of liquidation, the corporation pays an account payable due to the shareholder. In *Braddock Land Co., Inc.*, the shareholder's forgiveness of a corporate indebtedness for accrued compensation and interest after the corporation had adopted a plan of liquidation was ignored because the court determined that there was no "business purpose" for the forgiveness. Payment of the indebtedness was not part of a liquidation distribution and was treated as ordinary income to the shareholder. See also Dwyer v. United States, 622 F.2d 460 (9th Cir.1980) (shareholder who purportedly forgave accrued interest on debt owed to him by corporation realized ordinary income equal to "forgiven" interest upon liquidation). Furthermore, if a shareholder contributes to the corporation a corporate debt owed to the shareholder,

---

[5]   But see Howard v. United States, 106 A.F.T.R.2d 2010–5533 (E. D. Wa. 2010), aff'd, 448 Fed. Appx. 752 (9th Cir. 2011), holding that compensation for a noncompetition clause signed by a selling shareholder on sale of his dental practice was ordinary income rather than capital gain on the sale of personal goodwill. The court held that because the taxpayer was the corporation's employee with a covenant not to compete with it, any goodwill generated during that time period was the corporation's goodwill. The court also rested its holding that the goodwill was a corporate asset on its conclusion that the income associated with the practice was earned by the corporation and the covenant not to compete, which extended for three years after the taxpayer no longer owned stock in the corporation rendered any personal goodwill "likely [of] little value."

§ 108(e)(6) might require the corporation to recognize income. The result may not be so clear where a cash method shareholder forgives a corporate indebtedness prior to adoption of a plan of liquidation, but shortly before the corporation liquidates.

5. "RECEIPT" OF DISTRIBUTION

A liquidation distribution need not actually be received for a shareholder to be taxed on the gain realized. Rev.Rul. 80–177, 1980–2 C.B. 109, held that a cash method shareholder had constructively received a liquidating distribution on the date announced by the corporation as the date on which it would make a liquidating distribution to any shareholder presenting a stock certificate for surrender. If a shareholder makes a gift of stock in a liquidating corporation after a plan of liquidation has been adopted but prior to receiving the liquidating distribution, the gain generally will be taxed to the donor, even though the distribution is received by the donee. See Kinsey v. Commissioner, 477 F.2d 1058 (2d Cir.1973) (charitable contribution of stock following adoption of plan of liquidation); Dayton Hydraulic Co. v. United States, 592 F.2d 937 (6th Cir.1979) (corporation taxed on gain of stock of another corporation distributed to shareholder).

Typically, distributions in complete liquidation of a corporation are pro rata in amount to the shareholders. If, however, a non-pro rata distribution occurs in a § 331 liquidation, a shareholder who receives less than a pro rata share of the value of the liquidating distribution is treated as having received a pro rata share and then, in a separate transaction, having conveyed a portion of the liquidating distribution (equal to the difference between a pro rata share and the share actually received) to the other shareholders as compensation, gifts, in satisfaction of obligations, or the like, as the facts indicate. Rev.Rul. 79–10, 1979–1 C.B. 140.

In some cases a liquidating distribution may be made to a trust for the benefit of the shareholders rather than directly to the shareholders. A liquidation often is structured in this manner to facilitate a post-liquidation sale of assets that are not readily divisible where there are numerous shareholders. Generally, the shareholders will be treated as receiving a liquidating distribution when the assets are transferred to the trust. See Rev.Rul. 72–137, 1972–1 C.B. 101. The trust is then treated as a grantor trust for income tax purposes. However, if a liquidation involving a liquidating trust is unreasonably prolonged or the business activities of the trust are significant enough to obscure its stated purpose of facilitating an orderly liquidation, the trust may be reclassified as an association taxable as a corporation or as a partnership. Treas.Reg. § 301.7701–4(d). See also Rev.Proc. 82–58, 1982–2 C.B. 847, amplified, Rev.Proc. 91–15, 1991–1 C.B. 484, modified and amplified, Rev.Proc. 94–45, 1994–2 C.B. 685 (requirements for advance ruling on classification of liquidating trust).

SECTION 4.   LIQUIDATION OF SUBSIDIARY CORPORATIONS—SECTION 332

INTERNAL REVENUE CODE: Sections 332; 334(b); 337(a), (b)(1), (c), (d); 381(a), (c)(1)(A), (c)(2)–(c)(7); 453B(d).

REGULATIONS: Sections 1.332–2, –5, –7.

Pursuant to § 332, where a parent corporation completely liquidates a subsidiary corporation, no gain or loss is recognized to the parent if the parent owns a requisite amount of stock of the subsidiary. This provision also applies if a controlled subsidiary merges into its parent corporation. Treas.Reg. § 1.332–2(d). Under § 334(b) the basis of the assets in the parent corporation's hands remains the same as the basis of the assets to the subsidiary corporation.

Section 332(b)(1), through a cross reference to § 1504(a)(2), limits nonrecognition to situations in which the parent corporation's stock ownership of the subsidiary constitutes both (1) 80 percent or more of the voting power of the subsidiary's stock, and (2) 80 percent or more of the total value of all stock of the subsidiary corporation, except that pursuant to § 1504(a)(4), nonparticipating, nonconvertible, nonvoting preferred stock is not counted in determining control. When the nonrecognition rule of § 332 applies, the parent's basis in the stock of the subsidiary is irrelevant, and any potential gain or loss inherent in the stock disappears.[6] This treatment differs from the exchanged basis rule that is more commonly encountered in tax free transactions and is the same as the transferred basis rule generally applied to the transferee corporation in a § 351 exchange or a corporate reorganization. Elimination of the potential gain inherent in the subsidiary's stock prevents two levels of taxation of corporate profits that have not been distributed out of corporate solution. In this regard, § 332 serves a purpose analogous to the dividends received deduction under § 243 (see page 223). The theory behind § 332 is also reflected in the consolidated return provisions of §§ 1501 through 1504, discussed in Chapter 9, which permit affiliated corporations (defined with reference to the 80 percent control test) to file a single income tax return reflecting their combined incomes. Although § 332 governs the liquidation in both cases, the results of liquidating a subsidiary with which the parent did not file a consolidated return, however, are not always the same as the results of a liquidation of a subsidiary in a group filing a consolidated return.

Under § 332, the term "property" includes money. Rev.Rul. 69–379, 1969–2 C.B. 48. Thus the parent corporation recognizes neither gain nor loss even though only cash is received on the liquidation. International Investment Corp. v. Commissioner, 11 T.C. 678 (1948), aff'd per curiam, 175 F.2d 772 (3d Cir.1949). Taxable gain or loss would have been recognized previously by the subsidiary on the conversion of its assets to cash.

When § 332 applies to the parent of a liquidating corporation, § 337 provides a general exception to the basic rule of § 336 that a liquidating

---

[6]   Additional considerations come to bear when the parent and subsidiary have been filing a consolidated return.

corporation recognizes gain or loss on liquidating distributions.[7] Under § 337(a), no gain or loss is recognized on a distribution to an "80 percent distributee," defined in § 337(c) as a corporation that meets the stock ownership requirements of § 332(b). The final sentence of § 337(c), referring to the consolidated return regulations, requires that a single corporation meet the 80 percent requirement; it is not sufficient for two or more affiliated corporations to have aggregate holdings meeting the 80 percent test. In concert, §§ 332 and 337 provide for complete nonrecognition of gain or loss at the corporate level on the liquidation of a wholly owned subsidiary.

As a corollary to the nonrecognition treatment accorded to both the liquidating subsidiary and the distributee parent corporation, § 381(a), discussed in Chapter 15, provides that the tax attributes of the subsidiary carry over to the parent. The most notable of these attributes are net operating loss carryovers, capital loss carryovers, and the earnings and profits accumulations or deficits. Even if the parent corporation owns less than 100 percent of the subsidiary, the parent succeeds only to the portion of the subsidiary's earnings and profits not allocable to distributions to minority shareholders. Treas.Reg. § 1.381(c)(2)–1(c)(2). If either the parent or the subsidiary has a deficit in its earnings and profits accounts, after a § 332 liquidation the parent must maintain separate earnings and profits accounts; the deficit of one corporation cannot be used to offset the surplus in the earnings and profits account of the other. I.R.C. § 381(c)(2); Luckman v. Commissioner, 56 T.C. 1216 (1971). Earnings and profits accumulated by the parent after the liquidation are used to exhaust the deficit account before the accumulated earnings and profits account of the parent is increased. Treas.Reg. § 1.312–11(b)(2), (c).

DETAILED ANALYSIS

1. EIGHTY PERCENT CONTROL REQUIREMENT AND TAX PLANNING

1.1. *Breaking Control Prior to Completion of Liquidation*

Section 332 is not by its terms elective. But if the taxpayer desires to avoid §§ 332 and 337 to obtain loss deductions on the parent's stock investment and the subsidiary's liquidating distributions, it may do so by a sale of stock that reduces the parent's stock ownership below the 80 percent control line prior to the adoption of the plan of liquidation. In Granite Trust Co. v. United States, 238 F.2d 670 (1st Cir.1956), after the plan of liquidation was adopted, the parent corporation made some sales and charitable gifts of stock to cause the parent's ownership of the subsidiary to drop below 80 percent. It thus sought to avoid § 332 and recognize a loss. The IRS argued that the transfers should have been ignored and § 332 applied. The court, however, found the stock transfers to be real in substance, not just form, and gave effect to them. The court stated:

---

[7]   To prevent the complete avoidance of tax on appreciation in the subsidiary's assets, subject to certain exceptions, § 337 does not apply to a liquidation of a subsidiary of a tax-exempt organization. I.R.C. § 337(b)(2). This provision is necessary because notwithstanding a carryover basis under § 334(b), a subsequent sale of the former subsidiary's assets generally would not be taxable.

As for the Commissioner's "end-result" argument, the very terms of [§ 332(b)] make it evident that it is not an "end-result" provision, but rather one which prescribes specific conditions for the nonrecognition of realized gains or losses, conditions which if not strictly met, make the section inapplicable. * * *

In the present case the question is whether or not there actually were sales. Why the parties may wish to enter into a sale is one thing, but that is irrelevant under the *Gregory* case so long as the consummated agreement was no different from what it purported to be.

Even the Commissioner concedes that "[l]egal title" passed to the several transferees on December 13, 1943, but he asserts that "beneficial ownership" never passed. We find no basis on which to vitiate the purported sales, for the record is absolutely devoid of any evidence indicating an understanding by the parties to the transfers that any interest in the stock transferred was to be retained by the taxpayer. * * *

In addition to what we have said, there are persuasive reasons of a general nature which lend weight to the taxpayer's position. To strike down these sales on the alleged defect that they took place between friends and for tax motives would only tend to promote duplicity and result in extensive litigation as taxpayers led courts into hair-splitting investigations to decide when a sale was not a sale. It is no answer to argue that, under Gregory v. Helvering, there is an inescapable judicial duty to examine into the actuality of purported corporate reorganizations, for that was a special sort of transaction whose bona fides could readily be ascertained by inquiring whether the ephemeral new corporation was in fact transacting business, or whether there was in fact a continuance of the proprietary interests under an altered corporate form. * * *

In short, though the facts in this case show a tax avoidance, they also show legal transactions not fictitious or so lacking in substance as to be anything different from what they purported to be, and we believe they must be given effect in the administration of [§ 332(b)]as well as for all other purposes.

A similar result was reached in Commissioner v. Day & Zimmerman, 151 F.2d 517 (3d Cir.1945), in which the parent corporation sold at public auction a sufficient number of shares to reduce to less than 80 percent its ownership in a subsidiary that it planned to liquidate. The fact that the purchaser at the auction was the parent corporation's treasurer did not affect the result, because the court found that he purchased the stock with his own funds and assumed an actual economic risk with respect to the value he ultimately might realize. See also Associated Wholesale Grocers, Inc. v. United States, 927 F.2d 1517 (10th Cir.1991) (step transaction doctrine applied to disallow loss claimed on a taxable merger, the transaction treated instead as a § 332 liquidation followed by an asset sale).

1.2. *Acquisition of Control Prior to Adoption of Plan of Liquidation*

In the opposite situation, in Estate of Glass v. Commissioner, 55 T.C. 543 (1970) (Acq.), aff'd per curiam, 453 F.2d 1375 (5th Cir.1972), § 332 was held not to apply where a parent corporation owned only 75 percent of the stock of the subsidiary at the time of adoption of the plan of liquidation and thereafter acquired the balance of the stock. The difference in result between *Granite Trust Co. and Day & Zimmermann, Inc.*, on the one hand, and *Estate of Glass*, on the other hand, can be explained by the statutory requirement of § 332(b)(1) that the parent meet the 80 percent control test at the time of adoption of the plan and at all times until receipt of the distribution. Thus, although control may be broken after adoption of the plan, control acquired after adoption of the plan does not meet the statutory prerequisite.

Because control acquired after adoption of a plan of liquidation does not bring the liquidation under § 332, it is important to determine when the plan was adopted. In Rev.Rul. 70–106, 1970–1 C.B. 70, the parent corporation owned 75 percent of the stock of its subsidiary and desired to liquidate the subsidiary under § 332. Pursuant to an agreement with the minority shareholders, their stock was redeemed and the subsidiary corporation was then liquidated. The ruling held that the plan of liquidation was adopted at the time the agreement was reached with the minority shareholders and the transaction therefore did not qualify under § 332, since at that time the parent corporation owned only 75 percent of the stock of the subsidiary. All shareholders thus were taxed under § 331. On the other hand, Rev.Rul. 75–521, 1975–2 C.B. 120, applied § 332 where the parent corporation first purchased the stock of the minority shareholders and then liquidated the subsidiary. Rev.Rul. 75–521 distinguished Rev.Rul. 70–106 on the grounds that in the earlier ruling the entire distribution was a distribution in liquidation; in Rev.Rul. 75–521, however, the purchase by the parent corporation was not a part of a distribution in liquidation and the mere sale between shareholders did not constitute the adoption of a plan of liquidation.

In George L. Riggs, Inc. v. Commissioner, 64 T.C. 474 (1975) (Acq.), a corporation, during the time that it owned less than 80 percent of the stock of its subsidiary, voted in favor of selling substantially all of the assets of the subsidiary and took various other steps evidencing an intention to liquidate the subsidiary. Subsequently, by virtue of a redemption by the subsidiary, the parent corporation obtained 80 percent control of the subsidiary. Thereafter the subsidiary formally adopted a plan of liquidation. The IRS asserted that a plan of liquidation had been adopted prior to obtaining 80 percent control and thus § 332 was inapplicable. The court held, however, that although the actions taken prior to formal adoption of the plan of liquidation may have evidenced an intention to liquidate the subsidiary, the intent to liquidate is not tantamount to adoption of a plan of liquidation. The date of adoption of the plan of liquidation controlled and § 332 therefore provided nonrecognition treatment to the liquidation. The court stated that "section 332 is elective in the sense that with advance planning and properly structured transactions, a corporation should be able to render section 332 applicable or inapplicable". The court distinguished Rev.Rul. 70–106 on the basis that the plan of liquidation in the revenue ruling was adopted when the agreement regarding the redemption was reached with the minority shareholders. The distinction is difficult to understand.

Thus, if liquidation of a subsidiary is contemplated, the tax advisor has a choice of recommending a taxable or tax-free liquidation of the subsidiary. In choosing between the alternatives, the effect of §§ 336 and 337 often will be more important than the effect of § 332. Because the parent's basis in the stock of the subsidiary is unaffected by the subsidiary's earnings and profits history (unless a consolidated return has been filed), the parent may realize little or no gain on the liquidation while the subsidiary realizes a substantial gain or loss on the liquidating distribution. In general, a taxable liquidation will be advisable where the subsidiary has depreciated assets and both the subsidiary and the parent will realize a loss or the subsidiary's loss exceeds the parent's gain, or where the parent's loss exceeds the subsidiary's gain. On the other hand, the tax-free route of § 332 ordinarily will be advisable where the subsidiary's gain exceeds the parent's loss or both corporations realize a gain. Where the subsidiary has a net operating loss carryover that would be available to the parent, the determination is more complex. If the net operating loss carryover is large enough, the tax benefit to the parent of acquiring the carryover may compensate for denial of otherwise available losses, but in other cases, current loss recognition may yield a greater benefit.

Even if the parent corporation cannot acquire 80 percent control of the subsidiary, a tax-free combination of the subsidiary and the parent can be achieved by merging the subsidiary into the parent under state law corporate merger statutes, if the prerequisites for nonrecognition prescribed § 368(a)(1)(A) have been met. See Treas.Reg. § 1.368–1(e)(8), Ex. 7. Tax-free reorganizations are discussed in Chapter 12.

2. STATUTORILY REQUIRED TIME LIMITS ON COMPLETING THE LIQUIDATION

A liquidation qualifies under § 332 either (1) if it is completed within a single taxable year or (2) if the plan requires completion of the liquidation within three years from the close of the year in which the first distribution is made *and* the liquidation is in fact completed within that period. Neither timetable requires that distributions commence within any particular period after the plan is adopted. Rev.Rul. 71–326, 1971–2 C.B. 177, held that § 332 applied where a subsidiary for valid business reasons did not make a liquidating distribution until February, 1966, pursuant to a plan of liquidation adopted on July 1, 1963, because the phrase "within the taxable year" in § 332(b)(2) refers to the year in which liquidating distributions are made and not to the year of the adoption of the plan of liquidation. Rev.Rul. 76–317, 1976–2 C.B. 98 held that the "taxable year" referred to in § 332(b)(2) and (3) is the taxable year of the subsidiary corporation. No formal plan is required if a liquidation actually is completed within a single year. Burnside Veneer Co. v. Commissioner, 167 F.2d 214 (6th Cir.1948).

If the liquidation takes more than a year to complete, the IRS may require the corporation to post a bond. See Treas.Reg. § 1.332–4. The statute provides that if the liquidation is not completed within the required period, none of the distributions are treated as liquidating distributions within the meaning of § 332(a). However, the last sentence of Treas.Reg. § 1.332–4(b) provides that the distributions remain liquidating distributions within the meaning of §§ 331 and 336. Thus, if the conditions of § 332 are not met, both the liquidating subsidiary corporation and the parent corporation will recognize gain or loss on the liquidation. The property received by the parent would take a fair market value basis under § 334(a) rather than a transferred basis.

In general, retention of any property by a subsidiary, regardless of amount, for the purpose of continuing the operation of a business or of engaging in a new business will prevent the application of § 332. Rev.Rul. 76–525, 1976–2 C.B. 98. But Rev.Rul. 84–2, 1984–1 C.B. 92, held that the transfer to a new subsidiary by the parent of a nominal amount of the liquidated subsidiary's assets for the purpose of protecting the corporate name of the subsidiary did not disqualify the liquidation.

Sections 332 and 337 might be avoided by intentionally spreading liquidating distributions out over a long period in order for both the parent and subsidiary to recognize losses. There is no direct authority on this issue. In Cherry-Burrell Corp. v. United States, 367 F.2d 669 (8th Cir.1966), a U.S. parent received the first liquidating distribution from its British subsidiary in 1952. However, because claims were pending against the subsidiary and British law prohibited further distributions until the claims were finally settled in 1968, the court held that § 332 applied because the corporation had de facto liquidated within the required time period and the delay in distributing the remaining assets was involuntary; all the assets were converted to cash in 1952, only an amount necessary for a reasonable reserve for the claims asserted was retained as required by British law, no commercial activity was engaged in during the interim period, and the final liquidating distribution was made immediately after the settlement of claims.

3. DISTRIBUTION MADE ON "ALL ITS STOCK"

3.1. *Generally*

For § 332 to apply there must be some distribution applicable to the common stock, so as to supply the "cancellation or redemption of *all* [the] stock" required by § 332(b)(2). Thus, if the assets of the subsidiary are insufficient to pay its debts or do not exceed the amount necessary to both pay its debts and satisfy the liquidation preference of its preferred shares, including those held by the parent, the common stock simply becomes worthless rather than being cancelled or redeemed, and § 332 is therefore inapplicable. In such a case, the tax consequences of the liquidation depend on whether the subsidiary is insolvent, and thus makes no distributions with respect to any class of its stock, or, while solvent, has net assets sufficient only to make a distribution on its preferred stock.

3.2. *Distribution Only on Preferred Stock*

In H.K. Porter Co. v. Commissioner, 87 T.C. 689 (1986), the parent corporation owned all the outstanding common and preferred stock of its Australian subsidiary. The subsidiary sold all its assets and distributed the cash to the taxpayer in liquidation. The amount received by the parent was less than the liquidation preference in the preferred stock; no distribution therefore was made on the common stock. The taxpayer claimed a § 165 loss deduction. The court rejected the Commissioner's argument that § 332 applied to the transaction and allowed the taxpayer's loss. The court

A second tier of distribution rules applies to an S corporation that has accumulated earnings and profits from taxable years in which it was a C corporation in order to preserve the "double" tax pattern for earnings originally generated in a C corporation. The corporation must maintain an "accumulated adjustments account" that reflects net corporate income items that have been passed through to shareholders. Distributions to the extent of this accumulated adjustments account are received by the shareholders without tax. I.R.C. § 1368(b) and (c). To the extent that distributions exceed the accumulated adjustments account, the distributions are treated as distributions of earnings and profits, to the extent thereof, and are taxed to the shareholders as dividends. Any further distributions are received by the shareholders as a reduction of basis, then as capital gain to the extent that a distribution exceeds the recipient shareholder's basis.

Comparison of S Corporations and Partnerships (Including LLCs). Although Subchapter S in general adopts the partnership model for passing through S corporation income, there are significant differences between the taxation of S corporations and partnerships that affect a taxpayer's choice between the two entities. (Since an LLC usually will elect to be taxed as a partnership, the following considerations are applicable to LLCs as well.) As discussed previously, beneficial ownership of an S corporation nominally is limited to 100 shareholders, while there is no limit on the number of persons who may be partners in a partnership. Nor is there any restriction upon the types of entities that may be partners. The partnership form provides a significant advantage in the case of leveraged investments if losses are anticipated. Partners are allowed to include their shares of partnership debt in the bases of their partnership interests, which in turn allows partners to deduct partnership losses attributable to partnership level debt. In contrast, the shareholder's basis in Subchapter S stock or debt is limited to the shareholder's actual investment in the corporation. This limitation also means that while untaxed entity level cash, e.g., from a refinancing, can be distributed by a partnership free of tax, the same distribution by an S corporation may trigger gain recognition. For these reasons, S corporations generally have not been used for leveraged investments such as real estate.

Subchapter S also differs from Subchapter K in its treatment of distributions of appreciated property. An S corporation is required by §§ 311(b) and 336 to recognize gain on a distribution of appreciated property to shareholders. The recognized gain is passed through to the shareholders, who increase the basis of their stock accordingly. The distributee shareholder obtains a fair market value basis in the distributed property, and decreases the basis of the S corporation stock by the same amount. Subject to some exceptions, distributions of appreciated property by a partnership generally do not trigger recognition of gain. Instead, the distributee partner takes the partnership's basis in the property and recognition of gain is deferred until the distributee disposes of the property. The Code is thus not completely neutral as to the choice between a Subchapter S corporation and a partnership.

As a corporation, an S corporation can terminate its election and offer shares to the public without tax consequence. In addition, an S stock of an electing corporation even though the person was not included on the corporate books as a shareholder of record); Cabintaxi Corp. v. Commissioner, T.C. Memo. 1994–316, aff'd, 63 F.3d 614 (7th Cir.1995) (election must be joined in by all persons who have contributed equity capital, not merely those to whom stock certificates have been issued; whether a person is a shareholder for this purpose depends on whether the person would have been required to report income from the S corporation if it were profitable and a valid election had been made). See Treas.Reg. § 1.1362–6 for procedural aspects of shareholder consents and extensions of time for filing consents.

Although husband and wife are treated as a single shareholder, Treas.Reg. § 1.1362–6(b)(2)(i) requires that both consent to the election if they own the stock as community property, tenants in common, joint tenants, or as tenants by the entirety. In Wilson v. Commissioner, 560 F.2d 687 (5th Cir.1977), the record owner of a single share of stock who lived in a community property state, held the stock as an accommodation to other shareholders. He filed a consent to the corporation's S election but his wife did not. The court held that the husband had no beneficial interest in the stock and was therefore not required to consent to the corporation's S election. Thus his wife's consent was also unnecessary.

Section 1362(f) authorizes the IRS to waive a defect rendering an election ineffective because all of the required shareholder consents (including QSST elections) were not obtained in a timely manner if (1) the defect was inadvertent, (2) within a reasonable period of time the corporation obtains the shareholder consents, and (3) the corporation and the shareholders all agree to report as if the S corporation had been effective originally. See also Treas.Reg. § 1.1362–6(b)(3)(iii), providing for a waiver of the timely shareholder consent requirement in certain circumstances for years prior to the amendment of § 1362(f) to deal with this problem.

2.   CORPORATE ELECTION

It is necessary to identify the date on which the taxable year of a newly formed corporation begins in order to determine whether an election has been filed on or before the fifteenth day of the third month of the taxable year. Treas.Reg. § 1.1362–6(a)(2)(ii)(C) provides that the taxable year of a new corporation begins on the date the corporation has shareholders, acquires assets, or begins doing business, whichever is the first to occur. See Bone v. Commissioner, 52 T.C. 913 (1969) (first taxable year had begun when the corporation acquired assets and engaged in business even though no stock had been issued to shareholders; under state law the issuance of stock was not a prerequisite to corporate existence).

Treas.Reg. § 1.1362–6(a)(2)(ii)(C) provides that a month is measured from the first day of the corporation's taxable year to the day preceding the same numerical date of the following month, or the last day of the month if there is no corresponding date in the succeeding month. Treas.Reg. § 1.1362–6(a)(2)(iii), Ex. 1, promulgated before the 1996 amendments to § 1362(f), indicates that an election filed before the corporation begins its first taxable year will not be valid. Presumably, the 1996 amendments to § 1362(f) now permit the IRS to treat such a premature election as an effective election.

Section 1362(b)(5) permits the IRS to waive a late election for "reasonable cause." Rev.Proc. 98–55, 1998–2 C.B. 643, provides detailed procedures for seeking relief from a late election under § 1362(b)(5). If the only defect was a late filed Form 2553 (the corporate election itself) and the due date for the first corporate tax return (excluding extensions) has not passed, relief is virtually automatic if the election is filed within twelve months of the original due date and there was reasonable cause for the failure to file a timely S Corporation election. Otherwise, a private letter ruling seeking relief under § 1362(b)(5) must be requested.

Under Rev.Proc. 97–48, 1997–2 C.B. 521, later is better. Rev.Proc. 97–48 provides automatic relief for late filed elections that are made at least six months after the date on which the corporation filed its tax return for the first year the corporation intended to be treated as an S corporation. Automatic relief is provided under Rev.Proc. 97–48 if the corporation fails to qualify as an S corporation because its election was not timely, and the corporation and all of its shareholders reported their income consistent with S corporation status for the year in which the election should have been made and for all subsequent years. Automatic relief is available to the corporation and its shareholders even where the IRS has notified the corporation of an invalid election and has indicated that the corporation must file as a C corporation, as long as the statute of limitations has not lapsed with respect to either the corporation or any of its shareholders for years that the corporation intended to be treated as an S corporation. In order to seek automatic relief from a late filed election, the election must be signed by a corporate officer and all persons who were shareholders during the period the corporation is to be treated as an S corporation. The corporation and the shareholders must certify that returns were filed consistent with S corporation status, or in the case of a corporation notified by the IRS that its S status in invalid, the corporation and shareholders must agree to amend their returns to reflect S corporation status.

Rev. Proc. 2003–43, 2003–1 C.B. 998, provides a simplified procedure for relief from late Subchapter S elections, QSST elections, and ESBT elections. Relief is available if the request is filed within 24 months of the original due date of the election and there is a showing that a late S Corporation election was due to reasonable cause, or the failure to make a valid S Corporation election, an inadvertent termination of an S Corporation election, or failure to make a timely ESBT or QSST election was inadvertent. In addition to other requirements, the application for relief must be filed no later than six months after the due date of a tax return for the year of the election, and all shareholders must report their taxes consistent with a valid election. If the conditions for relief under Rev. Proc. 2003–43 are not met, the taxpayer may seek relief through application for a private letter ruling. Rev. Proc. 2007–62, 2007–2 C.B. 786, provides an additional simplified procedure to request relief from a failure to make a timely S Corporation election that is due to a failure to file the required Form 2553. The simplified method is available if the corporation files the Form 2553 within six-months of the due date of the first return of the corporation (including extensions) and the shareholders have reported the S corporation items consistent with a valid election.

D. REVOCATION OR TERMINATION OF S CORPORATION STATUS

INTERNAL REVENUE CODE: Section 1362(d), (e), (f) and (g).

REGULATIONS: Section 1.1362–2(a) and (b), –3 (a), –4, –5.

An S corporation election is effective for the taxable year to which it first applies and all succeeding taxable years until revoked or terminated. S corporation status may be ended in three ways: voluntary revocation by shareholders holding a majority of the S corporation stock, failure to comply with the requirements for S corporation status, or receipt of passive investment income in excess of 25 percent of gross income for three consecutive years if the corporation has Subchapter C previously accumulated and undistributed earnings and profits in those years.[14] Section 1362(d)(1) provides that a voluntary revocation of S corporation status by shareholders can be effective on the date specified by the revocation. Termination of S corporation status because the corporation or its shareholders subsequently fail to meet the initial requirements for eligibility is effective on the date the corporation ceases to qualify as an S corporation. I.R.C. § 1362(d)(2). The S corporation's taxable year ends on the day preceding the effective date of a revocation or termination and a new taxable year begins for the corporation as a C corporation on the following day. I.R.C. § 1362(e). Items of income and deduction must be allocated between the corporation's short Subchapter S and Subchapter C taxable years.

DETAILED ANALYSIS

1.   TERMINATION BY VOLUNTARY REVOCATION

Section 1362(d)(1) allows revocation of an S election by shareholders owning a majority of outstanding stock. A revocation made on or before the fifteenth day of the third month of the taxable year will be retroactively effective as of the first day of the taxable year. Otherwise, a revocation is effective on the first day of the next taxable year. Alternatively, the revocation may specify an effective date as long as the date specified is subsequent to the date of the revocation. Treas.Reg. § 1.1362–2(a)(2)(ii) requires that the date be specified in terms of a day, month, and year, rather than in terms of a particular event. Treas.Reg. § 1.1362–2(a)(4) also allows rescission of a voluntary prospective revocation at any time before the revocation becomes effective. Rescission requires the consent of any person who consented to the revocation and any person who became a shareholder of the corporation after the revocation was filed.

Section 1362(e) requires that in any taxable year in which the S corporation election terminates effective on a date other than the first day of the taxable year, income and deduction items must be allocated between the portion of the year the corporation is qualified as an S corporation and the portion of the year the corporation is treated as a C corporation. This rule is discussed at page 392.

---

[14] The rules governing an S corporation with a prior history as a C corporation are discussed in Section 5 of this Chapter.

2. INADVERTENT TERMINATION

A corporation's S election terminates immediately upon an event that disqualifies the corporation or one of its shareholders under the initial requirements for S corporation status. I.R.C. § 1361(d)(2). However, the savings clause of § 1362(f) allows the IRS to overlook an inadvertent termination if (1) the IRS determines that disqualification was inadvertent, (2) the corporation and/or its shareholders take steps to remedy the disqualifying event within a reasonable period after discovery, and (3) the corporation and each shareholder agree to such adjustments as the IRS may prescribe. The Senate Finance Committee indicated that it "intends that the Internal Revenue Service be reasonable in granting waivers, so that corporations whose Subchapter S eligibility requirements have been inadvertently violated do not suffer the tax consequences of a termination if no tax avoidance would result from the continued Subchapter S treatment."[15]

Treas.Reg. § 1.1362–4(b) provides that the burden is on the corporation to establish that termination is inadvertent under the facts and circumstances. The regulations add: "The fact that the terminating event or invalidity of the election was not reasonably within the control of the corporation and, in the case of a termination, was not part of a plan to terminate the election, or the fact that the terminating event or circumstance took place without the knowledge of the corporation, notwithstanding its due diligence to safeguard itself against such an event or circumstance, tends to establish that the termination or invalidity of the election was inadvertent." See Rev. Proc. 2003–43, 2003–1 C.B. 998 (granting automatic inadvertent termination relief to S corporations when stock is transferred to a QSST whose beneficiary inadvertently fails to file a timely election or an ESBT whose trustee fails to file a timely election, if the beneficiary or trustee files the election within 24 months of the original due date and the corporation and all shareholders report income as if a timely election had been filed). Rev.Rul. 86–110, 1986–2 C.B. 150, granted inadvertent termination relief to an S corporation that lost its eligibility because the majority shareholder transferred stock to trusts for the shareholder's children. The shareholder acted on the advice of counsel that the transfer would not disqualify the corporation's S election and would not have made the transfer but for the advice of counsel. Private letter rulings issued by the IRS indicate that it is quite lenient in applying the authority granted under § 1362(f).

3. TRANSFER TO INELIGIBLE OWNER BY MINORITY SHAREHOLDER

A minority shareholder may intentionally and unilaterally, to the detriment of other shareholders, terminate an S election by transferring stock to a disqualified person or by otherwise taking action to fail the requirements for S corporation status. In T.J. Henry Associates, Inc. v. Commissioner, 80 T.C. 886 (1983) (Acq.), the controlling shareholder of a Subchapter S corporation transferred a single share of stock to himself as custodian for his children under a Uniform Gifts to Minors statute. The

---

[15]   S.Rep. No. 97–640, 97th Cong., 2d Sess. 10 (1982).

transfer was intended to terminate the corporation's S election.[16] The Tax Court rejected the IRS's assertion that the transfer was not a bona fide transfer of beneficial ownership of the stock and that the shareholder acted as a custodian for his children merely as an accommodation. The Tax Court further held that, so long as there is a bona fide transfer of beneficial ownership, a transfer deliberately made to disqualify an S election should be recognized. The IRS has acquiesced in this result. 1984–2 C.B. 1.

Provisions in corporate documents and shareholder agreements often seek to limit the shareholder's ability to make a stock transfer that would terminate the corporation's S election. While not always effective to prevent termination, such provisions might give rise to civil liability for shareholders undertaking disqualifying events.

4. ELECTION FOLLOWING REVOCATION OR TERMINATION OF S CORPORATION STATUS

Under § 1362(g), if an S corporation election is revoked or terminated the corporation or its successor is not eligible to make a new election for five years unless the IRS consents to an earlier election. Treas.Reg. § 1.1362–5(a) provides that consent ordinarily will be denied unless it can be shown that the event causing termination was not reasonably within the control of the corporation or shareholders having a substantial interest in the corporation and was not part of a plan to terminate the election. The regulations also provide that consent should be granted if more than 50 percent of the corporation's stock is owned by persons who were not shareholders at the time the election was terminated. Private letter rulings reflect a rather relaxed approach on the part of the IRS in granting the requisite consent.

E. COORDINATION WITH SUBCHAPTER C

INTERNAL REVENUE CODE: Section 1371.

Section 1371(a) provides that, except when specifically displaced, the normal Subchapter C rules, including the rules governing corporate distributions, are applicable to Subchapter S corporations. This is in contrast to § 1363(b), which provides that subject to certain exceptions, the taxable income of an S corporation is computed in the same manner as an individual's taxable income.

Section 1371 also contains rules coordinating the treatment of items that affect both Subchapter S and Subchapter C years when a former C corporation elects S corporation status or an S corporation revokes or terminates its Subchapter S election.

There are no carrybacks or carryovers of loss or other items from Subchapter C years to Subchapter S years and vice versa. I.R.C. § 1371(b). Thus, a carryover of net operating losses incurred in a Subchapter C year will not be available to reduce S corporation income taxable to the shareholders. See Rosenberg v. Commissioner, 96 T.C. 451 (1991) (shareholders of former C corporation that elected S corporation status when it had unused net operating loss carryovers attributable to the development of condominiums could not exclude gain

---

[16] With respect to the taxable year involved, § 1372(e)(1) required an affirmative consent to the election by a new shareholder in order to maintain S corporation status. The shareholder in *T.J. Henry Assoc., Inc.* did not file the requisite consent.

from the subsequent sale of the condominium units under the tax benefit rule). See also Frederick v. Commissioner, 101 T.C. 35 (1993) (shareholders of an S corporation were required to include under the tax benefit rule of § 111 a "recovery" of accrued but unpaid interest expense by an S corporation deducted in a prior year when the corporation was a C corporation).

The period during which the S election is in effect will be counted in determining the number of years during which a carryforward or carryback is available. I.R.C. § 1371(b)(3). In the case of a former S corporation, however, losses will have passed through to shareholders who may carryover losses on their individual returns to a year following revocation of the S election.

SECTION 3.   EFFECT OF THE SUBCHAPTER S ELECTION BY A CORPORATION WITH NO C CORPORATION HISTORY

A. PASSTHROUGH OF INCOME AND LOSS

(1) GENERAL PRINCIPLES

INTERNAL REVENUE CODE: Sections 1363; 1366(a)–(e); 1367; 1378; 444.

REGULATIONS: Sections 1.1366–1, –2, 1.1367–1, –2, 1.1368–1(e)(2) and (g).

Senate Finance Committee Report, Subchapter S Revision Act of 1982

S.Rep. No. 97–640, 97th Cong., 2d Sess. 15–18 (1982).

2.   Treatment of shareholders (secs. 1363(b) and (c), 1366, 1367, 1371(b) and 1373)

In general

The bill sets forth new rules for the taxation of income earned by, and the allowance of losses incurred by, subchapter S corporations. These rules generally follow the * * * rules governing the taxation of partners with respect to items of partnership income and loss.

Computation of corporate items

A subchapter S corporation's taxable income will be computed under the same rules presently applicable to partnerships under section 703, except that the amortization of organization expenditures under section 248 will be an allowable deduction. As in the case of partnerships, deductions generally allowable to individuals will be allowed to subchapter S corporations, but provisions of the Code governing the computation of taxable income which are applicable only to corporations, such as the dividends received deduction (sec. 243) or the special rules relating to corporate tax preferences (sec. 291), will not apply. Items, the separate treatment which could affect the liability of any shareholder (such as investment interest) will be treated separately. Elections will generally be made at the corporate level, except for those elections which the partners of a partnership may make separately (such as the election to claim the foreign tax credit).

Generally subchapter C will apply, except that a subchapter S corporation will be treated in the same manner as an individual in transactions, such as the treatment of dividends received under section 301, where the corporation is a shareholder in a regular corporation. Provisions relating to transactions by a subchapter S corporation with respect to its own stock will be treated as if the S corporation were a regular corporation. However, the subchapter C rules are not to apply where the result would be inconsistent with the purpose of the subchapter S rules which treat the corporation as a passthrough entity.

Passthrough of items

The following examples illustrate the operation of the bill's passthrough rules:

   a.   *Capital gains and losses.*—Gains or losses from sales or exchanges of capital assets will pass through to the shareholders as capital gains or losses. Net capital gains will [not] be offset by ordinary losses at the corporate level.

   b.   *Section 1231 gains and losses.*—The gains and losses on certain property used in a trade or business will be passed through separately and will be aggregated with the shareholder's other section 1231 gains and losses. Thus, section 1231 gains will [not] be aggregated with capital gains at the corporate level and passed through as capital gains.

   c.   *Charitable contributions.*—The corporate 10–percent limitation will no longer apply to contributions by the corporation. As in the case of partnerships, the contributions will pass through to the shareholders, at which level they will be subject to thc individual limitations on deductibility.

   d.   *Tax-exempt interest.*—Tax-exempt interest will pass through to the shareholders as such and will increase the shareholders' basis in their subchapter S stock. Subsequent distributions by a corporation will not result in taxation of the tax-exempt income. (See discussion below for rules relating to corporate distributions.)

* * *

   f.   *Credits.*—As with partnerships, items involved in the determination of credits, * * * will pass through to the subchapter S corporation's shareholders.

* * *

   i.   *Other items.*—Limitations on the * * * expensing of certain depreciable business assets (sec. 179), and the amortization of reforestation expenditures (sec. 194) will apply at both the corporate level and shareholder level, as in the case of partnerships. * * *

Carryovers from years in which the corporation was not a subchapter S corporation will not be allowed to the corporation while in subchapter S status.

Shareholders treatment of items

In general.—As with the partners of a partnership, each shareholder of a subchapter S corporation will take into account separately his or her pro rata share of items of income, deduction, credit, etc., of the corporation. These rules parallel the partnership rules under section 702.

Each shareholder's share of the items will be taken into account in the shareholder's taxable year in which the corporation's year ends. In the case of the death of a shareholder, the shareholder's portion of subchapter S items will be taken into account on the shareholder's final income tax return. Items from the portion of the corporation's taxable year after the shareholder's death will be taken into account by the estate or other person acquiring the stock.

* * * In cases of transfers of subchapter S stock during the taxable year, income, losses, and credits will be allocated in essentially the same manner as when the election terminates during the year. Thus, the allocation generally will be made on a per-share, per-day basis unless the corporation, with the consent of its shareholders, elected to allocate according to its permanent records (including work papers).

A "conduit" rule for determining the character of items realized by the corporation and included in the shareholder's pro rata share will be the same as the partnership rule (sec. 702(b)). Under the partnership rules, this has generally resulted in an entity level characterization. Also, the "gross income" determinations made by a shareholder will parallel the partnership rule (sec. 702(c)).

Worthless stock.—If the corporation's stock becomes worthless in any taxable year of the corporation or shareholder, the corporate items for that year will be taken into account by the shareholders and the adjustments to the stock's basis will be made before the stock's worthlessness is taken into account under section 165(g).

Family members.—Under [section 1366(e)], items taken into account by members of the family (whether or not themselves shareholders) wherever it is necessary to reflect reasonable compensation to the shareholder for services rendered or capital furnished to the corporation may be properly adjusted. Both the amount of compensation and the timing of the compensation can be so adjusted.

Loss limitations.—As under [pre-1983] law, a shareholder's allowable pro rata share of the corporation's loss will be limited to the sum of the shareholder's adjusted basis in the stock of the corporation plus the shareholder's adjusted basis of any indebtedness of the corporation to the shareholder. However, unlike [pre-1983] law, disallowed losses can be carried forward or allowed in any subsequent year in which the shareholder has adequate basis in such stock or debt.

* * *

Terminated election.—Subsequent to a termination of a subchapter S election, these disallowed losses will be allowed if the shareholder's basis in his stock in the corporation is restored by the later of the following dates:

(1) One year after the effective date of the termination, or the due date for the last subchapter S return, whichever is later; or

(2) 120 days after a determination that the corporation's subchapter S election had terminated for a previous year. (A determination will be defined as a court decision which becomes final, a closing agreement, or an agreement between the corporation and the Internal Revenue Service that the corporation failed to qualify.)

3. Basis adjustment (sec. 1367)

Under [section 1367(a)], both taxable and nontaxable income and deductible and nondeductible expenses will serve, respectively, to increase and decrease a subchapter S shareholder's basis in the stock of the corporation. These rules generally will be analogous to those provided for partnerships under section 705. [Section 1368(d) requires that adjustments to basis as a result of distributions be taken into account under section 1367(a) prior to applying the rule of section 1366(d) limiting shareholder loss deductions to basis.]* Unlike the partnership rules, however, to the extent property distributions are treated as a return of basis, basis will be reduced by the fair market value of these properties * * *. Any passthrough of income for a particular year (allocated according to the proportion of stock held in the corporation) will first increase the shareholder's basis in loans to the corporation to the extent the basis was previously reduced by the passthrough of losses.

DETAILED ANALYSIS

1.   PASS THROUGH OF CHARACTER OF INCOME AND LOSS

Although the individual shareholders report the items of gain or loss on their own returns, the character of items is determined at the corporate level and passed through to the shareholders pursuant to § 1366(b), a provision analogous to § 702(b), which requires that partnership items be characterized at the partnership level. In Rath v. Commissioner, 101 T.C. 196 (1993), the Tax Court held that § 1244, discussed at page 159, cannot apply to allow an ordinary loss to be recognized on the sale of stock in another corporation held by an S corporation. Even though the loss ultimately will be reported by individuals, under § 1366(b) the character of the loss is determined at the corporate level. An S corporation shareholder does not "step into the shoes of the corporation for purposes of determining the character of a loss." Since Treas.Reg. § 1.1244(a)–1(b) provides that a corporation cannot claim an ordinary loss for § 1244 stock, the loss passes through to the shareholders as a capital loss. On the other hand, Rev.Rul. 2000–43, 2000–2 C.B. 333, held that an accrual-method S corporation could not elect under § 170(a)(2) to treat a charitable contribution as paid in the year that it was authorized by its board of directors when the contribution was paid by the S corporation after the close of the taxable year. This result was required because § 1363(b) generally requires S corporations to

---

*   [Ed.: The material in brackets reflects amendments to §§ 1366 and 1368 made in the Small Business Job Protection Act of 1996.]

compute their taxable income in the same manner as individuals, subject to certain specified exceptions.

Trugman v. Commissioner, 138 T.C. 390 (2012) held that the first time homebuyer's credit under now-expired § 36, which was available to an "individual" who had no present ownership interest in a principal residence during the three year period ending on the date of the purchase, was not allowable to an S corporation that purchased a home for its shareholders, notwithstanding that the § 36 credit was not one of the listed exceptions in § 1363(b). The court held that a corporation could not be an "individual" for purposes of § 36, and election of subchapter S status did not change that characterization. The court reasoned that only individuals can have a principal residence—a corporation has a principal place of business. Thus, before concluding that a provisions that applies to individuals also applies to S corporations, the statutory provision in question must be carefully examined.

After the character of an item is determined at the corporate level, whether it must be separately stated depends on whether the characterization may affect the computation of tax at the shareholder level. Thus, Rev.Rul. 93–36, 1993–1 C.B. 187, held that a nonbusiness bad debt must be separately stated as a short term capital loss under § 166(d) and passed through to its shareholders as such. Because § 166 is not an enumerated exception to § 1363(b), § 166 applies in the same manner as it does for an individual in computing the taxable income of an S corporation.

Treas.Reg. § 1.1366–1(b)(2) and (3) contain exceptions to the general rule that gains and losses are characterized at the corporate level in cases where the corporation is formed or availed of by any shareholder, or group of shareholders, for the purpose of converting ordinary gain at the shareholder level on property contributed to the corporation, which holds the property as a capital asset, or, conversely, converting a capital loss at the shareholder level on contributed property to an ordinary loss on sale of the property by the corporation.

2.   PERMITTED TAXABLE YEAR

Under § 1366(a), shareholders account for their share of an S corporation's items in the taxable year of the shareholder in which the taxable year of the S corporation ends. Before the enactment of § 1378 in 1982, calendar year shareholders of a profitable S corporation generally preferred a taxable year for the corporation ending on January 31, which permitted calendar year shareholder to defer income for up to eleven months. If, on the other hand, the S corporation was passing through losses to the shareholders, the shareholders preferred a calendar year so as to avoid any deferral of deductions.

Section 1378(b)(1) generally requires an S corporation to report on the calendar year. Although § 1378(b) allows an S corporation to adopt a different taxable year with the permission of the IRS if the corporation can establish a business purpose for the fiscal year, the last sentence of 1378(b) prohibits shareholder tax deferral from being treated as a business purpose for adopting a fiscal year.

Rev.Proc. 87–32, 1987–2 C.B. 396, modified by Rev.Proc. 92–85, 1992–2 C.B. 490, and Rev.Proc. 93–28, 1993–2 C.B. 344, set forth procedures to obtain the IRS's approval of a different taxable year that coincides with the

S corporation's "natural business year." An S corporation's natural business year is any twelve month period in the last two months of which the corporation realizes twenty-five percent of its gross receipts (under the method of accounting used to prepare its tax returns) for three consecutive years. If the corporation has more than one natural business year, it may only adopt the one in which the highest percentage of gross receipts are received in the last two months. Rev.Rul. 87–57, 1987–2 C.B. 117, explains the factors to be considered and deals with eight fact patterns in which the corporation does not have a natural business year under Rev.Proc. 87–32 or desires a taxable year different from its natural business year. Under the facts and circumstances test of Rev.Rul. 87–57, a business purpose for a particular year is not established merely by the use of a particular year for regulatory, financial accounting, or administrative purposes. If the desired taxable year creates deferral or distortion, which according to the ruling always occurs if the requested year differs from the calendar year, the corporation "must demonstrate compelling reasons for the requested tax year."

The rigid rules of § 1378, limiting flexibility in choosing the S corporation's taxable year, are ameliorated by § 444. This provision allows an S corporation to elect a taxable year other than that required by § 1378, provided that the selected year does not end more than three months before the end of the required year, even if there is no business purpose for the selected year. Thus, for example, if an S corporation otherwise is required to use the calendar year because it either has no natural business year or no business purpose for a different year, it nevertheless may elect to adopt a fiscal year ending in September, October, or November. If an election is made under § 444, the corporation must make a payment computed under § 7519 to compensate the Treasury for the deferral of taxes. This is a nondeductible entity level payment which is not credited against the shareholders' individual tax liabilities. (This payment in effect converts the interest free loan generated by any tax deferral resulting from the use of a fiscal year into an interest-bearing loan.)

3.   SHAREHOLDER'S BASIS

3.1. *General*

The shareholder's basis in S corporation stock initially is determined in the same manner as the basis of any other stock. Thereafter, in general, the shareholder's basis is increased by items included in the shareholder's income (and the shareholder's share of the corporation's tax-exempt income) and reduced by deductions allocated and distributions made to the shareholder. I.R.C. § 1367. Treas. Regs. §§ 1.1367–1(b)(2) and (c)(3) provide that increases and decreases to the basis of Subchapter S stock are determined on a per share per day basis. Basis adjustments generally are made at the close of the taxable year, Treas.Reg. § 1.1367–1(d)(1), but if a shareholder sells stock during the year, the adjustment to the basis of the stock sold is effective immediately prior to the disposition. Treas.Reg. § 1.1367–1(d)(1). Adjustments to the basis of the stock are made in the following order: (1) increases for income items; (2) decreases for distributions; (3) decreases for noncapital nondeductible expenses; and (4) decreases for losses. See Treas.Reg. § 1.1367–1(f). Treas.Reg. § 1.1366–2(a)(5)(ii) requires that losses incurred during the year of a transfer between spouses or former spouses be prorated on the basis of stock ownership at the beginning of the following taxable year.

Section 1367(a)(2)(D) requires a reduction in basis for expenses that are neither deductible nor chargeable to capital account. Treas.Reg. § 1.1367–1(c)(2) clarifies this language as applying only to expenses for which no loss or deduction is allowable, and as not applying to expenses that are deferred to a later taxable year. The regulations describe expenses to which § 1367(a)(2)(D) apply as including such things as fines, penalties, illegal bribes and kickbacks and other items disallowed under § 162(c) and (f); expenses incurred to earn tax-exempt income disallowed under § 265; losses disallowed under § 267 relating to related party transactions; and the nondeductible portion of meal and entertainment expenses under § 274. This adjustment is necessary to prevent the shareholder from in effect recognizing the disallowed deduction by realizing less gain or greater loss on the subsequent sale of the stock.

3.2. *Effect of Corporate Level Cancellation of Indebtedness Income*

Sections 1366(a)(1) and 1367(a)(1) provide for an increase in a shareholder's basis with respect to the shareholder's separately stated and non-separately stated income items, including "tax-exempt" income. The committee reports accompanying the enactment of these rules give as an example of tax-exempt income interest excluded under § 103. See S. Rep. No. 97–640, page 376. Neither the Code nor the regulations, however, clearly define "tax-exempt" income for this purpose, and the question arises regarding what is "tax-exempt income," which results in a current basis adjustment, versus what is "tax-deferred income," which does not result in a current basis increase. However, a 2002 Act amendment to § 108(d)(7) specifically provides that cancellation of indebtedness income excluded under § 108(a) will not be taken into account as tax-exempt income under § 1366(a).[17]

The 2002 amendment to § 108(d)(7) was enacted to reverse the result in Gitlitz v. Commissioner, 531 U.S. 206 (2001). The taxpayer in *Gitlitz* was the sole shareholder of an S corporation that realized cancellation of indebtedness (COD) income while it was insolvent. The corporation properly excluded the COD income under § 108(a). Upon the subsequent disposition of the stock (in the same year) the taxpayer shareholder claimed an increase in the basis of his stock in the corporation pursuant to §§ 1366(a)(1)(A) and 1367(a)(1)(A) on the theory that the COD income was passed-through "exempt" income, and reported a long-term capital loss. The IRS disallowed the portion of the loss attributable to the untaxed COD income. The Tax Court, 110 T.C. 114 (1998), and the Court of Appeals, 182 F.3d 1143 (10th Cir. 1999), upheld the IRS's position and denied the basis increase. The Supreme Court reversed on the basis of its reading of the "plain meaning" of the statutory scheme. First, the Court concluded that COD was "income" within the meaning of § 1366(a)(1)(A), which increases shareholder basis under § 1367(a)(1)(A). The fact that COD may be "tax-deferred" because of the insolvency exclusion of § 108(a)(1)(B) does not take the income out of the definition of income under § 1366(a)(1)(A). In addition, although § 108(d)(7)(A), as in effect for the year in question, provided that the exclusions of § 108(a) and the attribute reductions

---

[17] See also, Treas.Reg. § 1.1366–1(a)(2)(viii), promulgated in 1999 before *Gitlitz* was decided by the Supreme Court, providing that cancellation of indebtedness income excluded at the corporate level under § 108(d)(7)(A) is not "tax-exempt" income for purposes of §§ 1366 and 1367. Although the validity of the regulation was questionable after *Gitlitz,* the regulation is consistent with the 2002 statutory change.

required by § 108(b) were to be applied to an S corporation at the corporate level, the Court concluded that § 108(b)(4)(A), which provides that attribute reduction under § 108(b)(2) takes place "after the determination of the tax imposed by this chapter," expressly requires that the S corporation's shareholder's pass-through of income and basis adjustment must be taken into account before the COD income is reduced by corporate level net operating losses. As a result of this reasoning, the S corporation shareholder in *Gitlitz* received a tax-free step-up in basis, which he was able to convert into a deductible capital loss. The Court addressed this concern by stating:

> Second, courts have discussed the policy concern that, if shareholders were permitted to pass through the discharge of indebtedness before reducing any tax attributes, the shareholders would wrongly experience a "double windfall": They would be exempted from paying taxes on the full amount of the discharge of indebtedness, and they would be able to increase basis and deduct their previously suspended losses. See, e.g., 182 F.3d at 1147– 1148. Because the Code's plain text permits the taxpayers here to receive these benefits, we need not address this policy concern.

4. LIMITATION OF LOSS DEDUCTIONS TO BASIS

4.1. *General*

When net losses have reduced a shareholder's basis to zero, additional allocations of deduction and loss items reduce the basis of any indebtedness of the S corporation held by the shareholder. I.R.C. § 1367(b)(2)(A). See also Treas.Reg. § 1.1366–2. (If an S corporation has a qualified S corporation subsidiary, any indebtedness of the subsidiary to a shareholder of the parent is treated as indebtedness of the parent S corporation to the shareholder for this purpose. I.R.C. § 1361(b)(3)(A)(ii); H.R. Rep. No. 104– 586, 104th Cong., 2d Sess. 89 (1996).) When the basis of both the shareholder's stock and corporate indebtedness have been reduced to zero, passed through losses no longer can be deducted by the shareholder. The losses are suspended and may be deducted in a later year in which the shareholder acquires basis. I.R.C. § 1366(d). Treas.Reg. § 1.1367–2(b)(3) provides that if the shareholder holds multiple debts of the S Corporation, the reduction in basis is applied to each debt in proportion to the relative bases of the indebtedness. The legislative history of the Small Business Job Protection Act directs the IRS to promulgate regulations governing the order in which the basis of indebtedness is reduced if a shareholder holds indebtedness of both an S corporation and the corporation's qualified Subchapter S subsidiary. H.R. Rep. No. 104–586, 104th Cong., 2d Sess. 89 (1996).

The reduction in basis occurs notwithstanding the taxpayer's inability to use the losses on the taxpayer's own tax return. In Hudspeth v. Commissioner, 914 F.2d 1207 (9th Cir.1990), the shareholders were required to reduce the basis of bonds because of the corporation's net operating losses. However, because the shareholders' shares of losses exceeded their incomes in the taxable year of the losses and in subsequent years, they received no tax benefit with respect to the losses. The court rejected the shareholders' assertion that under the tax benefit rule the basis of the bonds should not be reduced to the extent that the corporation's losses did not produce a tax benefit. The court indicated that to so hold would nullify the limited carryback and carryforward provisions of § 172.

For purposes of the loss limitation of § 1366(d), the basis of stock received as a gift is limited under the transferred basis rules of § 1015(a) for determining loss. Treas.Reg. § 1.1366–2(a)(6). Thus the transferee's basis for purposes of § 1366(d) is the lesser of the fair market value or adjusted basis of the stock at the time of the gift.

4.2. *Restoration of Basis*

If a shareholder has reduced the basis in S corporation stock to zero and also has reduced the basis of corporate indebtedness by any amount, any "net increase in basis" attributable to passed-through income in a subsequent year (i.e., basis increase minus distributions for the year) will be applied to restore the basis of indebtedness before there is any increase in the basis of the stock. I.R.C. § 1367(b)(2)(B); Treas.Reg. § 1.1367–2(c). Assume for example, that A is the sole shareholder of X Corp., which has an S election in effect. The basis of A's stock in X Corp. is $10,000 and A holds a $5,000 promissory note from X Corp. In 2014, X Corp. passes a $14,000 loss through to A, and A reduces the basis of the X Corp. stock to zero and the basis of the promissory note to $1,000. In 2015, X Corp. has $6,500 of income and distributes $3,000 to A. To the extent of the $3,000 distribution, the passed through income is allocated to increase the basis of A's stock, and because the positive and negative adjustments to the stock basis offset, its basis remains zero. The remaining $3,500 of passed-through income increases the basis of the debt to $4,500. See Treas.Reg. § 1.1367–2(e), Ex. 2.

Nevertheless, § 1367(b)(2)(B) can produce an unexpected consequence to the shareholder. To the extent that corporate earnings passed through to the shareholder under § 1366 are allocated to increase the basis of shareholder debt, the shareholder's stock basis will not be adjusted to reflect income previously taxed to the shareholder. Distributions of these earnings in a subsequent year might be taxed to the shareholder to the extent distributions exceed the shareholder's stock basis even though the shareholder has basis in the debt. Thus, if in the immediately preceding example, in 2016 X Corp. realized neither income nor loss and distributed $2,000 to A, A would recognize a $2,000 gain under § 1368. (But if X Corp. had distributed $5,000 to A in 2015, A would have recognized no gain under § 1368 and the basis of the debt would have been increased to only $2,500.) As a consequence, the shareholder appears to be taxed twice on the same income; once as the shareholder is allocated a proportionate share of the income under § 1366, and a second time to the extent the distribution of that income exceeds the shareholder's stock basis. The "second" tax, however, can be viewed as a consequence of the pass through of losses in excess of stock basis, which has reduced the basis in the debt; the statute in effect requires those losses to be "recaptured" when distributions are made on the stock before the full basis of the debt has been accounted for.

Treas.Reg. § 1.1367–2(d) provides that adjustments to debt obligations held by shareholders are generally determined at the close of the taxable year, but if the debt is repaid during the year, its basis is adjusted immediately before the repayment. Suppose, for example, that in 2014 a shareholder-creditor is allocated a loss that exceeds the basis of the shareholder's stock by $600, and as a result reduces the basis of a $1,000 corporate debt obligation to $400. In July 2015, the corporation repays the debt and for 2015, the shareholder's share of the S corporation's income is $700. If the debt had not been repaid until January 1, 2016, its basis would have been increased from $400 to $1,000 as a result of the 2015 income, and no gain would have been recognized upon repayment. Under Treas.Reg. § 1.1367–2(d), the shareholder's basis in the debt obligation is adjusted immediately before repayment to reflect the shareholder's share of the corporation's 2015 income. As a result, the shareholder realizes no gain in 2015.

4.3. *Carryover of Disallowed Losses*

The loss limitation of § 1366(d)(1) prevents a shareholder from claiming losses in excess of the shareholder's investment in the S corporation. Losses disallowed by § 1366(d)(1) may be carried over indefinitely to future years and deducted whenever the shareholder has sufficient basis to support the deduction. I.R.C. § 1366(d)(2). The loss carryover is personal to each individual shareholder and is not a loss carryover to the corporation. I.R.C. § 1366(d)(2); Treas.Reg. § 1.1366–2(a)(5). Thus, disposition of S corporation stock by the shareholder, including a disposition by gift that has a transferred basis to the donee under § 1015, generally terminates the loss carryforward attributable to that stock. However, § 1366(d)(2)(B) provides that if stock of an S corporation with respect to which there is a suspended loss is transferred between spouses or pursuant to a divorce, the suspended loss follows the stock and is available to the transferee spouse.

If pursuant to § 108(a)(1)(A), (B), or (C) cancellation of debt income realized by the S corporation was not recognized, Treas.Reg. § 1.108–7(d) treats any shareholder losses from the current year and prior years that have been suspended under the limitation-on-losses rule of § 1366(d) as net operating losses that are subject to attribute reduction under § 108(b). If the S corporation has more than one shareholder during the taxable year of the debt cancellation, each shareholder's disallowed losses or deductions is a pro rata share of the total losses and deductions allocated to the shareholder under § 1366(a) during the corporation's taxable year. The deemed NOL allocated to a shareholder consists of a proportionate amount of each item of the shareholder's loss or deduction that was disallowed under § 1366(d)(1) in the year of the debt cancellation.

A shareholder may have losses carried into the last taxable year of the S corporation. In such a case, the loss is treated as a loss incurred by the shareholder on the last day of a "post-termination transition period." The post-termination transition period is defined in § 1377(b) as the period beginning on the last day of the corporation's taxable year as an S corporation and ending on the later of (1) one year after the last day of the S corporation taxable year, (2) the due date for the tax return for the last taxable year as an S corporation (including extensions), (3) 120 days after any determination pursuant to a post-termination audit of a shareholder that adjusts any item of S corporation income, loss, or deduction for the period the corporation was an S corporation, or (4) if there is a judicial determination or administrative agreement that the corporation's S election terminated in an earlier taxable year, 120 days after the date of the determination. See also Treas.Reg. § 1.1377–2.

4.4. *Additional Shareholder Contributions to Capital*

Cash or property contributions to capital will increase the shareholder's stock basis, thereby allowing the shareholder to deduct losses otherwise in excess of basis. In Rev.Rul. 81–187, 1981–2 C.B. 167, the shareholder of an S corporation attempted to increase basis for purposes of deducting a net operating loss by transferring the shareholder's own promissory note to the corporation. The IRS ruled that the note did not increase the shareholder's basis because the shareholder incurred no cost in executing the note; the shareholder's basis in the note was zero. But see Peracchi v. Commissioner, 143 F.3d 487 (9th Cir.1998), page 83; Lessinger v. Commissioner, 872 F.2d 519 (2d Cir.1989), page 92.

A contribution of additional assets will not necessarily increase basis, however, if the assets are encumbered or the corporation assumes liabilities of the shareholder in connection with the transfer. In Wiebusch v. Commissioner, 59 T.C. 777 (1973), aff'd per curiam, 487 F.2d 515 (8th Cir.1973), the taxpayer transferred the assets of a sole proprietorship to an existing S corporation that also assumed certain of the transferor's liabilities. The liabilities exceeded the taxpayer's basis for the assets, which resulted in gain to the taxpayer under § 357(c) and, as a result of § 358(d)(1), the taxpayer's basis in the stock was reduced to zero. Accordingly, the corporation's current losses could not be deducted by the taxpayer. As a result of the contribution, the taxpayer recognized gain and lost the benefit of a current loss deduction, neither of which would have occurred had the business continued to be operated in a sole proprietorship form.

A shareholder contribution to capital excluded from the corporation's gross income under § 118 is not tax-exempt income that provides an increase in basis under §§ 1366(a)(1)(A) and 1367. In Nathel v. Commissioner, 131 T.C. 262 (2008), aff'd, 615 F.3d 83 (2d Cir. 2010), the taxpayer received loan repayments from an S corporation in excess of his basis in the debt. In an attempt to avoid gain recognition, the taxpayer argued that under Gitlitz v. Commissioner, page 382, capital contributions are permanently excludable from income and thereby constitute tax-exempt income under Treas.Reg. § 1.1366–1(a)(2)(viii), which would first restore basis to the taxpayer's outstanding loans to the corporation under § 1367(b)(2)(B) before increasing basis of the taxpayer's stock. The court concluded that under long standing principles shareholder contributions to capital are added to the shareholder's basis in stock (Treas.Reg. § 1.118–1), that equity contributions and debt are treated differently, and that in any event, contributions to capital are not "income" treated as tax-exempt

4.5. *Shareholder Advances*

As discussed in paragraph 4.1 of the *DETAILED ANALYSIS*, after stock basis is reduced to zero, an S corporation shareholder may claim losses against the basis of any indebtedness of the S corporation held by the shareholder. Repayment of a corporate indebtedness before the basis is restored will result in gain recognition. However, open account advances and payments are netted at the close of the taxable year so that only net repayment of open account advances during the year (where basis has not been restored) will result in recognized gain. Treas.Reg. § 1.1367–2(a)(2) limits open account debt for this purpose to advances not represented by a written instrument that do not exceed $25,000. Any advance not evidenced by a written instrument that results in the total running net open account advances exceeding $25,000, and each subsequent advance not evidenced by a written instrument, is treated as a separate indebtedness evidenced by a written instrument, subject to the rules of Treas.Reg. § 1.1367–2(d), rather than as open account indebtedness. Treas.Reg. § 1.1367–2(d)(2). In making this determination, Treas.Reg. § 1.1367–2(d)(2) requires that advances and payments on open account debt be netted continually as they occur. Under the regulations, a shareholder may not offset the repayment of one shareholder advance with the basis of another shareholder advance. Treas.Reg. § 1.1367–2(c)(2). Treas.Reg. § 1.1367–2(c)(2) provides that any net increase in basis is applied first to restore the basis of any indebtedness (including open account indebtedness not exceeding $25,000) repaid during the taxable year to the extent necessary to offset any gain that would be realized on the repayment, then to restore the basis of each outstanding indebtedness in proportion to the amount that the basis of each indebtedness had been reduced by losses allowed under § 1367(b)(2)(A). Treas.Reg. § 1.1367–2(d)(1) provides that adjustments to basis of indebtedness are determined and effective as of the close of the taxable year (except as provided in Treas.Reg. § 1.1367–2(d)(2) for the purpose of determining if advances not evidenced by a written instrument exceed $25,000). Thus, the effect of the net advances and repayments is determined at the close of the year, or earlier if the taxpayer has disposed of the open account debt or the debt is repaid.

The regulations reverse the result of the Tax Court's decision in Brooks v. Commissioner, T.C. Memo 2005–204. Together, the Brooks brothers owned 100 percent of Brooks AG Company, a Subchapter S corporation. The stock basis of each shareholder was zero. In 1997 the Brooks brothers each advanced $500,000 to the company in open account transactions, then claimed losses that reduced their respective bases in the indebtedness to zero. On January 5, 1999, the company repaid each shareholder for the $500,000 advance. On December 31, 1999, each Brooks brother advanced $800,000 to the company on open account, which was sufficient to offset any gain on repayment of the first advance and to allow the Brooks brothers to claim additional losses thereby reducing their basis in the indebtedness to zero. The Brooks brothers repeated the pattern in 2000. The company made an $800,000 repayment to each shareholder on January 3, 2000. On December 29, 2000, the Brooks brothers each advanced $1.1 million to the company, which again offset any gain on the repayment that year and permitted the shareholders to deduct losses from the company to the extent of the remaining basis in the advance. The cycle of advances and repayment thus permitted the Brooks brothers to perpetually defer recognition of gain. The Tax Court endorsed this scheme by treating the Brooks brothers' multiple advances and repayments as a single open account indebtedness. Thus, the shareholders were permitted to net the advances and repayments as of the close of the taxable year and avoid recognition of gain on the repayment that occurred early in each taxable year. Under the post-*Brooks* regulations, however, open account indebtedness in excess of $25,000 is treated as a separate indebtedness. Thus, under the current regulations, repayment of the Brooks brothers' zero basis advances each January would produce recognized income in the amount of the repayment.

5. ALLOCATIONS IF STOCK OWNERSHIP CHANGES DURING THE YEAR

5.1. *In General*

Section 1377(a) provides that each shareholder's pro rata share of an S corporation's items passed through under § 1366 is determined on a day-by-day, share-by-share method if the ownership of shares changes during the year. See Treas.Reg. § 1.1377–1(a), (c), Ex. 1. This rule is similar to the proration method available to partnerships under § 706(d), except that in the case of an S corporation, the proration method is the normal rule. Pursuant to authority granted in § 1377(a)(2), Treas.Reg. § 1.1377–1(b) allows an S corporation to close its year for purposes of allocating income among shareholders if a shareholder completely terminates the shareholder's interest and the corporation and all of the shareholders who are affected consent. If stock is sold, the affected shareholders are the seller and the purchaser(s); if stock is redeemed by the corporation, however, all shareholders are affected and must consent. I.R.C. § 1377(a)(2)(B); Treas.Reg. § 1.1377–1(b)(2). Treas.Reg. § 1.1368–1(g) provides a similar election if any shareholder disposes of more than 20 percent of the outstanding stock of the corporation during the taxable year but has not disposed of all of the shareholder's stock. Treas.Reg. § 1.1368–1(g) requires consent of all shareholders, not just the "affected shareholders." The Treasury has not amended Treas.Reg. § 1.1368–1(g) to conform to the consent requirements in § 1377(a)(2), apparently because it was not promulgated under authority of that Code section, although the policy considerations are identical. The proration method is not applicable, however, and allocations based on the closing corporate books method are required if there is a sale or exchange of more than 50 percent of the corporation's stock during a year in which the corporation's S election terminates. I.R.C. § 1362(e)(6)(D).

If items are allocated by closing the corporation's books, the corporation prorates its income within each segment of the year among the shareholders in proportion to their ownership during that segment of the year and then cumulates the share of items for each shareholder for all of the segments of the year.[18] If two or more qualifying dispositions occur during the year, it apparently would be possible for the corporation to terminate its year with respect to one but to pro rate income with respect to the other.

These principles are illustrated by the following example. Assume that A, B, C, D, and E each owned 100 shares of stock of X Corp., which had made an S election. X Corp.'s income for the year was $182,500, but by quarters it was as follows: 1st quarter, ($90,000); 2nd quarter, $90,000; 3rd quarter, $229,000; 4th quarter, ($46,500). On March 31st, A sold A's stock to F, and on September 30, B sold B's stock to G.[19]

Under the normal method in § 1377(a), $500 of the corporation's $182,500 of income would be allocated to each day, and then $1 would be allocated to each share. The shareholders' income would be as follows:

---

[18] See Treas.Reg. § 1.1377–1(b), (c)(2) (method of making the election to allocate items under this method; illustrating method of making computations).

[19] On the day of the sale the selling shareholder rather than the purchaser is counted as the shareholder. Treas.Reg. § 1.1377–1(a)(2)(ii).

Shareholder	Days	Shares	Income/Share/Day	Total
A	90	100	$1	$ 9,000
B	273	100	$1	$27,300
C	365	100	$1	$36,500
D	365	100	$1	$36,500
E	365	100	$1	$36,500
F	275	100	$1	$27,500
G	92	100	$1	$ 9,200

If, however, all affected shareholders consented to closing the books as of March 31, $18,000 of the corporation's $90,000 loss for the first quarter would be allocated to A and $54,450 of the corporation's $272,500 income for the last three quarters (rounded off to $2.00 per share-per day) would be allocated to F. Section 1377(a)(2)(B) and Treas.Reg. § 1.1377–1(b)(2) define affected shareholders as including only the seller and purchaser. Thus, A and F are the only affected shareholders with respect to the March 31 sale and only A and F need consent to closing the books on March 31. The overall annual $1 per share per day profit would be allocated among B, C, D, E, and G without regard to the closing of the books with respect to A and F. The results are as follows:

Shareholder	Days	Shares	Income/Share/Day	Total
A	90	100	($2)	($18,000)
B	273	100	$1	$ 27,300
C	365	100	$1	$ 36,500
D	365	100	$1	$ 36,500
E	365	100	$1	$ 36,500
F	275	100	$2	$ 54,500
G	92	100	$1	$ 9,200

Since F realizes significantly greater income by closing the books at the end of the first quarter than under the proration method, F is not likely to consent unless F is compensated in some manner. B's and G's shares are computed without reference to the March 31 closing of the books, which applies only to A and F. B and G could, however, make their own election to close the books with respect to their shares on September 30.

5.2. *Bankruptcy Situations*

In Williams v. Commissioner, 123 T.C. 144 (2004), the taxpayer owned all of the stock of two S corporations that incurred losses for the year. He filed a personal bankruptcy petition at the beginning of December and reported a pro rata share of the losses on his personal return. The court disallowed the passed-through losses on the grounds that § 1377(a) did not apply and that § 1398 allocated all of the losses to the bankruptcy estate. It reasoned that under § 1398(f)(1) "a transfer of an asset from the debtor to the bankruptcy estate when the debtor files for bankruptcy is not a disposition triggering tax consequences, and the estate is treated as the debtor would be treated with respect to that asset." Thus the bankruptcy estate was treated as if it had owned all of the shares of the S corporations for the entire year and was entitled to all of the passed-through losses.

In contrast, Mourad v. Commissioner, 387 F.3d 27 (1st Cir. 2004), aff'g 121 T.C. 1 (2003), held that when an individual's wholly-owned S corporation filed for a bankruptcy chapter 11 plan of reorganization and an independent trustee was appointed by the Bankruptcy Court, the individual remained liable for the tax on any income or gain recognized by the S corporation.

6. ALLOCATIONS AMONG FAMILY GROUPS

The IRS is given authority to allocate items described in § 1366 among those shareholders who are members of the shareholder's family (spouse, ancestors, and lineal descendants) if the IRS determines that reallocation is necessary to reflect the value of services rendered by any of those persons. I.R.C. § 1366(e). See also Treas.Reg. § 1.1366–3. Thus, if a parent works for a low salary in an effort to shift income to the parent's shareholder-children, the IRS may allocate additional income to the parent or reduce the deduction for salary allocable to the parent. Unlike § 704(e)(3), which reallocates partnership income in the case of an interest purchased from a related person, § 1366(e) permits reallocation of S corporation income among family members who purchased their stock from the corporation or from an outsider in an arm's length transaction. On the other hand, § 1366(e) is more restrictive than § 704(e)(1) and (2) (which provide for reallocation of partnership income in the case of transfers by gift) in the sense that it permits reallocation only among family members.

In Davis v. Commissioner, 64 T.C. 1034 (1975), the Tax Court held that the IRS abused its discretion under the predecessor to § 1366(e) by allocating 100 percent of the income of two S corporations to the taxpayer. The taxpayer was an orthopedic surgeon who organized two corporations to perform X-ray and physical therapy services related to his medical practice. Ninety percent of the stock of each corporation was owned by the taxpayer's three minor children. The Tax Court indicated that the value of the taxpayer's services depended upon factors such as the nature of the services, the responsibilities involved, the time spent, the size and complexity of the business, economic conditions, compensation paid by others for comparable services, and salary paid to company officers in prior years. The court held that the 20 or so hours per year that the taxpayer spent directly performing services for the corporations was minimal and rejected the IRS's argument that the taxpayer's referral of patients to the corporations was personal service rendered by him to the corporations. Thus, the fees earned by the corporations were the result of the use of equipment owned by the corporations and the services of corporate employees, and not the result of services rendered by the taxpayer. The Tax Court also rejected the IRS's claim that income was allocable to the taxpayer under § 482 and assignment of income principles.

7. APPLICABILITY OF AT RISK AND PASSIVE ACTIVITY LOSS LIMITATION RULES

The at-risk rules of § 465 apply to the shareholder of an S corporation. As a result, a loss that is passed through to a shareholder may be deducted only to the extent that the shareholder is at risk with respect to the activities that generated the loss. Under the aggregation rules of § 465(c)(3)(B), an S corporation may be treated as engaged in a single activity if its activities constitute a trade or business and 65 percent or more of the losses are allocable to persons who actively participate in the management of the trade or business. If passed through losses have been suspended by the at-risk rules and they have not been used by the shareholder prior to the termination of the corporation's S election, the suspended losses may be carried forward to the post-termination transition period (as defined in § 1377(b)) and can be deducted in the year or years within the post-termination transition period to the extent the taxpayer's at-risk amount is increased.

In Van Wyk v. Commissioner, 113 T.C. 440 (1999), the taxpayer together with another person each owned 50 percent of the stock of an S corporation engaged in the farming business. The taxpayer and his wife borrowed funds from the other shareholder and his wife and re-lent them to the corporation, after which the taxpayer attempted to claim passed-through losses against the debt basis under § 1366(d)(1)(B). The court held that pursuant to § 465(b)(3), the taxpayer shareholder was not at risk for amounts lent to the corporation because he borrowed the funds from another shareholder (and that shareholder's spouse, from whom borrowing is treated in the same manner as borrowing from the husband under § 465(b)(3)(C)) to re-lend them to the corporation. The taxpayer was thus denied a current deduction for losses passed through under § 1366. Money that is borrowed from a third party by the taxpayer on his own credit and then invested or contributed by the taxpayer to an activity is not governed by § 465(b)(1)(A), but rather is treated as borrowing with respect to the activity and will be considered to be at risk only if the borrowing transaction passes muster under the several other subsections of § 465 dealing with the treatment of borrowed funds. Treas. Regs. §§ 1.465–8 and 1.465–20, promulgated in 2004, extend to all activities the rule that amounts borrowed from another party with an interest in the activity (other than a creditor) are not at risk, even if the borrowing is with full recourse. This rule does not apply, however, to amounts that are qualified nonrecourse borrowing under § 465(b)(6), or that would have been qualified nonrecourse borrowing if the debt had been nonrecourse.

The passive activity loss limitations of § 469 apply to losses passed through to S corporation shareholders in the same manner as to partners. Thus net losses of an activity operated by an S corporation in which the shareholder does not materially participate are deductible by the shareholder only to the extent of the shareholder's passive activity income. Disallowed losses are carried forward and treated as passive activity deductions in the next succeeding year until offset by the taxpayer's passive activity income. Complete disposition of the activity of the S corporation allows the taxpayer to deduct the unused loss attributable to the specific activity.

St. Charles Investment Co. v. Commissioner, 110 T.C. 46 (1998), rev'd 232 F.3d 773 (10th Cir. 2000), involved an S corporation that prior to making its S election had been subject to § 469 as a closely held C corporation. The corporation had unused passive activity loss carryovers from the period that it had been a C corporation. The Tax Court held that under § 1371(b)(1), the passive activity loss carryovers from C corporation years could not be claimed against passive activity income recognized in S corporation years. The Court of Appeals reversed and allowed the suspended losses to be carried over and applied to reduce the passive activity income passed through to the shareholders in years for which the S election was in effect.

8.   SHORT SUBCHAPTER S AND SUBCHAPTER C TAXABLE YEARS ON TERMINATION

Section 1362(e) requires that in any taxable year in which the S corporation election terminates effective on a date other than the first day of the taxable year, income and deduction items must be allocated between the portion of the year the corporation is qualified as an S corporation and the portion of the year the corporation is treated as a C corporation.[20] The Senate Finance Committee Report explained the allocation rule as follows:

> The day before the day on which the terminating event occurs will be treated as the last day of a short Subchapter S taxable year, and the day on which the terminating event occurs will be treated as the first day of a short regular (i.e., Subchapter C) taxable year. There will be no requirement that the books of a corporation be closed as of the termination date. Instead the corporation will allocate the income or loss for the entire year (i.e., both short years) on a proration basis.

S.Rep. No. 97–640, 97th Cong., 2d Sess. 11 (1982).

Each separately stated item of the corporation's income and loss during the short Subchapter S year must be allocated to each day of the short taxable year and taken into account by the shareholders. I.R.C. § 1362(e)(2). The remaining taxable income for the taxable year is allocated to the short C corporation year. Taxable income for the short Subchapter C year is then annualized for purposes of computing the tax under § 11. First, the corporation's tax for the short Subchapter C year is determined as if it had earned a proportionate amount of taxable income for a full taxable year; then the corporation pays only the proportionate amount of the tax that corresponds to the portion of a full taxable year that it is deemed a C corporation. See Treas.Reg. § 1.1362–3(a) and (c)(2). For example, suppose S Corporation has taxable income of $100,000 in 2014. Its Subchapter S election terminates effective April 1, 2014. There have been 90 days in S Corporation's short taxable year ending on March 31, 2014, and there are 275 days in S Corporation's short Subchapter C year beginning on April 1, 2014. As a result, $24,658 of S Corporation's $100,000 taxable income is allocated to the short S corporation year ($100,000 × 90/365) and the remaining $75,342 of taxable income is allocated to S Corporation's Subchapter C year. The $75,342 of taxable income is annualized so that S Corp. is deemed to have $100,000 of taxable income for purposes of determining its corporate tax for the short Subchapter C year ($75,342 × 365/275). The tax under § 11 on $100,000 of taxable income is $22,250. S Corporation's actual tax liability for the short Subchapter C year then is calculated to be $16,764 ($22,250 × 275/365).

In lieu of a pro rata allocation of income between the short Subchapter S and C years, the corporation may elect, with the consent of *all* shareholders at any time during the S year and all shareholders on the first day of the C year, to report income and deductions on the basis of actual amounts shown on the corporate books. I.R.C. § 1362(e)(3). Allocation of amounts based on the corporate books is required if the corporation's stock

---

[20] Section 1362(e)(6)(A) provides that the short taxable years required by § 1362(e) will be treated as only one year for purposes of the carryback and carryforward of corporate items such as net operating losses.

is acquired by a corporation, thereby terminating the S election, if the acquiring corporation elects to treat the acquisition as an asset purchase under § 338, see page 484. I.R.C. § 1362(e)(6)(C). The "closing of the books" method may be desirable in situations in which the parties do not want events occurring after termination to affect income determination for the S corporation portion of the year. Note, however, that a single shareholder, who may be adversely affected, can prevent the use of the closing of the books method.

(2) EFFECT OF INDIRECT CONTRIBUTIONS ON LIMITATION OF LOSS DEDUCTIONS TO SHAREHOLDER BASIS

Estate of Leavitt v. Commissioner

Court of Appeals, United States, Fourth Circuit, 1989.
875 F.2d 420.

■ MURNAGHAN, CIRCUIT JUDGE:

The appellants, Anthony D. and Marjorie F. Cuzzocrea and the Estate of Daniel Leavitt, Deceased, et al., appeal the Tax Court's decision holding them liable for tax deficiencies for the tax years 1979, 1980 and 1981. Finding the appellants' arguments unpersuasive, we affirm the Tax Court.

I.

As shareholders of VAFLA Corporation,[1] a subchapter S corporation during the years at issue, the appellants claimed deductions under § 1374 of the Internal Revenue Code of 1954 to reflect the corporation's operating losses during the three years in question. The Commissioner disallowed deductions above the $10,000 bases each appellant had from their original investments.

The appellants contend, however, that the adjusted bases in their stock should be increased to reflect a $300,000 loan which VAFLA obtained from the Bank of Virginia ("Bank") on September 12, 1979, after the appellants, along with five other shareholders ("Shareholders-Guarantors"), had signed guarantee agreements whereby each agreed to be jointly and severally liable for all indebtedness of the corporation to the Bank.[5] At the time of the loan, VAFLA's liability exceeded its assets, it could not meet its cash flow requirements and it had virtually no assets to use as collateral. The appellants assert that the Bank would not have lent the $300,000 without their personal guarantees.

VAFLA's financial statements and tax returns indicated that the bank loan was a loan from the Shareholders-Guarantors. Despite the representation to that effect, VAFLA made all of the loan payments, principal and interest, to the Bank. The appellants made no such payments. In addition, neither VAFLA nor the Shareholders-

---

[1]   VAFLA is a Virginia corporation incorporated in February 1979 to acquire and operate the Six-Gun Territory Amusement Park near Tampa, Florida. At that time, both Cuzzocrea and Leavitt each paid $10,000 for their respective shares of VAFLA. Therefore, the adjusted bases of their stock amounted to $10,000 each, the cost of the stock.

[5]   All the guarantees to the Bank were unlimited except the guarantee of Cuzzocrea which was limited to $300,000. The Shareholders-Guarantors had an aggregate net worth of $3,407,286 and immediate liquidity of $382,542.

Guarantors treated the corporate payments on the loan as constructive income taxable to the Shareholders-Guarantors.

The appellants present the question whether the $300,000 bank loan is really, despite its form as a borrowing from the Bank, a capital contribution from the appellants to VAFLA. They contend that if the bank loan is characterized as equity, they are entitled to add a *pro rata* share of the $300,000 bank loan to their adjusted bases, thereby increasing the size of their operating loss deductions.[7] Implicit in the appellants' characterization of the bank loan as equity in VAFLA is a determination that the Bank lent the $300,000 to the Shareholders-Guarantors who then contributed the funds to the corporation. The appellants' approach fails to realize that the $300,000 transaction, regardless of whether it is equity or debt, would permit them to adjust the bases in their stock if, indeed, the appellants, and not the Bank, had advanced VAFLA the money. The more precise question, which the appellants fail initially to ask, is whether the guaranteed loan from the Bank to VAFLA is an economic outlay of any kind by the Shareholders-Guarantors. To decide this question, we must determine whether the transaction involving the $300,000 was a loan from the Bank to VAFLA or was it instead a loan to the Shareholders-Guarantors who then gave it to VAFLA, as either a loan or a capital contribution.

Finding no economic outlay, we need not address the question, which is extensively addressed in the briefs, of whether the characterization of the $300,000 was debt or equity.

II.

To increase the basis in the stock of a subchapter S corporation, there must be an economic outlay on the part of the shareholder. See Brown v. Commissioner, 706 F.2d 755, 756 (6th Cir.1983), affg. T.C. Memo. 1981–608 ("In similar cases, the courts have consistently required some economic outlay by the guarantor in order to convert a mere loan guarantee into an investment."); Blum v. Commissioner, 59 T.C. 436, 440 (1972) (bank expected repayment of its loan from the corporation and not the taxpayers, i.e., no economic outlay from taxpayers).[8] A guarantee, in and of itself, cannot fulfill that requirement. The guarantee is merely a promise to pay in the future if certain unfortunate events should occur. At the present time, the appellants have experienced no such call as guarantors, have engaged in no economic outlay, and have suffered no cost.

The situation would be different if VAFLA had defaulted on the loan payments and the Shareholders-Guarantors had made actual disbursements on the corporate indebtedness. Those payments would represent corporate indebtedness to the shareholders which would

---

[7] Former § 1374 of the 1954 tax code which was in effect during the years in issue provides that a shareholder of an electing small business corporation may deduct from gross income an amount equal to his or her portion of the corporation's net operating loss to the extent provided for in § 1374(c)(2). Such deduction is limited, however, to the sum of (a) the adjusted basis of the shareholder's stock in the corporation, and (b) the adjusted basis of any indebtedness of the corporation to the shareholder, as determined as of the close of the corporation's taxable year.

[8] Even the Eleventh Circuit case on which the appellants heavily rely applies this first step. See Selfe v. United States, 778 F.2d 769, 772 (11th Cir.1985) ("We agree with *Brown* inasmuch as that court reaffirms that economic outlay is required before a stockholder in a Subchapter S corporation may increase her basis.").

increase their bases for the purpose of deducting net operating losses under § 1374(c)(2)(B). Brown, 706 F.2d at 757. See also Raynor v. Commissioner, 50 T.C. 762, 770–71 (1968) ("No form of indirect borrowing, be it guaranty, surety, accommodation, co-making or otherwise, gives rise to indebtedness from the corporation to the shareholders until and unless the shareholders pay part or all of the obligation.").

The appellants accuse the Tax Court of not recognizing the critical distinction between § [1366(d)(1)(A)] (adjusted basis in stock) and § [1366(d)(1)(B)] (adjusted basis in indebtedness of corporation to shareholder). They argue that the "loan" is not really a loan, but is a capital contribution (equity). Therefore, they conclude, § [1366(d)(1)(A)] applies and § [1366(d)(1)(B)] is irrelevant. However, the appellants once again fail to distinguish between the initial question of economic outlay and the secondary issue of debt or equity. Only if the first question had an affirmative answer, would the second arise.

The majority opinion of the Tax Court, focusing on the first issue of economic outlay, determined that a guarantee, in and of itself, is not an event for which basis can be adjusted. It distinguished the situation presented to it from one where the guarantee is triggered *and actual payments are made.* In the latter scenario, the first question of economic outlay is answered affirmatively (and the second issue is apparent on its face, i.e., the payments represent indebtedness from the corporation to the shareholder as opposed to capital contribution from the shareholder to the corporation). To the contrary is the situation presented here. The Tax Court, far from confusing the issue by discussing irrelevant matters, was comprehensively explaining why the transaction before it could not represent any kind of economic outlay by the appellants.

The Tax Court correctly determined that the appellants' guarantees, unaccompanied by further acts, in and of themselves, have not constituted contributions of cash or other property which might increase the bases of the appellants' stock in the corporation.

The appellants, while they do not disagree with the Tax Court that the guarantees, standing alone, cannot adjust their bases in the stock, nevertheless argue that the "loan" to VAFLA was in its "true sense" a loan to the Shareholders-Guarantors who then theoretically advanced the $300,000 to the corporation as a capital contribution. The Tax Court declined the invitation to treat a loan and its uncalled-on security, the guarantee, as identical and to adopt the appellants' view of the "substance" of the transaction over the "form" of the transaction they took. The Tax Court did not err in doing so.

Generally, taxpayers are liable for the tax consequences of the transaction they actually execute and may not reap the benefit of recasting the transaction into another one substantially different in economic effect that they might have made. They are bound by the "form" of their transaction and may not argue that the "substance" of their transaction triggers different tax consequences. Don E. Williams Co. v. Commissioner, 429 U.S. 569, 579–80 (1977) * * *.[10] In the

---

[10] On the other hand, the Commissioner is not so bound and may recharacterize the nature of the transaction according to its substance while overlooking the form selected by the

Without this rule, assets could be distributed tax-free (except for recapture in certain instances) and subsequently sold without income recognition to the selling shareholder because of the stepped-up fair market value basis.

DETAILED ANALYSIS

1. DISTRIBUTIONS OF APPRECIATED PROPERTY

1.1. *Generally*

Section 311(b) requires recognition of gain at the corporate level on the distribution of appreciated property to shareholders, which is a significant departure from the partnership provisions on which treatment of S corporation distributions is generally based. (In the corresponding partnership situation, gain recognition is postponed through the rules on basis adjustments.[22] Presumably, Congress believed that the partnership approach would have been too complex to apply in a corporate context.) Technically, this result is reached under § 1371(a), which provides that, except when specifically displaced, the normal Subchapter C rules, including the rules governing corporate distributions, are applicable to Subchapter S corporations. Thus, § 311(b) requires recognition of corporate level gain on the distribution of appreciated property as if the property were sold for its fair market value.[23] The recognized gain is passed through to shareholders who report the gain as income under § 1366. Under § 1368, the distribution of the property itself is tax-free to the shareholder to the extent of the shareholder's basis in the stock. The shareholder's basis in the property received is its fair market value, I.R.C. § 301(d), and the shareholder reduces by a like amount the basis of the stock with respect to which the distribution was made. Thus, in comparison to the treatment accorded distributions by a partnership, the distribution of appreciated property by an S corporation accelerates the payment of tax, although there is still only one level of tax.

1.2. *Liquidating Distributions*

Liquidating distributions by an S corporation are also subject to the liquidation rules of Subchapter C. Section 336 requires recognition of gain or loss at the corporate level as if the property were sold for its fair market value. The gain or loss is passed through to shareholders under § 1366 and the shareholders' bases in their stock are adjusted accordingly pursuant to § 1367. Under § 331 liquidating distributions are treated as received by the shareholders in exchange for their stock; gain is recognized to the extent the distribution exceeds basis, or loss is recognized if the distribution is less than the shareholder's basis. Gain or loss is recognized in situations where the shareholder's stock basis is not the same as the shareholder's ratable share of the corporation's asset bases, e.g., where the shareholder acquired the stock by purchase or bequest.

Distribution of a § 453 installment obligation generally results in immediate recognition of gain to the corporation under either or both of §§ 311 and 453B, and the gain will be passed through to the shareholders.

---

[22] Except to the extent required by § 751, no gain is recognized by a partnership on a distribution of appreciated property. The partnership basis carries over to the distributee partner to the extent of the partner's basis in the partner's partnership interest.

[23] H.Rep.No. 100–795, 100th Cong., 2d Sess. 64 (1988).

Section 453B(h), however, provides a very narrow exception for the distribution of an installment obligation acquired by an S corporation on the sale of its assets within twelve months preceding complete liquidation of the corporation. Corporate level gain is not triggered by the distribution in liquidation of the installment obligation,[24] and the shareholder does not treat receipt of the installment obligation itself as a payment in exchange for the shareholder's stock in the liquidation. I.R.C. § 453(h). Instead, the receipt of each installment payment by the shareholder is a taxable event. Thus, S corporation shareholders are permitted to defer recognition of liquidation gain in the same manner that § 453(h) permits deferral of recognition by C corporation shareholders. But § 453B(h) requires that the character of the shareholder's gain be determined as if the corporation had recognized the gain and the gain had passed through to the shareholders under § 1366.

2.   TIMING OF BASIS ADJUSTMENTS FOR GAIN AND LOSS AND DISTRIBUTIONS

Section 1368(d) requires that positive adjustments to a shareholder's stock basis under § 1367(a)(1) reflecting the shareholder's share of corporate income, be taken into account before applying the distribution rules of § 1368(b). On the other hand, § 1368(d) requires distributions to be taken into account before negative adjustments to a shareholder's stock basis reflecting the shareholder's share of corporate loss are made under § 1367(a)(2). See also Treas.Reg. § 1.1367–1(f), (h), Ex. 2. This asymmetrical rule works to the shareholder's advantage by preventing interim distributions of profits during the year from being treated as distributions in excess of basis, thereby triggering gain under § 1368(b)(2). Conversely, if the corporation loses money, distributions will not be taxed to the extent they did not exceed the shareholder's basis at the beginning of the year (subject to adjustment for items other than passed-through corporate losses).

Prior to 1997, adjustments to stock basis to reflect passed-through losses were taken into account before the distribution rules were applied. Thus, if the corporation lost money, distributions that did not exceed basis on the date of the distribution could result in recognition of capital gain when taken into account after the shareholder's basis had been reduced by the loss for the year. While this result may appear to have been detrimental to the shareholder, it was in some cases quite beneficial because it could create capital gains and ordinary losses that offset in amounts but not in character.

Suppose that A is a fifty percent shareholder of X Corp., an S Corporation. A's adjusted basis in the X Corp. stock on January 1, 1996, was $1,000. During 1996, A's share of X Corp.'s items of income and loss was a capital gain of $200 and an operating loss of $900, and during the year X Corp. distributed $700 to A. Under the pre-1997 rules, A would have recognized both the $200 capital gain and the $900 ordinary loss under § 1366; as a result A's stock basis would be reduced to $300 under § 1367. A

---

[24] Section 453B(h) does not apply for purposes of determining the corporation's tax liability under Subchapter S. Thus the corporation is not relieved from recognition of gain on the distribution of an installment obligation that triggers the built-in gain tax of § 1374, discussed at page 415, or the tax on passive investment income of § 1375, discussed at page 422.

also would have recognized a $400 gain on the distribution. The net result would have been that A recognized $600 of capital gain and $900 of ordinary loss.

Under the post-1996 rules, the loss is taken into account last. A's basis in the X Corp. stock first is increased to $1,200 ($1,000 plus $200 capital gain). The distribution then reduces A's stock basis to $500, with no gain being recognized. Finally, A is able to deduct currently $500 of the $900 loss that passed through, reducing A's basis to zero. The remaining $400 loss is carried forward pursuant to § 1366(d)(2). The net result is that A recognizes currently $200 of capital gain and $500 of ordinary loss. See Staff of the Joint Committee on Taxation, General Explanation of Tax Legislation Enacted in the 104th Congress 122–124 (Comm. Prt. 1996).

3. DISTRIBUTIONS FOLLOWING TERMINATION OF S CORPORATION STATUS

Following termination of an S election, distributions of money may be received by shareholders as a tax-free reduction of basis to the extent of the undistributed taxable income of the S corporation that has been passed through to the shareholders. I.R.C. § 1371(e)(1). The distribution must be made within the "post-termination transition period" as defined in § 1377(b), generally at least a one year period after termination of S corporation status, although the period may differ in certain specified circumstances. See Treas.Reg. § 1.1377–2. If the shareholders fail to withdraw previously taxed income from the corporation within the applicable period, the privilege of tax-free distribution under § 1368 is lost and subsequent corporate distributions are taxable under § 301, i.e., subsequent distributions are taxable dividends if supported by sufficient earnings and profits. (If the corporation has always been an S corporation, earnings and profits will arise only in the period following termination of the election.)

Section 1371(e)(1) prescribes that only distributions of "money" may be tax-free during the post-termination transition period. Under a requirement of the pre-1983 Subchapter S rules, distributions of money during the first two and one-half months of the taxable year were received tax-free by the shareholders as distributions of previously taxed income of the prior taxable year.[25] Taxpayers attempted various devices to circumvent this "money" distribution requirement, but with a marked lack of success. This case law remains relevant under § 1371(e)(1). See, e.g., Roesel v. Commissioner, 56 T.C. 14 (1971) (Nonacq.) (cash distribution and subsequent loan to corporation by shareholders were disregarded and the transaction was treated as a taxable distribution of the debt obligations); DeTreville v. United States, 445 F.2d 1306 (4th Cir.1971) (two transactions treated as one because the shareholders purported to receive cash distributions and immediately purchased property from the corporation; the transactions were in substance a distribution of property); Stein v. Commissioner, 65 T.C. 336 (1975) (fact that shareholders were in constructive receipt of amounts credited to their accounts on the books of the corporation did not satisfy the money requirement).

---

[25] Otherwise, distributions during the taxable year were taxed as dividends to the extent of the current year's earnings and profits. After current earnings were distributed, distributions of prior years' undistributed taxable income were also received tax-free by shareholders.

4.   SHAREHOLDER-EMPLOYEE FRINGE BENEFITS

For purposes of employee fringe benefit provisions, § 1372 treats an S corporation as a partnership and each more than 2 percent shareholder as a partner. As a result, S corporation shareholders holding more than 2 percent of the stock are not eligible to receive employee fringe benefits tax-free. Revenue Ruling 91–26, 1991–1 C.B. 184, holds that payments of health and accident insurance premiums with respect to a more than two percent shareholder/employee of an S corporation must be included in income by the shareholder/employee and are not subject to exclusion from gross income under § 106. The corporation may deduct the premiums under § 162 and is required to report the premiums as compensation to the employee/shareholder on a Form W-2.

Section 1372 does not affect the treatment of a qualified pension plan maintained by an S corporation. If an S corporation had a qualified pension plan, a shareholder of the corporation who is also an employee may participate in the corporation's qualified pension plan regardless of the amount of stock that the shareholder-employee owns. But if the shareholder is not also an employee, the shareholder may not participate in the qualified pension plan. Passed-through S corporation income is not self-employment income for purposes of maintaining an H.R. 10 Plan.

SECTION 4.   QUALIFIED SUBCHAPTER S SUBSIDIARIES

INTERNAL REVENUE CODE: Sections 1361(b)(3).

REGULATIONS: Sections 1.1361–3,–4.

Prior to 1997, an S corporation could not be part of an affiliated group of corporations as defined in § 1504. This meant that an S corporation could not own stock of an 80 percent or more controlled subsidiary. The limitation was repealed by the 1996 Act, thereby permitting an S corporation to own 80 percent or more of the stock of a subsidiary that is a C corporation. Such a C corporation subsidiary may elect to join in the filing of a consolidated return with its affiliated C corporations (chains of controlled corporations of which the subsidiary is the common parent), but the S corporation parent is not allowed to join in the consolidated return. See I.R.C. § 1504(b)(8). On the other hand, because a corporation that has another corporation as a shareholder is not eligible to make an S election, a subsidiary of another corporation may not be an S corporation. However, § 1361(b)(3) provides a special rule for "qualified Subchapter S subsidiaries."

A qualified subchapter S subsidiary (QSub) is any domestic corporation that (1) is not an ineligible corporation, (2) is wholly owned by an S corporation, and (3) for which the parent S corporation elects to treat as a QSub. I.R.C. § 1361(b)(3)(B). Election procedures are described in Treas.Reg. § 1.1361–3(a). A corporation for which a QSub election is made is not treated as a separate corporation. The existence of the stock of a QSub is disregarded for tax purposes. Treas.Reg. § 1.1361–4(a)(4). All assets, liabilities, and items of income, deduction, and credit of the QSub are treated as assets, liabilities, and items of income, deduction, and credit of the parent S corporation. Treas.Reg. § 1.1361–4(a)(1). Transactions between the S corporation parent and the qualified S corporation subsidiary are not taken into account for tax purposes.

under § 1, which varies depending on the shareholders' marginal tax rates and whether or not the asset was an ordinary income asset, capital asset, or § 1231 asset. Before the introduction in 2003 of the preferential rate for dividends, the total taxes would have been the same as would have been imposed on a C corporation selling the assets and distributing the after-tax proceeds as a dividend, thus preserving the effects of the double tax regime. After 2003, when an S corporation that formerly was a C corporation sells assets with a built-in gain, § 1374 tax can impose a higher total tax burden than is imposed on a C corporation selling assets and distributing the after-tax proceeds as a dividend.

Section 1374(e) grants to the Treasury Department broad authority to promulgate regulations to ensure that the double tax on assets that were appreciated at the time the corporation converted from C to S corporation status is not circumvented. Treas. Regs. §§ 1.1374–1 through 1.1374–10 provide detailed rules governing the application of § 1374.

2.   AMOUNT OF GAIN SUBJECT TO THE BUILT-IN GAIN TAX

The technical operation of § 1374 is somewhat convoluted. Section 1374(a) imposes the tax on the corporation's "net recognized built-in gain." The term net recognized built-in gain is, in turn, defined in § 1374(d)(2)(A) as the amount that would be the corporation's taxable income for the year if only "recognized built-in gains" and "recognized built-in losses" were taken into account (but not more than the corporation's actual taxable income for the year). "Recognized built-in gain" is defined in § 1374(d)(3) as the amount of the gain recognized with respect to any asset disposed of during the year that was held by the corporation on the first day of its first taxable year as an S corporation to the extent the property's fair market value exceeded its basis on that day. Similarly, recognized built-in loss is defined in § 1374(d)(4) as the loss recognized with respect to any asset disposed of during the year that was held by the corporation on the first day of its first taxable year as an S corporation to the extent the fair market value of the property was less than its basis on that day. Section 1374(c)(2) then limits the net recognized built-in gain taxable under § 1374(a) for the year to the excess of the corporation's "net unrealized built-in gain" over the net recognized built-in gain for previous years. "Net unrealized built-in gain" is defined in § 1374(d)(1) as the excess of the fair market value of the corporation's assets on the first day of its first taxable year as an S corporation over the aggregate basis of those assets on that day.

The purpose of this maze of statutory rules is to assure that the aggregate amount taxed under § 1374 if assets held on the day the S election was made are sold over a number of years does not exceed the gain that would have been recognized if the corporation had sold all of its assets immediately before making the S election. Furthermore, since the precise wording of § 1374(d)(3) creates rebuttable presumptions that all recognized gain on any asset sold during the ten year recognition period is built-in gain and that no loss recognized during the period is built-in loss, it is incumbent on the corporation to appraise all of its assets as of the effective date of an S election.

The limitation in § 1374(c) is illustrated in the following example. Assume that X Corporation made an S election on July 1, 2012. At that time X Corporation had the following assets:

Asset	Basis	Fair Market Value	Built-in Gain/Loss
Blackacre	$150	$225	$ 75
Whiteacre	$300	$550	$ 250
Greenacre	$450	$350	($100)
			$ 225

In 2014, when it has operating profits of $500, X Corporation sells Whiteacre for $650 and Greenacre for $300. The corporation recognizes a gain of $350 on Whiteacre and a loss of $150 on Greenacre. Assuming that X Corporation satisfies its burden of proof as to the properties' fair market values on July 1, 2012, the recognized built-in gain on Whiteacre is $250 and the recognized built-in loss on Greenacre is $100. The net recognized built-in gain for the year is $150. Since the corporation's net unrealized built-in gain with respect to all of its assets is $225, the entire net recognized built-in gain is taxed under § 1374(a) in 2014. If Blackacre is sold the following year for $225, the entire gain is net recognized built-in gain, and since the ceiling in § 1374(c)(2) is $75 ($225 net unrealized built-in gain minus $150 net recognized built-in gain from 2014), the entire $75 gain is taxed at the corporate level under § 1374(a).

Now assume alternatively that in 2014, X Corporation sells Blackacre for $225 and Greenacre for $300. X Corporation recognizes a gain of $75 on Blackacre and a loss of $150 on Greenacre. Assuming that X Corporation satisfies its burden of proof as to the properties' fair market values on July 1, 2012, the recognized built-in gain on Blackacre is $75 and the recognized built-in loss on Greenacre is $100. Its net recognized built-in loss for the year is $25, and no tax is due under § 1374(a). If Whiteacre is sold the following year for $650, the corporation recognizes a gain of $350, of which $250 is net recognized built-in gain. But since the corporation's net unrealized built-in gain is only $225, only $225 of that gain is subject to corporate level tax under § 1374(a).

Although § 1371(b) generally proscribes the use by an S corporation of net operating loss carryovers from years when it was a C corporation, there is an exception if built-in gains are required to be recognized and taxed to the S corporation under § 1374. Section 1374(b) permits Subchapter C NOL carryovers to offset net recognized built-in gain for a Subchapter S year solely for the purpose of computing the § 1374 tax.

Treas. Regs. §§ 1.1374–9 and 1.1374–10(b)(3) provide anti-abuse rules directed to the acquisition of property for the purpose of avoiding the § 1374 tax.

3.   EFFECT OF ACCOUNTING METHOD ON APPLICATION OF SECTION 1374 TO GAINS FROM PROPERTY

Treas.Reg. § 1.1374–7 provides that the inventory method maintained by a corporation will be used to determine whether goods required to be included in inventory were on hand with built-in gain at the time of conversion to S corporation status. Reliable Steel Fabricators, Inc. v. Commissioner, T.C. Memo. 1995–293, held that the valuation of inventory work in progress on the effective date of an S election must include some profit margin for completed work, but not for raw materials.

Treas.Reg. § 1.1374–4(h) imposes the tax under § 1374 on all gains from an installment sale under § 453 recognized during or after the 120

The treatment of intercompany transactions under § 482 should be compared with the approach in the consolidated return context where a deferred accounting technique is used to postpone the recognition of gain or loss on intercompany sales until the property is sold outside the group.

SECTION 2.   CONSOLIDATED RETURNS

INTERNAL REVENUE CODE: Sections 1501; 1503(b); 1504(a)–(b).

REGULATIONS: Sections 1.1502–1(f), (g), –2, –11(a), –12, –13(a), (b), (c)(7)(ii), Exs. 1–4, (d), –19(a)–(g), –21(a), (b)(1), –22(a)–(b), –32(a) and (b), –33(a), (b), (c), (d)(1), (e)(1), –34.

Virtually all publicly owned corporations that have subsidiaries, as well as the handful of large privately owned corporations that have subsidiaries and cannot (or chose not to) make an election under subchapter S, as well as the domestic subsidiary groups of foreign corporations, elect to report their income for federal tax purposes as part of a consolidated group rather than as separate entities. In one form or another, the consolidated return regime dates back to 1917, although the current regime is far more sophisticated than its early forerunners. The modern consolidated return regime is highly complex and articulated by voluminous regulations. Nevertheless, judging by the paucity of litigation in the area, one must conclude that the regime works surprisingly well.

Election to file a consolidated return—Section 1501 provides that all members of an affiliated group of corporations may elect to file a consolidated income tax return. A consolidated return permits the includible corporations (as defined in § 1504(b)) that are members of an affiliated group of corporations to combine their incomes, net operating losses, credits, and other items into a single return. Section 1502 authorizes the Treasury to promulgate Regulations as necessary in order "that the tax liability of any affiliated group of corporations making a consolidated return and of each corporation in the group * * * may be returned, determined, computed, assessed, collected, and adjusted, in such manner as clearly to reflect the income tax liability and the various factors necessary for the determination of such liability, and in order to prevent avoidance of such tax liability." As amended in 2004, § 1502 specifically provides that the consolidated return Regulations may contain "rules that are different from the provisions . . . that would apply if such corporations filed separate returns." The detailed rules for filing consolidated returns are found in Regulations promulgated pursuant to this broad delegation of authority. Broadly speaking, the Regulations reflect a "single entity" approach to dealings within the group, which attempts to treat the several members of a consolidated group in the same manner as divisions of a single corporation. However, in certain instances a separate-corporation approach applies to coordinate separate-return and consolidated-return years and to properly associate certain tax attributes with particular members of the group.

The members of an affiliated group includible in a consolidated return are identified under § 1504(a) as the common parent corporation and one or more corporations affiliated through a chain (or chains) of corporations connected by ownership of stock representing 80 percent of the voting power and value of each affiliated member.[2] Unless otherwise excluded by statutory provision, any corporation that is connected to the common parent or another member of an affiliated group by meeting this ownership requirement is treated as an "includible corporation" and must be included on the consolidated return. I.R.C. § 1501. Foreign subsidiaries are specifically excluded from the definition of "includible corporation" and thus are almost never included in a consolidated return. I.R.C. § 1504(b)(3).

Advantages of Filing a Consolidated Return: Net Operating Losses—The principal advantage of filing consolidated returns is the ability to combine the income and loss of each member of an affiliated group into a single taxable income. Treas.Reg. § 1.1502–11(a). Thus, net operating losses of one member of the group can be used to offset the taxable income of another member. This ability to offset losses of one member of the group against income of another member of the group does not extend to affiliated corporations that do not file a consolidated return.

In addition, net operating losses of a member of the group incurred during consolidated return years of the group in which the group as a whole operates at a loss contribute to the overall net operating loss of the group, which may be carried back or forward to other consolidated return years, offsetting income of any member of the group. There are, however, limitations on carryovers of losses incurred by a corporation in separate return years before the corporation became a member of the affiliated group. Treas.Reg. § 1.1502–21(c). Filing a consolidated return also permits the members of the affiliated group to exclude intercompany dividends from gross income in computing taxable income and to defer recognition of gain or loss on intercompany transactions. The basis of stock of one member of a consolidated group held by another member is adjusted to reflect taxable income, loss and the other items of the lower-tier member. Intercompany distributions and contributions also affect the basis of stock of a member of an affiliated group that is held by the common parent or other members, thereby increasing or decreasing gain or loss on disposition of the stock. In addition, deferred intercompany gains and losses may be taken into account in the event that a member leaves the consolidated group, even if the transaction otherwise would be accorded nonrecognition treatment as a tax-free reorganization. Filing consolidated returns requires that all members of the consolidated group use the taxable year of the common parent, but, subject to an anti-abuse rule, the individual members may use different accounting methods. Treas. Regs. §§ 1.1502–76(a), –17.

Advantages of Filing a Consolidated Return: Intercompany Transactions—The treatment of intercompany transactions within members of a consolidated group also offers significant advantages in many instances. In general, the tax consequences of intercompany transactions between members of the same consolidated group are accounted for in consolidated taxable income as transactions between divisions of a single corporation. Treas.Reg. § 1.1502–13(a)(2). In the

---

[2] The value determination is made without regard to certain non-voting, non-convertible preferred stock. I.R.C. § 1504(a)(4).

case of payment for services or a sale or exchange of property, gain or loss that is recognized by the selling member under its method of accounting is deferred until the item can be matched with the buying member's accounting of its corresponding item in the form of a deduction or a recovery of basis when the expenditure is capitalized. Treas.Reg. § 1.1502–13(c)(2). Thus, in the case of an intercompany sale of property, the selling member defers accounting for its recognized gain or loss until the date on which the buying member sells the property outside of the consolidated group or an analogous event requiring acceleration occurs. In this manner, the gain or loss is deferred until the property is disposed of outside of the consolidated group, as would be the case with respect to an exchange of property between divisions of a single corporation. The character of the selling member's deferred gain and the buying member's recognized gain on sale outside of the group also will be determined by single entity principles. The activities of each, therefore, may affect the character of the other's gain. Treas.Reg. § 1.1502–13(c)(1)(i). For example, assume that S Corporation and B Corporation are members of an affiliated group filing a consolidated return. S Corporation sells appreciated investment real estate to B Corporation. Subsequently, B Corporation develops the land as residential real estate for sale to customers in the ordinary course of B Corporation's trade or business. When B Corporation disposes of the land, S Corporation must recognize its deferred gain. Even though S Corporation held the land for investment at the time of its sale to B Corporation, both S Corporation and B Corporation's gain will be treated as ordinary income. Treas.Reg. § 1.1502–13(c)(7)(ii), Ex. 2.

In the case of a sale of depreciable property, the selling member will defer its gain or loss to the time when the buying member claims increased capital cost recovery deductions. Treas.Reg. § 1.1502–13(c)(7)(ii), Ex. 4. For example, under the single entity approach of the Regulations, if the selling member sells depreciable property at a gain, the increased capital recovery deductions that result from the buying member's cost basis will be offset by the corresponding gain taken into account by the selling member. In this fashion, these transactions have no net effect on the overall taxable income of the group, which is the same result that would have occurred if the selling and buying members had been divisions of a single corporation, rather than separate corporations filing a consolidated return. Any increased deduction or basis recovery by the buying member will be offset on the consolidated return by an equivalent recognition of deferred gain by the selling member.

Deferred gain or loss from intercompany transactions is accelerated into a year in which it becomes no longer possible to match the buying member's corresponding item with the selling member's deferred gain or loss. Treas.Reg. § 1.1502–13(d). Thus, gain or loss deferred by the selling member will be accounted for if either the buying member or the selling member ceases to be a member of the consolidated group before the buying member accounts for its matching item corresponding to the selling member's deferred gain or loss.

Distributions—Distributions from one member of an affiliated group to another are also treated under the single entity principle. Distributions are not included in the income of the recipient, Treas.Reg.

§ 1.1502–13(f)(2)(ii), but only so long as there is a matching reduction in the basis of the stock of the distributing member held by the recipient member under the investment adjustment rules of Treas.Reg. § 1.1502–32. Gain recognized by the distributing member under § 311(b) is deferred under the matching principle until the property is sold outside the group, the property is depreciated by the distributee member, or either the distributing or distributee corporation leaves the group. Treas.Reg. § 1.1502–13(f)(2).

Aggregate versus Entity Theory—Even though the federal tax liability of an affiliated group filing a consolidated return is based on the combined taxable incomes of the members of the affiliated group, the separate tax identity of each member of the group is respected through maintenance of individual earnings and profits accounts and basis adjustments with respect to the stock of each member. Treas. Regs. §§ 1.1502–19, –31, –32, and –33. As a result, while accounting for certain intercompany transactions is deferred for purposes of computing taxable income of the group under the consolidated return rules, those transactions will affect the earnings and profits and stock basis of the component members. Accounting for the separate tax identity of each member is required to determine tax consequences in the event that an includible corporation enters or leaves the affiliated group.

Investment Adjustment Accounts—The Regulations require a series of "investment adjustments" to the basis of stock of subsidiaries held by other members of an affiliated group. Treas.Reg. § 1.1502–32. These adjustments are intended to eliminate potential double tax consequences as the separate taxable income or loss of each member of the consolidated group is reflected on the consolidated return. Treas.Reg. § 1.1502–32(a)(1). Investment adjustments begin with the stock of the lowest-tier subsidiary in a chain and work their way up to stock of includible corporations held by the common parent. Treas.Reg. § 1.1502–32(a)(3)(iii). Positive adjustments increase the basis of the stock of a subsidiary member of the group held by another member, and negative adjustments decrease basis. Treas.Reg. § 1.1502–32(b)(2). Adjustments are made for the net amount of the subsidiary's taxable income or loss, expired loss carryover, tax-exempt income, non-deductible non-capital expenses (e.g. fines and disallowed losses), and distributions with respect to the stock of the subsidiary. Losses of a subsidiary and/or distributions may exceed the upper-tier corporation's basis in the stock of the subsidiary. In that case, Treas.Reg. § 1.1502–32(a)(3)(ii) provides for the creation of an "excess loss account," which is the equivalent of a negative basis in the subsidiary's stock.[3] The amount of an excess loss account attributable to the stock of an includible subsidiary is recognized as income (1) on a sale of the stock, (2) whenever either the subsidiary or the includible corporation holding the stock ceases to be a member of the consolidated group, or (3) if the subsidiary's stock becomes worthless (as defined in the Regulations). Treas.Reg. § 1.1502–19(a)(1), (b). The gain is generally treated as gain from the disposition of stock, and is thus capital gain. However, to the extent that the subsidiary is insolvent (or deemed to be insolvent), gain

---

[3]   Reg. § 1.1502–19(a)(2)(B)(ii) refers to the amount of an excess loss account as "basis that is negative in amount."

is ordinary except to the extent that the excess loss account is attributable to distributions. Treas.Reg. § 1.1502–19(b)(4).

Elections—In the first year that a group files a consolidated return, each member of the affiliated group for any part of that year must consent to filing the return; generally that consent must be demonstrated by the member filing a Form 1122 with the first return. Treas.Reg. § 1.1502–75(a)(1), (b)(2). The common parent consents to the return by filing the return. After the first year, each member is deemed to consent to the return, even if it joins the group after that first year. Treas.Reg. § 1.1502–75(a)(2).

An election to file a consolidated return may not be revoked without the consent of the IRS. Permission to discontinue filing a consolidated return will be granted only on a showing of good cause. Treas.Reg. § 1.1502–75(c). Treas.Reg. § 1.1502–75(c)(1)(ii) describes "good cause" as including a change in the Code, Regulations, or other law which has a "substantial adverse effect" on the tax liability of an affiliated group relative to the aggregate tax liability of the members of the group filing separate returns. The IRS has additional authority to grant blanket permission to discontinue filing consolidated returns to all groups, or to a class of groups, in the event of a change in the law of the type that will have a "substantial adverse effect on the filing of consolidated returns." Treas.Reg. § 1.1502–75(c)(2). The election to file a consolidated return will, therefore, affect the tax liability of an affiliated group for the current and future tax years, and a proposal to file a consolidated return must be carefully analyzed.

DETAILED ANALYSIS

1. ELIGIBILITY AND INCLUDIBLE CORPORATIONS

1.1. *Stock Ownership*

An affiliated group consists of the common parent and one or more chains of corporations connected through stock ownership with the common parent. I.R.C. § 1504(a)(1). The common parent must own stock of at least one other corporation that represents at least 80 percent of the total voting power of the stock of that corporation and has value equal to at least 80 percent of the total value of the stock of that corporation. I.R.C. § 1504(a)(1), (2). In addition, each includible corporation must be connected to the common parent or to one or more corporations owned by the common parent with the requisite 80 percent of voting power and value. Thus, a single chain of connected corporations or parallel brother-sister corporations connected to a common parent corporation can qualify as an affiliated group. All shares of stock within a class are treated as having the same value. Control premiums, minority discounts, and blockage discounts are not taken into account. Treas.Reg. § 1.1504–4(b)(2)(iv).

Generally, voting power relates to the right to elect members of the board of directors, although other factors may be considered for complicated voting arrangements. In Alumax Inc. v. Commissioner, 109 T.C. 133 (1997), *aff'd*, 165 F.3d 822 (11th Cir. 1999), the court was required to interpret the 80 percent voting power requirement of § 1502(a)(2) in the face of a complicated voting arrangement. Alumax had two classes of stock outstanding. The class C stock, which was owned by an affiliated group claiming control, was entitled to elect four of six voting members of the

Alumax Board. The class B stock was entitled to elect two of six voting members. The class B and class C directors, in the aggregate and not voting by class, elected one of two special non-voting directors. By agreement between the two classes of stockholders, the class B directors were permitted to name this special director. The other special non-voting director was the CEO of Alumax. Each of the two class B directors had one vote. Each of the four class C directors had two votes. However, a majority of the directors of each of the two classes was required to approve certain corporate actions. Likewise, with respect to shareholder votes, each share of class C stock had four votes while each share of class B stock had one vote. A majority vote of each class of stock was required with respect to a number of restricted stockholder matters. The court rejected the taxpayer's assertion that a mechanical application of these voting formulae represented 80 percent voting control. The court held that the impact of various restrictions on the actions of elected directors must be taken into account in assessing the existence of voting power under § 1502(a)(2). Accordingly, the control test was not met and Alumax was not part of the affiliated group.

Certain stock that possesses more "debt-like" features than equity features is not included for purposes of determining whether the voting power and value tests of § 1504(a)(2) are satisfied. Section 1504(a)(4) provides that "stock" does not include non-voting stock that is limited and preferred as to dividends and does not participate in corporate growth to any significant extent, if its liquidation and redemption rights do not exceed its issue price (except for a reasonable liquidation or redemption premium), and it is not convertible into another class of stock. In addition, § 1504(a)(5) authorizes Regulations that treat certain convertible instruments as not constituting stock.

The Regulations provide in general that options will not be treated as stock, or as deemed to have been exercised unless it can be reasonably anticipated that the issue or transfer of the underlying stock will result in a substantial federal income tax saving and it is reasonably certain that the option will be exercised. Treas.Reg. § 1.1504–4(b)(1), (2)(i). The Regulations broadly define options as including any instrument that provides for the transfer of stock. Treas.Reg. § 1.1504–4(d)(1). This definition, therefore, includes convertible stock. The inquiry is undertaken at the time of issue or transfer of an option, the "measurement date," with some exceptions.[4] If an option is treated as exercised, it will be taken into account in determining the percentage of the value of stock held by the option holder relative to other parties, but not for purposes of determining the option holder's voting power. Treas.Reg. § 1.1504–4(c)(4).

1.2. *Includible Corporations*

An includible corporation is any domestic corporation that is a member of the affiliated group at any time during the taxable year under the stock ownership tests of § 1504(a) that is not excluded under § 1504(b). Includible corporations do not include, among others, tax-exempt corporations,

---

[4] A "measurement date" does not include a transfer between spouses that is covered by § 1041, or a transfer between persons none of whom is a member (or related to a member) of an affiliated group that includes the issuing corporation. Treas.Reg. § 1.1504–4(c)(4)(ii).

insurance companies,[5] possessions corporations under § 936 (certain U.S. owned corporations doing business in Puerto Rico), regulated investment companies (mutual funds) and real estate investment trusts. An includible corporation must be included in the consolidated return of an affiliated group for the part of any year during which the includible corporation meets the stock ownership tests. I.R.C. § 1501. If a corporation ceases to be a member of an affiliated group, absent the consent of the IRS, the corporation may not again be included within the consolidated return of the affiliated group for five years after the close of the taxable year in which the corporation ceased to be a member of the group. I.R.C. § 1504(a)(3). See also Rev. Proc. 2002–32, 2002–1 C.B. 959 (permitting certain qualifying corporations to obtain a waiver of the § 1504(a)(3) bar).

In *Elko Realty Co. v. Commissioner*, 29 T.C. 1012 (1958), aff'd per curiam, 260 F.2d 949 (3d Cir.1958), the court held that two subsidiaries acquired for the purpose of using losses to offset income of the profitable acquiring corporation were not includible on a consolidated return. The court indicated that if ownership of a subsidiary's stock serves no business purpose other than a tax reduction purpose, the subsidiary is not an affiliate for purposes of the consolidated return provisions. The court also disallowed loss deductions under the predecessor to § 269.

2.   CONSOLIDATED TAXABLE INCOME

2.1. *Generally*

The consolidated group computes its regular federal income tax liability on the basis of its consolidated taxable income, which combines the income and loss of each member of the consolidated group into a single taxable income. The computation of consolidated taxable income begins with the determination of the separate taxable incomes of each member of the consolidated group. Treas.Reg. § 1.1502–11(a)(1). In general, each member of the consolidated group computes its separate taxable income as a separate corporation. Treas.Reg. § 1.1502–12(a).

In determining separate taxable income, with limited exceptions all of the generally applicable rules of the Code apply, except as modified by the consolidated return regulations themselves. Treas.Reg. § 1.1502–80. However, separate taxable income excludes distributions with respect to the stock of other members of the group, deferred gains and losses from intercompany transactions, capital gains and losses, § 1231 gains and losses, and charitable contributions. Items excluded from the taxable income of members are separately consolidated and accounted for in consolidated taxable income as provided in specific Regulations. Treas.Reg. § 1.1502–11(a)(2)–(8). Tax liability for the consolidated group is determined by applying the rates of § 11, and other relevant provisions of the Code, to the consolidated taxable income of the group. Tax liability is reduced by consolidated credits attributable to members of the group. Treas.Reg. § 1.1502–6(a). The members of the group typically provide for each member to contribute to the payment of the consolidated tax liability, which is remitted by the parent. Nevertheless, vis-à-vis the IRS, each member of a

---

[5]   Section 1504(c) permits insurance companies to form a consolidated group that includes only affiliated insurance companies. In addition, the common parent of an affiliated group can elect to include an insurance company on the consolidated return of the group after the insurance company has been a member of the affiliated group for five consecutive years.

consolidated group is severally liable for the tax on consolidated taxable income.

2.2. *Consolidated Net Operating Losses*

In some instances, it may be important to determine whether a particular item is characterized separately by a member corporation, whose net taxable income or loss is then separately calculated based on that characterization and aggregated with the net taxable income or loss of other member corporations, or whether the item must be characterized with reference to the overall income and expense items of the consolidated group viewed as a single entity without regard to how it would separately be taken into account by a member in computing the member's separately taxable income. In other words, it can be important whether the consolidated group computes its income with respect to certain items on a "single entity" basis in which all such items are consolidated, or whether the different impact of an item on the taxable income of separate entities is taken into account.

In *United Dominion Industries, Inc. v. United States*, 532 U.S. 822 (2001), the Supreme Court adopted the single entity approach regarding consolidated net operating losses, making it clear that there is only a consolidated net operating loss, not a collection of the separate members' losses, although separate member losses must be identified when members enter and leave a group. United Dominion Industries was the parent of an affiliated group that reported a consolidated net operating loss in each of three years. The consolidated net operating losses included losses attributable to so-called product liability expenses that gave rise to product liability losses. Product liability losses can be carried back under § 172(b)(1)(I) for ten years, rather than the much shorter carryback allowed under § 172(b)(1)(A). Five of the corporate members of the affiliated group, which collectively generated $3.1 million of product liability expenses over three years, had sufficient income to offset their product liability expenses, thereby producing positive separate taxable income in each entity. The government argued that the consolidated group could not carry back product liability expenses incurred by a profitable member because the product liability expenses that were offset with positive income did not enter into the consolidated net operating loss of the group. The Supreme Court reasoned that there is only a single definition of consolidated net operating loss in Treas.Reg. § 1.1502–21(f) and no definition in the Regulations of a separate NOL for a single member of the consolidated group. The subsidiary's specified liability loss deduction items reduced the subsidiary's separate taxable income dollar-for-dollar and thereby contributed to the overall consolidated net operating loss of the affiliated group. A product liability loss subject to the special ten year carryback is the lesser of product liability expenses or the taxpayer's NOL for the taxable year. I.R.C. § 172(j)(1). Identifying the product liability loss first requires calculation of the consolidated group's consolidated net operating loss, the only NOL available under the consolidated return Regulations, then determining product liability loss from all of the product liability expenses within the consolidated group. Thus, a portion of the consolidated NOL could be carried back ten years.

The consolidated net operating loss of a consolidated group generally includes the consolidated net operating loss carrybacks and carryovers of the consolidated group. Treas.Reg. § 1.1502–21(a). In addition, the net operating losses of a member of a consolidated group can be carried over from a pre-consolidation return period against the consolidated income of the group. Treas.Reg. § 1.1502–21(b). This general rule, is, however, subject to two limitations: (1) if the loss year was a "separate return limitation year" (SRLY), then the loss may be carried over only against the income of the member of the group that generated the loss, Treas.Reg. §§ 1.1502–21 and –22(c) (applicable to capital loss carryovers) or (2) if § 382 is applicable, then the carryovers are limited accordingly. Treas.Reg. § 1.1502–91. The SRLY rule does not apply in the case of an acquisition of a new member of a consolidated group if the net operating loss limitation of § 382 applies to the losses of the new member. Treas.Reg. § 1.1502–21(g). Section 382 and the SRLY rules are discussed in Chapter 15.

3.   INVESTMENT ADJUSTMENTS

3.1. *Stock Basis: Investment Adjustment Rules*

3.1.1.   *Generally*

Treas.Reg. § 1.1502–32 requires each member of the group owning stock in another member of the group to adjust its basis for that stock to account for income, losses, and other items attributable to the subsidiary that are reflected in consolidated taxable income. The purpose of the investment adjustment rule is to prevent gain or loss which has been recognized by the subsidiary from being recognized a second time as investment gain or loss by the parent upon disposition of the subsidiary's stock. These rules treat the consolidated group as a single entity by accounting for gains and losses within the consolidated group only once.

A parent corporation's basis in the stock of its consolidated subsidiary is increased or decreased annually by the net amount of the subsidiary's taxable income or loss, tax exempt income, nondeductible noncapital expenses, and distributions to the parent corporation. Treas.Reg. § 1.1502–32(a) and (b). This rule applies with respect to both the common parent and subsidiaries that are in turn parents of lower-tier subsidiaries. A positive adjustment increases basis, while a negative adjustment decreases basis. These items cause an adjustment to the parent's basis in subsidiary stock in the taxable year in which the item is taken into account in determining consolidated taxable income. Thus, items of income and loss, and distributions, will result in adjustments to the parent's basis in the stock of a consolidated subsidiary. Adjustments to the basis of a member's stock are taken into account in determining the basis adjustments of higher-tier members; the adjustments are applied in the order of the tiers, from lowest to highest. If a parent corporation does not own all of the common stock of a subsidiary, only a proportionate part of the subsidiary's income or loss is taken into account in making investment adjustments. For example, if P Corporation owns 90 percent of the stock of S Corporation and S Corporation has $100 of taxable income included on the consolidated return, P Corporation increase its basis in the S Corporation stock by only $90. See Treas.Reg. § 1.1502–32(b)(5)(ii), Ex. 6. The basis adjustment is made at the end of the year unless an interim basis adjustment is necessary to determine a tax liability, for example, as a result of the sale of some of the stock. Treas.Reg. § 1.1504–32(b)(1).

Negative adjustments are allocated only to common stock and then among the shares to reflect the manner in which the shares suffer the economic loss. Positive adjustments are allocated first to preferred stock to reflect distributions and dividend arrearages accrued during the period the subsidiary was a member of the group, Treas.Reg. § 1.1504–32(c)(1)(iii), (c)(3), and then to the common stock. Treas.Reg. § 1.1504–32(c)(2). Adjustments to the common stock generally are made equally to each share, but if any shares have an excess loss account, the adjustments are first allocated among the shares with an excess loss account to equalize and then to eliminate the excess loss accounts. Treas.Reg. § 1.1504–32(c)(2). Basis adjustments attributable to distributions are allocated to the shares on which the distribution was made. Treas.Reg. § 1.1504–32(c)(1)(i).

For purposes of the investment adjustment rules, a member's taxable income or loss includes items of income or loss attributable to the member that are included in the consolidated taxable income of the group. Treas.Reg. § 1.1502–32(b)(3)(i). Operating losses are included in the investment adjustment in the year the loss is absorbed into consolidated taxable income. Thus, a net operating loss carryforward is reflected in a basis adjustment for the year to which the loss is carried. A carryback loss is reflected as an adjustment in the year in which it arose. Treas.Reg. § 1.1502–32(b)(3)(i)(A) and (B).

3.1.2. *Adjustment for Tax Liabilities*

A lower-tier member's federal taxes are nondeductible noncapital expenditures that result in a negative basis adjustment for the stock of the lower-tier member held by a higher-tier member. Treas.Reg. § 1.1502–32(b)(3)(iii)(A). In general, the Regulations require a negative adjustment to the basis of the stock of each group member to reflect its tax liability under the method applied to determine earnings and profits under § 1552, discussed in paragraph 4. Treas.Reg. § 1.1502–32(b)(3)(iv)(D). The basic rule apportions the tax liability of the consolidated group among the members in proportion to each member's contribution to consolidated taxable income, as a percentage of the total tax attributable to the member if the tax of each member were computed on a separate return basis, on the basis of each member's actual contribution to consolidated taxable income including reductions in income. However, the group may select another method. Many consolidated groups enter into what are called "tax sharing agreements," which are contracts that specifically provide for payments by members with a positive separate tax liability to members with net operating losses and to the member—generally the common parent—that remits the group's taxes to the IRS. Regardless of whether the group has a tax sharing agreement, when one member owes a payment to a second member (as determined under the regulations or pursuant to a tax sharing agreement), the first member is treated as indebted to the second member. The right to receive a payment is treated as a positive adjustment, and the obligation to make a payment is treated as a negative adjustment under paragraph (b)(3)(iii) of this section. If the obligation is not paid, the amount not paid generally is treated as a distribution, contribution, or both, depending on the relationship between the members. Thus, stock basis is determined by the actual payment or receipt of cash by one member from another member. If no amount is actually paid, no stock basis adjustment is made.

3.2. *Excess Loss Accounts*

Under Treas.Reg. § 1.1502–11, the utilization by the consolidated group of the operating losses of a subsidiary is not limited by the group's current investment in the subsidiary. When the losses are utilized, however, the parent's investment adjustments under Treas.Reg. § 1.1502–32 may reduce the basis in the subsidiary stock below zero. This negative basis creates an "excess loss account" with respect to the subsidiary's stock. Treas.Reg. § 1.1502–32(a)(3)(ii). The purpose of the excess loss account is to allow losses in excess of basis and to ensure the subsequent recapture in consolidated taxable income of negative adjustments to the stock of a subsidiary upon the occurrence of specified events. Treas.Reg. § 1.1502–19(a)(1). The excess loss account is treated as a "negative basis" reflecting the fact that the group has been able to utilize current deductions in excess of the investment in the subsidiary. The negative basis reflected in an excess loss account is used as adjusted basis to determine the tax consequence of transactions involving the stock. Treas.Reg. § 1.1502–19(a)(2)(ii).

The existence of an excess loss account has an important impact on a number of corporate transactions involving the stock of the subsidiary. For example, if the stock of the subsidiary is sold to a third party outside the group, under Treas.Reg. § 1.1502–19 the amount of gain realized by the parent on the transaction includes not only the sales proceeds received but also the amount of the parent's excess loss account for the subsidiary. Treas.Reg. § 1.1502–19(b)(1).

The amount of gain on the sale resulting from the excess loss account is treated as capital gain. Arguably, the gain attributable to the excess loss account should be treated as ordinary income when it represents deductions previously taken against ordinary income. However, the Regulations allow capital gain treatment, apparently on the theory that, had the subsidiary realized the appreciation in its assets prior to the disposition, the earnings and profits so generated would have eliminated the excess loss account and this is in effect what is happening when the parent sells the stock at a gain. If the subsidiary is insolvent at the time of the disposition, however, then ordinary income results from the transaction to the extent of the insolvency. Treas.Reg. § 1.1502–19(b)(4)(i).[6] The amount treated as ordinary income is limited to the amount of the excess loss account redetermined to exclude distributions to the parent. Treas.Reg. § 1.1502–19(b)(4)(ii).

The existence of an excess loss account also can affect transactions that otherwise would be tax-free. For example, the disposition of stock in a reorganization involving an unrelated corporation will trigger recognition of gain if the subsidiary involved had generated an excess loss account. Treas.Reg. § 1.1502–19(b)(2)(ii) and (c)(1)(ii). On the other hand, tax-free reorganizations within the group generally do not require the inclusion of the excess loss account in income; instead the excess loss account is applied to the stock received without recognition of gain or loss under § 354, either reducing the basis of the stock received or adding to the excess loss account of that stock. Treas.Reg. § 1.1502–19(b)(2)(i). (Tax-free reorganizations are discussed in Chapter 12). A liquidation to which §§ 332 and 334(b)

---

[6]   Covil Insulation Co. v. Commissioner, 65 T.C. 364 (1975), upheld the validity of Treas.Reg. § 1.1502–19, and required the parent corporation to include as ordinary income the excess loss account with respect to a subsidiary whose stock had become worthless. Both the treatment of the stock's worthlessness as an income generating event with respect to the excess loss account and characterization of the gain as ordinary were "permissible exercise[s] of the rulemaking power granted by section 1502."

5. INTERCON

5.1. *Transaction*

5.1.1. *Genera*

Treas.Reg.
members of the
property, the pr
the licensing or
of money. The
distributions wit
13(f). The inter
accounting that
accounting. Tre
intercompany t
methods, howev
that the consol
§ 446(e).

The Regul;
transaction in sc
divisions of a sin
items related to
corporations. For
the seller recogn
basis in the as
character, and of
as divisions of a
does not take it
takes its basis i;
may depend on t
accomplish thes
acceleration rule

5.1.2. *Matchii*
Losses

Under Trea
selling member
selling member u
consolidated taxa
§ 1.1502–13(b)(3)
the buying meml
of property, the
consolidated tax
property outside
corresponding b
resulting from a
manner that pro
income as if the t
a member sells a
member later s
purchasing mem
purchase price p;
income by the s
principle, the cl

(discussed in Chapter 7, section 4) apply eliminates the excess loss account. The transaction is in effect treated as if the parent had owned the subsidiary's assets directly from the beginning; triggering the excess loss account in this situation could lead to duplication of gain.

Other events, such as the deconsolidation of a subsidiary (e.g., by virtue of a stock issuance or sale that results in failure to meet the stock ownership requirements), the discontinuation of filing consolidated returns, or the worthlessness of the stock of the subsidiary, also require the inclusion in income of the amount of the excess loss account. Treas.Reg. § 1.1502–19(c)(1)(iii) and (2). Recognition of gain attributable to an excess loss account of a worthless subsidiary is deferred from the date the stock becomes worthless under the normal facts and circumstances test of § 165(g) to the date on which substantially all of the subsidiary's assets are disposed of or abandoned or the date on which the subsidiary realizes cancellation of indebtedness income that is accorded nonrecognition under § 108(a) by virtue of insolvency or in a bankruptcy proceeding. Treas.Reg. § 1.1502–19(c)(1)(iii).

In *Garvey, Inc. v. United States*, 726 F.2d 1569 (Fed. Cir. 1984), the parent corporation acquired stock of a subsidiary in a tax-free type (B) reorganization (an exchange of stock for stock under § 368(a)(1)(B) pursuant to which under § 354 no gain or loss is recognized) that resulted in a $250,000 basis in the subsidiary stock for the common parent under § 358. Subsequent to acquisition, the subsidiary distributed $4.9 million in dividends out of pre-affiliation earnings and profits. Under the predecessor of Treas. Regs. §§ 1.1502–32(b)(2)(iv) and 1.1502–19(a)(2), the dividend distribution created an excess loss account of $4.65 million which was required to be recognized as income when the group disaffiliated. The court rejected the taxpayer's argument that application of the Regulations unfairly created phantom income that would not have existed had the group filed separate tax returns. The court pointed out that in electing consolidated treatment the taxpayer "must now take the bitter with the sweet."

3.3. *Section 357(c) Situations*

In the consolidated return context, Treas.Reg. § 1.1502–80(d) provides that § 357(c) does not apply to an intercompany transaction. Instead, § 358 applies, sometimes resulting in a negative basis (*i.e.*, excess loss account), due to investment adjustments. Suppose that P Corporation, the parent of a consolidated group, forms S Corporation, which immediately becomes a member of the P Corporation consolidated group. In exchange for all of the stock of S Corporation P contributes to S an asset with a basis of $100, subject to a liability of $130, which S corporation assumes. Apart from the consolidated return rules, § 357(c) would require P to recognize gain of $30—an amount equal to the excess of the liabilities assumed over the basis of the property transferred. But P Corporation takes a basis of negative $30 in the stock of S Corporation, and S Corporation's basis in the asset remains $100.

4. EARNINGS AND PROFITS

Earnings and profits are tracked on a separate member basis because it is necessary to know when each member pays a dividend. However, in a consolidated group special adjustments are required in the earnings and profits accounts of the parent corporation to reflect the consolidated transactions are determined with reference to the activities of both the selling and buying members of the consolidated group. Treas.Reg. § 1.1502–13(c)(1). However, for purposes of identifying the amount and location of specific items, each party to an intercompany transaction is treated as a separate entity. Treas.Reg. § 1.1502–13(a)(2).

The Regulations illustrate the single entity approach with the following example. Treas.Reg. § 1.1502–13(c)(7)(ii), Ex. 1(f). In year one, S Corporation sells property for $100 that it has held for investment with a basis of $70 to B Corporation, which is a member of the consolidated group that includes S Corporation. The accounting in consolidated taxable income for S Corporation's recognized gain on the sale is deferred. As a separate entity, B Corporation holds the property with an adjusted basis of $100 and S Corporation will be required to recognize its deferred gain when B Corporation takes advantage of the $30 basis increase. Treas.Reg. § 1.1502–13(a)(2). In year three B Corporation resells the property for $90 to a customer in the ordinary course of B Corporation's business. If S Corporation and B Corporation were divisions of a single entity, B Corporation would succeed to S Corporation's $70 basis in the land and realize $20 of gain. Under the matching principle of Treas.Reg. § 1.1502–13(c), in the year of B Corporation's sale, S Corporation must take into income an amount that reflects the difference for the year between the "corresponding item," which is the amount actually taken into account by B Corporation as a separate entity, a $10 loss ($90 − $100), Treas.Reg. § 1.1502–13(b)(3), and the "recomputed corresponding item," a $20 gain ($90 − $70), which is the amount that B Corporation would take into account if S Corporation and B Corporation were divisions of a single entity. Treas.Reg. § 1.1502–13(b)(4); see Treas.Reg. § 1.1502–13(c)(7)(ii), Ex. 1(d). Thus, in year three, S Corporation is required to recognize $30 ($20 − ($10) = $30). Treas.Reg. § 1.1502–13(c)(2)(ii). B Corporation recognizes its $10 loss in year three. Treas.Reg. § 1.1502–13(c)(2)(i). The net effect on consolidated taxable income is $20 gain. The character of S Corporation's and B Corporation's gain (or loss) is also determined as if S Corporation and B Corporation were divisions of a single entity. Thus, if B Corporation's activities with respect to the property convert the property from investment property into property described in § 1221(a)(1), both S Corporation's and B Corporation's gain or loss will be ordinary. Treas.Reg. § 1.1502–13(c)(1) and (7)(ii), Ex. 2. The gain and loss taken into account by S Corporation and B Corporation will be preserved on a separate entity basis for purposes of stock basis and earnings and profits adjustments as required by Treas. Regs. §§ 1.1502–32 and –33. See Treas.Reg. § 1.1502–13(a)(2).

The matching principle of the Regulations also requires an accounting for the selling member's deferred gain as the buying member claims capital recovery deductions on its purchase price basis of depreciable property in an intercompany transaction. Assume for example, that S Corporation and B Corporation are members of the same consolidated group. In 2008, S Corporation acquires depreciable five year property for $150 and properly claims capital recovery deductions of $30 in 2008 and $48 in 2009. On the first day of its 2010 taxable year, S Corporation sells the property to B Corporation for $110. At the time of sale, S Corporation's basis in the property is $72 ($150 − [$30 + 48]). S Corporation recognizes $38 of gain, which is deferred. Under § 168(i)(7), B Corporation must use the same depreciation rate as S Corporation with respect to so much of the adjusted

corporation recognizes gain or lo
§ 337(a), no gain or loss is recogni
distributee," defined in § 337(c) a
ownership requirements of § 332(b)

In determining whether a me
to qualify for nonrecognition under
the group is taken into account
example, that Y Corporation and Z
same consolidated group, owned 60
the stock of S Corporation, and S C
percent of its assets to Y Corpora
Section 332 accords nonrecogniti
Corporation. However, § 337(c) pro
a corporation receiving a liquid
distributee," distributions to whic
liquidating corporation under § 337
consolidated return regulation. T
Corporation nor Z Corporation n
requirement of § 332(b) and S Co
loss. I.R.C. § 336(d)(3). However, th
to S's deferred gain. Treas.Reg. §
13(j)(9), Ex. 7. But the manner in
between the distributee corporation

An intercompany sale of the
group, followed by a liquidation o
problem under the single entity a
stock of the member gives rise to
exceptions to the matching pr
intercompany items being redeterr
nondeductible, noncapital amount,
rule does not apply to gain on the
followed by a § 332 liquidation in
gain. Treas.Reg. §§ 1.1502–13(c)(6
illustrated by the following exampl
Ex. 6(c). B Corporation, S Corpora
the same consolidated group. S Co
stock, which has a fair market valu
Corporation stock is $70. The fair m
$100 and the assets have a basis of
purchases the T Corporation sto
Corporation's $30 gain on the interc
is deferred in determining consolic
July 1 of Year 3, when T Corpor
Corporation distributes all of its a
liquidation governed by § 332. B C
stock is $100. On liquidation of T
$100 distribution and thus has
Corporation recognizes no gain or lo
transfer of T Corporation stock fro
been between divisions of a single
liquidation of T Corporation would
have been recognized under § 33
corresponding item is $30 of unreco

basis of the property in B Corporation's hands as does not exceed S Corporation's adjusted basis at the time of the transfer. Thus, in taxable year 2010, B Corporation deducts $28.80, which is the depreciation deduction that would have been available to S Corporation under § 168. In addition, B Corporation is permitted to recover its remaining basis as if the property were new five-year property. Thus, in 2010 B Corporation claims an additional $7.60 depreciation deduction (20 percent of adjusted basis of $38, applying the half-year convention as if the property were new five-year property). The additional depreciation deduction claimed by B Corporation requires that S Corporation take into account $7.60 of its deferred intercompany gain in 2010. In 2011, B Corporation deducts $17.28 of depreciation with respect to the basis that would have been its basis had it taken a transferred basis from S Corporation, plus $12.16 of depreciation based on its $28 basis increase from the intercompany transaction. S Corporation is required to take into account $12.16 of its deferred intercompany gain in 2011. Treas.Reg. § 1.1502–13(c)(7)(ii), Ex. 4. Under the single entity principle, which treats S Corporation and B Corporation as divisions of a single corporation, the character of S Corporation's recognized gain will reflect the tax consequence of B Corporation's depreciation. Treas.Reg. § 1.1502–13(c)(1)(i) and (c)(4). Thus, because S Corporation's deferred gain offsets B Corporation's increased depreciation, S Corporation's gain is treated as ordinary income. Treas.Reg. § 1.1502–13(c)(7)(ii), Ex. 4(d). In this fashion, the Regulations recognize separate entity aspects of the transaction as reflected in B Corporation's increased basis and depreciation, but treat the overall consequence to consolidated taxable income as though the property were transferred between divisions of a single entity through the matching of B Corporation's increased depreciation deductions with restoration of S Corporation's deferred intercompany gain.

If, on the first day of its 2012 taxable year, B Corporation sells the property to X Corporation, which is not a member of the S-B consolidated group, for $120 payable in two annual installments with adequate interest, both B Corporation and S Corporation must account for recognized gain. B Corporation recognizes gain of $75.84 ($120 – $44.16).[7] As a consequence of B Corporation's sale, S Corporation must also recognize recapture gain. If S and B Corporations were divisions of a single entity, on its 2012 sale of the property the Corporation would have realized $94.08 of gain, determined by subtracting from the $120 amount realized an adjusted basis of $25.92 computed without regard to B Corporation's purchase from S Corporation ($150 original cost less four year's capital recovery deductions totaling $94.08). The difference between the gain recognized on a single entity basis and the gain recognized by B Corporation as a separate entity, $18.24 ($94.08 – $75.84), is B Corporation's "recomputed corresponding item," which must be accounted for by S Corporation at the time of B Corporation's disposition.[8] As a consequence, the consolidated taxable income of the group reflects the tax consequence of the sale of the property on a single entity basis; S Corporation's gain of $18.24 plus B Corporation's gain of $75.84 is the equivalent of the gain that would have been recognized

---

[7] B Corporation's adjusted basis is its $110 purchase price minus $65.84 of depreciation for 2010 and 2011.

[8] The recomputed corresponding item is equivalent to S's deferred gain of $38 less gain recognized by S Corporation in 2010 and 2011 as B Corporation claimed increased capital recovery deductions.

Year 9, T issu
a nonmember

(b) Dividend e
P's $100 of di
and its $10 of
included in gr

(c) Matching
when T beco
amount of its
excess loss ac
item from the
divisions of a
have a $10
under § 1.150
and $5 of ear
excess loss a
corresponding
matching rule
as a result of
between P's §
gain. S's rem
matching anc
example, und
stock, or unde

In the examp
result of S's distrik
have resulted in a
single entity bas
original $10 of ba:
by the $90 distrib
of deferred gain v
The remaining $
which can be ma
accelerated if eith
group. Treas.Reg.

5.2.3. *Liquidat*

Section 332,
upon the compl
consolidated retu
regime.[11] The sto
§§ 332 and 337 is
the ownership sto
When § 332 ap|
corporation recei
subsidiary's asset

When § 332
provides a genera

---

[11] Section 332 al
Treas.Reg. § 1.332–2(c

amount loaned and the fair market value of the obligation will be treated as transferred between the creditor member and the debtor member, as appropriate (for example, as a distribution or a contribution to capital). Treas.Reg. § 1.1502–13(g)(3)(i)(C).

5.2.7. *Anti-Abuse Rules*

In language designed to force tax practitioners to bang their heads against a brick wall for pleasure, Treas.Reg. § 1.1502–13(h)(1) provides that, "If a transaction is structured with a principal purpose to avoid the purposes of this section, (including, for example, by avoiding treatment as an intercompany transaction), adjustments must be made to carry out the purposes of this section." Specific examples of abusive transactions described in the Regulation include the transfer of property to a partnership to avoid the SRLY limitation, the use of corporations formed under § 351 or partnerships to mix assets for the purpose of avoiding gain on disposition of appreciated property, and the use of a sale-leaseback transaction to create gain for the purpose of absorbing losses subject to the SRLY limitation. Treas.Reg. § 1.1502–13(h)(2). Similar anti-abuse language is attached to other consolidated return Regulations. *See e.g.*, Regs. §§ 1.1502–19(e), –32(e), and –33(g).

6. SALES OF SUBSIDIARY STOCK: THE UNIFIED LOSS RULES

6.1. *Generally*

In some cases, application of the investment adjustment rules conflicts with the principles of §§ 311 and 336, which require recognition of gain on the distribution by a corporation of appreciated property, and permit the recognition of loss on the distribution of depreciated property by a liquidating corporation, because it permits assets that are sold out of the consolidated group to obtain a step up in basis without the payment of a current corporate level tax. Suppose, for example, that S Corporation holds a single asset with a basis of $100 and a fair market value of $300. P Corporation purchases all of the stock of S Corporation for $300, P and S do not make a § 338 election, and P and S Corporations elect to file a consolidated return. S Corporation then sells the asset for $300. S Corporation recognizes a $200 gain, and P Corporation increases its basis in the S Corporation stock from $300 to $500. P Corporation then sells the stock of S Corporation for $300, realizing a $200 loss, which offsets the $200 gain. Absent a limitation on the recognition of this loss, tax on the gain realized from the sale of the assets effectively would be eliminated by P Corporation's loss on the sale of the stock of S. P Corporation's tax loss is artificial; it does not reflect an economic loss. The same problem arises if the asset is a depreciable asset which is consumed in the course of S Corporation's business.

To deal with this issue, Treas.Reg. § 1.1502–36 provides unified rules for loss on subsidiary stock transferred by a member of an affiliated group filing a consolidated return. A transfer of a loss share of stock (defined as a share of stock of an affiliate having a basis in excess of fair market value) includes any event in which (1) gain or loss would be recognized (apart from the rules in the Regulations), (2) the holder of a share and the subsidiary cease to be members of the same group, (3) a nonmember acquires an outstanding share from a member, or (4) the share is treated as worthless. The purpose of these rules is twofold, to prevent the consolidated return provisions from creating non-economic losses on the sale of subsidiary stock and to prevent members of the affiliated group filing the consolidated return from claiming more than one tax benefit from a single economic loss. Under the Regulations, any transfer of a loss share requires the application in sequence of three basis rules.

First, under Treas.Reg. § 1.1502–36(b), a basis redetermination rule is applied to deal with tax losses attributable to investment adjustment account allocations among different shares of stock that result in disproportionate reflection of gain or loss in shares' basis. Second, if any share is a loss share after application of the basis redetermination rule, a basis reduction rule is applied under Treas.Reg. § 1.1502–36(c) to deal with artificial loss attributable to investment adjustment account adjustments, but this reduction does not exceed the share's "disconformity amount." Third, if any duplicated losses remain after application of the basis reduction rule, under Treas.Reg. § 1.1502–36(d) an attribute reduction rule is applied to the corporation the stock of which was sold to prevent the duplication of a loss recognized on the transfer or preserved in the basis of the stock. If a chain of subsidiaries is transferred (rather than a single subsidiary) the order in which the rules are applied is modified. In this case, the basis redetermination rule and the basis reduction rule are applied sequentially, working down the chain, and the attribute reduction rule is then applied working up the chain, starting with the lowest tier subsidiary.

6.2. *The Basis Redetermination Rule*

The basis redetermination rule in Treas.Reg. § 1.1502–36(b) does not apply when all of the stock of the subsidiary has been transferred in a taxable transaction; thus often it is not applicable. When the basis redetermination rule does apply, investment adjustments (exclusive of distributions) that were previously applied to members' bases in subsidiary stock are reallocated in a manner that, to the greatest extent possible, first eliminates loss on preferred shares and then eliminates basis disparity on all shares. This rule affects both positive and negative adjustments, and thus addresses both noneconomic and duplicated losses. First, the basis of any transferred loss share is reduced by any positive investment adjustments, but the basis will not be reduced to less than the value of the loss share. Second, to the extent of any remaining loss on the transferred shares, negative investment adjustments are removed from shares that are not transferred loss shares and are applied to reduce the loss on transferred loss shares. Third, the positive adjustments removed from the transferred loss shares are allocated to increase basis of other shares only after the negative adjustments have been reallocated. This rule does not affect the aggregate basis of the shares, and thus does not apply if all of the shares of a subsidiary are sold or become worthless; it is important only when some, but not all, shares are sold. A number of special limitations on basis reallocation also must be considered in various specific circumstances.

6.3. *The Basis Reduction Rule*

If, after applying the basis redetermination rule in step one, any transferred share is a loss share (even if the share only became a loss share as a result of the application of the basis redetermination rule), the basis of that share is subject to reduction. The basis reduction rule in Treas.Reg. § 1.1502–36(c) eliminates noneconomic losses that arise from the operation of the investment adjustment account rules. Under this rule, the basis of each transferred loss share is reduced (but not below its value) by the lesser of (1) the share's disconformity amount, or (2) the share's net positive adjustment.

The "disconformity amount" with respect to a subsidiary's share is the excess of its basis over the share's allocable portion of the subsidiary's inside tax attributes (determined at the time of the transfer). Every share within a single class of stock has an identical allocable portion. Between shares of different classes of stock, allocable portions are determined by taking into account the economic arrangements represented by the terms of the stock. "Net inside attributes" is the sum of the subsidiary's loss carryovers, deferred deductions, cash, and asset bases, minus the subsidiary's liabilities. The disconformity amount identifies the net amount of unrealized appreciation reflected in the basis of the share.

A share's net positive adjustment is computed as the greater of (1) zero, or (2) the sum of all investment adjustments (excluding distributions) applied to the basis of the transferred loss share, including investment adjustments attributable to prior basis reallocations under the basis reallocation rule. The net positive adjustment identifies the extent to which a share's basis has been increased by the investment adjustment provisions for items of income, gain, deduction and loss (whether taxable or not) that have been taken into account by the group. Special rules apply when the subsidiary the stock of which is transferred itself holds stock of a lower-tier subsidiary.

The application of the basis reduction rule is illustrated by the following example. Assume that P purchased all the stock of S for $500 at a time when S had a single capital asset with a basis of $400. During the period P owned S, S earned $50 (after taxes) and purchased a second capital assets. P sells all of the stock of S for $380, when P's basis in the S stock is $550, thereby realizing a $170 loss. At that time the fair market value of S's assets is $380, and the basis of S's assets is $450. The disconformity amount is $100, the excess of P's $550 basis in the S stock over S's $450 basis in its assets, and the net positive basis adjustment is $50. The lesser of the two is $50. Thus, P's $550 basis in the S stock is reduced by $50 to $500 and only $120 of the loss is allowed.

6.4. *The Attribute Reduction Rule*

If any transferred share remains a loss share after application of the basis reallocation and basis reduction rules, any loss recognized with respect to the transferred share is allowed. However, in this instance, the subsidiary's tax attributes (including the consolidated attributes, e.g., loss carryovers, attributable to the subsidiary) are reduced pursuant to Treas.Reg. § 1.1502–36(d). The attribute reduction rule addresses the duplication of loss by members of consolidated groups, and is designed to prevent the group from recognizing more than one tax loss with respect to a single economic loss, regardless of whether the group disposes of the subsidiary stock before or after the subsidiary recognizes the loss with respect to its assets or operations. However, under a type of *de minimis* rule, unless the group so elects, the attribute reduction rule does not apply if the aggregate attribute reduction amount in the transaction is less than five percent of the total value of the shares transferred by members in the transaction. Treas.Reg. § 1.1502–36(d)(2)(ii).

Under the attribute reduction rule, the subsidiary's attributes are reduced by the "attribute reduction amount," which equals the lesser of (1) the net stock loss, or (2) the aggregate inside loss. The "attribute reduction amount" reflects the total amount of unrecognized loss that is reflected in both the basis of the subsidiary stock and the subsidiary's attributes. "Net stock loss" is the amount by which the sum of the bases (after application of the basis reduction rule) of all of the shares in the subsidiary transferred by members of the group in the same transaction exceeds the aggregate value of those shares. Treas.Reg. § 1.1502–36(d)(3)(ii). The subsidiary's "aggregate inside loss" is the excess of its net inside attributes over the aggregate value of all of the shares in the subsidiary. Treas.Reg. § 1.1502–36(d)(3)(iii). (Net inside attributes generally has the same meaning as in the basis reduction rule, subject to special rules for lower-tier subsidiaries.)

The attribute reduction amount is first applied to reduce or eliminate items that represent actual realized losses, such as operating loss carryovers (Category A), capital loss carryovers (Category B), and deferred deductions (Category C) in that order unless the taxpayer elects to make a different allocation. If the subsidiary does not hold stock of any lower-tier subsidiaries, any excess attribute reduction amount is then applied to reduce the basis of assets (Category D) in the asset classes specified in Treas.Reg. § 1.338–6(b) other than Class I (cash and general deposit accounts, other than certificates of deposit held in depository institutions), but in the reverse order from the order specified in that section. Thus, the basis in any purchased goodwill is the first item reduced. If the subsidiary holds stock of one or more lower-tier subsidiaries, the Category D attribute reduction is first allocated between the subsidiary's basis in any stock of lower-tier subsidiaries and the subsidiary's other assets (treating the non-stock Category D assets as one asset) in proportion to the subsidiary's basis in the stock of each lower-tier subsidiary and its basis in the Category D assets other than subsidiary stock. Only the portion of the attribute reduction amount not allocated to lower-tier subsidiary stock is applied under the reverse residual method. (Additional special rules apply to prevent excessive reduction of attributes when the subsidiary itself holds stock of a lower-tier subsidiary. Treas.Reg. § 1.1502–36(d)(4)(ii).) If the attribute reduction amount exceeds all of the attributes available for reduction, that excess amount generally has no effect. If, however, cash or other liquid assets are held to fund payment of a liability that has not yet been deducted but will be deductible in the future (e.g., a liability the deduction for which is subject to the economic performance rules of § 461(h)), loss could be duplicated later, when the liability is taken into account. To prevent such loss duplication, the excess attribute reduction amount will be held in suspense and applied to prevent the deduction or capitalization of later payments with respect to the liability. Treas.Reg. § 1.1502–36(d)(4)(ii)(C). Additional special rules apply to prevent excessive reduction of attributes when the subsidiary itself holds stock of a lower-tier subsidiary.

The application of the attribute reduction rule is illustrated by continuing the preceding example. The "net stock loss" when P sold the stock of S was $120. The "aggregate inside loss"—the excess of the basis of S's assets ($450) over the value of the S stock ($380) is $70. The lesser of the two is $70. Thus the basis of S's assets is reduced by $70, from $450 to $380. No gain or loss would be realized on the sale of S' assets for $380.

In cases where as a result of the stock transfer the subsidiary ceases to be a member of the group, an election may be made to reattribute attributes (other than asset basis) and/or to reduce stock basis (and thereby reduce stock loss) in order to avoid attribute reduction. Treas.Reg. § 1.1502–36(d)(4). If an election is made and it is ultimately determined that the subsidiary has no attribute reduction amount the election will have no effect (or if the election is made for an amount that exceeds the finally determined attribute reduction amount, the election will have no effect to the extent of that excess). In addition, taxpayers may elect to reduce (or not reduce) stock basis, or to reattribute (or not reattribute) attributes, or some combination thereof, in any amount that does not exceed the subsidiary's attribute reduction amount.[13]

Finally, if the subsidiary ceases to be a member of the consolidated group as a result of the transfer, the common parent of the group can elect to reduce stock basis (thereby reducing an otherwise allowable loss on the sale of the stock), reattribute attributes, or apply some combination of basis reduction and attribute reattribution after the otherwise required attribute reduction.

6.5. *Worthlessness*

If a member treats stock of the subsidiary as worthless under § 165(g) and the subsidiary continues as a member, or if a member recognizes a loss on subsidiary stock and on the following day the subsidiary is not a member and does not have a separate return year following the recognition of the loss, all Category A, Category B, and Category C attributes (i.e., capital loss carryovers, net operating loss carryovers, and deferred deductions) that have not otherwise been eliminated or reattributed, as well as any credit carryovers, are eliminated. Treas.Reg. § 1.1502–36(d)(7). A worthlessness determination must take into account the rules in Treas.Reg. § 1.1502–80(c), as well as under § 165.

---

[13] The reattribution election may be made only if the subsidiary ceases to be a group member.

PART 4

CORPORATE ACQUISITION TECHNIQUES

CHAPTER 10

TAXABLE ACQUISITIONS: THE PURCHASE AND SALE OF A CORPORATE BUSINESS

The material considered up to this point has focused on the provisions of Subchapter C from the perspective of their function in the statutory structure provided for the taxation of corporations and shareholders. The material in this Part changes from this structural focus to concentrate on the application of the corporate rules to a specific transaction, the purchase and sale of a corporate business. This Chapter and Chapter 11 deal with the tax aspects of a taxable purchase and sale of the corporate business.[1] The various forms of tax-free acquisitions are considered in Chapter 12.

A taxable purchase and sale of a business involves the application of the general principles of taxation of sales and exchanges of property, supplemented by a limited number of special rules. The exact application of the principles depends on the form of the transaction. There are basically three approaches to the sale of a corporate business: A corporation may sell its assets and distribute the proceeds to its shareholders in liquidation; the corporation may distribute its assets to its shareholders in liquidation, following which the shareholders sell the assets; or the shareholders might simply sell the stock of the corporation, which continues in existence.

Suppose that A owns all of the stock of X Corporation, which operates a business consisting of two assets, Asset #1, having a fair market value of $500 and a basis of $50, and Asset #2, having a fair market value of $200 and a basis of $250. Also assume that the basis of A's stock is $200. If Y Corporation desires to acquire the business of X Corporation it might purchase the assets of X Corporation for $700. X Corporation would realize a net gain of $450 on the sale of Asset #1 and a loss of $50 on Asset #2. Assuming that the gain and loss could be offset (which would be true unless Asset #2 was a capital asset and Asset #1 was not), X Corporation's net gain on the sale of its assets would be $400. If this gain were taxed at the maximum corporate rate of 35 percent, X Corporation would pay taxes of $140 and make a $560 liquidating distribution to A, who would recognize a capital gain of $360. A would pay a tax, at the preferential capital gains rate of 20 percent (assuming that A otherwise would be in the highest income tax bracket), of $72 and would receive net after-tax proceeds of $488. Y Corporation would take a basis of $500 for Asset #1 and $200 for Asset #2. On a subsequent sale of the assets, assuming that their fair market values were unchanged, Y Corporation would realize neither gain nor loss. In some situations, however, issues peculiar to the sale of a

---

[1] Chapter 11 examines the problems that arise when corporate distributions are made in connection with the sale of a corporate business.

corporate business have arisen and rules have been fashioned, either by the Congress or by the courts, to deal with these problems. The materials in Section 1 deal with the sale of a business that takes the form of a sale of corporate assets and explore the problems that this form of transaction historically has generated and the currently applicable rules.

Rather than purchasing the X Corporation's assets, Y Corporation might purchase the stock of X Corporation from A. If Y Corporation paid $700 for the stock, A would recognize a gain of $500. The basis of the assets in X Corporation's hands would be unaffected by the sale of the stock, and on a subsequent sale of the assets, X Corporation would recognize an aggregate gain of $400. Since the economic burden of the tax on this gain would be borne by Y Corporation, presumably it would offer A less than $700 for the stock of X Corporation to reflect this inherent tax burden. If the gain were to be realized and taxed contemporaneously with the purchase, it could be expected that Y Corporation would offer A only $560 for the stock, the same amount that A would receive in a liquidating distribution following a taxable sale of its assets by X Corporation. But if the gain were not expected to be realized until sometime in the future, Y Corporation could be expected to be willing to pay somewhat more for the stock.

Section 2 of this Chapter focuses on this second basic alternative form for the sale of a corporate business, the sale of the shares of stock of the corporation and again focuses on the corporate tax rules designed for this form of transaction.

The manner in which the parties have structured transactions involving the sale of a corporate business is influenced by two significant tax factors: the seller's desire to maximize the portion of the gain that would be taxed as capital gain rather than as ordinary income; the buyer's desire to obtain as high a basis as possible for the corporation's assets, particularly inventory and depreciable property.[2] In addition, asset sales and stock sales often have significantly different consequences under state tax law.

Tax results are not the only factors that influence the form of a sale and purchase of a corporate business. Indeed, tax results in many cases are of lesser importance than nontax factors. In many cases, a single purchaser for all of the corporation's business activities cannot be located, and one line of business is sold to one purchaser while another line of business is sold to a second purchaser. In other cases, a purchaser might be unwilling to acquire the stock of a corporation because of concerns regarding contingent or unascertained liabilities. On the other hand, an asset purchase might be ruled out if the acquired business owns contract rights that are not assignable; in such a case the

---

[2]   Before 1987 the sale of a corporate business was structured around the ability to avoid recognition of gain at the corporate level under either the *General Utilities* doctrine or the pre-1987 version of § 337. The elimination of this last factor by the 1986 Tax Reform Act significantly altered the stakes in many transactions, but important issues remain. The general rule of former § 337, as in effect from 1954–1987, was that a corporation recognized neither gain nor loss on the sale or exchange of assets after the adoption of a plan of liquidation, if all of the assets (including proceeds from the sale of assets) were distributed in liquidation within twelve months of adoption of the plan. Elimination of the corporate tax through nonrecognition of gain depended, however, on following mechanical formulae involving time intervals, bulk inventory sales of a certain nature, and the like.

acquisition must be structured as a sale and purchase of stock. In addition, the impact of various potential liabilities, including contingent liabilities such as environmental remediation obligations and product liability claims, influences the form of the transaction. Other important factors to be considered include state law rights of dissenting shareholders, federal and state securities laws, and the authority of state and federal regulatory agencies to approve or disapprove a transaction.

SECTION 1.   ASSETS SALES AND ACQUISITIONS

INTERNAL REVENUE CODE: Sections 197(a)–(e), (f)(1), (3), (7); 453(h)(1)(A)–(C), (2); 1060.

REGULATIONS: Sections 1.1001–1(g); 1.1001–2; 1.1060–1(a)(1), (b)(1)–(3), (6), (7), (c)–(e); 1.338–6(b).

If a corporation sells its business by selling its assets to the purchaser, it recognizes gain or loss with respect to each separate asset, as would a partnership or sole proprietorship selling its business. On liquidation the shareholders recognize capital gain or loss under the rules governing complete liquidations, discussed in Chapter 7, subject to the exception under § 332 for liquidations of controlled subsidiaries. Thus, gain or loss generally results to both the corporation and the shareholders. The same tax results follow if the corporation liquidates first, recognizing gain or loss under § 336, with the shareholders again taxable under § 331. In this case the shareholders take a fair market value basis in the corporation's assets pursuant to § 334(a), and they realize no gain or loss upon the immediate sale of the assets.

In an asset sale, both buyer and seller must allocate the purchase price to the various assets transferred, the seller in order to determine the amount of gain or loss on each asset and the buyer to establish the tax basis for each of the newly acquired assets. These allocations generally present no problem if the parties have bargained on an asset-by-asset basis, but that is rarely the case. More commonly, the parties bargain for the sale and purchase based on a lump sum price. After the total purchase price has been determined, the parties often then bargain as to the allocation of the price among all of the assets. The parties' objectives in this *ex post* allocation are to a large extent determined by tax considerations. Generally, allocations of the purchase price agreed upon by the parties have been respected by the IRS and the courts on the theory that the parties had adverse tax interests and that a bargained-for allocation is therefore presumptively correct.

Historically, however, there was the danger that the Treasury could be "whipsawed" by inconsistent allocations in which each party allocated the purchase price in the manner most advantageous to that party and differently from the other party. This was a particularly serious problem prior to the enactment in 1993 of § 197, which allows 15–year amortization of almost all purchased intangible assets. Prior to the enactment of § 197, goodwill and going concern value were not depreciable. Thus, purchasers preferred to minimize the amount allocated to those assets and maximize the amount allocated to depreciable assets and inventory. From the seller's perspective, however, it was more desirable to allocate purchase price to goodwill and going concern value, because the gain on those assets was capital gain, rather than to inventory and depreciable equipment subject to § 1245 recapture, which resulted in ordinary income. In addition, purchasers attempted to allocate all or part of a "premium" payment in excess of the value of the assets among all of the assets, rather than allocating the premium solely to goodwill or going concern value.[3] Congress responded to these problems with the enactment in 1986 of § 1060, requiring the use by both the buyer and the seller on the sale of a trade or business of the "residual method" of valuing goodwill. This provision was intended not only to prevent the allocation of any purchase price premium to depreciable assets, but to help ensure that the seller and purchaser allocate the price consistently.

With the enactment of § 197, providing for uniform amortization of purchased intangible assets over 15 years, however, the former function of § 1060 has diminished in importance and the latter function has become more significant. Pursuant to its statutory authority, the Treasury Department has promulgated regulations requiring both parties to file information returns with respect to the purchase price allocation, thus allowing the IRS to identify situations in which allocations have been made on an inconsistent basis. See Treas.Reg. § 1.1060–1(e).

DETAILED ANALYSIS

1.   ALLOCATION OF PURCHASE PRICE

1.1. *General*

Section 1060 refers to preexisting regulations under § 338(b)(5), which contain a detailed set of rules for the allocation of the purchase price among acquired assets. Treas.Reg. § 1.1060–1(a)(1) adopts the allocation rules of Treas. Regs. §§ 1.338–6, which divide all assets into seven classes. Class I includes cash and general deposit accounts, not including certificates of deposit; Class II includes actively traded personal property, such as marketable stocks and securities, and certificates of deposit and foreign currency (but stock of target corporation affiliates is excluded); Class III assets are (1) assets that the taxpayer marks-to-market annually for tax purposes, and (2) debt instruments, including accounts receivable, mortgages, and credit card receivables which arise in the ordinary course of a business; Class IV includes stock in trade, inventory, and property held for sale to customers in the ordinary course of a trade or business; Class V includes all assets not specifically assigned to the other classes (including stock of target affiliates); Class VI includes all § 197 intangibles except for goodwill and going concern value; and Class VII includes goodwill and going concern value (whether or not amortizable under § 197). The term "§ 197 intangibles" is intended to be broader than the term "amortizable § 197 intangibles" and includes, for example, § 197 intangibles that are amortizable by the buyer but not by the seller. See T.D. 8711, 1997–1 C.B.

---

[3] Purchasers had sometimes applied a so-called "proportional allocation method" in determining purchase price premiums. Under this approach, an independent value was established for goodwill, often by a capitalization of earnings method, and then the premium was allocated proportionately to all assets, including goodwill. See United States v. Cornish, 348 F.2d 175 (9th Cir.1965) (allowing premium paid for partnership interest to be allocated among partnership assets in making basis adjustment under § 743).

85, 86. Class V contains most tangible assets, including depreciable buildings and equipment, as well as land (which is not depreciable) and some depreciable intangible assets, such as computer software, while Class VI typically contains intangible assets, such as patents, copyrights, trademarks, tradenames, franchises, customer lists, and covenants not to compete. Class VI assets are amortizable over 15 years under § 197.

The purchase price is allocated first to Class I assets based on their aggregate fair market value, then to Class II assets, and so on through Class VI. Within each class, the price is allocated among assets relative to their respective fair market values. Since each asset in Classes I-VI should be allocated a portion of the purchase price equal to its fair market value, any amount designated as paid for goodwill or going concern value, as well as the entire premium, if any, is allocated to Class VII. Conversely, if a going business is purchased for less than its liquidation value, the Class VI assets, and the Class V assets if the Class VI assets are insufficient enough or the discount is deep enough, are allocated an amount less than their individual fair market values.

Nevertheless, even after the enactment of § 197, under Treas.Reg. § 1.338–6, some conflict of interest between buyer and seller remains.

Class V contains both depreciable and nondepreciable assets, such as land. Purchasers will want to establish as high a fair market value as is possible for depreciable assets, but for the seller such an allocation may give rise to ordinary income (including § 1245 recapture income) instead of capital gain.

The interests of buyer and seller may vary with respect to allocations to Class V versus Class VI because Class V contains many assets for which cost recovery under § 168 is more rapid than is cost recovery under § 197 for Class VI and Class VII assets, but it also contains important assets, e.g., real property, for which cost recovery under § 168 is not as rapid as cost recovery for intangibles under § 197. Generalizations as to which of the seller or purchaser is benefitted by an allocation to Class V versus Class VI are impossible because the analysis is fact specific.

Since all § 197 intangibles are amortized over 15 years, the division of § 197 amortizable intangibles between two classes—Class VI and Class VII—for purposes of determining basis is significant only if some, but not all, of the amortizable intangibles acquired in a single transaction are subsequently sold at a gain, necessitating calculation of individual bases of the intangibles that were sold. From the seller's side, however, it is more likely that § 1245 recapture will apply with respect to Class VI assets than with respect to Class VII assets, since Class VI may contain amortizable self-created intangibles, but Class VII intangibles are amortizable, and thus subject to § 1245 on sale, only if purchased.

1.1.1.   *Covenants Not to Compete*

The purchase and sale of a corporate business often is accompanied by the shareholders' agreement not to compete with the buyer in the field of business involved. Like goodwill, the cost of a covenant not to compete must be capitalized and amortized by the buyer. See I.R.C. § 197(f)(3). Section 1060 did not completely address the problem of artificial allocations between goodwill and covenants not to compete. A covenant not to compete, even though created in the sale transaction, is a Class VI asset. Treas.Reg.

§ 1.1060–1(b)(7), (d), Ex. 2. Goodwill, however, is a Class VII asset. Because a covenant not to compete is as difficult to value as goodwill itself, the tension has continued after the enactment of § 197. Both a covenant not to compete and purchased goodwill must be amortized over 15 years under § 197, regardless of the term of the covenant or the payment schedule, and no loss deduction is allowed for the basis allocated to one as long as the other is retained, I.R.C. § 197(f)(1). The buyer is thus indifferent as to the allocation between the two. As to the seller, however, payments received for a covenant not to compete are ordinary income, Hamlin's Trust v. Commissioner, 209 F.2d 761 (10th Cir.1954); Rev.Rul. 69–643, 1969–2 C.B. 10, while amounts received for self-created goodwill produce capital gain and amounts received for purchased goodwill produce § 1231 gain (subject to § 1245 recapture for prior amortization), see I.R.C. § 197(f)(7), which might result in capital gain treatment. Thus, if the seller is an individual (or partnership of individuals) that unlike a corporation enjoys a preferential rate for capital gains, the seller will want as much as possible of the purchase price that exceeds the fair market value of other assets allocated to goodwill rather than to a covenant not to compete. If, however, the covenant not to compete involves the shareholders of the corporation whose assets are acquired, they might prefer an allocation to a covenant not to compete because, although the payments are taxed as ordinary income rather than capital gain, they will not be subject to the double tax regime as they would be if the payments were allocated to goodwill of the corporate business. Bemidji Distributing Company v. Commissioner, T.C. Memo. 2001–260, aff'd sub nom. Langdon v. Commissioner, 59 Fed.Appx. 168 (8th Cir. 2003), involved a taxable year before enactment of § 197, where the parties allocated $1,000,000 to the individual shareholder's covenant not to compete, and nothing to corporate level goodwill. Based on all the facts and circumstances, e.g., the seller's ability to compete and expert witnesses' valuation testimony, the Tax Court found that the value of the covenant was only $334,000 and that $666,000 allocated to the covenant by the taxpayer was really the price of goodwill. The reallocation resulted in corporate level recognition of gain on the sale of goodwill. In addition, $666,000 of the amount paid to the shareholder for the covenant was treated as a constructive dividend to the shareholder.

In many cases the buyer's business need for an enforceable covenant not to compete will prevent the parties from omitting a covenant not to compete from the transaction entirely. See Beaver Bolt, Inc. v. Commissioner, T.C. Memo. 1995–549 (buyer's allocation of $380,000 of price to seller's covenant not to compete was reduced to $324,000; a substantial allocation was proper, even though the parties had no adverse tax interests, because seller had the ability to compete and realistically might have competed in the absence of the covenant). However, artificial allocations nevertheless might continue to be a problem.

1.1.2.   *Shareholder Owned Goodwill*

In the overwhelming number of transactions there is no doubt that business goodwill is owned by the corporation and not by the shareholders. However, a few cases suggest that occasionally, in transactions involving the sale of the assets of a closely held corporation in which the shareholders are also the primary entrepreneurs and key employees, some or all of the business goodwill might be owned by shareholder/employees individually. In Martin Ice Cream Co. v. Commissioner, 110 T.C. 189 (1998), Häagen-

Dazs repurchased the rights to distribute Häagen-Dazs ice cream in the United States from the business that had been distributing Häagen-Dazs under an oral agreement between Häagen-Dazs and the majority shareholder. The IRS treated the amounts received in consideration of the distributorship rights as an amount realized by the corporation, but the corporation and its majority shareholder argued that the amounts were received directly by the shareholder. The Tax Court agreed with the taxpayer, holding that the shareholder, rather than the corporation, owned the distribution rights and sold them back to Häagen-Dazs, reasoning that the rights were based on personal relationships with supermarket chains and the shareholder's personal oral agreement with the founder of Häagen-Dazs, which had never become corporate property. The court emphasized that ownership of the distribution rights could not be attributed to the corporation because the shareholder, who owned the rights before he began conducting the business through the corporation, never entered into a covenant not to compete with the corporation or any other agreement—not even an employment contract—by which any of the shareholder's distribution agreements with Häagen-Dazs, the shareholder's relationships with supermarkets, or his ice cream distribution expertise became the property of the corporation. " '[P]ersonal relationships' of a shareholder-employee are not corporate assets when the employee has no employment contract with the corporation. Those personal assets are entirely distinct from the intangible corporate asset of corporate goodwill."

A similar result was reached in Norwalk v. Commissioner, T.C. Memo 1998–279, which involved a CPA professional services corporation that dissolved and distributed its assets to its two CPA shareholders, who in turn contributed the assets to a partnership that they joined in that year. The IRS asserted that in addition to the tangible assets expressly distributed, the corporation distributed various customer-based intangible assets, including goodwill, which resulted in a gain to the corporation under § 336 and also increased the capital gain realized by the shareholders on the liquidation. The Tax Court upheld the taxpayer's contention that the corporation's earning were entirely attributable to the CPA-shareholders—any clients would have followed the individual CPAs—and that it owned no goodwill that could be separately sold. The court reasoned that on the facts clients sought the personal ability, personality, and reputation of the individual CPAs, and these assets did not belong to the corporation; the corporation's name and its business location did not contribute to goodwill.

More recent cases reflect hesitation on the part of courts to liberally apply the holding of *Martin Ice Cream*. In Solomon v. Commissioner, T.C. Memo. 2008–102, the taxpayers argued that the principles of *Martin Ice Cream Co.* and *Norwalk* should apply, but the Tax Court found those cases to be distinguishable on the facts. In *Solomon*, the corporation (Solomon Colors), of which the taxpayers (father and son) were dominant, but not sole, shareholders and key employees, sold one of its several lines of business. In connection with the sale, the taxpayers entered into covenants not to compete. Provisions in the contracts described payments received by the taxpayers as consideration for their entering into covenants not to compete, but other documents allocating the purchase price and payments among assets described those payments as consideration for the shareholders' ownership interest in the customer list for the line of business that was sold. The court rejected the taxpayers' argument that, like in *Martin Ice Cream Co.*, the payments were consideration for the sale of goodwill owned by the shareholders. The *Solomon* court found that the value of the Solomon Colors' business was not attributable to the quality of service and customer relationships developed by the shareholders, which distinguished the facts from *Martin Ice Cream Co.* Because the Solomon Colors' business involved processing, manufacturing, and sale of a product, rather than the provision of services, the corporation's success did not depend entirely on the personal goodwill of its shareholder/employees. Furthermore, the fact that the purchaser did not require the shareholders to enter into employment or consulting agreements made it unlikely that it was purchasing their personal goodwill. Accordingly, the payments were entirely consideration for the shareholders' covenants not to compete and thus were ordinary income, not capital gain.

In Howard v. United States, 448 Fed. Appx. 752 (9th Cir. 2011), aff'g 106 A.F.T.R.2d 2010–5533 (E.D. Wash. 2010), the taxpayer was a dentist who practiced through a solely owned (before taking into account community property law) professional corporation until the practice was sold to a third party. He had an employment agreement with the corporation that included a noncompetition clause that survived for three years after the termination of his stock ownership. The purchase and sale agreement allocated approximately $550,000 of the total $600,000 price to the taxpayer-shareholder's personal goodwill. The IRS recharacterized the goodwill as a corporate asset and treated the amount received by the taxpayer from the sale to the third party as a dividend from the taxpayer's professional service corporation (which had not been liquidated in the year of the sale). The government argued that (1) the goodwill was a corporate asset, because the taxpayer was a corporate employee with a covenant not to compete for three years after he no longer owned any stock, (2) the corporation earned the income, and correspondingly earned the goodwill, and (3) attributing the goodwill to the taxpayer-shareholder did not comport with the economic reality of his relationship with the corporation. After reviewing the principles of *Norwalk* and *Martin Ice Cream Co.*, the District Court held that because the taxpayer was the corporation's employee with a covenant not to compete with it, any goodwill generated during that time period was the corporation's goodwill. The court also reasoned that the goodwill was a corporate asset based on its conclusions that the income associated with the practice was earned by the corporation and the covenant not to compete, which extended for three years after the taxpayer no longer owned stock in the corporation, rendered any personal goodwill "likely [of] little value." In affirming the District Court, the Ninth Circuit concisely summarized the current state of the law.

> Goodwill "is the sum total of those imponderable qualities which attract the custom of a business,—what brings patronage to the business." *Grace Brothers v. Comm'r*, 173 F.2d 170, 175–76 (9th Cir. 1949). For purposes of federal income taxation, the goodwill of a professional practice may attach to both the professional as well as the practice. * * * Where the success of the venture depends entirely upon the personal relationships of the practitioner, the practice does not generally accumulate goodwill. See *Martin Ice Cream Co. v. Comm'r*, 110 T.C. 189 at 207–08 (1998). The professional may, however, transfer his or her goodwill to the practice by entering into an employment contract

or covenant not to compete with the business. See, e.g., *Norwalk v. Comm'r*, 76 T.C.M. (CCH) 208, (1998) (finding that there is no corporate goodwill where "the business of a corporation is dependent upon its key employees, unless they enter into a covenant not to compete with the corporation or other agreement whereby their personal relationships with clients become property of the corporation") (emphasis added); *Martin Ice Cream Co.*, 110 T.C. at 207–08 (finding that "personal relationships . . . are not corporate assets when the employee has no employment contract [or covenant not to compete] with the corporation") (emphasis added); *Macdonald v. Comm'r*, 3 T.C. 720, 727 (1944) (finding "no authority which holds that an individual's personal ability is part of the assets of a corporation . . . where . . . the corporation does not have a right by contract or otherwise to the future services of that individual") (emphasis added). In determining whether goodwill has been transferred to a professional practice, we are especially mindful that "each case depends upon particular facts. And in arriving at a particular conclusion . . . we . . . take into consideration all the circumstances . . . [of] the case and draw from them such legitimate inferences as the occasion warrants." *Grace Brothers v. Comm'r*, 173 F.2d 170, 176 (9th Cir. 1949).

Looking at the facts as found by the District Court, the Ninth Circuit concluded that "while the relationships that Dr. Howard developed with his patients may be accurately described as personal, the economic value of those relationships did not belong to him, because he had conveyed control of them to the Howard Corporation." This conclusion regarding "personal relationships" of shareholder-employees is markedly different than the conclusion in *Martin Ice Cream Co.*

In H&M, Inc. v. Commissioner, T.C. Memo. 2012–290, the Tax Court rejected the IRS's assertion that a portion of amounts paid to the selling sole shareholder of an incorporated insurance business represented an amount realized by the corporation for corporate goodwill. A bank purchased H&M's insurance business for $20,000 and entered into an employment agreement with the corporation's sole shareholder pursuant to which he was paid total compensation of over $600,000 over a six-year period for continuing to run the insurance business on behalf of the bank. The IRS asserted a deficiency against H&M, Inc. based on the "substance over form" theory that a significant portion of the compensation paid to the shareholder by the bank under the employment agreement actually was a payment to H&M, Inc. for the sale of the insurance business, and that H&M, Inc. thus realized significant capital gains and interest income over the period the compensation was paid to the shareholder. Applying the holding of *Martin Ice Cream Co.*, the court stated that payments by a purchaser of a corporate business to a controlling shareholder for that shareholder's customer relationships were not taxable to the corporation "where the business of a corporation depends on the personal relationships of a key individual [i.e., the controlling shareholder], unless he transfers his goodwill to the corporation by entering into a covenant not to compete or other agreement so that his relationships become property of the corporation." The court concluded that the insurance business was " 'extremely personal,' and the development of [the] business before the sale was due to the shareholder's ability to form relationships with customers and keep big insurance companies interested in a small insurance market." Furthermore, the compensation paid to the shareholder was reasonable, and there were no other intangibles to be accounted for in the purchase price.

1.1.3.   *Effect of Parties Agreement on Price Allocation*

Section 1060(a) binds both the transferor and transferee to any written agreement between them with respect to the allocation of the purchase price or the fair market value of the assets, unless the IRS determines that the allocation is not appropriate. Treas.Reg. § 1.1060–1(c)(4) provides that the agreement will be binding on both parties unless a party is able to refute the allocation under the standards of Commissioner v. Danielson, 378 F.2d 771 (3d Cir. 1967). See also H.Rep. 101–964, 101st Cong., 2d Sess. 95 (1990). *Danielson* allows a party to refute an agreement only on proof admissible in an action to show unenforceability because of mistake, undue influence, fraud, or duress. In Peco Foods, Inc. v. Commissioner, T.C. Memo. 2012–18, the taxpayer purchased poultry processing plants pursuant to contracts that allocated a large portion of the purchase price to nonresidential real property (with a cost recovery period of 39 years). Following the purchase, the taxpayer attempted to classify certain components of the poultry processing plants as equipment and machinery and claim accelerated depreciation on the basis of shorter § 168 cost recovery periods. The court held that under § 1060(a), the taxpayer was bound by the purchase price allocation agreement and could not change the classification of those components of the poultry processing plants to machinery and equipment with shorter cost recovery periods.

The IRS, however, is not restricted from challenging the taxpayers' allocations. Treas.Reg. § 1.1060–1(c)(4); see also S.Rep. No. 99–313, 99th Cong., 2d Sess. 255 (1986). Both the buyer and seller are required to file information returns reporting the amount of consideration in the transaction and its allocation among the assets transferred. Treas.Reg. § 1.1060–1(e). In general, there is no requirement in § 1060 or in the regulations that the parties agree on an allocation or that they file consistent information returns. As a practical matter, however, the purchaser often requires a contractual provision that consistent information returns be filed.

1.2. *Applicable Asset Acquisition*

The legislative history indicates that § 1060 applies to any sale and purchase of assets that constitute an active trade or business under § 355, discussed in the text at page 713, or to which "goodwill or going concern value could under any circumstances attach." S.Rep. No. 99–313, 99th Cong., 2d Sess. 255 (1986). Treas.Reg. § 1.1060–1(b)(2) and (3), Exs. 1–4 indicates that the term "applicable asset acquisition" is to be broadly construed. Thus, if a liquidating corporation sells a portion of its assets to each of several purchasers, several applicable asset acquisitions may have occurred. Conversely, if a purchasing corporation acquires assets of a seller that constitute a trade or business of the seller, an applicable asset acquisition has occurred even though the purchaser discontinues the seller's trade or business and uses the assets in a different trade or business conducted by it. Section 1060 does not apply to a stock purchase treated as an asset purchase under § 338, discussed in Section 2 of this Chapter. See H.Rep. 101–882, 101st Cong., 2d Sess. 102 (1990). A transfer of assets from seller to buyer in a series of related transactions also will be treated as an applicable asset acquisition. Treas.Reg. § 1.1060–1(b)(5). Assets acquired in an acquisition that includes more than one trade or business are treated as a single trade or business in order to avoid allocations of purchase price among two or more trades or businesses. Treas.Reg. § 1.1060–1(b)(6).

2. LIABILITIES

Assumption by the buyer of the seller's liabilities is generally treated as a payment received by the seller. Treas.Reg. § 1.1001–2. This is true even in cases in which those liabilities would have given rise to a deduction when paid. In Commercial Security Bank v. Commissioner, 77 T.C. 145 (1981) (Acq.), the purchaser of all of the business assets of a cash method corporation assumed the seller's accounts payable as part of the consideration paid. The court held that the selling corporation must include the payables in the amount realized on the sale but is entitled to an offsetting deduction because the seller in effect paid the liabilities at the time of the sale through the receipt of less cash on the sale to account for the liabilities. The court stated that the purchaser was required to capitalize the assumed liabilities into the basis of acquired assets and could not deduct them when paid.[4] See also Pacific Transport Co. v. Commissioner, 483 F.2d 209 (9th Cir.1973) (requiring capitalization by the purchaser of payments that would have been deductible by the seller); Holdcroft Transportation Co. v. Commissioner, 153 F.2d 323 (8th Cir. 1946) (where the taxpayer acquired the business and assets of a partnership in a taxable transaction in exchange for the taxpayer's common stock and the assumption of the partnership's liabilities that would have been deductible by the partnership if paid, the payment of the liabilities by the taxpayer was capitalized).

Corporate acquisitions may involve the assumption of contingent liabilities, such as environmental damage, products liability, pension plan, and other employment related claims. Such contingent liabilities also raise tax issues. For example, In Illinois Tool Works Inc. v. Commissioner, 355 F.3d 997 (7th Cir. 2004), aff'g 117 T.C. 39 (2001), the taxpayer acquired the assets of another corporation (for approximately $126 million) in a taxable transaction in which the taxpayer assumed the target's liabilities, including a contingent liability for a patent infringement claim, (Lemelson v. Champion Spark Plug Co., 975 F.2d 869 (1992)), for which it established a reserve of $350,000. Subsequently, the taxpayer, as the target's successor, was held liable for damages, interest, and court costs (totaling over $17 million), which it paid. The court upheld the IRS's treatment requiring capitalization of the payments by the purchaser as a cost of acquiring the assets rather than a deductible expense, even though the parties had not

---

[4] A different approach was taken in Focht v. Commissioner, 68 T.C. 223 (1977) (Acq.), with respect to liabilities under § 357(c) before adoption of § 357(c)(3) treating assumed payables of a cash method taxpayer as not constituting liabilities, discussed at page 100. The court determined that since the liabilities would be deductible when paid, the assumption of liabilities could be treated as a receipt of payment followed by the deduction. The court in Crane v. Commissioner, 331 U.S. 1, 13 n. 34 (1947), similarly held that liabilities for accrued but unpaid interest deductible by the seller were not included in the amount realized on the sale of assets This view reflects the current policy of the IRS in § 351 transactions, see Rev. Rul. 95–74, page 96. There are fundamental differences between a nonrecognition transaction in which a transferee can be viewed as "stepping into the transferor's shoes" and a taxable transaction to which such a perspective is not logically applicable.

adjusted the purchase price to reflect the contingent liability. The liability was known, was considered in setting the price, and was expressly assumed. The fact that the taxpayer considered it highly unlikely that it would be called upon to pay was not relevant. *Holdcroft Transportation Co.*, supra, reached the same result with respect to contingent liabilities for tort claims.

When a contingent obligation related to the acquisition of property is satisfied, the amount of the satisfied debt is added to the purchaser's basis in the acquired assets of the target. In Albany Car Wheel Co. v. Commissioner, 40 T.C. 831 (1963), aff'd per curiam, 333 F.2d 653 (2d Cir.1964), the purchaser of a business assumed the seller's contingent liability for severance pay under a union contract if the purchased factory was closed. Because the obligation was "speculative," the court held that it could not be taken into account in determining the basis of the purchased assets until the liability was paid. If the property is depreciable (or amortizable), the taxpayer may depreciate (or amortize) the increased basis over the property's remaining cost recovery period; a new cost recovery period is not commenced. See Meredith Corp. v. Commissioner, 102 T.C. 406, 462–463 (1994). If the property's cost recovery period has expired prior to the contingent obligation having been satisfied, however, an ordinary loss deduction is allowable. See Meredith Corp. v. Commissioner, 108 T.C. 89 (1997). In most cases, noncontingent consideration paid by the purchaser exceeds the value of all of the assets in Classes I-IV and the amount of the contingent obligation that is capitalized when it is paid is added to the basis of the Class VII asset—goodwill, which is amortizable over fifteen years.

3. TAXABLE "CASH" MERGERS

The use of a statutory merger under state law allows an acquisition to take place on a tax-free basis if the various requirements of § 368, discussed in Chapter 12, are met. The statutory merger technique sometimes is used instead of a direct asset sale to carry out a taxable acquisition in which the acquiring corporation pays the shareholders of the target corporation cash, corporate bonds (installment obligations), or a combination of cash and installment obligations in connection with the merger. One of the reasons for using a "cash" merger is to effect a transfer of the properties of the acquired corporation directly to the acquiring corporation as a matter of state law, avoiding the need to document separately each transfer. In addition, a merger forces out any minority shareholders in the acquired corporation who dissented from the merger. Furthermore, if the acquisition takes the form of a "reverse" merger in which the acquired corporation is the surviving corporation, problems can be avoided with regard to assets which cannot be assigned or transferred, for example, assets subject to a restriction on transferability in connection with a loan agreement.

To take the simplest case, suppose T Corporation is merged into A Corporation in a transaction in which the T Corporation shareholders all receive cash or debt instruments of A Corporation. For tax purposes, the transaction is treated as a sale of assets followed by the liquidation of T Corporation. See West Shore Fuel, Inc. v. United States, 598 F.2d 1236 (2d Cir.1979) (all-debt merger treated as corporate assets sale); Rev.Rul. 69–6, 1969–1 C.B. 104 (merger of mutual savings banks). Thus, both the acquired corporation and its shareholders recognize gain or loss on the transaction.

This double tax treatment of cash mergers may be avoided through the use of a "reverse" triangular merger, the merger of a subsidiary of the acquiring corporation into the target corporation, with the shareholders of the target receiving cash from the parent. Rev.Rul. 90–95, 1990–2 C.B. 67, and Rev.Rul. 79–273, 1979–2 C.B. 125, indicate that this transaction will be treated as a sale and purchase of shares of the target corporation.

4. SALE OF WHOLLY OWNED LIMITED LIABILITY COMPANY

There has been an increasing trend to operate different divisions of a corporation's business through a number of separately organized limited liability companies (LLCs). Under the so-called "check-the-box" regulations, unless an LLC with a single owner elects to be taxed as a corporation, Treas.Reg. § 301.7701–3(a), it will be disregarded as an entity separate from its owner. Treas.Reg. § 301.7701–3(b)(1)(ii). When a LLC is a disregarded entity, its assets, liabilities, income items, and deduction items are treated as owned, owed, received, and incurred directly by its owner. Thus, if a corporation sells the membership units of a wholly owned LLC that is a disregarded entity—as virtually all wholly owned LLCs are—the transaction will be treated as an asset sale and purchase.

In Dover Corp. v. Commissioner, 122 T.C. 324 (2004), the taxpayer corporation had complete ownership of a business entity organized under the laws of a foreign jurisdiction. Under Treas.Reg. § 301.7701–3, the entity was taxable as a corporation unless it elected to be a disregarded entity.[5] The taxpayer sold the subsidiary entity to another party and solely for the purpose of reducing the taxes on the sale, elected effective immediately before the sale to treat the subsidiary entity as a disregarded entity. As a result, the subsidiary corporation was treated as having been liquidated in a transaction to which § 332, discussed at page 342, applied to provide nonrecognition. The transaction was thus transmuted from a stock sale and purchase to an asset sale and purchase. The Tax Court upheld the taxpayer's treatment of the sale as an asset sale rather than a stock sale. The proposition that a non-tax business purpose is not a prerequisite for a check-the-box election was implicit in the Tax Court's holding.

Applying *Dover* in the domestic context, the owner of an LLC that is a disregarded entity has the last minute option of structuring the sale of the entity's business as either an asset sale and purchase, by simply selling the membership units of the LLC, or as a stock sale and purchase by first electing to treat the LLC as a corporation, which would be an incorporation governed by § 351, discussed at page 53, and then selling the membership units of the LLC, which as a result of the election are treated as stock.

5. INSTALLMENT REPORTING BY ACQUIRED CORPORATION'S SHAREHOLDERS

5.1. *Generally*

If the consideration in an asset sale consists in whole or in part of the acquiring corporation's bonds or other debt instruments, the installment method of § 453 may apply in some circumstances. In situations in which the selling corporation liquidates, the possibilities for installment reporting are limited. Installment reporting of gains from inventory and depreciation

---

[5]   For certain foreign entities with limited liability that are not per se corporations, the default rule is that the entity is a corporation unless it elects to be a disregarded entity—the opposite of the rule for domestic entities.

recapture is not permitted in any event. See I.R.C. § 453(b)(2), (i)(2). In addition, as a result of distribution of installment obligations in liquidation, under § 453B the corporation must recognize all of its gain on any installment notes for which § 453 installment sale accounting otherwise would have been available. Then the question is whether the shareholders may report their gain on the installment method when they receive the purchaser's debt obligations in the liquidating distribution. If the seller receives purchaser's bonds that are readily tradable, § 453(f)(4) precludes installment sale reporting. Furthermore, if the stock of the selling liquidating corporation was publicly traded, § 453(k)(2) might deny installment sale treatment. If neither of these disqualifying facts is involved and if the conditions of § 453(h) are satisfied, the shareholders of the selling corporation may be eligible to report gain using the installment method in either an asset sale followed by a liquidation or a taxable merger.

Suppose that under the terms of the merger agreement, the shareholders of T Corporation may elect to receive either cash or installment obligations of A Corporation. Will those shareholders electing to receive the installment obligations nonetheless be found to be in constructive receipt of cash and thus currently taxable? Rev.Rul. 73–396, 1973–2 C.B. 160, held that the constructive receipt doctrine did not apply in a situation in which the purchaser was willing to pay cash but the seller insisted on deferred payments.

5.2. *Section 453(h)*

Section 453(h) provides a limited exception to the shareholder recognition rule (but not to the rules requiring recognition by the corporation upon distribution of the note) when the shareholders receive installment obligations arising from a sale or exchange of corporate assets occurring after the adoption of a plan of complete liquidation that is completed within twelve months after it was adopted,[6] and it applies whether the installment sale is pursuant to a complete acquisition of the seller's business or a dispersal sale. This provision applies only if the liquidation is completed within twelve months following adoption of the plan.[7] If this requirement is met, shareholders recognize gain on the liquidation with respect to the notes under the installment method of § 453 as they receive payments on the obligations. If an installment obligation arises from the sale of inventory, however, deferred recognition is available only if substantially all of the inventory attributable to a particular trade or business of the corporation was sold in bulk to a single purchaser. Section 453(h) is discussed in further detail at page 337.

---

[6]   Section 453(k)(2), denying installment sale treatment for sales of marketable stock and securities, might render § 453(h) unavailable in the liquidation of a publicly traded corporation, but it is highly unlikely that a publicly traded corporation ever would liquidate in a manner to which § 453(h) could apply.

[7]   Section 453(h) is a vestige of the pre-1987 rules under which a corporation did not recognize gain or loss on the sale or exchange of certain assets if the assets were sold after the adoption of a plan of liquidation and the liquidation was completed within twelve months. Although those rules were repealed by the Tax Reform Act of 1986, installment reporting of shareholder gain was continued.

6. USE OF PARENT CORPORATION'S STOCK AS PAYMENT MEDIUM

Treas.Reg. § 1.1032–3 deals with the treatment of a subsidiary that uses the stock of its parent corporation as the medium of payment in a taxable transaction. If a subsidiary receives its parent's stock as a contribution to capital or in a § 351 transaction (i.e., a transaction in which the subsidiary's basis in acquired property otherwise is determined under § 362(a)), and immediately transfers the stock for money, other property, or services in a purchase-type transaction, then the transaction is treated as if the acquiring subsidiary corporation had purchased its parent corporation's stock at fair market value with cash contributed by the parent corporation immediately before the transaction. If the subsidiary actually pays the parent for the stock, then the amount of cash deemed to have been contributed by the parent to the subsidiary in the cash purchase equals the difference between the fair market value of the parent's stock and the fair market value of the money or other property received by the parent from the subsidiary (or the subsidiary's employee in certain option situations). Notwithstanding the rules of Treas.Reg. § 1.1032–3, however, if the subsidiary transfers the newly acquired parent stock to acquire or satisfy the subsidiary corporation's indebtedness, the subsidiary may recognize cancellation of indebtedness income under §§ 61(a)(12) and 108. These regulations overturn the application of International Freighting Corp. v. Commissioner, 135 F.2d 310 (2d Cir. 1943), when the specified conditions of the regulation are met (but do not do so on the facts of International Freighting Corp. itself).

If the stringent conditions of § 368(a)(1)(C), discussed at page 627, have been met, an asset purchase using stock of either the acquiring corporation or its parent, will be treated as a tax free reorganization rather than as a taxable sale and purchase.

SECTION 2. STOCK SALES AND ACQUISITIONS

INTERNAL REVENUE CODE: Sections 338.

REGULATIONS: Sections 1.338(h)(10)–1(a)–(d).

In the transactions considered in Section 1, the purchaser of the corporate business desired to acquire assets and the seller agreed to this form of the transaction. Often, however, an individual seller may desire to structure the transaction as a sale of corporate stock in order to take advantage of the preferential tax rate accorded to long-term capital gains—currently a maximum rate of 20 percent pursuant to § 1(h)—that applies to the entire recognized gain.[8] (Corporations that

---

[8] Alternatively, § 1202 provides a special preference for gain recognized by a noncorporate taxpayer on a sale or exchange of "qualified small business stock" issued after August 10, 1993. If the stock is held for more than five years, fifty percent of the gain is excluded from gross income. The remaining 50 percent of the gain continues to be eligible for the 28 percent maximum rate on long-term capital gains, but not for the even more preferential 0, 15, or 20 percent capital gains rates. Thus the effective maximum rate of tax on gains from qualified small business stock is only 14 percent. Section 1202(b)(1) limits the amount excludable with respect to the stock of a particular corporation in any year to the lesser of (a) $10,000,000 ($5,000,000 for married taxpayers filing separately), minus any amount excluded with respect to that corporation's stock in prior years, or (b) ten times the aggregate basis of stock of the qualified corporation sold during the year. Section 1202

sell stock do not have a preferential rate for capital gains.) In addition, depending on the extent to which the purchaser reduces the offering price to reflect the lower asset basis attendant to a stock purchase and sale, by avoiding double taxation the seller may expect to net a larger after-tax profit even without taking the capital gains preference into account.

On the other hand, for a variety of reasons the purchaser often prefers to purchase the assets directly. First, the corporation may have liabilities that the purchaser does not wish to assume indirectly. Second, if the assets have a basis lower than their market value, and hence lower than the price to be paid for the business, the assets will retain that low basis when the ownership of the corporation changes hands. This basis result may be unsatisfactory to the purchaser, especially with respect to inventory or depreciable property. Third, a stock purchase involves taking over other tax attributes, such as accumulated earnings and profits. However, a stock purchase will permit the use of the acquired corporation's net operating loss carryovers, subject to the limitations of § 382, discussed in Chapter 15.

A purchaser, desiring to buy the assets but unable to persuade the seller to agree, may purchase the stock and then proceed to liquidate the corporation to obtain the assets, thereby making it clear that the purchase of the stock was but a step in the direction of an asset purchase. Under current law, unless the purchaser is a corporation that controls 80 percent of the acquired corporation, the liquidation of the acquired corporation will require corporate-level recognition of built-in gains and losses on the liquidation distribution under § 336 plus potential additional recognition of gain or loss under § 331 if the value of the liquidation distribution varies from the purchaser's stock basis. In the case of a corporate purchaser in control of the liquidated corporation there is no gain or loss recognized on the liquidation distribution under §§ 332 and 337, but the distributed assets retain their historic basis under § 334(b)(2) and the purchaser's stock basis disappears.

In general, as a consequence of all of this, a seller prefers to sell stock, while the purchaser often prefers to acquire assets. This conflicting preference has generated a significant evolution of judicial and statutory approaches to the problem. The history of the statutory development is important to understand the current state of the law.

In Kimbell-Diamond Milling Company v. Commissioner, 14 T.C. 74 (1950), aff'd per curiam, 187 F.2d 718 (5th Cir.1951), the IRS successfully contended that the stock purchase followed by liquidation of the acquired corporation should be disregarded. In that case, and cases following it, the courts took the view that if the liquidation was part of an overall plan for the acquisition of assets, the stock purchase and liquidation would in effect be disregarded, no gain or loss would result to the purchaser, and the purchaser's basis for the assets would be the price paid for the stock. Prior to the 1986 repeal of the *General Utilities* doctrine, which prevented corporate level recognition on the

---

excludes 100 percent of gain recognized on the sale of qualified small business stock acquired after September 27, 2010 and before January 1, 2014.

distribution of property, if the purchaser was an individual, the result would have been the same whether the liquidation was held to have substance or not, since the price paid for the stock would generally reflect the value of the assets and thus there would be no additional gain in the liquidation transaction. But if a corporation was the purchaser and § 332(a) governed the liquidation, the basis of the assets would remain the same under § 334(b) and would be unaffected by the amount paid for the stock; hence the need for the step-transaction approach of *Kimbell-Diamond*.

The *Kimbell-Diamond* approach proved to be unsatisfactory because it relied on the intent of a corporate purchaser to acquire assets. This subjective approach was difficult to administer, and it was replaced in 1954 by an objective standard codified in former § 334(b)(2). That section replaced the subjective intent test of *Kimbell-Diamond* with a set of objective standards to determine whether a stock purchase would be treated as a purchase of assets for tax purposes. In general terms, under § 334(b)(2), if a corporation "purchased" 80 percent or more of the stock of another corporation and then liquidated it within two years, the basis of the assets acquired in the liquidation would be determined by the purchase price of the stock, i.e., in the same manner as if the assets had been purchased directly.

Although nominally not elective, § 334(b)(2) in fact provided significant flexibility to the purchasing corporation to obtain a purchase price basis for only selected assets, particularly where the acquired corporation was the parent of an affiliated group. In addition, the computations of asset basis if the liquidation was delayed raised problems of their own. For these reasons, in 1982 § 334(b)(2) was repealed and replaced by § 338.

Section 338 permits an election by a corporate purchaser following a "qualified stock purchase" of another corporation to treat the acquired subsidiary as if it sold all its assets pursuant to a plan of complete liquidation at the close of the stock acquisition date. That deemed asset sale results in the recognition of gain (or loss) with respect to all of the acquired corporation's assets. The acquired corporation is then deemed to re-acquire its assets on the next day, thereby providing a basis for the acquired assets determined with reference to the stock purchase price, which is intended to approximate the fair market value of the assets. A qualified stock purchase is defined, through a cross reference to § 1504(a) (discussed at page 442), as the acquisition within a twelve month period of stock representing 80 percent of voting power and 80 percent of the value of all stock, excluding nonvoting stock that is limited and preferred as to dividends and does not participate in corporate growth to any significant extent, of the acquired corporation.

Before 1987, former § 337 provided for nonrecognition of gain or loss on the deemed disposition of the acquired corporation's assets so that § 338 was a useful device for providing a basis for corporate assets in a stock acquisition to reflect the acquiring corporation's stock purchase price. After 1986, because of the required recognition of gain on the deemed asset sale, § 338 elections are rarely beneficial except in some special circumstances.

DETAILED ANALYSIS

1. GENERAL

In many important respects, § 338 eliminated or resolved the problems and discontinuities that arose under former § 334(b)(2). An acquiring corporation may obtain a step-up in basis without liquidating a newly acquired subsidiary which for independent business reasons the acquiring corporation wishes to continue to operate as a subsidiary. Conversely, a newly acquired subsidiary may be liquidated for independent business reasons either with or without a step-up (or step-down) in the basis of its assets. Inevitably, § 338 has given rise to its own complexity: new interpretive issues have been raised and different avenues for manipulation of the rules governing taxable acquisitions have been created.

One by-product of § 338 has been to create a form of corporate acquisition which was not previously possible—the purchase of the stock in the target corporation followed by immediate liquidation of the target in which all tax attributes of the target corporation are preserved. Under the mechanical rules of former § 334(b)(2), the transaction resulted in a step-up in basis of the acquired assets, but elimination of all the tax attributes of the target corporation. If no § 338 election is made with respect to the acquisition, the liquidation of the target will be governed by § 332, the acquired corporation's basis in the assets will be carried over under § 334(b), and all corporate attributes such as earnings and profits, net operating loss carryovers, etc., will be preserved under § 381(a). Such a procedure might be preferable to the § 338 route where, for example, the target corporation's basis in its assets is high relative to the stock purchase price and the target has net operating loss carryovers that could be utilized by the acquiring corporation. (See Chapter 15 for limitations that are applicable to the use of such carryover items following a corporate acquisition.)

2. IMPACT OF *GENERAL UTILITIES* REPEAL

2.1. *General*

When § 338 originally was enacted, the pre-1987 version of § 337 provided nonrecognition to the target corporation on the deemed sale of its assets under § 338(a) when a § 338 election was made. Thus, except to the extent that one of the exceptions to former § 337 required that gain be recognized on the sale of a liquidating corporation's assets, the effect of a § 338 election was to secure a step-up in basis without an attendant gain. Because of this highly advantageous treatment, § 338 elections frequently were made when the qualifying conditions were satisfied. Section 338 was amended by the 1986 Act to conform it with the repeal of the *General Utilities* doctrine. Since then, § 338 elections (other than § 338(h)(10) elections, discussed infra) have been rare.

Section 338(a)(1) provides that if an election is made under § 338(g), the target corporation will be treated as having sold all of its assets in a transaction in which gain or loss is fully recognized. This corresponds to the treatment that the target corporation would have received if it had distributed all of its assets in liquidation or had made a direct sale of the assets. Thus, in all circumstances in which the purchaser obtains, directly or indirectly, a step-up in basis for the target corporation's assets, the target corporation will be required to recognize gain currently. This change substantially reduces the advantage of a § 338 election. The tax benefit of increased future depreciation or amortization deductions generated by the step-up in basis must be "purchased" at the price of a present tax liability with respect to any appreciation in the acquired corporation's assets. And since there is no preferential treatment for corporate capital gains, the tax price is at full rates. Thus, only in very unusual circumstances, for example, where the target corporation has a net operating loss which would shield the gain required to be recognized under § 338, would an election make economic sense from the point of view of the purchaser. See I.R.C. § 382(h)(1)(C), permitting the net operating loss of an acquired corporation to be used to offset recognized built-in gain without regard to the limitations otherwise imposed by § 382, discussed in Chapter 15.

2.2. *Example*

Generally, as long as the parties take into account tax burdens in negotiating the price and the seller does not have otherwise unusable capital loss deductions, from a tax perspective it makes no difference to either the seller or the buyer whether a purchase and sale is structured as an asset sale or as a stock sale followed by a § 338 election and a § 332 liquidation.

Suppose that individual C owns all of the stock of T Corporation. C's basis for the stock is $2,000. T Corporation's sole asset has a basis of $1,000 and a fair market value of $4,000. If T Corporation sold the asset to A Corporation for $4,000, it would owe taxes of $1,050 on its $3,000 gain (assuming that T Corporation was subject to a flat corporate tax of 35 percent) and would distribute $2,950 to C in a liquidating distribution. C would pay taxes of $190 (assuming a 20 percent rate) on the $950 gain, leaving C with $2,760 of net proceeds.

Alternatively, A Corporation could pay C $2,950 in cash for the stock, again leaving C with $2,760 after taxes. A Corporation could make a § 338 election, which would give rise to a $1,050 tax liability on the deemed sale of T Corporation's asset. The asset would acquire a $4,000 basis, which under § 334(b) would carry over to A corporation if it liquidated T Corporation pursuant to § 332. Again, A Corporation has paid a total of $4,000 to acquire T Corporation's asset with a basis of $4,000.

In actual practice, however, things will work somewhat differently. Although the two levels of tax theoretically cannot be avoided, the corporate level tax can be deferred through a sale and purchase of stock without a § 338 election. Alternatively, one level of tax can be deferred through an installment purchase of assets coupled either with continuation of the selling corporation or the use of § 453(h). If the acquiring corporation is willing to buy stock, it will not likely be willing to make the § 338 election; hence it will not pay the shareholders of the target corporation the full net asset value (including goodwill and going concern value) of the target corporation, but will discount the offset for the corporate level tax to reflect the deferral of that tax. Thus, in the preceding example, A Corporation likely would pay C more than $2,950 but less than $4,000 for the stock of T Corporation. Thus § 338 is something of an anachronism after 1986, providing a complex solution to a situation that seldom arises.

outstanding (for example, nonvoting limited preferred stock that is not counted in determining whether a qualified stock purchase has occurred) reduces the denominator of the faction, thereby increasing the grossed-up basis to a value greater than the amount paid for the stock. The grossed-up basis is then increased by acquisition costs of the recently purchased stock, which are not themselves grossed-up. Treas.Reg. § 1.338–5(c)(3). "Grossed-up basis" for purposes of determining AGUB under Treas.Reg. § 1.338–5 differs from the definition of "grossed-up amount realized" for computing ADSP under Treas.Reg. § 1.338–4 in that the former includes the old basis of nonrecently purchased stock where grossed up amount realized is adjusted to reflect the fair market value of all of the target stock. Section 338(b)(3) permits the acquiring corporation to elect to recognize gain attributable to any nonrecently purchased stock and add that amount to its deemed purchase price. In such a case, the basis of nonrecently purchased stock is adjusted to reflect the recognized gain. Treas.Reg. § 1.338–5(d)(3).

The purpose of the "grossed-up basis" concept is to assign to the target's assets a basis equal to the aggregate fair market value of the target corporation's stock where the acquiring corporation purchases more than 80 percent but less than all of the target corporation's stock. For example, assume that P Corporation, which previously owned none of the stock of T Corporation, purchases 85 percent of the T Corporation stock for $850. The grossed-up basis of the stock is $1,000, computed as follows: $850 × (100–0)/85.

Section 338(b)(2) provides for an adjustment to the deemed purchase price in computing AGUB to reflect the acquired corporation's liabilities that would have been included in the purchaser's basis if the transaction had been an asset purchase. Treas.Reg. § 1.338–5(b)(1)(iii). Target liabilities that increase basis are those liabilities that would be included in the basis of the target's assets under general principles of tax law if the target had acquired its assets from an unrelated person for consideration that would have included the assumption of or taking property subject to the liabilities. Treas.Reg. § 1.338–5(e). These liabilities include the target corporation's tax liability arising from the deemed sale of its assets under § 338(a)(1). Treas.Reg. § 1.338–5(g), Ex. 1.

6. COMPUTATION AND ALLOCATION OF TAX LIABILITY

A § 338 election results in closing the taxable year of the target. As long as the target corporation was not purchased from a parent that was a member of an affiliated group filing a consolidated return, the old target's final return includes the deemed sale. Treas.Reg. § 1.338–10(a)(1). Section 338(h)(9) provides that except as provided in § 338(h)(10) a target corporation is not treated as a member of any affiliated group with respect to the deemed sale of its assets. As a general rule, if the target corporation otherwise would have been included in a consolidated return, it is required to file a special "deemed sale return" reporting the items from the § 338 sale. Treas.Reg. § 1.338–10(a)(2). Section 338(h)(9) requires that the target not be treated as a member of an affiliated group for purposes of reporting the sale, thereby precluding the use of net operating losses or capital losses of the purchaser (or its consolidated group) to offset the gain recognized on the deemed sale. However, if the acquiring corporation on the same acquisition date made qualified stock purchases with respect to two or more corporations that were members of the same consolidated group prior to the purchases, a consolidated deemed sale return covering all of such corporations may be filed. I.R.C. § 338(h)(15); Treas.Reg. § 1.338–10(a)(4).

While the target corporation nominally bears the liability for any taxes generated by the § 338 deemed sale, economically the burden is borne by the purchasing corporation, except to the extent that the purchase price is reduced to reflect the tax burden.

7. ACQUISITION OF SUBSIDIARY FROM AFFILIATED GROUP

7.1. *Section 338(h)(10): Purchase of Stock of Subsidiary from Consolidated Group*

A special rule applies when a corporation makes a qualified stock purchase of the stock of a controlled subsidiary of another corporation and the target corporation and the selling parent corporation filed a consolidated return or were members of an affiliated group filing separate returns. Section 338(h)(10) allows a joint election by the acquiring corporation and the former consolidated (or affiliated) group of the target corporation pursuant to which the gain or loss on the sale of the stock will not be recognized by the selling parent, but the selling group or parent will include on its tax return the gain and loss recognized under § 338(a)(1) by virtue of the § 338 election. In essence, this election permits the selling corporation to treat the sale as if its subsidiary first had made a taxable sale of its assets that, in most cases, was followed by a § 332 liquidation. Treas.Reg. § 1.338(h)(10)–1(d)(3) – (5). The regulations treat both the parent and the subsidiary corporations as if the subsidiary actually had been liquidated, Treas.Reg. § 1.338(h)(10)–1(d)(5)(i), which, as long as the subsidiary is solvent, will be governed by §§ 332 and 337, discussed in Chapter 7, Section 4. As a result, the affiliated group of the selling shareholder corporation bears the tax liability for any gain recognized with respect to the § 338 election. Thus, in the case of a § 338(h)(10) election, neither the ADSP nor the AGUB reflects the tax liability resulting from the deemed sale of the target S corporation's assets. See Treas.Reg. § 1.338(h)(10)–1(e), Ex. 5.

If the § 338(h)(10) route is followed, the tax attributes of the target corporation are inherited by the selling parent corporation. Treas.Reg. § 1.338(h)(10)–1(d)(4)(i). The election results in both corporations being treated as if the subsidiary actually had been liquidated. As long as the subsidiary is solvent, the liquidation will be governed by § 332 with the result that the subsidiary's earnings and profits and NOLs will carry over to the parent under § 381.

The existence of § 338(h)(10) allows the parties to keep the form of the transaction as a sale of stock but have the tax results of an asset sale. Since this situation does not involve a double tax on the sale of the stock and the deemed liquidating sale of assets, a § 338 election remains a viable tax planning technique when § 338(h)(10) is available, despite the repeal of the *General Utilities* doctrine. It is a particularly attractive planning device when the selling group has losses from other activities which will offset the gains on the consolidated return, since § 338(h)(9) does not apply where a § 338(h)(10) election has been made.

survivor would purchase them. The same result follows where A agrees that if B desires to sell his shares, A will purchase the shares or cause another person to purchase the shares, and A causes the corporation to purchase the shares.

The results in individual cases turn on whether under state contract law the continuing shareholder has a contractual obligation. For example, in Apschnikat v. United States, 421 F.2d 910 (6th Cir.1970), the court found that the negotiations and correspondence between the purchaser and the sellers resulted in a binding obligation on the purchaser to purchase the stock and were not simply pre-contract dealings. Accordingly, payments for the stock by a corporation to which the purchaser had transferred the sales contract resulted in dividends to him.

If a shareholder of X Corporation is obligated to purchase stock of Y Corporation and, rather than purchasing the Y Corporation stock directly, the shareholder assigns the contractual obligation to X Corporation, which purchases the stock, there is no dividend to the shareholder. In this case X Corporation has not redeemed its own stock. Rather it has received fair value for the amount paid and thus it is not a distribution. See Citizens Bank & Trust Co. v. United States, 580 F.2d 442 (Ct.Cl.1978).

2.1.2. *Continuing Shareholder as Agent of Corporation*

In situations in which the shares first pass through the continuing shareholder, the courts sometimes may regard the continuing shareholder as an agent acquiring the stock on behalf of the corporation, which was the real purchaser, so that no dividend results. In Bennett v. Commissioner, 58 T.C. 381 (1972) (Acq.), the majority shareholder in the corporation wished to terminate his interest. The taxpayer, a minority shareholder, suggested that the corporation redeem the shares but the retiring shareholder (in order not to incur a possible liability to creditors of the corporation because of a depletion of corporate assets) insisted that the taxpayer appear as the purchaser of the shares. It was agreed that the corporation would borrow money to advance to the taxpayer, the latter would then purchase the shares from the retiring shareholder and the corporation would immediately redeem. The transaction was consummated in this manner and the Tax Court found no dividend, distinguishing the *Wall* case, relied on by the IRS, as follows:

> In *Wall*, the taxpayer in one transaction acquired stock, paid an amount of cash, and obligated himself personally to pay additional amounts; in a subsequent, separate transaction the corporation paid the notes. In contrast, [the taxpayer here] never intended to acquire personal ownership of the Jones stock and never incurred any personal obligation to do so; at all times, he was serving as a conduit or agent for the Corporation in a single, integrated transaction in which it acquired the stock.

A similar result was reached in Ciaio v. Commissioner, 47 T.C. 447 (1967) (Acq.), where, as a result of disagreements, two shareholders agreed to sell their stock to the corporation, leaving the taxpayer as the sole shareholder. To finance the transaction, the corporation obtained a bank loan. The bank, as a condition of the loan (imposed under banking law), required that the stock be deposited with it as security and that the documents reflect the continuing shareholder and not the corporation as the buyer of the stock. The continuing shareholder was also required to guarantee the bank loan. The loan proceeds were used to redeem the shares of the two retiring shareholders. The court found no dividend to the continuing shareholder on account of the redemption since he was at all times acting as an agent for the corporation. Compare Deutsch v. Commissioner, 38 T.C. 118 (1962), rejecting the agency argument where the contract for the purchase of the stock was at all times between the individual taxpayer and the seller, and Glacier State Electric Supply Co. v. Commissioner, 80 T.C. 1047 (1983), holding that a parent corporation was the true owner of redeemed stock of its wholly owned subsidiary, rather than an agent of the parent corporation's shareholders who were asserted to be the beneficial owners of the stock of the subsidiary.

In Schroeder v. Commissioner, 831 F.2d 856 (9th Cir.1987), the selling shareholder, after initially agreeing to cause the corporation to redeem 90 percent of her stock and to sell 10 percent of her stock to the purchaser, on the advice of counsel changed her mind and insisted on selling all of the stock to the purchaser. The bank which was financing the acquisition, however, required that the permanent loan be made to the corporation as primary obligor and be guaranteed by the purchaser. In order to effect the acquisition of all of the stock directly by the purchaser a "bridge" loan was made directly to the purchaser, subject to an agreement between the purchaser and the bank that immediately after the acquisition, the corporation would assume primary responsibility for the loan in consideration of a redemption of a proportionate amount of its stock. In fact, the corporation assumed approximately two-thirds of the loan two months after the acquisition, and it redeemed a proportionate amount of stock. The taxpayer argued that the purchase and the redemption were part of a single transaction which should have been treated as a redemption from the seller. The court rejected this argument as follows:

> The Tax Court found that "there was no common or mutually agreed plan of action between the estate of Fred Collins [the seller], Schroeder [the buyer], and Skyline [the corporation] whose object was the ultimate redemption by Skyline of a part of its stock." * * * We agree with the Tax Court. The record confirms Schroeder's stated intentions, but also shows that this intention was particular to him. Donna Collins, as the personal representative of her husband's estate and as the seller of Skyline's stock, made it clear to Schroeder by April 13, 1976, that she would not agree to Skyline redeeming its stock as part of a bootstrap acquisition of Skyline proposed by Schroeder. Instead, she insisted that Schroeder buy the stock personally, which Schroeder undertook to do. In addition, Skyline cannot have had any intention different from Donna's, since she controlled 100 percent of Skyline's stock.

> Schroeder, because of Donna's insistence, could not undertake a bootstrap acquisition and had to buy the Skyline stock himself. He had business reasons for choosing the form of the transaction that he did. He cannot now argue that he is immunized from tax because the transaction was really something that never occurred. * * *

Schroeder's contention that he acted as an agent or conduit of the corporation pursuant to a prearranged plan is without merit. First, as noted above, there was no mutually agreed plan between Collins and Schroeder or between Schroeder and Skyline. The intention to have the corporation redeem its own stock was Schroeder's intention alone. Second, when he acquired the stock on April 30, 1976, "Schroeder was neither an officer, director nor a shareholder of Skyline, and he had no apparent authority to bind or commit Skyline to acquire its own stock or to borrow $600,000 from the bank in Skyline's name." * * * It was not until he acquired sole ownership of the Skyline stock, on July 1, 1976, when the debt to State Bank was restructured, and on August 1, 1976, when Skyline redeemed his stock, that Schroeder caused his intention to become Skyline's as well. Schroeder was not Skyline's agent or conduit on April 30, 1976.

Can *Schroeder* be distinguished from *Bennett* and *Ciaio?*

2.1.3.   *Post-Acquisition Redemption From Purchaser*

As discussed at page 501, as long as dividends and capital gains are taxed at the same rate, the issue in *Zenz* is of limited importance—it arises only with respect to the ability to offset basis against a distribution by the corporation where the selling shareholder does not completely terminate the shareholder's interest in the corporation and is seeking redemption treatment under § 302(b)(1) or (2) rather than under § 302(b)(3). With respect to post-acquisition redemptions from the purchaser, however, even with the tax rates on dividends and long-term capital gains equalized, the issue remains important. First, if a redemption occurs within a year after the stock purchase and § 302(a) applies, there will be basis recovery, but any resulting short-term capital gain will be taxed at the same rates as ordinary income, while if the redemption is treated as a dividend under § 302(d) the entire distribution will be taxed, albeit at a preferential rate. Second, if a redemption occurs more than a year after the stock purchase, basis recovery will be allowed if § 302(a) applies, but not if the redemption is treated as a dividend under § 302(d).

While a well-tailored plan for the purchase of a corporate business can use part of the corporation's assets to finance the transaction, the formalities generally must be observed. If an agency argument fails, a distribution to the purchaser following the acquisition of all of the stock, for the purpose of reducing the net out-of-pocket purchase price paid for the corporate business, will be a dividend to the purchaser. In Television Industries, Inc. v. Commissioner, 284 F.2d 322 (2d Cir.1960), the purchasing shareholder borrowed money to complete the purchase of all the shares then had some of the shares redeemed to obtain funds to repay the loan; a dividend resulted. See also Adams v. Commissioner, 594 F.2d 657 (8th Cir.1979) (pro-rata redemption of shares following purchase taxed as dividend even though pursuant to prearranged plan of which sellers had knowledge). Even though in economic effect and intent this transaction may not differ from a pre-acquisition redemption from the seller, the form of the transaction will control for tax purposes. See Jacobs v. Commissioner, T.C. Memo. 1981–81, aff'd, 698 F.2d 850 (6th Cir.1983), in which upon finding that the corporation acted as the continuing shareholders' agent in acquiring the seller's shares, the Tax Court observed as follows: "Petitioners could very easily have avoided dividend treatment of this transaction had they obtained tax advice from the start. * * * Unfortunately, this is another area of the law in which 'the formalities of handling a particular transaction assume a disproportionate importance and * * * a premium is placed upon consulting one's lawyer early enough in the game.' * * * Petitioners have chosen the wrong form and consequently must suffer the consequences." Is the agency theory employed in *Bennett* and *Ciaio* inconsistent with the "form controls" theory of *Jacobs*?

2.2. *Section 305 Aspects*

While the case law after *Holsey* was unanimous in rejecting the Government's argument that the continuing shareholder's increase in his proportionate interest in the corporation as a result of the redemption of other shareholders constituted a taxable dividend to him, increase in proportionate interest again became relevant with the amendments to § 305 in 1969, see page 296. Under § 305(b)(2) the increase in the proportionate interests of some shareholders in the earnings or assets of the corporation caused by a stock dividend, when coupled with the receipt of property by other shareholders, can result in a taxable distribution to the former group. Under § 305(c), the increase in proportionate interest caused by a redemption can be treated as a constructive stock dividend for purposes of § 305(b)(2). The regulations, however, provide that in a situation like *Holsey,* where the redemption distribution is entitled to capital gains treatment under § 302(b), no constructive dividend will result to the continuing shareholders. Treas.Reg. § 1.305–3(b)(2). In addition, an isolated redemption will not trigger a constructive stock dividend under § 305(c). Treas.Reg. § 1.305–7(a). See Treas.Reg. § 1.305–3(b)(3), (e) , Ex. 10 (no constructive dividend as a result of isolated redemption even though redemption was treated as a § 301 distribution). For an example of a redemption situation in which § 305(b)(2) was applicable by virtue of § 305(c), see Rev.Rul. 78–60, 1978–1 C.B. 81.

3. TREATMENT OF THE REDEEMED SHAREHOLDER

Where a prospective purchaser of the stock is unwilling to pay for all the stock at its present value and the parties arrange for the corporation to redeem some of the shares of the existing shareholders contemporaneously with the sale of the balance of their stock to the purchaser, who thus is required to pay a lesser figure (but who also receives a corporation with fewer assets), the courts generally have followed the approach of Zenz v. Quinlivan. See Auto Finance Co. v. Commissioner, 24 T.C. 416 (1955), aff'd per curiam, 229 F.2d 318 (4th Cir.1956); In re Lukens' Estate, 246 F.2d 403 (3d Cir.1957) (father had part of his stock redeemed at book value and gave the balance to his adult children, who also were shareholders and who managed the corporation). The IRS has ruled that it will follow *Zenz,* Rev.Rul. 55–745, 1955–2 C.B. 223, and that the actual sequence of the redemption and the sale will be ignored in a *Zenz*-type corporate sale as long as the two steps are both part of an integrated plan to reduce the outgoing shareholders' interest. Thus, the fact that the redemption precedes the sale of the shares will not cause the outgoing shareholder to receive dividend treatment; the formal order of the steps in the transaction is not crucial. Rev.Rul. 75–447, 1975–2 C.B. 113; accord Monson v. Commissioner, 79 T.C. 827 (1982). See also Rev.Rul. 77–226, 1977–2 C.B. 90 (corporate shareholder tendered part of its shares for redemption and sold the remaining shares of stock on the market; it treated the redemption as a § 301 distribution under § 302(d) qualifying for the intercorporate dividends deduction and claimed a capital loss on the disposition of the remaining shares which were attributed the basis of the shares which were redeemed; held, the entire transaction resulted in a termination of the corporate shareholder's interest and hence a taxable capital gain).

It is not necessary for the selling shareholder's interest to be completely terminated in order for the *Zenz* principle to apply. Rev.Rul. 75–447, 1975–2 C.B. 113, held that the reduction in interest effected through a combined sale and redemption should be aggregated to determine whether the redemption qualified for sale or exchange treatment under § 302(b)(2), discussed at page 235. Furthermore, in private letter rulings the IRS has applied *Zenz* to qualify a redemption under § 302(b)(1). See Ltr.Rul. 8540074.

A variation on Zenz v. Quinlivan was involved in McDonald v. Commissioner, 52 T.C. 82 (1969). There the shareholder, who owned all of the preferred stock and most of the common stock in a corporation, had the preferred stock redeemed and, as part of a prior arrangement, exchanged his common stock for the common stock of a public corporation in a tax-free exchange. The IRS argued that the preferred stock redemption constituted a dividend, distinguishing *Zenz,* since in this situation the shareholder retained a continuing interest in the assets of old corporation by virtue of his stock ownership in the acquiring corporation. The court found the redemption and subsequent reorganization effected a "substantial change" in the shareholder's interest and refused to treat the redemption as a dividend.

An interesting twist on the *Zenz* principle is found in Estate of Durkin v. Commissioner, 99 T.C. 561 (1992). The taxpayer purchased a corporate asset for a price substantially below fair market value. At the same time, the taxpayer's stock was redeemed by the corporation for a price equal to its basis, the taxpayer reporting no gain or loss on the redemption. The IRS asserted that the bargain sale of corporate assets was a constructive dividend to the taxpayer. The taxpayer argued that the substance of the transaction was a redemption qualified under § 302(b)(3) under *Zenz*. The Tax Court sustained the IRS's assertion of dividend treatment with respect to the bargain purchase holding that the taxpayer is to be held to the form of the transaction that he chose, which was selected in an attempt to avoid recognition of gain on the redemption.

4. REDEMPTIONS IN CONNECTION WITH SHAREHOLDER'S DIVORCE

Often in a divorce, corporate assets are used to acquire the stock of a closely held corporation held by one spouse while the other spouse continues to own the remaining stock of the corporation. The use of corporate assets to acquire the stock of one spouse may result in a constructive dividend to the continuing shareholder who is treated as transferring property to the selling spouse in a tax-free settlement under § 1041, or the transaction may be treated as a taxable redemption of the selling spouse. Under Treas.Reg. § 1.1041–2(a), promulgated in 2003 to resolve conflicting case law, the determination of whether there is a constructive dividend to the continuing shareholder is based on "applicable tax law," meaning the unconditional obligation test of *Wall* and *Sullivan*. Treas.Reg. § 1.1041–2(a)(2) provides that, if under the *Wall* and *Sullivan* principles, the redemption of stock from one spouse (the transferor spouse whose stock is redeemed) is treated as a constructive dividend to the other spouse (the non-transferor spouse, who continues as a shareholder), the transferor spouse is treated as transferring the stock to the other, non-transferor, spouse in exchange for the redemption proceeds in a nonrecognition exchange under § 1041. The transferor spouse does not recognize gain or loss. The non-transferor spouse is treated as receiving a distribution subject to § 302, which generally results in a dividend under § 301, and then transferring the distributed money or property to the transferor spouse. Treas.Reg. § 1.1041–2(b)(2). Thus, for example, if husband and wife own all of the stock of X Corporation, and pursuant to a decree of divorce husband is obligated to acquire wife's X Corporation stock and causes the corporation to redeem the stock, the husband is treated as receiving a constructive § 302 distribution, which will most likely be treated as a dividend under § 301. The wife is treated as transferring the X corporation stock to the husband in a nontaxable transfer under § 1041.

If the non-transferor spouse is not obligated to acquire the stock of the transferor spouse so that the redemption is not treated as a constructive dividend to the non-transferor spouse under the principles of *Wall* and *Sullivan*, then the transaction will be taxed in accordance with its form; the transferor spouse will be treated as receiving a taxable distribution under § 302. Treas.Reg. § 1.1041–2(a)(1) and (b)(1). Thus, in the above example, if the husband is not obligated to acquire wife's X Corporation stock under the standards of *Wall* and *Sullivan,* the transaction is treated as a redemption distribution to the wife who recognizes the gain or loss on disposition of her stock. The husband is not treated as receiving a taxable distribution.

The regulations permit the spouses to designate the tax treatment of the redemption by agreeing to treat the redemption inconsistently with the generally applicable tax law regarding constructive dividends. Treas.Reg. § 1.1041–2(c)(1) provides that even though the redemption results in a constructive dividend distribution to the non-transferor spouse under applicable tax law, if the spouses agree in the divorce or separation instrument (or other valid written agreement) that the redemption will be treated as a redemption distribution to the transferor spouse, then the redemption will be treated as a redemption taxable to the transferor spouse notwithstanding that the redemption otherwise would result in a constructive dividend distribution to the non-transferor spouse. Conversely, Treas.Reg. § 1.1041–2(c)(2) provides that even though the redemption does not result in a constructive dividend distribution to the non-transferor spouse under applicable tax law, if the spouses agree in the divorce or separation instrument (or other valid written agreement) that the redemption will be treated as a dividend distribution to the non-transferor spouse, then the redemption will be treated as a transfer by the transferor spouse of the redeemed stock to the non-transferor spouse in exchange for the redemption proceeds, and the receipt of the redemption proceeds by the non-transferor spouse as a distribution from the corporation. Thus, the spouses can agree to nonrecognition treatment for the transferor spouse who is redeemed, coupled with constructive dividend treatment for the non-transferor spouse who continues as a shareholder.

5.   DIVIDENDS DISTRIBUTED IN CONNECTION WITH THE SALE
      OF A CORPORATE BUSINESS

While the treatment of redemptions made as part of the sale of a corporate business is fairly well established since the initial decisions in *Holsey* and *Zenz,* the appropriate treatment of dividend distributions in similar situations raises a different question. Some question remains whether a dividend distribution to a selling shareholder that is made as an integral part of the sale and purchase of stock is to be recharacterized as a dividend distribution to the purchaser, and taxed to the purchaser, with the same amount being, in turn, treated as having been paid by the purchaser to the selling shareholder as part of the purchase price.

In Casner v. Commissioner, 450 F.2d 379 (5th Cir.1971), substantial shareholders in the corporation wished to withdraw by selling their stock to the remaining shareholders. The buyers did not have enough cash to finance the transaction. It was agreed that a distribution of some of the cash of the corporation would be made pro rata to all the shareholders, thus reducing the value of the corporation and giving the continuing shareholders some cash to pay a portion of the purchase price. Accordingly, the corporation made a cash distribution and contemporaneously the retiring shareholders sold their shares. The selling shareholders treated all the payments, including the distributions, as sales proceeds; the buying shareholders regarded themselves as conduits for the distributions to the selling shareholders. The Tax Court treated the corporate distributions to both the selling and buying shareholders as dividends. T.C. Memo. 1969–98. The Court of Appeals reversed, finding that the distributions to the *selling* shareholders were in fact part of the payment of the purchase price and as such resulted in constructive dividends to the *buying* shareholders (in addition to the latter's own direct dividends). The court found alternatively that the buying stockholders were the beneficial owners of the stock at the time of the dividend distribution.[1]

The *Casner* treatment of the distributions to the selling shareholders as dividends to the buying shareholders followed by a payment of the purchase price to the sellers is inconsistent with the obligation-to-purchase standard of the *Wall and Sullivan* line of cases dealing with a similar factual pattern. The IRS will not apply *Casner* to tax the buyer where the payment of the dividend to the selling shareholder does not reduce the buyer's obligation to pay an agreed upon purchase price, Rev.Rul. 75–493, 1975–2 C.B. 108. This position is consistent with the redemption cases which likewise focus on the question of whether the distribution by the corporation discharges the buying shareholder's personal obligation. It similarly places a premium on the careful timing of the transactions since very different tax consequences result depending on whether the distribution is made before or after entering into a binding purchase agreement.

Even where the dividend does not reduce the buying shareholder's obligation under the purchase agreement, a dividend to the buyer may still be found on the theory that the buyer had become the beneficial owner of the stock at the time the dividend was declared. See Steel Improvement

---

[1]   The *Casner* result is advantageous where the seller and purchaser are corporations that can take advantage of the dividends received deduction of § 243 as discussed in Section 2.

and Forge Co. v. Commissioner, 314 F.2d 96 (6th Cir.1963); Walker v. Commissioner, 544 F.2d 419 (9th Cir.1976).

SECTION 2.   BOOTSTRAP TRANSACTIONS INVOLVING CORPORATIONS

Different problems arise where a dividend in connection with a sale is paid to a selling shareholder which is itself a corporation and thus able to take advantage of the reduction or elimination of tax on intercorporate dividends under § 243. Suppose that X Corporation owns 100 percent of the stock of Y Corporation, which has a basis of $200 and a fair market value of $500. (Also assume that X Corporation and Y Corporation do not file a consolidated return.) If X Corporation sold the stock of Y Corporation to Z Corporation for $500, after paying taxes (at 35 percent) on its $300 gain, X Corporation would have net after-tax proceeds of $395. Now suppose that prior to the sale Y Corporation declared a dividend of $200, which was eligible for 100 percent exclusion under § 243(a)(3), following which X Corporation sold the stock of Y Corporation for $300. In this case, X Corporation would pay taxes on only a $100 gain, and after taxes it would receive $465.

The IRS generally argues that such a dividend payment was in fact additional purchase price, and therefore constituted capital gain which was not eligible for the § 243 deduction. See Rev.Rul. 75–493, 1975–2 C.B. 108, characterizing such a transaction as a "sham designed to disguise the true substance of the transaction." The IRS has had mixed success with this argument in the courts.

Litton Industries, Inc. v. Commissioner

Tax Court of the United States, 1987.
89 T.C. 1086.

[The taxpayer's board of directors began to consider a sale of its subsidiary, Stouffer, in July of 1972. In late August, Stouffer declared a $30 million dividend, which was paid in the form of a negotiable promissory note for $30 million; and on September 7, Litton announced that it was interested in selling Stouffer. After considering a public offering of the Stouffer stock in late 1972, on March 1, 1973, Litton sold its Stouffer stock to Nestle for $75 million; simultaneously, it sold the promissory note to Nestle for $30 million. The IRS contended that the $30 million "dividend" was in fact part of the purchase price and disallowed Litton's dividends received deduction.]

OPINION

* * *

The instant case is substantially governed by Waterman Steamship Corp. v. Commissioner, 50 T.C. 650 (1968), revd. 430 F.2d 1185 (5th Cir.1970), cert. denied 401 U.S. 939 (1971). [The Commissioner] urges us to follow the opinion of the Fifth Circuit * * *. [Taxpayer] contends that the reasoning of the Fifth Circuit in *Waterman Steamship* should not apply since the facts here are more favorable to petitioner. Additionally, petitioner points out that several business purposes were served by the distribution here which provide additional support for recognition of the distribution as a dividend. For the reasons set forth below, we conclude that the $30 million distribution constituted a dividend which should be recognized as such for tax purposes. * * *

In many respects, the facts of this case and those of *Waterman Steamship* are parallel. The principal difference, and the one which we find to be most significant, is the timing of the dividend action. In *Waterman Steamship,* the taxpayer corporation received an offer to purchase the stock of two of its wholly owned subsidiary corporations, Pan-Atlantic and Gulf Florida, for $3,500,000. The board of directors of Waterman Steamship rejected that offer but countered with an offer to sell the two subsidiaries for $700,000 after the subsidiaries declared and arranged for payments of dividends to Waterman Steamship amounting in the aggregate to $2,800,000. Negotiations between the parties ensued, and the agreements which resulted therefrom included, in specific detail, provisions for the declaration of a dividend by Pan-Atlantic to Waterman Steamship prior to the signing of the sales agreement and the closing of that transaction. Furthermore, the agreements called for the purchaser to loan or otherwise advance funds to Pan-Atlantic promptly in order to pay off the promissory note by which the dividend had been paid. Once the agreement was reached, the entire transaction was carried out by a series of meetings commencing at 12 noon on January 21, 1955, and ending at 1:30 p.m. the same day. * * *

As the Fifth Circuit pointed out, "By the end of the day and within a ninety minute period, the financial cycle had been completed. Waterman had $3,500,000, hopefully tax-free, all of which came from Securities and McLean, the buyers of the stock." 430 F.2d at 1190. This Court concluded that the distribution from Pan-Atlantic to Waterman was a dividend. The Fifth Circuit reversed, concluding that the dividend and sale were one transaction. 430 F.2d at 1192.

The timing in the instant case was markedly different. The dividend was declared by Stouffer on August 23, 1972, at which time the promissory note in payment of the dividend was issued to Litton. There had been some general preliminary discussions about the sale of Stouffer, and it was expected that Stouffer would be a very marketable company which would sell quickly. However, at the time the dividend was declared, no formal action had been taken to initiate the sale of Stouffer. It was not until 2 weeks later that Litton publicly announced that Stouffer was for sale. There ensued over the next 6 months many discussions with various corporations, investment banking houses, business brokers, and underwriters regarding Litton's disposition of Stouffer through sale of all or part of the business to a particular buyer, or through full or partial public offerings of the Stouffer stock. All of this culminated on March 1, 1973, over 6 months after the dividend was declared, with the purchase by Nestle of all of Stouffer's stock. * * *

In the instant case, the declaration of the dividend and the sale of the stock were substantially separated in time in contrast to *Waterman Steamship* where the different transactions occurred essentially simultaneously. In *Waterman Steamship,* it seems quite clear that no dividend would have been declared if all of the remaining steps in the transaction had not been lined up in order on the closing table and did not in fact take place. Here, however, Stouffer declared the dividend, issued the promissory note, and definitely committed itself to the dividend before even making a public announcement that Stouffer was for sale. Respondent argues that the only way petitioner could ever receive the dividend was by raising revenue through a sale of Stouffer. Therefore, respondent asserts the two events (the declaration of the dividend and then the sale of the company) were inextricably tied together and should be treated as one transaction for tax purposes. In our view, respondent ignores the fact that Stouffer could have raised sufficient revenue for the dividend from other avenues, such as a partial public offering or borrowing. Admittedly, there had been discussions at Litton about the sale of Stouffer which was considered to be a very salable company. However, there are many slips between the cup and the lip, and it does not take much of a stretch of the imagination to picture a variety of circumstances under which Stouffer might have been taken off the market and no sale consummated. Under these circumstances, it is unlikely that respondent would have considered the dividend to be a nullity. On the contrary, it would seem quite clear that petitioner would be charged with a dividend on which it would have to pay a substantial tax. Petitioner committed itself to the dividend and, thereby, accepted the consequences regardless of the outcome of the proposed sale of Stouffer stock. See Crellin v. Commissioner, 17 T.C. 781, 785 (1951), affd. 203 F.2d 812 (9th Cir.1953), cert. denied 346 U.S. 873 * * * (1953).

Since the facts here are distinguishable in important respects and are so much stronger in petitioner's favor, we do not consider it necessary to consider further the opinion of the Fifth Circuit in *Waterman Steamship.*

* * * [T]he $30 million distribution by Stouffer would clearly constitute a dividend if the sale of Stouffer had not occurred. We are not persuaded that the subsequent sale of Stouffer to Nestle changes that result merely because it was more advantageous to Litton from a tax perspective.

It is well established that a taxpayer is entitled to structure his affairs and transactions in order to minimize his taxes. This proposition does not give a taxpayer carte blanche to set up a transaction in any form which will avoid tax consequences, regardless of whether the transaction has substance. Gregory v. Helvering, 293 U.S. 465, 55 S.Ct. 266 (1935). A variety of factors present here preclude a finding of sham or subterfuge. Although the record in this case clearly shows that Litton intended at the time the dividend was declared to sell Stouffer, no formal action had been taken and no announcement had been made. There was no definite purchaser waiting in the wings with the terms and conditions of sale already agreed upon. At that time, Litton had not even decided upon the form of sale of Stouffer. Nothing in the record here suggests that there was any prearranged sale agreement, formal or informal, at the time the dividend was declared.

Petitioner further supports its argument that the transaction was not a sham by pointing out Litton's legitimate business purposes in declaring the dividend. Although the Code and case law do not require a dividend to have a business purpose, it is a factor to be considered in determining whether the overall transaction was a sham. T.S.N.

Liquidating Corp. v. United States, 624 F.2d 1328 (5th Cir.1980). Petitioner argues that * * * since Litton was considering disposing of all or part of Stouffer through a public or private offering, the payment of a dividend by a promissory note prior to any sale had two advantages. First, Litton hoped to avoid materially diminishing the market value of the Stouffer stock. At that time, one of the factors considered in valuing a stock, and in determining the market value of a stock was the "multiple of earnings" criterion. Payment of the dividend by issuance of a promissory note would not substantially alter Stouffer's earnings. Since many investors were relatively unsophisticated, Litton may have been quite right that it could increase its investment in Stouffer by at least some portion of the $30 million dividend. Second, by declaring a dividend and paying it by a promissory note prior to an anticipated public offering, Litton could avoid sharing the earnings with future additional shareholders while not diminishing to the full extent of the pro rata dividend, the amount received for the stock. Whether Litton could have come out ahead after Stouffer paid the promissory note is at this point merely speculation about a public offering which never occurred. The point, however, is that Litton hoped to achieve some business purpose, and not just tax benefits, in structuring the transaction as it did.

Under these facts, where the dividend was declared 6 months prior to the sale of Stouffer, where the sale was not pre-arranged, and since Stouffer had earnings and profits exceeding $30 million at the time the dividend was declared, we cannot conclude that the distribution was merely a device designed to give the appearance of a dividend to a part of the sales proceeds. In this case, the form and substance of the transaction coincide; it was not a transaction entered into solely for tax reasons, and it should be recognized as structured by petitioner.

DETAILED ANALYSIS

1. OTHER JUDICIAL DECISIONS

As in *Waterman Steamship,* discussed in the excerpt from *Litton Industries,* the IRS met with success in the District Court in TSN Liquidating Corp. v. United States, 77–2 U.S.T.C. ¶ 9741 (N.D.Tex.1977), but on appeal the decision was reversed, 624 F.2d 1328 (5th Cir.1980). In that case, Union Mutual agreed to purchase from TSN the stock of TSN's subsidiary, CLIC, but Union Mutual insisted that prior to the acquisition CLIC distribute to TSN certain securities, primarily stock of closely held corporations, constituting some 78 percent of CLIC's total assets. Although Union Mutual did not desire CLIC to hold the particular securities distributed pursuant to the agreement, neither did it desire to own a "smaller" corporation. To the contrary, for reasons having to do with state law it desired to maintain the net assets of CLIC, and shortly after the closing, Union Mutual contributed to CLIC cash and marketable securities slightly in excess of the amount distributed to TSN.

Emphasizing that the distribution of investment assets immediately prior to the sale of the stock was matched by a post-acquisition infusion of investment assets, the IRS argued that the conduit rationale of *Waterman Steamship* applied. Although it agreed with the District Court that "the substance of the transaction controls over the form," the Court of Appeals found *Waterman Steamship,* upon which the District Court had relied, to be distinguishable. The earlier case involved a "sham transaction," which even the IRS did not argue was the case in *TSN Liquidating.* Instead, the IRS argued, successfully in the District Court, that from CLIC's perspective there was no business purpose for the distribution which could not have occurred other than in the context of the sale. The Court of Appeals, however, concluded as follows:

> We agree that the transaction must be viewed as a whole and we accept the district court's finding of fact that the dividend of the unwanted assets was "part and parcel of the purchase arrangement with Union Mutual," motivated specifically by Union Mutual's unwillingness to take and pay for such assets. That being the case, we decline to focus on the business purpose of one participant in the transaction—a corporation controlled by the taxpayer—and instead find that the business purpose for the transaction as a whole, viewed from the standpoint of the taxpayer, controls. The facts found by the district court clearly demonstrate a business purpose for the presale dividend of the unwanted assets which fully explains that dividend. We note that there is no suggestion in the district court's opinion of any tax avoidance motivation on the part of the taxpayer TSN. The fact that the dividend may have had incidental tax benefit to the taxpayer, without more, does not necessitate the disallowance of dividend treatment.

In Basic Inc. v. United States, 549 F.2d 740 (Ct.Cl.1977), the court refused to respect the taxpayers' structure of the transaction even though payment of an intercorporate dividend was not in effect a conduit device to transfer funds from the purchaser to the seller. Basic owned all the shares of Falls which in turn owned all the shares of Carbon. A corporate purchaser was interested in buying the shares of Falls and Carbon but, in order to take advantage of a now repealed provision governing a subsequent liquidation of the subsidiaries, it desired to purchase the stock of both Falls and Carbon directly rather than simply purchasing the Falls stock and obtaining the Carbon stock on a liquidation of Falls. After an irrevocable offer by the purchaser to purchase the Falls and Carbon stock, Falls distributed the Carbon stock to Basic as a dividend. The dividend of the stock was entitled to the dividends received deduction under § 243(a)(1) but because under § 301(d) the basis of the Carbon stock was not reduced to reflect the dividends received deduction, Basic acquired an essentially "cost free" basis in the Carbon stock against which to offset the sales price to be paid for the stock of the two corporations. The Court of Claims held that the transfer of the Carbon stock to Basic did not qualify as a dividend. The court rested its decision on general notions of tax avoidance, citing Gregory v. Helvering, 293 U.S. 465 (1935), and took the position that for a corporate distribution to qualify as a dividend it must have an independent "business purpose":

> These facts leave no room for a conclusion that a business interest was served by the claimed dividend. From all that appears, the case is plain that Falls, through its controlling parent, was caused to transfer the property whose sale the parent had decided upon for its own separate purposes. Nothing therefore

remains save the obvious: the transaction reduced the tax that Basic would otherwise have incurred in the sale of its own property, i.e., the shares of Falls. * * *

Under the facts and circumstances presented here, plaintiff has not shown that there was a reason for the transfer of the Carbon stock from Falls to Basic aside from the tax consequences attributable to that move. Accordingly, for purposes of taxation, the transfer was not a dividend within the meaning of § 316(a)(1). Instead, it should be regarded as a transfer that avoided part of the gain to be expected from the sale of the business to Carborundum, and should, therefore, be now taxed accordingly. Such a treatment is in keeping with the results reached in like situations. Waterman Steamship Corp. v. Commissioner, supra; Steel Improvement & Forge Co. v. Commissioner, 314 F.2d 96, 98 (6th Cir.1963) * * *.

The *Basic, Inc.* opinion cannot be reconciled with *Litton Industries* and *TSN Liquidating. Basic, Inc.* appears to require that the payor have a business purpose for paying the dividend totally apart from the business purpose of the parent. It will be difficult, if not impossible, ever to establish an independent business purpose for the payment of an extraordinary dividend by a controlled subsidiary.

The cases involving intercorporate dividends associated with a bootstrap acquisition requiring that a dividend distribution must have a "business purpose" are in marked contrast to the cases in the redemption area in which the form which the taxpayer has selected for the extraction of corporate assets prior to a sale of the corporation is in general respected without regard to any inquiry into purposes. Does the fact that intercorporate dividends are in general either tax free or subject to reduced taxation mean that special safeguards are required with respect to such distributions in the context of corporate acquisitions? If so, is the introduction of a "business purpose" doctrine an appropriate response? Compare the treatment given intercorporate dividends in the consolidated return situation discussed at page 455, where the parent corporation upon receipt of an excluded intercorporate dividend must reduce its basis in the stock of the subsidiary by an amount equal to the dividend. Thus, in a consolidated return context, the intercorporate dividend prior to the sale does not produce a tax advantage to the seller.

2.   SECTION 1059

Section 1059 requires that a corporate shareholder that receives an "extraordinary dividend" under certain circumstances must, in computing the gain or loss realized upon the sale of the stock, reduce the basis of the stock by the amount of the untaxed portion of the dividend. See page 226. As long as the stock has been held for more than two years prior to the dividend announcement date, however, only a distribution in partial liquidation of the corporation (as defined in § 302(e), discussed at page 261) or a non-pro rata redemption distribution generally will be treated as an extraordinary distribution.

Section 1059 generally does not apply to "qualifying dividends" (as defined in § 243(b), page 223) received by a corporation from an 80 percent controlled subsidiary, except to the extent that the dividends were attributable to pre-affiliation earnings and profits. I.R.C. § 1059(e)(2). Section 1059 also applies to qualifying dividends that are the proceeds of a partial liquidation as defined in § 302(e). Treas.Reg. § 1.1059(e)–1(a) provides that the exception for qualifying dividends in § 1059(e)(2) does not apply to § 1059(e)(1), which treats a dividend distribution to a corporation in partial liquidation of its interest in another corporation as an extraordinary dividend. Nevertheless, § 1059 would not apply, for example, to a transaction identical to that in *Litton*, because the distribution was not a partial liquidation.

Section 1059 was not enacted for the purpose of dealing with *Litton* type transactions, but the mechanical approach of § 1059 could be extended to apply to such transactions if Congress considered bootstrap acquisitions involving intercorporate dividends to involve inappropriate tax avoidance.

CHAPTER 12

TAX-FREE ACQUISITIVE REORGANIZATIONS

SECTION 1.   EARLY JUDICIAL BACKGROUND

Marr v. United States

Supreme Court of the United States, 1925.
268 U.S. 536.

■ MR. JUSTICE BRANDEIS delivered the opinion of the Court.

Prior to March 1, 1913, Marr and wife purchased 339 shares of the preferred and 425 shares of the common stock of the General Motors Company of New Jersey for $76,400. In 1916, they received in exchange for this stock 451 shares of the preferred and 2,125 shares of the common stock of the General Motors Corporation of Delaware which (including a small cash payment) had the aggregate market value of $400,866.57. The difference between the cost of their stock in the New Jersey corporation and the value of the stock in the Delaware corporation was $324,466.57. The Treasury Department ruled that this difference was gain or income * * *.

The exchange of securities was effected in this way. The New Jersey corporation had outstanding $15,000,000 of 7 per cent. preferred stock and $15,000,000 of the common stock; all shares being of the par value of $100. It had accumulated from profits a large surplus. The actual value of the common stock was then $842.50 a share. Its officers caused to be organized the Delaware corporation with an authorized capital of $20,000,000 in 6 percent nonvoting preferred stock and $82,600,000 in common stock; all shares being of the par value of $100. The Delaware corporation made to stockholders in the New Jersey corporation the following offer for exchange of securities: For every share of common stock of the New Jersey corporation, five shares of common stock of the Delaware corporation. For every share of the preferred stock of the New Jersey corporation, one and one-third shares of preferred stock of the Delaware corporation. In lieu of a certificate for fractional shares of stock in the Delaware corporation, payment was to be made in cash at the rate of $100 a share for its preferred and at the rate of $150 a share for its common stock. On this basis all the common stock of the New Jersey corporation was exchanged and all the preferred stock except a few shares. These few were redeemed in cash. For acquiring the stock of the New Jersey corporation only $75,000,000 of the common stock of the Delaware corporation was needed. The remaining $7,600,000 of the authorized common stock was either sold or held for sale as additional capital should be desired. The Delaware corporation, having thus become the owner of all the outstanding stock of the New Jersey corporation, took a transfer of its assets and assumed its liabilities. The latter was then dissolved.

It is clear that all new securities issued in excess of an amount equal to the capitalization of the New Jersey corporation represented income earned by it; that the new securities received by the Marrs in excess of the cost of the securities of the New Jersey corporation theretofore held were financially the equivalent of $324,466.51 in cash; and that Congress intended to tax as income of stockholders such gains when so distributed. The serious question for decision is whether it had power to do so. Marr contends that, since the new corporation was organized to take over the assets and continue the business of the old, and his capital remained invested in the same business enterprise, the additional securities distributed were in legal effect a stock dividend; and that under the rule of Eisner v. Macomber, 252 U.S. 189, 40 S.Ct. 189, applied in Weiss v. Stearn, 265 U.S. 242, 44 S.Ct. 490, he was not taxable thereon as income, because he still held the whole investment. The government insists that identity of the business enterprise is not conclusive; that gain in value resulting from profits is taxable as income, not only when it is represented by an interest in a different business enterprise or property, but also when it is represented by an essentially different interest in the same business enterprise or property; that, in the case at bar, the gain actually made is represented by securities with essentially different characteristics in an essentially different corporation; and that, consequently, the additional value of the new securities, although they are still held by the Marrs, is income under the rule applied in United States v. Phellis, 257 U.S. 156, 42 S.Ct. 63; Rockefeller v. United States, 257 U.S. 176, 42 S.Ct. 68; and Cullinan v. Walker, 262 U.S. 134, 43 S.Ct. 495. In our opinion the government is right.

In each of the five cases named, as in the case at bar, the business enterprise actually conducted remained exactly the same. In United States v. Phellis, in Rockefeller v. United States, and in Cullinan v. Walker, where the additional value in new securities distributed was held to be taxable as income, there had been changes of corporate identity. That is, the corporate property, or a part thereof, was no longer held and operated by the same corporation; and, after the distribution, the stockholders no longer owned merely the same proportional interest of the same character in the same corporation. In Eisner v. Macomber and in Weiss v. Stearn, where the additional value in new securities was held not to be taxable, the identity was deemed to have been preserved. In Eisner v. Macomber the identity was literally maintained. There was no new corporate entity. The same interest in the same corporation was represented after the distribution by more shares of precisely the same character. It was as if the par value of the stock had been reduced, and three shares of reduced par value stock had been issued in place of every two old shares. That is, there was an exchange of certificates but not of interests. In Weiss v. Stearn a new corporation had, in fact, been organized to take over the assets and business of the old. Technically there was a new entity; but the corporate identity was deemed to have been substantially maintained because the new corporation was organized under the laws of the same state, with presumably the same powers as the old. There was also no change in the character of securities issued. By reason of these facts, the proportional interest of the stockholder after the distribution of the new securities was deemed to be exactly the same as if the par value of the stock in the old corporation had been reduced, and five shares of reduced par value stock had been issued in place of every two shares of the old stock. Thus, in Weiss v. Stearn, as in Eisner v. Macomber, the transaction was considered, in essence, an exchange of certificates representing the same interest, not an exchange of interests.

In the case at bar, the new corporation is essentially different from the old. A corporation organized under the laws of Delaware does not have the same rights and powers as one organized under the laws of New Jersey. Because of these inherent differences in rights and powers, both the preferred and the common stock of the old corporation is an essentially different thing from stock of the same general kind in the new. But there are also adventitious differences, substantial in character. A 6 per cent. nonvoting preferred stock is an essentially different thing from a 7 per cent. voting preferred stock. A common stock subject to the priority of $20,000,000 preferred and a $1,200,000 annual dividend charge is an essentially different thing from a common stock subject only to $15,000,000 preferred and a $1,050,000 annual dividend charge. The case at bar is not one in which after the distribution the stockholders have the same proportional interest of the same kind in essentially the same corporation.

Affirmed.

■ The separate opinion of MR. JUSTICE VAN DEVANTER, MR. JUSTICE McREYNOLDS, MR. JUSTICE SUTHERLAND, and MR. JUSTICE BUTLER.

We think this cause falls within the doctrine of Weiss v. Stearn, 265 U.S. 242, 44 S.Ct. 490, and that the judgment below should be reversed. The practical result of the things done was but the reorganization of a going concern. The business and assets were not materially changed, and the stockholder received nothing actually severed from his original capital interest—nothing differing in substance from what he already had.

Weiss v. Stearn did not turn upon the relatively unimportant circumstance that the new and old corporations were organized under the laws of the same state, but upon the approved definition of income from capital as something severed therefrom and received by the taxpayer for his separate use and benefit. Here stockholders got nothing from the old business or assets except new statements of their undivided interests, and this, as we carefully pointed out, is not enough to create taxable income.

DETAILED ANALYSIS

1.   STATUTORY NONRECOGNITION

By the time *Marr* was decided the Internal Revenue Code already contained rudimentary provisions for nonrecognition in certain corporate reorganizations. The first such provisions were enacted in 1918 (and thus did not apply to the transaction in *Marr,* which occurred in 1916), and these early statutes were exceedingly simplistic. For example, both the 1924 and 1928 Acts defined a tax-free reorganization as follows:

> [A] merger or consolidation (including the acquisition by one corporation of at least a majority of the voting stock and at least a majority of the total number of shares of all other classes of stock

of another corporation, or substantially all the properties of another corporation).

The statutory definition of reorganization was expanded and refined through the 1930's. Most of the basic principles regarding nonrecognition, however, were in place by 1928. Further changes were made when the 1954 Code was adopted, and a number of refinements have been enacted since that time.

SECTION 2.   THE FUNDAMENTAL RULES GOVERNING REORGANIZATIONS

A.   THE BASIC STATUTORY SCHEME

INTERNAL REVENUE CODE: Sections 1001; 354(a), (b); 356(a), (c), (d)–(f); 357(a); 358(a), (b), (f); 361(a); 362(b); 368 (omitting (a)(2)(F) and (a)(3)); see also 336(c).

REGULATIONS: Section 1.368–1(a)–(c); –2(a), (b), (f), (g).

PROPOSED REGULATIONS: Section 1.368–1(f)(1)–(4).

The corporate reorganization sections cover a variety of corporate transformations. In general these sections are designed to permit business transactions involving certain corporate acquisitions and readjustments to be carried out without a tax being incurred by the participating corporations or their shareholders at the time of the transaction. The policy rationale for according nonrecognition to these transactions, however over-inclusive and unrealistic that rationale might be, is that although such acquisitions and readjustments change the form of a business enterprise, these changes do not alter the nature or character of the relationship of the enterprise's owners to the enterprise sufficiently to warrant taxation of gain (generally capital gain) or allowance of loss. Because these sections, like the other nonrecognition provisions, permit nonrecognition and hence postponement of gain and loss, special provisions are needed to reflect such nonrecognition in the basis of the corporate assets and stock involved.

This Chapter deals with the application of the provisions permitting deferral of gain recognition upon the sale and purchase of a corporate business. Such transactions are usually referred to as "tax-free" reorganizations. The transactions covered are the same in form as those considered in Chapter 10, i.e., the sale may be effected by the transfer of stock or assets of the target corporation. But in the case of "tax-free" reorganizations, the consideration for the purchase medium is different. In general, the acquiring corporation uses its own stock (or in some cases the stock of its parent corporation), rather than cash or notes, to make the acquisition. As a policy matter, consider whether this difference justifies such a radical difference in tax treatment, particularly where publicly traded corporations are involved. Further, within the tax free reorganization provisions themselves, small differences in form can produce significantly different tax results. Consider whether these differences are either justified or necessary. Perhaps in no other area of corporate taxation is Professor Eustice's dictum more apt: "In subchapter C, form *is* the substance."

In addition to "acquisitive" reorganizations, there are a number of other corporate readjustments that are governed by the reorganization provisions. Although the acquisition of one corporation by another may be furthered by one of these types of reorganization, more frequently they involve a realignment of the ownership of a single corporation. Such nonacquisitive reorganizations are considered in subsequent chapters.

1. *Definition of Reorganization*

The essential nonrecognition provisions are in § 354(a) and § 361(a). However, these provisions apply only after it has been determined that a "reorganization" has occurred. The term "reorganization" is narrowly defined in § 368(a) as encompassing seven basic transactions. Section 368(a)(1) states that the term "reorganization" "*means*" the seven specifically described transactions rather than "*includes*" those transaction, thus precluding other transactions from qualifying under the statute.

The reorganizations considered in this Chapter are defined as follows:

Type (A) Reorganization: Statutory Merger. Section 368(a)(1)(A) describes a merger or consolidation in compliance with the substantive corporation law statutes permitting such transactions—as where the target corporation merges into the acquiring corporation or two corporations and consolidate into a new corporation.[1] The target and acquiring corporations may be existing parent and subsidiary corporations, or may be corporations that have not previously been related. Where the acquiring corporation acquires the assets of the target corporation in a statutory merger, the acquiring corporation may then transfer part or all of the assets to its controlled subsidiary without disqualifying the (A) reorganization. See I.R.C. § 368(a)(2)(C).

Type (B) Reorganization: Stock-for-Stock Exchange. Section 368(a)(1)(B) defines as a tax-free reorganization the acquisition of stock of the target corporation solely in exchange for the stock of the acquiring corporation if, following the exchange, the acquiring corporation is in control of the target corporation. The shareholders of the target corporation become shareholders in the acquiring corporation. They may be minority or majority shareholders, depending on the amount of stock issued by the acquiring corporation, which depends on the relative size of the target and acquiring corporations. If the target corporation is liquidated (which may be accomplished under § 332 without recognition of gain or loss), the end result is the same as either a statutory merger under (A) above or a stock-for-assets acquisition under (C), below.

In order to qualify as a (B) reorganization, after the stock-for-stock exchange, the acquiring corporation must have *control* of the target corporation, which is defined in § 368(c) as ownership of 80 percent of the total combined voting power of all classes of stock entitled to vote and 80 percent of the total number of shares of all other classes of stock. Rev.Rul. 59–259, 1959–2 C.B. 115, interpreted the statute to require

---

[1] See Treas.Reg. § 1.368–2(b); Russell v. Commissioner, 40 T.C. 810, 822 (1963), aff'd per curiam, 345 F.2d 534 (5th Cir.1965) (failure to follow state merger laws prevented a type (A) reorganization).

ownership of 80 percent of each class of nonvoting stock. In addition, to qualify as a reorganization the acquisition of stock of the target corporation must be *solely* in return for *voting stock* of the acquiring corporation. No other consideration is permissible.

There is no requirement that 80 percent or more of the stock of the target corporation be acquired in one transaction. Thus, any particular acquisition is a reorganization if after that acquisition the acquiring corporation has "control" of the target corporation. Hence, while a previous acquisition of some shares of the target corporation for cash or non-voting stock, or for voting stock but without "control," would not constitute a reorganization, the earlier acquisition would not prevent a later separate acquisition for voting stock from being a reorganization if after the latter acquisition the requisite 80 percent of the shares of the target corporation are held by the acquiring corporation as a result of the several acquisitions. This acquisition of control over a period of time is called a "creeping acquisition." Even though this rule has been in the statute for nearly fifty years, its application is uncertain, in that an acquisition for cash related in time or by plan to an acquisition for stock may be treated as one transaction and prevent a reorganization, since the "acquisition" would not be solely for voting stock. Treas.Reg. § 1.368–2(c).

A controlled subsidiary corporation may acquire the stock of the target corporation solely in return for the *voting* stock of its parent corporation. In addition, a transaction is not disqualified as a (B) reorganization if, after the transaction, the acquiring corporation in turn transfers the stock of the target corporation to its subsidiary. I.R.C. § 368(a)(2)(C).

Type (C) Reorganization: Stock-for-Assets Exchange. The acquisition by one corporation of substantially all the assets of another corporation—as where the acquiring corporation acquires the assets of the target corporation rather than its stock (as in (B) above)—may qualify as a reorganization under § 368(a)(1)(C). Subject to a limited exception, the acquisition must be *solely* by means of the *voting* stock of the acquiring corporation. This asset acquisition is sometimes referred to as a "practical merger." Because of this analogy to a merger, the acquiring corporation must obtain all or substantially all of the target corporation's assets. The IRS considers a transfer of 90 percent of the net assets and 70 percent of the gross assets as clearly qualified under the "substantially all the assets" requirement.[2] Depending on the circumstances, however, lower percentages may qualify, particularly if the retained assets are used to pay creditors. Also, analogous to a statutory merger, as part of the overall transaction the target corporation must be liquidated, distributing the acquiring corporation stock it receives, as well as any other assets it has retained, to the target corporation's shareholders. See I.R.C. § 368(a)(2)(G).

While the acquisition in general must be solely for the voting stock of the acquiring corporation, several exceptions allow the use of other consideration. First, the assumption by the acquiring corporation of the liabilities of the target corporation or the acquisition subject to its liabilities does not prevent the acquisition from being regarded as solely

---

[2]   See Rev.Proc. 77–37, 1977–2 C.B. 568.

for voting stock. Second, cash or other property may be used if at least 80 percent of *all* of the assets of the target corporation are acquired for voting stock. Any additional assets may be acquired for cash, other property, or other stock. However, in applying the 20 percent limitation, liabilities of the target corporation that are assumed are treated as cash. See I.R.C. § 368(a)(2)(B).

Section 368(a)(1)(C) also permits the assets of the target corporation to be acquired by a controlled subsidiary corporation in exchange for the voting stock of its parent. Finally, whether the acquisition was made directly by the acquiring corporation or by a controlled subsidiary corporation in exchange for voting stock of its controlling parent corporation, the corporation that initially acquired the assets may then transfer the assets to a controlled subsidiary corporation without destroying the reorganization treatment. See I.R.C. § 368(a)(2)(C).

Forward Triangular Merger. Section § 368(a)(2)(D) permits a subsidiary corporation, which may either be an existing or a newly-created subsidiary, to acquire the assets of the target corporation in a statutory merger between the subsidiary corporation and target corporation in which the shareholders of the target corporation receive the stock of the acquiring subsidiary's parent corporation, for "substantially all" of the properties of the target corporation if (1) the transaction would have qualified as an (A) reorganization if the merger had been directly into the parent corporation,[3] and (2) no stock of the acquiring subsidiary corporation is used in the transaction. If these conditions are met, the transaction will be treated as a type (A) reorganization. The § 368(a)(2)(D) transaction frequently is referred to as a "forward" triangular reorganization.

Reverse Triangular Merger. Section 368(a)(2)(E) permits a "reverse" triangular merger to qualify under certain specified conditions. Here, rather than a merger of the target corporation into the acquiring subsidiary corporation (using the stock of the parent corporation), the acquiring subsidiary corporation is merged into the target corporation (which survives the transaction), with the shareholders of the target corporation receiving stock of the acquiring subsidiary's parent corporation. This transaction qualifies if (1) after the transaction the surviving target corporation holds substantially all of its properties and the properties of the acquiring subsidiary corporation (other than stock of the parent corporation that may have been issued to the subsidiary corporation to be distributed in the transaction to the shareholders of the target corporation), and (2) in the transaction the former shareholders of the target corporation exchange for voting stock of the acquiring subsidiary's parent corporation an amount of stock in the target corporation that constitutes *control* of the target corporation. If these conditions are met, the transaction will qualify as an (A) reorganization.

---

[3]　The restriction that the transaction "would have qualified" as an (A) reorganization if it had involved the acquiring corporation directly does not require that the hypothetical merger would have been permissible under state merger statutes; it has reference to qualification under judicially developed restrictions on tax-free reorganizations such as "business purpose," "continuity of interest," etc., discussed at page 539; see Treas.Reg. § 1.368–2(b)(2).

Under § 368(a)(2)(E), the target corporation ends up as a subsidiary of the acquiring parent corporation, replacing the original subsidiary corporation. In contrast, in a § 368(a)(2)(D) transaction, the target corporation ends up as a part of the acquiring subsidiary corporation. In both cases, however, the shareholders of the target corporation become shareholders of the acquiring parent corporation. The "triangular merger" leaves the shareholders of the target corporation in the same position as in the "two corporation" direct merger of the target corporation and acquiring parent corporation, but with the assets of the target corporation transferred to a subsidiary of the acquiring corporation. The same result occurs under § 368(a)(2)(C), which permits the acquiring corporation to transfer the target corporation's assets to a subsidiary after the merger. In effect, all of the subparagraphs are designed to qualify as tax-free the differing merger mechanics utilized to obtain the same end result. However, the statutory development has not been an orderly one and as outlined above, there are different technical requirements to be satisfied depending on the route chosen to reach the end result. These technical differences are of such a magnitude—for example the requirement in § 368(a)(2)(E) that the acquiring corporation use its voting stock as consideration as opposed to the allowance of the use of nonvoting stock in a § 368(a)(2)(D) transaction—that it is often more useful to think of § 368(a)(2)(D) and (E) transactions as representing two separate and independent forms of corporate reorganization.

Type (D) Reorganization: Transfer of Assets for Stock. The transfer of some or all of a corporation's assets to a newly created or existing corporation followed by the distribution of the stock of the transferee corporation to the shareholders of the transferor corporation is a type (D) reorganization if, the stock distribution meets the requirements of § 354, § 355, or § 356. Thus, for example, if X corporation transfers some or all of its assets to a new or existing Y corporation followed by a distribution of a controlling amount of the Y corporation stock to the X corporation shareholders in a distribution that qualifies under §§ 354, 355, or 356, the asset transfer is a type (D) reorganization. The requirements for a type (D) reorganization differ significantly depending on whether the distribution to the shareholders of the transferor corporation qualifies for nonrecognition under § 354 and/or § 356, on the one hand, or § 355 and/or § 356, on the other hand. For the distribution to the shareholders to qualify under § 354, the transferor corporation (X) must transfer "substantially all" of its assets to the transferee (Y) and liquidate (I.R.C. § 354(b)(1)). Neither of these requirements is a prerequisite for the stock distribution to the shareholders to qualify under § 355 (discussed in Chapter 14). Furthermore, if the transferor corporation (X) transfers all of its assets and liquidates, so that the stock distribution to the shareholders might qualify under § 354, the transferor need not distribute a controlling amount of stock of the transferee corporation in the liquidation; rather all that is required is that the shareholders of the transferor corporation (X) control the transferee corporation (Y) after the transaction. Further, for a transaction to qualify as a type (D) reorganization via § 354, under § 368(a)(h), through a cross reference to § 304(c), the control requirement is met if at least 50 percent of the combined voting power or 50 percent of the total value of shares of stock are distributed to the shareholders of the transferor. If, however, the transferor corporation (X) has transferred less than substantially all of its assets to the transferee corporation (Y), whether or not the transferor corporation (X) liquidates, for the asset transfer to constitute a type (D) reorganization and the distribution to the shareholders to qualify under § 355, the transferor corporation (X) must distribute a controlling amount of stock of the transferee corporation (Y), as defined by the normal rule in § 368(c)—80 percent of combined voting power and 80 percent of each other class of stock. As a result of these varying requirements, a wide variety of transactions constitute type (D) reorganizations.

For example, if X Corporation, the stock of which was owned equally by A and B, transferred all of its assets to Y Corporation, in which A, B, and C each owned 10 shares, in exchange for 30 shares of voting stock, which X Corporation distributed equally between A and B in a liquidating distribution qualifying under § 354, the transaction is a type (D) reorganization. In this, case, after the reorganization, Y Corporation's shares are owned as follows: A owns 25, B owns 25, and C owns 10. Alternatively, if Y Corporation, the stock of which was owned equally by D and E, transferred all of its assets to Z Corporation, all 50 of the shares of which were owned by F in exchange for 50 shares of voting stock, which Y Corporation distributed to D and E in a liquidating distribution qualifying under § 354, the transaction also is a type (D) reorganization. In this case, after the reorganization, Z Corporation's shares are owned as follows: A, 25, B, 25, and C 50. In both instances the reorganization is a type of acquisitive reorganization.

A type (D) reorganization also can be found in transactions in which there is little or no change in beneficial ownership. For example, if D and E equally own all of each of V Corporation and W Corporation, and V Corporation transfers all of its assets to W Corporation, following which V Corporation liquidates, the transaction is a type (D) reorganization.

Finally, a type (D) reorganization can be the first step in dividing a corporate enterprise into two separate corporations by a distribution of stock of the subsidiary to the parent's shareholders in a transaction subject to § 355. This aspect of type (D) reorganizations is discussed in Chapter 14.

Type (G) Reorganization: Bankruptcy Reorganization. A transfer of the assets of a corporation involved in a bankruptcy reorganization, or a receivership, foreclosure, or similar judicial proceeding in a federal or state court is a tax-free reorganization under § 368(a)(1)(G) if the stock or securities received from the insolvent corporation are distributed pursuant to a plan of reorganization in a transaction that qualifies under §§ 354, 355 or 356. Section 368(a)(1)(G) applies only to judicially supervised insolvency proceedings. Thus a nonjudicial reorganization of an insolvent corporation must qualify under one of the other provisions of § 368 in order to achieve reorganization status. But, where a transaction qualifies both as a type (G) and, as a result of its form, as another type of reorganization, for example a type (C), it will be qualified as a type (G). I.R.C. § 368(a)(3)(C).

Subparagraphs (A), (B), (C), (D), and (G) of § 368(a)(1), together with subparagraphs (D) and (E) of § 368(a)(2), cover various methods by which several corporations may be combined into one ownership, e.g., a national chain store swallowing a locally owned store (obtaining its assets directly under (C), or obtaining its stock under (B) and then liquidating it or keeping it alive as a subsidiary, or pursuing a statutory merger under (A)), so that the owners of the grocery are really "selling" their business for stock. The types (A), (C), (D), and (G) reorganizations, and the forward triangular merger under § 368(a)(2)(D) are analogous to asset acquisitions, while the type (B) reorganization and the reverse merger under § 368(a)(2)(E) are analogous to a stock acquisition. While the various statutorily defined reorganizations overlap to a considerable extent, there are differences among them that can influence the choice of the particular reorganization route to be utilized and that may present traps to disqualify a reorganization that fails the proper form.

2.   *Corporate Transferors and Transferees: Nonrecognition and Basis*

Section 368 does not govern the tax consequences of a reorganization; it merely defines a reorganization. The operative provisions providing nonrecognition and the attendant basis consequences appear in other sections of the Code. Section 361(a) provides for nonrecognition of gain or loss to the corporation transferring its assets, the target corporation, in the situations constituting reorganizations under § 368(a). The target corporation does not recognize gain or loss with respect to the assets transferred by it in type (A) and (C) reorganizations.[4] Section 361(a) is applicable only if the exchange is solely for stock or securities. Qualification as an (A) reorganization does not guarantee complete nonrecognition under § 361(a) since property other than stock or securities may form part of the consideration under the merger or consolidation (as long as enough stock is present). If the reorganization qualifies as a type (C) reorganization, however, this condition usually is satisfied because in most cases only voting stock will be involved. An assumption of liabilities does not violate either the "solely for voting stock" or "solely for stock or securities" requirements under the express provisions of §§ 368(a)(1)(C) and 357(a). However, because in a type (C) reorganization a limited amount of property other than voting stock may pass from the acquiring corporation to the target corporation under § 368(a)(2)(B), qualification as a type (C) reorganization does not automatically guarantee compliance with § 361(a).

If money, property, or obligations not qualifying as stock, or securities (collectively boot) is received by the target corporation, § 361(a) does not apply and § 361(b) and (c) determine the consequences to the target corporation.[5] Under § 361(b), no gain is recognized by the target corporation as a result of the receipt of the boot if the boot is transferred to its shareholders or creditors pursuant to the plan of reorganization. In a type (A) reorganization such transfer takes place automatically under the state law merger statute. In a type (C) reorganization, the requirement in § 368(a)(2)(G) that the target corporation be liquidated generally will insure the required

---

[4]   A merger under § 368(a)(1)(A) is regarded as involving such a transfer of property. See Rev.Rul. 69–6, 1969–1 C.B. 104.

[5]   Technically speaking, § 361(c)(2) permits the distribution of stock, rights to acquire stock, or "obligations" of "another corporation which is a party to the reorganization." The scope of the term "obligations" presumably is broader than the term "securities."

distribution. If the boot is distributed, the target corporation recognizes no gain on receipt of the boot, but under § 361(c), it recognizes gain (but not loss) upon the distribution of the boot if at the time of the distribution the boot property has a fair market value in excess of basis.

Section 358 prescribes the basis that the target corporation takes in the stock, securities, and boot received in the exchange in type (A), (C) and (G) reorganizations. Under § 358 the basis of property allowed to be received without recognition of gain or loss is the same as the basis of the property transferred, increased by gain recognized and decreased by the amount of any cash and the fair market value of other property. Because the target corporation disappears in a type (A) reorganization, and must be liquidated in a type (C) reorganization, this basis is seldom of any consequence.

Section 362(b) prescribes the basis for property received by the acquiring corporation in type (A), including § 368(a)(2)(D) and (E) triangular reorganizations, type (C), and type (D) reorganizations. Both the acquiring and target corporations end up with the original basis of the target corporation for the assets (aside from adjustments where boot is involved), so that possibilities of two gains or two losses exist. While § 362(b), transferring the target corporation's basis in its property to the acquiring corporation, adds to that basis any gain recognized to the target corporation on the transfer, as indicated above, the reorganization provisions allow little room for gain to be recognized to the target corporation. By virtue of the second clause of its second sentence, § 362(b) also applies to carry over to the acquiring corporation the basis of the target shareholders in the stock of the target corporation acquired in a type (B) reorganization. If a reorganization does not exist, then the general rule of "cost" applies to fix the basis for the acquiring corporation. Treas.Reg. § 1.1032–1(d).

3. Shareholders and Security Holders: Extent of Nonrecognition and Basis

Sections 354 and 356 control taxation of the shareholders in acquisitive reorganization transactions. Section 358(a) prescribes exchanged basis rules for the shareholders in § 354 and § 356 exchanges.

In type (A), including § 368(a)(2)(D) and (E) triangular reorganizations, type (B), type (C), and type (D) reorganizations, the shareholders of the target corporation are exchanging their target corporation stock for stock of the acquiring corporation. In type (A) and type (B) reorganizations, the stock exchange is made between the target corporation's shareholders and the acquiring corporation; in type (C) and Type (D) reorganizations, the stock exchange is made upon the liquidation of the target corporation. The acquiring and target corporations are both parties to the reorganization under § 368(b). In type (A), type (C), and type (D) reorganizations, the target corporation's shareholders also may receive securities of the acquiring corporation (although the receipt of securities in a type (C) reorganization is limited by § 368(a)(2)(B)). These exchanges are covered by § 354 and generally any gain or loss realized by the shareholders will not be recognized.

Section 354(a) applies only to an exchange *solely* for stock or securities, so that the presence of boot prevents its application. Section

356(a)(1) operates to provide partial nonrecognition; any realized gain is recognized but only to the extent of the boot. Loss may not be recognized. Thus, if the target corporation transfers its assets to the acquiring corporation for stock of the acquiring corporation and cash in a transaction that qualifies as a type (C) reorganization by virtue of § 368(a)(2)(B), pursuant to § 361(b), the target corporation avoids recognition of gain by distributing the cash. This distribution, however, constitutes boot to the distributee shareholders. When the target corporation liquidates, as is required to qualify the transaction as a (C) reorganization, the accompanying exchange by the shareholders of their target corporation stock for the acquiring corporation stock is not accorded complete nonrecognition under § 354(a). Section 356(a)(1) operates to provide partial nonrecognition; any realized gain is recognized but only to the extent of the boot. Loss may not be recognized.

Determination of the gain that must be recognized under the rule of § 356(a)(1) is illustrated as follows. Suppose that in a type (A) reorganization (statutory merger) individual A, a shareholder of the target corporation, surrendered shares of stock of the target corporation having a basis to A of $100 in exchange for $40 of cash and shares of the acquiring corporation having a fair market value of $110. A realizes a gain of $50, but only $40, an amount equal to the cash boot, must be recognized. Under § 358(a), A's basis in the acquiring corporation stock would be $100, thus accounting for the $10 of realized but unrecognized gain. If A's basis for the target corporation stock were $120, then A would realize a gain of only $30, all of which would be recognized. The receipt of the other $10 of cash "tax-free" would be taken into account by reducing the basis of the acquiring corporation stock received in the exchange from $120 to $110 pursuant to § 358(a)(1)(A).

In all of these situations, the transfer of boot to shareholders of the target corporation constitutes a distribution by a corporation to its shareholders. Section 356(a)(2) provides generally that if the distribution of boot pursuant to the plan of reorganization has the *effect of the distribution of a dividend*, the amount of the gain shall be taxed as a dividend and not as part of the exchange transaction. This provision is necessary as a safeguard to insure that distributions that in substance are dividends rather than additional consideration for the exchange of stock will be appropriately taxed. The resemblance to § 302 is apparent, but there are some differences. The dividend rule is considered at page 601.

An exchange of securities other than stock gives rise to boot under § 354(a)(2) if the corporation distributes securities with a principal amount in excess of the securities received in return. In such a case the amount of the boot as determined under § 356(d) is the fair market value of the excess principal amount, which, due to the operation of the OID rules, in most cases equals the excess principal amount.[6]

Section 357(a) does not apply to § 356(a), so that if any liabilities of the shareholders of the target corporation are assumed by the acquiring corporation, the liabilities are boot. If the initial corporate transaction

---

[6] Note that application of the original issue discount rules can produce a principal amount that differs from the face amount of the bond.

involves a situation that will qualify as a reorganization only if the exchange is solely for voting stock, such as a type (B) reorganization, then the presence of boot will prevent a reorganization and §§ 354(a) and 356 will not be applicable at all.

If §§ 354 and 356 do not apply, then the distributions are considered under §§ 301, 302 and 331. Sections 354 and 356 thus operate as exceptions to these other provisions respecting corporate distributions and exchanges, though the other sections do not contain any explicit references to the reorganization exceptions.

DETAILED ANALYSIS

1.   THE DEFINITION OF "STATUTORY MERGER"

1.1. *Mergers Involving a Disregarded Entity*

Treas.Reg. § 1.368–2(b)(1) provides that a statutory merger or consolidation under § 368(a)(1)(A) is limited to transactions pursuant to a statute (whether domestic or foreign) that effects the merger or consolidation and that results in one corporation that is not a disregarded entity,[7] and all of its related disregarded entities (defined as a "combining unit"), acquiring the assets and liabilities of each member of another combining unit. Subject to very limited exceptions, each member of the acquired combining unit must simultaneously cease its separate legal existence for all purposes.[8] The regulations describe the acquiring and target corporations as "combining units" in order to provide that a merger of a target corporation into a disregarded entity that is owned by a corporation will be treated as a statutory merger of the target corporation into the corporation owning the acquiring disregarded entity. The transactions that most commonly will qualify as type (A) mergers under Treas.Reg. § 1.368–2(b)(1) are: (1) a merger of a corporation (which might or might not own one or more limited liability companies that are disregarded entities, or, if the target corporation is an S corporation, one or more qualified Subchapter S subsidiaries (QSub) under § 1361(b)) into a limited liability company (LLC) that is wholly owned by another corporation and which is a disregarded entity, and (2) mergers of a corporation (which might or might not own any disregarded entity) into a QSub owned by an S corporation. The preamble to the proposed regulations indicated that this result is consistent with the theory that all of the assets of a disregarded entity are treated as directly owned by the corporate owner of the disregarded entity. See Reg.–126485–01, Statutory Mergers and Consolidations, 66 F.R. 57400 (Nov. 15, 2001). Otherwise, as provided by Treas.Reg. § 1.368–2(b)(1)(iii), a state law merger involving an entity that is disregarded for federal tax purposes under Treas.Reg. § 301.7701–3(b)(ii), such as a single member LLC that has not elected to be taxed as a corporation, cannot qualify as a merger under § 368(a)(1)(A). However, mergers involving disregarded entities that do not qualify as a type (A)

---

[7]   Disregarded entities, including single member limited liability companies that have not elected to be treated as a corporation and qualified subchapter S subsidiaries (QSubs), are generally ignored as entities separate from their owners and their assets are treated as held directly by their owners. See pages 23, 409.

[8]   The requirements that all of the assets and liabilities of the target entity be acquired and that the acquired entity cease to exist prevent divisive transactions, which are governed by § 355, discussed in Chapter 14, from qualifying for nonrecognition as a statutory merger.

reorganization under Treas.Reg. § 1.368–2(b)(1) might qualify as a reorganization under another subsection of § 368, such as § 368(a)(1)(C), dealing with voting-stock-for-asset reorganizations, if all the applicable requirements are met. Likewise, a merger of a disregarded entity into an acquiring corporation might qualify as a reorganization under § 368(a)(1)(D) or (F) if all relevant requirements are met. But the merger of a disregarded entity owned by one corporation into another corporation, or into a disregarded entity owned by another corporation, generally cannot qualify as a reorganization under § 368; rather, such a transaction must be tested under § 355, discussed in Chapter 14, under which it rarely will qualify for nonrecognition.

1.2. *Merger of Controlled Subsidiary into Parent*

If an 80 percent controlled subsidiary is merged into its parent, Treas.Reg. § 1.332–2(d) and (e) provide that the transaction will be taxed as if the subsidiary had been liquidated. Prop.Reg. § 1.332–2(b) (2005) would provide that § 332 applies only to those cases in which the recipient corporation receives at least partial payment for each class of stock that it owns in the liquidating corporation. The proposed regulations note, however, that even though a liquidation of a subsidiary might not qualify under § 332, the transaction nevertheless might qualify as a tax-free reorganization under § 368. Prop.Reg. § 1.332–2(e), Ex. 2 (2005). See page 348.

In Rev.Rul. 69–617, 1969–2 C.B. 57, a parent corporation owned more than 80 percent of the stock of its subsidiary. In order to operate its subsidiary as a wholly-owned subsidiary, it merged the subsidiary into itself and the minority shareholders of the subsidiary received the parent's stock. The parent then transferred all of the assets acquired from the subsidiary to a newly created wholly-owned subsidiary. The ruling held that the transaction constituted an (A) reorganization; § 332 was not applicable because the immediate transfer of the subsidiary's assets to the newly created subsidiary meant that there was not a complete liquidation of the former subsidiary. Thus the minority shareholders of the former subsidiary received tax-free reorganization treatment, whereas under liquidation treatment, gain would have resulted to them.

In Kass v. Commissioner, 60 T.C. 218 (1973), aff'd by order, 491 F.2d 749 (3d Cir.1974), the IRS conceded that "theoretically" it would be possible for the same transaction to be treated as a liquidation under § 332 and § 334(b) at the corporate level and as a reorganization from the point of view of minority shareholders. While no case has expressly so held, such treatment was implicit in King Enterprises, Inc. v. United States, 418 F.2d 511 (Ct.Cl.1969), page 580. Treas.Reg. § 1.332–2(d) also strongly infers that a statutory merger treated as a liquidation under § 332 as far as the corporations are concerned can be a reorganization under § 368 as far as minority shareholders are concerned. In certain cases, however, *Kass* will require that minority shareholders of the subsidiary who receive parent corporation stock in the merger recognize gain or loss on the exchange of their shares. See page 563.

2. "TRANSFER OF NET VALUE" REQUIREMENT

Proposed amendments to Treas.Reg. § 1.368–1(b)(1) would add a requirement that there be "an exchange of net value" as a prerequisite for finding a reorganization under § 368(a)(1)(A)–(D), including triangular mergers under § 368(a)(2)(D) and (E). Prop.Reg. § 1.368–1(b)(1) (2005). Prop.Reg. § 1.368–1(f) (2005) would provide separate rules for determining whether there has been "an exchange of net value" in asset acquisitions and stock acquisitions, respectively. For an asset acquisition to qualify under § 368(a)(1)(A), (C), (D) or § 368(a)(2)(D):, (1) the value of the transferred assets of the target corporation must exceed the sum of the liabilities of the target corporation assumed by the acquiring corporation plus the amount of boot (cash and property other than stock) paid by the acquiring corporation, and (2) immediately after the acquisition the fair market value of the assets of the acquiring corporation must exceed its liabilities. Prop.Reg. § 1.368–1(f)(2) (2005). This rule would assure that a target corporation transfers property in exchange for stock and that the stock is not worthless. For a stock acquisition to qualify under § 368(a)(1)(B) or § 368(a)(2)(E), the rule for computing whether net value has been surrendered would be modified to reflect the fact that the target corporation remains in existence, but the rule assuring that the stock received is not worthless would remain the same. Under Prop.Reg. § 1.368–1(f)(3) (2005), for a stock acquisition (under either § 368(a)(1)(B) or § 368(a)(2)(E)) to qualify, the fair market value of the target corporation's assets would be required to exceed the sum of the target corporation's liabilities immediately prior to the exchange plus the amount of any boot (other than nonqualified preferred stock within the meaning of section 351(g)) received by the target corporation's shareholders in the exchange. Although the proposed regulations do not define the term "liability," according to the preamble, the Treasury Department intends the term to be interpreted broadly. The preamble states, "for purposes of the proposed regulations, a liability should include any obligation of a taxpayer, whether the obligation is debt for federal income tax purposes or whether the obligation is taken into account for the purpose of any other Code section. Generally, an obligation is something that reduces the net worth of the obligor." REG–163314–03, Transactions Involving the Transfer of Net Value, 70 F.R. 11903 (March 10, 2005). The proposed regulations will apply to transactions entered into after the publication date of final regulations.

B. THE CONTINUITY OF SHAREHOLDER INTEREST REQUIREMENT

(1) QUALITATIVE AND QUANTITATIVE ASPECTS

REGULATIONS: Sections 1.368–1(a), (b), (e) (excluding (e)(2)(iv), Exs. 4–6, 8–12),–2(a).

Le Tulle v. Scofield

Supreme Court of the United States, 1940.
308 U.S. 415.

■ MR. JUSTICE ROBERTS delivered the opinion of the court.

* * *

The Gulf Coast Irrigation Company was the owner of irrigation properties. Petitioner was its sole stockholder. He personally owned certain lands and other irrigation properties. November 4, 1931, the

Irrigation Company, the Gulf Coast Water Company, and the petitioner, entered into an agreement which recited that the petitioner owned all of the stock of the Irrigation Company; described the company's properties, and stated that, prior to conveyance to be made pursuant to the contract, the Irrigation Company would be the owner of certain other lands and irrigation properties. These other lands and properties were those which the petitioner individually owned. The contract called for a conveyance of all the properties owned, and to be owned, by the Irrigation Company for $50,000 in cash and $750,000 in bonds of the Water Company, payable serially over the period January 1, 1933, to January 1, 1944. The petitioner joined in this agreement as a guarantor of the title of the Irrigation Company and for the purpose of covenanting that he would not personally enter into the irrigation business within a fixed area during a specified period after the execution of the contract. Three days later, at a special meeting of stockholders of the Irrigation Company, the proposed reorganization was approved, the minutes stating that the taxpayer, "desiring also to reorganize his interest in the properties," had consented to be a party to the reorganization. The capital stock of the Irrigation Company was increased and thereupon the taxpayer subscribed for the new stock and paid for it by conveyance of his individual properties.

The contract between the two corporations was carried out November 18, with the result that the Water Company became owner of all the properties then owned by the Irrigation Company including the property theretofore owned by the petitioner individually. Subsequently all of its assets, including the bonds received from the Water Company, were distributed to the petitioner. The company was then dissolved. The petitioner and his wife filed a tax return * * * in which they reported no gain as a result of the receipt of the liquidating dividend from the Irrigation Company. The latter reported no gain for the taxable year in virtue of its receipt of bonds and cash from the Water Company. The Commissioner of Internal Revenue assessed additional taxes against the * * * taxpayers, by reason of the receipt of the liquidating dividend, and against the petitioner as transferee of the Irrigation Company's assets in virtue of the gain realized by the company on the sale of its property. The tax was paid and claims for refund were filed. * * * [The taxpayer] alleged that the transaction constituted a tax-exempt reorganization as defined by the Revenue Act. The * * * causes were * * * tried by the District Court without a jury. The respondent's contention that the transaction amounted merely to a sale of assets by the petitioner and the Irrigation Company and did not fall within the statutory definition of a tax-free reorganization was overruled by the District Court and judgment was entered for the petitioner.

* * *

The Circuit Court of Appeals concluded that, as the Water Company acquired substantially all the properties of the Irrigation Company, there was a merger of the latter within the literal language of the statute, but held that, in the light of the construction this Court has put upon the statute, the transaction would not be a reorganization unless the transferor retained a definite and substantial interest in the affairs of the transferee. It thought this requirement was satisfied by

CHAPTER 12 · TAX-FREE ACQUISITIVE REORGANIZATIONS · 541

the taking of the bonds of the Water Company, and, therefore, agreed with the District Court that a reorganization had been consummated. * * *

[Ed.: The Circuit Court then reversed the District Court as to part of the petitioner's tax liability on grounds that had not been raised by the parties. The Circuit Court concluded that the petitioner was taxable on the gain attributable to the transfer of his individually owned assets to the Irrigation Company for transfer to the Water Company. The petitioner sought to overturn the Circuit Court decision on this ground. The Commissioner, having won in the Circuit Court, did not seek certiorari.]

We find it unnecessary to consider petitioner's contention that the Circuit Court of Appeals erred in deciding the case on a ground not raised by the pleadings, not before the trial court, not suggested or argued in the Circuit Court of Appeals, and one as to which the petitioner had never had the opportunity to present his evidence, since we are of opinion that the transaction did not amount to a reorganization and that, therefore, the petitioner cannot complain, as the judgment must be affirmed on the ground that no tax-free reorganization was effected within the meaning of the statute.

Section 112(i) provides, so far as material: "(1) The term 'reorganization' means (A) a merger or consolidation (including the acquisition by one corporation of at least a majority of the voting stock and at least a majority of the total number of shares of all other classes of stock of another corporation, or substantially all the properties of another corporation) * * * "

As the court below properly stated, the section is not to be read literally, as denominating the transfer of all the assets of one company for what amounts to a cash consideration given by the other a reorganization. We have held that where the consideration consists of cash and short term notes the transfer does not amount to a reorganization within the true meaning of the statute, but is a sale upon which gain or loss must be reckoned.[3] We have said that the statute was not satisfied unless the transferor retained a substantial stake in the enterprise and such a stake was thought to be retained where a large proportion of the consideration was in common stock of the transferee,[4] or where the transferor took cash and the entire issue of preferred stock of the transferee corporation.[5] And, where the consideration is represented by a substantial proportion of stock, and the balance in bonds, the total consideration received is exempt from tax under § 112(b)(4) and 112(g).[6]

In applying our decision in the Pinellas case the courts have generally held that receipt of long term bonds as distinguished from short term notes constitutes the retention of an interest in the

---

[3]   Pinellas Ice & Cold Storage Co. v. Commissioner, 287 U.S. 462.

[4]   Helvering v. Minnesota Tea Co., 296 U.S. 378.

[5]   Nelson Co. v. Helvering, 296 U.S. 374.

[6]   45 Stat. 816, 818. See Helvering v. Watts, 296 U.S. 387.

purchasing corporation. There has naturally been some difficulty in classifying the securities involved in various cases.[7]

We are of opinion that the term of the obligations is not material. Where the consideration is wholly in the transferee's bonds, or part cash and part such bonds, we think it cannot be said that the transferor retains any proprietary interest in the enterprise. On the contrary, he becomes a creditor of the transferee; and we do not think that the fact referred to by the Circuit Court of Appeals, that the bonds were secured solely by the assets transferred and that, upon default, the bondholder would retake only the property sold, changes his status from that of a creditor to one having a proprietary stake, within the purview of the statute.

We conclude that the Circuit Court of Appeals was in error in holding that, as respects any of the property transferred to the Water Company, the transaction was other than a sale or exchange upon which gain or loss must be reckoned in accordance with the provisions of the revenue act dealing with the recognition of gain or loss upon a sale or exchange.

Had the respondent sought and been granted certiorari the petitioner's tax liability would, in the view we have expressed, be substantially increased over the amount found due by the Circuit Court of Appeals. Since the respondent has not drawn into question so much of the judgment as exempts from taxation gain to the irrigation Company arising from transfer of its assets owned by it on and prior to November 4, 1931, and the part of the liquidating dividend attributable thereto, we cannot afford him relief from that portion of the judgment which was adverse to him.

* * *

The judgment of the Circuit Court of Appeals is affirmed * * *.

John A. Nelson Co. v. Helvering

Supreme Court of the United States, 1935.
296 U.S. 374.

MR. JUSTICE MCREYNOLDS delivered the opinion of the Court.

The petitioner contests a deficiency income assessment made on account of alleged gains during 1926. It claims that the transaction out of which the assessment arose was reorganization within the statute. Section 203, Revenue Act, 1926 * * * is relied upon.

In 1926, under an agreement with petitioner, the Elliott-Fisher Corporation organized a new corporation with 12,500 shares non-voting preferred stock and 30,000 shares of common stock. It purchased the latter for $2,000,000 cash. This new corporation then acquired substantially all of petitioner's property, except $100,000, in return for $2,000,000 cash and the entire issue of preferred stock. Part of this cash was used to retire petitioner's own preferred shares, and the remainder

---

[7]   Worcester Salt Co. v. Commissioner, 75 F.2d 251; Lilienthal v. Commissioner, 80 F.2d 411, 413; Burnham v. Commissioner, 86 F.2d 776; Commissioner v. Kitselman, 89 F.2d 458; Commissioner v. Freund, 98 F.2d 201; * * * L. & E. Stirn, Inc. v. Commissioner, 107 F.2d 390.

and the preferred stock of the new company went to its stockholders. It retained its franchise and $100,000, and continued to be liable for certain obligations. The preferred stock so distributed, except in case of default, had no voice in the control of the issuing corporation.

The Commissioner, Board of Tax Appeals, and the court all concluded there was no reorganization. This, we think, was error.

The court below thought the facts showed "that the transaction essentially constituted a sale of the greater part of petitioner's assets for cash and the preferred stock in the new corporation, leaving the Elliott-Fisher Company in entire control of the new corporation by virtue of its ownership of the common stock."

"The controlling facts leading to this conclusion are that petitioner continued its corporate existence and its franchise and retained a portion of its assets; that it acquired no controlling interest in the corporation to which it delivered the greater portion of its assets; that there was no continuity of interest from the old corporation to the new; that the control of the property conveyed passed to a stranger, in the management of which petitioner retained no voice.

"It follows that the transaction was not part of a strict merger or consolidation or part of something that partakes of the nature of a merger or consolidation and has a real semblance to a merger or consolidation involving a continuance of essentially the same interests through a new modified corporate structure. Mere acquisition by one corporation of a majority of the stock or all the assets of another corporation does not of itself constitute a reorganization, where such acquisition takes the form of a purchase and sale and does not result in or bear some material resemblance to a merger or consolidation."

True, the mere acquisition of the assets of one corporation by another does not amount to reorganization within the statutory definition. Pinellas, Ice & Cold Storage Co. v. Commissioner of Internal Revenue, 287 U.S. 462 * * * so affirmed. But where, as here, the seller acquires a definite and substantial interest in the affairs of the purchasing corporation, a wholly different situation arises. The owner of preferred stock is not without substantial interest in the affairs of the issuing corporation, although denied voting rights. The statute does not require participation in the management of the purchaser; nor does it demand that the conveying corporation be dissolved. A controlling interest in the transferee corporation is not made a requisite by section 203(h)(1)(A). * * *

The judgment below must be reversed.

DETAILED ANALYSIS

1.   QUALITATIVE ASPECTS

1.1. *Generally*

Le Tulle v. Scofield is one of a long line of Supreme Court decisions developing the "continuity of interest" doctrine. The first pronouncement by the Supreme Court regarding the requisite consideration in a reorganization was in Pinellas Ice & Cold Storage Co. v. Commissioner, 287 U.S. 462 (1933). In that case, on December 15, 1926, the taxpayer corporation transferred all of its assets to the acquiring corporation in consideration of $400,000 cash (which was used to pay off debts) and promissory notes for $500,000, due on January 31, 1927, $250,000, due on March 1, 1927, and $250,000, due on April 1, 1927. As the notes were paid, the taxpayer distributed the proceeds to its shareholders in liquidation.

The IRS asserted that the taxpayer was required to recognize a gain on the sale of its assets, but the taxpayer contended that the transaction was a "reorganization" as defined in the Revenue Act of 1926, and that, accordingly, the predecessor of § 361 provided for nonrecognition of the gain. Notwithstanding that the statutory provision imposed no requirements or limits on the nature of the consideration required to qualify the transaction as a reorganization, the Court rejected the taxpayer's argument: "[T]he mere purchase for money of the assets of one company by another is beyond the evident purpose of the provision, and has no real semblance to a merger or consolidation. Certainly, we think that to be within the exemption the seller must acquire an interest in the affairs of the purchasing company more definite than that incident to ownership of its short-term purchase-money notes."

In Helvering v. Minnesota Tea Co., 296 U.S. 378 (1935), a transfer of assets for 18,000 shares of common worth approximately $540,000, amounting to 7 ½ percent of the transferee's outstanding stock, and cash of $426,842.52 was found to be a reorganization. The IRS argued that the shareholders of the target corporation had not acquired a sufficiently large enough percentage interest in the acquiring corporation for the transaction to qualify. After referring to the *Pinellas* statement that an "interest" must be acquired in the transferee, the Court said:

> And we now add that this interest must be definite and material; it must represent a substantial part of the value of the thing transferred. This much is necessary in order that the result accomplished may genuinely partake of the nature of merger or consolidation. * * *

> The transaction here was no sale, but partook of the nature of a reorganization, in that the seller acquired a definite and substantial interest in the purchaser.

> True it is that the relationship of the taxpayer to the assets conveyed was substantially changed, but this is not inhibited by the statute. Also, a large part of the consideration was cash. This, we think, is permissible so long as the taxpayer received an interest in the affairs of the transferee which represented a material part of the value of the transferred assets.

In its most recent pronouncement in this area, Paulsen v. Commissioner, 469 U.S. 131 (1985), the Supreme Court held that an exchange of stock in a savings and loan association for certificates of deposit in a mutual savings and loan (where the certificates of deposit represented ownership interests in the mutual savings and loan association) lacked the requisite continuity of interest. The court concluded that the debt aspects of the certificates of deposit, which permitted withdrawal of cash after one year, outweighed their equity characteristics and that the certificates of deposit were cash equivalents.[9] The Court

---

[9]   In Estate of Silverman v. Commissioner, 98 T.C. 54 (1992), the taxpayers exchanged stock in a state chartered savings and loan association for certificates of deposit in the

acknowledged that when two mutual associations merge, an exchange of interests in deposits in one mutual savings for an equivalent interest in the other, notwithstanding the slight equity interest reflected in the shares, will be treated as a reorganization because the shares received are essentially equivalent to the shares given up as long as the cash value of the shares on each side of the exchange is the same. Rev.Rul. 78–286, 1978–2 C.B. 145, reaches this result.

As a result of these opinions, an ownership interest cannot be turned into a creditor interest, though long-term in nature, and still have the exchange qualify as a reorganization. *A fortiori*, the ownership interest cannot be turned into cash or its equivalent in the form of notes or other evidences of a short-lived creditor status. See *Le Tulle v. Scofield*, supra. Thus, an equity interest in the transferee has to be obtained by the transferor of the property. The equity interest obtained, moreover, has to be substantial, so that a non-equity interest that is too extensive might disqualify the exchange. However, the nature of the equity interest can be either that of a common stockholder or that of a preferred stockholder, whether voting or non-voting. Obviously, the line drawn between preferred stock and bonds may in some instances come very close to one of form since the participation in earnings and assets and effective control can be drafted nearly alike for both types of instruments. For example, in Roebling v. Commissioner, 143 F.2d 810 (3d Cir.1944), the target corporation had leased all its properties to the acquiring corporation for 900 years. As a result of a merger, the former shareholders of the target corporation received 100 year bonds of the acquiring corporation that paid annual interest equal to the amount previously paid as rent. The court rejected the taxpayer's argument that the former shareholders' interests after the merger were substantially equivalent to their interests before the merger and applied *Le Tulle v. Scofield* to find that there was not a reorganization.

1.2. *Nonqualified Preferred Stock*

Section 356(d) treats certain "nonqualified preferred stock" as property other than stock, requiring recognition of gain under § 356(a) if such nonqualified preferred stock is received in a reorganization other than in exchange for nonqualified preferred stock of the target corporation. See page 609. Nonqualified preferred stock is defined in § 351(g)(2), page 75. Preferred stock is stock that is limited and preferred as to dividends and which does not participate in corporate growth. I.R.C. § 351(g)(3)(A). Preferred stock is "nonqualified" only if within 20 years after issue, the issuer or a related person (1) may be required by the holder to redeem the stock, (2) is required to redeem the stock, or (3) has a right to redeem the stock, and it is more likely than not that the right to redeem will be exercised. I.R.C. § 351(g)(2). Preferred stock also is nonqualified preferred stock if the dividend rate is determined in whole or in part by reference to interest rates, commodity prices, or similar indices. However, unless and "[u]ntil regulations are issued, [nonqualified] preferred stock * * * shall

---

acquiring federally chartered mutual savings and loan association. The certificates of deposit could not be withdrawn for six years and were subject to limitations on transfer. After *Paulsen* was decided, the taxpayers filed an amended return reporting their gain on the sale of the stock using the installment sales method under § 453. The Tax Court rejected the IRS's argument that the certificates of deposit were equivalent to cash and allowed the taxpayers to report gain on the installment method.

continue to be treated as stock under other provisions of the Code." Staff of the Joint Committee on Taxation, General Explanation of Tax Legislation Enacted in 1997, 213 (JCS–23–97, Dec. 17, 1997). Thus, such nonqualified preferred stock presumably meets the qualitative requirements for continuity of interest, even though a debt instrument with a much longer maturity does not qualify. Apparently, the continuity of interest doctrine, which found its origins in a type of substance over form analysis, has been transmuted at least partially into a form over substance type analysis.

2.   QUANTITATIVE ASPECTS

2.1. *Generally*

The statutory provisions for type (B) and type (C) reorganizations provide for continuity of interest with requirements that the stock or assets of the target corporation be acquired *solely* for voting stock. There are no specific statutory requirements concerning continuity of interest in an (A) reorganization, although to qualify a reverse triangular merger as a type (A) reorganization though § 368(a)(2)(E) at least eighty percent of the consideration must be in the form of voting stock. The subjective standards developed by the Supreme Court require an exploration of the sufficiency of equity consideration in type (A) statutory mergers, including § 368(a)(2)(D) forward triangular mergers, as well as type (D) reorganizations.

In Southwest Natural Gas Company v. Commissioner, 189 F.2d 332 (5th Cir.1951), continuity of interest was held to be lacking in a statutory merger in a situation in which those shareholders of the transferor (target) corporation who chose to receive some stock in the merger had received about 16 percent of the common stock of the acquiring corporation, but such interest was worth only about $5,500 out of a total consideration of about $660,000 in bonds, cash, assumptions of liabilities, and stock. However, prior to the merger a group that owned 35 percent of the common stock of the target corporation also held 85 percent of the acquiring corporation's common stock and after the merger this group owned 88 percent of the acquiring corporation's stock. Thus, an underlying equity interest in the acquiring corporation actually existed, as a dissent pointed out, though "control" did not exist because 80 percent of the preferred stock was not held by the group.

The opinion in *Southwest Natural Gas* phrased the continuity of interest test as follows:

> Where no precise formula has been expressed for determining whether there has been retention of the requisite interest, it seems clear that the requirement of continuity of interest consistent with the statutory intent is not fulfilled in the absence of a showing: (1) that the transferor corporation or its shareholders retained a substantial proprietary stake in the enterprise represented by a material interest in the affairs of the transferee corporation, and, (2) that such retained interest represents a substantial part of the value of the property transferred.

Taken literally, the first requirement would in general depend on the relative size of the two corporations that are merged. This measure of the *quantitative* aspect was rejected, however, in *Minnesota Tea*, page 544 and never has been a significant factor in either IRS policy or judicial decisions.

The focus instead is primarily on the second factor, the relation between the value of the stock received and the value of the equity interest in the target corporation.

The case law never clearly established a specific minimum percentage of the total consideration that must be received in the form of stock of the acquiring corporation. Note, however, that although the issue before the Supreme Court in John A. Nelson Co. v. Helvering, 296 U.S. 374 (1935), page 542, was whether preferred stock, as opposed to common stock, provided adequate *qualitative* continuity of interest, which the Supreme Court answered affirmatively, finding the continuity of interest requirement to have been satisfied, on the facts only 38.46 percent of the consideration received by the former shareholders of the target corporation was stock of the acquiring corporation. Although the IRS did not argue that the quantitative aspect of the continuity of interest requirement was not met in *John A. Nelson Co.*, the case came to be cited by taxpayers for the proposition that 38.46 percent was adequate quantitative continuity of interest. However, Civic Center Finance Co. v. Kuhl, 83 F.Supp. 251 (E.D.Wis.1948), aff'd per curiam, 177 F.2d 706 (7th Cir.1949), held that participation by 40 percent of the former stockholders was insufficient to provide continuity of interest. See also Kass v. Commissioner, 60 T.C. 218 (1973), aff'd by order, 491 F.2d 749 (3d Cir.1974) (16 percent insufficient); Yoc Heating Corp. v. Commissioner, 61 T.C. 168 (1973) (15 percent insufficient);

In 2005, the Treasury Department promulgated regulations that include an example that sets the administratively sanctioned threshold for adequate quantitative continuity of interest at 40 percent stock consideration. Treas.Reg. § 1.368–1(e)(2)(v), Ex. 1. Conversely, Treas.Reg. § 1.368–1(e)(2)(v), Ex. 2, indicates that stock consideration of 25 percent is insufficient. Note, however, that because of the existence of statutory quantitative continuity of interest requirements for type (B), type (C), and § 368(a)(2)(E) reverse triangular mergers, this 40 percent continuity of interest safe harbor generally applies only to type (A) and § 368(a)(2)(D) forward triangular merger reorganizations. Type (D) reorganizations have unique continuity of interest requirements.

Rev.Rul. 66–224, 1966–2 C.B. 114, held that the continuity of interest requirement is to be applied with reference to the aggregate consideration received by the entire group of the shareholders of the acquired corporation. Thus, for example, if A, B, C, D and E each owns 20 percent of the stock of the target corporation, and the target corporation is merged into the acquiring corporation in consideration of $80,000 worth of the acquiring corporation stock and $120,000 of cash, the transaction will qualify as a type (A) reorganization regardless of how the consideration is distributed among A, B, C, D, and E. Thus A and B could receive only stock while C, D, and E received only cash. The gain attributable to the cash boot that must be recognized by each shareholder, however, will be determined individually. In this regard, note, however, that if a particular shareholder receives only cash (or debt instruments) in exchange for the shareholder's stock, § 356 does not apply to that particular shareholder; rather, § 1001 applies to that shareholder.

2.2. *Date of Valuation*

Treas.Reg. § 1.368–1(e)(2) provides that if the consideration to be provided to the target corporation shareholders is fixed in the binding contract and includes only stock of the issuing corporation and money, the determination of whether the continuity of interest requirement is satisfied is based on the value of the consideration to be exchanged for the proprietary interests in the target corporation as of the end of the last business day before the first date there is a binding contract to effect the potential reorganization. The number of shares of stock of the acquiring corporation that will be exchanged for stock of the target corporation generally is fixed by agreement at a time significantly in advance of the actual closing of the transaction. The regulation is intended to eliminate uncertainty where the target corporation shareholders receive cash (or debt instruments) in addition to acquiring corporation stock and, at the time the transaction is agreed upon, the amount of the boot equals the value of the agreed upon number of shares of the acquiring corporation stock to be received. Otherwise, the transaction might fail to satisfy the continuity of interest requirement if the value of the acquiring corporation's stock declined between the date the parties agreed to the terms of the transaction (the signing date) and the date the transaction closed if the quantitative aspect of the continuity of interest requirement were tested on the closing date rather than the signing date.

Under Treas.Reg. § 1.368–1(e)(2)(iii)(A), a contract provides for fixed consideration if it specifies the number of shares of the acquiring corporation, the amount of money, and the other property (identified by value or by description) that is to be exchanged for the stock of the target corporation. With an Orwellian flourish, Treas.Reg. § 1.368–1(e)(2)(iii)(C)(1) states that "a contract that provides for contingent consideration will be treated as providing for fixed consideration if it would satisfy the requirements of paragraph (e)(2)(iii)(A) of this section without the contingent adjustment provision." Treas.Reg. § 1.368–1(e)(2)(iii)(C)(2) adds that contingent consideration will not be fixed consideration if the adjustments prevent the target shareholders from being subject to the economic benefits and burdens of ownership of the acquiring corporation stock as of the last business day before a binding contract. Thus, adjustments that reflect changes in the value of the stock or assets of the acquiring corporation at a later date will prevent the contract from being treated as providing for fixed consideration. The preamble to the almost identical temporary regulations that preceded the current regulations suggests that the contingent consideration provision allows adjustments to the consideration that do not decrease the ratio of the value of the shares of the acquiring corporation to the value of money or other property delivered to the target shareholders relative to the ratio of the value of the target stock to the value of the money or other property that would be delivered to the target shareholders if none of the contingent consideration were delivered. See T.D. 9316, 72 F.R. 12974 (2007).

Under Treas.Reg. § 1.368–1(e)(2)(iii)(B), if the target corporation's shareholders may elect to receive either stock or money, the contract provides for fixed consideration if the determination of the number of shares of issuing corporation stock to be provided to the target corporation shareholder is based on the value of the issuing corporation stock on the last business day before the first date there is a binding contract. The preamble to the identical temporary regulations indicated that the IRS and Treasury believe that if shareholders have an election to receive stock of the acquiring corporation at an exchange rate based on the value of the acquiring corporation stock on the date of a binding contract, the target shareholders are at risk for the economic benefits and burdens of ownership of the acquiring corporation stock as of the contract date. Thus, the preamble concluded that it is appropriate to value the stock of the acquiring corporation as of the signing date for purposes of testing continuity of interest. Treas.Reg. § 1.368–1(e)(2)(v), Ex. 9, provides an example of the application of the shareholder election.

On January 3 of year 1, P and T sign a binding contract pursuant to which T will be merged with and into P on June 1 of year 1. On January 2 of year 1, the value of the P stock and the T stock is $1 per share. Pursuant to the contract, at the shareholders' election, each share of T's 100 shares will be exchanged for cash of $1, or alternatively, P stock. The contract provides that the determination of the number of shares of P stock to be exchanged for a share of T stock is made using the value of the P stock on the last business day before the first date there is a binding contract (that is, $1 per share). The contract further provides that, in the aggregate, 40 shares of P stock and $60 will be delivered, and contains a proration mechanism in the event that either item of consideration is oversubscribed. On the closing date, the value of the P stock is $.20 per share, and all target shareholders elect to receive cash. Pursuant to the proration provision, each target share is exchanged for $.60 of cash and $.08 of P stock. Pursuant to paragraph (e)(2)(iii)(A) of this section, the contract provides for fixed consideration because it provides for the number of shares of P stock and the amount of money to be exchanged for all the proprietary interests in the target corporation. Furthermore, pursuant to paragraph (e)(2)(iii)(B) of this section, the contract provides for fixed consideration because the number of shares of issuing corporation stock to be provided to the target corporation shareholders is determined using the pre-signing date value of P stock. Accordingly, whether the transaction satisfies the continuity of interest requirement is determined by reference to the value of the P stock on January 2 of year 1. Because, for continuity purposes, the T stock is exchanged for $40 of P stock and $60 of cash, the transaction preserves a substantial part of the value of the proprietary interest in T. Therefore, the transaction satisfies the continuity of interest requirement.

Treas.Reg. § 1.368–1(e)(2)(ii)(A) provides that a binding contract is an instrument enforceable under applicable law. However, the presence of a condition outside of the control of the parties, such as a requirement for regulatory approval, will not prevent an instrument from being treated as a binding contract. Treas.Reg. § 1.368–1(e)(2)(ii)(C) provides rules pursuant to which a tender offer can be considered to be a binding contract, even though it is not enforceable against the offerees, if certain conditions are met. The regulations also provide for modifications of a binding contract. If the contract is modified to change the amount or type of consideration that the target shareholders would receive, the date of the modification becomes a new signing date for purposes of testing for continuity of interest. Treas.Reg. § 1.368–1(e)(2)(ii)(B)(1). However, if in a transaction that provides for adequate continuity of interest, the contract is modified to increase the amount of stock of the acquiring corporation to be delivered to the target shareholders, or to decrease the amount of cash or value of other property, then the modification will not be treated as a modification of the binding contract. Treas.Reg. § 1.368–1(e)(2)(ii)(B)(2). Similarly, in a transaction that does not qualify as a reorganization for failure to meet the continuity of interest requirement, a modification that reduces the number of shares of stock to be received by the target shareholders, or increases the amount of money or value of property, will not be treated as a modification of the binding contract so that the consideration will continue to be valued as of the signing date. Treas.Reg. § 1.368–1(e)(2)(ii)(B)(3).

Treas.Reg. § 1.368–1(e)(2)(iii)(D) provides that stock that is escrowed to secure customary pre-closing covenants and representations and warranties is not treated as contingent consideration, which would render the safe harbor unavailable. However, escrowed consideration that is forfeited is not taken into account in determining whether the continuity of interest requirement has been met. Treas.Reg. § 1.368–1(e)(2)(iv), Ex. 2.

On the same day that the above described rules in Treas.Reg. § 1.368–1(e) were promulgated, the Treasury Department published Prop.Reg. § 1.368–1(e)(2)(vi) (2012), under which application of the signing date principles for determining whether continuity of interest is satisfied would be expanded. The proposed regulations would also permit the use of an average value for issuing corporation stock, in lieu of the value of issuing corporation stock on the closing date, in certain circumstances. An average value could "be used if it is based on issuing corporation stock values occurring after the signing date and before the closing date, and the binding contract utilizes the average price, so computed, in determining the number of shares of each class of stock of the issuing corporation, the amount of money, and the other property to be exchanged for all the proprietary interests in the target corporation, or to be exchanged for each proprietary interest in the target corporation." This rule applies signing date rule "principles," because "the target shareholders become subject to the fortunes of the issuer's stock across the range of dates being averaged."

2.3. *Insolvent Target*

In Helvering v. Alabama Asphaltic Limestone Co., 315 U.S. 179 (1942), the Supreme Court held that a transfer of assets pursuant to which creditors of a bankrupt concern became the controlling stockholders of a new corporation provided the requisite continuity of interest. Although the old continuity of proprietary interest was broken when the creditors took steps to enforce their demands against the insolvent concern, by such action they stepped into the shoes of the stockholders and hence continuity was present on the subsequent exchange. Similarly, in Norman Scott, Inc. v. Commissioner, 48 T.C. 598 (1967), the court held that a statutory merger between the surviving corporation and its insolvent sister corporation qualified as an (A) reorganization; the continuity of interest test was satisfied since the principal shareholder-creditors of the insolvent corporation received stock in the surviving corporation.

Treas.Reg. § 1.368–1(e)(6), promulgated in 2009, deals with the issues raised in cases such as *Alabama Asphaltic Limestone* and *Norman Scott, Inc.* and describes the circumstances in which a corporation's creditors will be treated as holding a proprietary interest in a target corporation immediately before a potential reorganization. A creditor has a proprietary interest only if the target corporation's liabilities exceed the fair market value of its assets immediately prior to the potential reorganization (or the target corporation is in a title 11 or similar case, as defined in § 368(a)(3)). If any creditor receives a proprietary interest in the acquiring corporation, every claim of that class of creditors and every claim of all equal and junior classes of creditors (in addition to the claims of shareholders) is a proprietary interest in the target corporation immediately prior to the potential reorganization. Generally, in applying continuity of interest principles, the value of a creditor's proprietary interest is the fair market value of the creditor's claim. A special rule applies to the most senior class of creditors receiving stock of the acquirer (and claims of any equal class of creditors). The value of those most senior creditors' proprietary interests in the target is determined by multiplying the fair market value of the claim by a fraction, the numerator of which is the aggregate fair market value of the acquirer's stock received in exchange for claims of those classes of creditors and the denominator of which is the total amount of money and the fair market value of all other consideration (including acquirer stock) received in exchange for such claims.

Furthermore, Prop.Reg. § 1.368–1(f) (2005) would require that there be "an exchange of net value," pursuant to which an acquisition of an insolvent target corporation involving an exchange of outstanding debt instruments for stock will qualify as a reorganization only if the target corporation is rendered solvent in the transaction.

The special aspects of reorganizations involving insolvent corporations are considered in Section 7 of this Chapter.

(2) "REMOTE CONTINUITY OF INTEREST" AND "PARTY TO A REORGANIZATION"

REGULATIONS: Section 1.268–2(k).

Section 368(a)(2)(C) permits the acquiring corporation to drop assets or stock of the target corporation down to a controlled subsidiary following the initial acquisition. In addition, § 368(a)(2)(D) includes within the definition of a reorganization a "triangular merger," a merger in which the shareholders of the acquired corporation receive stock of the acquiring corporation's parent (and in which they receive no stock of the acquiring subsidiary), and § 368(a)(2)(E) permits "reverse triangular mergers" subject to several restrictive conditions. Triangular acquisitions are considered in detail at page 638.

These statutory provisions are in response to cases that restricted the ability to bring triangular acquisitions within the definition of a "reorganization." In Groman v. Commissioner, 302 U.S. 82 (1937), P Corporation desired to acquire T Corporation. Accordingly, P Corporation organized S Corporation, and held all of its common stock. The shareholders of T Corporation transferred their T stock to S Corporation in return for preferred stock of S Corporation, preferred stock of P Corporation, and cash. S Corporation then liquidated T

Corporation. In effect, the assets of T Corporation went to a newly-formed subsidiary of P Corporation. The Court held that the preferred stock of P Corporation was not stock in a "party to a reorganization" and hence was boot received by the T Corporation shareholders. The Court relied on the continuity of interest doctrine and stated that since P Corporation had not received the T Corporation assets, the possession of the P stock by the T shareholders did not represent a continuing interest in those assets. *Groman* was followed in Helvering v. Bashford, 302 U.S. 454 (1938), where there was a transitory ownership of the T Corporation stock by P Corporation but it was then immediately transferred by P Corporation to its subsidiary S Corporation. The T Corporation shareholders received some common stock of S Corporation and some preferred and common stock of P Corporation. Since the ownership of the T stock by P Corporation was only transitory and the transfer to S Corporation was part of a plan, the transitory ownership did not serve to distinguish the *Groman* case.

In the *Groman* and *Bashford* cases the former stockholders had divided their ownership—they now owned some stock (preferred stock in the *Groman* case, minority common stock in the *Bashford* case) in the corporation to which the assets had been transferred and also some stock (preferred in the *Groman* case, preferred and minority common in the *Bashford* case) in the parent corporation of the corporation to which the assets had been transferred. They were thus free to dispose of one interest without the other. Suppose, however, that the assets had gone to a wholly-owned subsidiary of the parent and the former owners had received only stock in the parent? The courts held that the results were the same; stock of the parent does not provide continuity of interest and make the parent a party to the reorganization where the assets go to another corporation even though it is a wholly owned subsidiary of the parent and even though a reorganization would obviously be present if the assets had gone to the parent. This was also the result under some decisions where the assets were first transferred to the parent and then by it transferred to the subsidiary if the latter step was contemplated as part of the plan of reorganization. Anheuser-Busch, Inc. v. Helvering, 115 F.2d 662 (8th Cir.1940); Hedden v. Commissioner, 105 F.2d 311 (3d Cir.1939); Mellon v. Commissioner, 12 T.C. 90 (1949) (Nonacq.), aff'd on other issues 184 F.2d 157 (3d Cir.1950); Campbell v. Commissioner, 15 T.C. 312 (1950) (Acq.).

Sections 368(a)(2)(C), (D) and (E) have changed the results in these cases. However, § 368(a)(2)(D), but not § 368(a)(2)(C) and (E), prohibits the splitting of interests, as was present in the *Groman* and *Bashford* cases themselves.

Nevertheless, the statutory provisions do not expressly deal with a variety of situations that can give rise to "remote continuity of interest" issues. For a number of years the IRS dealt with these situations on an *ad hoc* basis through revenue rulings, prior to the promulgation of Treas.Reg. § 1.368–2(k), which provides a more comprehensive, but still incomplete set of rules for dealing with situations not addressed by the statute. Rev.Rul. 2002–85, which follows, is an example of the IRS's reasoning in such cases.

Revenue Ruling 2002–85

2002–2 C.B. 986.

ISSUE

Whether an acquiring corporation's transfer of a target corporation's assets to a subsidiary controlled by the acquiring corporation as part of a plan of reorganization will prevent a transaction that otherwise qualifies as a reorganization under § 368(a)(1)(D) of the Internal Revenue Code from so qualifying.

FACTS

A, an individual, owns 100 percent of T, a state X corporation. A also owns 100 percent of P, a state Y corporation. For valid business reasons and pursuant to a plan of reorganization, (i) T transfers all of its assets to P in exchange for consideration consisting of 70 percent P voting stock and 30 percent cash, (ii) T then liquidates, distributing the P voting stock and cash to A, and (iii) P subsequently transfers all of the T assets to S, a preexisting, wholly owned state X subsidiary of P, in exchange for stock of S. S will continue T's historic business after the transfer and P will retain the S stock. Without regard to P's transfer of all the T assets to S, the transaction qualifies as a reorganization under § 368(a)(1)(D).

LAW

Section 368(a)(1)(D) provides that the term reorganization means a transfer by a corporation of all or a part of its assets to another corporation if immediately after the transfer the transferor, or one or more of its shareholders (including persons who were shareholders immediately before the transfer), or any combination thereof, is in control of the corporation to which the assets are transferred; but only if, in pursuance of the plan, stock or securities of the corporation to which the assets are transferred are distributed in a transaction which qualifies under § 354, 355, or 356.

Section 354(a) provides that, in general, no gain or loss shall be recognized if stock or securities in a corporation a party to a reorganization are, in pursuance of the plan of reorganization, exchanged solely for stock or securities in such corporation or in another corporation a party to the reorganization. Section 354(b)(1) provides that § 354(a) shall not apply to an exchange in pursuance of a plan of reorganization within the meaning of subparagraph (D) or (G) of § 368(a)(1) unless (A) the corporation to which the assets are transferred acquires substantially all of the assets of the transferor of such assets; and (B) the stock, securities, and other properties received by such transferor, as well as the other properties of such transferor, are distributed in pursuance of the plan of reorganization.

Section 368(a)(2)(A) provides that if a transaction is described in both §§ 368(a)(1)(C) and 368(a)(1)(D) , then, for purposes of subchapter C (other than for purposes of § 368(a)(2)(C)), such transaction shall be treated as described only in § 368(a)(1)(D).

Section 368(a)(2)(C) provides that a transaction otherwise qualifying under § 368(a)(1)(A), (B), (C), or (G) shall not be disqualified by reason of the fact that part or all of the assets or stock which were acquired in the transaction are transferred to a corporation controlled (as defined in § 368(c)) by the corporation acquiring such assets or stock.

Section 368(b) provides that the term "a party to a reorganization" includes a corporation resulting from a reorganization, and both corporations in the case of a reorganization resulting from the acquisition by one corporation of the properties of another.

Congress enacted § 368(a)(2)(C) in response to the Supreme Court decisions in Groman v. Commissioner, 302 U.S. 82 (1937), and Helvering v. Bashford, 302 U.S. 454 (1938). In *Groman*, the shareholders of one corporation (Target) entered into an agreement with another corporation (Parent) pursuant to which Target would merge into Parent's newly formed subsidiary (Sub). In the transaction, the Target shareholders transferred their Target shares to Sub in exchange for shares of Parent, shares of Sub, and cash, and Target liquidated. The Court concluded that, even though the statutory definition of "party to a reorganization" was not exclusive, Parent was not a party to the reorganization because it received nothing in the exchange. The Court then stated that an exchange that is pursuant to a plan of reorganization is not taxable to the extent the interest of the stockholders of a corporation continue to be definitely represented in substantial measure in a new or different corporation. The stock of Parent, however, did not represent a continued substantial interest in the assets conveyed to Sub. Because Parent was not a party to the reorganization, the Court held that the receipt of the stock of Parent was taxable.

In *Bashford*, a corporation (Parent) wished to acquire three competitors (Targets). Pursuant to a plan, Parent formed a new corporation (Sub) and acquired all the preferred shares and a majority of the common shares of Sub. Sub became the owner of the stock and assets of the Targets. The former stockholders of the Targets exchanged their shares in the Targets for shares of Sub, shares of Parent, and cash. Because any direct ownership by Parent of the Targets was transitory and without real substance, the Court saw no significant distinction between this transaction and the transaction in *Groman*. Therefore, the Court concluded that Parent was not a party to the reorganization. Hence, the Parent stock received by the shareholders of the Targets did not confer the requisite continuity of interest.

In 1954, Congress enacted § 368(a)(2)(C) in response to *Groman* and *Bashford*. See S. Rep. No. 1622, 83d Cong., 2d Sess. 52, 273, 275 (1954). As originally enacted, § 368(a)(2)(C) applied only to reorganizations under §§ 368(a)(1)(A) and 368(a)(1)(C), but Congress has since amended the statute to apply to other reorganizations. Specifically, Congress amended § 368(a)(2)(C) in 1964 to apply to reorganizations under § 368(a)(1)(B), and, in 1980, to reorganizations under § 368(a)(1)(G).

Section 1.368–2(k)(1) of the Income Tax Regulations restates the general rule of § 368(a)(2)(C) but permits the assets or stock acquired in certain types of reorganizations to be successively transferred to one or more corporations controlled (as defined in § 368(c)) in each transfer by the transferor corporation without disqualifying the reorganization.

Section 1.368–2(f) provides that, if a transaction otherwise qualifies as a reorganization, a corporation remains a party to the reorganization even though the stock or assets acquired in the reorganization are transferred in a transaction described in § 1.368–2(k).

To qualify as a reorganization under § 368, a transaction must satisfy the continuity of business enterprise (COBE) requirement. The COBE requirement is intended to ensure that reorganizations are limited to readjustments of continuing interests in property under modified corporate form. Section 1.368–1(d)(1). Section 1.368–1(d)(1) provides that COBE requires the issuing corporation (generally the acquiring corporation) in a potential reorganization to either continue the target corporation's historic business or use a significant portion of the target's historic business assets in a business. Pursuant to § 1.368–1(d)(4)(i), the issuing corporation is treated as holding all of the businesses and assets of all members of its qualified group. Section 1.368–1(d)(4)(ii) defines a qualified group as one or more chains of corporations connected through stock ownership with the issuing corporation, but only if the issuing corporation owns directly stock meeting the requirements of § 368(c) in at least one other corporation, and stock meeting the requirements of § 368(c) in each of the corporations (except the issuing corporation) is owned directly by one of the other corporations.

In Rev.Rul. 88–48, 1988–1 C.B. 117, in a taxable transaction, corporation X sold 50 percent of its historic business assets to unrelated purchasers for cash. Immediately afterwards, pursuant to an overall plan, X transferred to corporation Y, a corporation unrelated to X and the purchasers, all of its assets, including the cash from the sale. The ruling holds that X's transfer of assets to Y satisfied the substantially all requirement of § 368(a)(1)(C).

In Rev.Rul. 2001–25, 2001–1 C.B. 1291, pursuant to a plan, corporation S, a wholly owned subsidiary of corporation P, merged with and into corporation T in a state law merger. Immediately after the merger and as part of a plan that included the merger, T sold 50 percent of its operating assets for cash to an unrelated corporation. After the sale of the assets to corporation X, T retained the sales proceeds. Without regard to the requirement that T hold substantially all of the assets of T and S immediately after the merger, the merger satisfied all the other requirements applicable to reorganizations under §§ 368(a)(1)(A) and 368(a)(2)(E). The IRS ruled that even though T's post-merger sale of 50 percent of its operating assets prevented T from holding substantially all of its historic business assets immediately after the merger, because the sales proceeds continued to be held by T, the merger did not violate the requirement of § 368(a)(2)(E) that the surviving corporation hold substantially all of its properties after the transaction.

In Rev.Rul. 2001–24, 2001–1 C.B. 1290, corporation X merged with and into corporation S, a newly organized, wholly owned subsidiary of corporation P, in a transaction intended to qualify as a reorganization under §§ 368(a)(1)(A) and 368(a)(2)(D). S continued the historic business of X following the merger. Following the merger and as part of the plan of reorganization, P transferred the S stock to corporation S1, a preexisting, wholly owned subsidiary of P. The IRS ruled that the transaction satisfied the continuity of business enterprise requirement of § 1.368–1(d). Analyzing whether P's transfer of the S stock to S1 caused P to fail to control S for purposes of § 368(a)(2)(D) and caused P to fail to be a party to the reorganization, the IRS noted that the legislative history of § 368(a)(2)(E) suggests that forward and reverse triangular mergers should be treated similarly. Section 1.368–2(k)(2) permits the transfer of stock or assets to a controlled corporation following a reverse triangular merger under §§ 368(a)(1)(A) and 368(a)(2)(E), which supports permitting P to transfer the S stock to S1 without causing the transaction to fail to qualify as a reorganization under §§ 368(a)(1)(A) and 368(a)(2)(D). Furthermore, although §§ 368(a)(2)(C) and 1.368–2(k) do not specifically address P's transfer of S stock to S1 following a reorganization under §§ 368(a)(1)(A) and 368(a)(2)(D), § 368(a)(2)(C) is permissive rather than exclusive or restrictive. Accordingly, the IRS concluded that the transfer of the S stock to S1 would not cause P to be treated as not in control of S for purposes of § 368(a)(2)(D) and would not cause P to fail to be treated as a party to the reorganization.

ANALYSIS

Neither § 368(a)(2)(C) nor § 368(a)(2)(A) indicates that an acquiring corporation's transfer of assets to a controlled subsidiary necessarily prevents a transaction that otherwise qualifies as a reorganization under § 368(a)(1)(D) from so qualifying. Because § 368(a)(2)(C) is permissive and not exclusive or restrictive, the absence of § 368(a)(1)(D) from § 368(a)(2)(C) does not indicate that such a transfer following a transaction that otherwise qualifies as a reorganization under § 368(a)(1)(D) will prevent the transaction from qualifying as such. Furthermore, although § 368(a)(2)(A) contains the parenthetical exception "other than for purposes of [§ 368(a)(2)(C)]," that exception appears to have been provided in the same spirit as § 368(a)(2)(C), i.e., to resolve doubts about the qualification of transactions as reorganizations, and does not indicate that the transfer of assets to a controlled subsidiary necessarily prevents a transaction from qualifying as a reorganization under § 368(a)(1)(D). See S. Rep. No. 313, 99th Cong., 2d Sess. 914 (1986).

Accordingly, an acquiring corporation's transfer of assets to a controlled subsidiary following a transaction that otherwise qualifies as a reorganization under § 368(a)(1)(D) will not cause a transaction to fail to qualify as such, provided that the original transferee is treated as acquiring substantially all of the assets of the target corporation, the transaction satisfies the COBE requirement and does not fail under the remote continuity principle of *Groman* and *Bashford*, and the transfer of assets to a controlled corporation does not prevent the original transferee from being a "party to the reorganization."

Section 354(b)(1)(A) requires that, in a reorganization under § 368(a)(1)(D), the corporation to which the assets are transferred acquire substantially all of the assets of the transferor of such assets. In this case, the requirement that P acquire substantially all of T's assets is satisfied because P retains the stock of S. See Rev.Rul. 2001–24; Rev.Rul. 88–48.

To qualify as a reorganization under § 368(a)(1)(D), a transaction must satisfy the COBE requirement of § 1.368–1(d). In the present transaction, P and S constitute a qualified group, and S will continue T's historic business after the transfer. Therefore, the transaction satisfies the COBE requirement.

As described above, Congress enacted § 368(a)(2)(C) in response to the Supreme Court's holdings in *Groman* and *Bashford*. After the enactment of § 368(a)(2)(C), however, the IRS continued to apply the principles of *Groman* and *Bashford* to transactions that otherwise qualified as reorganizations under § 368(a)(1)(B). See Rev.Rul. 63–234, 1963–2 C.B. 148. In response to this position, Congress expanded the scope of § 368(a)(2)(C) to include reorganizations under § 368(a)(1)(B). Congress' response to the application of the principles of *Groman* and *Bashford* has been to limit the application of those principles. Implicit in Congress' enactment and expansion of § 368(a)(2)(C) is a rejection of the principle that the transfer of acquired stock or assets to a controlled subsidiary of the acquiring corporation creates a remote continuity problem that causes a transaction that otherwise qualifies as a reorganization to fail to so qualify. See H.R. Rep. No. 1337, 83d Cong., 2d Sess. A134 (1954) (stating, after citing *Groman* and *Bashford* in reference to proposed legislation that ultimately became § 368(a)(2)(C), "a corporation may not acquire assets with the intention of transferring them to a stranger").

Under the COBE regulations, stock or assets acquired in transactions that satisfy certain provisions of § 368(a)(1) may be transferred without limitation to successive lower-tier controlled subsidiaries within a qualified group. The Preamble to the final COBE regulations states that "the IRS and Treasury believe the COBE requirements adequately address the issues raised in *Groman* and *Bashford* and their progeny. Thus, [the final COBE regulations] do not separately articulate rules addressing remote continuity of interest." T.D. 8760, 1998–1 C.B. 803, Supplementary Information (Explanation of Provisions). Accordingly, a transfer of acquired stock or assets will not cause a transaction to fail for remote continuity if it satisfies the COBE requirement.

Under the facts described above, P's transfer of the T assets to S pursuant to the plan of reorganization satisfies the COBE requirement. Therefore, the transaction does not fail for remote continuity.

Section 368(b) provides that the term "a party to a reorganization" includes a corporation resulting from a reorganization, and both corporations in the case of a reorganization resulting from the acquisition by one corporation of the properties of another. The use of the word "includes" in § 368(b) indicates that the definition of "party to a reorganization" is not exclusive. See § 7701(c); *Groman*, supra, at 86 (stating that "when an exclusive definition is intended the word 'means' is employed * * * whereas [in the definition of 'party to a reorganization'] the word used is 'includes'"). Furthermore, § 1.368–2(f), which interprets § 368(b), provides that, if a transaction otherwise qualifies as a reorganization, a corporation remains a party to a reorganization even though the stock or assets acquired in the reorganization are transferred in a transaction described in § 1.368–2(k). Section 1.368–2(k) does not reference § 368(a)(1)(D). Nonetheless, because § 1.368–2(k) restates and interprets § 368(a)(2)(C), which is a permissive and not an exclusive or restrictive provision, § 1.368–2(k) also should be viewed as permissive and not exclusive or restrictive. Therefore, because §§ 368(b), 1.368–2(f), and 1.368–2(k) are not exclusive or restrictive provisions, the absence of § 368(a)(1)(D) from § 1.368–2(k) does not prevent a corporation from remaining a party to a reorganization even if the acquired stock or assets are transferred to a controlled subsidiary.

Reorganizations under § 368(a)(1)(D), like reorganizations under §§ 368(a)(1)(A) and 368(a)(1)(C), are asset reorganizations. In reorganizations under §§ 368(a)(1)(A) and 368(a)(1)(C), the original transferee is treated as a party to a reorganization, even if the acquired assets are transferred to a controlled subsidiary of the original transferee. The differences between reorganizations under § 368(a)(1)(D) on the one hand and reorganizations under §§ 368(a)(1)(A) and 368(a)(1)(C) on the other hand do not warrant treating the original transferee in a transaction that otherwise satisfies the requirements of a reorganization under § 368(a)(1)(D) differently from the original transferee in a reorganization under § 368(a)(1)(A) or 368(a)(1)(C) for purposes of § 368(b). Therefore, the original transferee in a transaction that otherwise satisfies the requirements of a reorganization under § 368(a)(1)(D) is treated as a party to the reorganization, notwithstanding the original transferee's transfer of acquired assets to a controlled subsidiary of the original transferee.

For the reasons set forth above, P's transfer of the T assets to S will not prevent P's acquisition of those assets from T in exchange for P voting stock and cash from qualifying as a reorganization under § 368(a)(1)(D).

HOLDING

An acquiring corporation's transfer of the target corporation's assets to a subsidiary controlled by the acquiring corporation as part of a plan of reorganization will not prevent a transaction that otherwise qualifies as a reorganization under § 368(a)(1)(D) from so qualifying.

* * *

DETAILED ANALYSIS

1.   DROP-DOWNS AND PUSH-UPS FOLLOWING ACQUISITIONS

Treas.Reg. § 1.368–2(k) provides that a transaction otherwise qualifying as a reorganization under § 368(a) will not be disqualified as a result of the transfer or successive transfers ("drop-downs") to one or more corporations controlled in each transfer by the transferor corporation of part or all of either (1) the assets of any party to the reorganization, or (2) the stock of any party to the reorganization (other than the acquiring corporation whose stock is issued). Consonantly, Treas.Reg. § 1.368–2(f), dealing with the definition of a "party to a reorganization" requirement, and Treas.Reg. § 1.368–1(d)(4)(i)(A) and (B), dealing with the continuity of business enterprise requirement, provide that a post-acquisition distribution ("push-up") by an acquisition subsidiary that is member of the acquiring corporation's group to a corporation that controls the acquiring corporation of either (1) the target corporation's stock (following a § 368(a)(1)(B) or § 368(a)(2)(E) reorganization) or (2) the target corporation's assets (following a § 368(a)(1)(A), 368(a)(1)(C), or

§ 368(a)(2)(E) reorganization) does not disqualify the acquisition from reorganization treatment, even though there is no statutory provision expressly providing that such transfers do not affect the validity of reorganization treatment. The combined effect of these provisions is to permit the acquiring corporation to rearrange ownership of the target corporation's assets or stock, as the case may be, in almost any manner it desires among all of the members of its qualified group (based on § 368(c) control) without disqualifying the reorganization.

(3) TEMPORAL ASPECTS

REGULATIONS: Sections 1.368–1(a), (b), (e)(1), (3)–(7), –2(a). See also section 1.338–2(c)(3).

Rules and Regulations, Department of the Treasury, Internal Revenue Service, Continuity of Interest and Continuity of Business Enterprise

T.D. 8760, 1998–1 C.B. 803.

Explanation of Provisions

The Internal Revenue Code of 1986 provides general nonrecognition treatment for reorganizations specifically described in section 368. In addition to complying with the statutory requirements and certain other requirements, a transaction generally must satisfy the continuity of interest requirement and the continuity of business enterprise requirement.

A. *Continuity of Interest*

The purpose of the continuity of interest requirement is to prevent transactions that resemble sales from qualifying for nonrecognition of gain or loss available to corporate reorganizations. The final regulations provide that the COI requirement is satisfied if in substance a substantial part of the value of the proprietary interest in the target corporation (T) is preserved in the reorganization. A proprietary interest in T is preserved if, in a potential reorganization, it is exchanged for a proprietary interest in the issuing corporation (P), it is exchanged by the acquiring corporation for a direct interest in the T enterprise, or it otherwise continues as a proprietary interest in T. The issuing corporation means the acquiring corporation (as the term is used in section 368(a)), except that, in determining whether a reorganization qualifies as a triangular reorganization (as defined in § 1.358–6(b)(2)), the issuing corporation means the corporation in control of the acquiring corporation. However, a proprietary interest in T is not preserved if, in connection with the potential reorganization, it is acquired by P for consideration other than P stock, or P stock furnished in exchange for a proprietary interest in T if the potential reorganization is redeemed. All facts and circumstances must be considered in determining whether, in substance, a proprietary interest in T is preserved.

Rationale for the COI Regulations

The * * * regulations permit former T shareholders to sell P stock received in a potential reorganization to third parties without causing the reorganization to fail to satisfy the COI requirement. Some commentators have questioned whether the regulations are consistent with existing authorities.

The COI requirement was applied first to reorganization provisions that did not specify that P exchange a proprietary interest in P for a proprietary interest in T. Supreme Court cases imposed the COI requirement to further Congressional intent that tax-free status be accorded only to transactions where P exchanges a substantial proprietary interest in P for a proprietary interest in T held by the T shareholders rather than to transactions resembling sales. See LeTulle v. Scofield, 308 U.S. 415 (1940); Helvering v. Minnesota Tea Co., 296 U.S. 378 (1935); Pinellas Ice & Cold Storage Co. v. Commissioner, 287 U.S. 462 (1933). * * *

None of the Supreme Court cases establishing the COI requirement addressed the issue of whether sales by former T shareholders of P stock received in exchange for T stock in the potential reorganization cause the COI requirement to fail to be satisfied. Since then, however, some courts have premised decisions on the assumption that sales of P stock received in exchange for T stock in the potential reorganization may cause the COI requirement to fail to be satisfied. McDonald's Restaurants of Illinois, Inc. v. Commissioner, 688 F.2d 520 (7th Cir.1982); Penrod v. Commissioner, 88 T.C. 1415 (1987); Heintz v. Commissioner, 25 T.C. 132 (1955), nonacq., 1958–2 C.B. 9 * * *. The apparent focus of these cases is on whether the T shareholders intended on the date of the potential reorganization to sell their P stock and the degree, if any, to which P facilitates the sale. Based on an intensive inquiry into nearly identical facts, some of these cases held that as a result of the subsequent sale the potential reorganization did not satisfy the COI requirement; others held that satisfaction of the COI requirement was not adversely affected by the subsequent sale. The IRS and Treasury Department have concluded that the law as reflected in these cases does not further the principles of reorganization treatment and is difficult for both taxpayers and the IRS to apply consistently.

Therefore, consistent with Congressional intent and the Supreme Court precedent which distinguishes between sales and reorganizations, the final regulations focus the COI requirement generally on exchanges between the T shareholders and P. Under this approach, sales of P stock by former T shareholders generally are disregarded.

The final regulations will greatly enhance administrability in this area by both taxpayers and the government. The regulations will prevent "whipsaw" of the government, such as where the former T shareholders treat the transaction as a tax-free reorganization, and P later disavows reorganization treatment to step up its basis in the T assets based on the position that sales of P stock by the former T shareholders did not satisfy the COI requirement. See, e.g., *McDonald's Restaurants*, supra. In addition, this approach will prevent unilateral sales of P stock by former majority T shareholders from adversely affecting the section 354 nonrecognition treatment expected by former minority T shareholders.

Dispositions of T Stock

* * * The IRS and Treasury Department believe that issues concerning the COI requirement raised by dispositions of T stock before a potential reorganization correspond to those raised by subsequent dispositions of P stock furnished in exchange for T stock in the potential reorganization. * * * [T]he final regulations apply the rationale of the proposed COI regulations to transactions occurring both prior to and after a potential reorganization. Cf. J.E. Seagram Corp. v. Commissioner, 104 T.C. 75 (1995) (sales of T stock prior to a potential reorganization do not affect COI if not part of the plan of reorganization). The final regulations provide that, for COI purposes, a mere disposition of T stock prior to a potential reorganization to persons not related to P is disregarded and a mere disposition of P stock received in a potential reorganization to persons not related to P is disregarded. * * *

In soliciting comments on the effect upon COI of dispositions of T stock prior to a potential reorganization, the preamble to the proposed COI regulations specifically requests comments on King Enterprises, Inc. v. United States, 418 F.2d 511 (Ct.Cl.1969) (COI requirement satisfied where, pursuant to a plan, P acquires the T stock for 51 percent P stock and 49 percent debt and cash, and T merges upstream into P), and Yoc Heating Corp. v. Commissioner, 61 T.C. 168 (1973) (COI requirement not satisfied where, pursuant to a plan, P acquires 85 percent of the T stock for cash and notes, and T merges into P's newly formed subsidiary with minority shareholders receiving cash). Consistent with these cases, where the step transaction doctrine applies to link T stock purchases with later acquisitions of T, the final regulations provide that a proprietary interest in T is not preserved if, in connection with the potential reorganization, it is acquired by P for consideration other than P stock. Whether a stock acquisition is made in connection with a potential reorganization will be determined based on the facts and circumstances of each case. See generally § 1.368–1(a). This regulation does not address the effect, if any, of section 338 on corporate transactions * * *. See generally § 1.338–[3(d)] (certain tax effects of a qualified stock purchase without a section 338 election on the post-acquisition elimination of T).

Related Person Rule

* * * The final regulations provide * * * that a proprietary interest in T is not preserved if, in connection with a potential reorganization, a person related (as defined below) to P acquires, with consideration other than a proprietary interest in P, T stock or P stock furnished in exchange for a proprietary interest in T in the potential reorganization. The IRS and Treasury Department believe, however, that certain related party acquisitions preserve a proprietary interest in T and therefore, the rule includes an exception to the related party rule. Under this exception, a proprietary interest in T is preserved to the extent those persons who were the direct or indirect owners of T prior to the potential reorganization maintain a direct or indirect proprietary interest in P. See, e.g., Rev.Rul. 84–30 (1984–1 C.B. 114).

* * * [The] regulations adopt a * * * related person definition which has two components in order to address two separate concerns.

First, the IRS and Treasury Department were concerned that acquisitions of T or P stock by a member of P's affiliated group were no different in substance from an acquisition or redemption by P, because of the existence of various provisions in the Code that permit members to transfer funds to other members without significant tax consequences. Accordingly, § [1.368–1(e)(4)(i)(A)] includes as related persons corporations that are members of the same affiliated group under section 1504, without regard to the exceptions in section 1504(b).

Second, because the final regulations take into account whether, in substance, P has redeemed the stock it exchanged for T stock in the potential reorganization, the final regulations treat two corporations as related persons if a purchase of the stock of one corporation by another corporation would be treated as a distribution in redemption of the stock of the first corporation under section 304(a)(2) (determined without regard to § 1.1502–80(b)).

Because the final regulations focus generally on the consideration P exchanges, related persons do not include individual or other noncorporate shareholders. * * *

T Stock Not Acquired in Connection With a Potential Reorganization

* * * The final regulations provide that a proprietary interest in T is preserved if it is exchanged by the acquiring corporation (which may or may not also be P) for a direct interest in the T enterprise, or otherwise continues as a proprietary interest in T.

* * *

Transactions Following a Qualified Stock Purchase

As stated above, these final regulations focus the COI requirement generally on exchanges between the T shareholders and P. Accordingly, the language of § 1.338–[3(d)] is conformed to these final COI regulations to treat the stock of T acquired by the purchasing corporation in the qualified stock purchase as though it was not acquired in connection with the transfer of the T assets.

* * *

DETAILED ANALYSIS

1. CONTINUITY OF INTEREST AND HISTORIC SHAREHOLDERS

1.1. *Generally*

As discussed in T.D. 8760, prior to 1998, usually at the IRS's behest, a number of decisions imposed the requirement that continuity of interest be tested with respect to the "historic" shareholders of the acquired corporation, not those persons who owned the stock of the acquired corporation immediately before the merger. In Superior Coach of Florida, Inc. v. Commissioner, 80 T.C. 895 (1983), the court held that for shareholders to be considered historic shareholders the acquired corporation's shares must be "old and cold" in the hands of the shareholders participating in the reorganization. A contrary result was reached in J.E. Seagram Corp. v. Commissioner, 104 T.C. 75 (1995), in which the Tax Court held that the pre-reorganization sales and purchases of a publicly held target corporation's stock did not vitiate the continuity of interest requirement, thereby largely abandoning any "historic shareholder" continuity of interest requirement. In adopting current Treas.Reg. § 1.368–1(e), the Treasury rejected the *Superior Coach* approach in favor of the *J.E. Seagram* approach. But if the acquiring corporation (or a related corporation) itself purchases stock of the target corporation prior to the reorganization, as noted in T.D. 8760, vestiges of the historic shareholder continuity of interest requirement come into play.

Rev.Rul. 99–58, 1999–2 C.B. 701, held that the open market purchase of its shares by a publicly traded corporation following a tax free reorganization in which the shareholders of the target corporation received 50 percent cash and 50 percent stock did not violate the continuity of interest requirement under Treas.Reg. § 1.368–1(e), even though the acquiring corporation's intent to repurchase shares (to prevent dilution) had been announced prior to the reorganization, because the repurchase was not negotiated with the target or its shareholders and there was no "understanding" between the acquiring corporation and the target shareholders that their ownership would be transitory.

1.2. *Reorganizations Immediately Following Stock Purchases*

In Kass v. Commissioner, 60 T.C. 218 (1973), aff'd by order, 491 F.2d 749 (3d Cir.1974), individuals A and B, minority shareholders in the target corporation, desired to obtain control of the target corporation. To accomplish this goal, A and B organized the acquiring corporation and contributed their target corporation stock to the acquiring corporation. As a result, the acquiring corporation held 10.23 percent of the stock of the target corporation. Shortly thereafter, the acquiring corporation purchased for cash an additional 83.95 percent of the stock of the target corporation. Finally, the target corporation was merged into the acquiring corporation, with the remaining shareholders of the target corporation stock, who held 5.82 percent of the target corporation stock, receiving the acquiring corporation stock. The taxpayer, who was one of the minority shareholders who received the acquiring corporation stock in the merger, claimed that the transaction was a type (A) reorganization. The court agreed with the IRS's argument that as far as the taxpayer was concerned, the transaction was a taxable sale because more than 80 percent of the shares of the target corporation prior to the commencement of the series of transactions culminating in the merger of the target corporation had been sold for cash. Thus the continuity of interest requirement was not satisfied. A similar result was reached on similar facts in Yoc Heating Corp. v. Commissioner, 61 T.C. 168 (1973), which involved the tax treatment of the target corporation.

As noted in T.D. 8760, under Treas.Reg. § 1.368–1(e), the shareholders in cases such as *Kass* and *Yoc Heating* generally will not be considered to have participated in a reorganization if the cash purchases by the acquiring corporation are of such a magnitude relative to the stock consideration that the continuity of interest requirement has not been met. See Treas.Reg. § 1.368–1(e)(1) and (e)(8) , Ex. 2. As far as the corporations themselves are concerned, however, Treas.Reg. § 1.338–3(d) might produce a different result. Suppose P Corporation makes a qualified stock purchase of T Corporation, i.e., it purchases at least 80 percent (by vote and value) of the stock of T, but does not make a § 338 election, see page 486. P then causes the assets of T to be transferred to P (or another member of P's affiliated group, such as another subsidiary) in a reorganization defined in § 368. The regulation states that P will be treated as the relevant owner, i.e., "historic owner" of the T stock for purposes of testing continuity of interest under Treas.Reg. § 1.368–1(b) and (e). Any minority shareholders of T, however, will continue to be tested under generally applicable principles. As a result of the treatment under the regulations, the reorganization may qualify as a tax-free reorganization under § 368 for the acquiring corporation's controlled group; it will not be a "taxable merger" (see page 478). T will not recognize gain or loss on the transfer of its assets, and P (or a related corporation that acquires T's assets in the reorganization) will not obtain a step-up in basis for the T assets. Thus, the result in *Yoc Heating* has been changed by the regulations, but the result in *Kass* has not been affected. The position of the regulations that a reorganization can exist with respect to some shareholders but not with respect to other shareholders is difficult to justify.

2. EFFECT OF PRE-ACQUISITION DISTRIBUTIONS BY TARGET CORPORATION

Treas.Reg. § 1.368–1(e)(1)(ii) deals with effect on the continuity of interest requirement of pre-acquisition redemptions of one or more of the target corporation's shareholders. The regulation in effect provides that stock of the target corporation's shareholders that is redeemed prior to the acquisition will not be taken into account in determining whether continuity of interest has been preserved to the extent that the consideration received by those shareholders prior to the potential reorganization is not treated as boot received from the acquirer (or from a related party) in exchange for target stock for purposes of § 356 (or would have been so treated if the target shareholder also had received acquirer stock in exchange for target stock owned by the shareholder, thus dealing with pre-acquisition complete redemptions of one or more target shareholders). Treas.Reg. § 1.368–1(e)(1)(ii) also provides that extraordinary pre-acquisition distributions to the shareholders of the target—which have the economic effect of reducing the amount of acquirer stock necessary to effect the acquisition—likewise will not be taken into account in determining the percentage of the target corporation's' stock that has been surrendered in the acquisition unless the amount received in the distribution is treated as boot received from the acquirer. The only example of the application of these rules, which is in Treas.Reg. § 1.368–1(e)(8), Ex. 9, is not particularly illuminating, because it provides no guidance regarding how to determine whether the pre-acquisition consideration provided to target shareholders is treated as boot received from the acquirer.

C. THE CONTINUITY OF BUSINESS ENTERPRISE REQUIREMENT

REGULATIONS: Sections 1.368–1(d),–2(k)(1).

Honbarrier v. Commissioner

United States Tax Court, 2000.
115 T.C. 300.

■ RUWE, JUDGE:

* * *

The sole issue for decision is whether the merger of Colonial into Central Transport, Inc. (Central), on December 31, 1993, qualifies as a tax-free reorganization within the meaning of section 368(a)(1)(A).

FINDINGS OF FACT

* * *

Colonial was a trucking company that operated as a common carrier of packaged freight. * * * When the trucking industry was deregulated at the Federal level in the 1980's, Colonial was subjected to competition from small individual truckers, with low overhead costs. As a result, Colonial's ICC operating authority became worthless, and the company experienced significant business reversals. * * * In 1988, as a result of its financial losses, Colonial stopped hauling freight and began selling its operating assets. By December 31, 1990, Colonial had sold all of its operating assets, except for the ICC and North Carolina operating authorities, for cash and cash equivalents. On August 21, 1992, Colonial sold its North Carolina authority for $5,000 but retained its ICC authority.

Colonial invested the proceeds from the sale of its operating assets almost exclusively in tax-exempt bonds and a municipal bond fund. Colonial held 18 tax-exempt bonds, 16 of which were purchased in 1990 and 1991, and 2 of which were purchased in 1992. One bond was redeemed in 1991, and three bonds were redeemed in 1992 and 1993. Colonial continued to hold the remaining 14 bonds as of the end of 1993.

As of October 31, 1993, 2 months prior to the merger, Colonial held approximately $7.35 million in tax-exempt bonds and a municipal bond fund and approximately $1,500 in cash. On December 31, 1993, Colonial liquidated one of its tax-exempt bonds and its municipal bond fund. The proceeds of this liquidation together totaled more than $2,550,000. * * *

From 1985 to December 31, 1993, Mr. Honbarrier owned 100 percent of Colonial's issued and outstanding shares. * * *

From 1951 through 1997, Central was a trucking company that operated as a bulk carrier of liquid and dry chemicals. Some of the chemicals that Central hauled were toxic. Central transported bulk chemicals in tanker trailers pulled by tractors. * * * Central was an S corporation. Central was highly successful in its bulk chemical hauling business * * *. [At the end of 1993, the balance in Central's accumulated adjustments account exceeded $10,000,000.]

Unlike Colonial, Central did not invest in tax-exempt bonds. Central held passive investments in the form of short-term liquid investments, such as certificates of deposit, because it needed cash and cash equivalents to operate its business. * * *

From 1982 through 1997, all of Central's stock was owned by Mr. and Mrs. Honbarrier and their children * * *.

On December 31, 1993, Colonial merged into Central in accordance with the laws of North Carolina. Central was the surviving corporation. * * * Pursuant to the merger, Mr. Honbarrier's 245 shares of Colonial stock were exchanged for 17,840 shares of Central stock.

On December 22, 1993, the board of directors of Central also declared a $7 million distribution payable to its shareholders on December 31, 1993. The shareholder distribution was allocated on a pro rata basis among the shareholders based on their stock ownership in Central on December 22, 1993. * * * With the exception of the amount allocable to Mr. Honbarrier, all of the declared distributions were paid by check on December 31, 1993. Central made the $5,042,772 distribution to Mr. Honbarrier in two parts. The first part was paid via a $493,626 check drawn on Central's account on December 31, 1993. * * * The second part of the distribution to Mr. Honbarrier was made on January 3, 1994, and consisted of $4,549,146 in tax-exempt bonds. The tax-exempt bonds distributed to Mr. Honbarrier on January 3, 1994, were the same bonds acquired by Central from Colonial in the merger.

For Federal income tax purposes, petitioners treated the merger as a tax-free reorganization within the meaning of section 368(a)(1)(A) and treated the $7 million distribution as a payment of previously taxed income reflected in Central's accumulated adjustments account.

OPINION

* * *

Section 368(a)(1)(A) defines a reorganization as "a statutory merger or consolidation". A statutory merger or consolidation is one effected pursuant to the corporate laws of the United States, a State, a territory, or the District of Columbia. See sec. 1.368–2(b)(1), Income Tax Regs. The merger of Colonial into Central meets this literal requirement. Petitioners argue that they are entitled to tax-free treatment under the Code because the merger was a complete and valid transaction for State law purposes.

It has long been held that qualification as a merger under State law is not, by itself, sufficient to qualify as a reorganization under section 368(a)(1)(A). Courts have interpreted section 368 as imposing three additional requirements for a merger to be treated as a reorganization under section 368(a)(1)(A). These are: (1) Business purpose; (2) continuity of business enterprise; and (3) continuity of interest. * * * Following judicial precedent, the regulations also require that there be a business purpose for the transaction, continuity of business enterprise, and continuity of interest, in order for a merger to qualify as a reorganization under section 368(a)(1)(A). See sec. 1.368–1(b), Income Tax Regs.; T.D. 7745, 1981–1 C.B. 134. Failure to comply

returns, Pacific had distributed the remainder of the stock. * * *.

The opinion in Gordon contains not the slightest indication that the Supreme Court intended the binding commitment requirement as the touchstone of the step transaction doctrine in tax law. Nor is there any indication that the Court intended to overrule any prior decisions applying the step transaction doctrine to other types of transactions where there were no binding commitments. On the contrary, the opinion addressed a narrow situation (a D reorganization) involving a specific statutory requirement (divestiture of control), and limited the potential for dilution and circumvention of that requirement by prohibiting the indefinite extension of divestiture distributions. Its interpretation should be so limited.[8] Clearly, the step transaction doctrine would be a dead letter if restricted to situations where the parties were bound to take certain steps.

The doctrine derives vitality, rather, from its application where the form of a transaction does not require a particular further step be taken; but, once taken, the substance of the transaction reveals that the ultimate result was intended from the outset. * * * In the majority of cases, it is the Government that relies on the step transaction doctrine for tax characterization. General application of the binding commitment requirement would effectively insure taxpayers of virtual exemption from the doctrine merely by refraining from such commitments. Such an untoward result cannot be intended by the Gordon opinion; indeed, defendant acknowledges as much in its brief by stating "the Supreme Court seems to have restricted the step transaction doctrine at least in one type of transaction, a corporate distribution of stock in a controlled corporation". The present case involves no such transaction.

In the alternative, the Government asserts that the step transaction doctrine has no application to this case because the merger of Tenco into Minute Maid was not the intended end result from the outset. Although the appropriate standard is invoked, defendant's assertion is inconsistent with the inferences to be drawn from the record.

The operative facts emerging from the record in this case suggest that Minute Maid, desirous of diversifying its operations in order to stabilize its income, was presented with the opportunity to acquire the entire stock of Tenco for a bargain "price". Tenco's record of financial success and its asking price for Tenco stock of seven or eight times its earnings (while other companies were asking 20 times their earnings), without more, constituted an attractive investment. After the stock acquisition, moreover, Minute Maid was at liberty to operate Tenco as a wholly owned subsidiary, if it so desired. There is no persuasive evidence, however, that Minute Maid's appetite was limited to these

---

8   See Mintz v. Plumb, supra, at 285, where in regard to the similarly restrictive interdependence test it is concluded:

> [The interdependence test] applies * * * in cases * * * where the concept of a "plan or reorganization" is not pertinent. In reorganization cases, except possibly in applying the "control" requirement * * * the determinative test seems to be whether the step was intended, or even contemplated as an alternative possibility, under the plan or reorganization, and the test of "interdependence" has not been applied.

goals, though worthy, when there was more in sight. On the contrary, the record reveals that, prior to the acquisition of Tenco stock, the officers of Minute Maid considered merging its existing subsidiaries into the parent in order to eliminate some of the general ledgers and extra taxes, and to bring about other savings. In fact, the merger of subsidiaries as a money-saving device was Mr. Speeler's (Minute Maid's vice president and general counsel) pet idea, which he discussed with Minute Maid's President Fox before the initial agreement with Tenco.

Shortly after the stock acquisition, Minute Maid instituted steps to consummate the merger of Tenco into Minute Maid. The proposed merger was motivated by a desire to avoid additional income tax on intercorporate dividends, to eliminate duplicate costs in the approximate amount of $50,000, and to obtain a stepped-up basis for stock in foreign corporations and other assets owned by Tenco. The potential step-up in basis for the foreign stock was estimated at $750,000 and the step-up for Tenco's other assets, although unable to be precisely ascertained, was considerable and probably sufficient as a justification for the merger independent of the other assigned reasons.[10]

Minute Maid applied for on January 5, 1960, and received on February 25, 1960, a ruling by the Internal Revenue Service that Minute Maid's basis in property received upon the complete liquidation of Tenco would be determined under section 334(b)(2) by reference to the adjusted basis of Tenco stock in Minute Maid's hands. Subsequently, on April 30 and May 2, 1960, in accordance with applicable state laws, Tenco and certain other subsidiaries were merged into Minute Maid.

No express intention on the part of Minute Maid to effect a merger of Tenco surfaces in the record until after the initial agreement to exchange stock. It strains credulity, however, to believe other than that the plan to merge was something more than inchoate, if something less than announced, at the time of such exchange. One gains the impression that the record of intentions is edited, so in reconstruction we must lean heavily on the logic of tell-tale facts and lightly on chameleon words. It is difficult to believe that sophisticated businessmen arranging a multimillion dollar transaction fraught with tax potentials were so innocent of knowledge of the tax consequences as the testimony purports. Perhaps testimony from private tax authorities serving the parties would have yielded more explicit knowledge of the questions asked and the advice given, but a trial record is rarely perfect in retrospect and a decision must be reached on an objective appraisal of the facts, including the inferences to be squeezed from them.

The operative facts in this case clearly justify the inference that the merger of Tenco into Minute Maid was the intended result of the transaction in question from the outset, the initial exchange of stock constituting a mere transitory step. Accordingly, it is concluded that the initial exchange and subsequent merger were steps in a unified transaction qualifying as a Type A reorganization, and that petitioner

---

[10] Petitioner asserts that the potential step-up in basis of Tenco assets is approximately $5,525,000. There is also evidence that Minute Maid believed such step-up to be approximately $5,950,000. The actual step-up, though undisclosed by the available facts, is probably at least several million dollars.

received its Minute Maid stock pursuant to the plan of reorganization shown by the facts and circumstances above to have existed.[11]

* * *

Bruce v. Helvering

Court of Appeals for the District of Columbia, 1935.
76 F.2d 442.

■ GRONER, ASSOCIATE JUSTICE.

In January, 1928, E. E. Bruce & Co. was a Nebraska corporation conducting business in Omaha in that state. Its capital structure consisted of 2,380 shares of common stock. Petitioner owned 700 shares, her sister owned 700 shares, and the remaining 980 shares were owned by employees and former employees of the corporation. The Board found as a fact that petitioner and her sister, as of the time mentioned, desired to sell a part of their Bruce stock, in order to reduce their investment in that company and bring it more in line, as to amount, with their other investments.

On January 27, 1928, Churchill Drug Company, also a Nebraska corporation, determined, if possible, to acquire the entire capital stock of Bruce Company, and to that end authorized its president and secretary to purchase the stock on such terms and conditions as they thought advisable.

On January 28, the president and secretary of Churchill Company offered to purchase from petitioner and her sister 400 shares of the capital stock of Bruce Company for $96,000 cash. Each sister accepted the offer for 200 shares. Immediately after the sale had been agreed to, the president of Churchill Company stated to the two sisters that his company desired and intended to obtain all the outstanding stock of Bruce Company in order to merge the two corporations, and then offered on behalf of Churchill Company to exchange 2,400 shares of its preferred stock for the remaining 1,000 shares of Bruce stock then owned by the two sisters. The sisters had never before received such an offer, nor were they previously aware of Churchill Company's purpose, but after considering the offer for a part of that day, they accepted it. Within a few days thereafter the exchange of stocks was consummated, and at the same time the payment of the purchase money on account of the 400 shares was duly made.

On or before April 18 following, Churchill Company had acquired all the outstanding shares of Bruce Company, and on that day the board of directors of Bruce Company authorized the transfer to Churchill Company of all its assets; and thereupon Bruce Company was dissolved. The Commissioner treated the sale of the 200 shares and the exchange of the 500 shares of Bruce stock belonging to petitioner as a single transaction and determined gain from the transaction to the extent of the $48,000 of cash which petitioner received. Petitioner, in her tax return for 1928, treated the two transactions as separate, and reported the $48,000 cash received by her for 200 shares of Bruce stock

---

[11] A formal plan or reorganization is not necessary if the facts of the case show a plan to have existed. See William H. Redfield, 34 B.T.A. 967 (1936).

and paid the tax on the basis of the difference in its cost price and sale price. She treated the exchange of the 500 shares of Bruce stock for 1,200 shares of Churchill stock as a tax exempt exchange under [the predecessor of § 354]. The result of the Commissioner's action was to increase the tax liability some $4,000. The Board sustained the Commissioner's determination, and this appeal resulted. * * *

The Board, after finding the facts to be as we have stated them, was of opinion that despite the fact petitioner had entered into a binding agreement for the sale of 200 shares of her Bruce stock before she had heard of the plan of reorganization, and therefore before she negotiated for the exchange of her remaining shares, "still both transactions were made pursuant to the same plan of reorganization," and the Board apparently thought this was conclusive even though, as it suggests, the plan of reorganization was not her plan, and even though, likewise, she had not heard of it when she sold her 200 shares of stock for money.

The Board says: "Here the petitioner, pursuant to the plan of reorganization, gave up her rights to 700 shares of the stock of E. E. Bruce & Co. and received not only stock of the Churchill Drug Co., but also cash. Thus [the predecessor of § 354] does not apply, but the exchange which she made of the 700 shares would have been within the provisions of [the predecessor of § 354] if it were not for the fact that the property received in the exchange consisted not only of property permitted by such paragraph to be received without the recognition of gain, but also of money."

Our criticism of this statement is that its foundation is without factual support. Petitioner did not give up her rights to 700 shares of Bruce Company stock for stock in Churchill Company and cash. On the contrary, she sold 200 shares of stock for money. When that was done, she had but 500 shares remaining, and only these she exchanged for Churchill stock. Unless, therefore, the Commissioner is right in treating the two separate transactions as one, it follows necessarily the Board's conclusion is wrong.

The Commissioner gives no reason for his holding, nor does the Board, and we ourselves are unable to supply one. If petitioner, after making a binding contract for the sale of 200 shares of stock, had declined the subsequent offer of exchange, it is perfectly obvious the transaction would have been just an ordinary sale of stock for money with no relation to the reorganization plan. On the other hand, if the sale of her 200 shares of stock for money had been conditioned on the exchange of her 500 shares of stock for stock in the other company, the transaction would have been one directly under the provisions of [the predecessor of § 356]. And so also it would have been if the separation of the transactions were a fraud or a trick; but neither of these conditions is even contended for. Petitioner, as all agree, determined, entirely for investment purposes, to sell part of her share holdings in Bruce Company. With that purpose in view, she bargained with the president of Churchill Company for the sale of a limited number of shares at so much per share in money. She committed herself and was bound. The transaction was a completed one; the minds of the parties met and carried with it unconditional liability each to the other. It was a closed sale, and beneficial ownership passed. Not until then was petitioner informed by the purchaser he intended, on behalf of his company, to buy all other shares of Bruce stock outstanding, except those belonging to petitioner and her sister; and that for these he was willing to deliver, in exchange, 2,400 shares of the preferred stock of his company. That this proposal was accepted later in the same day is neither significant nor, as we think, important. There being no challenge to the good faith of petitioner or to the verity of the facts on which she relies, the result would be the same if the two transactions had been thirty or sixty days apart, and we think it certainly would not be contended in the latter case there was but a single transaction involving, as to all 700 shares, an exchange of stock in one corporation for stock and money in another.

The case we have would be wholly different if it appeared the plan was one designed to defeat the payment of taxes. In such a case it would be just as subject to condemnation as was the fictitious transfer of assets by one corporation to another, and thence to the sole stockholder, which, though accomplished in strict conformity with the statute, the Supreme Court denounced in Gregory v. Helvering, [293 U.S. 465 (1935)].

But here there is not a suspicious circumstance suggesting that what was done was a sham. The sale on the one hand, and the exchange on the other, stand on the admitted facts separate and apart; and as the Supreme Court has said, and as we also have said time and again, in such circumstances the correct rule is to give effect to what actually was done, for that, after all, is the test.

Revenue Ruling. 2001–46

2001–2 C.B. 223.

ISSUE

Under the facts described below, what is the proper tax treatment if, pursuant to an integrated plan, a newly formed wholly owned subsidiary of an acquiring corporation merges into a target corporation, followed by the merger of the target corporation into the acquiring corporation?

FACTS

Situation (1). Corporation X owns all the stock of Corporation Y, a newly formed wholly owned subsidiary. Pursuant to an integrated plan, X acquires all of the stock of Corporation T, an unrelated corporation, in a statutory merger of Y into T (the "Acquisition Merger"), with T surviving. In the Acquisition Merger, the T shareholders exchange their T stock for consideration, 70 percent of which is X voting stock and 30 percent of which is cash. Following the Acquisition Merger and as part of the plan, T merges into X in a statutory merger (the "Upstream Merger"). Assume that, absent some prohibition against the application of the step transaction doctrine, the step transaction doctrine would apply to treat the Acquisition Merger and the Upstream Merger as a single integrated acquisition by X of all the assets of T. Also assume that the single integrated transaction would satisfy the nonstatutory requirements of a reorganization under § 368(a) of the Internal Revenue Code.

* * *

LAW

Section 338(a) provides that if a corporation makes a qualified stock purchase and makes an election under that section, then the target corporation (i) shall be treated as having sold all of its assets at the close of the acquisition date at fair market value and (ii) shall be treated as a new corporation which purchased all of its assets as of the beginning of the day after the acquisition date. Section 338(d)(3) defines a qualified stock purchase as any transaction or series of transactions in which stock (meeting the requirements of § 1504(a)(2)) of one corporation is acquired by another corporation by purchase during a 12–month acquisition period. Section 338(h)(3) defines a purchase generally as any acquisition of stock, but excludes acquisitions of stock in exchanges to which § 351, § 354, § 355, or § 356 applies.

Rev.Rul. 90–95 (1990–2 C.B. 67) (Situation 2), holds that the merger of a newly formed wholly owned domestic subsidiary into a target corporation with the target corporation shareholders receiving solely cash in exchange for their stock, immediately followed by the merger of the target corporation into the domestic parent of the merged subsidiary, will be treated as a qualified stock purchase of the target corporation followed by a § 332 liquidation of the target corporation. As a result, the parent's basis in the target corporation's assets will be the same as the basis of the assets in the target corporation's hands. The ruling explains that even though "the step-transaction doctrine is properly applied to disregard the existence of the [merged subsidiary]," so that the first step is treated as a stock purchase, the acquisition of the target corporation's stock is accorded independent significance from the subsequent liquidation of the target corporation and, therefore, is treated as a qualified stock purchase regardless of whether a § 338 election is made.

Section 1.338–3(d) of the Income Tax Regulations incorporates the approach of Rev.Rul. 90–95 into the regulations by requiring the purchasing corporation (or a member of its affiliated group) to treat certain asset transfers following a qualified stock purchase (where no § 338 election is made) independently of the qualified stock purchase. In the example in § 1.338–3(d)(5), the purchase for cash of 85 percent of the stock of a target corporation, followed by the merger of the target corporation into a wholly owned subsidiary of the purchasing corporation, is treated (other than by certain minority shareholders) as a qualified stock purchase of the stock of the target corporation followed by a § 368 reorganization of the target corporation into the subsidiary. As a result, the subsidiary's basis in the target corporation's assets is the same as the basis of the assets in the target corporation's hands.

Section 368(a)(1)(A) defines the term "reorganization" as a statutory merger or consolidation. Section 368(a)(2)(E) provides that a transaction otherwise qualifying under § 368(a)(1)(A) shall not be disqualified by reason of the fact that stock of a corporation (controlling corporation), which before the merger was in control of the merged corporation, is used in the transaction if (i) after the transaction, the corporation surviving the merger holds substantially all of its properties and the properties of the merged corporation, and (ii) in the transaction, former shareholders of the surviving corporation exchange, for an amount of voting stock of the controlling corporation, an amount of stock in the surviving corporation which constitutes control of such corporation.

In Rev.Rul. 67–274 (1967–2 C.B. 141), Corporation Y acquires all of the stock of Corporation X in exchange for some of the voting stock of Y and, thereafter, X completely liquidates into Y. The ruling holds that because the two steps are parts of a plan of reorganization, they cannot be considered independently of each other. Thus, the steps do not qualify as a reorganization under § 368(a)(1)(B) followed by a liquidation under § 332, but instead qualify as an acquisition of X's assets in a reorganization under § 368(a)(1)(C).

ANALYSIS

Situation (1)

Because of the amount of cash consideration paid to the T shareholders, the Acquisition Merger could not qualify as a reorganization under § 368(a)(1)(A) and § 368(a)(2)(E). If the Acquisition Merger and the Upstream Merger in Situation (1) were treated as separate from each other, as were the steps in Situation (2) of Rev.Rul. 90–95, the Acquisition Merger would be treated as a stock acquisition that is a qualified stock purchase, because the stock is not acquired in a § 354 or § 356 exchange. The Upstream Merger would qualify as a liquidation under § 332. However, if the approach reflected in Rev.Rul. 67–274 were applied to Situation (1), the transaction would be treated as an integrated acquisition of T's assets by X in a single statutory merger (without a preliminary stock acquisition). Accordingly, unless the policies underlying § 338 dictate otherwise, the integrated asset acquisition in Situation (1) is properly treated as a statutory merger of T into X that qualifies as a reorganization under § 368(a)(1)(A). See King Enterprises, Inc. v. United States, 418 F.2d 511 (Ct. Cl. 1969) (in a case that predated § 338, the court applied the step transaction doctrine to treat the acquisition of the stock of a target corporation followed by the merger of the target corporation into the acquiring corporation as a reorganization under § 368(a)(1)(A)); J.E. Seagram Corp. v. Commissioner, 104 T.C. 75 (1995) (same). Therefore, it is necessary to determine whether the approach reflected in Rev.Rul. 90–95 applies where the step transaction doctrine would otherwise apply to treat the transaction as an asset acquisition that qualifies as a reorganization under § 368(a).

Rev.Rul. 90–95 and § 1.338–3(d) reject the approach reflected in Rev.Rul. 67–274 where the application of that approach would treat the purchase of a target corporation's stock without a § 338 election followed by the liquidation or merger of the target corporation as the purchase of the target corporation's assets resulting in a cost basis in the assets under § 1012. The rejection of step integration in Rev.Rul. 90–95 and § 1.338–3(d) is based on Congressional intent that § 338 "replace any nonstatutory treatment of a stock purchase as an asset purchase under the *Kimbell-Diamond* doctrine." H.R. Rep. No. 760, 97th Cong., 2d Sess. 536 (1982), 1982–2 C.B. 600, 632. (In Kimbell-Diamond Milling Co. v. Commissioner, 14 T.C. 74, *aff'd per curiam*, 187 F.2d 718 (1951), *cert. denied*, 342 U.S. 827 (1951), the court held that the purchase of the stock of a target corporation for the purpose of obtaining its assets through a prompt liquidation should be treated by the purchaser as a purchase of the target corporation's assets with the purchaser receiving a cost basis in the assets.) Rev.Rul. 90–95 and § 1.338–3(d) treat the acquisition of the stock of the target corporation as a qualified stock purchase followed by a separate carryover basis transaction in order to preclude any nonstatutory treatment of the steps as an integrated asset purchase.

The policy underlying § 338 is not violated by treating Situation (1) as a single statutory merger of T into X because such treatment results in a transaction that qualifies as a reorganization under § 368(a) (1)(A) in which X acquires the assets of T with a carryover basis under § 362, and does not result in a cost basis for those assets under § 1012. Thus, in Situation (1), the step transaction doctrine applies to treat the Acquisition Merger and the Upstream Merger not as a stock acquisition that is a qualified stock purchase followed by a § 332 liquidation, but instead as an acquisition of T's assets through a single statutory merger of T into X that qualifies as a reorganization under § 368(a)(1)(A). Accordingly, a § 338 election may not be made in such a situation.

* * *

HOLDING

Under the facts presented, if, pursuant to an integrated plan, a newly formed wholly owned subsidiary of an acquiring corporation merges into a target corporation, followed by the merger of the target corporation into the acquiring corporation, the transaction is treated as a single statutory merger of the target corporation into the acquiring corporation that qualifies as a reorganization under § 368(a)(1)(A).

* * *

DETAILED ANALYSIS

1.   VARIATIONS OF THE STEP TRANSACTION DOCTRINE

As should be evident from the opinion in *King Enterprises, Inc.*, the difficulty in predicting when the step transaction doctrine will be applied is compounded by the fact that there are several different variations of the step transaction doctrine. It is likewise difficult to predict which variation of the doctrine will be applied. These variations on a theme were summarized by the Tax Court in Penrod v. Commissioner, 88 T.C. 1415 (1987):

> * * * There is no universally accepted test as to when and how the step transaction doctrine should be applied to a given set of facts. Courts have applied three alternative tests in deciding whether to invoke the step transaction doctrine in a particular situation.
>
> The narrowest alternative is the "binding commitment" test, under which a series of transactions are collapsed if, at the time the first step is entered into, there was a binding commitment to undertake the later step. See Commissioner v. Gordon, 391 U.S. 83, 96 (1968) * * *. The binding commitment test has the advantage of promoting certainty in the tax planning of shareholders. Under such test, a court must make an objective

determination as to whether the acquired shareholders were bound by an obligation to sell the shares received in an acquisition. Other factors, such as intent by such shareholders to sell their shares, are not considered. However, there have been objections to that test on the ground that the result is easily manipulable by taxpayers. * * *

At the other extreme, the most far-reaching alternative is the "end result" test. Under this test, the step transaction doctrine will be invoked if it appears that a series of formally separate steps are really prearranged parts of a single transaction intended from the outset to reach the ultimate result. See King Enterprises, Inc. v. United States, 418 F.2d at 516 * * *. The end result test is based upon the actual intent of the parties as of the time of the merger. It can be argued that any test which requires a court to make a factual determination as to a party's intent promotes uncertainty and therefore impedes effective tax planning. However, in contrast to the binding commitment test, the end result test is flexible and bases tax consequences on the real substance of the transactions, not on the formalisms chosen by the participants.

The third test is the "interdependence" test, which focuses on whether "the steps are so interdependent that the legal relations created by one transaction would have been fruitless without a completion of the series." Redding v. Commissioner, 630 F.2d at 1177 * * * American Bantam Car Co. v. Commissioner, 11 T.C. 397 (1948), affd. 177 F.2d 513 (3d Cir.1949). This test concentrates on the relationship between the steps, rather than on their "end result." * * * However, since the interdependence test requires a court to find whether the individual steps had independent significance or whether they had meaning only as part of the larger transaction, the court may be called upon to determine the result the participants hoped to achieve. Thus, the interdependence test is a variation of the end result test.

Courts have applied each of these three alternatives to a variety of transactions to determine whether the transactions should be "stepped." * * *

The impact of the variation of the step transaction doctrine that the court chooses to apply can be significant. For example, if the court in *King Enterprises, Inc.* had determined that the mutual interdependence test or the binding commitment test ought to have been applied, rather than the end result test, Tenco and its shareholder, King Enterprises, Inc., would not have been involved in a reorganization.

2. OTHER EXAMPLES OF APPLICATION OF THE STEP TRANSACTION DOCTRINE

As in *King Enterprises, Inc.*, in some cases the step transaction doctrine is applied to find a reorganization where none would have existed if each step of the overall transaction were viewed independently. Unlike in the *King Enterprises* case, however, in most of these cases, the step transaction doctrine is applied at the IRS's behest to produce a tax-free reorganization, thereby denying a loss deduction, where following the form of the several steps would have produced a taxable transaction. For example, in Heller v. Commissioner, 2 T.C. 371 (1943), aff'd, 147 F.2d 376 (9th Cir.1945), the shareholders of a Delaware corporation organized a California corporation, contributing borrowed cash for the stock of the California corporation. The California corporation then borrowed additional cash and purchased the assets of the Delaware corporation, which paid its existing indebtedness and distributed the balance of the cash to its shareholders in liquidation. The taxpayer claimed a deductible loss on the liquidation of the Delaware corporation because his basis for his stock in that corporation exceeded the amount of the liquidating distribution. The IRS disallowed the loss, asserting that the series of steps was in fact a single transaction which was a reorganization under the predecessors of § 368(a)(1)(D) or § 368(a)(1)(F) and that, accordingly, pursuant to the predecessor of § 354(a)(1), no loss was recognizable. In response, the taxpayer argued that even if the transaction had the same result as a reorganization, no exchange of stock for stock as required by the predecessor of § 354(a)(1), had occurred.

The Tax Court held for the IRS, reasoning as follows:

> In determining the substance of a transaction it is proper to consider the situation as it existed at the beginning and end of the series of steps as well as the object sought to be accomplished, the means employed, and the relation between the various steps. * * *

> Petitioner and two others, the stockholders and directors of the Delaware corporation, decided to have the business, assets, and liabilities of that company taken over by a new California corporation. The desired end was accomplished by a series of steps, all of which were planned in advance. * * * The net result was that petitioner and the other two stockholders had substituted their interest in the Delaware corporation for substantially the same interest in the California corporation. The nonrecognition of gain or loss provisions of the statute are "intended to apply to cases where a corporation in form transfers its property, but in substance it or its stockholders retain the same or practically the same interest after the transfer." * * *

> The result achieved under the plan could have been accomplished by having the California corporation acquire the assets of the Delaware corporation for its stock, and by having the latter distribute the stock to its stockholders in complete liquidation. Petitioner and his associates apparently chose the longer route, hoping that they might thereby become entitled to a loss deduction. However, as the Supreme Court pointed out in Minnesota Tea Co. v. Helvering, 302 U.S. 609, 613, "a given result at the end of a straight path is not made a different result because reached by following a devious path." The effect of all the steps taken was that petitioner made an exchange of stock of one corporation for stock of another pursuant to a plan of reorganization."

In Rev.Rul. 67–448, 1967–2 C.B. 144, P Corporation formed a subsidiary, S Corporation, and contributed P's stock to the subsidiary. S

Corporation was then merged into unrelated corporation Y with shareholders of Y receiving P Corporation stock in the merger. The ruling treated the series of transactions as the direct acquisition by P of the Y stock in exchange for its own shares, thereby qualifying the transaction as a type (B) reorganization. "It is evident that the shortest route to the end result described above would have been achieved by a transfer of P voting stock directly to the shareholders of Y in exchange for their stock. This result is not negated because the transaction was cast in the form of a series of interrelated steps. The transitory existence of the new subsidiary, S, will be disregarded. The effect of all the steps taken in the series is that Y became a wholly owned subsidiary of P, and P transferred solely its voting stock to the former shareholders of Y." The ruling dealt with a situation arising before the enactment of § 368(a)(2)(E).

In some cases, a reorganization undoubtedly has occurred, but the question is the scope of the reorganization and the identification of the transactions that will be accorded nonrecognition as occurring "pursuant to the plan of reorganization." This type of issue was the question addressed in *King Enterprises, Inc.* Another case raising a similar issue was J.E. Seagram Corp. v. Commissioner, 104 T.C. 75 (1995). This case involved a battle of corporate giants for control of Conoco. J.E. Seagram Corp. approached Conoco to negotiate a friendly takeover. After negotiations broke down, Seagram made a public tender offer to acquire for cash at least 33 percent of the Conoco shares. In the meantime, Conoco entered into an agreement with DuPont pursuant to which DuPont agreed to acquire at least 51 percent of Conoco's shares for either stock or cash, provided a minimum number of shares had been acquired for stock. Pursuant to the agreement, after the requisite number of shares had been acquired, Conoco would then be merged into a subsidiary of DuPont and Conoco shareholders would receive DuPont stock. Mobil Oil then entered the fray and an escalating round of purchase price increases ensued. Seagram acquired 32 percent of the Conoco stock for cash. Mobil dropped out. DuPont's tender offer was successful, and it acquired 51 percent of the Conoco shares for either stock or cash, including approximately 16 million newly issued Conoco shares acquired pursuant to an option granted by Conoco to DuPont. At this point, Seagram decided to accept DuPont stock, which constituted a little over 20 percent of the outstanding stock of DuPont, in exchange for its Conoco stock, and this exchange was completed pursuant to the tender offer. DuPont then completed its agreement with Conoco by merging Conoco into a DuPont subsidiary. Seagram claimed a loss on the exchange, on the theory that because approximately 78 percent of the original Conoco shareholders had sold their stock for cash, the transaction lacked the requisite continuity of interest to qualify as a reorganization, even though approximately 54 percent of the Conoco shares were acquired by DuPont in exchange for its own shares. The IRS denied the loss, claiming that there was an integrated plan of reorganization and § 354 was thus applicable.

The first issue in *J.E. Seagram Corp.* was whether the exchange of Conoco stock held by J.E. Seagram for DuPont stock was "in pursuance of the plan of reorganization," as required by § 354 as a condition for nonrecognition. J.E. Seagram argued that the exchange of its Conoco common stock for DuPont common stock was not done in pursuance of a plan of reorganization, as required by § 354, and that therefore it could recognize a loss on the exchange. It claimed that DuPont's tender offer and the subsequent merger were separate independent transactions.

The Tax Court rejected J.E. Seagram's argument:

> The concept of "plan of reorganization" * * *is one of substantial elasticity. * * * One commentator has stated that
>
>> The courts, and the Service where it has served its purposes, have adopted a functional approach to the problem that is undoubtedly consistent with congressional intent. They have held that a plan of reorganization is a series of transactions intended to accomplish a transaction described as a reorganization in section 368, regardless of how and in what form the plan is expressed and whether the parties intended tax free treatment. * * * [Faber, "The Use and Misuse of the Plan of Reorganization Concept," 38 Tax L. Rev. 515, 523 (1982–1983).]
>
> The DuPont/Conoco Agreement was the definitive vehicle spelling out the interrelated steps by which DuPont would acquire 100 percent of Conoco's stock. To explain the mechanics of the type of procedure utilized by DuPont and Conoco, respondent submitted an Expert Affidavit of Bernard S. Black. Black is a Professor of Law at the Columbia University School of Law, where he teaches courses in Corporate Finance, Securities and Capital Markets Regulations, and Corporate Acquisitions. * * *
>
> In the affidavit, Professor Black states that
>
>> In substance, DuPont's bid for Conoco was a minor variant on a standard two-step acquisition, in which the parties sign a merger agreement that contemplates a first-step cash tender offer, to be followed by a second-step merger. The parties to an acquisition often use this transaction form, rather than a single-step merger (without a tender offer), because a tender offer can close faster than a merger, which increases the likelihood that the acquisition will be completed. * * *
>
> Professor Black goes on to observe that "DuPont added a third step to this transaction form—an exchange offer of DuPont stock for Conoco stock."
>
> The DuPont/Conoco Agreement, which definitively states the terms for "the acquisition of [Conoco] by [DuPont] * * * ", sets out the steps referred to by Professor Black in his affidavit—the series of transactions which in their totality were intended to accomplish a section 368 reorganization. * * *
>
> It has been said that "reorganizations, like other commercial events, must have a discrete start and a finish." See Bittker & Eustice, Federal Income Taxation of Corporations and Shareholders, par. 12.21.[10]. Uncertainty in this regard can present questions as to whether various steps can be considered together as a unified transaction constituting a reorganization. * * *

The Agreement provides a discrete start and finish, and the record discloses no steps agreed to outside the Agreement, or pre-Agreement activity by DuPont or its shareholders, that would invalidate the contemplated reorganization. * * *

In Commissioner v. Gordon, supra * * *, the Supreme Court held that the requirement that the character of a transaction be determinable means that "if one transaction is to be characterized as a 'first step' there must be a binding commitment to take the later steps." This requirement has been met. While DuPont's acquisition of control of Conoco by means of the tender offer unquestionably had economic significance, "independent" or not, and unquestionably was not a "meaningless step," DuPont * * * [was] under a binding and irrevocable commitment to complete the culminating merger—the second step—upon the successful completion of the DuPont tender offer—the first step.

Petitioner argues that DuPont had a "plan" to engage in a series of transactions that might "ultimately may include a reorganization," but not a "plan of reorganization". For reasons already discussed, we disagree. We hold that, because DuPont was contractually committed to undertake and complete the second step merger once it had undertaken and completed the first step tender offer, these carefully integrated transactions together constituted a plan of reorganization within the contemplation of section 354(a).

Despite the existence of the step transaction doctrine, in some situations, the tax result may in the end become one turning purely on form alone, with one route leading to one tax consequence and another route leading to a different tax consequence, though the non-tax end result is the same. See Granite Trust Co. v. United States, 238 F.2d 670 (1st Cir.1956), page 343. In the end, determining when the form of a particular transaction will be respected and when a step transaction approach will be applied is a complex process that resists a simple verbal formulation. Nonetheless, it is central to understanding the reorganization provisions and corporate taxation generally.

3. TURNING OFF THE STEP TRANSACTION DOCTRINE

Treas.Reg. § 1.338(h)(10)–1(c)(2) provides that the step transaction doctrine will not be applied if a valid § 338(h)(10) election, discussed at page 491, has been made with respect to a stock acquisition that, standing alone, is a qualified stock purchase, even if the transaction is part of a multi-step transaction that would otherwise qualify as a reorganization. This provision generally can apply only in the case of the acquisition by a corporation from another corporation of one of its controlled subsidiaries or of an S corporation.

In Rev.Rul. 84–71, 1984–1 C.B. 106, P Corporation, a public corporation, wanted to acquire the stock of T Corporation. A, who held 14 percent of T's stock, was willing to participate only in a nonrecognition transaction. The remainder of T's stockholders would accept cash. P and A formed new S Corporation. P transferred sufficient cash to purchase 86 percent of the T stock and A transferred his T stock to S Corporation in exchange for S Corporation preferred stock in a transaction that qualified under § 351. S transferred the cash to a new subsidiary, again under § 351. The new subsidiary used the cash to acquire T stock from the remaining T stockholders. The transaction could not have qualified for tax-free reorganization treatment to A because of a lack of continuity of interest. The ruling, however, states that application of § 351 to transfers that are part of the larger transaction will not be precluded by the fact that the larger acquisitive reorganization is taxable due to the absence of the continuity of interest in transferred assets that is required in corporate reorganizations.

4. THE STEP TRANSACTION DOCTRINE AND THE CONTINUITY OF INTEREST REGULATIONS

Treas.Reg. § 1.368–1(e), promulgated in 1998, eliminated the application of the step transaction doctrine in determining whether pre-reorganization sales of target corporation stock and post-reorganization sales of acquired corporation stock by former shareholders of the target affect whether the continuity of interest requirement is satisfied. At the same time, however, Treas.Reg. § 1.368–1(a) was amended specifically to require that "[i]n determining whether a transaction qualifies as a reorganization under section 368(a), the transaction must be evaluated under the relevant provisions of law, including the step transaction doctrine." An example of the application of the step transaction that results in failure to meet the continuity of interest requirement even though the acquiring corporation putatively acquires 100 percent of the stock of the target in exchange for stock is provided in Treas.Reg. § 1.368–1(e)(8), Ex. 5:

> Redemption in substance by issuing corporation. A owns 100 percent of the stock of T and none of the stock of P. T merges into P. In the merger, A receives P stock. In connection with the merger, B buys all of the P stock received by A in the merger for cash. Shortly thereafter, in connection with the merger, P redeems the stock held by B for cash. Based on all the facts and circumstances, P in substance has exchanged solely cash for T stock in the merger. The continuity of interest requirement is not satisfied, because in substance P redeemed the stock exchanged for a proprietary interest in T, and a substantial part of the value of the proprietary interest in T is not preserved.

E. TAX RESULTS TO THE PARTIES TO A REORGANIZATION

The consequences to the parties to a reorganization generally do not vary significantly as a result of which of the several different subsections of § 368 defines the reorganization. The type (A) reorganization represents the simplest type of acquisitive reorganization. Section 368(a)(1)(A) defines an (A) reorganization as a "statutory merger or consolidation." See Treas.Reg. § 1.368–2(b)(1)(ii). Thus, generally speaking, any type of amalgamation or consolidation of corporate entities under state or federal merger statutes meets the statutory definition. The assets and liabilities of the target corporation are transferred to the acquiring corporation by operation of state law; the shareholders of the target corporation receive the consideration agreed upon in the merger agreement in exchange for their stock. The consideration may include property other than stock or securities. There are no statutory requirements regarding the proportion of the consideration that must include stock. Thus, the judicially developed continuity of interest requirement, now incorporated in the regulations, is determinative in qualification as a type (A) reorganization.

The type (C) reorganization is treated very similarly to a statutory merger, and the forward triangular merger (§ 368(a)(2)(D)) and reverse triangular merger (§ 368(a)(2)(E)) reorganizations are merely variations of the type (A) reorganization as far as treatment of the parties to the reorganization is concerned. The type (B) reorganization, however, is the only form of tax free reorganization that involves a direct transaction between the acquiring corporation and the shareholders of the target corporation. In addition, it is the only reorganization that does not involve at least one corporation that disappears in the transaction. As a result, it can produce somewhat different tax results to the parties to the reorganization.

This section examines the overarching principles involving taxation of the parties to a reorganization and deals comprehensively with the tax treatment of parties to a type (A) reorganization. Special aspects of the treatment of parties to other forms of reorganizations are discussed in succeeding sections, along with the detailed rules for qualifying as a tax-free reorganization under those subsections of § 368.

(1) SHAREHOLDERS AND SECURITY HOLDERS

INTERNAL REVENUE CODE: Sections 354(a); 356(a), (c), (d), (e); 358(a), (b) (f); 368(b).

REGULATIONS: Sections 1.354–1(a), (b), (e); 1.356–1, –3, –4; 1.358–1, –2(a)(1), (2)(i)–(ii), (vii), (b), (c), Exs. 1–7; 1.368–2(f), (g).

Section 354 provides for nonrecognition of gain or loss to shareholders of the acquired corporation to the extent they receive stock of the acquiring corporation. Where cash or other non-qualifying property, including debt securities, is received in addition to stock, the shareholders will recognize gain under § 356, but only to the extent of the amount of cash or the fair market value of the other property received. If a loss has been realized, it may not be recognized even though boot has been received. I.R.C. § 356(c).

Section 358(a) prescribes exchanged basis rules for the shareholders in § 354 and § 356 exchanges. If gain is recognized under § 356, the exchanged basis is adjusted through an increase for gain recognized and a decrease equal to the amount of the boot received.

Section 362(b) prescribes a transferred basis for property received by the acquiring corporation in a reorganization.

Section 356(a)(2) provides that gain recognized under § 356(a) sometimes may be treated as a dividend depending upon the characterization of boot. However, as long as dividends and capital gains are taxed at the same rate, the question of whether boot is characterized as a dividend under § 356(a)(2) is of limited importance to individual shareholders of the target corporation. It matters primarily because capital gains can be offset by unrelated capital losses, but dividends cannot be offset by capital losses in computing taxable income. For corporate shareholders of the target corporation, however, the issue remains critical. Characterization of boot as a dividend, rather than a capital gain, is advantageous to the corporate shareholder because of the consequent availability of the § 243 dividends received deduction, discussed at page 223.

DETAILED ANALYSIS

1.   RECOGNITION OF GAIN

If a shareholder exchanges more than one block of stock in exchange for stock and boot with respect to each block of stock, the gain must be computed separately on each block. Gain may be recognized on one block of stock while an unrecognized loss is realized on the other. Treas.Reg. § 1.356–1(b); Rev.Rul. 68–23, 1968–1 C.B. 144. If a loss has been realized with respect to a particular block of stock, it may not be recognized even though boot has been received. I.R.C. § 356(c).

Current Treas.Reg. § 1.356–1(b) provides that if a shareholder exchanges stock of more than one class for stock and boot, for purposes of computing gain recognized on an exchange, the terms of the plan of reorganization will determine the extent to which the other property or money has been received in exchange for a particular share of stock or security, provided that such terms are economically reasonable. See Treas.Reg. § 1.356–1(d), Ex. 4. If the plan of reorganization does not specify the stock and boot received in exchange for a particular share of stock or security surrendered, a pro rata portion of the other property and money received is treated as received in exchange for each share of stock and security surrendered, based on the fair market value of such surrendered share of stock or security. Treas.Reg. § 1.356–1(b), (d) , Ex. 3.

Prop.Reg. § 1.356–1(b) (2009) would restate these rules by referring to Prop.Reg. § 1.354–1(d)(1) (2009), providing a default rule under which a pro rata portion of property and money received will be treated as received in exchange for each share of stock or security surrendered based on the fair market value of the surrendered stock or security. However, the proposed regulations would modify the rule of current Treas.Reg. § 1.356–1(b) by providing, in Prop.Reg. § 1.354–1(d)(1) (2009), that the terms of the exchange agreement specifying the other property or money that is received in exchange for a particular share of stock or security surrendered or a particular class of stock or securities surrendered will control the allocation if the terms are economically reasonable, unless the shareholder's exchange has the effect of a distribution of a dividend. Thus, as long as the exchange does not have the effect of a dividend under § 356(a)(2), if no stock is received with respect to a particular block of stock and only cash (or debt instruments) is received with respect to that block of stock, gain or loss will be recognized under § 1001; neither § 354 nor § 356 applies to that block of stock.

Where the distribution has the effect of a distribution of a dividend, the proposed regulations would respect an economically reasonable allocation among classes of stock, but not permit an allocation among shares within the same class. The exchange of a class of stock solely for cash (or debt instruments) boot will not be treated as an exchange to which §§ 354 or 356 applies, but will be treated as an exchange to which § 302(d) applies (redemption distributions treated as § 301 distributions). Prop.Reg. § 1.354–1(d)(2) (2009).

For the nonrecognition protection of § 354 to apply the stock must be received as part of the reorganization exchange. Thus, in Rev.Rul. 73–233, 1973–1 C.B. 179, where minority shareholders in a merger refused to vote in favor of the merger unless they received a disproportionate amount of stock in the acquiring corporation, the amount of stock received in excess of their proportionate interest was taxable under § 61. A contribution to capital by the majority shareholder was disregarded and the transaction was treated as if all of the parties had received their proportionate shares of stock in the acquiring corporation with the majority shareholder then transferring to the minority shareholders additional shares of stock as consideration for their voting in favor of the merger.

2.   CHARACTERIZATION OF GAIN

2.1. *Dividend versus Capital Gain*

Section 356(a)(2) treats recognized gain on the distribution of boot as a dividend if the exchange "has the effect of the distribution of a dividend." The characterization of recognized gain as a dividend was important when dividends were subject to a significantly higher tax rate than were capital gains. However, under current law, which taxes dividends at the same rate as long-term capital gains, characterizing boot as a dividend under § 356(a)(2) or as capital gain has no significance in many instances. Since the amount of the dividend under § 356(a)(2) is limited to the lesser of the amount of the boot or the gain realized, a basis offset automatically occurs in either case. Thus for a noncorporate shareholder receiving boot, the only important difference is that gain recognized with respect to boot received in a reorganization can be offset by capital losses, while § 356(a)(2) dividend income can be offset by capital losses only to a very limited extent under § 1211. For a corporation that is a shareholder of the target corporation, however, characterization of boot as a dividend, rather than a capital gain, remains important. In this case characterization as a dividend is advantageous because of the consequent availability of the § 243 dividends received deduction, discussed at page 223.

In Commissioner v. Clark, 489 U.S. 726 (1989), the Supreme Court settled a long-standing dispute regarding the manner in which dividend equivalency under § 356(a)(2) is to be tested. In *Clark*, the sole shareholder of the target corporation in a triangular merger, in which target was merged into a subsidiary of the acquiring corporation, received 300,000 shares of the acquiring corporation's stock plus $3,250,000 of cash. The IRS asserted that the gain from the boot was a dividend to the extent of the target corporation's earnings and profits at the time of the merger. The Supreme Court addressed a conflict among the Circuit Courts of Appeal regarding whether the tests for redemption under § 302 (discussed in Chapter 5) should be applied by treating the boot as received in exchange for a redemption of stock of the target corporation prior to the reorganization, or by treating the distribution of boot as a redemption of the stock of the surviving corporation after the reorganization. In Shimberg v. United States, 577 F.2d 283 (5th Cir. 1978), adopting the position of the IRS, the court held that the distribution of boot is treated as though it were made in a hypothetical redemption by the acquired corporation immediately prior to the reorganization. Under this approach, any pro rata distribution (including a distribution to a sole shareholder) would fail the disproportionate distribution tests of § 302(b) and result in dividend treatment. On the other hand, the Fourth Circuit in *Clark*, following

Wright v. United States, 482 F.2d 600 (8th Cir. 1973), held that the distribution should be tested for redemption status under § 302 as if the acquiring corporation issued and then redeemed a number of shares equivalent in value to the boot. Under this approach redemption status is tested by the reduction in ownership of the acquiring corporation represented by the hypothetical issue and redemption of shares represented by the boot. The Supreme Court adopted the approach of the Fourth and Eighth Circuits in *Clark* and *Shimberg*. The Court indicated that the post-redemption approach more accurately reflected Congressional intent to treat a reorganization as an integrated transaction, rather than analyzing the payment of boot as an isolated distribution by the target corporation prior to the reorganization. Thus, under the Court's analysis, the shareholder in *Clark* was treated as if he had received an additional 125,000 shares of the acquiring corporation stock, the number of shares foregone in favor of the boot, which the acquiring corporation redeemed for the $3,250,000 cash payment. The hypothetical redemption of 125,000 shares reduced the shareholder's interest in the acquiring corporation from 1.3 percent of the outstanding stock to 0.9 percent. As a result, the taxpayer held less than 80 percent of his previous interest in the acquiring corporation and less than 50 percent of voting stock, thereby satisfying the disproportionate distribution test of § 302(b)(2), and resulting in capital gain treatment.

The pre-reorganization redemption analysis urged by the IRS, which was rejected by the Court in *Clark,* would lead to a dividend in all cases in which the boot is paid pro rata to the shareholders of the acquired corporation. The dissent in *Clark* described the distribution of boot as a pro rata redemption of stock to the shareholder of the target corporation that should be taxed as a dividend under United States v. Davis, 397 U.S. 306 (1970), page 250. Justice White observed in the dissent that "[t]ransporting § 302 from its purpose to frustrate shareholder sales of equity back to their own corporation, to § 356(a)(2)'s reorganization context, however, is problematic. Neither the majority nor the Court of Appeals explains why § 302 should obscure the core attribute of a dividend as a pro rata distribution to a corporation's shareholders, nor offers insight into the mechanics of valuing hypothetical stock transfers and equity reductions; nor answers the Commissioner's observations that the sole shareholder of an acquired corporation will always have a smaller interest in the continuing enterprise when cash payments combine with a stock exchange."

Contrary to the protestations of the dissent, however, the post-reorganization constructive redemption analysis adopted in *Clark* does not eliminate dividend treatment in all cases. Under the analysis adopted in *Clark*, proportionately larger cash distributions to the shareholders of the target corporation are more likely to receive capital gains treatment than relatively smaller amounts of boot, which remain susceptible to dividend characterization. Suppose that A and B each own 200 shares of common stock of T Corporation, which has outstanding 400 shares. Each of their blocks of stock has a basis of $50,000 and a fair market value of $200,000. In a valid type (A) reorganization, T Corporation is merged into P Corporation. Prior to the merger, P Corporation had outstanding 800 shares of common stock, which had an aggregate fair market value of $400,000. Each corporation has retained earnings and profits in excess of $200,000. Pursuant to the merger, A and B each receive in exchange for their T stock 240 newly issued shares of P Corporation common stock having a fair market value of $120,000 plus $80,000 of cash. Under the analysis of *Clark*, if A and B had received stock instead of cash, they each would have received 400 shares of P stock. Each would have held 25 percent of the outstanding P stock (400/1600 shares). After the $80,000 cash redemption, A and B each would have had 18.75 percent of the outstanding P stock (240/1280 shares). The boot thus qualifies for capital gain treatment as a redemption under § 302(b)(2) (18.75% is less than 80% of 25%). If A and B each were to receive $25,000 of cash and 350 shares of P stock, the boot is more likely to be treated as a dividend. A and B each would own 23.33 percent of the outstanding P stock (350 of 1500 outstanding shares). Under the analysis of *Clark*, the reduction in their interest from the 25 percent interest they would have held if they had received all stock to 23.33 percent is not enough to qualify the distribution as a redemption under § 302(b)(2). However, the boot might qualify for capital gain treatment under § 302(b)(1), although that result is anything but clear. See Rev.Rul. 76–364, 1976–2 C.B. 91 and Rev.Rul. 75–512, 1975–2 C.B. 112, page 257, both of which involved additional circumstances.

Prop.Reg. § 1.354–1(d)(1) (2009) would provide that whether the receipt of boot has the effect of a dividend is to be determined by taking into account the overall exchange of all stock. However, in order to maintain the distinction between different classes of stock, for purposes of determining gain, any boot is allocated pro rata among the shares of a class. If the distribution has the effect of a dividend, the proposed regulations would allow the terms of an exchange to provide economically reasonable allocations of consideration among different classes of stock, but not among shares within a class.

2.2. *Earnings and Profits*

If the position of the IRS argued in *Clark* (the *Shimberg* approach) had been upheld, the logical implication would have been that only the earnings and profits of the acquired corporation would have been relevant in determining dividend equivalency under § 356(a)(2). Although there have been no cases or rulings involving the computation of earnings and profits in mergers for purposes of applying § 356(a)(2), prior to *Clark* in cases involving type (D) reorganizations the courts reached conflicting decisions. In Davant v. Commissioner, 366 F.2d 874 (5th Cir.1966), the Fifth Circuit looked to the earnings and profits of both corporations where there was identity of ownership. However, in Atlas Tool Co. v. Commissioner, 70 T.C. 86 (1978), aff'd, 614 F.2d 860 (3d Cir. 1980), the Tax Court and the Third Circuit both held that dividend status was measured by the earnings and profits of the target (transferor) corporation, rejecting the IRS's argument that dividend status should be determined from the combined earnings and profits of the acquiring and target corporations. The *Davant* approach was specifically rejected. In American Manufacturing Co. v. Commissioner, 55 T.C. 204 (1970), which reached a result similar to that in *Atlas Tool*, the Tax Court reasoned that "[t]he legislative history of the section leads to the conclusion that Congress was concerned with a bailout of the earnings and profits of the transferor corporation, and Congress did not seem to consider that there could be, under certain circumstances, a bailout of those of the transferee as well."

Following the post-acquisition redemption analysis of *Clark*, which views the exchange as an integrated whole, the distribution that is treated as a post-acquisition distribution by the acquiring corporation logically should be treated as coming from the earnings and profits of the acquiring corporation, as enhanced by the earnings and profits of the target corporation pursuant to § 381. Under § 381(a) and (c)(2), discussed at page 795, the acquiring corporation in a type (A) or type (C) reorganization inherits the earnings and profits of the target corporation. The earlier authorities may be distinguished as predating *Clark* and by differences between type (A) and type (D) reorganizations, particularly in the context of the liquidation/reincorporation transactions at issue. See page 660. However, the opinion in *Clark* does not directly address which corporation's earnings and profits are to be used to determine whether a distribution of boot is a dividend under § 316.

What if neither the target corporation nor the acquiring corporation has accumulated earnings and profits as of the date of a reorganization, but the acquiring corporation has current earnings and profits for the taxable year in which it distributes boot that is taxable as a dividend under § 356(a)(2)? The reference of § 356(a)(2) to the distributee's "ratable share of earnings and profits accumulated after February 28, 1913," suggests that dividend status is dependent upon earnings and profits accumulated to the date of the distribution. See also Treas.Reg. § 1.356–1(b)(1).

3. BASIS CONSIDERATIONS

The basis for the stock of the acquiring corporation received by the shareholders of the target corporation without recognition of gain under § 354 is determined under § 358(a). That section provides that the basis of the stock is the same as the stock in the target corporation that was surrendered in the reorganization transaction. If, in addition to stock or securities of the acquiring corporation, nonqualifying "boot" is received, the basis of the stock received is the same as the basis of the stock surrendered, decreased by the amount of money and the fair market value of property treated as boot that is received and increased by the amount of gain recognized including the amount of gain treated as a dividend. I.R.C. § 358(a)(1). Property received as boot is assigned a basis equal to its fair market value. I.R.C. § 358(a)(1).

The basis of stock and securities received without recognition of gain is allocated among the qualified stock and securities, as provided in Treas.Reg. § 1.358–2. Generally speaking, Treas.Reg. § 1.358–2 requires that the basis be allocated among the stock or securities received in proportion to their fair market values. Where a single class of stock or securities has been surrendered, the regulations permit the aggregate basis of the stock or securities to be used as the starting point in a single computation. Treas.Reg. § 1.358–2(a)(2) and (3), (c), Ex. 2. But where multiple classes or blocks of stock, or both stock and securities, have been exchanged, the basis for each class of stock or securities surrendered must be assigned to the particular stock and securities received in exchange therefor. Treas.Reg. § 1.358–2(a)(2)(i).

In a reorganization shareholders often exchange blocks of the same class of stock in the target corporation that were acquired at different times for different prices for shares of the acquiring corporation. Treas.Reg. § 1.358–2 provides that the basis of each share of stock (or each security) received in a reorganization will be the same as the basis of the share or shares of stock (or security or securities) surrendered. Thus, under the regulation, a particular share or block of shares of the acquiring corporation received in the exchange is traced to a particular share or block of shares of the target corporation surrendered in the reorganization exchange. The regulations thus prevent a reorganization from triggering averaging of the bases of the exchanged blocks of stock. According to the preamble to the proposed regulations that preceded the final regulations, the IRS was "concerned that averaging the bases of the exchanged blocks of stock may inappropriately limit the ability of taxpayers to arrange their affairs or may afford opportunities for the avoidance of certain provisions of the Code."

If more than one share of stock or more than one security (or a combination of shares of stock and securities) is received in exchange for one share of stock or one security, the basis of the share of stock or security surrendered is allocated to the shares and/or securities received based on the fair market value of the shares and/or securities received. In addition, if one share of stock or security is received in respect of more than one share of stock or security or a fraction of a share of stock or security is received, the basis of the shares of stock or securities surrendered must be allocated to the shares of stock or securities received in a manner that, to the greatest extent possible, reflects that a share of stock or security received is received in respect of shares of stock or securities acquired on the same date and at the same price. Treas.Reg. § 1.358–2(a)(2)(i). Suppose, for example, that B acquired 100 shares of stock of T Corporation in 2012 for $4,000 and 200 shares of stock of the target corporation in 2013 for $6,000 and pursuant to a reorganization in a subsequent year shareholder exchanges those shares for 150 shares of P Corporation. Under the regulations, 50 shares of P Corporation are treated as acquired for the 100 shares of T Corporation the shareholder acquired in 2012 and 100 shares of P Corporation are treated as acquired for the 200 shares of T Corporation acquired in 2013. Accordingly, 50 shares will have a basis of $4,000 and the other 100 shares will have a basis of $6,000. This rule minimizes the chances of creating shares or securities with split holding periods.

If a shareholder cannot identify the specific shares (i.e., block of stock) of the target corporation involved in an exchange for specific shares of the acquiring corporation, the shareholder may designate the particular share or shares surrendered in exchange for the new share or shares (or securities for securities). Treas.Reg. § 1.358–2(a)(2)(vii). However, the designation must be consistent with the terms of the exchange or distribution and must be made on or before the first date on which the basis of a share or security received is relevant. In instances where a shareholder holds two or more blocks of a single class of stock of the target that are exchanged for stock of the acquiring corporation, this will almost always be the case.

If the terms of the plan of reorganization specify which shares of stock or securities are received in exchange for a particular share of stock or security or a particular class of stock or securities, the terms of the plan will control for purposes of determining the basis of the stock or securities received, provided that such terms are economically reasonable. Treas.Reg. § 1.358–2(a)(2)(ii). This rule is important primarily in reorganizations pursuant to which a shareholder or security holder surrenders shares of stock of one or more classes (or a security) and receives shares of stock (or securities) of more than one class, or receives "other property" or money in addition to shares of stock or securities. If the terms of the plan do not specify which shares of stock or securities are received in exchange for a particular share of stock or security or a particular class of stock or securities, a pro rata portion of the shares of stock and securities of each class received is treated as received in exchange for each share of stock and security surrendered, based on the fair market value of the surrendered stock and securities. Treas.Reg. § 1.358–2(a)(2)(i) and (ii).

Proposed amendments to Treas.Reg. § 1.358–2 published in 2009 would revise the section numbering and headings, but would not make any significant substantive changes. See Prop.Reg. §§ 1.358–1, –2 (2009).

4.   RECEIPT OF SECURITIES

4.1. *Amount of Boot*

Section 354(a) extends nonrecognition treatment to an exchange of "stock or securities * * * for stock or securities."[14] Thus, where the target corporation's securities become securities of the acquiring corporation under state law in a statutory merger, no gain or loss is recognized. However, § 354(a)(2) and § 356(d) treat the receipt of securities as boot if the principal amount of securities received is greater than the principal amount of any securities surrendered. The fair market value of the excess principal amount of securities received is treated as "other property." Where securities are received in exchange for only stock, the entire fair market value of the securities is treated as boot. Treas.Reg. § 1.356–3(c), Ex. 1. Where securities are received in exchange for other securities, only the fair market value of the excess principal amount constitutes boot. The value of the excess principal amount is determined by the following formula:

$$\text{Fair Market Value of Securities Received} \times \frac{\text{Principal Amount of Securities Received} \quad \text{Minus} \quad \text{Principal Amount of Securities Surrendered}}{\text{Principal Amount of Securities Received}}$$

In determining the "principal amount" of securities exchanged in the reorganization, the original issue discount (OID) rules of §§ 1272 and 1274, discussed in Chapter 3, Section 2, must be taken into account. If the OID rules do not apply, generally speaking, the amount of any excess face value of a security received over the face value of securities surrendered also will be the value of the excess. However, if the OID rules apply the principal amount of the securities exchanged must be reduced as required by those rules to an amount less than their face value when computing gain under § 356. Thus, receipt of a security having a *face* value in excess of the principal amount of the security surrendered will not give rise to boot under § 356 if under the OID rules the imputed principal amount of the security received does not exceed the principal amount of the security surrendered. Section 1273(b) applies to the determination of the amount of

---

[14] Generally under state law in a statutory merger outstanding securities of the target corporation become liabilities of the acquiring corporation. Without intervention of a nonrecognition provision the exchange of securities may be a taxable transaction. See Treas.Reg. § 1.1001–3. However, Treas.Reg. § 1.1001–3(e)(4)(i)(B) provides that a change in the obligor of a debt instrument in a transaction to which § 381 applies, which includes reorganizations qualified under § 368(a)(1)(A), is not a significant modification of the debt resulting in a taxable exchange.

OID if either the securities surrendered or the securities received are publicly traded. If the securities received are publicly traded, their "issue price," and thus "principal amount," is their fair market value, i.e. trading price, on the day they are issued. Treas.Reg. § 1.1273–2(b)(1). Thus, if new publicly traded bonds are issued for outstanding publicly traded bonds, the principal amount of the new bonds is their trading price, not the trading price of the old bonds. But if securities that are not publicly traded are issued for publicly traded securities, the issue price, and thus principal amount, of the new securities is the trading price of the old securities. Treas.Reg. § 1.1273–2(c)(1). Section 1274 controls if the securities involved in the exchange are not publicly traded. See also Treas.Reg. § 1.356–3(c), Exs. 2–6. The application of these rules is discussed in greater detail at page 687.

Not all debt instruments qualify as "securities" for purposes of § 354. In Neville Coke & Chemical Co. v. Commissioner, 148 F.2d 599 (3d Cir.1945), the taxpayer held stock, bonds, three-, four-, and five-year notes, and accounts receivable of an insolvent corporation. In a reorganization involving the debtor corporation, the taxpayer received new common stock for its stock, new debentures for its bonds, and new debentures and common stock for its notes and accounts receivable. The IRS asserted that the taxpayer recognized a gain on the exchange of the notes and accounts receivable for debentures and common stock. The taxpayer asserted that the notes and accounts receivable were "securities" within the meaning of the predecessor of § 354(a)(1) and that it had exchanged "securities" for "stock and securities," thereby entitling it to nonrecognition on the exchange. In holding for the IRS, the court held that "securities" has the same meaning in the context of the interest surrendered as it does in the context of the interest received, that a "security" entails having a "proprietary" interest in the corporation, and that the rights of the taxpayer as a note holder were merely those of a creditor.

Conventional wisdom is that debt instruments with a term of more than five years generally qualify as "securities." Camp Wolters Enterprises v. Commissioner, 230 F.2d 555 (5th Cir. 1956), held that a series of notes issued by a corporation that were payable between the fifth and ninth year after issuance constituted "securities." Nevertheless, quoting the Tax Court opinion that it affirmed, the court noted as follows:

> The test as to whether notes are securities is not a mechanical determination of the time period of the note. Though time is an important factor, the controlling consideration is an overall evaluation of the nature of the debt, degree of participation and continuing interest in the business, the extent of proprietary interest compared with the similarity of the note to a cash payment, the purpose of the advances, etc.

See also Rev.Rul. 59–98, 1959–1 C.B. 76 (first mortgage bonds with a term of six and one-half years were securities).

However, Rev.Rul. 2004–78, 2004–2 C.B. 108, held that debt instruments with a term of two years received in a merger qualified as securities under the particular circumstances in which they were received. That ruling involved a merger that qualified as a reorganization under § 368(a)(1)(A) in which the holders of the target corporation's long-term securities that had only two years remaining before maturity received in exchange for those securities debt instruments of the acquirer that matured in two years and which, except for the interest rate, bore identical rights to the surrendered securities. Nevertheless, the ruling described the case law as concluding that an instrument with a term of less than five years generally is not a security.

4.2. *Installment Reporting*

Gain recognized on the receipt of securities in a reorganization may be reported using the installment method under § 453 unless either the stock or securities surrendered were readily tradable on an established securities market (§ 453(h)(1)) or the securities received are readily tradable (§ 453(f)(4)). See Prop.Reg. § 1.453–1(f)(2) (1984). In the case of gain reported under the installment method, the basis of the stock received in the reorganization is computed under Prop.Reg. § 1.453–1(f)(2) (1984) in the same manner that the basis of stock received in a § 351 transaction is computed if an installment note is received as boot. See page 73.

5.   STOCK RIGHTS AND WARRANTS

Treas. Regs. §§ 1.354–1(e) and 1.356–3(b) treat rights to acquire stock (options and warrants) of a corporation that is a party to a reorganization as securities of the corporation having no principal amount. The term "rights to acquire stock" of an issuing corporation has the same meaning as for purposes of §§ 305(d)(1) and 317(a). Thus, an exchange of options to purchase stock of the target corporation for options to purchase stock of the acquiring corporation is accorded nonrecognition, as is an exchange of target corporation bonds for acquiring corporation options. Likewise, an exchange of stock for stock and an option, or an exchange of an option for stock and an option, is not taxable. See Treas.Reg. § 1.356–3(b) and (c), Exs. 7 and 8. If, however, warrants are exchanged for debt securities, gain must be recognized. Treas.Reg. § 1.356–3(c), Ex. 9. Arguably, however, because the receipt solely of warrants in exchange for stock is not covered by § 354, see Treas.Reg. § 1.354–1(d), Ex. 4, and § 356 technically applies only if some permissible consideration under § 354 is received in the exchange, an exchange of target stock solely for options to purchase stock of the acquiring corporation is not entitled to nonrecognition. The regulations do not address this point and it is not clear whether or not the ambiguity was intended. (In any event, a purported reorganization involving the exchange of target stock for only options to purchase stock of the acquiring corporation would fail the continuity of interest requirement.)

Rights exercisable against persons other than the issuer of the stock are not covered by Treas.Reg. § 1.354–1(e). Rev.Rul. 69–265, 1969–1 C.B. 109, held that a conversion privilege contained in a stock or debt instrument generally is not considered to be a separate property right received in the reorganization, and the regulations do not change that result. Treas. Regs. §§ 1.354–1(e) and 1.356–3(b) apply only in determining the amount of gain recognized in an otherwise qualifying reorganization. Thus, the regulations do not affect pre-existing law under which stock rights are not taken into account in determining whether the continuity of shareholder interest test has been satisfied. See Notice of Proposed Rulemaking and Notice of Public Hearings, Reorganizations, Receipt of Securities, REG–249819–96, 1997–1 C.B. 793, 794.

6.   PREFERRED STOCK

6.1. *Nonqualified Preferred Stock*

Sections 354(a)(2)(C) and 356(e) require that "nonqualified preferred stock" be treated as boot for purposes of §§ 354 and 356. Nonqualified preferred stock is defined in § 351(g)(2), page 75. Preferred stock is stock that is limited and preferred as to dividends and which does not participate in corporate growth. I.R.C. § 351(g)(3)(A). Preferred stock is "nonqualified" only if within 20 years after issue, the issuer or a related person (1) may be required by the holder to redeem the stock, (2) is required to redeem the stock, or (3) has a right to redeem the stock and it is more likely than not that the right to redeem will be exercised. I.R.C. § 351(g)(2). Preferred stock is also nonqualified preferred stock if the dividend rate is determined in whole or in part by reference to interest rates, commodity prices, or similar indices.

Because nonqualified preferred stock received in an exchange will not be treated as stock or securities but, instead, will be treated as boot, the receipt of nonqualified preferred stock will result in recognition of gain under § 356 unless a specified exception applies. Sections 354(a)(2)(C) and 356(e)(2) provide that nonqualified preferred stock is treated as stock rather than as other property in cases where the nonqualified preferred stock is received in exchange for other nonqualified preferred stock. In these cases, the receipt of nonqualified preferred stock will not result in recognition of gain under § 356. Treas. Regs. §§ 1.354–1(f) and 1.356–7(b) provide additional rules to deal with various aspects of exchanges of nonqualified preferred stock in reorganizations. Under the general rule in the regulations, the nonrecognition rules apply only if nonqualified preferred stock is received with respect to "substantially identical" nonqualified preferred stock. Stock is considered to be substantially identical if two conditions are met: First, the stock received does not contain any terms which, in relation to the terms of the stock previously held, decrease the period in which a redemption or purchase right will be exercised, increase the likelihood that such a right will be exercised, or accelerate the timing of the returns from the stock instrument (including the receipt of dividends or other distributions). Second, as a result of the receipt of the stock, the exercise of the right or obligation does not become more likely than not to occur within a 20-year period beginning on the issue date of the stock previously held.

6.2. *Section 306 Aspects*

If pursuant to the reorganization the shareholders of the acquired corporation surrender common stock and receive both common stock and preferred stock, the preferred stock will be characterized as § 306 stock pursuant to § 306(c)(1)(B) if "the effect of the transaction was substantially the same as the receipt of a stock dividend." See Treas.Reg. § 1.306–3(d). (Section 306 is discussed in Chapter 6.) The regulations indicate that unless a cash distribution in lieu of the preferred stock would have been a dividend under § 356(a)(2), the stock will not be § 306 stock. As a result of the decision in Commissioner v. Clark, page 601, classification of preferred stock received in an acquisitive reorganization as § 306 stock depends on the ratio of common stock to preferred stock received by the shareholder in the reorganization. Generally speaking, the higher the ratio of common to preferred, the more likely the preferred stock will be characterized as § 306 stock and the lower the ratio the more likely the preferred stock will not be so characterized.

Rev.Rul. 89–63, 1989–1 C.B. 90, held that where both common and preferred stock of a publicly held acquiring corporation were issued to the former holders of the common stock of a publicly held target corporation in a type (A) statutory merger, the preferred stock was § 306 stock. The ruling did not provide any rationale for its conclusion that the stock was § 306 stock, and if cash had been distributed in lieu of the preferred stock, under *Clark* the cash would not have been substantially equivalent to a dividend. The fact that the corporations were publicly held, standing alone, was not sufficient to bring the preferred stock within the § 306(b)(4) exception for transactions not involving tax avoidance.

Preferred stock received for preferred stock in acquisitive reorganizations will not be § 306 stock if it is of equal value to the preferred stock surrendered, the terms of the new preferred stock are not substantially different from the terms of the old preferred stock, and the preferred stock surrendered in the exchange was not itself § 306 stock. Rev.Rul. 88–100, 1988–2 C.B. 46 (holding that Treas.Reg. § 1.306–3(d), Ex. (2), applies to acquisitive reorganizations); Rev.Rul. 82–118, 1982–1 C.B. 56. The rulings emphasize that in such cases the new preferred stock is merely a substitute for the old preferred stock, and the distribution therefore does not have the effect of a distribution of earnings and profits. However, if the surrendered preferred stock was § 306 stock, then any preferred stock (or common stock) received in exchange for the tainted preferred stock will be § 306 stock. I.R.C. § 306(c)(1)(C).

7.   CONTINGENT STOCK PAYOUTS

The shareholders of the target corporation also may receive the right to obtain additional voting shares in the future if specified conditions are met, e.g., the earnings of the target corporation reaching a certain level. Generally, such contingent stock payout agreements are utilized in situations in which the parties to the reorganization are unable to agree on the fair market value of the target corporation's stock. The right to receive voting shares in the future is not the same as the present receipt of voting shares as such and hence arguably could violate the solely for voting stock restriction.

Carlberg v. United States, 281 F.2d 507 (8th Cir.1960), held that certificates representing a contingent interest in shares in the acquiring corporation should be treated as "stock" for purposes of nonrecognition under § 354 (a result disputed by the IRS because the certificates in question were negotiable). In Hamrick v. Commissioner, 43 T.C. 21 (1964), the court treated a nonnegotiable contingent right to receive additional shares of stock as the equivalent of stock for purposes of § 351. Neither case had to decide whether the contingent interest represented "voting stock," a somewhat more difficult question. Subsequently, Rev.Rul. 66–112, 1966–1 C.B. 68, held that the receipt of a contingent contractual right to additional voting shares that was not assignable and could only ripen into additional voting shares did not violate the solely for voting stock requirement in a type (B) reorganization. The holding in Rev.Rul. 66–112 is also relevant in the context of type (C) reorganization and with respect to reverse triangular mergers under § 368(a)(2)(E).

Rev.Proc. 77–37, § 3.03, 1977–2 C.B. 568, amplified by Rev.Proc. 84–42, 1984–1 C.B. 521, sets forth nine conditions under which a favorable ruling will be issued on the solely for voting stock question in a contingent stock payout situation. The principal requirements are that all the additional stock must be issued within five years from the date of the original reorganization transaction, there must be a valid business reason for not issuing all the stock immediately, such as the difficulty of valuing the stock of one or both of the corporations, the maximum number of shares that may be issued is stated, and at least one-half of the total number of shares to be issued must be issued in the initial distribution.

The OID regulations under §§ 1272 through 1275 (governing the imputation of interest, see page 162) do not deal with contingent stock payout situations because the OID rules apply only to "debt instruments," and a contingent stock right is not a debt instrument. Section 483, however, applies to impute interest on "contingent payments," and Treas.Reg. § 1.483–4(b), Ex. 2 applies § 483 to a contingent stock payout. As a result, upon receipt of the contingent stock, a portion of the stock will be characterized as interest taxable as ordinary income and not entitled to nonrecognition under § 354.

Rev.Rul. 75–94, 1975–1 C.B. 111, dealt with a variation on a contingent stock payout situation. In 1973, a type (B) reorganization took place. In the following year it was discovered that the acquiring corporation had misrepresented its earnings because of an improper accounting practice. Upon correction of the improper practice, the earnings were reduced and the target corporation's stockholders asserted that they were entitled to additional stock of the acquiring corporation to satisfy the negotiated acquisition price. After discussions between the parties, the acquiring corporation did issue additional stock. The ruling concluded that the additional shares received were part of the original "plan of reorganization" and hence qualified as part of the (B) reorganization.

Another technique that is employed where the parties cannot agree upon the value of the corporations is the "escrowed stock" arrangement. Under such an arrangement, the acquiring corporation issues its stock to the shareholders of the target corporation, but part of the stock is placed in escrow to be returned to the acquiring corporation upon the occurrence of a specified event, for example, the failure of the target corporation to reach a specified earnings level. If the earnings level is reached, the stock is transferred out of escrow to the former shareholders of the target corporation. Since the stock is actually issued, subject to subsequent forfeiture, some problems of contingent stock payouts are avoided. For example, interest will not be imputed under § 483 if the transaction is properly structured. Rev.Rul. 70–120, 1970–1 C.B. 124 (shareholders entitled to unrestricted voting rights and received dividends on stock); Feifer v. United States, 500 F.Supp. 102 (N.D.Ga.1980) (same even though voting rights were restricted).

Rev.Rul. 76–42, 1976–1 C.B. 102, held that no gain or loss is recognized by the shareholders of the target corporation if the escrowed stock is returned to the acquiring corporation where the number of shares to be returned was based on their initially negotiated value. The adjusted basis of the returned shares is added to the basis of those received by the shareholders of the target corporation. Compare Rev.Rul. 78–376, 1978–2 C.B. 149 (because the number of shares to be returned from the escrow to discharge an indemnity obligation was based on the value of the shares on the date of the return from escrow and not on the initially negotiated price, the taxpayer was required to realize gain since he received a benefit from the appreciation in value that was used to discharge his obligations).

Rev.Proc. 77–37, § 3.06, 1977–2 C.B. 568, amplified by Rev.Proc. 84–42, 1984–1 C.B. 521, sets forth nine conditions under which a favorable ruling will be issued in escrowed stock transactions. The principal requirements are that there must be a valid reason for establishing the arrangement, the stock subject to the escrow agreement must be treated as issued and outstanding stock of the acquiring corporation for all purposes, voting rights must be exercisable by the shareholders or their agent, all shares must be released from the escrow within five years, and not more than 50 percent of the total number of shares to be issued may be subject to the escrow.

Contingent stock and escrowed stock arrangements are not unique to any particular type of reorganization. They may be used in connection with any type of acquisition, but different problems may arise with respect to qualifying the transaction under different provisions of § 368. For example, Rev.Rul. 76–334, 1976–2 C.B. 108, involved the use of an escrow arrangement in a type (C) reorganization in which the transferor corporation liquidated and distributed all rights in the escrowed stock to its shareholders. The purpose of the escrow was to protect the acquiring corporation from a breach of representations and warranties made by the target corporation as a part of the reorganization transaction. The acquiring corporation asserted a breach and the escrow agent returned part of the escrowed stock to the acquiring corporation, with the balance being distributed to the target corporation's shareholders. However, those shareholders disputed the validity of the acquiring corporation's claim to a return of part of the escrowed stock. Negotiations between the parties resulted in a settlement pursuant to which the acquiring corporation paid cash equal to one-half the value of the escrowed shares distributed to the shareholders and the shareholders returned the balance of the escrowed shares to the acquiring corporation. The ruling held that the cash payment was separate from, and did not violate the solely for voting stock requirement of, the (C) reorganization. There was a redemption of one-half the escrowed stock under § 302 and the other one-half was simply returned pursuant to the escrow arrangement with no gain or loss being recognized by the target corporation's shareholders under the principles of Rev.Rul. 76–42.

(2) TREATMENT OF THE CORPORATIONS PARTICIPATING IN AN (A) REORGANIZATION

INTERNAL REVENUE CODE: Sections 357(a), (b); 358(a), (b)(1), (e), (f); 361; 362(b); 368(b).

DETAILED ANALYSIS

1. TARGET CORPORATION

Section 361 protects the target corporation from gain recognition in a type (A) reorganization transaction regardless of the nature of the consideration received from the acquiring corporation. If only stock or securities of the acquiring corporation are received in the reorganization, § 361(a) provides nonrecognition upon receipt of the stock or securities. (Section 361(b)(2) bars the recognition of any loss.) In addition, no gain or loss is recognized by the target corporation on the distribution of the acquiring corporation's stock or securities. I.R.C. § 361(c)(1), (2)(B). If boot is received, § 361(b)(1) requires that the target corporation recognize gain upon receipt only if that boot is not distributed to either its shareholders or creditors pursuant to the plan of reorganization. See also § 361(c). Since in an (A) reorganization the target corporation disappears by operation of law, all of the boot must be distributed and no gain will be recognized under § 361(b).

Section 361(c)(2) provides for recognition of gain to the target corporation upon the distribution of appreciated boot. However, because § 358(a)(2) provides the target corporation with a fair market value basis in any boot received in the reorganization transaction, no gain will be realized.

2.   ACQUIRING CORPORATION

2.1. *Nonrecognition of Gain*

The acquiring corporation in an (A) reorganization is protected from gain recognition on the issue of its stock by § 1032. However, if the acquiring corporation also transfers non-qualifying "boot" (other than its own securities) that has appreciated in value, neither § 1032 nor any of the reorganization nonrecognition provisions apply to the acquiring corporation with respect to the boot, and gain must be recognized on the transfer. Rev.Rul. 72–327, 1972–2 C.B. 197. Loss is similarly recognized if the basis of the boot property is less than its fair market value.

2.2. *Basis of Assets*

Under § 362(b), the acquiring corporation takes as its basis in the acquired assets the basis that the assets had in the hands of the transferor corporation. The statute provides that the basis of the assets in the hands of the acquiring corporation is increased by any gain recognized by the target-transferor corporation in the reorganization transaction, but since gain is only recognized if the property received is not distributed in a type (A) reorganization, the acquiring corporation always takes a transferred basis in the assets without any increase for gain recognized to the transferor.

2.3. *Carryover of Corporate Attributes*

Under § 381, the tax attributes of the target corporation, e.g., net operating loss carryovers, earnings and profits accounts, etc., carry over to the acquiring corporation. However, § 382 limits the post-acquisition use of any net operating loss carryovers of the target corporation. See Chapter 15.

SECTION 3.   STOCK FOR STOCK ACQUISITIONS: TYPE (B) REORGANIZATIONS

INTERNAL REVENUE CODE: Sections 354; 362(b); 368(a)(1)(B), (a)(2)(C), (c).

REGULATIONS: Section 1.368–2(c).

Chapman v. Commissioner

United States Court of Appeals, First Circuit, 1980.
618 F.2d 856.

■ LEVIN H. CAMPBELL, CIRCUIT JUDGE.

* * * We must decide whether the requirement of Section 368(a)(1)(B) that the acquisition of stock in one corporation by another be solely in exchange for voting stock of the acquiring corporation is met where, in related transactions, the acquiring corporation first acquires 8 percent of the acquiree's stock for cash and then acquires more than 80 percent of the acquiree in an exchange for voting stock. The Tax Court agreed with the taxpayers that the latter exchange constituted a valid tax-free reorganization. Reeves v. Commissioner, 71 T.C. 727 (1979).

THE FACTS

Appellees were among the more than 17,000 shareholders of the Hartford Fire Insurance Company who exchanged their Hartford stock for shares of the voting stock of International Telephone and Telegraph Corporation pursuant to a formal exchange offer from ITT dated May 26, 1970. On their 1970 tax returns, appellees did not report any gain or loss from these exchanges. * * *

* * * In October 1968, ITT executives approached Hartford about the possibility of merging the two corporations. This proposal was spurned by Hartford, which at the time was considering acquisitions of its own. In November 1968, ITT learned that approximately 1.3 million shares of Hartford, representing some 6 percent of Hartford's voting stock, were available for purchase from a mutual fund. After assuring Hartford's directors that ITT would not attempt to acquire Hartford against its will, ITT consummated the $63.7 million purchase from the mutual fund with Hartford's blessing. From November 13, 1968 to January 10, 1969, ITT also made a series of purchases on the open market totaling 458,000 shares which it acquired for approximately $24.4 million. A further purchase of 400 shares from an ITT subsidiary in March 1969 brought ITT's holdings to about 8 percent of Hartford's outstanding stock, all of which had been bought for cash.

In the midst of this flurry of stock-buying, ITT submitted a written proposal to the Hartford Board of Directors for the merger of Hartford into an ITT subsidiary, based on an exchange of Hartford stock for ITT's $2 cumulative convertible voting preferred stock. * * * [O]n April 9, 1969 a provisional plan and agreement of merger was executed by the two corporations. * * *

* * * By private letter ruling, the Service notified the parties on October 13, 1969 that the proposed merger would constitute a nontaxable reorganization, provided ITT unconditionally sold its 8

percent interest in Hartford to a third party before Hartford's shareholders voted to approve or disapprove the proposal. On October 21, the Service ruled that a proposed sale of the stock to Mediobanca, an Italian bank, would satisfy this condition, and such a sale was made on November 9.

On November 10, 1969, the shareholders of Hartford approved the merger, which had already won the support of ITT's shareholders in June. On December 13, 1969, however, the merger plan ground to a halt, as the Connecticut Insurance Commissioner refused to endorse the arrangement. ITT then proposed to proceed with a voluntary exchange offer to the shareholders of Hartford on essentially the same terms they would have obtained under the merger plan. * * * More than 95 percent of Hartford's outstanding stock was exchanged for shares of ITT's $2.25 cumulative convertible voting preferred stock. The Italian bank to which ITT had conveyed its original 8 percent interest was among those tendering shares, as were the taxpayers in this case.

In March 1974, the Internal Revenue Service retroactively revoked its ruling approving the sale of Hartford stock to Mediobanca, on the ground that the request on which the ruling was based had misrepresented the nature of the proposed sale. Concluding that the entire transaction no longer constituted a nontaxable reorganization, the Service assessed tax deficiencies against a number of former Hartford shareholders who had accepted the exchange offer. Appellees, along with other taxpayers, contested this action in the Tax Court, where the case was decided on appellees' motion for summary judgment. For purposes of this motion, the taxpayers conceded that questions of the merits of the revocation of the IRS rulings were not to be considered; the facts were to be viewed as though ITT had not sold the shares previously acquired for cash to Mediobanca. The taxpayers also conceded, solely for purposes of their motion for summary judgment, that the initial cash purchases of Hartford stock had been made for the purpose of furthering ITT's efforts to acquire Hartford.

THE ISSUE

Taxpayers advanced two arguments in support of their motion for summary judgment. Their first argument related to the severability of the cash purchases from the 1970 exchange offer. Because 14 months had elapsed between the last of the cash purchases and the effective date of the exchange offer, and because the cash purchases were not part of the formal plan of reorganization entered into by ITT and Hartford, the taxpayers argued that the 1970 exchange offer should be examined in isolation to determine whether it satisfied the terms of Section 368(a)(1)(B) of the 1954 Code. The Service countered that the two sets of transactions—the cash purchases and the exchange offer—were linked by a common acquisitive purpose, and that they should be considered together for the purpose of determining whether the arrangement met the statutory requirement that the stock of the acquired corporation be exchanged "solely for * * * voting stock" of the acquiring corporation. The Tax Court did not reach this argument; in granting summary judgment it relied entirely on the taxpayers' second argument.

For purposes of the second argument, the taxpayers conceded arguendo that the 1968 and 1969 cash purchases should be considered "parts of the 1970 exchange offer reorganization." Even so, they insisted upon a right to judgment on the basis that the 1970 exchange of stock for stock satisfied the statutory requirements for a reorganization without regard to the presence of related cash purchases. The Tax Court agreed with the taxpayers, holding that the 1970 exchange in which ITT acquired more than 80 percent of Hartford's single class of stock for ITT voting stock satisfied the requirements of Section 368(a)(1)(B), so that no gain or loss need be recognized on the exchange under section 354(a)(1). The sole issue on appeal is whether the Tax Court was correct in so holding.

I.

* * *

The single issue raised on this appeal is whether "the acquisition" in this case complied with the requirement that it be "solely for * * * voting stock." It is well settled that the "solely" requirement is mandatory; if any part of "the acquisition" includes a form of consideration other than voting stock, the transaction will not qualify as a (B) reorganization. See Helvering v. Southwest Consolidated Corp., 315 U.S. 194, 198, 62 S.Ct. 546, 550 (1942) (" 'Solely' leaves no leeway. Voting stock plus some other consideration does not meet the statutory requirement"). The precise issue before us is thus how broadly to read the term "acquisition." The Internal Revenue Service argues that "the acquisition * * * of stock of another corporation" must be understood to encompass the 1968–69 cash purchases as well as the 1970 exchange offer. If the IRS is correct, "the acquisition" here fails as a (B) reorganization. The taxpayers, on the other hand, would limit "the acquisition" to the part of a sequential transaction of this nature which meets the requirements of subsection (B). They argue that the 1970 exchange of stock for stock was itself an "acquisition" by ITT of stock in Hartford solely in exchange for ITT's voting stock, such that after the exchange took place ITT controlled Hartford. Taxpayers contend that the earlier cash purchases of 8 percent, even if conceded to be part of the same acquisitive plan, are essentially irrelevant to the tax-free reorganization otherwise effected.

The Tax Court accepted the taxpayers' reading of the statute, effectively overruling its own prior decision in Howard v. Commissioner, 24 T.C. 792 (1955), rev'd on other grounds, 238 F.2d 943 (7th Cir.1956). The plurality opinion stated its "narrow" holding as follows:

> "We hold that where, as is the case herein, 80 percent or more of the stock of a corporation is acquired in one transaction,[18] in exchange for which only voting stock is furnished as consideration, the 'solely for voting stock' requirement of section 368(a)(1)(B) is satisfied.
>
> [18]   In determining what constitutes 'one transaction,' we include all the acquisitions from shareholders which were clearly part of the same transaction."

71 T.C. at 741. The plurality treated as "irrelevant" the 8 percent of Hartford's stock purchased for cash, although the opinion left somewhat ambiguous the question whether the 8 percent was irrelevant because of the 14–month time interval separating the transactions or because the statute was not concerned with transactions over and above those

the net assets and at least 70 percent of the fair market value of the gross assets of the corporation immediately prior to the transfer. This test is only a guideline for advance rulings, and does not "define, as a matter of law, the lower limits of 'continuity of interest' or 'substantially all of the properties'." Rev.Proc. 77–37 also stated that payments to dissenters and pre-acquisition redemptions and extraordinary dividends that are part of the plan of reorganization are considered assets held immediately prior to the transfer for purposes of determining whether substantially all the assets are transferred to the acquiring corporation. See also Rev.Rul. 74–457, 1974–2 C.B. 122 (cash used in payment of regular cash dividend prior to the reorganization by the target corporation is not taken into account in applying the "substantially all" test; however, if the payment occurred after the reorganization, the cash required to pay the dividend and the liability for payment of the dividend are taken into account).

Rev.Rul. 88–48, 1988–1 C.B. 117, found the "substantially all" requirement to have been met where the target corporation sold for cash one of its two historic businesses, which represented 50 percent of its historic business assets, and then transferred the cash and all its remaining assets to the acquiring corporation for the acquiring corporation's voting stock and assumption of the target corporation's liabilities. The sale of the assets was pursuant to the overall plan because the acquiring corporation did not wish to acquire the business that was sold. The ruling stressed that the IRS views the purpose of the "substantially all" requirement as preventing the use of § 368(a)(1)(C) to effect a divisive reorganization. Since the sale was to unrelated persons and no part of the proceeds was directly or indirectly retained by the shareholders of the target corporation, the test was met.

In Helvering v. Elkhorn Coal Co., 95 F.2d 732 (4th Cir.1937), the Elkhorn Coal and Coke Co. desired to transfer a part of its mining property to Mill Creek Company for stock. To qualify as a reorganization, since Mill Creek would not obtain control of Elkhorn Coal Co., Elkhorn would have had to transfer substantially all its assets. To accomplish this, Elkhorn first formed a new company, transferred the other Elkhorn properties to it for its stock, and distributed such stock to its shareholders, this distribution being nontaxable under the predecessors of §§ 368(a)(1)(D) and 355. It then transferred the mining properties, now "all its properties," to Mill Creek for stock, technically a reorganization. The new company then acquired the Elkhorn stock for its stock and dissolved Elkhorn so that the old Elkhorn stockholders ended up as the shareholders of a corporation that owned the remaining Elkhorn properties and stock of Mill Creek. The transaction predated the enactment of the liquidation requirement in § 368(a)(2)(G). Applying *Gregory* principles, the court disregarded the distribution of the stock of the new company and held that Elkhorn had not transferred substantially all of its assets to Mill Creek. Hence no reorganization had occurred and the transaction was taxable. Compare Rev.Rul. 70–434, 1970–2 C.B. 83 (preacquisition spin-off of assets does not preclude type (B) reorganization treatment).

Rev.Rul. 2003–79, 2003–2 C.B. 80, found a valid type (C) reorganization in a transaction that reached substantially the same end result as *Elkhorn Coal* but which was structured slightly differently. In this ruling, X Corporation transferred a business consisting of one-half of its assets to newly formed subsidiary Y Corporation, following which X

Corporation distributed all of the stock of Y Corporation to its shareholders in a transaction governed by § 355, page 705. After the distribution, P, an unrelated acquiring corporation, acquired all of the assets of Y in a stock-for-assets reorganization. The ruling held that the acquisition was a valid type (C) reorganization, even though an acquisition of the same properties from the X Corporation would have failed the substantially all the properties requirement if those properties had not been transferred to Y Corporation.

3. LIQUIDATION REQUIREMENT

Section 368(a)(2)(G) requires that the target corporation liquidate and distribute the stock and securities it receives in the reorganization as well as its other properties to its shareholders in pursuance of the plan of reorganization. This requirement was added in 1984 to forestall tax avoidance effected by keeping the target corporation in existence as an investment company following the acquisition. The tax avoidance potential arose because under § 381 all of the target corporation's tax attributes are transferred to the acquiring corporation as a result of the reorganization. See Chapter 15. Thus if not required to liquidate, the target corporation would have substantial assets, against which it might borrow to make distributions, but would have no earnings and profits to support dividend treatment. See H.Rep. No. 98–861, 98th Cong., 2d Sess. 205 (1984).

The distribution requirement may be waived by the IRS in circumstances in which an actual distribution would result in substantial hardship. However, the waiver will be granted only on the condition that the target corporation and its shareholders are treated as if the retained assets were distributed and then recontributed to a new corporation. See H.Rep. No. 98–861, 98th Cong., 2d Sess. 845–46 (1984). This constructive liquidation and contribution will trigger recognition of gain and loss to the target corporation under § 361(c)(2)(A) as well as recognition of gain to the shareholders of the target corporation under § 356(a).

As a further safeguard, § 312(h)(2) authorizes the Treasury to promulgate regulations requiring that the earnings and profits of the target corporation be allocated between the acquiring and the target corporations.

4. MULTI-STEP ACQUISITIONS

4.1. *Treated as Separate Transactions*

The problems of "creeping acquisitions," as in the case of a (B) reorganization, discussed at page 624, might also arise in the (C) reorganization context. Treas.Reg. § 1.368–2(d)(4) provides that preexisting ownership of a portion of a target corporation's stock by an acquiring corporation generally does not negate satisfaction of the solely for voting stock requirement in a (C) reorganization. Thus, for example, if P Corporation acquires the assets of S Corporation, in which P corporation already owns 60 percent of the stock, in exchange for sufficient P Corporation stock to make a liquidating distribution to the 40 percent minority shareholders of S Corporation (with P corporation receiving nothing in the liquidation of S Corporation), the transaction can qualify as a type (C) reorganization. If, however, in connection with a potential (C) reorganization the acquiring corporation acquires any of the target corporation's stock for consideration other than its own voting stock (or its parent's voting stock if the parent's stock is used in an attempted triangular (C) reorganization), whether from a shareholder of the target corporation or from the target corporation itself, such consideration will be treated as money or other property exchanged by the acquiring corporation for the target corporation's assets for purposes of applying the boot limitation in § 368(a)(2)(B). Whether there has been an acquisition in connection with a potential (C) reorganization of a target corporation's stock for consideration other than voting stock will be made on the basis of all of the facts and circumstances.

Treas.Reg. § 1.368–2(d)(4) should provide tax-free treatment to minority shareholders who receive P stock in a type C reorganization in which a subsidiary is acquired by its parent. Compare Kass v. Commissioner, 60 T.C. 218 (1973), aff'd by order, 491 F.2d 749 (3d Cir.1974), in which the minority shareholders in an upstream type (A) reorganization closely following a cash purchase of over 80 percent of the stock of T were required to recognize gain.

Treas.Reg. § 1.368–2(d)(4) also provides nonrecognition treatment for liquidations of corporate subsidiaries that do not qualify for nonrecognition under § 332 and 337. Such transactions are commonly termed "an upstream § 368(a)(1)(C) reorganization." See Notice of Proposed Rulemaking and Notice of Public Hearing, The Solely for Voting Stock Requirement in Certain Corporate Reorganizations, REG–115086–98, 64 Fed. Reg. 31770 (June 14, 2001); see also Treas.Reg. § 1.368–2(e)(1); Treas.Reg. § 1.368–2(e)(6), Ex. 7.

Treas.Reg. § 1.368–2(d)(4)(i), Ex. 1, illustrates a tax-free upstream § 368(a)(1)(C) reorganization.

> Corporation P (P) holds 60 percent of the Corporation T (T) stock that P purchased several years ago in an unrelated transaction. T has 100 shares of stock outstanding. The other 40 percent of the T stock is owned by Corporation X (X), an unrelated corporation. T has properties with a fair market value of $110 and liabilities of $10. T transfers all of its properties to P. In exchange, P assumes the $10 of liabilities, and transfers to T $30 of P voting stock and $10 of cash. T distributes the P voting stock and $10 of cash to X and liquidates.

While this example does not deal with a "liquidation" under corporate law, it is sufficiently analogous to support treatment as a type (C) reorganization of a liquidation of a corporate subsidiary that does not qualify for nonrecognition under § 332 and 337.

4.2. *Treated as a Single Transaction*

The IRS may regard a stock-for-stock type (B) acquisition followed by the liquidation of the target corporation as a type (C) reorganization. Rev.Rul. 67–274, 1967–2 C.B. 141; Resorts International, Inc. v. Commissioner, 60 T.C. 778 (1973), aff'd on this issue, 511 F.2d 107 (5th Cir.1975) (no intention to operate target corporations as subsidiaries; the liquidations were part of a series of continuing transactions that constituted a (C) reorganization); American Potash & Chemical Corp. v. United States, 399 F.2d 194 (Ct.Cl.1968).

The IRS's recharacterization of a (B) reorganization-liquidation as a (C) reorganization is grounded on the theory that under Kimbell-Diamond

Milling Co. v. Commissioner, 14 T.C. 74 (1950), aff'd per curiam 187 F.2d 718 (5th Cir.1951), the transaction is actually an asset acquisition (see page 482). See Rev.Rul. 74–35, 1974–1 C.B. 85 (holding that *Kimbell-Diamond* reasoning and Rev.Rul. 67–274 do not apply to recast a (B) reorganization where the target corporation does not transfer substantially all its assets to the acquiring corporation); Rev.Rul. 72–405, 1972–2 C.B. 217 ((C) reorganization upheld where a newly-created subsidiary acquired the assets of another corporation in a merger utilizing the parent corporation's stock, followed by a liquidation of the subsidiary).

Where one of the steps in a multi-step acquisition is a cash purchase of stock of the target corporation, which is followed by an asset acquisition using voting stock, the transaction may fail to qualify as a (C) reorganization because the "solely for voting stock" requirement has been violated. In Rev.Rul. 85–138, 1985–2 C.B. 122, P Corporation owned all of the stock of S1 and S2. Pursuant to a plan by which S1 would acquire substantially all the properties of the target corporation in consideration of P voting stock and the assumption by S1 of the target corporation's liabilities, S2 purchased some of the outstanding stock of the target corporation for cash in order to eliminate any possible adverse minority interest in the target corporation. The liabilities of the target corporation assumed by S1 exceeded 20 percent of the value of the target corporation's assets. Because the cash purchases of stock by S2 were part of a prearranged plan, the cash was treated as additional consideration provided by S1 and, since the cash and liabilities together exceeded the 20 percent limit in § 368(a)(2)(B), the acquisition did not qualify as a (C) reorganization.

5. PARTIES TO THE REORGANIZATION

Section 368(a)(2)(C) allows the acquiring corporation in a (C) reorganization to transfer the target's assets to a controlled subsidiary. Treas.Reg. § 1.368–2(k) provides detailed rule regarding permissible drop downs of assets to lower tier subsidiaries in chains of subsidiaries meeting the 80 percent control test of § 368(c), as well as to certain partnerships. See also Treas.Reg. § 1.368–1(d)(4). The regulations also permit assets acquired in a reorganization to be transferred to certain partnerships of which the acquiring corporation is a partner. See also Rev.Rul. 68–261, 1968–1 C.B. 147 (where the target corporation operated through six divisions and merged into the acquiring corporation, which then transferred each division to six wholly-owned subsidiaries, § 368(a)(2)(C) applied).

In addition, by virtue of the parenthetical clause in § 368(a)(1)(C), a subsidiary can be utilized as the acquiring corporation, exchanging voting stock of its parent for substantially all the assets of the target corporation.

6. RELATIONSHIP OF TYPE (C) REORGANIZATIONS TO OTHER PROVISIONS

Section 368(a)(2)(A) provides that if a (C) reorganization also constitutes a (D) reorganization it will be treated only as a (D) reorganization, thus insuring that the (C) reorganization provisions cannot be used to accomplish a disguised tax-free division of a corporation that does not comply with the requirements of § 355. See Chapter 14.

Rev.Rul. 2007–8, 2007–1 C.B. 469, provides that § 357(c)(1), discussed at page 82, will not apply to an acquisitive reorganization notwithstanding the fact that the transaction might also qualify as a § 351 transaction. Rev.Rul. 2007–8 declares obsolete Rev.Rul. 76–188, 1976–1 C.B. 99, which involved a transaction in which a parent corporation transferred all its assets to its wholly-owned subsidiary and the subsidiary assumed all of the parent corporation's liabilities. The liabilities assumed exceeded the basis of the assets transferred to the subsidiary. Section 357(c) was held to be applicable, since the transaction was one "described in" § 351 (a provision to which § 357(c) applies). The prior ruling concluded that the fact that it also constituted a (C) reorganization did not prevent the application of § 357(c) and the parent corporation accordingly recognized a gain on the transaction. Rev.Rul. 2007–8 concludes that since the transferor corporation ceases to exist, it cannot be enriched by the assumption of liabilities.

If brother-sister corporations are involved, it is possible for a (C) reorganization to overlap with § 304, discussed at page 272. It is not clear which provision will control.

7.   TREATMENT OF PARTIES TO A TYPE (C) REORGANIZATION

7.1.   *Target Corporation and Shareholders*

Normally, no gain or loss is recognized by the target corporation on the exchange with the acquiring corporation regardless of the nature of the property received from the acquiring corporation. If only stock or securities of the acquiring corporation is received in the reorganization, § 361(a) provides nonrecognition. If nonqualifying boot is received, § 361(b) requires that the target corporation recognize gain upon receipt only if the boot is not distributed to either its shareholders or creditors pursuant to the plan of reorganization. Because § 368(a)(2)(G) requires the target corporation to liquidate, all of the boot must be distributed and, in general, no gain can be recognized under § 361(b). However, if boot is received and expended, for example to pay ongoing expenses, so that it is not distributed, then gain will be recognized.

As for the liquidating distributions, no gain or loss is recognized by the target corporation on the distribution of qualified stock or securities. I.R.C. § 361(c)(1), (2)(B). Distribution of appreciated boot in the liquidation results in recognition of gain (but not loss) under § 361(c)(2), but because § 358(a)(2) provides the target corporation with a fair market value basis in any boot received in the reorganization transaction, no gain will be realized unless there is a change in value between the receipt and the liquidating distribution. If any property was retained by the target corporation, gain may be recognized by the corporation as a result of distributing such property in the liquidation.

The operative rules of § 361 leave little room for the target corporation to recognize gain in a (C) reorganization. However, although § 361(c)(3) accords tax free treatment to the receipt and distribution of stock in satisfaction of creditors' claims, if stock of the acquiring corporation received in the reorganization is *sold* by the target corporation and the proceeds used to pay creditors' claims, the target corporation must recognize gain on the sale; the receipt of the stock remains nontaxable.

For the shareholders of the target corporation, the tax results are similar to those in an (A) reorganization. No gain or loss is recognized if they receive solely the stock of the acquiring corporation in exchange for their stock in the target corporation. I.R.C. § 354(a). If the permissible amount of "boot" is involved and it is distributed to the shareholders, they may recognize gain under § 356, either as capital gain or as a dividend, depending on the circumstances, as discussed at page 600. Section 358 then provides an exchanged basis for the acquiring corporation's stock. If any boot is received, however, the basis is determined by first increasing the basis by the amount of any gain recognized by the shareholders as the result of the receipt of boot, and then decreasing it by the amount of cash or the fair market value of any other property received.

7.2. *Acquiring Corporation*

Pursuant to § 1032, the acquiring corporation recognizes no gain or loss on the transfer of its shares in a (C) reorganization. If, however, the acquiring corporation transfers any boot other than cash or its own stock or securities, it must recognize gain or loss with respect to the boot transferred.

Under § 362(b) the acquiring corporation's basis in the acquired assets is equal to the target corporation's basis in those assets. Although § 362(b) provides that the acquiring corporation's basis in the assets is to be increased by any gain recognized under § 361(b) by the target corporation on the transfer of its assets to the acquiring corporation, it is not likely that the target corporation will recognize gain as a result of the transfer of its assets to the acquiring corporation because the target liquidates and distributes all of its property to shareholders.

Under § 381, the tax attributes of the target corporation, e.g., net operating loss carryovers, earnings and profits accounts, etc., carry over to the acquiring corporation. However, § 382 limits the post-acquisition use of any net operating loss carryovers of the target corporation. See Chapter 15.

SECTION 5. TRIANGULAR REORGANIZATIONS

INTERNAL REVENUE CODE: Sections 368(a)(2)(D), (E); 368(c).

REGULATIONS: Sections 1.358–6; 1.368–2(b)(2), (j), (k); 1.1032–2. See also 1.1032–3.

The early reorganization statutes did not permit tax-free triangular mergers, as was explained in the discussion of Groman v. Commissioner, 302 U.S. 82 (1937), and Helvering v. Bashford, 302 U.S. 454 (1938), at page 552. There is no policy reason, however, not to allow acquisitions by a subsidiary using the stock of a parent corporation to qualify for tax-free reorganization treatment. As discussed in the preceding materials, a series of amendments to the reorganization definitions made it possible to transfer assets or stock acquired in a reorganization transaction to a controlled subsidiary (§ 368(a)(2)(C)) or to employ the subsidiary itself as the acquiring vehicle in a type (B) or type (C) reorganization, using stock of the parent company as consideration for the acquisition. However, these amendments did not cover two situations that were important in practice. In the first place, a direct acquisition by the subsidiary of the target company's assets in an (A) reorganization in exchange for the parent stock was not possible since the parent was not considered to be a party to the reorganization under § 368(b). In addition, though the subsidiary could acquire assets in a (C) reorganization for the parent stock, the parent could not assume liabilities of the target corporation directly since § 368(a)(1)(C) applies only to liabilities assumed by the "acquiring" corporation, in this case the subsidiary. The desired results could have been obtained through other somewhat complicated means, such as the acquisition by the parent of the assets in a (C) reorganization and the subsequent transfer of the target assets to a newly formed subsidiary under § 368(a)(2)(C), with the parent assuming the liabilities of the target corporation.

In successive amendments to § 368 in 1968 and 1971, described in the following Senate Finance Committee Report, Congress made such arrangements unnecessary. In 1968 Congress added § 368(a)(2)(D), which, together with a corresponding amendment to the § 368(b) definition of "party to a reorganization," permits the direct use of the parent's stock by the subsidiary as consideration for assets acquired in an (A) reorganization. See Treas.Reg. § 1.368–2(b)(2).

Section § 368(a)(2)(E), added in 1971, covers the so-called "reverse triangular merger" situation by allowing the subsidiary to be merged into the target corporation using stock of the parent in an (A) reorganization. Thus, the target corporation becomes a subsidiary of the acquiring parent corporation. The stockholders of the target corporation exchange their target corporation stock for the stock of the acquiring parent corporation.

Senate Finance Committee Report, Public Law 91–693

S.Rep. No. 91–1533, 91st Cong., 2d Sess. 622–23 (1971).

[H.R. 19562] amends the tax law to permit a tax-free statutory merger when stock of a parent corporation is used in a merger between a controlled subsidiary of the parent and another corporation, and the other corporation survives—here called a "reverse merger."

In 1968 Congress added a provision to the tax laws permitting statutory mergers where the stock of the parent of the corporation making the acquisition was used in the acquisition (sec. 368(a)(2)(D)). At the time that statute was enacted, the use of stock of a parent corporation was permitted in the type of reorganization involving the acquisition of stock (subparagraph (B)) and in the type of reorganization involving the acquisition of assets (subparagraph (C)) but was not permitted in the case of a statutory merger of a subsidiary. After noting this fact, the House committee report went on to explain the reasons for the amendment as follows:

> Apparently the use of a parent's stock in statutory mergers was not initially provided for because there was no special concern with the problem at the time of the adoption of the 1954 code. However, this is no longer true. A case has been called to the attention of your committee in which it is desired to have an operating company merged into an operating subsidiary in exchange for the stock of the parent holding

company. Your committee sees no reason why tax-free treatment should be denied in cases of this type where for any reason the parent cannot or, for business or legal reasons, does not want to acquire the assets (even temporarily) through a merger.

For the reasons set forth above your committee concluded that it was desirable to permit the use of the stock of the parent corporation in a statutory merger in acquiring a corporation in essentially the same manner as presently is available in the case of other tax-free acquisitions. (House report on H.R. 18942 (90th Cong.))

Thus, under existing law, corporation X (an unrelated corporation) may be merged into corporation S (a subsidiary) in exchange for the stock in corporation P (the parent of S) in a tax-free statutory merger. However, if for business and legal reasons (wholly unrelated to Federal income taxation) it is considered more desirable to merge S into X (rather than merging X into S), so that X is the surviving corporation—a "reverse merger"—the transaction is not a tax-free statutory merger.

Although the reverse merger does not qualify as a tax-free statutory merger, it may, in appropriate circumstances, be treated as tax-free as a stock-for-stock reorganization (subparagraph (B)). However, in order to qualify as a tax-free stock-for-stock reorganization it is necessary that the acquisition be *solely* for voting stock and that no stock be target for cash or other consideration. Thus, if a small amount of the stock of X (the unrelated corporation) is acquired for cash before the merger of S into X, there often may be doubt as to whether or not the transaction will meet the statutory requirements of a stock-for-stock reorganization.

The committee agrees with the House, that there is no reason why a merger in one direction (S into X in the above example) should be taxable, when the merger in the other direction (X into S), under identical circumstances, is tax-free. Moreover, it sees no reason why in cases of this type the acquisition needs to be made solely for stock. For these reasons the amendment makes statutory mergers tax-free in the circumstances described above.

In discussions on this bill, the Treasury Department has expressed concern that the corporate reorganization provisions need review and modification. The committee in agreeing to this amendment does not intend to foreclose consideration of any substantive changes which the Treasury may propose in the corporate reorganization provisions in any future presentations.

Revenue Ruling 2001–26

2001–1 C.B.1297.

ISSUE

On the facts described below, is the control-for-voting-stock requirement of section 368(a)(2)(E) of the Internal Revenue Code satisfied, so that a series of integrated steps constitutes a tax-free reorganization under sections 368(a)(1)(A) and 368(a)(2)(E) and section 354 or section 356 applies to each exchanging shareholder?

FACTS

Situation 1. Corporation P and Corporation T are widely held, manufacturing corporations organized under the laws of state A. T has only voting common stock outstanding, none of which is owned by P. P seeks to acquire all of the outstanding stock of T. For valid business reasons, the acquisition will be effected by a tender offer for at least 51 percent of the stock of T, to be acquired solely for P voting stock, followed by a merger of a subsidiary of P into T. P initiates a tender offer for T stock conditioned on the tender of at least 51 percent of the T shares. Pursuant to the tender offer, P acquires 51 percent of the T stock from T's shareholders for P voting stock. P forms S and S merges into T under the merger laws of state A. In the statutory merger, P's S stock is converted into T stock and each of the T shareholders holding the remaining 49 percent of the outstanding T stock exchanges its shares of T stock for a combination of consideration, two-thirds of which is P voting stock and one-third of which is cash. Assume that under general principles of tax law, including the step transaction doctrine, the tender offer and the statutory merger are treated as an integrated acquisition by P of all of the T stock. Also assume that all nonstatutory requirements for a reorganization under sections 368(a)(1)(A) and 368(a)(2)(E) and all statutory requirements of section 368(a)(2)(E), other than the requirement under section 368(a)(2)(E)(ii) that P acquire control of T in exchange for its voting stock in the transaction, are satisfied.

Situation 2. The facts are the same as in Situation 1, except that S initiates the tender offer for T stock and, in the tender offer, acquires 51 percent of the T stock for P stock provided by P.

LAW AND ANALYSIS

Section 368(a)(1)(A) states that the term "reorganization" means a statutory merger or consolidation. Section 368(a)(2)(E) provides that a transaction otherwise qualifying under section 368(a)(1)(A) will not be disqualified by reason of the fact that stock of a corporation (the "controlling corporation") that before the merger was in control of the merged corporation is used in the transaction, if (1) after the transaction, the corporation surviving the merger holds substantially all of its properties and of the properties of the merged corporation (other than stock of the controlling corporation distributed in the transaction), and (2) in the transaction, former shareholders of the surviving corporation exchanged, for an amount of voting stock of the controlling corporation, an amount of stock in the surviving corporation that constitutes control of such corporation (the "control-for-voting-stock requirement"). For this purpose, control is defined in section 368(c).

In King Enterprises, Inc. v. United States, 418 F.2d 511 (Ct. Cl. 1969), as part of an integrated plan, a corporation acquired all of the stock of a target corporation from the target corporation's shareholders for consideration, in excess of 50 percent of which was acquiring corporation stock, and subsequently merged the target corporation into the acquiring corporation. The court held that, because the merger was the intended result of the stock acquisition, the acquiring corporation's acquisition of the target corporation qualified as a reorganization under section 368(a)(1)(A).

* * *

Section 1.368–1(c) of the Income Tax Regulations provides that a plan of reorganization must contemplate the bona fide execution of one of the transactions specifically described as a reorganization in section 368(a) and the bona fide consummation of each of the requisite acts under which nonrecognition of gain is claimed. Section 1.368–2(g) provides that the term plan of reorganization is not to be construed as broadening the definition of reorganization as set forth in section 368(a), but is to be taken as limiting the nonrecognition of gain or loss to such exchanges or distributions as are directly a part of the transaction specifically described as a reorganization in section 368(a).

As assumed in the facts, under general principles of tax law, including the step transaction doctrine, the tender offer and the statutory merger in both Situations 1 and 2 are treated as an integrated acquisition by P of all of the T stock. The principles of King Enterprises support the conclusion that, because the tender offer is integrated with the statutory merger in both Situations 1 and 2, the tender offer exchange is treated as part of the statutory merger (hereinafter the "Transaction") for purposes of the reorganization provisions. Cf. J.E. Seagram Corp. v. Commissioner, 104 T.C. 75 (1995) (treating a tender offer that was an integrated step in a plan that included a forward triangular merger as part of the merger transaction). Consequently, the integrated steps, which result in P acquiring all of the stock of T, must be examined together to determine whether the requirements of section 368(a)(2)(E) are satisfied. Cf. section 1.368–2(j)(3)(i); section 1.368–2(j)(6), Ex. 3 (suggesting that, absent a special exception, steps that are prior to the merger, but are part of the transaction intended to qualify as a reorganization under sections 368(a)(1)(A) and 368(a)(2)(E), should be considered for purposes of determining whether the control-for-voting-stock requirement is satisfied).

In both situations, in the Transaction, the shareholders of T exchange, for P voting stock, an amount of T stock constituting in excess of 80 percent of the voting stock of T. Therefore, the control-for-voting-stock requirement is satisfied. Accordingly, in both Situations 1 and 2, the Transaction qualifies as a reorganization under sections 368(a)(1)(A) and 368(a)(2)(E).

Under sections 1.368–1(c) and 1.368–2(g), all of the T shareholders that exchange their T stock for P stock in the Transaction will be treated as exchanging their T stock for P stock in pursuance of a plan of reorganization. Therefore, T shareholders that exchange their T stock only for P stock in the Transaction will recognize no gain or loss under section 354. T shareholders that exchange their T stock for P stock and cash in the Transaction will recognize gain to the extent provided in section 356. In both Situations 1 and 2, none of P, S, or T will recognize any gain or loss in the Transaction, and P's basis in the T stock will be determined under section 1.358–6(c)(2) by treating P as acquiring all of the T stock in the Transaction and not acquiring any of the T stock before the Transaction.

* * *

DETAILED ANALYSIS

1.   GENERAL

The Senate Finance Committee report suggests that a merger in one direction, the target corporation into the acquiring subsidiary, should not be treated differently than the reverse, the acquiring subsidiary into the target corporation. Note however, that in the case of a reverse triangular merger, § 368(a)(2)(E)(ii) requires that the original shareholders of the surviving corporation must receive voting stock of the acquiring parent corporation in exchange for stock representing control, as defined in § 368(c), of the surviving corporation. There is no such limitation applicable to a forward triangular merger under § 368(a)(2)(D). The reason for this requirement in § 368(a)(2)(E) is not grounded in a policy distinction between the two forms but rather on the difference in structures used by the taxpayers who sought the remedial legislation to effect these transactions before the remedial legislation was enacted. As noted in the Senate Finance Committee Report, a reverse triangular merger is functionally equivalent to a stock-for-stock exchange under § 368(a)(1)(B), but the reverse triangular merger allows somewhat more latitude with respect to non-stock consideration. The relationship of § 368(a)(2)(E) to § 368(a)(1)(B) is highlighted by Rev.Rul. 67–448, 1967–2 C.B. 144, which, prior to the enactment of § 368(a)(2)(E), held that a reverse triangular merger into corporate shell subsidiary in consideration solely for the parent's voting stock was a type (B) reorganization. There really is no continuing justification for the stricter statutory continuity of interest requirements of § 368(a)(2)(E).

On the other hand, the prohibition against a splitting of interests, reflected in the *Groman* and *Bashford* decisions, discussed at page 552, is present in the requirement in § 368(a)(2)(D) that no stock of the subsidiary corporation be used in the transaction. In contrast, § 368(a)(2)(E) contains no such express prohibition, although the stricter continuity of interest requirement leaves little room for shareholders of the target corporation to continue to hold a minority interest in it after the acquisition.

2.   FORWARD TRIANGULAR MERGERS

2.1. *Permissible Consideration*

Since § 368(a)(2)(D) is grafted onto the basic type (A) reorganization definition, there is no restriction on the consideration that may be used by the subsidiary in the acquisition other than the general continuity of interest limitation in an (A) reorganization (see discussion at page 539) and the express statutory restriction that no stock of the subsidiary be used. Thus, as long as 40 percent of the consideration paid to the target corporation's shareholders is stock of the acquiring subsidiary's parent corporation, which may be of any class and either voting or nonvoting, the remainder of the consideration for the acquisition maybe cash or debt obligations of either the acquiring subsidiary or its parent. Treas.Reg. § 1.368–2(b)(2). Under the principles of Rev.Rul. 66–224, 1966–2 C.B. 114, discussed at page 547 the continuity of interest requirement is to be applied with reference to the aggregate consideration received by the entire group of the shareholders of the acquired corporation.

The assumption of liabilities of the target corporation by the parent will not prevent the transaction from qualifying as a reorganization, nor will the assumption be treated as "boot" under § 361(b). In Rev.Rul. 79–155, 1979–1 C.B. 153, the holders of convertible securities of the target corporation in a forward triangular merger received securities on which the parent and the subsidiary were jointly and severally liable and which were convertible into stock of the parent, unless the parent sold the subsidiary, in which case the securities were convertible into stock of the subsidiary. The ruling held that the exchange of securities, which had identical principal amounts, was tax-free under § 354; in addition, conversion of the securities into stock of the parent was not a realization event. It is likely that the result in the ruling would have differed if the securities had been convertible into stock of the subsidiary from the outset.

2.2. *Substantially all of the Properties*

In a § 368(a)(2)(D) acquisition, the acquiring subsidiary must *acquire* substantially all of the properties of the target corporation. Treas.Reg. § 1.368–2(b)(2) indicates that the "substantially all" criteria developed in the context of (C) reorganizations (page 632) are to be applied.

2.3. *Hypothetical Merger Requirement*

The requirement in § 368(a)(2)(D) that the merger "would have qualified" as an (A) reorganization if the transaction had taken place between the target corporation and the parent is not interpreted literally. It need not be established that the merger actually could have taken place under state or federal law; it is sufficient that the "general requirements of a reorganization (such as a business purpose, continuity of business enterprise and continuity of interest)" are met. Treas.Reg. § 1.368–2(b)(2). Section 368(a)(2)(D) applies only to a merger; a consolidation of the target corporation with the acquiring subsidiary in a new corporation is not covered. See e.g. Rev.Rul. 84–104, 1984–2 C.B. 94 (§ 368(a)(2)(E) applies only to state law mergers, not to "consolidations" involving a subsidiary, but consolidation under federal banking law where the target corporation survived was treated as a merger).

3.   REVERSE TRIANGULAR MERGERS

3.1. *Permissible Consideration*

The requirement of § 368(a)(2)(E)(ii) that former shareholders of the surviving corporation exchange a controlling interest in the target corporation for voting stock of the acquiring parent corporation assures that the continuity of interest test will be satisfied. While this requirement is reminiscent of the (B) reorganization, which is the antecedent to the reverse triangular merger, it also has aspects of a (C) reorganization in that a 20 percent leeway for other consideration is permissible. Within this exception there are no limits on the character of the boot that may be exchanged; theoretically stock of the surviving subsidiary, i.e. new stock of the target, is permissible. See also Treas.Reg. § 1.368–2(j)(4), permitting the acquiring parent to assume the target corporation's liabilities.

State law requirements that shareholders exercising statutory dissenters rights be redeemed for cash can present problems with respect to the 80 percent requirement of § 368(a)(2)(E)(ii). Treas.Reg. § 1.368–2(j)(3)(i) provides that stock of the target corporation that is redeemed for cash or property of the target corporation (in contrast to cash or property provided by the acquiring parent or its subsidiary) is not counted as outstanding immediately prior to the reorganization. Thus, for example, if the holders of

100 out of 1000 shares of the target corporation dissent from the merger, the target corporation may redeem those shares, and to qualify under § 368(a)(2)(E) the acquiring parent's stock need be exchanged only for 80 percent of the remaining 900 shares, or 720 shares; the remaining 180 shares may be acquired for cash. But if the funds to redeem the stock are provided by the acquiring parent or subsidiary, then all 1000 shares are taken into account and 800 shares must be acquired for the parent's voting stock. Not only does a redemption of stock by the target corporation not prevent compliance with the continuity of interest requirement, but the regulations indicate that the redeemed stock is disregarded for purposes of determining continuity of interest even if the pre-reorganization redemption is of an extraordinary amount of target corporation stock. See Treas.Reg. § 1.368–1(e)(1)(ii), (e)(8), Ex. 9. However, cash and property of the target corporation used to redeem the stock of its own dissenting shareholders are taken into account in determining whether the "substantially all the properties" test has been met. Treas.Reg. § 1.368–2(j)(6), Ex. 3. If the cash or property distributed in redemption of the dissenting stockholders' shares constitutes too high a percentage of the target corporation's assets, the transaction may fail to meet the "substantially all of the properties" test.

3.2. *Substantially all of the Properties*

In the case of a § 368(a)(2)(E) acquisition, the surviving corporation must *hold* substantially all of its properties and the properties of the merged subsidiary corporation (other than the stock of the parent distributed in the acquisition). Treas.Reg. § 1.368–2(j)(3)(iii) indicates that the "substantially all" criteria developed in the context of (C) reorganizations are to be applied, but assets transferred from the controlling corporation to the merged corporation pursuant to the plan of reorganization are not taken into account. Thus, for example, cash transferred from the controlling corporation to the merged corporation to pay dissenting shareholders of the surviving corporation pursuant to state law or to pay reorganization expenses would not be considered in determining whether the resulting corporation held "substantially all" the assets of the two corporations involved in the acquisition transaction.

Rev.Rul. 2001–25, 2001–1 C.B. 1291, addressed the application of the substantially all the properties requirement in § 368(a)(2)(E). That revenue ruling deals with whether a reverse triangular merger that otherwise qualified under § 368(a)(2)(E) was disqualified because immediately after the merger and as part of a plan that included the merger, T sold fifty percent of its operating assets to an unrelated corporation for cash. The IRS applied Rev.Rul. 88–48, 1988–1 C.B. 117, page 633, to conclude that the "substantially all of the properties requirement had been met." The reasoning of Rev.Rul. 2001–25 was as follows.

> Section 368(a)(2)(E) uses the term "holds" rather than the term "acquisition" as do §§ 368(a)(1)(C) and 368(a)(2)(D) because it would be inapposite to require the surviving corporation to "acquire" its own properties. The "holds" requirement of § 368(a)(2)(E) does not impose requirements on the surviving corporation before and after the merger that would not have applied had such corporation transferred its properties to another

corporation in a reorganization under § 368(a)(1)(C) or a reorganization under §§ 368(a)(1)(A) and 368(a)(2)(D).

In this case, T's post-merger sale of 50 percent of its operating assets for cash to X prevents T from holding substantially all of its historic business assets immediately after the merger. As in Rev.Rul. 88–48, however, the sales proceeds continue to be held by T. Therefore, the post-acquisition sale of 50 percent of T's operating assets where T holds the proceeds of such sale along with its other operating assets does not cause the merger to violate the requirement of § 368(a)(2)(E) that the surviving corporation hold substantially all of its properties after the transaction. Accordingly, the merger qualifies as a reorganization under §§ 368(a)(1)(A) and 368(a)(2)(E), notwithstanding the sale by T of a portion of its assets to X immediately after the merger and as part of a plan that includes the merger.

Rev.Rul. 2008–25, 2008–2 C.B. 986, dealt with the application of the step transaction doctrine where the target corporation was liquidated after a reverse triangular merger that otherwise would have qualified as a tax-free reorganization. In the ruling, all of the stock of T Corporation was owned by individual A. T had $150x of assets and $50x dollars of liabilities. P Corporation was unrelated to A or T Corporation, and was worth over four times the value of T Corporation. P Corporation formed a controlled subsidiary solely to effect the acquisition, and the subsidiary merged into T Corporation. As a result of the merger, P Corporation became the owner of all of the stock of T Corporation (which was newly issued by T in exchange for P's stock in the subsidiary), and A exchanged the T Corporation stock (which was cancelled) for P Corporation voting stock worth $90x and $10x in cash. As part of an integrated plan, following the merger, T Corporation was completely liquidated by P Corporation; T Corporation transferred all of its assets to P Corporation, which assumed all of T Corporation's liabilities. P Corporation continued to conduct the business previously conducted by T Corporation. Apart from the liquidation, the reverse triangular merger otherwise would have qualified as a tax-free reorganization under § 368(a)(2)(E). Because of the presence of the cash boot, the merger transaction, standing alone, could not have qualified as a tax-free reorganization under § 368(a)(1)(B), or (after taking into account T Corporation's debt) under § 368(a)(1)(C), or under § 368(a)(1)(D) because A did not own sufficient stock of P Corporation after the merger. The ruling reached two conclusions. First, because both the reverse triangular merger and liquidation occurred pursuant to an "integrated plan," the step transaction doctrine applied and the safe harbor in Treas.Reg. § 1.368–2(k) did not apply—the safe harbor in Treas.Reg. § 1.368–2(k) applies only if the target corporation, in this case T Corporation is not liquidated—and the reverse triangular merger did not qualify as a § 368(a)(2)(E) tax-free reorganization, because after the acquisition and liquidation, T Corporation, which no longer existed, did not hold substantially all of its properties. The ruling then held, in a feat of Orwellian reasoning, that in characterizing the transactions as other than a reorganization, the step transaction doctrine would not apply. Thus, the first step—the reverse triangular merger—was treated as a § 338(d)(3) qualified stock purchase under Treas.Reg. § 1.338–3(d) and Rev.Rul. 90–95, 1990–2 C.B. 67, discussed at page 479. The liquidation was a § 332 liquidation, with P Corporation taking a transferred basis under § 334(b) in T Corporation's assets, and T Corporation not recognizing gain or loss pursuant to § 337. In this regard, the ruling reasoned "integrating the acquisition of T stock with the liquidation of T would result in treating the acquisition of T stock as a taxable purchase of T's assets. Such treatment would violate the policy underlying § 338 that a cost basis in acquired assets should not be obtained through the purchase of stock where no § 338 election is made. Accordingly, consistent with the analysis set forth in Rev.Rul. 90–95, the acquisition of the stock of T is treated as a qualified stock purchase by P followed by the liquidation of T into P under § 332." It is interesting that disqualifying the initial transaction from reorganization status and recharacterizing it as a qualified stock purchase followed by a § 332 liquidation did not affect the ultimate tax treatment of either T Corporation or P Corporation. Only individual A, the shareholder of T Corporation, was affected because A was required to recognize all of the gain or loss. This was so even though apart from tax results, individual A has no interest in or reason to be concerned with whether P Corporation continued to operate T Corporation's business in a continuing T Corporation or as a division of P Corporation, and furthermore, individual A had little or no power over whether or not P Corporation liquidated T Corporation. Note that while the ruling describes the events as occurring pursuant to an "integrated plan," the ruling is silent regarding whether individual A had any knowledge or control over the plan, and it also fails to specify which version of the step transaction doctrine it applied.

3.3. *"Creeping" Acquisitions*

There is no such thing as a "creeping" reverse triangular merger under § 368(a)(2)(E). If the parent corporation already owns over 20 percent of the stock of the target corporation, a § 368(a)(2)(E) reorganization is not possible because of the statutory requirement that an amount of stock constituting "control" in the target corporation be exchanged in the reorganization transaction for voting stock of the acquiring parent corporation. Rev.Rul. 74–564, 1974–2 C.B. 124. However, a failed § 368(a)(2)(E) reverse triangular merger may be recharacterized as a (B) reorganization under the principles of Rev.Rul. 67–448, page 643, if the requirements for a (B) reorganization have been met. See Treas.Reg. § 1.368–2(j)(6), Exs. 4 and 5. This recharacterization will save the reorganization only if the sole consideration used is voting stock of the parent.

These problems are not presented in a § 368(a)(2)(D) forward triangular merger situation. Indeed, a forward triangular merger often is used as the second step in a "two-step acquisition" in which the acquiring corporation first purchases a majority of the stock of the target corporation and then causes the target to be merged into another subsidiary with the minority shareholders of the target receiving stock of the acquiring parent corporation. See, e.g., J.E. Seagram Corp. v. Commissioner, 104 T.C. 75 (1995), page 595.

4. "REMOTE" "CONTINUITY"

4.1. *Use of "Grandparent" Stock Prohibited*

While various subsections of § 368 permit the use by a first tier subsidiary of its parent's stock in a reorganization acquisition, the problem of "remote" continuity of interest still exists where stock of a corporation further removed in the chain of ownership is used in the acquisition transaction. Thus, Rev.Rul. 74–565, 1974–2 C.B. 125, held that an acquisition made by a second tier subsidiary using the stock of its "grandparent" did not qualify under § 368(a)(2)(E). However, since the second tier subsidiary that formally made the acquisition was formed solely for the purpose of the acquisition and disappeared as a result of the "reverse" merger, its existence was ignored; because the sole consideration was now the parent's voting stock the transaction was viewed as an acquisition by the now first tier subsidiary of the stock of the target company in exchange for its parent's stock that qualified as a (B) reorganization under the principles of Rev.Rul. 67–448, page 643.

4.2. *Drop-Downs Following Acquisitions*

Treas.Reg. §§ 1.368–1(d)(4) and 1.368–2(k) permit certain post-reorganization transfers by the acquiring corporation of the target corporation's assets or stock to controlled corporations or to partnerships without violating the continuity of interest or continuity of business enterprise requirements. One of the purposes of these regulations is to reflect the relaxation by Congress, in § 368(a)(2)(D) and (E), among other provisions, of the judicially developed doctrine, discussed at page 551, that remote continuity of interest did not suffice to support reorganization treatment. See Notice of Proposed Rulemaking and Notice of Public Hearing, Continuity of Interest and Continuity of Business Enterprise, REG–252233–96, 1997–1 C.B. 802. Thus, for example, a forward triangular merger followed by a transfer of the acquired corporation's assets to a sister corporation can qualify under § 368. However, the regulations do not permit an acquisition using stock of a grandparent or higher tier corporation to qualify. Rev.Rul. 74–565, supra, continues to disqualify such transactions.

5. TREATMENT OF PARTIES TO A TRIANGULAR REORGANIZATION

5.1. *Section 368(a)(2)(D) Forward Triangular Merger*

5.1.1. *Target Corporation and Shareholders*

No gain or loss is recognized by the target corporation on the exchange with the acquiring corporation regardless of the nature of the property received from the acquiring corporation. Because the target corporation disappears by operation of state law, any nonqualifying boot not directly distributed to its shareholders or creditors is deemed to have been distributed to its shareholders or creditors, and thus no gain can be recognized under § 361(b).

As to the shareholders of the target corporation, no gain or loss will be recognized if they receive solely the stock of the acquiring parent corporation in exchange for their stock in the target corporation. I.R.C. § 354(a). If "boot" is involved, the shareholders may recognize gain under § 356, either as capital gain or as a dividend, depending on the circumstances. See page 600. Section 358 provides an exchanged basis for the acquiring parent corporation's stock. If any boot is received, however, the basis is determined by first increasing the basis by the amount of any gain recognized by the shareholders as the result of the receipt of boot, and then decreasing it by the amount of cash and the fair market value of any other property received.

5.1.2. *Acquiring Corporation*

Neither the acquiring subsidiary nor its parent generally recognizes any gain or loss on the transfer of the parent's shares in a forward triangular merger. Treas.Reg. § 1.1032–2 prevents gain recognition to the acquiring subsidiary corporation so long as the parent corporation stock was received by the subsidiary pursuant to the plan or reorganization. The acquiring subsidiary would be required to recognize gain, however, if it acquired some of its parent corporation's stock in a prior unrelated transaction and used that stock in the reorganization. If the acquiring subsidiary or its parent transfers any boot other than cash or its own securities, gain or loss must be recognized with respect to the boot transferred. Under § 362(b) the acquiring corporation's basis in the assets is equal to the target corporation's basis in those assets. The acquiring parent corporation's basis in its subsidiary's stock is determined under Treas.Reg. § 1.358–6, which is discussed in item 6, below.

Under § 381, the tax attributes of the target corporation e.g., net operating loss carryovers, earnings and profits accounts, etc., carryover to the acquiring subsidiary corporation. However, § 382 limits the post-acquisition use of any net operating loss carryovers of the target corporation. See Chapter 15.

5.2. *Section 368(a)(2)(E) Reverse Triangular Merger*

5.2.1. *Target Corporation and Shareholders*

No gain or loss can be realized by the surviving target corporation as a result of the merger because it has not disposed of any of its assets. No statutory provision is necessary to shield it from recognition of gain or loss. The bases of all of its assets remain unchanged; the assets retain their historic bases.

The shareholders of the target corporation recognize no gain or loss if they receive solely the stock of the parent of the acquiring corporation in exchange for their stock in the target corporation. I.R.C. § 354(a). If "boot" is involved, the shareholders may recognize gain under § 356, as in the case of a forward triangular merger. Section 358 provides the stock received in the reorganization with an exchanged basis determined with reference to the basis of the target shares surrendered, subject to the same adjustments as are made in a forward triangular merger if boot is involved.

5.2.2. *Acquiring Corporation*

Neither the acquiring subsidiary corporation nor its parent generally recognizes any gain or loss on the transfer of the parent's shares in a § 368(a)(2)(E) reorganization. Although § 1032 on its face applies only to provide nonrecognition to the issuing parent corporation in a triangular merger, § 361 provides nonrecognition to the merged subsidiary of the parent in a § 368(a)(2)(E) reverse triangular merger. If the acquiring corporation or its parent transfers any boot other than cash or its own securities, gain or loss must be recognized with respect to the boot transferred. Because the target corporation remains in existence, its basis for its assets is unchanged. The acquiring parent corporation's basis in the stock of the surviving subsidiary is generally determined in the same manner as in a forward triangular merger.

Under § 381, the target corporation retains its tax attributes, but the § 382 limitations are applicable. See infra, Chapter 15.

6. THE PARENT CORPORATION'S BASIS FOR THE STOCK OF THE SUBSIDIARY

There is no statutory provision to adjust the basis of the acquiring parent corporation in the stock of its subsidiary to reflect the subsidiary's basis in property acquired in a reorganization described in § 368(a)(2)(D) or (E). Presumably the parent corporation's basis in its own shares is zero. As a consequence, Rev.Rul. 74–503, 1974–2 C.B. 117, revoked by Rev.Rul. 2006–2, 2006–2 C.B. 261, held the parent's basis in the stock of the acquiring subsidiary formed by the transfer of the parent's stock would also be zero and that the subsidiary similarly would have a zero basis in shares of the parent's stock transferred to the shareholders of the target corporation. In revoking Rev.Rul. 74–503, however, the IRS did not change the conclusion in the earlier ruling; Rev Rul. 2006–2 merely states that "the conclusions that X's basis in the Y stock received in the exchange and Y's basis in the X stock received in the exchange are zero, are under study." To the extent the conclusions in Rev.Rul. 74–503 are correct, it would mean that in a § 368(a)(2)(E) transaction the parent corporation has a zero basis in the shares it holds in the surviving corporation. Furthermore § 1032, which generally provides nonrecognition treatment to the acquiring corporation in a reorganization transaction on the issuance of its shares for property, does not apply to the subsidiary corporation's transfer of its parent's shares in a reorganization.

The statutory lacuna in the triangular reorganization area arose because of the grafting of §§ 368(a)(2)(D) and (E) onto the preexisting reorganization structure without adequate analysis of the implications of the change in structure. The issues are addressed in Treas.Reg. §§ 1.358–6 and 1.1032–2, which apply a common set of rules to forward and reverse triangular mergers, triangular (B) reorganizations (page 626) and triangular (C) reorganizations (page 636). In general, the regulations adopt an "over-the-top" model, i.e., the basis and gain results parallel those that occur if the parent corporation were to acquire the stock or assets of the target corporation and transfer them to its controlled subsidiary.

In a forward triangular merger and a triangular (C) reorganization, the acquiring parent corporation's basis in its subsidiary's stock after the transaction is adjusted as if the parent corporation had acquired the target corporation's assets in a transaction in which the parent corporation's basis in the assets was determined under § 362(b) and the parent corporation then transferred those assets to its subsidiary in a transaction in which the parent corporation's basis in the subsidiary corporation's stock was determined under § 358. As provided in § 358(d), the target corporation's liabilities must be taken into account in calculating the parent's basis in the acquiring subsidiary, but § 357(c) does not apply for these purposes. Treas.Reg. § 1.358–6(c). Thus, assuming that the subsidiary was a shell formed for purposes of the merger and the parent had a zero basis in the subsidiary immediately before the forward triangular merger, after the reorganization, the parent's basis in the subsidiary will be an amount equal to the subsidiary's basis for its assets acquired from the target minus the subsidiary's liabilities acquired from the target. See Treas.Reg. § 1.358–6(c)(1)(i), (c)(4), Ex. 1(e). Because § 357(c) does not apply, however, if the target's liabilities exceed its basis in the acquired assets, the parent's adjustment to the basis of its stock in the subsidiary equals zero, but the parent recognizes no gain. See Treas.Reg. § 1.358–6(c)(1)(ii), (c)(4), Ex. 1(f). Similar rules apply to a triangular (B) reorganization, i.e., the parent corporation is treated as having acquired the target corporation's stock directly and as having dropped the stock down to its subsidiary.

The acquiring parent corporation's basis in the surviving subsidiary in a reverse triangular merger is also determined as if the target corporation's assets were acquired directly by the parent corporation and transferred to a subsidiary in a forward triangular merger. Treas.Reg. § 1.358–6(c)(2)(i)(A). If the acquiring parent corporation acquires less than all of the target corporation's stock in a reverse triangular merger, the parent corporation's basis in the surviving subsidiary is adjusted to reflect an allocable portion of the target corporation's basis in its assets. Treas.Reg. § 1.358–6(c)(2)(i)(B). A special rule applies if a reverse triangular merger is effected using a shell subsidiary corporation, organized for purposes of the merger, and the parent's voting stock is the only consideration. Because under Rev.Rul. 67–448, 1967–2 C.B. 144, such a transaction qualifies as a type (B) reorganization, the parent corporation may elect to take a basis in the target corporation's stock computed with reference to the aggregate basis of the former target corporation's shareholders. Treas.Reg. § 1.358–6(c)(2)(ii).

The regulations for triangular reorganizations also apply in the consolidated return context. Treas.Reg. § 1.1502–30. However, in the consolidated return context, liabilities are taken into account in determining the parent corporation's basis in the stock of the acquiring subsidiary. As a result, the parent corporation will have an excess loss account (see page 447) to the extent liabilities exceed basis. This adjustment is possible in the consolidated return context because the excess loss account rules in effect permit the use of negative basis. Outside of consolidated returns, negative basis is not permitted.

SECTION 6.　ACQUISITIVE TYPE (D) REORGANIZATIONS

INTERNAL REVENUE CODE: Sections 354(b); 357(a); 368(a)(1)(D), (a)(2)(A), (a)(2)(H), (c); 312(h)(2).

REGULATIONS: Section 1.368–2(k)(2), Ex. 6, –2(l)

A type (D) reorganization occurs upon the transfer of some or all of a corporation's assets to a newly created or existing corporation, for example, where X Corporation transfers some of its assets to new or existing Y Corporation, if, following the transfer, the transferor corporation (X Corporation) distributes the stock of the transferee corporation (Y Corporation) to its shareholders in a distribution that meets the requirements of § 354, § 355, or § 356. The requirements for a type (D) reorganization differ significantly, however, depending on whether the distribution to the shareholders of the transferor corporation qualifies for nonrecognition under § 354 and/or § 356, on the one hand, or § 355 and/or § 356, on the other hand. As a result, there are many different types of transactions, some of which are quite dissimilar, that qualify as type (D) reorganizations.

For the distribution to the shareholders to qualify under § 354, the transferor corporation (X) must transfer "*substantially all*" of its assets to the transferee (Y) and liquidate (I.R.C. § 354(b)(1)). Neither of these requirements is prerequisite for the stock distribution to the shareholders to qualify under § 355, however. In addition, one or more of the transferor corporation's shareholder's must "control" the transferree corporation after the transaction. A type (D) reorganization that results by virtue of a distribution of stock that qualifies under § 354 is commonly termed a "nondivisive" or "acquisitive" type (D) "reorganization," while a type (D) reorganization that results by virtue of a distribution of stock that qualifies under § 355 is commonly termed a "divisive" type (D) reorganization. The asset distribution and liquidation requirements of § 354(b) are designed to prevent a corporate division that does not qualify for nonrecognition under § 355 to qualify under as a reorganization under § 368.

Acquisitive and divisive type (D) reorganizations differ in a second significant aspect. In an acquisitive type (D) reorganization "*control*" of the transferee corporation (Y), which after the transaction must be held by the transferor corporation's (X's) shareholders, is defined by § 368(a)(2)(H), through a cross reference to § 304(c), as *at least 50 percent* of combined voting power *or* at least 50 percent of total value of shares of all classes of stock, rather than by § 368(c). But in a divisive type (D) reorganization, whether or not the transferor corporation (X) liquidates, for the distribution to the shareholders to qualify under § 355, and thus for the asset transfer to constitute a type (D) reorganization, control is defined by the normal rule in § 368(c), requiring 80 percent of combined voting power and 80 percent of each other class of stock.

A variety of transactions fall under the rubric of "nondivisive" type (D) reorganizations. These transactions can be quite dissimilar. A nondivisive type (D) reorganization often involves little or no change in beneficial ownership. For example, if A and B equally own all of each of X Corporation and Y Corporation, and X Corporation transfers all of its assets to Y Corporation, following which X Corporation liquidates, the transaction is a type (D) reorganization. Other type (D) reorganizations, however, can effect a substantial change in beneficial ownership.

(1) If W Corporation, the stock of which was owned equally by E and F, transferred all of its assets to Z Corporation, in which E, F, and G each owned 10 shares, in exchange for 30 shares of voting stock, which W Corporation distributed to E and F in a liquidation distribution qualifying under § 354, the transaction is a type (D) reorganization. In this, case, after the reorganization Z Corporation's shares are owned as follows: E owns 25, F owns 25, and G owns 10. E and F have substantially increased their ownership of Z Corporation.

(2) If T Corporation, the stock of which was owned equally by E and F, transferred all of its assets to Q Corporation, all 50 of the shares of which were owned by G in exchange for 50 shares of voting stock, which T Corporation distributed to E and F in a liquidation distribution qualifying under § 354, the transaction also is a type (D) reorganization. In this, case, after the reorganization Q Corporation's shares are owned as follows: E

owns 25, F owns 25, and G owns 50. G has acquired a substantial interest in T Corporation.

Finally, as noted previously, a type (D) reorganization can be the first step in dividing a corporate enterprise into two separate corporations by a distribution of stock of the subsidiary to the parent's shareholders in a transaction subject to § 355. A divisive type (D) reorganization generally involves the transfer of some, but not all, of a corporation's assets to a newly created or existing 80–percent controlled subsidiary corporation, following which the transferor corporation distributes all (or at least 80–percent) of the stock of the subsidiary to its shareholders in a distribution that meets the requirements of § 355. This aspect of type (D) reorganizations is discussed in Chapter 14.

The asset transfer in both acquisitive and divisive type (D) reorganizations can overlap with a § 351 incorporation transfer, which, like a reorganization, is a nonrecognition event. There is not an overlap, however, in the case of acquisitive type (D) reorganizations that depend on the 50 percent control test rather than the 80-percent control test. The liquidation of the transferor corporation, the second step in an acquisitive type (D) reorganization, overlaps with the liquidation provisions, which, when they apply, require corporate and shareholder gain or loss recognition. However, when the liquidation is pursuant to a plan of reorganization, § 354 provides nonrecognition to the shareholders, except to the extent of boot, which is governed by § 356. Section 361 displaces § 336 to provide nonrecognition to the liquidating corporation. However, § 361(c) requires that the liquidating corporation recognize gain (but not loss) with respect to all other property distributed in the liquidation.

Atlas Tool Co., Inc. v. Commissioner

United States Court of Appeals, Third Circuit, 1980.
614 F.2d 860.

■ GIBBONS, CIRCUIT JUDGE.

* * * Stephan Schaffan is the sole stockholder of Atlas, a New Jersey corporation still in existence, and of Fletcher, also a New Jersey corporation, which was dissolved in 1970. The deficiency assessed against the Schaffans involves the tax treatment of over $400,000 in cash distributed to Schaffan upon the dissolution of Fletcher. The Schaffans reported this distribution as a long-term capital gain but the Commissioner of Internal Revenue and the Tax Court treated it as a dividend, taxable as ordinary income. The individual taxpayers contend that the distribution from Fletcher qualified for capital gains treatment, while the Commissioner urges that the Tax Court erred in calculating the amount of the dividend, and that a higher tax is due. * * * We affirm the Tax Court in all respects.

I.   The Schaffan's Individual Tax Liability

In October 1970, Schaffan owned all the stock of Atlas and of Fletcher. Atlas was then engaged in the business of designing and selling products for the hobby industry, principally model railroads. Prior to 1960, Atlas also manufactured such products. In 1960, Fletcher was incorporated, acquired Atlas' plastic molding machines, and thereafter, conducted the manufacturing operations previously conducted by Atlas. * * * Atlas was virtually the only customer of Fletcher.

During the 1960's, Atlas continually increased its purchase of foreign manufactured components, which were cheaper than those domestically manufactured. Eventually, Schaffan decided that the manufacturing operations being performed by Fletcher were no longer essential since the same quality components could be acquired at a lower cost from foreign sources. Accordingly, in October 1970, at the directors' and stockholders' meetings, it was voted that Fletcher liquidate * * *.

On November 5, 1970, Fletcher transferred to Atlas all its machinery and equipment for an appraised price of $100,250, and all its inventory for its $14,600 cost. * * * On November 19, 1970, Schaffan received from Fletcher a cash distribution of $482,246.82 which represented all of its remaining assets. * * *

The machinery and equipment transferred to Atlas remained in place in the building otherwise occupied by Atlas. Fletcher's former employees were employed by Atlas, initially in its packing and shipping departments. The machinery and equipment, left in place, was idle for a time. However, by December 1970, Atlas began experiencing delivery and quality difficulties with its foreign suppliers, and to keep its inventory adequate, it soon started operating some of the Fletcher machines. By the end of 1971, all the machinery and equipment acquired from Fletcher were in operation.

On the Schaffan's 1970 federal income tax return they reported $400,000 as a distribution from Fletcher in complete liquidation under section 331 * * *. They claimed an adjusted basis of $10,000 for the Fletcher stock, and paid tax on a long-term capital gain of $390,000. In the notice of deficiency, the Commissioner asserted that the amount distributed to Schaffan was actually $482,246.82 (an amount not contested by the taxpayer) and that the transaction was not a section 331–337 liquidation, but a reorganization within the meaning of 26 U.S.C. § 368(a)(1)(D). * * * [I]f the transaction was a reorganization, the distribution by Fletcher to Schaffan would be covered by the "boot" provision of section 356, and thus be treated as ordinary income rather than as a capital gain pursuant to section 331.

Section 356(a)(2) provides that money distributed to stockholders in a reorganization shall, to the extent of the stockholders' gain, be treated as a dividend out of earnings and profits of "the corporation." The Commissioner contends that when, as here, there is complete identity of shareholders in the two corporate parties to a D reorganization, the earnings and profits of both corporations should be taken into account to determine how much of the cash distributed by either is the equivalent of a dividend. The combined earnings and profits of Fletcher and Atlas exceeded $5 million, and thus the Commissioner proposes to treat the entire $482,246.82, less Schaffan's $10,000 basis for his Fletcher stock, as a section 356(a)(2) dividend.

The Tax Court held that the transaction was a D reorganization, and therefore section 356(a)(2) applied, but that the dividend treatment was authorized only to the extent of earnings and profits of Fletcher. It computed those earnings and profits as $440,342.56, and determined that the difference between that sum and $472,246.82 was taxable as a long-term capital gain. The Schaffans contend that the entire $472,262.82 was a long-term capital gain. The Commissioner contends it was all a section 356(a)(2) dividend.

We turn first to the Schaffan's contention. They point to the adoption by appropriate corporate resolution of a plan of complete liquidation of Fletcher * * *, to the accomplishment of both the disposition and distribution of Fletcher's assets * * *, and to Fletcher's dissolution. * * * [T]hey argue that the distribution is "in complete liquidation" of Fletcher and should, therefore, "be treated as in full payment in exchange for (Fletcher) stock" pursuant to section 331. Taxpayers contend that in the absence of any proof of an intent to avoid taxes, it was error for the Tax Court to characterize the transaction as a D reorganization instead of a complete liquidation.

Our starting point is the text of section 368(a)(1)(D) * * *. Clearly there was, as that section requires, a transfer by Fletcher of all or part of its assets in this case all its machinery, equipment and inventory were transferred to another corporation, Atlas. In addition, Schaffan, the sole stockholder of Fletcher, was in control of Atlas "immediately after" the transfer. No stock or securities of Atlas were distributed to Schaffan. But despite the language in section 368(a)(1)(D) to that effect, it has been held that a distribution is not necessary where the ownership of the transferor and transferee is identical because such a distribution would be a mere formality.[3]

A distribution pursuant to section 368(a)(1)(D) must also qualify under section 354 or section 355 in order for section 356 to be applicable. Section 355, which concerns the distribution of stock and securities of a controlled corporation, does not come into play in the Fletcher-Atlas transaction. Section 354, however, is applicable to the facts in this case. It provides for the nonrecognition of gain or loss on an exchange of stock or securities solely for stock or securities. Where there is complete identity of ownership, section 354, like section 368(a)(1)(D), has been construed not to require the meaningless formality of such an exchange.[4] However, section 354(a):

> shall not apply to an exchange in pursuance of a plan of reorganization within the meaning of section 368(a)(1)(D), unless—
>
> (A) the corporation to (Atlas) which the (Fletcher) assets are transferred acquires substantially all of the assets of the transferor of such assets. . . .

26 U.S.C. § 354(b)(1)(A). The "substantially all" requirement is chiefly determined by focusing on the transfer of the operating assets by the transferor, and not on the unneeded liquid assets such as cash and

---

[3] See Davant v. Commissioner, 366 F.2d 874, 886–87 (5th Cir. 1966) cert. denied, 386 U.S. 1022 * * * (1967); James Armour, Inc. v. Commissioner, 43 T.C. 295, 307 (1964); Commissioner v. Morgan, 288 F.2d 676, 680 (3d Cir. 1961) * * *.

[4] Wilson v. Commissioner, 46 T.C. 334, 344 (1966); James Armour, Inc. v. Commissioner, 43 T.C. at 307; cf. Commissioner v. Morgan, 288 F.2d at 680.

accounts receivable.[5] In light of the facts that all of Fletcher's assets except cash and accounts receivable went to Atlas, that Atlas had hired all of Fletcher's employees, that the operating assets never changed location, and were utilized within four months to manufacture the same products, we conclude that the "substantially all" assets requirement of section 354(b)(1)(A) was satisfied.

Section 354(b)(1)(B) requires, as well, that the distribution of securities in a D reorganization be "in pursuance of a plan of reorganization." The transfer was certainly a part of an overall plan. The controlling shareholder chose to call the transaction a plan of liquidation. If what resulted was a plan of reorganization, the chosen label is not dispositive.

We conclude, as did the Tax Court, that the transaction which resulted in Fletcher's distribution of $482,246.82 to Schaffan met all the statutory requisites of a D reorganization. The Schaffans urge, however, that two nonstatutory requirements must be satisfied before a transaction, characterized by a taxpayer as a liquidation, may be treated as a reorganization: tax avoidance motive and a continuity of business enterprise.

The Tax Court, while expressing some skepticism about the absence of a tax avoidance motive in structuring the transaction, held that a finding of such a motive was not required. The Schaffans, in advancing their tax avoidance motive argument, rely on cases such as Gregory v. Helvering, 293 U.S. 465 * * * (1935), which held that taxpayers cannot take advantage of the tax-free reorganization provisions of the Code in the absence of a business purpose for the transaction other than a purpose to avoid taxes. That requirement was imposed to prevent the resort to liquidation and reincorporation as a way of bailing out earnings and profits without appropriate payment of taxes.

There is no disagreement among the parties that a business purpose is required for a reorganization. The Schaffans contend that there was a business purpose for liquidation as opposed to reincorporation, and that from this business purpose for liquidation one can infer a non-tax avoidance motive for the overall transaction. However, the liquidation-reincorporation doctrine is aimed at recharacterizing liquidations in light of the entire transaction, notwithstanding liquidation motives. Thus the liquidation purpose alone, and therefore the inference of a non-tax avoidance motive from it, cannot by definition be dispositive, and certainly does not prevent the characterization of the transaction as a D reorganization.

The Treasury Regulations state the essence of the requirement as:

---

[5]   See American Mfg. Co. v. Commissioner, 55 T.C. 204, 221–22 (1970) (transfer of operating assets sufficient; receivables and cash not necessary to conduct business); Reef Corp. v. Commissioner, 368 F.2d 125, 131 (5th Cir. 1966) * * * (transfer of operating assets without liquid cash assets qualified as substantially all); Moffat v. Commissioner, 363 F.2d 262, 268 (9th Cir. 1966) * * * (transfer of key personnel and operating assets qualified as substantially all); James Armour, Inc. v. Commissioner, 43 T.C. at 309 (transfer of cash and receivables not necessary to qualify as substantially all); cf. DeGroff v. Commissioner, 444 F.2d 1385, 1386 (10th Cir. 1971) (substantially all requirement met without actual transfer where taxpayer owned and controlled both corporations). * * *

[t]he readjustments involved in the exchanges or distributions effected in the consumation (of a plan of reorganization) must be undertaken for reasons germane to the continuance of the business of a corporation a party to the reorganization.

26 C.F.R. § 1.368–2(g) (1979). The focus of the nonstatutory test is not, therefore, whether there were tax avoidance motives, but whether, objectively, there was continuity of business rather than termination of business. It is not significant that one party to the transaction was liquidated since that is a fairly common feature of a reorganization. What is critical is whether the new corporation carries forward the business enterprise of the old. The continuity of interest concept is "at the heart of the nonrecognition provisions."[12]

Sometimes, a taxpayer will seek to establish that the reorganization took place, thus postponing payment of any tax. In other cases, especially where, as here, there is a distribution of liquid assets, the taxpayer will prefer to have the liquidation aspect separated from the rest of the transaction so as to qualify for capital gains treatment. In response, the Commissioner will seek to treat all the events as one transaction and thus characterize it as a reorganization in order to tax the distribution under section 356(a) at ordinary income rates. The subjective motivation of neither the taxpayer nor the Commissioner is relevant. The test must be whether, objectively, the transferee corporation, if it otherwise qualifies for reorganization treatment, has a continuity of business enterprise with the transferor corporation. Thus we agree with the Tax Court that there was no requirement that it find a tax avoidance motive in order to classify the transaction as a D reorganization.

While the Schaffans urge that there was no continuity of business enterprise, the record establishes otherwise. * * * Within four months, the machinery and equipment was placed in operation and within a year all of it was utilized to make the same products as formerly. Atlas retained all of Fletcher's employees. The business enterprise which Atlas conducted was substantially the same as that formerly conducted by Fletcher. Complete identity of business operations is not required.* * * The Tax Court did not err in holding that the Fletcher-Atlas transaction provided the continuity of business enterprise referred to in the Treasury Regulations. Since both the statutory requirements for a D reorganization and the nonstatutory continuity of business enterprise test are on this record satisfied, we must affirm the Tax Court's determination that there was a reorganization and that section 356(a) applies to the distribution of cash from Fletcher to Schaffan.

DETAILED ANALYSIS

1.   CONSEQUENCES OF (D) REORGANIZATION CLASSIFICATION

As in *Atlas Tool Co.*, a type (D) reorganization frequently is found where the form of the transaction under state law is something else, such as an asset sale and purchase. Because there are no statutory restrictions

---

[12]   B. Bittker & J. Eustice, Federal Income Taxation of Corporations and Shareholders, P 14.01 at 14–3 (abridged ed. 1971).

If an all-cash transaction subject to Treas.Reg. § 1.368–2(*l*) occurs between members of an affiliated group filing a consolidated return, the selling member (S) is treated as receiving the deemed share of stock and any additional stock of the buying member (B) under Treas.Reg. § 1.1502–13(f)(3), which it distributes to its shareholder member (M) in liquidation. Immediately after the sale, the B stock (with the exception of the nominal share which is still held by M) received by M is treated as redeemed in a distribution to which § 301 applies. M's basis in the B stock is reduced under Treas.Reg. § 1.1502–32(b)(3)(v), and under Treas.Reg. § 1.302–2(c), any remaining basis attaches to the nominal share.

2.3. *Reorganization Versus Stock Sale and Purchase*

A type (D) reorganization sometimes can be found in purported "cross-chain" sales of corporate subsidiaries. In Rev.Rul. 2004–83, 2004–2 C.B. 157, a parent corporation (P) sold the stock of a wholly owned subsidiary (T) for cash to another wholly owned subsidiary (S), following which the acquired subsidiary (T) was completely liquidated into the acquiring subsidiary (S). The ruling held that if the events occurred pursuant to an integrated plan, the transaction would be treated as a type (D) reorganization. As a consequence, § 338 could not apply to step-up the basis in the T assets because there was no stock purchase within the meaning of § 338(h)(3)(A). Note that if P, S, and T are not members of a consolidated group and the step transaction doctrine does not apply to step together the stock sale and liquidation, the stock sale would be treated as a distribution in redemption of the S stock under § 304(a)(1) and the liquidation of T into S would qualify as a liquidation under § 332. In this regard, the ruling concluded as follows: "There is no policy that requires § 304 to be applied when § 368(a)(1)(D) would otherwise apply. See J. Comm. on Tax'n., 98th Cong. 2nd Sess., General Explanation of the Revenue Provisions of the Deficit Reduction Act of 1984 192 (Comm. Print 1984). Moreover, the legislative history to the Deficit Reduction Act of 1984, P.L. 98–369, 1984–3 (Vol. 1) C.B. 1, indicates that § 304 was not intended to override reorganization treatment."

3. LIQUIDATION-REINCORPORATION TRANSACTIONS AND THE TYPE (D) REORGANIZATION PROVISIONS

3.1. *Background*

Historically, the nondivisive (D) reorganization provision was used principally by the IRS as a weapon to attack the liquidation-reincorporation transactions described at page 702, in connection with (F) reorganizations. Indeed, the definition of "control" for purposes of (D) reorganizations subject to § 354 is reduced from the 80 percent benchmark in § 368(c) to 50 percent (§ 368(a)(2)(H)), making it easier to fit liquidation-reincorporation transactions under the (D) reorganization definition when there is a change in the shareholder ownership between the "new" and "old" corporations. See S.Rep. No. 98–169, 98th Cong., 2d Sess. 207–209 (1984).

In general, the courts were quite liberal in interpreting the (D) reorganization requirements in order to find a reorganization with an accompanying dividend in order to block the tax avoidance possibilities in the liquidation-reincorporation situations. In testing whether "substantially all" the assets have been transferred, as is required by § 354(b)(1)(A), the focus has been on the operating assets of the corporation. See, e.g., Smothers v. United States, 642 F.2d 894 (5th Cir.1981):

To maintain the integrity of the dividend provisions of the Code, "substantially all assets" in this context must be interpreted as an inartistic way of expressing the concept of "transfer of a continuing business." * * * Properly interpreted, therefore, the assets looked to when making the "substantially all assets" determination should be all the assets, and only the assets, necessary to operate the corporate business—whether or not those assets would appear on a corporate balance sheet. * * * Inclusion of assets unnecessary to the operation of the business in the "substantially all assets" assessment would open the way for the shareholders of any enterprise to turn dividends into capital gains at will. * * * [E]xclusion of assets not shown on a balance sheet * * * would offer an unjustified windfall to owners of service businesses conducted in the corporate form. The most important assets of such a business may be its reputation and the availability of skilled management and trained employees * * *. [F]or example a sole legal practitioner who owns nothing but a desk and chair could incorporate himself, accumulate earnings, and then set up a new corporation and liquidate the old at capital gain rates—as long as he is careful to buy a new desk and chair for the new corporation, rather than transferring the old.

3.2. *Control and Continuity of Interest*

The requirement that the transferor corporation or its shareholders be in control of the transferee corporation after the transfer has been strictly construed. For example, in Breech v. United States, 439 F.2d 409 (9th Cir.1971), a corporation sold all of its assets to a second corporation the stock of which was owned 20 percent by one of its shareholders and 80 percent by a third corporation in which its shareholders had a 75 percent interest. The court refused to ignore the separate existence of the third corporation or to apply the attribution rules in § 318 (which by their terms did not then apply) to find control of the transferee in the shareholders of the transferor. Hence a (D) reorganization was not present. A similar result was reached in Commissioner v. Berghash 361 F.2d 257 (2d Cir.1966). Section 368(a)(2)(H) now incorporates the attribution rules of § 318 for purposes of determining controlling stock ownership.

Can a "functionally unrelated" concept be applied to "disaggregate" a transaction in order to create a reorganization in which the continuity of interest requirement has been met? Suppose for example that X Corporation transfers its operating assets to Y Corporation in exchange for Y Corporation stock. Y Corporation is controlled by a group of X Corporation shareholders who own less than 50 percent of the X stock. X Corporation then liquidates, distributing the Y Corporation stock to its shareholders who control Y and liquid assets to its shareholders who do not own Y stock. Could this be treated as a (D) reorganization and a separate redemption of the stock owned by the shareholders who received the liquid assets? A type (D) (or an (F)) reorganization could be present since, under this analysis, there would be no change in the continuing shareholders of the corporation.

The IRS attempted to fit liquidation-reorganization transactions into the (D) reorganization definition by considering pieces of the transaction that might defeat reorganization treatment as "functionally unrelated" to shareholders and creditors. Thus, for example, short-term creditors who do not hold "securities" will have a taxable exchange; shareholders and other securities holders will be subject to the usual pattern of reorganization taxation.

3.   CONTINUITY OF INTEREST IN A BANKRUPTCY
      REORGANIZATION

In Helvering v. Alabama Asphaltic Limestone Co., 315 U.S. 179 (1942), a creditors' committee formed a new corporation to acquire the assets of an insolvent corporation. An involuntary bankruptcy proceeding was instituted in which the creditors' claims were satisfied by the transfer of assets to the new corporation pursuant to a judicial sale. Ninety-five percent of the stock of the new corporation was issued to note holders and the balance was issued to unsecured creditors of the insolvent corporation. The new corporation claimed depreciation based on a transferred basis from the old corporation, arguing that a reorganization had taken place. The IRS contended that the assets were acquired by purchase because the continuity of shareholder interest requirement had not been satisfied. Citing LeTulle v. Scofield, 308 U.S. 415 (1940), page 539, the IRS argued that for a transaction to qualify as a reorganization, a substantial ownership interest in the transferee company must be retained by the holders of the ownership interest in the transferor. In holding that the assets had been acquired in a tax-free reorganization, the Supreme Court explained the application of the continuity of interest rules to insolvent acquired corporations as follows:

> We conclude, however, that it is immaterial that the transfer shifted the ownership of the equity in the property from the stockholders to the creditors of the old corporation. Plainly, the old continuity of interest was broken. Technically, that did not occur in this proceeding until the judicial sale took place. For practical purposes, however, it took place not later than the time when the creditors took steps to enforce their demands against the insolvent debtor. In this case, that was the date of the institution of the bankruptcy proceedings. From that time on, they had effective command over the disposition of the property. The full priority rule * * * in bankruptcy * * * gives creditors, whether secured or unsecured, the right to exclude the stockholders entirely from the reorganization plan when the debtor is insolvent. When the equity owners are excluded and the old creditors become the stockholders of the new corporation, it conforms to realities to date their equity ownership from the time when they invoked the process of the law to enforce their rights to full priority. At the time they stepped into the shoes of the old stockholders. * * *

> That conclusion involves no conflict with the principals of the *Le Tulle* case. A bondholder interest in a solvent corporation plainly is not the equivalent of a proprietary interest * * *.

This approach continues under the (G) reorganization provisions. In testing for continuity, all classes of creditors who receive stock in the reorganized corporation are considered to be the historic shareholders of the corporation. In addition, if the shareholders receive anything for their shares, they too will be taken into account in the continuity test. Thus, for example, if all the stock in the reorganized company is received by junior creditors, with the secured creditors receiving cash and the shareholders receiving nothing, continuity of interest would be present. On the other hand, if the secured creditors also receive stock, they too would be counted in testing for continuity, which might be lacking if the amount of the cash payment is too large in relation to the stock. If shareholders receive cash, the Committee Report indicates that the transaction may be considered a purchase rather than a reorganization.

Treas.Reg. § 1.368–1(e)(6), promulgated in 2009, describes the circumstances in which a corporation's creditors will be treated as holding a proprietary interest in a target corporation immediately before a potential reorganization. A creditor has a proprietary interest only if the target corporation's liabilities exceed the fair market value of its assets immediately prior to the potential reorganization (or the target corporation is in a title 11 or similar case, as defined in § 368(a)(3)). If any creditor receives a proprietary interest in the acquiring corporation, every claim of that class of creditors and every claim of all equal and junior classes of creditors (in addition to the claims of shareholders) is a proprietary interest in the target corporation immediately prior to the potential reorganization. Generally, in applying continuity of interest principles, the value of a creditor's proprietary interest is the fair market value of the creditor's claim. A special rule applies to the most senior class of creditors receiving stock of the acquirer (and claims of any equal class of creditors). The value of those creditors' proprietary interests in the target is determined by multiplying the fair market value of the claim by a fraction, the numerator of which is the aggregate fair market value of the acquirer's stock received in exchange for claims of those classes of creditors and the denominator of which is the total amount of money and the fair market value of all other consideration (including acquirer stock) received in exchange for such claims.

4. SECURITIES

Neither § 354 nor the regulations under § 354 define the term "securities." In Neville Coke & Chemical Co. v. Commissioner, 148 F.2d 599 (3d Cir.1945), the taxpayer held stock, bonds, three-, four-, and five-year notes, and accounts receivable of an insolvent corporation. Pursuant to a bankruptcy proceeding the debtor corporation was recapitalized and the taxpayer received new common stock for its stock, new debentures for its bonds, and new debentures and common stock for its notes and accounts receivable. The IRS asserted that the taxpayer recognized a gain on the exchange of the notes and accounts receivable for debentures and common stock. The taxpayer asserted that the notes and accounts receivable were "securities" within the meaning of the predecessor of § 354(a)(1) and that it had exchanged "securities" for "stock and securities," thereby entitling it to nonrecognition on the exchange. In holding for the IRS, the court held that "securities" has the same meaning in the context of the interest surrendered as it does in the context of the interest received, that a "security" entails having a "proprietary" interest in the corporation, and that the rights of the taxpayer as a note holder were merely those of a creditor.

Rev.Rul. 2004–78, 2004–2 C.B. 108, described the case law as concluding that an instrument with a term of less than five years generally is not a security, although on the particular facts of that ruling, it concluded that two year instruments were securities. See page 607.

Under § 368(a)(1)(G), while short-term creditors who receive stock in the reorganization will be counted for continuity purposes, the exchange of their debt claims for stock presumably will be a taxable transaction, because the "securities" test has not been met.

5.   TREATMENT OF PARTIES TO A TYPE (G) REORGANIZATION

5.1. *Target Corporation and Shareholders*

Normally no gain or loss is recognized by the target corporation on the exchange with the acquiring corporation regardless of the nature of the property received from the acquiring corporation. If only stock or securities of the acquiring corporation are received in the reorganization, § 361(a) provides nonrecognition. If nonqualifying boot is received, § 361(b) requires that the target corporation recognize gain upon receipt only if the boot is not distributed to either its shareholders or creditors pursuant to the plan of reorganization.

The target corporation may realize discharge of indebtedness income, but because a type (G) reorganization is limited to a corporation involved in a bankruptcy proceeding, discharge of indebtedness income is excluded under § 108(a)(1)(A).

As for the liquidating distributions, no gain or loss is recognized by the target corporation on the distribution of qualified stock or securities. I.R.C. § 361(c)(1), (2)(B). Distribution of appreciated boot in the liquidation results in recognition of gain (but not loss) under § 361(c)(2), but because § 358(a)(2) provides the target corporation with a fair market value basis in any boot received in the reorganization, no gain will be realized unless there is a change in value between the receipt and the liquidating distribution. If any property was retained by the target corporation, gain may be recognized by the corporation as a result of distributing such property in the liquidation.

For the shareholders of the target corporation, the tax results are similar to those in an (A) reorganization. No gain or loss will be recognized if they receive solely the stock of the acquiring corporation in exchange for their stock in the target corporation. I.R.C. § 354(a). If the permissible amount of "boot" is involved and it is distributed to the shareholders, they may recognize gain under § 356, either as capital gain or as a dividend, depending on the circumstances, as discussed at page 600. Section 358 then provides an exchanged basis for the acquiring corporation's stock. If any boot is received, however, the basis is determined by first increasing the basis by the amount of any gain recognized by the shareholders as the result of the receipt of boot, and then decreasing it by the amount of cash or the fair market value of any other property received. If, as may be the case, the shareholders of the target corporation receive nothing in the reorganization, they may recognize losses under § 165(g).

5.2. *Acquiring Corporation*

Pursuant to § 1032, the acquiring corporation recognizes no gain or loss on the transfer of its shares in a (G) reorganization. If, however, the acquiring corporation transfers any boot other than cash or its own stock or securities, it must recognize gain or loss with respect to the boot transferred.

Under § 362(b) the acquiring corporation's basis in the assets is equal to the target corporation's basis in those assets. Although § 362(b) provides that the acquiring corporation's basis in the assets is to be increased by any gain recognized under § 361(b) by the target corporation on the transfer of its assets to the acquiring corporation, the target corporation will not recognize gain as a result of the transfer of its assets if the target corporation distributes all of its property to shareholders.

In Washington Mutual Inc. v. United States, 636 F.3d 1207 (9th Cir. 2011), the Court of Appeals appears to have disregarded the transferred basis rule of § 362(b) to allow a cost basis for certain rights acquired in a § 368(a)(1)(G) reorganization. The taxpayer, as the successor corporation to Home Savings of America, filed a refund action claiming amortization deductions for certain rights, and loss deductions for abandonment of branching rights, created in a § 368(a)(1)(G) reorganization by the Federal Savings and Loan Insurance Corporation (FSLIC) in which Home Savings acquired three failed savings and loan associations. The District Court granted summary judgment for the government, concluding that Home Savings had no basis in the rights. The Ninth Circuit reversed and remanded, disagreeing with the District Court's conclusion regarding basis. As part of the acquisition of the three failed thrifts in a supervisory merger transaction structured as a type G reorganization, FSLIC entered into an "Assistance Agreement" with Home Savings that included, among other things, approval for Home Savings to establish branches in Florida and Missouri as if Home Savings maintained its home office in those states, and approval of the purchase method of accounting under which Home Savings was permitted to apply a percentage of acquired intangible assets in its deposit base and for amortization of the remainder over 40 years. The Ninth Circuit concluded that the excess of liabilities of the acquired thrifts over the value of assets represented a cost that was consideration for the rights created in the assistance agreement in the integrated transaction, and that allowing the taxpayer a cost basis was not inconsistent with characterizing the transaction as a § 368(a)(1)(G) reorganization, notwithstanding the transferred basis rule of § 362(b). The Ninth Circuit rejected the government's assertion that "recognizing Home Savings a cost basis in the Rights based on the assumption of FSLIC's liabilities requires characterizing some of the acquired thrifts' liabilities as FSLIC's liabilities, because Home Savings did not pay FSLIC or the Bank Board separate consideration for the Rights." The District Court had concurred with the government's position holding that the excess liabilities of the acquired thrifts were the same as FSLIC's insurance liabilities that remained liabilities of FSLIC. The Ninth Circuit reasoned that Home Savings received a generous incentive package, the cost of which was the excess of the failing thrifts liabilities over the value of their assets. A concurring opinion argued that the acquired rights had a fair market value basis as acquired directly from FSLIC in exchange for taking over the liabilities of the failed thrifts. The Ninth Circuit remanded the case to the District Court to determine the proper amortization amounts for the intangibles and the amount of abandonment loss for the branch rights.

Under § 381, the tax attributes of the target corporation, most significantly net operating loss carryovers, which may be an important asset of the target corporation, carry over to the acquiring corporation. The limitations of § 382(b) are, however, applicable. Under § 382, a corporation's net operating loss carryover is limited if there has been a greater than 50 percent change in ownership over a three year testing period (an "ownership change"). See Chapter 15. However, as discussed in greater detail beginning at page 836, in the case of a bankruptcy or insolvency proceeding, the § 382 limitation is not applied if, following an ownership change, the creditors and former stockholders of the loss corporation own at least 50 percent of the loss corporation stock. I.R.C. § 382(*l*)(5)(A).

PART 5

NONACQUISITIVE REORGANIZATIONS

CHAPTER 13

SINGLE-CORPORATION REORGANIZATIONS

SECTION 1.   STATUTORY STRUCTURE

While the reorganization provisions are most important in the context of acquisition transactions, several forms of reorganizations allow exchanges of stock or securities to modify some aspects of the corporate capital structure of a single corporation without requiring the current recognition of gain (or allowing the recognition of loss). The present statutory structure provides for reorganization treatment in two situations. Section 368(a)(1)(E) deals with corporate "recapitalizations", i.e., adjustments to the corporation's capital structure, as when a bondholder exchanges bonds for stock in the corporation or a shareholder exchanges stock of one class for stock of another class in the same corporation. Section 368(a)(1)(F) deals with a change in corporate structure involving a change in the place of incorporation or form of organization, as when a California corporation reincorporates in Delaware.

The controversies involving these nonacquisitive reorganizations have primarily involved attempts by taxpayers to avoid dividend treatment on cash or other property extracted from the corporation. When dividends are taxed at ordinary rates rather than the preferential rates imposed on capital gains, as was the case in years prior to 2004, generally the issue has been whether the reorganization rules themselves, as properly applied, should result in the receipt of a dividend when a shareholder receives property (often debt instruments issued by the corporation) in the context of an admitted reorganization. With the introduction in the 2003 Act of a preferential rate for dividends that mirrors the preferential rate for capital gains, generally a maximum rate of 20 percent, the stakes in this regard were greatly reduced. In other cases, the question is whether the transaction is in fact a reorganization at all, or whether it is more appropriately characterized as some form of sale or liquidation transaction, which qualifies for capital gain treatment at the shareholder level and results in recognition of gain or loss by the corporation. In these latter cases, it often has been the IRS that was arguing for characterization as a reorganization in order to apply the reorganization rules requiring dividend treatment.

The requirements of § 311 and § 336 that the corporation recognize gain on the distribution of appreciated property have curtailed taxpayer attempts to convert potential dividend income into capital gain by distributing property from the corporation. There remains, however, the fundamental question of whether an otherwise taxable transaction should be given nonrecognition treatment when it takes place in the context of a corporate adjustment or restructuring.

Section 368 provides the following definitions of the reorganizations considered in this Chapter:

Type (E) Recapitalizations. Section 368(a)(1)(E) covers the recapitalization of an existing corporation, such as the exchange of one type of common stock for another, or of one type of preferred stock for another, or of new preferred stock for old bonds, of new preferred stock for old stock or of new common stock for old preferred stock, or of new bonds for old bonds. Here only one corporation and its shareholders (or bondholders) are involved. These same transactions, however, can be implemented under sections 368(a)(1)(A), (B) or (C), for example, by a corporation that creates a new subsidiary corporation and has the new corporation issue to the parent, in return for the parent's assets, stock and securities of the nature desired, which the parent will then distribute to its shareholders on its liquidation. Type (E) reorganizations are considered in Section 2.

Type (F) Change of Identity, Form, or Place of Organization. A mere change in identity, form, or place of organization of one corporation, however effected, is governed by § 368(a)(1)(F). For example, X Corporation may change its state of incorporation from New Jersey to Delaware by forming Y Corporation, a Delaware subsidiary into which X Corporation merges with the shareholders (and bondholders) of X Corporation receiving identical securities of Y Corporation in exchange for their interests in X Corporation. But if X Corporation simultaneously effects a recapitalization, for example, by exchanging both common and preferred shares of Y Corporation for X Corporation common stock (as was the case in Marr v. United States, 268 U.S. 536 (1925), page 525), then the transaction might not be an (F) reorganization. Such a transaction is not easily characterized as an (E) reorganization either. In this case, unless the single transaction can be bifurcated into simultaneous but separate (E) and (F) reorganizations, the transaction will be a reorganization only if it fits within the definition of one of the other subparagraphs, such as type (A). Type (F) reorganizations are considered in Section 3.

SECTION 2.   RECAPITALIZATIONS

INTERNAL REVENUE CODE: Sections 108(e)(8), (10); 368(a)(1)(E); 354(a); 356(a), (c)–(f); 306(c)(1)(B), (C).

REGULATIONS: Sections 1.354–1(d), (e); 1.356–1, –3, –4, –5; 1.368–1(b); 1.368–2(e); 1.306–3(d), (e); 1.301–1(*1*).

Bazley v. Commissioner*
Supreme Court of the United States, 1947.
331 U.S. 737.

■ MR. JUSTICE FRANKFURTER delivered the opinion of the Court.

The proper construction of provisions of the Internal Revenue Code relating to corporate reorganizations is involved in both these cases. Their importance to the Treasury as well as to corporate enterprise led us to grant certiorari, 329 U.S. 695, 67 S.Ct. 62; 329 U.S. 701, 67 S.Ct.

---

*   Together with No. 209, Adams v. Commissioner of Internal Revenue.

77. While there are differences in detail to which we shall refer, the two cases may be disposed of in one opinion.

In the Bazley case, No. 287, the Commissioner of Internal Revenue assessed an income tax deficiency against the taxpayer for the year 1939. Its validity depends on the legal significance of the recapitalization in that year of a family corporation in which the taxpayer and his wife owned all but one of the Company's one thousand shares. These had a par value of $100. Under the plan of reorganization the taxpayer, his wife, and the holder of the additional share were to turn in their old shares and receive in exchange for each old share five new shares of no par value, but of a stated value of $60, and new debenture bonds, having a total face value of $400,000, payable in ten years but callable at any time. Accordingly, the taxpayer received 3,990 shares of the new stock for the 798 shares of his old holding and debentures in the amount of $319,200. At the time of these transactions the earned surplus of the corporation was $855,783.82.

The Commissioner charged to the taxpayer as income the full value of the debentures. The Tax Court affirmed the Commissioner's determination, against the taxpayer's contention that as a "recapitalization" the transaction was a tax-free "reorganization" and that the debentures were "securities in a corporation a party to a reorganization," "exchanged solely for stock or securities in such corporation" "in pursuance of a plan of reorganization," and as such no gain is recognized for income tax purposes. [The Court cites the predecessors of §§ 368(a)(1)(E) and 354(a)(1)].** The Tax Court found that the recapitalization had "no legitimate corporate business purpose" and was therefore not a "reorganization" within the statute. The distribution of debentures, it concluded, was a disguised dividend, taxable as earned income under [the predecessors of §§ 61(a), 301, 302 and 318(a)]. 4 T.C. 897. The Circuit Court of Appeals for the Third Circuit, sitting en banc, affirmed, two judges dissenting. 155 F.2d 237.

Unless a transaction is a reorganization contemplated by [the predecessor of § 368(a)(1)], any exchange of "stock or securities" in connection with such transaction, cannot be "in pursuance of the plan of reorganization" under [the predecessor of § 354(a)(1)]. While [§ 368(a)(1)] informs us that "reorganization" means, among other things, "a recapitalization," it does not inform us what "recapitalization" means. "Recapitalization" in connection with the income tax has been part of the revenue laws since 1921. Congress has never defined it and the Treasury Regulations shed only limited light. [Citing the predecessor of Treas.Reg. § 1.368–2(e).] One thing is certain. Congress did not incorporate some technical concept, whether that of accountants or of other specialists, into [§ 368(a)(1)], assuming that there is agreement among specialists as to the meaning of recapitalization. And so, recapitalization as used in [§ 368(a)(1)] must draw its meaning from its function in that section. It is one of the forms of reorganization which obtains the privileges afforded by [§ 368(a)(1)]. Therefore, "recapitalization" must be construed with reference to the presuppositions and purpose of [§ 368(a)(1)]. It was not the purpose of

---

** [Ed.: The case arose under the 1939 Code which did not contain provisions corresponding to §§ 354(a)(2) and 356(d), which treat the excess principal amount of securities received in a reorganization as boot.]

the reorganization provision to exempt from payment of a tax what as a practical matter is realized gain. Normally, a distribution by a corporation, whatever form it takes, is a definite and rather unambiguous event. It furnishes the proper occasion for the determination and taxation of gain. But there are circumstances where a formal distribution, directly or through exchange of securities, represents merely a new form of the previous participation in an enterprise, involving no change of substance in the rights and relations of the interested parties one to another or to the corporate assets. As to these, Congress has said that they are not to be deemed significant occasions for determining taxable gain.

These considerations underlie [§ 368(a)(1)] and they should dominate the scope to be given to the various sections, all of which converge toward a common purpose. Application of the language of such a revenue provision is not an exercise in framing abstract definitions. In a series of cases this Court has withheld the benefits of the reorganization provision in situations which might have satisfied provisions of the section treated as inert language, because they were not reorganizations of the kind with which [§ 368] in its purpose and particulars, concerns itself. See Pinellas Ice & Cold Storage Co. v. Commissioner, 287 U.S. 462, 53 S.Ct. 257; Gregory v. Helvering, 293 U.S. 465, 55 S.Ct. 266; Le Tulle v. Scofield, 308 U.S. 415, 60 S.Ct. 313.

Congress has not attempted a definition of what is recapitalization and we shall follow its example. The search for relevant meaning is often satisfied not by a futile attempt at abstract definition but by pricking a line through concrete applications. Meaning frequently is built up by assured recognition of what does not come within a concept the content of which is in controversy. Since a recapitalization within the scope of [§ 368(a)(1)] is an aspect of reorganization nothing can be a recapitalization for this purpose unless it partakes of those characteristics of a reorganization which underlie the purpose of Congress in postponing the tax liability.

No doubt there was a recapitalization of the Bazley corporation in the sense that the symbols that represented its capital were changed, so that the fiscal basis of its operations would appear very differently on its books. But the form of a transaction as reflected by correct corporate accounting opens questions as to the proper application of a taxing statute; it does not close them. Corporate accounting may represent that correspondence between change in the form of capital structure and essential identity in fact which is of the essence of a transaction relieved from taxation as a reorganization. What is controlling is that a new arrangement intrinsically partake of the elements of reorganization which underlie the Congressional exemption and not merely give the appearance of it to accomplish a distribution of earnings. In the case of a corporation which has undistributed earnings, the creation of new corporate obligations which are transferred to stockholders in relation to their former holdings, so as to produce, for all practical purposes, the same result as a distribution of cash earnings of equivalent value, cannot obtain tax immunity because cast in the form of a recapitalization-reorganization. The governing legal rule can hardly be stated more narrowly. To attempt to do so would only challenge astuteness in evading it. And so it is hard to escape the conclusion that whether in a particular case a paper recapitalization is no more than an admissible attempt to avoid the consequences of an outright distribution of earnings turns on details of corporate affairs, judgment on which must be left to the Tax Court. See Dobson v. Commissioner, 320 U.S. 489, 64 S.Ct. 239.

What have we here? No doubt, if the Bazley corporation had issued the debentures to Bazley and his wife without any recapitalization, it would have made a taxable distribution. Instead, these debentures were issued as part of a family arrangement, the only additional ingredient being an unrelated modification of the capital account. The debentures were found to be worth at least their principal amount, and they were virtually cash because they were callable at the will of the corporation which in this case was the will of the taxpayer. One does not have to pursue the motives behind actions, even in the more ascertainable forms of purpose, to find, as did the Tax Court, that the whole arrangement took this form instead of an outright distribution of cash or debentures, because the latter would undoubtedly have been taxable income whereas what was done could, with a show of reason, claim the shelter of the immunity of a recapitalization-reorganization.

The Commissioner, the Tax Court and the Circuit Court of Appeals agree that nothing was accomplished that would not have been accomplished by an outright debenture dividend. And since we find no misconception of law on the part of the Tax Court and the Circuit Court of Appeals, whatever may have been their choice of phrasing, their application of the law to the facts of this case must stand. A "reorganization" which is merely a vehicle, however elaborate or elegant, for conveying earnings from accumulations to the stockholders is not a reorganization under [§ 368(a)(1)]. This disposes of the case as a matter of law, since the facts as found by the Tax Court bring them within it. And even if this transaction were deemed a reorganization, the facts would equally sustain the imposition of the tax on the debentures under [the predecessors of § 356(a)(1) and (2)]. Commissioner v. Estate of Bedford, 325 U.S. 283, 65 S.Ct. 1157.

In the Adams case, No. 209, the taxpayer owned all but a few of the 5914 shares of stock outstanding out of an authorized 6000, par value $100. By a plan of reorganization, the authorized capital was reduced by half, to $295,700, divided into 5914 shares of no par value but having a stated value of $50 per share. The 5914 old shares were cancelled and the corporation issued in exchange therefor 5914 shares of the new no-par common stock and 6 per cent 20 year debenture bonds in the principal amount of $295,700. The exchange was made on the basis of one new share of stock and one $50 bond for each old share. The old capital account was debited in the sum of $591,400, a new no-par capital account was credited with $295,700, and the balance of $295,700 was credited to a "Debenture Payable" account. The corporation at this time had accumulated earnings available for distribution in a sum not less than $164,514.82, and this account was left unchanged. At the time of the exchange, the debentures had a value not less than $164,208.82.

The Commissioner determined an income tax deficiency by treating the debenture bonds as a distribution of the corporation's accumulated earnings. The Tax Court sustained the Commissioner's determination, 5 T.C. 351, and the Circuit Court of Appeals affirmed. 155 F.2d 246.

The case is governed by our treatment of the Bazley case. The finding by the Tax Court that the reorganization had no purpose other than to achieve the distribution of the earnings, is unaffected by the bookkeeping detail of leaving the surplus account unaffected. See [the predecessor to § 316(a), second sentence], and Commissioner v. Wheeler, 324 U.S. 542, 546, 65 S.Ct. 799.

* * *

Judgments affirmed.

Revenue Ruling 84–114

1984–2 C.B. 90.

ISSUE

When nonvoting preferred stock and cash are received in an integrated transaction by a shareholder in exchange for voting common stock in a recapitalization described in section 368(a)(1)(E) of the Internal Revenue Code, does the receipt of cash have the effect of the distribution of a dividend within the meaning of section 356(a)(2)?

FACTS

Corporation X had outstanding 420 shares of voting common stock of which A owned 120 shares and B, C and D each owned 100 shares. A, B, C and D were not related within the meaning of section 318(a) of the Code. X adopted a plan of recapitalization that permitted a shareholder to exchange each of 30 shares of voting common stock for either one share of nonvoting preferred stock or cash. Pursuant to the plan, A first exchanged 15 shares of voting common stock for cash and then exchanged 15 shares of voting common stock for 15 shares of nonvoting preferred stock. The facts and circumstances surrounding these exchanges were such that the exchanges constituted two steps in a single integrated transaction for purposes of sections 368(a)(1)(E) and 356(a)(2). The nonvoting preferred stock had no conversion features. In addition, the dividend and liquidation rights payable to A on 15 shares of nonvoting preferred stock were substantially less than the dividend and liquidation rights payable to A on 30 shares of voting common stock. B, C, and D did not participate in the exchange and will retain all their voting common stock in X. X had a substantial amount of post-1913 earnings and profits.

The exchange by A of voting common stock for nonvoting preferred stock and cash qualified as a recapitalization within the meaning of section 368(a)(1)(E) of the Code.

LAW AND ANALYSIS

Section 354(a)(1) of the Code provides that no gain or loss will be recognized if stock or securities in a corporation a party to a reorganization are, in pursuance of the plan of reorganization, exchanged solely for stock or securities in such corporation or in another corporation a party to the reorganization.

Section 356(a)(1) of the Code provides that if section 354 would apply to an exchange but for the fact that the property received in the exchange consists not only of property permitted by section 354 to be received without the recognition of gain but also of other property or money, then the gain, if any, will be recognized, but in an amount not in excess of the sum of the money and fair market value of the other property. Section 356(a)(2) provides that if such exchange has the effect of the distribution of a dividend (determined with the application of section 318(a)), then there will be treated as a dividend to each distributee such an amount of the gain recognized under section 356(a)(1) as is not in excess of each distributee's ratable share of the undistributed earnings and profits of the corporation accumulated after February 28, 1913.

Under section 302(b)(1) and section 302(a) of the Code a redemption will be treated as a distribution in part or full payment in exchange for stock if it is not essentially equivalent to a dividend to the shareholder.

Rev.Rul. 74–515, 1974–2 C.B. 118, and Rev.Rul. 74–516, 1974–2 C.B. 121, state that whether a reorganization distribution to which section 356 of the Code applies has the effect of a dividend must be determined by examining the facts and circumstances surrounding the distribution and looking to the principles for determining dividend equivalency developed under section 356(a)(2) and other provisions of the Code. * * * Rev.Rul. 74–516 indicates that in making a dividend equivalency determination under section 356(a)(2), it is proper to analogize to section 302 in appropriate cases. * * *

In United States v. Davis, 397 U.S. 301 (1970), rehearing denied, 397 U.S. 1071 (1970), 1970–1 C.B. 62, the Supreme Court of the United States held that a redemption must result in a meaningful reduction of the shareholder's proportionate interest in the corporation in order not to be essentially equivalent to a dividend under section 302(b)(1) of the Code.

Rev.Rul. 75–502, 1975–2 C.B. 111, sets forth factors to be considered in determining whether a reduction in a shareholder's proportionate interest in a corporation is meaningful within the meaning of *Davis*. The factors considered are a shareholder's right to vote and exercise control, to participate in current earnings and accumulated surplus, and to share in net assets on liquidation. The reduction in the right to vote is of particular significance when a redemption causes a redeemed shareholder to lose the potential for controlling the redeeming corporation by acting in concert with only one other shareholder. See Rev.Rul. 76–364, 1976–2 C.B. 91.

The specific issue is whether, in determining dividend equivalency under section 356(a)(2) of the Code, it is proper to look solely at the change in A's proportionate interest in X that resulted from A's exchange of voting common stock for cash, or instead, whether consideration should be given to the total change in A's proportionate interest in X that resulted from the exchange of voting common stock for both cash and nonvoting preferred stock.

In Rev.Rul. 55–745, 1955–2 C.B. 223, the Internal Revenue Service announced that for purposes of section 302(b)(3) of the Code, it would follow the decision in Zenz v. Quinlivan, 213 F.2d 914 (6th Cir.1954), that a complete termination of shareholder interest may be achieved when a shareholder's entire stock interest in a corporation is disposed of partly through redemption and partly through sale. See also Rev.Rul. 75–447, 1975–2 C.B. 113, in which the *Zenz* rationale was applied to section 302(b)(2).

Since the exchange of voting common stock for cash and the exchange of voting common stock for nonvoting preferred stock constitute an integrated transaction, in this situation involving a single corporation it is proper to apply the *Zenz* rationale so that both exchanges are taken into consideration in determining whether there has been a meaningful reduction of A's proportionate interest in X within the meaning of *Davis.* * * *

If the exchange of voting common stock for preferred stock and cash in this situation had been tested under section 302 of the Code as a redemption, it would not have qualified under section 302(b)(2) or (3) because there was neither an adequate reduction in A's voting stock interest nor a complete termination of that interest. In determining whether this situation is analogous to a redemption meeting the requirements of section 302(b)(1), it is significant that A's interest in the voting common stock of X was reduced from 28.57 percent (120/420) to 23.08 percent (90/390) so that A went from a position of holding a number of shares of voting common stock that afforded A control of X if A acted in concert with only one other shareholder, to a position where such action was not possible. Moreover, it is significant that A no longer holds the largest voting stock interest in X. In addition, although A received dividend and liquidation rights from the 15 shares of nonvoting preferred stock, these were substantially less than the dividend and liquidation rights of the 30 shares of voting common stock A surrendered. Accordingly, the requirements of section 302(b)(1) would have been met if the transaction had been tested under section 302, and, therefore, the cash received by A did not have the effect of the distribution of a dividend within the meaning of section 356(a)(2).

HOLDING

When A received cash and nonvoting preferred stock of X in an integrated transaction in exchange for voting common stock of X in a recapitalization described in section 368(a)(1)(E) of the Code, the receipt of cash did not have the effect of the distribution of a dividend within the meaning of section 356(a)(2).

DETAILED ANALYSIS

1.   DEFINITION OF "RECAPITALIZATION" IN GENERAL

Section 368(a)(1)(E) includes within the definition of a reorganization a "recapitalization." The term "recapitalization" is not defined in either the Code or regulations, however, and its scope and contours have been left to judicial development. Speaking generally, a recapitalization involves a "reshuffling of a capital structure within the framework of an existing corporation," Helvering v. Southwest Consolidated Corporation, 315 U.S. 194, 202 (1942), and encompasses transactions involving exchanges of one class of stock or securities in a corporation for another class issued by the same corporation. Treas.Reg. § 1.368–2(e) provides examples of five different recapitalization exchanges, but those examples are not exhaustive.

The Courts of Appeals and the Tax Court held in the *Bazley* and *Adams* cases that no corporate business purpose existed and that the business purpose test must be viewed in terms of the corporation qua corporation and apart from the shareholders. Dissenting opinions in both courts contended that the shareholders had persuasive business reasons for the transaction (obtaining a more marketable security and one that could be sold without reducing stock control of the corporation, an equal footing with creditors to the extent of the debentures, and a more permanent dedication of the accumulated profits to the business). They rejected the view that shareholder business purposes do not supply the necessary corporate business purpose, stating that such a distinction between "corporate" and "shareholder" purposes lacked substance since a corporation did not have purposes apart from its shareholders. The Government's brief stressed the argument that the transaction was not actuated by a purpose germane to the corporation's business, relied strongly on the *Gregory* case, and stated in effect that the stockholders' purposes were not relevant. In the light of this background, note the Supreme Court's avoidance of direct "business purpose" terminology. For a similar issue in the context of divisive reorganizations, see page 749.

Rev.Rul. 77–238, 1977–2 C.B. 115, found an (E) reorganization existed where the certificate of incorporation required retiring employees owning common stock to exchange that stock for preferred. The purpose of the provision was to eliminate common stockholdings by employees no longer with the corporation, thus supplying the business purpose necessary to support the reorganization.

Treas.Reg. § 1.368–1(b) provides that neither the continuity of shareholder interest doctrine nor the continuity of business enterprise doctrine embodied in Treas.Reg. § 1.368–1(d) apply to a recapitalization. Thus, for example, a recapitalization might convert all of the shareholders to creditors and some or all of the corporation's creditors to shareholders; although § 356 would require gain recognition by the shareholders who became creditors, § 354 would accord nonrecognition of gain or loss to security holders who became shareholders. Likewise, incident to a recapitalization a corporation may sell all of its assets and purchase new assets to engage in a different line of business. Presumably, the corporation also could sell its assets and acquire investment assets, thereby becoming a holding company.

2. EXCHANGE OF OUTSTANDING STOCK FOR NEW STOCK OR NEW BONDS

2.1. *General*

The exchange of outstanding preferred stock for new preferred stock or of outstanding common stock for new common stock constitutes a recapitalization.[1] The exchange of outstanding preferred stock for common stock is likewise a recapitalization as is an exchange of common stock for common and preferred stock. Treas.Reg. § 1.368–2(e). In the latter

---

[1]   Where the exchange is of stock for stock, there is an overlap of § 368(a)(1)(E) and § 1036. That section applies both to an exchange between shareholders and one between the shareholder and the issuing corporation. See Treas.Reg. § 1.1036–1(a). However, both sections produce the same result, at least where no boot is involved. Rev.Rul. 72–57, 1972–1 C.B. 103, held that where boot is involved, only the reorganization provisions apply.

situation, however, special rules apply to limit the "bailout" potential of the transaction.

It is not necessary that all shareholders in a recapitalization exchange their stock. Thus, a valid (E) reorganization results where only one of three shareholders exchanges common stock for preferred stock and the fair market value of the preferred equals the fair market value of the common stock exchanged. If there is a difference in value between the common and the preferred stock, the difference may constitute a gift, compensation, etc. Rev.Rul. 74–269, 1974–1 C.B. 87. See also Rev.Rul. 89–3, 1989–1 C.B. 278 (recapitalization whereby shareholder who had acquired shares by gift from controlling shareholder exchanged common stock for new voting common and donor shareholder exchanged common stock for new common stock with restricted voting rights resulted in a taxable gift).

2.2. *Basis Aspects*

If a taxpayer acquires a corporation's stock at different times and at different prices and exchanges the acquired stock in a recapitalization, the bases of the acquired stock are not blended or averaged in computing the basis of the stock received in the recapitalization. Under Treas.Reg. §§ 1.358–1(a) and 1.358–2(a)(2), the basis of each share of stock (or each security) received in a reorganization is the same as the basis of the share or shares of stock (or security or securities) surrendered. Assume, for example, that a shareholder purchased 200 shares of X corporation common stock for $1,000 and at another time purchased 100 shares of X Corporation common stock for $3,000. If in a recapitalization the shareholder exchanges the 300 shares of X Corporation common stock for 60 shares of preferred stock, 20 shares of the preferred stock will have a basis of $1,000 and 40 shares will have a basis of $3,000.

Special rules in Treas.Reg. § 1.358–2(a)(2) deal with more complex exchanges. If more than one share of stock or security is received in exchange for one share of stock or security, the basis of the share of stock (or security) surrendered is allocated among the shares of stock (or securities) received in the exchange in proportion to the fair market value of the shares of stock (or securities) received. If one share of stock or security is received in respect of more than one share of stock or security or a fraction of a share of stock or security is received, the basis of each share of stock or security surrendered must be allocated to the shares of stock or securities received in a manner that reflects, to the greatest extent possible, that a share of stock or security received is received in respect of shares of stock or securities acquired on the same date and at the same price. The regulations also provide rules for situations in which a share of stock is received in exchange for more than one share of stock (or a fraction of a share of stock is received).

2.3. *Stock Surrendered in Exchange for Securities*

2.3.1.   *General—Continuity of Interest*

In Hickok v. Commissioner, 32 T.C. 80 (1959) (Acq.), the Tax Court held that the continuity of interest doctrine, discussed at page 539, does not apply to recapitalizations. For many years the IRS followed this principle in Revenue Rulings. See Rev.Rul. 77–415, 1977–2 C.B. 311, obsoleted by T.D. 8182, 2005–11 I.R.B. 713. Finally, in 2005, Treas.Reg. § 1.368–1(b) was amended to expressly provide that the continuity of interest doctrine, does not apply to recapitalizations. Thus, for example, if A, B, C, and D each held 25 percent of the stock of X Corporation, a transaction in which A exchanged common stock for new common stock and new preferred stock, while B, C, and D exchanged their stock for debentures, would qualify as a recapitalization. B, C, and D would recognize gain, but A would be entitled to nonrecognition. Likewise, a pre-arranged sale of newly issued stock received in an (E) reorganization does not impair the validity of the reorganization. Rev.Rul. 77–479, 1977–2 C.B. 119.

2.3.2. *Security Bailouts*

Sections 354(a)(2) and 356(d) extend the rationale of the *Bazley* case to all recapitalization and other reorganization exchanges since the value of the excess in principal amount of securities received by the shareholder over the principal amount of securities given up is considered "other property" or "boot." Hence if a shareholder exchanges stock, whether common or preferred, for new stock, whether common or preferred, and debt securities, the securities will be boot and governed by § 356(a). If stock is exchanged for securities alone, § 354(a)(2) renders § 354(a)(1) inapplicable entirely, § 356(a)(1)(B) does not come into play, and the treatment of the exchange is determined under §§ 301, 302, and 331. Treas.Reg. § 1.354–1(d), Ex. 3.

Thus, although lack of continuity of equity interest does not destroy the validity of a type (E) reorganization, § 354(a)(2) in effect applies a continuity of interest concept on a shareholder by shareholder basis. Where the recapitalization exchange "has the effect" of a dividend distribution, dividend income is recognized to the extent of the gain realized on the exchange. I.R.C. § 356(a)(2).[2] See Commissioner v. Estate of Bedford, 325 U.S. 283 (1945). As discussed in Rev.Rul. 84–114, page 680, dividend equivalency of boot distributions made in connection with a recapitalization is determined by applying the principles of § 302, which governs redemptions (discussed in Chapter 5). See also Johnson v. Commissioner, 78 T.C. 564 (1982) ($850 per share boot in recapitalization which converted nonvoting common stock into voting common stock was a dividend because it was pro rata and compensated nonvoting shareholders for dividends previously withheld). The reasoning in *Clark,* page 601, which significantly limits the application of § 356(a)(2) in the case of acquisitive reorganizations, should not affect the application of that section to recapitalizations because only a single corporation is involved. The IRS has so ruled in the context of a divisive reorganization of a single corporation under § 355. See Rev.Rul. 93–62, 1993–2 C.B. 118, page 768. In addition, in the appropriate circumstances, the IRS might argue that under the approach of *Bazley,* the full amount of the boot was a dividend. Treas.Reg. § 1.301–1(*l*) preserves this contention.

---

[2] The effect of § 1036 must also be considered. On the face of the statute, there is an overlap of § 368(a)(1)(E) and § 1036 in these various situations. Where boot is involved in a § 1036 exchange, § 1031(b), which applies to § 1036 transactions, controls taxation of the boot. But in cases of an overlap between § 1036 and § 368(a)(1)(E), Treas.Reg. § 1.1031(b)–1(a)(3) defers to the reorganization provisions, See Rev.Rul. 72–57, 1972–1 C.B. 103 (exchange of outstanding stock for stock and cash as part of a transaction to eliminate minority shareholders was a recapitalization and therefore, under Treas.Reg. § 1.1031(b)–1(a)(3), was not a § 1036 exchange coupled with the receipt of nonqualifying property by the majority shareholder under § 1031(b)); Rev.Rul. 78–351, 1978–2 C.B. 148, modifying Rev.Rul. 72–57, held the cash was a § 356(a)(2) dividend to the majority shareholder.

2.4. *Preferred Stock Bailouts—Exchange of Outstanding Common Stock for New Preferred Stock*

In a recapitalization variant of the preferred stock dividend bailout, dealt with by § 306, holders of common stock may exchange some common stock for new preferred, or exchange all of their common stock for new common stock and new preferred, so that after the exchange they own both common stock and preferred stock. Section 306(c)(1)(B) extends the § 306 solution to the recapitalization exchange if "the effect of the transaction was substantially the same as the receipt of a stock dividend." Treas.Reg. § 1.306–3(d) refers to § 356(a)(2) and states that if any cash received in lieu of the stock would have been a dividend under § 356(a)(2), then the stock is § 306 stock. If a cash distribution would not have been taxable under § 356(a)(2) because of the "dividend within the gain" limitation, then the stock apparently is not § 306 stock.

Rev.Rul. 81–186, 1981–2 C.B. 85, suggests that the § 318 attribution of ownership rules do not apply in determining whether preferred stock received in a recapitalization is § 306 stock. For example, if a husband retains his common stock but his wife receives preferred stock in a recapitalization, the preferred stock is not § 306 stock. That ruling held that where a sole shareholder exchanged some of his common stock for preferred stock in a recapitalization and gave his remaining common stock to his children, the preferred stock was not § 306 stock; if the shareholder had received cash it would not have been a dividend because he would have terminated his entire interest in the corporation. See Zenz v. Quinlivan, 213 F.2d 914 (6th Cir.1954), page 505.

Where, in a reorganization, boot is distributed in exchange for § 306 stock, § 356(f) applies to treat the boot under § 301. In Rev.Rul. 76–14, 1976–1 C.B. 97, the majority shareholder desired to transfer control of the business to an employee-minority shareholder. Under a recapitalization plan, the majority shareholder turned in his common stock for cash and his preferred stock (which was § 306 stock) for a new class of nonvoting common stock. The ruling held § 356(f) applied; thus the cash received was applied first to the § 306 stock, with a resulting dividend. But if cash is distributed to minority shareholders in lieu of fractional shares, the exception in § 306(b)(4)(A) applies, and the cash will be treated as received in a redemption subject to § 302. Rev.Rul. 81–81, 1981–1 C.B. 122. If in the reorganization, stock which is other than common stock is issued for § 306 stock under § 306(c)(1)(B), the new stock is § 306 stock.

A recapitalization exchange can occur without a direct exchange of stock. Thus, in Rev.Rul. 56–654, 1956–2 C.B. 216, a corporation with outstanding common and preferred stock amended its charter to increase the liquidation value of the preferred stock. The ruling states that this represented an exchange of all preferred stock and a portion of the common stock for new preferred stock; presumably the increase in value of the preferred stock is § 306 stock. Rev.Rul. 66–332, 1966–2 C.B. 108, modified by Rev.Rul. 81–91, 1981–1 C.B. 123, held that a "reclassification" of outstanding common stock together with the issuance of additional classes of stock could result in the reclassified stock being treated as § 306 stock if as a result of the change in its rights under the reclassification it ceased to be common stock.

2.5. *Relation of Security Bailout to Preferred Stock Bailout*

The IRS's view of *Bazley* type recapitalizations prior to the 1954 Code was that the vice lay in splitting a common stockholder's interest into common stock which could be retained and another interest, preferred stock or debt, which could be sold, thereby obtaining capital gain treatment for a part of the accumulated earnings without reducing the shareholder's common stock interest. The current Code embodies the view that an exchange of outstanding stock for debt must meet the tests of the dividend sections. It is akin to the policy of § 306 respecting preferred stock bailouts, in that it seeks to block the efforts to convert situations having potential dividend taxation into situations involving capital gain potential only. The solution for the "security bailout," however, is that of an immediate tax, while under § 306 the solution for the "preferred stock bailout" is that of "tainting" by giving the preferred stock an ordinary income status on future disposition.

3. EXCHANGE OF DEBT SECURITIES FOR DEBT SECURITIES

3.1. *Qualification as a Recapitalization*

The regulations under § 368(a)(1)(E) and its predecessors never have expressly provided that an exchange of only debt securities qualifies as a recapitalization. See Treas.Reg. § 1.368–2(e). Treatment of the exchange of outstanding debentures for new corporate debentures as a recapitalization was first established judicially.

Commissioner v. Neustadt's Trust, 131 F.2d 528 (2d Cir.1942), involved the exchange of outstanding 20 year, 6 percent debentures for a like face amount of 10 year, 3¼ percent convertible debentures of the corporation. The IRS contended that a taxable gain resulted, but the court disagreed and applied the reorganization provisions:

> The first question is whether the debentures are "securities" within the meaning of [the predecessor of § 354(a)(1)]. The word is used in contrast to "stock"; it necessarily refers to bonds of some sort, since bonds are the most usual, if not the only, form of corporate securities to contrast with stock. * * * [It] is usual financial practice to speak of debentures as "securities" and the term should be given its ordinary meaning. In Helvering v. Watts, 296 U.S. 387, 56 S.Ct. 275, bonds with a maximum maturity of seven years were held to be "securities" within the corresponding provision of the Revenue Act of 1924. We do not understand that the authority of this case has been destroyed by the subsequent decision in LeTulle v. Scofield, 308 U.S. 415, 60 S.Ct. 313. There it was held that continuity of proprietary interest must be found if the transaction is to be deemed within the definition of reorganization, and that a transfer of all the assets of one corporation to another in exchange for cash and bonds of the latter did not fall within such a definition. It was not held that an exchange of bonds for bonds pursuant to a plan of reorganization is not an exchange of "securities" within the meaning of [the predecessor of § 354(a)(1)]. * * * We think the debentures involved in the case at bar are "securities" within that section.

It remains to determine whether they were exchanged pursuant to a plan of reorganization and this turns on whether the exchange amounts to a "recapitalization," as that word is used in [the predecessor of § 368(a)(1)(E)]. * * * The Commissioner contends that only a change in authorized or outstanding capital stock of a corporation can properly be denominated a recapitalization or a reshuffling of the capital structure. He describes an exchange of old debentures for new debentures in the same corporation as a mere refinancing operation. * * * But in common financial parlance the long term funded debt of a corporation is usually regarded as forming part of its capital structure. * * * The Security and Exchange Commission has required the funded debt of a corporation to be listed under the caption of "capital securities." The Interstate Commerce Commission treats funded debt as part of the corporate capital structure. St. Louis, San Francisco Ry. Co., Reorganization, 240 I.C.C. 383, 406 * * *. [T]he purpose of the statutory nonrecognition of gain or loss from reorganization transactions, favors ascribing to the word "recapitalization" a broad rather than a restricted meaning. Such purpose, as indicated by the Congressional reports * * * was apparently twofold: To encourage legitimate reorganizations required to strengthen the financial condition of a corporation, and to prevent losses being established by bondholders, as well as stockholders, who have received the new securities without substantially changing their original investment. The transaction in the case at bar meets both of these tests. By changing the interest rate and date of maturity of its old bonds and adding a conversion option to the holders of the new, the corporation could strengthen its financial condition, while the bondholders would not substantially change their original investments by making the exchange. "Recapitalization" seems a most appropriate word to describe that type of reorganization and it is the very kind of transaction were Congress meant the recognition of gain or loss to be held in suspense until a more substantial change in the taxpayer's original investment should occur. We hold that the exchange of securities was made pursuant to a plan of "recapitalization."

The Committee Reports under the 1954 Act approve the *Neustadt* rule. Senate Finance Committee Report, S.Rep. No. 83–1622, 83rd Cong., 2d Sess. 51 (1954). Rev.Rul. 77–415, 1977–2 C.B. 311,[3] accepted the principle that an exchange of new debentures for outstanding debentures is a recapitalization under § 368(a)(1)(E). Thus, the exchange of new ten-year, 10 percent debentures for outstanding 20–year, 8 percent debentures did not result in gain or loss to the exchanging debenture holders since the principal amounts of the two issues were the same.

---

[3]   Rev.Rul. 77–415 was obsoleted by T.D. 8182, 2005–11 I.R.B. 713 because the primary holding in the ruling, which dealt with continuity of interest issues, has been superseded by regulations.

3.2. *Treatment of Bondholders*

Although an exchange of bonds for bonds qualifies as a recapitalization, § 354(a)(2) excludes from the complete nonrecognition rule the receipt of securities in a principal amount greater than the principal amount of any securities surrendered. In such a case, § 356(d) treats the fair market value of the excess principal amount as boot. See Treas.Reg. § 1.356–3(c), Exs. 2–6. The value of the "excess principal amount" is determined by the following formula:

$$\text{Fair Market Value of Securities Received} \times \frac{\text{Principal Amount of Securities Received} \quad minus \quad \text{Principal Amount of Securities Surrendered}}{\text{Principal Amount of Securities Received}}$$

In determining the "principal amount" of securities received in the reorganization, the original issue discount rules of §§ 1272 through 1274, discussed in Chapter 3, Section 2, must be taken into account. If the securities received are publicly traded, their "issue price," and thus "principal amount," is their fair market value, i.e. trading price, on the day they are issued. I.R.C. § 1273(b); Treas.Reg. § 1.1273–2(b)(1). Thus, if new publicly traded bonds are issued for outstanding publicly traded bonds, the issue price of the new bonds is their trading price, not the trading price of the old bonds. But if bonds that are not publicly traded are issued for publicly traded bonds (or stock) the issue price, and thus principal amount, of the new bonds is the trading price of the old bonds (or stock). Treas.Reg. § 1.1273–2(c)(1). Where neither security is publicly traded, whether a security issued in a recapitalization is an OID instrument is determined by treating the instrument as issued for property. I.R.C. § 1275(a)(4). Thus, the issue price (and principal amount) is determined by discounting to net present value the payments due on the instrument (including both principal and interest), using the appropriate "applicable federal rate." See I.R.C. § 1274, discussed at page 169. In either case, if the stated principal amount exceeds the issue price, the principal amount of the securities received will be an amount less than their face value when computing gain under § 356. Thus, receipt of a security having a *face* value in excess of the principal amount of the security surrendered will not give rise to boot under § 356 if under the OID rules the imputed principal amount of the security received does not exceed the principal amount of the security surrendered.

Boot can result under § 354(a)(2) and give rise to taxable gain under § 356(d) even where the value of the securities given up is the same as the value of those received. For example, if a 9½ percent, $100 face amount bond with basis of $100 is exchanged for a new 6 percent, $120 face amount publicly traded bond, and the value of each is $120, the value of the excess $20 in principal amount, i.e., $120 × $^{20}/_{120}$, is boot. See Treas.Reg. § 1.356–3. The new bond has a basis under § 358 of $120 ($100 basis of old bond + $20 gain).

Under Rev.Rul. 60–37, 1960–1 C.B. 309, if the old bonds had an original issue discount element, the new bonds were to be similarly treated. This rule is now embodied in the "issue price" rules in § 1273(b)(3) where either security is publicly traded.

A single transaction can involve recognition of gain attributable to boot, the creation of OID, and the preservation of market discount. Suppose a publicly traded 9½ percent, $100 face amount bond with a basis of $90 (because it was purchased at a discount in the secondary market) is exchanged for a new 6 percent, $130 face amount publicly traded bond and the values of both are $120. The issue price, and thus the principal amount, of the new bond is $120. The value of the excess $20 of principal amount, i.e., $20 ($120 × ($20/$120)), is boot, and that amount of gain must be recognized currently. Because the face amount of the security received ($130) exceeds the fair market value of the security surrendered ($120) the excess amount ($10) is OID. The new bond has a basis under § 358 of $110 ($90 basis of the old bond plus $20 gain), and upon redemption at maturity the holder will recognize gain of $10. This gain will be ordinary income under § 1276 because it is market discount. See I.R.C. § 1278(a)(1)(D)(iii).

If the excess principal amount is in satisfaction of accrued interest, § 354(a)(2)(B) requires that the entire amount of the excess so attributable be recognized as ordinary income. To the extent the excess is not attributable to accrued interest, the value of the excess principal amount is treated as boot taxable under § 356(a), and the boot gain should be treated as capital gain under § 356(a)(1).

3.3. *Treatment of the Corporation*

If a corporation issues new bonds in exchange for outstanding bonds having a higher principal amount, an (E) reorganization exists but the corporation may have to recognize cancellation of indebtedness income under § 61(a)(12), subject to the exceptions and technical rules of § 108. Neither § 361(a) nor § 1032 applies to relieve the corporation from tax. Rev.Rul. 77–437, 1977–2 C.B. 28. If the corporation is solvent and not in bankruptcy at the time of the recapitalization it must recognize cancellation of indebtedness income equal to the amount by which the principal amount of the obligations surrendered, plus accrued but unpaid interest, exceeds the issue price/principal amount of the newly issued securities. See I.R.C. § 108(e)(10). Note that the amount of cancellation of indebtedness income realized by the corporation is determined by comparing the amount owed on the surrendered obligations to the issue price/principal amount of the newly issued bonds, while the creation of OID is determined by comparing the fair market value of the surrendered obligations with the stated principal amount of the newly issued obligations. Thus, both cancellation of indebtedness income and OID may be created simultaneously in a debt-for-debt recapitalization. This result would occur, for example, if outstanding publicly traded bonds with a stated principal amount of $100 and a fair market value of $80 were exchanged for new bonds with a stated principal amount of $90.

If the corporation is *insolvent* (as defined in § 108(d)(3)) both before and after the recapitalization, no cancellation of indebtedness income is recognized. If an insolvent corporation is rendered solvent, cancellation of indebtedness income results only to the extent the recapitalization results in a positive net worth. See I.R.C. § 108(a)(1)(B) and (3). In either case, the insolvent corporation is required to reduce its tax attributes, such as net operating loss carryovers, by the amount of income excluded by the insolvency exception, and in the order specified in § 108(b)(2). The corporation may elect to reduce the basis of depreciable assets under § 1017 in lieu of the tax attribute reduction. I.R.C. § 108(b)(5). If the recapitalization was pursuant to a bankruptcy proceeding, the corporation is not required to recognize any cancellation of indebtedness income that might result from debt restructuring, even if the reorganization renders the corporation solvent. I.R.C. § 108(a)(1)(A). As in the case of an insolvent corporation, however, the reorganized corporation's tax attributes must be reduced under § 108(b).

Regardless of the reorganized corporation's financial status, if the new bonds have a *higher principal amount* than the old bonds (determined under OID principles), the corporation may deduct the retirement premium as an additional cost of borrowing, unless a portion of the premium is attributable to extinguishment of a conversion feature in the old bonds. See I.R.C. § 249, discussed at page 174.

4. EXCHANGE OF OUTSTANDING BONDS FOR NEW STOCK

Treas.Reg. § 1.368–2(e)(1) provides that the issuance by a corporation of new preferred stock in exchange for existing bonds is a recapitalization. See also Commissioner v. Capento Securities Corporation, 140 F.2d 382 (1st Cir.1944). An exchange of outstanding bonds for new common stock would likewise be a recapitalization. In either case, the former security owners are accorded nonrecognition under § 354 (subject to recognition under § 354(a)(2)(B) to the extent that the stock is attributable to interest arrearages). From the corporation's perspective, however, if the corporation is solvent, the transaction gives rise to taxable discharge of indebtedness income to the extent that the sum of the principal amount of the securities plus accrued but unpaid interest exceeds the fair market value of the stock issued in the transaction. I.R.C. § 108(e)(8). To the extent of the fair market value of the stock, § 1032 provides nonrecognition to the corporation.

If the holder of a security that is an OID instrument receives stock in exchange for the instrument in a recapitalization, the balance of the original issue discount will not be included in the income of the exchanging bondholder. See Rev.Rul. 75–39, 1975–1 C.B. 272. The stock will take a basis under § 358 equal to the basis of the debt instrument, which includes all previously accrued OID.

On a related point, the exercise of a conversion privilege of a bond convertible into stock of the same corporation is not an "exchange" and hence the recapitalization provision and § 354 are not involved, Rev.Rul. 72–265, 1972–1 C.B. 222. See also Rev.Rul. 79–155, 1979–1 C.B. 153 (parent of subsidiary that issued debt obligations convertible into stock of parent was treated as a joint obligor on debt, thereby resulting in conversion not being a taxable event).

5. SECTION 305 ASPECTS

A recapitalization, which would be tax-free under the reorganization provisions, is one of the transactions that can result in a constructive stock dividend under § 305(c). See page 307. For example, in a recapitalization in which a shareholder exchanges preferred stock with dividend arrearages for new common and preferred stock, the exchange would be a tax-free recapitalization under § 368. See e.g., Kaufman v. Commissioner, 55 T.C. 1046 (1971) (Acq.). When viewed from the perspective of § 305, however, the recapitalization has the effect of a distribution of additional shares of stock to the preferred stockholder which would result in a taxable dividend under sections 305(c) and 305(b)(4). Treas.Reg. § 1.305–5(d), Ex. 1 (taxable stock dividend if arrearages are eliminated). However, see Treas.Reg. § 1.305–3(e), Ex. 12, illustrating that § 305 is inapplicable to a "single and isolated" recapitalization transaction.

SECTION 3.   CHANGES IN IDENTITY, FORM, OR PLACE OF ORGANIZATION: TYPE (F) REORGANIZATIONS

INTERNAL REVENUE CODE: Section 368(a)(1)(F).

PROPOSED REGULATIONS: Section 1.368–2(m).

Section 368(a)(1)(F) treats as a reorganization a change in "identity, form or place of organization of one corporation." The definition of an (F) reorganization focuses on purpose and effect, not the form of the transaction. Thus, the (F) reorganization definition overlaps with other forms of reorganizations. For example, in order to change its state of incorporation, X Corporation might form a new Y Corporation in another jurisdiction and then merge into it. The transaction is both an (A) and an (F) reorganization, but the IRS has indicated that in these circumstances the transaction will be characterized as an (F) reorganization. Rev.Rul. 57–276, 1957–C.B. 126.[4] The phrase "of one corporation" in § 368(a)(1)(F) precludes treating a merger of two or more pre-existing operating companies as a type (F) reorganization.[5]

Classifying a transaction as a type (F) reorganization has two principal effects: (1) the old corporation's taxable year does not end; and, (2) the new corporation is entitled under § 172 to carry back to taxable years of the old corporation post-reorganization net operating losses.[6] See I.R.C. § 381(b). These results reflect the fact that the reorganized corporation is "really" unchanged by the reorganizing transaction. In other respects, the new (or acquiring) corporation succeeds to the old (or acquired) corporation's tax attributes under § 381, discussed in Chapter 15, in the same manner as in any other reorganization.

The Treasury Department has published proposed regulations, Prop.Reg. § 1.368–2(m) (2005), dealing with the definition of a

---

[4] See also Rev.Rul. 88–25, 1988–1 C.B. 116 (conversion of foreign corporation to domestic corporation by filing domestication certificate under state law); Rev.Rul. 87–27, 1987–1 C.B. 134 (reincorporation of domestic corporation in foreign country is a type (F) reorganization); Rev.Rul. 87–66, 1987–2 C.B. 168 (reincorporation of foreign corporation in U.S. is a type (F) reorganization); Rev.Rul. 80–105, 1980–1 C.B. 78 (conversion of federal mutual savings and loan association to state stock savings and loan association was a type (F) reorganization).

[5] Section 368(a)(1)(E) was amended in 1982 to add the phrase "of one corporation" to make it clear that the provision does not apply to the merger of pre-existing operating companies. See H.Rep. No. 97–760, 97th Cong., 2d Sess. 540–541 (1982). Prior to the amendment, some courts had permitted (F) reorganization treatment in such circumstances. See, e.g., Home Construction Corp. v. United States, 439 F.2d 1165 (5th Cir.1971).

[6] In cases where the type (F) and type (D) reorganization overlap, classification as a type (F) has an additional effect. Type (F) reorganizations differ from Type (D) reorganizations in that § 357(c) applies to type (D) reorganizations but not to type (F) reorganizations. Rev.Rul. 79–289, 1979–2 C.B. 145 (§ 357(c) does not apply to reorganization meeting requirements for both (D) and (F)). For example, if X Corporation, whose sole asset is land and a building which has a basis of $50,000 and is subject to a $70,000 mortgage, reincorporates in a different state by merging into Y Corporation, a wholly owned subsidiary formed solely for the reincorporation transaction, no gain is recognized to X Corporation and Y Corporation takes a $50,000 basis in the land and building.

reorganization under § 368(a)(1)(F). The preamble to the proposed regulations, which follows, describes the scope of (F) reorganizations.

Proposed Rules, Department of the Treasury, Reorganizations Under Section 368(a)(1)(E) or (F), REG–106889–04.

69 F.R. 49836 (Aug. 12. 2004).

Section 368(a)(1)(F) provides that the term reorganization includes a mere change in identity, form, or place of organization of one corporation, however effected (an F reorganization). One court has described the F reorganization as follows:

> [The F reorganization] encompass[es] only the simplest and least significant of corporate changes. The (F)-type reorganization presumes that the surviving corporation is the same corporation as the predecessor in every respect, except for minor or technical differences. For instance, the (F) reorganization typically has been understood to comprehend only such insignificant modifications as the reincorporation of the same corporate business with the same assets and the same stockholders surviving under a new charter either in the same or in a different State, the renewal of a corporate charter having a limited life, or the conversion of a U.S.-chartered savings and loan association to a State-chartered institution.

Berghash v. Commissioner, 43 T.C. 743, 752 (1965) (citation and footnotes omitted), aff'd, 361 F.2d 257 (2nd Cir. 1966).

To qualify as a reorganization, a transaction must generally satisfy not only the statutory requirements of the reorganization provisions but also certain nonstatutory requirements, including the continuity of interest and continuity of business enterprise requirements. See § 1.368–1(b) . The purpose of the continuity requirements is to ensure that reorganizations are limited to readjustments of continuing interests in property under modified corporate form and to prevent transactions that resemble sales from qualifying for nonrecognition of gain or loss available to corporate reorganizations. § 1.368–1(d)(1) and (e)(1); see also LeTulle v. Scofield, 308 U.S. 415 (1940); Helvering v. Minnesota Tea Co., 296 U.S. 378 (1935); Pinellas Ice & Cold Storage Co. v. Commissioner, 287 U.S. 462 (1933).

Despite the general rule, the courts and the Service have taken the position that the continuity of interest and continuity of business enterprise requirements need not be satisfied for a transaction to qualify as an E reorganization. See Hickok v. Commissioner, 32 T.C. 80 (1959); Rev.Rul. 82–34 (1982–1 C.B. 59); Rev.Rul. 77–415 (1977–2 C.B. 311). In Revenue Rulings 77–415 and 82–34, the IRS reasoned that the continuity of interest and continuity of business enterprise requirements are necessary in an acquisitive reorganization to ensure that the transaction does not involve an otherwise taxable transfer of stock or assets, but that they are not necessary when the transaction involves only a single corporation.

Although an F reorganization may involve an actual or deemed transfer of assets from one corporation to another, such a transaction effectively involves only one corporation. In this way, an F reorganization is much like an E reorganization, which can only involve one corporation even in form. As a result, an F reorganization is treated for most purposes of the Code as if the reorganized corporation were the same entity as the corporation in existence before the reorganization. Consequently, the taxable year of the corporation does not end on the date of the transfer, and the losses of the reorganized corporation can be carried back to offset income of its predecessor. See [Treas.Reg.] § 1.381(b)–1(a)(2). Nonetheless, courts have applied the continuity requirements in determining whether a transaction qualifies as an F reorganization. See, e.g., Pridemark, Inc. v. Commissioner, 345 F.2d 35 (4th Cir. 1965) (stating that the application of the F reorganization statute is limited to cases where the corporate enterprise continues uninterrupted, except perhaps for a distribution of some of its liquid assets); Yoc Heating Corp. v. Commissioner, 61 T.C. 168 (1973) (holding that continuity of interest is required for an F reorganization).

The Service and the Treasury Department have considered whether continuity of interest and continuity of business enterprise should be requirements of an F reorganization. Because F reorganizations involve only the slightest change in a corporation and do not resemble sales, the Service and the Treasury Department have concluded that applying the continuity of interest and continuity of business enterprise requirements to transactions that would otherwise qualify as F reorganizations is not necessary to protect the policies underlying the reorganization provisions. Therefore, these * * * regulations [Treas.Reg. § 1.368–1(b)] provide that a continuity of interest and a continuity of business enterprise are not required for a transaction to qualify as an F reorganization.* * *

Consistent with section 368(a)(1)(F), the * * * regulations provide that, to qualify as an F reorganization, a transaction must result in a mere change in identity, form, or place of organization of one corporation. The * * * regulations further provide that a transaction that involves an actual or deemed transfer is a mere change only if four requirements are satisfied. First, all the stock of the resulting corporation, including stock issued before the transfer, must be issued in respect of stock of the transferring corporation. Second, there must be no change in the ownership of the corporation in the transaction, except a change that has no effect other than that of a redemption of less than all the shares of the corporation. Third, the transferring corporation must completely liquidate in the transaction. Fourth, the resulting corporation must not hold any property or have any tax attributes (including those specified in section 381(c)) immediately before the transfer.

The first two requirements reflect the Supreme Court's holding in Helvering v. Southwest Consolidated, 315 U.S. 194 (1942), that a transaction that shifts the ownership of the proprietary interests in a corporation cannot be a mere change. These requirements prevent a transaction that involves the introduction of a new shareholder or new capital into the corporation from qualifying as an F reorganization. Such an introduction may occur, for example, when a new shareholder contributes assets to the resulting corporation in exchange for stock before a merger of the transferring corporation into the resulting corporation. Notwithstanding these requirements, the * * * regulations permit the resulting corporation's issuance of a nominal amount of stock not in respect of stock of the transferring corporation to facilitate the organization of the resulting corporation. This rule is designed to permit reincorporation in a jurisdiction that requires, for example, minimum capitalization, two or more shareholders, or ownership of shares by directors. It is also intended to permit a transfer of assets to certain pre-existing entities.

The second requirement allows changes of ownership that have no effect other than a redemption of less than all the shares of the corporation to reflect the case law holding that certain transactions qualify as F reorganizations even if shareholders are redeemed in the transaction. See Reef Corp. v. U.S., 368 F.2d 125 (5th Cir. 1966) (holding that a redemption of 48 percent of the stock of a corporation that occurred during a change in place of incorporation did not cause the transaction to fail to qualify as an F reorganization); cf. Casco Products Corp. v. Commissioner, 49 T.C. 32 (1967) (holding that the surviving corporation in a merger was the continuation of the merging corporation for purposes of allowing a loss carryback, despite the forced redemption of nine percent of the stock of the merging corporation).

The third requirement (providing for the liquidation of the transferring corporation) and the fourth requirement (limiting the assets the resulting corporation may hold immediately before the transfer) reflect the statutory requirement that an F reorganization involve only one corporation. Although the * * * regulations generally require that the transferring corporation completely liquidate in the transaction, they do not require the transferring corporation to legally dissolve, thereby facilitating preservation of the value of the transferring corporation's charter. Further, to accommodate transactions in jurisdictions where it is customary to preserve pre-existing entities for future use rather than create new ones, the proposed regulations permit the retention of a nominal amount of assets for the sole purpose of preserving the transferring corporation's legal existence.

Although the * * * regulations generally require that the resulting corporation not hold any property or have any tax attributes immediately before the transfer, they do allow the resulting corporation to hold or to have held a nominal amount of assets to facilitate its organization or preserve its existence, and to have tax attributes related to these assets. In addition, to accommodate transactions involving the refinancing of debt or the leveraged redemption of shareholders, the * * * regulations provide that this requirement will not be violated if, before the transfer, the resulting corporation holds the proceeds of borrowings undertaken in connection with the transaction.

As described above, section 368(a)(1)(F) provides that an F reorganization includes a mere change in identity, form, or place of organization of one corporation, however effected. The IRS and the Treasury Department believe that the inclusion of the words "however effected" in the statutory definition of an F reorganization reflects a Congressional intent to treat as an F reorganization a series of transactions that together result in a mere change. The * * * regulations reflect this view by providing that a series of related transactions that together result in a mere change may qualify as an F reorganization.

The IRS and the Treasury Department also recognize that a reorganization qualifying under section 368(a)(1)(F) may be a step in a larger transaction that effects more than a mere change. For example, in Revenue Ruling 96–29 (1996–1 C.B. 50), the IRS ruled that a reincorporation qualified as an F reorganization even though it was a step in a transaction in which the reincorporated entity issued common stock in a public offering and redeemed stock having a value of 40 percent of the aggregate value of its outstanding stock before the offering. In the same ruling, the IRS ruled that a reincorporation of a corporation in another state qualified as an F reorganization even though it was a step in a transaction in which the reincorporated entity acquired the business of another entity.

Consistent with Revenue Ruling 96–29, the * * * regulations provide that related events preceding or following the transaction or series of transactions that constitute a mere change do not cause that transaction or series of transactions to fail to qualify as an F reorganization. The * * * regulations further provide that the qualification of the mere change as an F reorganization does not alter the treatment of the larger transaction. For example, if a redemption of stock occurs in a transaction that qualifies as an F reorganization and the F reorganization is part of a plan that includes a subsequent merger, the step or series of steps constituting the F reorganization will not alter the tax consequences of the subsequent merger.

A number of commentators have questioned whether distributions of money or other property in an F reorganization are distributions to which section 356 applies. The IRS and the Treasury Department believe it is appropriate to treat such distributions as transactions separate from the F reorganization, even if they occur during the F reorganization. See, e.g., § 1.301–1(*l*). Accordingly, these * * * regulations provide that if a shareholder receives money or other property (including in exchange for its shares) from the transferring or resulting corporation in a transaction that constitutes an F reorganization, the money or other property is treated as distributed by the transferring corporation immediately before the transaction. The tax treatment of such distributions is governed by sections 301 and 302, and section 356 does not apply to such distributions. * * *

Revenue Ruling 96–29

1996–1 C.B. 50.

ISSUE

Do the transactions described below qualify as reorganizations under § 368(a)(1)(F) of the Internal Revenue Code?

FACTS

Situation 1. Q is a manufacturing corporation all of the common stock of which is owned by twelve individuals. One class of nonvoting preferred stock, representing 40 percent of the aggregate value of Q, is held by a variety of corporate and noncorporate shareholders. Q is incorporated in state M. Pursuant to a plan to raise immediate additional capital and to enhance its ability to raise capital in the future by issuing additional stock, Q proposes to make a public offering of newly issued stock and to cause its stock to become publicly traded. Q entered into an underwriting agreement providing for the public offering and a change in its state of incorporation. The change in the state of incorporation was undertaken, in part, to enable the corporation to avail itself of the advantages that the corporate laws of state N afford to public companies and their officers and directors. In the absence of the public offering, Q would not have changed its state of incorporation. Pursuant to the underwriting agreement, Q changed its place of incorporation by merging with and into R, a newly organized corporation incorporated in state N. The shares of Q stock were converted into the right to receive an identical number of shares of R stock. Immediately thereafter, R sold additional shares of its stock to the public and redeemed all of the outstanding shares of nonvoting preferred stock. The number of new shares sold was equal to 60 percent of all the outstanding R stock following the sale and redemption.

Situation 2. W, a state M corporation, is a manufacturing corporation all of the stock of which is owned by two individuals. W conducted its business through several wholly owned subsidiaries. The management of W determined that it would be in the best interest of W to acquire the business of Z, an unrelated corporation, and combine it with the business of Y, one of its subsidiaries, and to change the state of incorporation of W. In order to accomplish these objectives, and pursuant to an overall plan, W entered into a plan and agreement of merger with Y and Z. In accordance with the agreement, Z merged with and into Y pursuant to the law of state M, with the former Z shareholders receiving shares of newly issued W preferred stock in exchange for their shares of Z stock. Immediately following the acquisition of Z, W changed its place of organization by merging with and into N, a newly organized corporation incorporated in state R. Upon W's change of place of organization, the holders of W common and preferred stock surrendered their W stock in exchange for identical N common and preferred stock, respectively.

LAW AND ANALYSIS

Section 368(a)(1)(F) provides that a reorganization includes a mere change in identity, form, or place of organization of one corporation, however effected. This provision was amended by the Tax Equity and Fiscal Responsibility Act of 1982, Pub.L. No. 97–248, in order to limit its application to one corporation. Certain limitations contained in § 381(b), including those precluding the corporation acquiring property in a reorganization from carrying back a net operating loss or a net capital loss for a taxable year ending after the date of transfer to a taxable year of the transferor, do not apply to reorganizations described in § 368(a)(1)(F) "in recognition of the intended scope of such reorganizations as embracing only formal changes in a single operating corporation." H.R.Rep. No. 760, 97th Cong., 2d Sess. 540, 541 (1982). Although a change in the place of organization usually must be effected through the merger of one corporation into another, such a transaction qualifies as a reorganization under § 368(a)(1)(F) because it involves only one operating corporation. The 1982 amendment of § 368(a)(1)(F) thus overruled several cases in which a merger of two or more operating corporations could be treated as a reorganization under § 368(a)(1)(F). See, e.g., Estate of Stauffer v. Commissioner, 403 F.2d 611 (9th Cir.1968); Associated Machine, Inc. v. Commissioner, 403 F.2d 622 (9th Cir.1968); and Davant v. Commissioner, 366 F.2d 874 (5th Cir.1966).

* * *

The rules applicable to corporate reorganizations as well as other provisions recognize the unique characteristics of reorganizations qualifying under § 368(a)(1)(F). In contrast to other types of reorganizations, which can involve two or more operating corporations, a reorganization of a corporation under § 368(a)(1)(F) is treated for most purposes of the Code as if there had been no change in the corporation and, thus, as if the reorganized corporation is the same entity as the corporation that was in existence prior to the reorganization. See § 381(b); § 1.381(b)–1(a)(2); see also 87–110, 1987–2 C.B. 159; 80–168, 1980–1 C.B. 178; 73–526, 1973–2 C.B. 404; 64–250, 1964–2 C.B. 333.

In Rev.Rul. 69–516, 1969–2 C.B. 56, the Internal Revenue Service treated as two separate transactions a reorganization under § 368(a)(1)(F) and a reorganization under § 368(a)(1)(C) undertaken as part of the same plan. Specifically, a corporation changed its place of organization by merging into a corporation formed under the laws of another state and, immediately thereafter, it transferred substantially all of its assets in exchange for stock of an unrelated corporation. The ruling holds that the change in place of organization qualified as a reorganization under § 368(a)(1)(F).

Accordingly, in *Situation 1*, the reincorporation by Q in state N qualifies as a reorganization under § 368(a)(1)(F) even though it was a step in the transaction in which Q was issuing common stock in a public offering and redeeming stock having a value of 40 percent of the aggregate value of its outstanding stock prior to the offering.

In *Situation 2*, the reincorporation by W in state N qualifies as a reorganization under § 368(a)(1)(F) even though it was a step in the transaction in which W acquired the business of Z.

HOLDING

On the facts set forth in this ruling, in each of *Situations 1* and *2*, the reincorporation transaction qualifies as a reorganization under § 368(a)(1)(F), notwithstanding the other transactions effected pursuant to the same plan.

EFFECT ON OTHER REVENUE RULINGS

Rev.Rul. 79–250, 1979–2 C.B. 156, addressed a similar issue on facts that are substantially similar, in all material respects, to those of *Situation 2*. The ruling holds that a merger of Z with and into Y in exchange for the stock of W qualifies as a reorganization under § 368(a)(1)(A) by reason of § 368(a)(2)(D), even though W is reincorporated in another state immediately after the merger. The ruling also holds that the reincorporation qualifies as a reorganization under § 368(a)(1)(F). Rev.Rul. 79–250 did not apply the step transaction doctrine in order to combine the two transactions, stating that the merger and the subsequent reincorporation were separate transactions because "the economic motivation supporting each transaction is sufficiently meaningful on its own account, and is not dependent upon the other transaction for its substantiation."

Although the holding of Rev.Rul. 79–250 is correct on the facts presented therein, in order to emphasize that central to the holding in Rev.Rul. 79–250 is the unique status of reorganizations under § 368(a)(1)(F), and that Rev.Rul. 79–250 is not intended to reflect the application of the step-transaction doctrine in other contexts, Rev.Rul. 79–250 is modified.

DETAILED ANALYSIS

1.   (F) REORGANIZATION FOLLOWING OR PRECEDING AN ACQUISITION

Suppose that X Corporation purchases all of the stock of Y Corporation and immediately thereafter merges Y Corporation into Z Corporation, a subsidiary of X Corporation with no assets which was formed solely for the purpose of changing the state of incorporation of Y Corporation. Does the merger qualify as an (F) reorganization?

In Security Industrial Insurance Co. v. United States, 702 F.2d 1234 (5th Cir.1983), OIC, a holding company, purchased all of the stock of Southern, following which OIC liquidated Southern and then contributed OIC's operating assets to Security, another subsidiary of OIC. The taxpayer argued that the transaction was an (F) reorganization. Applying the step transaction doctrine, the court held that no (F) reorganization had occurred because the end result of the transaction was an acquisition of the assets of Southern for cash. The court tested shareholder continuity of interest by comparing ownership of Southern before the acquisition with ownership of OIC after the entire transaction had been completed. Since the historic shareholders of Southern corporation had been eliminated, the transaction failed to meet the continuity of interest requirement. The application of the step transaction doctrine was a key element in the reasoning of *Security Industrial Insurance Co.* See also Cannonsburg Skiing Corporation v. Commissioner, T.C. Memo. 1986–150, aff'd sub nom. Russell v. Commissioner, 832 F.2d 349 (6th Cir.1987) (step transaction doctrine applied to treat the overall transaction as an asset acquisition, and concluded that no (F) reorganization had occurred because there was a 98 percent shift in ownership "which clearly violates the identity of shareholders and their proprietary interests as required for an F reorganization").

Treas.Reg. § 1.338–3(d)(2) ameliorates these problems to a large extent by providing that for purposes of applying the continuity of interest requirement, an acquiring corporation will be treated as the historic shareholder of a target corporation if it made a "qualified stock purchase," as defined in § 338(d)(3). In addition, Treas.Reg. § 1.368–1(b) now provides that continuity of interest no longer applies to an F reorganization. The merger of Y Corporation into Z Corporation in the above example could qualify as a type (F) reorganization. The result in *Security Industrial Insurance Co.* is unchanged, however, with respect to the holding that the transaction was a cash acquisition of assets. The transaction would fail to qualify for F reorganization status under Prop.Reg. § 1.368–2(m)(1)(i)(B) (2005) because of the change in ownership of Southern. Although the regulation does not apply to purchases by individual shareholders, it would be incongruous not to apply the same principle if individual A (or a group of individuals) purchased 100 percent of the stock of X Corporation and then merged X Corporation into Y Corporation, a shell corporation wholly owned by A (or the group who purchased X), for the purpose of changing the state of incorporation.

In Dunlap & Associates, Inc. v. Commissioner, 47 T.C. 542 (1967), the merger of a New York corporation into its Delaware subsidiary as part of an overall plan subsequently to acquire stock of two other corporations in type (B) reorganizations prior to making a public offering of stock in the Delaware corporation, was held to be an (F) reorganization.

Rev.Rul. 2003–19, 2003–1 C.B. 468, held that the validity of a type (F) reorganization that converted a mutual insurance company to a stock insurance company, followed by a prearranged acquisitive reorganization that interposed a new holding corporation between the operating insurance company and its original shareholders was not affected by the subsequent transaction. Rev.Rul. 2003–48, 2003–1 C.B. 863, reached a similar result where a mutual savings bank was converted to a stock savings bank, which was then acquired by a holding company according to a prearranged plan. In one situation, the original owners of the mutual savings bank held a majority of the stock of the holding company, but less than 80 percent, with the remainder of the holding company stock having been sold to the public in a public offering. In the other situation, the original owners of the mutual savings bank held more than 80 percent of the stock of the holding company, with less than 20 percent having been sold to the public. The final step in the first situation was a § 351 transaction, while the final step in the second transaction was a reorganization. In neither situation, however, was the validity of the (F) reorganization affected.

2.   "FUNCTIONALLY UNRELATED" TRANSACTIONS

Suppose that X Corporation, which is incorporated in California, wishes to reincorporate in Delaware and simultaneously to redeem the stock of A, a 20 percent shareholder. To this end, X Corporation forms Y Corporation (a Delaware corporation) and then merges into Y Corporation with A receiving cash and all of the other X shareholders receiving Y Corporation stock. Does the transaction qualify as an (F) reorganization or does it qualify only as an (A) reorganization? This will be an important issue if, for example, Y Corporation incurs a net operating loss, which can be carried back to an X Corporation year only if the transaction qualifies as an (F) reorganization.

If the payment of cash to A can be viewed as functionally unrelated to the merger effected to change the place of organization, then the transaction might be divided into a redemption and an (F) reorganization. This analysis is suggested by Rev.Rul. 61–156, 1961–2 C.B. 62. In that ruling, X Corporation liquidated and distributed its assets to its shareholders, who in turn contributed the operating assets received in the liquidation to newly formed Y Corporation, but who retained liquid assets received in the liquidation. Other individuals who had not been shareholders of X Corporation also contributed property to Y Corporation. To treat the shareholders of X Corporation as receiving a dividend with respect to the liquid assets, the IRS held that the issuance of stock to the new shareholders was "functionally unrelated" to the "liquidation-reincorporation" and did not prevent the finding of an (F) reorganization.

There is also some support in the case law for application of the "functionally unrelated" analysis. In Reef Corp. v. Commissioner, 368 F.2d 125 (5th Cir.1966), two groups of shareholders controlled a corporation. One group desired to buy out the other and a plan was developed whereby a new corporation was formed and then it issued stock in exchange for a portion of the stock in the old corporation held by the shareholders desiring to continue in the business. Both groups then sold the remaining stock in the old corporation to a third party with the outgoing shareholders receiving cash and notes. The old corporation then sold its assets to the new corporation in exchange for notes of the new corporation. Those notes were then distributed to the old shareholders in discharge of the third party's obligation for the purchase price. The outgoing group was thus left with notes of the new corporation and cash while the continuing group now controlled the new corporation and held its notes as well. The court found that an (F) reorganization had occurred:

> Distilled to their pure substance, two distinct and unrelated events transpired. First, the holders of 48 percent of the stock in Reef Fields had their stockholdings completely redeemed. Second, new Reef was formed and the assets of Reef Fields were transferred to new Reef. The business enterprise continued without interruption during both the redemption and the change in corporate vehicles.

> Much confusion flows from the fact that the corporate reorganization took place simultaneously with the stock redemption. But taking the Code as a standard, these two elements were functionally unrelated. Reef Fields could have completely redeemed the stock of 48 percent of its shareholders without changing the state of its incorporation. A complete redemption is not a characteristic of a reorganization. Congress clearly indicated this when it defined reorganization in section 368. Section 368(a)(1)(A) speaks of a "merger or consolidation" which looks to the joining of two or more corporations. Section 368(a)(1)(B) and (C) look to one corporation acquiring the assets of another or control of another corporation solely for its voting stock. Section 368(a)(1)(D) looks to the consolidation of two or more corporations or the division of two or more going businesses into separate corporations. Only sections 368(a)(1)(E) and (F) look to adjustments within a corporation. But none of these provisions focuses on a complete redemption as a characteristic of a reorganization. Congress did not have redemption of stock as a primary purpose of any of the forms of a reorganization. That subject came under consideration when it undertook to enact specific legislation on complete and partial redemptions, section 302.

> The boot provision, section 356, is adequate to cover a complete redemption when it occurs incident to a reorganization * * *. When the primary characteristics of the reorganization conform to those described by 368(a)(1)(F) , we should parse the

occurrences into their functional elements. * * * To effectuate the intention of Congress manifested in the Code, we must separate this transaction into its two distinctly separate functional parts. The test of whether events should be viewed separately or together as part of a single plan is not temporal but is functional.

Applying this test to the instant case, it is clear that the redemption and the change of corporate vehicles must be viewed as separate and distinct occurrences. Cf. Bazley v. Commissioner, 1947, 331 U.S. 737, 67 S.Ct. 1489.

In The Aetna Casualty and Surety Co. v. United States, 568 F.2d 811 (2d Cir.1976), Aetna Life, which held 61 percent of the stock of Old Aetna, formed a new corporation, New Aetna, to which it transferred its stock of Old Aetna. Old Aetna was then merged into New Aetna with the minority shareholders in Old Aetna receiving shares of Aetna Life. The minority shareholders of Old Aetna thus became shareholders of Aetna Life and New Aetna became a wholly owned subsidiary of Aetna Life. Subsequent to the reorganization, New Aetna operated at a loss and attempted to carry that loss back against part of Old Aetna's taxable income, arguing that the transaction constituted an (F) reorganization and that the carryback was permitted under § 381(b)(3). The court held that the transaction constituted an (F) reorganization despite the fact that the minority shareholders in Old Aetna emerged from the transaction with a substantially changed interest in the reorganized corporate structure. The court treated the transaction as if the minority shareholders' interests in Old Aetna had been redeemed (i.e., by exchanging their Old Aetna shares for shares in Aetna Life) in the course of an (F) reorganization: "Clearly a corporation which merely redeems its minority shareholders' stock has not undergone a reorganization at all under § 368(a)(1) and is entitled to carryback its losses under § 172. We see no reason why the result should be different simply because the redemption occurs in the course of merging one corporation into a different shell. * * * If the redemption, reorganization and carryback provisions were not intended to preclude carrybacks where there has been a simple redemption, we do not believe those provisions should be construed to preclude the carryback here involved."

In Casco Products Corp. v. Commissioner, 49 T.C. 32 (1967), "New Casco" corporation acquired 91 percent of the stock of "Old Casco" by means of a public tender. Solely to acquire 100 percent ownership of Old Casco, New Casco formed a subsidiary and Old Casco was merged into it, with the dissenting shareholders receiving cash. The Tax Court treated the overall transaction, including the merger, as a "reorganization in form" only, and regarded the subsidiary as "merely a meaningless detour" to accomplish the effect of a redemption of the remaining 9 percent of the shares. Thus a net operating loss of the now wholly owned subsidiary was allowed to be carried back to the taxable years of Old Casco.

Treas.Reg. § 1.368–1(b), as amended in 2005, adopts the reasoning of this line of cases, as does Prop.Reg. § 1.368–2(m) (2005).

3.   "LIQUIDATION-REINCORPORATION" TRANSACTIONS AND THE TYPE (F) REORGANIZATION

Prior to 1986, when the *General Utilities* doctrine permitted corporations to distribute appreciated property without recognizing gain, shareholders often attempted to extract property from corporate solution at capital gains rates while continuing to operate the business in corporate form. In a typical transaction, the corporation would be liquidated and simultaneously or within a short period the operating assets of the corporation would be reincorporated in a new corporation with the shareholders retaining the liquid assets. If the form of the transaction was respected, the liquidation would generate capital gains to the shareholders under § 331 and the incorporation would be tax-free under § 351.

In attacking such transactions, the IRS often argued that the overall effect of the transaction was an (F) reorganization, with the retained assets representing "boot" that was taxable as a dividend. This argument was generally successful where the shareholders in the "old" and "new" corporations were substantially identical. See, e.g., Pridemark v. Commissioner, 42 T.C. 510 (1964) (Acq.), aff'd in part and rev'd in part, 345 F.2d 35 (4th Cir.1965). However, where some shareholders were eliminated in the transaction, it was harder to characterize the transaction as a "mere" change of form. In these cases, the IRS argued that the aspect of the transaction which resulted in the change in share ownership was "unrelated" to the (F) reorganization transaction. See, e.g., Rev.Rul. 61–156, page 700. The IRS's approach had only mixed success in the courts, with the Tax Court insisting on complete identity of share ownership as a precondition for finding an (F) reorganization. See, e.g., Gallagher v. Commissioner, 39 T.C. 144 (1962); Reef Corp. v. Commissioner, T.C. Memo. 1965–72, rev'd, 368 F.2d 125 (5th Cir.1966). Type (D) reorganization aspects of the liquidation-reincorporation transaction are discussed at page 660.

Because § 336 now requires that gain be recognized by a corporation distributing appreciated assets in liquidation, intentionally structured transactions of this sort no longer occur. However, the case law developed in connection with liquidation-reincorporation transactions has had some effect on the case law involving "normal" (F) reorganizations. Compare Romy Hammes, Inc. v. Commissioner, 68 T.C. 900, 906 note 8 (1977) ("The (F) reorganization received relatively little judicial or administrative attention until [the government] began to use the (F) reorganization as a weapon in the liquidation-reincorporation area. * * * Although the litigating positions of the Service and the taxpayer are reversed when the scope of the (F) reorganization is to be determined for purposes of § 381(b)(3) loss carryback, the judicial interpretation of § 368(a)(1)(F) must obviously be consistent."); The Aetna Casualty and Surety Co. v. United States, 568 F.2d 811, 823 (2d Cir.1976) ("We specifically declin[e] to decide whether classifying a reorganization as an (F) reorganization for purposes of § 381(b)(3) will necessarily mean it is an (F) reorganization for purposes of other provisions of the Code.").

of the stock of the controlled subsidia
of a split-up) being displaced by one
provisions. If the controlled corporat
existing subsidiary to which asse
§ 368(a)(1)(D) reorganization prior to
nonrecognition to the distributing cor
of the controlled corporation. If th
transfer of assets from the distribut
corporation in a § 368(a)(1)(D) reorga
provides nonrecognition for the distrib
controlled corporation assumes liabilit
or takes property subject to liabilities
transferred to the controlled corpora
subject to nonrecognition under § 3
recognition of gain by the distributin
excess of the liabilities over the ba
controlled corporation even though th
§ 368(a)(1)(D) reorganization rather th

The essence of a § 355 division
stockholder level of the corporate
businesses are already divided or sep
the stockholders. In the first example
could have been conducted as sepa
Corporation; in the third example,
through parent-subsidiary operatior
example, could separate the businesse
new Y Corporation under § 351 and o
desired separation is a degree of ins
other, it will be accomplished throu
Section 355 applies to a different typ
ownership at the stockholder level.

The separate ownership at the
distribution of the controlled corporati
pro rata to the ownership of the
depending on the specific facts o
potentially applies to very different
Suppose X Corporation is owned
Corporation distributes the stock of
rata in a spin-off, each individual
stockholder owned before—a one-half
stockholders have separated the
Corporations have been transmuted f
brother-sister corporations. If the di
stock is completely non-pro rata, as wl
stock in X Corporation for all the stoc
then a complete division of ownershi
stockholder level in addition to the di

---

¹ Note that § 357(c) does not apply to an as
of liabilities in excess of basis in a § 368(a)(1)(D)
distribution by the transferor corporation of tra
requirements of § 354, discussed at page 651.

CHAPTER 14

CORPORATE DIVISIONS: SPIN-OFFS, SPLIT-OFFS, AND SPLIT-UPS

SECTION 1.   CORPORATE DIVISIONS: GENERAL RULES

INTERNAL REVENUE CODE: Sections 355(a)(1), (2); 368(a)(1)(D), (2)(A), (2)(H)(ii); 354(b); 356(a) and (b); 358(a)–(c).

REGULATIONS: Sections 1.355–1(b); –2(a); (b)(1)–(3); –3(a); –4.

In contrast to provisions for acquisitive reorganizations, which allow the merger or consolidation of separate corporate entities, § 355 provides nonrecognition treatment for the division of a corporation's existing business into separate corporate entities owned by the shareholders. A divisive transaction under § 355 may take one of three basic forms.

1.   *Spin-Off.* A spin-off occurs when a corporation distributes the stock of an existing subsidiary to its stockholders pro rata or transfers assets to a controlled subsidiary in a type (D) reorganization and distributes the stock of the subsidiary pro rata to its stockholders. Thus, X Corporation, which conducts business A, and which own all of the stock of Y Corporation, which conducts business B, may spin-off Y Corporation by distributing the Y corporation stock to X Corporation's stockholders. Alternatively, X Corporation, conducting businesses A and B, may divide by transferring business B to a newly formed subsidiary, Y Corporation, and then distributing the stock of Y Corporation pro rata to the stockholders of X Corporation. A division may also be undertaken by a corporation operating a single business that is capable of division into two separate independently functioning trades or businesses. X Corporation divides its single business into two parts by transferring some of its assets to Y Corporation which, following the transaction, is also actively engaged in the conduct of a trade or business. X Corporation then distributes all of the stock of Y Corporation to the X Corporation stockholders. In each of these transactions the shareholders of the distributing corporation, which formerly owned multiple businesses (or a single business capable of division), own the same businesses but the businesses are now in separate corporations.

2.   *Split-off.* In a split-off, the distributing corporation distributes the stock of a new or existing subsidiary to its stockholders in exchange for a portion of the outstanding stock of the distributing corporation. For example, X Corporation, conducting business A, owns the stock of Y Corporation, which conducts business B. X Corporation distributes the stock of Y

Corporation to so
exchange for some
While this transac
Corporation or Y (
changed as a resu
which conducts be
business B to r
reorganization an
stockholders in ex
A split-off distribu
among the stoc
functionally equiv
however, results i
businesses. In the
the distributing c
corporation in ex
conducting a bu
ownership of the d

3. *Split-Up.*
separate trade or
type (D) reorganiz
the stock of the
Each separate tra
distributed to difi
owns businesses
Corporation and b
then liquidates c
stockholders, anc
stockholders. Alte
its businesses th
the stock of its
liquidation. Thus
distributing corp
businesses among
the distributing co

As noted above, e
the initial step a tran
a distribution of the
transaction that invol
is a type (D) reorganiz
corporation if immedi
more of its sharehold
assets are transfer
§ 368(a)(1)(D), the dis
the pivotal section i
accomplish a corporat
is preceded by the tra
either a new or pre-ex
been met, § 355(a) pi
receipt of the stock of

Subject to a n
corporation also is ent

corporations are no longer related in any way, assuming there is no family or other special relationship between C and D.

Prior to 1987, and between 1992 and 2003, when dividends were taxed at higher rates than capital gains, the pro rata corporate division into brother-sister corporations presented the potential for a bail-out of corporate profits taxable to the stockholders at capital gains rates. Thus, in the examples above, if the stockholders of X and Y Corporations sell the stock of Y Corporation, they end up with stock of X Corporation and cash taxed at capital gain rates. This situation, it will be recalled, is also the end result of a "preferred stock bail-out" or a "security bail-out." Section 355 imposes limitations intended to ensure that the tax-free corporate division privilege was not abused. Currently, with individual dividend rates the same as individual long-term capital gain rates, the incentive to "bail-out" earnings and profits by means of a corporate division is significantly reduced. In this situation, the tax stakes for the distributee shareholders in a corporate division are whether they receive a current taxable dividend equal to the fair market value of the stock received or a distribution of stock on which tax is deferred until a subsequent sale. Even though the tax rate may be the same in both cases, deferral of tax can be a great financial benefit. In addition, the gain realized on the sale would be reduced by some portion of original basis in the stock of the distributing corporation.

The limitations of § 355 also play a key role in ensuring that a corporate division is not used to avoid corporate level tax on appreciated assets the gain on which otherwise would be recognized under § 311(b) or § 336. Over the past several decades, Congress has enacted several detailed amendments to § 355 that are intended to limit corporate tax planning to avoid §§ 311(b) and § 336 by channeling transactions through § 355. These statutory provisions are implemented through some of the more complex and detailed regulations promulgated under the Code. Whether those limitations are necessary to achieve that objective is a matter that warrants further attention by tax policymakers.

The basic framework of § 355 evolved during periods when dividends were taxed at ordinary income rates greater than the preferential rates for long-term capital gains. Thus, most of the statutory pattern for qualifying a division as a tax-free transaction can be understood in terms of its attempt to prevent the bail-out of corporate earnings as capital gains. These safeguards are found in both § 355 itself and in other sections governing corporate reorganizations under § 368(a)(1)(D).

With respect to § 355:

1. The transaction must not be used principally as a *device* for the distribution of the earnings and profits of either of the corporations. I.R.C. § 355(a)(1)(B).

2. To prevent the isolation of cash or passive investments into a separate corporation with its potential for ready sale at capital gains rates, each corporation after the division must be operating an active trade or business. In addition, to prevent either the distributing corporation or the controlled corporation from utilizing accumulated

earnings to acquire the active business, the active businesses must have been operated for five years preceding the distribution and must not have been acquired in a taxable transaction within the five-year period. I.R.C. § 355(a)(1)(C), (b).

3.   All of the stock and securities that the distributing parent owns in the controlled corporation being separated must be distributed to the stockholders (or at least 80 percent of the stock of the controlled corporation if retention of the balance of stock and securities can be justified). I.R.C. § 355(a)(1)(D). This requirement was originally designed to differentiate between genuine separations and incidental distributions of a controlled corporation's stock that took the place of current cash dividends. If, in addition, boot is distributed, pursuant to either § 356(a)(2) or § 356(b) the distribution may be taxed as a dividend to the extent of the boot. The distributing corporation also must recognize gain with respect to appreciated property distributed as boot. I.R.C. §§ 355(c); 361(c). Further, the distributing corporation is required to recognize gain on the distribution of stock of the controlled corporation to a person who, by virtue of an acquisition by purchase of the stock of either the distributing or the controlled corporation within the five-year period ending on the date of the distribution, holds a 50 percent or greater interest in either the distributing corporation or the controlled corporation. I.R.C. § 355(d). This requirement is aimed at preventing a transfer of ownership of the distributed corporation that avoids corporate level recognition of gain on the disposition.

4.   A "security bail-out" is not permitted as part of a corporate division, and rules similar to § 354(a)(2) are utilized to treat the excess principal amount of securities received over the principal amount of securities surrendered as boot. I.R.C. §§ 355(a)(3), (a)(4)(A); 356(b), (d)(2)(C).

With respect to § 368(a)(1)(D) reorganizations:

Due to the statutory requirements of the various specific forms of corporate reorganizations, only the § 368(a)(1)(D) reorganization has the potential for a corporate division. For a transaction to constitute a reorganization under § 368(a)(1)(D), it must either (1) comply with the requirement of § 354(b)(1)(A) that substantially all of the assets of the distributing corporation be transferred to the controlled corporation so as to eliminate the effect of a division, or (2) constitute a step in a series of transactions culminating in a distribution qualifying under § 355. This pattern is found in the addition of the last clause in § 368(a)(1)(D), which requires that a corporation forming a controlled subsidiary must, to qualify as a reorganization, distribute the stock of the subsidiary to its stockholders in a transaction qualifying under §§ 354 or 355 (and § 356). The reference to § 355 thus brings into play the tests for qualifying corporate divisions. The reference to § 354 brings into play § 354(b), which makes § 354 inapplicable unless substantially all the assets are transferred and the transferor liquidates. As a result, a transfer that divides assets of the distributing corporation cannot qualify under § 354. If the requirements of § 354(b) are not met, as where only some of the assets are transferred or where the transferor does not liquidate, then a corporate division is present since the stockholders will now own stock in the old and the new corporations. Section 354(a) is not applicable, and the exchange with the stockholders

Ridge and Sunbelt

Ridge was incorporated in 1959 by Richard B. Craney (Craney). From 1977 until July 25, 1993, the sole, equal shareholders of Ridge were McLaulin, King (Craney's stepson), and Holland. Ridge was engaged in the forest products business. Ridge was profitable, with more than $13 million in retained earnings as of July 25, 1993.

On December 31, 1986, Ridge elected to become an S corporation as that term is defined by section 1361(a)(1) (S corporation), effective for its taxable year ended July 25, 1988. Ridge qualified as an S corporation for each taxable year thereafter, through and including its taxable year ended July 25, 1994.

Sunbelt was incorporated in 1981. Initially, its sole, equal shareholders were Craney, Ridge, and an otherwise unrelated individual, John L. Hutto (Hutto). In 1986, Craney's shares of stock were redeemed by Sunbelt, and, from then until January 15, 1993, Ridge and Hutto were the sole, equal shareholders of Sunbelt. Hutto was president of Sunbelt and chairman of its board of directors. He was responsible for all executive functions of Sunbelt. Sunbelt produced and sold pressure-treated lumber. That business was profitable. In February 1989, based on Hutto's experience in the millwork business (manufacturing doors and window frames), Sunbelt entered the millwork business (the millwork division). The millwork division lost money from its inception to its shutdown in mid-1990. Because of Sunbelt's management's focus on the millwork division, Sunbelt's core business (pressure-treating lumber) also suffered. Nonetheless, Sunbelt had over $1.8 million in retained earnings as of the close of its fiscal taxable year ended June 26, 1993.

Events Leading to Ridge's Distribution of the Sunbelt Stock to Ridge's Shareholders

In 1982, Sunbelt began to borrow money from Citrus and Chemical Bank, in Bartow, Florida (the Bank), pursuant to a series of renewable notes (the notes). Beginning in 1984, and until 1989, Ridge stood as a guarantor of the notes. Borrowings pursuant to the notes reached $2 million by 1989. On February 26, 1990, the board of directors of Ridge (the Ridge board) authorized the withdrawal of Ridge's guaranty of Sunbelt's debt to the bank (the Ridge guaranty) if there was not "a prompt cessation and controlled liquidation of the millwork division." Ridge could not force a shutdown of the millwork division because it was unable to outvote Hutto, who, like Ridge, was a 50–percent shareholder in Sunbelt. The Ridge board reasoned that, without the Ridge guaranty, Sunbelt would be unable to obtain new funds to cover future losses, and, as a result, Hutto would be forced to shut down the millwork division.

On May 18, 1990, Ridge withdrew the Ridge guaranty and, shortly thereafter, the millwork division was liquidated. On September 17, 1990, Ridge purchased Sunbelt's 1989 note (the 1989 note) from the Bank for $630,000, the balance due. Thereafter, Ridge financed Sunbelt directly by extending and modifying the 1989 note on numerous occasions. In that way, Ridge was able to exercise control over the management of Sunbelt.

In mid-1992, Hutto decided to sell his shares in Sunbelt and leave the company. Hutto's decision culminated several months of negotiations between Ridge and Hutto, in which Ridge sought either to purchase Hutto's interest in Sunbelt or sell its interest to Hutto. Ridge instigated those negotiations because of its dissatisfaction with Hutto's management of Sunbelt. Earlier in 1992, Ridge and Hutto had tentatively agreed to a price of $825,000 for a 50–percent stock interest in Sunbelt, applicable whether Hutto was the buyer or the seller. Ridge and Hutto finally agreed that Ridge and Hutto would cause Sunbelt to redeem Hutto's shares in Sunbelt (the redemption) in exchange for $828,943.75 in cash and real estate valued at $101,000. The redemption was accomplished on January 15, 1993. Immediately thereafter, Ridge owned the only outstanding shares of Sunbelt.

Also on January 15, 1993, subsequent to the redemption, Ridge made a distribution with respect to its stock of all of its shares in Sunbelt (the distribution and the Sunbelt shares, respectively). The distribution was to petitioners, the sole shareholders of Ridge, pro rata. * * *

Funding the Redemption

Sunbelt needed cash in the amount of $828,243.74 to fund the redemption. Although Sunbelt had assets and accumulated earnings in excess of that amount, it did not have the necessary cash. On January 14, 1993, the amount available to Sunbelt pursuant to the 1989 note was increased from $2 million to $3 million, and, on that same date, Sunbelt took advantage of its increased borrowing power under the 1989 note and borrowed $900,000 from Ridge, which, in part, it used to make the redemption.

OPINION

I. *Introduction*

The fundamental question we must answer is whether gain is to be recognized to Ridge on account of the distribution. If so, then, since, for Ridge's taxable year ending July 25, 1993, it was an S corporation, petitioners must take into account their pro rata shares of such gain. See sec. 1366(a). No gain will be recognized to Ridge on account of the distribution if that transaction qualifies for nonrecognition treatment pursuant to section 355. * * * If the distribution does not qualify for section 355 nonrecognition treatment, then gain will be recognized to Ridge pursuant to section 311(b). * * * Respondent argues that the distribution does not qualify for section 355 nonrecognition treatment on two separate and independent grounds:

(1) The contemporaneous redemption and distribution fail to satisfy the requirements of section 355(b) as to active trade or business. Specifically, respondent argues that, although Sunbelt had been engaged in an active trade or business for more than 5 years on the date of the distribution, control of Sunbelt was acquired by the distributing corporation (Ridge), within such 5–year period, in a transaction (the redemption) in which gain was recognized, thereby violating the requirements of section 355(b)(2)(D)(ii).

(2) Petitioners have failed to prove that the distribution was designed to achieve a corporate business purpose, as required by section 1.355–2(b), Income Tax Regs.

Because we agree with respondent's first ground, we do not address respondent's second ground.

II.   *Active Business Requirement*

A.   *Pertinent Provisions of the Internal Revenue Code*

One of the specific requirements for section 355 nonrecognition treatment on the pro rata distribution of the shares of a controlled corporation (a so-called spinoff) is that "the requirements of subsection (b) [of section 355] (relating to active businesses) are satisfied". Sec. 355(a)(1)(C). Section 355(b)(1)(A) provides that both the distributing and the controlled corporation must be "engaged immediately after the distribution in the active conduct of a trade or business". Section 355(b)(2) defines the circumstances under which "a corporation shall be treated as engaged in the active conduct of a trade or business". Section 355(b)(2)(B) provides that the trade or business must have been "actively conducted throughout the 5–year period ending on the date of the distribution" (the 5–year period). Section 355(b)(2)(D) provides, in pertinent part, that control of the corporation engaged in the active conduct of a trade or business on the date of acquisition of control must not have been acquired within the 5–year period or, if acquired within such period, it must have been acquired "only by reason of transactions in which gain or loss was not recognized in whole or in part, or only by reason of such transactions combined with acquisitions before the beginning of such period." Sec. 355(b)(2)(D)(ii).

B.   *Arguments of the Parties*

Respondent does not dispute that both Ridge and Sunbelt were engaged in the active conduct of a trade or business immediately after the distribution. Nor does he dispute that both businesses had been actively conducted throughout the 5–year period. Respondent argues, however, that Ridge violated the conditions of section 355(b)(2)(D)(ii) because it acquired control of Sunbelt within the 5–year period in a transaction (the redemption) in which gain or loss was recognized. In reaching that conclusion, respondent relies upon the statutory language and upon Rev. Rul. 57–144, 1957–1 C.B. 123, in which respondent determined that a personal holding company's distribution to its shareholders of the stock of one of its two controlled operating subsidiaries does not qualify as a tax-free spinoff where control of the parent's other operating subsidiary (which was merged into the parent after the distribution) was obtained during the 5–year period as a result of that subsidiary's redemption of a portion of a more than 20–percent minority interest.

Petitioners respond that this case simply does not involve tax avoidance of a kind that the active business requirement of section 355(b) and, in particular, section 355(b)(2)(D) is designed to combat. In that regard, petitioners argue that (1) Ridge's accumulated adjustment account under section 1368(e)(1) (in this case, Ridge's undistributed, previously taxed earnings) exceeded the value of the distributed Sunbelt stock so that the distribution could not have constituted a taxable dividend to petitioners even if it had taken the form of a cash distribution (see sec. 1368(c)(1)), and 2) the redemption was not an acquisition of control by Ridge for purposes of section 355(b)(2)(D). Alternatively, petitioners argue that, even if the combined redemption-distribution is deemed to have violated the literal terms of the statute (since gain was, in fact, recognized to Hutto), respondent has allowed tax-free treatment for other transactions that failed to meet the literal statutory requirements for nonrecognition of gain. Petitioners claim that nonrecognition of gain is equally justified in this case. Petitioners also argue that the facts of Rev.Rul. 57–144, supra, are distinguishable from the facts of this case, and, therefore, it is not germane.

C.   *Discussion*

1.   *Acquisition of Control*

We generally treat a revenue ruling as merely the Commissioner's litigating position not entitled to any judicial deference or precedential weight. See, e.g., Norfolk S.S. Corp. v. Commissioner, 104 T.C. 13, 45–46 (1995), supplemented by 104 T.C. 417 (1995), affd. 140 F.3d 240 (4th Cir. 1998) * * *. We may, however, take a revenue ruling into account where we judge the underlying rationale to be sound. See Spiegelman v. Commissioner, 102 T.C. 394, 405 (1994) * * *. The degree to which we must respect the Respondent's longstanding position in Rev.Rul. 57–144, supra, is of no concern, however, because, in the circumstances of this case, we reach the same result.

First of all, we do not agree with petitioners that the facts in Rev.Rul. 57–144, supra, are distinguishable from the facts in this case in any significant way. While it is true that the ruling involves (1) a parent holding company and two operating subsidiaries rather than, as in this case, a parent operating company and a single operating subsidiary, and (2) a taxable stock redemption by the retained rather than by the distributed subsidiary, those are distinctions of no legal significance. The key determination by respondent in Rev.Rul. 57–144, supra, which is relevant to this case, is the determination that a parent corporation is considered to acquire control of its subsidiary by virtue of the subsidiary's redemption of the stock of another shareholder whose interest in the subsidiary before the redemption exceeded 20 percent.

In opposition to that determination by respondent, petitioners argue that, where control of the subsidiary is the result of the subsidiary's redemption of its own stock, there is no "acquisition" of control by the parent distributing corporation as contemplated by section 355(b)(2)(D). Again, we disagree with that blanket assertion. As one commentator has noted:

> The literal statutory language supports the redemption rule of Rev.Rul. 57–144, since P acquired control of S as a result of a taxable transaction. Although the purpose of section 355(b)(2)(D) to prevent Distributing from using its liquid assets to buy a corporation conducting an active business would not at first blush seem to be violated by a redemption of S stock before a spin-off (because P is not using any of its own assets in a way contrary to the purpose of section 355(b)(2)(D)), the *fungibility of cash makes such a redemption problematic.* It may be difficult to determine whether, in true economic effect, the cash used in the redemption could be attributed to P—as,

for instance, if S used all of its cash normally used for its working capital requirements for the redemption, which P made up to S after the redemption. * * *

Ridgway, 776–2d Tax Mgmt. (BNA), Corporate Separations at A–42, A–43 (2000) (fn. refs. & citations omitted; emphasis added).

In this case, all of the cash needed to accomplish the redemption came directly from Ridge, the parent distributing corporation. On January 14, 1993, Sunbelt borrowed $900,000 from Ridge. On the following day, Sunbelt redeemed all of Hutto's stock for $828,943.75, in cash, plus real estate with a value of $101,000. Petitioners specifically acknowledge that Sunbelt lacked sufficient liquidity to fund the redemption and, therefore, needed to borrow the necessary funds. Although, as petitioners point out, Sunbelt might have borrowed the funds from a third-party lender, it did not. Moreover, the negotiations between Hutto and Ridge prior to the redemption, whereby the two parties sought to terminate their joint ownership of Sunbelt by having one buy the stock of the other, clearly indicate that Ridge was the motivating force for the buyout of Hutto's interest in Sunbelt and that Sunbelt was, in effect, serving Ridge's purpose in accomplishing this goal. Any distinction between that series of transactions and an outright purchase of the stock by Ridge, the distributing corporation, is illusory for purposes of section 355(b)(2)(D)(ii).[8]

Under Rev.Rul. 57–144, 1957–1 C.B. 123, section 355(b)(2)(D) applies to any taxable redemption during the 5–year period that results in control of the subsidiary by the distributing corporation. We need not and do not decide whether we would reach the same result as Rev.Rul. 57–144, supra, in all such cases. We decide only that we reach the same result under the circumstances of this case.

2. *Additional Arguments*

In reaching our decision, we find none of petitioners' additional arguments persuasive.

a. *Active Business Test*

Petitioners argue that the fundamental goal of the active business test is to prevent shareholder withdrawal of accumulated earnings at capital gain rates, and that, because Ridge's accumulated adjustment account under section 1368(e)(1) exceeded the value of the distributed Sunbelt stock, an otherwise taxable distribution (including a cash dividend) would not have been taxable to petitioners. Therefore, petitioners continue, there could not have been any conversion of ordinary income into capital gain. Additionally, petitioners argue that the issue in this case, the taxation of corporate level gain, is not addressed by section 355(b)(2)(D).

Petitioners' first argument ignores the fact that, pursuant to sections 1367(a)(2)(A) and 1368(e)(1)(A), the accumulated adjustment account is reduced by the amount of the distribution (the value of the

---

[8] See Waterman S.S. Corp. v. Commissioner, 430 F.2d 1185 (5th Cir. 1970), revg. 50 T.C. 650 (1968), in which the court held that, where a subsidiary-payor distributed a promissory note to its shareholder-payee in the form of an intercompany dividend, the payor's discharge of the note with funds borrowed from the purchaser of the payor's stock from the payee was, in substance, the purchaser's payment of additional purchase price for the stock.

distributed Sunbelt stock) thereby reducing the interval before additional distributions by Ridge would become taxable to petitioners. Moreover, petitioners' argument proves too much, as it would also apply to Ridge's purchase of Hutto's Sunbelt stock directly from Hutto during the 5–year period.

Petitioners' additional argument (section 355(b)(2)(D) does not deal with corporate level gain) ignores the post-1986 evolution of section 355 (including amendments to section 355(b)(2)(D)) into a weapon against avoidance of the repeal of the *General Utilities*[9] doctrine, which, prior to its repeal by the Tax Reform Act of 1986, Pub. L. 99–514, sec. 631(c), 100 Stat. 2085, 2272, generally provided for the nonrecognition of gain realized by a corporation on the distribution of appreciated property to its shareholders. As noted by one commentator:

> It should not be surprising that more attention has been directed toward Section 355 today than was ever the case in the past. From a tax perspective, its attraction is grounded on the fact that it is one of the few (some might say the only) viable opportunity to escape the repeal of the *General Utilities* doctrine. * * *

Gould, "Spinoffs: Divesting in a Post-General Utilities World, with Emphasis on Practical Problems", 69 TAXES 889 (Dec. 1991); (fn. refs. omitted). Indeed, petitioners themselves place obvious reliance upon section 355 to avoid taxation pursuant to section 311(b).

B.   *Literal Compliance with Section 355 Not Always Required*

Petitioners also argue that nonrecognition treatment is justified herein on the basis of case law and respondent's pronouncements in which nonrecognition of gain was afforded to a transaction despite a failure to satisfy the literal terms of the governing statute. * * *

The other authorities relied upon by petitioners are also distinguishable because, in each, either the taxable acquisition (or incorporation) of the subsidiary to be spun off within the 5–year period or the spinoff itself less than 5 years after a taxable purchase of the subsidiary occurred within the context of an affiliated group of corporations. Thus, Commissioner v. Gordon, supra, involves a subsidiary spun off within 5 years of its incorporation in a transaction involving the receipt of "boot" (a demand note) taxable to the transferor parent. The Court of Appeals for the Second Circuit held that the section 355(b)(2)(C) and (D) prohibition against acquiring a business or a corporation in a taxable transaction within the 5–year period must be restricted to acquisitions from outside the affiliated group in order to carry out the legislative intent of section 355(b), which, it concluded, was to prevent "the temporary investment of liquid assets in a new business in preparation for a 355(a) division." Id. at 506 (emphasis added).[10] Respondent adopted that reasoning in Rev.Rul. 78–442,

---

[9]   See General Utils. & Operating Co. v. Helvering, 296 U.S. 200, * * * 56 S. Ct. 185 (1935).

[10]   In Baan v. Commissioner, 45 T.C. 71 (1965), revd. and remanded 382 F.2d 485 (9th Cir. 1967), we reached the same result as the Court of Appeals for the Second Circuit, but on the ground (rejected by the Court of Appeals) that the incorporation of the subsidiary was, in fact, a nonrecognition transaction because the gain attributable to the receipt of boot was eliminated in consolidation.

supra, and Counsel did so in G.C.M. 35633, supra, both of which involve the incorporation of an operating division preparatory to a spinoff of the newly formed subsidiary in a transaction intended to qualify as a tax-free reorganization under section 368(a)(1)(D). In both pronouncements, the incorporation of the more-than-5-year-old division involves the assumption of liabilities in excess of the transferor's basis, resulting in gain recognized to the transferor under section 357(c). Respondent and Counsel, like the Court of Appeals for the Second Circuit in Commissioner v. Gordon, supra, determined that section 355(b)(2)(C) is intended to prevent the acquisition of a new business from outside the affiliated group within the 5–year period. Therefore, they found no violation of that provision by virtue of the section 357(c) gain on the distributing corporation's incorporation of an existing business.[11]

In Rev.Rul. 69–461, supra, respondent determined that a distribution by a subsidiary to its parent of the stock of the former's subsidiary, within 5 years of the first-tier subsidiary's purchase of such stock, does not violate section 355(b)(2)(D). Respondent reasoned that section 355(b)(2)(D) is not intended to apply to a distribution "that merely has the effect of converting indirect control into direct control", but, rather, "applies to a transaction in which stock is acquired from outside a direct chain of ownership." Rev.Rul. 69–461, 1969–2 C.B. at 53. * * *

In this case, the redemption accomplished more than merely the conversion of indirect to direct control of Sunbelt. It accomplished the acquisition of control where none had existed previously. For that reason, it represents, in the language of the Court of Appeals for the Second Circuit in Commissioner v. Gordon, 382 F.2d at 506, "the temporary investment of liquid assets in a new business in preparation for * * * [a spinoff]". We hold that, in contrast to the circumstances involved in the pronouncements cited by petitioners, the distribution within 5 years of the redemption is precisely the type of transaction section 355(b)(2)(D) is designed to eliminate from nonrecognition treatment under section 355(a).

III. *Conclusion*

Respondent's deficiencies against petitioners are sustained.

DETAILED ANALYSIS

1.   ACTIVE TRADE OR BUSINESS

1.1. *What is a Trade or Business?*

For purposes of § 355, Treas.Reg. § 1.355–1(b)(2)(ii) defines a "business" as a specific group of activities consisting of the operations necessary to the process of earning income or profit. Activities that merely contributed to the process of earning income before the distribution may themselves constitute a business. Treas.Reg. § 1.355–3(c), Ex. (9), provides that a research department of a manufacturing activity may be spun-off as

---

[11] Sec. 1.355–3(b)(4)(iii), Income Tax Regs., applicable to acquisitions prior to the Revenue Act of 1987, Pub. L. 100–203, 101 Stat. 1330, and the Technical and Miscellaneous Revenue Act of 1988, Pub. L. 100–647, 102 Stat. 3342, also provides that sec. 355(b)(2)(C) and (D) does not apply to an acquisition of assets or stock by one member of an affiliated group from another member of the same group, even if the acquisition is taxable.

a separate business. The Example states that the status of the research department as a separate business is independent of whether it furnishes services solely to the distributing corporation or undertakes to contract with others. The Example cautions, however, that if the research department continues to function as a secondary business providing service solely to the distributing corporation, that fact is evidence of a "device" under Treas.Reg. § 1.355–2(d)(2)(iv), discussed at page 748. See also Treas.Reg. § 1.355–3(c), Ex. (10) (sales function separated from manufacturing function), and Ex. (11) (captive coal mine separated from steel products manufacturing). Treas.Reg. § 1.355–2(d)(2)(iv)(C) indicates that the functional relationship between the active trade or businesses of the distributing and controlled corporations may be evidence of a "device."

1.2. *Rental Real Estate and Other Activities as an "Active" Trade or Business?*

The operation and maintenance of owner-occupied rental real estate, as well as other rental property, may be classified as the operation of a trade or business depending upon whether the nature of the relationship of the distributing corporation to the rental activity is the *active* conduct of that business. The pre-1989 regulations refused to find an active trade or business if owner-occupied real estate was involved unless the rental activities with respect to, and the rental income from, third parties were substantial. Some cases used a similar approach; see, e.g. Appleby v. Commissioner, 35 T.C. 755 (1961), aff'd per curiam, 296 F.2d 925 (3d Cir.1962) (rental of less than 50 percent of space in building occupied by insurance agency where rentals were small part of total income did not constitute an active trade or business); Bonsall v. Commissioner, 317 F.2d 61 (2d Cir.1963) (lease of small part of owner-occupied building as an accommodation to a supplier and rental of another building was not a trade or business where rental income small).

Furthermore, the IRS held the view that if "investment" property was involved, no amount of activity with respect to the investment would constitute an active trade or business. See Rev.Rul. 66–204, 1966–2 C.B. 113 (substantial activity in managing an investment portfolio of a broker-dealer not an active trade or business).

But *Rafferty* signaled a new approach to the treatment of investment property and property used in the trade or business of the owner under the active trade or business test of § 355. Under *Rafferty,* the satisfaction of the active trade or business test turns on the question whether the corporation engaged "in entrepreneurial endeavors of such a nature and to such an extent as to qualitatively distinguish its operations from mere investments." Under the *Rafferty* approach, it is possible for the operation of owner-occupied real estate to constitute an active trade or business under § 355, even though no renting of the property to third parties is present. In *Rafferty* the real property was owned and operated in a subsidiary. The IRS appears to regard the parent-subsidiary rental situation as a variation on the owner-occupied real estate situation and uses the same tests in each to determine whether the requisite level of business activity is present. Thus, the analysis should not be altered by the form in which property is held. The result in *Rafferty* would be the same if the property had been owned directly by the parent and managed and operated as a real estate division, with the real estate division "charging" rent to the operating division for internal accounting purposes.

King v. Commissioner, 458 F.2d 245 (6th Cir.1972), applied the *Rafferty* approach in a transaction in which a transportation company owned three subsidiaries formed earlier to acquire real estate, erect terminals, and lease the terminals on a net lease basis to the parent company. To facilitate a merger with another operating company, the transportation company decided to put all of the transportation operations in one corporate group and the nonoperating corporations in a separate corporate group. The stock of the real estate subsidiaries was distributed to the stockholders of the transportation company who then transferred the stock to a sister corporation and the business activities were operated as before. In reversing the Tax Court, the Court of Appeals concluded that the financing and construction activities of the real estate group constituted an active trade or business, even though performed by the identical persons who were employees of the operational group and no third party leasing was involved.

Rev.Rul. 73–234, 1973–1 C.B. 180, reflected a shift in the IRS's interpretation of the active conduct of a trade or business requirement. The ruling stated that an actively conducted business denoted "substantial management and operational activities directly carried on by the corporation itself." A corporation that engaged in farming through tenant farmers, who were independent contractors, was held to be engaged in an active trade or business because it performed substantial management activities with respect to the farm business.

Rev.Rul. 89–27, 1989–1 C.B. 106, discussed the role of services performed by outside contractors:

> "[I]n order for a trade or business to be actively conducted, substantial management and operational activities generally must be directly carried on by the corporation itself and such activities generally do not include the activities of others outside the corporation, including independent contractors. However, the fact that a portion of a corporation's business activities is performed by others will not preclude the corporation from being engaged in the active conduct of a trade or business if the corporation itself directly performs active and substantial management and operational functions."

The ruling held that the owner of a working interest in an oil lease was actively engaged in the conduct of a business despite outside work by independent contractors. See also Rev.Rul. 73–237, 1973–1 C.B. 184 (construction corporation acting as a general contractor was in an active trade or business even though it utilized independent subcontractors for actual construction work; the general contractor's activities were substantial). However, in Rev.Rul. 86–125, 1986–2 C.B. 57, the IRS held that a subsidiary's ownership of an office building that was operated and managed by an independent real estate management company was not the active conduct of a business. The subsidiary's limited managerial and operational activities were compared to those of a prudent investor.

Treas.Reg. § 1.355–3(b)(2)(iii) incorporates a requirement that to satisfy the "active conduct" test the corporation must "perform active and substantial management and operational functions." The current regulations modify the strict rule of the prior regulations by stating that the holding of real or personal property used in a trade or business can satisfy the active conduct test if the owner performs significant services with respect to the operation and management of the property. Treas.Reg. § 1.355–3(b)(2)(iv)(B). See also Rev.Rul. 92–17, 1992–1 C.B. 142 (a corporation that was a general partner of a real estate limited partnership, and whose officers performed active and substantial management functions for the partnership, was engaged in an active trade or business), amplified by Rev.Rul. 2002–49, 2002–2 C.B. 288 (dealing with a similar situation involving a corporation that was a managing member of an LLC taxed as a partnership).

In Rev.Rul. 2007–42, 2007–2 C.B. 44, the IRS held that a distributing corporation that owned a one-third interest in an LLC that was engaged in the active conduct of a trade or business was itself engaged in the active conduct of a trade or business. The ruling reasons that ownership of a one-third interest in the LLC was significant and that the LLC itself performed the requisite management functions constituting an active trade or business. The ruling also held, however, that ownership of a 20 percent interest in an LLC is not sufficient to constitute the distributing corporation as engaged in an active trade or business.

Despite the modification in principle of the IRS's prior strict rule regarding investment property (other than stocks, securities and similar portfolio type investments) and owner-occupied real estate, however, Exs. (1)–(3), (12), and (13) in Treas.Reg. § 1.355–3(c) indicate that the IRS will continue to closely scrutinize divisive transactions involving investment assets and owner-occupied real estate. Indeed, only one of the examples, Example (12), concludes that an active trade or business is involved. In that example, the owner of a building occupied only one of eleven floors and the spun-off corporation continued the prior practice of renting the other ten floors to unrelated tenants. Example (13) indicates that if the controlled corporation leases the property it owns back to the distributing corporation, it will be difficult to establish that an active trade or business is present.

1.3. *Vertical Division of a Single Business Activity*

As noted by the court in *Rafferty,* the IRS position for many years was that § 355 could not be applied to divide a single business, which did have the requisite five-year active trade or business history, into two separate corporations. The IRS position was rejected in Coady v. Commissioner, 33 T.C. 771 (1960) (Acq.), aff'd per curiam, 289 F.2d 490 (6th Cir.1961), holding invalid regulations providing that § 355 did not apply to the separation of a single business. Accord, United States v. Marett, 325 F.2d 28 (5th Cir.1963). In Rev.Rul. 64–147, 1964–1 C.B. 136, the IRS announced that it would follow *Coady* and *Marett.*

Treas.Reg. § 1.355–3(c), Ex. (4) and (5), now specifically sanction the use of § 355 to divide a single business with the requisite five-year pre-distribution history. See also Treas.Reg. § 1.355–1(b) and –3(c), Exs. (6) and (7).

1.4. *Single Business Versus Two Separate Businesses*

As a result of the *Coady* and *Marett* cases, the IRS and taxpayers tended to shift sides in the single business versus separate businesses controversy. The IRS contended that an activity involved two separate businesses, and one of the two did not satisfy the five-year rule; the taxpayer argued that the activities constituted a single business, which could be divided under *Coady*. The question of whether an activity constitutes a single business or two separate businesses may arise in several different contexts.

1.4.1.   *Geographical Division*

The creation of branches in each of its market areas by a multi-state business may be treated as an expansion of a single business with a continuing history. In Burke v. Commissioner, 42 T.C. 1021 (1964), the IRS asserted that establishing a second retail store in another town constituted the creation of a separate trade or business as to which the five-year rule was not satisfied. The court upheld the taxpayer's assertion that under the *Coady* rule the second store constituted a branch of a single retail business that satisfied the five-year rule. In Lockwood's Estate v. Commissioner, 350 F.2d 712 (8th Cir.1965), a corporation operated in the Midwest through branches that were ultimately separately incorporated and spun-off. In 1949 it began to make sales in New England and in 1954 established a branch office in Maine. In 1956, the branch was incorporated separately and the stock distributed. No sales activity was present in Maine from 1951 to 1953 and the IRS asserted that the business had not been actively conducted in the Maine location for the five years preceding the division in 1956. The court rejected the IRS's reliance on its "geographical area" test:

> Nothing in the language of § 355 suggests that prior business activity is only to be measured by looking at the business performed in a geographical area where the controlled corporation is eventually formed. In this case, when the entire Lockwood market is viewed, it can be seen that Lockwood was engaged in active business as required by § 355 for the five years prior to the incorporation of Maine, Inc. Since its incorporation Maine, Inc. has carried on the same kind of manufacturing and selling business previously and concurrently performed by Lockwood. Thus all § 355 prerequisites are met. * * *

> Since there is no Congressional intent evidenced to the contrary, the test, restated, is not whether active business had been carried out in the geographic area later served by the controlled corporation. But, simply, whether the distributing corporation, for five years prior to distribution, had been actively conducting the type of business now performed by the controlled corporation without reference to the geographic area.

Treas.Reg. § 1.355–3(c), Ex. (7), now follows the *Burke* and *Estate of Lockwood* cases. Example (6) likewise approves the separation of the downtown and suburban branches of a retail clothing store. See also Treas.Reg. § 1.355–3(c), Ex. (8).

1.4.2.   *Separate Lines of Business*

In Lester v. Commissioner, 40 T.C. 947 (1963) (Acq.), a corporation was both a warehouse distributor (in which capacity it sold to "jobbers") and a "jobber" (in which capacity it sold to retailers). Jobber customers objected to purchasing from a corporation that was also a competitor, and the warehouse activity was spun-off. The court reaffirmed *Coady,* but in any event found that the activities constituted two separate businesses, each with its own five-year history. See also Wilson v. Commissioner, 42 T.C. 914 (1964), rev'd on other grounds, 353 F.2d 184 (9th Cir.1965) (furniture business and its financing activities were two separate businesses). In Rev.Rul. 56–451, 1956–2 C.B. 208, the IRS ruled that the publication of a trade magazine for one industry was a business separate from the publication of three magazines for another industry, and the former could be spun-off since the requirements of § 355 were met.

The problems in this area are closely related to the "functional division" situations discussed above, and the position in the regulations that there can be a valid functional division of a single business under § 355 will presumably have an impact in the single business-two separate businesses context as well. As discussed below, Treas.Reg. § 1.355–2(d)(2)(iv)(C), focuses on the device test in this context.

2.   FIVE-YEAR HISTORY

2.1. *Acquisitions of a Going Business Within the Five-Year Period*

The active trades or businesses of the distributing corporation must be the historic trades or businesses of the distributing corporation or its subsidiary. Section 355(b)(2)(C) and (D) stand as barriers to bailing out corporate earnings and profits through the acquisition of a new business shortly before it is distributed. Section 355(b)(2)(C) disqualifies an active trade or business that was acquired in a taxable transaction within the five-year period ending on the date of the distribution. Section 355(b)(2)(D) disqualifies a trade or business in a controlled corporation that was acquired by the distributing corporation or any distributee corporation in a taxable transaction within the five-year period.

In Rev.Rul. 78–442, 1978–2 C.B. 143, a corporation transferred assets and liabilities of one of its businesses to a newly formed corporation, which assumed the liabilities associated with the transferred business, and then distributed the stock. The parent corporation recognized gain on the transfer of the assets to the subsidiary under § 357(c) because the liabilities assumed exceeded the bases of the assets transferred. The ruling held that despite the fact that gain was recognized on the transfer of the business to the subsidiary, § 355(b)(2)(C) did not disqualify the distribution from qualifying under § 355, because § 355(b)(2)(C) was not intended to apply to an acquisition of a trade or business by a controlled corporation from the distributing corporation.

Rev.Rul. 2002–49, 2002–2 C.B. 288, dealt with whether the five-year active conduct of a trade or business requirement of § 355(b) was satisfied when, during the five-year period prior to a transaction that otherwise met the requirements of § 355, a corporation holding a membership interest in a member-managed limited liability company (LLC), which was taxed as a partnership, purchased the remaining interests in the LLC, contributed a portion of the LLC's business to a newly formed controlled subsidiary, and then distributed the stock of the controlled subsidiary to its shareholders. In *Situation 1*, originally *D* Corporation's sole asset was 20 percent of the LLC, which operated numerous rental properties. *D*'s officers actively participated in the management of the LLC, along with the officers of another 20 percent owner; none of the other owners participated in management. (As a result, under Rev.Rul. 92–17, page 729, *D* was engaged in the active conduct of the leasing business for the first two years.) After two years, *D* purchased the other 80 percent of the interests, and the LLC became a disregarded entity. On the first day of year 6, the LLC distributed forty percent of the rental properties to *D,* which contributed the properties

month period prior to the distribution and the new corporation itself had not engaged in the business until after the distribution. The court upheld the taxpayer's argument that § 355 nonetheless applied since it concluded that there was no requirement that the business in the five-year period preceding the distribution be conducted by either the distributing corporation or the distributee corporation. It was sufficient that the business itself was conducted during the five-year period, and the taxpayer was permitted to add on the 14-month operation as a sole proprietorship to the time when the businesses had been conducted by the distributing corporation for the purpose of satisfying the five-year requirement.

In Rev.Rul. 82–219, 1982–2 C.B. 82, a subsidiary corporation that manufactured pollution control equipment for a single unrelated automobile manufacturer was required to cease its production activities for a year when the automobile manufacturer unexpectedly filed for bankruptcy. During the year in which it was shut down, the subsidiary pursued new customers for its products. The subsidiary was spun-off by its parent corporation for valid business reasons. The fact that the subsidiary had income in only four of the five years preceding the distribution of its stock to its parent's stockholders did not defeat the five-year active conduct of business requirement.

3.   SALE OF ASSETS FOLLOWING DISTRIBUTION

Suppose that shortly after the distribution, the distributed corporation sells all of its operating assets and winds up its business. Martin Ice Cream Co. v. Commissioner, 110 T.C. 189 (1998), held that a post-distribution sale of all of the assets of the distributed controlled corporation six weeks after a split-off, but pursuant to a pre-arranged plan, resulted in the distribution failing to qualify under § 355 because the active business requirement of § 355(a)(1)(A) had not been met after the distribution. The same result should occur if the distributing corporation sells all of its assets and liquidates immediately after the distribution.

4.   HOLDING COMPANIES

Section 355(b)(2)(A) provides that a holding company will be engaged in the active conduct of a trade or business if "substantially all" of its assets consists of stock or securities of controlled corporations that are each actively engaged in the conduct of a business. For advance ruling purposes, the "substantially all" requirement is met if at least 90 percent of the fair market value of the *gross* corporate assets consist of stock and securities in controlled corporations that have actively been engaged in a trade or business for the requisite five-year period. Rev.Proc. 96–30, § 4.03(5), 1996–1 C.B. 696; Rev.Proc. 77–37, § 3.04, 1977–2 C.B. 568, 570. See also Rev.Rul. 74–382, 1974–2 C.B. 120 (same result where first tier subsidiary is a holding company but all the second tier subsidiaries are actively engaged in a trade or business); Rev.Rul. 74–79, 1974–1 C.B. 81 (operating subsidiaries acquired in taxable transactions within five-year period are treated as stock in corporations not actively engaged in a trade or business).

5.   ACTIVE TRADE OR BUSINESS OF AFFILIATED CORPORATIONS

For purposes of determining whether the active business requirement of § 355(b)(1) has been met, § 355(b)(3) provides that all members of a corporation's separate affiliated group (SAG) will be treated as a single corporation. A corporation's SAG is the affiliated group that would be determined under § 1504(a) if the corporation were the common parent (and § 1504(b) did not apply). See page 442. Prop.Reg. § 1.355–3(b) (2007) would treat all of the subsidiaries of the common parent of a SAG as divisions of the common parent for purposes of determining whether either the distributing or controlled SAG is engaged in a qualified trade or business. The separate affiliated group of the distributing corporation (DSAG) is the affiliated group consisting of the distributing corporation and all of its affiliated corporations. The separate affiliated group of a controlled corporation (CSAG) is determined in a similar manner, but by treating the controlled corporation as the common parent. Accordingly, prior to a distribution, the DSAG includes CSAG members if the ownership requirements are met. Prop.Reg. § 1.355–3(b)(1)(iii) (2007).

The SAG rule is applied for purposes of determining whether a corporation has conducted a trade or business throughout the requisite five-year period preceding the distribution and whether the distributing and controlled corporations are actively conducting a trade or business following distribution. These proposed regulations will affect the application of the active business requirement in a number of respects.

First, if ownership requirements are met, members of the distributing corporation DSAG and the controlled corporation SAG will be treated as belonging to a single SAG during the pre-distribution period, which facilitates identifying the appropriate trades or businesses regardless of how the assets are distributed among the SAG members. See Prop.Reg. § 1.355–3(b)(3)(i) (2007).

Second, the SAG rule applies for purposes of determining whether there has been a taxable acquisition of the trade or business within the five years preceding the distribution under § 355(b)(2)(C) or (D). Because, the subsidiaries of the common parent of a SAG are treated as divisions of the common parent, a stock acquisition of a corporation that becomes a member of a SAG is treated as an asset acquisition (which affects the application of § 355(b)(2)(D) regarding acquisition of control of a corporation conducting an active business). Prop.Reg. § 1.355–3(b)(1)(ii) (2007).

Third, Prop.Reg. § 1.355–3(b)(4)(iii) (2007) permits certain taxable acquisitions of the assets of a trade or business by the distributing corporation from affiliated corporations without violating the restrictions of § 355(b)(2)(C) and (D), which are interpreted as preventing the use of the assets of the distributing corporation to acquire a trade or business in lieu of dividend distributions. The proposed regulations disregard a taxable acquisition by the controlled SAG from the distributing SAG, disregard the use of cash to pay off fractional shares, and to a limited extent, disregard taxable acquisitions from members of the same SAG. However, the proposed regulations do not disregard the recognition of gain or loss in transactions between affiliated corporations unless the affiliates are members of the same SAG. (Analogous to current regulations, taxable acquisitions to expand an existing business within a SAG are disregarded. Prop.Reg. § 1.355–3(b)(3)(ii) (2007).)

Fourth, the application of § 355(b)(2)(D)(i) (control acquired by any distributee corporation) is limited to situations designed to avoid the impact of the repeal of the *General Utilities* doctrine. Thus, the proposed regulations allow a taxable acquisition by a distributee corporation of control of the distributing corporation in a transaction where the basis of the acquired distributing stock is determined in whole or by reference to the transferor's basis. Prop.Reg. § 1.355–3(b)(4)(iii)(C) (2007).

Fifth, the proposed regulations interpret § 355(b)(2)(C) and (D) to have the common purpose of preventing the direct or indirect acquisition of the trade or business (to be relied on a distribution to which § 355 would otherwise apply) by a corporation in exchange for assets other than its stock. Thus, if (1) a DSAG member or controlled corporation acquires the trade or business solely for the distributing corporation's stock, (2) the distributing corporation acquires control of the controlled corporation solely for the distributing corporation's stock, or (3) the controlled corporation acquires the trade or business from the distributing corporation solely in exchange for stock of the controlled corporation, in a transaction in which no gain or loss was recognized, § 355(b)(2)(C) and (D) are satisfied. However, if the trade or business is acquired in exchange for assets of the distributing corporation (other than stock of a corporation in control of the distributing corporation used in a reorganization) § 355(b)(2)(C) and (D) are not satisfied. Under this rule, for example, an acquisition by a controlled corporation (while controlled by the distributing corporation) from an unrelated party in exchange for the controlled corporation stock has the effect of an indirect acquisition by the distributing corporation in exchange for its assets. Such an acquisition violates the purpose of § 355(b)(2)(C), and will be treated as one in which gain or loss is recognized. Prop.Reg. § 1.355–3(b)(4)(ii) (2007).

6. ACQUISITION OF CONTROL OF THE DISTRIBUTING CORPORATION BY A DISTRIBUTEE CORPORATION

Section 355(b)(2)(D) was amended in 1987 to apply the five-year rule to the acquisition of control by the distributee corporation of a corporation conducting a trade or business. Following repeal of the *General Utilities* doctrine by the 1986 Act, there was concern that a § 355 division could be used to thwart recognition of corporate level gain in a corporate acquisition followed by a disposition of unwanted assets. For example, T Corporation operates two separate businesses. X Corporation wishes to acquire business number 1, but not business number 2. T is not willing to dispose of the businesses separately. To accomplish the transaction, T transfers each business into separate subsidiaries, S1 and S2, in a nontaxable transaction under § 351. X acquires the T stock from the T stockholders. X causes T to distribute the stock of S1, the wanted subsidiary, to it in a § 355 distribution. Subsequently, X sells the T stock thereby disposing of the unwanted assets of business number 2 (held in S2) without corporate level recognition of unrealized gain in the assets of business number 2.[6] In the example, because X, the distributee of the S1 stock, indirectly acquired control of S1 and S2 within the five-year period preceding the distribution,

---

[6]   This transaction was thought to have been approved by Rev.Rul. 74–5, 1974–1 C.B. 82, obsoleted by Rev.Rul. 89–37, 1989–1 C.B. 107, in which P Corporation in 1969 acquired all of the stock of X Corporation for cash. X Corporation in turn owned all of the stock of Y Corporation that it had acquired in 1965. In 1971, X distributed the Y stock to P and in 1972 P distributed the Y stock to its stockholders. The Ruling held that the 1971 distribution satisfied § 355(b)(2)(D), since P was neither the distributing nor the controlled corporation but simply the stockholder of the distributing corporation. On the other hand, the 1972 distribution did not satisfy § 355(b)(2)(D), since the business of controlled Corporation Y was acquired indirectly by P through another Corporation (X) in a transaction within five years in which gain or loss had been recognized. See also Rev.Rul. 69–461, 1969–2 C.B. 52.

under § 355(b)(2)(D), § 355 would not apply to the distribution of S1 stock to X. T will be required to recognize gain on the distribution of S1 stock to X under § 311.

Note that the transaction as described above would have difficulty satisfying both the business purpose and continuity of interest requirements. Section 355(b)(2)(D) was amended to avoid the need to rely on these general subjective tests.

C. THE "DEVICE" LIMITATION

INTERNAL REVENUE CODE: Section 355(a)(1)(B).

REGULATIONS: Section 1.355–2(d).

The "device" language of § 355(a)(1)(B) permits nonrecognition in a divisive transaction only if the transaction is not used principally as a "device" for the distribution of earnings and profits of either the distributing or controlled corporations, or both. The restriction is aimed at preventing a division from being merely a step in a bail-out of earnings and profits through the sale of the stock or liquidation of one of the corporations. The division of a part of one corporation into distributed stock of another corporation provides an opportunity to dispose of the distributed assets in a stock sale that produces capital gains and basis recovery deferred to the date of sale, in contrast to immediate recognition of ordinary income in the amount of the full fair market value of the distributed property in the form of a dividend. Thus, as previously noted, the reason for the presence of the "device" restriction in § 355 has been diminished by the equalization of the income tax rates on dividends and capital gains in years after the 2003 Act because with dividends and long-term capital gains taxed at the same rates rate-arbitrage based bailout *per se* is no longer a relevant concern. Nevertheless, bailout issues remain. First, basis recovery upon the sale of the stock of either the distributing or controlled corporation after the distribution effects a bailout. Second, because §§ 311(b) and 336, enacted in 1986 to repeal the *General Utilities* doctrine, see pages 197 and 326, impose tax at the corporate level on asset appreciation in corporate redemptions and liquidations, § 355 remains important in this regime because it draws the line between distributions that trigger corporate level recognition and those distributions that are permitted to enjoy corporate level tax deferral.

What constitutes a "device" is far from clear. Is it akin to a distribution essentially equivalent to a dividend? Or does it refer to tax avoidance of the Gregory v. Helvering type? Treas.Reg. § 1.355–2(d)(1) states: "Section 355 recognizes that a tax-free distribution of the stock of a controlled corporation presents a potential for tax avoidance by facilitating the avoidance of the dividend provisions of the Code through the subsequent sale or exchange of stock of one corporation and the retention of the stock of another corporation." The presence of the "device" test in § 355 focuses the inquiry on the circumstances under which the corporate division has taken place. Since every corporate division carries with it the potential for extracting earnings from the corporation with no dividend consequences, the problem is how to identify those situations in which dividend treatment is nonetheless proper. Compare, however, the treatment of partial liquidations under

§ 302(b)(4) and (e)(2), page 261, in which a corporate "division" is involved, but no "device" limitation is imposed.

South Tulsa Pathology
Laboratory, Inc. v. Commissioner

United States Tax Court, 2002.
118 T.C. 84.

■ MARVEL, JUDGE

[Ed. The taxpayer corporation provided pathology related medical services including anatomic pathology and clinical pathology. In 1993 the taxpayer's shareholders agreed to sell the clinical pathology business to National Health Laboratories, Inc. (NHL). The assets of the clinical pathology business were transferred to a newly formed corporation, Clinpath, in exchange for the Clinpath stock. The Clinpath stock was then distributed to taxpayer's shareholders. As part of a plan the shareholders sold the Clinpath stock to NHL. The transaction predated § 355(e), page 774. The distributing corporation had accumulated earnings and profits of at least $236,347 as of its taxable year beginning July 1, 1993. There was no proof that either the taxpayer or the controlled corporation had current earnings and profits as of October 30, 1993.]

OPINION

I.   *The Statutory Framework*

Section 361(a) provides that "No gain or loss shall be recognized to a corporation if such corporation is a party to a reorganization and exchanges property, in pursuance of the plan of reorganization, solely for stock or securities in another corporation a party to the reorganization." Section 368(a)(1) defines reorganization for purposes of section 361 to include:

> (D) a transfer by a corporation of all or a part of its assets to another corporation if immediately after the transfer the transferor, or one or more of its shareholders (including persons who were shareholders immediately before the transfer), or any combination thereof, is in control of the corporation to which the assets are transferred; but only if, in pursuance of the plan, stock or securities of the corporation to which the assets are transferred are distributed in a transaction which qualifies under section 354, 355, or 356;
> * * *

The above-described transaction, commonly referred to as a "D" reorganization, is sometimes used to divide an existing corporation on a tax-deferred basis into more than one corporation for corporate business purposes. In order for a divisive D reorganization to qualify for tax-deferred treatment at the corporate level under section 361, however, there must be a qualifying distribution of stock under section 355.

In this case, petitioner divided its existing business into two parts by way of a spinoff. It transferred its clinical business to a newly formed subsidiary, Clinpath, in exchange for 100 percent of Clinpath's stock. Petitioner then immediately distributed the Clinpath stock to its shareholders in a transaction petitioner claims met the requirements of section 355.

If a spinoff does not qualify under section 355, it could result in a taxable dividend to the distributing corporation's shareholders under section 301 to the extent of corporate earnings and profits and in tax to the distributing corporation computed in accordance with sections 311(b)(1) and 312. Secs. 355(c), 361(c). Section 311(b)(1) provides that, if a corporation distributes property to a shareholder in a transaction governed by sections 301 through 307 and the fair market value of such property exceeds its adjusted basis in the hands of the distributing corporation, then gain shall be recognized to the distributing corporation as if such property were sold to the distributee at its fair market value. Section 312(b) provides that, on a distribution of appreciated property by a corporation with respect to its stock, earnings and profits of the corporation are increased by the excess of the fair market value of the property over its basis.

II. *The Parties' Arguments*

The primary issue in this case is whether petitioner's spinoff of Clinpath qualified as a valid reorganization under section 368(a)(1)(D). Respondent claims it did not so qualify because the distribution of Clinpath's stock to petitioner's shareholders did not qualify as a nontaxable distribution under section 355. Respondent asserts that the spinoff of Clinpath and the subsequent sale of Clinpath stock to NHL were, in reality, a prearranged sale by petitioner of its clinical business which failed to qualify as a reorganization under section 368 and a nontaxable distribution of stock to petitioner's shareholders under section 355. Consequently, respondent contends petitioner realized and must recognize gain on the distribution of Clinpath stock. Sec. 311(b)(1). Petitioner disagrees, urging us to conclude that it structured the spinoff of its clinical business and the subsequent sale of Clinpath's stock for legitimate corporate business purposes and that the spinoff satisfied the requirements of sections 368(a)(1)(D) and 355. Therefore, petitioner contends, it is not required to recognize gain on the distribution of Clinpath stock to its shareholders.

* * *

In order to resolve these disputes, we must first decide whether the distribution of Clinpath stock to petitioner's shareholders met the section 355 requirements. We conclude that it did not for the reasons set forth below.

III. *Section 355 Distribution*

Section 355(a)(1) permits a nontaxable distribution by a corporation to its shareholders of stock in a controlled corporation if the distribution meets four statutory requirements: (1) Solely stock of a controlled corporation is distributed to shareholders with respect to their stock in the distributing corporation; (2) the distribution is not used principally as a device for the distribution of earnings and profits of the distributing corporation or the controlled corporation or both; (3) the requirements of section 355(b) (relating to active businesses) are satisfied; and (4) all of the controlled corporation's stock held by the distributing corporation, or an amount constituting control, is distributed. Sec. 355(a)(1). In addition to these statutory requirements, the regulations under section 355 require that the distribution have an independent corporate business purpose and that there be continuity of proprietary interest after the distribution. Sec. 1.355–2(b) and (c), Income Tax Regs.

* * *

A.   *Nondevice Requirement of Section 355(a)(1)(B)*

A transaction fails to qualify under section 355 if that transaction is used principally as a device for the distribution of the earnings and profits of the distributing corporation, the controlled corporation, or both. Sec. 355(a)(1)(B); see also Sec. 1.355–2(d)(1), Income Tax Regs. We analyze whether a transaction was used principally as a device for distributing earnings and profits by examining all the facts and circumstances, including, but not limited to, the presence of the device factors listed in section 1.355–2(d)(2), Income Tax Regs., and the presence of the nondevice factors listed in section 1.355–2(d)(3), Income Tax Regs.

Petitioner essentially concedes that there is evidence of device as described in section 1.355–2(d)(2), Income Tax Regs.; however, it argues that a lack of substantial earnings and profits, Sec. 1.355–2(d)(5), Income Tax Regs., and a corporate business purpose, Sec. 1.355–2(d)(3), Income Tax Regs., outweigh any evidence of device.

1.   *Device Factors*

Section 1.355–2(d)(2), Income Tax Regs., identifies the following factors as evidence that a transaction was a device for the distribution of a corporation's earnings and profits: (1) Pro rata distribution among the shareholders of the distributing corporation and (2) subsequent sale or exchange of stock of the distributing or the controlled corporation. Our analysis of these factors is set forth below.

A distribution that is pro rata or substantially pro rata among shareholders of the distributing corporation is more likely to be used principally as a device and is evidence of device. Sec. 1.355–2(d)(2)(ii), Income Tax Regs. Petitioner does not dispute that the Clinpath stock was distributed pro rata to petitioner's shareholders. The parties stipulated that pursuant to the reorganization agreement, petitioner would and did distribute all the Clinpath stock to its shareholders in proportion to their stock ownership in petitioner. This factor is evidence of device.

A sale or exchange of the distributing or controlled corporation's stock after a distribution is also evidence of device. Sec. 1.355–2(d)(2)(iii)(A), Income Tax Regs. Generally, the greater the percentage of stock sold and the shorter the period of time between the distribution and the sale or exchange, the stronger the evidence of device. Id. On brief, petitioner concedes "100% of Clinpath's stock was sold to NHL, and the distribution and the subsequent sale of stock occurred on" October 30, 1993.

In addition, a sale or exchange negotiated or agreed upon before the distribution is substantial evidence of device. Sec. 1.355–2(d)(2)(iii)(B), Income Tax Regs. On brief, petitioner concedes that "there is no question that the sale of the Clinpath stock to NHL was prearranged prior to the spin-off transaction in which the clinical laboratory assets of Petitioner were transferred to Clinpath." Indeed, the sale of Clinpath stock to NHL was discussed, negotiated, and agreed upon by NHL and petitioner and was anticipated by both parties well before the distribution. Sec. 1.355–2(d)(2)(iii)(D), Income Tax Regs. This factor is substantial evidence of device.

We conclude, based on a review of the applicable factors, that the facts and circumstances of this case present substantial evidence of device within the meaning of section 355(a)(1)(B).

2.   *Nondevice Factors and Absence of Earnings and Profits*

In order to overcome the substantial evidence of device, petitioner argues that: (1) Although both petitioner and Clinpath had some accumulated earnings and profits during the periods in question, these amounts were not significant enough to warrant the conclusion that the spinoff of Clinpath was a device in contravention of section 355(a)(1)(B), and (2) several compelling corporate business purposes drove the entire transaction.

a.   *Earnings and Profits*

Section 1.355–2(d)(5), Income Tax Regs., specifies three types of distributions that ordinarily do not present the potential for tax avoidance and will not be considered to have been used principally as a device for the distribution of earnings and profits even if there is other evidence of device. A distribution that takes place at a time when neither the distributing nor the controlled corporation has earnings or profits is one of the distributions described in section 1.355–2(d)(5), Income Tax Regs., and is the only type of distribution thus described that petitioner argues applies in this case.

A distribution ordinarily is considered not to have been used principally as a device if: (1) The distributing and controlled corporations have no accumulated earnings and profits at the beginning of their respective taxable years; (2) the distributing and controlled corporations have no current earnings and profits as of the date of the distribution; and (3) no distribution of property by the distributing corporation immediately before the separation would require recognition of gain resulting in current earnings and profits for the taxable year of the distribution. Sec. 1.355–2(d)(5)(ii), Income Tax Regs. Petitioner claims that the distribution at issue here satisfies these requirements.

In its opening brief, petitioner concedes, "that the balance sheet for * * * [petitioner] as of June 30, 1993, reflected current and accumulated earnings and profits of $252,928.64, for both the anatomic and clinical pathology portions of * * * [petitioner's] business." Petitioner argues, however, that:

> While petitioner concedes that it and Clinpath had some earnings and profits during the periods in question, these amounts were not meaningful and certainly do not provide a basis for a "bailout" of these earnings and profits amounts in order to avoid dividend treatment to Petitioner's shareholders.

Respondent disagrees, contending that the presence of any earnings and profits precludes petitioner from utilizing section 1.355–2(d)(5)(ii),

Income Tax Regs., and that there is no credible evidence that petitioner lacked accumulated or current earnings and profits on the distribution date.

We agree with respondent for several reasons. First, petitioner reported it had over $230,000 of accumulated earnings and profits as of July 1, 1993, and petitioner did not introduce any evidence to prove that it had no current earnings and profits as of October 30, 1993. Section 1.355–2(d)(5)(ii)(A) and (B), Income Tax Regs., emphasizes that a distribution ordinarily will not be considered to have been used principally as a device if the distributing and controlled corporations have "no accumulated earnings and profits at the beginning of their respective taxable years" and "no current earnings and profits as of the date of the distribution". (Emphasis added.) Section 1.355–2(d)(5)(ii), Income Tax Regs., does not provide a safe harbor for corporations with "insignificant" or "minimal" earnings and profits, as petitioner contends.

Second, petitioner ignores the fact that the spinoff enabled it to claim that the substantial gain on the distribution of Clinpath stock to its shareholders, which ordinarily would have increased its current and accumulated earnings and profits, need not be recognized for corporate income tax purposes or reflected in the calculation of its earnings and profits as of October 30, 1993 and at year end. * * *

Neither party disputes that, if the spinoff of Clinpath does not qualify as a tax-free transaction under sections 368 and 355, petitioner must realize and recognize substantial gain as of the date of distribution, Sec. 311(b)(1), which will substantially increase petitioner's earnings and profits, Sec. 312(b). Nevertheless, petitioner dismisses the prospect that it would have substantial current earnings and profits as a result of the spinoff and overlooks what respondent describes as "the conspicuous fact that the corporate profits petitioner's shareholders clearly intended to bail out were the anticipated profits of the prearranged sale." Despite petitioner's efforts to suggest otherwise, we simply are not convinced that the decision to structure this transaction as a spinoff and subsequent stock sale was prompted by NHL; NHL usually structured its acquisitions as asset sales to minimize its exposure to liabilities that can arise from the purchase of an active business. Petitioner's protestations notwithstanding, the spinoff of Clinpath followed immediately by a prearranged sale of the Clinpath stock on the same day appears to have been designed to eliminate the corporate-level tax that would have been due had petitioner sold its clinical business to NHL directly or distributed its clinical business to its shareholders prior to any sale.

For the reasons set forth above, petitioner has failed to prove that it did not have accumulated or current earnings and profits as of the date of the distribution within the meaning of section 1.355–2(d)(5)(ii), Income Tax Regs.

b.   *Corporate Business Purpose*

The presence of a valid corporate business purpose may trump a conclusion that the transaction was used principally as a device for the distribution of earnings and profits. Sec. 1.355–2(b)(4), (d)(3)(ii), Income Tax Regs. Section 1.355–2(b)(2), Income Tax Regs., defines "corporate business purpose" as a "real and substantial non-Federal tax purpose germane to the business of the distributing corporation, the controlled corporation, or the affiliated group * * * to which the distributing corporation belongs."

The stronger the evidence of device, such as the presence of the device factors specified in section 1.355–2(d)(2), Income Tax Regs., the stronger the corporate business purpose required to prevent the conclusion that the transaction was used principally as a device. Sec. 1.355–2(d)(3), Income Tax Regs. The assessment of the strength of the business purpose must be made based upon all the facts and circumstances, including, but not limited to: (1) The importance of achieving the purpose to the success of the business; (2) the extent to which the transaction is prompted by a person not having a proprietary interest in either corporation, or by other outside factors beyond the control of the distributing corporation; and (3) the immediacy of the conditions prompting the transaction. Sec. 1.355–2(d)(3)(i) and (ii), Income Tax Regs.

Petitioner identifies three purported corporate business purposes for the disputed distribution: (1) Increased competition caused by a changing economic environment that favored the larger, national laboratories; (2) Oklahoma State law restricting the ownership of petitioner to licensed physicians or physician-owned entities licensed to practice medicine within Oklahoma; and (3) NHL's requirement that each of petitioner's physician-shareholders sign binding and enforceable covenants not to compete in the clinical laboratory business. Respondent contends there was no valid corporate business purpose for the distribution. We consider each of the purported corporate business purposes below.

i.   *Increased Competition*

The first purported corporate business purpose asserted by petitioner is that the changing economic environment in the clinical laboratory market in 1993 favored the large, national laboratories over the smaller clinical laboratories, such as petitioner's. * * * We do not question, and respondent does not dispute, that the economic factors cited by petitioner may have forced it out of the clinical business within a few years. Although these factors may have been the impetus behind the decision to sell the clinical business in the first instance, such factors do not demonstrate a corporate business purpose for petitioner's decision to distribute the Clinpath stock to its shareholders before selling the stock to NHL. A transfer of the clinical laboratory assets directly to Clinpath would have sufficed to achieve petitioner's desired result; i.e., to create a new company containing solely the assets of the clinical business in order to sell the clinical business with minimum liability to the buyer. Minimizing the effect of the economic factors cited by petitioner, however, did not require the nearly simultaneous distribution of Clinpath stock to its shareholders. The purpose of separating the clinical laboratory assets in preparation for the sale to NHL and shielding NHL from liability was achieved as soon as the clinical business was contributed to Clinpath by petitioner in exchange for Clinpath stock. See generally Sec. 1.355–2(b)(5), *Example (3)*, Income Tax Regs.

* * *

ii.   *Petitioner's Status as a Professional Corporation*

The second purported corporate business purpose arises from petitioner's claim that Oklahoma State law mandated the final structure of the spinoff transaction. Petitioner essentially argues that it was constrained from selling, and NHL was prevented from purchasing, petitioner's stock because petitioner's status as a professional corporation prevented NHL from owning any interest in it. * * *

Even if petitioner were precluded from selling its stock to nonphysicians as petitioner contends, such a bar would justify only petitioner's decision to transfer its clinical business to a separate general business corporation, i.e., Clinpath; it would not lend support to petitioner's decision to distribute Clinpath stock to petitioner's shareholders. * * *

iii.   *Covenants Not To Compete*

The third purported corporate business purpose cited by petitioner is NHL's requirement that each of Clinpath's physician-shareholders sign a binding and enforceable covenant not to compete. * * * [P]etitioner contends that representatives for both petitioner and NHL believed that a covenant not to compete would be enforced under Oklahoma State law only if it were entered into in connection with the sale of goodwill or the dissolution of a partnership. Petitioner contends that the final structure of the transaction as a sale of Clinpath stock by Clinpath's shareholders, and not by petitioner, was mandated by NHL's desire to obtain from the shareholders valid and enforceable covenants not to compete. Therefore, a corporate business purpose existed for the distribution of Clinpath stock to the shareholders.

We do not agree. Even if we were to conclude that NHL's desire to obtain enforceable covenants not to compete qualified as a corporate business purpose of either petitioner or Clinpath, as section 1.355–2(b)(2), Income Tax Regs., requires, we would still reject petitioner's argument. Okla. Stat. Ann. tit. 15, Sec. 217 (West 1986 and Supp. 2000), provides that "Every contract by which any one is restrained from exercising a lawful profession, trade or business of any kind, otherwise than as provided by Sections 218 and 219 of this title, is to that extent void." Oklahoma State courts interpret Okla. Stat. Ann. tit. 15, Sec. 217, to prohibit only unreasonable restraints on the exercise of a lawful profession, trade, or business. * * * Even unreasonable contracts in restraint of trade, which are normally void and unenforceable under Oklahoma State law, are enforceable if they fall within one of the two statutorily created exceptions to the general rule—covenants given in connection with the sale of goodwill or covenants given in connection with the dissolution of a partnership. Okla. Stat. Ann. tit. 15, Secs. 218 and 219 (West 1986 and Supp. 2000) * * *. Assuming the covenants in this case were reasonable and/or were given in connection with the sale of goodwill, it was unnecessary to first distribute the Clinpath stock to petitioner's shareholders. Petitioner has failed to demonstrate either that the covenants in question were unreasonable or that they were not adequately tied to the sale of goodwill under Oklahoma State law.

We conclude, therefore, that NHL's demand for binding and enforceable covenants not to compete does not constitute a corporate business purpose within the meaning of section 1.355–2(d)(3)(ii), Income Tax Regs., and, therefore, is insufficient to overcome the substantial evidence of device in this case.

3.   *Conclusion*

There is substantial evidence of device in this case, which is not overcome by substantial evidence of nondevice or by proof that petitioner and Clinpath lacked current or accumulated earnings and profits. We hold, therefore, that the distribution of Clinpath stock failed to satisfy the requirements of section 355(a)(1).

* * *

DETAILED ANALYSIS

1.   NON-PRO RATA DISTRIBUTIONS

Pro rata divisions represent a clear situation in which there is a bail-out potential in a divisive distribution. Thus, Treas.Reg. § 1.355–2(d)(2)(ii) treats the fact that a distribution is pro rata, or substantially pro rata, as evidence that the transaction is used as a device to effect a distribution of earnings and profits. At the other extreme, however, Treas.Reg. § 1.355–2(d)(5) provides that a non-pro rata distribution that qualifies as a redemption under § 302(a), page 231, ordinarily will not be considered to be a device. There is no "bail-out" potential in a transaction that would produce capital gains in any event. See also Rev.Rul. 64–102, 1964–1 C.B. 136 (transfer to a previously existing subsidiary of assets representing more than 50 percent of the value of the subsidiary to equalize the value of the subsidiary stock with the value of the parent company stock owned by a minority stockholder, followed by a distribution of the subsidiary stock in exchange for the minority stockholder's parent stock, did not amount to a "device" since the transaction as to the minority stockholder would have entitled him to capital gain treatment under § 302(b)(3)); Rev.Rul. 71–383, 1971–2 C.B. 180 (a distribution that was substantially disproportionate under § 302(b)(2) did not constitute a "device" since under that section the taxpayer was entitled to capital gain treatment). For the same reason, Treas.Reg. § 1.355–2(d)(5)(ii) provides that there is ordinarily no device present if neither the distributing nor controlled corporations have earnings and profits (including built-in gain property that would create earnings if distributed) that would cause taxable dividend treatment on a distribution to stockholders. In these situations, however, the "business purpose" and "continuity of interest" requirements of the regulations still must be met.

2.   POST-DISTRIBUTION SALE OR EXCHANGE

Treas.Reg. § 1.355–2(d)(2)(iii) provides that a sale or exchange of the stock of either the distributing or the spun-off corporation following a division is evidence that the transaction was used principally as a device for distribution of the earnings and profits of either or both of the corporations. The percentage of stock sold and the period of time before the stock sale affect the strength of this evidence of a "device." If the stock sale is negotiated or agreed upon before the § 355 division occurs, the evidence of a "device" is elevated by the regulations to the level of "substantial evidence", while a sale or exchange arranged only after the division is merely "evidence" of a "device." Treas.Reg. § 1.355–2(d)(2)(iii)(B) and (C).

Treas.Reg. § 1.355–2(d)(2)(iii)(E) also provides that a post-distribution exchange of stock of either the distributing or the controlled corporation in a reorganization in which no more than an insubstantial amount of gain is recognized will not be treated as a subsequent sale or exchange constituting evidence of a "device." This portion of the regulations adopts the holding of Commissioner v. Morris Trust, 367 F.2d 794 (4th Cir.1966). In *Morris Trust,* a state bank desired to merge into a national bank. However, the state bank operated an insurance department, an operation that could not be continued by the national bank. To avoid a violation of the national banking laws, the state bank organized a new corporation to which it transferred the insurance business assets and then distributed the stock in the insurance corporation to its stockholders. Following the distribution, the state bank was merged into the national bank. The IRS argued in part that there was "an inherent incompatibility in substantially simultaneous divisive and amalgamating reorganizations." The court rejected the IRS's argument, holding that there was no "discontinuance of the [distributing corporation's] banking business" even though conducted in a different corporate form, and that the stockholders of the distributing corporation retained the requisite continuity of interest through their majority stock interest in the resulting national bank.[7] See also Rev.Rul. 70–434, 1970–2 C.B. 83, in which the stockholders of the distributing corporation, after receiving the stock of the spun-off corporation, then exchanged their stock in the distributing corporation in a (B) reorganization. Helvering v. Elkhorn Coal Company, 95 F.2d 732 (4th Cir.1937), indicates, however, that a (C) reorganization is not available following a spin-off because of the requirement that the acquired corporation transfer "substantially all" its assets in the (C) reorganization.

In Rev.Rul. 77–377, 1977–2 C.B. 111, an estate owned 80 percent of the stock of X Corporation. In a split-up transaction, X transferred its assets to new Y and Z Corporations, and then liquidated. Prior to the split-up, the estate had contemplated a § 303 redemption of a part of its X stock to pay estate taxes. The § 303 redemption could not be completed before the split-up. Therefore, after the split-up, new Y and Z Corporations redeemed part of the estate's stock in each under § 303. The ruling held that no "device" was involved since the dividend provisions of the Code had not

---

[7]   Curtis v. United States, 336 F.2d 714 (6th Cir.1964), was to the contrary, holding that § 355 did not apply where following the distribution of the stock of the corporation holding the unwanted assets, the distributing corporation merged into another corporation. It construed § 355 to require the distributing corporation to stay in existence.

The IRS also argued in *Morris Trust* that the active business requirements of § 355(b)(1)(A) were not met since the state bank's business was not continued in unaltered corporate form. The court found no specific limitation in § 355 preventing continuation of the active conduct of the business of the distributing corporation in altered corporate form and concluded that permitting nonrecognition under § 355 did not violate the principles underlying the provision.

In Rev.Rul. 68–603, 1968–2 C.B. 148, the IRS announced that it would follow the *Morris Trust* decision to the extent that it held (1) the active trade or business requirement is met even though the distributing corporation merges following the distribution; (2) the control requirement of a (D) reorganization implies no limits on the reorganization of the distributing corporation after the spin-off; and (3) there is a business purpose for the spin-off and the merger.

been avoided. See Treas.Reg. § 1.355–2(d)(5)(iii) (a transaction is generally not considered to be a device if the distribution would have been treated as a redemption under § 303).

Finally, the 1997 Act added §§ 355(e) and (f), which are colloquially referred to as "the anti-*Morris Trust* rules," even though they would not actually apply to the specific transaction in that case if it were to occur today. If pursuant to a plan or arrangement in connection with a corporate division there is a change of ownership of 50 percent or more of either the distributing corporation or the controlled corporation, under § 355(e) the distributing corporation generally must recognize gain as if the stock of the controlled corporation had been sold for fair market value on the date of distribution. The distributee shareholders, however, continue to receive nonrecognition treatment if § 355 otherwise applies. Acquisitions occurring within two years before or after the date of the distribution are presumed to have occurred pursuant to a plan or arrangement. Special rules under § 355(f) apply to divisive distributions of stock from one member of an affiliated group of corporations (as defined in § 1504(a)) to another member of the group followed by a sale outside the group. These provisions, which are discussed in greater detail in Section 5, are primarily designed to prevent selective disposition of corporate assets without recognizing gain under §§ 311 or 336.

3.   NATURE AND USE OF ASSETS

Treas.Reg. § 1.355–2(d)(2)(iv)(A) provides that in determining whether a transaction is principally a device for the distribution of earnings and profits, consideration will be given to the "nature, kind, amount, and use" of the assets of both corporations immediately after the transaction. There are two aspects to this consideration.

3.1. *Nonbusiness Assets*

The presence of assets not related to the trade or business of one of the corporations, such as cash and other liquid assets, is evidence of a device. Treas.Reg. § 1.355–2(d)(2)(iv)(B). The presence of unrelated assets is particularly damaging if the amount of unrelated assets transferred to or retained by one corporation is disproportionate to the relative value of the business assets in that corporation. See Treas.Reg. § 1.355–2(d)(4), Ex. (3). In Rev.Rul. 86–4, 1986–1 C.B. 174, the IRS held that the transfer of investment assets to the controlled corporation in a spin-off is a factor to be considered in determining whether the transaction is a device regardless of the percentage of the investment assets relative to the total amount of assets transferred to the controlled corporation.

In Rev.Rul. 73–44, 1973–1 C.B. 182, clarified by Rev.Rul. 76–54, 1976–1 C.B. 96, the distributing corporation conducted three businesses: (1) a manufacturing and distribution business that it had conducted for more than five years and that constituted over one-half the value of the corporation's total business assets; (2) a newspaper business, acquired in a taxable transaction within the preceding five years, which had been transferred to a newly created subsidiary in a nontaxable transaction; and (3) a separate manufacturing business conducted for more than five years. The distributing corporation transferred business (3) to the newspaper subsidiary and then distributed all the stock of the subsidiary to its shareholders. Business (3) represented a "substantial portion" of the value of the spun-off corporation, but less than one-half. The ruling held that a "device" was not present since the newspaper business acquired in the taxable transaction represented "operating businesses and not assets that would be used" as a device.

A contribution to the capital of the controlled corporation preceding a spin-off of the subsidiary's stock also may provide an opportunity for the distribution of earnings to stockholders. In Rev.Rul. 83–114, 1983–2 C.B. 66, the IRS held that a predistribution capital contribution to the controlled corporation was not per se a device. P was required by an antitrust decree to divest itself of its subsidiary S. In order to improve S's capital and expand S's business opportunities, P discharged S's indebtedness to it. The debt discharge increased S's net worth by more than 100 percent. P distributed S stock to P stockholders. The ruling concluded that there was no device since both the distribution of S stock and the discharge of S's indebtedness were undertaken for valid business reasons.

3.2. *Related Business Activities*

The second part of the inquiry into the nature of transferred assets concerns the relationship of the businesses of the two corporations. Although the regulations recognize that § 355 can be employed to divide a single business or to effect a functional division of the business, there is evidence of a device if the businesses of the distributing and controlled corporations are functionally related in the sense that one of the businesses is a secondary business of the other, and the secondary business can be sold without adversely affecting the other. Treas.Reg. § 1.355–2(d)(2)(iv)(C). Example (10) of Treas.Reg. § 1.355–3(c), illustrates this concept. A corporation engaged in the manufacture of steel products spins off a subsidiary that owns a coal mine supplying the steel plant. Evidence of a device exists if the principal function of the coal mine is to satisfy the requirements of the steel business for coal and the stock of the coal mine could be sold without adversely affecting the steel business by depriving it of the supply of coal from the mine.

The related function test of Treas.Reg. § 1.355–2(d)(2)(iv)(C) is closely related to the spin-off of real estate involved in *Rafferty*, and is not wholly inconsistent with the result in that case. In King v. Commissioner, 458 F.2d 245 (6th Cir.1972), a transportation company distributed stock of subsidiaries that owned and leased terminals and other real estate necessary to the operation of the distributing corporation's business. Distinguishing *Rafferty*, the court in *King* rejected the IRS's argument that the distribution failed the device requirement, pointing out that a sale or liquidation of the spun-off corporation would have hindered the business operation of the distributing corporation.

The *Rafferty* court's reliance on the factor of "readily realizable value" to determine the bail-out potential refers to the division of liquid from illiquid assets; even if the spun-off corporation is in an active trade or business, the bail-out potential may be high because of the nature of the assets (as would be the case with real estate). But further, if the sale or liquidation of the spun-off corporation would seriously impair the ability of the distributing corporation to operate, then a "device" is not likely to be present. Thus, the court in *King* upheld § 355 treatment for the spin-off of real estate leased solely to the distributing corporation on the ground that, while the real estate operations were highly liquid (net leases were involved), the properties were uniquely suited to the distributing company's needs and a sale would have impaired the company's ability to obtain financing. Under the *Rafferty* approach, transactions involving real estate must be closely scrutinized. For example, long-term leases on the real estate may make possible a sale of the stock of the distributed corporation without impairing in any way the operating functions of the distributing corporation. In such a case, the transaction should constitute a "device" under the *Rafferty* test.

D. THE "BUSINESS PURPOSE" REQUIREMENT

REGULATIONS: Sections 1.355–2(b) and (d)(3)(ii).

The role of "business purpose" in the § 355 framework is important and has several aspects. Under Treas.Reg. § 1.355–2(d)(3)(ii) the presence of a corporate business purpose for the transaction is evidence that a "device" is not present. The stronger the device factors, the stronger the evidence of business purpose necessary to overcome the presence of a device. In addition, Treas.Reg. § 1.355–2(b) independently requires a corporate business purpose for nonrecognition treatment in order to limit nonrecognition to "distributions that are incident to readjustments of corporate structures required by business exigencies and that effect only readjustments of continuing interests in property under modified corporate forms." This business purpose test is independent of the "device" language, so that even upon a finding of no "device," the transaction nonetheless may fail to qualify for want of a "business purpose." The regulations are consistent with the decision in Commissioner v. Wilson, 353 F.2d 184 (9th Cir.1965), holding that § 355 was inapplicable where, although the transaction was not a "device" because there was no tax avoidance motive, no affirmative business purpose was demonstrated for the transaction, and that under the *Gregory* doctrine "business purpose" is an essential ingredient of the law. *Rafferty,* on the other hand, appears to deal with "business purpose" only as a factor under the "device" prohibition.

Revenue Ruling 2003–52

2003–2 C.B. 960.

ISSUE

Whether, in the situation described below, the distribution of the stock of a controlled corporation satisfies the business purpose requirement of § 1.355–2(b) of the Income Tax Regulations.

FACTS

Corporation X is a domestic corporation that has been engaged in the farming business for more than five years. The stock of X is owned 25 percent each by Father, age 68, Mother, age 67, Son, and Daughter. Although Father and Mother participate in some major management decisions, most of the management and all of the operational activities are performed by Son, Daughter, and several farmhands. The farm operation consists of breeding and raising livestock and growing grain.

Son and Daughter disagree over the appropriate future direction of X's farming business. Son wishes to expand the livestock business, but Daughter is opposed because this would require substantial borrowing by X. Daughter would prefer to sell the livestock business and concentrate on the grain business. Despite the disagreement, the two siblings have cooperated on the operation of the farm in its historical manner without disruption. Nevertheless, it has prevented each sibling from developing, as he or she sees fit, the business in which he or she is most interested.

Having transferred most of the responsibility for running the farm to the children, Father and Mother remain neutral on the disagreement between their children. However, because of the disagreement, Father and Mother would prefer to bequeath separate interests in the farm business to their children.

For reasons unrelated to X's farm business, Son and Daughter's husband dislike each other. Although this has not impaired the farm's operation to date, Father and Mother believe that requiring Son and Daughter to run a single business together is likely to cause family discord over the long run.

To enable Son and Daughter each to devote his or her undivided attention to, and apply a consistent business strategy to, the farming business in which he or she is most interested, to further the estate planning goals of Father and Mother, and to promote family harmony, X transfers the livestock business to newly formed, wholly owned domestic corporation Y and distributes 50 percent of the Y stock to Son in exchange for all of his stock in X. X distributes the remaining Y stock equally to Father and Mother in exchange for half of their X stock. Going forward, Daughter will manage and operate X and have no stock interest in Y, and Son will manage and operate Y and have no stock interest in X. Father and Mother will also amend their wills to provide that Son and Daughter will inherit stock only in Y and X, respectively. After the distribution, Father and Mother will still each own 25 percent of the outstanding stock of X and Y and will continue to participate in some major management decisions related to the business of each corporation.

Apart from the issue of whether the business purpose requirement of § 1.355–2(b) is satisfied, the distribution meets all of the requirements of §§ 368(a)(1)(D) and 355 of the Internal Revenue Code.

LAW

Section 355 provides that if certain requirements are met, a corporation may distribute stock and securities in a controlled corporation to its shareholders and security holders without causing the distributing corporation or the distributees to recognize gain or loss.

To qualify as a distribution described in § 355, a distribution must, in addition to satisfying the statutory requirements of § 355, satisfy certain requirements in the regulations, including the business purpose requirement. Section 1.355–2(b)(1) provides that a distribution must be motivated, in whole or substantial part, by one or more corporate business purposes. A corporate business purpose is a real and substantial non-Federal tax purpose germane to the business of the distributing corporation, the controlled corporation, or the affiliated group to which the distributing corporation belongs. Section 1.355–2(b)(2). A shareholder purpose (for example, the personal planning purposes of a shareholder) is not a corporate business purpose. Id.

Depending upon the facts of a particular case, however, a shareholder purpose for a transaction may be so nearly coextensive with a corporate business purpose as to preclude any distinction between them. Id. In such a case, the transaction is carried out for one or more corporate business purposes. Id. A transaction motivated in substantial part by a corporate business purpose does not fail the business purpose requirement merely because it is motivated in part by non-Federal tax shareholder purposes. Preamble to the § 355 regulations, T.D. 8238, 1989–1 C.B. 92, 94.

In Example (2) of § 1.355–2(b)(5), Corporation X is engaged in two businesses: the manufacture and sale of furniture and the sale of jewelry. The businesses are of equal value. The outstanding stock of X is owned equally by unrelated individuals A and B. A is more interested in the furniture business, while B is more interested in the jewelry business. A and B decide to split up the businesses and go their separate ways. A and B expect that the operations of each business will be enhanced by the separation because each shareholder will be able to devote his undivided attention to the business in which he is more interested and more proficient. Accordingly, X transfers the jewelry business to new corporation Y and distributes the stock of Y to B in exchange for all of B's stock in X. The example concludes that the distribution is carried out for a corporate business purpose, notwithstanding that it is also carried out in part for shareholder purposes.

ANALYSIS

The disagreement of Son and Daughter over the farm's future direction has prevented each sibling from developing, as he or she sees fit, the business in which he or she is most interested. The distribution will eliminate this disagreement and allow each sibling to devote his or her undivided attention to, and apply a consistent business strategy to, the farming business in which he or she is most interested, with the expectation that each business will benefit. Therefore, although the distribution is intended, in part, to further the personal estate planning of Father and Mother and to promote family harmony, it is motivated in substantial part by a real and substantial non-Federal tax purpose that is germane to the business of X. Hence, the business purpose requirement of § 1.355–2(b) is satisfied.

HOLDING

In the situation described above, the distribution of the stock of a controlled corporation satisfies the business purpose requirement of § 1.355–2(b).

Revenue Ruling 2003–55

2003–2 C.B. 961.

ISSUE

Is the business purpose requirement of § 1.355–2(b) of the Income Tax Regulations satisfied if the distribution of the stock of a controlled corporation is, at the time of the distribution, motivated, in whole or substantial part, by a corporate business purpose, but that purpose cannot be achieved as the result of an unexpected change in circumstances following the distribution?

FACTS

D is a publicly traded corporation that conducts Business A and Business B directly and Business C through its wholly owned subsidiary C. Business C needs to raise a substantial amount of capital in the near future to invest in plant and equipment and to make acquisitions. D has been advised by its investment banker that the best way to raise this capital is through an initial public offering of C stock after C has been separated from D. The investment banker believes, based on its analysis of comparable situations, and taking into account the current market climate, that such an offering would be more efficient than a stock offering by C or D without first separating from the other because it would raise the needed capital with significantly less dilution of the existing shareholders' interests in the combined enterprises.

In reliance on the investment banker's opinion, D distributes the stock of C to its shareholders, and C prepares to offer its stock to the public as soon as practicable but with a target date approximately six months after the distribution. Following the distribution and before the offering can be undertaken, market conditions unexpectedly deteriorate to such an extent that, in the judgment of C and its advisors, the offering should be postponed. One year after the distribution, conditions have not improved sufficiently to permit the offering to go forward and C funds its capital needs through the sale of debentures.

Apart from the issue of whether the business purpose requirement of § 1.355–2(b) is satisfied, the distribution meets all of the requirements of § 355 of the Internal Revenue Code.

LAW

Section 355 provides that if certain requirements are met, a corporation may distribute stock and securities in a controlled corporation to its shareholders and security holders without causing the distributing corporation or the distributees to recognize gain or loss.

To qualify as a distribution described in § 355, a distribution must, in addition to satisfying the statutory requirements of § 355, satisfy certain requirements in the regulations, including the business purpose requirement. Section 1.355–2(b)(1) provides that a distribution must be motivated, in whole or substantial part, by one or more corporate business purposes. A corporate business purpose is a real and substantial non-Federal tax purpose germane to the business of the distributing corporation, the controlled corporation, or the affiliated group to which the distributing corporation belongs. Section 1.355–2(b)(2). The principal reason for the business purpose requirement is to provide nonrecognition treatment only to distributions that are incident to readjustments of corporate structures required by business exigencies and that effect only readjustments of continuing interests in property under modified corporate forms. Section 1.355–2(b)(1).

ANALYSIS

To satisfy the business purpose requirement of § 1.355–2(b)(1), a distribution of controlled corporation stock must be motivated, in whole

SECTION 3.   DISTRIBUTION OF "CONTROL" AND CONTINUITY OF INTEREST REQUIREMENTS

INTERNAL REVENUE CODE: Section 355(a)(1)(A), and (D); 368(a)(2)(H)(ii).

REGULATIONS: Section 1.355–2(a),–2(c).

The nonrecognition principles of § 355 apply to the distribution of stock of a corporation that is "controlled" by the distributing corporation immediately before the distribution. Control is defined in § 368(c) as ownership of 80 percent of voting power and 80 percent of each other classes of stock of a corporation. In addition, § 355(a)(1)(D) requires the distributing corporation to distribute all of the stock or securities of the controlled corporation held by it immediately before the distribution, or, with the permission of the IRS, at least a controlling amount of the stock of the controlled corporation. This distribution requirement results, at least initially, in continued ownership of the business of the controlled corporation by the shareholders of the distributing corporation. This rule is bolstered by a requirement in Treas.Reg. § 1.355–2(c) that the shareholders of the distributing corporation maintain a continuing interest in the business of both the distributing and controlled corporations. However, § 368(a)(2)(H)(ii) provides that in determining whether a transfer of assets to a subsidiary prior to a distribution of stock qualifying under § 355 meets the requirements of § 368(a)(1)(D), the fact that the shareholders of the distributing corporation dispose of all or part of the stock of the distributed corporation, or whether the distributed corporation issues additional stock, shall not be taken into account.[8] Since a § 368(a)(1)(D) reorganization cannot occur without a subsequent distribution that qualifies under either § 354, which cannot occur in a divisive (D) reorganization, or § 355, the inference is that there is no requirement that the shareholders of the distributing corporation maintain any interest in the distributed corporation following the distribution.

The Supreme Court addressed the control requirement in Commissioner v. Gordon, 391 U.S. 83 (1968). The taxpayers were minority shareholders in the Pacific Telephone and Telegraph Company (Pacific). Ninety percent of the Pacific stock was owned by A.T. & T. In 1961, A.T. & T. decided to split Pacific into two separate corporations, Pacific and Pacific Northwest Bell. Pacific transferred all of the assets and liabilities related to its business in Oregon, Washington and Idaho to Northwest Bell in exchange for all of the Northwest Bell stock and some debt instruments. Pacific retained assets related to its business in California. Also in 1961, Pacific distributed warrants entitling Pacific stockholders to purchase Pacific Northwest Bell stock representing 57 percent of the outstanding stock at a price substantially below the market price at which the stock traded on a public exchange. In 1963, Pacific distributed additional warrants to its stockholders entitling the Pacific stockholders to purchase the remaining 43 percent of Pacific

---

8   The purpose of § 368(a)(2)(H)(ii) is to assure that assets transferred to a subsidiary prior the distribution of the stock of the subsidiary to the transferor corporation's shareholders retain a transferred basis under § 362 and do not take a fair market value basis. This result is reinforced by § 351(c), which has the same effect as § 368(a)(2)(H), regardless of whether the subsequent stock distribution qualifies under § 355 or is controlled by another section.

Northwest Bell. The IRS argued that the transaction failed the requirements of § 355 because Pacific did not distribute enough stock of Pacific Northwestern Bell in 1961 to constitute control. The IRS thus asserted that the taxpayers realized ordinary income in an amount equal to the difference between the value of the Pacific Northwest Bell stock and the purchase price paid on exercise of the warrants. The Supreme Court agreed with the IRS, rejecting the taxpayers' argument that in combination the 1961 and 1963 distributions satisfied the requirements of § 355(a)(1)(D).[9]

> * * * The Code requires that "the distribution" divest the controlling corporation of all of, or 80% control of, the controlled corporation. Clearly, if an initial transfer of less than a controlling interest in the controlled corporation is to be treated for tax purposes as a mere first step in the divestiture of control, it must at least be identifiable as such at the time it is made. Absent other specific directions from Congress, Code provisions must be interpreted so as to conform to the basic premise of annual tax accounting. It would be wholly inconsistent with this premise to hold that the essential character of a transaction, and its tax impact, should remain not only undeterminable but unfixed for an indefinite and unlimited period in the future, awaiting events that might or might not happen. This requirement that the character of a transaction be determinable does not mean that the entire divestiture must necessarily occur within a single tax year. It does, however, mean that if one transaction is to be characterized as a "first step" there must be a binding commitment to take the later steps.

The continuity of interest requirement of Treas.Reg. § 1.355–2(c) is closely related to the "device" provision in terms of preventing post-distribution sales.[10] Nonetheless, under the regulations continuity of interest is an independent requirement aimed at limiting nonrecognition in corporate separations to transactions in which shareholders of the original corporation maintain a continuing interest in each of the corporations surviving a division. However, 1998 amendments to § 368(a)(2)(H)(ii), noted above and discussed further at page 763, indicate that post-distribution sales of stock of the controlled corporation by shareholders of the distributing corporation, which may terminate the interest of the former shareholders in the controlled corporation, should not be taken into account in determining whether the requirements of § 355 are met. This provision may have eliminated shareholder continuity of interest, at least with respect to the business transferred to the controlled corporation.

---

[9]   The IRS also argued that the transaction failed under § 355 because the Pacific Northwestern Bell stock received by the taxpayers was not distributed to them by Pacific, but was instead sold to the taxpayers for cash under the terms of the warrants. The Court declined to address this argument.

One of the taxpayers sold some warrants for cash. The taxpayer was required to treat the sales proceeds as ordinary income.

[10]   See Rev.Rul. 59–197, 1959–1 C.B. 77, treating a pre-distribution sale of a minority interest in the stock of the distributing corporation as in effect a binding contract to sell stock in the newly-created corporation after the distribution; but the transaction did not constitute a "device" in view of the valid business purpose for the spin-off, i.e., to permit a key employee to obtain a proprietary interest in the spun-off business.

The regulatory continuity of interest doctrine in the divisive distribution context never required that every stockholder in the distributing corporation maintain a continuing interest in each corporation surviving the division. A non-pro rata division may result in some of the stockholders of the divided corporation owning no interest at all in a business in which they were stockholders prior to the divisive reorganization.

The continuity of interest requirement of Treas.Reg. § 1.355–2(c) is satisfied in a divisive reorganization as long as one or more of the stockholders of the original corporation retain sufficient continuing interest in each of the divided corporations, but not necessarily in both. Thus, the regulations indicate that the continuity of interest requirement is satisfied in the following example: A and B own all of the stock of X Corporation. X in turn owns the stock of S Corporation. C acquires 49 percent of A's stock in X. Immediately thereafter, and as part of a prearranged plan, X distributes its S stock to B in exchange for B's stock in X. There is sufficient continuity of interest for nonrecognition treatment under § 355 since the former stockholders of X have a continuing interest in one of the businesses formerly undertaken by X. A has a 51 percent continuing interest in X, B has 100 percent continuing interest in S. Treas.Reg. § 1.355–2(c)(2), Ex. (2).[11]

Treas.Reg. § 1.355–2(c)(2), Exs. (3) and (4), further indicate that if C purchased all of A's X stock, or purchased 80 percent of A's X stock, before the division, continuity would not exist because the original stockholders of X would have an insufficient continuing interest in one of the two corporations following division. However, this result also is indirectly precluded by § 355(d), discussed at page 772, which was enacted after the examples in Treas.Reg. § 1.355–2(c)(2) were promulgated. Section 355(d) would require recognition of gain by the distributing corporation, X, on the distribution of S stock to B, because C acquired by purchase within the five-year period ending on the date of distribution stock representing a 50 percent interest in the distributing corporation immediately after the distribution. Section 355(d) thus indirectly creates a limited continuity of interest requirement with respect to corporate nonrecognition in certain circumstances.

DETAILED ANALYSIS

1.   THE DISTRIBUTION REQUIREMENT

1.1. *General*

In Redding v. Commissioner, 630 F.2d 1169 (7th Cir.1980), rev'g. 71 T.C. 597 (1979), the court was presented with a transaction similar to that before the Supreme Court in *Gordon*. In *Redding,* the parent corporation distributed transferable rights to its stockholders that enabled the stockholders to subscribe to shares of stock of the parent corporation's wholly owned subsidiary. The rights could be exercised only for a two-week period. A stockholder could receive one share of the subsidiary's stock for

---

[11]   The example in the regulations provides that B acquires 50% of A's stock. In that case, however, § 355(d)(3) would require recognition of gain by the distributing corporation, X, on distribution of stock to B.

two rights plus $5. During the two-week period the fair market value of the subsidiary's stock ranged from $5.70 per share to $7 per share. An over-the-counter market for the warrants developed during this subscription period. After the two-week period, the warrants became worthless. The IRS and the taxpayers stipulated that, as the result of the exercise of the stock rights, more than 80 percent of the subsidiary's stock was distributed in the offering. The parties stipulated further that there was a good business purpose for the distribution of the subsidiary stock, the distribution was not a device for the distribution of earnings and profits, and the 20 percent of the subsidiary's stock retained by the parent corporation was not held for tax avoidance purposes under § 355(a)(1)(D)(ii).

The IRS asserted that the rights distribution constituted a taxable dividend under § 301, relying on Rev.Rul. 70–521, 1970–2 C.B. 72, to that effect. The taxpayers, on the other hand, asserted that the transaction was an integrated transaction and qualified under § 355. The Tax Court held that the requirements of § 355(a)(1)(A) and (D) were met. The issuance of the rights by the distributing corporation "was merely a procedural device to give [the distributing corporation] stockholders the opportunity to be included or excluded from the [subsidiary] stock distribution." Having found that the distribution of the stock rights was "merely a brief transitory phase of the corporate separation," the Tax Court concluded that the requirements of § 355(a)(1)(A) and (D) were met. The requisite 80 percent of the subsidiary stock was in fact distributed and after the transaction the stockholders held only stock of the subsidiary.

The Court of Appeals disagreed with the Tax Court's finding that the issuance of the warrants was only a procedural step and concluded that the warrants had independent economic significance in light of their readily ascertainable market value and transferability on an open market. The issuance of the warrants could not, therefore, be disregarded as a mere transitory step in the distribution of the stock of the subsidiary to stockholders of the distributing corporation. The Court of Appeals concluded further that the distribution of the stock of the subsidiary failed the requirement of § 355(a)(1)(A) that the stock of the controlled corporation be distributed with respect to the stock of the distributing corporation. Since the warrants had independent significance, the distribution of the subsidiary's stock was made with respect to the warrants rather than the stock of the distributing corporation. The court held that the distribution of warrants was a dividend to the stockholders.[12]

Although it felt bound by the parties' stipulation that 80 percent control of the subsidiary was distributed to the stockholders of the distributing corporation, the Court of Appeals in *Redding* questioned whether the control requirement of § 355(a)(1)(D) was in fact satisfied. For valid business reasons the distributing corporation retained 1 share less than 20 percent of the subsidiary's stock. Fifty thousand shares of the subsidiary's stock were distributed to underwriters. The remaining shares distributed with respect to exercised warrants represented approximately 76 percent of the subsidiary's stock. The Court of Appeals read § 355(a)(1)(D) in conjunction with § 355(a)(1)(A) to require the distribution of control to persons who were the stockholders of the distributing

---

[12] Receipt of the warrants was not sheltered from dividend treatment under § 305 because the warrants did not represent rights to acquire the stock of the distributing corporation. 630 F.2d at 1181.

corporation before the division. That requirement was not satisfied in *Redding* because of the distribution of stock to the underwriters.

The IRS has indicated that it will use the step transaction doctrine to find a qualifying distribution in a § 355 transaction in appropriate cases. In Rev.Rul. 83–142, 1983–2 C.B. 68, a foreign subsidiary of a United States parent corporation distributed assets to a new subsidiary, the controlled corporation, in exchange for stock. To satisfy a requirement of the foreign country in which it was incorporated, the subsidiary sold the stock of the controlled corporation to its parent for cash. The subsidiary thereupon redistributed the cash to its parent as a dividend. The IRS held that the transfer of stock of the controlled corporation to the parent was a § 355 distribution by the subsidiary. The subsidiary's sale of stock and subsequent return of cash as a dividend were disregarded for Federal tax purposes as transitory steps taken for the purpose of complying with local law.

1.2. *Retention of Stock or Securities*

Section 355(a)(1)(D) permits the distributing corporation to retain some of the stock of the distributed corporation if it is established that the retention of the stock was not motivated by tax avoidance purposes. Treas.Reg. § 1.355–2(e)(2) warns, however, that ordinarily the corporate business purpose for a divisive reorganization will require the distribution of all the stock and securities of the controlled corporation. The IRS, in addition to examining whether there is a good business purpose for retention of any stock or securities, also looks to whether the retained stock gives the distributing corporation "practical control" over the spun-off corporation. See Rev.Rul. 75–321, 1975–2 C.B. 123 (pursuant to federal banking laws, distributing corporation was required to divest itself of at least 95 percent of the stock of a bank subsidiary; retention of a percent of the bank stock to use as collateral for short-term financing for the distributing corporation's remaining business enterprises was for a valid business purpose and the retained interest did not give the distributing corporation practical control); Rev.Rul. 75–469, 1975–2 C.B. 126 (stock of controlled corporation was pledged as collateral for bank loan; to eliminate dissident stockholders, the distributing corporation desired to spin-off the subsidiary's stock, but the bank required substitute collateral for the loan; debenture issued by the subsidiary to the parent, which was pledged to the bank to secure the loan, could be retained since it gave the distributing corporation no practical control over the spun-off corporation).

2.   CONTROL AND CONTINUITY OF INTEREST

Treas.Reg. § 1.355–2(c) requires as an independent qualification for nonrecognition under § 355 "that one or more persons who, directly or indirectly, were the owners of the enterprise prior to the distribution or exchange own, in the aggregate, an amount of stock establishing a continuity of interest in each of the modified corporate forms in which the enterprise is conducted after the separation." Two statutory provisions impact application of the continuity of interest rules.

First, § 368(a)(2)(H)(ii), enacted in 1998, provides that in determining whether a transfer of assets to a subsidiary prior to a distribution of stock qualifying under § 355 meets the requirements of § 368(a)(1)(D), the fact that the shareholders of the distributing corporation dispose of all or part of the stock of either the controlled corporation or the distributing corporation, or whether the controlled corporation issues additional stock, shall not be taken into account. This infers that a post-distribution sale or exchange of the stock of either corporation will not defeat either the control requirement and or the continuity of interest requirement for purposes of shielding the shareholders from recognition of gain under § 355(a).[13] Since a § 368(a)(1)(D) reorganization cannot occur without a subsequent distribution that qualifies under either § 354, which cannot occur in a divisive (D) reorganization, or § 355, the inference is that there is no requirement that the shareholders of the distributing corporation maintain any interest in the distributed corporation following the distribution.

Another wrinkle on the applicability of the continuity of interest requirement in Treas.Reg. § 1.355–2(c) was added by the enactment of § 355(d), (e) and (f) after promulgation of Treas.Reg. § 1.355–2(c). Sections 355(d), (e), and (f), discussed at pages 775 and 789, require recognition of gain by the distributing corporation in the case of pre- and post-distribution acquisitions of a 50 percent or greater interest in one of the corporations. Although these provisions do not directly affect recognition of gain or loss by the shareholders under § 355(a), the imposition of a recognition requirement on the distributing corporation in the case of a 50 percent ownership change by historic shareholders is in effect a statutory continuity of interest requirement for completely tax-free divisive restructuring.

The legislative history accompanying § 355(e) states as follows:

> The House bill does not change the present law requirement under section 355 that the distributing corporation must distribute 80 percent of the voting power and 80 percent of each other class of stock of the controlled corporation. It is expected that this requirement will be applied by the Internal Revenue Service taking account of the provisions of the proposal regarding plans that permit certain types of planned restructuring of the distributing corporation following the distribution, and to treat similar restructurings of the controlled corporation in a similar manner. Thus, the 80–percent control requirement is expected to be administered in a manner that would prevent the tax-free spin-off of a less-than-80-percent controlled subsidiary, but would not generally impose additional restrictions on post-distribution restructurings of the controlled corporation if such restrictions would not apply to the distributing corporation.

H.R.Rep. No. 105–220, at 529–30 (1997). In Rev.Rul. 98–27, 1998–1 C.B. 1159, the IRS interpreted this language as follows:

> [T]he Service will not apply *Court Holding* [324 U.S. 331 (1945)] (or any formulation of the step transaction doctrine) to determine whether the distributed corporation was a controlled corporation immediately before the distribution under § 355(a) solely because of any post distribution acquisition or restructuring of the distributed corporation, whether prearranged or not. In otherwise applying the step transaction doctrine, the Service will continue to consider all facts and circumstances. See, e.g.,

---

[13] This result is reinforced by § 351(c), which is the same effect as § 368(a)(2)(H)(ii), regardless of whether the subsequent stock distribution qualifies under § 355 or is controlled by another section.

Rev.Rul. 63–260, 1963–2 C.B. 147. An independent shareholder vote is only one relevant factor to be considered.

It is unclear whether this statement means that the IRS believes that there no longer is any post-distribution continuity of interest requirement, apart from the "device" and business purpose tests, that must be satisfied in order to qualify for § 355 treatment. But at first blush, it appears to be difficult to understand how the enactment of § 355(e), which affects only the treatment of the distributing corporation under § 355(a) and (c), could be interpreted to eliminate a requirement for qualifying the shareholders for nonrecognition under § 355(a).

However, the legislative history of the 1998 amendments to §§ 351(c)(2) and 368(a)(2)(H)(ii), which are related to the enactment of § 355(e) the prior year, also infers that there no longer should be any shareholder continuity of interest requirement imposed with respect to § 355 transactions. S.Rep. No. 105–174, 105th Cong., 2d Sess. (1998) describes the 1998 amendments as follows:

> [I]n the case of certain divisive transactions in which a corporation contributes assets to a controlled corporation and then distributes the stock of the controlled corporation in a transaction that meets the requirements of section 355 (or so much of section 356 as relates to section 355), solely for purposes of determining the tax treatment of the transfers of property to the controlled corporation by the distributing corporation, the fact that the shareholders of the distributing corporation dispose of part or all of the distributed stock shall not be taken into account for purposes of the control immediately after requirement of section 351(a) or 368(a)(1)(D). For purposes of determining the tax treatment of transfers of property to the controlled corporation by parties other than the distributing corporation, the disposition of part or all of the distributed stock continues to be taken into account, as under prior law, in determining whether the control immediately after requirement is satisfied.

> *Example 1*: Distributing corporation D transfers appreciated business X to subsidiary C in exchange for 100 percent of C stock. D distributes its stock of C to D shareholders. As part of a plan or series of related transactions, C merges into unrelated acquiring corporation A, and the C shareholders receive 25 percent of the vote or value of A stock. If the requirements of section 355 are met with respect to the distribution, then the control immediately after requirement will be satisfied solely for purposes of determining the tax treatment of the transfers of property by D to C. Accordingly, the business X assets transferred to C and held by A after the merger will have a carryover basis from D. Section 355(e) will require D to recognize gain as if the C stock had been sold at fair market value.

> *Example 2*: Distributing corporation D transfers appreciated business X to subsidiary C in exchange for 85 percent of C stock. Unrelated persons transfer appreciated assets to C in exchange for the remaining 15 percent of C stock. D distributes all its stock of C to D shareholders. As part of a plan or series of related

transactions, C merges into acquiring corporation A; and the interests attributable to the D shareholders' receipt of C stock with respect to their D stock in the distribution represent 25 percent of the vote and value of A stock. If the requirements of section 355 are met with respect to the distribution, then the control immediately after requirement will satisfied solely for purposes of determining the tax treatment of the transfers of property by D to C. Section 355(e) will require recognition of gain as if the C stock had been sold for fair market value. The business X assets transferred to C and held by A after the merger will have a carryover basis from D. The persons other than D who transferred assets to C for 15 percent of C stock will recognize gain on the appreciation in their assets transferred to C if the control immediately after requirement is not satisfied after taking into account any post spin-off dispositions that would have been taken into account under prior law.

Example 3: The facts are the same as in example 2, except that the interests attributable to the D shareholders' receipt of C stock with respect to their D stock in the distribution represent 55 percent of the vote and value of A stock in the merger. If the requirements of section 355 are met with respect to the distribution, then the control immediately after requirement will be satisfied solely for purposes of determining the tax treatment of the transfers by D to C. The business X assets in C (and in A after the merger) will therefore have a carryover basis from D. Because the D shareholders retain more than 50 percent of the stock of A, section 355(e) will not apply. The persons other than D who transferred property for the 15 percent of C stock will recognize gain on the appreciation in their assets transferred to C if the control immediately after requirement is not satisfied after taking into account any post-spin-off dispositions that would have been taken into account under prior law.

Although the introductory paragraph of the legislative history quoted above refers only to the impact of the amendments with respect to the treatment of the transfer of assets to the controlled subsidiary, the examples presume that a post-distribution disposition of the stock received in the spin-off does not necessarily destroy the § 355 treatment of the distribution by the shareholders even though the shareholders who received the distribution do not indirectly retain a majority interest in the distributed corporation. If this is so, the continuity of interest requirement in Treas.Reg. § 1.355–2(c) has been *sub silentio* repealed with respect to the controlled corporation.

To treat Treas.Reg. § 1.368–2(c) as having been effectively repealed by events subsequent to its promulgation is also consistent with the 1998 revisions to the continuity of interest requirement in Treas.Reg. § 1.368–1(e)(1) applicable to acquisitive reorganizations, discussed at page 559. Treas.Reg. § 1.368–1(e)(1) provides that "a mere disposition of stock of the target corporation prior to a potential reorganization . . . and a mere disposition of stock of the issuing corporation received in a potential reorganization . . . is disregarded."[14] If "continuity of interest" has the same meaning under Treas.Reg. § 1.368–2(c) as it does under Treas.Reg. § 1.368–1(e)(1), neither a pre-distribution nor a post-distribution sale or exchange of the stock of either the distributing corporation or the controlled corporation should affect the application of § 355(a) to the shareholders if all of the other conditions of § 355 have been met. Nevertheless, such transactions could result in recognition to the distributing corporation under § 355(d) or (e).

There are no authorities directly applying the Treas.Reg. § 1.355–2(c) continuity of interest provision since its promulgation. Some rulings issued before the current regulations were promulgated illustrate the historic application of the continuity of interest requirement under § 355. These authorities have any current relevance only if the Treas.Reg. § 1.355–2(c) continuity of interest requirement has survived the enactment of §§ 355(e) and 368(a)(2)(H)(ii) and the 1998 revisions to the continuity of interest requirement in Treas.Reg. § 1.368–1(e)(1) applicable to acquisitive reorganizations.

A number of authorities pre-dating the 1997 and 1998 statutory revisions addressed continuity of interest in the context of post-distribution dispositions of stock of the distributing or controlled corporations. Commissioner v. Morris Trust, 367 F.2d 794 (4th Cir.1966), discussed at page 746, held that a post-distribution tax-free reorganization of the distributing corporation in which its shareholders received a majority of the stock of the surviving corporation did not invalidate a § 355 transaction. On the other hand, in Rev.Rul. 79–273, 1979–2 C.B. 125, continuity of interest was found lacking where P Corporation distributed the stock of its subsidiary to P stockholders as part of a reverse cash merger in which P was acquired by an unrelated corporation. Since the former P stockholders had no continuing interest in P, the distribution of S stock to the P stockholders did not qualify for nonrecognition treatment under § 355.

A result similar to that in Rev.Rul. 79–273 was reached on different reasoning in Rev.Rul. 70–225, 1970–1 C.B. 80, obsoleted by Rev.Rul. 98–44, 1998–2 C.B. 315. In Rev.Rul. 70–225, the IRS held that an attempted post-distribution (B) reorganization involving the stock of the controlled subsidiary defeated nonrecognition treatment because of the control requirement of § 368(a)(1)(D). T Corporation desired to acquire one of two businesses of R Corporation. Pursuant to a prearranged plan, R Corporation transferred the assets of the desired business to a newly created subsidiary and then distributed the stock of the subsidiary to its sole stockholder. The stockholder then immediately exchanged the stock of the subsidiary for stock of T Corporation in an attempted (B) reorganization. The spin-off failed because the stockholder did not acquire control of the distributed corporation. The transaction was treated in effect as a transfer by R Corporation of part of its assets in exchange for stock of T Corporation, followed by a distribution of the T Corporation stock as a dividend to the sole stockholder of R Corporation. The result in Rev.Rul. 70–225 appears to have been reversed by the 1998 amendment to § 368(a)(2)(H)(ii), which led the IRS to declare Rev.Rul. 70–225 and Rev.Rul. 96–30 obsolete. Rev.Rul. 98–27, 1998–1 C.B. 1159, supra. On the other hand, Rev.Rul. 75–406, 1975–2 C.B. 125, modified by Rev.Rul. 96–30,

---

[14]   However, the disposition cannot be to a person related to the acquirer or the issuer.

1996–1 C.B. 36, held that a spin-off prior to the merger of the distributing corporation into another corporation was a valid § 355 transaction as long as the shareholders were free to vote either for or against the merger after the spin-off.

Rev.Rul. 69–293, 1969–1 C.B. 102, disqualified a putative § 355 distribution for lack of continuity of interest where two stockholders who owned all of the stock of a private university spun off a subsidiary trade school and then converted the distributing corporation into a § 501(c)(3) organization in order to qualify for federal financial aid; the stockholders' proprietary interests were converted into non-proprietary interests and the requisite continuity of interests was therefore lacking.

On the other hand, in Rev.Rul. 62–138, 1962–2 C.B. 95, regulatory authorities required the subsidiary of a bank to divest itself of two apartment buildings that it owned. The subsidiary transferred the two apartment buildings to a new corporation and distributed the stock of that corporation to the bank, which in turn distributed the stock to its stockholders. The required continuity of interest was found to exist. See also Rev.Rul. 70–18, 1970–1 C.B. 74 (A, an individual, owned 100 percent of the stock of X and Y Corporations; Y Corporation owned 60 percent and X Corporation owned 40 percent of Z Corporation; Y Corporation was required to divest itself of its interest in Z Corporation; Y Corporation merged into X Corporation, which then distributed all of the Z stock to A; continuity of interest was satisfied under these circumstances); Rev.Rul. 76–528, 1976–2 C.B. 103 (continuity of interest requirement satisfied despite pre-split-up dissolution of partnership that owned 60 percent of the stock of the distributing corporation).

3.   COMPARISON WITH PARTIAL LIQUIDATIONS

Apart from the principal focus of § 355 as preventing a corporate bail-out of earnings and profits, § 355 is significant with respect to the question of recognition of corporate level gain on appreciated assets when there is a change of ownership. A comparison of the tax treatment of the spin-off or split-off of a trade or business under § 355 with the tax consequence of the distribution of a trade or business to stockholders in a partial liquidation under § 302(b)(4), page 261, is illustrative. Both transactions involve the distribution of a trade or business with a five-year history. If appreciated property is distributed to stockholders in a partial liquidation, gain is recognized at both the corporate and stockholder levels. However, under § 355, if the distributed trade or business is housed in a corporation, no gain or loss is recognized at either level. This different treatment is justified in a § 355 transaction by the stockholders' continued interest in business assets that remain in corporate solution. The double tax regime is protected because gain or loss will ultimately be recognized at the stockholder and corporate levels on disposition of the stock and assets, respectively. A distribution in partial liquidation removes the business assets from corporate solution thus eliminating the opportunity for future taxation of corporate level appreciation. See Simon and Simmons, The Future of Section 355, 40 Tax Notes 291, 296–7 (1988).

SECTION 4.   CONSEQUENCES TO PARTIES TO A CORPORATE DIVISION

INTERNAL REVENUE CODE: Sections 355(a)(1), (2), (c); 361(c); 368(a)(1)(D), (2)(A), (2)(H)(ii); 354(b); 356(a) and (b); 358(a)–(c); 312(h).

REGULATIONS: Sections 1.356–1, –2; 1.358–1(a), –2(a), (c), Ex. 13.

As noted previously, if the conditions of § 355 have been met, § 355(a) provides nonrecognition to the shareholders upon receipt of the stock of the controlled corporation. Pursuant to § 358, the shareholders take a transferred basis in the stock of the distributed corporation. If the shareholder continues to hold stock of the distributing corporation, as well as holding stock of the controlled corporation after the distribution, the shareholder's basis in the stock of the distributing corporation immediately prior to the distribution (as adjusted for gain recognition and the receipt of boot) is apportioned between the basis of the stock in the distributing and controlled corporation held immediately after the distribution in proportion to fair market value.

Subject to a number of special exceptions, the distributing corporation also is entitled to nonrecognition of gain on the distribution of the stock of the controlled subsidiary, § 311(b) (and § 336) being displaced by one of two operative nonrecognition provisions. Section 355(c) provides nonrecognition to the distributing corporation with respect to the stock of the controlled corporation if the controlled corporation that is distributed is a pre-existing subsidiary to which assets were not transferred in a § 368(a)(1)(D) reorganization prior to the distribution. If the distribution is preceded by a transfer of assets from the distributing corporation to the controlled corporation in a § 368(a)(1)(D) reorganization, then § 361(c) generally provides nonrecognition for the distributing corporation. If, however, prior to a distribution otherwise qualifying under § 355, the distributing corporation transfers property to the controlled corporation and the controlled corporation assumes liabilities of the distributing corporation in excess of the basis of the transferred assets, § 357(c) applies to require recognition of gain to the distributing corporation on the asset transfer, even though the transfer might be classified as a § 368(a)(1)(D) reorganization rather than as a § 351 transfer.[15]

DETAILED ANALYSIS

1.   BOOT IN A SECTION 355 TRANSACTION

1.1. *Distributions of Cash or Other Property*

The shareholder nonrecognition rule of § 355(a) is limited to the distribution of stock or securities of the controlled corporation, or the exchange of stock or securities solely for stock or securities of the controlled corporation. However, § 356 allows for the receipt of cash or other property (including the receipt of securities in excess of the securities transferred)

---

[15] Note that § 357(c) does not apply to an asset transfer accompanied by an assumption of liabilities in excess of basis in a § 368(a)(1)(D) reorganization that qualifies by virtue of a distribution by the transferor corporation of transferee corporation stock that meets the requirements of § 354, discussed at page 651.

with the recognition of gain to the extent of the boot. In the case of a non-pro rata split-off, which involves an exchange by the shareholder of the distributing corporation's shares for the controlled corporation's shares, § 356(a)(2) provides for ordinary income treatment of recognized gain to the extent of the distributee's pro rata share of earnings and profits if the distribution is essentially equivalent to a dividend. Rev.Rul. 93–62, 1993–2 C.B. 118, requires that the distribution of boot be tested for dividend equivalency under § 302 as if the boot were distributed prior to the divisive transaction in redemption of an amount of stock of the distributing corporation equal to the value of the boot. If, however, the distribution does not involve an exchange, as would be the case in a pro rata spin-off, § 356(b) provides that any boot will be treated as a distribution under § 301. In that case, since there has been no exchange, the amount of the dividend is not limited to gain realized on the exchange of stock of the distributing corporation for stock of the controlled corporation plus boot.

1.2. *Stock of the Controlled Corporation as Boot*

Section 355(a)(3)(B) provides that stock of the controlled corporation that has been acquired by the distributing corporation in a taxable transaction within the five-year period preceding distribution to stockholders will be treated as other property taxable to the stockholders as boot.

Trust of E.L. Dunn v. Commissioner, 86 T.C. 745 (1986) (Acq. in result), narrowly interpreted the meaning of "acquired" in a taxable transaction. In a taxable reverse triangular merger consummated on May 12, 1982, AT&T acquired all of the stock of Pacific Telephone and Telegraph with the exception of nonvoting preferred stock held by institutional investors. Following this transaction, AT&T owned the only share of Pacific common stock outstanding. The reverse triangular merger was a taxable transaction because, by virtue of the outstanding nonvoting preferred stock, AT&T did not meet the control requirement of § 368(c). On August 24, 1982, a long standing antitrust action between AT&T and the United States government was settled with a judicially approved agreement that AT&T would divest itself of each of its regional telephone operating companies, including Pacific. At that time, AT&T was the common parent of a group of corporations known as the Bell System. The divestiture plan required AT&T to group its 22 operating companies into seven regional holding companies. The stock of the regional holding companies was distributed to AT&T stockholders pro rata. As part of this plan, Pacific was reorganized under § 368(a)(1)(E) to convert the single share of Pacific stock held by AT&T into 224,504,982 shares of voting common stock (the number of shares outstanding before AT&T's taxable reorganization of Pacific) and to convert the nonvoting preferred stock into voting preferred stock. By virtue of this transaction the holding company to which Pacific was transferred, the PacTel Group, would acquire control of Pacific within the meaning of § 368(c). AT&T transferred its Pacific stock along with other assets to the PacTel Group in exchange for all of the stock of the PacTel Group, which was then distributed to AT&T stockholders in the divestiture.

The IRS asserted that the receipt of PacTel Group stock was taxable in part to the AT&T stockholders as a dividend under § 355(a)(3)(B) because a portion of the value of the PacTel Group stock represented the stock of Pacific that was acquired by AT&T in a taxable merger within five years of the distribution. The Tax Court rejected the IRS's argument and held that the distribution was completely tax-free to the AT&T stockholders. The court read § 355(a)(3)(B) literally, concluding that the provision applied only to the stock of the controlled corporation that is distributed to the stockholders of the distributing corporation. The controlled corporation is the corporation that the distributing corporation controls immediately before the distribution. The Tax Court refused to look through the controlled corporation, in this case the PacTel Group, to examine the stock of its subsidiaries for purposes of applying the boot rule of § 355(a)(3)(B). The court reasoned in part that since Congress carefully provided a look-through rule for purposes of identifying under § 355(b)(2)(D) whether a trade or business had been acquired "directly (or through 1 or more corporations)" in a taxable transaction by the controlled corporation, Congress would have specifically provided a similar look-through rule in subdivision (a)(3)(B) if it had intended such a rule to be applied.

As amended in 2011, Treas.Reg. § 1.355–2(g), conforms the "hot stock" rule of § 355(a)(3)(B) to the 2005 amendments of § 355(b)(3) (discussed at page 734) that treat a "separate affiliated group" (SAG) as a single corporation for purposes of determining whether the active trade or business requirements of § 355 have been met. The regulations generally provide that the hot stock rule does not apply to any acquisition of stock of the controlled corporation where the controlled corporation is a member of the separate affiliated group of the distributing corporation (DSAG) at any time after the acquisition (but prior to the distribution of controlled). Taxable transfers of controlled corporation stock owned by DSAG members immediately before and immediately after the transfer are disregarded and are not treated as acquisitions for purposes of the hot stock rule. The amended regulations also contain the exception of the prior version of Treas.Reg. § 1.355–2(g), which provides that the hot stock rule does not apply to acquisitions of controlled corporation stock by the distributing corporation from a member of the affiliated group (as defined in Treas.Reg. § 1.355–3(b)(4)(iii)) of which the distributing corporation was a member.

2.   SHAREHOLDER BASIS ISSUES

Pursuant to § 358(b)(2) and Treas.Reg. § 1.358–1(a) and –2(a)(2)(iv), in a spin-off in which shareholders of the distributing corporation receive a distribution of stock in the controlled corporation without surrendering any stock of the distributing corporation, each shareholder allocates the original basis of the shareholder's stock of the distributing corporation between the stock of the controlled corporation received in the distribution and the retained stock of the distributing corporation in proportion to the respective fair market values of the stockholdings *after* the distribution. Suppose, for example, that A owned 100 shares of X Corporation, with a basis of $1,000 and a fair market value of $5,000. A received 50 shares of Y Corporation in a spin-off. After the distribution, A's 100 shares of X Corporation had a fair market value of $2,000 and A's 50 shares of Y Corporation had a fair market value of $3,000. A's basis in the 100 shares of X Corporation is $400 ($1,000 × $2,000/($3,000 + $2,000)); A's basis in the 50 shares of Y Corporation is $600 ($1,000 × $3,000/($3,000 + $2,000)).

If the shareholder holds two or more blocks of stock acquired at different times or for different prices, then the basis of each share of stock of the distributing corporation will be allocated between the share of stock of the distributing corporation and the share of stock received with respect to that share of stock of the distributing corporation in proportion to their fair market values. For an example of the application of this rule, see Treas.Reg. § 1.358–2(c), Ex. 13. If one share of stock is received in respect of more than one share of stock or a fraction of a share of stock is received, the basis of each share of stock or security of the distributing corporation must be allocated to the shares of stock or securities received in a manner that reflects, to the greatest extent possible, that a share of stock or security received is received in respect of shares of stock or securities acquired on the same date and at the same price.

In a non-pro rata split-off subject to § 355 involving a complete redemption of a shareholder's interest in the distributing corporation, § 358(a) provides the shareholder an exchanged basis (increased by any gain or dividends recognized pursuant to § 356 and reduced by the amount of any boot received) in the shares of the controlled corporation received in the exchange. Suppose, for example, B owned 100 shares of Z Corporation, with a basis of $5,000, and B received 400 shares of W Corporation in a complete redemption of B's Z Corporation stock pursuant to a split-off governed by § 355. B's basis in the 400 shares of W Corporation is $5,000. Treas.Reg. § 1.355–2(a)(2)(ii) provides that the basis of each share of stock received in the exchange is the same as the basis of the share or shares of stock (or allocable portions thereof) exchanged, as adjusted for gain under Treas.Reg. § 1.358–1. If more than one share of stock is received in exchange for one share of stock, the basis of the share of stock surrendered is allocated among the shares of stock received in the exchange in proportion to the fair market value of the shares of stock received. If one share of stock or security is received in respect of more than one share of stock or security or a fraction of a share of stock or security is received, the basis of each share of stock or security of the distributing corporation must be allocated to the shares of stock or securities received in a manner that reflects, to the greatest extent possible, that a share of stock or security received is received in respect of shares of stock or securities acquired on the same date and at the same price. The regulations provide more detailed rules for situations in which a share of stock is received in exchange for more than one share of stock (or a fraction of a share of stock is received).

The same principles control in a non-pro rata split-off subject to § 355 that involves less than a complete redemption of a shareholder's interest in the distributing corporation. Section § 358(a) provides the shareholder an exchanged basis (increased by any gain or dividends recognized pursuant to § 356 and reduced by the amount of any boot received) in the shares of the controlled corporation received in the exchange. Suppose, for example, C owned 200 shares of Q Corporation, with a basis of $6,000, and C received 300 shares of V Corporation in redemption of 150 of C's 200 shares of Q Corporation stock pursuant to a split-off governed by § 355. C's basis in the 300 shares of V Corporation should be $4,500 ($6,000 × 150/200); C's basis in the remaining 50 shares of Q Corporation should be $1,500 ($6,000 × 50/200).

If in a split-off a shareholder surrenders a share of stock in the distributing corporation in exchange for stock of more than one class of the distributing corporation, or receives money or other boot in addition to stock, then, to the extent the plan specifies that shares of stock of a particular class or boot is received in exchange for a particular share of stock, the terms of the plan control, provided the terms are economically reasonable. If the plan does not specify the exchange, a pro rata portion of the shares of each class of controlled corporation stock received and a pro rata portion of the boot shall be treated as received in exchange for each share of stock surrendered, based on the fair market value of the stock surrendered. Treas.Reg. § 1.355–2(a)(2)(ii).

3. EXCHANGES OF OPTIONS TO PURCHASE STOCK OF DISTRIBUTING AND CONTROLLED CORPORATION

Treas. Regs. §§ 1.355–1(c) and 1.356–3(b) treat rights to acquire stock of a corporation (options and warrants) issued by either the distributing corporation or the controlled corporation as securities of the respective corporations having no principal amount. The term "rights to acquire stock" of an issuing corporation has the same meaning for purposes of §§ 355 and 356 as for purposes of §§ 305(d)(1) and 317(a). Accordingly, as long as the other requirements of § 355, particularly the "distribution" of stock constituting "control" of the distributed corporation, have been met, the recipient of stock rights in either corporation is not required to recognize gain under § 356(d)(2)(B). Thus, for example, a shareholder of the distributing corporation who surrenders stock in the distributing corporation for stock of the controlled corporation in a split-off and also exchanges options to purchase stock of the distributing corporation in exchange for options to purchase stock of the controlled corporation does not recognize any gain or loss on the exchange of options. Likewise, nonrecognition is available in the case of a split-up of a corporation having outstanding options, which must be replaced by options to purchase stock of the distributed corporations. Rights exercisable against persons other than the issuer of the stock are not covered by Treas.Reg. § 1.355–1(c).

4. RECOGNITION OF GAIN BY THE DISTRIBUTING CORPORATION

4.1. *Distributions of Property*

Generally, under § 361(b) the distributing corporation can avoid recognition of gain with respect to money or other property received from the controlled corporation in a § 368(a)(1)(D) reorganization that precedes a § 355 divisive transaction as long as the money or other property is distributed pursuant to the plan of reorganization. Section 361(b)(3) also permits a corporation that is a party to a reorganization to avoid recognition on the receipt of boot if the money or other property is transferred to the creditors of the distributing corporation. However, the last sentence of § 361(b)(3) requires recognition of gain on the transfer of money or other property to creditors by the distributing corporation to the extent that the amount of money and the fair market value of the distributed property exceeds the basis of assets transferred to the controlled corporation.

The recognition rule applicable to distributions to creditors is necessary to prevent avoidance of the otherwise required gain recognition under § 357(c) applicable to a § 368(a)(1)(D) reorganization qualified for nonrecognition under § 355. For example, assume that D transfers assets with a basis of $100 and subject to a liability of $150 to C in a transaction meeting the requirements of § 368(a)(1)(D), and D distributes the C stock to D's shareholders in a transaction that meets the requirements of § 355. Section 357(c) would require D to recognize $50 of gain. Instead of transferring the assets subject to the liability, D causes C to borrow $150 which C distributes to D along with C stock. D distributes the $150 to creditors to pay the liability. Thus, C does not assume any liabilities subject to § 357(c). However, under § 361(b)(3), D is required to recognize the $50 gain triggered by the receipt of boot in excess of the basis of the transferred assets.

4.2. *Distributions of Appreciated Property as Boot*

Under either § 355(c) or § 361(c), whichever may be applicable, the distributing corporation must recognize gain on the distribution of appreciated property as boot. The statute requires recognition of gain with respect to the distribution of any property with a fair market value in excess of basis that is not "qualified property." Qualified property is limited to stock or securities of the controlled corporation. I.R.C. § 355(c)(2)(B). Gain is recognized as if the nonqualified property were sold to the distributee for its fair market value. If the distributed property is subject to liabilities (or liabilities are assumed by the distributee), the fair market value of distributed property is deemed to be at least the amount of the liabilities. I.R.C. § 355(c)(2)(C).

4.3. *Stockholder's Disqualified Stock*

Section 355(d) requires recognition of gain by the distributing corporation (but not the stockholder) on all of the stock of the controlled corporation distributed in a transaction that otherwise qualifies under § 355 if *any* stockholder holds "disqualified stock." See Treas.Reg. § 1.355–6(b)(4)(ii), Ex. The shareholders receiving the distribution, including the shareholder holding the disqualified stock, nevertheless are entitled to nonrecognition under § 355(a). A stockholder holds disqualified stock if immediately after the distribution the stockholder holds stock that constitutes either (1) a 50 percent or greater interest in the distributing corporation acquired by purchase within the five-year period ending on the date of the distribution, or (2) a 50 percent or greater interest in the controlled corporation that was received as a distribution on stock of the distributing corporation that was purchased within the five-year period. I.R.C. § 355(d)(3). An acquisition by purchase is generally defined as any acquisition in which the basis of the stock in the hands of the acquiring stockholder is not determined by reference to its basis in the hands of the transferor. I.R.C. § 355(d)(5)(A). However, acquisition by purchase includes the acquisition of stock in a § 351 exchange to the extent that the stock is acquired in exchange for cash, marketable securities, or debt of the transferor. In the case of a transferred basis acquisition from a person who acquired the stock by purchase, the five-year period begins with the date of purchase by the person transferring the stock to the stockholder. The five-year period is suspended during any period in which the holder's risk of loss is substantially diminished by an arrangement such as an option, short sale, a special class of stock or any other such device or transaction. I.R.C. § 355(c)(6).

The legislative history explains that the purpose of these provisions is to prevent avoidance of corporate level tax in a manner that is inconsistent with repeal of the *General Utilities* doctrine by precluding acquisition of a corporate subsidiary by an individual purchaser, or a corporate purchaser who acquires less than 80 percent of the stock of the parent corporation, without recognition of gain by the selling parent corporation. H.R.Rep. No. 101–882, 101st Cong., 2d Sess. 90–92 (1990).

For the myriad of complex technical details regarding application of § 355(d), see Treas.Reg. § 1.355–6. The regulations indicate that a distribution will not be treated as a disqualified distribution under § 355(d)(2) if the distribution and any related transactions do not violate the purpose of § 355(d). Distributions that do not violate that purpose are described as distributions that neither increase direct or indirect ownership in the distributing corporation or any controlled corporation by a disqualified person, nor provide a disqualified person with a cost basis in the stock of any controlled corporation. Treas.Reg. § 1.355–6(b)(3)(i). For an example of a distribution and related transactions that do not violate the purpose of § 355(d), see Treas.Reg. § 1.355–6(b)(3)(vi), Ex. 1.

4.4. *Post-Distribution Dispositions of Distributee Corporation*

Sections 355(e) and (f) require corporate level recognition of gain with respect to the stock of the controlled distributee corporation if pursuant to a plan or arrangement in connection with a corporate division there is a change of ownership of a 50 percent or greater interest of either the distributing corporation or the controlled corporation. In such cases, the distributing corporation generally must recognize gain as if the stock of the controlled corporation had been sold for fair market value on the date of distribution. (If the distributee corporation was formed in a § 368(a)(1)(D) reorganization in contemplation of the distribution, § 368(a)(2)(H)(ii) preserves the tax-free status of that transaction for the asset transfer from D to C, thus assuring that the assets retain a transferred basis, even if the controlling corporation's shareholders dispose of the stock of the distributed corporation in a transaction subject to § 355(e).) Acquisitions occurring within two years before or after the date of the distribution are presumed to have occurred pursuant to a plan or arrangement. If, however, a divisive distribution of stock is from one member of an affiliated group of corporations (as defined in § 1504(a)) to another member of the group, e.g., S1 distributes the stock of its subsidiary, S2 to S1's parent, P, § 355(f) provides that § 355 does not apply at all if the distribution is part of a plan or series of related transactions pursuant to which a 50 percent or greater interest in the distributing corporation or controlled corporation will be transferred to new owners. The effects of § 355(e) and (f) are discussed in Section 5 of this Chapter.

5.   TREATMENT OF CORPORATE ATTRIBUTES

5.1. *Earnings and Profits*

Section 381, which provides for the carryover of corporate attributes (including earnings and profits) in certain reorganizations and liquidations, discussed in Chapter 15, is not applicable to a corporate division under § 355. However, § 312(h) provides that the earnings and profits of the two corporations must be allocated as provided in regulations. In the case of a § 355 transaction that is a § 368(a)(1)(D) reorganization with a newly created controlled corporation, earnings and profits are allocated between the distributing corporation and the controlled corporation in proportion to the fair market value of assets transferred to the controlled corporation. In the case of a divisive type (D) reorganization involving the transfer of trade or business assets to an existing controlled corporation, earnings and profits may be allocated with respect to the relative net bases of assets transferred to the controlled corporation and assets retained by the distributing corporation, or by some other appropriate method. Treas.Reg. § 1.312–10(a).

In a § 355 division that involves an existing controlled corporation and thus is not a type (D) reorganization, the earnings and profits of the distributing corporation are decreased by the lesser of the amount by which earnings and profits would be decreased by allocating earnings and profits to the controlled corporation in proportion to the value of the stock of the controlled corporation as if the stock were a newly created corporation under the rules of Treas.Reg. § 1.312–10(a), or in an amount equal to the net worth of the controlled corporation. If the earnings and profits of the controlled corporation immediately before the transaction are less than the decrease of earnings and profits of the distributing corporation, the earnings and profits of the controlled corporation after the transaction will be the same as the amount of the decrease of earnings and profits to the distribution corporation. If the earnings and profits of the controlled corporation are greater than the amount of the decrease, the earnings and profits of the controlled corporation are not changed. Treas.Reg. § 1.312–10(b).

5.2. *Net Operating Losses*

The treatment of net operating loss carryovers in a § 355 transaction is discussed in Rev.Rul. 77–133, 1977–1 C.B. 96. In a split-off under § 355, M Corporation transferred assets constituting a business to S, a newly formed corporation, and distributed all of the S stock to one of M's two stockholders in exchange for all of stockholder's M stock. The IRS held that no part of M's net operating loss carryover was transferred to S in the split-off but that M could continue to use its loss carryover. However, where the transaction is a split-up under § 355 in which the loss corporation transfers separate businesses to each of two new corporations and distributes the stock of each corporation to different stockholders in complete liquidation, Rev.Rul. 56–373, 1956–2 C.B. 217, held that neither of the successor corporations can take advantage of the distributing corporation's unused net operating loss carryover. The ruling concluded that because all of the assets of the distributing corporation were transferred to two corporations, the type (D) reorganization is not a transaction described by § 354(b)(1) and therefore was not subject to attribute carryover under § 381(a)(2). Thus the survival of net operating loss carryovers in a divisive type (D) reorganization depends upon whether the transaction is structured as a split-off or a split-up, even though the economic results of the two transactions may be identical.

The limitations on net operating loss carryovers of § 382, discussed in Chapter 15, will apply to unused net operating loss carryovers that survive a split-off as described in Rev.Rul. 77–133 if the continuing stockholders of the loss corporation increase their ownership interest by more than 50 percentage points.

SECTION 5.   DIVISIVE DISTRIBUTIONS IN CONNECTION WITH ACQUISITIONS

INTERNAL REVENUE CODE: Sections 351(c)(2), 355(e), (f); 368(a)(2)(H)(ii).

As is evident from the preceding material, a source of continuing tension has been whether, and the extent to which, tax-free treatment under § 355 is warranted in the case of a divisive transaction prior to and in contemplation of a subsequent acquisition (whether by taxable purchase or tax-free reorganization) of either the distributing or distributed corporation. Generally speaking, a prearranged spin-off of the corporation to be acquired was denied § 355 nonrecognition. On the other hand, as illustrated by Commissioner v. Morris Trust, page 746, a spin-off followed by a merger in which the distributing corporation's shareholders retained more than 50 percent of the merged entity could be tax-free under § 355. The controversial issue was whether a corporation that was the target of an acquisition could be "customized" by spinning-off to its pre-acquisition shareholders the stock of a subsidiary that the acquiring corporation did not want to acquire. Nevertheless, a number of highly publicized transactions of this nature in the mid-1990s led to congressional concerns that "customizing" tax-free spin-offs were inappropriate, and Congress responded to this issue in 1997 by enacting §§ 355(e) and (f).

General Explanation of Tax Legislation Enacted in 1997

Staff of the Joint Committee on Taxation, 197–203, 205 (1997).

2. Require Gain Recognition on Certain Distributions of Controlled Corporation Stock (Sec. 1012 of the Act and Secs. 355, 358, 351(c), and 368(a)(2)(H) of the Code)

Prior Law

A corporation generally is required to recognize gain on the distribution of property (including stock of a subsidiary) as if such property had been sold for its fair market value. The shareholders generally treat the receipt of property as a taxable event as well. Section 355 of the Internal Revenue Code provides an exception to this rule for certain "spin-off" type distributions of stock of a controlled corporation, provided that various requirements are met, including certain restrictions relating to acquisitions and dispositions of stock of the distributing corporation ("distributing") or the controlled corporation ("controlled") prior and subsequent to a distribution.

In cases where the form of the transaction involves a contribution of assets to the particular controlled corporation that is distributed in connection with the distribution, there are specific Code requirements that distributing corporation's shareholders own "control" of the corporation immediately after the distribution. Control is defined for this purpose as 80 percent of the voting power of all classes of stock entitled to vote and 80 percent of each other class of stock (secs. 368(a)(1)(D), 368(c), and 351(a) and (c)). In addition, it is a requirement for qualification of any section 355 distribution that the distributing corporation distribute control of the controlled corporation (defined by reference to the same 80–percent test). [Pre-1997] law has the effect of imposing more restrictive requirements on certain types of acquisitions or other transfers following a distribution if the company acquired is the controlled corporation rather than the distributing corporation.

* * *

Reasons for Change

The Congress believed that section 355 was intended to permit the tax-free division of existing business arrangements among existing shareholders. In cases in which it is intended that new shareholders will acquire ownership of a business in connection with a spin-off, the transaction more closely resembles a corporate level disposition of the portion of the business that is acquired.

The Congress also believed that the difference in treatment of certain transactions following a spin-off, depending upon whether the distributing or controlled corporation engages in the transaction, should be minimized.

* * *

Explanation of Provision

The Act adopts additional restrictions under section 355 on acquisitions and dispositions of the stock of the distributing or controlled corporation.

Under [section 355(e)], if either the controlled or distributing corporation is acquired pursuant to a plan or arrangement in existence on the date of distribution, gain is recognized as of the date of the distribution.

In the case of an acquisition of either the distributing corporation or the controlled corporation, the amount of gain recognized is the amount that the distributing corporation would have recognized had the stock of the controlled corporation been sold for fair market value on the date of the distribution. Such gain is recognized immediately before the distribution and is treated as long-term capital gain. No adjustment to the basis of the stock or assets of either corporation is allowed by reason of the recognition of the gain.

Whether a corporation is acquired is determined under rules similar to those of * * * section 355(d), except that acquisitions would not be restricted to "purchase" transactions. Thus, an acquisition occurs if one or more persons acquire 50 percent or more of the vote or value of the stock of the controlled or distributing corporation pursuant to a plan or arrangement. For example, assume a corporation ("P") distributes the stock of its wholly owned subsidiary ("S") to its shareholders in a transaction that otherwise qualifies as a section 355 spin-off. If, pursuant to a plan or arrangement, 50 percent or more of the vote or value of either P or S is acquired by one or more persons, the Act requires gain recognition by the distributing corporation. Except as provided in Treasury regulations, if the assets of the distributing or controlled corporation are acquired by a successor in a merger or other transaction under section 368(a)(1)(A), (C) or (D) of the Code, the shareholders (immediately before the acquisition) of the corporation acquiring such assets are treated as acquiring stock in the corporation from which the assets were acquired. Under Treasury regulations, other asset transfers also could be subject to this rule.

Under [section 355(e)(4)(C)], certain aggregation and attribution rules apply for determining whether one or more persons has acquired a 50–percent or greater interest in distributing or controlled. * * *

A public offering of sufficient size can result in an acquisition that causes gain recognition under the provision.

Acquisitions occurring within the four-year period beginning two years before the date of distribution are presumed to have occurred pursuant to a plan or arrangement. Taxpayers can avoid gain recognition by showing that an acquisition occurring during this four-year period was unrelated to the distribution.

* * *

Certain transactions not considered acquisitions

Under the Act, certain specific types of transactions do not cause gain recognition or are not counted as acquisitions for purposes of determining whether there has been an acquisition of a 50–percent or greater interest in the distributing or the controlled corporation.

Single affiliated group

Under [section 355(e)(2)(C)], a plan (or series of related transactions) is not one that will cause gain recognition if, immediately after the completion of such plan or transactions, the distributing corporation and all controlled corporations are members of a single affiliated group of corporations (as defined in section 1504 without regard to subsection (b) thereof).

* * *

Continuing direct or indirect ownership

Under [section 355(e)(3)(A)], except as provided in Treasury regulations, certain acquisitions are not taken into account in determining whether a 50 percent or greater interest in distributing or controlled has been acquired. Generally, in any transaction, stock received directly or indirectly by former shareholders of distributing or controlled, in a successor or new controlling corporation of either, is not treated as acquired stock if it is attributable to such shareholders' stock in distributing or controlled that was not acquired as part of a plan or arrangement to acquire 50 percent or more of such successor or other corporation.

* * *

Example 2: Individual A owns all the stock of P corporation. P owns all the stock of a subsidiary corporation, S. Subsidiary S is distributed to individual A in a transaction that otherwise qualifies under section 355. As part of a plan, P then merges with corporation X, also owned entirely by individual A. There is not an acquisition that requires gain recognition under the provision, because individual A owns directly or indirectly 100 percent of all the stock of both X, the successor to P, and S before and after the transaction.[225] * * *

Example 3: Assume the facts are the same as in Example 2 except that corporations P and X are each owned by the same 20 individual 5–

---

[225] The example assumes that A did not acquire his or her stock in P as part of a plan or series of related transactions that results in the direct or indirect ownership of 50 percent or more of S or P separately by A. If A's stock in P was acquired as part of such a plan, the transaction would be one requiring gain recognition on the spin-off of S.

percent shareholders (rather than wholly by individual A). The transaction described in Example 2, in which S is spun off by P to P's shareholders and P is acquired by X, would not cause gain recognition, because each shareholder that owned stock of distributing and controlled before the transaction continues to own the same percentage of stock of each corporation after the transaction.

* * *

Except as provided in Treasury regulations, certain other acquisitions also are not taken into account. For example, under section 355(e)(3)(A), the following other types of acquisitions of stock are not subject to the provision, provided that the stock owned before the acquisition was not acquired pursuant to a plan or series of related transactions to acquire a 50–percent or greater ownership interest in either distributing or controlled:

* * *

[Section 355(e)] does not apply to distributions that would otherwise be subject to section 355(d) * * *, which imposes corporate level tax on certain disqualified distributions.

[Section 355(e)] does not apply to a distribution pursuant to a title 11 or similar case.

Section 355(f)

[Section 355(f)] provides that, except as provided in Treasury regulations, section 355 (or so much of section 356 as relates to section 355) shall not apply to the distribution of stock from one member of an affiliated group of corporations (as defined in section 1504(a)) to another member of such group (an "intragroup spin-off") if such distribution is part of a plan (or series of related transactions) described in subsection (e)(2)(A)(ii), pursuant to which one or more persons acquire directly or indirectly stock representing a 50–percent or greater interest in the distributing corporation or any controlled corporation.

Example 5: P corporation owns all the stock of subsidiary corporation S. S owns all the stock of subsidiary corporation T. S distributes the stock of T corporation to P as part of a plan or series of related transactions in which P then distributes S to its shareholders and then P is merged into unrelated X corporation. After the merger, former shareholders of X corporation own 50 percent or more of the voting power or value of the stock of the merged corporation. Because the distribution of T by S is part of a plan or series of related transactions in which S is distributed by P outside the P affiliated group and P is then acquired under section 355(e), section 355 in its entirety does not apply to the intragroup spin-off of T to P, under section 355(f). Also, the distribution of S by P is subject to section 355(e).

In determining whether an acquisition described in subsection (e)(2)(A)(ii) occurs, all the provisions of new subsection 355(e) are applied. For example, an intragroup spin-off in connection with an overall transaction that does not cause gain recognition under section 355(e) because it is described in section 355(e)(2)(C), or because of section 355(e)(3), * * * is not subject to the rule of section 355(f).

* * *

Revenue Ruling 2005–65

2005–2 C.B.. 684.

ISSUE

Under the facts described below, is a distribution of a controlled corporation by a distributing corporation part of a plan pursuant to which one or more persons acquire stock in the distributing corporation under § 355(e) of the Internal Revenue Code and § 1.355–7 of the Income Tax Regulations?

FACTS

Distributing is a publicly traded corporation that conducts a pharmaceuticals business. Controlled, a wholly owned subsidiary of Distributing, conducts a cosmetics business. Distributing does all of the borrowing for both Distributing and Controlled and makes all decisions regarding the allocation of capital spending between the pharmaceuticals and cosmetics businesses. Because Distributing's capital spending in recent years for both the pharmaceuticals and cosmetics businesses has outpaced internally generated cash flow from the businesses, it has had to limit total expenditures to maintain its credit ratings. Although the decisions reached by Distributing's senior management regarding the allocation of capital spending usually favor the pharmaceuticals business due to its higher rate of growth and profit margin, the competition for capital prevents both businesses from consistently pursuing development strategies that the management of each business believes are appropriate.

To eliminate this competition for capital, and in light of the unavailability of nontaxable alternatives, Distributing decides and publicly announces that it intends to distribute all the stock of Controlled pro rata to Distributing's shareholders. It is expected that both businesses will benefit in a real and substantial way from the distribution. This business purpose is a corporate business purpose (within the meaning of § 1.355–2(b)). The distribution is substantially motivated by this business purpose, and not by a business purpose to facilitate an acquisition.

After the announcement but before the distribution, X, a widely held corporation that is engaged in the pharmaceuticals business, and Distributing begin discussions regarding an acquisition. There were no discussions between Distributing or Controlled and X or its shareholders regarding an acquisition or a distribution before the announcement. In addition, Distributing would have been able to continue the successful operation of its pharmaceuticals business without combining with X. During its negotiations with Distributing, X indicates that it favors the distribution. X merges into Distributing before the distribution but nothing in the merger agreement requires the distribution.

As a result of the merger, X's former shareholders receive 55 percent of Distributing's stock. In addition, X's chairman of the board and chief executive officer become the chairman of the board and chief executive officer, respectively, of Distributing. Six months after the merger, Distributing distributes the stock of Controlled pro rata in a distribution to which § 355 applies and to which § 355(d) does not apply. At the time of the distribution, the distribution continues to be substantially motivated by the business purpose of eliminating the competition for capital between the pharmaceuticals and cosmetics businesses.

LAW

Section 355(c) generally provides that no gain or loss is recognized to the distributing corporation on a distribution of stock in a controlled corporation to which § 355 (or so much of § 356 as relates to § 355) applies and which is not in pursuance of a plan of reorganization. Section 355(e) generally denies nonrecognition treatment under § 355(c) if the distribution is part of a plan (or series of related transactions) (a plan) pursuant to which one or more persons acquire directly or indirectly stock representing a 50–percent or greater interest in the distributing corporation or any controlled corporation.

Section 1.355–7(b)(1) provides that whether a distribution and an acquisition are part of a plan is determined based on all the facts and circumstances, including those set forth in § 1.355–7(b)(3) (plan factors) and (4) (non-plan factors). The weight to be given each of the facts and circumstances depends on the particular case. The determination does not depend on the relative number of plan factors compared to the number of non-plan factors that are present.

Section 1.355–7(b)(3)(iii) provides that, in the case of an acquisition (other than involving a public offering) before a distribution, if at some time during the two-year period ending on the date of the acquisition there were discussions by Distributing or Controlled with the acquirer regarding a distribution, such discussions tend to show that the distribution and the acquisition are part of a plan. The weight to be accorded this fact depends on the nature, extent, and timing of the discussions. In addition, the fact that the acquirer intends to cause a distribution and, immediately after the acquisition, can meaningfully participate in the decision regarding whether to make a distribution, tends to show that the distribution and the acquisition are part of a plan.

Section 1.355–7(b)(4)(iii) provides that, in the case of an acquisition (other than involving a public offering) before a distribution, the absence of discussions by Distributing or Controlled with the acquirer regarding a distribution during the two-year period ending on the date of the earlier to occur of the acquisition or the first public announcement regarding the distribution tends to show that the distribution and the acquisition are not part of a plan. However, this factor does not apply to an acquisition where the acquirer intends to cause a distribution and, immediately after the acquisition, can meaningfully participate in the decision regarding whether to make a distribution.

Section 1.355–7(b)(4)(v) provides that the fact that the distribution was motivated in whole or substantial part by a corporate business purpose (within the meaning of § 1.355–2(b)) other than a business purpose to facilitate the acquisition or a similar acquisition tends to show that the distribution and the acquisition are not part of a plan.

Section 1.355–7(b)(4)(vi) provides that the fact that the distribution would have occurred at approximately the same time and in similar form regardless of the acquisition or a similar acquisition tends to show that the distribution and the acquisition are not part of a plan.

Section 1.355–7(h)(6) provides that discussions with the acquirer generally include discussions with persons with the implicit permission of the acquirer.

Section 1.355–7(h)(9) provides that a corporation is treated as having the implicit permission of its shareholders when it engages in discussions.

ANALYSIS

Whether the X shareholders' acquisition of Distributing stock and Distributing's distribution of Controlled are part of a plan depends on all the facts and circumstances, including those described in § 1.355–7(b). The fact that Distributing discussed the distribution with X during the two-year period ending on the date of the acquisition tends to show that the distribution and the acquisition are part of a plan. See § 1.355–7(b)(3)(iii). In addition, X's shareholders may constitute acquirers who intend to cause a distribution and who, immediately after the acquisition, can meaningfully participate (through X's chairman of the board and chief executive officer who become D's chairman of the board and chief executive officer) in the decision regarding whether to distribute Controlled. See id. However, the fact that Distributing publicly announced the distribution before discussions with X regarding both an acquisition and a distribution began suggests that the plan factor in § 1.355–7(b)(3)(iii) should be accorded less weight than it would have been accorded had there been such discussions before the public announcement.

With respect to those factors that tend to show that the distribution and the acquisition are not part of a plan, the absence of discussions by Distributing or Controlled with X or its shareholders during the two-year period ending on the date of the public announcement regarding the distribution would tend to show that the distribution and the acquisition are not part of a plan only if X's shareholders are not acquirers who intend to cause a distribution and who, immediately after the acquisition, can meaningfully participate in the decision regarding whether to distribute Controlled. See § 1.355–7(b)(4)(iii). Because X's chairman of the board and chief executive officer become the chairman and chief executive officer, respectively, of Distributing, X's shareholders may have the ability to meaningfully participate in the decision whether to distribute Controlled. Therefore, the absence of discussions by Distributing or Controlled with X or its shareholders during the two-year period ending on the date of the public announcement regarding the distribution may not tend to show that the distribution and the acquisition are not part of a plan.

Nonetheless, the fact that the distribution was substantially motivated by a corporate business purpose (within the meaning of § 1.355–2(b)) other than a business purpose to facilitate the acquisition or a similar acquisition, and the fact that the distribution would have occurred at approximately the same time and in similar form regardless of the acquisition or a similar acquisition, tend to show that the distribution and the acquisition are not part of a plan. See § 1.355–7(b)(4)(v), (vi). The fact that the public announcement of the distribution preceded discussions by Distributing or Controlled with X or its shareholders, and the fact that Distributing's business would have continued to operate successfully even if the merger had not occurred, evidence that the distribution originally was not substantially motivated by a business purpose to facilitate the acquisition or a similar acquisition. Moreover, after the merger, Distributing continued to be substantially motivated by the same corporate business purpose (within the meaning of § 1.355–2(b)) other than a business purpose to facilitate the acquisition or a similar acquisition (§ 1.355–7(b)(4)(v)). In addition, the fact that Distributing decided to distribute Controlled and announced that decision before it began discussions with X regarding the combination suggests that the distribution would have occurred at approximately the same time and in similar form regardless of Distributing's combination with X and the corresponding acquisition of Distributing stock by the X shareholders.

Considering all the facts and circumstances, particularly the fact that the distribution was motivated by a corporate business purpose (within the meaning of § 1.355–2(b)) other than a business purpose to facilitate the acquisition or a similar acquisition, and the fact that the distribution would have occurred at approximately the same time and in similar form regardless of the acquisition or a similar acquisition, the acquisition and distribution are not part of a plan under § 355(e) and § 1.355–7(b).

HOLDING

Under the facts described above, the acquisition and the distribution are not part of a plan under § 355(e) and § 1.355–7(b).

DETAILED ANALYSIS

1.   ASPECTS OF SECTION 355(e)

1.1. *Plan or Series of Related Transactions*

The recognition rule of § 355(e) applies to a divisive distribution that is part of a plan or a series of related transactions in which one or more persons acquire stock representing a 50 percent or greater interest in either the distributing or any controlled corporation. I.R.C. § 355(e)(2)(A)(ii). Section 355(e)(2)(B) provides that if one or more persons acquires a 50 percent or greater interest in the distributing or any controlled corporation within a four-year period beginning two-years before the date of the distribution and ending two-years after the date of the distribution "such acquisition *shall* be treated as pursuant to a plan * * * unless it is established that the distribution and the acquisition are not pursuant to a plan or series of related transactions." As the legislative history indicates, "taxpayers can avoid gain recognition by showing that an acquisition occurring during this four-year period was unrelated to the distribution." See page 776.

A perceived need for certainty has spawned complicated regulations providing guidance for identifying the presence of the prohibited plan. After promulgating a series of ever changing temporary regulations over the course of the years since the enactment of § 355(e), in 2005 the Treasury Department promulgated final regulations. The regulations disregard the presumption of § 355(e)(2)(B) and provide that "whether a distribution and an acquisition are part of a plan is determined based on all the facts and circumstances." Treas.Reg. § 1.355–7(b)(1). In the case of an acquisition not involving a public offering that occurs within two-years following the date of a distribution, the distribution and acquisition "will be treated as part of a plan *only* if there was an agreement, understanding, arrangement, or substantial negotiations regarding the acquisition or a similar acquisition at some time during the two-year period ending on the date of the distribution." Treas.Reg. § 1.355–7(b)(2) (italics added). The "super safe harbor" implicit in this rule trumps all other facts and circumstances. The regulations add that the existence of an agreement, understanding, arrangement, or substantial negotiations during the two-year period preceding the distribution tends to show that the distribution and acquisition are part of a plan, and further describe such an understanding etc., as merely a factor among the facts and circumstances to be evaluated. See Treas.Reg. § 1.355–7(b)(3)(i). If the acquisition involves a public offering after the distribution, the presence of discussions during the two-year period preceding the distribution with an investment banker regarding a distribution is a factor indicating the existence of a plan. Treas.Reg. § 1.355–7(b)(3)(ii). The regulations add that in the case of an acquisition involving a public offering after the distribution, the absence of discussions with an investment banker within the two-year period ending on the date of the distribution is a factor indicating the absence of a plan. Treas.Reg. § 1.355–7(b)(4)(i).

Whether there is an agreement, understanding, or arrangement also is a question of facts and circumstances. Treas.Reg. § 1.355–7(h)(1)(iii). A binding agreement is not required, but an agreement, understanding, or arrangement "clearly exists if a binding contract to acquire stock exists." Also, an agreement may exist even though the parties have not reached agreement on all significant economic terms. "Substantial negotiations" are said to "require discussions of significant economic terms . . . by one or more officers or directors acting on behalf of [the corporations], . . . controlling shareholders" or "another person or persons with the implicit or explicit permission of one or more of such officers, directors, or controlling shareholders." Treas.Reg. § 1.355–7(h)(1)(iv). A "controlling shareholder" with respect to a publicly traded corporation is a five percent shareholder who actively participates in the management or operation of the corporation. Treas.Reg. § 1.355–7(h)(3)(i). With respect to a corporation the stock of which is not publicly traded, a controlling shareholder is any person that owns stock possessing voting power representing a meaningful voice in the governance of the corporation. Treas.Reg. § 1.355–7(h)(3)(ii). In the case of an acquisition involving a public offering, the existence of an agreement, etc., depends on discussions with investment bankers by one or more officers, directors, or controlling shareholders of either the distributing or controlled corporations. Treas.Reg. § 1.355–7(h)(1)(vi).

Under Treas.Reg. § 1.355–7(e) the acquisition of stock pursuant to an option will result in the option agreement being treated as an agreement to acquire the stock as of the date the option was written, transferred, or modified if the option is more likely than not to be exercised as of such date.

In the case of an acquisition that precedes the distribution, the existence of a plan is indicated by discussions within the two-year period preceding the acquisition by either the controlled or distributing corporation with the acquirer regarding a distribution. Treas.Reg. § 1.355–7(b)(3)(iii). The absence of discussions regarding a distribution during the two-year period ending on the earlier to occur of (a) the acquisition, or (b) the first public announcement regarding the distribution, is a factor indicating that the acquisition and distribution were not part of a plan. Treas.Reg. § 1.355–7(b)(4)(iii). If the acquisition involves a public offering before the distribution, the presence of discussions during the two-year period preceding the acquisition with an investment banker regarding a distribution is a factor indicating the existence of a plan. Treas.Reg. § 1.355–7(b)(3)(iv). A change in the market or business conditions after the acquisition that results in a distribution that was otherwise unexpected is a factor that indicates that the acquisition and distribution are not part of a plan. Treas.Reg. § 1.355–7(b)(4)(iv).

In the case of a distribution either before or after the acquisition, the regulations provide that the existence of a corporate business purpose, as defined in Treas.Reg. § 1.355–2(b), other than a business purpose to facilitate the acquisition, is a factor indicating the absence of a plan. Treas.Reg. § 1.355–7(b)(4)(v). Discussions by either the distributing or controlled corporation with outside advisors, as well as internal discussions of either corporation provide an indication of a business purpose for the distribution. Treas.Reg. § 1.355–7(c)(1). Similarly, the absence of a plan is indicated if the distribution would have occurred at approximately the same time and in similar form regardless of the acquisition. Treas.Reg. § 1.355–7(b)(4)(vi). Treas.Reg. § 1.355–7(c)(2) provides that discussions with the acquirer regarding a distribution to decrease the likelihood of an acquisition of either the distributing or controlled corporation by separating it from the corporation that is likely to be acquired will be treated as having a business purpose to facilitate acquisition of the corporation that is likely to be acquired. Nonetheless, a distribution that facilitated trading in the stock of the distributing or controlled corporation will not be taken into account in determining whether a distribution and acquisition are part of a plan. Treas.Reg. § 1.355–7(c)(3).

Treas.Reg. § 1.355–7(d) provides nine safe harbors from the stormy seas of prohibited plans. A distribution and an acquisition are not part of a plan if they are described in one of the following safe harbors:

1.   An acquisition occurs more than six months after a distribution, there was no agreement, understanding, arrangement, or substantial negotiations concerning the acquisition during a period from one year before the distribution to six months following the distribution, and the distribution was motivated in whole or substantial part by a corporate business purpose other than a business purpose to facilitate an acquisition.

2.   An acquisition occurs more than six months after a distribution for which there was no agreement, understanding, arrangement, or substantial negotiations concerning the acquisition during a period from one year before the distribution to six months following the distribution. This safe harbor applies where the distribution was not motivated by a business purpose to

facilitate an acquisition of either the distributing or controlled corporations, and no more than twenty-five percent of the stock of the corporation whose stock was acquired in the acquisition was either acquired or the subject of an agreement, understanding, arrangement, or substantial negotiations during a period from one year before the distribution to six months following the distribution.

3.   An acquisition occurs after the distribution and there was no agreement, understanding, arrangement, or substantial negotiations concerning the acquisition at the time of the distribution or within one-year thereafter. This provision disregards the two-year post-distribution presumption of the statute and replaces it with a one-year safe harbor.

4.   An acquisition occurs before a distribution but before the first "disclosure event" regarding the distribution. A "disclosure event" is any communication to the acquirer or any other third person by an officer, director, controlling shareholder, or employee of any of the distributing corporation, the controlled corporation, or a corporation related to either of them, or an outside advisor to any of those corporations regarding the distribution, or the possibility thereof. To assure that this safe harbor is not available for acquisitions by a person who could participate in the decision to effect a distribution, it does not apply to acquisitions by a person that was a controlling shareholder or a ten-percent shareholder of the acquired corporation at any time during the period beginning immediately after the acquisition and ending on the date of the distribution. The safe harbor is also unavailable if the acquisition occurs in connection with a transaction in which the aggregate acquisitions represent 20 percent or more (by vote or value) of the stock of the acquired corporation.

5.   An acquisition of the distributing corporation (not involving a public offering) that occurs prior to a pro rata distribution, if the acquisition occurs after the date of a public announcement regarding the distribution, but there were no discussions by the distributing corporation or the controlled corporation with the acquirer regarding a distribution on or before the date of the first public announcement regarding the distribution. To assure that this safe harbor is not available for acquisitions by a person who could participate in the decision to effect a distribution, it does not apply to acquisitions by a person that was a controlling shareholder or a ten-percent shareholder of the acquired corporation at any time during the period beginning immediately after the acquisition and ending on the date of the distribution. The safe harbor is also unavailable if the acquisition occurs in connection with a transaction in which the aggregate acquisitions represent 20 percent or more (by vote or value) of the stock of the acquired distributing corporation.

6.   A distribution and an acquisition involving a public offering occurring before the distribution if: (1) in the case of an acquisition of stock that is not listed on an established market, the acquisition occurs before the first disclosure event regarding the distribution, or (2) in the case of an acquisition of stock that is listed on an established market, the acquisition occurs before the date of the first public announcement regarding the distribution. This safe harbor is based on the view that a public offering and a distribution are not likely to be part of a plan if the acquirers in the offering are unaware that a distribution will occur.

7.   An acquisition (other than through a public offering) of stock of the distributing or controlled corporation that is listed on an established market that occurs because of transfers involving shareholders of distributing or controlled who are not controlling shareholders (five percent shareholders who participate in management) or ten percent shareholders. This safe harbor is not available if the transferor or transferee of the stock is a corporation that is controlled by the acquired corporation, is a member of a controlled group that includes the acquired corporation, or is an underwriter with respect to the acquisition.

8.   An acquisition of stock by an employee, director, or independent contractor in connection with the performance of services. The safe harbor does not apply to acquisitions by controlling shareholders or ten percent shareholders.

9.   Certain acquisitions by qualified pension or retirement plans.

Section 355(e) may well be considered the wrong solution to a problem that does not exist. Nonetheless, the presumption that an acquisition and distribution within two-years of each other are part of a plan is contained in statutory language enacted by the Congress and signed into law by the President. Is it appropriate for the Treasury Department to write the presumption out of the statute by regulations where Treasury thinks the provision does not represent good policy?

1.2. *Corporate Level Issues*

Even though § 355(e) requires corporate level recognition of gain with respect to stock in transactions that otherwise qualify for nonrecognition under § 355, nonrecognition at the shareholder level is still the order of the day. What is the precise tax policy justification for § 355(e)? Section 355(e) can, and often will, apply even though neither the distributing corporation nor the distributed corporation has itself received any consideration, let alone any cash consideration, and the only consideration that the shareholders have received is stock in one or more corporations. Furthermore, none of the assets held in corporate solution has received a step-up in basis. Given these parameters, why should the distributing corporation recognize gain with respect to the stock of the distributed corporation?

Nevertheless, customizing spin-offs do have the potential for abuse. Assume, for example, that T manufactures toys and airplanes. P wants to acquire the airplane business, but not the toy business, and is willing to pay in stock and deferred cash. To effectuate the transaction, T borrows an amount equal to one-half of the negotiated purchase price. T then contributes the cash and the toy business to S, which is spun-off to the T shareholders. Thereafter, T, which retained the liability for the borrowed money that has been transferred to S, is merged into P and the T shareholders (who also are the S shareholders) receive P stock. Since S holds cash equal to one half of the total consideration effectively provided by P, the transaction has significant overtones of a sale of the airplane division at the corporate level. If this perceived abuse is the real problem with which Congress was concerned, could it have drafted a more narrowly targeted remedy?

Another strange aspect of § 355(e) is the measure of gain. Regardless of whether the distributing corporation or the controlled corporation is the corporation that is subsequently acquired, the recognized gain is measured with reference to the stock of the controlled corporation.[16] This might be a reasonable measure of the gain to be recognized in cases where the controlled corporation is the subsequently acquired corporation. However, if the distributing corporation is the corporation that is acquired, as in the above example, it is difficult to understand why Congress considered the proper measure of gain to be the appreciation in the stock of the controlled corporation, which is retained by the shareholders of the acquired target corporation.

1.2.1.   *Section 336(e) Election*

A distribution subject to either § 355(d), page 772 (50 percent shareholder with disqualified stock), or § 355(e) carries the potential for gain recognition at three levels: gain recognized by the distributing corporation on distribution of the stock of the controlled corporation, gain recognized by the controlled corporation on disposition of appreciated assets, and gain recognized by the shareholders of the controlled corporation. Section 336(e) provides in the case of a sale or distribution of stock representing control under § 1504(a)(2), page 442 (80 percent of voting stock and value), the selling or distributing corporation may elect to treat the sale or distribution as a sale of the assets of the distributed corporation rather than as a stock sale. Section 336(e) is discussed at page 495. Treas.Reg. § 1.336–2(b)(2) provides rules for a § 336(e) election when the distributing corporation distributes stock of the controlled corporation representing control under § 1504(a)(2) (a "qualified stock disposition") and is required to recognize its realized gain under § 355(d) or (e). If a § 336(e) election is made by the distributing corporation, the controlled corporation is deemed to have sold its assets in a taxable transaction to an unrelated person for an aggregate deemed asset disposition price (Treas.Reg. § 1.336–3, discussed at page 498), which, in general, reflects the net fair market value of the assets plus liabilities grossed-up to reflect non-recently disposed-of stock. The gain or loss is recognized while the controlled corporation is controlled by the distributing corporation.

---

[16] If the controlled corporation was formed in a § 368(a)(1)(D) reorganization in contemplation of the distribution, § 368(a)(2)(H)(ii) preserves the tax-free status of that transaction even if the distributing corporation's shareholders dispose of the stock of the controlled corporation in a transaction subject to § 355(e).

Net losses from the deemed asset sale are recognized only in relation to the amount of stock sold or exchanged in the qualified stock disposition during the 12–month disposition period. Treas.Reg. § 1.336–2(b)(2)(i)(B)(2)(iii). However, if the controlled corporation has any subsidiaries for which a § 336(e) election is made, the general deemed asset disposition methodology shall apply. This prevents taxpayers from effectively electing whether the attributes of the lower tier subsidiary become those of target, by doing an actual sale of target subsidiary's assets followed by a liquidation of target subsidiary, or remain with target subsidiary, by making a § 336(e) election for target subsidiary.

The controlled corporation is deemed to have repurchased its assets for an amount equal to the adjusted grossed basis, determined under the rules of Treas.Reg. § 1.338–5, discussed at page 489. Treas.Reg. § 1.336–2(b)(2)(ii). The controlled corporation is not deemed to liquidate into the distributing corporation, but is treated as acquiring all of its assets from an unrelated person and the distributing corporation is treated as distributing the stock of the controlled corporation to its shareholders. Treas.Reg. § 1.336–2(b)(2)(i)(A). Because the controlled corporation is not treated as liquidating, it retains its tax attributes despite the § 336(e) election. Furthermore, the controlled corporation will take into account the effects of the deemed asset disposition to adjust its earnings and profits immediately before allocating earnings and profits pursuant to Treas. Reg. § 1.312–10. Treas.Reg. § 1.336–2(b)(2)(vi).

The distributing corporation does not recognize gain or loss on the qualified stock disposition of the stock of the controlled corporation. Treas.Reg. § 1.336–2(b)(2)(iii). The deemed sale and repurchase of assets by the controlled corporation does not cause the distribution to fail the requirements of § 355. Treas.Reg. § 1.336–2(b)(2)(v).

1.3. *Shareholder Level Issues*

In Rev.Rul. 96–30, 1996–1 C.B. 36, obsoleted by Rev.Rul. 98–27, 1998–1 C.B. 1159, D Corporation distributed the stock of a controlled subsidiary, C Corporation, to its shareholders. Soon after the distribution, Y Corporation proposed to acquire C Corporation and subsequently C Corporation was merged into Y Corporation in a tax-free merger in which the former C Corporation shareholders received 25 percent of the stock of Y Corporation. No negotiations had occurred between D Corporation and Y Corporation, and the C Corporation shareholders were free to vote their stock as they saw fit. The IRS ruled that the step transaction doctrine must be applied to determine whether the substance of the transaction was the same as its form or whether in substance C Corporation had been merged into Y Corporation prior to the distribution by D Corporation, followed by a constructive distribution by D Corporation to its shareholders of the Y Corporation stock received in the merger. In the latter case, the transaction would not have qualified under § 355. Based on the facts and circumstances, particularly the fact that there had been no pre-distribution negotiations regarding the acquisition of C Corporation by Y Corporation, the IRS ruled that the form of the transaction would be respected and § 355 thus applied.

Following the enactment of § 355(e), in Rev.Rul. 98–27, 1998–1 C.B. 1159, the IRS obsoleted Rev.Rul. 96–30. Rev.Rul. 98–27 states that the IRS will no longer apply *Court Holding Company* principles (or any other variant of the step transaction doctrine) to determine whether for purposes of § 355(a) the distributed corporation qualifies as a controlled corporation solely because of any post-distribution acquisition or restructuring of the distributed corporation, whether prearranged or not. According to the ruling, any implication that § 355(a) restricts post-distribution acquisitions or restructurings of a controlled corporation is inconsistent with § 355(e) and its legislative history (citing H.R.Rep. No. 105–220, at 529–30). In applying the step transaction doctrine to divisive transactions for other purposes, however, the IRS will continue to consider all facts and circumstances.

2.   ASPECTS OF SECTION 355(f)

2.1. *Background*

The effect of § 355(e), which triggers gain to the distributing corporation if it applies, is rather straightforward. The effect of § 335(f), which removes the transaction from the ambit of § 355 entirely, however, is not so clear. Section 355(f) provides that a transaction is not subject to § 355 when the distributee shareholders are one or more corporations that are members of the same affiliated group of corporations as the distributing and controlled corporations and the transaction is part of a plan to transfer ownership as described in § 355(e)(2). Special rules control the taxation of the distribution even though § 355 does not apply. The precise treatment of the transaction depends on whether or not the corporations involved in the transaction file consolidated returns, which are discussed in Chapter 9.

2.2. *Effect of Section 355(f)*

2.2.1.   *Corporations That Do Not File Consolidated Returns*

If the corporations involved in the transaction do not file consolidated returns, the distributing corporation generally must recognize gain (but not loss) under § 311 (discussed at page 197) with respect to the distributed stock of the controlled corporation.[17] The distributee corporation recognizes dividend income equal to the fair market value of the stock, but the income item is entirely offset by a 100 percent dividends received deduction under § 243 (discussed at page 223). Nevertheless, pursuant to § 301(d), the distributee corporation takes a fair market value basis in the stock of the controlled corporation. The distributee corporation's basis in the distributing corporation stock that it continues to hold is not affected. See I.R.C. § 1059(e)(2). Thus, whether the distributing corporation or the controlled corporation is acquired after the spin-off, the tax consequence of the spin-off is limited to recognition of gain by the distributing corporation with respect to the controlled corporation's stock.

2.2.2.   *Corporations That File Consolidated Returns*

The effect of § 355(f) is different if the distributing and distributee shareholder corporation file consolidated returns. First, although the distributing corporation recognizes gain on the distribution of the controlled corporation under § 311(a), the dividend distribution is a deferred intercompany transaction, and pursuant to Treas.Reg. § 1.1502–13(f)(2)(iii), discussed at page 455, the gain is not immediately recognized.

---

[17] If, however, the distributing corporation liquidates as part of the transaction, § 337 (discussed at page 342) may provide nonrecognition of gain or loss with respect to the stock of the controlled corporation.

The distributee corporation excludes the dividend from gross income, Treas.Reg. §§ 1.1502–13(f)(2)(iii), but must reduce its basis in the stock of the distributing corporation by the amount of the excluded dividend, i.e., the fair market value of the stock of the controlled corporation received in the distribution. Treas.Reg. §§ 1.1502–32 (discussed at page 446). If the distributee corporation subsequently disposes of the controlled corporation received in the spin-off, the distributing corporation must recognize its deferred gain without regard to whether the disposition is a sale or a tax-free reorganization. Treas.Reg. §§ 1.1502–13. The same result occurs if the distributee corporation disposes of the stock of the distributing corporation.

2.2.3.   *Pyramiding Sections 355(e) and 355(f)*

It is possible for both § 355(e) and § 355(f) to apply to a series of transactions involving an intragroup spin-off followed by a spin-off out of the group as part of a plan by which a majority interest in either of the distributing corporations or the distributed controlled corporation subsequently is acquired by new owners. Assume that X Corporation is publicly held and owns all of the stock of Y Corporation, which in turn owns all of the stock of Z Corporation. The corporations file a consolidated return. To facilitate the acquisition of X Corporation by P Corporation, Y Corporation distributes all of the stock of Z Corporation to X Corporation, which in turn distributes the Z Corporation stock to its public shareholders. Thereafter, X Corporation is merged into P Corporation. After the merger the former shareholders of X Corporation hold less than 50 percent of the P Corporation stock. Pursuant to § 355(f), § 355 does not apply to the distribution of Z Corporation stock to X Corporation by Y Corporation. The distribution is a taxable distribution, but Y Corporation can defer its intercompany gain and X Corporation can eliminate the dividend from gross income. X Corporation takes a fair market value basis in the Z Corporation stock, but must reduce its basis in its Y Corporation stock by a like amount. Section 355(e) applies to the distribution by X Corporation to its shareholders of the Z Corporation stock, but because X Corporation's basis in the Z Corporation stock equals its fair market value on the day it was received, if the distribution follows promptly, it is likely that little, if any, gain will be realized. As a result of the spin-off of Z Corporation by X Corporation, Y Corporation recognizes its deferred intercompany gain, and X Corporation increases its basis in Y Corporation by the amount of gain recognized. The same consequences would follow if P acquired Z Corporation.

3.   SPECIAL BASIS PROBLEMS IN INTRAGROUP SPIN-OFFS

In the case of an intragroup spin-off, i.e., a divisive distribution of stock from one member of an affiliated group of corporations (as defined in § 1504(a)) to another member of the group, the issues involving the appropriate effects on basis are essentially the same whether or not the spin-off is part of an acquisition. Spin-offs in the consolidated return context present special problems even if an acquisition is not in the wind. In this case, the basis of the distributed corporation is generally determined with reference to the basis of the distributing corporation. The basis allocation rules generally eliminate any excess loss account in the stock of a controlled corporation that is distributed within the group. See I.R.C. §§ 355(c), 358; Treas.Reg. § 1.1502–19(b)(2)(i). Congress also was concerned that a § 355 distribution within an affiliated group that does not file a consolidated return also could result in similar basis results, which it considered inappropriate. Congress addressed these issues by giving the Treasury Department broad regulatory authority in § 358(g), which is discussed in the following excerpt from Staff of the Joint Committee on Taxation, General Explanation of Tax Legislation Enacted in 1997, 203–204 (1997).

[Section 358(g)] provides that in the case of any distribution of stock of one member of an affiliated group of corporations to another member under section 355 ("intragroup spin-off"), the Secretary of the Treasury is authorized under section 358(g) to provide adjustments to the basis of any stock in a corporation which is a member of such group, to reflect appropriately the proper treatment of such distribution. It is understood that the approach of any such regulations applied to intragroup spinoffs that do not involve an acquisition may also be applied under the Treasury regulatory authority to modify the rule of section 355(f) as may be appropriate.

Congress believed that the concerns relating to basis adjustments in the case of intragroup spin-offs are essentially similar, whether or not an acquisition is currently intended as part of a plan or series of related transactions. The concerns include the following. First, under present law consolidated return regulations, it is possible that an excess loss account of a lower tier subsidiary may be eliminated. This creates the potential for the subsidiary to leave the group without recapture of the excess loss account, even though the group has benefitted from the losses or distributions in excess of basis that led to the existence of the excess loss account.

Second, under present law, a shareholder's stock basis in its stock of the distributing corporation is allocated after a spin-off between the stock of the distributing and controlled corporations, in proportion to the relative fair market values of the stock of those companies. If a disproportionate amount of asset basis (as compared to value) is in one of the companies (including but not limited to a shift of value and basis through a borrowing by one company and contribution of the borrowed cash to the other), present law rules under section 358(c) can produce an increase in stock basis relative to asset basis in one corporation, and a corresponding decrease in stock basis relative to asset basis in the other company. Because the spin-off has occurred within the corporate group, the group can continue to benefit from high inside asset basis either for purposes of sale or depreciation, while also choosing to benefit from the disproportionately high stock basis in the other corporation. If, for example, both corporations were sold at a later date, a prior distribution can result in a significant decrease in the amount of gain recognized than would have occurred if the two corporations had been sold together without a prior spin off (or separately, without a prior spin-off).

Example 6: P owns all the stock of S1 and S1 owns all the stock of S2. P's basis in the stock of S1 is 50; the inside asset basis of S1's assets is 50; and the total value of S1's stock and assets (including the value of S2) is 150. S1's basis in the stock of S2 is 0; the inside basis of S2's assets is 0; and the value of S2's stock and assets is 100. If S1 were sold, holding S2, the total gain would be 100. S1 distributes S2 to P in a section 355 transaction. After this spin-off, under present law, P's basis in the stock of S1 is approximately 17 (50/150 times the total 50 stock basis in S1 prior to the spin-off) and the inside asset basis of S1 is 50. P's basis in the stock of S2 is 33 (100/150 times the total 50 stock basis in S1 prior to the spin-off) and the inside asset basis of S2 is 0. After a period of time, S2 can be sold for its value of 100, with a gain of 67 rather than 100. Also, since S1 remains in the corporate group, the full 50 inside asset basis can continue to be used. S1's assets could be sold for 50 with no gain or loss. Thus, S1 and S2 can be sold later at a total gain of 67, rather than the total gain of 100 that would have occurred had they been sold without the spin-off.

As one variation on the foregoing concern, taxpayers have attempted to utilize spin-offs to extract significant amounts of asset value and basis, (including but not limited to transactions in which one corporation decreases its value by incurring debt, and increases the asset basis and value of the other corporation by contributing the proceeds of the debt to the other corporation) without creation of an excess loss account or triggering of gain, even when the extraction is in excess of the basis in the distributing corporation's stock.

The Treasury Department may promulgate any regulations necessary to address these concerns and other collateral issues. As one example, the Treasury Department may consider providing rules that require a carryover basis within the group (or stock basis conforming to asset basis as appropriate) for the distributed corporation (including a carryover of an excess loss account, if any, in a consolidated return). Similarly, the Treasury Department may provide a reduction in the basis of the stock of the distributing corporation to reflect the change in the value and basis of the distributing corporation's assets. The Treasury Department may determine that the aggregate stock basis of distributing and controlled after the distribution may be adjusted to an amount that is less than the aggregate basis of the stock of the distributing corporation before the distribution, to prevent inappropriate potential for artificial losses or diminishment of gain on disposition of any of the corporations involved in the spin-off. The Treasury Department may provide separate regulations for corporations in affiliated groups filing a consolidated return and for affiliated groups not filing a consolidated return, as appropriate to each situation.

PART 6

Corporate Attributes in Reorganizations and Other Transactions

CHAPTER 15

CARRY OVER AND LIMITATION OF CORPORATE TAX ATTRIBUTES

SECTION 1. CARRY OVER OF TAX ATTRIBUTES

INTERNAL REVENUE CODE: Section 381.

REGULATIONS: Section 1.381(a)–1(a), (b)(1) and (2).

Commissioner v. Sansome

United States Court of Appeals, Second Circuit, 1932.
60 F.2d 931.

[In 1921 Corporation X transferred all its assets to newly-formed Corporation Y in return for all of the latter's stock, which went to the Corporation X shareholders. Corporation X had a large amount of earnings and profits. Corporation Y did not earn profits after its formation but instead suffered some losses. Corporation Y then made cash distributions in 1923 which under the applicable statute, § 201 of the 1921 Act, were taxable if those distributions were out of "its earnings and profits." If the earnings and profits of Corporation X were taken into account, then the distributions would be taxable. The 1921 transaction was a reorganization under the applicable statute, § 202(c)(2) of the 1921 Act.]

■ L. Hand, Circuit Judge. * * * It seems to us that [§ 202(c)(2) of the 1921 Act] should be read as a gloss upon [§ 201 of the 1921 Act]. That section provides for cases of corporate "reorganization" which shall not result in any "gain or loss" to the shareholder participating in them, and it defines them with some particularity. He must wait until he has disposed of the new shares, and use his original cost as the "base" to subtract from what he gets upon the sale. Such a change in the form of the shares is "an exchange of property," not a "sale or other disposition" of them * * *. It appears to us extremely unlikely that what was not "recognized" as a sale or disposition for the purpose of fixing gain or loss, should be "recognized" as changing accumulated profits into capital in a section which so far overlapped the latter. That in substance declared that some corporate transactions should not break the continuity of the corporate life, a troublesome question that the courts had beclouded by recourse to such vague alternatives as "form" and "substance," anodynes for the pains of reasoning. The effort was at least to narrow the limits of judicial inspiration, and we cannot think that the same issue was left at large in the earlier section. Hence we hold that a corporate reorganization which results in no "gain or loss" under [§ 202(c)(2) of the 1921 Act], does not toll the company's life as a continued venture under [§ 201 of the 1921 Act], and that what were "earnings or profits" of the original * * * company remain, for purposes of distribution, "earnings and profits" of the successor * * *.

Order reversed; cause remanded for further proceedings in accord with the foregoing.

DETAILED ANALYSIS

1.   GENERAL

The *Sansome* doctrine respecting earnings and profits is but one facet of the larger problem of the extent to which the acquiring corporation is to be regarded as succeeding to the tax characteristics, benefits, and obligations possessed by the transferor corporation, where both are parties to a tax-free reorganization. Prior to 1954, the rules regarding carry over of corporate attributes were found mainly in court decisions.

Section 381, enacted in 1954, contains detailed but non-exclusive statutory rules regarding the carry over of items in corporate liquidations and reorganizations in which the acquiring corporation steps into the shoes of the transferor or distributing corporation. Under § 381(a), corporate attributes carry over on the liquidation of a controlled subsidiary in which the parent takes the basis of the subsidiary's assets pursuant to §§ 332 and 334(b), discussed at page 342, and in type (A), (C), and (F) reorganizations and nondivisive type (D) and (G) reorganizations. In general, § 381 applies to transactions in which the transferor corporation is absorbed by the acquiring corporation in a tax free transaction, such as a reorganization. Section 381 does not apply to taxable acquisitions, for example, a "cash merger."

Under Treas.Reg. § 1.381(a)–1(b)(2), the acquiring corporation that succeeds to tax attributes of the transferor is the corporation that acquires directly or indirectly all of the assets transferred by the transferor. Under the regulations, there may be only one acquiring corporation. Thus, if X Corporation acquires all of the assets of T in a type (C) reorganization and thereafter transfers one-half of the assets to its wholly owned subsidiary, S1 and the remaining one-half of the T assets to a wholly owned subsidiary S2, X, as the corporation which first acquired all of T's assets, is treated as the acquiring corporation so that neither S1 nor S2 succeeds to T's corporate attributes. See Treas.Reg. § 1.381(a)–1(b)(2)(ii), Ex. (4).

2.   CARRY OVER OF EARNINGS AND PROFITS

Sections 381(a) and 381(c)(2) provide in general that in the transactions covered under § 381(a) the earnings and profits, or deficit in earnings and profits, of the transferor or distributing corporation carry over to the acquiring corporation, but that any deficit in earnings and profits of the corporations involved shall be used only to offset earnings and profits accumulated after the date of transfer or distribution. Treas.Reg. § 1.381(c)(2)–1(a)(5). Thus, a deficit earnings account of one corporation cannot be used to offset pre-transfer accumulated earnings of the other. Treas.Reg. § 1.381(c)(2)–1(a)(2). If both corporations either have accumulated earnings, or a deficit in accumulated earnings, the earnings and profits accounts are consolidated into a single account in the surviving corporation. Treas.Reg. § 1.381(c)(2)–1(a)(4). Treas.Reg. § 1.381(c)(2)–1(a)(2) also provides that earnings and profits inherited by the acquiring corporation become part of its accumulated earnings and profits, but not part of current earnings and profits for purposes of § 316(a)(2).

The rule that a deficit in accumulated earnings can offset only profits accumulated after the date of transfer requires identification of the transfer date. Treas.Reg. § 1.381(b)–1(b)(1) provides that the relevant date is the date on which the transfer is finally completed. Treas.Reg. § 1.381(b)–1(b)(2) and (3) also allow the taxpayer to specify a transfer date by filing a statement indicating the date on which substantially all of the assets of the transferor are transferred and the transferor has ceased business operations.

Prop.Reg. § 1.312–11(a) (2012) would promulgate the long-standing administrative position that only the acquiring corporation, as defined in Treas.Reg. § 1.381(a)–1(b)(2), in a transaction described in § 381 succeeds to the earnings and profits of the distributing or transferor corporation. Thus, if the acquired assets are divided among more than one corporation, the acquiring corporation in the § 381 transaction succeeds to the full earnings and profits of the transferor corporation. If all of the target corporation's assets are transferred to a subsidiary of the acquiring corporation, the subsidiary will inherit all of the target's assets, but if the acquiring corporation retains any of the target assets, the full earnings and profits of the target will remain with the acquiring corporation. The proposed regulation does not apply to divisive reorganizations under § 355, which are covered by Treas.Reg. § 1.312–10, discussed at page 773.

Treas.Reg. § 1.381(c)(2)–1(c) requires an adjustment to the earnings and profits of the transferor corporation to reflect distributions. In the case of a reorganization in which the transferor distributes other property along with stock or securities allowed to be received under § 354 without recognition of gain, the earnings and profits of the transferor corporation as of the transfer date are reduced by the amount attributable to the distribution. In the case of a liquidation of the transferor corporation under § 332, the earnings and profits of the transferor must be adjusted to account for distributions of property to minority stockholders. In both cases, the adjustments are required whether the distributions are made before or after the transfer date.

3. CARRY OVER OF NET OPERATING LOSSES

3.1. *General*

Net operating losses are probably the most significant corporate tax attribute affected by § 381. Normally a corporation with a net operating loss for the taxable year is entitled to carryback its loss to the two taxable years preceding the loss year, and then forward for the next twenty taxable years. I.R.C. § 172(b)(1)(A), (B). Section 381(c)(1) allows the transfer of an acquired corporation's net operating loss carryover to the acquiring corporation in a transaction covered by § 381(a), but limits the carryover to taxable income of the acquiring corporation attributable to the period following the transfer date. If the transfer date is any day other than the last day of the acquiring corporation's taxable year, the taxable year of the acquiring corporation is divided into two periods and taxable income is allocated to each period on a daily basis. An inherited loss carryover may be deducted by the acquiring corporation in the year of the transfer only against income allocated to the period subsequent to the transfer date. This rule results in the creation of two separate years for carry over purposes;

one carryover year for the transferor corporation ending on the transfer date, and a second period ending on the last day of the acquiring corporation's taxable year. If the acquiring corporation acquires several loss corporations during a taxable year, the taxable year of the acquiring corporation will be divided into several short periods, one for the transfer date of each acquisition. Treas.Reg. § 1.381(c)(1)–2(b)(2). If the transfer occurs on the last day of the acquiring corporation's taxable year, the inherited loss carryover may be used only in subsequent taxable years.

Even though § 381 provides for the carry over of net operating losses to the acquiring corporation, § 382, discussed in Section 2, restricts the rate at which those losses may be claimed against post-acquisition income, including income that is derived from the business of the acquired corporation.

The taxable year of the transferor corporation ends on the transfer date. I.R.C. § 381(b)(1). Under § 381(b)(3), net operating losses of the acquiring corporation may not be carried back to taxable years of the transferor corporation preceding the transfer date, except in an (F) reorganization. Thus, for example, if X Corporation acquires the assets of Y Corporation in a statutory merger, and following the transfer date the combined enterprise incurs a net operating loss, the loss cannot be carried back to pre-acquisition profitable years of Y, even if the loss is attributable entirely to a trade or business acquired from Y. The loss may be carried back, however, and deducted from pre-acquisition taxable income of X, the acquiring corporation.

In Bercy Industries v. Commissioner, 640 F.2d 1058 (9th Cir.1981), the Court of Appeals declined to strictly interpret § 381(b)(3). The taxpayer was acquired by another corporation in a reverse triangular merger in which the newly formed subsidiary acquired all of the assets of the taxpayer in exchange for its parent corporation's stock. Immediately after the acquisition the acquiring subsidiary corporation changed its name to that of the taxpayer (the transaction occurred prior to enactment of § 368(a)(2)(E)). The court held that the purpose of § 381(b)(3) was to avoid accounting difficulties in allocating post acquisition losses of the surviving corporation between pre-acquisition carryback years of the acquired corporation and the surviving corporation. The court concluded that when the acquiring corporation in a triangular reorganization is merely a shell corporation formed for the purpose of the acquisition, the policy of § 381(b)(3) is not violated. (640 F.2d at 1061–1062.) Thus, post-reorganization losses of the surviving corporation were allowed to be carried back to pre-reorganization years of the acquired corporation. The court also noted that the surviving corporation was essentially the same entity as the acquired corporation. See also Aetna Casualty & Sur. Co. v. United States, 568 F.2d 811 (2d Cir.1976).

3.2. *Liquidation of a Worthless Subsidiary*

In the case of a parent-subsidiary relationship, there is an interplay between § 381 and § 165(g)(3). If § 332 applies to the liquidation of a controlled subsidiary, see page 342, § 381 provides that the subsidiary's tax attributes are carried over to the parent. However, § 332 does not apply to the liquidation of an 80 percent controlled subsidiary unless some assets of the liquidating subsidiary are allocable to the common stock after payment of all creditors and preferred stockholders including the parent. If the common stock of the subsidiary is worthless, then § 332 is not applicable and § 381(a) does not permit a carry over of net operating losses. See Rev.Rul. 68–359, 1968–2 C.B. 161; Rev.Rul. 68–602, 1968–2 C.B. 135. If, however, the parent directly or indirectly owns at least 80 percent of the aggregate voting power and 80 percent of the aggregate value of the subsidiary, excluding nonvoting stock that is limited and preferred as to dividends and liquidating distributions, and the subsidiary was operating a business, then § 165 applies to give the parent an ordinary loss on its stock and security investment in the subsidiary. In this context, the term "securities" means any debt obligation that is in registered form or with interest coupons.[1] If the debt obligation is not a security, an ordinary loss still results under § 166. These ordinary losses in turn can create both loss carrybacks and carryovers for the parent under § 172. If § 165(g)(3) does not apply, the parent's worthless stock and security losses are capital losses.

In Marwais Steel Co. v. Commissioner, 354 F.2d 997 (9th Cir.1965), a subsidiary corporation borrowed operating capital from its parent and incurred net operating losses. The parent claimed bad debt deductions with respect to loans made to the subsidiary. The subsidiary was subsequently liquidated and the parent attempted to use the subsidiary's net operating losses under § 381. Despite the literal satisfaction of § 381, the court denied the carryover since the net operating losses had formed the rationale for the previous bad debt deductions, and a double deduction was not permitted. But in Textron, Inc. v. United States, 561 F.2d 1023 (1st Cir.1977), a parent corporation was allowed to claim a deduction for the worthless stock of its subsidiary despite the fact that the subsidiary was subsequently able to acquire a new profitable business and use its net operating loss carryovers to offset the income from the new business. Section 382(g)(4)(D) now limits the use of net operating losses in a Textron type situation. See page 834.

4.   CAPITAL LOSS CARRYOVERS

Under § 381(c)(3), the transferor's excess capital losses carry over to the acquiring corporation on much the same terms as net operating losses. The inherited capital loss carryover becomes a capital loss carryover of the acquiring corporation for purposes of § 1212, the capital loss carryover provision. The transferor's capital losses are available to the acquiring corporation in the acquiring corporation's first taxable year ending after the transfer date. I.R.C. § 381(c)(3)(A). The amount of the transferor's capital loss that can be utilized by the acquiring corporation in the year of the transfer is limited to the proportion of the acquiring corporation's capital gain net income that is allocable on a daily basis to the portion of the acquiring corporation's taxable year remaining after the transfer date. I.R.C. § 381(c)(3)(B). In addition, under § 381(b)(3), any net capital loss of the acquiring corporation incurred after the transfer date cannot be carried back to offset capital gain net income of the transferor derived in a taxable year ending on or prior to the transfer date.

5.   CARRY OVER OF OTHER ATTRIBUTES

In addition to earnings and profits and loss carryovers, § 381(c) lists a number of separate corporate attributes that carry over in a transaction

---

[1]   Securities rarely are issued in bearer form with interest coupons. See page 152.

described by § 381(a). Several of these provisions deal with accounting issues. In general, § 381(c)(4) provides for continuation of the transferor's method of accounting, but authorizes regulations to prescribe the method to be used if the parties to the transfer use different methods. Under Treas.Reg. § 1.381(c)(4)–1(b)(2), if the acquiring corporation maintains the assets of the transferor as a separate and distinct trade or business, the acquiring corporation must continue to use the accounting method of the transferor with respect to that trade or business. If the transferor's assets are integrated into a trade or business of the acquiring corporation, the acquiring corporation must adopt whichever accounting method is determined to be the "principal method of accounting" based on a comparison of the relative asset bases and gross receipts of the component businesses immediately preceding the transfer date. Treas.Reg. § 1.381(c)(4)–1(b)(2), (c). In any event, the method adopted must clearly reflect income of the acquiring corporation and the acquiring corporation may apply for permission from the IRS to adopt a different method of accounting. Any change in a method of accounting under these provisions may require adjustments under § 481, which is intended to avoid double counting of income and deduction items. A method of accounting for purposes of § 381(c)(4) includes, under § 446, the accounting treatment of any material item of income or deduction in addition to the taxpayer's overall method of accounting. Treas.Reg. § 1.382(c)(4)–1(a)(2). Thus, § 381(c)(4) applies broadly to numerous items not specifically enumerated in § 381(c).

Several accounting matters are specifically described in § 381(c): inventory accounting carries over under rules similar to accounting methods, § 381(c)(5); the acquiring corporation inherits the transferor's depreciation and capital recovery elections and methods, § 381(c)(6); the transferor's installment sales reporting continues without change, § 381(c)(8); amortization of premium and discount on the transferor's bonds for which the acquiring corporation becomes liable are reported by the acquiring corporation as they would have been by the transferor, § 381(c)(9); and the acquiring corporation is entitled to the benefits of § 111 with respect to the recovery of items previously deducted by the transferor, § 381(c)(12).

The acquiring corporation steps directly into the shoes of the transferor with respect to some deduction and credit items: the acquiring corporation may deduct contributions to employee benefit plans under § 404, § 381(c)(11); the acquiring corporation inherits an obligation to replace property involuntarily converted if nonrecognition treatment was claimed by the transferor under § 1033, § 381(c)(13); the acquiring corporation becomes entitled to general business credit carryovers and is potentially liable for credit recapture, § 381(c)(24); and the acquiring corporation becomes entitled to the transferor's § 53 credit for prior year alternative minimum tax liability, § 381(c)(25).

Section 381(c)(16) allows the acquiring corporation to deduct payments of liabilities that result from obligations of the transferor that are assumed by the acquiring corporation if the liability would have been deductible by the transferor if paid by it. This provision permits the acquiring corporation to avoid capitalization of such liabilities as part of the cost of the acquired assets. However, § 381(c)(16) provides that deductibility is available only if the assumed obligation is not reflected in the amount of stock or securities transferred by the acquiring corporation for the assets of the transferor. Treas.Reg. § 1.381(c)(16)–1(a)(5) provides that if the liability is known at the time of transfer, and the amount of consideration transferred by the acquiring corporation is reduced to account for the liability, the liability will be treated as reflected in the stock transfer. Otherwise, it is presumed that a liability is not reflected in the consideration transferred. Treas.Reg. § 1.381(c)(16)–1(a)(1) provides that a liability not subject to § 381(c)(16) is subject to the general accounting provision of § 381(c)(4). Although this reference may be read to require that a liability assumed as part of the consideration for the acquisition must be capitalized, that is not necessarily the case. In Rev.Rul. 83–73, 1983–1 C.B. 84, the taxpayer acquired the assets of Y Corporation in a type (A) reorganization. The assets were subject to an outstanding contingent claim against Y which the taxpayer settled for $700x. Pursuant to an agreement entered into at the time of the reorganization, the former stockholders of Y reimbursed the taxpayer for $500x. The $500x reimbursement was based on the taxpayer's cost of settling the claim, taking into account the taxpayer's § 162 deduction for the payment. The IRS held that, because of the former stockholders' indemnity agreement, the contingent liability was reflected in the consideration given for the transfer of the assets. Thus, payment of the liability was not covered by § 381(c)(16). The ruling further held, however, that the $500x reimbursement from Y's former stockholders was to be deemed a nontaxable contribution by them to Y's capital, and that the taxpayer's satisfaction of the claim was deductible under Y's accounting method which carried over to the taxpayer under § 381(c)(4) and Treas.Reg. § 1.381(c)(4)–1(a)(1).

SECTION 2.   LIMITATIONS ON NET OPERATING LOSS CARRYOVERS FOLLOWING A CHANGE IN CORPORATE OWNERSHIP

INTERNAL REVENUE CODE: Sections 382; 383; 384; 269.

REGULATIONS: Sections 1.382–2T(a)(1) and (2)(i).

General Explanation of the Tax Reform Act of 1986

Staff of the Joint Committee on Taxation 288–299 (1987).

Overview

In general, a corporate taxpayer is allowed to carry a net operating loss ("NOL(s)") forward for deduction in a future taxable year, as long as the corporation's legal identity is maintained. After certain nontaxable asset acquisitions in which the acquired corporation goes out of existence, the acquired corporation's NOL carryforwards are inherited by the acquiring corporation. Similar rules apply to tax attributes other than NOLs, such as net capital losses and unused tax credits. Historically, the use of NOL and other carryforwards has been subject to special limitations after specified transactions involving the corporation in which the carryforwards arose (referred to as the "loss corporation"). [Pre-1986] law also provided other rules that were intended to limit tax-motivated acquisitions of loss corporations.

The operation of the special limitations on the use of carryforwards turned on whether the transaction that caused the limitations to apply took the form of a taxable sale or exchange of stock in the loss corporation or one of certain specified tax-free reorganizations in which the loss corporation's tax attributes carried over to a corporate successor. After a purchase (or other taxable acquisition) of a controlling stock interest in a loss corporation, NOL and other carryforwards were disallowed unless the loss corporation continued to conduct its historical trade or business. In the case of a tax-free reorganization, NOL and other carryforwards were generally allowed in full if the loss corporation's shareholders received stock representing at least 20 percent of the value of the acquiring corporation.

NOL and other carryforwards

Although the Federal income tax system generally requires an annual accounting, a corporate taxpayer was allowed to carry NOLs back to the three taxable years preceding the loss and then forward to each of the 15 taxable years following the loss year (sec. 172). The rationale for allowing the deduction of NOL carryforwards (and carrybacks) was that a taxpayer should be able to average income and losses over a period of years to reduce the disparity between the taxation of businesses that have stable income and businesses that experience fluctuations in income.

In addition to NOLs, other tax attributes eligible to be carried back or forward include unused investment tax credits (secs. 30 and 39), excess foreign tax credits (sec. 904(c)), and net capital losses (sec. 1212). Like NOLs, unused investment tax credits were allowed a three-year carryback and a 15–year carryforward. Subject to an overall limitation based on a taxpayer's U.S. tax attributable to foreign-source income, excess foreign tax credits were allowed a two-year carryback and a five-year carryforward. For net capital losses, generally, corporations had a three-year carryback (but only to the extent the carrybacks did not increase or create a NOL) and a five-year carryforward.

NOL and other carryforwards that were not used before the end of a carryforward period expired.

Carryovers to corporate successors

In general, a corporation's tax history (e.g., carryforwards and asset basis) was preserved as long as the corporation's legal identity was continued. Thus, under the general rules of [pre-1986] law, changes in the stock ownership of a corporation did not affect the corporation's tax attributes. Following are examples of transactions that effected ownership changes without altering the legal identity of a corporation:

(1) A taxable purchase of a corporation's stock from its shareholders (a "purchase"),

(2) A type "B" reorganization, in which stock representing control of the acquired corporation is acquired solely in exchange for voting stock of the acquiring corporation (or a corporation in control of the acquiring corporation) (sec. 368(a)(1)(B)),

(3) A transfer of property to a corporation after which the transferors own 80 percent or more of the corporation's stock (a "section 351 exchange"),

(4) A contribution to the capital of a corporation, in exchange for the issuance of stock, and

(5) A type "E" reorganization, in which interests of investors (shareholders and bondholders) are restructured (sec. 368(a)(1)(E)).

Statutory rules also provided for the carry over of tax attributes (including NOL and other carryforwards) from one corporation to another in certain tax-free acquisitions in which the acquired corporation went out of existence (sec. 381). These rules applied if a corporation's assets were acquired by another corporation in one of the following transactions:

(1) The liquidation of an 80–percent owned subsidiary (sec. 332),

(2) A statutory merger or consolidation, or type "A" reorganization (sec. 368(a)(1)(A)),

(3) A type "C" reorganization, in which substantially all of the assets of one corporation is transferred to another corporation in exchange for voting stock, and the transferor completely liquidates (sec. 368(a)(1)(C)),

(4) A "nondivisive D reorganization," in which substantially all of a corporation's assets are transferred to a controlled corporation, and the transferor completely liquidates (secs. 368(a)(1)(D) and 354(b)(1)),

(5) A mere change in identity, form, or place of organization of a single corporation, or type "F" reorganization (sec. 368(a)(1)(F)), and

(6) A type "G" reorganization, in which substantially all of a corporation's assets are transferred to another corporation pursuant to a court approved insolvency or bankruptcy reorganization plan, and stock or securities of the transferee are distributed pursuant to the plan (sec. 368(a)(1)(G)).

In general, to qualify an acquisitive transaction (including a B reorganization) as a tax-free reorganization, the shareholders of the acquired corporation had to retain "continuity of interest." Thus, a principal part of the consideration used by the acquiring corporation had to consist of stock, and the holdings of all shareholders had to be traced. Further, a tax-free reorganization was required to satisfy a "continuity of business enterprise" test. Generally, continuity of business enterprise requires that a significant portion of an acquired corporation's assets be used in a business activity (see Treas.Reg. sec. 1.368–1(d)).

Acquisitions to evade or avoid income tax

The Secretary of the Treasury was authorized to disallow deductions, credits, or other allowances following an acquisition of control of a corporation or a tax-free acquisition of a corporation's assets if the principal purpose of the acquisition was tax avoidance (sec. 269). This provision applied in the following cases:

(1) where any person or persons acquired (by purchase or in a tax-free transaction) at least 50 percent of a corporation's voting stock, or stock representing 50 percent of the value of the corporation's outstanding stock;

(2) where a corporation acquired property from a previously unrelated corporation and the acquiring corporation's basis for the property was determined by reference to the transferor's basis; and

(3) where a corporation purchased the stock of another corporation in a transaction that qualified for elective treatment as a direct asset purchase (sec. 338), a section 338 election was not made, and the acquired corporation was liquidated into the acquiring corporation (under sec. 332).

Treasury regulations under section 269 provided that the acquisition of assets with an aggregate basis that is materially greater than their value (i.e., assets with built-in losses), coupled with the utilization of the basis to create tax-reducing losses, is indicative of a tax-avoidance motive (Treas.Reg. § 1.269–3(c)(1)).

* * *

1954 Code special limitations

The application of the special limitations on NOL carryforwards was triggered under the 1954 Code by specified changes in stock ownership of the loss corporation (sec. 382). In measuring changes in stock ownership, section 382(c) specifically excluded "nonvoting stock which is limited and preferred as to dividends." Different rules were provided for the application of special limitations on the use of carryovers after a purchase and after a tax-free reorganization. Section 382 did not address the treatment of built-in losses.

If the principal purpose of the acquisition of a loss corporation was tax avoidance, section 269 would apply to disallow NOL carryforwards even if section 382 was inapplicable.

* * *

Special limitations on other tax attributes

Section 383 incorporated by reference the same limitations contained in section 382 for carryforwards of investment credits, foreign tax credits, and capital losses.

* * *

Reasons for Change

* * *

Preservation of the averaging function of carryovers

The primary purpose of the special limitations is the preservation of the integrity of the carryover provisions. The carryover provisions perform a needed averaging function by reducing the distortions caused by the annual accounting system. If, on the other hand, carryovers can be transferred in a way that permits a loss to offset unrelated income, no legitimate averaging function is performed. With completely free transferability of tax losses, the carryover provisions become a mechanism for partial recoupment of losses through the tax system. Under such a system, the Federal Government would effectively be required to reimburse a portion of all corporate tax losses. Regardless of the merits of such a reimbursement program, the carryover rules appear to be an inappropriate and inefficient mechanism for delivery of the reimbursement.

Appropriate matching of loss to income

[Amendments to § 382 enacted in 1976 which never became effective] reflect the view that the relationship of one year's loss to another year's income should be largely a function of whether and how much the stock ownership changed in the interim, while the *Libson Shops* business continuation rule[*] measures the relationship according to whether the loss and the income were generated by the same business. The Act acknowledges the merit in both approaches, while seeking to avoid the economic distortions and administrative problems that a strict application of either approach would entail.

A limitation based strictly on ownership would create a tax bias against sales of corporate businesses, and could prevent sales that would increase economic efficiency. For example, if a prospective buyer could increase the income from a corporate business to a moderate extent, but not enough to overcome the loss of all carryovers, no sale would take place because the business would be worth more to the less-efficient current owner than the prospective buyer would reasonably pay. A strict ownership limitation also would distort the measurement of taxable income generated by capital assets purchased before the corporation was acquired, if the tax deductions for capital costs economically allocable to post-acquisition years were accelerated into pre-acquisition years, creating carryovers that would be lost as a result of the acquisition.

Strict application of a business continuation rule would also be undesirable, because it would discourage efforts to rehabilitate troubled businesses. Such a rule would create an incentive to maintain obsolete and inefficient business practices if the needed changes would create the risk of discontinuing the old business for tax purposes, thus losing the benefit of the carryovers.

Permitting the carry over of all losses following an acquisition, as is permitted under the 1954 Code if the loss business is continued following a purchase, provides an improper matching of income and loss. Income generated under different corporate owners, from capital

---

*   [Ed.: In Libson Shops, Inc. v. Koehler, 353 U.S. 382 (1957), the Court held that following a merger of seventeen separate entities (all of which were engaged in the same line of business and owned by the same stockholders) into a single corporation, the loss carryovers of three of the merged entities could not be deducted from the income of the combined enterprise. The Court held that the prior year's loss could be offset against the current year's income only to the extent that income was derived from the operation of substantially the same business that produced the loss. The Court stated that it could find no indication in the legislative history to the predecessor of § 172 that it was intended "to permit the averaging of the pre-merger losses of one business with the post-merger income of some other business which had been operated and taxed separately before the merger."

Maxwell Hardware Company v. Commissioner, 343 F.2d 713 (9th Cir.1965), held that enactment of the predecessor to § 382 in the 1954 Code destroyed the precedential value of *Libson Shops. Maxwell Hardware* was followed in Frederick Steel Co. v. Commissioner, 375 F.2d 351 (6th Cir.1967); Euclid-Tennessee, Inc. v. Commissioner, 352 F.2d 991 (6th Cir.1965); United States v. Adkins-Phelps, Inc., 400 F.2d 737 (8th Cir.1968). However, the IRS announced that it would continue to apply the *Libson Shops* doctrine to any loss carryover case under the 1954 Code where there has been both a 50 percent or more shift in beneficial interests in a loss carryover and a change of business. T.I.R. No. 773, 657 CCH 6751 (1965).]

In addition, the Treasury Department will promulgate regulations regarding the extent to which stock that is not described in section 1504(a)(4) should nevertheless not be considered stock. For example, the Treasury Department may issue regulations providing that preferred stock otherwise described in section 1504(a)(4) will not be considered stock simply because the dividends are in arrears and the preferred shareholders thus become entitled to vote.

Owner shift involving a 5–percent shareholder

An owner shift involving a 5–percent shareholder is defined as any change in the respective ownership of stock of a corporation that affects the percentage of stock held by any person who holds five percent or more of the stock of the corporation (a "5–percent shareholder") before or after the change (new sec. 382(g)(2)). For purposes of this rule, all less-than-5-percent shareholders are aggregated and treated as one 5–percent shareholder. Thus, an owner shift involving a 5–percent shareholder includes (but is not limited to) the following transactions:

(1) A taxable purchase of loss corporation stock by a person who holds at least five percent of the stock before the purchase;

(2) A disposition of stock by a person who holds at least five percent of stock of the loss corporation either before or after the disposition;

(3) A taxable purchase of loss corporation stock by a person who becomes a 5–percent shareholder as a result of the purchase;

(4) A section 351 exchange that affects the percentage of stock ownership of a loss corporation by one or more 5–percent shareholders;

(5) A decrease in the outstanding stock of a loss corporation (e.g., by virtue of a redemption) that affects the percentage of stock ownership of the loss corporation by one or more 5–percent shareholders;

(6) A conversion of debt (or pure preferred stock that is excluded from the definition of stock) to stock where the percentage of stock ownership of the loss corporation by one or more 5–percent shareholders is affected; and

(7) An issuance of stock by a loss corporation that affects the percentage of stock ownership by one or more 5–percent shareholders.

* * *

Equity structure shift

An equity structure shift is defined as any tax-free reorganization within the meaning of section 368, other than a divisive "D" or "G" reorganization or an "F" reorganization (new sec. 382(g)(3)(A)). In addition, to the extent provided in regulations, the term equity structure shift may include other transactions, such as public offerings not involving a 5–percent shareholder or taxable reorganization-type transactions (e.g., mergers or other reorganization-type transactions that do not qualify for tax-free treatment due to the nature of the consideration or the failure to satisfy any of the other requirements for a tax-free transaction) (new secs. 382(g)(3)(B), (g)(4), and [(m)(4))]. A purpose of the provision that considers only owner shifts involving a 5–percent shareholder is to relieve widely held companies from the burden of keeping track of trades among less-than-5-percent shareholders. For example, a publicly traded company that is 60 percent owned by less-than-5-percent shareholders would not experience an ownership change merely because, within a three-year period, every one of such shareholders sold his stock to a person who was not a 5–percent shareholder. There are situations involving transfers of stock involving less-than-5-percent shareholders, other than tax-free reorganizations (for example, public offerings), in which it will be feasible to identify changes in ownership involving such shareholders, because, unlike public trading, the changes occur as part of a single, integrated transaction. Where identification is reasonably feasible or a reasonable presumption can be applied, the Treasury Department is expected to treat such transactions under the rules applicable to equity structure shifts.

For purposes of determining whether an ownership change has occurred following an equity structure shift, the less-than-5-percent shareholders of each corporation that was a party to the reorganization will be segregated and treated as a single, separate 5-percent shareholder (new sec. 382(g)(4)(B)(i)). The Act contemplates that this segregation rule will similarly apply to acquisitions by groups of less-than-5-percent shareholders through corporations as well as other entities (e.g., partnerships) and in transactions that do not constitute equity structure shifts (new sec. 382(g)(4)(C)). Moreover, the Act provides regulatory authority to apply similar segregation rules to segregate groups of less than 5–percent shareholders in cases that involve only a single corporation, (for example, a public offering or a recapitalization). (new sec. [382(m)(4)]).

* * *

To the extent provided in regulations that will apply prospectively from the date the regulations are issued, a public offering can be treated, in effect, as an equity structure shift with the result that the offering is a measuring event, even if there is otherwise no change in ownership of a person who owns 5–percent of the stock before or after the transaction. Rules also would be provided to segregate the group of less-than-5-percent shareholders prior to the offering and the new group of less than-5-percent shareholders that acquire stock pursuant to the offering. Under such regulations, therefore, the less-than-5-percent shareholders who receive stock in the public offering could be segregated and treated as a separate 5–percent shareholder. * * * The Act contemplates that the regulations may provide rules to allow the corporation to establish the extent, if any, to which existing shareholders acquire stock in the public offering.

Attribution and aggregation of stock ownership

Attribution from entities.—In determining whether an ownership change has occurred, the constructive ownership rules of section 318, with several modifications, are applied (new sec. 382(l)(3)). Except to the extent provided in regulations, the rules for attributing ownership of stock (within the meaning of new section 382(k)(6)) from corporations to their shareholders are applied without regard to the extent of the shareholders' ownership in the corporation. Thus, any stock owned by a corporation is treated as being owned proportionately by its shareholders. Moreover, except as provided in regulations, any stock attributed to a corporation's shareholders is not treated as being held by such corporation. Stock attributed from a partnership, estate or trust similarly shall not be treated as being held by such entity. The effect of the attribution rules is to prevent application of the special limitations after an acquisition that does not result in a more than 50 percent change in the ultimate beneficial ownership of a loss corporation. Conversely, the attribution rules result in an ownership change where more than 50 percent of a loss corporation's stock is acquired indirectly through an acquisition of stock in the corporation's parent corporation.

* * *

3–year testing period

In general, the relevant testing period for determining whether an ownership change has occurred is the three-year period preceding any owner shift involving a 5–percent shareholder or any equity structure shift (new sec. 382(i)(1)). Thus, a series of unrelated transactions occurring during a three-year period may constitute an ownership change. A shorter period, however, may be applicable following any ownership change. In such a case, the testing period for determining whether a second ownership change has occurred does not begin before the day following the first ownership change (new sec. 382(i)(2)).

In addition, the testing period does not begin before the first day of the first taxable year from which there is a loss carryforward (including a current NOL that is defined as a pre-change loss) or excess credit (new sec. 382(i)(3)). Thus, transactions that occur prior to the creation of any attribute subject to limitation under section 382 or section 383 are disregarded. Except as provided in regulations, the special rule described above does not apply to any corporation with a net unrealized built-in loss. The Act contemplates, however, that the regulations will permit such corporations to disregard transactions that occur before the year for which such a corporation establishes that a net unrealized built-in loss first arose.

Effect of ownership change

Section 382 limitation

For any taxable year ending after the change date (i.e., the date on which an owner shift resulting in an ownership change occurs or the date of the reorganization in the case of an equity structure shift resulting in an ownership change), the amount of a loss corporation's (or a successor corporation's) taxable income that can be offset by a pre-change loss (described below) cannot exceed the section 382 limitation for such year (new sec. 382(a)). The section 382 limitation for any taxable year is generally the amount equal to the value of the loss corporation immediately before the ownership change multiplied by the long-term tax-exempt rate (described below) (new sec. 382(b)(1)).

The Treasury Department is required to prescribe regulations regarding the application of the section 382 limitation in the case of a short taxable year. These regulations will generally provide that the section 382 limitation applicable in a short taxable year will be determined by multiplying the full section 382 limitation by the ratio of the number of days in the year to 365. Thus, taxable income realized by a new loss corporation during a short taxable year may be offset by pre-change losses not exceeding a ratable portion of the full section 382 limitation.

If there is a net unrealized built-in gain, the section 382 limitation for any taxable year is increased by the amount of any recognized built-in gains (determined under rules described below). Also, the section 382 limitation is increased by built-in gain recognized by virtue of a section 338 election (to the extent such gain is not otherwise taken into account as a built-in gain). Finally, if the section 382 limitation for a taxable year exceeds the taxable income for the year, the section 382 limitation for the next taxable year is increased by such excess.

If two or more loss corporations are merged or otherwise reorganized into a single entity, separate section 382 limitations are determined and applied to each loss corporation that experiences an ownership change.

* * *

Special rule for post-change year that includes the change date.—In general, the section 382 limitation with respect to an ownership change that occurs during a taxable year does not apply to the utilization of losses against the portion of the loss corporation's taxable income, if any, allocable to the period before the change. For this purpose, except as provided in regulations, taxable income (not including built-in gains or losses, if there is a net unrealized built-in gain or loss) realized during the change year is allocated ratably to each day in the year. The regulations may provide that income realized before the change date from discrete sales of assets would be excluded from the ratable allocation and could be offset without limit by pre-change losses. Moreover, these regulations may provide a loss corporation with an option to determine the taxable income allocable to the period before the change by closing its books on the change date and thus forgoing the ratable allocation.

Value of loss corporation

The value of a loss corporation is generally the fair market value of the corporation's stock (including preferred stock described in section 1504(a)(4)) immediately before the ownership change (new sec. 382(e)(1)). If a redemption occurs in connection with an ownership change-either before or after the change-the value of the loss corporation is determined after taking the redemption into account (new sec. 382(e)(2)). The Treasury Department is given regulatory authority to treat other corporate contractions in the same manner as redemptions for purposes of determining the loss corporation's value. The Treasury Department also is required to prescribe such regulations as are necessary to treat warrants, options, contracts to acquire stock, convertible debt, and similar interests as stock for purposes of determining the value of the loss corporation (new sec. 382(k)(6)(B)(i)).

In determining value, the price at which loss corporation stock changes hands in an arms-length transaction would be evidence, but not conclusive evidence, of the value of the stock. Assume, for example, that an acquiring corporation purchased 40 percent of loss corporation stock over a 12–month period. Six months following this 40 percent acquisition, the acquiring corporation purchased an additional 20 percent of loss corporation stock at a price that reflected a premium over the stock's proportionate amount of the value of all the loss corporation stock; the premium is paid because the 20–percent block carries with it effective control of the loss corporation. Based on these facts, it would be inappropriate to simply gross-up the amount paid for the 20–percent interest to determine the value of the corporation's stock. Under regulations, it is anticipated that the Treasury Department will permit the loss corporation to be valued based upon a formula that grosses up the purchase price of all of the acquired loss corporation stock if a control block of such stock is acquired within a 12–month period.

* * *

Long-term tax-exempt rate

The long-term tax-exempt rate is defined as the highest of the Federal long-term rates determined under section 1274(d), as adjusted to reflect differences between rates on long-term taxable and tax-exempt obligations, in effect for the month in which the change date occurs or the two prior months (new sec. 382(f)). The Treasury Department will publish the long-term tax-exempt rate by revenue ruling within 30 days after the date of enactment and monthly thereafter. The long-term tax-exempt rate will be computed as the yield on a diversified pool of prime, general obligation tax-exempt bonds with remaining periods to maturity of more than nine years.

The use of a rate lower than the long-term Federal rate is necessary to ensure that the value of NOL carryforwards to the buying corporation is not more than their value to the loss corporation. Otherwise there would be a tax incentive to acquire loss corporations. If the loss corporation were to sell its assets and invest in long-term Treasury obligations, it could absorb its NOL carryforwards at a rate equal to the yield on long-term government obligations. Since the price paid by the buyer is larger than the value of the loss company's assets (because the value of NOL carryforwards are taken into account), applying the long-term Treasury rate to the purchase price would result in faster utilization of NOL carryforwards by the buying corporation. The long-term tax-exempt rate normally will fall between 66 (1 minus the maximum corporate tax rate of 34 percent) and 100 percent of the long-term Federal rate.

* * *

Continuity of business enterprise requirements

Following an ownership change, a loss corporation's NOL carryforwards (including any recognized built-in losses, described below) are subject to complete disallowance (except to the extent of any recognized built-in gains or section 338 gain, described below), unless the loss corporation's business enterprise is continued at all times during the two-year period following the ownership change. If a loss corporation fails to satisfy the continuity of business enterprise requirements, no NOL carryforwards would be allowed to the new loss corporation for any post-change year. This continuity of business enterprise requirement is the same requirement that must be satisfied to qualify a transaction as a tax-free reorganization under section 368. (See Treasury regulation section 1.368–1(d)). Under these continuity of business enterprise requirements, a loss corporation (or a successor corporation) must either continue the old loss corporation's historic business or use a significant portion of the old loss corporation's assets in a business. Thus, the requirements may be satisfied even though the old loss corporation discontinues more than a minor portion of its historic business. Changes in the location of a loss corporation's business or the loss corporation's key employees, in contrast to the results under the business-continuation rule in the 1954 Code version of section 382(a), will not constitute a failure to satisfy the continuity of business enterprise requirements under the conference agreement.

Reduction in loss corporation's value for certain capital contributions

Any capital contribution (including a section 351 transfer) that is made to a loss corporation as part of a plan a principal purpose of which is to avoid any of the special limitations under section 382 shall not be taken into account for any purpose under section 382. For purposes of this rule, except as provided in regulations, a capital contribution made during the two-year period ending on the change date is irrebuttably presumed to be part of a plan to avoid the limitations. The application of this rule will result in a reduction of a loss corporation's value for purposes of determining the section 382 limitation. The term "capital contribution" is to be interpreted broadly to encompass any direct or indirect infusion of capital into a loss corporation (e.g., the merger of one corporation into a commonly owned loss corporation). Regulations generally will except (i) capital contributions received on the formation of a loss corporation (not accompanied by the incorporation of assets with a net unrealized built-in loss) where an ownership change occurs within two years of incorporation, (ii) capital contributions received before the first year from which there is an NOL or excess credit carryforward (or in which a net unrealized built-in loss arose), and (iii) capital contributions made to continue basic operations of the corporation's business (e.g., to meet the monthly payroll or fund other operating expenses of the loss corporation). The regulations also may take into account, under appropriate circumstances, the existence of substantial nonbusiness assets on the change date (as described below) and distributions made to shareholders subsequent to capital contributions, as offsets to such contributions.

* * *

Losses subject to limitation

The term "pre-change loss" includes (i) for the taxable year in which an ownership change occurs, the portion of the loss corporation's NOL that is allocable (determined on a daily pro rata basis, without regard to recognized built-in gains or losses, as described below) to the period in such year before the change date, (ii) NOL carryforwards that arose in a taxable year preceding the taxable year of the ownership change and (iii) certain recognized built-in losses and deductions (described below).

For any taxable year in which a corporation has income that, under section 172, may be offset by both a pre-change loss (i.e., an NOL subject to limitation) and an NOL that is not subject to limitation, taxable income is treated as having been first offset by the pre-change loss (new sec. 382(l)(2)(B)). This rule minimizes the NOLs that are subject to the special limitations. For purposes of determining the amount of a pre-change loss that may be carried to a taxable year (under section 172(b)), taxable income for a taxable year is treated as not greater than the section 382 limitation for such year reduced by the unused pre-change losses for prior taxable years. (New sec. 382(l)(2)(A)).

Built-in losses

If a loss corporation has a net unrealized built-in loss, the recognized built-in loss for any taxable year ending within the five-year period ending at the close of the fifth post-change year (the "recognition period") is treated as a pre-change loss (new sec. 382(h)(1)(B)).

Net unrealized built-in losses.—The term "net unrealized built-in loss" is defined as the amount by which the fair market value of the loss corporation's assets immediately before the ownership change is less than the aggregate adjusted bases of a corporation's assets at that time. Under a de minimis exception, the special rule for built-in losses is not applied if the amount of a net unrealized built-in loss does not exceed [15] percent of the value of the corporation's assets immediately before the ownership change. For purposes of the de minimis exception, the value of a corporation's assets is determined by excluding any (1) cash, (2) cash items (as determined for purposes of section 368(a)(2)(F)(iv)), or (3) marketable securities that have a value that does not substantially differ from adjusted basis.

* * *

Recognized built-in losses.—The term "recognized built-in loss" is defined as any loss that is recognized on the disposition of an asset during the recognition period, except to the extent that the new loss corporation establishes that (1) the asset was not held by the loss corporation immediately before the change date, or (2) the loss (or a portion of such loss) is greater than the excess of the adjusted basis of the asset on the change date over the asset's fair market value on that date. The recognized built-in loss for a taxable year cannot exceed the net unrealized built-in loss reduced by recognized built-in losses for prior taxable years ending in the recognition period.

The amount of any recognized built-in loss that exceeds the section 382 limitation for any post-change year must be carried forward (not carried back) under rules similar to the rules applicable to net operating loss carryforwards and will be subject to the special limitations in the same manner as a pre-change loss.

* * *

Built-in gains

If a loss corporation has a net unrealized built-in gain, the section 382 limitation for any taxable year ending within the five-year recognition period is increased by the recognized built-in gain for the taxable year (new sec. 382(h)(1)(A)).

Net unrealized built-in gains.—The term "net unrealized built-in gain" is defined as the amount by which the value of a corporation's assets exceeds the aggregate bases of such assets immediately before the ownership change. Under the de minimis exception described above, the special rule for built-in gains is not applied if the amount of a net unrealized built-in gain does not exceed [15] percent of the value of a loss corporation's assets.

Recognized built-in gains.—The term "recognized built-in gain" is defined as any gain recognized on the disposition of an asset during the recognition period, if the taxpayer establishes that the asset was held by the loss corporation immediately before the change date, to the extent the gain does not exceed the excess of the fair market value of such asset on the change date over the adjusted basis of the asset on that date. The recognized built-in gain for a taxable year cannot exceed the net unrealized built-in gain reduced by the recognized built-in gains for prior years in the recognition period.

* * *

Carryforwards other than NOLs

The Act also amends section 383, relating to special limitations on unused business credits and research credits, excess foreign tax credits, and capital loss carryforwards. Under regulations to be prescribed by the Secretary, capital loss carryforwards will be limited to an amount determined on the basis of the tax liability that is attributable to so much of the taxable income as does not exceed the section 382 limitation for the taxable year, with the same ordering rules that apply under present law. Thus, any capital loss carryforward used in a post-change year will reduce the section 382 limitation that is applied to pre-change losses. In addition, the amount of any excess credit that may be used following an ownership change will be limited, under regulations, on the basis of the tax liability attributable to an amount of taxable income that does not exceed the applicable section 382 limitation, after any NOL carryforwards, capital loss carryforwards, or foreign tax credits are taken into account. The Act also expands the scope of section 383 to include passive activity losses and credits and minimum tax credits.

* * *

DETAILED ANALYSIS

1.   GENERAL

The *General Explanation* indicates that net operating loss carryovers are provided to average the loss years of a business with a fluctuating income against its profitable years. The averaging rationale is not applicable to the new owners of a loss business who have not borne the burden of pre-acquisition losses. The existence of a net operating loss carryover that is transferable to new owners, however, allows the previous owners to recoup a portion of their loss from the new owners who are willing to pay for the future tax savings available from an acquired net operating carryover.[2] The *General Explanation* indicates that eliminating net operating loss carryovers completely following a substantial ownership change would discourage the sale of a loss corporation and hence the partial recoupment of the losses by the historic shareholders who have borne the losses. Thus, Congress adopted the "limitation of earnings" approach which focuses on the market value of the loss to the loss corporation.

In general terms, the market value of a net operating loss carryover to a loss corporation (and indirectly to its existing shareholders) is the present value of its anticipated tax savings on future earnings. The present value of a loss carryover is dependent on the net return the loss corporation can expect to derive from its invested capital. Likewise the value of a loss carryover to a purchaser is the present value of anticipated tax savings on the future earnings which will be offset by acquired losses. Since a profitable enterprise may be expected to achieve a higher rate of return on its investment than a loss corporation (whose rate of return may be negative), an unlimited loss carryover will be more valuable to a profitable purchaser than to the loss corporation. The difference in value may result in a sale of loss carryovers for a price substantially less than the value of the carryover to the purchaser or, in any event, at a price somewhere between the value to the purchaser and the value to the loss corporation. Thus, an unlimited loss carryover not only provides a form of recoupment of prior losses for the seller of a loss corporation, but also provides a windfall profit for the purchaser financed by the Treasury. Section 382 is intended to eliminate this windfall potential by limiting the value of a loss carryover following a substantial ownership change to an approximation of the value of the carryover to the loss corporation. So limited, the carryover has the same value to both seller and purchaser. The cost of this limitation falls, in part, on the loss corporation which is limited in the amount it can receive for the transfer of loss carryovers.

Theoretically, because the loss carryover has the same value to each, the seller and the purchaser should be neutral with respect to the presence of a loss carryover as part of an asset transfer. This "neutrality" principle works only if the limitation on the use of acquired loss carryovers does not reduce the value of loss carryovers to an amount less than the present value of the losses to the loss corporation. An overly restrictive limitation will inhibit the transfer of assets to more efficient operators. A limitation that is too generous, however, will provide a windfall profit to one of the parties. Section 382 attempts to strike a balance by limiting the annual recovery of a net operating loss carryover following an ownership change to the fair market value of the equity interests in the loss corporation multiplied by a federal tax exempt rate. This formula is based on the theory that a loss corporation could dispose of its assets and invest the proceeds in risk-free taxable government bonds thereby earning an annual rate of return at least equal to the rate on long-term federal instruments. Senate Finance Committee, Final Report on Subchapter C, The Subchapter C Revision Act of 1985 (Staff Report), S. Prt. 99–47, 99th Cong., 1st Sess. 71 (1985). The Conference Report on the 1986 Act indicates that the rate is

---

[2]   In re Prudential Lines Inc., 928 F.2d 565 (2d Cir.1991), recognized a corporate net operating loss carryforward as a property interest of the loss corporation's bankruptcy estate and enjoined the loss corporation's parent corporation from taking an action (claiming a worthless stock deduction) that would jeopardize the subsidiary's loss carryforward.

reduced to a tax-exempt rate, in part, because Congress believed that the fair market value of the loss corporation includes the value of the loss carryover itself. The loss carryover is an asset which could not be individually sold and the proceeds reinvested. See H. Rep. No. 99–841, 99th Cong., 2d Sess. II–188 (1986). In addition, Congressional studies have indicated that loss corporations typically have absorbed net operating losses at the rate of 4.4 percent of book net worth.[3] Senate Finance Committee, Final Report on Subchapter C, The Subchapter C Revision Act of 1985 (Staff Report), S. Prt. 99–47, 99th Cong., 1st Sess. 71 (1985). The federal tax-exempt rate, which has varied between approximately 8 percent and 2.7 percent since § 382 was enacted,[4] is generous when compared with actual experience. Some commentators have argued, however, that the limitation based on the federal exempt rate is too low thereby undervaluing the loss corporation's loss carryovers. See, e.g., N.Y. State Bar Ass'n Tax Section, Comm. on Net Operating Losses, The Net Operating Loss and Excess Credit Carryforwards Under H.R. 3838, 31 Tax Notes 725, 729 (1986).

2. OWNERSHIP CHANGE

2.1. *In General*

The limitation on loss carryovers in § 382 is triggered by an "ownership change," which in general is a greater than 50 percentage point increase in the ownership of the stock of a loss corporation by one or more five percent stockholders over a three year testing period. I.R.C. § 382(g)(1). Disposition of a corporate business by a majority of the investors who suffered the burden of losses terminates the averaging function of loss carryovers as to those investors and thus eliminates this particular justification for further loss carryovers. The only remaining justification for allowing loss carryovers to the new owners of a loss corporation is to provide the former investors with some recovery of a portion of their loss in the form of consideration paid for the carryover. Thus, a more than 50 percentage point change of ownership of the loss corporation is deemed an appropriate trigger for imposing limitations on loss carryovers.

Under the statutory language, an ownership change may result from an "owner shift," defined as any change in ownership of a loss corporation's stock involving a five percent stockholder, or an "equity structure shift," which is a reorganization of a loss corporation (with the exception of divisive (D) and (G) reorganizations, and (F) reorganizations). Under the statutory definitions, an equity structure shift that results in an ownership change also will qualify as an owner shift. This is true even for a publicly held corporation with no single five percent stockholder because of rules that aggregate the stock ownership of non-five percent stockholders. I.R.C. § 382(g)(4)(B) and (C). The preamble to the § 382 temporary regulations states that there are no substantive differences (except for some transitional rule purposes) between classifying a transaction as an owner shift or an equity structure shift. T.D. 8149, 52 Fed. Reg. 29,668, 29,670 (1987); See also Temp.Reg. § 1.382–2T(e)(2)(iii) (an equity structure shift which affects the stock ownership of a five percent stockholder is also an

---

[3]   This rate will itself overstate the true rate of recovery on the fair market value of assets if book values are less than fair market value.

[4]   The federal tax-exempt rate is determined monthly by the IRS and announced in Revenue Rulings.

owner shift). There is no apparent reason for the distinction, which appears to be attributable to an early version of the statute that was changed during the drafting process.

The recipient of stock by reason of death, as a gift, or in a transfer from a spouse by reason of divorce or separation, is treated as the owner of the stock for the period the stock was held by the transferor. I.R.C. § 382(l)(3)(B). These transfers, therefore, are not counted in testing for an ownership change.

Technically, the § 382 limitation applies to losses carried over to any "post change year" of a "new loss corporation." I.R.C. § 382(a). A new loss corporation is defined as a corporation entitled to a net operating loss carryover following an ownership change. I.R.C. § 382(k)(1) and (3). A "post change year" is any taxable year ending after the date of an ownership change. I.R.C. § 382(d)(2). A loss corporation to which the limitation applies following an ownership change is any corporation entitled to a net operating loss carryover or which incurred a net operating loss in the year of an ownership change. I.R.C. § 382(k)(1). The term "loss corporation" also includes a corporation with built-in losses, page 833, which are also subject to the § 382 limitation. A corporation which is a loss corporation before the date of an ownership change is referred to as an "old loss corporation." I.R.C. § 382(k)(2).

2.2. *Counting Owner Shifts During the Testing Period*

An ownership change occurs if the percentage stock ownership of five percent stockholders on the date of any owner shift or equity structure shift (the "testing date") has increased by more than 50 percentage points over the lowest percentage of stock ownership of five percent stockholders at any time within the three-year period preceding the testing date. I.R.C. § 382(g)(1). An ownership change may result from the sum of unrelated stock transfers by five percent stockholders and transfers from less than five percent stockholders to persons who become five percent stockholders. A loss corporation is thus required during a rolling three-year period to keep track of all stock transfers from or to persons who are or who become five percent stockholders.

A full three year look-back is not necessary in all cases. The testing period does not begin until the first day of a taxable year in which a loss corporation incurs a net operating loss that is carried over into a taxable year ending after the testing date. I.R.C. § 382(i)(3). Thus, stock transfers occurring in a year in which a corporation has neither a net operating loss nor loss carryover do not count towards an ownership change. In addition, a new testing period begins following an ownership change. I.R.C. § 382(i)(2). Stock transfers predating an ownership change will not be counted again towards a subsequent ownership change.

The basic operation of these rules is illustrated by the following example. As of January 1, 2010, A, B, C, D, and E each owned 20 of the 100 outstanding shares of L Corporation. L Corporation had no net operating loss carryovers as of that date and did not incur a net operating loss in 2010. On July 1, 2010, A sold A's 20 shares of L Corporation stock to P Corporation, which previously owned no L Corporation stock. In 2011, L Corporation incurred a net operating loss which is carried forward. On January 1, 2011, B sold B's 20 shares to P Corporation, and on June 30, 2013, C sold C's 20 shares to P Corporation. Although P has increased its stock ownership of L from zero percent to 60 percent during the three-year period ending on June 30, 2013, because L Corporation did not have any net operating loss carryovers from 2010 or earlier years, the owner shift effected by the July 1, 2010 purchase from A is not counted in determining whether there has been an ownership change. On December 31, 2013, D sold D's 20 shares to P Corporation. Looking backwards from December 31, 2013, P has increased its stock ownership by 60 percentage points, from 20 percent to 80 percent. Because L had a net operating loss in 2011 that was carried forward to subsequent years, the purchases from B, C, and D are taken into account and an ownership change has occurred. Because the ownership change starts a new testing period, if E were to sell E's stock to F on June 1, 2016, there would be no ownership change, even though in the three-year period ending June 1, 2016, P Corporation would have increased its stock ownership by 40 percentage points (from 40 percent to 80 percent) and F would have increased his stock ownership by 20 percentage points, for a total shift of 60 percentage points.

In some circumstances, the requirement of § 382(g)(1)(B) that an ownership change be tested with respect to the lowest percentage of stock owned by a five percent stockholder during the testing period can have a surprising result. For example, L Corporation has 200 shares of stock outstanding of which A owns 100 shares and B and C each own 50 shares. On January 2, 2013, A sells 60 shares of L stock to B. B's ownership interest increases by 30 percentage points, from 25 percent of L stock to 55 percent. A's interest drops to 20 percent. On January 1, 2014, A acquires all of C's L stock. A and B have in the aggregate increased their percentage ownership of L by only 25 percentage points during the testing period; B's interest has increased by 30 percentage points and A's percentage interest has declined by five percentage points. Nonetheless, Temp.Reg. § 1.382–2T(c)(4)(i) treats A's acquisition of C's stock as an ownership change. The temporary regulation concludes that, as a result of A's purchase of C's stock, A's percentage interest increased from a low of 20 percent, the lowest percentage of A's ownership interest during the testing period, to 45 percent. A's 25 percentage points increase plus B's 30 percentage points increase within the testing period are sufficient to trigger an ownership change despite the fact that their aggregate overall increase in stock ownership during the testing period is only 25 percentage points. The temporary regulation reaches this result even if A's sale to B and purchase from C are part of an integrated plan. Temp.Reg. § 1.382–2T(c)(3).

Arguably, the temporary regulation misreads § 382(g)(1) and reaches an unduly harsh result. Section 382(g)(1) can be interpreted as requiring that the increased interests of A and B be aggregated for purposes of both subsections (A) and (B). To paraphrase the statutory language, A and B's stock ownership of L has increased by only 25 percentage points over the lowest percentage of stock owned by A and B together ("such shareholders") at any time during the testing period (from a low of 75% [20% plus 55%] to 100%). Given the Treasury's broad regulatory authority under § 382(m) to interpret § 382, however, it is not likely that its interpretation of § 382(g)(1) could be challenged successfully.

2.3. *Stock Ownership and Five Percent Stockholders*

2.3.1.   *Identifying Five Percent Stockholders*

The § 382 trigger focuses on stock transfers to or by persons who own five percent or more of the loss corporation stock. Proportionate stock ownership is determined by the value of stock held by the stockholder. I.R.C. § 382(k)(6)(C). A person is treated as a five percent stockholder if the person was a five percent stockholder at any time during the testing period, even though the person may not own five percent of the loss corporation stock on the testing date. Temp.Reg. § 1.382–2T(g)(1)(iv). The five percent figure was chosen to relieve companies from the burden of keeping track of trades among stockholders with a minor interest. H.Rep. No. 99–841, 99th Cong., 2d Sess. II–176 (1986).[5] Thus stock transfers between less than five percent stockholders are not counted in testing for an ownership change. Temp.Reg. § 1.382–2T(e)(1)(ii). The less than five percent stockholders as a group, however, are treated as a single five percent stockholder regardless of the percentage interest held by such persons. I.R.C. § 382(g)(4)(A). Temp.Reg. § 1.382–2T(f)(13) refers to the group of less than five percent stockholders as a "public group." As a single five percent stockholder, transfers to or by a public group can trigger an ownership change. Thus, for example, a public issue of more than 50 percent of the stock of a closely held loss corporation to less than five percent stockholders will trigger an ownership change because the public group of new stockholders increases its ownership interest from zero preceding the public offering to more than 50 percent following the public offering. See Temp.Reg. § 1.382–2T(e)(1)(iii), Ex. (5). Various groups of less than five percent stockholders separately may represent five percent stockholders and transfers between those groups can be an ownership change. See page 827.

Notice 2010–50, 2010–27 I.R.B. 12, provides guidance for measuring owner shifts of loss corporations that have more than one class of stock outstanding when the value of one class of stock fluctuates relative to another class of stock. The IRS will accept use of the "full value methodology," under which all shares are "marked to market" on each testing date. Under this method, the percentage of stock owned by any person is determined with reference to "the relative fair market value of the stock owned by such person to the total fair market value of the outstanding stock of the corporation.... [C]hanges in percentage ownership as a result of fluctuations in value are taken into account if a testing date occurs, regardless of whether a particular shareholder actively participates or is otherwise party to the transaction that causes the testing date to occur...." The IRS also will accept use of the "hold-constant principle." Under this methodology, "the value of a share, relative to the value of all other stock of the corporation, is established on the date that share is acquired by a particular shareholder. On subsequent testing dates, the percentage interest represented by that share (the "tested share") is then determined by factoring out fluctuations in the relative values of the loss corporation's share classes that have occurred since the acquisition date of the tested share. Thus, as applied, the hold constant principle is individualized for each acquisition of stock by each shareholder." The "hold-

---

[5]   In general, any person who acquires five percent or more of the stock of a publicly traded corporation is required to register the acquisition with the Securities and Exchange Commission.

constant principle" has several variations that the notice identifies as acceptable. An acquisition is not an event upon which the acquiring shareholder marks to fair market value other shares that it holds under any hold-constant principle variation. To be acceptable, whichever methodology is selected must measure the increased percentage ownership represented by a stock acquisition by dividing the fair market value of that stock on the acquisition date by the fair market value of all of the outstanding stock of the loss corporation on that date. Any alternative treatment of an acquisition is inconsistent with § 382(*l*)(3)(C) and is not acceptable. Any method selected, whether the "full value methodology" or a particular variation of the "hold-constant principle" must be applied consistently to all testing dates in a "consistency period." With respect to any testing date, the consistency period includes all prior testing dates, beginning with the latest of: (1) the first date on which the taxpayer had more than one class of stock; (2) the first day following an ownership change; or (3) the date six years before that testing date.

2.3.2.   *Attribution Rules*

With certain modifications, the attribution rules of § 318 apply to identify proportionate stock ownership. I.R.C. § 382(l)(3). In general, the modifications to § 318 have two effects. First, members of a family who are subject to stock attribution under § 318(a)(1) are treated as a single individual. Thus, stock transfers among family members to whom stock is attributable will not trigger an ownership change.[6] If an individual is a member of more than one family group under the attribution rules, that individual will be treated as a member of the family which results in the smallest increase in stock held by five percent stockholders on a testing date. Temp.Reg. § 1.382–2T(h)(6)(iv). The regulations also provide that an individual who is not otherwise a five percent stockholder will not be treated as a five percent stockholder as a result of family attribution. Second, stock of a loss corporation owned by any entity (corporation, partnership or trust) which has a five percent or greater interest is attributed up the ownership chain to the last person from whom no further attribution is possible. I.R.C. § 382(l)(3)(A)(ii)(II); Temp.Reg. § 1.382–2T(g)(2), (h)(2)(i). Intermediate entities are disregarded. Temp.Reg. § 1.382–2T(h)(2)(i)(A). Treas.Reg. § 1.382–3(a)(1)(i) includes as an entity for this purpose any group of less than five percent shareholders who act pursuant to a plan to acquire five percent of the stock of a loss corporation.

Temp.Reg. § 1.382–2T(g)(4), Ex. (1), illustrates application of these attribution rules as follows. The stock of L, a loss corporation is owned 20 percent by A, 10 percent by corporation P1, and 20 percent by E, a joint venture. The remaining 50 percent of L stock is publicly held ("Public

---

[6]   Garber Industries Holding Co., Inc. v. Commissioner, 124 T.C. 1 (2005), aff'd, 435 F.3d 555 (5th Cir. 2006), held that the family aggregation rule of § 382(*l*)(3)(A)(i) applies solely from the perspective of individuals who are shareholders (as determined under the attribution rules of § 382(*l*)(3)(A)) of the loss corporation. Thus, the sale of stock from one sibling to another that resulted in a more than 50 percent increase in stock ownership by the purchasing sibling triggered the application of § 382. The fact that each sibling and either of their parents would be viewed as a single shareholder did not result in the siblings being treated as a single shareholder where neither of their parents was a shareholder. The court recognized the possibility that the rule it announced might result in arbitrary distinctions between cases in which a parent of the siblings also was a shareholder and cases in which the parent was not a shareholder, but concluded that the announced rule was the one most compatible with the statutory language and legislative history.

Group L"). B owns 15 percent of the stock of P1 Corporation. The remaining 85 percent of the shares of P1 are publicly held ("Public Group P1"). E, the joint venture, is owned 30 percent by corporation P2 and 70 percent by corporation P3. Both P2 and P3 are publicly held ("Public Group P2" and "Public Group P3"). L's ownership structure is illustrated as follows:

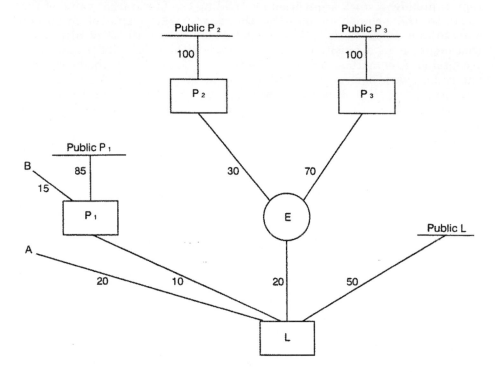

A is a five percent stockholder of L because of A's direct ownership of 20 percent of L stock. Public Group L is a single five percent stockholder by virtue of its collective 50 percent interest in L.

B is not a five percent stockholder. Although B is a five percent stockholder of P1, and thereby indirectly owns the L stock owned by P1, Temp.Reg. § 1.382–2T(g)(2), B's ownership interest in L is only 1.5 percent (15% of P1's 10%). Because B is not a five percent stockholder of L, B is treated as a member of the Public Group P1. See Temp.Reg. § 1.382–2T(j)(1)(iv). P1 is not a five percent stockholder because its interest is attributable to its stockholders. P1's public stockholders, Public P1, are treated as a single five percent stockholder of L owning 10 percent of the L stock, 8.5 percent plus B's 1.5 percent.

Public Group P2 is also a five percent stockholder. P2 has a six percent interest attributed from P2's 30 percent interest in E, which in turn owns 20 percent of L (30% × 20% = 6%). P2's six percent interest is attributed to the P2 public group which owns 100 percent of P2. Public Group P3 is also a five percent stockholder with a 14 percent interest attributed to it ([20% × 70%] × 100%).

2.3.3.   Option Attribution

Even in the absence of a direct stock transfer, outstanding options and other rights to acquire stock (including convertible debt) may create an owner shift that must be taken into account in determining whether there is an ownership change during a testing period. Section 382(l)(3)(A)(iv) provides that, except to the extent provided in the regulations, an option or other right to acquire stock will be treated as exercised if the deemed exercise results in an ownership change. However, Treas.Reg. § 1.382–4(d)(2) provides that an option will be treated as exercised on the date of its issue, transfer, or on a subsequent testing date, only if the option satisfies one of three tests, an ownership test, a control test, or an income test.

Under the *ownership* test of Treas.Reg. § 1.382–4(d)(3), an option will be treated as exercised if a principal purpose of the issuance, transfer, or structure of the option is to avoid or ameliorate the impact of an ownership change by providing its holder with a substantial portion of the attributes of ownership of the underlying stock. Under Treas.Reg. § 1.382–4(d)(6)(i), factors that indicate the presence or absence of a purpose to avoid or ameliorate the impact of an ownership change (under all three of the tests) include whether there are business purposes for the issuance, transfer or structure of the option, the likelihood of exercise of the option, and the consequences of treating the option as having been exercised. Treas.Reg. § 1.382–4(d)(6)(ii) specifically identifies additional factors that indicate that an option provides its holder with the attributes of ownership. These include the relationship between the exercise price of the option at the time of its issue or transfer and the value of the underlying stock, whether the option provides a right to participate in management or other rights that ordinarily would be held by stock owners, and the existence of reciprocal options (e.g. offsetting put and call options held by the prospective seller and purchaser). The ability of the option holder to participate in future appreciation in the value of the underlying stock may be considered, but is not of itself sufficient to satisfy the ownership test. Conversely, the absence of risk of loss does not preclude treating an option as exercised.

An option will be treated as exercised under the control test of Treas.Reg. § 1.382–4(d)(4) if a principal purpose of the issuance, transfer, or structure of the option is to avoid or ameliorate the impact of an ownership change and the option holder (or a related person) directly or indirectly has a more than 50 percent interest in the loss corporation determined by including the ownership interest that would result from exercise of the option. Treas.Reg. § 1.382–4(d)(6)(iii) indicates that economic interests in the loss corporation and influence over management of the loss corporation held by the holder and related persons will be taken into account in applying the control test.

The *income* test of Treas.Reg. § 1.382–4(d)(5) treats an option as exercised if a principal purpose of the issuance, transfer, or structure of the option is to avoid or ameliorate the impact of an ownership change of the loss corporation by facilitating the creation of income or value in the loss corporation prior to the exercise of the option. Under this test, an option will be treated as exercised if in connection with the issuance or transfer of an option the loss corporation engages in transactions that accelerate income thereby utilizing loss carryovers prior to an ownership change, or the option holder or related person purchases stock or makes a capital contribution that increases the value of the loss corporation. Treas.Reg. § 1.382–4(d)(6)(iv).

Treas.Reg. § 1.382–4(d)(7) contains a list of safe harbors that exclude some options from the deemed exercise rules. Commercially reasonable

amounts of stock of a loss corporation. Treas.Reg. § 1.382–3(j)(13) provides that transfer of a direct ownership in the loss corporation by a first-tier five percent entity, or a transfer by a five percent shareholder, to public shareholders will not create a new segregated public group. Instead, existing public groups will be treated as acquiring the transferred interest. In addition, Treas.Reg. § 1.382–3(j)(14) provides a special exception under which a loss corporation may annually redeem ten percent of the value of its stock, or ten percent of the shares of a particular class of stock, without triggering the segregation rules and the creation of new five percent groups. Under the regulations, transactions that result in the creation of a new public group, and thus a possible owner shift, simply will be folded into the existing public groups, thereby reducing the chance of an ownership change.

Once an ownership change has occurred following a transaction that requires segregation of different groups of less than five percent stockholders, the groups are no longer treated as separate five percent stockholders. Temp.Reg. § 1.382–2T(j)(2)(iii)(B)(2), Ex. (3)(iv).

Treas.Reg. § 1.382–3(j) exempts certain small stock issues from the segregation requirement so that the loss corporation is not required to treat recipients of a small stock issue as a separate group of less than five percent stockholders. A stock issue is subject to the exception if the value of all stock issued during the taxable year does not exceed ten percent of the total value of outstanding stock at the beginning of the year, or if, on a class-by-class basis, the total number of shares of any class of stock issued during the taxable year does not exceed ten percent of the number of shares of stock of that class outstanding at the beginning of the taxable year. Treas.Reg. § 1.382–3(j)(2).

In addition, Treas.Reg. § 1.382–3(j)(3) exempts from the segregation rules stock issued for cash if the total amount of the newly issued stock does not exceed one-half of the stock ownership of direct public groups immediately preceding the stock issue. Stock exempted from the segregation rules under these provisions is treated as acquired by existing direct public groups in proportion to the existing public groups' pre-issuance ownership interests. Treas.Reg. § 1.382–3(j)(5). However, if the loss corporation has actual knowledge that a particular direct public group acquired a greater percentage of newly issued stock than its proportionate share, the loss corporation may treat that public group as receiving the higher percentage. Treas.Reg. § 1.382–3(j)(5)(ii).

The small issue and cash issue exemptions from the segregation rules also apply to stock issues of first tier and higher tier entities. Treas.Reg. § 1.382–3(j)(11).

The operation of the aggregation and segregation rules is illustrated by the following example:

L, a loss corporation, P1, and P2 each have 1000 shares of stock outstanding. The stock of L is owned 600 shares by P1, 200 shares by P2, and 170 shares by a public group, none of whom owns more than five percent of the L stock, and A who owns 30 shares. A owns 50 shares of the P1 stock. The remaining 950 shares of P1 stock are owned by public stockholders none of whom owns more than five percent of P1 stock. A owns 100 shares of P2 stock. The remaining 900 shares of P2 stock are held by public stockholders none of whom owns more than five percent of P2 stock. The ownership structure of L is as follows:

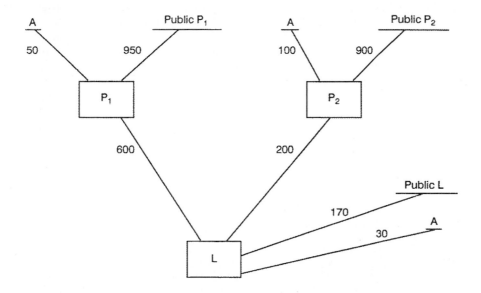

L's stock is held by three separate public groups, each of which is treated as a single five percent stockholder: the public group that directly holds L stock, the public group of P1 stockholders which by attribution holds 60 percent of L stock, and the public group of P2 stockholders which by attribution holds 20 percent of L stock.

Although A directly and indirectly owns more than five percent of L stock, A is not a five percent stockholder of L. A owns 3 percent of L directly. As a five percent owner of P1, A is attributed a proportionate share of P1's L stock, an interest of 3 percent (5% × 60%). Since A's interest is less than five percent, A is treated as a member of the P1 public group. Temp.Reg. § 1.382–2T(j)(1)(iv)(A). As a 10 percent owner of P2, A indirectly owns an additional 2 percent of L, but again A's stock interest is included as part of the interest of the P2 public group. Temp .Reg. § 1.382–2T(j)(1)(iii) contains a presumption that stockholders, including five percent owners of a higher tier entity which owns stock in a loss corporation, who are not five percent stockholders of a loss corporation are not members of more than one public group. Thus, A's three percent direct interest, A's three percent interest through P1, and A's two percent interest through P2 are not accumulated to make A a five percent stockholder of L. Because L is required to keep track of only five percent stockholders who can be traced through a chain of at least five percent ownership interests, L is presumed not to have knowledge of A's existence as a five percent stockholder. However, A will be treated as a five percent stockholder if L has actual knowledge of A's ownership interests. Temp.Reg. § 1.382–2T(j)(1)(iii), (k)(2). As the example demonstrates, this distinction can be significant.

On April 1, 2011, L issues 111 shares of new stock to the public. The stock is not purchased by any person who owns five percent of L stock. The issue of L stock to less than five percent stockholders creates a new public group which is treated as a five percent stockholder.[7] This new group ("New Public L") increased its interest in L during the testing period from 0 percent before the stock offering to 10 percent (111/1111) afterwards. Temp.Reg. § 1.382–2T(j)(1)(iii) presumes that there is no cross-ownership between the old public stockholders of L and the new public stockholders. Thus, absent actual knowledge by L, any acquisition of the newly issued L stock by existing stockholders will be ignored. The stock issue is, therefore, a 10 percent owner shift.

On April 1, 2012, all of the assets of P1, including the L stock, are acquired by P2 in a statutory merger. The P1 stockholders receive one share of P2 stock for every four shares of P1 stock. A receives 12.5 shares of P2 stock, the remaining P1 stockholders receive 237.5 shares of P2 stock. P2 now owns 72 percent (800/1111 shares) of L. The transaction is tested for an ownership change by segregating the post-merger stockholders of P2 into two public groups, the original P2 stockholders, who now own 72 percent of P2 ("Old Public P2"), and the pre-merger P1 stockholders ("New Public P2"). (As will be discussed below, A has become a five percent stockholder of L and is therefore no longer included in a P2 public group.) Before the reorganization, the original P2 public group, including A, owned 18 percent of L by attribution from P2 ([200/1111] × 100%). After the reorganization, the original P2 public group owns 51.8 percent of L ([800/1111] × [900/1250]). Thus, Old Public P2 has increased its ownership interest in L by 33.8 percent.

Following the merger, the ownership structure of L is as follows:

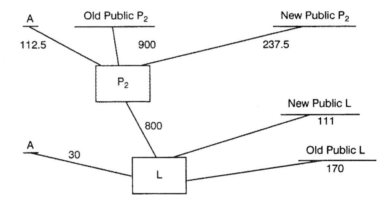

Within the testing period, the 33.8 percent owner shift in L from New Public P2 to Old Public P2, plus the 10 percent owner shift from Old Public L to New Public L, are not sufficient to trigger an ownership change of L. However, A's interest in the transaction causes an ownership change to be triggered. Before the merger of P1 into P2, A's cross-ownership was disregarded under the presumption of Temp.Reg. § 1.382–2T(j)(1)(iii), and A was treated as a less than five percent stockholder whose stock interests are part of public groups. In contrast to A's pre-merger ownership interests, after the merger A has an identifiable interest greater than five percent that is traceable through a connection of five percent ownership interests.

---

7   Treas.Reg. § 1.382–3(j) does not prevent segregation of the new public group because the stock issue exceeds ten percent of the outstanding stock and is more than one-half of the stock held by direct public groups immediately preceding the stock issue.

A thus becomes a distinct five percent stockholder who must be counted. After the merger A owns 112.5 shares of P2 stock, 9 percent of P2. A is, therefore, deemed to own 6.5 percent of L by attribution from P2 (9% × 72%). Even though A is now identified as a five percent stockholder, A's ownership interest is presumed to include only A's 6.5 percent interest through P2. A's 2.7 percent direct interest in L is still treated as part of the Old Public L group. Temp.Reg. § 1.382–2T(j)(1)(vi), Ex. (5). As a result, A's interest as an identified five percent stockholder increased from zero before the transaction to 6.5 percent after the merger. A's 6.5 percent owner shift, when added to the increased interests of Old Public P2 and New Public L, result in an increased interest by five percent stockholders of 50.3 percent, sufficient to trigger an ownership change.

If L has actual knowledge of A's pre-merger stock ownership interest, L may overcome the presumption of Temp.Reg. § 1.382–2T(j)(1)(iii), and avoid the ownership change. See Temp.Reg. § 1.382–2T(k)(2). After L's public offering, but before the merger of P1 and P2, A's lowest actual percentage interest during the testing period was 7.2 percent, 2.7 percent direct interest in L stock, 2.7 percent attributed through P1, and 1.8 percent attributed through P2. A's percentage interest in L after the merger is 9.2, of which 6.5 percent is attributed from P2 and 2.7 percent is direct. Based on actual knowledge, the owner shift attributable to A is only two percent. In addition, without A as a member, Public P2's ownership interest goes from 16.2 percent (200/1111 × 90%) to 51.8 percent, an ownership change of 35.6 percent. That is not sufficient to trigger an ownership change on the merger of P1 into P2 (35.6% + 10% + 2% = 47.6%).

2.3.6.   *Reporting Requirements*

Temp.Reg. § 1.382–2T(a)(2)(ii) and (iii) impose extensive information reporting and record keeping requirements that require the corporation to monitor its status under § 382 even if there is only a remote possibility of an ownership change. In any taxable year in which a corporation is a loss corporation (see § 382(k)(1)), the corporation must file a statement with its tax return indicating whether there has been a testing date during the year, identifying any testing dates on which an ownership change occurred, identifying testing dates that occurred closest to the end of each calendar quarter of the taxable year, indicating the percentage stock ownership of each five percent stockholder on each testing date reported and the percentage increase of each five percent stockholder during the testing period, and identifying the extent to which the corporation relied on presumptions provided in Temp.Reg. § 1.382–2T(k)(1). Temp.Reg. § 1.382–2T(k)(1) allows a publicly held loss corporation to rely on filings with the Securities and Exchange Commission to disclose the existence of five percent stockholders. A loss corporation is also allowed to rely on statements by responsible persons (such as officers, trustees, partners, etc.), signed under penalties of perjury, which disclose the ownership interests and changes in interest of the owners of an upper-tier entity that owns an interest in the loss corporation. The temporary regulations also require a loss corporation to maintain records adequate to identify five percent stockholders and ascertain whether an ownership change has occurred. In many cases, it is possible that the cost of providing information returns will outweigh the value of loss carryovers.

3.   COMPUTING THE SECTION 382 LIMITATION

3.1. *Valuing the Loss Corporation*

The annual limitation on income of a loss corporation that can be offset by net operating loss carryovers following an ownership change is computed by multiplying the value of the loss corporation by the federal long-term tax-exempt rate. I.R.C. § 382(b)(1). Value is based on the value of the stock of the loss corporation on the date immediately preceding an ownership change. I.R.C. § 382(e)(1). As noted in the *General Explanation*, the value of a loss corporation includes the value of interests that are not treated as stock under § 1504(a)(4). The value of the loss corporation also includes nonstock that is treated as stock under Temp.Reg. § 1.382–2T(f)(18)(iii).

To prevent a loss corporation from artificially enhancing its value on the eve of an ownership change, § 382(*l*) provides that any capital contributed to the loss corporation as part of a plan to increase the limitation shall not be taken into account in determining value. Section 382(*l*)(2) provides that, except as otherwise provided in regulations, any capital contribution within 2 years of the date of an ownership change shall be treated as part of a forbidden plan.

Additional anti-abuse rules are found in § 382(*l*)(4), which reduces the value of a loss corporation that has substantial nonbusiness assets. The value of the loss corporation is reduced by the fair market value of nonbusiness assets, less liabilities attributable to such assets. A loss corporation has substantial nonbusiness assets if more than one-third of the total value of the loss corporation consists of investment assets. This limitation is intended to prevent the sale of carryovers by a loss corporation which has disposed of its operating assets. However, given the severity of the limitation imposed by § 382, a market for shell corporations with loss carryovers is not likely to exist in any event. The provision ultimately works only to reduce the sales price of a loss corporation with substantial investment assets.

Under § 382(e)(2), if an ownership change occurs in connection with a redemption or other corporate contraction, the value of the loss corporation immediately before the ownership change must be adjusted to account for assets distributed in the redemption.

3.2. *Valuing Members of Controlled Groups of Corporations*

Treas.Reg. § 1.382–8 contains rules for the valuation of a loss corporation that is a member of a controlled group of corporations (as defined in § 1563(a), page 435). These rules are designed to avoid duplication of the value of assets of one member of a controlled group by including in the value of the stock of an upper-tier corporation the value of stock of a subsidiary member of the controlled group held directly by the upper-tier corporation. Thus, in general, for purposes of determining the § 382 limitation with respect to a loss of a controlled group, the value of the stock of each component member of the controlled group (as defined in § 1563(b), page 435) is reduced by the value of the stock of any other member of the controlled group held directly by the component member of the controlled group. Treas.Reg. § 1.382–8(c)(1).

3.3. *Built-in Gains and Losses*

Section 382 also deals with unrealized losses of a loss corporation that could be utilized to offset future income following an ownership change in the same manner as a net operating loss carryforward. Without application of the limitation, the loss corporation could realize the losses after an ownership change to offset post-change income. Net unrealized losses existing at the time of an ownership change are subject to the annual § 382 limitation in the taxable year the losses are recognized. I.R.C. § 382(h)(1)(B). Recognized built-in losses that are not deductible in the taxable year because of the § 382 limitation are carried forward into subsequent taxable years (subject to the limitation in future years) in the same manner as a net operating loss which arose in the year of recognition. I.R.C. § 382(h)(4).

With respect to built-in gains, § 382 takes into account the fact that a loss corporation could at any time absorb its loss carryovers by disposing of assets with unrealized appreciation. Section 382(h)(1)(A) thus allows a loss corporation to increase its annual limitation following an ownership change by built-in gain recognized during the taxable year.

The built-in gain or loss rules of § 382(h) apply only to unrealized gains or losses recognized by the loss corporation within five years of an ownership change, and only if the corporation has net unrealized gain or loss on the date of an ownership change. Net unrealized built-in gains and losses are based on the difference between the fair market value and adjusted bases of the assets of a loss corporation immediately before an ownership change. I.R.C. § 382(h)(3)(A). Net unrealized loss also includes any depreciation or other capital recovery deductions attributable to the excess of the adjusted basis of an asset over its fair market value on the date of an ownership change. I.R.C. § 382(h)(2)(B). Thus, a valuation of the corporation's assets is required as of the date of an ownership change. Net unrealized built-in gain or loss is ignored, however, if the amount of unrealized gain or loss is not greater than the lesser of $10,000,000 or 15 percent of the fair market value of the loss corporation's assets (computed without regard to cash or marketable securities the value of which approximates cost) immediately prior to the date of an ownership change. I.R.C. § 382(h)(3)(B). In the case of a corporation with respect to which a § 338 election (discussed at page 484) is in effect following an ownership change, the § 382 limitation is increased by the lesser of gain recognized by reason of the § 338 election, or built-in gain determined without regard to the limitation of § 382(h)(3)(B). I.R.C. § 382(h)(1)(C).

Pending the issuance of regulations, Notice 2003–65, 2003–2 C.B. 747, provides two optional methods for calculating net unrealized built-in gains and losses and recognized built-in gains and losses under the rules of § 382(h). Under the "§ 1374 approach" adopted in the notice, net unrealized built-in gain or loss is determined under rules derived from § 1374, which is applicable to determining built-in gain or loss of a subchapter S corporation (discussed at page 415). Net unrealized built-in gain or loss is the gain or loss that would be recognized on a hypothetical sale of the assets of the loss corporation immediately before an ownership change. Recognized built-in gains, which increase the § 382 limitation, and recognized built-in losses subject to the § 382 limitation for any year are the actual gains and losses recognized by the loss corporation during the year. Under the "§ 338 approach" of the notice, net unrealized gain and loss is calculated in the

5. LIMITATIONS ON CARRYOVERS UNDER SECTION 383

Section 383 applies the limitation of § 382 following an ownership change to capital loss carryovers, general business credits, minimum tax credits under the alternative minimum tax, and foreign tax credits. Section 383(b) states that regulations are to be issued to provide that capital losses carried forward from a year pre-dating an ownership change are limited under § 382 principles and shall reduce the § 382 limitation on net operating losses. Section 383(a) and (c) provide for regulations to limit the use of tax credit carryforwards to tax liability computed on income up to the § 382 limitation. Tax credits are thereby converted into their taxable income equivalents for limitation purposes. See Treas.Reg. § 1.383–1.

6. APPLICATION OF SECTION 382 IN BANKRUPTCY AND INSOLVENCY PROCEEDINGS

6.1. *Stock for Debt Exchange*

In the case of a loss corporation involved in a Title 11 or similar bankruptcy proceeding, the § 382 limitation is not applied if, following an ownership change, the creditors and former stockholders of the loss corporation own at least 50 percent of the loss corporation stock. I.R.C. § 382(*l*)(5)(A). In effect, the creditors of the financially distressed corporation are treated as stockholders for purposes of testing for an ownership change. Under this provision, an exchange of debt for stock by creditors does not trigger the § 382 limitation. The relief of § 382(*l*)(5)(A) is available only with respect to an exchange of stock for indebtedness that has been held by the creditor for at least eighteen months preceding the date of filing of the bankruptcy or insolvency proceeding, or with respect to indebtedness incurred in the ordinary course of business of the old loss corporation which at all times has been held by the same person. I.R.C. § 382(*l*)(5)(E).

There is a substantial cost imposed for avoiding the general § 382 limitation under the exception provided by § 382(*l*)(5)(A). Section 382(*1*)(5)(B) requires that loss carryovers be reduced by the amount of interest on indebtedness converted into stock that has been paid or accrued during the taxable year of the ownership change and the three year period preceding the taxable year of the ownership change. Theoretically, debt of the bankrupt corporation has had the characteristics of equity during this period so that the interest deduction should not be available to increase loss carryovers.

Under § 382(*l*)(5)(C), cancelled indebtedness for interest that is taken into account to reduce net operating loss carryovers does not create cancellation of indebtedness income under § 108(e)(8). Cancellation of indebtedness income is created under § 108(e)(8) in the amount by which the fair market value of stock issued in exchange for debt is less than the amount of the debt.

If there is a second ownership change within two years with respect to a corporation that avoided the § 382 limitation under § 382(*l*)(5)(A), the § 382 limitation following the second ownership change will be zero. I.R.C. § 382(*l*)(5)(D).

6.2. *Qualified Debt Holders*

Relief from an ownership change under § 382(*l*)(5) is available only with respect to debt held by the creditor for eighteen months preceding the ownership change, or trade or business debt held at all times by the same person. Under Treas.Reg. § 1.382–9(d)(3), debt held by a person who is a less than five percent shareholder after the ownership change will be treated as owned by the same creditor for the 18 month period preceding the filing of a bankruptcy or insolvency petition. Thus, qualification under § 385(*l*)(5) does not require tracing of ownership during this "continuity period" of widely held debt that is converted into equity. This provision does not apply to an entity through which a five percent shareholder owns an indirect ownership interest in the loss corporation. In addition, if the loss corporation has knowledge of the acquisition of its debt by a group of persons with the principal purpose of exchanging the debt for stock, the indebtedness and stock will be treated as owned by an entity. Treas.Reg. § 1.382–9(d)(3)(ii)(A). Treas.Reg. § 1.382–9(d)(4) also provides that indebtedness held by a beneficial owner that is a five percent shareholder after the ownership change of the loss corporation and which is a corporation (or other entity) that has itself experienced an ownership change, will not be treated as indebtedness qualified for § 385(*l*)(5) treatment if the indebtedness represents more than 25 percent of the beneficial owner's gross assets on the beneficial owner's ownership change date.

For purposes of determining whether the eighteen month holding period is met, Treas.Reg. § 1.382–9(d)(5) provides that the transferee of indebtedness in certain transactions is treated as holding the indebtedness during the transferor's holding period. Transfers subject to this "tacking rule" include (1) transfers between related parties, (2) transfers pursuant to customary loan syndications, (3) transfers by an underwriter in the course of an underwriting, (4) transfers in which the transferee's basis is determined under § 1014 (death-time transfers), § 1015 (gifts), or with reference to the transferor's basis (nonrecognition transactions in general), (5) transfers in satisfaction of a pecuniary bequest, (6) transfers pursuant to a divorce or separation agreement, and (7) transfers by reason of subrogation. The tacking rule does not apply, however, if the transfer is for the principal purpose of taking advantage of the losses of the loss corporation. In addition, Treas.Reg. § 1.382–9(d)(5)(iv) provides for tacking of the holding period and character of indebtedness incurred in the course of a trade or business in the case of indebtedness received from the loss corporation in exchange for old indebtedness. This tacking rule also applies to a change in the terms of an indebtedness which constitutes an exchange under § 1001.

6.3. *Election Out*

A loss corporation may elect under § 382(*l*)(5)(H) not to have § 382(*l*)(5) apply to it. Treas.Reg. § 1.383–9(i) provides that the election is irrevocable and specifies the language that must be filed with the electing corporation's tax return by the due date (including extensions) for the loss corporation's return for the taxable year that includes the change date.

If an ownership change in a bankruptcy reorganization or Title 11 case does not qualify for the benefits of § 382(*l*)(5), or the loss corporation has elected out of the provision, under § 382(*l*)(6) the value of the loss

Treas.Reg. § 1.1502–21(b)(2) to a separate return year of a member of the consolidated group. In Amorient, Inc. v. Commissioner, 103 T.C. 161 (1994), the taxpayer incurred a consolidated net operating loss that was allocable in part to separate return years of a corporation that had been a Subchapter S corporation prior to acquisition by the consolidated group. The Tax Court held that the portion of the taxpayer's consolidated net operating loss allocable to separate return years of the former S corporation was to be carried back to the S corporation's separate return year even though deduction of net operating losses by an S corporation is barred by § 1373(d). The Tax Court justified its result in part on its conclusion that losses that are not deductible in carryback separate return years of the S corporation are to be carried forward to a year when either the former S corporation or the consolidated group can utilize the loss. Treas.Reg. § 1.1502–21(b)(2)(i) partially addresses the issues raised in *Amorient* by providing that the portion of a consolidated net operating loss that is apportioned to a member and carried back to a separate return year of the member may not be carried back to an equivalent or earlier year of the consolidated group. Likewise, if a consolidated net operating loss is carried forward to a separate return year of a member of the group, that carryforward loss may not be used in an equivalent or later consolidated return year of the group.

PART 7

SPECIAL RULES TO PREVENT AVOIDANCE OF SHAREHOLDER LEVEL TAX

CHAPTER 16

PENALTY TAXES

The Code contains two sets of provisions to prevent the use of a corporation to accumulate income in avoidance of progressive individual tax rates on dividend distributions and to convert ordinary income at the corporate level into stockholder capital gain. First, the accumulated earnings tax of §§ 531–537 imposes a penalty tax on corporate earnings that are accumulated beyond the reasonable needs of the business. Second, the personal holding company tax of §§ 541–547 imposes a penalty tax on undistributed passive investment income of closely held holding companies.

The changes in corporate and individual income taxation resulting from various tax acts in recent decades have reduced or even eliminated the significance of these penalty tax provisions. Until the 1980s, the higher individual marginal rates were substantially higher than the top rate on corporate income and dividends were taxed at higher rates than capital gains, thereby creating an incentive for accumulating earnings at the corporate level. However, from 2003 through 2012, the highest rate—35 percent—was the same for individuals and corporations, and since 2003 dividends have been taxed at the same rates as long-term capital gains, with the highest rate now 20 percent. Nevertheless, there remains some incentive to accumulate corporate income. Distribution of a dividend results in a combined rate on income earned in corporate form of 48 percent. In addition to reducing tax rates on accumulated earnings, if corporate income is accumulated the resulting increase in value may go untaxed on the death of an individual shareholder as a result of § 1014.

SECTION 1.   THE ACCUMULATED EARNINGS TAX

INTERNAL REVENUE CODE: Sections 531–537.

REGULATIONS: Sections 1.532–1(a); 1.533–1(a); 1.537–1(a), (b), –2, –3.

Sections 531 and 532 impose a tax of 20 percent on the "accumulated taxable income" of a corporation that has been formed or availed of for the purpose of avoiding the imposition of income tax on its shareholders, or the shareholders of another corporation, by permitting earnings and profits to accumulate instead of being distributed. In Ivan Allen Company v. United States, 422 U.S. 617 (1975), at a time when the top individual rate was significantly higher than the top corporate rate, the Court described the purpose and function of the accumulated earnings tax as follows:

> Under our system of income taxation, corporate earnings are subject to tax at two levels. First, there is the tax imposed upon the income of the corporation. Second, when the corporation, by way of a dividend, distributes its earnings to its shareholders, the distribution is subject to the tax imposed upon the income of the shareholders. Because of the disparity between the corporate tax rates and the higher gradations of

the rates on individuals, a corporation may be utilized to reduce significantly its shareholders' overall tax liability by accumulating earnings beyond the reasonable needs of the business. Without some method to force the distribution of unneeded corporate earnings, a controlling shareholder would be able to postpone the full impact of income taxes on his share of the corporation's earnings in excess of its needs. * * *

In order to foreclose this possibility of using the corporation as a means of avoiding the income tax on dividends to the shareholders, every revenue act since the adoption of the Sixteenth Amendment in 1913 has imposed a tax upon unnecessary accumulations of corporate earnings effected for the purpose of insulating shareholders.

The Court has acknowledged the obvious purpose of the accumulation provisions of the successive acts:

> As the theory of the revenue acts has been to tax corporate profits to the corporation, and their receipt only when distributed to the stockholders, the purpose of the legislation is to compel the company to distribute any profits not needed for the conduct of its business so that, when so distributed, individual stockholders will become liable not only for normal but for surtax on the dividends received. Helvering v. Chicago Stock Yards Co., 318 U.S. 693, 699, * * * (1943).

This was reaffirmed in United States v. Donruss Co., 393 U.S. 297 * * * (1969).

It is to be noted that the focus and impositions of the accumulated earnings tax is upon "accumulated taxable income," § 531. This is defined in § 535(a) to mean the corporation's "taxable income," as adjusted. The adjustments consist of the various items described in § 535(b), including federal income tax, the deduction for dividends paid defined in § 561, and the accumulated earnings credit defined in § 535(c). The adjustments prescribed by § 535(a) and (b) are designed generally to assure that a corporation's "accumulated taxable income" reflects more accurately than "taxable income" the amount actually available to the corporation for business purposes. This explains the deductions for dividends paid and for federal income taxes; neither of these enters into the computation of taxable income. Obviously, dividends paid and federal income taxes deplete corporate resources and must be recognized if the corporation's economic condition is to be properly perceived. Conversely, § 535(b)(3) disallows, for example, the deduction, available to a corporation for income tax purposes under § 243, on account of dividends received; dividends received are freely available for use in the corporation's business.

The purport of the accumulated earnings tax structure established by §§ 531–537, therefore, is to determine the corporation's true economic condition before its liability for tax upon "accumulated taxable income" is determined. The tax, although a penalty and therefore to be strictly construed, Commissioner v. Acker, 361 U.S. 87, 91, * * * (1959), is directed at economic reality.

* * *

Accumulation beyond the reasonable needs of the business, by the language of § 533(a), is "determinative of the purpose" to avoid tax with respect to shareholders unless the corporation proves the contrary by a preponderance of the evidence. The burden of proof, thus, is on the taxpayer. A rebuttable presumption is statutorily imposed. To be sure, we deal here, in a sense, with a state of mind. But it has been said that the statute, without the support of the presumption, would "be practically unenforceable without it." United Business Corp. v. Commissioner, 62 F.2d 754, 755 (CA2), cert. denied, 290 U.S. 635 * * * (1933). What is required, then, is a comparison of accumulated earnings and profits with "the reasonable needs of the business." Business needs are critical. And need, plainly, to use mathematical terminology, is a function of a corporation's liquidity, that is, the amount of idle current assets at its disposal. The question, therefore, is not how much capital of all sorts, but how much in the way of quick or liquid assets, it is reasonable to keep on hand for the business.

Generally, the IRS has attempted to apply the accumulated earnings tax only to closely held corporations. The requirement that the corporation be formed or availed of to avoid shareholder tax is less likely to exist in the case of publicly owned companies. In some instances, the tax has been applied to widely held companies that were controlled by a small group of stockholders;[1] and since 1984 § 532(c) has provided that the accumulated earnings tax is to be applied without regard to the number of stockholders.

---

[1]   See Trico Products Corp. v. Commissioner, 137 F.2d 424 (2d Cir.1943) and Trico Products v. McGowan, 169 F.2d 343 (2d Cir.1948) (corporation owned by 2,000 stockholders but 74% of the stock was held by six stockholders). But in Golconda Mining Corp. v. Commissioner, 507 F.2d 594 (9th Cir.1974), the appellate court reversed the Tax Court's holding that the accumulated earnings tax was applicable to a corporation whose management group owned from 12% to 17% of the stock. The court held that the accumulated earnings tax could apply only if a relatively small group of stockholders exercised control, a situation which could exist only if a small group of stockholders owned more than 50% of the stock of the corporation.

In Technalysis Corp. v. Commissioner, 101 T.C. 397 (1993), the court held that the accumulated earnings tax is applicable to a publicly held corporation without regard to whether control was exercised by a relatively small group of shareholders. However, the court concluded that although the corporation's accumulations were beyond the reasonable needs of the business, the corporation was not formed or availed of to avoid income tax with respect to its shareholders.

DETAILED ANALYSIS

1. THE RELATIONSHIP BETWEEN THE PROSCRIBED ACCUMULATION "PURPOSE" AND THE REASONABLE NEEDS OF THE BUSINESS

In United States v. Donruss Co., 393 U.S. 297 (1969), the Court resolved a conflict as to whether, as urged by the government, a taxpayer to rebut the presumption contained in § 533(a) must establish that tax avoidance with respect to the shareholders was not "one" of the purposes for the accumulation or whether, as some Courts of Appeals had held, the presumption could be rebutted by demonstrating that tax avoidance was not the "dominant, controlling, or impelling" purpose for the accumulation. The Court sustained the Government's position.

To understand the impact of the holding in *Donruss*, consider the situation of the taxpayer in that case on remand. Since the jury that decided the case below had already found that the accumulation was beyond the reasonable needs of the business, the presumption in § 533(a) that the purpose was to avoid income taxes with respect to the shareholders had been brought into play. It would thus now be up to the taxpayer to prove by a preponderance of the evidence the negative proposition that not one of the purposes of the accumulation was tax avoidance, an almost impossible task. Though the statute makes a finding of the proscribed purpose the crucial event for the imposition of the tax, the *Donruss* holding made the finding as to the reasonableness of the accumulation the determinative factor in the vast majority of cases. See e.g., Bahan Textile Machinery Co., Inc. v. United States, 453 F.2d 1100 (4th Cir.1972) (after an accumulation beyond the reasonable needs of the business was established, the taxpayer unsuccessfully tried to overcome the presumption as to purpose by showing that the controlling shareholder was "an overly cautious man, fearful of long-term debt and conservative in financial outlook"). Compare Bremerton Sun Publishing Co. v. Commissioner, 44 T.C. 566 (1965) ("Although we feel that the total accumulation was somewhat beyond the reasonable foreseeable business needs of petitioner, we are convinced that the only reason for the excessive retention of earnings was the conservative policies of the directors and not their concern for the surtax liability of [the shareholders]."); Starman Investment, Inc. v. United States, 534 F.2d 834 (9th Cir.1976) (even if accumulation beyond reasonable needs, lack of tax avoidance motive precludes imposition of tax).

In Magic Mart, Inc. v. Commissioner, 51 T.C. 775 (1969), the court concluded that since accumulations beyond the reasonable needs of the business were not present, a finding as to the purpose of the accumulations was unnecessary in light of the credit in § 535(c) for reasonable accumulation, and the *Donruss* issue was not reached. In contrast to Magic Mart, some courts have apparently been of the view that, to escape tax, the accumulations, in addition to being reasonable in an objective sense, must have been motivated by business needs and not tax avoidance purposes. Apollo Industries, Inc. v. Commissioner, 358 F.2d 867 (1st Cir.1966), remanded the case to the Tax Court for an answer to the following question: "[E]ven if accumulated earnings did not exceed reasonably anticipated business needs in one or both years, was avoidance of taxes on shareholders nevertheless a dominant purpose?" The Court of Appeals in

Donruss apparently was of the same view (384 F.2d 292, 294 (6th Cir.1967)), though the cases it cited for this proposition were decided prior to the enactment of § 535(c). The Tax Court uniformly has taken the view that if the accumulations do not exceed the reasonable needs of the business so that a sufficient credit would be present quite apart from any issue as to the purpose for the accumulation, the issue as to the purpose of the accumulations is irrelevant. John P. Scripps Newspapers v. Commissioner, 44 T.C. 453 (1965); Dielectric Materials Co. v. Commissioner, 57 T.C. 587 (1972).

2.   FACTORS BEARING ON REASONABLE BUSINESS NEEDS

2.1. *General*

Determining the "reasonable business needs" involves a complex factual inquiry into all aspects of the corporation's business. Courts generally start with the statement that they are reluctant to substitute their judgment for the business judgment of the management as to the need for the accumulations (see e.g., Dielectric Materials Co. v. Commissioner, 57 T.C. 587 (1972)), and then proceed with an exhaustive analysis of the corporation's financial and business history. While the cases are not easily classified, each turning on its own facts, they typically involve the factors discussed below.

2.2. *Accumulations for Expansion or Diversification*

The expansion or replacement of existing business facilities often is given as a justification for accumulations. Treas.Reg. § 1.537–1(b)(1) requires that the corporation "must have specific, definite, and feasible plans for the use of such accumulations." The courts have applied this requirement with varying degrees of strictness. See, e.g., Faber Cement Block Co., Inc. v. Commissioner, 50 T.C. 317 (1968) (Acq.) (taxpayer's operations on its property constituted a nonconforming use under the local zoning ordinances and any expansion would have required an additional variance; accumulations over a long period of time for a proposed expansion were justified).

In addition to expansion of facilities, accumulations often are justified on the ground that they are needed to diversify the existing business. Treas.Reg. § 1.537–3(a) defines the "business" of a corporation very broadly as "not merely that which it has previously carried on but includ[ing], in general, any line of business which it may undertake." On the other hand, investments that are "unrelated" to the activities of the business of the taxpayer are an indication of unreasonable accumulations, Treas.Reg. § 1.537–2(c)(4), and the line between an "unrelated investment" and the beginning of a new "business" is not a clear one. See, e.g., Electric Regulator Corp. v. Commissioner, 336 F.2d 339 (2d Cir.1964) (taxpayer produced a small patented voltage regulator that was successful commercially, resulting in large accumulated profits; taxpayer's justification for the accumulation based on the desire to develop new products was sustained); Hughes Inc. v. Commissioner, 90 T.C. 1 (1988) (purchase of an orange grove and interests in partnerships holding real estate were justified as part of efforts to diversify the business of owning and leasing improved real and tangible personal properties); J. Gordon Turnbull, Inc. v. Commissioner, 41 T.C. 358 (1963) (fact that an architectural and engineering firm invested large sums in real estate was found indicative of an accumulation beyond the reasonable needs of its business); Cataphote Corp. of Miss. v. United States, 535 F.2d 1225 (Ct.Cl.1976) (acquisition of 26 fractional working interests in oil and gas ventures by a corporation in the truck leasing business did not mean that the corporation was also in the oil and gas business for accumulated earnings tax purposes; the corporation did not have the necessary business responsibilities and the interests constituted mere investments unrelated to the active business of the corporation).

2.3. *Working Capital Needs*

Treas.Reg. § 1.537–2(b)(4) recognizes the need to accumulate earnings "to provide necessary working capital for the business." The courts have struggled to develop standards for the determination of a reasonable allowance for working capital. Earlier cases allowed an accumulation of working capital to cover some arbitrary period of time, such as one year, or stressed the relationship between current liabilities and current assets in assessing working capital needs. More recent cases, following the approach taken initially in Bardahl Mfg. Corp. v. Commissioner, T.C. Memo. 1965–200, attempt to relate the corporation's need for working capital to its "operating cycle." In J.H. Rutter Rex Mfg. Co. v. Commissioner, 853 F.2d 1275 (5th Cir.1988), the court described the operating cycle approach as follows:

> An operating cycle for a manufacturing business like Rutter Rex is the period of time needed to convert cash into raw materials, raw materials into inventory, inventory into accounts receivable, and accounts receivable into cash. In other words, an operating cycle is the time a corporation's working capital is tied up in producing and selling its product. * * *

> The "operating cycle" as originally formulated in *Bardahl Manufacturing* is broken down into two sub-cycles: an inventory cycle and an accounts receivable cycle. These cycles are measured in terms of days. An inventory cycle is the time necessary to convert raw materials into finished goods and to sell those goods. An accounts receivable cycle is the time necessary to convert the accounts receivable created by the sale of finished goods into cash. These two cycles are added together to determine the total number of days in the operating cycle. The number of days in the operating cycle is then divided by 365; the resulting fraction is multiplied by the amount of the corporation's operating expenses for one year, including costs of goods sold, selling expenses, general and administrative expenses, and estimated federal and state income tax payments (but excluding depreciation). The resulting figure is the amount of liquid assets necessary to meet the ordinary operating expenses for the complete operating cycle.

The *Bardahl* formula is also applied by taking account of a credit cycle. The credit cycle is based on the amount of time between the corporation's receipt of raw materials, supplies, labor, and other inputs, and the corporation's payment for these items. The deferral of payment reduces the corporation's need for capital and thus the credit cycle is subtracted from the operating cycle determined from inventory and receivables cycles. See C.E. Hooper, Inc. v. United States, 539 F.2d 1276 (Ct.Cl.1976). In *J.H. Rutter Rex Mfg. Co.*, supra, the taxpayer convinced the appellate court that application of a credit cycle to reduce its working capital needs was inappropriate because of the lack of evidence that the corporation utilized an extension of credit from its major suppliers to any significant degree.

Despite the seeming exactness of the operating cycle formula, its limitations must be recognized. See Dielectric Materials Co. v. Commissioner, 57 T.C. 587 (1972) (*Bardahl* not strictly applied because the formula was not sufficiently "flexible" to take into account the fact that taxpayer had additional working capital needs in the light of a threatened labor dispute); Ready Paving and Construction Co. v. Commissioner, 61 T.C. 826 (1974) ("special investment warrants" received as payment for contracting work done for municipal governments constituted assets available for use as working capital under the *Bardahl* formula; correspondingly, the warrants did not constitute accounts receivable for determining the amount of accumulated earnings needed for working capital; consistent treatment of the items was required in both aspects of the *Bardahl* formula).

2.4. *Provision for Contingencies*

Fears, both real and imagined, of contingent liabilities also have been used to justify accumulations of earnings. In Halby Chemical Co., Inc. v. United States, 180 Ct.Cl. 584 (1967), the court allowed accumulations for self-insurance against the "enduring possibility of a disastrous fire or explosion" which could not adequately be covered by insurance because of the risk of taxpayer's operations. In Hughes Inc. v. Commissioner, 90 T.C. 1 (1988), a closely held corporation which rented warehouses to a publicly held corporation used accumulated earnings to purchase stock of the public corporation in order to prevent a hostile takeover of its lessee. The court said that investments in marketable securities which bear some relationship to a corporation's business are considered a proper business application of funds and may be accumulated with impunity. On the other hand, in Oyster Shell Products Corp. v. Commissioner, 313 F.2d 449 (2d Cir.1963), the taxpayer unsuccessfully attempted to justify accumulations on the ground that possible flooding of the river on which its operations were located could result in large expenses; the court rejected the argument as "conjured up" after the accumulated earnings tax issue was first raised by the Government.

In Otto Candies, LLC v. United States, 288 F. Supp. 2d 730 (E.D. La. 2003), an accumulation of between $15 and $21 million during the years in question by a closely held corporation (an LLC that elected to be taxed as a corporation) was found to meet the reasonable needs of the business. The taxpayer, a family corporation with three shareholders, was "one of the leading providers of marine transportation in the Gulf of Mexico." The corporation was found to be engaged in a volatile business and the dominant shareholder was conservative and avoided debt. The accumulations were required to fund necessary periodic fleet replacement, including newer vessels with modern technology meeting customer demands, new ventures into related businesses, and to internally fund future redemptions under a shareholder buy/sell agreement upon the death of a shareholder.

Section 537(b)(4) specifically provides for the accumulation of a reserve for reasonably anticipated product liability losses.

2.5. *Accumulations to Fund Stock Redemptions*

If a redemption is treated as a dividend under § 301, no accumulated earnings tax issue arises because the distribution is fully taxed at the shareholder level. But redemptions qualifying under § 302(b) or § 303 are not treated as dividends and thus raise an accumulated earnings tax issue. Pelton Steel Casting Co. v. Commissioner, 251 F.2d 278 (7th Cir.1958), held that the accumulated earnings tax applied in a case in which the corporation accumulated income to redeem the stock of two of its three shareholders rather than paying its earnings out as dividends to all of the shareholders and, presumably, then redeeming the stock at a lower price. The purpose of the redemption was to prevent the redeemed shareholders from selling their stock to outsiders, which was found not to be a corporate business purpose.

Mountain State Steel Foundries, Inc. v. Commissioner, 284 F.2d 737 (4th Cir.1960), held that the accumulated earnings tax did not apply to earnings in 1951 through 1954 used to pay a promissory note issued by the corporation in redemption of 50 percent of its shares in 1950. The Court emphasized that there was a business purpose for the redemption because the redeemed shareholders, who were inactive, had conflicting interests regarding corporate management with the continuing shareholders, who were active.

Is a business purpose such as was found in *Mountain State Steel Foundries* sufficient to justify a pre-redemption accumulation, as occurred in *Pelton Steel Casting Co.?* The lower courts have found a proper "corporate purpose" sufficient to avoid the accumulated earnings tax in a number of situations involving minority shareholders or retiring employee-shareholders. See Ted Bates & Co., Inc. v. Commissioner, T.C.Memo. 1965–251 (redemption made in order to assure "continuity of [taxpayer's] management"); Farmers & Merchants Investment Co. v. Commissioner, T.C.Memo. 1970–161 ("promotion of harmony in the conduct of the business"). In contrast, accumulations to redeem uncontentious large shareholders have been held subject to the tax. See John B. Lambert & Associates v. United States, 76–2 U.S.T.C. ¶ 9776 (Ct.Cl.1976); Lamark Shipping Agency, Inc. v. Commissioner, T.C.Memo. 1981–284.

Section 537(a)(2) specifically provides that accumulations to fund redemptions which qualify under § 303 are to meet the reasonable need of the business. However, § 537(b)(1) limits qualification under this rule to accumulations in the year the shareholder dies and subsequent years. Accumulations in years prior to the year of death cannot be justified by subsequent use for a § 303 redemption. See S.Rep. No. 91–522, 91st Cong., 1st Sess. 291 (1969).

2.6. *Shareholder Loans, Dividend Record, and Shareholder Tax Bracket*

While the fact that the corporation has paid no dividends is, of course, not conclusive on the issue of the proscribed purpose, it is a factor. Failure to pay dividends, together with loans to shareholders by the corporation, indicates an availability of funds to make dividend distributions. See, e.g., Bahan Textile Machinery Co. v. United States, 453 F.2d 1100 (4th Cir.1972) (loans to shareholders and relatives "show not only that the company was dissipating funds which it claimed were needed for the business, but also indicated a purpose to distribute corporate profits indirectly rather than as dividends that would be taxable to the recipients").

In GPD, Inc. v. Commissioner, 60 T.C. 480 (1973), rev'd, 508 F.2d 1076 (6th Cir.1974), the Tax Court held that the corporation was subject to the accumulated earnings tax for a year in which there had been a decrease in the corporation's earnings and profits. The Tax Court took the position that since there was no accumulation of earnings and profits, the accumulated earnings tax could not apply, even though in that year, the corporation did have accumulated taxable income under § 535.[2] The Court of Appeals reversed the Tax Court, holding that the legislative history of the accumulated earnings tax did not show any intent to require the accumulations of earnings and profits in the current year as a condition precedent to the imposition of the tax. The Court of Appeals observed that if the Tax Court position were adopted, and a corporation distributed the exact amount of its earnings and profits for a year, no accumulated earnings tax could be imposed on accumulated taxable income of the corporation in that year; on the other hand, one cent of undistributed earnings and profits for the year would subject the entire accumulated taxable income to the tax. Moreover, the Court of Appeals observed that the Tax Court rule in effect gave a corporation a double accumulated earnings tax credit, since a corporation would be protected both in the year of accumulation and also in the year in which the actual redemption reduced earnings and profits.

Atlantic Properties, Inc. v. Commissioner, 519 F.2d 1233 (1st Cir.1975), involved a corporation owned by four equal shareholders but whose corporate charter required an 80 percent vote of the shareholders for any corporate action. Three of the shareholders desired to have the corporation adopt a policy of dividend distributions; one shareholder did not, in part because of the adverse tax consequences of the dividend distribution to him. The court held that the accumulated earnings tax applied since the corporation was availed of for a proscribed purpose, even though a majority of the shareholders did not agree with that purpose.

2.7. *Accumulations by and for Subsidiaries*

Treas.Reg. § 1.537–3(b) provides that under certain circumstances the accumulated earnings of a parent corporation may be justified by the reasonably anticipated business needs of its subsidiary. In the converse situation, the Court of Appeals in Inland Terminals, Inc. v. United States, 477 F.2d 836 (4th Cir.1973), held that it was also possible to justify a controlled subsidiary's accumulated earnings with reference to the parent corporation's reasonably anticipated business needs which the parent corporation itself could not satisfy. On remand, the District Court held that the parent corporation's alternative diversification or relocation plans were such as would take all or substantially all of its own earnings and those of the subsidiary; thus the combined earnings of the two corporations did not exceed the reasonable needs of the parent's business. 73–2 U.S.T.C. ¶ 9724 (D.Md.1973).

In Chaney & Hope, Inc. v. Commissioner, 80 T.C. 263 (1983), the court held that accumulations for the business needs of a brother or sister

---

[2] Accumulated taxable income was present despite a reduction in earnings and profits because stock redemptions, not being dividends, had no effect on the determination of accumulated taxable income.

corporation cannot generally be considered as accumulations to meet reasonable business needs because the business of the sister corporation is not the business of the brother corporation. The court also held, however, that the taxpayer could accumulate its earnings to meet the reasonably anticipated future needs of an expanded business to be conducted by its successor corporation, a sister corporation into which the taxpayer would be merged. Permissible accumulations were limited to earnings accumulated after the time plans for the merger became definite.

In Advanced Delivery and Chemical Systems of Nevada, Inc. v. Commissioner, T.C. Memo 2003–250, a holding company was found not to be liable for accumulated earnings tax where the business activities of its subsidiaries and partnerships in which it was a partner were attributed to it under Treas.Reg. § 1.537–3(b). Because of the rapid growth of the affiliates' businesses, the accumulations did not exceed the holding company's reasonable needs for expansion of the affiliates. Furthermore, on the particular facts, even if the accumulations did exceed the taxpayers' reasonable needs, there was not a tax avoidance purpose.

2.8. *Valuation Aspects*

In Ivan Allen v. United States, 422 U.S. 617 (1975), page 849, the issue was whether in determining the reasonable needs of the business marketable securities owned by the corporation should be counted at cost, as the taxpayer asserted, or their net liquidation value as claimed by the IRS. The Court pointed out that the accumulated earnings tax itself is imposed only on accumulated taxable income, which includes only realized gains. The Court held, however, that in determining whether accumulations exceed the reasonable needs of the business the full value of readily available liquid assets should be taken into account.

The decision of the Supreme Court in *Ivan Allen* was correct from the standpoint of the policy behind the accumulated earnings tax. The actual value which the corporation could realize from its investments and distribute to its shareholders is the best measure of the amount and reasonableness of its total accumulation; the cost basis of the investments is not relevant to that determination. Nevertheless, there are some difficulties in implementing the Court's decision. The majority in *Ivan Allen* assumed that the proper time for valuation of the securities was the end of the taxable year of the corporation. In some instances, other dates, for example, the date on which the Board of Directors makes its dividend decision for the year, might be more appropriate. There are also some technical problems. In other areas of the tax law, valuation of securities is made by taking a "blockage" factor into account, i.e., the size of the block of stock held by a particular shareholder can reduce the total value below a fair market value based on the quoted per share value because a single sale of the entire stock would depress the market. Valuation of closely held stock will present similar difficulties.

The majority in *Ivan Allen* went to some length to emphasize that its opinion was directed toward "readily marketable portfolio securities." But, as the dissenters pointed out, the majority's "rationale is not so easily contained." If a corporation holds securities which are not readily marketable but are still unrelated to its business, the majority's reasoning appears equally applicable; the lack of marketability or difficulties in disposition would be relevant to the valuation issue but do not lead to the conclusion that cost basis should be employed. Likewise, a finding that investments in real estate, timber land, and other such assets are unrelated to the business of the corporation should call into play the fair market value approach adopted by the majority.

In footnote 9 of the opinion, the majority stated that it was expressing no view with respect to the valuation of items such as inventory or accounts receivable. Motor Fuel Carriers, Inc. v. Commissioner, 559 F.2d 1348 (5th Cir.1977), held that accounts receivable should be treated as liquid assets for accumulated earnings tax purposes and valued at fair market value.

3.   PROCEDURAL ASPECTS

In addition to the presumptions in § 533, discussed above, § 534 sets forth a complicated allocation of the burden of proof on certain issues in Tax Court proceedings. The provision is intended to ease the burden on the taxpayer in an accumulated earnings tax case. See, Senate Finance Committee Report, S.Rep. No. 83–1622, 83rd Cong., 2d Sess. 70–71 (1954). The provision, however, has not been of much help to taxpayers because the Tax Court has been quite strict regarding the required content of the taxpayer's statement under § 534(c). It must contain adequate factual material and not simply "conclusory" statements. See, J.H. Rutter Rex Mfg. Co. v. Commissioner, 853 F.2d 1275, 1283 (5th Cir.1988), in which the taxpayer's statement was found wanting because of its failure to quantify working capital needs and provide financial information supporting its claim: "Obviously the statute does not contemplate shifting the burden of proof when a taxpayer merely tells the Commissioner it is going to challenge the imposition of the accumulated earnings tax. There must be notice of the specific grounds and contentions." See also, Hughes Inc. v. Commissioner, supra, 90 T.C. 1 (1988) (taxpayer provided sufficient detail which, if proven, would support the alleged business needs for the accumulation with respect to some but not all of the grounds asserted). The significance of the shift in the burden of proof provided by § 534 is reduced by § 7491, enacted in 1998, which shifts the burden of proof to the IRS after the taxpayer has produced credible evidence in support of the taxpayer's position, but only if the taxpayer has cooperated with the IRS.

Sections 561–563 provide a deduction for dividends paid within two and one-half months of the close of the taxable year, which dividends reduce the taxpayer's accumulated earnings and profits for the prior year for purposes of the accumulated earnings tax.

SECTION 2.   THE PERSONAL HOLDING COMPANY TAX

INTERNAL REVENUE CODE: Sections 541–547; 6501(f).

Section 541 imposes a special tax on the undistributed personal holding company income of a corporation that qualifies as a personal holding company. For most of its history, the personal holding company tax was imposed on corporate income at the highest individual tax rate. Under current law, a 20 percent tax—the same rate as the maximum rate that applies to dividends—is imposed by § 541 on the undistributed personal holding company income of a personal holding company. A corporation is classified as a personal holding company under § 542(a) if at least 60 percent of its adjusted ordinary gross income is personal

1.3. *Incorporated Personal Use Assets*

The third device targeted by the personal holding company provisions is incorporation of personal use property such as a yacht or vacation home. Individuals would put personal use property in a corporation along with passive investments producing sufficient income to maintain the personal use property. The more aggressive taxpayer would then attempt to deduct the cost of maintaining the personal use property from income produced by the passive investment, thereby maintaining the personal use property with tax-free income. In a modified form, the taxpayer might rent the personal use property from the corporation for an arm's-length rental which was less than the cost of maintenance, and fund the difference with income from passive assets. To combat these attempts, § 543(a)(6) includes as personal holding company income amounts received as compensation for the use of tangible property of the corporation if a 25 percent or greater shareholder is entitled to personal use of the property. In addition, § 545(b)(6) provides that in computing taxable income subject to the personal holding company tax, no deduction for depreciation and maintenance expense shall be allowed against rental income from property held by a personal holding company unless the corporation can establish (A) that the rent received was the highest rent attainable, (B) that the property is held in the course of a business carried on for bona fide profit, and (C) that there is either an expectation that operation of the property would produce a profit or that the property is necessary for the conduct of the business. Section 545(b)(6) is intended to insure that deductions attributable to property used by a shareholder do not reduce other personal holding company income.

2.   COMPUTING THE PERSONAL HOLDING COMPANY TAX BASE

Section 541 imposes the personal holding company tax on the corporation's "undistributed personal holding company income." Section 545 defines this undistributed taxable income as the current year's taxable income less deductions for other taxes,[7] dividends[8] (including consent dividends not involving actual distributions), and other disbursements. In addition, § 547 allows a deficiency dividend deduction under which a deficiency in personal holding company tax may be avoided by a dividend distribution to shareholders after a determination of the deficiency. This device is helpful, for example, if the corporation does not realize it is a personal holding company or if, even though it realizes it is a personal holding company, believes that it has distributed all of its income only to

---

[7]   The deduction for taxes paid is limited to taxes accrued during the taxable year. Contested tax liabilities are not properly accrued and therefore not allowed as a deduction in computing income subject to the personal holding company tax. Kluger Associates, Inc. v. Commissioner, 617 F.2d 323 (2d Cir.1980); LX Cattle Company v. United States, 629 F.2d 1096 (5th Cir.1980).

[8]   Treas.Reg. § 1.562–1(a) provides that the reduction in income for dividends if appreciated property is distributed as a dividend in kind is limited to the adjusted basis of the property. The Supreme Court in Fulman v. United States, 434 U.S. 528 (1978), resolving a conflict in the Circuits, upheld the regulation as it applies to distributions of appreciated property. The Court, after describing a rather confusing legislative history, found a "reasonable basis" for the regulation limiting the corporate deduction to the basis of the property despite the fact that the full fair market value of the property is included in the income of the shareholder as a dividend. The limitation to adjusted basis no longer may be appropriate as the distributing corporation is required to recognize gain on the distribution of appreciated property.

find that undistributed income exists either because the IRS has found additional income items or has disallowed deductions. This device is not available, however, if fraud is present or there was a willful failure to file an income tax return.

3. ADDITIONAL ASPECTS OF THE PERSONAL HOLDING COMPANY PROVISIONS

There are several facets of the relationship between the accumulated earnings tax and the personal holding company tax. A corporation may escape the accumulated earnings tax, which is based upon the accumulation of earnings and profits, but still be subject to the personal holding company tax, because the latter tax depends upon the existence of undistributed personal holding company income, a concept entirely distinct from earnings and profits. Also the concept of "accumulation" is essentially absent from the personal holding company tax. On the other hand, if the corporation is a personal holding company, the accumulated earnings tax does not apply. § 532(b)(1). But, a corporation that avoids personal holding company status must still face the possibility that its accumulations will be reached under the accumulated earnings tax.

An active manufacturing company with some investment income may fall accidentally into personal holding company status. For manufacturing companies, "gross income" is not "gross receipts," but instead constitutes gross receipts less cost of goods sold. Thus, in a bad year in which the cost of goods sold exceeded gross receipts, the corporation might find itself with less than 40 percent of its adjusted ordinary gross income from non-personal holding income sources.

The at-risk provisions of § 465, limiting the taxpayer's ability to take deductions in connection with nonrecourse financing, apply to "closely held" corporations that meet the stock ownership requirements of § 542(a)(2). This limitation in turn can have an impact on the calculation of adjusted ordinary gross income and thus on the status of the corporation as a personal holding company.

INDEX